INFORMATION TRANSMISSION, MODULATION, AND NOISE

McGraw-Hill Series in Electrical Engineering

Stephen W. Director, Carnegie-Mellon University
Consulting Editor

Circuits and Systems
Communications and Signal Processing
Control Theory
Electronics and Electronic Circuits
Power and Energy
Electromagnetics
Computer Engineering
Introductory
Radar and Antennas
VLSI

Previous Consulting Editors

Communications and Signal Processing

Stephen W. Director, Carnegie-Mellon University
Consulting Editor

Communications and Signal Processing

Stephen W. Director, Carnegie Mellon University
Consulting Editor

Antoniou: *Digital Filters: Analysis and Design*

Candy: *Signal Processing: The Model-Based Approach*

Candy: *Signal Processing: The Modern Approach*

Carlson: *Communication Systems: An Introduction to Signals and Noise in Electrical Communication*

Cherin: *An Introduction to Optical Fibers*

Cooper and McGillem: *Modern Communications and Spread Spectrum*

Davenport: *Probability and Random Processes: An Introduction for Applied Scientists and Engineers*

Drake: *Fundamentals of Applied Probability Theory*

Gardner: *Introduction to Random Processes: With Applications...*

Keiser: *Local Area Networks*

Keiser: *Optical Fiber Communications*

Kuc: *Introduction to Digital Signal Processing*

Papoulis: *Probability, Random Variables, and Stochastic Processes*

Papoulis: *Signal Analysis*

Papoulis: *The Fourier Integral and Its Applications*

Peebles: *Probability, Random Variables, and Random Signal Principles*

Proakis: *Digital Communications*

Schwartz: *Information Transmission, Modulation, and Noise*

Schwartz and Shaw: *Signal Processing*

Smith: *Modern Communication Circuits*

Taub and Schilling: *Principles of Communication Systems*

INFORMATION TRANSMISSION, MODULATION, AND NOISE

Fourth Edition

Mischa Schwartz

*Department of Electrical Engineering
and
Center for Telecommunications Research
Columbia University*

McGraw-Hill Publishing Company

New York   St. Louis   San Francisco   Auckland   Bogotá   Caracas
Hamburg   Lisbon   London   Madrid   Mexico   Milan   Montreal
New Delhi   Oklahoma City   Paris   San Juan   São Paulo   Singapore
Sydney   Tokyo   Toronto

INFORMATION TRANSMISSION, MODULATION AND NOISE

INTERNATIONAL EDITION

1 2 3 4 5 6 7 8 9 0 KHL PMP 9 4 3 2 1 0

This book was set in Times Roman by Science Typographer, Inc.
The editors were Lyn Beamesderfer and John M. Morris;
The production supervisor was Janelle S. Travers.
The cover was designed by Warren Infield.
Project supervision was done by Science Typographers, Inc.

Library of Congress Cataloging-in-Publication Data

Schwartz, Mischa
    Information transmission, modulation and noise/Mischa Schwartz
    4th ed
      p.   cm — (McGraw-Hill series in electrical engineering)
      (Communications and signal processing)
      ISBN 0-07-055909-0
      1. Telecommunication.   2. Digital communications
3. Modulation (Electronics)   4. Electronic noise   I. Title
II. Series   III. Series; McGraw-Hill series in electrical engineering
Communications and signal processing

TK5101.83   1990
621.382-dc20   89-27692

When ordering this title use ISBN 0-07-100931-0

Printed in Singapore

CONTENTS

4 Modulation Techniques

PREFACE

This book has again undergone substantial revisions for this fourth edition. The past decade has seen two major developments in the field of telecommunications: the widespread introduction of fiber optics for long-haul transmission over telephone facilities worldwide, and the explosive use of local area networks (LANs) for business and campus. This book reflects these new developments, as well as a number of others noted later.

A complete new chapter, Chapter 5, is devoted to telecommunication networks, with particular emphasis on LANs. In keeping with the most modern trends, the discussion of LANs is oriented to the IEEE 802 LAN standards. There is some discussion as well of the optically based FDDI standard. All of this material is in turn related within the book to the OSI (Open Systems Interconnection) Reference Model for data networks, providing a good introduction to the concept of layered communications architectures. Packet and circuit switching are discussed as well in this chapter.

In addition to much descriptive material on data and circuit-switched networks, performance considerations are introduced. Simple queueing concepts are developed for this purpose. The networking knowledge of the reader is thus enhanced. The discussion of queuing builds on, and provides good application for, the concepts of probability the reader is assumed to have just acquired.

The widespread deployment of fiber optics is reflected in this edition throughout the book. The 45-Mbit/s DS3 transmission format, which is widely used over fiber-optic facilities, is discussed at length in Sec. 3-8 as part of the discussion on time-division multiplexing. This material is followed in Sec. 3-9 by a discussion of SONET, the digital multiplexing hierarchy specifically geared to fiber-optic transmission. A quantitative discussion of digital light-wave (fiber-optic) systems appears in Chapter 6. Direct detection and coherent detection systems are introduced, and limits on their performance which are widely quoted in the literature are obtained.

Other new developments in the field of telecommunications are introduced in this edition: high-bit-rate digital radio is discussed in Chapters 4 and 7 as an added example of the use of QAM over band-limited channels; a new section (4-4) appears on minimum-shift keying; new material on Reed–Solomon codes, convolutional coding, and trellis-coded modulation appears in Chapter 7. Much of this material is self-contained and is quantitatively presented where possible at this introductory level. New application examples introduced in this edition include the compact-disc system, the new CCITT delta modulation and DPCM voice standards, examples of digital radio systems, and recent developments in space and satellite communications.

The book assumes no prior knowledge of communication systems. It is designed to provide the reader with a solid foundation in point-to-point communications (the physical layer in networks), telecommunication networks, and communication theory. A reader completing the material in the book is equipped to go on to further advanced study, or to begin work in various aspects of the field of communications. The material progresses gradually from the simpler ideas to the more complex. Theoretical concepts are explained in terms of concrete, real-life examples. This blend of theory and practice has always been the hallmark of the previous editions.

At Columbia University the material in the book is covered in two successive courses. The first course, on Communication Systems and Networks, covers the first five chapters. Chapter 2, on Linear Systems, is gone over quite rapidly, since most of this has been covered in a junior-level Signals and Systems course. A course in probability is a corequisite, and the use of probability is deferred until Chapter 5, on Networks. That chapter is covered in the latter third of the course and, as already noted, provides some welcome applications for the parallel study of probability.

The second course, on Digital Communications, which is taken by many first-year graduate students as well as seniors, covers the appropriate material of Chapters 6 and 7. Interestingly, most of the graduate students taking this second course come from universities other than Columbia. They generally have not had the same first course on Communications, but experience no trouble learning the material.

With appropriate selection of material, the book should lend itself to various types of courses. A full-year course similar to that at Columbia would cover most of the book. A single-semester course on digital communications or an introductory course in communication theory would cover Chapters 6 and 7, following some brief introduction drawn from portions of Chaps. 3 and 4. A one-quarter course on networks could be based on Chapter 5. Courses focusing on analog communications could select from Chapters 3, 4, and 6.

ACKNOWLEDGEMENTS

The author has always found his research and professional practice in the field of telecommunications to provide an incomparable source of knowledge in this rapidly developing field. He is grateful to the hospitable facilities provided by the Center for Telecommunications Research, an Engineering Research Center supported by the National Science Foundation. Close contact with students, colleagues, and industrial participants in the Center has provided an exciting atmosphere of learning, and has provided the impetus for developing the new material introduced in this edition.

The preparation of this revision would not have been possible without the dedicated help of Betty Lim, Editorial Assistant in the Department of Electrical Engineering, and Leila Thomson, the author's secretary. He is grateful for their support.

Finally, acknowledgement is due to the author's many students and readers of the book over the years, who, through probing questions in class, on the phone, and by mail, have helped immeasurably in clarifying the concepts presented here.

Mischa Schwartz

INFORMATION TRANSMISSION, MODULATION, AND NOISE

CHAPTER
1

INTRODUCTION TO INFORMATION TRANSMISSION

1-1 INTRODUCTION

Information-handling systems in the millions are deployed worldwide—on the ground, in space, and even underwater. They include the ubiquitous telephone with which we are all familiar, data sets and intelligent terminals, computers of various types and sizes, facsimile systems, graphics and video display terminals, intelligent workstations and word-processing systems, even the TV sets appearing in almost all homes. Remote-sensing and telemetering systems, robots on factory floors—these and many others could be included as well. The list is almost endless.

Communications between such systems is of paramount importance. Most often these systems are connected together through networks to avoid the problem of having a "user" (a human using such a system, a system itself, or a program running on a system) require a specific, dedicated connection to every other user with which it might want to communicate. (Just think of the number of wires, cables, or fibers you might require in your home if your telephone and PC were each required to be connected separately to all other telephones and PCs in the world!) An idealized example of such a telecommunications network appears in Fig. 1-1. The most common real example is the set of telephone networks worldwide, handling primarily voice traffic, but with data traffic playing a larger and larger role. Packet-switching networks, deployed worldwide over the past two decades, carry data primarily. Studies underway worldwide are consider-

1

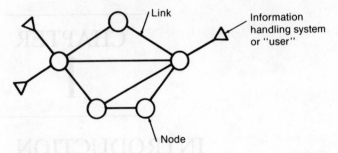

FIGURE 1-1
Idealized telecommunications network.

ing newer types of networks, designed to carry all types of traffic—data, voice, graphics, video, among other examples—in an integrated fashion.

All have the general form of Fig. 1-1. The information-handling systems or users are connected to *nodes*, or switches, in the network. These switches in turn are interconnected via communication *links*. Links—between users and network nodes and between nodes themselves—can be twisted wire pairs; radio connections, including microwave and satellite communications; coaxial cable; optical fibers; etc. The links can be on land, in space, or underwater.

The engineering design of these networks is a complex subject for study. There are three basic sets of issues to be considered. The first is that of topological design: How many switching stations (nodes) does one need, how many links are required, and how should they be interconnected? The second is that of switching the communications traffic appropriately through the networks to ensure a given set of "users" are connected together and can carry on a "conversation". We purposely put the words "users" and "conversations" in quotes because it is clear from our earlier comment that "users" do not necessarily have to be humans. Machines are required to communicate as well and carry on "conversations" with one another. This leads to the third set of issues to be addressed—how does one ensure that two or more users, even if appropriately connected, can carry on an "understandable conversation"? In a voice network it is up to the users themselves, the humans carrying on the conversation, to resolve any such problem. With communicating machines this issue must be addressed by embedding the necessary intelligence within the machines themselves.

This book addresses only a small, albeit extremely vital, portion of this overall telecommunications problem. It focuses principally on link communication or on communications between neighboring nodes or between end users and nodes in the picture of Fig. 1-1. This is the area of point-to-point communications. In Chap. 5 of this book we do probe further, albeit quite briefly, into some of the other (network) issues as well. In the next few paragraphs we outline some of these other areas in the broad field of telecommunications and information handling. We point out in more detail where the material of this book fits in.

Readers interested in pursuing in detail questions related to network topological design are referred to [SCHW 1977].[1] The other two issues raised above are addressed in more detail in [SCHW 1987][2] and [TANE 1989].[3]

1-2   LAYERED COMMUNICATION ARCHITECTURES

The question of having disparate machines, of different types and from different manufacturers, able to communicate openly and understandably, began to be addressed more than a decade ago by many engineers and computer scientists meeting under the auspices of an international standards body, the International Organization for Standardization ISO. Building on earlier work of computer manufacturers and designers of data networks, they standardized on a communications architecture called the Reference Model for Open Systems Interconnection (OSI Reference Model), the implementation of which would enable disparate intelligent systems to communicate. This architecture, represented schematically in Fig. 1-2, is an example of a layered architecture, with different functions of the complete communications process allocated to different layers. Implicit in this architecture is the assumption that all communication is digital, with information carried in binary (bit) format. We shall see later, however, that point-to-point communications over the physical medium can be carried out by analog as well as digital signaling.

Note that the seven layers indicated are classified into two types. The lowest three layers, labeled *network services*, are assumed to reside within each of the nodes of Fig. 1-1. Alternatively, an information-handling system could serve as a network node as well as an end user, in which case it would have the ability to carry out network services. These services, taken together, ensure that blocks of data (usually called *packets*) leaving one end node, a source node, are routed properly to the other end node, the destination node. As shown in both Figs. 1-1 and 1-2, intermediate network nodes may be involved in this process. Three types of tasks are involved: The network layer carries out the routing or switching along an appropriate path through the network. The data link layer's function is to ensure that packets moving along a link from one node to its neighbor arrive at the receiving node error-free, and in sequence. The physical layer's function is to ensure communication on the link between nodes. It provides the means by which a binary symbol (a bit, if digital signaling of the binary type is used) is transmitted to the other node of the link.

---

[1][SCHW 1977] M. Schwartz, *Computer Communication Network Design and Analysis*, Prentice-Hall, Englewood Cliffs, N.J., 1977.

[2][SCHW 1987] M. Schwartz, *Telecommunication Networks: Protocols, Modeling, and Analysis*, Addison-Wesley, Reading, Mass., 1987.

[3][TANE 1989] A. Tanenbaum, *Computer Networks*, Prentice-Hall, Englewood Cliffs, N.J., 1989.

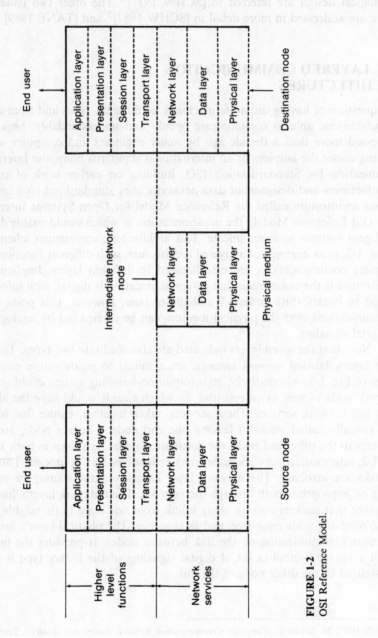

FIGURE 1-2
OSI Reference Model.

The higher layers, on the other hand, ensure that the information sent from one user to another not only arrives there, but arrives there correctly, in the proper sequence if blocked into packets, and, most important, in understandable form. The key work *understandable* implies that information addressed to a particular machine or user reaches that machine with the appropriate syntax and semantic structure. (As a simple example, consider the problem of having the output of a Pascal program running on a computer drive a laser printer thousands of miles away, or suppose the program output is to drive a multicolored graphics terminal or workstation.) It is the function of the presentation layer in this model to ensure presentation of the appropriate character string at the destination machine, i.e., to do appropriate mapping of one sequence of characters into another. This is the syntactical function noted above. The application layer handles the semantics of the information interchange. Finally, the session and transport layers shown in Fig. 1-2 are concerned, respectively, with maintaining an appropriate dialog, if necessary (e.g. allowing each end user to take its turn at an appropriate time in transmitting information) and ensuring correct, sequenced, and timely delivery of packets to the destination end users [SCHW 1987].

Where does this book fit into this complex communications process? As noted earlier, we focus principally on the lowest layer, the physical layer, although we do return briefly to networks in Chap. 5. As already stated, the physical layer is the one that ensures communication between end user and a node in the network, or between adjacent nodes in a network. Without this "workhorse" activity, no network could exist. The physical layer must provide this service whether the link is meters long or millions of meters long, as in communications between a distant space probe and a ground-based computer network. It must provide this service in the presence of noise, interference, and other deleterious effects. It may require communication over free space, over a microwave link, over an optical fiber, or underwater. Appropriate signals, transmitters, and receivers must be designed for this purpose.

Physical-layer communication embodies by its very nature *point-to-point communications*. Much of the work on these facilities either predates the development of packet switching and computer networks, or has developed alongside it. It is clearly necessary to the proper functioning of these networks, however. Telephone networks have contributed heavily to the development of point-to-point communications. Satellite and space communications have been major driving forces as well.

In the past, point-to-point communications could be studied in isolation, without the need to involve the concept of networks. This is no longer the case. Networks of all types have begun to proliferate. These include local-area, fiber-optic metropolitan, and wide-area networks. They involve CATV networks, satellite networks, space-earth networks. Ships at sea are tied into networks. We may someday see large-scale home entertainment networks, with video movies transmitted on demand to the home. Integrated networks are expected to proliferate. It is clear that telecommunication networks play an increasingly

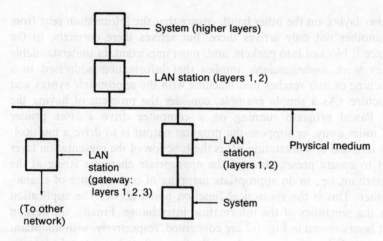

FIGURE 1-3
Example of a bus-type LAN.

larger role in this information/telecommunications age we are entering. Point-to-point communications can no longer be considered as an isolated subject for study. It must be seen as an integral part of the communication architectures, to wit, the very important physical layer.

Consider a concrete example of a local-area network (LAN), to be discussed in more detail in Chap. 5. LANs have proliferated rapidly in past years in almost all countries of the world. They are used to interconnect terminals, PCs, workstations, host computers, printers, and other devices within a small private environment (an office, a building, or a campus, for example). The physical media used to interconnect these systems are twisted wire pairs, coaxial cables, and, quite recently, optical fibers. Access to the medium is provided via a LAN station. These stations all handle the physical-layer and data-link functions of Fig. 1-2; some implement layer-3 functions if they interconnect a number of LANs, or connect a given LAN to a larger, external network. They are thus the nodes in the network. The systems connected to the LAN stations—the terminals, printers, computers, and other devices—incorporate the higher-level functions of Fig. 1-2.

An example of a bus-type LAN appears in Fig. 1-3 (ring structures are also used commonly and are discussed in Chap. 5). Each station in general transmits to, and receives from, another station. The station incorporating functions of layers 1, 2, and 3, connecting this network to another, is often called a *gateway* as shown. The physical-layer portion of the station has two major functions: it encodes (and decodes) data into a form appropriate for transmission over the physical medium, and it provides a transmit/receive function for actually supplying energy to and receiving energy from the medium. These encoding/decoding and transmit/receive functions are precisely those we shall be stressing throughout this book.

1-3 PHYSICAL LAYER: POINT-TO-POINT COMMUNICATIONS

As already noted a number of times, the bulk of this book deals with point-to-point communications, as exemplified in the study of the physical layer of modern telecommunication networks. In this section we outline the basic engineering questions arising in the design of a good point-to-point link. Many of these are raised again in detail in the chapters following.

The basic problem is that of transmitting signals representing information varying with time over a physical medium connecting one side, the transmitter, with the other side, the receiver. The LAN of Fig. 1-3 provides one simple example. The medium could in general be free space, the atmosphere, a pair of wires or a coaxial cable, or, more and more commonly these days, an optical fiber. Each medium tends to distort the signals in a characteristic way: noise and interference will be introduced, nonlinearities may be present, or the medium may have a physical limit on the rate at which communications over it can take place. The transmitter and receiver themselves may introduce distortion effects. How does one then design the signals introduced at the transmitter to overcome these problems? How does one design transmitter–receiver combinations that operate effectively together despite the effect of the medium? The encode/decode and transmit/receive functions of the LAN stations of Fig. 1-3 provide an example.

Generalizing the LAN-station example, consider the point-to-point communication system shown in Fig. 1-4. This adds the ability to launch a sinusoidal signal called a *carrier* into the medium. As we shall see later, this is done for a number of reasons: antennas may be used to focus the signal energy, allowing more power to converge on the receiver; multiple signals, each at a different frequency, may be carried simultaneously without interference over the same medium. The actual information to be transmitted is then imposed as a time variation or modulation of the carrier. The receiver must *demodulate*, or retrieve, the information from the time-varying carrier. The information-carrying signal is commonly called the *modulating* signal, to distinguish it from the carrier. We are of course all familiar with amplitude and frequency modulation of carriers; other techniques are used as well, and we shall compare a number of these in this book. (The LAN of Fig. 1-3 is an example of a *baseband* system, with no sinusoidal carrier used).

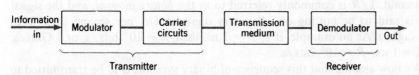

FIGURE 1-4
Communication system.

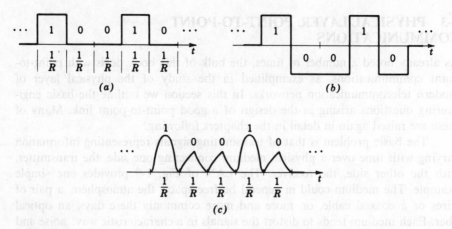

FIGURE 1-5
Binary signal transmission. (*a*) On-off sequence. (*b*) Polar sequence. (*c*) Arbitrary waveshapes.

The primary stress in this book will be on *digital* communications because of their ever-increasing importance in modern telecommunications. (As we shall see, modern voice communication systems deal with voice signals in digital form. Facsimile systems operate digitally. Video, or picture, signals will some day be transmitted in digital form as well. Telecommunications networks, as already noted, are moving rapidly to an all-digital environment.) We therefore provide an example of some of the ideas raised above through the study of a typical digital message as it is transmitted over a point-to-point link connecting a transmitter–receiver combination. We further focus on a *binary* signal, since this is the simplest form of a digital signal. This binary signal will then be utilized, as a particularly simple form of information-bearing signal, throughout this book.

By a binary message or signal we mean a sequence of two types of pulses of known shape, occurring at regularly spaced intervals, as shown in Fig. 1-5. Although the shape of the pulses is presumed known in advance, the occurrence of one or the other, say the 1 or 0 in Fig. 1-5, is not known beforehand, and the information carried is actually given by the particular sequence of binary 1's and 0's coming in. We shall most commonly use the rectangular pulse shapes of Fig. 1-5*a* and *b* in this book for simplicity's sake, but other types of signal shape could be or are being used as well.

These pulses are shown occurring regularly every $1/R$ seconds, or at a rate of R/second. $1/R$ is commonly referred to as the *binary interval*, and the signal source is said to be putting out R binary digits or *bits* per second (*bits* from *bi*nary digi*ts*). As an example, if $1/R = 1$ ns, then $R = 10^9$ bits/s, or 1 Gbit/s. If $1/R = 1$ μs, $R = 10^6$ bits/s.

We now assume that this sequence of binary symbols is to be transmitted to a distant destination. A typical system block diagram, a more detailed version of Fig. 1-4, is shown in Fig. 1-6. The two filters shown, one at the transmitter and

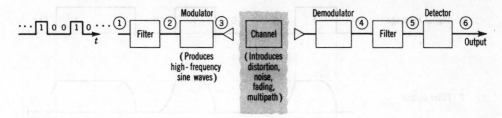

FIGURE 1-6
Transmission of digital message.

the other at the receiver, represent the filtering of the signals either innately present in the system circuitry or purposely introduced as part of the design. The demodulator at the receiver serves to strip away the high-frequency sine-wave modulation introduced at the transmitter modulator. The modulation process is necessary to enable the signals to be effectively radiated into space (or whatever other medium is represented by the channel shown). The purpose of the detector at the receiver is to reproduce, as well as possible, the original signal sequence representing the digital data to be transmitted.

Some typical waveshapes, corresponding to the numbered points in Fig. 1-6, are shown sketched in Fig. 1-7. Note that the filters cause symbols to overlap into adjacent time slots. If carried too far, these interfere with symbols actually transmitted in the adjacent time slots, leading to confusion in symbol interpretation and possible errors at the system output. *Intersymbol interference* is a significant problem in many data communication systems, being particularly troublesome in the transmission of data via telephone lines. We shall have occasion to discuss the problem further in later chapters, and will indicate some design techniques used to overcome it.

The modulator chosen in this example happens to be of the amplitude-modulation (AM) type, in which a sine-wave oscillator adjusts its amplitude to the incoming signals. We could equally well have depicted the output of a frequency-shift-keyed (FSK) modulator, in which the carrier frequency alternates between two frequencies, depending on the symbol coming in (this is the digital version of an FM signal), or a phase-shift-keyed (PSK) output, in which the polarity ($\pm$) of the sine wave depends on the incoming signal.

In this example the channel is shown as having introduced noise during transmission, so that the demodulator output represents the sum of signal plus noise waveshapes. Note that the noise introduced tends to obscure the signal if the two are comparable in magnitude. Some channels (the telephone line, for example) introduce signal distortion as well (although this effect could be modeled by incorporating it in the filter following the demodulator). Others introduce signal fading, in which the received signal amplitude is found to fluctuate randomly, or so-called *multipath* effects, in which the radiated transmitter energy for one signal symbol, following several alternative paths to the

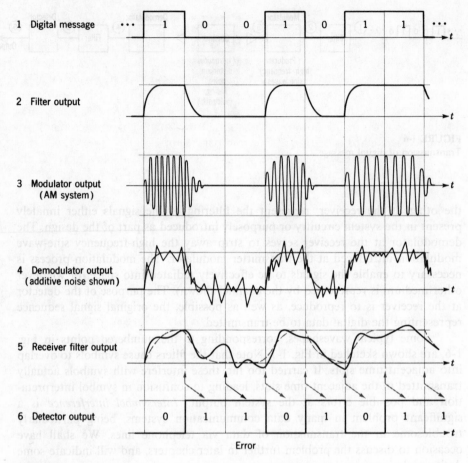

FIGURE 1-7
Waveshapes in digital system.

receiver appears at the receiver as a sequence of received symbols. Examples of this latter type of randomly fading channel include some microwave links, short-wave radio transmission via the ionosphere, and underwater and seismic communications, among others. For simplicity's sake we shall stress additive noise effects in this book [SCHW 1966].[4]

The receiver filter serves to eliminate some of the noise, at the expense, however, of further distorting the signal transmitted. This is shown pictorially in

---

[4]See [SCHW 1966], M. Schwartz, W. R. Bennett, and S. Stein, *Communication Systems and Techniques*, McGraw-Hill, New York, 1966, for a comprehensive treatment of such channels.

Fig. 1-7, in which the dashed lines of parts (4) and (5) represent the signal term, while the solid lines represent the composite sum of signal and noise.

To finally reproduce the original signal message, the detector must sample the receiver filter output once every bit interval and decide *as well as possible* whether a 1 or 0 was transmitted. It is apparent from part (5) of Fig. 1-7 that the appropriate sampling times, in this example, occur at the end of each bit interval, since it is there that the filtered signals reach their maximum amplitudes. Mistakes can be made, however, with noise obscuring the correct symbol. An example of an error occurring is shown in part (6) of Fig. 1-7.

We have purposely used the words "as well as possible" twice in the discussion above because they play a key role in the overall design of any communication system. In the context of the simple digital communication system we have been describing, these words have a rather precise meaning. It is apparent that we would like to transmit any arbitrary sequence of data symbols with as small a number of errors occurring as is possible, costwise. The fact that errors will occur is apparent. Noise is always introduced in a system (we shall have a great deal to say on this subject later in the book), physical transmitters have power limitations so that one cannot generally increase the signal strength as much as necessary in order to overcome the noise, intersymbol interference is generally a problem, signal fluctuations during transmission give rise to possible errors, etc.

A comprehensive engineering design of a data system such as this one would have to take into account all possible sources of error and try to minimize their effect. This includes appropriate design of the signals at the transmitter. That is: How does one shape the signals or design the transmitter filter? Given various means of transmitting the binary symbols at the required high frequency —the AM technique shown in Fig. 1-7, FSK, PSK, etc.—which is most appropriate for the problem at hand, including the particular channel over which transmission will take place? We shall find in discussing this particular question later in the book that there is the usual engineering trade-off between the various modulation techniques. Thus PSK, although generally most effective in terms of conserving power or minimizing errors, is difficult to use over fading channels, and its use introduces severe phase-control problems. FSK is generally less effective in the presence of noise and requires wider system bandwidths (a term to be defined in the next chapter), but is more effective over fading channels. Current optical fiber (lightwave) systems use the AM (on–off keyed, or OOK) technique. Work is going on on introducing PSK and FSK techniques as well.

With a specific modulation scheme chosen, how does one design the receiver? How does one minimize intersymbol interference and noise? How does one design the detector and the decision-making circuitry associated with it?

These are just a few of the design questions that arise in the actual development of a digital system of the type we have been considering. (We have, for example, ignored timing problems associated with the sequential transmission of 1's and 0's every $1/R$ s. This is particularly important in the design of systems with the transmitter and receiver located thousands and even millions of miles apart, where the receiver must nonetheless always maintain the same timing as the transmitter.)

It is one of the purposes of this book to approach problems such as these systematically, indicating how one does go about designing a particular system. Although we shall stress for simplicity's sake the effects of noise and filtering, since their effect is important in every communication system, some of the other problems noted will be treated as well.

Now assume the system has been "optimally" designed. We have minimized the number of errors that will occur, on the average, by appropriate design at both transmitter and receiver. How good is it? Is the resultant design appropriate for our needs (i.e., for the particular application for which intended)? This requires a quantitative system evaluation, modeling the presumed effect of the channel, noise introduced, etc., and such an evaluation will be one of the subjects treated in this book. For this purpose we shall find it necessary to introduce statistical concepts and approach the combined problems of system design and evaluation statistically.

If the error rate of the system, the average number of errors occurring per unit time, is too high, more complex system configurations, with their attendant increased cost, may be called for. These include signal coding techniques, sophisticated error detection and correction procedures, etc.

This raises another extremely important question: For a given channel over which we desire to communicate, is it possible to keep improving the system performance, i.e., reduce its error rate, as much as we like, with appropriate increased complexity of the system design? This is obviously a basic question in all communications design, for if the answer is "no," there is no sense in even trying to design more complex systems.

To answer this question we choose to phrase it in somewhat more precise fashion. The question is now: With the rate of transmission of binary symbols, R bits/s, fixed, as is the power available at the transmitter, is it possible, for a given channel, to reduce the error rate as much as desired (with appropriate system design and complexity)? The answer, as first established by Claude Shannon in 1948 to 1949 in a monumental piece of work [SHAN 1948], [SHAN 1949],[5] is "yes," with one qualification. That is, his work was restricted to the study of a channel introducing noise only (intersymbol interference and fading effects were not included). This has since been extended to a few other channels by other investigators.

Shannon found that the chance of an error occurring may ideally be reduced as low as one likes by appropriate coding of the incoming signals, provided the binary signaling rate R, in bits per second, is less than a specified number determined by the transmitter power, channel noise, and channel re-

---

[5][SHAN 1948] C. E. Shannon, "A Mathematical Theory of Communication," *Bell System Tech. J.*, vol. 27, pp. 379–423, July 1948; pp. 623–656, October 1948. [SHAN 1949] C. E. Shannon, "Communication in the Presence of Noise," *Proc. IRE*, vol. 37, pp. 10–21, January 1949.

sponse time or bandwidth (this latter concept will be discussed in detail in the next chapter). If one tries to push too many bits per second over the channel, the errors begin to mount up rapidly. The maximum rate of transmission of signals over the channel is referred to as the *channel capacity*.

Since the channel capacity is obviously an important concept in systems design (one can determine from this whether it pays to develop more complex systems), we shall devote some time to exploring its significance. The remainder of this chapter is devoted to a qualitative discussion of this concept, indicating why one physically expects a channel capacity to exist. There is a semantic difficulty that must be mentioned, however. We choose to use the word *channel* here most often to denote the physical medium, or link, over which transmission takes place. Many authors include in the channel various portions of the transmitter and receiver as well. Generally the meaning is clear from the context of the discussion. Shannon's channel capacity actually refers to this more general class of channels. To avoid confusion, we shall use the term *system capacity*, and, as we explain in the next section, all portions of the transmitter and receiver, as well as the physical channel, contribute to determining the capacity.

Since the maximum rate of transmission of binary symbols over a given channel is fixed, one would like to know what the binary rate R of a given signal source is. This is particularly true in the case of sources that are initially nonbinary in nature and that must be converted to binary symbols. These include speech, TV or facsimile, telemetry signals, etc. The concept of information content of a given message, in terms of the bits needed to represent it, is thus also explored in this chapter.

One last word before we close this section. We have emphasized digital communications here because of its relative simplicity as well as its technological importance. The questions raised here hold as well for the other types of communication systems. Thus one is always interested in "optimizing" system performance. The major difficulty arising in much of communication system design and evaluation, however, is that no simple criterion exists as to "optimum performance." How does one determine whether a particular speech signal is reproduced as effectively as possible? When does a TV picture have an "optimum" appearance? It is apparent that for continuously varying (analog) signals such as these, simple performance measures may be hard to justify, since much of the essential system evaluation can only be done subjectively. Yet the techniques of minimizing noise or of appropriate signal filtering that we shall discuss are significant in these types of systems as well as in strictly digital ones, and we will be able to establish some measure of their performance.

1-4 INFORMATION AND SYSTEM CAPACITY

As we mentioned in the previous section, the information content of a message to be transmitted must be established in order to determine whether or not the message may be transmitted over a given channel. By the information content we mean the number of binary symbols that will ultimately be necessary, on the average, to transmit it. Although we may in actuality not transmit binary symbols, but choose to transmit a more complex signal pattern, we prefer to normalize all signal messages to their binary equivalents for simplicity's sake. (This conversion to a binary equivalent will be discussed further both in this chapter and in chapters that follow.)

Since all communication systems transmit *information* in one form or another and since we desire some measure of the information content of messages to be transmitted, it is important first to establish some measure of what is actually meant by the concept *information*. Although a precise mathematical definition can be set up for this concept, we shall rely on our intuitive sense in this introductory text.

Consider a student attending a class in which the teacher spends the entire time whistling one continuous note. Obviously, attending such a class would be a waste of time. What could one possibly learn from the one note? (Even if it were important for the student to repeat the sound exactly, he would be better off staying at home listening to a recording.) Perhaps in the next class the teacher chooses to devote the entire hour to a reading, word for word, from the text: no time for questions, no pauses, no original thoughts. Again why come to class (aside from the irrelevant fact that many persons might not then take the opportunity to read the book for themselves)?

What is the point to these hypothetical and obviously made-up stories? A student comes to class to receive *information*. That is, the teacher and student are in class to discuss new material or, at least, review old material in a new way.

The words and phrases used should thus be *changing* continuously; they should, in most cases, be *unpredictable* (otherwise—why come to class?).

The key phrase here is *unpredictable* change. If information is to be conveyed, we must presumably have sounds or, more generally, signals changing unpredictably with time. A continuous trilling of one note conveys no information to you. If the note is varied in a manner that you can interpret, however, the "signal" begins to convey meaning and information.

The binary sequence of the previous section was one simple example of a signal to be transmitted that is changing unpredictably in time. There the specific sequences of 1's and 0's were unknown beforehand and corresponded to the message to be transmitted.

So the transmission of information is related to signals changing with time, and changing in an unpredictable way. (For a well-known melody or old story conveys no new information although made up of changing notes or words.)

Why is it so important to stress these points? As noted previously, if we, as engineers, are to design systems to transmit information and are interested in the best possible type of system given practical equipment and a limited budget, we must know (at least intuitively) what it is we are transmitting and the effect of the system on this quantity.

To see how these concepts fit into our work in communication, consider the voltage-time diagram of Fig. 1-8. Assume that we have an interval of time T

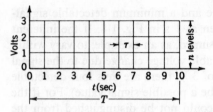

FIGURE 1-8
Voltage–time diagram.

seconds long in which to transmit information and a maximum voltage amplitude (because of power limitations) that we can use. (In Fig. 1-8, T is 10 s, and the maximum voltage is 3 V.) A natural question to ask is: How much information can be transmit in this interval? Can we put a tag on the amount, and how does it depend on our system? (Note that the system has already introduced one limitation—that of power.)

The next question is: Why a limit to the amount of information? If information transmission is related to signals changing unpredictably with time, why not just change the signal as rapidly as we like and over as many subdivisions of the maximum amplitude as we like? This would imply increasing the information content indefinitely.

We deal with physical systems, however, and these systems do not allow us to increase the rate of signal change indefinitely and to distinguish indefinitely many voltage amplitudes, or levels:

1. All our systems have energy-storage devices present, and changing the signal implies changing the energy content. There is a limit on the rate of doing this determined by the particular system.
2. Every system provides inherent (even if small) variations or fluctuations in voltage, or whatever parameter is used to measure the signal amplitude, and we cannot subdivide amplitudes indefinitely. These unwanted fluctuations of a parameter to be varied are called noise. This noise is exactly the noise we noted as being introduced during transmission over a channel in the previous section. The channels discussed there are all examples of physical systems of the type with which we deal.

Consider some simple examples: the twisted-wire pair that is used for telephone communications to the home is capable of transmitting binary signals at a rate of several hundred thousand bits/s over distances that are not too long; local area networks, covering short distances, transmit at millions of bits/s (Mbits/s); optical fibers can, however, transmit at the rate of billions of bits/s (Gbits/s) for much longer distances. (Electronic devices interfacing with the optics will tend to reduce these numbers.) Coaxial cable used in CATV systems can transmit hundreds of Mbits/s. Optical fibers tend to be less noisy than wire and cable as well.

For any of these and other media together with their transmitter/receiver pairs, generically encompassed by the term physical *system*, say there is a *minimum* time τ required for energy change and a minimum detectable signal-amplitude change. As an example, τ is given as 1 s in Fig. 1-8. If the inherent voltage fluctuations of the system may be assumed, as an example, to vary within ± 1 V most of the time, the minimum detectable voltage change due to the signal is 1 V. With a maximum voltage amplitude of 3 V, there are thus four detectable levels of signal (0 voltage being assumed to be a possible signal value). For if the signal were to change by less than 1 V, it could not be distinguished from the undesired noise fluctuations introduced by the system.

If the "amount of information" transmitted in T seconds is related to the number of different and distinguishable signal–amplitude combinations we can transmit in that time—as we might intuitively feel to be the case—it is apparent that the information capacity of the system is limited. It is exactly these arguments, phrased in a much more quantitative manner, that were used by Shannon in developing his capacity expression referred to in the previous section. (Recall that the word *channel* was used in that section to refer to the physical medium over which signals are transmitted. Limitations on signal-time response may be produced anywhere in the systems of Figs. 1-4 or 1-6. The filters shown in Fig. 1-6, for example, definitely introduce specific time responses. Also, noise is often introduced at the receiver as well as during transmission. We shall thus refer here to *system capacity*, considering the effect of the overall system, rather than *channel capacity*, as commonly done in the literature.)

The capacity of the system, or maximum rate at which it can transmit information, should be measurable in terms of τ and n, the number of distinguishable amplitude levels. (Both limitations may be produced again anywhere in the system of Fig. 1-4, but we are speaking of the effect of the overall system.)

We can derive a more quantitative measure of system capacity in the following manner. We assume that the information transmitted in the 10-s interval of Fig. 1-8 is directly related to the number of different signal-amplitude combinations in that time. For example, two different signals that might be transmitted are shown in Fig. 1-9. They differ over the first two intervals and have the same amplitudes over the remaining 8 s. How many such combinations can we specify? There are four different possibilities in the first interval, and corresponding to each such possibility there are four more in the second interval,

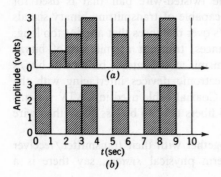

FIGURE 1-9
Two different signals.

or a total of $4^2 = 16$ possibilities in two intervals. (The reader should tabulate the different combinations to check this result.) Repeating this procedure, we find that there are 4^{10} combinations of different signal amplitudes in 10 s.

If, instead of 4, we had had n levels and, instead of 1-s, τ-s intervals, the number of combinations in T seconds would have been

$$n^{T/\tau}$$

Under our basic assumption the information transmitted in T seconds is related to this number of signal combinations. We might feel intuitively, however, that information should be proportional to the length of time of transmission. Doubling T (10 s here) should double the information content of a message. The information content can be made proportional to T by taking the logarithm of $n^{T/\tau}$, giving us

$$\text{Information transmitted in } T \text{ seconds} \propto \frac{T}{\tau} \log n \qquad (1\text{-}1)$$

The proportionality factor will depend on the base of logarithm used. The most common choice is the base 2, or

$$\text{Information} = \frac{T}{\tau} \log_2 n \qquad (1\text{-}2)$$

The unit of information defined in this manner is the *bit* (mentioned earlier and to be explained in the next section). The information content of the 10-s strip of Fig. 1-8 is, for example,

$$10 \log_2 4 = 20 \text{ bits}$$

A 5-s strip would have 10 bits of information. If there had been only two possible voltage levels (say 0 and 1), the information conveyed in 10 s would have been 10 bits.

The system capacity can be defined as the maximum *rate* of transmitting information. From Eq. (1-2) this is simply

$$C = \frac{\text{information}}{T} = \frac{1}{\tau} \log_2 n \qquad (1\text{-}3)$$

and the units are bits per second.

System capacity is thus inversely proportional to the minimum interval τ over which signals can change and proportional to the logarithm of n.

We shall show in Chap. 2, in reviewing some simple concepts of networks, that there is an intimate inverse relationship between time response and frequency response. This will enable us to relate information transmitted and system capacity to the system "bandwidth."

These two parameters of system behavior, τ (or its inverse, bandwidth) and n (or, as we shall see, the signal-to-noise ration in a system), are basic in any study of communication systems. Much of the material of this book will thus be devoted to a study of the time (or frequency) and noise characteristics of different networks and the frequency–noise characteristics of various practical communication systems.

1-5 BINARY DIGITS IN INFORMATION TRANSMISSION

The information content of a signal was defined in the previous section by Eq. (1-2),

$$\text{Information} = \frac{T}{\tau}\log_2 n \quad \text{bits}$$

The use of the logarithm to the base 2 in defining the unit of information can be justified in an alternative and instructive way. Assume that a signal to be transmitted will vary anywhere from 0 to 7 V with any one voltage range as likely as the next. Because of the system limitations described in Sec. 1-4, the signal can be uniquely defined only at the integral voltage values and will not change appreciably over an interval τ seconds long. (The noise fluctuations are assumed to have the same magnitudes on the average as in the example of Sec. 1-4.)

The signal can thus be replaced by a signal of the type shown in Fig. 1-9; during any interval τ s long it will occupy one of eight voltage levels (0 to 7 V), each one equally likely to be occupied.

The process of replacing a continuous signal by such a discrete signal is called the *quantizing process*. A typical signal and its quantized equivalent are shown in Fig. 1-10.

The signal can of course be transmitted by simply sending the successive integral voltage values as they appear. In any one interval any one of eight different voltages must be sent. The informational content of the signal is thus related to these eight different voltage levels (i.e., one of eight choices).

We ask ourselves, however: Is there another way of sending this information so that fewer than eight numbers are needed completely to specify the signal in any one interval? The informational content will then be assumed equal to the smallest number needed. The answer is "yes": the simplest way uniquely to label

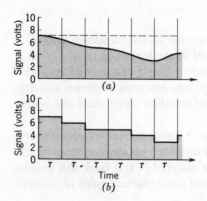

(a)

(b)

Time

FIGURE 1-10
Quantization of a signal. (a) Original signal. (b) Quantized signal.

a particular level and to indicate its selection is by means of a series of yes–no instructions. For this particular type of signal with eight levels three such yes–no instructions are needed.

To indicate the procedure followed, assume that the signal is at 7 V during a particular instant. We first decide whether the proper level lies among the first four or the last four levels. If "yes," we use a designating symbol 1 for each level in the group of four; if "no," a designating symbol 0. In this case, then, levels 0 to 3 are labeled 0, and levels 4 to 7 are labeled 1 (see Fig. 1-11a). We can thus immediately reject the 0 levels and concentrate on choosing one of the remaining four. Our area of choice has been reduced considerably.

Again we separate the remaining levels into two parts. That half which does not contain the desired level (7 in this case) is labeled "no," or 0; the other, "yes," or 1. This is shown in Fig. 1-11b. Again half the levels are eliminated, leaving only 6 and 7. This time we find level 7 uniquely singled out. Note that this method required three consecutive yes–no responses.

Proceeding in a similar way, we could single out any one of the eight possible voltages. They can thus be uniquely identified by means of three 0 or 1 labels. This method of identification is called *binary coding*. A typical identification table would appear as follows:

	Binary coding
7	111
6	110
5	101
4	100
3	011
2	010
1	001
0	000

Instead of transmitting this signal as one of eight different voltage levels, we need transmit only three successive yes–no (voltage–no-voltage) voltages during a particular interval. Any one yes–no label is a *bit*. Three bits are thus required to transmit the desired information as to a particular voltage level occupied for the eight-level signal under discussion.

This process of binary coding is the simplest one that can be devised for uniquely tagging a signal. With binary selection only three consecutive numbers,

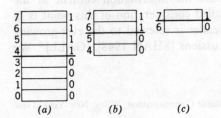

(a)   (b)   (c)

FIGURE 1-11
Binary selection of a signal. (*a*) First choice. (*b*) Second choice. (*c*) Third choice.

or 3 bits, are needed to transmit the informational content of this particular signal in any one time interval. For 16 levels 4 bits are required, for 32 levels 5 bits, and so on. For n levels $\log_2 n$ bits are required.

If the information in three successive intervals, each containing eight possible levels, is to be transmitted, then 3 bits for each interval, or 9 in all, are required for the signal transmission.

For T/τ intervals and n levels, $T/\tau \log_2 n$ bits must be transmitted. The information content of a signal is defined to be equal to the number of bits, or binary choices, needed for transmission.

1-6   RELATION BETWEEN SYSTEM CAPACITY AND INFORMATION CONTENT OF MESSAGES

In Sec. 1-4 we pointed out that the capacity (or ability) of a system to transmit information depended on the system time response and its ability to distinguish among different levels of a signal.

The capacity of a given system is defined as the maximum amount of information per second (in bits per second) that the system can transmit. Much of the rest of this book will be devoted to relating the system limitations on information transmission to bandwidth and system noise properties. Here we take time to consider the relation between system capacity and the information content of signals to be transmitted.

Being able to measure the ability of a particular system to transmit information is not enough. The more basic question in information transmission should perhaps be phrased: Which system or group of systems will have sufficient capacity to transmit a specified class of signals or information-bearing messages? In order to answer this question, we must be able to measure the information content of a signal.

For example, assume that we are interested in transmitting a speech delivered in the English language. In order to choose a system for transmission, we must be able to determine the information content of the speech and the rate at which it is to be transmitted. The system chosen will then obviously have to accommodate the rate of information to be transmitted, or will have to possess a capacity greater than the rate of information transmission desired. The system must thus be "matched" to the class of signals being transmitted.

In order to choose a system or group of systems with the proper information capacity, we first determine or measure the information content of the signals that are to be transmitted. The detailed consideration of this point is in the realm of information theory, and the reader is referred to the ever-growing literature on this subject for thorough discussions [SHAN 1948], [GALL].[6] We

---

[6] [GALL] R. G. Gallager, *Information Theory and Reliable Communication*, Wiley, New York, 1968.

shall, however, indicate the approach used, and we shall find some of the material of value in our later work.

We have already shown, in Secs. 1-4 and 1-5, that, where different values of a signal are *equally likely* and where the signal appears at discrete voltage levels the information content of a signal is readily evaluated. It is simply the logarithm of the number of equally likely signal combinations possible in a given interval. [In the example we considered, $n^{T/\tau}$ was the number of equally likely signal combinations in T seconds, since each signal level was as likely to be occupied as any other. The information content of the strip T seconds long was thus $\log_2 n^{T/\tau} = (T/\tau)\log_2 n$.]

The equally likely case is a very restricted one, however. For example, if we were transmitting a speech in the English language by transmitting the different letters in the successive words uttered, this would correspond to assuming that each letter was equally likely to occur. This assumption is obviously not true, since we know, for example, that the letter e occurs much more frequently than the letter z, or any other letter for that matter. We could guess that a particular letter to come would be an e and be much more sure that we were right than if we had guessed q, z, or u.

But this prior knowledge of the greater chance of e rather than z occurring reduces the information content of the speech being transmitted. For, as we noted in Sec. 1-4, the amount of information transmitted depends on the *uncertainty* of the message. In particular, if e were known to be the only letter occurring in this speech, no information at all would be transmitted, since all uncertainty as to the message would vanish.

Thus, although the different number of signals in any one interval is still the gamut of all letters from a to z, the fact that some occur more frequently than other reduces the information content of the message. In T seconds the different signal combinations possible occur with differing relative frequencies, and the information content of the T-second message is reduced as compared with the equally likely case.

The same considerations obviously hold true in our representation of different signals by different voltage levels in Sec. 1-4. If a 3-V signal were to be the only signal transmitted, it would carry no information and transmission might just as well cease. If the 3-V signal were to be expected more often than any other, a message T seconds long would carry information, but the *information content* of the message would be less than if all voltage levels were equally likely. (Those signal combinations containing the 3-V level would be expected to occur more frequently than any of the others.)

The information content of a message thus relates not only to the number of possible signal combinations in the message but also to their *relative frequency of occurrence*. This in turn depends on the source of the message. The information content of a message in the English language depends on a knowledge of the structure of the language and its alphabet: the relative frequency of occurrence of each letter, of different combinations of letters, of word combinations, of sentence combinations, etc. All these structural properties of English affect the different possible signal combinations and their relative frequency of occurrence, and hence the information content of a particular signal.

The decrease in the information content of a message due to unequally likely signals results in the requirement of a correspondingly reduced system capacity for information transmission. Telegraph transmission of messages in the English language has long taken this into account by coding the letter e with the shortest telegraph symbol. This thus reduces the average time required for transmission of a message.

But how do we *quantitatively* measure the information content of a message in this more general case of signals with differing frequencies of occurrence? To study this case, we shall first assume that successive signals (the individual letters in the case of English) are independent of one another and then attempt some further generalization. The assumption of *independence* implies that the occurrence of any one signal does not affect in any way the occurrence of any other signal. In the case of a message in the English language this assumption implies that the occurrence of one letter does not affect the occurrence of any other. (A q coming up could then be followed by an x or a z, as well as by a u.) This assumption of independence is thus an oversimplification of a much more complicated situation in the case of English, but it does serve to simplify the analysis.

To develop a quantitative measure of the information content of a message, we shall first rewrite our result for the "equally likely" case in a different form. We recall that we showed that $n^{T/\tau}$ was the total possible number of signal combinations in T seconds if each signal lasted τ seconds and there were n possible levels in each interval.

If we were to look at many messages, each T seconds long, we would find that on the average each possible signal combination would occur with a relative frequency of $1/n^{T/\tau}$. For example, with $\tau = 1$ s and $n = 4$, 64 different combinations are possible in an interval 3 s long. The relative frequency of occurrence of each 3-s message would be $\frac{1}{64}$. In 10,000 such 3-s messages there would be approximately 10,000/64 messages of each of the 64 possibilities. The greater the number of 3-s messages we were to look at, the more closely any one signal combination would approach a relative frequency of $\frac{1}{64}$.

The relative frequency of occurrence of any one combination, or *event*, we define to be its probability of occurrence, or, symbolically, P. Thus

$$P \equiv \frac{\text{number of times event occurs}}{\text{total number of possibilities}} \qquad (1\text{-}4)$$

where the total number of possibilities must be very large compared with the number of possible events (10,000 as compared with 64 in the example just cited) if we are to have an accurate measure of the relative frequency.

For example, if we were interested in the probability of occurrence of a letter in the English alphabet, we would pick letters at random (say, from words on successive pages of a book to ensure independence of choice) and determine the number of times a given letter showed. We would have to pick many more than 26 total letters for our results to be valid, however.

If n possible events are specified to be the n possible signal levels, at any instant, of Sec. 1-4, then $P = 1/n$ for equally likely events. The information carried by the appearance of any one event in one interval is then

$$H_1 = \log_2 n = -\log_2 P \qquad \text{bits/interval} \tag{1-5}$$

Over m intervals of time (an interval is τ sec long) we should have m times as much information, assuming that each signal or event in time is independent. Therefore,

$$H = mH_1 = -m \log_2 P \qquad \text{bits in } m \text{ intervals} \tag{1-6}$$

The information available in T s is thus $(m = T/\tau)$

$$H = -\frac{T}{\tau} \log_2 P = \frac{T}{\tau} \log_2 n \qquad \text{bits in } T \text{ seconds} \tag{1-7}$$

as in Sec. 1-4.

Now consider the case where the different signal levels (or events) are not equally likely. For the sake of simplicity we first assume just two levels to be transmitted, 0 or 1, the first with probability p, the second with probability q. Then

$$p \equiv \frac{\text{number of times 0 occurs}}{\text{total number of possibilities}} \tag{1-8}$$

$$q \equiv \frac{\text{number of times 1 occurs}}{\text{total number of possibilities}} \tag{1-9}$$

Since either a 0 or a 1 must always come up, $p + q = 1$. (The number of times 0 comes up plus the number of times 1 comes up equals the total number of possibilities.)

For example, say that the message to be transmitted by this two-level signal device represents the birth of either a boy or a girl in the United States; 1 corresponds to boy, 0 to girl. After counting 1,000,000 births, we find that 480,000 boys and 520,000 girls were born. Then we estimate $p = 0.52$, $q = 0.48$, and $p + q = 1$.

What is now the information content of a particular message consisting of a group of 0's and 1's? Each time a 0 appears, we gain $-\log_2 p$ bits of information, and each time 1 appears we gain $-\log_2 q$ bits. If p and q are approximately each 0.5, either event occurring (0 or 1) carries almost the same amount of information. The two events are nearly equally likely. This is of course the case in the births of boys and girls in the United States to which we referred. But now assume that $p \gg q$ (0 occurs more frequently, on the average). Since $-\log_2 q \gg -\log_2 p$, the occurrence of a 1, the more *rarely occurring* event, carries *more* information.

This seems to agree with our previous discussion, where we point out that, the greater the uncertainty of an event occurring, the more the information carried. Does this again agree with intuition? We use births as an example once more, but this time consider the case of a family with five sons and no daughters. The father has given up all hope of a daughter, especially since both his family and that of his wife have a long history of a preponderance of male children. The father, waiting expectantly for his wife to give birth again, receives word that his wife has given birth to—a *boy*. So? That is nothing new. A boy was expected. But suppose his wife had given birth to—a *girl*! This news would be something tremendously different, it would carry much more information; it would be the completely unexpected.

More rarely occurring events thus carry more information than frequently occurring events in an intuitive sense, and our use of the $-\log_2 p$, $-\log_2 q$ formulation for information agrees with the intuitive concept.

The information carried by a group of 0 or 1 symbols should now be the sum of the bits of information carried by each appearance of 0 or of 1. If $p = 0.8$ and $q = 0.2$ and if p occurs 802 times in 1,000 possibilities, q occurring 198 times, the information content of the 1,000 appearances of a 0 or 1 is

$$H = -(802\log_2 0.8 + 198\log_2 0.2)$$

$$\doteq -1,000(0.8\log_2 0.8 + 0.2\log_2 0.2)$$

$$= -1,000(p\log_2 p + q\log_2 q)$$

(The dot over the equal sign indicates "approximately equal to.")

The information content of a longer message made up of many 0's and 1's thus depends on $p\log_2 p + q\log_2 q$, the information in bits per occurrence of a 0 or 1 times the relative frequency of occurrence of 0 or 1.

Generalizing for this case of two possible signals, we again consider a time interval T seconds long, subdivided into intervals τ seconds long. There are then $m = T/\tau$ possibilities for a 0 or 1 to occur. On the average ($m \gg 1/p$ and $1/q$) the 0 will appear $mp = (T/\tau)p$ times, the 1, $mq = (T/\tau)q$ times in the T-second interval. (Remember again that q and p represent, respectively, the probability or relative frequency of occurrence of a 1 and a 0.)

The information content of a message T seconds long is thus, on the average,

$$H = m(-p\log_2 p - q\log_2 q) \qquad \text{bits in } T \text{ seconds} \qquad (1\text{-}10)$$

The average information per interval τ seconds long is

$$H_{av} = \frac{H}{m} = -p\log_2 p - q\log_2 q \qquad \text{bits/interval} \qquad (1\text{-}11)$$

A communication system capable of transmitting this information should thus have an average capacity

$$C_{av} \geq \frac{H_{av}}{\tau} = \frac{1}{\tau}(-p\log_2 p - q\log_2 q) \qquad \text{bits/s} \qquad (1\text{-}12)$$

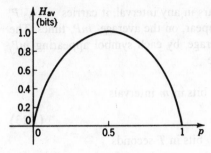

As a check consider the two possibilities, 0 or 1, equally likely. Then $p = q = 0.5$, and

$$H_{av} = \log_2 2 = 1 \text{ bit/interval}$$

or

$$\frac{T}{\tau}\log_2 2 = \frac{T}{\tau} \quad \text{bits in } T \text{ seconds}$$

(Note that $n = 2$ here.)

As a further check, $p = 1$, $q = 0$ or $q = 1$, $p = 0$ gives $H_{av} = 0$. This corresponds to the case of a completely determined message (all 0's or 1's), which should carry no information according to our previous intuitive ideas.

Since $q = 1 - p$ in this simple case, H_{av} may be plotted as a function of p to give the curve of Fig. 1-12 [SHAN 1948]. H_{av} reaches its maximum value of 1 bit per interval when $p = q = \frac{1}{2}$, or the two possibilities are equally likely. This is of course also in accord with our intuitive ideas that the maximum information should be transmitted when events are completely random, or equally likely to occur.

We can now generalize to the case of n possible signals or signal levels in any one signal interval τ seconds long. This could be the n levels of Sec. 1-4, the 26 possible letters in the English alphabet, any group of symbols or numbers of which one appears at a time, etc. We again seek an expression for the information content of a message T seconds long ($T > \tau$) and the average information in bits for the interval τ seconds long.

Let the relative frequency of occurrence, or probability, of each possible signal level or symbol be $P_1, P_2, \ldots, P_n$, respectively,

$$P_1 + P_2 + \cdots + P_n = 1$$

and, for the jth symbol, $0 \le P_j \le 1$. If we again assume that occurrences in adjacent intervals are independent (i.e., that any particular symbol occurring in any one interval does not affect the relative rate of occurrence of any of the symbols in any other interval), we can find the information carried by a particular selection in any one interval, the total information (on the average) in T seconds or $m = T/\tau$ intervals, and the average per τ-second interval, as before.

As before, if level (or symbol) j appears in any interval, it carries $-\log_2 P_j$ bits of information. In m intervals j will appear, on the average, mP_j times. The information in bits contributed, on the average, by each symbol appearing mP_j times in m intervals is then summed to give

$$H = -m \sum_{j=1}^{n} P_j \log P_j \qquad \text{bits in } m \text{ intervals}$$

$$= -\frac{T}{\tau} \sum_{j=1}^{n} P_j \log P_j \qquad \text{bits in } T \text{ seconds} \tag{1-13}$$

The *average* information per single symbol interval (τ seconds long) of a message with n possible symbols or levels, of probability P_1 to P_n, respectively, is then

$$H_{\text{av}} = -\sum_{j=1}^{n} P_j \log P_j \qquad \text{bits/interval} \tag{1-14}$$

With τ-second intervals the rate of transmission of information is $1/\tau$ symbols per second. The capacity required of a system to transmit this information would thus be

$$C_{\text{av}} \geq -\frac{1}{\tau} \sum_{j=1}^{n} P_j \log P_j \qquad \text{bits/s} \tag{1-15}$$

As a check, let $P_1 = P_2 = \cdots = P_n = 1/n$ (equally likely events). Then

$$H = m \log_2 n \qquad \text{bits in } m \text{ intervals} \tag{1-16}$$

as before.

As an example of the application of these results, we again consider the problem of determining the information content of a typical message of English speech. This is of course important knowledge required in determining the capacity of a communication system to be used for transmission of messages in English.

If we assume that the occurrence of any letter in the English alphabet is independent of preceding letters or words (a gross approximation), we may use a table of the relative frequency of occurrence of letters in the English alphabet to get an approximate idea of the information content of English speech or writing. This in turn can give us some estimate of the system capacity needed to transmit English at any specified rate (letters or words per second). Such a table appears in a book by Fletcher Pratt [PRAT][7] and has been reprinted by S. Goldman [GOLD 1953][8] in his book *Information Theory*. C. E. Shannon, in the article already referred to, reproduces some of the information available [SHAN 1948].

---

[7][PRAT] Fletcher Pratt, *Secret and Urgent*, Doubleday, Garden City Books, New York, 1942.

[8][GOLD 1953] S. Goldman, *Information Theory*, Prentice-Hall, Englewood Cliffs, N.J., 1953.

The relative frequency of occurrence of the letter e is found to be 0.131 (131 times in 1,000 letters), t occurs 0.105 of the time, a 0.086 of the time, etc., all the way down to z with a probability of 0.00077 (0.77 times in 1,000 letters). Equation (1-14) then gives, as a first approximation to the information content of English, 4.15 bits per letter. Had the letters been equally likely to occur ($P_j = \frac{1}{26}$ for all 26 letters), we would have had $H_{av} = \log_2 26 = 4.7$ bits per letter. The fact that some letters are more likely to occur than others has thus *reduced* the information content of English from 4.7 bits to 4.15 bits per letter. If six letters are to be transmitted every second, we require a system with a capacity of at least $6 \times 4.15 = 25$ bits/s. Doubling the number of letters to be transmitted doubles the required capacity as well.

The information content of English is actually much less than the 4.15 bits per letter figure because there is of course some dependence between successive letters, words, and even groups of words. Thus, if the letter q occurs, it is almost certain to be followed by a u. These two occurrences (q and then u) are thus not independent, and the uncertainty of a message with a q occurring is reduced, and with it the message information content. Similarly, t is frequently followed by an h, r, or e and almost never by a q or an x. Certain patterns of letters in groups of two thus occur much more frequently than others. The same holds true for groups of three letters. (The group *ter* frequently occurs in that order, while *rtn*, as an example, rarely appears.) Patterns also exist for four- and even five-letter combinations (*mani-*, *semi-*, etc). In addition, there is dependence between successive words. The word *the* is almost always followed by a noun or adjective, a noun is frequently followed by a verb, etc. Various other words commonly occur together.

All these constraints on different letter and word combinations in English tend to reduce its information content. This reduction in information content of a message from the maximum possible (equally likely and independent symbols) is called the *redundancy* of the message. The redundancy of English, as an example, has been estimated to be considerably more than 50 percent [GOLD 1953, p. 45].

To calculate the information content of English more accurately, one would have to consider the influence of the different letters and words on one another. This requires additional knowledge of the statistics of the language, for example, the probability that e occurring would be followed by a or b or any of the other letters, the probability that a th would be followed by a or b, etc. These probabilities can also be calculated from the relative frequencies of occurrence of the different combinations. They are called *conditional probabilities* because they relate the occurrence of an event to the previous occurrence of another event.

The existence of redundancy in message transmission can also be demonstrated very simply in the case of black-and-white TV pictures. Here one signal element or interval corresponds to one spot on the screen, and the time taken for the electron beam to move one element corresponds to the time interval τ in our previous example. The number of levels, n, then corresponds to the number of intensity levels from white to gray to black that can be distinguished. In the case of TV one does not expect adjacent elements to change drastically very often from black to white as the beam sweeps across the screen (usually there is a gradual change from black through gray to white). In addition, a particular element will not be expected to change very much from one sweep interval to the next ($\frac{1}{30}$ s). More than likely a given picture will persist for a while, backgrounds may remain the same for long intervals, small areas of black will remain black for a while, etc. The signal message considered as a time sequence, with various voltage levels corresponding to the different brightness levels and τ to the time to move across one element, will thus not consist of equally likely voltage levels, with the possibility of completely independent changes from one τ interval to the next. These constraints reduce the different number of signal combinations possible and thus quite markedly the average information content of a TV picture. (The limiting case again corresponds to the one in which the picture remains unchanged indefinitely. This implies no information content: you might as well turn off your set and go to bed.) Television scenes have a high percentage of redundancy and for this reason require (at least theoretically) much less system capacity than under the assumption of equally likely and independently varying signal levels. (Various estimates have indicated the redundancy of a typical TV pattern to be as high as 99.9 percent.)

PROBLEMS

1-1. In facsimile transmission, 2.25×10^6 square picture elements are needed to provide proper picture resolution. (This corresponds to 1,500 lines in each dimension.) Find the maximum information content if 12 brightness levels are required for good reproduction.

1-2. An automatic translator, with a capacity of 15×10^3 bits/s, converts information from one coding system to another. Its input is a train of uniformly spaced variable-amplitude pulses, 2.71×10^5 pulses occurring each minute. Its output is another uniformly spaced variable-amplitude pulse train, with one-fifth the number of possible amplitude levels as in the input. Find the repetition rate of the output pulses.

1-3. (a) Find the capacity in bits per second that would be required to transmit black-and-white TV picture signals if 500,000 picture elements were required for good resolution and 10 different brightness levels were specified for proper contrast. Thirty pictures per second are to be transmitted. All picture elements are assumed to vary independently, with equal likelihood of occurrence.

(b) In addition to the above requirements for a monochrome system a particular color TV system must provide 30 different shades of color. Show that transmission in this color system requires almost $2\frac{1}{2}$ times as much capacity as the monochrome system.

1-4. Refer to Prob. 1-3b. If 10 of the 30 color shades require only 7 brightness levels instead of 10, what is the capacity of the system? How many times greater is this capacity than that required for the monochrome system described in Prob. 1-3a?

1-5. Express the following decimal numbers in the binary system of notation: 6, 16, 0, 33, 1, 63, 127, 255, 117.

1-6. A system can send out a group of four pulses, each of 1-ms width, and each equally likely to have a height of 0, 1, 2, or 3 V. The four pulses are always followed by a pulse of height -1, to separate the groups. A typical sequence of groups is shown in Fig. P1-6. What is the average rate of information in bits per second that is transmitted with this system?

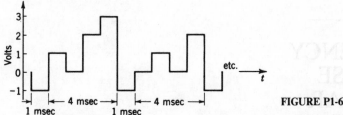

FIGURE P1-6

1-7. In the system of Prob. 1-6 the zero voltage level occurs one-half of the time on the average, the 1-V level occurs one-fourth the time on the average, and the remaining two levels occur one-eighth of the time each on the average. Find the average rate of transmission of information.

1-8. An alphabet consists of the letters A, B, C, D. For transmission each letter is coded into a sequence of two binary (on–off) pulses. The A is represented by 00, the B by 01, the C by 10, the D by 11. Each individual pulse interval is 5 ms.

  (*a*) Calculate the average rate of transmission of information if the different letters are equally likely to occur.

  (*b*) The probability of occurrence of each letter is, respectively, $P_A = \frac{1}{5}$, $P_B = \frac{1}{4}$, $P_C = \frac{1}{4}$, $P_D = \frac{3}{10}$. Find the average rate of transmission of information in bits/s.

1-9. Repeat Prob. 1-8 with the letters coded into single pulses of 0-, 1-, 2-, or 3-V amplitude and of 10-ms duration.

1-10. A communication system is used to transmit one of 16 possible signals. Suppose that the point-to-point transmission is accomplished by encoding the signals into binary digits.

  (*a*) What will be the pulse sequence for the thirteenth symbol; for the seventh symbol?

  (*b*) If each binary digit requires 1 μs for transmission, how much information in bits does the system transmit in 8 μs? Assume that the signals are equally likely to occur.

  (*c*) If the symbols are sent directly without encoding, it is found that each symbol requires 3 μs for transmission. What is the information rate in bits/s in this case?

CHAPTER
2

FREQUENCY
RESPONSE
OF LINEAR
SYSTEMS

We indicated in Chap. 1 that the system capacity, or rate of information transmission through a communication system, is related to the rapidity with which signals may change with time. From studies of the transient behavior of networks we know that in all networks with energy-storage elements (L and C), the currents, or voltages as the case may be, cannot change instantaneously with time. A specified length of time is required (depending on the network) to reach a desired amplitude level.

In all networks inherent capacitance and inductance limit the time response. In many networks additional limitations are purposely imposed by adding filtering circuits which include inductance and capacitance. From our previous studies we also know that the time, or transient, response is inherently related to the familiar frequency, or steady-state sine-wave, response.

Since frequency concepts are widely used in radio and communication practice, and since frequency analysis of networks frequently simplifies the study of a system, we shall review and extend, in detail, the relation between frequency and time response. The importance of these concepts can be seen from some typical examples:

1. Radio-broadcasting stations are required to operate at their assigned frequency with very tight tolerances. Channels are spaced every 10 kHz in the amplitude-modulation (AM) broadcast band. This 10-kHz spacing is specified

30

in order to prevent overlapping of stations and to allow as many stations as possible to be "squeezed into" the available frequency spectrum. As we shall see later, these severe restrictions limit the maximum rate of information transmission.

2. CATV cables are limited in their transient response (or, alternatively, in their frequency response). For a given cable to accommodate as many signal channels as possible, a limitation must be placed upon the frequency extent, or bandwidth, of each channel. This again limits the rate of information transmission in a specified channel.

3. Television stations are limited to 6-MHz bandwidth, again to conserve available frequency space. This in turn imposes limitations on information-transmission capabilities.

Note that in all these simple examples it is the *frequency response* of the network that is specified. This has become common practice, and so it is important to study in detail the relation between frequency and time response, relating both in turn to the particular networks involved.

Consider the simplest set of examples of familiar time functions,

$$f(t) = a_1 \sin \omega_0 t, \, a_2 \sin 2\omega_0 t, \, a_3 \sin 3\omega_0 t, \ldots, \, a_n \sin n\omega_0 t \qquad (2\text{-}1)$$

The first two functions are shown in Fig. 2-1. As n increases, the rates of variation with time become more rapid. This may also be seen easily by comparing the different derivatives,

$$\frac{df(t)}{dt} = a_n n\omega_0 \cos n\omega_0 t \qquad (2\text{-}2)$$

As n increases, the maximum rate of change of $f(t)$ increases.

We can represent these functions in a different way by plotting the amplitude a_n versus angular frequency, as in Fig. 2-2. As the frequency increases, the time function varies more rapidly.

Now consider a simple example of an amplitude-modulated signal,

$$f(t) = A(1 + \cos \omega_m t)\cos \omega_0 t \qquad \omega_m \ll \omega_0 \qquad (2\text{-}3)$$

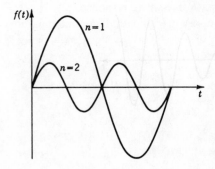

FIGURE 2-1
Amplitude–frequency plot, modulated carrier.

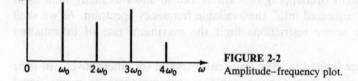

FIGURE 2-2
Amplitude–frequency plot.

The amplitude varies slowly (as compared with $\cos \omega_0 t$ time variations) between 0 and $2A$. Its rate of variation is given by ω_m, the modulating frequency. ω_0 is the carrier frequency. Figure 2-3 is a plot of one cycle of this function. The amplitude variations form the envelope of the complete signal and represent any information being transmitted. (In a practical situation the envelope would actually be a more complex function of time.)

A simple trigonometric manipulation of Eq. (2-3) gives

$$A(1 + \cos \omega_m t)\cos \omega_0 t$$

$$= A \cos \omega_0 t + \frac{A}{2}\left[\cos(\omega_0 - \omega_m)t + \cos(\omega_0 + \omega_m)t\right] \qquad (2\text{-}4)$$

The complete function can thus be represented as the sum of three sinusoidal functions and be plotted on an amplitude–frequency graph (Fig. 2-4). The two smaller lines are called the sideband frequencies; the larger, central line, the carrier. As the amplitude-modulating signal varies more rapidly, ω_m increases and the sideband frequencies move farther away from the carrier. We therefore again have the notion that more rapid variations correspond to wider frequency swings.

These simple examples have all been cases of sinusoidal variations. As such, they are presumed to exist for all time and so carry no information. (Information-carrying signals are continuously varying in an unpredictable manner.) They are valuable in studying networks and systems, however, since any physical time function existing over a finite time interval can be expanded into a Fourier series of sinusoidal functions. Such a series will then represent that function over the interval desired. (Because of the periodic nature of sinusoidal functions the

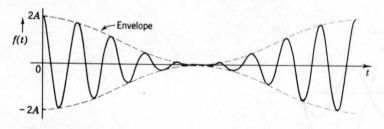

FIGURE 2-3
Amplitude–modulated wave.

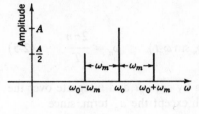

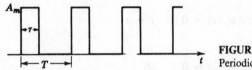

FIGURE 2-4
Amplitude–frequency plot, modulated carrier.

FIGURE 2-5
Periodic pulse sequence.

Fourier series representation will then repeat itself regularly outside the specified time interval.)

It is this concept that makes the frequency approach so useful in the communication field. We are quite familiar with the steady-state sinusoidal response of networks. It is also a fact that sinusoidal analysis is frequently much simpler than a time, or transient, analysis. The ability to relate time to frequency response will thus simplify the solution of many problems.

The two examples previously discussed indicated that as the rate of time variation increased the frequency increased also. To generalize this concept somewhat, consider the series of periodic rectangular pulses shown in Fig. 2-5. Note that these pulses are related to the binary pulse sequence introduced in Sec. 1-3. We shall be dealing with such rectangular pulse sequences throughout most of the book because of their widespread occurrence in digital communications. Such a sequence of pulses can of course be expanded into a Fourier series. We ask the question: What is the amplitude–frequency plot of this sequence? This will further fix the time–frequency connection and will then enable us to go further into an examination of the effect of networks on time functions. Before treating this particular problem we review the Fourier-series concept.

2-1   REVIEW OF FOURIER SERIES

Let $f(t)$ be a periodic function of time with period T. Then $f(t)$ may be expanded into the following Fourier series[1] (we shall not deal here with the

---

[1]Many forms of the series may be written. For example,

$$f(t) = A_0 + \sum_{n=1}^{\infty} (A_n \cos \omega_n t + B_n \sin \omega_n t)$$

is commonly used. This is the same as Eq. (2-5) with

$$A_0 = \frac{a_0}{T} \qquad A_n = \frac{2a_n}{T} \qquad B_n = \frac{2b_n}{T}$$

mathematical conditions necessary):

$$f(t) = \frac{a_0}{T} + \frac{2}{T} \sum_{n=1}^{\infty} (a_n \cos \omega_n t + b_n \sin \omega_n t) \qquad \omega_n = \frac{2\pi n}{T} \qquad (2\text{-}5)$$

To find the constants a_n, we multiply through by $\cos \omega_n t$ and integrate over the period. All terms on the right-hand side vanish except the a_n term, since

$$\int_{-T/2}^{T/2} \cos \omega_j t \cos \omega_n t \, dt = 0 \qquad j \neq n$$

$$\int_{-T/2}^{T/2} \sin \omega_j t \cos \omega_n t \, dt = 0 \qquad \text{all } j$$

This gives us

$$\int_{-T/2}^{T/2} f(t) \cos \omega_n t \, dt = \frac{2a_n}{T} \int_{-T/2}^{T/2} \cos^2 \omega_n t \, dt = \frac{2a_n}{T} \frac{T}{2} = a_n \qquad (2\text{-}6)$$

[Remember that $\cos^2 \omega_n t = (1 + \cos 2\omega_n t)/2$.] Thus

$$a_n = \int_{-T/2}^{T/2} f(t) \cos \omega_n t \, dt \qquad n = 0, 1, 2, 3, \ldots \qquad (2\text{-}7)$$

Similarly,

$$b_n = \int_{-T/2}^{T/2} f(t) \sin \omega_n t \, dt \qquad n = 1, 2, \ldots \qquad (2\text{-}8)$$

The amplitude–frequency plot is proportional to a plot of $\sqrt{a_n^2 + b_n^2}$ versus ω_n. [The phase–frequency characteristic is a plot of $\tan^{-1}(-b_n/a_n)$ versus ω_n.] This plot of $\sqrt{a_n^2 + b_n^2}$ versus frequency will be referred to as the amplitude *spectrum* of the function.[2]

We know from our circuit analysis that, if the voltage across a 1-Ω resistor is given by

$$v_n(t) = A_n \cos \omega_n t + B_n \sin \omega_n t$$

the average power dissipated in the resistor is $(A_n^2 + B_n^2)/2$ watts. Alternatively, if $A_n = 2a_n/T$ and $b_n = 2b_n/T$, the average power dissipated can be written as

$$\left(\frac{2}{T}\right)^2 \frac{a_n^2 + b_n^2}{2}$$

The square of the amplitude spectrum is thus a measure of the power dissipated

---

[2] Note that this differs from the amplitude–frequency plot by the constant T.

in a 1-Ω resistor at the different frequencies ($n = 0, 1, 2, \ldots$). By adding the power dissipated at each frequency we get the total average power dissipated when a periodic voltage is impressed across a resistor.

In our work to follow we shall be more interested in the amplitude spectrum $\sqrt{a_n^2 + b_n^2}$ and the phase angle $\tan^{-1}(-b_n/a_n)$ than in the individual Fourier coefficients a_n and b_n. (Note that in general two quantities must be specified at each frequency in order completely to specify the Fourier series.) This implies writing our Fourier series in the form

$$f(t) = \frac{a_0}{T} + \frac{2}{T} \sum_{n=1}^{\infty} \sqrt{a_b^2 + b_n^2} \cos(\omega_n t + \theta_n) \qquad \theta_n = \tan^{-1} \frac{-b_n}{a_n} \qquad (2\text{-}9)$$

Equation (2-9) can of course be obtained from Eq. (2-5) by a simple trigonometric manipulation.

Since we shall frequently be interested in the amplitude and phase characteristics $\sqrt{a_n^2 + b_n^2}$ and θ_n of a periodic function, it would be much simpler to obtain these directly from $f(t)$, rather than by first finding a_n and b_n. We shall show that this can be done very simply by using yet another form of the Fourier series, the complex exponential form. This alternative form of the series may be written as

$$f(t) = \frac{1}{T} \sum_{n=-\infty}^{\infty} c_n e^{j\omega_n t} \qquad (2\text{-}10)$$

The Fourier coefficient c_n is then a complex number defined as

$$c_n \equiv a_n - jb_n = \sqrt{a_n^2 + b_n^2}\, e^{j\theta_n} = \int_{-T/2}^{T/2} f(t) e^{-j\omega_n t}\, dt \qquad (2\text{-}11)$$

$|c_n| = \sqrt{a_n^2 + b_n^2}$ is thus the desired amplitude spectrum, and

$$\theta_n = \tan^{-1} \frac{-b_n}{a_n}$$

represents the phase characteristic. The coefficient c_n gives the complete frequency spectrum.

Equations (2-10) and (2-11) are completely equivalent to Eqs. (2-5), (2-7), and (2-8). Not only does Eq. (2-11) give the amplitude and phase characteristics directly, but Eqs. (2-10) and (2-11) represent a much more compact form of the Fourier series,

$$f(t) = \frac{1}{T} \sum_{n=-\infty}^{\infty} c_n e^{j\omega_n t} \qquad (2\text{-}10a)$$

$$c_n = \int_{-T/2}^{T/2} f(t) e^{-j\omega_n t}\, dt \qquad (2\text{-}11a)$$

In rewriting Eqs. (2-5), (2-7), and (2-8) in this new form use has been made of the exponential form for the sine and cosine. Thus, in Eq. (2-5) let

$$\cos \omega_n t = \frac{e^{j\omega_n t} + e^{-j\omega_n t}}{2}$$

$$\sin \omega_n t = \frac{e^{j\omega_n t} - e^{-j\omega_n t}}{2j}$$

Regrouping terms in Eq. (2-5),

$$f(t) = \frac{a_0}{T} + \frac{1}{T} \sum_{n=1}^{\infty} \left[e^{j\omega_n t}(a_n - jb_n) + e^{-j\omega_n t}(a_n + jb_n) \right] \quad (2\text{-}12)$$

If $c_n \equiv a_n - jb_n$, $c_n^* \equiv a_n + jb_n$, where c_n^* is the complex conjugate of c_n. But

$$a_n - jb_n = \int_{-T/2}^{T/2} f(t)(\cos \omega_n t - j \sin \omega_n t)\, dt = \int_{-T/2}^{T/2} f(t)e^{-j\omega_n t}\, dt \quad (2\text{-}13)$$

from Eqs. (2-7) and (2-8). Since $\omega_n = 2\pi n/T$, we have $e^{-j\omega_n t} = e^{-j(2\pi n t/T)}$ and

$$e^{+j\omega_n t} = e^{-j(2\pi/T)(-n)t} = e^{-j\omega_{-n} t}$$

Therefore,

$$c_n^* = a_n + jb_n = \int_{-T/2}^{T/2} f(t)e^{j\omega_n t}\, dt = \int_{-T/2}^{T/2} f(t)e^{-j\omega_{-n} t}\, dt \quad (2\text{-}14)$$

[Remember again that $\omega_n = 2\pi n/T$, $\omega_{-n} \equiv 2\pi(-n)/T$.] From Eq. (2-14), then, assuming $f(t)$ real, $c_n^* = c_{-n}$. (That is, replacing n by $-n$ in c_n gives c_n^*.) Equation (2-12) can now be rewritten as

$$f(t) = \frac{a_0}{T} + \frac{1}{T} \sum_{n=1}^{\infty} \left(e^{j\omega_n t} c_n + e^{-j\omega_n t} c_{-n} \right) \quad (2\text{-}15)$$

But summing over $-n$ from 1 to ∞ is the same as summing over $+n$ from -1 to $-\infty$ ($c_{-3} \equiv c_n$, $n = -3$). Also,

$$c_0 = \int_{-T/2}^{T/2} f(t)e^{j0}\, dt = a_0$$

Equation (2-15) can thus be further simplified to

$$f(t) = \frac{1}{T} \sum_{n=-\infty}^{\infty} c_n e^{j\omega_n t} \quad (2\text{-}10)$$

$$c_n = \int_{-T/2}^{T/2} f(t)e^{-j\omega_n t}\, dt \quad (2\text{-}11)$$

Although "negative" frequencies seem to appear in Eq. (2-10), they are actually fictitious. For if Eq. (2-10) is rewritten in real form, Eq. (2-9) is obtained, in which the only frequencies appearing ($\omega_n = 2\pi n/T$) are positive. This is very

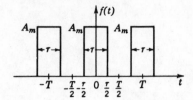

FIGURE 2-6
Fourier analysis of periodic pulses.

simply shown by writing $c_n = |c_n|e^{j\theta_n}$. Then Eq. (2-10) becomes

$$f(t) = \frac{1}{T} \sum_{n=-\infty}^{\infty} |c_n| e^{j(\omega_n t + \theta_n)}$$

$$= \frac{1}{T} \sum_{n=1}^{\infty} \left[|c_n| \left(e^{j(\omega_n t + \theta_n)} + e^{-j(\omega_n t + \theta_n)} \right) \right] + \frac{c_0}{T}$$

$$= \frac{a_0}{T} + \frac{2}{T} \sum_{n=1}^{\infty} |c_n| \cos(\omega_n t + \theta_n)$$

(Remember again that $-\omega_n = \omega_{-n}$, $-\theta_n = \theta_{-n}$.)

As an example of the utility of this complex form of the Fourier series, consider the series of pulses of Fig. 2-6. (The origin has been chosen to coincide with the center of one pulse.) Then

$$c_n = \int_{-\tau/2}^{\tau/2} A_m e^{-j\omega_n t}\, dt = \left. -\frac{A_m}{j\omega_n} e^{-j\omega_n t} \right]_{-\tau/2}^{\tau/2}$$

$$= A_m \frac{e^{j\omega_n \tau/2} - e^{-j\omega_n \tau/2}}{j\omega_n} = \frac{2A_m}{\omega_n} \sin \frac{\omega_n \tau}{2}$$

This may be written in the form

$$c_n = \tau A_m \frac{\sin(\omega_n \tau/2)}{\omega_n \tau/2} \tag{2-16}$$

If we define a normalized and dimensionless variable, $x = \omega_n \tau/2$,

$$c_n = \tau A_m \frac{\sin x}{x}$$

The $(\sin x)/x$ function will be occurring in many problems in the future and should be carefully studied. Note that it has its maximum value at $x = 0$, where $\sin x \to x$, $(\sin x)/x \to 1$. It approaches zero as $x \to \infty$, oscillating through positive and negative values. If x is a continuous variable, $(\sin x)/x$ has the form of Fig. 2-7.

In our particular problem n has discrete values only, ω_n takes on discrete values (harmonics of $\omega_1 = 2\pi/T$), and the normalized parameter x is thus also

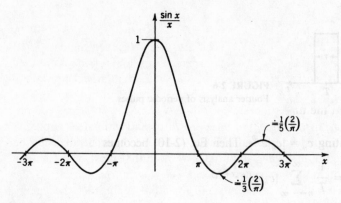

FIGURE 2-7
$(\sin x)/x$ versus x.

defined only at discrete points. The *envelope* of the plot of c_n will be exactly the curve of Fig. 2-7. The plot of c_n itself is shown in Fig. 2-8 ($\tau \ll T$). Since c_n is for this example a real number (alternatively positive and negative), there is no need to find $|c_n|$ and θ_n and plot each separately. (Note again that the "negative" frequencies shown are just a mathematical artifice, since $\omega_n = 2\pi n/T$ and $\omega_{-n} = -2\pi n/T$.) The spacing between the successive lines is

$$\Delta\omega_n = \frac{2\pi}{T}(n+1) - \frac{2\pi n}{T} = \frac{2\pi}{T}$$

or just the fundamental angular frequency. All lines of the frequency spectrum shown thus occur at multiples of this fundamental frequency. The "dc component" ($\omega_n = 0$) is of course just T times the average value.

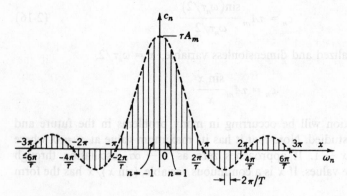

FIGURE 2-8
Frequency spectrum, rectangular pulses ($\tau \ll T$).

Time–Frequency Correspondence

Although the periodic function of Fig. 2-6 contains frequency components at all integral multiples of the fundamental frequency, the envelope of the amplitude decreases at higher frequencies. Note, however, that as the fundamental period T *decreases* (more pulses per second), the frequency lines move out farther. Again a *more rapid variation* in the time function corresponds to *higher-frequency* components. Alternatively, as T increases, the lines crowd in and ultimately approach an almost smooth frequency spectrum. Since the lines concentrated in the lower-frequency range are of higher amplitude, we note that most of the energy associated with this periodic wave is confined to the lower frequencies. As the function varies more rapidly (T decreases), the relative amount of the energy contained in the higher-frequency range increases.

Figure 2-8 and Eq. (2-16) emphasize another interesting phenomenon that will be very useful to us in later work. As the pulse width τ *decreases*, the frequency content of the signal extends out over a larger frequency range. The first zero crossing, at $\omega_n = 2\pi/\tau$, moves out in frequency. There is thus an *inverse relationship between pulse width, or duration, and the frequency spread of the pulses*.

If $\tau \ll T$ (that is, very narrow pulses), most of the signal energy will lie in the range

$$0 < \omega_n < \frac{2\pi}{\tau}$$

The first zero crossing is frequently a measure of the frequency spread of a signal (assuming, of course, that the envelope of the amplitude spectrum decreases with increasing frequency). In keeping with the notation for networks we can talk of the bandwidth of the signal as being a measure of its frequency spread.

As in the case of the frequency response of networks, the bandwidth occupied by the signal cannot be uniquely specified unless the signal is "band-limited" (i.e., occupies a finite range of frequencies with no frequency components beyond the range specified). However, some arbitrary (and frequently useful) criterion for bandwidth may be chosen to specify the range of frequencies in which most of the signal energy is concentrated. As an example, if the bandwidth B is specified as the frequency extent of the signal from zero frequency to the first zero crossing, then

$$B = \frac{1}{\tau} \tag{2-17}$$

where $\tau \ll T$. Any other criterion for bandwidth will still retain the inverse time-bandwidth relation, and, in general,

$$B = \frac{k}{\tau} \tag{2-18}$$

with k a constant depending on the choice of criterion. We shall return to this important concept later.

Power Considerations

We noted earlier that the average power dissipated in a 1-Ω resistor with a voltage

$$v_n(t) = A_n \cos \omega_n t + B_n \sin \omega_n t$$

impressed across it is just given by $(A_n^2 + B_n^2)/2$. If one deals with the complex exponential

$$v_n(t) = c_n e^{j\omega_n t}$$

instead, it is apparent that the average power is given by

$$\bar{P} = \frac{1}{T} \int_0^T |v_n(t)|^2 \, dt = |c_n|^2$$

This may be simply generalized to the case of an arbitrary periodic function $f(t)$ by using the Fourier-series expansion. Thus we recall that with an arbitrary (and possibly complex) voltage $f(t)$ impressed across a 1-Ω resistor the instantaneous power is just $|f(t)|^2$ and the average power is given by

$$\bar{P} = \frac{1}{T} \int_0^T |f(t)|^2 \, dt \tag{2-19}$$

[If $f(t)$ is real, as in most of the examples of this book, $|f(t)|$ is simply replaced by $f(t)$.] Substituting for $f(t)$ its Fourier-series expansion of Eq. (2-10), we get

$$\bar{P} = \frac{1}{T^3} \int_0^T \left[\sum_m \sum_n c_m^* c_n e^{j(\omega_n - \omega_m)t} \right] dt \tag{2-19a}$$

Interchanging the order of summation and integration and noting that

$$\int_0^T e^{j(\omega_n - \omega_m)t} \, dt = T \qquad \omega_n = \omega_m$$

$$= 0 \qquad \text{elsewhere}$$

(this is simply checked by expanding in sines or cosines or by noting that $e^{j\omega t}$, although complex, is periodic, and averages to zero over a period), we get

$$\bar{P} = \frac{1}{T} \int_0^T |f(t)|^2 \, dt = \sum_{n=-\infty}^{\infty} \left| \frac{c_n}{T} \right|^2 \tag{2-19b}$$

The average power is thus found by summing the power contribution at all frequencies in the Fourier-series expansion.

As an example, if we again consider the rectangular test pulses of Fig. 2-6, we have

$$\bar{P} = \frac{A_m^2 \tau}{T} = \sum_{n=-\infty}^{\infty} \left(\frac{\tau A_m}{T} \right)^2 \frac{\sin^2(\omega_n \tau/2)}{(\omega_n \tau/2)^2} \tag{2-20}$$

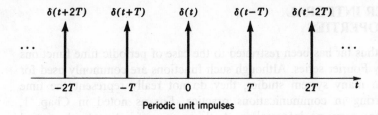

Periodic unit impulses

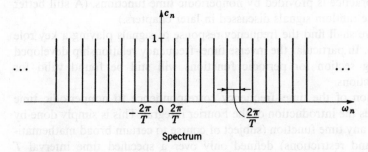

Spectrum

FIGURE 2-9
Spectrum of periodic impulses.

This expression enables us to determine the relative power contributions at the various frequencies. For example the dc power is just $(c_0/T)^2$ or $(\tau A_m/T)^2$ in the rectangular pulse case. (This is of course easily checked by noting that the dc power is $[(1/T)\int_0^T f(t)\,dt]^2$.) The power in the first harmonic, that at $\omega_1 = 2\pi/T$, is just

$$2\left(\frac{\tau A_m}{T}\right)^2 \frac{\sin^2(\omega_1\tau/2)}{(\omega_1\tau/2)^2} \qquad \text{etc.}$$

(The factor of 2 is due to the equal power contributions at ω_1 and $\omega_{-1} = -\omega_1$.)

Periodic Impulses

A special case of the rectangular pulse train, of great utility in both digital-communication analysis and modern digital computation, is obtained by letting the pulse width τ in Fig. 2-6 go to zero and the amplitude $A_m \to \infty$, with $A_m\tau = 1$. This results in the extremely useful set of periodic impulses of infinite height, zero width, and unit area. These unit impulses are shown sketched in Fig. 2-9. The symbol usually adopted for an impulse of unit area and centered at $t = \tau$ is $\delta(t - \tau)$. It is represented by an arrow, as indicated in Fig. 2-9. If the area $(A_m\tau)$ is some number k, one writes $k\delta(t - \tau)$.

We shall have more to say about the impulse function later, but note now that all spectral lines have the same height $A_m\tau$. The bandwidth thus approaches infinity. This agrees of course with the inverse time–bandwidth relation. As the width τ of the pulse $\to 0$, its bandwidth $1/\tau \to \infty$.

2-2 FOURIER INTEGRAL AND ITS PROPERTIES

The discussion thus far has been restricted to the case of periodic time functions representable by Fourier series. Although such functions are commonly used for test purposes in many system studies, they do not really represent the time functions occurring in communications practice. For as noted in Chap. 1, periodic functions carry no information. A closer approximation to the actual signals used in practice is provided by nonperiodic time functions. (A still better model will be the random signals discussed in later chapters.)

Here too we shall find the frequency response of signals playing a key role in the discussion. In particular the inverse time–frequency relationship developed in the preceding section for periodic functions will still be found valid for nonperiodic functions.

An extension of the time–frequency correspondence to nonperiodic time functions requires the introduction of the Fourier integral. This is simply done by recognizing that any time function (subject of course to certain broad mathematical definitions and restrictions) defined only over a specified time interval T seconds long may be expanded in a Fourier series of base period T. The time function is then artificially made to repeat itself outside the specified time interval. As the time interval of interest becomes greater, the Fourier period is correspondingly increased. Ultimately, as the region of interest is made to increase beyond bound, the resultant Fourier series becomes, in the limit, the Fourier integral.

Consider a periodic function $f(t)$,

$$f(t) = \frac{1}{T} \sum_{n=-\infty}^{\infty} c_n e^{j\omega_n t} \qquad \omega_n = \frac{2\pi n}{T} \tag{2-21}$$

$$c_n = \int_{-T/2}^{T/2} f(t) e^{-j\omega_n t} \, dt \tag{2-22}$$

A typical amplitude-spectrum plot would appear as in Fig. 2-10. The spacing between successive harmonics is just

$$\Delta\omega = \omega_{n+1} - \omega_n = \frac{2\pi}{T} \tag{2-23}$$

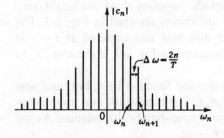

FIGURE 2-10
Amplitude spectrum, periodic function.

Equation (2-21) may be written as

$$f(t) = \frac{1}{2\pi} \sum_{n=-\infty}^{\infty} c_n e^{j\omega_n t} \Delta\omega \tag{2-24}$$

Now consider the limiting case as $T \to \infty$. Then $\Delta\omega \to 0$, the discrete lines in the spectrum of Fig. 2-10 merge, and we obtain a continuous-frequency spectrum. Mathematically, the infinite sum in Eq. (2-24) becomes the ordinary Riemann integral. c_n is now defined for *all* frequencies, not merely integral multiples of $2\pi/T$. In the limit, as $T \to \infty$, $\omega_n \to \omega$ and c_n becomes a continuous function $F(\omega)$:

$$F(\omega) = \lim_{T \to \infty} c_n \tag{2-25}$$

In the place of the Fourier series of Eq. (2-21) we now obtain as the Fourier-integral representation of a nonperiodic function $f(t)$

$$f(t) = \frac{1}{2\pi} \int_{-\infty}^{\infty} F(\omega) e^{j\omega t} \, d\omega \tag{2-26}$$

with

$$F(\omega) = \int_{-\infty}^{\infty} f(t) e^{-j\omega t} \, dt \tag{2-27}$$

from Eq. (2-22). $F(\omega)$ is, in general, a complex function of ω and may be written

$$F(\omega) = |F(\omega)| e^{j\theta(\omega)} \tag{2-28}$$

A typical time function and its Fourier spectrum $F(\omega)$ are shown in Fig. 2-11. The periodic pulses previously considered serve as a good example of the transition from the Fourier series to the Fourier integral. The pulses are shown in Fig. 2-12*a* and the corresponding spectrum in Fig. 2-12*b*.

The frequency spectrum of the periodic pulses is of course a plot of the Fourier coefficient c_n (normally amplitude and phase plots)

$$c_n = V\tau \frac{\sin(\omega_n \tau/2)}{\omega_n \tau/2} \qquad \omega_n = \frac{2\pi n}{T} \tag{2-29}$$

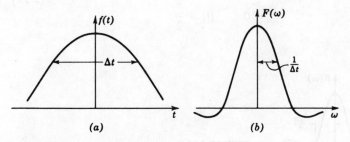

FIGURE 2-11
A typical time function and its spectrum. (*a*) $f(t)$. (*b*) $F(\omega)$.

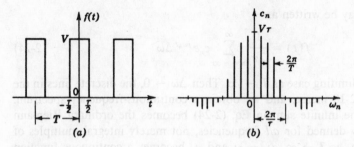

FIGURE 2-12
Periodic pulses and their spectrum.

As $T \to \infty$, all the pulses except for the one centered at $t = 0$ move out beyond bounds and we are left, in the time plot, with a single pulse of amplitude V and width τ seconds.

In the frequency plot $\omega_n \to \omega$ as $T \to \infty$, the lines move together and merge, and the spectrum becomes a continuous one (Fig. 2-13). Thus

$$F(\omega) = \lim_{T \to \infty} c_n = V_\tau \frac{\sin(\omega\tau/2)}{\omega\tau/2} \tag{2-30}$$

The single pulse of Fig. 2-13a has the continuous-frequency spectrum of Fig. 2-13b, defined for all frequencies.

Equation (2-30) can of course be obtained directly from the defining relation for $F(\omega)$ [Eq. (2-27)]:

$$F(\omega) = \int_{-\infty}^{\infty} f(t)e^{-j\omega t}\, dt$$

For a single pulse

$$f(t) = V \qquad |t| < \frac{\tau}{2}$$

$$= 0 \qquad |t| > \frac{\tau}{2} \tag{2-31}$$

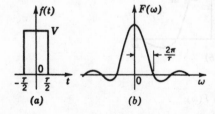

FIGURE 2-13
Rectangular pulse and its spectrum. (a) Time plane. (b) Frequency plane.

Then

$$F(\omega) = V\int_{-\tau/2}^{\tau/2} e^{-j\omega t}\, dt = \frac{V}{-j\omega}\left(e^{-j\omega\tau/2} - e^{j\omega\tau/2}\right) = V\tau\frac{\sin(\omega\tau/2)}{\omega\tau/2}$$

(2-32)

Note the inverse time–frequency relationship between the rectangular pulse and its spectrum (Fig. 2-13), exactly as pointed out earlier: as the pulse width τ decreases, the spectral spread moves out as $1/\tau$. The bandwidth B in hertz, measured to the first zero crossing, is again $B = 1/\tau$.

The Fourier integral $F(\omega)$ is frequently called the *Fourier transform* of $f(t)$. The two defining relations, (2-27) for the Fourier transform of $f(t)$ and (2-26) for the inverse Fourier transform, represent a Fourier transform pair. Note the complete duality between the integrals, particularly if $d\omega/2\pi$ is written as df, a differential frequency in hertz. If the two functions $f(t)$ and $F(\omega)$ are interchanged, their respective transforms interchange as well. For example, a rectangular spectrum $F(\omega)$ should have as its inverse transform a $(\sin x)/x$ function in time. We shall explore this point later, in more detail.

The introduction and use of the Fourier transform $F(\omega)$ enables us to readily determine the time response of linear networks. We shall find ourselves continually referring to the "frequency or spectral content" of signals and the "frequency properties" of communication systems. Communication engineers commonly refer to the "bandwidth" of a system with which they may be working. They have found the concept of frequency response to be an extremely useful one in the design and analysis of communication systems. We shall in fact be continually referring to spectrum and bandwidth throughout this book. With such continuous usage the concept of the "frequency property" of a network will tend to take on a physical meaning. But we must keep in mind that these frequency and spectral considerations are in reality mathematical abstractions. The frequency content of a signal $f(t)$ is obtained from the Fourier transform $F(\omega)$, an integral representation of $f(t)$.[3]

Before proceeding to discuss the properties of Fourier integrals and the response of linear systems to aperiodic time functions using the frequency concept, it is worthwhile examining some additional examples of Fourier integral pairs. The five examples that follow all focus on pulse-type signals in time, because of their common occurrence in communication practice. The calculation of some of the transforms is left for the reader as an exercise. Others are developed, in a somewhat different manner, later, using the properties of Fourier transforms.

---

[3] The discrete Fourier transform is often used nowadays to calculate the spectrum of a signal, because of the advent of high-speed digital processing. See [SCHW 1975] M. Schwartz and L. Shaw, *Signal Processing: Discrete Spectral Analysis, Detection, and Estimation*, McGraw-Hill, New York, 1975, chap. 2.

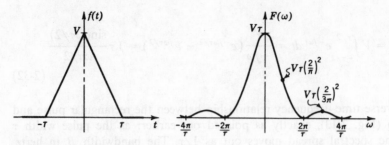

FIGURE 2-14
Triangular pulse and its spectrum.

1. Triangular pulse (Fig. 2-14). A triangular pulse of height V and base width 2τ has as its spectrum

$$F(\omega) = (V\tau)\left[\frac{\sin(\omega\tau/2)}{\omega\tau/2}\right]^2 \qquad (2\text{-}33)$$

Note that this pulse has the same amplitude and area as the rectangular pulse of Fig. 2-13. Its width, as measured at the half-amplitude points, is just that of the rectangular pulse. This triangular pulse and its spectrum obey the same inverse time–frequency relationship discussed previously: as the pulse width τ decreases, the bandwidth B, in hertz, measured to the first zero crossing, or any other comparable measure, increases as $1/\tau$.

Note, however, that the spectrum in this case is more tightly centered about the origin than in the previous rectangular pulse case. The spectrum here decreases as $1/f^2$ (or $1/\omega^2$ in radian measure), as contrasted with the $1/f$ decrease of the $(\sin x)/x$ spectrum of the rectangular pulse. The latter has a discontinuity in the function itself. The triangular pulse is a more smoothly varying function: it is continuous in the function itself and discontinuous in the derivative. We shall demonstrate further, by example, that the smoother the function, as exemplified by the continuity of higher and higher-order derivatives, the more rapidly the spectrum decreases with increasing frequency, packing more of the frequency content into a specified bandwidth. Integration of the triangle of Fig. 2-14 would result in a spectrum decreasing as $1/f^3$.

2. Cosine pulse (Fig. 2-15). Here

$$f(t) = V\cos\frac{\pi t}{\tau} \qquad |t| \le \frac{\tau}{2}$$

$$= 0 \qquad \text{elsewhere} \qquad (2\text{-}34)$$

One then finds that

$$F(\omega) = \frac{2\tau V}{\pi}\frac{\cos(\omega\tau/2)}{1 - (\omega\tau/\pi)^2} \qquad (2\text{-}35)$$

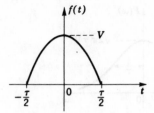
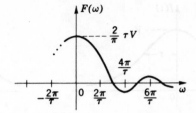

FIGURE 2-15
Cosine pulse and its Fourier transform.

Note that the spectrum here decreases as $1/f^2$ (or $1/\omega^2$) with increasing frequency. The cosine pulse is also continuous in time, while its first derivative is discontinuous at $\pm\tau/2$. The pulse width is again τ, while the first zero crossing, at $\omega\tau = 3\pi$, if chosen as a measure of the pulse bandwidth, corresponds to

$$B = \frac{3}{2\tau}$$

in hertz. The same inverse time–frequency relation again exists here.

3. Raised cosine pulse (Fig. 2-16). Let

$$f(t) = \frac{V}{2}\left(1 + \cos\frac{\pi t}{\tau}\right) \qquad |t| \le \tau$$

$$= 0 \qquad \text{elsewhere} \tag{2-36}$$

Then
$$F(\omega) = V\tau\frac{\sin\omega\tau}{\omega\tau\left[1 - (\omega\tau/\pi)^2\right]} \tag{2-37}$$

The spectrum here decreases as $1/f^3$ for large frequency, since the first derivative is continuous at all values of t. There is a discontinuity in the second derivative at $t = \pm\tau$. Note here that although the full pulse width is 2τ, its width to the half-amplitude points (indicated in Fig. 2-16 by the dashed lines), is τ. The bandwidth to the first zero crossing is $B = 1/\tau$.

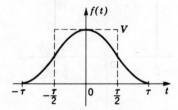
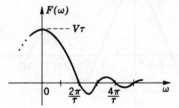

FIGURE 2-16
Raised cosine pulse and its Fourier transform.

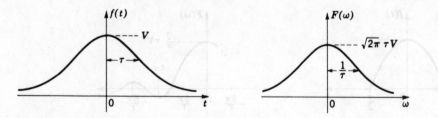

FIGURE 2-17
Gaussian pulse and its Fourier transform.

4. Gaussian pulse (Fig. 2-17). Let

$$f(t) = Ve^{-t^2/2\tau^2} \tag{2-38}$$

Then
$$F(\omega) = \sqrt{2\pi}\,\tau Ve^{-\tau^2\omega^2/2} \tag{2-38a}$$

Note that here τ is one possible measure of the width of the pulse. The width of $F(\omega)$, defined in an identical manner, is then $1/\tau$. The bandwidth of the signal thus increases inversely with its width, as expected. The Gaussian pulse is the smoothest of all those considered. All its derivatives exist and are continuous at all values of time. The rate of drop-off of the transform $F(\omega)$ is thus the greatest, dropping exponentially with ω^2 at frequencies higher than the bandwidth. Note, however, that the pulse is neither time-limited nor band-limited. Both the width in time and the width in frequency have to be arbitrarily defined. [As an interesting sidelight notice that $f(t)$ and $F(\omega)$ in this case have exactly the same shapes: a Gaussian pulse in time gives rise to a Gaussian pulse in frequency.]

5. $(\sin x)/x$ pulse (Fig. 2-18). Here

$$f(t) = V\frac{\sin(\pi t/T)}{\pi t/T} \tag{2-39}$$

This is just the dual of the rectangular pulse considered in Fig. 2-13. Since the Fourier transform pairs are reciprocal with respect to one another, it is apparent

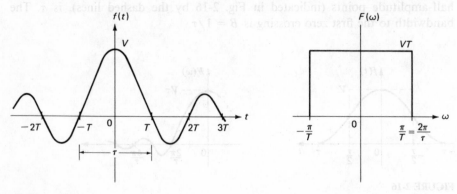

FIGURE 2-18
$(\sin x)/x$ pulse and its transform.

as noted earlier that this pulse must give rise to the rectangular transform shown in Fig. 2-18. Details are left to the reader. Note that in this example the frequency spectrum is precisely limited in frequency, although the function itself is not time-limited. If one takes as a measure of the pulse width τ the width between the two first zero crossings, as shown, the radian bandwidth is $\pi/T = 2\pi/\tau$, and the bandwidth in hertz is $B = 1/\tau$. Equation (2-39) can then also be written, with specific emphasis on bandwidth, in the form

$$f(t) = V\frac{\sin 2\pi Bt}{2\pi Bt} \qquad (2\text{-}39a)$$

In all the examples considered thus far there exists an inverse time–band-width relation: if a pulse width τ is defined, the bandwidth B in hertz is $\propto 1/\tau$. This is exactly the result noted earlier in our discussion of Fourier series and the spectra of periodic time functions [Eqs. (2-17) and (2-18)]. Thus, if the pulse width $\tau = 1\ \mu s$, $B = 1/\tau = 1$ MHz; if $\tau = 1$ ms, $B = 1/\tau = 1$ kHz; if $\tau = 10$ s, $B = 1/\tau = 0.1$ Hz. For simplicity's sake, and because this serves as a good rule of thumb, we shall often take $B = 1/\tau$ in this book. Although this generally serves as a good measure of the bandwidth, note that it is far from precise. The specific bandwidth in any particular case depends on the definition desired, or on the application itself. It may sometimes be defined as the frequency spacing between the half-power, or 3-dB, points; it may be related to the zero crossings of the frequency spectrum, as indicated in some of the examples considered here; it may be measured in terms of rms deviation about the center frequency (this is generally the case with the Gaussian pulse of Fig. 2-17). Other definitions are possible as well. Some of these will be considered elsewhere in this book. The concept of bandwidth will be particularly important in discussing the transmission of signals through linear systems. In Chap. 3, in discussing the transmission of digital symbols through band-limited channels, bandwidth will play a particularly significant role in determining appropriate bit rates to be allowed through these channels. We shall then discuss signal shaping to pack as many bits per second as possible through a given channel. But no matter what the definition of bandwidth, we shall always find that an inverse time–bandwidth relation exists. The particular definition used simply changes the proportionality constant k in Eq. (2-18): $B = k/\tau$.

The fact that there exists an inverse time–bandwidth relationship is due specifically to the Fourier-integral definition of Eq. (2-27). Thus it is readily shown for *any* time function that if the time scale is reduced by τ, the frequency is increased correspondingly by $1/\tau$. To demonstrate this relationship in the general case, consider time to be normalized to a parameter τ, written as t/τ. The Fourier integral of a function $f(t/\tau)$ is then given by

$$F'(\omega) = \int_{-\infty}^{\infty} f(t/\tau)e^{-j\omega t}\,dt$$

$$= \tau\int_{-\infty}^{\infty} f(x)e^{-j(\omega\tau)x}\,dx$$

$$= \tau F(\tau\omega) \qquad (2\text{-}40)$$

after introducing a dummy variable $x = t/\tau$, and recognizing that the resultant integral is again a Fourier transform, but with a radian frequency scale given by $\tau\omega$.

Equation (2-40) states, exactly as noted above, that if the time scale is *reduced* by a factor τ, the frequency scale is *increased* by $1/\tau$. If the pulse width in time is reduced from ms to μs, the bandwidth increases correspondingly, by a factor of 10^3, from kHz to MHz. The relationship (2-40) may be stated in a concise way by representing the Fourier-transform–inverse-Fourier-transform relationship with a doubleheaded arrow. Thus if we have

$$f(t) \leftrightarrow F(\omega) \tag{2-41}$$

then
$$f(t/\tau) \leftrightarrow \tau F(\tau\omega) \tag{2-42}$$

These expressions may be simply read as meaning that $F(\omega)$ is the Fourier transform of $f(t)$, and $f(t)$ the inverse transform of $F(\omega)$, or more simply, that the two form a Fourier transform pair.

Other properties of the Fourier integral may be deduced from the examples given above. Note for instance that in the case of both the rectangular pulse (Fig. 2-13) and the triangular pulse (Fig. 2-14), the dc content $F(0) = V\tau$, the *area* under each of the pulses. This is simply proven from Eq. (2-27), by setting $\omega = 0$:

$$F(0) = \int_{-\infty}^{\infty} f(t) \, dt \tag{2-43}$$

It is left to the reader to show that the other examples considered (see Figs. 2-14 to 2-16) do in fact obey this property.

The examples selected thus far have been *even* functions of time $[f(t) = f(-t)]$. The resultant Fourier transforms are all real and *even* functions of frequency. That this is a general property of even time functions is readily proven from Eq. (2-27). Thus, if $f(t) = f(-t)$, we have

$$F(\omega) = \int_{-\infty}^{\infty} f(t)e^{-j\omega t} \, dt = \int_{-\infty}^{\infty} f(t)(\cos \omega t - j \sin \omega t) \, dt$$
$$= \int_{-\infty}^{\infty} f(t)\cos \omega t \qquad f(t) \text{ even} \tag{2-44}$$

since the product of the even $f(t)$ and odd $\sin \omega t$ integrates to zero. Hence

$$F(\omega) = F(-\omega) \qquad f(t) \text{ even} \tag{2-45}$$

It is apparent as well that if $f(t)$ is an *odd* function in time, with $f(t) = -f(-t)$, $F(\omega)$ is imaginary and *odd* in frequency. In this case,

$$F(\omega) = -j\int_{-\infty}^{\infty} f(t)\sin \omega t \, dt \qquad f(t) \text{ odd} \tag{2-46}$$

and
$$F(\omega) = -F(-\omega) \qquad f(t) \text{ odd} \tag{2-47}$$

As an example, it is left for the reader to show that if $f(t)$ is given by

$$\begin{aligned} f(t) &= e^{-at} & t > 0 \\ &= -e^{at} & t < 0 \end{aligned} \tag{2-48}$$

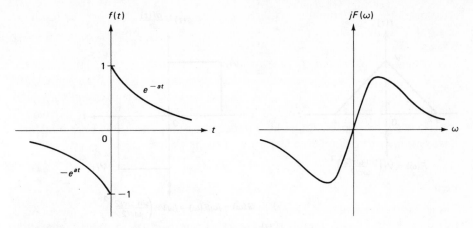

FIGURE 2-19
Example of an odd function in time and its Fourier transform.

as shown in Fig. 2-19, its Fourier transform is given by

$$F(\omega) = \frac{-2j\omega}{a^2 + \omega^2} \tag{2-49}$$

This is of course imaginary and an odd function of frequency, as also shown in Fig. 2-19.

Other useful Fourier-transform properties may be readily deduced from the defining Eqs. (2-26) and (2-27) of the Fourier transform pairs. We discuss just a few of these below. Others will be developed where needed in this book.

1. Fourier transform of a derivative. Let $f(t)$ be a differentiable function. The Fourier transform of $df(t)/dt$ is then $j\omega F(\omega)$. Thus, if

$$f(t) \leftrightarrow F(\omega)$$

then

$$\frac{df(t)}{dt} \leftrightarrow j\omega F(\omega) \tag{2-50}$$

To demonstrate this we simply differentiate Eq. (2-26) with respect to time. Then

$$\frac{df(t)}{dt} = \frac{1}{2\pi} \int_{-\infty}^{\infty} j\omega F(\omega) e^{j\omega t} \, d\omega$$

and Eq. (2-50) follows.

Equation (2-50) implies several things. Multiplication by ω increases $F(\omega)$ at the higher frequencies. Hence one can say that differentiation increases the high-frequency content of a signal. This generalizes the statement made earlier that successive discontinuities in a function and its derivatives reduce the rate of drop-off of the frequency spectrum. A pulse is essentially the derivative of a

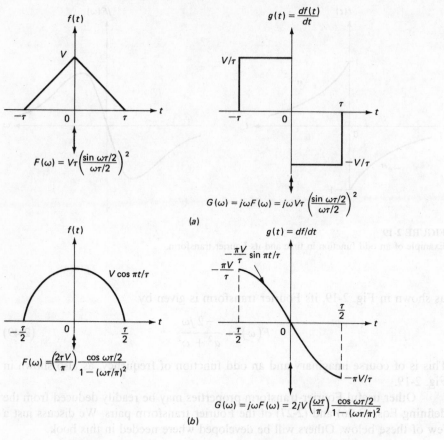

$$f(t)$$

$$V$$

$$-\tau \quad 0 \quad \tau \quad t$$

$$F(\omega) = V\tau \left(\frac{\sin \omega\tau/2}{\omega\tau/2}\right)^2$$

$$g(t) = \frac{df(t)}{dt}$$

$$V/\tau$$

$$-\tau \quad 0 \quad \tau \quad t$$

$$-V/\tau$$

$$G(\omega) = j\omega F(\omega) = j\omega V\tau \left(\frac{\sin \omega\tau/2}{\omega\tau/2}\right)^2$$

(a)

$$f(t)$$

$$V \cos \pi t/\tau$$

$$-\frac{\tau}{2} \quad 0 \quad \frac{\tau}{2} \quad t$$

$$F(\omega) = \left(\frac{2\tau V}{\pi}\right) \frac{\cos \omega\tau/2}{1 - (\omega\tau/\pi)^2}$$

$$g(t) = df/dt$$

$$-\frac{\pi V}{\tau} \sin \pi t/\tau$$

$$-\frac{\pi V}{\tau}$$

$$-\frac{\tau}{2} \quad 0 \quad \frac{\tau}{2} \quad t$$

$$-\pi V/\tau$$

$$G(\omega) = j\omega F(\omega) = 2jV\left(\frac{\omega\tau}{\pi}\right)\frac{\cos \omega\tau/2}{1 - (\omega\tau/\pi)^2}$$

(b)

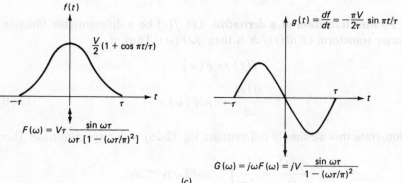

$$f(t)$$

$$\frac{V}{2}(1 + \cos \pi t/\tau)$$

$$-\tau \quad \tau \quad t$$

$$F(\omega) = V\tau \frac{\sin \omega\tau}{\omega\tau \left[1 - (\omega\tau/\pi)^2\right]}$$

$$g(t) = \frac{df}{dt} = -\frac{\pi V}{2\tau} \sin \pi t/\tau$$

$$-\tau \quad \tau \quad t$$

$$G(\omega) = j\omega F(\omega) = jV \frac{\sin \omega\tau}{1 - (\omega\tau/\pi)^2}$$

(c)

FIGURE 2-20
Fourier transforms of derivatives.

triangle. The latter has a frequency spectrum dropping off as $1/f^2$, the former as $1/f$. This will be noted again below in discussing some examples of the application of Eq. (2-50). Before we consider these examples, note also that the derivative of an even function in time must be odd. Hence the transform of the derivative must be odd and imaginary. This is of course borne out by Eq. (2-50).

If higher-order derivatives of $f(t)$ exist, we can proceed in a similar manner to find the transforms of those higher-order derivatives. For example, it is apparent from Eq. (2-50) that we also have

$$\frac{d^2f(t)}{dt^2} \leftrightarrow -\omega^2 F(\omega) \tag{2-51}$$

So as a general rule, successive differentiation increases the higher-frequency content of a signal. This observation is particularly important in following a signal through a linear system through which it propagates.

Equation (2-50) enables us to rapidly derive some other Fourier transform pairs, using some of the examples introduced earlier. Three such examples of pulses, their derivatives, and the resultant Fourier transforms appear in Fig. 2-20. Notice, as already pointed out, that the frequency spectrum of the derivative of the triangle drops off as $1/f$ with increasing frequency. The corresponding time function has a discontinuity at the origin. The same holds true for the derivative of the cosine pulse in Fig. 2-20b. The raised cosine of Fig. 2-20c has a continuous first derivative. The transform of the raised cosine itself drops off as $1/f^3$ at high frequencies, while the transform of its derivative drops off as $1/f^2$.

It is instructive to differentiate the derivative of the raised cosine once more. The resultant cosinusoidal pulse appears in Fig. 2-21. It is shown there that this may be considered as the superposition of a negative raised cosine pulse and a rectangular pulse of width 2τ. Multiplying the transform of the raised cosine

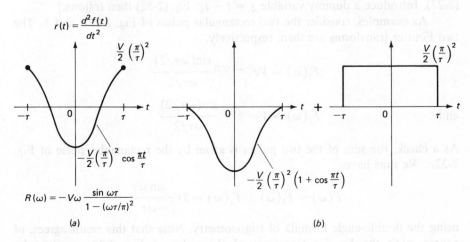

$$r(t) = \frac{d^2f(t)}{dt^2}$$

$$R(\omega) = -V\omega \frac{\sin \omega\tau}{1 - (\omega\tau/\pi)^2}$$

(a)

(b)

FIGURE 2-21
Decomposition of a cosinusoidal pulse.

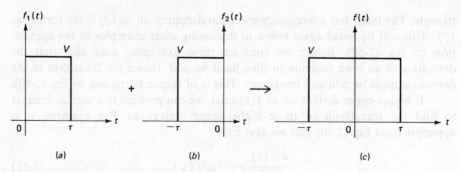

FIGURE 2-22
Examples of application of shifting theorem.

pulse by $-\omega^2$, one gets the transform $R(\omega)$ shown in Fig. 2-21. As a check, we can simply add the transforms of the two pulses shown in Fig. 2-21b. It is left to the reader to show that these are given by

$$R(\omega) = -V\tau\left(\frac{\pi}{\tau}\right)^2\frac{\sin\omega\tau}{\omega\tau\left[1 - (\omega\tau/\pi)^2\right]} + V\tau\left(\frac{\pi}{\tau}\right)^2\frac{\sin\omega\tau}{\omega\tau}$$

$$= -V\omega\frac{\sin\omega\tau}{1 - (\omega\tau/\pi)^2}$$

2. Shifting theorem. Let the origin of time be shifted from $t = 0$ to $t = t_0$. This then corresponds to a phase shift of $-j\omega t_0$ in $F(\omega)$. More precisely,

$$f(t - t_0) \leftrightarrow e^{-j\omega t_0}F(\omega) \tag{2-52}$$

The proof of this relation is left to the reader. [As a hint, use $f(t - t_0)$ in Eq. (2-27). Introduce a dummy variable $x = t - t_0$; Eq. (2-52) then follows.]

As examples, consider the two rectangular pulses of Fig. 2-22a and b. The two Fourier transforms are then, respectively,

$$F_1(\omega) = Ve^{-j\omega(\tau/2)}\frac{\sin(\omega\tau/2)}{\omega\tau/2}$$

and

$$F_2(\omega) = Ve^{j\omega(\tau/2)}\frac{\sin(\omega\tau/2)}{\omega\tau/2}$$

As a check, the sum of the two pulses is given by the rectangular pulse of Fig. 2-22c. We thus have

$$F(\omega) = F_1(\omega) + F_2(\omega) = 2V\tau\frac{\sin\omega\tau}{\omega\tau}$$

using the double-angle formula of trigonometry. Note that this result agrees, of course, with the Fourier transform of the pulse of Fig. 2-22c, written by inspection.

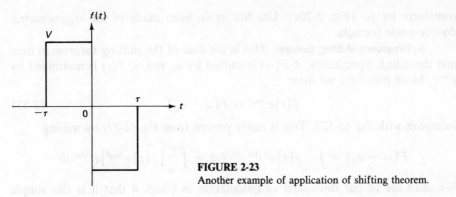

FIGURE 2-23
Another example of application of shifting theorem.

As another application of the shifting theorem, consider the function $f(t)$ of Fig. 2-23. This is obviously the superposition of the *difference* of the two pulses in Fig. 2-22a and b. Hence

$$f(t) = f_2(t) - f_1(t)$$

and

$$F(\omega) = F_2(\omega) - F_1(\omega)$$

$$= V\tau \frac{\sin(\omega\tau/2)}{\omega\tau/2} \underbrace{(e^{j\omega\tau/2} - e^{-j\omega\tau/2})}_{2j\sin(\omega\tau/2)}$$

$$= 2jV\tau \frac{\sin^2(\omega\tau/2)}{\omega\tau/2}$$

Note that this agrees with the results obtained for the transform of the derivative of the triangle in Fig. 2-20a. Since $f(t)$ in this case is odd, $F(\omega)$ is imaginary, and odd as well.

As a final example, consider the sinusoidal pulse

$$g(t) = -(\pi V/2\tau)\sin(\pi t/\tau) \qquad -\tau \le t \le \tau$$

shown sketched in Fig. 2-20c. Recall that this is the derivative of the raised cosine pulse shown in the same figure. A little thought will indicate that this sinusoidal pulse may be considered the difference of two cosine pulses, one centered at $t = -\tau/2$, the other at $t = \tau/2$, the amplitude of both being $\pi V/2\tau$. Using the shifting theorem, the Fourier transform of the difference of these two pulses is then

$$F(\omega) = \frac{2\tau}{\pi}\left(\frac{\pi V}{2\tau}\right)\frac{\cos(\omega\tau/2)}{1 - (\omega\tau/\pi)^2}\underbrace{(e^{j\omega\tau/2} - e^{-j\omega\tau/2})}_{2j\sin\omega\tau/2}$$

$$= jV\frac{\sin\omega\tau}{1 - (\omega\tau/\pi)^2}$$

in agreement with the transform obtained by multiplying the raised cosine transform by $j\omega$ (Fig. 2-20c). Use has again been made of the trigonometric double-angle formula.

3. Frequency-shifting theorem. This is the dual of the shifting theorem in time just described. Specifically, if $F(\omega)$ is shifted by ω_0 rad/s, $f(t)$ is multiplied by $e^{j\omega_0 t}$. More precisely, we have

$$f(t)e^{j\omega_0 t} \leftrightarrow F(\omega - \omega_0) \qquad (2\text{-}53)$$

[compare with Eq. (2-52)]. This is easily proven from Eq. (2-27) by writing

$$F(\omega - \omega_0) = \int_{-\infty}^{\infty} f(t)e^{-j(\omega - \omega_0)t}\, dt = \int_{-\infty}^{\infty} \left[f(t)e^{j\omega_0 t}\right]e^{-j\omega t}\, dt$$

We shall see in our discussion of modulation in Chap. 4 that it is this simple relation that accounts for the frequency shift incurred when a signal $f(t)$ is modulated onto a carrier. Specifically, we say that amplitude modulation of a carrier signal $\cos \omega_0 t$ by an information-bearing signal $f(t)$ is given by the simple multiplicative expression

$$f(t)\cos \omega_0 t$$

$f(t)$ is then called the *baseband* or *modulating* signal, and $f_0 = \omega_0/2\pi$ the carrier frequency. Writing $\cos \omega_0 t$ as the sum of two complex exponentials, and using Eq. (2-53) on each resultant term separately, we get $\frac{1}{2}[F(\omega - \omega_0) + F(\omega + \omega_0)]$ as the Fourier transform of the modulated signal. The effect of the multiplication by $\cos \omega_0 t$, the carrier signal, is to shift the spectrum by f_0 hertz. If $f(t)$ has a

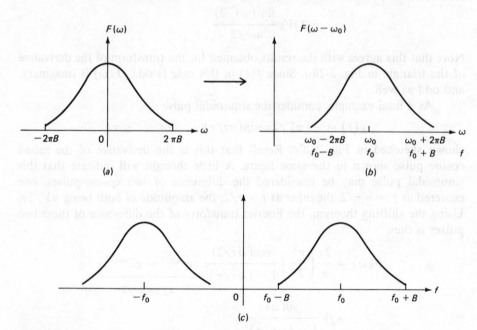

FIGURE 2-24
Illustration of frequency shift. (*a*) Original signal spectrum. (*b*) Shifted spectrum. (*c*) Spectrum of $f(t) \cos \omega_0 t$.

spectrum centered about 0, the modulated signal has its spectrum centered about the carrier, f_0. An example appears in Fig. 2-24.

4. Symmetry of amplitude and phase spectra. In general $F(\omega)$ is a complex function of frequency. Just as in the case of the Fourier spectra discussed earlier, $F(\omega)$ may be decomposed into an amplitude spectrum and a phase spectrum. For real time functions $f(t)$ (except for complex exponentials and the discussion in Chap. 4 dealing with representations of single-sideband signals, this is the only kind we shall be considering in this book), one finds that the *amplitude* spectrum is an *even* symmetrical function of frequency, and the phase spectrum is an *odd* symmetrical function of frequency.

To prove this statement we again invoke the defining Fourier integral relation (2-27). As noted previously in Eq. (2-28), we can write the generally complex $F(\omega)$ in the magnitude-phase complex form

$$F(\omega) = |F(\omega)| e^{j\theta(\omega)} \tag{2-28}$$

The magnitude term $|F(\omega)|$, written as a function of frequency, is just the amplitude spectrum; the variation of the phase angle $\theta(\omega)$ with frequency represents the phase spectrum. From Eq. (2-27),

$$F(\omega) = \int_{-\infty}^{\infty} f(t)\cos \omega t \, dt - j\int_{-\infty}^{\infty} f(t)\sin \omega t \, dt$$

Then
$$|F(\omega)|^2 = \left[\int_{-\infty}^{\infty} f(t)\cos \omega t \, dt\right]^2 + \left[\int_{-\infty}^{\infty} f(t)\sin \omega t \, dt\right]^2 \tag{2-54}$$

is an even function of frequency, and

$$\theta(\omega) = -\tan^{-1}\left[\int_{-\infty}^{\infty} f(t)\sin \omega t \, dt \Big/ \int_{-\infty}^{\infty} f(t)\cos \omega t \, dt\right] \tag{2-55}$$

is an odd function of frequency. (Why?)

As an example, consider the exponential time function of Fig. 2-25. It is readily shown that $F(\omega) = 1/(a + j\omega)$. Then $|F(\omega)| = 1/\sqrt{(a + \omega)^2}$, and $\theta(\omega) = -\tan^{-1}(\omega/a)$. Both $|F(\omega)|$ and $\theta(\omega)$ are sketched in Fig. 2-25. Notice

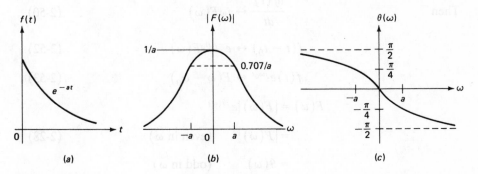

FIGURE 2-25
Amplitude and phase spectra of a signal. (*a*) Time function. (*b*) Amplitude spectrum. (*c*) Phase spectrum.

the even symmetry of the amplitude spectrum and the odd symmetry of the phase spectrum. The parameter a represents the 3-dB *radian* bandwidth (the 3-dB bandwidth in hertz is then $a/2\pi$), since $|F(a)|/F(0)| = 0.707$. The phase spectrum ranges between $\pm\pi/2$. The signal has zero phase angle at $\omega = 0$, has a $-\pi/4$-radian phase angle at $\omega = a$, and approaches $-\pi/2$ radians at large frequencies, $\omega \gg a$. The phase spectrum is generally nonlinear, but in the range $-a < \omega < a$ may be represented by the linear expression $\theta(\omega) \doteq -\omega/a$.

In discussing the concept of bandwidth earlier we focused exclusively on even symmetrical positive pulse-type time functions for which the Fourier transform is real and even, and exactly equal to the amplitude spectrum. (The phase spectrum is then zero for all ω. If the time function is negative, and even symmetrical, the phase spectrum is taken by definition to be π radians for negative frequency, and $-\pi$ radians for positive frequency. This keeps the phase spectrum odd symmetrical.) We then discussed various definitions of bandwidth in terms of the transform $F(\omega)$. More generally, the bandwidth is defined in terms of the amplitude spectrum, and everything noted earlier still holds true. The bandwidth may be taken as the 3-dB point of the amplitude spectrum as in the example of Fig. 2-25, it may be defined to be the frequency at which the amplitude spectrum first goes to zero, etc. In all cases, however, the same inverse time–frequency relation still holds. This is apparent from the exponential time function of Fig. 2-25: $1/a$ is a measure of the duration of the exponential, or its effective time constant. Its 3-dB bandwidth in hertz is then $a/2\pi$.

The Fourier-transform relations discussed above may be summarized as follows: Given

$$F(\omega) = \int_{-\infty}^{\infty} f(t) e^{-j\omega t}\, dt \tag{2-27}$$

$$f(t) = \frac{1}{2\pi} \int_{-\infty}^{\infty} F(\omega) e^{j\omega t}\, d\omega \tag{2-26}$$

or $$f(t) \leftrightarrow F(\omega) \tag{2-41}$$

Then $$\frac{df(t)}{dt} \leftrightarrow j\omega F(\omega) \tag{2-50}$$

$$f(t - t_0) \leftrightarrow e^{-j\omega t_0} F(\omega) \tag{2-52}$$

$$f(t) e^{j\omega_0 t} \leftrightarrow F(\omega - \omega_0) \tag{2-53}$$

$$F(\omega) = |F(\omega)| e^{j\theta(\omega)}$$

$$= |F(\omega)| \quad \text{(even in } \omega) \tag{2-28}$$

$$= \theta(\omega) \quad \text{(odd in } \omega)$$

Other relations will be developed at appropriate places in the book.

2-3 SIGNALS THROUGH LINEAR SYSTEMS: FREQUENCY RESPONSE

The use of the Fourier transform and the bandwidth or spectral occupancy concept developed from it enables us to readily assess the effect of passing communication signals through the systems. We commented on this point earlier. It is one of the reasons the frequency concept is so widely used in communication work. In this section we discuss the frequency response of linear systems in detail, focusing on the generally distorting effect of systems on signals passed through them. This distortion may be desired, as in the case of filters designed to produce certain controlled signal shapes at their output. The distortion may be undesirable, yet unavoidable, as in the transmission of various signal waveforms over their communication paths. (Both cases were first introduced in Sec. 1-3, Fig. 1-7, in discussing the transmission of a digital message over a communication path.)

In this section and throughout most of the book we take the system through which the signals are passed to be *linear*. This simplifies the analysis and enables us to readily assess the effect of the system on the signals in terms of frequency response. In later chapters, particularly Chaps. 4 and 6, we shall have occasion to deal with nonlinear responses as well. There too frequency analysis plays a useful role, but the analysis is much more complex and general results are hard to come by.

The simplest example of a linear system is the RC filter of Fig. 2-26. It is well known from elementary circuit analysis that a linear system has a frequency transfer function $H(\omega)$. This is a measure of the (complex) response to the complex exponential time function $e^{j\omega t}$. Depending on the input applied (voltage or current in electric circuits), and the output measured (again voltage or current in electric circuits), this transfer function may be the complex impedance, complex admittance, or transfer ratio. For example, in the RC filter of Fig. 2-26, $e^{j\omega t}$ applied at the input produces $H(\omega)e^{j\omega t}$ at the output. With the input–output ports indicated, $H(\omega)$, the voltage transfer ratio, is the ratio of the complex impedance $1/j\omega C$ at the output to the input impedance $R + 1/j\omega C$. This then gives

$$H(\omega) = \frac{1}{1 + j\omega RC} \tag{2-56}$$

as indicated in the figure. If the desired response were the voltage produced with a current $e^{j\omega t}$ applied at the input, $H(\omega)$ would be the input impedance

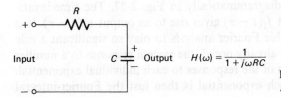

FIGURE 2-26
RC filter as example of linear system.

$R + 1/j\omega C$. More generally, for more complex networks or systems, one would have to *measure* the transfer function. One technique is to apply a fixed-amplitude and -phase sinusoidal signal at the input, and measure both amplitude and phase at the same frequency, as the input frequency is varied over the desired frequency range.

The response of a linear system to any arbitrary input signal $f(t)$ can be readily related to the transfer function, and hence to the frequency response of the network, because of the concept of superposition. For recall that by the inverse Fourier transform of Eq. (2-26) any time function $f(t)$ may be written as the sum of an infinitely dense number of complex exponentials. Each one of these exponentials gives rise to an exponential of the same frequency at the output, multiplied by the appropriate transfer function. Superposing these outputs, we find the desired output signal $g(t)$.

The concept of superposition is in fact the defining relation of a linear network, and it is because of this property that we confine ourselves to linear networks in this section. We also must invoke the assumption of time invariance or stationarity in order for the analysis to be valid. (Both nonlinear and time-varying networks generate new frequencies if a fixed-frequency sinusoidal signal is applied to them. This point is discussed further in Chaps. 4 and 5.)

Summarizing then, we deal in this section with linear stationary systems only. The RC network of Fig. 2-26 is probably the simplest example. Because of their importance to our work, we state the two basic properties in terms of which a linear stationary system is defined more precisely:

1. The response to a sum of excitations is equal to the sum of the responses to the excitations acting separately.

2. The relations between input and output are time-invariant or stationary.

The first condition is of course the statement of superposition noted above. The second condition implies that the system elements do not change with time.

Our familiar linear operations are those of multiplication by a constant, addition, subtraction, differentiation, and integration. The combination of these operations gives rise to a time-invariant linear system governed by constant-coefficient linear differential equations. The RC network of Fig. 2-26 is a particularly simple example of such a system.

The first condition cited above as defining a linear system may be summarized by saying that if an input $f_1(t)$ gives rise to an output $g_1(t)$, while an input $f_2(t)$ produces $g_2(t)$ at the output, the input $af_1(t) + bf_2(t)$ results in the output $ag_1(t) + bg_2(t)$. This is shown diagrammatically in Fig. 2-27. The time-invariance condition says that an input $f_1(t - \tau)$ gives rise to an output $g_1(t - \tau)$. It is these simple conditions that enable Fourier analysis to play so significant a role in linear system analysis. For, as already noted, the system response to a number of exponentials is simply the sum of the responses to each individual exponential. The sum of the responses to each exponential is then just the Fourier-integral

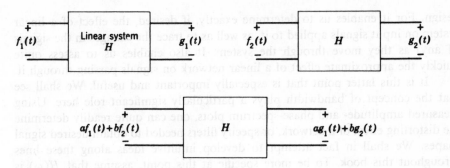

FIGURE 2-27
Linear system, defining relations.

representation of the output function $g(t)$, providing a powerful tool in linear system analysis.

To find the output response $g(t)$ of a stationary linear system with transfer function $H(\omega)$ to an input signal $f(t)$, we proceed as follows: From the inverse Fourier transform, Eq. (2-26), it is apparent that $f(t)$ is the sum of terms of the form $(1/2\pi)F(\omega)e^{j\omega t}$. Each such term produces an output $[H(\omega)/2\pi]F(\omega)e^{j\omega t}$. By superposition, then, we must have, as the response to the infinitely dense set of complex exponentials representing $f(t)$,

$$g(t) = \frac{1}{2\pi}\int_{-\infty}^{\infty}\underbrace{H(\omega)F(\omega)}_{G(\omega)}e^{j\omega t}\,d\omega \qquad (2\text{-}57)$$

Hence we have the well-known transfer function relation for linear systems,

$$G(\omega) = H(\omega)F(\omega) \qquad (2\text{-}58)$$

Here $G(\omega)$ is the Fourier transform of the desired output $g(t)$:

$$g(t) \leftrightarrow G(\omega) \qquad (2\text{-}59)$$

This transfer relationship is shown schematically in Fig. 2-28. We have of course by no means proven Eqs. (2-57) and (2-58) rigorously. We shall return to such a proof later using the convolution integral and the network impulse response.

Equation (2-58) is an extremely useful relation, and accounts in part for the widespread use of frequency concepts in communication system analysis and

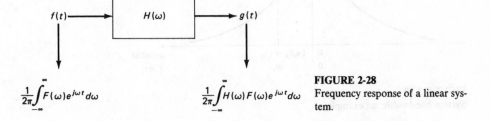

FIGURE 2-28
Frequency response of a linear system.

design. For it enables us to determine exactly, if desired, the effect of a linear system on input signals applied to it, as well as to trace the changes in the signals (if any) as they move through the system. It also enables us to assess quite quickly the approximate effect of a linear network on signals passing through it.

It is this latter point that is especially important and useful. We shall see that the concept of bandwidth plays a particularly significant role here. Using measured amplitude- and phase-spectrum plots, one can quite readily determine the distorting effect of a network, or specify filters needed to obtain desired signal shapes. We shall in fact attempt to develop intuitive ideas along these lines throughout this book. To be more specific at this point, assume that $H(\omega)$ is centered about the origin. Say that $|H(\omega)|$, the amplitude spectrum of the system transfer function, has a characteristic width, measured with respect to the origin, which we call the system bandwidth B_s in hertz, or $2\pi B_s$ in rad/s. A simple example might be

$$H(\omega) = \frac{1}{1 + j\omega/\omega_0} \tag{2-60}$$

$$|H(\omega)| = \frac{1}{\sqrt{1 + (\omega/\omega_0)^2}} \tag{2-60a}$$

This is of course just the transfer function and amplitude spectrum of the RC network of Fig. 2-26, with $RC \equiv 1/\omega_0$. $|H(\omega)|$ for this example is shown sketched in Fig. 2-29. (Note that it is identical in form to the amplitude spectrum of the exponential signal of Fig. 2-25.) If the 3-dB point is again chosen as a bandwidth measure in this case, we have $2\pi B_s = \omega_0$, or $B_s = \omega_0/2\pi$ Hz.

Now let a pulse signal $f(t)$ with bandwidth B be applied at the input to $H(\omega)$. Consider three cases:

1. $B > B_s$.
2. $B \sim B_s$.
3. $B < B_s$.

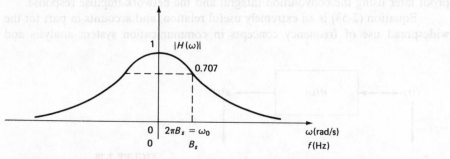

FIGURE 2-29
System bandwidth: an example.

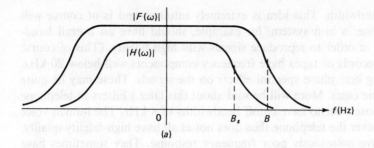

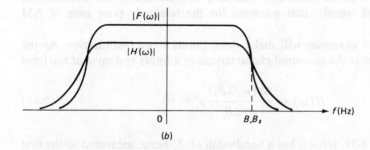

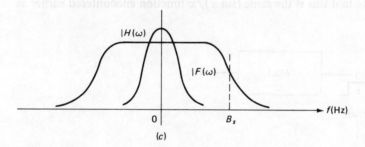

FIGURE 2-30
Effect of varying signal bandwidth. (*a*) $B > B_s$, high distortion. (*b*) $B \sim B_s$. (*c*) $B < B_s$, little distortion.

From the relation $G(\omega) = H(\omega)F(\omega)$ one would expect the output signal in case 3 to be a relatively undistorted replica of $f(t)$. In case 1 the output is highly distorted. In fact, in this case, with $B \gg B_s$, the characteristics of the input signal disappear, the output signal has a bandwidth $= B_s$, and the output signal shape is determined almost wholly by the characteristics of the linear system. Case 2 is of course intermediate between these. These three cases are shown schematically in Fig. 2-30, with the signal spectrum overlaid on the system spectrum in each case. Taking the product of the two spectra in each case, we see the reasoning behind the statements above.

It is thus apparent that to have relatively little distortion in a signal as it passes through a communication system, its bandwidth must be small compared to the system bandwidth. This idea is extremely intuitive and is of course well known to everyone: a hi-fi system, for example, should have an overall bandwidth of 20 kHz in order to reproduce signals with high fidelity. (This of course implies that all records or tapes have frequency components well below 20 kHz. We are neglecting here phase spectral effects on the signals. These may be quite significant in some cases. More will be said about this later.) Filters in telephone systems are purposely set to have cutoff bandwidths of 4 kHz. The human voice *or* music played over the telephone thus does not at all have high-fidelity quality. AM receivers have notoriously poor frequency response. They sometimes have bandwidths as low as 2.5 kHz. It is this fact, not necessarily the transmission bandwidth of AM signals, that accounts for the relatively poor tone of AM reception.

Some special examples will make these points more quantitative. As the first example say that the measured characteristic of a linear system is of the form

$$H(\omega) = \frac{\sin(\omega/2B_s)}{\omega/2B_s} e^{-j\omega/2B_s} \tag{2-61}$$

As shown in Fig. 2-31, $|H(\omega)|$ has a bandwidth of B_s hertz, measured to the first zero crossing. Note that this is the same $(\sin x)/x$ function encountered earlier as

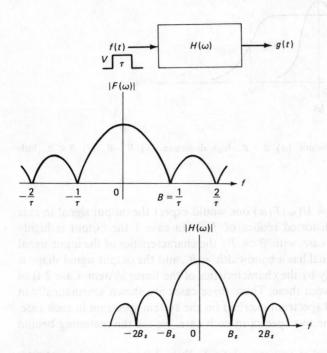

FIGURE 2-31
Response of linear system to a pulse.

the Fourier transform of a rectangular pulse (Fig. 2-13). Now consider a rectangular pulse signal $f(t)$ of width τ applied at the input to the same linear system. This is shown in Fig. 2-31. The bandwidth, in hertz, of the rectangular pulse, is $B = 1/\tau$, using the first zero crossing as a measure. $|F(\omega)|$ has the same $(\sin x)/x$ shape as $|H(\omega)|$, but with its bandwidth controlled by the pulse width τ. We now consider the three cases noted above:

1. $B \gg B_s$, or $\tau \ll 1/B_s$. The signal bandwidth is in this case much larger than the system bandwidth. The input pulse $f(t)$ is then very narrow compared to the characteristic time response of the system, which is the order of $1/B_s$. (As an example, say that $B_s = 100$ kHz and $\tau = 1$ μs. Then $B = 1$ MHz. The system time response is the order of 10 μs.) In this case the product $H(\omega)F(\omega)$ is dominated by the system transfer function $[|F(\omega)|$ is effectively constant and equal to $V\tau$ over most of the significant range of $|H(\omega)|]$. To a good approximation, then,

$$G(\omega) \doteq V\tau H(\omega) \qquad B \gg B_s \qquad (2\text{-}62)$$

and the output signal $g(t)$ is then the rectangular pulse shown in Fig. 2-32a. [Actually, $g(t)$ is not quite rectangular but has finite rise and fall times, as indicated in Fig. 2-32a, related to τ, the width of the input pulse. This will be discussed further in later sections.] The *shape* of $g(t)$ is to a good approximation determined by $H(\omega)$ only, although its amplitude $V\tau B_s$ depends on the input pulse $f(t)$ as well. As far as the system is concerned, $f(t)$ appears very much as an impulse, and $g(t)$ is then the *impulse response*. We shall have more to say about the impulse response of linear systems later, but note that a simple condition for a real excitation to approximate an impulse is exactly the relation assumed above:

$$B \gg B_s \qquad \text{or} \qquad 1/\tau \gg B_s$$

The excitation $[f(t)$ in this example] must have a frequency response that is wide compared to the system response.

2. $B = B_s$, or $\tau = 1/B_s$. In this case the signal and system bandwidths are the same. One would expect the output to be a distorted version of the input. In fact, in this case, because of the particular form of the transfer function assumed, we have

$$G(\omega) = H(\omega)F(\omega) = V\tau \left[\frac{\sin(\omega/2B_s)}{\omega/2B} \right]^2 e^{-j\omega/2B_s} \qquad (2\text{-}63)$$

From our previous discussion [Eqs. (2-33) and (2-52)] this represents the transform of a triangle centered at $\tau = 1/2B_s$. Both the input $f(t)$ and the output $g(t)$ for this case are sketched in Fig. 2-32b. Note that the distorting effect of the linear system has been to broaden the rectangular pulse out to the triangular shape shown. Alternatively, the rise time $\tau = 1/B_s$ is just half the width of the pulse.

3. $B \ll B_s$, or $\tau \gg 1/B_s$. In this case $|F(\omega)|$ is much more narrow than $|H(\omega)|$, all frequencies in the range $f < B_s$ are passed essentially unchanged, and

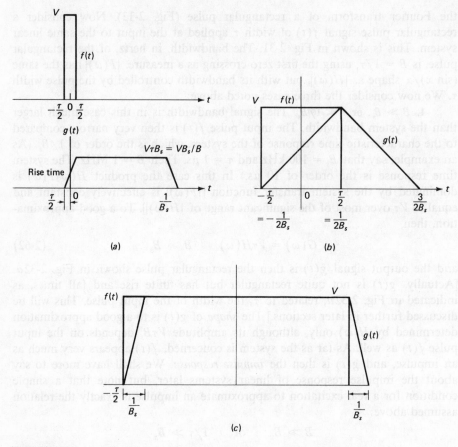

FIGURE 2-32
Effect of varying pulse width and bandwidth. (a) $B \gg B_s$ ($\tau \ll 1/B_s$). (b) $B = B_s$ ($\tau = 1/B_s$). (c) $B \ll B_s$ ($\tau \gg 1/B_s$).

$g(t)$ looks very much like the input $f(t)$:

$$G(\omega) \doteq F(\omega) \qquad B \ll B_s \qquad (2\text{-}64)$$

The resultant input and output pulses are shown sketched in Fig. 2-32c. They again differ only in the rise and fall portions. The output pulse has a rise time shown of about $1/B_s$ seconds. More-quantitative considerations relating to pulses passing through linear systems appear in the next section.

2-4 RESPONSE OF IDEALIZED NETWORKS

The example used in the previous section for determining the effect of linear filtering on a pulse-type signal was useful in showing the results of three extreme cases: the signal bandwidth much greater than the filter bandwidth, equal to the

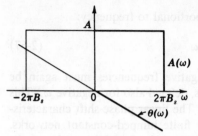

FIGURE 2-33
Ideal low-pass filter.

filter bandwidth, and much smaller than the filter bandwidth. It is less useful in intermediate cases because of the cumbersome mathematics involved in determining the output pulse response $g(t)$. More generally, one would like to *quantitatively* evaluate the response of a linear system or filter to a pulse-type signal. For this purpose numerical evaluation of the defining inverse transform relation (2-57) must be resorted to.[4] We repeat that relationship here for convenience:

$$g(t) = \frac{1}{2\pi} \underbrace{\int_{-\infty}^{\infty} H(\omega) F(\omega) e^{j\omega t} \, d\omega}_{G(\omega)} \tag{2-57}$$

This is the equation used to determine the effect of measured network amplitude and phase characteristics on signals.

Many examples of measured characteristics could be used for this purpose. It is more useful for us, since we are primarily interested in developing insight into the effect of filtering on signals, to consider instead an idealized network characteristic. This serves as a useful model of the filtering characteristics of many real networks, it enables us to demonstrate quantitatively the effect of filtering on a signal, and it focuses on the variation of only one parameter, the system bandwidth B_s. By varying B_s, we can thus see the effect of the network on the signal passing through it.

The example we shall study in detail is the ideal low-pass filter of Fig. 2-33. For simplicity of notation we define the amplitude characteristic of a linear system to be $|H(\omega)| = A(\omega)$. Hence we have, in general,

$$H(\omega) = A(\omega) e^{j\theta(\omega)} \tag{2-65}$$

For the ideal low-pass filter of Fig. 2-33, the amplitude characteristic is taken as a constant value A for all radian frequencies below the cutoff frequency $2\pi B_s$. Its bandwidth is thus precisely $2\pi B_s$ in radian measure, or B_s hertz. We thus have

$$\begin{aligned} A(\omega) &= A \qquad |\omega| \leq 2\pi B_s \\ &= 0 \qquad |\omega| > 2\pi B_s \end{aligned} \tag{2-66}$$

---

[4]In practice one often deals with discrete Fourier transforms instead, as already noted. See [SCHW 1975].

The phase shift $\theta(\omega)$ is assumed linearly proportional to frequency:

$$\theta(\omega) = -t_0\omega \qquad (2\text{-}67)$$

(t_0 is a constant of this ideal network. Negative frequencies must again be introduced in order to use the Fourier integrals, defined also for negative ω.) This amplitude response is physically unattainable. The linear phase-shift characteristic assumed is also physically impossible for finite lumped-constant networks. (Smooth transmission lines can have linear phase shift.) In addition, the amplitude and phase characteristics of a given network are connected together by the pole–zero plot of the network. They are thus normally not chosen independently, as was done here. (There do exist *all-pass* networks, synthesized from lattice structures, which provide phase variation with constant-amplitude response. These networks have their poles and zeros symmetrically arranged on either side of the $j\omega$ axis. Such networks can be included in an overall network to provide independent choice of amplitude and phase.)

The use of these idealizations to investigate the response of physical networks could thus lead to absurdities unless we are careful in interpreting our results.

We now investigate in detail the response of the ideal low-pass filter to a pulse. We shall vary the filter bandwidth B_s and determine the output signal $g(t)$ for several values of B_s. The results will of course be in agreement with those of the last section (Fig. 2-32), but more quantitatively specified.

If the input signal is a single rectangular pulse,

$$F(\omega) = V\tau\frac{\sin(\omega\tau/2)}{\omega\tau/2} \qquad (2\text{-}68)$$

(The time origin is chosen at the center of the pulse.) The transform of the output signal is

$$G(\omega) = V\tau\frac{\sin(\omega\tau/2)}{\omega\tau/2}Ae^{-jt_0\omega} \qquad -2\pi B_s < \omega < 2\pi B_s \qquad (2\text{-}69)$$

$$= 0 \qquad\qquad\qquad \text{elsewhere}$$

Then $g(t)$ will be

$$g(t) = \frac{AV\tau}{2\pi}\int_{-2\pi B_s}^{2\pi B_s}\frac{\sin(\omega\tau/2)}{\omega\tau/2}e^{j\omega(t-t_0)}\,d\omega \qquad (2\text{-}70)$$

To evaluate this integral, we recall that

$$e^{j\theta} = \cos\theta + j\sin\theta$$

Then

$$\int_{-2\pi B_s}^{2\pi B_s} \frac{\sin(\omega\tau/2)}{\omega\tau/2} e^{j\omega(t-t_0)} d\omega$$

$$= \int_{-2\pi B_s}^{2\pi B_s} \frac{\sin(\omega\tau/2)}{\omega\tau/2} [\cos\omega(t-t_0) + j\sin\omega(t-t_0)] d\omega$$

$$= \int_{-2\pi B_s}^{2\pi B_s} \frac{\sin(\omega\tau/2)}{\omega\tau/2} \cos\omega(t-t_0) d\omega$$

$$+ j\int_{-2\pi B_s}^{2\pi B_s} \frac{\sin(\omega\tau/2)}{\omega\tau/2} \sin\omega(t-t_0) d\omega \qquad (2\text{-}71)$$

The integrand of the first integral is an even function of ω. The integral is then just twice the integral from 0 to $2\pi B_s$. The integrand of the second integral is an odd function, and the integral, between equal negative and positive limits, vanishes. Equation (2-71) can thus be written

$$2\int_0^{2\pi B_s} \frac{\sin(\omega\tau/2)}{\omega\tau/2} \cos\omega(t-t_0) d\omega$$

$$= \int_0^{2\pi B_s} \left[\frac{\sin\omega(t-t_0+\tau/2)}{\omega\tau/2} - \frac{\sin\omega(t-t_0-\tau/2)}{\omega\tau/2} \right] d\omega \qquad (2\text{-}72)$$

using the trigonometric relation for sum and difference angles.

Breaking the integral up into two integrals and changing variables $[x = \omega(t - t_0 + \tau/2)$ in the first integral, $x = \omega(t - t_0 - \tau/2)$ in the second], we get finally for $g(t)$

$$g(t) = \frac{AV}{\pi} \int_0^{2\pi B_s(t-t_0+\tau/2)} \frac{\sin x}{x} dx - \frac{AV}{\pi} \int_0^{2\pi B_s(t-t_0-\tau/2)} \frac{\sin x}{x} dx \qquad (2\text{-}73)$$

Unfortunately, $\int_0^a [(\sin x)/x] dx$ cannot be evaluated in closed form but must be evaluated by expanding $(\sin x)/x$ in a power series in x and integrating term by term. Tables are available for the integral [JAHN],[5] however, and it is called the sine integral of x,

$$\text{Si } x \equiv \int_0^x \frac{\sin x}{x} dx \qquad (2\text{-}74)$$

Equation (2-73) can thus be written

$$g(t) = \frac{AV}{\pi} \left\{ \text{Si}\left[2\pi B_s\left(t - t_0 + \frac{\tau}{2}\right)\right] - \text{Si}\left[2\pi B_s\left(t - t_0 - \frac{\tau}{2}\right)\right] \right\} \qquad (2\text{-}75)$$

---

[5][JAHN] E. Jahnke and F. Emde, *Tables of Functions*, Dover, New York, 1945.

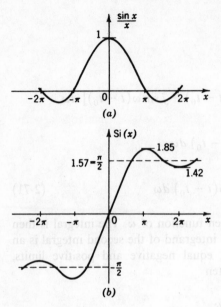

FIGURE 2-34

(a) $(\sin x)/x$. (b) Si x versus x.

The sine integral appears very frequently in the literature pertaining to pulse transmission through idealized networks. It represents the area under the $(\sin x)/x$ curve plotted previously and reproduced in Fig. 2-34a. It thus has its maxima and minima at multiples of π (the points at which $\sin x$ changes sign). The first maximum is 1.85 at $x = \pi$. The curve is odd-symmetrical about $x = 0$ and approaches $\pi/2 = 1.57$ for large values of x.

Since $(\sin x)/x$ is an even function and has zero slope at $x = 0$, the initial slope of Si x is linear and Si $x \doteq x$, $x \ll 1$. The sine integral is plotted in Fig. 2-34b.

The response of an idealized low-pass filter to a rectangular pulse of width τ sec is given by Eq. (2-75) in terms of the sine integral. Figure 2-35 shows Eq.

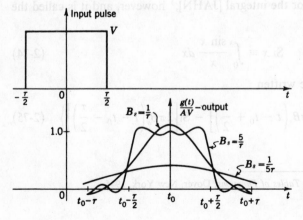

FIGURE 2-35

Response of low-pass filter.

(2-75) plotted for different filter bandwidths B_s:

1. $B_s = 1/5\tau$ ($B_s \ll 1/\tau$).
2. $B_s = 1/\tau$.
3. $B_s = 5/\tau$ ($B_s \gg 1/\tau$).

The three cases are shown superimposed and compared with the rectangular-pulse input.

What conclusions can we draw from the curves of Fig. 2-35?

1. All three output curves are displaced t_0 seconds from the input pulse and are symmetrical about $t = t_0$. The negative-linear-phase characteristic assumed for the filter has thus resulted in a *time delay* equal to the slope of the filter phase characteristic. This of course agrees with the shifting theorem of Eq. (2-52).

2. The curves bear out the filter-bandwidth–pulse-width relations developed previously.

   (*a*) $B_s \ll 1/\tau$. With the filter bandwidth much less than the reciprocal of the pulse width, the output is much broader than the input and peaks only slightly, i.e., is a grossly distorted version of the input. This approximates the impulse response of the filter.

   (*b*) $B_s = 1/\tau$. Here the output is a recognizable pulse, roughly τ sec in width, but far from rectangular. It is close to the triangle of Fig. 2-32*b*. The rise time is approximately half the pulse width.

   (*c*) $B_s \gg 1/\tau$. The output resembles the input closely and has approximately the same pulse width. There are several marked differences between output and input, however. To point these out, the curve for this case is replotted on an expanded time scale in Fig. 2-36. Note that the output pulse, although a delayed replica of the input, has a nonzero rise time.

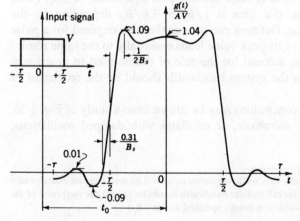

FIGURE 2-36
Signal transmission through ideal low-pass filter ($B_s \gg 1/\tau$).

This was first noted in the previous section. This rise time is inversely proportional to the filter bandwidth, as was to be expected. In particular, if the rise time here is defined as the time for a pulse to rise from zero to its maximum value of $1.09AV$,

$$\text{rise time} = 0.8\frac{1}{B_s} \tag{2-76}$$

Alternatively, if the rising curve is approximated by its tangent at the point $g(t) = 0.5AV$, the rise time of the resultant straight line $(0 \text{ to } AV)$ is

$$\text{rise time} = 0.5\frac{1}{B_s} \tag{2-77}$$

(Note that these results are valid only if $B_s \gg 1/\tau$, as is the case here.)

These results are in agreement with those obtained in the previous section for the $(\sin x)/x$ filter. If the object is merely to produce an output pulse which has about the same width as the input pulse, with fidelity unimportant, then the filter bandwidth required is approximately the inverse of the pulse width. This is the situation, for example, in a search radar system, where a recognizable signal pulse is required but its shape is of secondary interest.[6] If fidelity is required, then the bandwidth specified must be at least several times the reciprocal of the pulse width and is actually determined by rise-time considerations. For example, in tracking radars the time of arrival of individual pulses must be accurately known. The output pulse of the radar receiver must rise quite sharply so that the leading edge of the pulse may be accurately determined. The same considerations hold for navigational systems, where the time of arrival of each pulse, or its leading edge, must be accurately known. In some pulse-modulation systems the bandwidth is also determined by the specified pulse rise time. [Note that ordinarily i-f bandwidths, rather than a low-pass equivalent, are involved. As will be shown later, the i-f bandwidth is twice the low-pass equivalent, or $2B_s$. From Eqs. (2-76) and (2-77), then, rise time is $1/B_s$ or $1.6/B_s$, depending on the rise-time definition in this case. Defining rise time as the time required for a pulse to rise from 10 to 90 percent of its peak value leads essentially to the same result.]

These results, of course, account for the rule of thumb used in practice in most pulse system work that the system bandwidth should be the reciprocal of the pulse rise time.

Some other interesting conclusions may be drawn from a study of Fig. 2-36. Note that the output pulse *overshoots*, or oscillates with damped oscillations,

---

[6] Noise considerations lead to the same bandwidth requirement, as will be seen later on. Search-radar specifications thus indicate that the overall receiver bandwidth should be at least the reciprocal of the pulse width. (Actually the i-f bandwidth is normally specified and is $2B_s$.)

about the flat-top section of the pulse. This phenomenon is characteristic of filters with sharply cut-off amplitude response.

Figure 2-36 indicates that the output pulse actually has nonzero value for $t < -\tau/2$, *before* the input pulse has appeared. In fact, Eq. (2-75) gives nonzero values for negative time as well as positive time (although centered about $t = t_0$). This appearance of an output before the input producing it has appeared is obviously physically impossible and is due specifically to the non-physically-realizable filter characteristics assumed. Thus the rectangular amplitude characteristic of the idealized low-pass filter can never be realized with physical circuits. (It can be approached closely, but the number of elements required increases as the approximation becomes better. An exact fit requires an infinite number of elements theoretically. The filter phase-shift constant t_0 then becomes infinite, and the filter produces the amplitude of the pulse after infinite delay.) As pointed out previously, however, network idealizations are valuable in that they frequently provide insight into the system performance and enable general conclusions as to network response to be drawn.

In this section we have focused on the effect of amplitude spectral limiting on pulse transmission through a network. We chose an idealized low-pass filter with bandwidth B_s hertz and constant amplitude at frequencies $|f| < B_s$. We assumed the phase spectrum was linear with frequency.

It is left for the reader to show that a flat amplitude characteristic over all frequencies with linear phase shift results in a delayed replica of the input, although of possibly different magnitude. The delay is, of course, just given by the slope of the linear phase characteristic from the shifting theorem of Eq. (2-52). Thus if $\theta(\omega) = -\omega t_0$, the output pulse is delayed t_0 seconds with respect to the input one. A system in which the output is a delayed version of the input represents distortionless transmission, and is often very desirable in practice. It is again left for the reader to show that for distortionless transmission to occur, the amplitude and phase characteristics must be flat and linear with frequency, respectively, for all frequencies.

2-5 IMPULSES AND IMPULSE RESPONSE OF A NETWORK

In Sec. 2-3 we commented briefly on a pulse approximation to an impulse. We now pursue the concept of impulses and impulse response in more detail.

Specifically, let the input signal $f(t)$ to a network be the unit impulse function $\delta(t)$. Its Fourier transform is then

$$F(\omega) = \int_{-\infty}^{\infty} \delta(t) e^{-j\omega t} \, dt = 1 \qquad (2\text{-}78)$$

since

$$\int_{-\infty}^{\infty} \delta(t) r(t) \, dt = r(0) \qquad (2\text{-}79)$$

is the defining relation of the unit impulse function. An impulse function thus has a *flat* frequency characteristic, providing equal amplitude at all frequencies. If this impulse is applied to a linear system, it is equivalent to exciting the system with *all* frequencies simultaneously. The system selects the frequencies to be outputted according to its own characteristic transfer function $H(\omega)$ and outputs their weighted sum as the impulse response $h(t)$: with

$$G(\omega) = H(\omega)F(\omega) = H(\omega),$$

we have $\qquad g(t) = h(t) = \dfrac{1}{2\pi} \int_{-\infty}^{\infty} H(\omega)e^{j\omega t}\, d\omega \qquad$ (2-80)

The impulse response and the system transfer function represent a Fourier transform pair. This is an extremely useful relation in measuring the transfer function of any linear system. Instead of applying an oscillator and varying its frequency continuously, one can equally well excite the system with an impulse, measure the response $g(t) = h(t)$, and then take its Fourier transform $H(\omega)$:

$$H(\omega) = \int_{-\infty}^{\infty} h(t)e^{-j\omega t}\, dt \qquad (2\text{-}81)$$

Any pulse-type signal whose bandwidth $B \gg B_s$ can serve as a good approximation to an impulse. Alternatively, all we need is a pulse of width $\tau \ll 1/B_s$. For example,

$$\text{if} \quad B_s = 1 \text{ MHz} \qquad \tau \ll 1\ \mu s$$

$$\text{if} \quad B_s = 10 \text{ kHz} \qquad \tau \ll 100\ \mu s$$

$$\text{if} \quad B_s = 10 \text{ Hz} \qquad \tau \ll 0.1 \text{ s}$$

Two examples of the impulse response of a network have already been discussed. If $H(\omega)$ is of the $(\sin x)/x$ form, as shown in Fig. 2-31, $h(t)$ must be a rectangular pulse of width $1/B_s$ s (see Fig. 2-32a). If $H(\omega)$ is the ideal low-pass filter of Fig. 2-33, its impulse response must be of the $(\sin x)/x$ type:

$$h(t) = 2B_s A \frac{\sin 2\pi B_s(t - t_0)}{2\pi B_s(t - t_0)} \qquad (2\text{-}82)$$

(see Fig. 2-18). Details are left to the reader.

Convolution

Using the impulse response $h(t)$ and its Fourier transform $H(\omega)$, one can actually prove the transfer-function product form developed intuitively previously. Thus assume that we have a time-invariant linear system with impulse response $h(t)$. We can apply the convolution integral to obtain the response $g(t)$ to any input $f(t)$:

$$g(t) = \int_{-\infty}^{\infty} h(\tau)f(t - \tau)\, d\tau \qquad (2\text{-}83)$$

Take the Fourier transform of both sides of this equation. One then gets

$$G(\omega) = \int_{-\infty}^{\infty} \left[\int_{-\infty}^{\infty} h(\tau) f(t - \tau) \, d\tau \right] e^{-j\omega t} \, dt$$

Interchanging the order of integration on the right-hand side and using Fourier transform relations and the shifting theorem, one finds

$$G(\omega) = H(\omega) F(\omega) \tag{2-84}$$

where

$$H(\omega) \leftrightarrow h(t) \tag{2-85}$$

and

$$F(\omega) \leftrightarrow f(t) \tag{2-86}$$

As a check on the usefulness of the convolution integral and its direct connection to our frequency concepts, take the case where both $f(t)$ and $h(t)$ are rectangular pulses starting at $t = 0$, and lasting T seconds and $1/B_s$ seconds, respectively. This then corresponds to the example discussed earlier at the end of Sec. 2-3 (see Fig. 2-31). The convolution for the same three cases is carried out graphically in Fig. 2-37. Note the agreement with the previous results. Note also how the rise times arise naturally in this case.

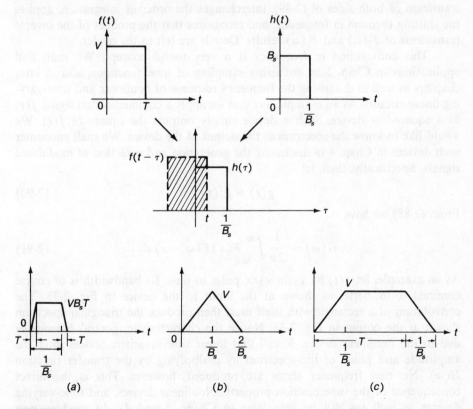

FIGURE 2-37
Convolution applied to example of Figs. 2-31 and 2-32. (a) $T < 1/B_s$. (b) $T = 1/B_s$. (c) $T > 1/B_s$.

The relations (2-83) and (2-84) may be written in more compact form by using an asterisk to represent the process of convolution. We then have the following equivalent Fourier transform pair representing the two equations:

$$g(t) = h(t) * f(t) \leftrightarrow G(\omega) = H(\omega)F(\omega) \qquad (2\text{-}87)$$

A little thought will indicate that because of the symmetry in the Fourier-transform–inverse-Fourier-transform relations there must exist an equivalent convolution in frequency when two time functions are multiplied together. The specific transform pair may be written concisely as follows:

$$g(t) = f_1(t)f_2(t) \leftrightarrow G(\omega) = \frac{1}{2\pi} F_1(\omega) * F_2(\omega) \qquad (2\text{-}88)$$

The shorthand asterisk form of the right-hand side of (2-88) implies, as above, the following convolution integral:

$$G(\omega) = \frac{1}{2\pi} \int_{-\infty}^{\infty} F_1(x) F_2(\omega - x) \, dx \qquad (2\text{-}89)$$

The proof of (2-88) is very similar to that of (2-87). One takes the inverse transform of both sides of (2-89), interchanges the order of integration, applies the shifting theorem in frequency, and recognizes that the product of the inverse transforms of $F_1(\omega)$ and $F_2(\omega)$ results. Details are left to the reader.

This convolution in frequency is a very useful concept. We shall find applications in Chap. 3 in discussing sampling of time functions, and in later chapters as well in discussing the frequency response of nonlinear and time-varying linear circuits. As an example, say that we apply a communication signal $f(t)$ to a square-law device. Such a device simply outputs the square of $f(t)$. We would like to know the spectrum at the output of the device. We shall encounter such devices in Chap. 4 in discussing the generation and detection of modulated signals. Specifically, then, let

$$g(t) = f^2(t) \qquad (2\text{-}90)$$

From (2-88) we have

$$G(\omega) = \frac{1}{2\pi} \int_{-\infty}^{\infty} F(x) F(\omega - x) \, dx \qquad (2\text{-}91)$$

As an example, let $f(t)$ be a $(\sin x)/x$ pulse in time. Its bandwidth is of course confined to B hertz, as shown at the input to the device in Fig. 2-38. The convolution of a rectangle with itself must then produce the triangular spectrum shown at the output in Fig. 2-38. Notice the characteristic spectral *broadening* due to the nonlinear device. Recall that linear time-invariant devices alter the amplitude and phase of the spectrum by multiplying by the transfer function $H(\omega)$. No new frequency terms are produced, however. This is the direct consequence of the superposition property. Nonlinear devices, and time-varying devices as well (as will be seen later in Chaps. 3 and 4), do produce new frequency terms. It is precisely this property that requires their use as modulators

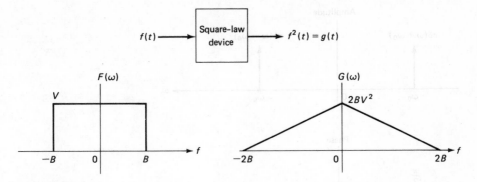

FIGURE 2-38
Spectrum at output of nonlinear device.

and demodulators (or detectors) in communication systems. [As a simple check on the result of Fig. 2-38, let $f(t) = \cos \omega_0 t$. Then $f^2(t) = \frac{1}{2} + \frac{1}{2} \cos 2\omega_0 t$. The single frequency term has been shifted down to dc and up to twice the frequency by the process of squaring. Figure 2-38 could in fact be obtained by approximating $f(t)$ as the dense sum of cosinusoidal terms, squaring the sum, and then using the trigonometric sum and difference formulas, term by term. This is just an approximate form of evaluating Fourier transforms.]

Periodic Signals

Impulse functions can be used to represent periodic signals, and from this representation, Fourier-series spectra can be represented naturally in terms of discrete-spectrum impulse functions. With this approach both periodic and aperiodic signals can be incorporated in a common Fourier-transform framework. To demonstrate this idea, recall that

$$\delta(t) \leftrightarrow 1 \tag{2-92}$$

and, from the shifting theorem,

$$\delta(t - t_0) \leftrightarrow e^{-j\omega t_0} \tag{2-93}$$

But recall as well the symmetry of the transforms in frequency and in time. Thus, let $F(\omega) = \delta(\omega - \omega_0)$. Then

$$f(t) = \frac{1}{2\pi} \int_{-\infty}^{\infty} F(\omega) e^{j\omega t} \, d\omega = \frac{1}{2\pi} e^{j\omega_0 t}$$

using the defining relation (2-79) for impulse functions. We thus have the following added transform pairs:

$$e^{j\omega_0 t} \leftrightarrow 2\pi \delta(\omega - \omega_0) \tag{2-94}$$

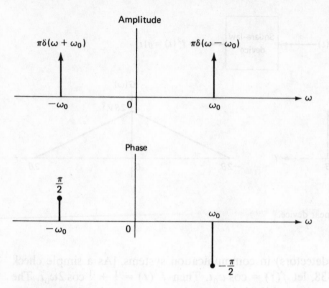

FIGURE 2-39
Fourier transform spectrum of $\sin \omega_0 t$.

and, in a similar manner,

$$e^{-j\omega_0 t} \leftrightarrow 2\pi\delta(\omega + \omega_0) \qquad (2\text{-}95)$$

In particular, then, both $\sin \omega_0 t$ and $\cos \omega_0 t$ may be presented by their Fourier transforms as well:

$$\sin \omega_0 t = \frac{e^{j\omega_0 t} - e^{-j\omega_0 t}}{2j} \leftrightarrow -j\pi[\delta(\omega - \omega_0) - \delta(\omega + \omega_0)] \qquad (2\text{-}96)$$

$$\cos \omega_0 t = \frac{e^{j\omega_0 t} + e^{-j\omega_0 t}}{2} \leftrightarrow \pi[\delta(\omega - \omega_0) + \delta(\omega + \omega_0)] \qquad (2\text{-}97)$$

The $\sin \omega_0 t$ amplitude spectrum thus consists of two impulse functions, each of weight π, at $\omega = -\omega_0$ and $\omega = +\omega_0$. Its phase spectrum is $\pi/2$ radians at $\omega = -\omega_0$ and $-\pi/2$ at $\omega = \omega_0$. These are shown in Fig. 2-39.

In general, we know that a periodic signal is representable by the complex Fourier series of Eq. (2-10). Taking Fourier transforms term by term and using (2-94) and (2-95), we get

$$f(t) = \frac{1}{T} \sum_{n=-\infty}^{\infty} c_n e^{j\omega_n t} \leftrightarrow F(\omega) = \frac{2\pi}{T} \sum_{n=-\infty}^{\infty} c_n \delta(\omega - \omega_n) \qquad (2\text{-}98)$$

Any periodic signal may thus be represented by a discrete-spectrum Fourier transform consisting of impulses at the harmonics of the periodic signal. This is

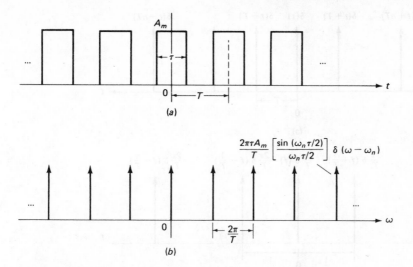

FIGURE 2-40
Fourier transform of rectangular pulse train. (a) Pulses. (b) Spectrum.

of course the same as the Fourier-series spectrum, except that weighted impulses are used here in place of the lines used previously. This is extremely useful in describing the Fourier transform of combined periodic and aperiodic signals. One simply invokes the impulses at the harmonics of the periodic signals to represent the periodic contribution.

As a simple example consider the periodic rectangular pulse train of Fig. 2-5. Taking these pulses to be centered at the time origin, we have

$$F(\omega) = \frac{2\pi\tau A_m}{T} \sum_{n=-\infty}^{\infty} \left[\frac{\sin(\omega_n\tau/2)}{\omega_n\tau/2}\right]\delta(\omega - \omega_n) \qquad \omega_n = \frac{2\pi n}{T} \qquad (2\text{-}99)$$

This is shown sketched in Fig. 2-40. As a special case, let $\tau \to 0$, $\tau A_m = 1$. The periodic pulses become a train of periodic impulses. For this case we get complete symmetry: periodic impulses in time are representable by a set of periodic impulses in frequency. Thus we have

$$f(t) = \sum_{n=-\infty}^{\infty} \delta(t - nT) \leftrightarrow F(\omega) = \frac{2\pi}{T} \sum_{n=-\infty}^{\infty} \delta(\omega - \omega_n) \qquad (2\text{-}100)$$

This Fourier-transform pair is shown sketched in Fig. 2-41. The reader is asked to compare this result with the equivalent result of Fig. 2-9. Note that the spectrum there is given by the Fourier-series coefficients. The spectrum of Fig. 2-41, on the other hand, is that of the Fourier integral or transform. It is left to the reader to show that the two results are identical.

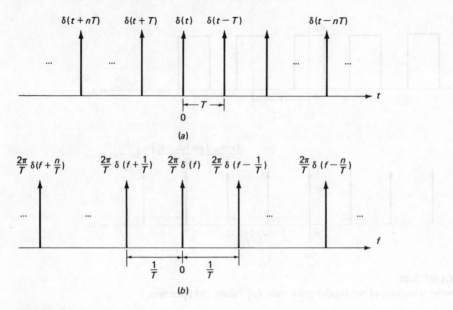

FIGURE 2-41
Fourier transform of periodic impulses. (*a*) $f(t)$: periodic impulses in time. (*b*) $F(\omega)$: periodic impulses in frequency.

2-6 TELEVISION BANDWIDTH REQUIREMENTS

Before concluding this chapter on signal transmission through linear networks, we give one further example—the calculation of the bandwidth needed to transmit a typical TV test pattern.

The pattern we choose consists of a series of alternating black and white spots. The pattern is 6 in high by 8 in wide, and the spots are 0.0121 in high and 0.0188 in wide. (These dimensions have been chosen as a compromise between the ability of the eye to resolve detail and the frequency bandwidth required.) There are then $6/0.0121 = 495$ horizontal lines that must be covered by a scanning beam of electrons. The equivalent of 30 additional lines is allowed to enable the beam to retrace from the final line back to the first again. (Actually, interlaced scanning is used in which even-numbered lines are first covered, then odd-number lines. This increases the time allotted for scanning the picture. The persistence of the eye is then relied on to give the effect of a more rapid scanning rate.) The total number of lines scanned is thus 525 (the time for the 30 additional lines is blanked out). The standard scanning rate is 30 frames per second, so that each line is scanned in

$$\frac{1}{30 \times 525} = 63.5 \ \mu\text{s}$$

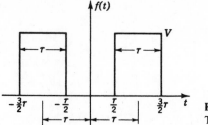

FIGURE 2-42
Two test pulses.

This represents the time in which the beam must sweep from left to right through the 8 in of the pattern and return to the left side again. Allowing 10 μs for the return, or horizontal, trace interval leaves 53.5 μs for the actual sweep. In this time $8/0.0188 = 425$ alternating black and white spots will be swept through. The electrical output will thus consist of a series of square waves of $53.5/425 = 0.125$ μs width.

Our problem is to determine how much bandwidth is needed to resolve these square-wave pulses of 0.125-μs duration, separated by the same time interval. We can relate this to the problem of resolving two pulses of width τ, separated by τ seconds (τ is 0.125 μs). These pulses are shown in Fig. 2-42.

The response of the idealized low-pass filter to a single pulse was given by Eq. (2-75). Since the system is assumed linear, superposition may be applied. The two pulses applied to the low-pass filter with bandwidth B_s hertz then produce a response at the output given by

$$g(t) = \frac{AV}{\pi}\left\{ \text{Si}\left[2\pi B_s(t - t_0) + \frac{3\tau}{2}\right] - \text{Si}\left[2\pi B_s(t - t_0) + \frac{\tau}{2}\right] \right.$$
$$\left. + \text{Si}\left[2\pi B_s(t - t_0) - \frac{\tau}{2}\right] - \text{Si}\left[2\pi B_s(t - t_0) - \frac{3\tau}{2}\right] \right\} \quad (2\text{-}101)$$

This equation has been plotted by S. Goldman in his book [GOLD 1948],[7] and some of these curves are reproduced in Fig. 2-43. (t_0 is assumed zero so that the input and output curves are superimposed for comparison.) These results indicate that for resolution of (the ability to separate) the two pulses we must have

$$B_s \geq \frac{1}{2\tau} \quad (2\text{-}102)$$

Note that this is a different situation from the one previously stressed in this chapter, in which it was desired to reproduce the pulse faithfully ($B_s \gg 1/\tau$). Here the problem is to distinguish between black and white spots or between an on and off signal. The signal detail as such is not important in this application.

[7][GOLD 1948] S. Goldman, *Frequency Analysis, Modulation, and Noise*, McGraw-Hill, New York, 1948.

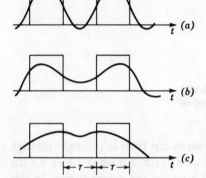

FIGURE 2-43
Low-pass filter response to TV test pattern (two pulses).
(a) $B_s = 1/\tau$. (b) $B_s = 1/2\tau$. (c) $B_s = 1/3\tau$. (From S. Goldman, *Frequency Analysis, Modulation, and Noise*, McGraw-Hill, New York, 1948.)

If $B_s < 1/2\tau$, the two pulses merge into one and the resolution disappears. If $B_s > 1/2\tau$, the sides of the pulses are sharpened, the rise times decreasing.

For the TV case outlined $\tau = 0.125\ \mu$s, and

$$B_s \geq 4 \text{ MHz}$$

It will be shown later that in order to transmit these signals at high frequencies bandwidths of $2B_s = 8$ MHz will be required. In practice some bandwidth compression is utilized (vestigial sideband transmission), and 6-MHz bandwidths are prescribed for home TV receivers.

2-8 SUMMARY

Major emphasis has been placed in this chapter on developing, through different examples, the inverse frequency–time relationship of signal transmission. We demonstrated, first through the use of the Fourier-series representation for periodic functions and then through the Fourier-integral representation of nonperiodic functions, that more rapid time variations in a signal give rise to the higher-frequency components in the signal spectrum. A general conclusion drawn from an analysis of signal transmission through linear networks was that the system bandwidth had to be approximately the reciprocal of the signal duration in order to produce at the system output a signal of the same general form as the input.

High-fidelity signal reproduction, or reproduction of detail, required bandwidths in excess of the reciprocal of the signal duration. The bandwidths needed were found to be about the reciprocal of the rise time, or the time taken for the signal to change from one level to another.

These conclusions are of importance in the design of practical system circuitry and are also of considerable theoretical importance in the study of information transmission through communication systems.

We recall that in Chap. 1 we discussed in a qualitative way the two system limitations on the amount of information per unit time (system capacity) a system could transmit:

1. Inability of the system to respond instantaneously to signal changes (due to the presence of energy-storage devices).
2. Inability of the system to distinguish infinitesimally small changes in signal level (due to inherent voltage fluctuations or noise).

These two limitations were tied together in a simple expression developed for system capacity,

$$C = \frac{1}{\tau}\log_2 n \qquad \text{bits/s} \tag{2-103}$$

where τ was the minimum time required for the system to respond to signal changes and n the number of distinguishable signal levels.

In this chapter we have found that this minimum response time is proportional to the reciprocal of the system bandwidth (two alternative ways of referring to the same phenomenon). The system capacity thus could be written

$$C = B \log_2 n \qquad \text{bits/s} \tag{2-104}$$

where B is the system bandwidth in hertz.

In the next two chapters we shall discuss some common point-to-point communication systems and their bandwidth requirements. We shall then return in Chap. 6 to a discussion of the second limitation on the system capacity—inherent noise.

PROBLEMS

2-1. (*a*) Find the Fourier-series representations of each of the pulse trains in Fig. P2-1. Choose the time origin so that a cosine series is obtained in each case.

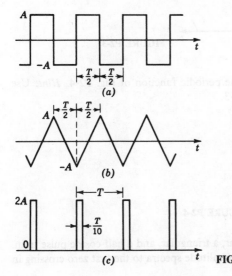

FIGURE P2-1

(b) Plot the first 10 Fourier coefficients vs. frequency for each pulse train. Compare the plot of Fig. P2-1a with each of the other two, paying particular attention to the rate of decrease of the higher-frequency components. Note that Fig. P2-1b represents in form the integral of Fig. P2-1a and has no discontinuities in the function. The pulses of Fig. P2-1c are much narrower than those of Fig. P2-1a.

2-2. (a) Find the cosine Fourier-series representation of the half-wave rectified sine wave of Fig. P2-2.

(b) Compare the successive Fourier coefficients and their rate of decrease with those of Fig. P2-1a.

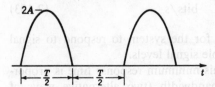

FIGURE P2-2

2-3. Find the complex Fourier series for the two pulse trains of Fig. P2-3. Plot and compare the two amplitude spectra. What is the significance of the term $e^{-j\omega_n t_0}(\omega_n = 2\pi n/T)$ in the expression for the complex Fourier coefficient for the rectangular pulses?

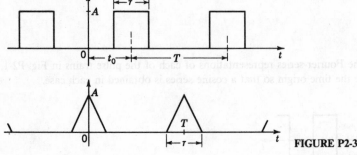

FIGURE P2-3

2-4. Find the complex Fourier series for the periodic function of Fig. P2-4. *Hint*: Use superposition and the result of Prob. 2-3.

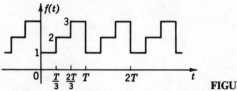

FIGURE P2-4

2-5. Consider the three cases of a rectangular, a triangular, and a half-cosine pulse train, all with $\tau/T = \frac{1}{10}$ (Fig. P2-5). Plot the amplitude spectra to the first zero crossing in each. What is the percentage of the total power in the first 10 frequency components?

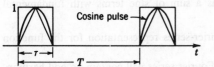

Cosine pulse

FIGURE P2-5

2-6. Find the complex Fourier series for the periodic function of Fig. P2-6. Find the percentage of power in the first six components.

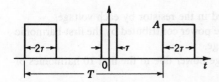

A

FIGURE P2-6

2-7. Plot the frequency spectra for the pulses of Fig. P2-7.

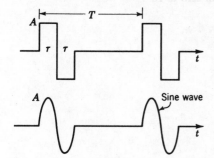

Sine wave

FIGURE P2-7

2-8. Find the complex Fourier series for the two periodic functions of Fig. P2-8.

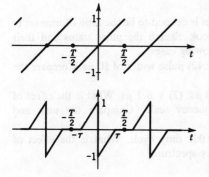

FIGURE P2-8

2-9. $f(t) = \sin \omega t$ for $0 \leq t \leq \pi/\omega$. It is undefined for values of t outside this interval.

(a) Express $f(t)$ inside the given interval as a sum of cosine terms with fundamental radian frequency ω.

(b) Express $f(t)$ in the same interval as a sum of sine terms with fundamental radian frequency ω.

2-10. T is the period of expansion in the Fourier-series representation for the function $f(t)$.

(a) Show that if $f(t) = f(t + T/2)$, the Fourier series will contain no odd harmonics.

(b) Show that if $f(t) = -f(t + T/2)$, the Fourier series will contain no even harmonics.

2-11. Each of the pulse trains shown in Fig. P2-11 represents a voltage $v(t)$ appearing across a load resistor of 1 Ω.

(a) Find the total average power dissipated in the resistor by each voltage.

(b) Find the percentage of the total average power contributed by the first-harmonic (fundamental) frequency of each voltage.

(c) Find the percentage of the total average power due to the first 10 harmonics of each voltage.

(d) Find the percentage of the total average power due to those harmonics of the voltage within the first zero-crossing interval of the amplitude spectrum.

(e) Add a fixed-bias (dc) level E volts to each of the pulse trains. Sketch the spectrum of each as E is increased from zero to 10 V.

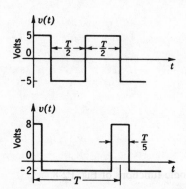

FIGURE P2-11

2-12. The duty cycle of a train of rectangular pulses is defined to be the ratio of time on to time off, or τ/T in the notation of this book. Sketch the pulse trains and their corresponding frequency spectra for the following cases:

(a) 0.1 duty cycle; (1) pulse width τ of 1 μs; (2) pulse width of 10 μs. Compare the frequency spectra.

(b) Repetition period T is 1 ms; (1) τ is 10 μs; (2) τ is 1 μs. What is the effect of varying τ, with T fixed, on the frequency scale? Compare the time and frequency plots.

(c) 10-μs pulses; (1) 0.1 duty cycle; (2) 0.001 duty cycle. What is the effect of varying T, with τ fixed, on the frequency spectrum?

2-13. Find the complex Fourier coefficient c_n, and write the Fourier series for the function shown in Fig. P2-13. Leave the coefficients in complex form.

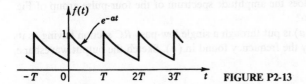

FIGURE P2-13

2-14. (a) Show that the complex Fourier coefficient c_n of the pulse train of Fig. P2-14 is given by $c_n = 2A\tau[\sin(\omega_n\tau/2)/(\omega_n\tau/2)]\cos \omega_n\tau$. *Hint*: Use the result of Prob. 2-3 and the principle of superposition.

(b) Sketch the spectrum envelope and indicate the location of the spectral lines for $\tau/T = 0.1$.

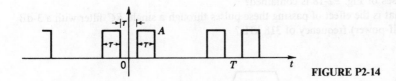

FIGURE P2-14

2-15. An ASCII terminal uses a code consisting of nine units or time intervals per character (letter). This includes start and stop pulses during the first and last time interval corresponding to each letter. During the remaining intervals the signal may be either on (a 1) or off (a 0). The average character has the form shown in Fig. P2-15. Assuming that the average word in the English language contains five letters and that one character is needed to transmit a space between words, there are on the average six characters per word. The rate of transmission is 60 words per minute.

(a) Find the length of one time interval.

(b) Find the bandwidth needed to transmit the first five harmonics of the pulse train of Fig. P2-15. What bandwidth would be needed if the rate of transmission were increased to 100 words per minute? Why are these bandwidths the maximum required to transmit a signal from this terminal?

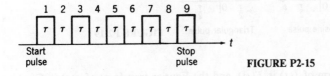

FIGURE P2-15

2-16. A pulse-code-modulation (PCM) system produces symmetrical trapezoidal-shaped pulses, 5 μs wide at the top and 5.5 μs wide at the base. The average spacing between pulses is 125 μs.

(a) What is the approximate system bandwidth required?

(b) If the average pulse spacing were halved, what bandwidth would be required?

(c) The pulses are passed through a low-pass filter cutting off at 200 kHz. Sketch the waveshape at the output of the filter.

2-17. (a) At what frequency does the amplitude spectrum of the four-pulse group of Fig. P2-17 first go to zero?

(b) The pulse group in (a) is put through a single low-pass RC section having as its half-power frequency the frequency found in (a). Sketch the output waveshape.

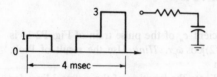

FIGURE P2-17

2-18. (a) What is the bandwidth in which 90 percent of the power in the trapezoidal pulses of Fig. P2-18 is contained?

(b) What is the effect of passing these pulses through a single RC filter with a 3-dB (half-power) frequency of 318 kHz?

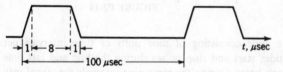

FIGURE P2-18

2-19. Find the Fourier transform of each of the pulses shown in Fig. P2-19. Compare with the complex Fourier coefficients of the corresponding pulse trains obtained in Prob. 2-5.

Rectangular pulse   Half-cosine pulse   Triangular pulse   **FIGURE P2-19**

2-20. The Fourier transform of $f(t)$ is $F(\omega)$, and the Fourier transform of $g(t)$ is $G(\omega)$. For each of the following cases, find $G(\omega)$ in terms of $F(\omega)$:

(a) $g(t) = f(3t)$.

(b) $g(t) = f(t + a)$.

2-21. (a) Show that for each of the pulses of Prob. 2-19 any "bandwidth" definition (e.g., the first zero crossing of the spectrum) would give $B = K/\tau$, K a constant.

(*b*) Superimpose sketches of $|F(\omega)|$ for each of these pulses, and compare the spectrum curves. Focus attention particularly on the l-f and h-f ends of the spectra.

2-22. Find the Fourier transform of each of the pulses of Fig. P2-22.

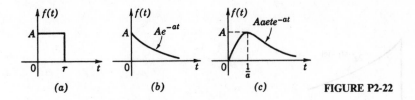

(*a*)   (*b*)   (*c*)   **FIGURE P2-22**

2-23. Find the Fourier transform of each of the functions of Fig. P2-23. The last two time functions are even and odd, respectively. What, therefore, is to be expected of their Fourier transforms?

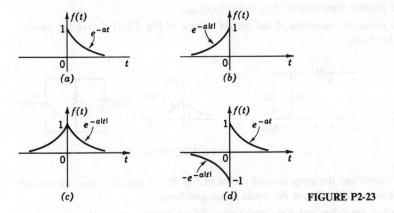

(*c*)   (*d*)   **FIGURE P2-23**

2-24. Find the Fourier transforms of the pulses of Figs. 2-14 to 2-16 and show they are given by (2-33), (2-35), and (2-37), respectively. *Hint*: Represent the cosine as the sum of two exponentials. Superimpose sketches of the spectra. Check the comments made in the text on the locations of the first zero crossings and variations of the spectra with frequency. Check that the dc content $F(0)$ is in each case given by the area under the curve [Eq. (2-43)].

2-25. Check that the inverse Fourier transform of the rectangular spectrum of Fig. 2-18 is given by the $(\sin x)/x$ time function of Eq. (2-39).

2-26. Use the Fourier-transform relation of Eq. (2-50), connecting the derivative of a function to the Fourier transform of that function, to verify the Fourier transforms of Figs. 2-20 and 2-21.

2-27. Prove the shifting theorem of Eq. (2-52).

2-28. Consider the delayed exponential $f(t) = 2e^{-5(t-10)}U(t-10)$ shown in Fig. P2-28 [$U(t)$ is the unit-step function]. Find its Fourier transform $F(\omega)$. Sketch both $|F(\omega)|$ and $\measuredangle F(\omega)$.

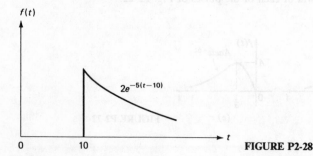

FIGURE P2-28

2-29. Find and sketch the spectrum of a cosinusoidal pulse, $A \cos \omega_0 t$, $-\tau/2 \le t \le \tau/2$; 0 elsewhere. Compare with the spectrum of a rectangular pulse of width τ, centered about $t = 0$. *Hint:* Show the cosinusoidal pulse is represented by a rectangular pulse $\times \cos \omega_0 t$.

2-30. Find the Fourier transform of $f(t) = e^{-a|t|} \cos \omega_0 t$.

2-31. Find the frequency spectrum of the output voltage of Fig. P2-31. Leave the answer in complex form.

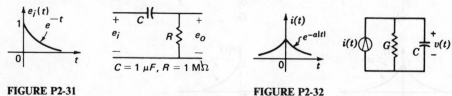

FIGURE P2-31   FIGURE P2-32

2-32. For the circuit and the input current shown in Fig. P2-32, find the capacitor voltage as a function of time. Leave the result in integral form.

2-33. "Integration smoothes out time variations; differentiation accentuates time variations." Verify this statement for the two circuits shown in Fig. P-33, by comparing the input and output spectra with an arbitrary input $v_i(t)$.

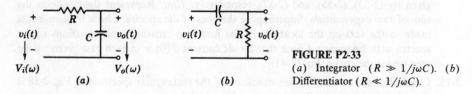

FIGURE P2-33

(a) Integrator ($R \gg 1/j\omega C$). (b) Differentiator ($R \ll 1/j\omega C$).

2-34. A delay line and integrating circuit, combined as shown in Fig. P2-34, are one example of a "holding circuit" commonly used in radar work, sampled-data servo systems, and pulse-modulation systems.

(a) Tracing through the circuit step by step, show that the frequency transfer function is $H(\omega) = [e^{-j\omega\tau/2} \sin(\omega\tau/2)]/(\omega\tau/2)$.

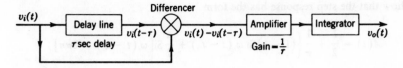

FIGURE P2-34
Holding circuit, $(\sin x)/x$ filter.

    (b) If $v_i(t)$ is a rectangular pulse of width τ seconds, show that the output is a triangular pulse of width 2τ seconds, by (1) actually performing the successive operations indicated in the figure, (2) using the spectrum approach, the results of (a), and Eq. (2-33).

2-35. A pulse of the form $e^{-at}u(t)$ with $u(t)$ the unit step function is applied to an idealized network with transfer characteristic $H(\omega) = Ae^{-jt_0\omega}$, $|\omega| \le \omega_c$; $H(\omega) = 0$, $|\omega| > \omega_c$.

    (a) Show that the output time response is given by

$$g(t) = \frac{A}{\pi}\int_0^{\omega_c}\left[\frac{a\cos\omega(t - t_0)}{a^2 + \omega^2} + \frac{\omega\sin\omega(t - t_0)}{a^2 + \omega^2}\right]d\omega$$

    (b) Show that, for $\omega_c \gg a$,

$$g(t) = \frac{A}{\pi}\,\text{Si}\,\omega_c(t - t_0) + \frac{A}{2}e^{-a|t - t_0|}$$

$$\text{Si}\,x \equiv \int_0^x\frac{\sin x}{x}\,dx$$

Note that $\int_0^\infty[(\cos mx)/(1 + x^2)]\,dx = (\pi/2)e^{-a|m|}$.

2-36. Using the results of Prob. 2-35, show that the *unit-step response* of an idealized network with amplitude A, cutoff frequency ω_c, and phase constant t_0 is given by

$$A(t) = A\left[\frac{1}{2} + \frac{1}{\pi}\,\text{Si}\,\omega_c(t - t_0)\right]$$

Sketch $A(t)/A$.

2-37. The unit-step response of the idealized network of Prob. 2-36 can also be obtained by first finding the response to a pulse of unit amplitude and width τ. As τ is allowed to get very large, the pulse approaches a unit step. Show that the network response approaches the unit-step response of Prob. 2-36.

2-38. A filter has the following amplitude and phase characteristics:

$$A(\omega) = 1 - \alpha + \alpha\cos 2\pi n\frac{\omega}{\omega_c} \qquad |\omega| \le \omega_c$$

$$= 0 \qquad |\omega| > \omega_c$$

$$\theta(\omega) = -t_0\omega$$

(This represents a filter with ripples in the passband.)

(a) Show that the step response has the form

$$A(t) = \frac{1}{2} + \frac{1}{\pi} \left\{ (1 - \alpha) \text{Si} \, \omega_c (t - t_0) + \frac{\alpha}{2} \text{Si}[\, \omega_c (t - t_0) + 2\pi n] \right.$$

$$\left. + \frac{\alpha}{2} \text{Si}[\, \omega_c (t - t_0) - 2\pi n] \right\}$$

(Use the approach of either Prob. 2-36 or Prob. 2-37.)

(b) Sketch $A(t)$ if $\alpha = \frac{1}{4}$, $n = 2$. Use the straight-line approximation for Si x indicated in Fig. P2-38.

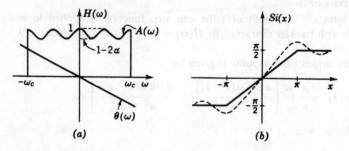

(a)   **(b)**

FIGURE P2-38
(a) Low-pass filter with ripples. (b) Linear approximation to Si x.

2-39. In the filter characteristic of Prob. 2-38 let $2n = 1$ and $\alpha = \frac{1}{2}$. Sketch the amplitude characteristic for this case. Find the step response of this filter, and compare with the step response of the idealized filter of Prob. 2-36. This shows the effect of rounding off the sharp corners of the ideal low-pass filter.

2-40. Two students were asked the effect of passing the square wave of Fig. P2-40 through the high-pass RC network shown. John reasoned that since the fundamental

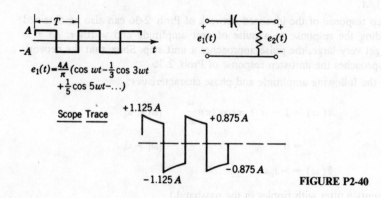

$$e_1(t) = \frac{4A}{\pi} \left(\cos wt - \frac{1}{3} \cos 3wt \right.$$
$$\left. + \frac{1}{5} \cos 5wt - \ldots \right)$$

FIGURE P2-40

frequency of the square wave was four octaves above the 3-dB falloff frequency of the filter, its attenuation and that of all the harmonics should be negligible. The output should thus look like the input. Conrad disagreed and to prove his point set up an experiment and obtained the oscilloscope trace for the output shown in the lower part of Fig. P2-40. Explain the fallacy (or fallacies) in John's argument. Describe the characteristics of a network to be connected in tandem with the RC network so that no overall distortion will result.

2-41. Suppose

$$H(\omega) = \frac{1}{a + j\omega} = |H(\omega)| e^{j\theta(\omega)}$$

(*a*) Sketch $|H(\omega)|$ and $\theta(\omega)$.
(*b*) Find and sketch the impulse response of a network with this transfer function.
(*c*) Show a simple RC circuit that has a transfer function of this type. Compare the impulse response of the RC circuit with the result of (*b*).

2-42. Show that the impulse response of the ideal low-pass filter of Fig. 2-33, with linear phase characteristic defined as in Eq. (2-67), is given by (2-82). Sketch this response, and relate the time difference between successive crossings to the bandwidth B_s.

2-43. Prove Eq. (2-88), relating convolution in frequency to the multiplication of two time functions. Use this transform pair, combined with (2-97), the Fourier transform of $\cos \omega_0 t$, to prove the frequency-shift property of $f(t)\cos \omega_0 t$.

2-44. Refer to Fig. P2-44, $RC = 1$ ms. Sketch the response $v_0(t)$ of the RC circuit to the excitation $f(t)$ over a 3-ms interval for four cases:
(*a*) $f(t)$ is a unit-amplitude rectangular pulse 1 ms wide.
(*b*) $f(t)$ is a unit-amplitude pulse 1 μs wide.
(*c*) $f(t)$ consists of two unit-amplitude pulses, each 1 μs apart wide, spaced 1 μs apart.
(*d*) $f(t)$ consists of two unit-amplitude pulses, each 1 μs wide, spaced 1 ms apart.
In which of these cases may $f(t)$ be approximated by an impulse function? Explain.

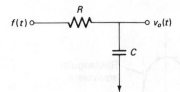

FIGURE P2-44

2-45. Repeat Prob. 2-44 if instead of the RC circuit an ideal low-pass filter of bandwidth $B_s = 1$ kHz is used.

2-46. Find the Fourier transforms of the two pulse trains of Prob. 2-3.

2-47. A time function $f(t)$ is multiplied by a periodic set of unit impulses, as shown in Fig. P2-47. The Fourier transform $F(\omega)$ is band-limited to (has no frequency components above) B hertz as shown. Use frequency convolution to find the spectrum at the multiplier output. Sketch the three cases $1/T = 4B$, $1/T = 2B$, and $1/T = B$.

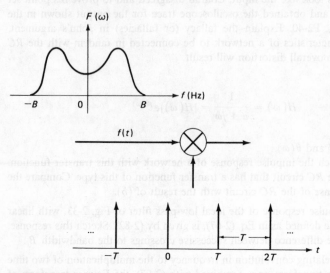

FIGURE P2-47

2-48. Following is an additional way of demonstrating the inverse time–bandwidth relation, given $f(t) \leftrightarrow F(\omega)$.

(a) $f(t)$ is an even pulse in time $[f(t) = f(-t)]$, as shown in Fig. P2-48a. Its width τ, in time, is defined to be the width of an equivalent rectangular pulse of the same area and the same height at $t = 0$, as shown in Fig. P2-48a. Show $\tau = F(0)/f(0)$.

(b) The width B, in Hz, of the spectrum $F(\omega)$, the bandwidth of $f(t)$, is defined to be the width of an equivalent rectangular spectrum of the same area as $F(\omega)$ and the same value at $f = 0$, as shown in Fig. P2-48b. Show $B = f(0)/2F(0)$. Hence show $B\tau = \frac{1}{2}$.

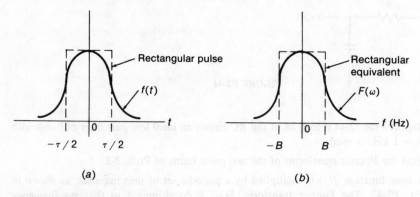

(a)

(b)

FIGURE P2-48

CHAPTER

3

DIGITAL
COMMUNICATION
SYSTEMS

3-1 INTRODUCTION

In this book we are basically interested in investigating the information-handling capabilities of different communication systems and networks, with stress on point-to-point (physical-layer) communication. We showed in Chap. 2 that one important parameter determining the system information capability is the system bandwidth. In Chap. 6 we shall discuss the limitations on system performance due to noise.

We pause at this stage in our discussion to describe some typical point-to-point digital communication systems, to compare them on the basis of bandwidth requirements, and to develop further the inverse frequency–time relationship of Chap. 2.

The stress here will be on digital systems because of their paramount importance in modern-day technology and because the concepts important to information transmission are so easily developed through the study of digital systems. This was first pointed out in Chap. 1, where the transmission of digital signals step by step through a typical system was discussed.

The current widespread use of digital signaling is the result of many factors:

1. The relative simplicity of digital circuit design and the ease with which one can apply integrated circuit techniques to digital circuitry.
2. The ever-increasing use and availability of digital processing techniques.

3. The widespread use of computers in handling all kinds of data.
4. The ability of digital signals to be coded to minimize the effects of noise and interference.

Although some communications signals are inherently digital in nature—e.g., terminal data, computer outputs, pulsed radar and sonar signals, etc., many signals are analog, or smooth, functions of time. If these signals are to be transmitted digitally, they first have to be sampled at a periodic rate and then further converted to discrete amplitude samples by quantization. The sampling procedure in this analog-to-digital (A/D) conversion process will be the first topic treated in this chapter. Speech, TV, facsimile, and telemetered data signals are all examples of analog signals that are often transmitted digitally.

We shall discuss time multiplexing of digital signals, in which signals from different sources are sequentially transmitted through the system. (Sine-wave carrier modulation by these signals for remote transmission will be discussed in Chap. 4.) Some of the problems arising in the use of digital systems will also be discussed. These include time synchronization, intersymbol interference, quantization noise, transmission bandwidth requirements, etc. Examples will be given of various types of digital systems in use.

3-2 NYQUIST SAMPLING

Consider a continuous varying signal $f(t)$ that is to be converted to digital form. We do this simply by first sampling $f(t)$ periodically at a rate of f_c samples per second. Although in practice this sampling process would presumably be carried out electronically by gating the signal on and off at the desired rate, we show the sampling process conceptually in Fig. 3-1 using a rotating mechanical switch.

Assume that the switch remains on the $f(t)$ line τ seconds, while rotating at the desired rate of $f_c = 1/T$ times per second ($\tau \ll T$). The switch output $f_s(t)$ is then a sampled version of $f(t)$. A typical input function $f(t)$, the sampling times, and the sampled output $f_s(t)$ are shown in Fig. 3-2. f_c is called the *sampling rate*, and T is the *sampling interval*.

The question that immediately arises is: What should the sampling rate be? Are there any limits to the rate at which we sample? One might intuitively feel that the process of sampling has irretrievably distorted the original signal $f(t)$. The process of sampling has been introduced to convert the signal $f(t)$ to a digital form for further processing and transmission. Yet eventually, and at a

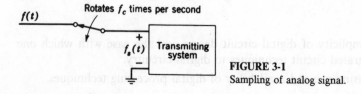

FIGURE 3-1
Sampling of analog signal.

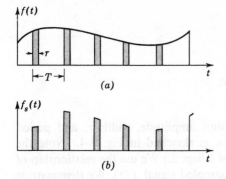

FIGURE 3-2
The sampling process. (τ = sampling time; $T = 1/f_c$ = sampling interval.) (*a*) Input $f(t)$. (*b*) Sampled output $f_s(t)$.

remote location, in most cases, one would like to retrieve $f(t)$ again. Have we lost valuable information in the sampling process?

The answer to this last question, and from this, to the other questions asked, is that under a rather simple assumption (closely approximated in practice), the sampled signal $f_s(t)$ contains within it *all* information about $f(t)$. Further, $f(t)$ can be uniquely extracted from $f_s(t)$. This amazing and not at all obvious result can be demonstrated through the use of the Fourier analysis of Chap. 2.

We first assume the signal $f(t)$ is *band-limited* to B hertz. This means there are absolutely no frequency components in its spectrum beyond $f = B$. The Fourier transform $F(\omega)$ of such a signal is shown in Fig. 3-3. Physically occurring signals generally do not have the sharp frequency cutoff implied by the concept of band-limitedness. Except for a few singular cases, examples of which were given in Chap. 2, real signals contain frequency components out to all frequencies. Yet we know from our discussion in Chap. 2 that the frequency content drops rapidly beyond some defined bandwidth. This approximation of real signals by band-limited ones introduces no significant error in the analysis and will therefore henceforth be assumed. (In practice, sharp-cutoff low-pass filters are frequently introduced before the sampling process to ensure that the band-limited condition is obeyed to the approximation desired.)

With the signal $f(t)$ band-limited to B hertz, it is then readily shown that sampling the signal does *not* destroy any information content, provided that the sampling rate $f_c \geq 2B$. The minimum sampling rate of $2B$ times per second is called the *Nyquist*[1] sampling rate, and $1/2B$ the Nyquist sampling interval.

To demonstrate this result through Fourier analysis we use a simple stratagem. It is apparent that the sampled signal $f_s(t)$ may be represented in terms of $f(t)$ by the simple relation

$$f_s(t) = f(t)S(t) \tag{3-1}$$

---

[1] After H. Nyquist of the Bell Telephone Laboratories.

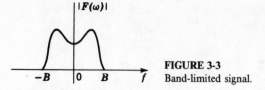

FIGURE 3-3
Band-limited signal.

with $S(t)$ a periodic series of pulses of unit amplitude, width τ, and period $T = 1/f_c$. This *switching* or *gating function* is sketched in Fig. 3-4. (Note the recurrence of our familiar periodic pulses of Chap. 2.) We use the relationship of (3-1) to derive the spectrum $F_s(\omega)$ of the sampled signal $f_s(t)$. We demonstrate two ways of doing this, both of which rely on Fourier-analysis relations developed in Chap. 2. First note that the periodic switching function $S(t)$ may be expanded in its Fourier series. It is apparent that the sampled signal $f_s(t)$ can be written in the form

$$f_s(t) = df(t)\left(1 + 2\sum_{n=1}^{\infty} \frac{\sin n\pi d}{n\pi d}\cos 2\pi nf_c t\right) \qquad (3\text{-}2)$$

Here $d = \tau/T$, the *duty cycle*. Note the typical term $f(t)\cos 2\pi nf_c t$ appearing. By the shifting theorem of Chap. 2, the Fourier transform $F_c(\omega)$ of this term represents $F(\omega)$, the transform of $f(t)$, shifted positively and negatively by $n\omega_c$, $\omega_c = 2\pi f_c$. Thus

$$F_c(\omega) = \tfrac{1}{2}F(\omega - n\omega_c) + \tfrac{1}{2}F(\omega + n\omega_c) \qquad (3\text{-}3)$$

If $F(\omega)$ was originally centered at 0, then $F_c(\omega)$ is centered at $\pm n\omega_c$. As pointed out in Chap. 2, the amplitude modulation of $\cos n\omega_c t$, the *carrier frequency*, by $f(t)$, the modulating signal, results in a new signal centered about the carrier.

Repeating this process for each value of n, weighting by the appropriate factors of (3-2), and then superposing all the terms, we have for the Fourier transform of $f_s(t)$

$$F_s(\omega) = dF(\omega) + d\sum_{\substack{n=-\infty \\ n\neq 0}}^{\infty} \frac{\sin n\pi d}{n\pi d}F(\omega - n\omega_c) \qquad (3\text{-}4)$$

This sum of individual Fourier transforms, each centered at a multiple of the sampling frequency, is shown sketched in Fig. 3-5. Note that the amplitude of each successive component decreases as $(\sin n\pi d)/n\pi d$. The effect of sampling

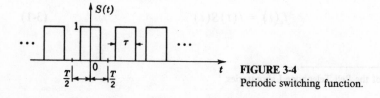

FIGURE 3-4
Periodic switching function.

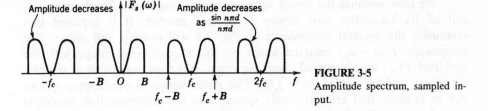

FIGURE 3-5
Amplitude spectrum, sampled input.

$f(t)$ has thus been to shift its spectrum up to all harmonics of the sampling frequency. Alternatively, we may say that the effect of multiplying the periodic sampling function $S(t)$ by the nonperiodic $f(t)$ has been to broaden its discrete-line spectrum into a continuous spectrum symmetrically situated about the original frequency lines.

Equation (3-4) for the spectrum of the sampled signal $f_s(t)$ may be derived in an alternative instructive fashion from the product relation of (3-1) by use of the frequency convolution theorem of Chap. 2. Recall from (2-88) that the product of two time functions results in a Fourier transform given by the convolution of the respective Fourier transforms. Specifically, we have, from (3-1),

$$F_s(\omega) = \frac{1}{2\pi} F(\omega) * S(\omega)$$

$$= \frac{1}{2\pi} \int_{-\infty}^{\infty} F(x) S(\omega - x) \, dx \qquad (3\text{-}5)$$

But the Fourier transform of the periodic sampling function $S(t)$ is, from (2-99), given by an infinite set of equally spaced impulse functions in frequency:

$$S(\omega) = 2\pi d \sum_{n=-\infty}^{\infty} \left(\frac{\sin n\pi d}{n\pi d} \right) \delta(\omega - n\omega_c) \qquad d = \frac{\tau}{T} \quad \omega_c = \frac{2\pi}{T} \qquad (3\text{-}6)$$

Inserting (3-6) in (3-5), and noting that

$$\int_{-\infty}^{\infty} F(x) \delta(\omega' - x) \, dx = F(\omega')$$

we get (3-4). Alternatively, the reader is asked to carry out a graphical convolution by plotting some arbitrary band-limited $F(x)$ and then sliding the impulse train of (3-6) past it. The spectrum of Fig. 3-5 results.

Consider Fig. 3-5 now. As long as the different spectra are separated, it is apparent that $f(t)$ can be filtered out from $f_s(t)$. This requires a low-pass filter, passing $F(\omega)$ but cutting off sharply before reaching the frequency-spectrum component centered at f_c. This answers the question previously raised about the possibility of retrieving $f(t)$, *undistorted*, from its sampled version $f_s(t)$. Systems transmitting these sampled values of the signal $f(t)$ are commonly called *sampled-data* or *pulse-modulation* systems.

We now visualize the switch rotation rate slowing down. The frequency f_c and all its harmonics start closing in on one another. It is apparent that eventually the spectral components in Fig. 3-5 will overlap and merge. The component $F(\omega - \omega_c)$ centered about f_c will in particular merge with the unshifted $F(\omega)$ term, centered about the origin. It is then impossible to separate out $F(\omega)$, and hence $f(t)$, from $f_s(t)$. This phenomenon of overlapping spectra due to samples that are too widely spaced, and the distortion that results, is termed *aliasing*. The limiting frequency at which $F(\omega)$ and $F(\omega - \omega_c)$ merges is, from Fig. 3-5, given by $f_c - B = B$, or

$$f_c = 2B \qquad (3-7)$$

which is just the Nyquist sampling rate introduced earlier.

Generally, one samples at a somewhat higher rate to ensure separation of the frequency spectra and to simplify the problem of low-pass filtering to retrieve $f(t)$. As an example, speech transmitted via telephone is generally filtered to $B = 3.3$ kHz. The Nyquist rate is thus 6.6 kHz. For digital transmission the speech is normally sampled at an 8-kHz rate, however. As another example, if the signal $f(t)$ to be sampled contains frequency components as high as 1 MHz, at least 2 million samples per second are needed. Analog TV signals, with bandwidths of 4 MHz (Chap. 2), require at least 8 million samples per second. The compact-disc (CD) digital audio system uses a sampling rate of 44,100 samples per second to allow a recorded audio bandwidth of 20 kHz [PEEK].[2] This bandwidth is perceived by most people to provide high-fidelity audio transcription.

Sampling Theorem—Further Discussion

The minimum Nyquist sampling rate, $2B$ samples per second, for signals band-limited to B hertz, is so important a concept in digital communications that it warrants further discussion and extension. In particular, we shall demonstrate rather simply that any $2B$ independent samples per second (not necessarily periodically obtained) suffice to represent the signal uniquely. One may thus sample aperiodically, if so desired; one may also sample a signal $f(t)$ and its successive derivatives, etc.

The lower (Nyquist) limit on the sampling rate in the case of periodic sampling is highly significant. Once we have satisfied ourselves that the sampled values of a signal $f(t)$ do in fact contain complete information about $f(t)$, we might logically feel that there must be a *minimum* value of f_c in order not to lose information or to be able eventually to reconstruct the continuous input signal. For we note that if we sample at too low a rate, the signal may change radically between sampling times. We thus lose information and eventually produce a

---

[2][PEEK] J. B. H. Peek, "Communications Aspects of the Compact Disc Digital Audio System," *IEEE Commun. Mag.*, vol. 23, no. 2, pp. 7–15, February 1985.

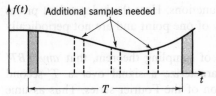

FIGURE 3-6
Sampling frequency too low.

distorted output. A sampling rate too low for the signal involved is shown in Fig. 3-6. In order not to lose the signal dips and rises, additional sampling pulses must be added as shown.

There is obviously a relation between the rate at which a signal varies and the number of pulses needed to reproduce it exactly. The rate at which a signal varies is of course related to its maximum frequency component, or bandwidth, B. Equation (3-7) tells us that at least $2B$ uniformly spaced samples are needed every second in order eventually to reproduce the signal without distortion.

This statement, arising quite naturally out of a consideration of the frequency spectrum of a periodically sampled signal, is the famous *sampling theorem*[3] of modern communication theory.

The theorem is of course particularly important in sampled-data and pulse-modulation systems, where sampling is inherent in the operation of the system. But it has deep significance in the modern concepts of information theory. For any measure of the information content of a specified signal must be related to the number of *independent* quantities needed to describe that signal completely (see Chap. 1). If the number is written in the form of binary units, the information content is measured in bits.

Although our statement of the sampling theorem, arising from Eq. (3-7), relates to the periodic sampling of a band-limited signal, the theorem can be generalized to *any* group of independent samples. Thus the more general theorem states that *any $2B$ independent samples per second will completely characterize a band-limited signal. Alternatively, any $2BT'$ unique (independent) pieces of information are needed to completely specify a signal over an interval T' seconds long.*

These statements should come as no surprise to us, for we use similar results constantly in applying the Taylor series expansion of calculus: a function, obeying certain conditions, may be expressed and completely specified at any point in terms of the value of the function and its successive derivatives at another point. All polynomials, for example $y = t, t^2, t^3, \ldots$, possess a finite number of nonzero derivatives, and so only a finite number of pieces of

[3][PAPO 1962] A. Papoulis, *The Fourier Integral and Its Applications*, McGraw-Hill, New York, 1962, and [PAPO 1968] A. Papoulis, *Systems and Transforms with Applications in Optics*, McGraw-Hill, New York, 1968. A tutorial paper stressing the history of the sampling theorem concept appears in [JERR] A. J. Jerri, "The Shannon Sampling Theorem—Its Various Extensions and Applications: A Tutorial Review," *Proc. IEEE*, vol. 65, no. 11, pp. 1565–1596, November 1977.

information are needed to describe these functions. Here the independent pieces of information are measured in the vicinity of one point and are not periodically spaced samples.

The proof of the more general form of sampling theorem, that *any* $2BT'$ pieces of information are needed to characterize a signal over a T'-second interval, follows readily from an application of the Fourier series. Thus assume that we are interested in a band-limited function $f(t)$ over an interval T' seconds long. We may then expand $f(t)$ in a Fourier series with T' as the base period. But with $f(t)$ band-limited to B hertz, we get only a finite number of terms in the Fourier series,

$$f(t) = \frac{c_0}{T'} + \frac{2}{T'} \sum_{n=1}^{BT'} |c_n| \cos(\omega_n t + \theta_n) \qquad \omega_n = \frac{2\pi n}{T'} \qquad (3\text{-}8)$$

or

$$f(t) = \frac{c_0}{T'} + \frac{2}{T'} \sum_{n=1}^{BT'} (a_n \cos \omega_n t + b_n \sin \omega_n t) \qquad (3\text{-}9)$$

with $|c_n| = \sqrt{a_n^2 + b_n^2}$, $\theta_n = -\tan^{-1}(b_n/a_n)$. [Since B is the maximum-frequency component of $f(t)$, ω_n has a maximum value

$$2\pi B = \frac{2\pi n}{T'}$$

The maximum value of n is thus BT'.]

The c_0 term is the dc term. It merely serves to shift the level of $f(t)$ and does not provide any new information. (Information implies signals *changing* with time, as pointed out in Chap. 1.) There are thus $2BT'$ independent Fourier coefficients (the sum of the c_n's and θ_n's or a_n's and b_n's), and any $2BT'$ independent samples of $f(t)$ suffice to specify $f(t)$ over the T'-second interval.

It is of interest to note at this point the connection between the sampling theorem just discussed and the equation for channel capacity developed in Chap. 1 and rephrased at the end of Chap. 2,

$$C = B \log_2 n \qquad \text{bits/s} \qquad (3\text{-}10)$$

where B is the channel bandwidth in hertz. In T' seconds the channel will allow the transmission of

$$BT' \log_2 n \qquad \text{bits}$$

This expression for system capacity includes possible effects of noise ($\log_2 n$), but, aside from noise considerations, it says simply that the information that can be transmitted over a band-limited system is proportional to the product of bandwidth and the time for transmission. The concept embodied in this last sentence was first developed by R. V. L. Hartley of Bell Laboratories in 1928 and is called *Hartley's law*. Modern communication theory has extended Hartley's law to include the effects of noise, giving rise to Eq. (3-10), the expression for system capacity.

Hartley's law and the sampling theorem (as developed by Nyquist in 1928) are in essence the same. For a band-limited signal may be viewed as having been "processed," or emitted, by a band-limited system. The information carried by this signal must thus be proportional to BT' by Hartley's law. This is the same result as that obtained from the sampling theorem. (The factor of 2 that appears to distinguish the expression for channel capacity and the results of the sampling theorem can be accounted for by using $\tau = 1/2B$ instead of $1/B$ in the development of the channel-capacity expression of Chap. 2.)

Demodulation of Sampled Signals

If $2BT'$ samples completely specify a signal, it should be possible to recover the signal from the samples. This is the demodulation process required for sampled-data or pulse-modulation systems. How do we accomplish it?

Note that the sampled output was expressed by Eq. (3-2) in the form

$$f_s(t) = df(t)\left(1 + 2\sum_{n=1}^{\infty} \frac{\sin n\pi d}{n\pi d} \cos \frac{2\pi nt}{T}\right) \tag{3-11}$$

As noted earlier, the simplest way to demodulate this output signal would be to pass the sampled signal through a low-pass filter of bandwidth B hertz. This is shown in Fig. 3-7.

If we sample at exactly the Nyquist rate ($f_c = 2B$), the filter required must have infinitely sharp cutoff characteristics, as shown in Fig. 3-7a. This requires an ideal filter, an impossibility in practice. A practical low-pass filter with sharp cutoff characteristics could of course be used, with resulting complexity in filtering and some residual distortion (part of the lower sideband about f_c would be transmitted). This situation can be relieved somewhat by sampling at a higher-rate, as shown in Fig. 3-7b. A guard band is thus made available, and filter requirements are less severe. The filter must cut off between B and $f_c - B$, its attenuation at $f_c - B$ being some prescribed quantity measured with respect to the passband.

In the example given previously of transmitting speech signals digitally, it was noted that the voice transmission is commonly band-limited to 3.3 kHz. The Nyquist sampling rate is then 6.6 kHz. A sampling rate of 8 kHz is most frequently used, however, so that the filter guard band is 1.4 kHz (from 3.3 to $8.0 - 3.3 = 4.7$ kHz).

It is instructive to consider a simple proof for the low-pass-filter demodulation of periodic samples [OLIV].[4] This will fill out in a more quantitative way our rather qualitative discussion based on Eq. (3-11) and Fig. 3-7. It also helps to clarify further the actual mechanism of filtering.

---

[4][OLIV] B. M. Oliver, J. R. Pierce, and C. E. Shannon, "Philosophy of PCM," *Proc. IRE*, vol. 36, no. 11, p. 1324, November 1948.

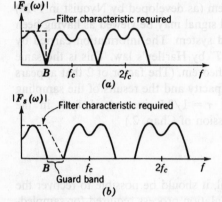

FIGURE 3-7

FIGURE 3-7
Sampled-data demodulation using low-pass filter. (a) $f_c = 2B$. (b) $f_c > 2B$.

Thus assume that a signal $f(t)$ band-limited to B hertz has been sampled at intervals of $1/2B$ seconds. We shall first show that $f(t)$ may be reconstructed from these samples (a necessary result from the sampling theorem) and shall then demonstrate that an ideal low-pass filter is called for in the reconstruction or demodulation process.

To show that the given samples suffice to reproduce $f(t)$, take the Fourier transform $F(\omega)$ of $f(t)$,

$$F(\omega) = \int_{-\infty}^{\infty} f(t)e^{-j\omega t}\, dt \qquad (3\text{-}12)$$

Then

$$F(\omega) = 0 \qquad |\omega| > 2\pi B \qquad (3\text{-}13)$$

by virtue of the band-limiting assumption on $f(t)$.

$F(\omega)$ can be arbitrarily made periodic with a period of $4\pi B$, as shown in Fig. 3-8. It can then be expanded in a Fourier series of period $4\pi B$ to be used within the interval $|\omega| \leq 2\pi B$. Thus

$$\begin{aligned}
F(\omega) &= \frac{1}{4\pi B} \sum_{-\infty}^{\infty} c_n e^{j(2\pi n/4\pi B)\omega} \\
&= \frac{1}{4\pi B} \sum_{-\infty}^{\infty} c_n e^{jn\omega/2B} \qquad |\omega| < 2\pi B \\
&= 0 \qquad |\omega| > 2\pi B
\end{aligned} \qquad (3\text{-}14)$$

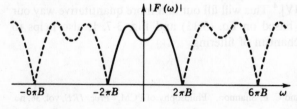

FIGURE 3-8
$F(\omega)$ represented as a periodic function.

with c_n defined by

$$c_n = \int_{-2\pi B}^{2\pi B} F(\omega)e^{-jn\omega/2B}\,d\omega \tag{3-15}$$

But, since $F(\omega)$ is the Fourier transform of $f(t)$, $f(t)$ can be written

$$f(t) = \frac{1}{2\pi}\int_{-\infty}^{\infty} F(\omega)e^{j\omega t}\,d\omega = \frac{1}{2\pi}\int_{-2\pi B}^{2\pi B} F(\omega)e^{j\omega t}\,d\omega \tag{3-16}$$

In particular, at time $t = -n/2B$

$$f\left(-\frac{n}{2B}\right) = \frac{1}{2\pi}\int_{-2\pi B}^{2\pi B} F(\omega)e^{-jn\omega/2B}\,d\omega = \frac{c_n}{2\pi} \tag{3-17}$$

from Eq. (3-15).

This means that if we are given $f(t)$ at the various sampling intervals (for example, $t = -3/2B, -2/2B, -1/2B, 0, 1/2B, \ldots$), we can find the corresponding Fourier coefficient c_n. But knowing c_n, we can in turn find $F(\omega)$ from the Fourier series of Eq. (3-14). Knowing $F(\omega)$, we find $f(t)$ for *all* possible times by Eq. (3-16). A knowledge of $f(t)$ at sampling intervals $1/2B$ seconds apart thus suffices to determine $f(t)$ at all times. This completes the first part of our proof. We have demonstrated that $f(t)$ may be reproduced completely, solely from a knowledge of $f(t)$ at the periodic sampling intervals. How do we now actually reconstruct $f(t)$ from these samples?

If we substitute the Fourier-series expansion for $F(\omega)$ [Eq. (3-14)] into Eq. (3-16), the Fourier-integral representation of $f(t)$, we get

$$f(t) = \frac{1}{2\pi}\int_{-2\pi B}^{2\pi B} F(\omega)e^{j\omega t}\,d\omega$$

$$= \frac{1}{2\pi}\int_{-2\pi B}^{2\pi B} \frac{1}{4\pi B}\left(\sum_n c_n e^{jn\omega/2B}\right)e^{j\omega t}\,d\omega \tag{3-18}$$

If the order of integration and summation are now interchanged (the integral is finite and no difficulties can arise because of improper integrals; the coefficients c_n also approach zero for n large enough), the resulting integral may be readily evaluated. We get

$$f(t) = \sum_n \frac{c_n}{2\pi}\frac{1}{4\pi B}\int_{-2\pi B}^{2\pi B} e^{j\omega(t+n/2B)}\,d\omega$$

$$= \sum_n \frac{c_n}{2\pi}\frac{\sin 2\pi B(t+n/2B)}{2\pi B(t+n/2B)} \tag{3-19}$$

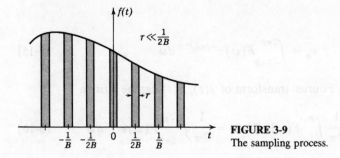

FIGURE 3-9
The sampling process.

But $c_n/2\pi = f(-n/2B)$, from Eq. (3-17). Therefore,

$$f(t) = \sum_{n=-\infty}^{\infty} f\left(-\frac{n}{2B}\right) \frac{\sin 2\pi B(t + n/2B)}{2\pi B(t + n/2B)}$$

$$= \sum_{n=-\infty}^{\infty} f\left(\frac{n}{2B}\right) \frac{\sin 2\pi B(t - n/2B)}{2\pi B(t - n/2B)} \tag{3-20}$$

since all positive and negative values of n are included in the summation. Mathematically, then, Eq. (3-20) indicates that we are to take each sample, multiply it by a $(\sin x)/x$ weighting factor centered at the sample's time of occurrence, and sum the resultant terms. This is exactly what is done, however, when we pass the samples through an ideal low-pass filter cutting off at B hertz.

We can demonstrate this very simply in the following manner: Assume $f(t)$ again limited to B hertz. We sample $f(t)$ for a length of time τ (the sampling time) periodically at intervals of $1/2B$ seconds. If $\tau \ll 1/2B$, then $f(t)$ may be assumed very nearly constant over the sampling time (Fig. 3-9).

The individual sample $f(n/2B)$ has a Fourier transform (or frequency spectrum) given by

$$F_n(\omega) = \int_{-\infty}^{\infty} f(t) e^{-j\omega t}\, dt \doteq \tau f\left(\frac{n}{2B}\right) e^{-jn\omega/2B} \tag{3-21}$$

since $f(t)$ is assumed constant over the τ-second interval and zero elsewhere. But note that this is just the Fourier transform of an impulse (delta function) of amplitude $\tau f(n/2B)$ and located at $t = n/2B$ in time. [See Eq. (2-78) plus the shifting theorem.]

The amplitude factor $\tau f(n/2B)$ represents the area under the curve of the individual sample. By assuming the sample duration τ to be very small, we have effectively approximated the sample by an impulse of the same area.

Assume that this impulse is now passed through an ideal low-pass filter of bandwidth B hertz with zero phase shift and unity amplitude assumed for simplicity. (The idealized linear phase shift just serves to delay the occurrence of the output signal, as pointed out in Chap. 2.) The response of this idealized filter to an impulse $K\delta(t - t_0)$ is, from (2-82), found to be given by

$$2KB\frac{\sin 2\pi B(t - t_0)}{2\pi B(t - t_0)}$$

The output response $g_n(t)$ of the ideal low-pass filter to the individual sample $f(n/2B)$ must thus be given by

$$g_n(t) = 2\tau f\left(\frac{n}{2B}\right)B\frac{\sin 2\pi B(t - n/2B)}{2\pi B(t - n/2B)} \tag{3-22}$$

This result can of course also be obtained directly from Eq. (3-21) and the assumed filter characteristic. Thus, for an ideal low-pass filter with zero phase shift and unit amplitude, the output response to the sample $f(n/2B)$ applied at the input is

$$g_n(t) = \frac{1}{2\pi}\int_{-2\pi B}^{2\pi B} F_n(\omega)e^{j\omega t}\,d\omega$$

$$= f\left(\frac{n}{2B}\right)\frac{\tau}{2\pi}\int_{-2\pi B}^{2\pi B} e^{j\omega(t - n/2B)}\,d\omega \tag{3-23}$$

Integrating, as indicated, we get for $g_n(t)$

$$g_n(t) = 2B\tau f\left(\frac{n}{2B}\right)\frac{\sin 2\pi B(t - n/2B)}{2\pi B(t - n/2B)}$$

as in Eq. (3-22). $g_n(t)$ is plotted in Fig. 3-10. Note that $g_n(t)$ has its maximum value at $t = n/2B$ (the filter was assumed to have zero phase shift), and precursors again appear because of the idealized filter characteristics assumed. The output is a maximum at the given sampling point, $t = n/2B$, and zero at all the other sampling points. At the sampling point $g_n(n/2B) = 2B\tau f(n/2B)$, so that g_n is just the input $f(n/2B)$ to within a constant. The next sample, occurring $1/2B$ seconds later, at $t = (n + 1)/2B$, likewise produces an output given by Eq. (3-22), but delayed $1/2B$ seconds, and proportional to $f[(n + 1)/2B]$.

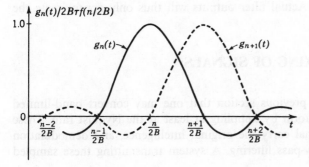

FIGURE 3-10
Filter response to sampled inputs.

The peak of each $(\sin x)/x$ term occurs at a sampling period where all other outputs are zero (Fig. 3-10), and the output at each of the sampling points is exactly proportional to the magnitude of the input sample at that point.

Since we have been assuming a linear ideal filter, the complete output is just the superposition of the individual sample outputs, or

$$g(t) = \sum_{n=-\infty}^{\infty} g_n(t)$$

$$= 2B\tau \sum_{n=-\infty}^{\infty} f\left(\frac{n}{2B}\right) \frac{\sin 2\pi B(t - n/2B)}{2\pi B(t - n/2B)}$$

$$= 2B\tau f(t) \tag{3-24}$$

by comparison with Eq. (3-20). The output of the low-pass filter, $g(t)$, is thus identically proportional to the original signal $f(t)$ at *all* instants of time, not only at the sampling points. [Had we included a linear phase-shift characteristic, we would of course have obtained a constant time delay for the output function. The output $g(t)$ would thus be a delayed replica of $f(t)$.]

The original input $f(t)$ may thus be reproduced from the samples by passing them through an ideal low-pass filter of bandwidth B hertz. The $2B\tau$ proportionality factor represents the ratio of the filter and sampling pulse bandwidths. Since we assumed $\tau \ll 1/2B$, and since the effective pulse "bandwidth" is proportional to $1/\tau$ (Chap. 2), the pulse spectral width is much greater than that of the filter. [We in fact assumed the pulse spectrum to be constant over the filter bandwidth, as shown by Eq. (3-21).] Most of the energy of the input sample thus lies outside the filter spectrum, as shown in Fig. 3-7. If the pulse width is so narrow that its spectrum is almost constant (again the justification for representing it by an impulse of the same area), the output amplitude is reduced by the ratio of bandwidths, or just $2B\tau$.

These considerations of filter operation from a frequency point of view of course agree with the time approach. For, as shown by Eq. (3-11), an ideal low-pass filter of unit amplitude and bandwidth B would produce $g(t) = df(t)$ at the output. But the pulse duty cycle d is simply τ/T, or $2B\tau$, with $T = 1/2B$, agreeing with the result of Eq. (3-24).

The ideal filter is of course a mathematical artifice and can only be approximated in practice. Actual filter outputs will thus only approximate the actual input $f(t)$.

3-3 THE MULTIPLEXING OF SIGNALS: AN INTRODUCTION

We have indicated in the previous section that one may convert band-limited analog data to a sampled form by sampling at least at the Nyquist rate. These sampled values of the signal carry the original intelligence, and demodulation may be carried out by low-pass filtering. A system transmitting these sampled values of the signal is commonly called a *pulse-amplitude-modulation* (PAM) system. For the sequence of samples may alternatively be visualized as a periodic sequence of pulses (the *carrier*) whose amplitude is modulated (or varied) in accordance with the intelligence to be transmitted. This is in fact apparent from the form of the sampled-data expression $f_s(t) = f(t)S(t)$. The switching function $S(t)$ represents the unmodulated pulse carrier, and $f(t)$ the intelligence modulating the carrier. This concept of amplitude modulation will be pursued further in Chap. 4.

Most pulse communication systems in use transmit many signals simultaneously, rather than just one. It is apparent from the sampling process, with a very narrow sample τ seconds wide taken every T seconds, that much of the time no information is being transmitted through the system (see Fig. 3-2). It is thus possible to transmit other information from other sources in the vacant intervals. The transmission of samples of information from several signal channels simultaneously through one communication system with different channel samples staggered in time is called *time-division multiplexing*, or *time multiplexing* for short.

Most time-multiplexed systems in use now are digital. This implies that analog signals are converted to digital format before transmission in multiplexed form. Digital signals (from data terminals, computers, printers, or any other digital source) are of course already in the form needed for multiplexing. In this introductory treatment we choose to separate the two ideas of time multiplexing and analog-to-digital conversion. In this section we discuss the basic idea of multiplexing of signals, without indicating whether they are digital or analog in form. In the next section we discuss the analog-to-digital (A/D) operation and its application to PCM systems. In Sec. 3-8 we return to time multiplexing, focusing there on digital systems only. We then describe the multiplexing process in more detail, drawing on examples of multiplexing techniques used in practice. In the digital-multiplexer case it is immaterial whether the signals to be multiplexed were digital to begin with, were analog and then converted using A/D techniques to digital format, or are combinations of both. All digital signals are handled in the same way once they are in that form.

In a typical time-multiplexing scheme, the various signals to be transmitted are sequentially sampled and combined for transmission over the one channel. Figure 3-11 shows a time diagram of a time-multiplexed signal system having four information carriers. It is apparent that all signals to be multiplexed must either be of the same bandwidth, or, if not, sampling must take place at a rate

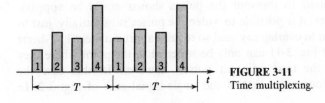

FIGURE 3-11
Time multiplexing.

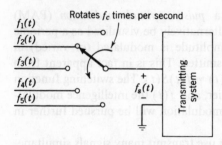

FIGURE 3-12
Sampler for time multiplexing.

determined by the maximum-bandwidth signal. (Alternatively, relatively low-bandwidth signals may be first combined before sampling, as will be noted later.) A sampler time-multiplexing a multichannel input sequentially into the transmission channel is shown in Fig. 3-12. A mechanical switch is again shown for simplicity, but in practice electronic switching would normally be used.

Time multiplexing has been widely used in the radio, data, and telephone fields, and for telemetering purposes. Experimental data from space probes are commonly sampled and transmitted sequentially, for example. A space vehicle transmitting back a variety of measured information such as temperature, electron density, magnetic intensity, and a multitude of other sensor outputs need only utilize one transmission channel, providing the sampling is carried out rapidly enough to accommodate the most rapidly varying signal to be transmitted.

If the various signals to be multiplexed have widely differing bandwidths, or, as is commonly the case with data sources, have widely different data rates, two approaches may be used. Proportionately more samples of the wider-bandwidth or higher-data-rate signals may be taken and combined with samples of the more slowly varying signals, or the more slowly varying signals may first be combined into a single wider-bandwidth analog signal by *frequency-multiplexing* techniques. This latter approach is discussed in Chap. 4. The former case, the direct time multiplexing of data sources with different data rates, is discussed briefly later in this chapter. In this section we assume, for simplicity, that all signals are sampled and combined at the same rate, as dictated by the most rapidly varying signal.

As is true with all engineering developments, one pays a price for introducing time multiplexing into a system. First, it is apparent that the necessary transmission bandwidth increases with the number of signals multiplexed, for the transmission bandwidth is proportional to the reciprocal of the width of the pulses transmitted (Chap. 2). Thus in the case of the single-signal pulses of Fig. 3-2, the bandwidth required to transmit the pulses shown would be approximately $1/\tau$ hertz. However, it is possible to widen the pulses substantially, just to the point where they begin to overlap say, and so require approximately $1/T$-hertz bandwidth. The pulses of Fig. 3-11 can only be widened to the point where they begin to interfere with the next adjacent pulses, however. In this case the minimum bandwidth is four times that of the single-signal case of Fig. 3-2. In

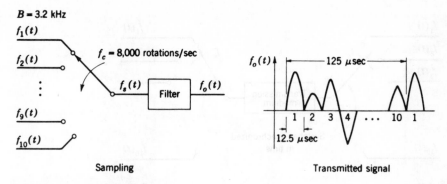

FIGURE 3-13
Time-multiplexed voice channels.

general, then, if N signals are time-multiplexed, the required transmission bandwidth is N times that for single-signal samples.

As an example, assume that 10 voice channels, each band-limited to 3.2 kHz, are sequentially sampled at an 8-kHz rate and time-multiplexed on one channel. The successive pulses are then spaced 12.5 μs apart, as shown in Fig. 3-13. The bandwidth required to transmit these pulses is roughly 80 kHz. (A more accurate determination of the filtering and bandwidth necessary to prevent pulse overlap will be considered later in Sec. 3-10 in the discussion of intersymbol interference.) The filter shown in Fig. 3-13 is used to widen the pulses as required. Filtering could be incorporated in the sampling operation as well, or it could be carried out further along the transmission path.

The other problem introduced by time multiplexing involves proper synchronization and registration of the successive pulses at the receiver. For it is apparent that the successive pulses must on reception be delivered to the appropriate destination. This implies that a switch is available at the receiver, is synchronized to the original transmitter switch, and deposits each sample in its appropriate signal channel. This is no mean task with high-speed data systems, and with receiver and transmitter located possibly thousands or millions of miles apart. Figure 3-14 shows a transmitter and receiver switching in a time-multiplexed system. The registration problem, with sample 1 placed in the 1 line at the destination and not in line 2 or 3, is particularly acute. (Although you might not mind eavesdropping on someone else's conversation, you in turn would not like to have your conversation picked up by a stranger!)

Various techniques have been utilized in practice to perform synchronization and registration of signals. The techniques have included: (1) the use of special marker pulses, tagged to be easily differentiable from regular signal pulses, and sent periodically at prescribed intervals; (2) continuous sine waves of known phase and frequency which can be filtered out at the receiver to provide the necessary timing information; and (3) schemes which derive timing information from the transmitted signal pulses themselves by averaging over long periods

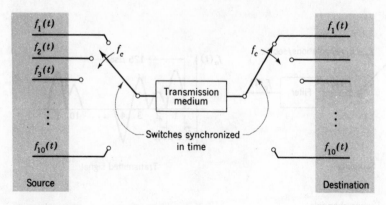

FIGURE 3-14
Switching in a time-multiplexed system.

of time, etc. Reference is made to the literature for details of various synchronizing techniques [STIF], [SKLA].[5] Some specific methods used in telephone systems are described in detail in Sec. 3-8.

3-4 ANALOG-TO-DIGITAL CONVERSION: APPLICATION TO PULSE CODE MODULATION

Very commonly in modern communication technology the sampled analog signals are further digitized before transmission. The digital signals may then be encoded into any equivalent form desired. Systems embodying the transmission of digitized and coded signals are commonly called *pulse-code-modulation* (PCM) systems. Binary digital systems constitute the most frequently encountered form of PCM systems.

There are many advantages to using PCM systems.

1. The signals may be regularly reshaped or regenerated during transmission, since information is no longer carried by continuously varying pulse amplitudes but by discrete symbols.
2. All-digital circuitry may be used throughout the system.
3. Signals may be digitally processed as desired.
4. Noise and interference may be minimized by appropriate coding of the signals, etc.

Some of these factors will be described in detail later in the book.

---

[5][STIF] J. J. Stiffler, *Theory of Synchronous Communications*, Prentice-Hall, Englewood Cliffs, N.J., 1971. [SKLA] B. Sklar, *Digital Communications*, Prentice-Hall, Englewood Cliffs, N.J., 1988, chap. 8.

The process of digitizing the original analog signals is called the *quantization* process. It consists of breaking the amplitudes of the signals up into a prescribed number of discrete amplitude levels. The resultant signals are said to be *quantized*. Unlike the sampling process, this results in an irretrievable loss of information, since it is impossible to reconstitute the original analog signal from its quantized version. However, as first noted in the discussion of the concept of information in Chap. 1, there is actually no need to transmit all possible signal amplitudes. Because of noise introduced during transmission and at the receiver, the demodulator or detector circuit will not be able to distinguish fine variations in signal amplitude. In addition, the ultimate recipient of the information—our ears in the case of speech or music, our eyes in the case of a picture—is limited with regard to the fine gradation of signal it can distinguish.

This ultimate limitation in distinguishing among all possible amplitudes thus makes quantization possible. In a specific system the sampled pulses may be quantized, or both quantization and sampling may be performed simultaneously. This latter process is portrayed in Fig. 3-15. The total amplitude swing of $A_0 = 7$

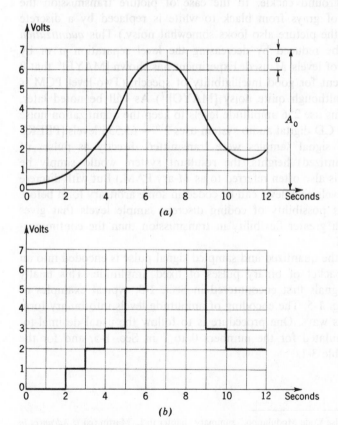

(a)

(b)

FIGURE 3-15
Quantization and sampling. (*a*) Given signal. (*b*) Quantized and sampled version.

V is divided into equally spaced amplitude levels $a = 1$ V apart. There are thus $M = A_0/a + 1$ possible amplitude levels, including zero. In Fig. 3-15 samples are shown taken every second and the nearest discrete amplitude level is selected as the one to be transmitted. The resultant quantized and sampled version of the signal of the smooth signal of Fig. 3-15a thus appears in Fig. 3-15b. (The signal of 0.3 V at 0 s is transmitted as 0 V, etc.)

Although the level separation is shown here as uniform, the separation is often tapered in practice to improve the system noise performance. In particular, the spacing of levels is decreased at low amplitude levels. This is done by a technique called *compression*. We shall discuss one common technique and its effect on performance in the next section. We shall assume equal spacing for simplicity, however, in this section.

Obviously, the quantizing process introduces some error in the eventual reproduction of the signal. The demodulated signal will differ somewhat from the derived signal, as noted earlier. The overall effect is as if additional noise had been introduced into the system. (In the case of sound transmission this manifests itself as a background cackle. In the case of picture transmission the continuous gradation of grays from black to white is replaced by a discrete number of grays, and the picture also looks somewhat noisy.) This *quantization noise* may of course be reduced by decreasing the level separation a or by increasing the number of levels M used. Experiment has shown [MAYE][6] that 8 to 16 levels are sufficient for good intelligibility of speech. (Two-level PCM is even understandable, although quite noisy [MAYO].[7]) As will be noted later, digital telephone systems use 256 amplitude levels to keep the quantization noise to tolerable levels. The CD digital audio system uses $2^{16} = 65,536$ levels [PEEK].

If the quantized signal samples were transmitted directly as pulses of varying (although quantized) heights, the resultant system would simply be quantized PAM. (This is also often referred to as M-ary PAM.) But with discrete or numbered voltage levels each level can be coded in some arbitrary form before transmission. It is this possibility of coding discrete sample levels that gives quantized signals much greater flexibility in transmission than the continuous-varying pulses of PAM.

Most commonly the quantized and sampled signal pulse is encoded into an equivalent group or packet of binary pulses of fixed amplitude. This finally provides the binary signals first encountered in Sect. 1-3, typical examples of which are shown in Fig. 1-5. The encoding of amplitude levels into binary form can be done in various ways. One procedure is to follow the usual decimal-to-binary conversion, tabulated for the numbers 0 to 7 in Sec. 1-5, and for the numbers 0 to 15 in Table 3-1.

---

[6][MAYE] H. F. Mayer, "Pulse Code Modulation," summary chapter in L. Martin (ed.), *Advances in Electronics*, Academic Press, New York, 1951, vol. III, pp. 221–260.

[7][MAYO] J. S. Mayo, "Pulse Code Modulation," *Electro-Technol.*, pp. 87–98, November 1962.

TABLE 3-1
Decimal-to-binary conversion

Digit	Binary code				Gray code			
	b_1	b_2	b_3	b_4	g_1	g_2	g_3	g_4
0	0	0	0	0	0	0	0	0
1	0	0	0	1	0	0	0	1
2	0	0	1	0	0	0	1	1
3	0	0	1	1	0	0	1	0
4	0	1	0	0	0	1	1	0
5	0	1	0	1	0	1	1	1
6	0	1	1	0	0	1	0	1
7	0	1	1	1	0	1	0	0
8	1	0	0	0	1	1	0	0
9	1	0	0	1	1	1	0	1
10	1	0	1	0	1	1	1	1
11	1	0	1	1	1	1	1	0
12	1	1	0	0	1	0	1	0
13	1	1	0	1	1	0	1	1
14	1	1	1	0	1	0	0	1
15	1	1	1	1	1	0	0	0

One difficulty with the normal decimal-to-binary conversion (labeled binary code in Table 3-1) is that in moving from one adjacent decimal digit to another the binary code changes by a variable number of binary digits. This is particularly apparent in changing from 3 to 4 and 7 to 8 in Table 3-1. In the first case three binary digits change, in the second case four digits change. In 7-bit PCM, handling levels 0 to 127, as many as seven binary digits may change. This makes the binary code highly susceptible to error in the A/D conversion. One would prefer a code in which only one binary digit at a time changed as the corresponding decimal digit changed by one level. The Gray code shown in Table 3-1 is an example of such a code.

The Gray code is easily obtained from the binary code by the following conversion equations. Say in general that an n-digit binary code is used. (This corresponds to 2^n possible decimal digits, including 0.) Call the successive bits in order, from the most significant to the least significant, $b_1 b_2 b_3 \ldots b_n$. (The digits in Table 3-1 are then $b_1 b_2 b_3 b_4$, as shown.) Let the corresponding Gray code digits be $g_1 g_2 g_3 \ldots g_n$. The reader can then check, using Table 3-1 as an example, that the following equations convert the binary code to the Gray code:

$$g_1 = b_1$$
$$g_k = b_k \oplus b_{k-1} \qquad k \geq 2 \tag{3-25}$$

The symbol $\oplus$ represents modulo-2, or exclusive-or addition of the binary numbers. ($0 \oplus 0 = 0$; $1 \oplus 0 = 1$; $0 \oplus 1 = 1$; $1 \oplus 1 = 0$.) Note that the procedure adds the current digit, b_k, to the next most significant one, b_{k-1}. Conversion from the Gray code to the binary code is easily accomplished by reversing

(3-25) (in mod-2 addition, subtracting two numbers is the same as adding them):

$$b_1 = g_1$$
$$b_k = g_k \oplus b_{k-1} \qquad k \geq 2 \tag{3-26}$$

For simplicity's sake we shall generally assume the usual decimal-to-binary conversion (the binary-code column of Table 3-1, for example) in discussing binary coding in this chapter. The appropriate conversion to the Gray code can then always be made using (3-25). In Chap. 7 we consider further encoding of these binary digits, with additional *parity bits* added for error detection and/or correction purposes.

It is apparent that in either case, the usual binary code or the Gray code, the number of binary digits used depends on the number of quantization levels used. Thus 8-level PCM requires three binary digits for transmission, 16-level requires four binary digits, and 128-level requires 7 binary digits, or bits, for the representation of each level. Since these binary digits must be transmitted in the sampling interval originally allotted to one quantized sample, the binary pulse widths are correspondingly narrower and the transmission bandwidth goes up proportionately to the number of binary pulses needed. An example of the binary encoding process is shown in Fig. 3-16. Here three binary pulses are transmitted in the original sampling interval, so that the bandwidth is increased by a factor of 3. (Note that if this represented a time-multiplexed system, the three samples of amplitudes 7, 6, and 5, respectively, would represent three separate signals.)

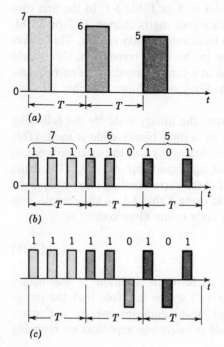

FIGURE 3-16
Binary coding of samples. (*a*) Given signal (already sampled and quantized). (*b*) Coded samples. (*c*) Another form of binary code: polar signals.

Two examples of binary signals are shown in Fig. 3-16: (1) an on–off signal, in which the 1 bit is represented by the presence of a pulse, the 0 bit by its absence; and (2) a signal with the 1 represented by a positive pulse, the 0 by a negative pulse.[8]

A binary code is just one special case of the coding theoretically possible in a PCM system. In general, any one quantized signal sample may be coded into a group of m pulses, each with n possible amplitude levels. These m pulses must be transmitted in the original sampling interval allotted to the quantized sample. Since the information carried by these m pulses is equivalent to the information carried by the original M amplitude levels, the number of possible amplitude combinations of the m pulses must equal M. Thus

$$M = n^m \tag{3-27}$$

(Recall from Chap. 1 that m pulses, each with n possible heights, may be combined in n^m different ways. Each combination must correspond to one of the original M levels.) If there are two possible levels, $n = 2$, and we have the binary code just mentioned. With $M = 8$, three binary pulses are necessary. If $n = 3$, a ternary code results. Obviously, if $m = 1$, then $n = M$ and we are back to our original uncoded but quantized samples. As the number n of levels chosen for the coded pulses increases, m decreases, as does the bandwidth required for transmission.

This ability to code back and forth is one of the reasons for the increased usage of PCM systems. Although most PCM systems in use are binary in form, so that the bandwidth required for transmission is wider than that required before binary encoding, bandwidth *reduction* schemes have been suggested in which successive M-level samples would be further collapsed into much higher-level samples. This is a reversal of the binary encoding process. For example, two successive binary pulses provide a total of four possible combinations, and so need four numbers to represent them. Similarly, two eight-level samples require 64 numbers to represent them. If combined into one *wider* pulse, covering the two adjacent time slots, the required bandwidth could be reduced by a factor of 2, but the one pulse used for transmission would take on 64 possible levels. This process of combining or collapsing successive pulses into one much wider pulse with many more amplitude levels can of course be continued indefinitely. [The m in Eq. (3-27) then represents the number of adjacent pulses, each with n amplitude levels, that are collapsed into one pulse with M levels. The bandwidth is then reduced by a factor of m.] There is one major difficulty, however; if the spacing between levels remains fixed, the required peak power goes up *exponentially* with the number of pulses combined. Alternatively, if the peak power or amplitude swing is to remain fixed, the levels must be spaced closer and closer together. This then makes it easier for noise in the system to obscure adjacent

---

[8]Different binary PCM waveforms are used in practice. Two examples, the nonreturn-to-zero (NRZ) and the bipolar signal sequences are discussed later in this chapter.

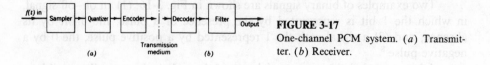

FIGURE 3-17
One-channel PCM system. (*a*) Transmitter. (*b*) Receiver.

levels. Such bandwidth reduction techniques are thus only possible in a sufficiently low-noise environment.

The binary form of transmission provides, on the other hand, the most noise immunity, and this is therefore the digital communication scheme with which we shall concern ourselves most in the chapters to follow. For, as indicated by the examples of Fig. 3-16, the information carried by the binary signals is represented either by the absence or presence of a pulse, or by its polarity. All the receiver has to do is to then correspondingly recognize the absence or presence of a pulse, or the polarity (plus or minus) of a pulse, and then decode into the original quantized form to reconstruct the signal. The pulse shape or exact amplitude is not significant as in the case of the original analog signal or a PAM signal. By transmitting binary pulses of high enough amplitude, we can ensure correct detection of the pulse in the presence of noise with as low an error rate (or possibly of mistakes) as required. We shall have more to say about this noise-improvement capability of PCM systems in later chapters of the book.[9]

As noted earlier, binary PCM lends itself readily as well to signal reshaping at periodic intervals during transmissions. This is a common practice in digital communication over telephone circuits. The reshaping of signals at these intermediate *repeaters* enhances the signal decisions when finally received at the receivers.

It is now of interest to tie together the processes of sampling, quantization, and binary encoding, as well as their reverse processes at the receiver. Figure 3-17 shows these various operations in block-diagram form for a complete one-channel PCM system. (Synchronizing circuitry, as well as modulation and demodulation circuits to be discussed later, are not shown.) In Fig. 3-18 we take a 10-channel PCM system and show the timing and pulse widths required as we progress through the system. Again, for simplicity's sake, necessary synchronizing pulses are not shown. (The insertion of additional synchronizing bits would of course require narrower pulses and hence wider bandwidths.) Thus if the original analog channels each have 3.2-kHz bandwidth, as shown, and a sampling rate of 8,000 samples per second is used, the time-multiplexed pulses at the sampler output [point (1), part (*a*)] appear at 12.5-μs intervals. Assuming an eight-level

---

[9]In Chap. 7 we consider encoding blocks of m successive binary digits into $M = 2^m$ possible signal symbols or code words for the purpose of reducing the probability of error. The resultant bandwidths then generally *increase* with m, or at best remain fixed. These encoding schemes for error reduction should not be confused with the binary to M-level amplitude transmission discussed here for bandwidth reduction.

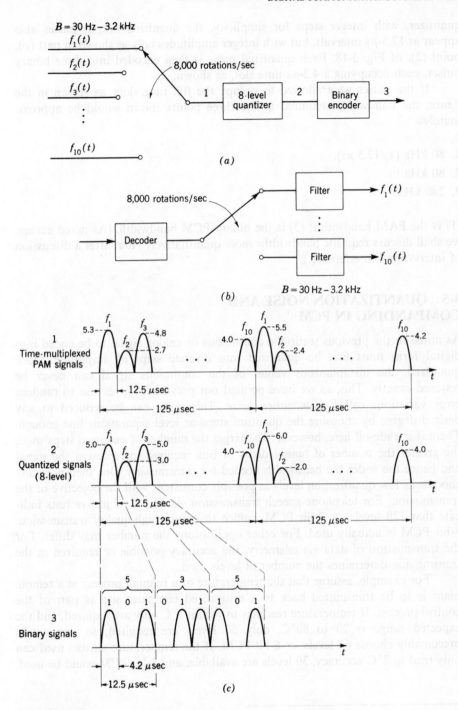

FIGURE 3-18
Ten-channel PCM system. (*a*) Transmitter. (*b*) Receiver. (*c*) Signal shapes.

quantizer, with integer steps for simplicity, the quantized output pulses also appear at 12.5-μs intervals, but with integer amplitudes only as shown in part (c), point (2), of Fig. 3-18. Each quantized pulse is then encoded into three binary pulses, each occupying a 4.2-μs time slot, as shown.

If the pulses were allowed to occupy the full time slots, as shown in the figure, the bandwidths required at the three points shown would be approximately

1. 80 kHz (1/12.5 μs),
2. 80 kHz,
3. 240 kHz.

(1) is the PAM bandwidth; (3) is the binary PCM bandwidth. (As noted earlier, we shall discuss requisite bandwidths more quantitatively later, after a discussion of intersymbol interference.)

3-5   QUANTIZATION NOISE AND COMPANDING IN PCM[10]

As noted in the previous section, a continuous or analog signal to be coded into digital form must first be quantized into discrete steps of amplitude. Once quantized, the instantaneous values of the continuous signal can never be restored exactly. This, as we have pointed out previously, gives rise to random error variations called *quantization noise*. This noise can be reduced to any desired degree by choosing the quantum steps or level separations fine enough. There is a trade-off here, however. The larger the number of quantum steps used, the greater the number of binary digits or bits required to represent the signal and hence the wider the bandwidth needed for transmission. One then normally chooses as few quantization levels as possible consistent with the objective of the transmission. For telephone speech transmission via PCM, subjective tests indicate that 128 levels, or 7-bit PCM, suffice to ensure high-quality transmission. 8-bit PCM is actually used. For other applications the number may differ. For the transmission of data via telemetry, the accuracy possible or required in the transmission determines the number of levels used.

For example, assume that the temperature of a refining process at a remote plant is to be transmitted back to a centralized computer site as part of the control process. If temperature readings to within 1°C only are required, and the expected range is 20 to 80°C, only 60 levels are required, so one would presumably choose 64 levels, or 6-bit PCM. If the temperature sensors used can only read to 2°C accuracy, 30 levels are available, and 5-bit PCM could be used.

---

[10]A detailed treatment appears in [CATT] K. W. Cattermole, *Principles of Pulse Code Modulation*, Illife, London, 1969; American Elsevier, New York, 1975.

If readings to within 0.5°C accuracy are required and sensors capable of this accuracy are available, 128 levels and 7-bit PCM would be used.

These rather qualitative remarks are useful to provide a first, intuitive understanding of the trade-offs among accuracy, quantization noise, and the number of quantization levels used. A more sophisticated treatment suitable for design purposes requires a quantitative approach, however. We have tacitly assumed to this point that the analog signal to be quantized has definite minimum and maximum values between which it ranges, and that it is equally likely to occupy any value in this range. We have thus taken the quantization levels to be equally spaced. For speech transmission via PCM telephony, this is far from the true situation, however. There one has talkers of different power and timbre. Some people shout, others speak very quietly on the telephone. If the 256 quantization levels assigned were to be equally spaced and cover the range from a soft whisper to a shout, it is apparent that good reproduction for all types of speakers would not be possible. One thus has to take into account the *statistics* of the signal and design the quantization scheme on this basis. The same problem arises in a telemetry situation: lower temperature readings may occur more frequently than high readings and may be required to be known with greater accuracy. One thus needs a *tapered* quantization level structure that is finer at the lower readings, and more coarse at the high readings.

To quantify these comments in this section we shall introduce the idea of a signal-to-quantization-noise ratio. This can be defined in various ways, as we shall see, but basically it establishes the idea, to be repeated many times throughout this book in discussing other kinds of noise, that the effect of noise on the performance of a system depends on the amount of noise relative to the signal. In a speech system quantization noise cackle, as heard by a listener, is only objectionable if it is noticeable compared to the signal intensity of the speaker. A given noise level is more objectionable when a quiet speaker is speaking than when a loud one is. We shall be calculating a mean-squared quantization noise, or its square root, the rms noise level, but shall relate it to some measure of the signal level (mean-squared value or peak value squared) to determine the quantization noise performance of a PCM system.

We shall also introduce a statistical model of the signal and see how tapering the quantization-level structure improves the performance compared to the equal-level case. We shall focus primarily on the speech-telephony application because of the availability of design procedures in this area, and because of its technological importance: the use of PCM in telephone transmission has increased dramatically since its introduction by the Bell System in the United States in the early 1960s. The ideas and concepts introduced are of course applicable to other application areas as well. (The CD audio system uses uniform spacing [PEEK].)

We first assume equally spaced quantization levels and calculate the signal-to-quantization-noise ratio for this case. In practice, rather than use tapered quantization levels to match the signal characteristics, the signals are first nonlinearly *compressed* in amplitude to force all signals to lie within a specified range. This compression characteristic is typically of a logarithmic form. Uniform quantization levels are then applied to this compressed signal. The effect is to provide proportionately more quantization levels at the smaller signal levels, as if the quantization-level spacing had been reduced at the lower signal levels. At the receiver the signal is *expanded* to its original amplitude through an inverse logarithmic form. The combination of compression and expansion is referred to as *companding* for short. Using some typical signal statistics for the speech example, we shall show that the effect of companding (or nonuniform tapering of quantization levels) is to provide a uniform signal-to-quantization-noise ratio over a much wider dynamic range of signals than in the noncompressed case.

Quantization Noise, Equal Level Spacing

To calculate the rms quantization noise in this case, prior to setting up an expression for the signal-to-quantization-noise ratio, let the signal at the transmitter be quantized into a total of M levels, with a the spacing in volts between adjacent levels. With a maximum plus–minus signal excursion of P volts, or a maximum excursion positively or negatively of V volts (see Fig. 3-19),

$$a = \frac{P}{M} = \frac{2V}{M} \tag{3-28}$$

(The continuous signal is assumed to have 0 average value, or no dc component.) The quantized amplitudes will be at $\pm a/2, \pm 3a/2, \ldots, \pm (M-1)(a/2)$, and the quantized samples will cover a range

$$A = (M-1)a \quad \text{volts}$$

As noted earlier, the quantization process introduces an irreducible error, since a sample appearing at the receiver output at quantized voltage A_j volts could have been due to any signal voltage in the range $A_j - a/2$ to $A_j + a/2$ volts. This region of uncertainty is shown in Fig. 3-20. As far as the ultimate recipient of the message is concerned, this region of uncertainty could just as well

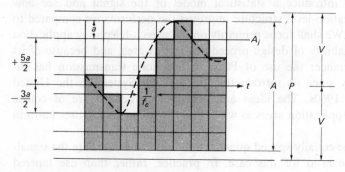

FIGURE 3-19
Quantized approximation to a signal: eight levels.

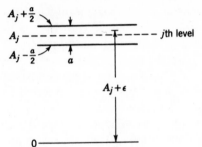

FIGURE 3-20
Region of uncertainty at system output.

have been due to additive noise masking the actual signal level. The one difference is that additive noise, as we shall see in Chap. 6, can theoretically take on all possible voltage values. The quantization noise, on the other hand, is limited to $\pm a/2$ volts. The distinction between these two will become clearer in Chap. 6.

We can calculate a mean-squared error voltage due to quantization. To do this, assume that over a long period of time all voltage values in the region of uncertainty eventually appear the same number of times. The instantaneous voltage of the signal will be $A_j + \epsilon$, with $-a/2 \le \epsilon \le a/2$. Here ϵ represents the error voltage between the instantaneous (actual) signal and its quantized equivalent. Under our assumption all values of ϵ are equally likely. The mean-squared value of ϵ will then be

$$E(\epsilon^2) = \frac{1}{a} \int_{-a/2}^{a/2} \epsilon^2 \, d\epsilon = \frac{a^2}{12} \qquad (3\text{-}29)$$

with the symbol $E(\cdot)$ representing statistical expectation. The average value of the error is zero with the assumption made. The rms error is then $a/\sqrt{12} = a/(2\sqrt{3})$ volts, and this represents the rms "noise" at the system output.

We now introduce the idea of the signal-to-quantization-noise ratio (SNR). We do this two ways, by defining two different SNRs, one in terms of the peak signal, V volts, the other in terms of the mean signal power, $S_0 = (M^2 - 1)a^2/12$.

PEAK SIGNAL. Since $V = aM/2$ is the peak signal excursion, the ratio of peak signal voltage to rms noise will be

$$\frac{S_{0v}}{N_{0v}} = \frac{V}{a/(2\sqrt{3})} = \sqrt{3}\,M \qquad (3\text{-}30)$$

The corresponding power ratio is

$$\frac{S_0}{N_0} = 3M^2 \qquad (3\text{-}31)$$

TABLE 3-2
Quantization SNR improvement
with number of levels

S_0 / N_0, dB	M	Relative bandwidth
11	2	1
17	4	2
23	8	3
29	16	4
35	32	5
41	64	6
47	128	7

or, in decibels,

$$\left(\frac{S_0}{N_0}\right)_{dB} = 4.8 + 20\log_{10} M \qquad (3\text{-}32)$$

The power ratio thus goes up as the square of the number of levels. The SNR decibel improvement with M is given in Table 3-2. Also indicated is the relative bandwidth as obtained from the discussion following.

Since M, the number of levels used, determines the number of pulses into which the quantized signal is encoded before transmission, increasing M increases the number of code pulses and hence the bandwidth. We can thus relate SNR to bandwidth. This is easily done by noting that $M = n^m$, with m the number of pulses in the code group and n the number of code levels. With this relation, Eqs. (3-31) and (3-32) become, respectively,

$$\frac{S_0}{N_0} = 3n^{2m} \qquad (3\text{-}33)$$

and

$$\left(\frac{S_0}{N_0}\right)_{dB} = 4.8 + 20m\log_{10} n \qquad (3\text{-}34)$$

In particular, for binary code ($n = 2$),

$$\left(\frac{S_0}{N_0}\right)_{dB} = 4.8 + 6m \qquad (3\text{-}35)$$

Since the bandwidth is proportional to m, the number of pulses in the code group, the output SNR increases exponentially with bandwidth. The decibel SNR increases linearly with bandwidth [Eq. (3-35)].

For a 256-level system $S_0/N_0 = 53$ dB, and eight-pulse binary-code groups are transmitted, requiring an eightfold bandwidth increase.

MEAN SIGNAL POWER. Essentially similar results are obtained upon defining a mean power SNR. With a quantized level spacing of a volts and signal swings of

$\pm V$ volts the mean signal power is readily found to be

$$S_0 = \tfrac{1}{12}(M^2 - 1)a^2$$

assuming all signal levels equally likely. Details are left to the reader as an exercise.

Since $N_0 = a^2/12$, the mean power output SNR is

$$\frac{S_0}{N_0} = M^2 - 1 \tag{3-36}$$

For $M \gg 1$ this differs only by a constant from the peak S_0/N_0 relation given by Eq. (3-31). For a system with 256 levels the quantization SNR is 48 dB. A binary-code group requires eight pulses ($2^8 = 256$), or eight times the bandwidth of the original quantized signal.

Signal-to-Noise Ratios with Companding

In the previous paragraph we tacitly assumed that a known peak signal amplitude V (or peak-to-peak excursion $P = 2V$) existed and chose the M quantization levels equally spaced to cover the total signal excursion. For many classes of signals there is no specified peak value and the signal level may in fact change in a random manner. The most common example is that of speech transmission, with different speakers using the same transmission facilities. The range of speech intensity may vary as much as 40 dB in going from a whisper to a bellow. It is apparent that to cover this dynamic range effectively nonuniform quantization-level spacing, or its equivalent, signal compression, must be used. If this is not done and equally spaced levels are chosen to cover the widest signal variation expected, the soft speakers will be penalized. The same problem obviously arises in the PCM transmission of any analog signals expected to cover a wide dynamic range.

We first demonstrate the effect of dynamic variation of the signal power on the SNR with uniform spacing of quantization levels by repeating the analysis of the previous paragraph somewhat differently. Say that the quantizer is again designed to accept a peak-to-peak signal excursion of $P = 2V$ volts, but that this corresponds to the maximum level of the highest-intensity signal expected. Let the actual signal appearing at the quantizer input have a mean power (mean-squared value) of σ^2. This should obviously be significantly less than V^2 to be accommodated by the quantizer. (As an example, if the signal is statistical in nature and follows the familiar gaussian probability distribution, σ^2 is the variance of the distribution. This is discussed in detail in Chaps. 6 and 7. Theoretically a gaussian random variable, in this case the signal amplitude, can take on any value whatsoever. There is no theoretical maximum. There is a 99.99 percent probability that the variable will lie within the range $\pm 4\sigma$, however. One can thus safely pick $V = 4\sigma$ in this case. In this example, then, $\sigma^2 = V^2/16$ is the maximum intensity signal that can be accommodated by the quantizer. If the

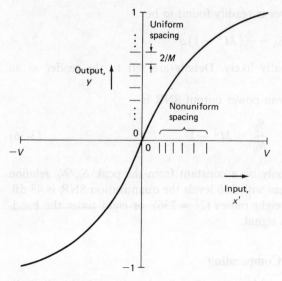

FIGURE 3-21
Nonlinear compressor characteristic.

signal covers the range $\pm V$ uniformly, however, $\sigma^2 = V^2/3$ is the maximum signal power that can be accommodated.)

As previously, we have for the mean-squared quantization noise

$$E(\epsilon^2) = \frac{a^2}{12}$$

$$= \frac{V^2}{3M^2} \qquad (3\text{-}37)$$

using the quantizer characteristic $a = 2V/M$. With an input signal power of σ^2 we have as the signal-to-noise ratio[11]

$$\text{SNR} = \frac{\sigma^2}{E(\epsilon^2)} = 3M^2\left(\frac{\sigma^2}{V^2}\right) \qquad (3\text{-}38)$$

Since the quantization noise is fixed, independent of σ^2, in the case of uniformly spaced levels, the SNR is proportional to σ^2. As a speaker reduces his intensity the SNR reduces correspondingly. The quantization noise becomes that much more noticeable. This is the problem mentioned above. To mitigate this and obtain a relatively fixed SNR over a wide dynamic range of signals it is necessary

---

[11] This definition of signal-to-noise ratio differs somewhat from those of the previous paragraph because it is the ratio of input signal power to mean-squared quantization noise. Previously, we used the output (quantized) power for the calculation. It is more convenient for our purpose now to refer to the input power, since it is this quantity that we will be varying. If the number of quantization levels $M \gg 1$, the difference between the input and output signal power, with equally spaced levels, is slight. Notice, for example, that $M^2 - 1$ appears in (3-36) rather than the factor M^2 in (3-38).

to introduce quantization-level tapering. Alternatively, as pointed out previously, it is simpler in practice to compress the signal nonlinearly and then apply uniform level spacing to the compressed output signal. At the receiver the signal is then expanded following an inverse nonlinear characteristic. It is apparent that this is exactly equivalent to nonuniform spacing of the levels. An example appears in Fig. 3-21. x' represents the input signal and y the output. For the characteristic chosen, the equivalent input levels move farther and farther apart as the input amplitude approaches $\pm V$. This is due to the compression of the higher input values into a correspondingly smaller range of output values.

A typical compression characteristic has a logarithmic form. A particularly common form implemented in practice for speech telephony is the *μ-law companding*. This has the specific form

$$y(x') = \frac{\ln(1 + \mu x'/V)}{\ln(1 + \mu)} \qquad 0 \le x' \le V \qquad (3\text{-}39)$$

It is odd symmetric with this characteristic about the $x' = 0$ point. $y(x')$ thus ranges between ± 1. The parameter μ appearing can be varied to obtain a variety of characteristics. Note that for $x' \ll V/\mu$ the characteristic is almost linear:

$$y(x') \doteq \frac{\mu x'}{V \ln(1 + \mu)} \qquad x' \ll \frac{V}{\mu} \qquad (3\text{-}40)$$

As x' increases beyond the point V/μ, the logarithmic characteristic takes over. For $\mu \ll 1$, $y(x') \doteq x'/V$, nonlinear compression disappears, and the uniform spacing of the output y corresponds to uniform spacing of the input x'. The telephone system in the United States uses a $\mu = 255$ companding law for its digital carrier systems [BELL 1982].[12] This particular characteristic is sketched, for $x' \ge 0$, in Fig. 3-22. We shall carry out a quantization-noise and SNR analysis for the μ-law compression characteristic. For this purpose it is useful to define a normalized input signal $x = x'/V$. In terms of this normalized signal, the μ-law compressor characteristic is given by

$$y(x) = \frac{\ln(1 + \mu x)}{\ln(1 + \mu)} \qquad 0 \le x \le 1 \qquad (3\text{-}41)$$

The normalized input form is the one actually sketched in Fig. 3-22. Our analysis will depend on the normalized signal power (or variance) $\sigma_x^2 = \sigma^2/V^2$. In terms of this parameter the SNR for uniform quantization levels (no compression) is given by

$$\text{SNR} = 3M^2 \sigma_x^2 \qquad (3\text{-}42)$$

We shall compare the SNR with compression with this expression.

---

[12][BELL 1982] Bell Telephone Laboratories, *Transmission Systems for Communications*, 5th ed., 1982.

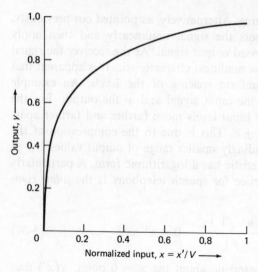

FIGURE 3-22
Compressor characteristic, μ-law companding, $\mu = 255$ (positive quadrant only.)

To analyze the effect of compression or nonlinear tapering on the quantization noise and hence the SNR, we note that the output signal y has values equally spaced $2/M$ units apart, from -1 to $+1$, as shown in Fig. 3-21. We focus on the analysis for positive x only. This uniform spacing projects into a nonuniform spacing Δ_j ($j = 1, 2, \ldots, M/2$) at the input which depends on the compressor characteristics. Consider a particular spacing Δ_j centered at x_j as shown in Fig. 3-23. It is apparent from the figure that for Δ_j small enough $(2/M \ll 1)$, $2/M \doteq (dy/dx)|_{x_j} \Delta_j$, or

$$\Delta_j \doteq \frac{2}{M} \left/ \left| \frac{dy}{dx} \right|_j \right. \tag{3-43}$$

All values of x in the range Δ_j centered at x_j will, after quantization of the compressed signal, correspond to one output value. Hence the mean-squared quantization error due to these values can be found by appropriately averaging

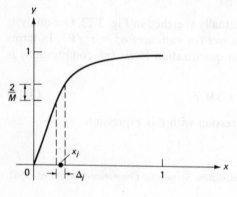

FIGURE 3-23
Compressor analysis.

over Δ_j. Assume that now the input signal is random with a known probability density function $f(x)$. The mean-squared variation about x_j is then, by definition, given by

$$E\left(\epsilon_j^2\right) = \int_{x_j-\Delta_j/2}^{x_j+\Delta_j/2}(x - x_j)^2 f(x)\, dx \qquad (3\text{-}44)$$

Since we have been assuming the number of quantization levels $M \gg 1$, it is a reasonable approximation that all values of x in the range Δ_j have the same probability of occurring. This corresponds to taking $f(x)$ constant over that range. We thus have

$$E\left(\epsilon_j^2\right) \doteq f(x_j)\int_{x_j-\Delta_j/2}^{x_j+\Delta_j/2}(x - x_j)^2\, dx$$

$$= f(x_j)\frac{\Delta_j^3}{12} \qquad (3\text{-}44a)$$

Note that this is similar to the analysis carried out in the previous paragraph, except that there the level spacing was a fixed value $\Delta_j = a$ [see Eq. (3-29)].

From (3-43) we can now write

$$E\left(\epsilon_j^2\right) \doteq \frac{1}{3M^2}\frac{f(x_j)}{\left[y'(x_j)\right]^2}\Delta_j \qquad (3\text{-}44b)$$

where we have used the shorthand notation $y'(x)$ to represent dy/dx. The total mean-squared quantization noise $E(\epsilon^2)$, including negative x_j, is twice the sum of all $M/2$ contributions, $E(\epsilon_j^2)$, $j = 1, 2, \ldots, M/2$:

$$E(\epsilon^2) = 2\sum_{j=1}^{M/2} E\left(\epsilon_j^2\right) \doteq \frac{2}{3M^2}\sum_{j=1}^{M/2}\frac{f(x)}{\left[y'(x)\right]^2}\bigg|_j \Delta_j \qquad (3\text{-}45)$$

For M large enough we can approximate the sum of (3-45) by the equivalent integral, and get

$$E(\epsilon^2) \doteq \frac{2}{3M^2}\int_0^1 \frac{f(x)}{\left[y'(x)\right]^2}\, dx \qquad (3\text{-}45a)$$

It is this expression that we use to evaluate the effect of the compression law. Note, as a check, that if there is no compression, then $y = x$, $y'(x) = 1$, and $E(\epsilon^2) = 1/3M^2$, as found previously. [See (3-37). Recall again that we are dealing here with the normalized input $x = x'/V$.] The effect of the compressor is thus given by the square of the derivative appearing in the denominator of the integral in (3-45a).

For the μ-law compander specifically, we have, from (3-41),

$$y'(x) = \frac{\mu}{\ln(1 + \mu)}\frac{1}{1 + \mu x} \qquad (3\text{-}46)$$

Inserting this in the denominator of (3-45a), we get

$$E(\epsilon^2) = \frac{2}{3M^2}\left(\frac{\ln(1+\mu)}{\mu}\right)^2 \int_0^1 f(x)(1+\mu x)^2\,dx$$

$$= \left[\frac{\ln(1+\mu)}{\mu}\right]^2 \frac{1}{3M^2}(1 + \mu^2\sigma_x^2 + 2\mu E[|x|]) \qquad (3\text{-}47)$$

where

$$\sigma_x^2 \doteq \int_{-1}^1 x^2 f(x)\,dx \qquad (3\text{-}48)$$

is the variance of the signal distribution to be quantized [$f(x)$ is assumed symmetrical about zero and concentrated in the range $-1, 1$], and

$$E[|x|] \doteq 2\int_0^1 x f(x)\,dx \qquad (3\text{-}49)$$

Equation (3-47) enables us to calculate the mean-squared quantization noise for the μ-law compressor characteristic for any set of signal statistics. The signal statistics required are the two parameters σ_x^2 and $E[|x|]$. The actual form of the signal probability density function $f(x)$ is not too critical. The ratio $E[|x|]/\sigma_x$ does not vary very much from one distribution to another, and hence $E(\epsilon^2)$ will be almost the same for various density functions. Three examples are tabulated below. The corresponding density functions are shown sketched in Fig. 3-24.

1. *Laplacian signal*:

$$f(x) = \frac{1}{\sqrt{2}\,\sigma_x} e^{-\sqrt{2}|x|/\sigma_x} \qquad (3\text{-}50)$$

$$\frac{2E[|x|]}{\sigma_x} = \sqrt{2} = 1.414 \qquad (3\text{-}51)$$

2. *Gaussian signal*:

$$f(x) = \frac{e^{-x^2/2\sigma_x^2}}{\sqrt{2\pi\sigma_x^2}} \qquad (3\text{-}52)$$

$$\frac{2E[|x|]}{\sigma_x} = 2\sqrt{\frac{2}{\pi}} = 1.6 \qquad (3\text{-}53)$$

3. *Uniformly distributed signal*:

$$f(x) = \frac{1}{2A} \qquad -A \le x \le A \qquad (3\text{-}54)$$

$$\sigma_x^2 = \frac{A^2}{3}$$

$$\frac{2E[|x|]}{\sigma_x} = \sqrt{3} = 1.732 \qquad (3\text{-}55)$$

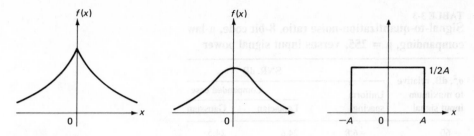

FIGURE 3-24
Examples of signal probability density functions. (*a*) Laplacian. (*b*) Gaussian. (*c*) Uniform.

The particular values of $E[|x|]$ given in each case are obtained by integrating (3-49) using the appropriate form of $f(x)$. It turns out that the laplacian density function of (3-50) is a relatively good model for speech [BELL 1982], so we will focus on it in making calculations of the SNR. The other density functions give almost identical results, however. The gaussian density function is the one most commonly appearing in the theory of probability, and we shall encounter it regularly in Chaps. 6 and 7 when modeling additive noise. The quadratic form in the exponential causes $f(x)$ to drop very rapidly for $|x| > \sigma_x$. It thus models signals that have a relatively low probability of exceeding σ_x. The laplacian density function serves as a good model of signals that have a higher probability of attaining high values. It is left to the reader to show, by integrating (3-50) from $4\sigma_x$ to ∞ and $-4\sigma_x$ to $-\infty$, that the probability that $|x|$ exceeds $4\sigma_x$, in that case, is 0.0035, contrasted with the equivalent probability for the gaussian case of 10^{-4}.

The signal-to-quantization noise ratio is now obtained, as previously, by defining it to be the mean-squared signal power σ_x^2 divided by $E(\epsilon^2)$. We thus get, for the μ-law compander,

$$\text{SNR} = \frac{\sigma_x^2}{E(\epsilon^2)} = \frac{3M^2}{[\ln(1 + \mu)]^2} \frac{1}{1 + 2E[|x|]/\mu\sigma_x^2 + 1/\mu^2\sigma_x^2} \quad (3\text{-}56)$$

Using this equation and various models for the signal statistics, one can obtain the SNR for various compander laws. For $\mu \to 0$ it is easy to see, as a check, that SNR $= 3M^2\sigma_x^2$, just the result for uniform level spacing obtained earlier [Eq. (3-42)]. In Table 3-3 we tabulate SNR in decibels ($10\log_{10}$ SNR) as a function of σ_x^2, in decibels also, for the $\mu = 255$ compander law and an 8-bit ($M = 256$) system. This is shown for both the laplacian and gaussian cases. Note that the results for the two are comparable, as expected from the discussion above. Also shown for comparison is the uniform-level-spacing case, obtained from (3-42). Since $\sigma_x^2 < 1$ because of the normalization, its value is indicated in dB relative to the maximum input signal. These results are sketched as well in Fig. 3-25. The

TABLE 3-3
Signal-to-quantization-noise ratio, 8-bit code, μ-law
companding, μ = 255, versus input signal power

σ_x^2, dB, relative to maximum input signal	SNR, dB		
	Uniform spacing	Companded case	
		Laplacian	Gaussian
− 60	− 6.8	24.6	24.5
− 56	− 2.8	27.8	27.6
− 50	3.2	31.7	31.5
− 46	7.2	33.6	33.3
− 40	13.2	35.7	35.5
− 26	27.2	37.5	37.5
− 20	33.2	37.8	37.8
− 14	39.2	38	38
− 8	45.2	38	38
0	53.2	38	38

important point to note is that over a broad range of input signals, the SNR is almost constant for the compander case. It is only when σ_x^2 reaches − 40 dB that the SNR begins to drop appreciably. The uniform-level SNR shows wide variations, however. For $\sigma_x^2 > -15$ dB, i.e., for higher-amplitude signals, it begins to exceed the compander result. But for all the other values shown (lower-level signals), it drops lower and lower with respect to the compander result. Uniform

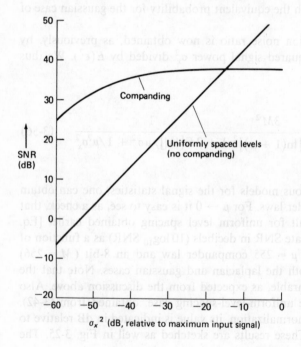

FIGURE 3-25
Signal-to-quantization-noise ratio, with companding, versus input signal power; $M = 256$ levels, $\mu = 225$.

spacing thus favors the higher-amplitude signals at the expense of the lower-amplitude signals. The companded SNR is of course almost constant over almost a 40-dB range of input amplitudes.

Other logarithmic companding laws have been proposed in addition to the μ-law characteristic discussed here. One example is the A law [BELL 1982], with the following characteristic (the input signal x is again normalized, relative to the maximum input signal):

$$
\begin{aligned}
y &= \frac{1 + \ln Ax}{1 + \ln A} \qquad \frac{1}{A} \le x \le 1 \\
&= \frac{Ax}{1 + \ln A} \qquad 0 \le x \le \frac{1}{A}
\end{aligned}
\tag{3-57}
$$

(The full characteristic is odd symmetric about $x = 0$.) A value of $A = 100$ is typical of practical companders using this characteristic. The SNR characteristic for this value of A is found to provide a somewhat wider dynamic range than the μ-law compander with $\mu = 255$, but its output SNR is somewhat smaller [BELL 1982].

Note that the A-law characteristic is defined to be linear for small x and logarithmic for large x. Both the μ-law and A-law characteristics are implemented in practice by piecewise linear approximations [BELL 1982].

3-6 EXAMPLES OF PAM AND PCM SYSTEMS

In this section we present some examples of specific PAM and PCM systems. The examples have been chosen to further focus attention on the elements of time multiplexing, quantization, and A/D conversion discussed earlier, as well as to present some typical engineering solutions to problems raised earlier. The emphasis here, as in previous sections, is on analog signals to be transmitted using digital techniques. Other examples of digital communication systems in use are described briefly in some of the sections following.

In Sec. 3-8 we stress the time multiplexing of signals already in digital format. These could be data terminal or computer signals, or they could be analog signals converted to digital form.

The applications described in this section include an older PAM system typical of those used for many years in radio telemetry, a PCM system developed for a meteorological satellite, a deep-space telemetry system, and the telephone T1 PCM system in common use for short-haul telephone communications. The techniques used in generating the time-multiplexed PAM or PCM signals in these examples are representative of those used in a broad variety of application areas requiring the telemetering of data. These include industrial telemetry for process control purposes, automatic monitoring of power-generation plants, biomedical telemetry, telemetry for geoseismic and geophysical exploration, etc. In the older systems the various sampling, A/D, and multiplexing operations were carried out using hard-wired logic. More recently, with the advent of programmable logic and microprocessor-controlled systems, the various operations have been brought under software control. This results in a flexibility of operation not possible with hard-wired logic. It often results in cheaper, more compact, and less power-consuming systems as well. Since the principles of multiplexing, commutation, and synchronization are independent of specific implementation, both older and newer systems can be described side by side to obtain insight into the operation of PAM and PCM systems. This is particularly true of the simple radio-telemetry PAM system to be described first. Although PCM systems have become much more common in telemetry, and have in many cases displaced older PAM systems, the techniques used to carry out the sampling and multiplexing operations are common to both PAM and PCM systems. This is apparent from our discussion in Sec. 3-3.

A Radio-Telemetry PAM System [GRUE][13]

The PAM system to be discussed is typical of those used for radio telemetry. It is of interest because it provides for the multiplexing of many data channels of greatly varying data rates or bandwidths. This is done by performing the multiplexing operations in two steps: low-data-rate channels are first time-multiplexed to form composite data channels of much wider bandwidths; the composite channels are then in turn time-multiplexed with wider-bandwidth channels to form the main multiplexed signal.

Specifically, in a typical application 318 different data channels are to be sampled, time-multiplexed, and transmitted via radio. The data rates involved range from a bandwidth of 1 Hz to one of 2 kHz. The main multiplexer is designed to handle 16 channels, with 2,500 samples per second for each. The low-data-rate signals must thus be combined in groups to provide the 2,500 samples per second required for any one channel. The various data channels, and their bandwidths, sampling rates, and group assignments, where necessary, are indicated in Table 3-4 [GRUE, p. 9–11].

The two 1-kHz channels, sampled at 2,500 samples per second, obviously can be tied directly to the main multiplexer. The channels in groups 3 to 7 must be combined, however. For ease in timing this combining is done by sampling at binary submultiples of the final 2,500-sample-per-second rate. The required sampling rates can then be obtained by successively dividing down by factors of 2 from a master clock. As an example, the 312.5-sample-per-second rate is obtained by dividing down by 8 from 2,500, and the 19.5-sample-per-second rate by dividing down by 128. Figure 3-26 shows the preliminary multiplexing at the 312.5-sample rate. Note that five data channels only are combined, leaving three

---

[13][GRUE] E. L. Gruenberg (ed.), *Handbook of Telemetry and Remote Control*, McGraw-Hill, New York, 1967, pp. 9-11 to 9-18.

TABLE 3-4
Multiplexing

Group	Number of data channels	Bandwidth per channel	Sampling rate, samples / second	Required accuracy, %	Main multiplexer position
1	3	2 kHz	5,000	10	2 and 10, 4 and 12, 5 and 13
2	2	1 kHz	2,500	5	3, 6
3	5	100 Hz	312.5	2	7
4	28	25 Hz	78	2	8
5	55	5 Hz	39	1	9
6	115	5 Hz	19.5	2	14
7	110	1 Hz	19.5	2	15

time slots available for synchronization, calibration, or inclusion of additional data channels later, if so desired.

It is apparent that such spare capacity exists in each of the low-data-rate groupings. Thus a sampling rate of 78 samples per second makes 32 time slots available. In this application there are only 28 channels (group 4) requiring this sampling rate. The 55 data channels of 5-Hz bandwidth (group 5) are grouped together and shown sampled at almost four times the Nyquist rate to meet the higher accuracy requirements in that case. Here nine spare time slots are available. The 110 channels of 1-Hz bandwidth are obviously highly oversampled, but system simplicity results.

The three high-bandwidth channels indicated as group 1 require 5,000 samples per second each. Two time slots, spaced $\frac{1}{5000}$ s apart, must be thus set aside, of the 16 available in the main multiplexer, for each of the three channels. These then use six time slots. Adding the two used by the two 1-kHz channels,

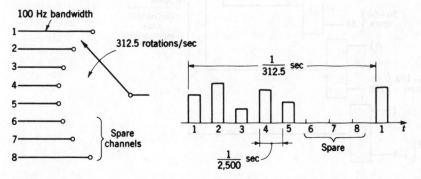

FIGURE 3-26
Preliminary multiplexing, group 3, PAM system.

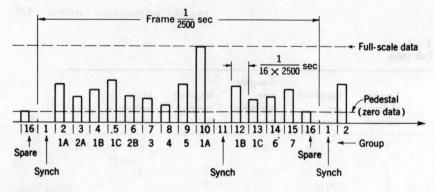

FIGURE 3-27
Composite signal format.

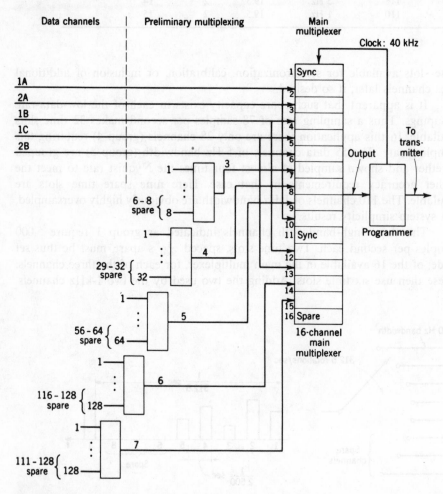

FIGURE 3-28
PAM system for radio telemetry. [From E. L. Gruenberg (ed.), *Handbook of Telemetry and Remote Control*, McGraw-Hill, New York, 1967, chap. 9, Fig. 11, simplified.]

and the five time slots required by the premultiplexed groups 3 to 7, we have 13 used in all. Two additional time slots in the final multiplexed signal are used for synchronization purposes, and one is left available as a spare. The main multiplexer assignments are indicated in the table.

The final multiplexed signal, following these assigned time slots, is shown in Fig. 3-27 [GRUE, p. 9-13, Fig. 12a]. The slots occupied by the three wide-bandwidth channels in group 1 are indicated by the labels 1A, 1B, and 1C, respectively, while the two 1-kHz channels are indicated by 2A and 2B. The entire sequence of 16 time slots shown is called a *frame*. In the format of Fig. 3-27 the composite data samples occupy 50 percent of each time slot. To provide synchronization all data samples are placed on a pedestal of about 20 percent of the full-scale data level. The absence of pulses in slots 1 and 11 then provides the necessary synchronization. Zero data corresponds to the pedestal height, as shown by the spare data slot 16. (In other systems synchronization may be provided by a specified digital code word inserted in the appropriate time slot [GRUE, p. 9-13, Fig. 12; pp. 5-34 and 5-35, Fig. 5a, b, c, d].)

The block diagram of the entire PAM system (transmitter only) is shown in Fig. 3-28 [GRUE, p. 9-12, Fig. 11]. The programmer shown provides the clock pulses for all multiplexers, starting with a clock rate of 40 kHz, and counting down by 2's, as indicated earlier.

The receiver for this PAM radio-telemetry system performs the necessary functions of demultiplexing the data samples, low-pass filtering them, and sending them to the appropriate receiving channel.

Commutation

The sampling and time-multiplexing operations, represented conceptually here and in previous sections by a rotating mechanical switch, represent the heart of PAM and PCM systems. Many electronic schemes have been devised to perform these operations. The process of sequentially sampling a group of input data channels is frequently referred to as a *commutation* process, and various electronic commutators have been devised to perform this function [GRUE, pp. 4-53–4-92]. The commutator is commonly divided into two parts: channel gates that sequentially open to allow one channel at a time through, performing the sequential sampling operation, and a sequential gate control generator, operated by a clock, that actually operates the gates. One common example is shown in Fig. 3-29a [GRUE, p. 4-79, Fig. 78a]. The sequential gate control generator here consists of a chain of flip-flops. The master pulse turns on the first element of the chain. The next channel pulse turns off the first flip-flop, and this in turn turns on the second element. This stepping continues to the end of the chain, when the master pulse again turns on the first element.

The counter-matrix arrangement of Fig. 3-29b provides another common form of commutation. The outputs shown open the corresponding gates sequentially. To perform the necessary sequencing, counter waveforms are combined appropriately. As an example consider the binary waveforms of Fig. 3-30. These correspond respectively to the appropriate binary counters of Fig. 3-29b. Thus

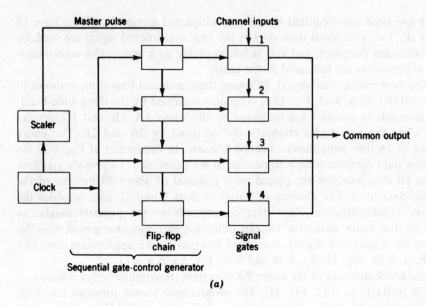

(a)

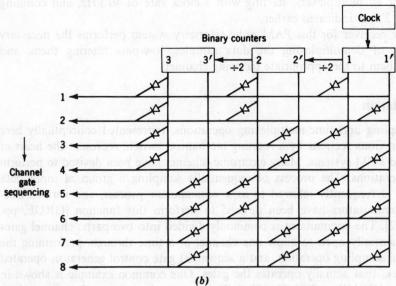

(b)

FIGURE 3-29
Typical electronic commutators. (*a*) Broken-ring commutator: four data channels. (*b*) Counter-matrix gate-control generator: eight channels. [From E. L. Gruenberg (ed.), *Handbook of Telemetry and Control*, McGraw-Hill, New York, 1967, chap. 4, Figs. 78*a* and 79, simplified.]

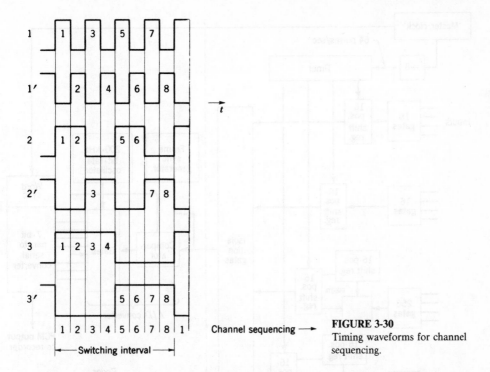

FIGURE 3-30
Timing waveforms for channel sequencing.

Channel sequencing ⟶

the basic binary sequence 1 and its phase-shifted version 1′ correspond to 1 and 1′, respectively, of Fig. 3-29b. Dividing down successively by 2, as indicated in Fig. 3-29b, we get the waveforms shown in Fig. 3-30. The three pairs of waveforms shown provide the $2^3 = 8$ possible connections needed for the eight channels indicated. Specifically, note from Fig. 3-30 that outputs 1, 2, and 3 are all simultaneously positive during the first $\frac{1}{8}$ of the switching cycle of Fig. 3-30. Connecting these outputs to channel 1 as shown in Fig. 3-29b, channel 1 is gated on during the first $\frac{1}{8}$ of the cycle only, being turned off during the remainder of the cycle. It is apparent from Fig. 3-30 that connecting the other seven channels appropriately, as shown in Fig. 3-29b, three simultaneously positive pulses are obtained in time sequence, providing the desired sequential gating action.

As noted above, sampling, multiplexing, and commutating functions just described can be implemented on LSI chips, or, with the addition of RAM and ROM memories, carried out using programmable logic. Microprocessor-controlled versions can be developed as well. In a deep-space telemetry system to be described later, programmed control is in fact used to carry out the multiplexing operations.

PCM Telemetry for the Nimbus Satellite

We turn to an example of a PCM system developed for space applications. The particular example we have chosen to describe very briefly is the telemetering

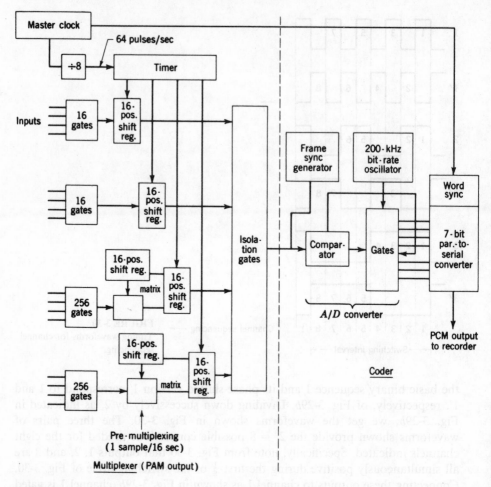

FIGURE 3-31
"A" telemeter, Nimbus PCM system, simplified. [Adapted from A. V. Balakrishnan (ed.), *Space Communications*, McGraw-Hill, New York, 1963, Fig. 18-4, pp. 372–373.]

system used aboard the NASA second-generation meteorological satellite, the Nimbus spacecraft. This spacecraft is designed to provide appropriate meteorological data (cloud measurements, distribution of rainfall, the earth's outgoing thermal radiation, heat balance, etc.) of the entire earth at least once a day.[14]

Two independent PCM telemetering systems are used. One, the so-called A system, records continuously on an endless-loop tape recorder; the other, the B system, may be commanded at any time. In the A system 544 inputs are

---

[14][STAM] R. Stampfl, in A. V. Balakrishnan (ed.), *Space Communications*, McGraw-Hill, New York, 1963, chap. 18. The telemetry systems are described on pp. 370–376 and 404–406.

multiplexed for recording and ultimate transmission on command. Thirty-two of these input channels, in two groups of 16 channels each, are sampled once per second; the remaining 512 channels, in two groups of 256 channels each, are sampled once every 16 s. Premultiplexing, just as in the PAM systems described in the previous paragraph, must thus be carried out on the two 256-channel groups, combining them first before combining with the 16-channel groups. A simplified block diagram of the system is shown in Fig. 3-31 [STAM, Fig. 18-4, pp. 372, 373].

Sampling and multiplexing are first carried out by means of the timer and 16-position shift registers shown. A pulse of the 64-pulse-per-second generator shown triggers the first position of the first (uppermost) shift register shown, gating on the first of the 16 upper channels. The second pulse, $\frac{1}{64}$ s later, triggers the first position of the second shift register, gating on the first of the 16 channels in the next group. One of the 256 multiplexed groups is then gated on, etc. The fifth pulse returns to the first shift register, opening its second position. The cycle thus continues for the full 64 pulses, returning to the first of the 16 upper channels 1 s later, as desired.

Premultiplexing of the 256 channel groups is done by using an additional 16-position shift register for each group to form a matrix with the shift registers mentioned above.

Each of the 64 outputs of the multiplexer constitutes a word $\frac{1}{64}$ s long. The 64 consecutive words in turn make up a frame 1 s long. Each word is quantized into $2^7 = 128$ levels and converted into a 7-bit sequence. A word sync bit (a zero) is added and the coded PCM stream fed out to the recorder. The complete frame 1 s long thus has $64 \times 8 = 512$ bits.

The A/D conversion is carried out by comparing the incoming (PAM) signal to a sequence of binary weighted reference voltages. The binary-coded signal is stored in a buffer where the word sync bit is added. Frame sync is also provided at the A/D converter input.

The Voyager 1977 Telemetry System [WOOD][15]

This telemetry system was originally developed to handle the telemetry requirements of NASA's spacecraft missions to Jupiter and Saturn (1.5×10^9 km from the earth). The mission later went on to Neptune and Uranus. The telemetry system is particularly interesting in that its requirements vary with the location of the spacecraft: during the launch period, during the interplanetary cruise period, during the planetary encounter period. Playback of data recorded on tape is also used when earth communications are interrupted.

Both engineering data and science data from a variety of instruments (including imaging data of the planets), at varying data rates, were telemetered

---

[15] [WOOD] G. E. Wood and T. Risa, "Design of the Mariner Jupiter/Saturn 1977 Telemetry System," *Proceedings, International Telemetry Conference*, Los Angeles, 1974, Vol. 10, pp. 606–615.

back as the vehicle moved through space. As an example, 1,200-bit/s high-rate engineering data were to be transmitted during the launch period, during periods of memory readout, and for anomaly diagnosis. During the encounter phase the engineering data rate was set at a normal rate of 40 bits/s. Science and engineering instrument data rates ranged from 80 to 2,560 bits/s during the cruise phase. Real-time engineering and science transmission during the encounter phase was transmitted at 7.2 kbits/s, while image information was transmitted at a maximum rate of 108 kbits/s. When this high rate of transmission is not possible, one of four selectable lower bit rates can be used, or the imaging data can be stored for retransmission later.

To accommodate this variety of data rates, computer control was used. Data from the science instruments and from engineering sensors were sampled and formatted at the proper rate and in the proper sequence by a special-purpose computer, called the Flight Data Subsystem. Data within a particular format were grouped into 8-bit bytes, or multiples thereof. More than 35 different programs were required to handle the different telemetry modes, depending upon the vehicle location and communication path conditions. Each of two memories containing 4,096 sixteen-bit words in the computer stored at least two separate programs. As the mission progressed, new programs required were transmitted to the spacecraft. The sequencing between the various instruments and sensors and data-format generation was controlled by these programs.

Note how the use of computer control makes adaptive telemetry relatively easy to handle. A 32-bit synchronization word and a nonambiguous time identification word were used to provide the appropriate timing and synchronization.

In Chap. 7 we discuss the data transmission requirements for Voyager 2 in more detail.

The T1 System: The North American PCM System for Short-Haul Telephone Communication

The Bell System in the United States pioneered in the early 1960s by its introduction of a PCM system for digital voice communication over short-haul distances of 10 to 50 mi. The T1 system, as it is called, has found widespread adoption throughout the United States, Canada, and Japan. It is the basis for a complete hierarchy of higher-order multiplexed systems, used either for longer-distance transmission or for transmission in heavily populated urban areas, to be described in Sec. 3-8. It forms the basis for many purely digital transmission systems as well. The 8-kHz sampling rate and the 8-bit-per-sample quantization currently in use form the basis for most digital PCM voice systems in use throughout the world, for both terrestrial and satellite communications. In the T1 system 24 telephone channels are time-multiplexed, sampled, and coded into 1.544-Mbit/s PCM for carrier transmission, or for further multiplexing for longer-distance transmission.

Since the development of the T1 system, worldwide standards calling for 30-channel time-division-multiplexed PCM systems with 2.048-Mbit/s transmis-

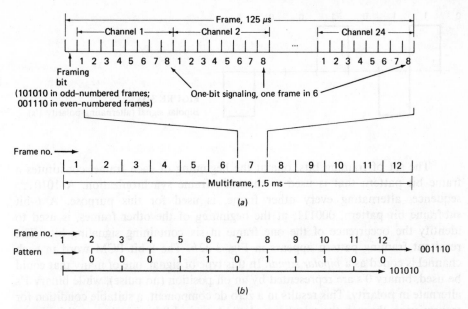

FIGURE 3-32
Signaling format, T1 system. (a) Frame structure, T1 system. (b) Framing bit pattern.

sion have been developed and implemented in many parts of the world.[16] Because of the earlier development of the 24-channel T1 system and its subsequent widespread adoption in certain parts of the world, two *de facto* standards now exist. Appropriate interfaces must be employed for PCM telephone signals moving from a 24-channel to a 30-channel system. The 30-channel PCM system is described briefly in Sec. 3-8 in a discussion of time-division-multiplexing hierarchies using this system as a base.

The T1 system, as originally conceived, used $2^7 = 128$ levels of quantization for each of the 24 voice channels multiplexed. More recently, 256 levels have been adopted, leading to a quieter system with less distortion. The signaling format for the system, called the DS1 format, groups twenty-four 8-bit PCM words, each corresponding to a coded PAM sample, sampled at a rate of 8,000 per second, plus a 1-bit framing bit, into a frame 125 μs long. The resultant transmission rate, corresponding to 193 bits transmitted in 125 μs, is thus 1.544 Mbits/s. Every sixth frame the eighth, least significant bit in each channel is deleted, or "robbed," and a signaling bit put into its place. The sequence of signaling bits, one every six frames, appearing thus at a rate of about 1,330 bits/s, is used to transmit dial pulses, as well as telephone off-hook/on-hook signals. The DS1 frame format thus has the form shown in Fig. 3-32a.

---

[16] The 30-channel system is the recommended CCITT standard. The CCITT (International Telegraph and Telephone Consultative Committee) is the international standards agency for telephone communications.

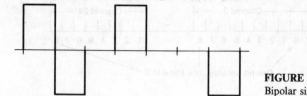

FIGURE 3-33
Bipolar signal (alternating-polarity 1's).

The set of framing bits, one at the beginning of each frame, constitutes a frame bit pattern that is used to maintain frame synchronization. A 1010... sequence, alternating every other frame, is used for this purpose. A 6-bit subframe bit pattern, 000111, at the beginning of the other frames, is used to identify the occurrence of the one frame in six containing signaling bits. The resultant framing pattern appears in Fig. 3-32b. The 8-bit PCM word in each channel is coded as a *bipolar signal*. In this type of signal, one of many that could be used, binary 0's are represented by an off position (no pulse), while binary 1's alternate in polarity. This results in a zero dc component, a suitable condition for transmission through the telephone plant. A typical 8-bit bipolar word is shown in Fig. 3-33.

The T1 system consists of two basic components: the PCM terminal, called the D3 channel bank, and a T1 line for transmitting the composite 1.544-Mbit/s data. The channel bank is the device that carries out the sampling, multiplexing, and nonlinear quantization operations required to form the transmitted T1 data stream, as well as the receiver operations, in the reverse direction, that reconstitute an analog voice signal on each of the 24 voice channels.

Some of the PCM operations in the D3 channel bank are carried out on a per-channel basis, for each of the 24 channels; the remainder are carried out in common [GAUN], [EVAN].[17] Specifically, filtering for band limiting, and sampling through the use of sampling gates to generate PAM signals, are done on a per-channel basis. A sampling rate of 8,000 samples per second is used. Each channel is sampled in sequence, and the PAM samples are passed on to the transmit portion of the common equipment. Here each sample is held momentarily while a PCM coder approximates it with an 8-bit digital code word. This thus represents the A/D process. Nonlinear quantization, using the μ-law compression characteristic described in the last section, is utilized. The common equipment generates the bipolar signal format, adds framing bits at the end of a frame, and inserts signaling bits in place of framing bits every sixth frame.

---

[17][GAUN] W. B. Gaunt and J. B. Evans, Jr., "The D3 Channel Bank," *Bell Lab. Rec.*, vol. 50, pp. 329–333, August 1972. [EVAN] J. B. Evans, Jr., and W. B. Gaunt, "The D3 Channel Bank," *Conference Record, International Conference on Communications*, Minneapolis, Minn., June 1974, pp. 7D-1 to 7D-5.

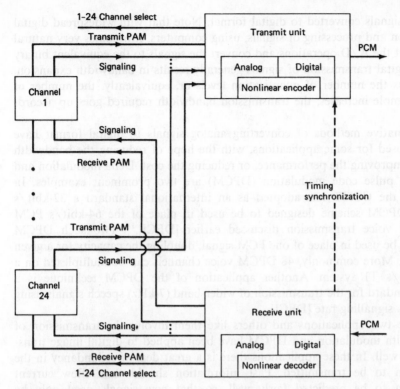

FIGURE 3-34
Simplified block diagram, D3 channel bank. (From J. B. Evans, Jr., and W. B. Gaunt, "The D3 Channel Bank," *Conference Record*, *International Conference on Communications*, Minneapolis, Minn., June 1974, Fig. 2, p. 7D-4; reprinted by permission.)

On reception a common receive unit processes the incoming bit pattern to extract clock information and develop frame synchronization, decodes the PCM words into PAM speech samples using an inverse nonlinear expansion characteristic, and then directs the PAM samples to the appropriate channel. Low-pass reconstruction filters are used in each channel to smooth the sequence of incoming PAM samples and to output the desired analog signal.

A simplified block diagram of the D3 channel bank units appears in Fig. 3-34.

3-7 DELTA AND DIFFERENTIAL PULSE CODE MODULATION

It has been pointed out in the foregoing two sections that PCM techniques have been widely applied in the digital transmission of speech (telephony) as well as in the transmission of various types of telemetry signals. They have been used for the transmission of images, both fixed-frame and TV, as well as for other forms

146 INFORMATION TRANSMISSION, MODULATION, AND NOISE

of analog signals converted to digital format. Note that with widespread digital transmission and processing of signals, using computers, it becomes very natural to carry out the A/D operations and convert the signals to the equivalent binary format. Digital transmission of signals generally results in bandwidth expansion, however: as the number of quantization levels or, equivalently, the number of bits per sample increases, the transmission bandwidth required goes up accordingly.

Alternative methods of converting analog signals to digital format have been proposed for some applications, with the hope of reducing the bandwidth required, improving the performance, or reducing the cost. Delta modulation and differential pulse code modulation (DPCM) are two prominent examples. In particular, the CCITT has adopted as an international standard a 32-kbit/s adaptive DPCM scheme designed to be used in place of the 64-kbit/s PCM system for voice transmission discussed earlier [DECI].[18] Two such DPCM signals can be used in place of one PCM signal, doubling the capacity for a given bandwidth. More commonly, 48 DPCM voice channels can be multiplexed on a 1.544-Mbit/s T1 system. Another application of the DPCM technique is a CCITT standard for the transmission of wider-band (7-kHz) speech signals using a 64-kbit/s signalling rate [DECI].

These two applications and others like them involve the transmission of speech. Delta modulation and DPCM have been applied to digital image transmission as well. In these applications there is a great deal of redundancy in the information to be transmitted. Past information should thus allow current information to be predicted fairly well, so that new signals need only be transmitted if a significant change in the signal occurs.

Consider the block diagram of a delta-modulation system shown in Fig. 3-35. Just as in the usual A/D conversion discussed earlier, the analog signal $x(t)$ must first be sampled periodically. These sampled values, designated x_j, $j = \ldots, -2, -1, 0, 1, 2, 3, \ldots$, are compared with a predicted sample value, designated g_j, and the *difference* ϵ_j is then passed to a quantizer. Obviously, if ϵ_j is small most of the time, so that the prediction is good, few bits will be needed to represent this difference signal. A delta modulator uses a two-level quantizer, so that one bit only is used to represent the signal. The two quantizer levels in Fig. 3-35 are designated $\pm k'$. At the receiver the quantized difference signal is added to the predictor output to obtain a discrete estimate $\hat{x}_j$ of the desired sampled signal x_j. These discrete estimates are then passed through a low-pass filter, for smoothing, to generate the desired estimate $\hat{x}(t)$.

It is apparent that improved performance could be obtained by using more than two levels for the quantizer. This more general scheme is the one called *differential pulse code modulation* (DPCM). Delta modulation is thus a special

[18][DECI] M. Decina and G. Modena, "CCITT Standards on Digital Speech Processing," *IEEE J. Selected Areas Commun.*, Special issue on voice coding for communications, Vol. 6, No. 2, pp. 227–234, February 1988.

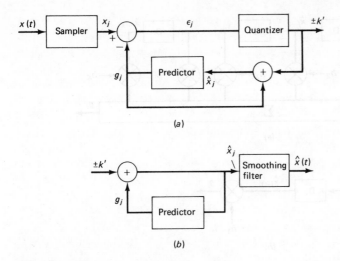

FIGURE 3-35
Delta modulation. (a) Transmitter. (b) Receiver.

case of DPCM, with two quantizer levels used. Both the 32-kbit/s and 64-kbit/s DPCM systems referred to above use 4-bit quantization. (The 32-kbit/s scheme, designed to operate over the normal telephone speech bandwidth of 3.2 kHz, uses the common sampling rate of 8000 samples/s. The 64-kbit/s system, designed for a 7-kHz bandwidth, uses 16,000 samples/s.) In the interest of simplicity, in this first treatment we focus on delta modulation with one-bit quantization. Reference is made later to detailed information on these DPCM systems.

The predictor used is generally a weighted sum of a number of past sample estimates. Specifically, with x_{j-1} the previous sample and $\hat{x}_{j-1}$ its estimate, $\hat{x}_{j-2}$ the estimate two time samples back, etc., the general form of a linear predictor may be written

$$g_j = \sum_{l=1}^{K} h_l \hat{x}_{j-l} \qquad (3\text{-}58)$$

The coefficients h_l are the weighting factors. The simplest predictor is one that uses the previous sample estimate only as an estimate of the current sample x_j. For this case we have

$$g_j = h_1 \hat{x}_{j-1} \qquad (3\text{-}59)$$

The coefficients h_l, $l = 1, 2, \ldots, K$, may be chosen to reduce some measure of the estimate errors to as small a value as possible. For example, one common measure of performance is the mean-squared error, averaged over many samples, or averaged statistically over the known statistics of the incoming samples x_j.

The linear predictor of (3-58) is an example of a transversal or nonrecursive digital filter [SCHW 1975]. It is readily implemented using shift-register elements.

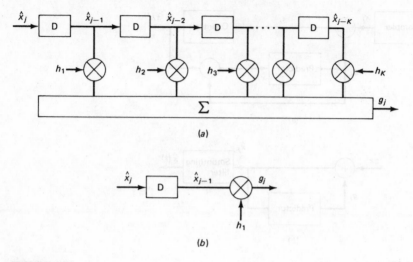

(a)

(b)

FIGURE 3-36
Predictor for DPCM and delta modulation. (*a*) General case (nonrecursive digital filter). (*b*) Previous-sample estimator.

A conceptual block diagram appears in Fig. 3-36*a*. The D boxes shown represent delay elements that delay the incoming samples by the required sampling interval. A block diagram for the special case of the previous-sample estimator of (3-59) appears in Fig. 3-36*b*.

How well does the delta modulator perform? This is rather difficult to determine in general, since the performance depends on the type of input signal, the sampling rate, the quantizer levels, and the form of predictor used. Although the device is conceptually simple, it is difficult to analyze because of the feedback implicit in its operation. Many studies of delta-modulator performance have been carried out in recent years. We shall focus here on some gross characteristics only, referring the interested reader to the literature for detailed studies of performance.

As is the case with PCM systems, noise is introduced by the use of delta modulation. Because the difference signal is quantized to two levels, granular or *quantization noise* similar to PCM quantization noise appears at the receiver output. This can clearly be reduced as in PCM, by using more quantization levels. This gives rise to the DPCM scheme. If one-bit delta modulation is used, the noise can only be reduced by sampling more often. One thus finds delta-modulation systems using sampling rates much higher than the Nyquist rate used with PCM. This means that the ultimate bit rate is higher than originally expected through the use of two-level quantization. In some cases the bit rate required may even be higher than that of PCM. For this reason adaptive delta-modulation schemes, to be described briefly later, have come into use.

In addition to quantization noise, another type of noise is encountered. This is called *overload noise* and occurs if the quantization levels $\pm k'$ are too small to

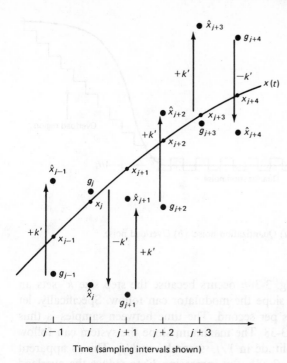

FIGURE 3-37
Operation of delta modulator.

Time (sampling intervals shown)

track a rapidly changing signal. To demonstrate the occurrence of both types of noise, consider a typical input signal and its predicted signal samples as shown in Fig. 3-37. For simplicity's sake previous-sample estimation is used. At sampling time $j - 1$ the predicted value g_{j-1} is found to be smaller than the actual signal sample x_{j-1}. Since $\epsilon_{j-1} = x_{j-1} - g_{j-1}$ is positive, the quantizer outputs $+k'$. This is then added to g_{j-1} to provide the estimate $\hat{x}_{j-1}$. The predicted signal at sampling time j is then $g_j = h_1 \hat{x}_{j-1}$. Assuming that h_1 is somewhat less than 1, one gets g_j as shown in the figure. Since $g_j > x_j$, the actual signal sample shown in the figure, $\epsilon_j < 0$, and $-k'$ is outputted. The resultant signal estimate is $\hat{x}_j = g_j - k'$, as shown. As one proceeds sample by sample, the sample estimates $\hat{x}_j$ tend to follow the curve of $x(t)$, sometimes lying above, sometimes lying below. The result is a received signal that tracks the original signal, but introduces quantization noise.

If a simple hold circuit is used at the receiver to provide the filtering, the resultant output signal appears as in Fig. 3-38a. It is apparent that the quantization noise introduced is proportional to the step size k'. By reducing k' the noise is reduced. Too small a value of k' results in the overload noise mentioned above, however. This is due to the inability of the modulator to track large changes of the input signal $x(t)$ in a small interval of time. An example appears in Fig. 3-38b. It is thus apparent that an optimum step size k' must exist: this depends on the characteristics of the input signal $x(t)$, the sampling rate, and the total noise that can be tolerated.

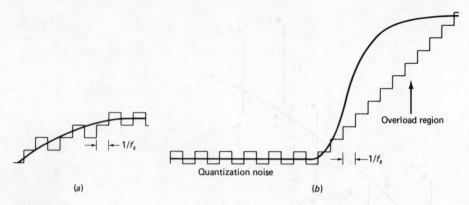

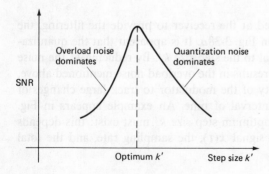

FIGURE 3-38
Sources of noise in delta modulation. (*a*) Quantization noise. (*b*) Overload noise.

The overload region of Fig. 3-38*b* occurs because the step size k' sets an upper limit on the input signal slope the modulator can follow. Specifically, let the sampling rate be f_s samples per second. The time between samples is thus $1/f_s$ seconds, as shown in Fig. 3-38. The maximum slope the system can follow corresponds to k' units of amplitude in $1/f_s$ seconds, or $k'f_s$. This is apparent from the overload region of Fig. 3-38*b*. But increasing k' to reduce the overload noise increases the quantization noise as well. This thus gives rise to the optimum choice of k' noted above.

This optimum choice of step size k' is shown graphically in Fig. 3-39, depicting a typical performance curve for delta modulation. The performance here is measured by the reciprocal of the noise, or the signal-to-noise ratio, which is proportional to this quantity. Obviously, as the noise is reduced, the performance improves.

These concepts may be made more quantitative by considering, as an example, a sine-wave test signal. Say that the signal $x(t)$ is given simply by

$$x(t) = A \sin \omega_m t \tag{3-60}$$

FIGURE 3-39
Typical performance curve for delta modulation.

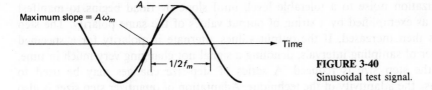

FIGURE 3-40
Sinusoidal test signal.

Its maximum slope, at $t = 0$ and times spaced multiples of half a period ($1/2f_m$ seconds) from this point, is just $A\omega_m = 2\pi Af_m$. This is shown in Fig. 3-40. Now let this signal be sampled *many* times in a period at a rate of f_s samples per second. Thus

$$f_s \gg f_m \tag{3-61}$$

As an example, we might use 10 to 20 samples in a period. This is of course a much higher sampling rate than that required by the Nyquist sampling theorem. With delta modulation we now compare the sampled values of $x(t)$ with the predicted values and transmit either of two levels, $+k'$ or $-k'$, as noted earlier. The delta modulator will track changes in $x(t)$ if they differ by no more than k' units in $1/f_s$ seconds. Hence for this sine wave, overload can be avoided if $k'f_s$ is greater than or equal to the maximum slope:

$$k'f_s \geq 2\pi Af_m \tag{3-62}$$

This is often shown in normalized form by defining a relative step size $k \equiv k'/A$, i.e., the ratio of the step size k' to the maximum signal level. For more realistic signals, often represented by randomly varying signals, as noted in Sec. 3-5, a definite maximum may not exist. As in that section, then, in discussing nonuniform quantization, one often arbitrarily selects as the maximum signal level a value four standard deviations (4σ) from the average. The relative step size would then be defined as $k \equiv k'/4\sigma$.

In terms of the relative step-size parameter k, then, one can avoid overload noise for the sine-wave test signal by selecting

$$kf_s \geq 2\pi f_m \tag{3-63}$$

But, as noted previously, large values of k' (or k) result in significant quantization noise. For example, if one chooses for the sine-wave test signal $kf_s = 2\pi f_m$, the minimum step size to eliminate overload noise, and then picks $f_s = 10f_m$, as noted earlier, one has $k \doteq 0.6$. The two quantization levels transmitted are each more than half the peak amplitude. This could lead to significant quantization noise. The noise can be reduced, however, by sampling at a higher rate. Or, since it is the *total* noise that counts, the quantization noise can be reduced, at the expense of introducing overload noise, by reducing k below the critical value, for a sine wave, of $2\pi f_m/f_s$. This is the trade-off noted earlier, as exemplified by Fig. 3-39.

Another procedure, adopted in practice, is to introduce *adaptive delta modulation*. In this scheme the quantization step sizes are kept small, to reduce quantization noise to a tolerable level, until slope overload begins to manifest itself, as exemplified by a string of output values of the same polarity. The step size is then increased. If the output values alternate in polarity for a specified number of sampling intervals, denoting a signal not changing very much in time, then the step size is reduced. A series of step-size changes may be used to increase the adaptivity of the technique. Adaptation of quantizer step sizes is also used in the two DPCM standards referred to above. They are thus termed *adaptive* DPCM or ADPCM schemes [BENV], [MAIT], [MERM].[19]

We can gain somewhat more insight into the slope-overload effect by actually calculating the mean-squared overload noise for the sine-wave test signal under some restricted conditions. We shall then quote results from the literature for overload-noise calculations for random-type signals more characteristic of signals encountered in practice. To do this we first define two normalizing parameters that allow a simplification of notation. The ratio of sampling rate f_s to sine-wave frequency f_m plays a key role in the determination of overload noise. For more general signals it is the ratio of f_s to the bandwidth B that plays the same role. We accordingly define a normalized sampling parameter

$$F_s \equiv \frac{f_s}{B}$$

For the sine-wave case B is just f_m. It is apparent from (3-63) that the quantity $kf_s/2\pi f_m = kF_s/2\pi$ plays a key role in the analysis of overload noise. This is a normalized slope parameter that we shall label α:

$$\alpha \equiv \frac{kF_s}{2\pi} = \frac{kf_s}{2\pi B} = \frac{k'f_s}{2\pi AB}$$

Although developed for a sine-wave test signal, this parameter is found to govern the delta-modulation overload-noise performance with other test signals as well. A little thought will indicate why this is so. As noted throughout Chap. 2, and as is exemplified by the simple sine-wave test signal, the bandwidth B is a measure of the rate of change of a signal. The larger B (f_m for the sine wave) is, the more rapidly the signal may change. Specifically, the minimum time required for a signal to change a "significant" amount is the order of $1/B$. This is shown in Fig. 3-41. (We cannot be more precise than this, as noted in Chap. 2, because of the variety of measures of bandwidth. But recall that the pulse rise time discussed in Chap. 2 was proportional to $1/B$.) If we let this "significant" amount be the amplitude A or the 4σ deviation noted earlier, the maximum slope of *any* signal

[19][BENV] N. Benvenuto et al., "The 32 kbit/s ADPCM Coding Standard," *AT&T Tech. J.*, Vol. 65, No. 5, pp. 12–22, September/October 1986. [MAIT] X. Maitre, "7 kHz Audio Coding within 64 kbits/s," *IEEE J. Selected Areas Commun.*, special issue on voice coding for communications, Vol. 6, No. 2, pp. 283–298, February 1988. [MERM] P. Mermelstein, "G. 722, A New CCITT Coding Standard for Digital Transmission of Wideband Audio Signals," *IEEE Commun. Mag.*, Vol. 26, No. 1, pp. 8–15, January 1988.

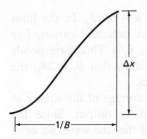

FIGURE 3-41
Rate of change of typical signal.

must be proportional to $4\sigma B = AB$. The maximum slope the delta modulator can follow is $k'f_s$. The parameter α is proportional to the ratio of these quantities. As α increases, the slope-overload noise decreases; as α decreases this noise increases.

Now consider the sine-wave test signal again. Say that the parameter $\alpha < 1$. From Eq. (3-63) overload noise will result. A typical case appears in Fig. 3-42. The sine wave is sketched there as a function of normalized time $\theta \equiv \omega_m t$. Assume that the quantization levels are chosen small enough so that quantization noise is negligible. A delta-modulator output thus tracks, or follows, the sine wave until the slope of the sine wave at some point $-\theta_1$ equals the value $k'f_s$. Beyond this point the modulator output can only rise at the maximum rate of $k'f_s$. This is shown by the straight line of the figure. The sine-wave slope exceeds this value for $\theta > -\theta_1$, and the overload-noise region is entered. The region ends at the point θ_2 when the modulator output intersects the signal. As $k'f_s$ increases θ_1 and θ_2 both decrease, and the overload-noise region is reduced correspond-

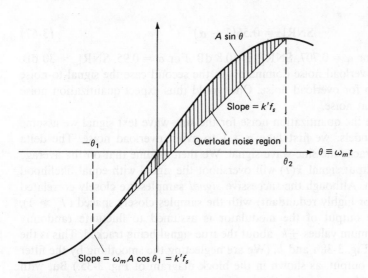

FIGURE 3-42
Calculation of overload noise, sine-wave signal.

ingly. From the figure θ_1 is defined by the expression $\alpha = \cos \theta_1$. In the limit when $\alpha \equiv k'f_s/\omega_m A = 1$, there is no overload noise, as indicated earlier. For simplicity of analysis we shall restrict θ_1 to the range $\leq \pi/4$. This corresponds to $\alpha \geq 0.707$. For this range it is left to the reader to show that $\theta_2 \doteq 2\theta_1$, the approximation improving as α increases and θ_1 decreases.

The slope overload noise N_o is now defined as the average of the square of the difference between the true signal and the modulator output. Since the overload region of Fig. 3-42 occurs twice in each cycle of the sine wave, we need only average over the one region shown to determine the overload noise. It is left to the reader to show that this is given by

$$N_o = \frac{1}{\pi} \int_{-\theta_1}^{\theta_2} \left\{ A \sin \theta - \left[\frac{k'f_s}{\omega_m}(\theta + \theta_1) - A \sin \theta_1 \right] \right\}^2 d\theta \qquad (3\text{-}64)$$

or

$$\frac{\pi N_o}{A^2} = \int_{-\theta_1}^{\theta_2} \left[(\sin \theta - \alpha\theta) + \sin \theta_1 - \alpha\theta_1 \right]^2 d\theta \qquad (3\text{-}65)$$

This may be integrated and evaluated to find N_o as a function of α. Doing this, and using the approximation $\theta_2 = 2\theta_1$, one finds, with $\theta_1 \leq \pi/4$, as assumed,

$$\frac{2N_o}{A^2} \doteq 0.32\theta_1^5 \doteq 1.8(1 - \alpha)^{5/2} \qquad (3\text{-}66)$$

(For this range of θ_1, $\alpha = \cos \theta_1 \doteq 1 - \theta_1^2/2$.) Note that the mean-squared signal itself is $A^2/2$. The expression in (3-66) is then just the reciprocal of the signal power to the overload-noise power, or the signal-to-noise ratio with overload noise only considered. Calling this $\text{SNR}|_o$, we get, for the sine-wave signal, with $0.7 \leq \alpha \leq 1$,

$$\text{SNR}|_o \doteq 0.56(1 - \alpha)^{-5/2} \qquad (3\text{-}67)$$

As an example, for $\alpha = 0.707$, $\text{SNR}|_o$ is 10.8 dB. For $\alpha = 0.95$, $\text{SNR}|_o = 30$ dB. In the first case overload noise dominates. In the second case the signal-to-noise ratio is quite high for overload noise. One would thus expect quantization noise to be the dominant noise.

To calculate the quantization noise for the sine-wave text signal we assume the crudest of models: we first take $\alpha \geq 1$ to avoid overload noise. The delta modulator thus tracks the sine-wave signal. We then assume that on the average the modulator output signal $\hat{x}(t)$ will overshoot the signal with equal likelihood in either direction. Although the successive *signal* samples are closely correlated (i.e., predictable or highly redundant) with the samples closely spaced ($F_s \gg 1$), the signal at the output of the modulator is assumed to fluctuate randomly between the maximum values $\pm k'$ about the true signal being tracked. This is the picture shown in Fig. 3-38a and b. (We are neglecting the smoothing by the filter at the modulator output, as shown in the block diagram of Fig. 3-35.) But with this crude model of quantization the mean-squared quantization noise is exactly that calculated for PCM in Sec. 3-5. This is just the mean-squared variation about the desired level given by (3-29). The level spacing a there is replaced by $2k'$ here. Denoting the quantization noise by N_q, we thus have

$$N_q = \frac{(2k')^2}{12} = \frac{k'^2}{3} \tag{3-68}$$

It is apparent, as noted previously in Sec. 3-5 and implicitly assumed in the discussion of overload noise here, that it is only the noise relative to the signal that has significance. For it is the perturbation in the signal that we call noise. We thus normalize to the mean signal power $A^2/2$ to obtain the relative quantization noise. This is exactly what we did in (3-66) with the overload noise. We thus have

$$\frac{2N_q}{A^2} = \frac{2}{3}k^2 \tag{3-69}$$

using the relative size parameter k introduced previously.

It is often assumed that with the quantization noise and overload noise each small enough, one can decouple their effects. They are assumed independent of one another. The total noise in the system is then taken as the sum of the two, or

$$N = N_o + N_q \tag{3-70}$$

The signal-to-noise ratio for the delta modulator with a sine-wave test signal at the input, involving the various assumptions made up to this point, may then be written as

$$\text{SNR} = \frac{A^2}{2N} = \frac{A^2}{2(N_o + N_q)} \tag{3-71}$$

Using (3-66) and (3-69) for N_o and N_q, respectively, one may evaluate the SNR as a function of k or kF_s for various values of the normalized sampling frequency F_s. Figure 3-43 shows the results of such a calculation. Note that this is of the general form indicated previously in Fig. 3-39. There is a narrow range of values of kF_s (or, equivalently, α) for which the signal-to-noise ratio is maximum. For smaller values the quantization noise is reduced but overload noise increases rapidly. For larger values the overload noise disappears but quantization noise begins to increase. The optimum value of kF_s is about 6 for the sine-wave test signal, under the assumptions made, for a value of α slightly less than 1. The curves for $F_s = 16, 32$, and 64, respectively, appear separate in the quantization-noise region because the SNR is plotted versus $kF_s = 2\pi\alpha$. With the assumptions made previously, quantization noise is independent of the sampling rate. It depends only on the quantization level k. (More accurate analyses do indicate a dependence on F_s, as will be noted later.) There is an indirect improvement with increasing sampling rate F_s, however, since, as noted earlier, increased sampling reduces the quantization level k required to maintain a specified overload-noise level. This in turn reduces the quantization noise.

More accurate analyses have been carried out for various classes of random signals. As an example, assume that the input signal $x(t)$ fed into the delta

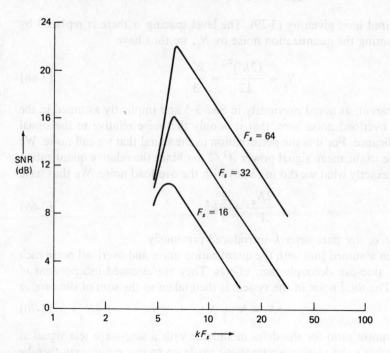

FIGURE 3-43
Delta-modulator SNR, sine-wave signal.

modulator is a gaussian random signal (this is then the model used in Sec. 3-5 in discussing nonuniform quantization in PCM) with a flat frequency spectrum out to a bandwidth of B hertz.[20] The overload-noise power is then found to be given by[21]

$$N_o = 0.83\alpha^{-5}e^{-1.5\alpha^2} \tag{3-72}$$

---

[20] The spectral properties of random signals, as contrasted with the *deterministic* signals discussed in Chap. 2, will be treated in detail in Chap. 6.

[21] There are a large number of papers in the field of delta modulation and DPCM in which both overload and quantization noise are analyzed. Examples include [ABAT] J. E. Abate, "Linear and Adaptive Delta Modulation," *Proc. IEEE*, vol. 55, no. 3, pp. 290–308, March 1967; [ONEA 1966a] J. B. O'Neal, "Delta Modulation Quantizing Noise, Analytical and Computer Simulation Results for Gaussian and Television Input Signals," *Bell System Tech. J.*, vol. 45, pp. 117–141, January 1966; [ONEA 1966b] J. B. O'Neal, "Predictive Quantizing Systems (Differential PCM) for the Transmission of Television Signals," *Bell System Tech. J.*, vol. 45, pp. 1023–1036, May–June 1966; [JAYA 1974] N. S. Jayant, "Digital Coding of Speech Waveforms: PCM, DPCM, and DM Quantizers," *Proc. IEEE*, vol. 62, no. 5, pp. 611–632, May 1974. The book [SPIL] James J. Spilker, Jr., *Digital Communications by Satellite*, Prentice-Hall, Englewood Cliffs, N.J., 1977, reproduces these derivations as well. A more detailed discussion of DPCM appears in [JAYA 1984] N. S. Jayant and P. Noll, *Digital Coding Waveforms*, Prentice-Hall, Englewood Cliffs, N.J., 1984.

with $\alpha \equiv kF_s/2\pi$ and $F_s = f_s/B$, as previously. This noise is actually normalized to the input variance, or signal power, σ_x^2. Alternatively, one may look on this as the overload-noise power, with $\sigma_x^2 = 1$. The step-size parameter k is the actual step size k' normalized to $4\sigma_x$, as noted previously. The overload noise thus drops extremely rapidly with increasing α.

The normalized quantization noise N_q is found to be given approximately by the expression

$$N_q \doteq \frac{2}{3} \frac{k^2}{F_s} \tag{3-73}$$

Note that this is of the form of our previous crude expression for N_q, (3-69), with the addition of the inverse dependence on the normalized sampling rate F_s. This reflects the correlation, or dependence, of successive input samples on one another, ignored in our previous assumption of completely random fluctuation of successive samples at the modulator output. The quantization noise here is also normalized to the input signal power, or variance, σ_x^2.

If we now assume, as we did earlier, that the overload noise occurs in short bursts, while the quantization noise is small enough in the vicinity of overload noise to be negligible, we can decouple the two noises and assume that they occur independently. The total noise power is then $N = N_o + N_q$. The signal-to-noise ratio is then $1/N = 1/(N_o + N_q)$, since $\sigma_x^2 = 1$ in writing (3-72) and (3-73). The resultant SNR, in dB, is shown plotted as a function of the normalized step size $kF_s = 2\pi\alpha$ in Fig. 3-44 [ONEA 1966a]. Note how similar the curve is to that for the sine-wave test signal discussed earlier (Fig. 3-43). The relative signal-to-noise ratios are different (both quantization and overload noise are smaller for the gaussian signal), but the main point made earlier still holds: there exists a narrow region of kF_s or α, for which the SNR is maximum. For larger values of kF_s or α, quantization noise dominates. For smaller values of kF_s, the slope-overload noise dominates. In the quantization-noise region an increase in sampling rate will reduce the quantization noise. This is apparent from the form of N_q in (3-73). The optimum value of kF_s varies from 10 for $F_s = 8$ to 15 for $F_s = 64$.

It is of interest, of course, to compare the performance of delta modulation with PCM. To do this assume that single-channel PCM is used, with uniform quantization (no companding). For a signal bandwidth of B hertz, the minimum sampling rate is of course $2B$ samples per second. With $M = 2^n$ quantization levels used, the *bit* rate is $2nB$ bits/s transmitted. This corresponds to the sampling rate f_s used with delta modulation. For comparison with delta modulation the *effective* normalized sampling rate is then $F_s = 2n$. From (3-38) the PCM signal-to-noise ratio with no companding is

$$SNR = 3M^2 \frac{\sigma_x^2}{V^2} \tag{3-38}$$

V is the maximum input signal intensity and σ_x^2 its average power, or variance. As noted several times previously, there is no theoretical maximum signal for

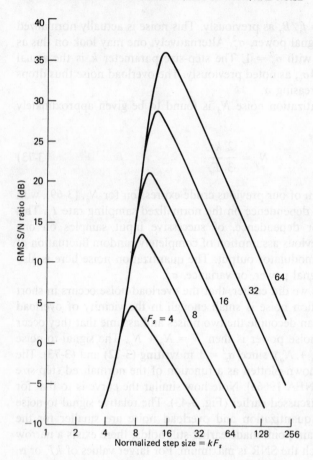

FIGURE 3-44
SNR for band-limited flat gaussian signals. (From J. B. O'Neal, "Delta Modulation Quantizing Noise, Analytical and Computer Simulation Results for Gaussian and Television Input Signals," *Bell System Tech. J.*, Vol. 45, p. 123, January 1966, Fig. 4. Copyright, 1966, The American Telephone and Telegraph Co.; reprinted by permission.)

gaussian random signals, the signal model assumed here. It is customary, as in the delta-modulation case just noted, to choose $V = 4\sigma_x$ quite arbitrarily. For gaussian statistics this is the signal intensity exceeded only 0.01 percent of the time, on the average. For this choice of V,

$$\text{SNR} = \frac{3M^2}{16} \tag{3-74}$$

Converting to decibels, letting $M = 2^n$, and then letting $F_s = 2n$, we have

$$\text{SNR}|_{dB} = 3F_s - 7.3 \tag{3-75}$$

This has been plotted in Fig. 3-45, together with two curves for delta modulation [ONEA 1966a]. The lower curve, labeled "flat signal," corresponds to the optimum SNR points in Fig. 3-44. The upper curve, a more accurate model for television signals, assumes that the input signal has the RC spectral characteristic $1/(1 + f/\beta)^2$, up to a maximum frequency of $B = 8\pi\beta$. β is thus the 3-dB bandwidth of this signal. Note the improvement in delta-modulation SNR of this type of smoothed input signal over the one with a flat spectral characteristic. For

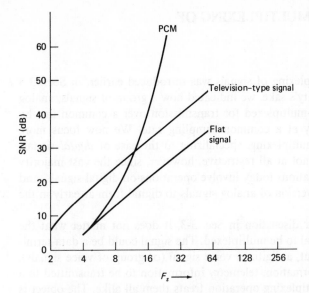

FIGURE 3-45
Comparison of delta modulation and standard PCM for band-limited gaussian signals. (From J. B. O'Neal, "Delta Modulation Quantizing Noise, Analytical and Computer Simulation Results for Gaussian and Television Input Signals," *Bell System Tech. J.*, Vol. 45, p. 127, January 1966, Fig. 7. Copyright, 1966, The American Telephone and Telegraph Co.; reprinted by permission.)

this class of signals delta modulation appears to provide an improvement in SNR at the lower sampling rates. This corresponds to situations in which simplicity and low cost dominate over performance. Where high-quality speech transmission or very accurate telemetering of data is not a prime consideration, nonadaptive delta modulation with relatively low sampling rates offers advantages. For higher-quality transmission, adaptive DPCM and delta modulation are used to improve the performance.

Consider the two adaptive DPCM (ADPCM) standards for digital voice telephony mentioned earlier. The 32-kbit/s ADPCM standard was adopted by the CCITT as a way of providing reduced-bit-rate transmission of 3.2-kHz telephone speech signals that approaches as closely as possible the performance of 64-kbit/s PCM. This recognizes the fact that much of the world's local-loop telephone communications, from subscriber to the telephone company's local office (exchange), is analog, with a bandwidth limitation of 3.2 kHz. As telephone companies introduce full digital communications end to end, to the subscriber's premises, the 3.2-kHz limitation will disappear. Instead, 64-kbit/s voice (as well as data) channels will become much more commonplace. With widespread use of 64-kbit/s channels end to end, it becomes appropriate to take this opportunity to introduce higher-quality speech communications. The 7-kHz 64-kbit/s ADPCM standard was adopted for this purpose by the CCITT.

The algorithms used in the two systems are similar. Both use adaptation for the predictor (Fig. 3-35); both use adaptive 4-bit quantization, replacing the single-bit quantizer for the delta-modulation system shown in Fig. 3-35. As noted earlier, the 32-kbit/s system samples at a rate of 8000 samples/s; the 64-kbit/s system uses 16,000 samples/s. Details of the two systems appear in [BENV], [MAIT], [MERM].

3-8 TIME-DIVISION MULTIPLEXING OF DIGITAL SIGNALS

Introduction

The concept of time multiplexing of signals was introduced earlier, in Secs. 3-3 and 3-4. There, for simplicity's sake, we indicated how a group of signals, analog and digital, might be time-multiplexed for transmission over a common line by sampling them sequentially at a common sampling rate. We now focus more deeply on the subject of multiplexing, specializing to the case of *digital* signals being multiplexed. This is not at all restrictive, however, since the vast majority of time-multiplexing applications today involve operations on digital signals, and the trend is moving to conversion of analog signals to digital form as early in the system as possible.

As noted in our prior discussion in Sec. 3-3, it does not matter what the source was of a digital signal to be multiplexed. The signal could be a data-terminal output, computer output, a digitized voice signal (or group of voice signals), digital facsimile or TV information, telemetry information to be transmitted to a remote point, etc. The multiplexing operation treats them all alike. The object is to combine digital signals of possibly varying bit rates and feed the combined signal stream out sequentially, at a correspondingly higher bit rate, over one higher-bandwidth, higher-bit-rate line. As an example, one might want to combine two 1,200-bit/s sources with three 2,400-bit/s sources and feed all five signals out sequentially at the combined nominal rate of 9,600 bits/s. Alternatively, one might want to combine several T1 signal streams into one correspondingly higher-bandwidth, higher-bit-rate stream. A conceptual diagram of the multiplexing–demultiplexing operation appears in Fig. 3-46.

The one distinction made that does indirectly distinguish between data (alphanumeric symbols) and other digital signals that might be transmitted is the interleaving of digital signals on either a character or a bit basis. Low-speed data terminals (up to 1,200 bits/s normally) generally transmit data asynchronously in character form, a character ranging from 5 to 10 bits in length, depending on the type of terminal and code used. Multiplexing of these terminals is generally carried out by interleaving characters. PCM signals, on the other hand, have no

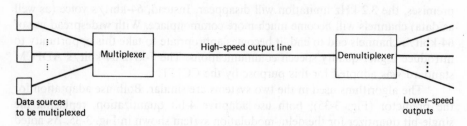

Data sources
to be multiplexed

High-speed output line

Lower-speed
outputs

FIGURE 3-46
Multiplexing operation.

natural character forms and are multiplexed by interleaving on a bit-by-bit basis. Higher-speed data terminals (1,200 bits/s and up) are sometimes also multiplexed by interleaving bits.

No matter how the multiplexing of digital signals may be carried out, several basic points can be made:

1. Some form of framing structure must be incorporated, a frame representing the smallest unit of time in which all signals to be multiplexed are serviced at least once.
2. The frame is slotted into time allocations, uniquely assigned to each data source connected. A timing procedure, comparable to the simple periodic sampling of individual channels in Sec. 3-3, must thus be developed to sample each data source at the appropriate time in the frame. (In Sec. 3-3 we focused on the sequential sampling of a group of channels to be combined. It is the procedure used in combining channels of the same bandwidth or bit rate. With widely differing bit rates or bandwidths, channels are sampled at correspondingly different rates.)
3. Framing and synchronization bits must be appended to enable the receiving system to uniquely synchronize in time with the beginning of each frame, with each slot in the frame, and with each bit within a slot. These bits may be collectively called control bits.
4. Provision must be made for handling small variations in the bit rates of the incoming digital signals to be multiplexed.

Although some variable-frame multiplexing schemes have appeared on the market [VAN],[22] we focus here on fixed-frame-size schemes only. A typical frame then might look as shown in Fig. 3-47. C_1 and C_2 represent sequences of control bits (in this example they are placed at the beginning and end of the frame, respectively), and four data sources are shown multiplexed. One of these transmits at twice the rate of the other three, so that it is allocated two slots per frame, as shown. As an example, say the basic slot contains 10 bits of data. Say control sequence C_1 is 3 bits, and C_2 is 2 bits long. The total frame length, in this example, is 55 bits long. Say units 2, 3, and 4 each transmit at 1,200 bits/s, while unit 1 transmits at 2,400 bits/s. The total data bit rate is then 6,000 bits/s. Because of the control bits used in this example, however, the multiplexer must actually be transmitting at a rate of 6,600 bits/s. This is of course a fictitious example, but it illustrates the point.

Two major classes of multiplexing appear in practice. The first group comprises multiplexers designed to combine lower-speed data signals, up to 4,800

---

[22][VAN] J. B. Van der Mey, "The Architecture of a Transparent Intelligent Network," *Conference Record, IEEE National Telecommunications Conference*, Dallas, Texas, December 1976, pp. 7.2.1–7.2.5.

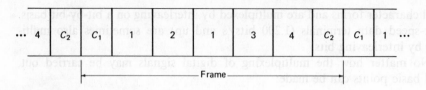

FIGURE 3-47
Typical framing structure.

bits/s maximum bit rate, into one higher-speed multiplexed signal of up to 9,600 bits/s data rate. These techniques are used primarily to transmit data over *voice-grade channels* of a telephone network. ("Voice grade" simply refers to the fact that these channels are nominally of the bandwidth required to transmit a single analog voice signal. These channels are exactly those of 3.3-kHz nominal bandwidth referred to previously in Sec. 3-3 in first discussing Nyquist sampling, and then again in Sec. 3-6 in discussing the T1 system. Modems, devices required to convert the digital format to the analog format required to transmit signals over the telephone channels, will be discussed in Chapter 4.) A customer with several data terminals to be connected to a geographically distant computer, or to equivalent terminals remotely located, can thus share the cost of a single voice channel among his terminals by multiplexing the signals into a single voice channel. The use of a multiplexer obviates the need for individual telephone connections for each terminal.

Multiplexers designed for this purpose normally transmit at output rates of 1,200, 2,400, 3,600, 4,800, 7,200, or 9,600 bits/s, depending on the application, and on whether the voice channel used is privately leased and specially conditioned (in which case higher bit rates can be used) or dialed, as in any telephone call. The input rates handled generally range as high as 7,200 bits/s. These multiplexers generally use character-interleaved multiplexing, as already noted. A detailed discussion of these lower-speed multiplexers, designed for transmission over telephone voice-grade channels, appears in [SCHW 1980].[23]

The second broad class of multiplexing occurs at much higher bit rates, and is part of the data transmission service generally provided by communication carriers. As an example, the North American telephone system uses a digital hierarchy based on the T1 carrier described in Sec. 3-6 [BELL 1982]. The hierarchy appears in schematic form in Fig. 3-48. Note that at any level a data signal at the input rate shown would be multiplexed with the other input signals at the same rate for more economical transmission as one combined higher-speed signal. The expression DSn is used to refer to the digital signal at level n. This generalizes the DS1 nomenclature introduced earlier (Fig. 3-32) in referring to the 1.544-Mbit/s T1 system. The 44.736-Mbit/s DS3 format will be discussed

[23][SCHW 1980] M. Schwartz, *Information Transmission*, *Modulation*, *and Noise*, 3rd ed., McGraw-Hill, New York, 1980.

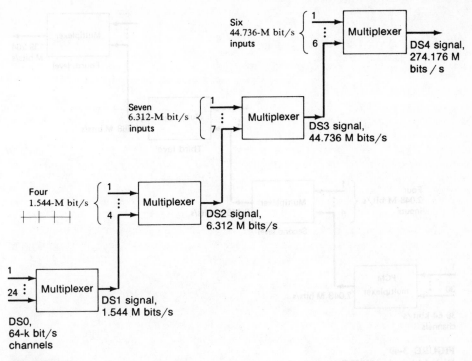

FIGURE 3-48
Digital hierarchy, North American telephone system.

later (Fig. 3-52). It is a particularly important example, since it is used extensively in digital lightwave systems.

The multiplexer at the DS1 level (used in the T1 system), although designed originally to handle 24 digitized voice circuits, is not restricted to multiplexing voice signals. Any 64-kbit/s signal, of the appropriate format (called a DS0 signal), could be transmitted as one of the 24 input channels shown. Similarly, at a higher level in the hierarchy, not all inputs need to have been derived from a lower-level multiplexer. At the DS3 level, for example, some of the 6.312-Mbit/s inputs could represent digitized TV inputs appearing directly at this bit rate; others could be multiplexed DS1 signals in groups of four (DS2 signals) transmitting voice information; others could be derived by multiplexing upward and combining appropriately some lower-speed data traffic.

A multiplexing hierarchy based on fiber optic transmission, referred to as SONET, and that extends the bit rates transmitted to the Gbit/s region and beyond, is described briefly in the next section.

The multiplexing of signals allows a given transmission channel to be shared by a number of users, reducing the cost. A similar hierarchy, but using different bit-rate levels, has been developed as an international standard by the CCITT, the international committee for standards relating to telephone and

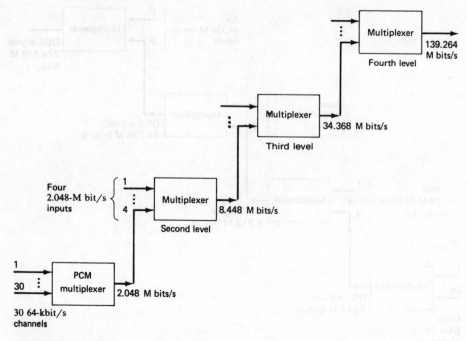

FIGURE 3-49
Digital hierarchy, CCITT recommendation.

telegraphy. This is used by most nations in the world outside North America and Japan. It is based on the lowest-level PCM international standard of 2.048 Mbits/s, which applies worldwide outside North America and Japan. This PCM standard multiplexes 30 channels at 64 kbits/s each, with two additional channels used for signaling and other purposes. It thus differs from the North American T1 standard. The CCITT-recommended digital hierarchy appears in Fig. 3-49 [IRME],[24] [BELL 1982]. This hierarchy consists of four levels of multiplexing as shown.

These very high-speed multiplexing hierarchies have been developed for use by the various national communications carriers. They are based historically on the PCM standards used to multiplex digitized voice channels, although other types of signals can be multiplexed as well.

In the following two subsections we discuss the time-multiplexing operation in more detail. We first focus on bit-interleaved multiplexers, and discuss design questions involved in combining independent bit streams of possibly differing rates, with statistical fluctuations in their rates. We then discuss questions relating to frame loss and acquisition, applicable to all types of multiplexers.

---

[24] [IRME] T. Irmer, "An Overview of Digital Hierarchies in the World Today," *Conference Record, IEEE International Conference on Communications*, San Francisco, June 1975, pp. 16-1 to 16-4.

Bit-Interleaved Multiplexers and Bit Stuffing

It was noted earlier that among the basic problems arising in the multiplexing of independent digital streams are those of framing, synchronization, and rate adjustment to accommodate small variations in the input data rates. We discuss the question of rate adjustment, by bit stuffing, in this subsection. This technique is used in bit-interleaved multiplexers.

In a bit-interleaved multiplexer the slots devoted to individual input channels (Fig. 3-47) are one or more bits in length. The multiplexer should presumably have the appropriate number of bits ready and available for transmission when an input data source's slot time arrives. Independent data sources will be expected to experience variations in their data rate, however. A nominal 2,400-bit/s input rate may occasionally drop to 2,390 bits/s, for example, or increase to 2,410 bits/s. A 9,600 bit/s multiplexer combining four such inputs must accommodate such variations. Otherwise, severe misalignment and synchronization problems can arise. The problem is handled in the bit-interleaved case by, first, running the multiplexed output at a speed slightly higher than the sum of the maximum expected rates of the input channels. Second, to accommodate small reductions in the input rates, as well as to handle the nominal rates, which have been designed to be somewhat below the multiplexer rate, *bit stuffing* on a per-channel basis is often used [JOHA].[25] The very fact that output pulses appear multiplexed at a higher rate than the expected input rate is equivalent to occasionally "stuffing" the output with additional non-information-carrying pulses.

To accomplish this, each input data stream feeds a buffer, or *elastic store*, at the multiplexer. The contents of this buffer are fed out, at the higher rate, onto the outgoing line when the appropriate slot interval appears. A simple schematic of the elastic-store operation appears in Fig. 3-50. The input is designated as R_1. The output rate is $R_1' > R_1$. If the input rate begins to drop relative to the multiplexer output rate, the store contents decrease. The multiplexer monitors the store contents, as indicated in Fig. 3-50, and when the number of bits stored drops below a specified threshold, the multiplexer disables readout of this store after a fixed time delay. The clock-inhibiting stuff signal shown in Fig. 3-50 is used for this purpose. This effectively inserts a "blank" into the corresponding slot position in the frame. This blank can be coded as a 1, if desired. When the store contents rise above the threshold, sampling of the store contents at the appropriate slot time is again resumed.

An example of the bit-stuffing process, using two multiplexed signals, appears in Fig. 3-51. Both input channels are assumed to operate at the same nominal bit rate. They are thus interleaved, bit by bit, in order, as shown. In this

---

[25][JOHA] V. I. Johannes and R. H. McCullough, "Multiplexing of Asynchronous Digital Signals Using Pulse Stuffing with Added-Bit Signaling," *IEEE Trans. Commun. Tech.*, vol. COM-14, no. 5, pp. 562–568, October 1966.

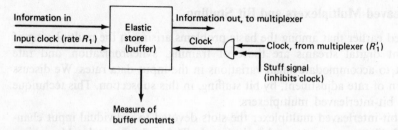

FIGURE 3-50
Elastic store for bit stuffing.

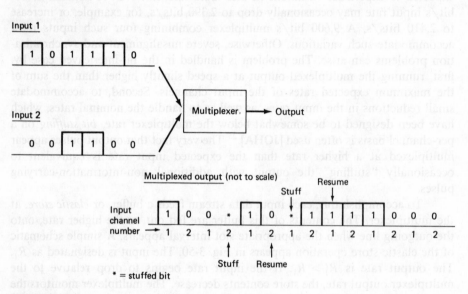

FIGURE 3-51
Bit-interleaved multiplexing using bit stuffing.

example first channel 2 and then channel 1 slow down somewhat, relative to the output rate, and stuffed bits are inserted. These could equally well be 0's or 1's, following an agreed-upon convention.

At the demultiplexer at the other end of the line, the stuffed bits must obviously be removed from the data stream. This requires a method of identifying the stuffed bits. Various techniques are possible. As an example, we present the approach used at the DS3 level of the North American digital hierarchy (Fig. 3-48), combining seven DS2 digital streams into one DS3 stream. This corresponds to the third level of the digital hierarchy of Fig. 3-48. This example also enables us to show one method of providing frame synchronization for a bit-interleaved system.

→ Order of transmission

X	(84)	F1	(84)	C11	(84)	F0	(84)	C12	(84)	F0	(84)	C13	(84)	F1(84)
X	(84)	F1	(84)	C21	(84)	F0	(84)	C22	(84)	F0	(84)	C23	(84)	F1(84)
P														
P														
M0														
M1	(84)	F1	(84)	C61	(84)	F0	(84)	C62	(84)	F0	(84)	C63	(84)	F1(84)
M0	(84)	F1	(84)	C71	(84)	F0	(84)	C72	(84)	F0	(84)	C73	(84)	F1(84)

FIGURE 3-52
DS3 frame format, North American digital hierarchy; numbers and symbols in bits.

Various levels of multiplexing are used to obtain the final DS3 signal [FLEU].[26] Seven incoming DS2 streams may actually be combined to form the composite DS3 signals. Alternatively, 28 incoming DS1 (1.544-Mbit/s) signals may be multiplexed up to the DS3 level. In this case, four at a time would first be multiplexed to form an internal DS2 signal. Seven such groups would then be combined internally to form the desired DS3 signal. Combinations of DS1, DS2, and other signals are possible as well. (The DS-1C signal, for example, operates at 3.152 Mbits/s, and accommodates 48 64-kbit/s channels). A simplified block diagram of a multistage DS3 multiplexer appears in Fig. 4 of [FLEU]. For simplicity's sake we focus on the final multiplexing stage only, combining seven DS2 signals to form the DS3 signal.

The DS3 frame contains 4704 data bits and 56 control bits, for a total of 4760 bits. Its efficiency (data bits/total bits) is thus 98.8 percent. The frame format appears in Fig. 3-52 [BELC].[27] The multiplexer uses bit-by-bit interleaving of the seven inputs, until a total of 84 bits, 12 from each input, is accumulated. A control bit is then inserted. The 56 control bits thus appear spread out throughout the frame, enclosing sequences of 84 data bits. Three types of control bits are used, as indicated in Fig. 3-52. They are there labeled the M series, the C series, and the F series. In addition, two bit pairs (X and P) are used to provide performance monitoring and alarm signaling, respectively. (These will be described briefly below.) The first line of the figure is transmitted, then the second, third, etc., in that order.

These three control signals are used to provide frame indication and synchronization and to identify which of the seven input signals has been stuffed. Only one stuffed bit per input channel is allowed per frame. As will be shown

---

[26][FLEU] B. Fleury, "Asynchronous High Speed Digital Multiplexing," *IEEE Commun. Mag.*, Vol. 24, No. 8, pp. 17–25, August 1988.

[27][BELC] "Asynchronous Digital Multiplexes: Requirements and Objectives," Technical Reference TR-TSY-000009, Bell Communications Research, Issue 1, May 1986.

shortly, this is sufficient to accommodate expected variations in the input signal rate.

A discerning reader will have noticed that the DS3 frame format (Fig. 3-52) is not based at all on the 125-μs frame structure of the DS1 signals (or, for that matter, of the basic 64-kbit/s DS0 signals—whether voice or data—on which the entire hierarchical structure is built). As a matter of fact, the frame length turns out to be 106.402 μs. Hierarchical organization of the DS3 frame, based on multiplexing 7 DS2 signals, makes it extremely difficult to extract the 1.544-Mbit/s DS1 (or 64-bit/s DS0) signals directly. Demultiplexing requires reversing the entire hierarchical multiplexing structure: First demultiplex the seven DS2 signals. Those that carry DS1 signals must then be further demultiplexed to extract the DS1 components.

In an effort to avoid this problem, a new DS3 format has been defined based on synchronous multiplexing. This new signal format, known as SYNTRAN (for SYNchronous TRANSmission), allows the direct multiplexing of bytes (8-bit characters) from 672 64-kbit/s DS0 or 28 DS1 signals. No intermediate DS2 multiplexing is required, as in the current DS3 scheme [RITC].[28] Because of the existence of many DS3 transmission facilities the new SYNTRAN format has been designed to be compatible with DS3. It uses the concept of a "superframe" made up of 699 DS3 frames in which to embed 595 SYNTRAN frames. (The superframe then occupies 74.575 ms [RITC]).

Returning to Fig. 3-52 for the DS3 format, the 0 or 1 following the M- and F-series control signals denotes the actual bit (0 or 1) transmitted. The F pattern, 1001, repeating every row (subframe), locates the position of the information and control bits, and provides the main framing pattern. The 010 pattern provided by the three M bits then locates the position of the seven subframes. Bit stuffing for each of the seven (DS2) input signals is restricted to the particular subframe (row) corresponding to the first integer following the C bits in that row. C51, as an example, refers to input channel 5; C32 refers to input channel 3, etc. The insertion of a stuffed pulse in any one subframe is denoted by setting all three C's in that row to 1. Three 0's in a row denote no stuffing. If a bit has been stuffed, it appears as the first information bit of the 12 for that input signal, following the end F1 in the same subframe. An example of a typical bit sequence appears in Fig. 3-53. C51, C52, C53 all equal to 1 denote one stuffed bit, as shown.

The 3-bit C sequence used to denote the presence or absence of a stuffed bit is necessary to reduce the chance of missing a stuffed bit to a tolerably low value. If a stuffed bit is mistakenly called an information bit and not deleted from the bit stream at the demultiplexer, all the bits for the entire frame in question will be in error. With three bits used to denote the stuffing, a single error in any one of the three bits will be recognized. Majority logic decoding is used. This simply

---

[28][RITC] G. R. Ritchie, "SYNTRAN—A New Direction for Digital Transmission Terminals," *IEEE Commun. Mag.*, Vol. 23, No. 11, pp. 20–25, November 1985.

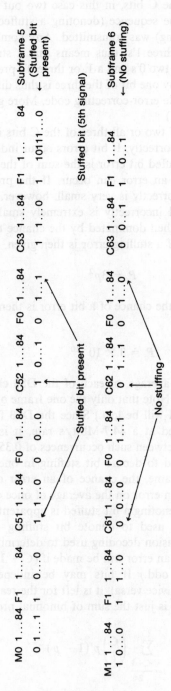

FIGURE 3-53
Example of the bit-stuffing process, DS3 frame.

means that the majority of the C bits, in this case two out of three, determine whether the all-zero or all-one sequence (denoting a stuffed bit present in the information sequence following) was transmitted. Any combination of two 1's and a 0, or the presence of three 1's, thus means that a stuffed bit is present. Similarly, any combination of two 0's and a 1, or three 0's present, means that no stuffing is used. An error in any one bit of the three is thus disregarded. (This is a very simple example of a single error-correcting code. More general codes of this type are discussed in Chap. 7.)

An error will be made if two or all three of the C bits in any subframe are misinterpreted or detected incorrectly. If bit errors occur independently from bit to bit, the probability of a stuffed bit error is the sum of the probabilities of the possible ways in which such an error can occur. If the probability p that an individual bit is detected incorrectly is very small, however, the chance that all three C bits will be detected incorrectly is extremely small. The chance of a stuffed-bit error occurring is then dominated by the chance that two bits will be transposed. The probability of a stuffing error is then given, very nearly, by

$$P_s \doteq 3p^2 \tag{3-76}$$

As an example, if $p = 10^{-5}$ (the chance of a bit error is then one in 100,000 bits transmitted, on the average),

$$P_s \doteq 3 \times 10^{-10}$$

Three frames in 10^{10}, on the average, of each of the DS3 channels will thus be lost because of this problem. (Note that only the one frame of the seven in a DS3 frame that is directly affected will be lost.) Since the DS3 frames are 4760 bits long and data are transmitted at a 44.7-Mbit/s rate, it is apparent that this converts to an average time between such occurrences of 0.35×10^6 s, or 97 h. If a *single* bit were used instead to denote bit stuffing in one of the seven input signal streams in any one frame, the chance of an error event would be just $p = 10^{-5}$. This would mean an error on the average of once every 10 s. The need for the longer bit sequence denoting a bit stuffed is apparent.

In general, for C bits used to denote bit stuffing in a bit-interleaved multiplexer, and majority-decision decoding used to determine the presence of a stuffed bit, it is apparent that an error will be made if $(C + 1)/2$ or more bits are transposed. (C is assumed odd.) If bits may be independently transposed (converted from a 0 to a 1, or vice versa), it is left for the reader to show that the probability of a stuffing error is just the sum of binomial probabilities, or

$$P_s = \sum_{i=\frac{C+1}{2}}^{C} \binom{C}{i} p^i (1 - p)^{C-i} \tag{3-77}$$

For $p \ll 1$, the leading term in this sum is dominant [i.e., $(C + 1)/2$ errors have a much higher probability of occurring than $(C + 1)/2 + 1$ errors], and

$$P_s \doteq \left(\begin{array}{c} C \\ \dfrac{C + 1}{2} \end{array} \right) p^{(C+1)/2} = \frac{C!}{\left(\dfrac{C - 1}{2} \right)! \left(\dfrac{C + 1}{2} \right)!} p^{(C+1)/2} \qquad (3\text{-}78)$$

For $C = 3$, this gives just the expression $3p^2$ written previously. For $C = 5$, $P_s \doteq 10p^3$, showing the improvement made possible by just adding two bits per C-series sequence. (Note, however, that all of this discussion assumes *independent* bit errors. Errors sometimes occur in bursts, and this assumption is no longer valid in that case.)

It has been noted above that the DS3 multiplexer we have been citing as an example of a bit-interleaved multiplexer allows only one bit per frame to be stuffed per input signal channel. Is this sufficient to accommodate expected variations in the input bit rates? Since a frame contains 672 bits per input channel (12 bits $\times$ 56 information-sequence positions per frame), the maximum fractional change in input bit rate that can be accommodated is $1/672$, or 0.15 percent. For a 6.3-Mbit/s DS2 channel this represents a 9.4-kbit/s variation, far more than the change in input bit rates actually expected.

This discussion of bit stuffing can be made somewhat more precise and generalized to include the extent of expected variations in the input clock (data) rate by the following argument. Say that m input signal streams (we sometimes use the word channels synonymously with this), each of the nominal bit rate R_1 bits/s, are multiplexed together. The frame consists of I information bits and X control bits. If the maximum expected fractional increase in R_1 is δ, the multiplexer output rate R_o required to accommodate the possible input clock rate increase is given by

$$R_o = mR_1(1 + \delta) \left(\frac{I + X}{I} \right) \qquad (3\text{-}79)$$

It is apparent that even if all m input channels are operating at the nominal data rates, stuffing will occasionally occur to offset the higher output rate R_o. If at most one stuffed bit per frame can be used per input channel, the average bit-stuffing rate must be less than 1 bit in the I/m information bits transmitted per channel in any one frame. Call the average number of bits stuffed per channel in any frame S. Then $S < 1$ is desired. As a matter of fact, it is desirable to have $S \leq \frac{1}{2}$ to accommodate input clock rates reduced by a fraction δ *below* the nominal rate. At $S = \frac{1}{2}$, bit stuffing will occur, on the average, once every two frames with the input clocks operating at their nominal values. In particular, we would like to have

$$S = \delta \left(\frac{I}{m} \right) \leq \frac{1}{2} \qquad (3\text{-}80)$$

Consider the DS3 multiplexer example again. Here $m = 7$, $(I + X)/I = 85/84$ (one control bit appears for every 84 information bits), and $I/m = 672$

(bits/frame)/input signal stream. Then

$$R_o = 7R_1 \times \frac{85}{84} \times \left(1 + \frac{S}{672}\right) \tag{3-81}$$

With $R_o = 44.736$ Mbits/s (the equivalent clock frequency is then a multiple of 8 kHz) and $R_1 = 6.312$ Mbits/s, we have $S = 0.39$. This choice of output bit rate thus satisfies the condition $S \leq \frac{1}{2}$ with some spare stuffing capacity.

It was noted earlier that two additional bit pairs, X and P, appear in the DS3 frame format (Fig. 3-52). The P bits must be identical and are used to transmit priority information for performance monitoring. (Parity check bits are used to detect errors in a binary message. This will be discussed in detail in chap. 7.) If the binary (modulo two) sum of the 4704 information bits on the previous frame is odd, the two P bits are both set to 1; if even, the bits are set to 0. The X bits must also be identical to avoid false framing and are normally set to 1. They can then be used to provide an alarm channel. As an example, if a DS3 multiplexer receives a signal for which the framing pattern cannot be found, it sets the X bits to 0 in the return signal. When bit stuffing is not used, the C bits can provide additional signaling channels as well.

Note that just as the DS3 signal bit rate is somewhat more than seven times the DS2 rate (Fig. 3-48) to accommodate added control bits and possible rate jitter (with bit stuffing used), the DS2 rate of 6.312 Mbits/s is somewhat more than four times the 1.544-Mbit/s DS1 rate. The multiplexer forming the DS2 signal itself inserts framing and synchronization bits, as well as bit-stuffing indication bits. The repeated patterns of 84 DS2 information bits shown in the DS3 format of Fig. 3-52 contain these control bits. The DS2 format, bit-stuffing process, and allowable-rate jitter analysis for the DS2 analysis are described in [SCHW 1980], paralleling the approach used here.

In the next subsection we consider the question of the appropriate choice of control bits for establishing and maintaining frame synchronization.

Frame Loss and Acquisition

As is apparent from the previous discussion and from our earlier discussion of time multiplexing in this chapter, framing and synchronization must be maintained for the corresponding transmitting and receiving data sources to stay in step with one another. Framing ensures that slots in the received time sequence will be correctly associated with the appropriate receiver terminals. Synchronization implies that the transmitter and receiver clocks are locked to one another, so that bit integrity is maintained. The subjects of framing and synchronization are quite broad and detailed in their own right. We have earlier mentioned typical ways in which synchronization and framing are maintained, without discussing the related design questions in detail. These include such questions as the length of the frame (in characters or bits) in fixed-frame systems, the length and type of framing pattern to be used, the design of the synchronization pattern, etc.

Rather than discuss these questions directly here, in this introductory text, we shall come at them indirectly, motivating them through a discussion of the way in which one maintains frame integrity. Specifically, we discuss in this concluding subsection on time-division multiplexing the questions of loss of frame and time required to acquire frame again, once a loss of frame has occurred. These will serve to introduce some of the quantitative aspects of synchronization and framing. The interested reader is referred to the literature for further study of the subject [STIF].

Specifically, there is a probability that a frame will be lost, owing to errors in the framing pattern. The longer the framing pattern generally, the higher the probability of a loss. Yet a longer frame pattern is easier for synchronization. So there is a trade-off in pattern length. One can add error-correction capability to the pattern, hence allowing a longer length to be used, but this reduces the efficiency of the frame (more overhead is introduced, at the expense of data), and results in increased complexity as well. Alternatively, one can require a frame error or violation detected to be repeated several times in a row before a firm decision is made that the frame is lost. This reduces the chance that a bit received in error due to noise will throw the framing procedure off. Thus the more repetitions required, the more accurate the final decision will be, but it will take the system correspondingly longer to reach a decision. If the system *is* out of frame, proportionately more data will be lost.

To quantify these statements say that a frame is L bits long, of which n bits represent the framing pattern. Let the probability of incorrectly detecting a bit again be $p \ll 1$. Assume that these bit errors are due to noise encountered during transmission, and that errors occur randomly, from bit to bit. For the simplest framing scheme an error in any of the n framing bits will be assumed to produce a framing error. For the n-bit pattern the probability P_f of a framing error is then

$$P_f = 1 - (1 - p)^n \doteq np \qquad p \ll 1 \qquad (3\text{-}82)$$

Now require k frames in succession to be declared in error before a frame loss is declared present. The probability P_l of a loss is then

$$P_l = (P_f)^k \doteq (np)^k \qquad (3\text{-}83)$$

If F frames per second are transmitted, the average time, in seconds, between frame losses is approximately

$$T_l = \frac{1}{P_l F} \qquad (3\text{-}84)$$

As an example, say that $p = 10^{-5}$, $n = 4$, and $k = 3$. The framing pattern is thus 4 bits long, and three repeats of a detected error are required before framing information is declared lost. Then $P_f \doteq 4 \times 10^{-5}$, and

$$P_l \doteq 0.64 \times 10^{-13}$$

On the average, then, 1 frame in 1.6×10^{13} frames transmitted is lost. If the bit rate is 1.6×10^6 bits/s and frames are $L = 10^3$ bits long, the frame rate is $F = 1,600$ frames per second. A frame will thus be lost, on the average, once every 10^{10} s, clearly a tolerable number. Now let p increase to 10^{-3}. Then $P_f \doteq 4 \times 10^{-3}$, and $P_l = 0.64 \times 10^{-7}$. A frame will now be lost, on the average, once every 10^4 s, or 3 h. This may or may not be tolerable.

Once a loss of frame has occurred, it requires some time to reacquire frame. One would like to reduce this time to as small a value as possible. Again trade-offs exist. There are two components to this time. One is the time required to detect the out-of-frame condition. This is the order of k frames. Hence now we want k small, yet previously we wanted k large to prevent the loss from occurring too often. The other component is the time required to acquire frame again, once it has been declared lost.

To quantify these comments, focus first on the time required to detect a lost frame. If the frame is lost, the receiving system may still not notice this, since the data are random, and there is a probability 2^{-n} that an n-bit data pattern will look like the expected frame pattern. Hence the probability the loss *is* detected in any one frame is $(1 - 2^{-n})$. The probability the frame loss is detected is then $(1 - 2^{-n})^k = 1 - k \times 2^{-n} + \cdots$. We want this to be close to 1, and hence we want

$$k \times 2^{-n} \ll 1$$

If this condition is satisfied, the time to detect a lost frame is very nearly k frames. In the example used earlier, with $k = 3$ and $n = 4$, $k \times 2^{-n} = \frac{3}{16}$.

Summarizing the conclusions thus far:

1. We want $np \ll 1$. This suggests picking n small, as noted earlier.
2. We want k *large* to keep random errors from establishing a frame loss.
3. We want k *small* to reduce the time to detect a lost frame.
4. We want $k \cdot 2^{-n} \ll 1$ to prevent a random data pattern from being mistaken for a framing pattern. Hence we want n *large*.

Note the trade-offs in n and k required here, as pointed out earlier.

Assuming it takes k frames to detect a frame loss, how long does it take to reframe? This is the time required to search through the data bits, n at a time, until a framing pattern is definitively detected as such. One simple procedure is to require a framing pattern, once detected, to appear at the same position in a frame m times in a row. m is normally chosen to be greater than 1 to prevent an n-bit data pattern from being (mistakenly) labeled as a frame pattern. Once such a mistake is made, a minimum of k frames is required to detect it, and to break out of the erroneous pattern. Using $m > 1$ reduces the chance of this occurrence. On the other hand, $m < k$ is desired to reduce the reframe time.

To calculate the average reframe or acquire time, once a frame loss is detected, consider the worst possible case—the one in which one starts searching at the opposite end of the frame from the location of the true frame pattern. It

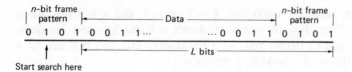

FIGURE 3-54
Worts-case search for n-bit frame pattern.

thus takes a minimum of $m + 1$ frames to acquire frame. A typical picture appears in Fig. 3-54. The 4-bit sequence 0101 is the frame pattern to be detected in this example. In the worst case the search begins at the second bit (the 1 in this sequence). The correct sequence is thus L bits away.

As the search proceeds, there is always a probability 2^{-n} that a frame pattern will be detected erroneously. If this occurs, search is suspended until the next frame, to check to see if the same pattern again appears at the same location in the frame. The chance of the frame pattern appearing erroneously at the same location during the next frame is again 2^{-n}. For $n > 2$ or 3 it is apparent that, on the average, only one frame interval will be required to detect the false pattern, with search then being resumed. Say that on the average h such suspensions of search or *holds* are encountered during the L-bit search. The worst-case acquire time is then

$$T_a = m + 1 + h \qquad \text{frames} \qquad (3\text{-}85)$$

To calculate h we note that in this worst case, $L + h$ patterns must be examined. Of these, h are detected as frame patterns. The ratio $h/(L + h)$ must thus be the same as the probability of detecting a frame pattern, so that

$$\frac{h}{L + h} = 2^{-n}$$

and

$$h = \frac{L}{2^n - 1} \qquad (3\text{-}86)$$

As an example, let $L = 1,000$ bits and $n = 4$ bits. Then $h = 1,000/15 \doteq 66$ frames. This is obviously much too big. The implication is that with such a large frame there are many opportunities, on the average, to (erroneously) detect frame patterns among the data bits. If n is increased to 8 bits, $h = 1,000/255 \doteq 4$ frames, a much more tolerable value.

The total average (worst case) time to detect a frame loss and acquire frame again can now be calculated as

$$T = k + m + 1 + \frac{L}{2^n - 1} \qquad \text{frames} \qquad (3\text{-}87)$$

As an example, take $L = 1,000$ bits, $k = 3$, $m = 2$, and $n = 8$ bits, as in the example above. Then $T = 10$ frames to detect a frame loss and reacquire frame. This corresponds to 10,000 bits. At a 1.5-Mbit/s rate, this is 6 ms. At a 50-kbit/s rate, it is 0.2 s. At a 10-kbit/s rate, it is 1 s.

If in this example we must take $n = 8$ to reduce the acquire time, what happens to the probability of losing a frame due to noise? Using $p = 10^{-5}$ again as the probability of erroneous bit detection, $P_f \doteq 8 \times 10^{-5}$ and $P_l \doteq 5 \times 10^{-13}$. For a trunk bit rate of 1.5 Mbits/s, and a corresponding frame rate of 1,500 frames per second, a frame will be lost, on the average, approximately once every 10^9 s, clearly a tolerable number again. If $p = 10^{-3}$ now, a frame will be lost, on the average, once every 1,000 s, or once every 16 min. This may no longer be tolerable. Hence one would require the use of low-noise lines in such a case.

3-9 MULTIPLEXING FOR FIBER-OPTIC TRANSMISSION: SONET

It has long been apparent that the digital hierarchy of Figs. 3-48 and 3-49, developed on the basis of long-haul telephone transmission over microwave radio and/or coaxial cable systems, no longer suffices for fiber-optic transmission systems. These systems run at Gbit/s bit rates, with the potential of going to terabit/s rates (Tbits/s or 10^{12} bits/s). The digital hierarchies of Figs. 3-48 and 3-49 were developed principally for voice communication, using a 64-kbit/s basic channel for that application. They are thus rated at multiples of 64-kbit/s (DS0) channels. Other, much wider-band applications are rapidly arising, however. As an example, local area networks (LANs, to be described in Chap. 5) running at 10 Mbits/s and 100 Mbits/s (these are generally fiber-based) are frequently interconnected. It would be appropriate to do this at much higher bit rates. Compressed high-definition digital TV to the home or business would require at least 150 Mbits/s. Broadband integrated-service digital networks (B-ISDN) of the future (integrated data, voice, and video) will operate at 150 Mbits/s and higher. Other applications will require hundreds of Mbits/s and possibly even Gbits/s. Fiber-optic communications will be used to provide the basic point-to-point transmission capability to support these services and applications. Standardization on a much higher-bit-rate digital multiplexing hierarchy, appropriate to optical transmission capability, is thus necessary.

Bell Communications Research (Bellcore) led an effort in the mid-1980s to develop such a standard [BOEH].[29] It has been informally called SONET for Synchronous Optical NETwork. The object has been to accommodate the lower, voice-channel-based digital hierarchies of both Figs. 3-48 and 3-49, and yet allow the introduction of newer, wider-band services, all using fiber optics as the

---

[29][BOEH] R. J. Boehm et al., "Standardized Fiber Optic Transmission Systems—A Synchronous Optical Network View," *IEEE J. Selected Areas Commun.*, Special issue on fiber optic systems for terrestrial applications, Vol. SAC-4, No. 9, pp. 1424–1431, December 1986.

transmission medium. The standard, as ultimately developed by a working group of the American National Standards Institute (ANSI) and refined, after extensive discussion, by CCITT, defines a base rate of 51.840 Mbits/s and multiples thereof on which to build a multiplexing hierarchy [ANSI] [BALL].[30] It also defines an equivalent set of optical signals, one for each level in the hierarchy. The optical signal, transmitted at an optical wavelength (frequency), serves as the "carrier," being "modulated" (for example, turned on and off) at the 51.840-Mbit/s rate. (The process of modulating a carrier is described in detail in the next chapter.) An example would be a 1.3-μm wavelength (2.3 $\times$ 10^{14}-Hz) optical carrier signal modulated at this rate.

The basic signal running at 51.840 Mbits/s is called STS-1, for Synchronous Transport Signal Level 1. Its optical counterpart is the Optical Carrier Level 1 signal, or OC-1 for short. Higher-level signals in the hierarchy are obtained by byte-interleaving the appropriate number of STS-1 signals. (This differs from the bit-interleaving approach used in the digital hierarchy of Fig. 3-48). Synchronous Transport Signal Level N (STS-N) then represents the multiplexing of N STS-1 signals, and runs at 51.840N Mbits/s. The corresponding optical signal resulting from the optical conversion of STS-N is called OC-N (Optical Carrier Level N). Examples of signals defined include, among others, STS-3 (and OC-3) at 155.520 Mbits/s, STS-9 (and OC-9) at 466.560 Mbits/s, STS-12 (and OC-12) at 662.080 Mbits/s, and STS-48 (OC-48) at 2.488320 Gbits/s. Note that the STS-3 signal could be used for compressed high-definition TV, as well as for multiplexed lower-bit-rate signals. A simplified example of transmission of an STS-N signal using an optical carrier (OC-N signal) appears in Fig. 3-55. The path shown represents the link between STS-N multiplexers.

The STS-1 frame is precisely 125 μs long, so there are 8000 frames/s. This enables DS0 (64 kbits/s) and DS1 (1.544 Mbits/s), as well as CCITT 30-channel (2.048 Mbits/s), signals (Figs. 3-48 and 3-49) to be readily accommodated by the STS-1 design. DS2 and DS3 signals are accommodated as well. The basic format of the STS-1 frame appears in Fig. 3-56 [ANSI, Fig. 5]. Note that there are 9 rows of 90 bytes each (1 byte = 8 bits). This thus gives 9 $\times$ 90 = 810 bytes or 6480 bits in a 125-μs frame. This results in the 51.840-Mbit/s rate mentioned. Of these, 27 bytes (the first 3 bytes in each row) are transport overhead bytes; the other 783 bytes are referred to as the *synchronous payload envelope* (SPE). The first column (9 bytes) of the SPE is also used for overhead and is called the *STS path* overhead. The remaining 774 bytes in the SPE represent "payload." The transport overhead bytes are used to carry out framing, scrambling, error monitoring, synchronization, and multiplexing functions, among others. The 9-byte path overhead within the SPE is used to provide end-to-end communica-

[30][ANSI] "American National Standard for Telecommunications-Digital Hierarchy Optical Interface Rates and Formats Specifications," ANSI T1.105-1988, American National Standards Inst., Inc., New York, Draft, March 10, 1988. [BALL] R. Ballart and Y.-C. Ching, "SONET: Now It's the Standard Optical Interface," *IEEE Commun. Mag.*, Vol. 29, No. 3, pp. 8–15, March 1989.

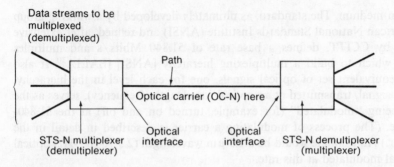

FIGURE 3-55
Optical path (no added multiplexing shown).

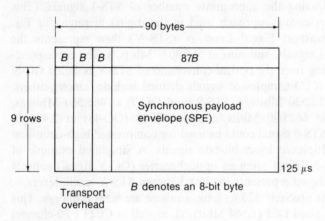

FIGURE 3-56
STS-1 frame.

tion between systems carrying the DS1, DS3, video, and other signals to be multiplexed onto the STS-1 signal. (A path is defined to end at the point at which the STS-1 signal is created or torn apart—demultiplexed—into its constituent lower-bit-rate signals).

The STS-1 SPE is not restricted to be contained within one frame. It may begin in one frame and end in another. A "payload pointer" within the transport overhead is used to designate the beginning of the SPE within that frame. This flexibility is needed to accommodate different bit rates and different services. To accommodate sub-STS-1 signal rates a *virtual tributary* (VT) structure is defined. Four sizes of VT are defined: VT1.5 occupies three columns of the synchronous payload envelope and hence runs at 3/90 of the STS-1 rate, or 1.728 Mbits/s. 1.544-Mbit/s signal streams are each mapped into a VT1.5 [ANSI, Sec. 12]. VT2 occupies four columns and runs at 2.304 Mbits/s. 2.048-Mbit/s signals (see Fig. 3-49) are each mapped into a VT2. Finally, VT3 occupies six columns and runs at 3.456 Mbits/s, while VT6 occupies twelve columns and runs at 6.912 Mbits/s.

The additional bits available for the DS1 (1.544 Mbits/s) and 2.048-Mbit/s signals are used for stuff control and other (communication) purposes.

44.736-Mbit/s DS3 signals are accommodated by the SONET structure in the following manner: 621 data (DS3) bits are mapped into each of the nine rows of the STS-1 synchronous payload envelope. Each row is now called a subframe. This provides a bit rate of $621 \times 9/(125\ \mu s) = 44.712$ Mbits/s. This is somewhat below the nominal 44.736-Mbit/s rate required. Stuffing bits are used to bring the bit rate up to the desired value. Specifically, each subframe (row) has, in addition to the 621 data bits, 1 stuff opportunity bit, 5 C (stuff control) bits, and 2 overhead communication channel bits. The remaining bits, called fixed stuff (R) bits, simply serve to pad out the subframe to the desired length and are ignored at the end of the path.

The stuff opportunity bit in each subframe can be used as an additional data bit by setting each of the 5 C bits to zero. If the bit has been stuffed, each of the C bits is set to 1. This adds an additional maximum of 72 kbits/s to the 44.712 Mbits/s specified, for a maximum possible data bit rate of 44.784 Mbits/s, above the nominal value required. By adding a data bit in any subframe when needed, the actual DS3 bit rate, as it fluctuates dynamically about its nominal value, can be made to fit into the synchronous STS-1 rate. Note that 5 C bits are used here, rather than the 3 cited in the DS3 multiplexer example of the previous section (Fig. 3-52). This reduces the chance of a stuffing error considerably. From (3-78) this is now approximately $10p^3$, with p the probability of a bit error.

The discussion thus far has focused on the STS-1 signal, running at 51.840 Mbits/s. It was noted above that the advent of fiber-optic transmission and wideband services makes the use of much higher bit rates extremely important.

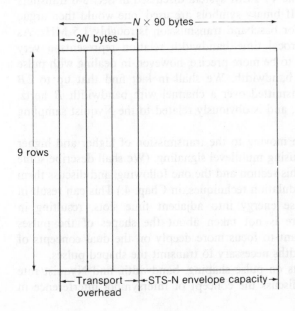

FIGURE 3-57
STS-N frame.

The use of STS-N signals (with the corresponding OC-N optical carrier signals) thus becomes of great significance. Formats for these signals have been defined as a simple extension of the STS-1 frame format. The STS-N frame format appears in Fig. 3-57 [ANSI, Fig. 24]. The STS-N signal is obtained by byte interleaving N STS-1 signals. The transport overhead bytes of each STS-1 (the first three single byte columns of each STS-1, as shown in Fig. 3-56) must be frame-aligned to create the 3N bytes of transport overhead shown in Fig. 3-57. The STS SPEs (synchronous payload envelopes) do not have to be aligned, however, since service payload pointers in the associated transport overhead bytes indicate the location of the SPEs.

3-10 WAVESHAPING AND BANDWIDTH CONSIDERATIONS

In discussing digital communication systems thus far, we have ignored the shapes of the pulses used to transmit the information. In many examples considered we have simply shown the digital pulses as rectangular in shape. In actual practice, where these pulses will modulate a carrier for transmission over relatively long distances, pulse shaping must be carried out. This is particularly true where constraints are placed on the channel bandwidth.

We have occasionally commented that the bandwidth is roughly given by the reciprocal of the time slot or interval in which a pulse is constrained to lie. Thus if 10 signals are sampled and time-multiplexed every 125 μs, each signal samples is constrained to lie within its 12.5-μs time slot. The bandwidth required to transmit the time-multiplexed signal train is then roughly $1/12.5$ μs, or 80 kHz. If eight-level quantization is now used, and binary signals sent, the bandwidth increases to 240 kHz. The T1 PCM system discussed in Sec. 3-6 transmits at the rate of 1.544 Mbits/s. If binary symbols are used, one would then argue that the bandwidth required for baseband transmission is roughly 1.5 MHz. As noted in Chap. 2, this reciprocal time–bandwidth relation represents a very useful rule of thumb. One has to be more precise, however, in dealing with pulse shaping to attain a specified bandwidth. We shall in fact find that up to $2B$ pulses per second can be transmitted over a channel with bandwidth B hertz. This is called the *Nyquist rate*, and is obviously related to the Nyquist sampling rate.

The technology has been moving to the transmission of higher and higher bit rates over given channels, using multilevel signaling. (We shall describe some of these techniques briefly in this section and the one following, and discuss them in more detail, in terms of modulation techniques, in Chap. 4.) This can result in considerable spillover of pulse energy into adjacent time slots, resulting in *intersymbol interference* if care is not taken about the shapes of the pulses transmitted. It is thus important to focus more deeply on the dual concepts of pulse shaping and the bandwidths necessary to transmit the shaped pulses.

To make these comments on pulse shaping, bandwidth, and Nyquist rate more precise, it is useful to discuss the concept of intersymbol interference in

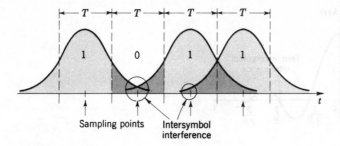

FIGURE 3-58
Intersymbol interference in digital transmission.

more detail. By choosing signal waveshapes to minimize or eliminate this phenomenon, we shall find the bandwidth necessary for their transmission.

Consider the sequence of pulses shown in Fig. 3-58. Although these are shown as binary pulses, they could equally well be pulses of identical shape, but of arbitrary height (PAM or quantized PAM). They are shown recurring at T-second intervals. T is the sampling interval in the PAM or quantized PAM case, the binary interval in the case of binary-encoded symbols. System filtering causes these pulses to spread out as they traverse the system, and they overlap into adjacent time slots as shown. At the receiver the original pulse message may be derived by sampling at the center of each time slot as shown, and then basing a decision on the amplitude of the signal measured at that point.

The signal overlap into adjacent time slots may, if too strong, result in an erroneous decision. Thus, as an example, in the case of Fig. 3-58 the 0 transmitted may appear as a 1 if the tails of the adjacent pulses add up to too high a value. (In practice there may be contributions due to the tails of several adjacent pulses rather than the one pair shown in Fig. 3-58.) This phenomenon of pulse overlap and the resultant difficulty with receiver decisions is termed *intersymbol interference*.

Note that this interference may be minimized by widening the transmission bandwidth as much as desired. This is unnecessarily wasteful of bandwidth, however, and if carried too far may introduce too much noise into the system (see Chap. 1). Instead we seek a way of *purposely* designing the signal waveshapes and hence transmission filters used to minimize or eliminate this interference with as small a transmission bandwidth as possible. One obvious signal waveshape to use is one that is maximum at the desired sampling point, yet goes through zero at all adjacent sampling points, multiples of T seconds away. This ideally provides zero intersymbol interference. With such a waveshape, chosen at the receiver, it should then be possible to design the overall system, back to the original sampling point at the transmitter, to provide this desired waveshape. (Recall that the original sampled pulses are essentially impulses if the time τ, during which the analog signal is sampled, is small compared to the sampling interval. The pulse broadening and shaping is then due to innate system filtering as well as filters purposely put in to achieve the final desired shape.)

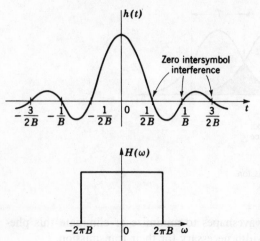

FIGURE 3-59
Pulse providing zero intersymbol interference.

One signal waveshape producing zero intersymbol interference is just the $(\sin x)/x$ pulse introduced in Chap. 2 as the impulse response of an ideal low-pass filter. Specifically, if the filter has a flat amplitude spectrum to B hertz, and is zero elsewhere, the impulse response is just $(\sin 2\pi Bt)/2\pi Bt$. This pulse is shown sketched in Fig. 3-59. Note that the pulse goes through zero at equally spaced intervals, multiples of $1/2B$ seconds away from the peak at the origin. If $1/2B$ is chosen as the sample interval T, it is apparent that pulses of the same shape and *arbitrary amplitude* that are spaced $T = 1/2B$ seconds apart will not interfere. This is shown in Fig. 3-60. $2B$ pulses per second may thus be transmitted over a bandwidth of B hertz if this waveshape is used. This is just the Nyquist rate noted earlier.

There are practical difficulties with this particular waveshape, however:

1. It implies that the overall characteristic between transmitter sampling and receiver decision point is that of an ideal low-pass filter. As noted in Chap. 2, this is physically unrealizable, and very difficult to approximate in practice because of the sharp cutoff in its amplitude spectrum at B hertz.
2. This particular pulse, if attainable, would require extremely precise synchronization. If the timing at the receiver varies somewhat from exact synchronization, the zero intersymbol interference condition disappears. In fact, under certain signal sequences, the tails of all adjacent pulses may add up as a divergent series, causing possible errors. Since some timing jitter will inevitably be present even with the most sophisticated synchronization systems, this pulse shape is obviously not the one to use.

It is, however, possible to derive from this waveshape related waveshapes with zero intersymbol interference that do overcome the two difficulties mentioned. They are much simpler to attain in practice, and the effects of timing jitter

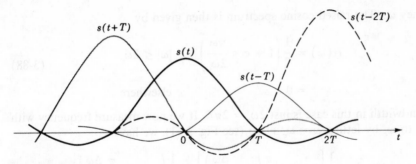

FIGURE 3-60
Sequence of pulses: zero intersymbol interference.

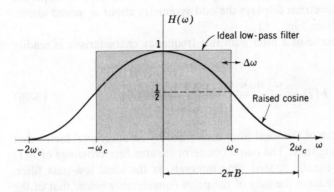

FIGURE 3-61
Raised cosine spectrum.

may be minimized. The particular class of such waveshapes we shall discuss is one of several first described by Nyquist [NYQU 1928a].[31]

To attain this particular class we start with the ideal low-pass filter of Fig. 3-59, but modify its characteristics at the cutoff frequency to attain a more gradual frequency cutoff, which is hence more readily realized. In particular, if the new frequency characteristic is designed to have odd symmetry about the low-pass cutoff point, it is readily shown, following Nyquist, that the resultant impulse response retains the derived property of having zeros at uniformly spaced time intervals. An example of such a spectrum often approximated in practice is the *raised cosine amplitude spectrum*. This particular spectrum and the original ideal low-pass spectrum are shown in Fig. 3-61. To avoid confusion with the transmission bandwidth B, we henceforth label the ideal low-pass cutoff

[31][NYQU 1982a] H. Nyquist, "Certain Topics in Telegraph Transmission Theory," *Trans. AIEE*, Vol. 47, pp. 617–644, April 1928.

frequency ω_c. The raised cosine spectrum is then given by

$$H(\omega) = \frac{1}{2}\left(1 + \cos\frac{\pi\omega}{2\omega_c}\right) \qquad |\omega| \leq 2\omega_c \tag{3-88}$$

$$= 0 \qquad \text{elsewhere}$$

The bandwidth in this case is just $2\omega_c = 2\pi B$. If we now measure frequency with respect to ω_c by letting $\omega = \omega_c + \Delta\omega$ (see Fig. 3-61), we have

$$H(\omega) = \frac{1}{2}\left[1 + \cos\frac{\pi}{2}\left(1 + \frac{\Delta\omega}{\omega_c}\right)\right] = \frac{1}{2}\left(1 - \sin\frac{\pi}{2}\frac{\Delta\omega}{\omega_c}\right) \tag{3-89}$$

Since the sine term has odd symmetry $[\sin(-x) = -\sin x]$, it is apparent that the raised cosine spectrum displays the odd symmetry about ω_c noted above. This is also apparent from Fig. 3-61.

The impulse response of a filter with this frequency characteristic is readily shown to be given by

$$h(t) = \frac{\omega_c}{\pi}\frac{\sin\omega_c t}{\omega_c t}\frac{\cos\omega_c t}{1 - (2\omega_c t/\pi)^2} \tag{3-90}$$

It has the $(\sin x)/x$ term of the ideal filter multiplied by an additional factor that decreases with increasing time. The $(\sin x)/x$ term ensures zero crossings of $h(t)$ at precisely the same equally spaced time intervals as the ideal low-pass filter. The additional factor reduces the tails of the pulse considerably below that of the $(\sin x)/x$ term, however, so that such pulses when used in digital transmission are relatively insensitive to timing jitter.

Letting the sampling interval $T = 1/2f_c = \pi/\omega_c$, so that the zeros of the pulse occur at T-second intervals as in the previous ideal low-pass case, we have the transmission bandwidth given by $B = 2f_c = 1/T$. This is just the bandwidth criterion adopted rather arbitrarily in previous sections. As an example, consider again an analog signal of 3.2 kHz sampled at an 8-kHz rate. If this signal only were transmitted by PAM, and the $(\sin x)/x$ ideal waveshape were used, the transmission bandwidth required would be $B = 1/2T = 4$ kHz. Using a raised cosine spectrum, however, the bandwidth required would be $B = 1/T = 8$ kHz. If 10 signals were time-multiplexed, the bandwidth would increase by a corresponding factor of 10. Thus although the $(\sin x)/x$ signal shape theoretically allows transmission at very nearly the original analog signal bandwidth (it would be the original bandwidth if the Nyquist sampling rate were used), the use of more realistic waveshapes results in an increase of the required bandwidth. The raised cosine spectrum doubles the bandwidth required. Other shapes to be discussed reduce this requirement.

The fact that the raised cosine spectrum is just one example of a class of spectra with odd symmetry about ω_c providing zero crossings at equally spaced sampling intervals is demonstrated as follows.

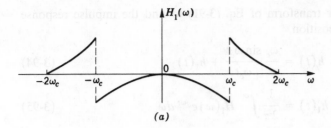

(a)

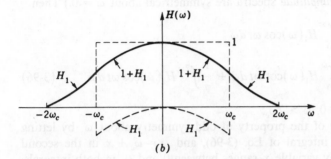

(b)

FIGURE 3-62
Nyquist filter. (a) Odd symmetry about ω_c. (b) Overall filter.

Assume a low-pass filter to have the characteristic

$$
\begin{aligned}
H(\omega) &= 1 + H_1(\omega) & |\omega| &< \omega_c \\
&= H_1(\omega) & \omega_c &< |\omega| < 2\omega_c \\
&= 0 & &\text{elsewhere}
\end{aligned} \tag{3-91}
$$

(If H_1 is zero, we have just the ideal low-pass filter.) As an example, let

$$
\begin{aligned}
H_1(\omega) &= \frac{1}{2}\left(\cos\frac{\pi}{2}\frac{\omega}{\omega_c} - 1\right) & |\omega| &< \omega_c \\
&= \frac{1}{2}\left(\cos\frac{\pi}{2}\frac{\omega}{\omega_c} + 1\right) & \omega_c &< |\omega| < 2\omega_c
\end{aligned} \tag{3-92}
$$

This is of course just the raised-cosine case.

Assume now for simplicity's sake that the overall filter has zero phase shift. (A linear phase term of course results in a corresponding pulse time delay.) Assume further that $H_1(\omega)$ has *odd symmetry* about ω_c. Then

$$
H_1(\omega_c + \Delta\omega) = -H_1(\omega_c - \Delta\omega) \tag{3-93}
$$

The raised cosine has this property. Another arbitrarily chosen example is shown in Fig. 3-62a, with the overall characteristic sketched in Fig. 3-62b.

Taking the Fourier transform of Eq. (3-91) to find the impulse response $h(t)$, we have, by superposition,

$$h(t) = \frac{\omega_c}{\pi} \frac{\sin \omega_c t}{\omega_c t} + h_1(t) \qquad (3\text{-}94)$$

where

$$h_1(t) = \frac{1}{2\pi} \int_{-\infty}^{\infty} H_1(\omega) e^{j\omega t} \, d\omega \qquad (3\text{-}95)$$

But $H_1(\omega)$, having zero (or linear) phase shift, must be even in ω (see Fig. 3-62a). (Recall that all *amplitude* spectra are symmetrical about $\omega = 0$.) Then

$$h_1(t) = \frac{1}{\pi} \int_0^{\infty} H_1(\omega) \cos \omega t \, d\omega$$

$$= \frac{1}{\pi} \int_0^{\omega_c} H_1(\omega) \cos \omega t \, d\omega + \frac{1}{\pi} \int_{\omega_c}^{2\omega_c} H_1(\omega) \cos \omega t \, d\omega \qquad (3\text{-}96)$$

using the fact that $H_1 = 0$, $\omega > 2\omega_c$.

We now make use of the property of odd symmetry about ω_c by letting $\omega = \omega_c - x$ in the first integral of Eq. (3-96), and $\omega = \omega_c + x$ in the second integral. The new dummy variable x ranges between 0 and ω_c in both integrals, and the two may be combined into the following one integral, after using the odd-symmetry property:

$$h_1(t) = \frac{1}{\pi} \int_0^{\omega_c} H_1(\omega_c - x)[\cos(\omega_c - x)t - \cos(\omega_c + x)t] \, dx \qquad (3\text{-}96a)$$

Now using the trigonometric identity

$$\cos(a - b) - \cos(a + b) = 2 \sin a \sin b$$

we finally obtain the following interesting result:

$$h_1(t) = \frac{2}{\pi} \sin \omega_c t \int_0^{\omega_c} H_1(\omega_c - x) \sin xt \, dx \qquad (3\text{-}96b)$$

Note that independently of the precise value of the integral (this will depend on the particular characteristic chosen for H_1), the $\sin \omega_c t$ preceding *guarantees* that $h_1(t)$ will be *zero* at intervals spaced $T = \pi/\omega_c$ seconds apart. But this is just the

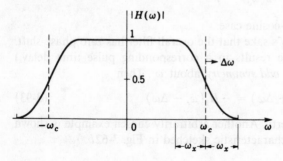

FIGURE 3-63
Sinusoidal roll-off spectrum.

original sampling interval T, so that $h(t)$ from Eq. (3-94) does go through zero at all intervals that are multiples of T away from the desired sampling point $t = 0$. This property of $h(t)$ is of course due to the odd-symmetric choice $H_1(\omega)$.

An interesting practical example of a spectrum satisfying the odd-symmetric property of (3-93) that leads theoretically to pulses with zero intersymbol interference is the *sinusoidal roll-off* spectrum of Fig. 3-63. Measuring frequency from ω_c, as shown in the figure, the amplitude spectrum for this example is specified by

$$|H(\Delta\omega)| = \frac{1}{2}\left(1 - \sin\frac{\pi}{2}\frac{\Delta\omega}{\omega_x}\right) \qquad |\Delta\omega| < \omega_x$$

$$= 0 \qquad |\Delta\omega| > \omega_x \qquad (3\text{-}97)$$

$$= 1 \qquad -\omega_c < \Delta\omega < -\omega_x$$

The design parameter ω_x represents the radian frequency by which the radian bandwidth exceeds ω_c. The ratio $r = \omega_x/\omega_c$ is called the *roll-off factor*. Smaller values of ω_x/ω_c lead to smaller bandwidth requirements, but require correspondingly tighter control on the design and more complex filter designs. The case of $\omega_x = 0$, or zero roll-off, is just the ideal low-pass filter case, and gives rise to the $(\sin x)/x$ pulse shape already discussed. Similarly, unity roll-off, with $\omega_x/\omega_c = 1$, results in the raised cosine spectrum discussed. By varying the roll-off factor a whole class of pulse shapes is generated. We shall have occasion to refer to examples of this spectral class later in the book in discussing spectral shaping for data transmission in various applications.

Note that in proving that the Nyquist odd-symmetry condition of (3-93) gives rise to a class of pulses capable (theoretically) of attaining zero intersymbol interference, we assumed zero phase shift. More generally, linear phase shift, $\theta(\omega) = -\omega t_0$, over the range of frequencies of interest ($|\omega| < \omega_c + \omega_x$) must be assumed. This of course makes the filter design more difficult. It is left to the reader to show that the impulse response for the sinusoidal roll-off spectrum with linear phase shift is given by

$$h(t) = \frac{\omega_c}{\pi}\frac{\sin\omega_c(t - t_0)}{\omega_c(t - t_0)}\frac{\cos\omega_x(t - t_0)}{1 - [2\omega_x(t - t_0)/\pi]^2} \qquad (3\text{-}98)$$

This is just a special case of (3-94) and (3-96b), and can of course be obtained from those equations by appropriate integration.

The bandwidth/pulse-rate trade-off using this sinusoidal roll-off spectrum (and other related spectra) depends of course on the roll-off factor chosen. What it does indicate is that if the desired rate of pulse transmission is $1/T$ pulses per second, the bandwidth B, in hertz, required is

$$B = \frac{1}{2T}\left(1 + \frac{f_x}{f_c}\right) = \frac{1}{2T}(1 + r) \qquad (3\text{-}99)$$

Alternatively, with B specified, the number of pulses per second that may be transmitted is given by

$$\frac{1}{T} = \frac{2B}{1 + f_x/f_c} = \frac{2B}{1 + r} \tag{3-100}$$

The number thus ranges from an unattainable maximum of $2B$ pulses per second to B pulses per second ($f_x/f_c = 1$), just the rule of thumb used up to now.

As an example, say that the allowable bandwidth is 2.4 kHz. (This is a number often used as a measure of the *available* bandwidth over telephone channels.) The maximum pulse rate over this channel is then $2B = 4800$ pulses per second. If a 25-percent roll-off factor is used, 3840 pulses per second may be transmitted. If the raised cosine spectrum is used, this reduces to 2400 pulses per second. In the chapters to come we shall often refer to the range B to $2B$ pulses per second, as the pulse rate that may be transmitted over a bandwidth of B hertz. Specific numbers in this range depend, as already noted, on design requirements, allowable costs, and various practical constraints introduced in any real application. As an example, timing jitter may play a prominent role in a particular application. If so, a roll-off factor close to zero may not be acceptable and a design close to the raised cosine spectrum may be necessary.

In addition, the discussion thus far has focused on eliminating intersymbol interference. The problem of minimizing intersymbol interference with digital transmission is a major one in the telephone plant, where the effects of additive noise are generally minimal. In digital systems designed for space communications, however, noise considerations play a highly significant role. Receiver design and signal shaping must take the effects of noise into account. We shall see, in considering this problem later, in Chap. 6, that the minimization of errors due to additive noise leads to *matched-filter* receivers. In an environment involving the minimization of both intersymbol interference and errors due to noise, some compromise between the two effects is generally necessary. Yet our discussion later will show that the receiver and signal-shaping problem is not too critical; in the matched-filter case, for example, we shall find that transmission bandwidths equal to the reciprocal of the interval T are close to optimum, so that one may simultaneously combat both intersymbol interference and noise without too much difficulty.[32]

---

[32] The minimization of errors due to both intersymbol interference and noise is considered in [LUCK] R. W. Lucky, J. Salz, and E. J. Weldon, *Principles of Data Communication*, McGraw-Hill, New York, 1968, Chap. 5. They show that if the channel may be assumed to introduce no distortion other than noise, the effect of both intersymbol interference and noise may be simultaneously minimized by splitting the Nyquist filter $H(\omega)$ equally into two parts, $H^{1/2}(\omega)$ at the transmitter, $H^{1/2}(\omega)$ at the receiver. As will be seen in Chap. 6, the receiver filter is then exactly the *matched filter* that minimizes errors due to noise.

For theoretical considerations it is often useful to use the maximum pulse rate, the Nyquist rate of $2B$ pulses per second, as the pulse rate to be expected with a bandwidth of B hertz. B is then referred to as the Nyquist bandwidth. More commonly, rather than speak of *pulses per second*, as we have been doing to this point, one refers to the number of *symbols per second* that one may transmit over a channel of B hertz. The use of the term "symbol" rather than "pulse" will become clear in Chap. 4 when we discuss modulated signals. Alternatively, one refers as well to the number of *symbols per hertz* that may be accommodated. Thus the Nyquist rate, with ideal low-pass shaping, provides 2 symbols/Hz; the raised cosine spectrum provides 1 symbol/Hz. The concept of symbols/Hz is particularly useful in that it enables us to compare various transmission schemes.

As noted earlier, the ideal transmission rate of $2B$ symbols per second agrees with the Nyquist sampling rate of Sec. 3-2. There is a close connection between the two concepts, one involving the number of samples required to uniquely represent a band-limited signal, the other the maximum rate of transmission of symbols over a band-limited channel. It is no accident that $(\sin x)/x$ filtering for signal reconstruction in the first case, and $(\sin x)/x$ pulses in time in the second, both appear. The maximum transmission rate of $2B$ symbols per second agrees as well with Hartley's law, mentioned in Sec. 3-2.

It is important at this point to distinguish between symbols/s and bits/s. We have already noted, in our discussion of the A/D or quantization process in Sec. 3-4, that a pulse may have a discrete number of amplitude levels. With the number of levels (generally a power of 2) specified, a unique conversion between a single multilevel pulse and the equivalent set of two-level, or binary, pulses exists. Specifically, a pulse of $M = 2^n$ levels is representable by n binary pulses. Generalizing to symbols, a multivalued symbol having $M = 2^n$ possible values is representable by n binary symbols. As an example, we shall see in Chap. 4, in discussing sine-wave signals, that amplitude, phase, and frequency can be varied independently. The discussion thus does not have to be restricted to *amplitude*-level variations. The symbol in that case is a sine wave with a particular amplitude, phase, and frequency.

More generally, different waveshapes can be used to transmit digital information. We use the word *symbol* to represent a specified waveshape which may or may not be of the simple pulse type assumed up to now, and refer generically to a class of M such specified waveshapes as the M symbols under consideration. One of these M symbols is assumed transmitted in an interval T seconds long, so that the transmission rate is 1 symbol/(T seconds). If a bandwidth B hertz is available, the Nyquist rate is $2B$ symbols/s. Since each symbol may be uniquely coded into $n = \log_2 M$ bits, the equivalent *bit rate* is $2Bn$ bits/s, or $2n$ bits/Hz. Transmission of the M-valued symbols, one at a time, is referred to as *M-ary transmission*. We shall have occasion to refer to specific schemes of this type in Chaps. 4 and 7. The simplest example is the one already referred to—the transmission of shaped pulses of varying amplitude. We have referred previously, in Sec. 3-4, to the bandwidth trade-off possible by coding between binary signals

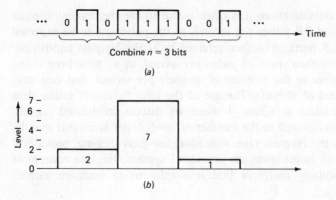

FIGURE 3-64

Binary–M-ary conversion. (a) Binary input sequence. (b) Output M-ary sequence.

and M-level signals in PCM. Thus a quantized PAM signal of M levels may be coded into binary PCM with $n = \log_2 M$ bits used to represent one of the M-level signals. The corresponding bandwidth is increased by a factor of n, since the binary digits each occupy $1/n$ of the original time. Conversely, n successive bits may be coded or collapsed into one symbol of n times the duration. The bandwidth is thus reduced by a factor of n. It is the latter concept that we have been exploiting in this current discussion. The bandwidth and *symbol* duration are inversely connected. If a symbol is one of $M = 2^n$ that could be transmitted in a specified interval, it represents $n = \log_2 M$ bits of information. By going to multivalued symbols one can increase the bit rate over a fixed bandwidth channel. An example of binary-to-M-ary conversion with $n = 3$ and $M = 8$ appears in Fig. 3-64.

Since it is the *symbol rate* that is determined by the bandwidth, one can theoretically increase the bit rate to be transmitted over a band-limited channel by going to higher- and higher-level M-ary schemes. In practice this is not always possible, however. As an example, take the case of M-level pulses. Figure 3-60 shows pulses of four different heights being transmitted in consecutive intervals T seconds long. In any real system some intersymbol interference must be present due to inaccuracies and tolerances in filter design, as well as to timing jitter. This is due to the tails of other pulses (those coming before and those coming after) having nonzero values at the sampling instants. It is apparent that the higher-level pulses in Fig. 3-60 will create more of a problem than will the lower-level ones. As the number of levels increases and the corresponding heights increase, the problem is exacerbated. One cannot indefinitely increase the pulse heights anyway because of power limitations. Trying to reduce the amplitude differences of the multilevel pulses is not helpful beyond a point, since ever-present noise means there should be some minimum amplitude separation or level spacing between the pulses. (The identical problem arises in attempting to distinguish between sine waves of varying phase or frequency.) So limits do exist on the bit rate possible over a channel of given bandwidth. As an example, the current state of the art for digital transmission over a telephone channel of 2,400 Hz bandwidth is 19.2 kbits/s. Two hundred fifty-six different sine waves, of differing amplitude and phase, are used for this purpose. The technique used is discussed in Chaps. 4 and 7. It has also been applied to much wider-bandwidth digital radio, as well as satellite communications. The combination of bandwidth, signal power, and noise in limiting the rate of transmission of signals over a given channel has already been noted briefly in Chaps. 1 and 2. In this section we have attempted to quantify the bandwidth limitation. In later chapters, after discussing the effects of noise on digital transmission, we shall come up with specific quantitative expressions that show how both bandwidth and noise affect the rate of data transmission. In Chap. 6 we shall develop a bit-rate expression for PCM that incorporates bandwidth, power, and noise. In Chap. 7 we shall discuss the celebrated Shannon capacity expression that provides a precise limit on the rate of data transmission over a channel obeying the assumptions in Shannon's model.

To further distinguish between symbols/s and bits/s the term *baud* is sometimes used to represent 1 symbol/s. If binary symbols are used, the number of bauds and the bit rate are identical. If multivalued symbols are used, however, the two differ. A device operating at 110 baud, for example, produces 110 symbols/s. If two such symbols only are used, the device outputs 110 bits/s. If eight such symbols are used, the bit rate is 330 bits/s. The term "baud" was

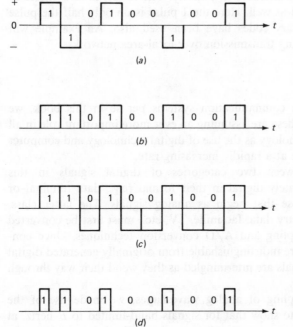

(a)

(b)

(c)

(d)

FIGURE 3-65
Examples of binary signals (wave-shaping not shown). (*a*) Bipolar signal. (*b*) Nonreturn-to-zero (NRZ) signal: on-off. (*c*) NRZ signal: polar. (*d*) Return-to-zero signal.

introduced historically in the telegraph field and is still used extensively to describe the transmission rates of lower-speed data terminals. They are often described by their baud characteristic. The higher-speed synchronous terminals are commonly rated in bits/s, however. (Some confusion occasionally arises, a 9,600-bit/s device, for example, being called, erroneously, a 9,600-baud device even though it may be outputting 2,400 symbols/s. The correct usage would be 2,400 baud, if baud usage were desired.)

Although the stress in this section thus far has been on waveshaping to reduce intersymbol interference, binary coding can be used as well to adjust the signal spectrum. One example, commonly used to reduce dc spectral components, is the *bipolar signal* discussed in Sec. 3-6 in connection with the Bell System T1 system. Recall that in this type of signal, successive 1's are represented by alternating polarity pulses. An example appears in Fig. 3-65a. (In practice, shaping as discussed up to this point in this section would be used in addition to get the desired pulse spectrum.) If a long sequence of 1's appears, the average of the signal is still 0, so that drift problems do not arise. This scheme is useful in cases where dc and low-frequency signal components cannot be tolerated.

The most common mode of binary transmission is the one called *nonreturn-to-zero* (NRZ) transmission. Two examples appear in Fig. 3-6b and c, respectively. These are the binary codes (again shown without shaping) we have been using thus far in this book. The first is also referred to as an *on-off signal*, since the 1 is represented by a positive pulse, the 0 by the absence of a pulse. This signal has a nonzero average value at half its positive amplitude (if 0's and 1's are equally likely), corresponding to its dc value. The second signal is often called a *polar signal*, since 1's and 0's alternate in polarity. The return-to-zero signal of Fig. 3-65d is sometimes used as well. Here the 1 pulse is on only half the pulse interval. Other types of binary codes have been used also. An example will appear in Chap. 5 in discussing transmission over local-area networks.

3-11 SUMMARY

In this chapter, the first on communication systems per se in this book, we focused on digital systems. These are assuming an ever more important role in all areas of communication technology as the use of digital technology and computer processing of data proliferate at a rapidly increasing rate.

We distinguished between two categories of digital signals in this chapter—those that are innately digital in their format (e.g., data terminal or computer outputs), and those that begin as analog signals. The latter class, whether voice signals, telemetry data, facsimile, TV, etc., must first be converted to digital format using sampling and A/D conversion techniques. Once converted to digital form, they are indistinguishable from originally generated digital data, and both classes of signals are intermingled as they wend their way through a communications network.

In discussing the sampling of analog waveshapes, we made use of the Fourier analysis of Chap. 2 to show that for signals band-limited to B hertz, at least $2B$ samples per second were necessary to retain all the information in the original (analog) signal. The sampling process is fundamental not only in preparing signals for digital transmission, but also in data analysis and processing by computer.

For the transmission of *digital data*, i.e., discrete numbers rather than continuous (analog) waveshapes, the signal samples must further be quantized into a specified number of amplitude levels. This results in quantization noise—the difference between the actual sample amplitude and its quantized approximation. The use of an appropriate number of levels makes this effect tolerable. The resultant stream of signal digits may then be coded into any number system desired. The binary system is the one most commonly used, since the resultant stream of binary pulses is least susceptible to noise and intersymbol interference. Where bandwidth limitations pose a problem, however, multilevel signaling may be used to pack higher data rates into a given bandwidth channel. This concept is explored in more detail in Chap. 4 in discussing multisymbol modulation techniques for digital communications.

For a fixed number of quantization levels, it is found appropriate to use nonuniform level spacing to accommodate a wider dynamic range of analog signals. This is carried out in practice by compressing the input signals prior to the quantization procedure. The reverse process of expansion is carried out at the receiver. The composite process is referred to as companding. In a brief analysis focusing on a particular nonlinear companding law used in practice, we demonstrated the improvement obtained using the companding technique.

Although most analog signals are transmitted using A/D conversion and time multiplexing in the overall process called pulse code modulation (PCM), DPCM, with delta modulation as a special case, has been adopted as an alternative procedure in a variety of existing systems. In this approach, the difference between the actual signal sample and its predicted estimate is quantized into multiple levels and the appropriate level transmitted. These systems generally require a higher sampling rate or some adaptive form to provide the same or better performance than the equivalent PCM system.

Time multiplexing of digital signals is commonly used to combine a multiplicity of signal sources over a common, shared channel. These signals can be either digital representations of analog signals or signals originally created in digital format. The time-multiplexing process serves as one important example of the efficient processing of signals that may be carried out if they are in digital form. Two types of multiplexing may be broadly distinguished, although boundaries are tending to disappear. One type combines digital streams bit by bit; the other combines blocks of bits, grouped into fixed-length characters. A common procedure is to periodically sample each of the input digital streams to be multiplexed, each at a rate commensurate with its own bit rate and that of the much higher output (multiplexed) rate. Known synchronization sequences must also be introduced periodically to enable demultiplexing to take place at a receiving destination.

Since the output bit stream, whether from a single digital source or a time-multiplexed output, must ultimately be transmitted over a channel to its destination point, the output pulses must be shaped appropriately to reduce intersymbol interference introduced due to signal distortion arising during transmission. A class of shaping referred to generically as Nyquist shaping was shown to eliminate intersymbol interference completely under ideal conditions. A special case, referred to as sinusoidal roll-off shaping, is used a great deal in practice, and was discussed in detail in this chapter. Reference will be made to this form of shaping in Chap. 4 and subsequent chapters. As a general conclusion, it is found that a channel with B-hertz bandwidth will allow from somewhat more than B to $2B$ symbols per second to be transmitted over the channel. Alternatively, if $1/T$ symbols (pulses) per second are to be transmitted, the bandwidth required ranges from an unattainable minimum of $B = 1/2T$ hertz to $B = 1/T$ hertz, depending on the shaping used. We use the word *symbol* here because multilevel signaling will allow correspondingly higher bit rates to be transmitted. This point is explored in more detail in Chap. 4.

The treatment in this chapter was devoted entirely to *baseband* signals, those that transmit the basic signals with no frequency translation carried out. In Chap. 4 we point out the common need for transmission of these digital signals at high frequencies, and discuss various ways of performing the requisite frequency translation up at the transmitter (*modulation*) and down at the receiver (*demodulation*). Again Fourier analysis and bandwidth concepts will be found to play a key role.

In Chap. 6 we return to baseband digital systems, calculating their performance in the presence of noise. We then discuss error-correction and error-detection coding in Chap. 7. These are methods for introducing additional noninformation bits, in a controlled way, at the transmitter, to detect and correct errors occurring due to noise during transmission.

PROBLEMS

3-1. A sinusoidal input at 1 Hz, $\sin 2\pi t$, is to be sampled periodically.
   (*a*) Find the maximum allowable interval between samples.
   (*b*) Samples are taken at intervals of $\frac{1}{3}$ s. Perform the sampling operation graphically, and show to your satisfaction that no other sine wave (or any other time function) of bandwidth less than 1.5 Hz can be represented by these samples.
   (*c*) The samples are spaced $\frac{2}{3}$ s apart. Show graphically that these may represent another sine wave of frequency less than 1.5 Hz.

3-2. A function $f_1(t)$ is band-limited to 2,000 Hz, another function $f_2(t)$ to 4,000 Hz. Determine the maximum sampling interval if these two signals are to be time-multiplexed, using a single sampling rate.

3-3. Consider the system shown in Fig. P3-3.
   (*a*) $P(t)$ is the periodic square pulse train shown in part (*a*) of the figure, with period $T = \pi/W$. Determine the parameters K and β of the ideal filter so that $g(t) = f(t)$.
   (*b*) Because of a failure in the pulse generator, the pulses of $P(t)$, although still periodic, come out nonflat and arbitrarily shaped, as shown in Fig. P3-3 (*b*). Can the shape of $f(t)$ still be recovered, to within a constant multiplier, at the output of the system? For simplicity, take $\beta = 0$.

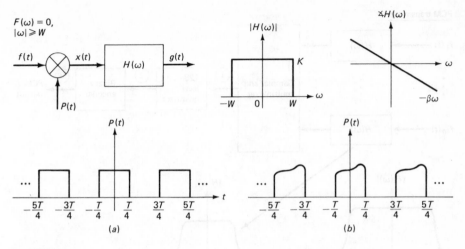

FIGURE P3-3

3-4. Twenty-four signal channels plus one synchronization (marker) channel, each band-limited to 3,300 Hz, are sampled and time-multiplexed at an 8-kHz rate. Calculate the minimum bandwidth needed to transmit this multiplexed signal in a PAM system.

3-5. Five signal channels are sampled at the same rate and time-multiplexed. The multiplexed signal is then passed through a low-pass filter. Three of the channels handle signals covering the frequency range 300 to 3,300 Hz. The other two carry signals covering the range 50 Hz to 10 kHz. Included is a synchronization signal.
   (*a*) What is the minimum sampling rate?
   (*b*) For this sampling rate what is the minimum bandwidth of the low-pass filter?

3-6. Temperature measurements covering the range -40 to $+40°C$, with $\frac{1}{2}°C$ accuracy, are taken at 1-s intervals. They are converted to binary format for PCM transmission. What is the bit rate required?

3-7. The readings from 100 pressure sensors, covering the range 10 to 50 psi, with 0.25-psi resolution, are taken every 10 s, and are then transmitted using time-multiplexed PCM techniques. What is the bit rate of the PCM output? Approximately what bandwidth is required to transmit the PCM signal?

3-8. Consider the PCM system shown in Fig. P3-8, which time-multiplexes 10 signal channels.
   (*a*) What is the minimum sampling rate?
   (*b*) 30,000 samples/s are taken.
      (1) What is the bit rate (bits/s) at the PCM output?
      (2) What are the *minimum* bandwidths required at points 1, 2, 3?

3-9. Ten 10-kHz signal channels are sampled and multiplexed at a rate of 25,000 samples/s per channel. Each sample is then coded into six binary digits.
   (*a*) Find the PCM output rate, in bits/s. Estimate the bandwidth needed to transmit the PCM stream.

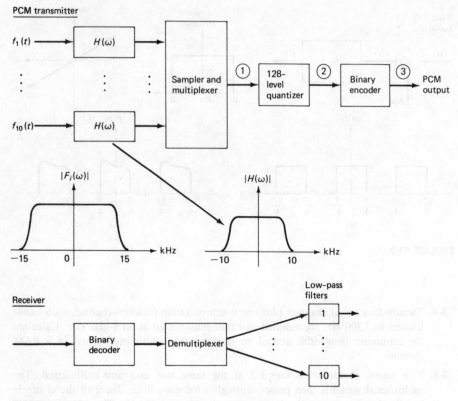

FIGURE P3-8

(b) Using the same number of quantization levels as above, each sample is now transmitted as a sequence of four-level pulses. What is the output rate, in bits/s? Estimate the transmission bandwidth required.

(c) Repeat (b) for the case in which each quantized sample is transmitted as a multilevel pulse without any further coding.

3-10. Three signal channels are sampled at a rate of 100 samples/s and then time-multiplexed. They have the following bandwidths:

Channel 1: 0–10 Hz.
Channel 2: 0–10 Hz.
Channel 3: 0–20 Hz.

(a) Sketch the multiplexed waveform if the signals in each of the channels is given, respectively, by $s_1(t) = 10\cos 20\pi t$, $s_2(t) = 0$, $s_3(t) = 5\sin 40\pi t$.

(b) Now assume that arbitrary signals of the appropriate bandwidth are present in each channel. After demultiplexing (separation) at the receiver, each signal is passed through a low-pass filter with transfer function $H_i(\omega)$ with characteristics as shown in Fig. P3-10 (f_1 and f_2 may differ from channel to channel). Determine the minimum permissible value of f_1 and maximum permissible value of f_2 for perfect signal recovery in each channel.

(*c*) Show, by means of a block diagram and waveforms, how the three channels could be time-multiplexed without loss of information into a single PAM signal with a composite pulse rate of 80 pulses/s.

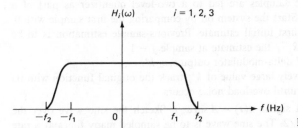

FIGURE P3-10

3-11. A single information channel carries voice frequencies in the range of 50 to 3,300 Hz. The channel is sampled at an 8-kHz rate, and the resulting pulses are transmitted over either a PAM system or a PCM system.

(*a*) Calculate the minimum bandwidth of the PAM system.

(*b*) In the PCM system the sampled pulses are quantized into eight levels and transmitted as binary digits. Find the transmission bandwidth of the PCM system, and compare with that of (*a*).

(*c*) Repeat (*b*) if 128 quantizing levels are used. Compare the rms quantization noise in the two cases if the peak-to-peak voltage swing at the quantizer is 2 V.

3-12. Repeat Prob. 3-11 for the case of 12 voice channels each carrying frequencies of 50 to 3,300 Hz, which are sampled and time-multiplexed. Include block diagrams of both the PAM and PCM systems.

3-13. The sinusoidal voltage $10 \sin 6,280t$ is sampled at $t = 0.33$ ms and thereafter periodically at a 3-kHz rate. The samples are then quantized into eight voltage levels and coded into binary digits. Draw the original voltage and below it to scale the outputs of the sampler, the quantizer, and the encoder. Calculate the rms quantization noise.

3-14. A signal voltage in the frequency range 100 to 4,000 Hz is limited to a peak-to-peak swing of 3 V. It is sampled at a uniform rate of 8 kHz, and the samples are quantized to 64 evenly spaced levels. Calculate and compare the bandwidths and ratios of peak signal to rms quantization noise if the quantized samples are transmitted either as binary digits or as four-level pulses.

3-15. Derive Eq. (3-47) for the mean-squared quantization noise using the μ-law compander.

3-16. Calculate the signal-to-quantization-noise ratio for an 8-bit code and a $\mu = 255$ companding law for several values of input signal power, checking the appropriate entries in Table 3-3. Consider both laplacian and gaussian statistics.

3-17. Repeat Prob. 3-16 for a $\mu = 100$ companding law. Plot the SNR calculated versus σ_x^2 for both values of μ and compare. How are the results affected if a 6-bit code is used? A 7-bit code?

3-18. A PCM system uses 7-bit quantization and a $\mu = 255$ companding law at its output. The maximum voltage at the input to the compressor is limited to 2 V. Compare the signal-to-quantization-noise ratio for two signals, both modeled by laplacian statistics, one with a standard deviation of 0.4 V, the other with a standard deviation of 0.02 V.

3-19. *Carefully* draw a slowly varying analog function. This function is to be sampled 10 times, with samples spaced somewhat closer together than the usual Nyquist interval. Assume that the samples are fed to a two-level quantizer as part of a delta-modulation system. Start the system off by comparing the first sample with 0. Zero is also used as the first initial estimate. Previous-sample estimation is to be used: $g_j = 0.9\hat{x}_{j-1}$, with $\hat{x}_{j-1}$ the estimate at sample $j - 1$.

(*a*) Show the sequence of delta-modulator outputs, $\pm k'$.

(*b*) Start off with a relatively large value of k'; track the original function with its estimates. Reduce k' until overload noise occurs.

3-20. Consider a sine-wave test signal $x(t) = A \sin \omega_m t$. Sketch the sine wave over the interval $-\pi/2 < \omega_m t < \pi/2$. The sine wave is to be sampled many times at a rate $f_s \gg f_m$.

(*a*) Demonstrate that if $k' f_s / 2\pi A f_m < 1$, overload noise will result. (k' is the delta-modulator step size.)

(*b*) Let $\alpha \equiv k' f_s / 2\pi A f_m = 0.707$. Show that the overload-noise region is entered at the point $\omega_m t = -\pi/4 \equiv -\theta_1$. Assuming that the quantization noise is negligible so that the delta-modulator receiver output is very nearly a straight line, draw the receiver output on top of the sine-wave curve and find the time $\omega_m t \equiv \theta_2$ at which the overload region ends.

(*c*) Verify Eq. (3-64) for the overload noise.

3-21. Refer to Prob. 3-19. Let the signal at the input to the delta-modulation system be $A \cos \omega_m t$. Sketch both the binary output sequence $\pm k'$ and the quantized estimate to the original signal, over several cycles of the cosine wave, for the following cases:

(*a*) $f_s = 10 f_m$, $A = 4k'$,

(*b*) $f_s = 30 f_m$, $A = 4k'$,

(*c*) $f_s = 30 f_m$, $A = 10k'$.

Comment on the effect of each of these cases on quantization noise and slope overload.

3-22. Consider the DS3 multiplexer described in the text. As pointed out there, it uses three 1's to denote a stuffed bit in one of the seven channels being multiplexed. Find the average time between losses of a frame in one of the channels due to a stuffing-bit error if the probability of a bit error is 10^{-5} and bit errors are assumed to be independent. Repeat for a bit-error probability of 10^{-9}. What would the average times between stuffing errors for the same two error probabilities be if one bit only were used to denote stuffing?

3-23. (*a*) The T1 PCM system multiplexes twenty-four 64-kbits/s channels. One framing bit is added at the beginning of each T1 frame for synchronization purposes. Show that the nominal bit rate of the T1 system is 1.544 Mbits/s.

(*b*) Four T1 (DS1) channels are combined to form a DS2 stream at 6.312 Mbits/s, as described in the text. Show these numbers provide a margin in the bit rate of each T1 channel of about 1.78 kbits/s. Show that the average bit stuffing rate per channel is 1 bit in three DS2 frames.

3-24. 12 voice signals covering the range 20 Hz–20 kHz are low-pass filtered to 7 kHz, and are then multiplexed into one binary stream as shown in Fig. P3-24a.

(*a*) What is the minimum sampling rate?

(*b*) The signals are each sampled at a rate of 16 ksamples/s. 256 levels of quantization are used. Framing bits are ignored. Show the output bit rate is 1.536 Mbits/s.

(*c*) The roll-off factor $r = 0.25$. Find the bandwidth required to transmit the baseband pulses.

(*d*) The receiver is diagrammed in Fig. P3-24*b*.
   (1) Specify the type of filter and its bandwidth.
   (2) Provide two reasons why $\hat{f}_i(t)$ differs from $f_i(t)$, $i = 1, \ldots, 12$.

(*e*) Frames are 125 μs long. Eight framing bits are added per frame. Repeat (*c*).

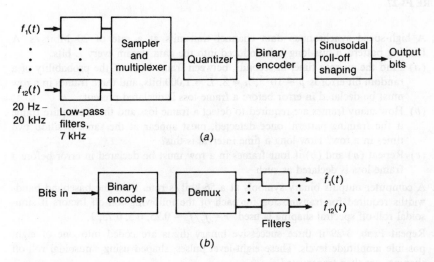

FIGURE P3-24

3-25. (*a*) 1000 seismic pressure sensors are sampled every 0.25 s. Readings are quantized to 0.1 psi, with a maximum range of ±0.8 psi about some nominal value. The quantized readings are multiplexed, and transmitted as binary digits. Show the output bit rate is 16 kbits/s.

   (*b*) Repeat (*a*) if the quantization spacing is reduced to 0.025 psi. Readings are taken every second. Again find the output bit rate.

3-26. The seismic binary output of Prob. 3-25*a* and two computer output bit streams, each running at 64 kbits/s, are time-multiplexed. The seismic signal stream uses one-fourth the number of slots of the computer outputs. A framing structure is imposed; frames are 1 ms long. Eight framing bits are added per frame. Find the baseband bandwidth of the multiplexed bit stream if sinusoidal roll-off shaping is used on the output bit stream; $r = 0.1$.

3-27. Five voice signals covering the range 30 Hz–25 kHz are filtered, and then multiplexed using PCM techniques as shown in Fig. P3-27. The filters $H_1(\omega)$ cover the range 20 Hz–20 kHz, as shown. Sampling is at the rate of 44,000 samples/s. Find the bandwidth of $H_2(\omega)$ for the following cases:
   (*a*) 256-level quantization, 50% roll-off.
   (*b*) $1024 = 2^{10}$ levels of quantization, 25% roll-off shaping.

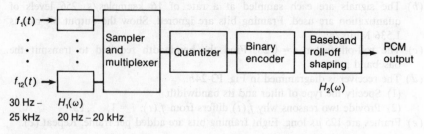

30 Hz – $H_1(\omega)$
25 kHz 20 Hz – 20 kHz

FIGURE P3-27

3-28. A high-speed synchronous data channel transmits at a rate of 20 Mbits/s. A framing pattern n bits long is introduced into the data stream every L bits.

(a) Find the average time, in seconds, between frame losses if the probability of a random bit error is $p = 10^{-5}$, $n = 8$, $L = 1,000$ bits, and three frames in a row must be declared in error before a frame loss is declared present.

(b) How many frames are required to detect a frame loss and then reacquire frame if the framing pattern, once detected, must appear at the same position two times in a row? How long a time interval is this?

(c) Repeat (a) and (b) if four frames in a row must be declared in error before a frame loss is declared as such.

3-29. A computer outputs binary symbols at a 56-kbit/s rate. Find the baseband bandwidths required for transmission for each of the following roll-off factors if sinusoidal roll-off spectral shaping is used: $r = f_x/f_c = 0.25, 0.5, 0.75, 1$.

3-30. Repeat Prob. 3-29 if three successive binary digits are coded into one of eight possible amplitude levels. These eight-level pulses, shaped using sinusoidal roll-off shaping, are then transmitted.

3-31. A baseband bandwidth of 3.6 kHz is available.

(a) Find the bit rates possible if binary pulses with sinusoidal roll-off shaping are to be transmitted. Consider the cases $r = f_x/f_c = 0.25, 0.5$, and 1.

(b) Repeat if four successive binary digits are combined into one pulse of 16 possible values.

3-32. Find the baseband bandwidth needed to transmit the DS1 and DS3 output streams of Prob. 3-23 if binary pulses with raised cosine shaping are used. Repeat if 25-percent roll-off shaping is used instead.

3-33. Consider the sinusoidal roll-off spectrum of Fig. 3-63 in the text. Assume linear phase shift, $\theta(\omega) = -\omega t_0$.

(a) Show that the impulse response is given by Eq. (3-98).

(b) Sketch $|H(\omega)|$ and $h(t)$ for the roll-off factor $\omega_x/\omega_c = 0.5, 0.75$, and 1.0, and compare. Pay specific attention to the bandwidth and pulse tails in each case. Sketch $h(t)$ for several symbol intervals.

(c) The raised cosine spectrum is given by $\omega_x/\omega_c = 1.0$. Show that the impulse response in this case has an additional zero halfway between the usual zero crossings. Discuss the possibility in this case of detecting successive pulses by "slicing" the received signal at the half-amplitude levels.

3-34. An analog source is sampled, quantized, and encoded into binary PCM. Four levels of quantization are used. The PCM pulses are transmitted over a bandwidth of 4,800 Hz using Nyquist shaping with 50-percent roll-off.

(a) Find the maximum possible PCM pulse rate.

(b) Find the maximum permissible source bandwidth.

3-35. A source is sampled, quantized, and encoded into PCM. Each sample is encoded into a "word" consisting of three information (data) pulses plus a synchronizing pulse. The information pulses can take on four possible levels. Transmission is accomplished over a channel of bandwidth 6,000 Hz using Nyquist pulses with 50-percent roll-off. Find:

(a) The maximum possible PCM pulse rate.

(b) The corresponding information rate of the PCM signal.

(c) The maximum permissible source bandwidth. It is desired to trade quantization levels for source bandwidth. If the number of quantization levels is reduced by a factor of 4, how large could the new source bandwidth be?

3-36. Refer to Prob. 3-9. Find the bandwidths required in all three parts of the problem if Nyquist shaping with 50-percent roll-off is used. How would these numbers change if 25-percent roll-off is used?

CHAPTER
4

MODULATION TECHNIQUES

4-1 INTRODUCTION

In Chap. 3 we focused on digital communication systems because of their great technological significance: digital data transmission is increasing at an extremely rapid rate, and analog signals are more and more frequently being converted to digital format before transmission. The stress in Chap. 3 was on the basic signals themselves, however. We described methods by which analog signals are converted to digital format (using, for example, normal A/D conversion or some form of DPCM). We also discussed ways in which digital signals are combined, using time-multiplexing techniques, to allow more efficient use of a transmission channel.

In all cases, however, the digital signals as well as the analog signals discussed were those originally generated. These are referred to generically as *baseband* signals. Although we discussed both the generation and reception of the baseband signals in Chap. 3, we had little to say about the actual medium over which the signals are ultimately transmitted. This channel separating the transmitter and receiver may in some cases be the air, in others, a set of wires, a coaxial cable, or a set of optical fibers. Efficiency of transmission requires that the information-bearing signals be processed in some manner before being transmitted over an intervening medium.

Most commonly, the baseband signals must be shifted to higher frequencies for efficient transmission. This is done by varying the amplitude, phase, or frequency (or combinations of these) of a high-frequency sine-wave carrier, in accordance with the information to be transmitted. This process of altering the characteristics of a sine-wave carrier is referred to as *sine-wave* or *continuous-wave* (c-w) modulation. The baseband signals constitute the modulating signal, and the resultant signal is a high-frequency modulated carrier. The use of higher frequencies provides more efficient radiation of electric energy and makes available wider bandwidths for increased information transfer than is possible at the lower frequencies. It is a well-known result of electromagnetic theory that an efficient radiator of electric energy (the antenna) must be at least the order of magnitude of a wavelength in size. Since the wavelength of a 1-kHz tone is 300 km, radio transmission is hardly practicable at audio frequencies. But a 1-MHz carrier wave could be (and is) transmitted efficiently with an antenna 300 ft high. Similarly, the outputs of low-speed data sets must be converted to c-w modulated signals for transmission over telephone channels, and 1.5-Mbit/s PCM signals must be converted to microwave c-w modulation for proper launching over a microwave transmission medium. Gbit/s signals are converted to optical frequencies (or wavelengths) and require the use of optical fibers for their transmission.

In this chapter we thus focus on sine-wave modulation techniques.

Although the term *modulation* in this chapter refers specifically to sine-wave or c-w modulation, it has been used more generally to refer to the procedure of processing a signal for more efficient transmission. We have already seen some examples of this use of the term in Chap. 3. There we referred to pulse amplitude modulation (PAM) and to pulse code modulation (PCM). In the first case an analog signal is sampled periodically to produce a series of pulses whose height varies in accordance with the analog signal value at the time of sampling. One may visualize this transmission scheme as one in which the height of a periodic set of pulses (the carrier) is altered in a definite pattern corresponding to the information to be transmitted. This form of modulation enables one to time-multiplex many information channels for sequential transmission over a single channel. In the case of pulse code modulation the PAM pulses are further processed by using A/D conversion (quantization) and then encoding into binary format. This serves the purpose of coding the signals to better overcome noise and distortion ultimately encountered on the channel (medium), as well as to enable digital processing to be utilized throughout the transmission path.

We have indicated above that pulse-modulation systems generally require some form of c-w modulation to finally transmit the signals over the desired channel; this is also true of analog signals that are to be transmitted, without conversion to pulse or digital forms, to remote points. Examples, of course, include the usual radio and TV broadcasts, as well as many telemetered signals where it is more expedient to transmit the data directly, without digitizing them. Although the modulation techniques used for digital (pulse-coded) signals and analog signals are conceptually the same, we shall distinguish between the two cases in this chapter. There are several reasons for this:

1. The increasing importance of the transmission of digital data, and the consequent development of a sizable industry devoted to the production of specialized digital modulation equipment, dictates emphasis on this area.
2. The resultant carrier systems are sufficiently distinct to warrant separate categorization in the literature. This is particularly true of multilevel or multisymbol digital carrier systems.

3. The study of digital carrier systems, particularly of the binary type, is often simpler than that of their analog counterparts. By focusing first on these we gain insight into the sine-wave modulation process that is then quite useful in understanding the operation of analog carrier systems. This is particularly true of the spectral properties of such systems. These can be obtained rather simply for digitally modulated sine-wave signals, particularly in the case of binary pulse modulation. The results can then readily be extended to more complex types of signals, involving analog modulating, or combinations of analog and digital modulating, signals.

We accordingly begin the chapter by focusing on binary communications, discussing the three basic ways of modulating sine-wave carriers, amplitude, phase, and frequency, using baseband binary signals as the modulating source. We then generalize this to include multisymbol modulation, with combinations of mu'tiple-phase and multiple-amplitude modulation as the prime practical example. As a special case we study an interesting digital modulation scheme called minimum-shift keying which provides a constant-amplitude signal and is spectrally (bandwidth) efficient. We then study various types of analog c-w modulation, with emphasis primarily on amplitude modulation (including both normal and single-sideband modulation) and frequency modulation.

Not only is c-w modulation necessary to launch signals effectively over a desired medium, but it also leads to the possibility of *frequency multiplexing*, or staggering of frequencies over the specified band. This is directly analogous to the *time-multiplexing* technique introduced in Chap. 3, in which many signal channels are sequentially sampled and transmitted serially in time. In the frequency-multiplexed case signal channels are transmitted over adjacent, nonoverlapping frequency bands. They are thus transmitted in parallel, simultaneously in time. This means that many telephone conversations can be transmitted over a single pair of wires (depending of course on the bandwidth allowed for each conversation and the total bandwidth of the system, including the wires). Very often a group of digital channels, each incorporating many time-multiplexed signals, may further be combined by frequency-multiplexing techniques. In current light-wave (fiber-optic) technology, wavelength multiplexing is the term used to designate the combined transmission of multiple optical signals of different wavelengths (frequencies) over a common optical fiber.

Operation at higher carrier frequencies makes more bandwidth available and hence leads to the possibility of frequency-multiplexing more signals or transmitting wider-band signals than is possible at lower frequencies. As an example, the amplitude-modulation (AM) broadcast band in this country is fixed at 550 to 1,600 kHz. This provides for 100 channels, spaced 10 kHz apart. This entire band, however, is just a fraction of the band, 6 MHz, needed for one TV channel. Operating TV broadcasts at the 60-MHz range and up (the VHF band) makes several channels available. Increasing the carrier frequency to 470 MHz and up (the UHF band) makes many more TV channels available. This is one reason for the current interest in optical frequencies for communication purposes.

In this chapter we shall concentrate, as in the previous chapter, on the spectral (bandwidth) characteristics of the various types of c-w systems, as well as on general systems aspects of their generation and reception. This will further solidify the Fourier analysis of Chap. 2. It parallels the approach used in Chap. 3 in discussing pulse-modulation systems. After introducing a discussion of noise effects in Chap. 6, we shall be in a position to further compare the various c-w systems, as well as the pulse systems already studied, on the basis of their performance in noise.

4-2 BINARY COMMUNICATIONS

As noted earlier, there are essentially three ways of modulating a sine-wave carrier: variation of its amplitude, phase, and frequency in accordance with the information being transmitted. In the binary case this corresponds to switching the three parameters between either of two possible values. Most commonly the amplitude switches between zero (the *off* state) and some predetermined amplitude level (the *on* state). Such systems are then called *on–off-keyed* (OOK) systems.[1] Similarly, in *phase-shift keying* (PSK), the phase of a carrier switches by π radians or 180°. Alternatively, one may think of switching the polarity of the carrier in accordance with the binary information stream. In *frequency-shift keying* (FSK), the carrier switches between two predetermined frequencies, either by modulating one sine-wave oscillator or by switching between two oscillators locked in phase. Although other types of binary sine-wave signaling schemes are in use as well, we shall concentrate here on the basic schemes. On–off keying is the technique used worldwide for digital communications over optical fibers.

On–Off Keying

Assume a sequence of binary pulses, as shown in Fig. 4-1a. The 1's turn on the carrier of amplitude A, the 0's turn it off (Fig. 4-1b). It is apparent that the spectrum of the OOK signal will depend on the particular binary sequence to be transmitted. Call a particular sequence of 1's and 0's $f(t)$. Then the amplitude-modulated or OOK signal is simply[2]

$$f_c(t) = Af(t)\cos \omega_c t \qquad (4-1)$$

where $f(t) = 1$ or 0, over intervals T seconds long. But note that this is in exactly the form of the modulated signal discussed in Chap. 2. As shown there, upon taking the Fourier transform of the amplitude-modulated (OOK) signal $f_c(t)$,

---

[1] The term *amplitude-shift keying* (ASK) is also used to denote this process.

[2] The carrier frequency ω_c should not be confused with the same symbol used for low-pass cutoff frequency in Sec. 3-10.

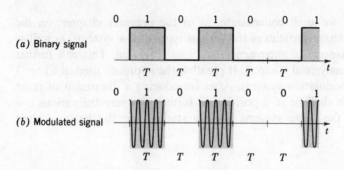

FIGURE 4-1
On–off-keyed signal.

and using the frequency-shifting theorem of (2-53), we have

$$F_c(\omega) = \frac{A}{2}\left[F(\omega - \omega_c) + F(\omega + \omega_c) \right] \qquad (4-2)$$

A similar example appeared in (3-3) in discussing sampling.

The effect of multiplication by $\cos \omega_c t$ is simply to shift the spectrum of the original binary signal (the baseband signal) up to frequency ω_c (Fig. 4-2). This is the general form of an AM signal. It contains upper and lower sidebands symmetrically distributed about the carrier or center frequency ω_c. Note the important fact that with an initial baseband bandwidth of $2\pi B$ rad/s (B hertz), the AM or transmission bandwidth is twice that, i.e., $\pm 2\pi B$ rad/s or $\pm B$ hertz about the carrier, for a total bandwidth of $2B$ hertz.

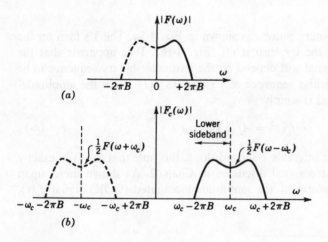

FIGURE 4-2
Amplitude spectrum of amplitude-modulated wave. (*a*) Spectrum of modulating signal. (*b*) Spectrum of amplitude-modulated wave.

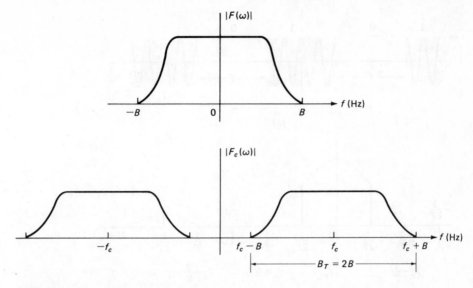

FIGURE 4-3
Example with sinusoidal roll-off shaping.

Although the signals of Fig. 4-1 are shown sketched as rectangular in shape for simplicity, they could equally well have any shaping desired. The baseband time function $f(t)$ would then incorporate the specific parameter used. Equation (4-2) and Fig. 4-2 then indicate that the shaped modulated signal of (4-1) would have the spectrum of the baseband signal shifted up to, and centered about, the carrier frequency. As an example, say that sinusoidal roll-off shaping is used, either by shaping the baseband pulses, or by shaping the high-frequency modulated pulses. The spectrum of the modulated signal looks like the baseband spectrum, shifted up to the carrier frequency f_c hertz and with a transmission bandwidth $B_T = 2B = (1/T)(1 + r)$, with r the roll-off factor [see (3-99)]. An example appears in Fig. 4-3.

Because of the form of (4-1), the frequency shift of a signal $f(t)$ due to multiplication by $\cos \omega_c t$ is a general result for AM signals. It is true for all modulating signals $f(t)$ and not just for the binary case we are in the process of considering. This will be stressed again in Sec. 4-5 in discussing AM signals in general. As an example, let $f(t) = \cos \omega_m t$, a single sine wave of frequency ω_m. Then, by trigonometry,

$$\cos \omega_m t \cos \omega_c t = \tfrac{1}{2} \cos(\omega_m + \omega_c)t + \tfrac{1}{2} \cos(\omega_m - \omega_c)t$$

The single-line spectral plot representing $\cos \omega_m t$ is thus replaced by *two* lines, symmetrically arrayed about ω_c. Similarly, if $f(t)$ is a finite sum of sine waves, each sine wave is translated up in frequency by ω_c.

As another special case, assume the signal $f(t)$ to be the single rectangular pulse of Chap. 2. (This is then the special case of a binary train in which all

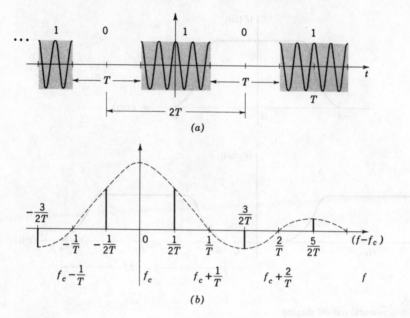

FIGURE 4-4
Spectrum, periodic OOK signal. (*a*) Periodic OOK signal. (*b*) Spectrum (positive frequencies only).

symbols are 0, except for one 1.) For a pulse of amplitude A and width T (the binary interval), the spectrum of the AM signal becomes simply

$$\frac{AT}{2}\left[\frac{\sin(\omega - \omega_c)T/2}{(\omega - \omega_c)T/2} + \frac{\sin(\omega + \omega_c)T/2}{(\omega + \omega_c)T/2}\right]$$

With an initial bandwidth of approximately $1/T$ hertz (from 0 frequency to the first zero crossing), we now have a transmission bandwidth of $2/T$ ($\pm 1/T$ about the carrier). Another special case is a binary train of alternating 1's and 0's, resulting in a periodically alternating OOK signal. The spectrum of this signal is just the $(\sin x)/x$ line spectrum of a pulse of width T, periodic with period $2T$, translated up to frequency f_c. This is shown in Fig. 4-4.

Frequency-Shift Keying

Here, if we first consider rectangular shaping for simplicity,

$$\left.\begin{array}{l} f_c(t) = A \cos \omega_1 t \\ f_c(t) = A \cos \omega_2 t \end{array}\right\} \qquad -\frac{T}{2} \le t \le \frac{T}{2} \qquad (4\text{-}3)$$

A 1 corresponds to frequency f_1, a zero to frequency f_2 (Fig. 4-5). (*Note*: Generally, f_1 and $f_2 \gg 1/T$. In some systems, particularly over 3-kHz telephone lines, f_1 and $f_2 \sim 1/T$, as shown here.) An alternative representation of the FSK

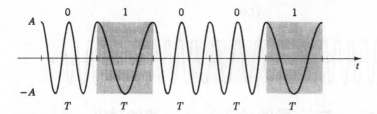

FIGURE 4-5
FSK wave.

wave consists of letting $f_1 = f_c - \Delta f$, $f_2 = f_c + \Delta f$. The two frequencies then differ by $2\,\Delta f$ hertz. Then

$$f_c(t) = A\cos(\omega_c \pm \Delta\omega)t \qquad -\frac{T}{2} \le t \le \frac{T}{2} \qquad (4\text{-}3a)$$

The frequency then deviates $\pm\Delta f$ about f_c. The quantity Δf is commonly called the *frequency deviation*. The frequency spectrum of the FSK wave $f_c(t)$ is in general difficult to obtain. We shall see this is a general characteristic of FM signals. However, one special case which provides insight into the spectral characteristics of more complex FM signals, and leads to a good rule of thumb regarding FM bandwidths, may be readily evaluated. Assume that the binary message consists of an alternating sequence of 1's and 0's. If the two frequencies are each multiples of the reciprocal of the binary period T (i.e., $f_1 = m/T$, $f_2 = n/T$, m and n integers), and are synchronized in phase, as assumed in Eq. (4-3), the FSK wave is the periodic function of Fig. 4-6. Note, however, that this may also be visualized as the linear superposition of two periodic OOK signals such as the one of Fig. 4-4, one delayed T seconds with respect to the other. The spectrum is then the linear superposition of two spectra such as the one in Fig. 4-4. Specifically, it is left for the reader to show that the positive frequency spectrum is of the form

$$\frac{\sin[(\omega_1 - \omega_n)T/2]}{(\omega_1 - \omega_n)T/2} + (-1)^n \frac{\sin[(\omega_2 - \omega_n)T/2]}{(\omega_2 - \omega_n)T/2}$$

with $\omega_n = \pi n/T$, $\omega_1 = \omega_c - \Delta\omega$, $\omega_2 = \omega_c + \Delta\omega$. This spectrum is shown sketched in Fig. 4-6 for the special case $\Delta f \gg 1/T$. The bandwidth of this periodic FSK signal is then $2\,\Delta f + 2B$, with B the bandwidth of the baseband signal. (The dashed lines shown in Fig. 4-6 are simply used to connect the discrete lines and have no significance.)

Two extreme cases are of interest:

1. If $\Delta f \gg B$, the bandwidth approaches $2\,\Delta f$. Thus, if one uses a wide separation of tones in an FSK system, the bandwidth is essentially just that separation. It is virtually independent of the bandwidth of the baseband binary signal. *This is distinctly different from the AM case.*

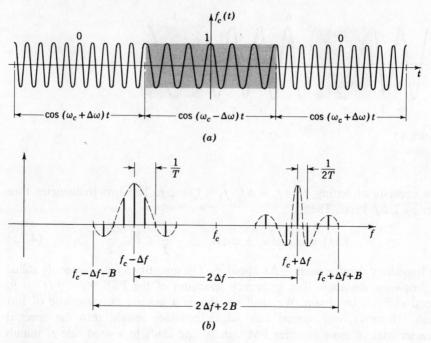

FIGURE 4-6
Spectrum, periodic FSK wave. (*a*) Periodic FSK signal. (*b*) Spectrum (positive frequencies only).

2. If $\Delta f \ll B$, the bandwidth approaches $2B$. In this case, even with the tones chosen very close together, the minimum bandwidth is still that required to transmit an OOK (AM) signal; here the bandwidth *is* determined by the baseband signal.

The first case is commonly called *wideband FM*, the second *narrowband FM*. We shall see shortly that the bandwidth $2\,\Delta f + 2B$ and its two extreme values are quite good approximations to FM bandwidths with complex modulating signals. This analysis through the use of simple binary signals provides, in addition, much more physical insight into FM bandwidth determination than is possible with complex signals. In particular, if the baseband signal is an arbitrary string of binary pulses, each shaped according to sinusoidal shaping with a roll-off factor, r, the approximate bandwidth of the corresponding FSK signal is given by $2\,\Delta f + 2B$, with $B = (1/2T)(1 + r)$, T being the baseband (or FSK) pulse width. The exact shape of the FSK spectrum is difficult to calculate, but its form would be roughly that shown in Fig. 4-7 [BENN 1965].[3]

---

[3][BENN 1965] W. R. Bennett and J. R. Davey, *Data Transmission*, McGraw-Hill, New York, 1965.

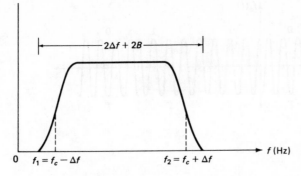

FIGURE 4-7
FSK spectrum, sinusoidal roll-off shaping (positive frequencies only).

Note that the FM transmission bandwidth is generally much greater than that for AM, which is always $2B$, that is, twice the baseband bandwidth. Then why use FM? We shall show in a later chapter that it is just this wideband property of FM that makes its performance generally far superior to AM in a noisy environment. This is analogous to the pulse-modulation results noted in Chap. 3. Encoding of pulse-amplitude-modulation (PAM) signals into binary pulse code modulation (PCM) results in an expansion of the system bandwidth, but the noise immunity increases considerably. A general characteristic of communication systems to which we shall refer after discussing noise in systems is that one can generally improve system performance in the presence of noise by encoding or modulating signals into equivalent wideband forms. Binary PCM and FM are examples of such wideband signals.

It is common in FM analysis to denote the dependence of transmission bandwidth on the relative magnitudes of the frequency deviation Δf and baseband bandwidth B by defining a parameter β, the *modulation index*, as the ratio of the two. Thus

$$\beta \equiv \frac{\Delta f}{B} \tag{4-4}$$

In terms of β the FM transmission bandwidth is

$$B_T = \text{FM bandwidth} = 2\Delta f + 2B$$

$$= 2B(1 + \beta) \tag{4-5}$$

Narrowband FM systems correspond to $\beta \ll 1$, wideband systems to $\beta \gg 1$. We shall find the modulation index β playing a significant role throughout our discussion of FM.

Phase-Shift Keying

In this case we have the phase-shift-keyed signal given as

$$f_c(t) = \pm \cos \omega_c t \qquad -\frac{T}{2} \leq t \leq \frac{T}{2} \tag{4-6}$$

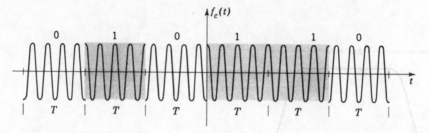

FIGURE 4-8
PSK signal.

if rectangular shaping is assumed. Here a 1 in the baseband binary stream corresponds to positive polarity, and a 0 to negative polarity. The PSK signal thus corresponds essentially to a polar NRZ binary stream (Fig. 3-65c), translated up in frequency. An example is shown in Fig. 4-8. The discontinuous-phase transitions shown at the beginning and end of each bit interval, whenever a transition from 1 to 0 or 0 to 1 takes place, are actually smoothed out during transmission because of the shaping used.[4] The information regarding polarity is, however, retained in the center of each interval, so that decoding at the receiver is normally timed to be carried out in the vicinity of the center. This is also true for OOK and FSK signals. The PSK signal has the same double-sideband characteristic as OOK transmission. Introducing roll-off shaping in the high-frequency pulses of (4-6) results in a spectrum centered at the carrier frequency f_c, with a bandwidth twice that of the shaped baseband spectrum.

Detection of Binary Signals

One may very well ask at this point which of the three binary signaling techniques discussed (and other possible ones as well) one would prefer using in practice. What are the relative advantages and disadvantages of the different techniques? We have already noted that FSK systems perform better in a noisy environment than do OOK systems. We shall show later in this book that PSK systems perform still better and, in fact, are the optimum possible for binary signaling in the presence of additive noise. (This ignores intersymbol interference and other types of distortion; it assumes that additive noise is the sole form of disturbance during transmission.)

Then why not always use PSK techniques? The answer lies in the detection process at the receiver. Recall that we modulate a sine-wave carrier with the baseband binary stream of necessity to shift the resultant modulated signal to an

---

[4] This results in a varying amplitude and can pose a problem in some systems. This leads to the need for constant-amplitude modulation schemes, a topic discussed later in Sec. 4-4.

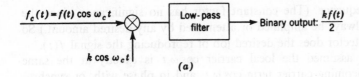

$f_c(t) = f(t) \cos \omega_c t$

Low-pass filter

Binary output: $\dfrac{kf(t)}{2}$

$k \cos \omega_c t$

(a)

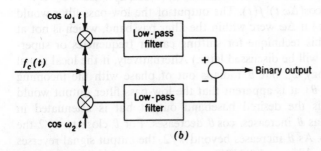

$\cos \omega_1 t$

Low-pass filter

$f_c(t)$

+

−

Binary output

$\cos \omega_2 t$

Low-pass filter

(b)

FIGURE 4-9
Synchronous detection. (a) OOK or PSK signals. (b) FSK signals.

appropriate frequency for transmission. At the receiver we must undo this process—*demodulate* the signal—to recover the original binary stream. This process of demodulation is often also called *detection*. (The binary stream must then be further processed as in Chap. 3 to eventually retrieve the individual signals contained within it.) There are essentially two common methods of demodulation. One, called *synchronous* or *coherent detection*, simply consists of multiplying the incoming signal by the carrier frequency, as locally generated at the receiver, and then low-pass-filtering the resultant multiplied signal. The other method is called *envelope detection*. The synchronous detection procedure is diagrammed in Fig. 4-9. Note that the FSK signals require *two* sine waves, one for each frequency transmitted. This is just the reverse of the original modulation process at the transmitter and serves to translate the binary signals back down to baseband.

To demonstrate the synchronous method, assume the high-frequency binary signal to have the AM form $f_c(t) = f(t)\cos \omega_c t$. [If $f(t) = \pm 1$, we have the PSK signal; if it is 1 or 0, we have the OOK case.] If we multiply this by $k \cos \omega_c t$ as indicated (k is an arbitrary constant of the multiplier), we get $kf(t)\cos^2 \omega_c t = (k/2)(1 + \cos 2\omega_c t)f(t)$.[5] But the term $f(t)\cos 2\omega_c t$ represents $f(t)$ translated up to frequency $2f_c$, the second harmonic of the carrier frequency f_c. This is rejected by the low-pass filter and the output is $(k/2)f(t)$, just the desired

---

[5]This discussion again assumes rectangular shaping for simplicity. Non-rectangular-shaped pulses are easily included by letting $f(t)$ provide the desired baseband shape.

baseband binary sequence. (The constant factor has no significance, since the output signal can always be amplified or attenuated by any desired amount.) So the synchronous detector does the desired job of reproducing the signal $f(t)$.

But we have assumed the local carrier $\cos \omega_c t$ is exactly at the same frequency as the incoming carrier term $\cos \omega_c t$, and in phase with, or synchronized to, it as well. If the locally generated sine wave were at a frequency $\cos(\omega_c + \Delta\omega)t$, the multiplication would generate $kf(t)\cos(\omega_c + \Delta\omega)t \cos \omega_c t = (k/2)[\cos(2\omega_c + \Delta\omega)t + \cos(\Delta\omega\, t)]f(t)$. The output of the low-pass filter would then be $[kf(t)/2]\cos(\Delta\omega\, t)$ if $\Delta\omega$ were within the filter passband, which is not at all the desired signal. (This technique for shifting carrier frequencies or superheterodyning AM signals will be discussed later.) Alternatively, if the local signal were at the right frequency ω_c, but θ radians out of phase with the incoming carrier, that is, $\cos(\omega_c t + \theta)$, it is apparent that the low-pass filter output would be $[kf(t)/2]\cos\theta$. This is the desired baseband output but is attenuated in amplitude. In particular, as θ increases, $\cos\theta$ decreases. For θ close to $\pi/2$ the output is very nearly zero. As θ increases beyond $\pi/2$, the output signal reverses sign. If the baseband signal is a polar NRZ sequence, the entire signal reverses polarity and all 1's become 0's, all 0's become 1's. So the locally generated carrier must be not only at the same frequency, but also synchronized in phase as well. This is the reason for the term *synchronous* detection.

Phase synchronism is quite difficult to attain, particularly if transmission takes place over long distances. This means that a receiver clock which provides the synchronism must be synchronized or slaved to the transmitter clock to within a fraction of a carrier cycle, no mean task. As an example, if transmission is at $f_c = 3$ MHz with a period $1/f_c = 0.3\ \mu s$ (this is in the so-called h-f band, used for short-wave broadcasting), a phase difference $\theta \ll \pi/2$ radians implies clock synchronization to within much less than a quarter of a period, or much less than $0.07\ \mu s$. At a carrier frequency of 100 MHz, $\pi/2$ radians corresponds to 2.5 ns, while at a carrier frequency of 1,000 MHz, this is 0.25 ns. Phase synchronization is thus quite a difficult task. It is particularly difficult if either the transmitter or receiver is mounted on a rapidly moving vehicle introducing doppler phase shifts proportional to the relative velocity between transmitter and receiver. If the relative velocities change rapidly enough, the phase shifts in turn change rapidly and synchronism cannot be maintained. The same problem arises if the signal transmission takes place through a fading medium in which randomly moving scatterers also introduce random doppler phase shifts. The problem is particularly acute in the case of digital lightwave (optical) transmission. Current lightwave technology uses on–off-keyed, noncoherent transmission, with envelope detection at the receiver. Coherent-optical-detection experiments have been carried out, however, demonstrating a significant improvement over the OOK technique [LINK].[6] Such systems, when improved to the point where they

---

[6][LINK] R. A. Linke and P. S. Henry, "Coherent Optical Detection: A Thousand Calls on One Circuit," *IEEE Spectrum*, February 1987, pp. 52–57.

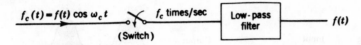

FIGURE 4-10
Another synchronous detector.

are commercially feasible and cost-effective, would clearly find a ready market. A comparative discussion of coherent and noncoherent light-wave transmission appears in Chap. 6.

The reader may have recognized already that this problem of maintaining synchronism is similar to that encountered in baseband binary transmission in Chap. 3. The problem here, however, is a much more difficult one; the synchronism previously considered was, for example, from bit interval to bit interval. With high carrier frequencies, $1/f_c \ll T$, the bit interval, so that the problem is compounded. As with the baseband digital synchronization case, various methods are available for obtaining the required phasing information.

1. A pilot carrier may be transmitted and superimposed on the high-frequency binary signal stream, which may be extracted at the receiver and used to synchronize the receiver local oscillator (this is similar to the marker or timing pulses transmitted with the baseband data stream to maintain bit interval, word, and frame synchronism).
2. A phase-locked loop, locking on either the data stream of a pilot tone, may be used at the receiver to drive the phase difference to zero [VITE 1966],[7] etc.

We shall have more to say about synchronous detection later in this chapter, as well as in the discussions on binary transmission in the presence of noise. It is interesting to note, however, that it is not really necessary to physically multiply by a pure sine wave to obtain the desired demodulated form $f(t)\cos^2 \omega_c t$. Switching or gating $f_c(t)\cos \omega_c t$ on and off at a rate of f_c times per second and then using low-pass filtering will accomplish the same job (see Fig. 4-10). This is apparent from a consideration of the switching function of Chap. 3. All-digital gating circuits are in fact often simpler to design and use for this purpose than is multiplication by a pure sine wave. [If the baseband binary stream contains time-multiplexed information, further switching (see Chap. 3) is then necessary to separate out the individual signals. But this switching, gating, or commutating function is of course carried out at the much slower baseband rate.]

The difficulty of maintaining phase synchronism notwithstanding, PSK transmission and phase-locked loop synchronous detection has been successfully used in space communications. The Pioneer V deep-space probe, as an example,

---

[7][VITE 1966] A. J. Viterbi, *Principles of Coherent Communication*, McGraw-Hill, New York, 1966, chap. 2.

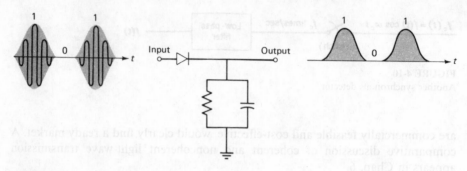

FIGURE 4-11
Envelope detector.

used biphase modulation in its telemetry system. As already noted, coherent communication has been successfully demonstrated in optical experiments.

The other common form of detection, *envelope detection*, avoids the timing and phasing problems of synchronous detection. Here the incoming high-frequency signal is passed through a nonlinear device and low-pass filter. Envelope detection will be considered later in this chapter in discussing more general AM signals and receivers. Suffice it to say at this point that one common form of envelope detector for radio communications is a diode half-wave rectifier (the nonlinear device) followed by an *RC* low-pass filter (Fig. 4-11). As the name indicates, the output of the detector represents the envelope of the incoming high-frequency wave. The *RC* time constant is long enough to hold the incoming amplitude over many carrier cycles, yet short enough compared to a binary period to discharge once the binary signal changes. For optical communications a photodetector is required. *p-i-n* diodes and avalanche photodiodes are used [HENR 1985b].[8] These will both be discussed briefly in Chap. 6 in determining the performance of optical communication systems.

Notice one difficulty in using envelope detection, however. The PSK signal has a *constant* envelope (Fig. 4-8), so that it cannot be used with an envelope detector. Thus the PSK system *requires* synchronous detection. As usual, there is a trade-off in economics. One may avoid using synchronous detection by adopting envelope detection, but at the price of requiring FSK or OOK transmission, rather than the more optimum (in the presence of noise) PSK system.[9] We shall also show in discussing the effects of noise, in later chapters, that envelope detection of OOK or FSK signals is somewhat inferior to synchronous detection

---

[8][HENR 1985b] P. S. Henry, "Lightwave Primer," *IEEE J. Quantum Electronics*, vol. QE-21, no. 12, pp. 1862–1879, December 1985.

[9]This is why the space communication systems have used synchronous detection, the cost notwithstanding. The reduction possible in transmitter power is worth the price there. This is also the reason for the great interest in coherent optical communication, as already noted.

of these signals. An additional price must thus be paid for this much simpler circuit, although in this case it can be demonstrated that the cost will not be too great.

The envelope-detection process requires the presence of an unchanging carrier term in addition to the varying high-frequency binary signal. This is the reason envelope detection cannot be used with PSK signals. To demonstrate this point consider an OOK signal $f_c(t) = Af(t)\cos \omega_c t$. Recall that $f(t)$ is a random sequence of 1's and 0's. Squaring the expression (this is the simplest nonlinear operation that demonstrates the envelope-detection process), we get $A^2 f^2(t)\cos^2 \omega_c t$. With rectangular shaping $f(t) = 1$ or 0, so $f^2(t) = 1$ or 0 as well. The output of a low-pass filter is then $A^2/2$ or 0, reproducing the derived 1, 0 sequence. In the case of the PSK signal, however, $f(t) = \pm 1$, $f^2(t) = 1$, and the output is *always* $A^2/2$. There are other ways of analyzing the envelope detector, and these are considered in discussions of AM systems, as well as in the problems at the end of this chapter.

To conclude the discussion of binary signaling at this point, we show in Fig. 4-12 a diagram of a complete time-multiplexed PCM system. This includes the initial time-multiplexing and A/D circuitry (the latter includes the quantization and binary encoding operations); the modulator which produces the high-frequency binary signals; then, at the receiver, the demodulator, which includes a synchronous or envelope detector, a binary decoder, and a switch or commutator circuitry for unscrambling the time-multiplexed signals; and finally low-pass filters in each output channel for providing the final output signals. Note that this is essentially the same set of blocks discussed in Chap. 3, but with the addition of the high-frequency modulator and demodulator.

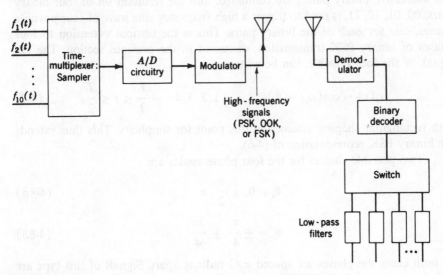

FIGURE 4-12
Complete PCM system.

4-3 MODULATION TECHNIQUES FOR DIGITAL COMMUNICATIONS: MULTISYMBOL SIGNALING

In the previous section we have focused on the simplest forms of digital carrier systems, those involving binary amplitude, phase, or frequency modulation. We noted in Chap. 3, particularly in Secs. 3-4 and 3-10, that the bandwidth required to transmit a baseband digital sequence could be reduced by going to multilevel signaling: combining successive binary pulses to form a longer pulse requiring a correspondingly smaller bandwidth for transmission. This was generalized in Sec. 3-10 to include the concept of multisymbol signaling. Specifically, with ideal Nyquist shaping 2 (symbols/s)/Hz can be transmitted over the Nyquist bandwidth of B hertz. If a set of $M = 2^k$ symbols is used, with k the number of successive binary digits combined to form the appropriate symbol to be transmitted, $2k$ (bits/s)/Hz may be transmitted using the Nyquist band.

In this section we specifically discuss multiphase, multiamplitude, and combined multiphase/multiamplitude signaling schemes as examples of multisymbol systems. These are used quite commonly in telephone, microwave, and satellite data communications, and we shall refer to examples from these application areas later in this section. Multifrequency schemes are also used in practice, but for a different purpose: they generally result in *larger*, rather than reduced bandwidths, because of the requirement to space multiple frequency carriers far enough apart. They provide improved noise immunity as a result, however, Multifrequency schemes will be discussed in Chap. 7. Multisymbol signals are often called *M*-ary signals.

As the first example of a multisymbol scheme, consider a system in which two successive binary pulses are combined, and the resultant set of four binary pairs, 00, 01, 10, 11, is used to trigger a high-frequency sine wave of four possible phases, one for each of the binary pairs. This is the obvious extension to four phases of binary PSK transmission, discussed in the previous section. The ith signal, of the four possible, can be written

$$s_i(t) = \cos(\omega_c t + \theta_i) \qquad i = 1, 2, 3, 4 \qquad -\frac{T}{2} \le t \le \frac{T}{2} \qquad (4\text{-}7)$$

with rectangular shaping assumed at this point for simplicity. This thus extends the binary PSK representation of (4-6).

Two possible choices for the four phase angles are

$$\theta_i = 0, \pm \frac{\pi}{2}, \pi \qquad (4\text{-}8a)$$

$$\theta_i = \pm \frac{\pi}{4}, \pm \frac{3\pi}{4} \qquad (4\text{-}8b)$$

In both cases the phases are spaced $\pi/2$ radians apart. Signals of this type are called *quaternary PSK* (QPSK) signals. They are a special case of multi-PSK (MPSK) signals. Binary PSK signals are sometimes labeled BPSK as well.

In general, as already noted, k successive binary pulses are stored up and one of $M = 2^k$ symbols is outputted. If the binary rate is R bits/s, each binary pulse interval is $1/R$ seconds long. The corresponding output symbol is then $T = k/R$ seconds long. The signals of (4-7) may be represented, by trigonometric expansion, in the following form:

$$s_i(t) = a_i \cos \omega_c t + b_i \sin \omega_c t \qquad -\frac{T}{2} \leq t \leq \frac{T}{2} \qquad (4\text{-}9)$$

For the case of (4-8a), the pairs (a_i, b_i) are given, corresponding respectively to the angles $\theta_i = 0$, $-\pi/2$, π, and $\pi/2$, by

$$(a_i, b_i) = (1, 0), (0, 1), (-1, 0), (0, -1) \qquad (4\text{-}10)$$

The corresponding sets of (a_i, b_i) for (4-8b) are given by

$$\left(\sqrt{2}\, a_i, \sqrt{2}\, b_i\right) = (1, 1), (-1, 1), (-1, -1), (1, -1) \qquad (4\text{-}11)$$

Transmission of this type is often called *quadrature transmission*, with two carriers in phase quadrature to one another ($\cos \omega_c t$ and $\sin \omega_c t$) transmitted simultaneously over the same channel.

It is useful to represent the signals of (4-9) in a two-dimensional diagram by locating the various points (a_i, b_i). The horizontal axis corresponding to the location of a_i is called the *inphase axis*. The vertical axis, along which b_i is located, is called the *quadrature axis*. The four signals of (4-10) then appear as shown in Fig. 4-13a, those of (4-11) in Fig. 4-13b. The signal points are said to represent a *signal constellation*.

The inphase (cosine) and quadrature (sine) representation of the QPSK signals $s_i(t)$ suggests one possible way of generating these signals: two successive binary input pulses are stored up, and the pair of numbers (a_i, b_i), taken every $T = 2/R$ seconds, is used to modulate two quadrature carrier terms, $\cos \omega_c t$ and $\sin \omega_c t$, respectively. Where one of the numbers is zero, that carrier is of course disabled. A modulator of this type is shown in Fig. 4-14a. An example, using the (a_i, b_i) pairs of (4-10), is shown in Fig. 4-14b.

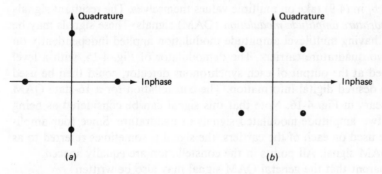

FIGURE 4-13
QPSK signal constellations.

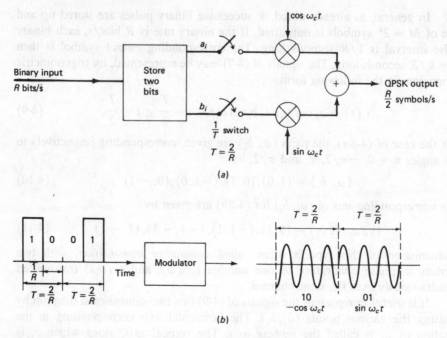

FIGURE 4-14
Generation of QPSK signals. (*a*) Modulator. (*b*) Example corresponding to Eq. (4-10).

It is apparent that demodulation is carried out by using two synchronous detectors in parallel, one in quadrature with the other. A comparison of the two detector outputs then determines the particular binary pair transmitted. A block diagram of such a demodulator appears in Fig. 4-15.

Quadrature Amplitude Modulation

More general types of multisymbol signaling schemes may be generated by letting a_i and b_i in (4-9) take on multiple values themselves. The resultant signals are called *quadrature amplitude modulation* (QAM) signals. These signals may be interpreted as having multilevel amplitude modulation applied independently on each of the two quadrature carriers. The demodulator of Fig. 4-15, with a level detector applied at the output of each synchronous detector, could then be used to recover the desired digital information. The constellation for a 16-state QAM signal set appears in Fig. 4-16. Note that this signal can be considered as being generated by two amplitude-modulated signals in quadrature. Since four amplitude levels are used on each of the carriers, the signal is sometimes referred to as a four-level QAM signal. All points in the constellation are equally spaced.

It is apparent that the general QAM signal may also be written

$$s_i(t) = r_i \cos(\omega_c t + \theta_i) \tag{4-12}$$

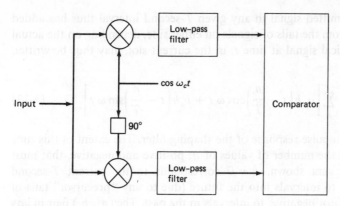

FIGURE 4-15
QPSK demodulator (a possible implementation).

with the amplitude r_i and phase angle θ_i given by the appropriate combinations of (a_i, b_i). A phase-detector–amplitude-level-detector combination could then also be used to extract the digital information.

We have neglected signal shaping up to now, just as in the previous section. This is apparent from the rectangular input signals and the sharp phase discontinuities shown in the output modulated signals of Fig. 4-14b. In practice, signal shaping, using, for example, the sinusoidal roll-off spectrum of Sec. 3-10 (Fig. 3-63) must be used to reduce intersymbol interference. This is particularly important for multilevel signaling, as already noted in Sec. 3-10. An actual modulator would thus have the input binary pulses shaped before modulating the carrier. Alternatively, the successive output signals of Fig. 4-14 would each be passed through an appropriate bandpass shaping filter before being transmitted.

As the result of shaping, an individual output symbol, nominally designed to fit into the interval T seconds long, may now span several T-second intervals. (The object is to shape the pulses, however, so that they go through zero at the decision points spaced T seconds apart in the other intervals. See Fig. 3-60, for

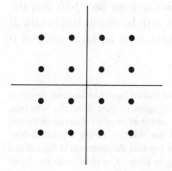

FIGURE 4-16
Four-level (16-symbol) QAM constellation.

example.) The transmitted signal in any given T-second interval thus has added to it contributions from the tails of signals on either side, depending on the actual shaping used. A typical signal at time t, in the current slot, may thus be written as

$$s(t) = \sum_n \left[a_n h\left(t - \frac{n}{T}\right) \cos \omega_c t + b_n h\left(t - \frac{n}{T}\right) \sin \omega_c t \right] \qquad (4\text{-}13)$$

$h(t)$ represents the impulse response of the shaping filter. The extent of this time response determines the number of values of n, positive and negative, that must be included in the sum shown. $n = 0$ corresponds to the current T-second interval; n positive, to intervals into the future (due to any "precursor" tails of symbols transmitted); n negative, to intervals in the past. The (a_n, b_n) pair in any interval represents the one of the possible pair values actually transmitted in that interval.

Letting $t = 0$ (the center of the interval) be the signal sampling point, $h(-n/T)$, $n \neq 0$, should be zero for intersymbol interference to be absent. If $h(-n/T) \neq 0$, (4-13) can be used to determine the extent of intersymbol interference.

From the form of (4-13) it is apparent that the general QAM signal must have a spectrum centered about the carrier frequency $f_c = \omega_c/2\pi$. There will be upper and lower sidebands extending a bandwidth B hertz, respectively, above and below the carrier frequency, corresponding to the baseband signal shifted up to frequency f_c. The shaping of the sidebands depends on the shaping filter $h(t)$.[10] An example appears in Fig. 4-17. The transmission bandwidth B_T is $2B$ hertz, as shown.

In practice, shaping is done both at the transmitter, as part of the modulation process, and at the receiver, in conjunction with the demodulation process. The Nyquist shaping characteristic to which we have referred many times, beginning in Chap. 3, represents the combination of these two filtering operations.

Using the discussion of Nyquist shaping in Sec. 3-10 and the discussion thus far in this section, one may determine the particular form of QAM, and the type of shaping required, to transmit specified bit rates over various channels. Specifically, say the transmission bandwidth is B_T hertz. This then corresponds to a baseband bandwidth of $B = B_T/2$ hertz. We know from Sec. 3-10 that the symbol rate that may be transmitted over a channel with baseband bandwidth B hertz is $2B/(1 + r)$, where the roll-off factor r varies from an ideal value of 0

---

[10] With no intersymbol interference the spectrum of an individual pulsed carrier in any one T-second interval is given exactly by the transform $H(\omega)$ of $h(t)$, the Nyquist shaping filter characteristic, shifted up to f_c. More generally, one must take into account the contribution of all intervals in finding the spectrum of the transmitted signal $s(t)$. This depends on the statistics of the amplitude-level sequence $\{a_n, b_n\}$. Details appear in [BENN 1965]. Suffice it to say that the spectrum is determined primarily by $H(\omega)$, so that we may still talk of Nyquist shaping in Chap. 3, applied to single digital pulses, as appropriate to a complete sequence of such pulses.

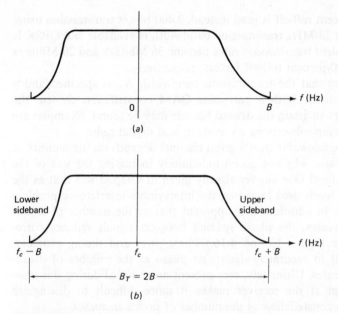

FIGURE 4-17
QAM spectrum. (*a*) Baseband spectrum. (*b*) QAM spectrum.

(for ideal low-pass filtering) to 1 (for raised-cosine filtering). The symbol rate allowable over the equivalent transmission channel of bandwidth B_T hertz is thus $B_T/(1 + r)$ symbols/s. For a QAM signal with $M = 2^k$ possible symbols or states, the allowable bit rate is $kB_T/(1 + r)$ bits/s, or $k/(1 + r)$ (bits/s)/Hz of *transmission* bandwidth. Some examples of the allowable bit rate per hertz appear in Table 4-1.

As an example, a channel with a 2.4-kHz bandwidth will allow $2,400 \times 1.8 = 4,300$ bits/s transmission if four-state QAM (equivalent to four-phase PSK or QPSK; see Fig. 4-13) is used, and pulse shaping with a 10-percent roll-off factor

TABLE 4-1
Allowable bit rates per unit transmission bandwidth, QAM transmission

	Allowable bit rate [(bits / s) / Hz]			
M (No. of states)	$r = 0.1^{\dagger}$	0.25	0.5	1
2	0.9	0.8	0.67	0.5
4	1.8	1.6	1.33	1.0
8	2.7	2.4	2.0	1.5
16	3.6	3.2	2.67	2.0

† Roll-off factor.

is adopted. If 100-percent roll-off is used instead, 2,400 bits/s transmission using QPSK is possible. If a 20-MHz transmission bandwidth is available and QPSK is again used, the equivalent transmission rates become 36 Mbits/s and 20 Mbits/s for 10-percent and 100-percent roll-off factors, respectively.

Alternatively, say that the transmission bandwidth B_T is specified and a certain bit rate is desired. With a particular QAM constellation chosen, the roll-off factor necessary to attain the desired bit rate may be found. Examples are provided in the following subsections on modems and digital radio.

Since the bit rate allowable over a given channel depends on the number of symbols or states chosen, why not go on indefinitely increasing the size of the QAM signal constellation? One answer already given in Chap. 3 was that as the number of amplitude levels used increases, the intersymbol-interference problem becomes more severe. In addition, it is apparent that as the number of distin-guishable phases increases, the phase spacing between signals reduces corre-spondingly. (Compare Figs. 4-13 and 4-16.) Phase jitter and timing problems make it more difficult to accurately determine phase as the number of distin-guishable phases increases. Ultimately, ever-present noise added during transmis-sion and in reception at the receiver makes it more difficult to distinguish individual points in a constellation as the number of points increases.

A little thought will indicate that the specific location of the points in the constellations of Figs. 4-13 and 4-16 depends on the actual amplitudes of the signals. As the amplitudes increase, the points move out. As they decrease, the points move in. For a fixed transmitter power level, the location of the points is restricted. The only way to add more states, or points in the constellation, is to put points between those already existing. The resultant points are spaced closer together, and noise and phase jitter will produce errors in detection more often. (The effect of noise will be considered in detail in Chap. 7.) There is thus a limit on the number of QAM states that may be used.

Modems: Application to Telephone Data Sets

A complete system for generating the modulated signals of (4-13), or the equivalent signal constellation as shown, for example, in Fig. 4-16, and then reproducing the baseband binary signals after reception, consists of a transmitter and a receiver. A simplified block diagram of a QAM transmitter–receiver combination, based on the discussion thus far, appears in Fig. 4-18. The trans-mitter shown there is often referred to as a modulator, even though the modula-tor itself may only represent a portion of the transmitter. It must contain input buffer memory to store the k successive binary pulses required to generate the particular output signal corresponding to the binary sequence, shaping filters, and an oscillator for generating the inphase and quadrature carrier terms.

Two-way transmission (either simultaneously or one way at a time) is commonly carried out over transmission channels. Binary digits are thus accepted by the transmitter for transmission over the channel, while modulated signals, coming from the other direction, are processed by a receiver and converted to a

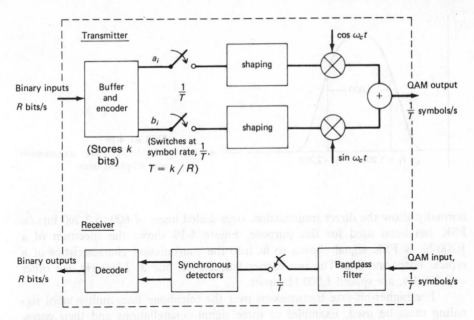

FIGURE 4-18
Simple diagram of a QAM modem.

desired binary output. Figure 4-18 shows such a receiver, often called a demodulator. The two devices, *mo*dulator and *dem*odulator, are most often packaged in one unit called a *modem*, as shown in Fig. 4-18. (The word "modem" is taken from the initial letters of both, shown italicized above.) Left out in the basic diagram of Fig. 4-18 are such important implementation details as carrier tracking and synchronization circuitry; a binary scrambler–descrambler combination if a Gray code is used (Sec. 3-4); additional adaptive filters at the receiver, called *adaptive equalizers* [LUCK] which automatically adjust their characteristics to compensate for intersymbol interference that may appear; etc.

Modems have been widely adopted for the transmission of digital data over various transmission media. In this subsection we provide examples of modems designed for use over the 3-kHz telephone voice band. In the next subsection we discuss much higher-bit-rate modems designed for use with digital radio (microwave) systems.

Voice-band modems have a long history, starting with research activities in the 1950s [PAHL].[11] Recall that the bandwidth properties of voice-band telephone lines were mentioned briefly in Secs. 3-2 to 3-4 in discussing the generation of PCM signals. They were referred to again in Sec. 3-10 when discussing Nyquist shaping. These lines accept signals in the range 300 to 3.3 kHz. They will

---

[11][PAHL] K. Pahlavan and J. L. Holsinger, "Voice-Band Data Communication Modems— A. Historical Review: 1919–1988," *IEEE Commun. Mag.*, vol. 26, no. 1, pp. 16–27, January 1988.

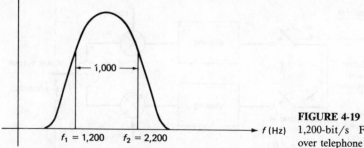

FIGURE 4-19
1,200-bit/s FSK transmission over telephone lines.

normally allow the direct transmission, over dialed lines, of 600 to 1,200 bits/s. FSK has been used for this purpose. Figure 4-19 shows the spectrum of a 1,200-bit/s FSK signal chosen to fit into the transmission characteristics of a typical telephone line. The two carrier frequencies, one at 1,200 Hz, the other at 2,200 Hz, are spaced 1,000 Hz apart.

For higher-bit-rate transmission over the telephone line, multisymbol signaling must be used. Examples of three signal constellations and their corresponding transmission spectra, used in 2,400-, 4,800-, and 9,600-bit/s modems, respectively, appear in Fig. 4-20 [KRET].[12] The amplitude spectra shown are scaled in decibels, the 6-dB points corresponding to one-half the peak amplitude. These points thus correspond to the cutoff frequency of the low-pass Nyquist shaping filters discussed in Sec. 3-10. The 2,400-bit/s modem uses a QPSK or four-phase PSK constellation, with raised-cosine signal shaping, as shown. The 4,800-bit/s modem uses eight-phase PSK (the signal points are spaced 45° apart on a circle) and a 50-percent roll-off filtering characteristic. A 16-point QAM signal constellation, with points equally spaced, as shown in Fig. 4-20c, is used for the 9,600-bit/s modem. The lower-bit-rate modems use the frequency range 600 to 3,000 Hz as the transmission bandwidth, with the carrier at the center. For the 9,600-bit/s modem a wider frequency range, from 300 to 3,000 Hz is needed. It is left to the reader to demonstrate that the signals of Fig. 4-20 do provide the transmission capabilities indicated.

9,600-bit/s modems of the type shown in Fig. 4-20 became commercially available in the 1970s, but could be used only over specially conditioned (filtered) lines leased from the telephone companies. They could not be used over the public switched telephone networks. In the 1980s AT & T introduced a 9,600-bit/s modem capable of operating over public switched networks. This used QAM plus *trellis coding*, a technique to be described in Chap. 7. The trellis-coding technique used has since been adopted as a CCITT Recommendation [PAHL].

---

[12][KRET] E. R. Kretzmer, "The Evolution of Techniques for Data Communication over Voiceband Channels," *IEEE Commun. Soc. Mag.*, vol. 16, no. 1, pp. 10–14, January 1978.

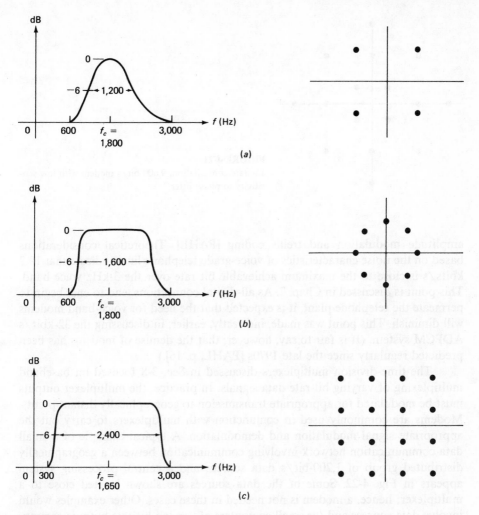

FIGURE 4-20
Spectra and constellations for higher-speed modems. (*a*) 2,400-bit/s, 4-phase PSK, raised cosine characteristic. (*b*) 4,800-bit/s, 8-phase PSK, 50-percent roll-off. (*c*) 16-state QAM, 9,600 bits/s, 10-percent roll-off.

Another 9,600-bit/s signal constellation, used by various modem manufacturers in the United States and adopted as an international standard by the CCITT for use with conditioned lines, appears in Fig. 4-21. This constellation, called a modified four-phase/four-amplitude system, has its points located at the relative distances of ±1, ±3, and ±5 units from the origin. It provides particularly low sensitivity to phase jitter.

Higher-bit-rate voice modems, operating at 14.4, 16.8, and 19.2 kbits/s, became available in the 1980s. These also use a combination of quadrature

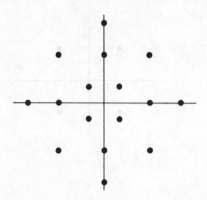

FIGURE 4-21
16-state constellation, 9,600-bit/s modem with low sensitivity to phase jitter.

amplitude modulation and trellis coding [PAHL]. Theoretical considerations based on the noise characteristics of voice-grade telephone lines indicate that 19.2 kbits/s is close to the maximum achievable bit rate over the 3-kHz voice band. This point is discussed in Chap. 7. As all-digital connections, end to end, begin to permeate the telephone plant, it is expected that the need for voice-band modems will diminish. This point was made, indirectly, earlier, in discussing the 32-kbit/s ADPCM system. (It is fair to say, however, that the demise of modems has been predicted regularly since the late 1970s [PAHL, p. 16].)

The time-division multiplexers discussed in Sec. 3-8 focused on baseband multiplexing of varying bit-rate data signals. In practice, the multiplexer outputs must be modulated for appropriate transmission to geographically distant points. Modems are commonly used in conjunction with multiplexers to carry out the appropriate signal modulation and demodulation. A typical example of a small data communication network involving communication between a geographically distributed group of 1,200-bit/s data sources and a central processing system appears in Fig. 4-22. Some of the data sources are shown located close to a multiplexer; hence, a modem is not needed in these cases. Other examples would involve data sources and/or small computers of varying bit-rate outputs communicating with one another, or with a large central computer [SCHW 1977, chaps. 2, 12; Appendix]. The use of multiplexers and the corresponding higher-speed modems, as shown in Fig. 4-22, results in reduced communications cost. Only one telephone line need be used, in this example, in linking terminals in the Midwest of the United States to the computer in New York City.

It was noted in Chap. 1 that much of modern telecommunications is network-oriented. The public switched telephone network with which we are all familiar is one example. The data network of Fig. 4-22, a portion of which could use the dialed public switched network (a portion of which might be overlaid on the telephone network, using lines and facilities leased from telephone companies), provides another example. Thus far in this book we have been discussing only the *point-to-point* aspects of communications over such a network, from modem to modem, or modems to TDM for digital multiplexing. In Chap. 5 we

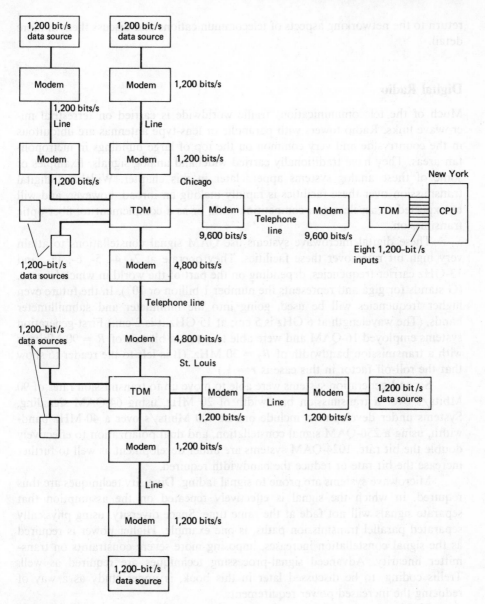

FIGURE 4-22
Example of a small data network: communication between terminals and central computer.

return to the networking aspects of telecommunications and discuss them in more detail.

Digital Radio

Much of the telecommunications traffic worldwide is carried on terrestrial microwave links. Radio towers with parabolic or lens-type antennas are ubiquitous in the countryside and very common on the top of large buildings in metropolitan areas. They have traditionally carried wideband analog signals. Examples of some of these analog systems appear later in this chapter. Wideband digital transmission over these facilities is rapidly making an inroad, however, and will be expected to accelerate in competition with, or as a complement to, fiber-optic transmission.

These digital microwave systems use QAM signal constellations to attain very high bit rates over these facilities. They operate at 2-, 4-, 5-, 6-, 11-, and 13-GHz carrier frequencies, depending on the part of the world in which located. (G stands for giga and represents the number 1 billion or 10^9). In the future even higher frequencies will be used, going into the millimeter and submillimeter bands. (The wavelength at 6 GHz is 5 cm; at 15 GHz it is 2 cm.) First-generation systems employed 16-QAM and were able to attain a bit rate of $R = 90$ Mbits/s with a transmission bandwidth of $B_T = 30$ MHz. (It is left to the reader to show that the roll-off factor in this case is $r = \frac{1}{3}$.)

Second-generation systems were able to move up to transmission rates of 90 Mbits/s over a transmission bandwidth of 20 MHz, using 64-QAM signaling. Systems under development include one at 400 Mbits/s over a 40-MHz bandwidth, using a 256-QAM signal constellation, and dual polarization to effectively double the bit rate. 1024-QAM systems are under development as well to further increase the bit rate or reduce the bandwidth required.

Microwave systems are prone to signal fading. Diversity techniques are thus required, in which the signal is effectively repeated on the assumption that separate signals will not fade at the same time. Space diversity, using physically separated parallel transmission paths, is one example. Higher power is required as the signal constellation increases, imposing more severe constraints on transmitter linearity. Advanced signal-processing techniques are required as well. Trellis coding, to be discussed later in this book, is under study as a way of reducing the increased power requirements.

The international radio communication standards body, the CCIR (the International Consultative Committee on Radio Communications), has proposed a digital microwave hierarchy. Portions of this hierarchy appear in Table 4-2, taken from a paper on future trends in microwave digital radio [HART].[13] This

---

[13][HART] G. Hart and J. A. Steinkamp, "Future Trends in Microwave Digital Radio: A View from Europe," *IEEE Commun. Mag.*, vol. 25, no. 2, pp. 49–52, February 1987.

TABLE 4-2
CCIR recommendations, digital microwave [HART, p. 50, Table 1]

Channel bandwidth	Recommended constellation			
B_T (MHz)	Bit rate: 64	140	280	560 Mbits / s
40	QPSK	16-QAM	256-QAM	256-QAM[†]
30	8-PSK	64-QAM	1024-QAM	
20	16-QAM	256-QAM	256-QAM[†]	

[†] Dual polarization.

paper is one of several describing the future of the field [IEEE 1987a].[14] A detailed discussion of digital radio systems appears in [IEEE 1987b].[15]

The performance of these digital microwave radio QAM systems is discussed later in this book, in Chap. 7, and is there compared with the "best possible" system for the same environment. The fact that additional power is required as the number of points in the signal constellation increases will be demonstrated quantitatively.

4-4 MINIMUM-SHIFT KEYING: CONSTANT-ENVELOPE MODULATION

It was noted earlier, in discussing PSK, that phase discontinuities may occur at the bit transition point. (See Fig. 4-8.) This would be smoothed out with appropriate signal shaping but would clearly result in a varying-amplitude signal. In communication systems with a nonlinearity following the signal generation point this would result in a broadened signal spectrum and hence increased signal bandwidth. This will be demonstrated in a later section. A similar problem arises in the generation and transmission of QPSK (4-phase PSK) signals, as will be demonstrated shortly. These signals are commonly used in satellite communication applications because of their reduced bandwidth requirements. Amplifiers in satellite systems are operated near their power saturation point for better efficiency. This is the highly nonlinear region and will result in a broadening of the signal spectrum unless the signal amplitude (envelope) is kept constant. Other high-power communication systems pose a similar problem. It is thus of interest to consider digital modulation schemes that maintain constant amplitude.

A series of such schemes have been invented and studied in recent years. These schemes are bandwidth-efficient and provide good performance in noise, both important attributes. We focus on one scheme only, called minimum-shift

[14][IEEE 1987a] "Future Trends in Microwave Digital Radio, Views from Asia, North America, and Europe," *IEEE Commun. Mag.*, vol. 25, no. 2, pp. 40–52, February 1987.

[15][IEEE 1987b] "Advances in Digital Communications by Radio," *IEEE J. Selected Areas Commun.*, vol. SAC-5, no. 3, April 1987.

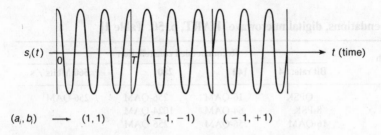

FIGURE 4-23
QPSK signal showing phase discontinuities.

keying (MSK). It is sometimes also called offset QPSK (OQPSK). Other schemes, including generalizations of MSK, are described in the literature [JAGE], [IEEE 1981], [SUND].[16]

To introduce the basic concepts of MSK we first start with QPSK [PASU].[17] Recall from Fig. 4-13, as well as (4-7) to (4-11), that in this system successive pairs of binary digits are combined to form four possible phases of a carrier. Alternatively, the system may be looked at as one transmitting simultaneously an inphase and a quadrature sinusoidal signal. This halves the bandwidth required to transmit the incoming bit stream. To simplify our discussion here we rewrite (4-9) in the following form:

$$s_i(t) = a_i \cos\left(\omega_c t + \frac{\pi}{4}\right) + b_i \sin\left(\omega_c t + \frac{\pi}{4}\right) \quad 0 < t < T \quad (4\text{-}14)$$

We have simply shifted the time origin by half a period and have added a phase factor of $\pi/4$.

In this representation we let both a_i and b_i be ± 1, a_i corresponding to the first bit of a pair, b_i to the second bit. Using this representation, we sketch in Fig. 4-23 a typical sequence of QPSK output signals, corresponding, respectively, to $(a_i, b_i) = (1, 1)$, $(-1, -1)$, and $(-1, +1)$. We have arbitrarily chosen the carrier frequency f_c to be $3/T$. Notice that when a_i and b_i *both* switch signal from one T-second interval to the next the phase of $s_i(t)$ shifts by π radians. (There is a $\pi/2$ phase shift when only one of the bits changes sign, as shown in Fig. 4-23.) The QPSK signal is typically smoothed or band-limited, resulting in a variable envelope in the vicinity of the phase discontinuity. The envelope would in fact go to zero as $s_i(t)$ changed sign. Hard-limiting this smoothed signal, as would be

[16][JAGE] F. de Jager and C. B. Dekker, "Tamed Frequency Modulation, a Novel Method to Achieve Spectrum Economy in Digital Transmission," *IEEE Trans. Commun.*, vol. COM-26, no. 5, pp. 534–542, May 1978. [IEEE 1981] Special Section on Combined Modulation and Coding, *IEEE Trans. Commun.*, vol. COM-29, no. 3, March 1981. [SUND] C.-E. Sundberg, "Continuous Phase Modulation," *IEEE Commun. Mag.*, vol. 24, no. 4, pp. 25–38, April 1986.

[17][PASU] S. Pasupathy, "Minimum Shift Keying: A Spectrally Efficient Modulation," *IEEE Commun. Mag.*, vol. 17, no. 4, pp. 14–22, July 1979.

done for power-efficiency reasons, brings the envelope back to a constant value, but spreads the envelope, as already noted.

In the QPSK signal representation of (4-14) both bits in a bit pair *simultaneously* modulate their respective carriers. (As shown in Fig. 4-14, the two successive bits are stored and then, when both are available, drive their respective carriers.) As a result, if both bits change sign, the π-rad shift of Fig. 4-23 occurs. If only one bit at a time is allowed to change, the maximum phase shift can only be $\pi/2$ rad, as shown in Fig. 4-23. This suggests offsetting the modulation by one of the two bits by half the T-second interval, so that at most a $\pi/2$-rad phase shift can occur. This gives rise to *offset* QPSK, or OQPSK, for which a simplified block diagram appears in Fig. 4-24. In this scheme each bit in a pair of successive bits still modulates its own carrier, but the application of the second (b_i) bit is delayed one-half the output interval. Since the maximum phase discontinuity is now limited to $\pi/2$ rad, there can be no zero crossing of the envelope. After band limiting, the resultant OQPSK signal shows some envelope drop at the phase-change point, but hard limiting no longer has such a large effect [PASU].

Minimum-shift keying (MSK) carries the offset approach one step further. Since real signals must always be shaped to attain the desired spectral (band-width) characteristic (see Sec. 3-10), consider multiplying both the inphase and (offset) quadrature terms of the OQPSK signal by a smoothing sine wave. Specifically, let the first bit a_i in a pair be multiplied by $\cos(\pi t/T)$; let the second bit b_i be multiplied by (the offset term) $\sin(\pi t/T)$. This is shown graphically in Fig. 4-25. Mathematically, we write, as the MSK signal,

$$s_i(t) = a_i \cos\left(\frac{\pi t}{T}\right)\cos \omega_c t + b_i \sin\left(\frac{\pi t}{T}\right)\sin \omega_c t \qquad a_i, b_i = \pm 1 \quad (4\text{-}15)$$

Note that the effect of the sinusoidal weighting terms is to multiply each carrier by a term going to zero at the bit transition point (Fig. 4-25). If the carrier has an integer number of half cycles within the symbol interval T, there is then no phase discontinuity at a bit transition point. This says that we should set

$$f_c = \frac{m}{2}\frac{1}{T} = \frac{mR}{4} \tag{4-16}$$

with m an integer, and $R = 2/T$ the input bit rate.

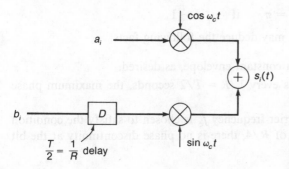

FIGURE 4-24
Generation of OQPSK.

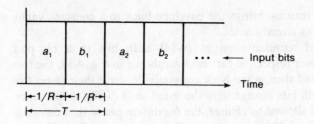

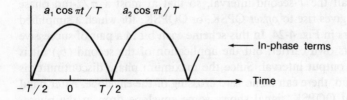

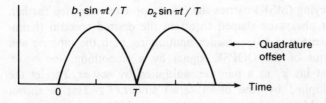

FIGURE 4-25
Development of MSK; a, $b = \pm 1$ (smoothing of OQPSK signal components).

From trigonometry we can rewrite (4-15) in two other equivalent forms:

$$s_i(t) = \cos\left(\omega_c t \mp \frac{\pi t}{T}\right) \qquad a_i = 1, \quad b_i = \pm 1$$

$$= \cos\left(\omega_c t \pm \frac{\pi t}{T} + \pi\right) \qquad a_i = -1, \quad b_i = \pm 1 \qquad (4\text{-}17a)$$

and
$$s_i(t) = \cos\left(\omega_c t - \frac{a_i b_i \pi t}{T} + \theta\right) \qquad (4\text{-}17b)$$

with
$$\theta = 0 \qquad \text{if} \quad a_i = 1$$
$$= \pi \qquad \text{if} \quad a_i = -1$$

From (4-17a) and (4-17b) one may deduce the following facts:

1. The MSK signal $s_i(t)$ has a constant envelope, as desired.
2. Since a_i or b_i only changes every $1/R = T/2$ seconds, the maximum phase change is $\pi/2$.
3. As already noted, if the carrier frequency f_c is chosen to satisfy the condition of (4-16), i.e., is a multiple of $R/4$, there is no phase discontinuity at the bit transition point.

Another interesting fact arises from studying (4-17b). Recall from (4-3a) that FSK uses the two signals $\cos(\omega_c t + \Delta\omega t)$ and $\cos(\omega_c t - \Delta\omega t)$. In particular, from (4-17b), we have

$$
\begin{aligned}
s_i(t) &= \cos(\omega_c t + \Delta\omega t + \theta) && \text{if} \quad a_i b_i = -1 \\
&= \cos(\omega_c t - \Delta\omega t + \theta) && \text{if} \quad a_i b_i = +1
\end{aligned}
\tag{4-18}
$$

Here $\qquad\qquad\qquad\qquad\qquad \Delta\omega = \pi/T$

or $$\Delta f = \frac{\Delta\omega}{2\pi} = \frac{1}{2T} = \frac{R}{4} \tag{4-19}$$

Minimum-shift keying may thus be interpreted as a form of FSK.

Why the use of the term *minimum* shift? Consider the synchronous or coherent detection of FSK signals diagrammed in Fig. 4-9b. One would like, as indicated, to obtain the correct binary signal at the output of the detection. Specifically, if a 1 has been inputted, corresponding, say, to $\cos \omega_1 t = \cos(\omega_c t - \Delta\omega t)$ transmitted, one would like to obtain a +1 as the binary output. This implies having zero output from the bottom low-pass filter of Fig. 4-9b. The simplest linear filter is an integrator, integrating over the binary interval $1/R$. To a good approximation, then, the output of the bottom low-pass filter is

$$\int_0^{1/R} f_c(t) \cos \omega_2 t\, dt \doteq 1/2 \int_0^{1/R} \cos(\omega_1 - \omega_2) t\, dt \tag{4-20}$$

writing $f_c(t) = \cos \omega_1 t$, using trigonometry, and then neglecting the integral of the sum term $\cos(\omega_1 + \omega_2)t$. (Why may this integral be neglected?) As noted, we want the result of the integration of (4-20) to be zero. Writing $\omega_1 - \omega_2 = 2\,\Delta\omega$ and carrying out the integration, we have, as the desired condition,

$$\sin\left(\frac{2\,\Delta\omega}{R}\right) = 0 \tag{4-21}$$

This is clearly obtainable if the quantity $2\,\Delta\omega/R$ is a multiple of π. The *minimum* possible value is

$$2\,\Delta\omega/R = \pi,$$

or $$\begin{aligned} 2\,\Delta f &= R/2 \\ \Delta f &= R/4 \end{aligned} \tag{4-22}$$

Note that this is exactly the condition of (4-19). The physical significance here is that (4-22) represents the minimum frequency spacing possible in FSK such that the synchronous detector output is unambiguously obtainable in the absence of noise. [As the two possible signals $\cos \omega_2 t = \cos(\omega_c + \Delta\omega)t$ and $\cos \omega_1 t = \cos(\omega_c - \Delta\omega)t$ are shifted further apart in frequency, requiring a correspondingly wider bandwidth for transmission, it becomes simpler to detect the presence of one or the other.] The smoothed OQPSK signal of Fig. 4-25 and (4-15) is found, alternatively, to be an FSK signal with minimum possible spacing of the two frequencies. This accounts for the designation minimum-shift keying.

Note was made, at the beginning of this section, that the constant-envelope (amplitude) digital signaling schemes investigated in recent years have the desirable property that they are bandwidth or spectrally efficient. This is readily demonstrated by comparing the spectrum of MSK with that of QPSK. We know that QPSK requires half the bandwidth of PSK, both operating at the same bit rate R. Does MSK retain this property? To compare the spectra of MSK and QPSK it suffices to calculate the spectra of their baseband equivalents [PASU]. For MSK this is the spectrum of the cosinusoidal shaping functions of (4-15). (See Fig. 4-25.) This is found from (2-35) in Chap. 2. For QPSK, neglecting any Nyquist shaping that might be used to reduce intersymbol interference, this is the familiar $(\sin x)/x$ spectrum of a rectangular pulse. This pulse is taken to have an amplitude of $1/\sqrt{2}$ to ensure it has the same "power" as the MSK cosinusoidal shaping function. The normalized square of the amplitude spectrum in each case is then given by the following equations:

MSK signal,

$$\frac{2|F(\omega)|^2}{T^2} = \frac{8}{\pi^2} \left| \frac{\cos(2\pi f/R)}{1 - 16(f/R)^2} \right|^2 \tag{4-23}$$

QPSK signal,

$$\frac{2|F(\omega)|^2}{T^2} = \left(\frac{\sin(2\pi f/R)}{2\pi f/R} \right)^2 \tag{4-24}$$

The MSK baseband signal has a broader first lobe, with the first zero crossing at $f = 0.75R = 3/2T$. [See the discussion following (2-35).] The actual MSK signal thus has a first lobe bandwidth, centered about the carrier frequency f_c, of $B_T = 1.5R = 3/T$. The QPSK signal has a corresponding baseband first zero crossing of $f = 0.5R = 1/T$. Its first-lobe transmission bandwidth, centered about f_c, is $B_T = R = 2/T$. The higher frequency content of the MSK signal drops off more rapidly, however. In fact its bandwidth to the 99-percent power point is $1.2R = 2.4/T$, while that for the QPSK signal is $8R = 16/T$ [PASU]. Additional comparative discussion of the two types of signal including further references to the literature appears in [PASU, p. 19].

4-5 AMPLITUDE MODULATION

In Sec. 4-2 we discussed sine-wave or c-w modulation systems in which the modulating signal consisted of a digital pulse train. Such systems are important in their own right because of the continuously increasing use of digital systems. The discussion was also important because it enabled us to introduce the basic concept of sine-wave modulation and demodulation (or detection), as well as to introduce spectrum considerations for AM and FM systems in which the modulating signal takes a particularly simple form. We now generalize our approach somewhat, and consider AM and FM systems designed to handle more complex signals than a sequence of binary digits. The signals could be voice or TV, as encountered in standard broadcasting, or complex combinations of both digital and analog waveshapes, obtained by time-multiplexing and frequency-multiplexing many individual signal channels into one master signal. This composite signal would in turn amplitude-modulate or frequency-modulate a sine-wave carrier.

In this section we concentrate on AM systems. Much of the material is identical to that already discussed previously, so that our treatment will be rather brief. We shall then go on to single-sideband (SSB) systems, concluding with a discussion of FM systems. Here too the material, particularly that relating to spectral considerations, will be similar to that presented previously.

Recall that when we talk of sine-wave modulation we imply that we have available a source of sinusoidal energy with an output voltage or current of the form

$$v(t) = A\cos(\omega_c t + \theta) \qquad (4\text{-}25)$$

This sinusoidal time function is called a *carrier*. Any one of the three quantities A, ω_c, or θ may be varied in accordance with the information-carrying, or modulating, signal. We restrict ourselves in this section to AM systems in which A only is assumed to be varied. A basic assumption to be adhered to in all the work to follow will be that the modulating signal varies slowly compared with the carrier. This then means that we can talk of an envelope variation, or variation of the locus of the carrier peaks. Figure 4-26 shows a typical modulating signal $f(t)$ and the carrier envelope variation corresponding to it. The amplitude-modulated carrier of Fig. 4-26 can be described in the form

$$f_c(t) = K[1 + mf(t)]\cos \omega_c t \qquad (4\text{-}26)$$

(We arbitrarily choose our time reference so that θ, the carrier phase angle, is zero.) Obviously, $|mf(t)| < 1$ in order to retain an undistorted envelope, in which case the envelope is a replica of the modulating signal. Note that in both Chap. 3 and Sec. 4-2 we discussed modulated carrier terms of the form

$$f_d(t) = f(t)\cos \omega_c t \qquad (4\text{-}27)$$

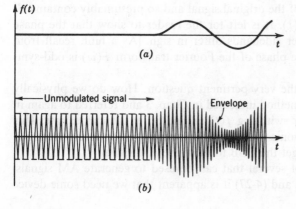

FIGURE 4-26
Amplitude modulation of a carrier. (*a*) Modulating signal. (*b*) Amplitude-modulated carrier.

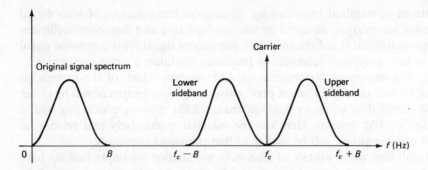

FIGURE 4-27
AM spectrum, including carrier (positive frequencies only are shown).

The present expression, Eq. (4-26), differs by the addition of the carrier term $K \cos \omega_c t$. This term is necessary to ensure the existence of an envelope, as shown in Fig. 4-26. This was no problem in the case of the OOK signals of Sec. 4-2, since the on–off sequence of pulses ensured the presence of an envelope. With more complex modulating signals $f(t)$, one must ensure this by adding the appropriate carrier term.

Some systems actually transmit signals of the form of Eq. (4-27). These are called *double-sideband* (DSB) or *suppressed-carrier* systems. As indicated earlier (Figs. 4-2 to 4-4), the effect of multiplying an arbitrary signal $f(t)$ by $\cos \omega_c t$ is to translate or shift the spectrum up to the range of frequencies surrounding the carrier frequency f_c. The further addition of the carrier term, as in Eq. (4-26), provides a discrete spectral line at frequency f_c as well. The resultant spectrum of the AM signal of (4-26) is thus similar to those of Figs. 4-2 to 4-4 with the addition of a discrete-line component at the carrier frequency f_c. An example appears in Fig. 4-27. The only stipulation here is that the bandwidth B of the modulating signal be less than the carrier frequency f_c. Two sets of side frequencies appear, as noted earlier: an upper and a lower set. Each set contains a band of frequencies corresponding to the band covered by the original signal and is called a *sideband*. Each sideband contains all the spectral components— both amplitude and phase—of the original signal and so presumably contains all the information carried by $f(t)$. It is left for the reader to show that the phase angles of the upper and lower sidebands differ in sign. [As a hint, recall from Chap. 2 that for real $f(t)$, the phase of the Fourier transform $F(\omega)$ is odd-symmetrical about the origin.]

We now ask ourselves the very pertinent question: How do we physically produce an AM signal? One method indicated in Chap. 3 and referred to again in Sec. 4-2 was that of gating or switching $f(t)$ on and off at the carrier rate. This translated $f(t)$ up to all harmonic multiples of frequency f_c. Bandpass filtering at one of these frequencies, we get the DSB form of the AM signal.

This technique is one of several that can be used to generate AM signals. From the form of Eqs. (4-26) and (4-27) it is apparent that we need some device that will provide at its output the product of the two input functions $f(t)$ and $\cos \omega_c t$. Such a device is called a *product modulator*. This generic device required for the generation of an AM signal is shown schematically in Fig. 4-28. If the baseband signal shown being applied at the input has the form $K[1 + mf(t)]$, as in (4-26), normal AM with a carrier present is produced at the output. If the input is simply $f(t)$, a baseband signal without the addition of a fixed constant (or dc value), suppressed-carrier DSB or AM results. Where DSB AM is specifically desired, two such modulators are often combined in a balanced configuration to ensure that no dc terms leak through to produce a carrier component. Details appear in the next section.

A simple example of a product modulator might be a galvanometer with separate windings for the magnet and the coil. The force on the coil is then proportional to the product of the currents in each winding. If

$$F \propto i_1 i_2 \tag{4-28}$$

$$i_i = a[1 + mf(t)] \tag{4-29}$$

(i.e., a dc bias plus the modulating signal), and

$$i_2 = b \cos \omega_c t \tag{4-30}$$

then the force on the coil, as a function of time, is of the same form as Eq. (4-26). The coil motion would then appear as an amplitude-modulated signal.

A motor with stator and rotor separately wound would give the same results. A loudspeaker, with the modulating signal and an appropriate dc bias applied to the voice coil and the carrier to the field winding, is again a similar device. These are all examples of *product* modulators.

These product modulators and other types of modulators commonly used may be classified in one of two categories:

1. Their terminal characteristics are nonlinear.
2. The modulation device contains a switch, as just described, which changes the system from one linear condition to another.

A *linear* time-invariant device by itself can never provide the product function needed. We may recall from our discussion of linear systems in Chap. 2 that *a non-time-varying linear system can generate no new frequencies.* The response to all sine-wave inputs may be superposed at the output. Such a system can therefore never be used as a modulator.

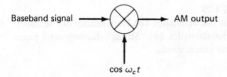

Baseband signal ⟶ ⊗ ⟶ AM output

$\cos \omega_c t$

FIGURE 4-28
Product modulator for generation of AM signals.

If we now add a switch to a linear system which switches the system in a specified manner from one linear condition to another (a simple example would be a switch turning the system on and off) and which does this independently of the signal, the system is still basically linear; the two basic characteristics of a linear system still apply. Such a system is still governed by linear differential equations, but the coefficients of the equations now vary with time according to the prescribed switching action. The system is now a linear time-varying system. As we shall see shortly, such a system can be used for modulation and will generate new frequencies. This is then a generalization of our previous switching process.

If instead of a switch we now introduce a device whose static terminal characteristics are nonlinear, the differential equations governing the system become nonlinear differential equations. Again, as we shall see, modulation or generation of new frequencies becomes possible. Two typical kinds of nonlinear characteristics are shown in Fig. 4-29. Actually, all physical devices have some curvature or nonlinearity in their static terminal characteristics, but we usually assume the region of operation to be small enough so that the characteristics are very nearly linear over this region.

Figure 4-29a might be the characteristic of a typical diode or transistor. Figure 4-29b might represent an approximation to a linear rectifier. The two curves differ in the type of nonlinearity. The linear rectifier of Fig. 4-29b has a strong nonlinearity at one point and is approximated by linear characteristics elsewhere. (The use of the term linear rectifier and the piecewise-linear characteristics assumed have sometimes led to the mistaken conclusion that the device is linear.) The characteristics of Fig. 4-29a have no one point of strong nonlinearity but are everywhere nonlinear, owing to the curvature of the characteristics.

Figure 4-29b can also be used as the representation of the characteristics of a switching device and, in fact, serves as a good example of the distinction between linear time-invariant, nonlinear, and switching characteristics. Thus, if the device is operated in one of the linear portions of the curve only, it behaves as a linear time-invariant device. Typically, the device would be biased to operate in a region far from the discontinuity, and the signals applied would be small enough to keep it in that region. The output is then a linear replica of the input, and if two signals are applied, the output is a superposition of the response to each. If the signal applied to the device is now increased to the point where the

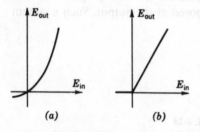

(a)   (b)

FIGURE 4-29
Nonlinear characteristics. (a) Nonlinearity due to curvature of characteristics. (b) "Strong" discontinuity; piecewise-linear characteristic.

discontinuity is crossed and the two linear regions are involved, the output is no longer a simple linear function of the input. If one signal is applied, the output is a distorted version, and if two signals are applied, the output no longer can be found by superposing the two input responses separately. The output is then a nonlinear function of the input; as the input amplitude changes, the output does not change proportionally.

If the input-signal level is now dropped back to its original small value but is somehow switched in a predetermined fashion between the two linear regions of Fig. 4-29b, we have a linear switch with the corresponding linear time-varying equations.

Most modulators in use can thus be classified as having one of the two types of characteristics of Fig. 4-29 if switches are included as represented by Fig. 4-29b.

We shall first analyze simple modulators incorporating the nonlinear characteristics of Fig. 4-29a. The analysis of the piecewise-linear characteristic of Fig. 4-29b will be very similar to that describing the switching operation in Chap. 3.

Nonlinear Modulator

The simplest form of this type of modulator appears in Fig. 4-30. e_o and e_i represent the incremental output and input variations, respectively, away from some fixed operating point (Fig. 4-30b). The nonlinear characteristics of this case are assumed continuous, so that e_o my be expanded in a power series in e_i,

$$e_o = a_1 e_i + a_2 e_i^2 + a_3 e_i^3 + \text{(higher-order terms)} \tag{4-31}$$

The quadratic term in the power series denotes the presence of curvature in the characteristics and is all-important in the modulation process. This nonlinear device is thus often called a *square-law* modulator.

For the circuit in Fig. 4-30a

$$e_i = \underbrace{\cos \omega_c t}_{\text{Carrier}} + \underbrace{f(t)}_{\substack{\text{Modulating} \\ \text{signal}}} \tag{4-32}$$

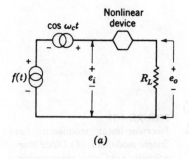

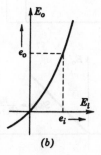

(a)   (b)

FIGURE 4-30
Simple modulator. (a) Simple circuit. (b) Terminal characteristics.

Then, retaining just the first two terms of the power series of Eq. (4-31), we get

$$e_o = a_1 \cos \omega_c t + a_1 f(t) + a_2 \left[\cos^2 \omega_c t + 2f(t) \cos \omega_c t + f^2(t) \right]$$

$$= \underbrace{a_1 f(t) + a_2 \cos^2 \omega_c t + a_2 f^2(t)}_{\text{Unwanted terms}} + \underbrace{a_1 \cos \omega_c t \left[1 + \frac{2a_2}{a_1} f(t) \right]}_{\substack{\text{Amplitude-modulated} \\ \text{terms}}} \quad (4\text{-}33)$$

The second term thus contains the desired AM signal. (Let $m \equiv 2a_2/a_1$, $K \equiv a_1$.) The first term contains unwanted terms that can be filtered out. $\cos^2 \omega_c t$ gives $\frac{1}{2}(1 + \cos 2\omega_c t)$, that is, dc and twice the carrier frequency. $f^2(t)$ contains frequency components from dc to twice the maximum-frequency component of $f(t)$, that is, $2B$. This is left as an exercise for the reader. It may be noted in passing that this device could also be used as a second-harmonic generator if $\cos \omega_c t$ only were introduced and its second harmonic retained.

Piecewise-Linear Modulator (Strong Nonlinearity)

A typical circuit (identical with the circuit of Fig. 4-30a) and the piecewise-linear characteristics for such a device (here chosen as a "linear" rectifier) are shown in Fig. 4-31. R_L is the load resistance; R_d, the diode forward resistance.

We should like to demonstrate that the piecewise-linear characteristics can also be used for simple AM. The discontinuity assumed in the terminal characteristics prevents the use of the power-series expansion as was done in the previous modulator.

We could, of course, approximate the characteristics by a polynomial. This would convert them to the continuous form of Fig. 4-30 with the discontinuity more pronounced at the origin. Both types of nonlinearity could thus be treated

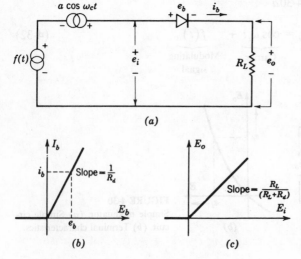

(a)

(b)

(c)

FIGURE 4-31
Piecewise-linear modulator. (a) Simple modulator. (b) Diode characteristic. (c) Circuit characteristic.

simultaneously. We prefer, however, to use a different approach similar to that used in discussing the switching operations in Chap. 3.

We shall assume that the carrier amplitude is much greater than the maximum value of $f(t)$,

$$|f(t)| \ll a$$

If the carrier alone were present, the rectifier would clip the negative halves of the carrier. Under the assumption of a strong carrier the clipping of the carrier plus modulating signal will occur approximately at the same point in the cycle as the carrier alone. We thus have

$$e_i = a \cos \omega_c t + f(t) \qquad |f(t)| \ll a$$

$$e_o \doteq \frac{R_L e_i}{R_L + R_d} = b e_i \qquad a \cos \omega_c t > 0 \qquad (4\text{-}34)$$

$$\doteq 0 \qquad a \cos \omega_c t < 0$$

Since the output now varies between two values ($b e_i$ and 0) periodically, at the frequency of the carrier, the input may be looked on as having been switched between two regions of the diode operation. By the simple expedient of assuming a weak signal compared with the carrier we have converted the nonlinear device into a linear switching device. Since the transitions from one region of operation to another are now variables of time independent of the signal $f(t)$, we have effectively replaced a nonlinear equation by a linear time-varying one. This approach is the one actually used in solving some types of nonlinear differential equations. It is to be emphasized, however, that this is an approximate technique, valid only for small signals. Equation (4-34) can be written mathematically as

$$e_o \doteq [a \cos \omega_c t + f(t)] S(t)$$

with
$$S(t) = b \qquad -\tfrac{1}{4}T < t < \tfrac{1}{4}T, \quad T = \frac{1}{f_c} \qquad (4\text{-}35)$$

$$= 0 \qquad t \text{ elsewhere}$$

and repeating at multiples of $T = 1/f_c$ seconds.

$S(t)$ is again our familiar periodic switching function as shown in Fig. 4-32. Again using the Fourier representation,

$$S(t) = b \left[\frac{1}{2} + \sum_{n=1}^{\infty} \frac{\sin(n\pi/2)}{n\pi/2} \cos n\omega_c t \right] \qquad (4\text{-}36)$$

But
$$e_o = [a \cos \omega_c t + f(t)] S(t)$$

By using the Fourier-series expansion for $S(t)$, performing the indicated multipli-

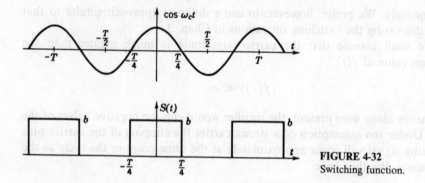

FIGURE 4-32
Switching function.

cation, and collecting terms, e_o can be written in the form

$$e_o(t) = b \left\{ \left\{ \frac{1}{2} f(t) + \frac{2}{\pi} a \cos^2 \omega_c t \right. \right.$$

$$\left. + \sum_{n=3}^{\infty} \frac{\sin(n\pi/2)}{n\pi/2} [f(t) + a \cos \omega_c t] \cos n\omega_c t \right\}$$

$$\left. + \frac{a}{2} \cos \omega_c t \left[1 + \frac{4}{\pi a} f(t) \right] \right\} \quad (4\text{-}37)$$

Again, we can filter this output. The terms in the braces give direct-current, low frequencies up to B [the maximum frequency component of $f(t)$], and then higher frequencies: $2f_c, 3f_c - B, 3f_c, 3f_c + B$, etc. After filtering,

$$e_o(t) \doteq K[1 + mf(t)] \cos \omega_c t$$

where
$$K = \frac{ab}{2}$$

$$m = \frac{4}{\pi a} \quad (4\text{-}38)$$

The piecewise-linear modulator of Fig. 4-31 thus produces an amplitude-modulated output upon proper filtering.

We have actually demonstrated this modulation property for the device considered as a switch rather than as a nonlinear device, under the assumption of a small signal (relative to the carrier). The truly nonlinear solution leads to harmonics of the signal $f(t)$ and higher-order modulation products of the carrier and its harmonics. These additional terms would be filtered out in an actual modulator, leaving Eq. (4-38) as the solution in the more exact analysis also.

The two nonlinear devices just discussed are representative of many types that are used for low-level (i.e., low-power) modulation purposes. Examples include nonlinear-resistance modulators, semiconductor diode modulators, mechanical-contact modulators (also called "choppers," or *vibrators*, which are

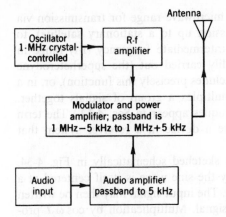

Antenna

Oscillator 1·MHz crystal-controlled → R-f amplifier

Modulator and power amplifier; passband is 1 MHz−5 kHz to 1 MHz+5 kHz

Audio input → Audio amplifier passband to 5 kHz

FIGURE 4-33
Standard high-level broadcast transmitter.

basically switching devices of the piecewise-linear type previously discussed), photodiodes for optical (light-wave) applications, magnetic modulators, nonlinear-capacitor modulators, transistor modulators, etc.

For standard radio-broadcast work these low-level modulators are highly inefficient. (Their use in balanced modulator circuits for SSB transmission or as parts of servo systems is discussed later in this chapter.) Class C amplifier operation provides higher efficiency of power generation and is commonly used for standard broadcast transmitters. The modulation process here involves the gross nonlinearity due to class C operation. A tuned circuit at the amplified output then provides the necessary filtering to obtain the desired amplitude-modulated wave: a carrier plus sidebands [CLAR 1971].[18] A modulator–power-amplifier combination provides the basic elements of the typical standard broadcast transmitter. A block diagram of the transmitter is shown in Fig. 4-33. This is a simplified version with only the essential elements shown.

Frequency Conversion

Multiplication by a sine wave, with its resultant shift in frequency, is used not only to generate AM signals, but to shift signals from one frequency band to another. Synchronous detection, described in Sec. 4-2 for the case of binary carrier transmission, and to be generalized in Sec. 4-8 to the case of any type of baseband signal, is an example in which high-frequency signals are shifted back down to baseband after multiplication by a sine wave at the carrier frequency.

More generally, the shift from one frequency band to another, using multiplication by a sine wave, is called *frequency conversion*. This process is often used to boost modulated carriers to a desired frequency range (one example

[18][CLAR 1971] K. K. Clarke and D. T. Hess, *Communication Circuits: Analysis and Design*, Addison-Wesley, Reading, Mass., 1971.

would be the shifting of signals up to the microwave range for transmission via terrestrial microwave links or for transmission up to a stationary satellite), to shift carrier signals down to a specified intermediate frequency (i-f) range in which filtering and amplification are readily carried out (the superheterodyne radio receiver to be described in Sec. 4-8 includes precisely this function), or, in a series of conversion steps, to frequency-multiplex a group of signals together. (Examples of frequency-multiplexing techniques appear in Sec. 4-12.) The term *mixer* is sometimes also used to designate a device in a receiver system that carries out frequency conversion.

The frequency conversion process is sketched schematically in Fig. 4-34. Assume that the signal to be multiplied by the sine wave is itself centered at a carrier frequency f_1, as shown in Fig. 4-34b. The input signal may then be written $g(t) = f(t)\cos \omega_1 t$, with $f(t)$ a baseband signal. Multiplication by $\cos \omega_2 t$ produces $f_M(t) = [f(t)/2][\cos(\omega_1 + \omega_2)t + \cos(\omega_1 - \omega_2)t]$, as shown in Fig. 4-34a. The spectrum of $f_M(t)$ is then shifted up and down by f_2 hertz, as shown in Fig. 4-34b. Either one of the two DSB signals, one centered at $f_1 + f_2$ hertz, the other at $f_1 - f_2$ hertz, may be selected by appropriate filtering. This process may be repeated if desired. As a special case, note that if $f_1 = 0$, we have just the product

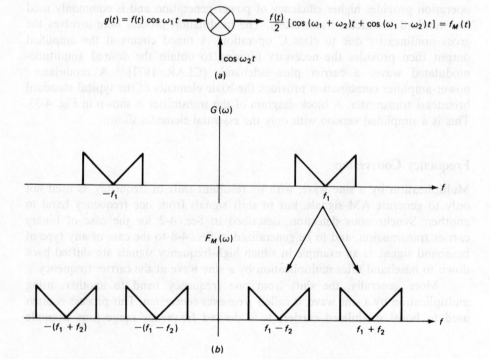

FIGURE 4-34
Frequency conversion. (*a*) Frequency converter. (*b*) Effect of conversion.

modulation discussed previously. If $f_2 = f_1$, we generate both the baseband signal $f(t)$ centered about 0 Hz and a signal at twice the original carrier frequency. If the carrier is to be doubled, we follow with a bandpass filter centered at $2f_1$. If we wish to select the baseband signal $f(t)$, we follow with a low-pass filter. The resultant process is the one we previously called synchronous detection. If $f_1 - f_2$ is required to be some specified intermediate frequency f_0, we must have $f_2 = f_1 + f_0$ or $f_1 - f_0$. (Note that f_2, the frequency of the sine wave multiplying the input signal, can thus be above f_1 or below f_1. Either case is possible.) If the output of the product modulator is followed by a bandpass filter centered at $f_0 = f_1 - f_2$, the difference frequency terms only are transmitted.

In modern systems the injected sine wave $\cos \omega_2 t$ is often synthesized digitally. Discrete samples of $\cos \omega_2 t$, enough to generate a full cycle of the sine wave, can be stored in tabular form in a random-access memory.

Specific examples of the frequency-conversion process appear in the sections following, as well as in problems at the end of the chapter.

4-6 SINGLE-SIDEBAND TRANSMISSION AND BALANCED MODULATORS

We note from the frequency plot of the amplitude-modulated carrier (Fig. 4-27) that the desired information to be transmitted [as originally given by variations of the modulating signal $f(t)$] is carried in one of the two sidebands. The carrier itself carries no information. Transmission of the entire spectrum thus represents a waste of frequency space, since transmitting both sidebands requires double the bandwidth needed for transmitting one sideband. It also represents a waste of power (especially power in the carrier). This has resulted in the widespread use of SSB transmission for transoceanic radiotelephone circuits and wire communications. In this type of transmission the carrier and one sideband are suppressed and only the remaining sideband transmitted. As an example, AT & T in the United States uses a single-sideband microwave radio, the AR6A, that allows 6,000 voice circuits to be transmitted over a 28.6-MHz-wide channel [MARK].[19] This is three times the number previously possible using FM techniques. Details will be presented later in this chapter in discussing frequency-division multiplexing.

With the apparent advantages of SSB over AM, why is it that SSB is not used for standard radio broadcasting? The answer is that the circuitry *required at the receiver* is quite complex. To demonstrate these statements more quantitatively, we must discuss methods of producing and then detecting SSB signals.

A method commonly used to generate an SSB signal is first to suppress the carrier of the AM signal. The resulting transmission is, as noted earlier, *sup-*

---

[19][MARK] R. E. Markle, "Single Sideband Triples Microwave Radio Route Capacity," *Bell Lab. Rec.*, vol. 56, no. 4, pp. 104–110, April 1978.

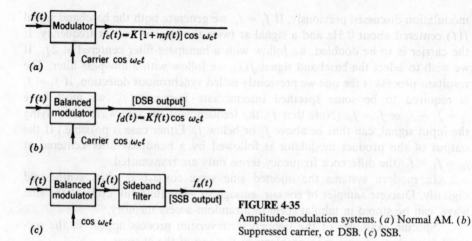

FIGURE 4-35
Amplitude-modulation systems. (a) Normal AM. (b) Suppressed carrier, or DSB. (c) SSB.

pressed-carrier, or *double-sideband* (DSB), transmission. One of the two sidebands is then filtered out. The carrier suppression is usually accomplished by means of a *balanced modulator*, as indicated in the block diagrams of Fig. 4-35.

A normal AM output has the form

$$f_c(t) = K[1 + mf(t)]\cos \omega_c t \tag{4-39}$$

while the corresponding mathematical expression for a DSB output is

$$f_d(t) = K'f(t)\cos \omega_c t \tag{4-40}$$

The DSB system differs from normal AM simply by suppressing the carrier term. This means that with no modulating signal applied the output should be zero. If we recall the nonlinear devices discussed previously, the carrier term arose because of a quiescent condition or dc bias somewhere in the modulator. If we can balance out this quiescent condition, we have a simple product modulator with the output given by Eq. (4-40). (In the case of the magnetic product modulators mentioned—the galvanometer, motor, loudspeaker—the assumption was that a dc term appeared in one of the currents. If we balance out this dc current, we have the desired suppressed-carrier output.)

One possible scheme for suppressing or balancing out the carrier term is shown in Fig. 4-36. This method uses two nonlinear elements of the types previously considered in a balanced arrangement. The resulting device is then an example of a *balanced modulator*.

To demonstrate the balancing effect, assume that the transformer between the load R and the modulator is ideal. The modulator then sees the resistor load. The upper and the lower sections of the balanced modulator are then each identical with Fig. 4-36a, and the previous analysis of such nonlinear circuits holds. In particular, the two currents flowing may be written in the form

$$i_1 = K[1 + mf(t)]\cos \omega_c t \tag{4-41}$$

and

$$i_2 = K[1 - mf(t)]\cos \omega_c t \tag{4-42}$$

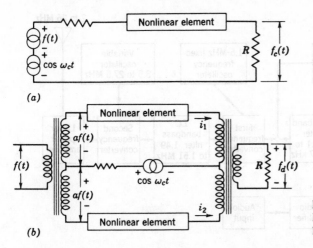

(a)

(b)

FIGURE 4-36
Balanced modulator. (*a*) Modulator. (*b*) Balanced modulator.

(the other terms generated in the nonlinear process are assumed filtered out). But the load voltage $f_d(t)$ is proportional to $i_1 - i_2$, or

$$f_d(t) = K'f(t)\cos \omega_c t \qquad (4\text{-}43)$$

Since the switching operation discussed in Chap. 3 in connection with sampling was shown to produce terms of exactly the DSB form, these switches may also be considered balanced modulators. One such switch, the shunt-bridge diode modulator, is shown in Fig. 4-37. The diodes in the bridge modulator may be treated as switches, switching on and off at the carrier rate. With the diodes assumed identical i.e., balanced), the bridge is balanced when $f(t) = 0$ and there is no output; with the carrier input of the polarity indicated the diodes are essentially short-circuited out, and the output is again zero. When the carrier reverses polarity, however, the diodes open and $f_d(t)$ is equal to $f(t)$. The output is thus alternately $f(t)$ and 0, switching at the carrier frequency rate, just as required here, and for the sampling function in Chap. 3 as well. Balanced modulators using p-i-n photodiodes or APDs have also been proposed for optical coherent detection.

The balanced modulator is essentially the heart of the SSB transmitter. The balanced modulators are operated at low power levels, with linear amplifiers then following to reach the required transmitted power. This is in contrast to ordinary AM (Fig. 4-33), where the modulation is frequently carried out at high power levels, with class C amplifiers.

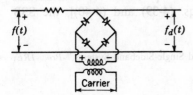

FIGURE 4-37
Balanced modulator: shunt-bridge diode modulator.

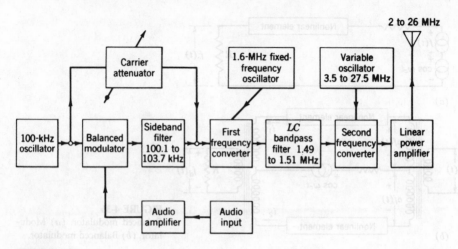

FIGURE 4-38
Single-sideband transmitter. (From B. Fisk and C. L. Spencer, "Synthesizer Stabilized Single-Sideband Systems," *Proc. IRE*, vol. 44, no. 12, p. 1680, December 1956, by permission.)

In addition to the balanced modulator, the SSB system requires a sideband filter with sharp cutoff characteristics at the edges of the passband. (Attenuation at the carrier frequency must be especially high.) Because of the stringent requirements on the fitter, the modulation is commonly performed at a relatively low fixed frequency at which it is possible to design the required sideband filter.

A typical SSB transmitter incorporating the two features mentioned—low-level balanced modulator and low-frequency (l-f) filtering—is shown in Fig. 4-38 [FISK].[20] The modulation process in this transmitter is carried out at 100 kHz. Two levels of frequency conversion, or mixing, are employed, with the signal successively shifted up in frequency by the frequency of the two injected signals (1.6 MHz and the final variable frequency).

In the discussion of SSB detection to follow, the need for reinjecting the suppressed carrier will be discussed. To ensure that the reinjected carrier is of precisely the right frequency a pilot carrier of known amplitude is transmitted (usually 10 to 20 dB below the carrier in normal AM). The carrier attenuator in Fig. 4-38 provides the pilot carrier.

4-7 SSB SIGNAL REPRESENTATION: HILBERT TRANSFORMS [SCHW 1966]

Note that although we have written mathematical expressions for both normal AM and DSB (suppressed-carrier) signals [Eqs. (4-39) and (4-40)], the SSB

---

[20][FISK] B. Fisk and C. L. Spencer, "Synthesizer Stabilized Single-Sideband Systems," *Proc. IRE*, vol. 44, no. 12, p. 1680, December 1956.

generation has been described only in terms of filtering out one of the sidebands of the DSB signal. It is of interest to develop an explicit expression for a SSB signal not only for its own sake, but because it also serves two other purposes: (1) as a by-product it indicates an alternative way of generating SSB signals (the *phase-shift method* of SSB generation); and (2) it enables us to discuss SSB detection in a quantitative way.

To obtain the desired expression for a single-sideband signal, assume we have available a baseband or low-frequency time function $z(t)$ whose Fourier transform $Z(\omega)$ is nonzero for positive frequencies only. This is admittedly not a real or physical possible time function, since we showed in Chap. 2 that all real-time functions had Fourier transforms defined over both negative and positive frequency ranges. [In fact, recall that $|F(\omega)| = |F(-\omega)|$ for real $f(t)$, while the phase angle of $F(\omega)$ is odd symmetric about zero frequency.] By definition, then,

$$Z(\omega) = 0 \qquad \omega < 0 \qquad (4\text{-}44)$$

An example of such a Fourier transform is shown in Fig. 4-39a. Now assume $z(t)$ multiplied by $e^{j\omega_c t}$. A little thought will indicate that this corresponds to a translation up by frequency ω_c, so that the transform of $z(t)e^{j\omega_c t}$ is just $Z(\omega - \omega_c)$. This is shown in Fig. 4-39b. It is apparent from the figure that this is just a SSB signal with *upper* sideband only present. A function $z(t)$ with the peculiar one-sided spectral property is called an *analytic signal* [SCHW 1966]. Since $z(t)e^{j\omega_c t}$ is complex, we simply take its real part to obtain the SSB signal $f_s(t)$:

$$f_s(t) = \text{Re}\big[z(t)e^{j\omega_c t}\big] \qquad (4\text{-}45)$$

Now given a modulating or information-bearing signal $f(t)$, how does one generate the analytic signal $z(t)$ from it? Once we shown this we have in essence closed the loop, indicating how one goes from $f(t)$ to its SSB version $f_s(t)$. Consider $f(t)$ passed through a $-90°$ phase shifter, a device which shifts the

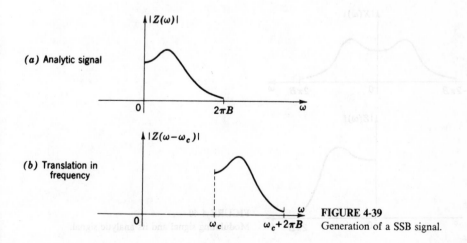

(*a*) Analytic signal

(*b*) Translation in frequency

FIGURE 4-39
Generation of a SSB signal.

phase of all positive frequency components of $f(t)$ by $-90°$ and all negative components by $90°$. (The phase characteristic is always an *odd* function of frequency.) Call the output of the phase shifter $\hat{f}(t)$. We then have

$$\hat{F}(\omega) = -jF(\omega) \qquad \omega \geq 0$$
$$= +jF(\omega) \qquad \omega < 0 \qquad (4\text{-}46)$$

Note now that $j\hat{F}(\omega) = F(\omega)$, $\omega \geq 0$; $= -F(\omega)$, $\omega < 0$. This indicates that we can generate the analytic signal $z(t)$ by adding $j\hat{f}(t)$ to $f(t)$:

$$z(t) = f(t) + j\hat{f}(t) \qquad (4\text{-}47)$$

For we then have

$$Z(\omega) = 2F(\omega) \qquad \omega \geq 0$$
$$= 0 \qquad \omega < 0 \qquad (4\text{-}48)$$

just as desired (Fig. 4-40). By this expedient of defining an analytic signal $z(t)$ and then showing how it may be generated from $f(t)$ and its 90°-phase-shifted version $\hat{f}(t)$, we have finally the desired SSB representation in terms of $f(t)$:

$$f_s(t) = \text{Re}\big[z(t)e^{j\omega_c t}\big] = \text{Re}\big\{\big[f(t) + j\hat{f}(t)\big]e^{j\omega_c t}\big\}$$
$$= f(t)\cos \omega_c t - \hat{f}(t)\sin \omega_c t \qquad (4\text{-}49)$$

Equation (4-49) is not only the explicit expression for a SSB signal in terms of the baseband signal $f(t)$; it tells us in addition how to generate $f_s(t)$; that is, we generate a DSB signal $f(t)\cos \omega_c t$ by using a product or balanced modulator, and we generate another DSB signal $\hat{f}(t)\sin \omega_c t$ by phase-shifting $f(t)$ by 90° and then multiplying by $\sin \omega_c t$ and then subtracting the two. This phase-shift method of generating SSB signals is diagrammed in Fig. 4-41.

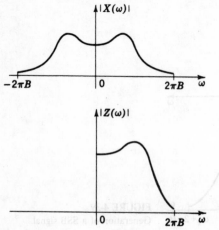

FIGURE 4-40
Modulating signal and its analytic signal.

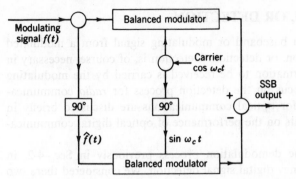

FIGURE 4-41
Phase-shift method of generating
SSB (upper-sideband case).

It is left to the reader to show that the *lower* sideband only may be similarly generated by writing

$$f_s(t) = f(t)\cos\omega_c t + \hat{f}(t)\sin\omega_c t \qquad (4\text{-}50)$$

As a simple example of these results, and to develop somewhat more insight into the significance of the operations indicated by Eqs. (4-49) and (4-50), consider $f(t)$ to be just the single-frequency term $\cos\omega_m t$. The DSB signal is then

$$f_{d1}(t) = \cos\omega_m t \cos\omega_c t = \tfrac{1}{2}[\cos(\omega_m + \omega_c)t + \cos(\omega_c - \omega_m)t] \qquad (4\text{-}51)$$

containing the expected two sideband frequencies. How do we now cancel one of these sideband terms? If it is desired to retain the upper-sideband term only, we must subtract from Eq. (4-51) an expression of the form

$$f_{d2}(t) = \tfrac{1}{2}[\cos(\omega_c - \omega_m)t - \cos(\omega_m + \omega_c)t] = \sin\omega_m t \sin\omega_c t \qquad (4\text{-}52)$$

Upon subtracting Eqs. (4-51) and (4-52), the lower sideband cancels, leaving the desired upper sideband,

$$\cos(\omega_c + \omega_m)t$$

Similarly, upon *adding* Eq. (4-51) and (4-52), the upper sideband cancels, leaving the lower sideband

$$\cos(\omega_c - \omega_m)t$$

These are, of course, the operations by Eqs. (4-49) and (4-50).

The 90° phase shift of all frequency components of $f(t)$ is commonly called a Hilbert transformation, and $\hat{f}(t)$ is called the *Hilbert transform* of $f(t)$. We shall use this transform in the next section in discussing the detection of SSB signals.

One major problem in the design of phase-shift SSB systems is the practical realization of the wideband 90° phase-shift network, for *all* the frequency components of the modulating signal $f(t)$ must be shifted by 90°.

4-8   DEMODULATION, OR DETECTION

The process of separating a baseband or modulating signal from a modulated carrier is called demodulation, or detection. Detection is, of course, necessary in all receivers where the information to be received is carried by the modulating signal. In this section we focus on the detection process for *radio* communications. Photodetectors used for optical communications are discussed briefly in Chap. 6, in determining limits on the performance of optical digital communication systems.

We have discussed the demodulation process previously in Sec. 4-2, in connection with high-frequency digital signal detection. We considered there two basic methods of demodulating high-frequency signals: envelope detection and synchronous (coherent) detection. Synchronous detection was also mentioned briefly in Sec. 4-5 in connection with frequency conversion. Both methods again appear here in discussing AM and SSB demodulation. In particular, we shall find that synchronous detection is generally required for SSB (or DSB) systems, while normal AM may use either detection method.[21] Since, as noted earlier, envelope detection is much more simply instrumented, this is the preferred method of AM detection.

Demodulation is basically the inverse of modulation and requires nonlinear or linear time-varying (switching) devices also. Since the nonlinear circuits used are essentially the same, the details of detector operation are left as exercises for the reader. (Again, two types of nonlinear detector may be considered: the square-law detector with the current–voltage characteristics represented by a power series, and the piecewise-linear detector with a nonlinearity concentrated at one point.)

Recall from Sec. 4-2 that envelope detection consisted of passing the amplitude-modulated carrier through a nonlinear device and then low-pass filtering the nonlinear output. One common configuration for radio communications, already noted in Sec. 4-2, consists of a half-wave diode rectifier followed by a parallel RC circuit. The circuit is diagrammed in Fig. 4-42. The rectified output is shown in the two cases of filtering and no filtering. Photodetectors used for optical communications are also envelope detectors. The operation and analysis of these devices differs somewhat from those discussed here. Their output is proportional to the envelope squared or average power of the incoming signal. As noted above, these devices will be discussed briefly in Chap. 6.

The analysis of the detector of Fig. 4-42a is carried out very simply by treating the diode either as a square-law device (as in Sec. 4-2),[22] or as a piecewise-linear device. In the former case, it is apparent that with the input

---

[21] Some thought will convince the reader that amplitude modulation is the generalized form of on–off keying, while double-sideband modulation corresponds to phase-shift keying in the binary case.

[22] Other nonlinear representations lead to essentially the same results, but with much more algebraic complexity and manipulation.

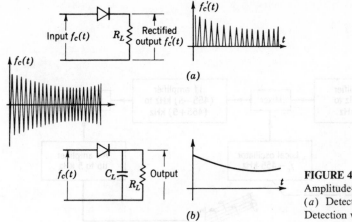

FIGURE 4-42
Amplitude-modulation detector.
(*a*) Detection, no filtering. (*b*)
Detection with filtering.

given by

$$f_c(t) = K[1 + mf(t)]\cos \omega_c t \qquad (4\text{-}53)$$

the output may be written

$$f_c'(t) = [f_c(t)]^2 = K^2[1 + mf(t)]^2 \cos^2 \omega_c t \qquad (4\text{-}54)$$

Expanding the expression and selecting the low-pass terms, it is easily shown that these latter contain the desired $f(t)$ plus distortion $[f^2(t)]$ components. Similarly, if the diode is approximated as a piecewise-linear device, switching at the carrier-frequency rate, the output may be written

$$f_c'(t) = K[1 + mf(t)]\cos \omega_c t\, S(t) \qquad (4\text{-}55)$$

with $S(t)$ the switching function previously defined. By again expanding $S(t)$ in its Fourier series, it can be shown very simply that the output contains a component proportional to $f(t)$ plus higher-frequency terms (sum and difference frequencies of carrier and modulating signal).

The capacitor of Fig. 4-42*b* serves to filter out these higher-frequency terms. Looked at another way, C_L is chosen so as to respond to envelope variations, but the circuit time constant (including the diode forward resistance) does not allow the circuit to follow the high-frequency (h-f) carrier variations [CLAR 1971]. A block diagram of a typical superheterodyne radio receiver incorporating such a detector is shown in Fig. 4-43.

The incoming signal passes first through a tuned radio-frequency (r-f) amplifier which can be tuned variably over the radio band 550 to 1,600 kHz. This signal is then mixed with a locally generated signal. The sum and difference frequencies generated contain a term centered about 455 kHz. (The local oscillator and r-f amplifier are tuned together so that there is always a difference frequency of 455 kHz between them.) The mixer acts as a frequency converter, shifting the incoming signal down to the fixed intermediate frequency of 455

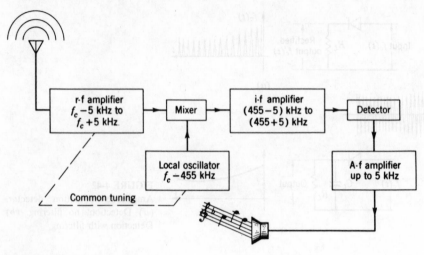

FIGURE 4-43
Superheterodyne AM receiver.

kHz. Several stages of amplification are ordinarily used, with double-tuned circuits providing the coupling between stages. The intermediate-frequency (i-f) signal is then detected as described above, amplified further in the audio-frequency (a-f) amplifiers and applied to the loudspeaker. The superheterodyning operation refers to the use of a frequency converter and fixed, tuned i-f amplifier before detection.

The synchronous detection operation as indicated in Secs. 4-2 and 4-5 consists simply of multiplying the incoming carrier signal by a locally generated carrier $\cos \omega_c t$ and low-pass-filtering the resultant. This is shown again in Fig. 4-44. Based on our discussion in the previous sections, it is apparent that the multiplication by $\cos \omega_c t$ serves to translate the frequency components in the incoming modulated carrier up and down by the carrier signal. The low-pass filter rejects the terms centered about $2f_c$, and passes those at baseband frequencies. The synchronous detection process can thus equally well be considered to consist of a frequency converter plus filter. This conversion process is diagrammed in Fig. 4-45, for the special case of SSB demodulation. The multiplication by $\cos \omega_c t$ may be accomplished in innumerable ways as noted previously: by the use of nonlinear devices, switching, digital synthesis, etc. The key factor, however, is the necessity of having available at the receiver the carrier-frequency term $\cos \omega_c t$.

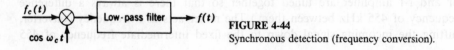

FIGURE 4-44
Synchronous detection (frequency conversion).

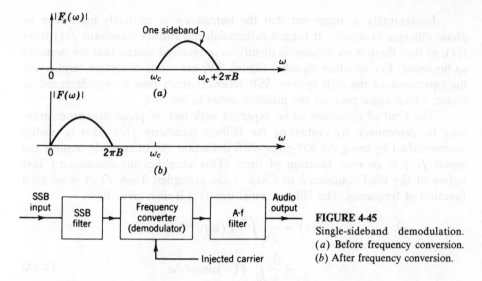

FIGURE 4-45
Single-sideband demodulation.
(a) Before frequency conversion.
(b) After frequency conversion.

In the case of normal AM it is apparent that multiplication by $\cos \omega_c t$ results in the prefiltered expression

$$K\left[1 + mf(t)\right]\cos^2 \omega_c t$$

For a DSB signal the equivalent expression is

$$f(t)\cos^2 \omega_c t$$

This latter expression is of course a special case of the one discussed in Sec. 4-5 in connection with frequency conversion (Fig. 4-34). For the SSB signal the pre-filtered term is, using Eq. (4-49),

$$f(t)\cos^2 \omega_c t - \hat{f}(t)\sin \omega_c t \cos \omega_c t$$

It is apparent that the desired term $f(t)$ appears at the filter output in all three cases.

For most types of baseband signals the local carrier must not only be of the right frequency but must be synchronized in phase with the carrier as well. This was emphasized in Sec. 4-2. If the carrier shifts in phase, the resultant output signal may be a considerably distorted version of the baseband signal $f(t)$. To demonstrate this for the SSB case, consider multiplication by a carrier term $\cos(\omega_c t + \theta)$. It is left for the reader to show that in this case the filtered output signal is given by

$$2f_o(t) = f(t)\cos \theta + \hat{f}(t)\sin \theta \qquad (4\text{-}56)$$

Note that not only is the desired output reduced as θ increases from 0, but a distortion term $\hat{f}(t)\sin \theta$ appears. If $\theta = \pi/2$, in particular, only $\hat{f}(t)$ appears at the output.

Interestingly, it turns out that the human ear is relatively insensitive to phase changes in signals. It cannot distinguish the Hilbert transform $\hat{f}(t)$ from $f(t)$, so that there is no noticeable distortion in received signals that are destined to be *heard*. For all other signals—digital, TV, etc.—this distortion term limits the operation of the SSB system. SSB receivers must thus be synchronized in phase, which again presents the problem noted in Sec. 4-2.

The kind of distortion to be expected with lack of phase synchronization may be determined by evaluating the Hilbert transform $\hat{f}(t)$. This is readily accomplished by using the 90°-phase-shift definition. As an example, assume the signal $f(t)$ is an *even* function of time. (This simplifies the discussion.) Test pulses of the kind considered in Chap. 2 are examples. Then $F(\omega)$ is an even function of frequency. The Hilbert transform $\hat{f}(t)$ is then given by

$$\hat{f}(t) = \frac{1}{2\pi} \int_{-\infty}^{\infty} \hat{F}(\omega) e^{j\omega t} \, d\omega$$

$$= \frac{1}{\pi} \int_0^{\infty} F(\omega) \sin \omega t \, d\omega \qquad (4\text{-}57)$$

Notice that $\hat{f}(t)$ is then an odd function of time. Using Eq. (4-57) we may calculate $\hat{f}(t)$ quite readily. Two simple examples are tabulated below, and sketched in Fig. 4-46:

1. $f(t) = 1/(1 + t^2)$. Then

$$F(\omega) = \pi e^{-|\omega|} \qquad \hat{f}(t) = \frac{t}{1 + t^2}$$

2. $f(t) =$ the unit pulse of Fig. 4-46b. Then

$$F(\omega) = 2 \frac{\sin \omega}{\omega} \qquad \hat{f}(t) = \frac{1}{\pi} \ln \frac{|t + 1|}{|t - 1|}$$

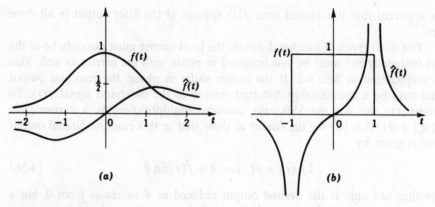

(a)   **(b)**

FIGURE 4-46
Examples of Hilbert transforms. (a) $f(t) = 1/(1 + t^2)$. (b) $f(t)$ a unit pulse.

Note that in the case of the sharply varying unit pulse the Hilbert transform becomes infinite at the points of sharp variation. In the case of the more realistic pulse of Fig. 4-46a, these peaks in the Hilbert transform are less pronounced but still quite high. This distortion becomes quite noticeable in TV and other signal receivers when the phase shift θ approaches $\pi/2$.

Various methods of synchronizing the local carrier exist, as noted in Sec. 4-2. A small amount of unmodulated carrier energy is commonly sent as a pilot signal and, after extraction at the receiver, is used to provide the necessary synchronization.

A typical SSB-receiver block diagram is shown in Fig. 4-47.

The carrier filter and sideband filter are used to separate the sideband and the pilot carrier. Double-frequency conversion (the first and the second mixers) is used, just as in the case of the SSB transmitter (Fig. 4-38), to obtain a convenient range of frequency for the filters. The output of the carrier filter is amplified and limited and used for automatic tuning controls, either directly as a reinsertion carrier or to lock the frequency of a local oscillator that furnishes a suitable insertion carrier.

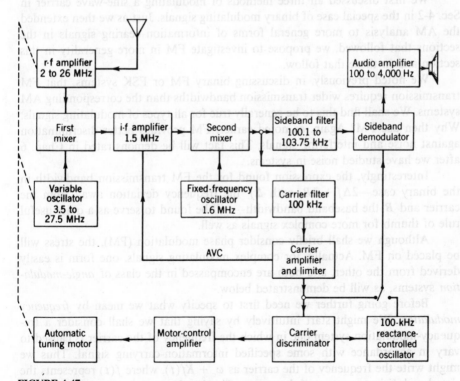

FIGURE 4-47

Single-sideband receiver. (From B. Fisk and C. L. Spencer, "Synthesizer Stabilized Single-Sideband Systems," *Proc. IRE*, vol. 44, no. 12, p. 1680, December 1956, by permission.)

4-9   FREQUENCY MODULATION

We have investigated thus far, in the past few sections, the effect of slowly varying the amplitude of a sinusoidal carrier in accordance with some information to be transmitted. The desired information is then found to be concentrated in sidebands about the carrier frequency. By choosing the carrier frequency high enough, information transmission by means of radio (through the air) becomes practicable. Alternatively, with AM the signal frequency spectrum may be shifted to a frequency range where circuit design becomes more feasible, where circuit components are more readily obtained and more economically built, or where equipment size and weight can be reduced.

In addition, many information channels may be transmitted simultaneously by means of frequency-multiplexing techniques.

For these reasons and others, AM systems of the standard, SSB or DSB type are commonly used in the communication field.

Amplitude modulation is, however, not the only means of modulating a sine-wave carrier. We could just as well modulate the phase and frequency of a sine wave in accordance with some information-bearing signal. And such frequency-modulation (FM) systems are of course also utilized quite commonly.

We first discussed all three methods of modulating a sine-wave carrier in Sec. 4-2 in the special case of binary modulating signals. Just as we then extended the AM analysis to more general forms of information-bearing signals in the sections that followed, we propose to investigate FM in more generality in this section and in those that follow.

We noted previously, in discussing binary FM or FSK systems, that FM transmission requires wider transmission bandwidths than the corresponding AM systems. We shall find this to be generally true for all types of modulating signals. Why then use FM? Again, as noted earlier, FM provides better discrimination against noise and interfering signals. This fact will be demonstrated in Chap. 6 after we have studied noise in systems.

Interestingly, the expression found for the FM transmission bandwidth in the binary case—$2\Delta f + 2B$, with Δf the frequency deviation away from the carrier and B the baseband bandwidth—will be found to serve as a quite useful rule of thumb for more complex signals as well.

Although we shall briefly consider phase modulation (PM), the stress will be placed on FM. Actually, for complex modulating signals, one form is easily derived from the other, and both are encompassed in the class of *angle-modulation* systems, as will be demonstrated below.

Before going further we need first to specify what we mean by *frequency modulation*. We might start intuitively by saying that we shall consider a frequency-modulation system one in which the frequency of the carrier is caused to vary in accordance with some specified information-carrying signal. Thus we might write the frequency of the carrier as $\omega_c + Kf(t)$, where $f(t)$ represents the signal and K is a constant of the system. This is, of course, analogous to the AM case, and was possible in the binary FM case. We run into some difficulty, however, when we attempt to express the more general frequency-modulated carrier mathematically. For we can talk about the frequency of a sine wave only when the frequency is constant and the sine wave persists for all time. Yet here we are attempting to discuss a variable frequency!

The difficulty lies in the fact that, strictly speaking, we can talk only of the sine (or cosine) of an *angle*. If this angle varies linearly with time, we can specifically interpret the frequency as the derivative of the angle. Thus, if

$$f_c(t) = \cos \theta(t) = \cos(\omega_c t + \theta_0) \tag{4-58}$$

the usual expression for a sine wave of frequency ω_c, we are implicitly assuming $\theta(t)$ to be linear with time, with ω_c its derivative.

When $\theta(t)$ does not vary linearly with time, we can no longer write Eq. (4-58) in the standard form shown, with a specified frequency term. To obviate this difficulty, we shall define an *instantaneous radian frequency* ω_i to be the derivative of the angle as a function of time. Thus with

$$f_c(t) = \cos \theta(t) \tag{4-59}$$

we have

$$\omega_i \equiv \frac{d\theta}{dt} \tag{4-60}$$

(This then agrees, of course, with the usual use of the word *frequency* if $\theta = \omega_c t + \theta_0$.)

If $\theta(t)$ in Eq. (4-59) is now made to vary in some manner with a modulating signal $f(t)$, we call the resulting form of modulation *angle modulation*. In particular, if

$$\theta(t) = \omega_c t + \theta_0 + K_1 f(t) \tag{4-61}$$

with K_1 a constant of the system, we say we are dealing with a *phase-modulation* system. Here the phase of the carrier wave varies linearly with the modulating signal. Binary signaling is a special case here.

Now let the *instantaneous frequency*, as defined by Eq. (4-60), vary linearly with the modulating signal,

$$\omega_i = \omega_c + K_2 f(t) \tag{4-60a}$$

Then $$\theta(t) = \int \omega_i \, dt = \omega_c t + \theta_0 + K_2 \int f(t) \, dt \tag{4-62}$$

This, of course, gives rise to an FM system. As an example, if we again consider binary FM (FSK), we have the baseband signal $f(t)$ switching between either of two states. Then $\omega_i = \omega_c \pm \Delta\omega$, and the instantaneous frequency switches correspondingly between two frequencies. The phase angle $\theta(t)$ increases linearly with time in any one binary interval T, switching back to its initial value θ_0 as a new interval begins.

Both phase modulation and frequency modulation are seen to be special cases of angle modulation. In the phase-modulation case the phase of the carrier

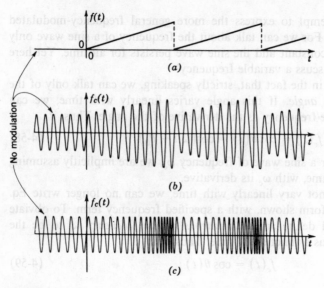

FIGURE 4-48

Frequency modulation. (*a*) Modulating wave. (*b*) AM carrier. (*c*) FM carrier.

varies with the modulating signal, and in the frequency-modulation case the phase of the carrier varies with the integral of the modulating signal. If we first integrate our modulating signal $f(t)$ and then allow it to phase-modulate a carrier, this gives rise to a frequency-modulated wave. This is the method used for producing a frequency-modulated carrier in the Armstrong indirect FM system.

A frequency-modulated carrier is shown sketched in Fig. 4-48c. The modulating signal is assumed to be a repetitive sawtooth of period T $(2\pi/T \ll \omega_c)$. Compare this with Fig. 4-6a, in which the modulating signal is a periodic square wave. As the sawtooth modulating signal increases in magnitude, the FM oscillates more rapidly. Its amplitude remains unchanged, however.

Frequency modulation is a nonlinear process, and so, as pointed out in previous sections, we would expect to see new frequencies generated by the modulation process. As indicated by Eqs. (4-60a) and (4-62), the FM signal oscillates more rapidly with increasing amplitude of the modulating signal. We would therefore expect the frequency spectrum of the FM wave, or its bandwidth, to widen correspondingly.

The analysis of the FM process is inherently much more complicated than that for AM, particularly in dealing with a general modulating signal. This is due to the nonlinearity of the FM process. Superposition cannot be used, so the analysis for one particular type of modulating signal cannot be readily applied to another. However, at the two extremes of small-amplitude modulating signal (narrowband FM) and large-amplitude modulating signal (wideband FM), it turns out that spectral analyses for different modulating signals produce the transmission bandwidth requirements: $2B$ hertz and $2\Delta f$ hertz, respectively, found in the binary-FSK case, while at intermediate amplitudes of modulating signal the bandwidth requirement obtained for the binary FSK signal serves as a good rule of thumb for all types of signals.

Because of the difficulty of analyzing general FM signals, we shall consider here only one nonbinary modulating signal; namely, we shall assume $f(t)$ a single sine wave. Although this is a poor "approximation" to information-carrying signals, which may vary randomly and unpredictably with time, the results obtained are in substantial agreement with the much simpler binary-FSK approach of Sec. 4-2, and will serve to further solidify the discussion there. (One would expect agreement between the two approaches, since a sine wave is similar in appearance to a square wave of the same frequency. The sine wave is in fact the first term in the square-wave Fourier series.)

Spectral analyses of other classes of modulating signals may be found in the literature [BLAC],[23] [GOLD 1948], [MIDD].[24] The results obtained are, as noted, not substantially different than those obtained here for square-wave (FSK) and sine-wave modulating signals. FM spectral analysis with a random or noiselike modulating signal (often used as a model for real signals) leads to similar results [SCHW 1966], [MIDD]. Assume then a sinusoidal modulating signal at frequency f_m:

$$f(t) = a \cos \omega_m t \qquad (4\text{-}63)$$

The instantaneous radian frequency ω_i is

$$\omega_i = \omega_c + \Delta\omega \cos \omega_m t \qquad \Delta\omega \ll \omega_c \qquad (4\text{-}64)$$

where $\Delta\omega$ is a constant depending on the amplitude a of the modulating signal and on the circuitry converting variations in signal amplitude to corresponding variations in carrier frequency.

The instantaneous radian frequency thus varies about the unmodulated carrier frequency ω_c, at the rate ω_m of the modulating signal and with a maximum deviation of $\Delta\omega$ radians. Just as in the binary case, $\Delta f = \Delta\omega/2\pi$ gives the maximum frequency deviation away from the carrier frequency and is called the *frequency deviation*.

The phase variation $\theta(t)$ for this special case is given by

$$\theta(t) = \int \omega_i \, dt = \omega_c t + \frac{\Delta\omega}{\omega_m} \sin \omega_m t + \theta_0 \qquad (4\text{-}65)$$

θ_0 may be taken as zero by referring to an appropriate phase reference, so that

[23][BLAC] H. S. Black, *Modulation Theory*, Van Nostrand, Princeton, N.J., 1955.

[24][MIDD] D. Middleton, *An Introduction to Statistical Communication Theory*, McGraw-Hill, New York, 1960, chap. 14.

the frequency-modulated carrier is given by

$$f_c(t) = \cos(\omega_c t + \beta \sin \omega_m t) \qquad (4\text{-}66)$$

with

$$\beta \equiv \frac{\Delta\omega}{\omega_m} = \frac{\Delta f}{f_m} \qquad (4\text{-}67)$$

Again, as in Sec. 4-2, for binary FSK, β is called the *modulation index* and is by definition the ratio of the frequency deviation to the baseband bandwidth. For a single sine wave of frequency f_m, the baseband bandwidth B is just f_m.

We noted previously that increasing the amplitude of the modulating signal should increase the bandwidth occupied by the FM signal. Increasing the modulating-signal amplitude corresponds to increasing the frequency deviation Δf or the modulation index β. We would thus expect the bandwidth of the FM wave to depend on β. This will be demonstrated in the sections to follow. The average power associated with the frequency-modulated carrier is independent of the modulating signal, however, and is in fact the same as the average power of the unmodulated carrier. This is again in contrast to the AM case, where the average power of the modulated carrier varies with the modulating-signal amplitude.

That this statement is true may be demonstrated by using Eq. (4-66) for a sinusoidal modulating signal. Assuming that $f_c(t)$ represents the instantaneous voltage impressed across a 1-Ω resistor, the average power over a cycle of the modulating frequency is given by

$$\frac{1}{T}\int_0^T f_c^2(t)\, dt = \frac{1}{T}\int_0^T \cos^2(\omega_c t + \beta \sin \omega_m t)\, dt$$

where $T = 1/f_m$. This expression may be rewritten as

$$\frac{1}{T}\int_0^T \frac{1 + \cos(2\omega_c t + 2\beta \sin \omega_m t)}{2}\, dt$$

The second term of the integral goes to zero, since it is periodic in T. This assumes $\omega_m = 2\pi/T \ll \omega_c$. The first term gives $\frac{1}{2}$ W. If the amplitude of the carrier had been written as A_c volts, the average power would have been found to be $A_c^2/2$ watts for a 1-Ω resistor.

Although shown only for a sinusoidal modulating signal, the foregoing result is true for any modulating signal whose highest frequency component B hertz is small compared with the carrier frequency f_c. This is left as an exercise for the reader.

Narrowband FM

To simplify the analysis of FM, we shall treat it in two parts. We shall first consider the sinusoidally modulated carrier with $\beta \ll \pi/2$, and then with $\beta > \pi/2$. Small β corresponds to narrow bandwidths, and FM systems with $\beta \ll \pi/2$ are thus called *narrowband FM systems*. The equations for narrowband FM appear in the form of the equations for the product modulator of the previous sections on AM and so give rise to sideband frequencies equally displaced about the carrier, just as in the case of AM.

To demonstrate this point, consider the sinusoidally modulated carrier of Eq. (4-66), and assume $\beta \ll \pi/2$. (This implies that the maximum phase shift of the carrier is much less than $\pi/2$ radians. This is ordinarily taken to mean $\beta < 0.2$ rad, although $\beta < 0.5$ rad is sometimes used as a criterion.) We have

$$f_c(t) = \cos(\omega_c t + \beta \sin \omega_m t)$$

$$= \cos \omega_c t \cos(\beta \sin \omega_m t) - \sin \omega_c t \sin(\beta \sin \omega_m t) \quad (4\text{-}68)$$

But, for $\beta \ll \pi/2$, $\cos(\beta \sin \omega_m t) \doteq 1$, and $\sin(\beta \sin \omega_m t) \doteq \beta \sin \omega_m t$.

The frequency-modulated wave for small modulation index thus appears in the form

$$f_c(t) \doteq \cos \omega_c t - \beta \sin \omega_m t \sin \omega_c t \qquad \beta \ll \frac{\pi}{2} \qquad (4\text{-}69)$$

Note that this expression for $f_c(t)$, the frequency-modulated carrier, has a form similar to that of the output of a product modulator; it contains the original unmodulated carrier term plus a term given by the product of the modulating signal and carrier. For the sinusoidal modulating signal, $\beta \sin \omega_m t$, this product term provides sideband frequencies displaced $\pm \omega_m$ radians from ω_c. The bandwidth of this narrowband FM signal is thus $2f_m = 2B$ hertz, agreeing with the FSK result.

If we had assumed a general modulating signal $f(t)$ instead of the sinusoidal modulating signal used here, we would have obtained similar results. For, as shown by Eqs. (4-60a) and (4-62), we then have

$$\omega_i = \omega_c + K_2 f(t)$$

$$\theta(t) = \int \omega_i \, dt = \omega_c t + \theta_0 + K_2 \int f(t) \, dt$$

Suppressing the arbitrary phase angle θ_0, and defining a new time function $g(t)$ to be the integral of $f(t)$, $g(t) \equiv \int f(t) \, dt$, we have, as the frequency-modulated carrier,

$$f_c(t) = \cos[\omega_c t + K_2 g(t)] \qquad (4\text{-}70)$$

If K_2 and the maximum amplitude of $g(t)$ are now chosen small enough so that $|K_2 g(t)| \ll \pi/2$,

$$f_c(t) = \cos \omega_c t - K_2 g(t)\sin \omega_c t \qquad (4\text{-}71)$$

Our previous discussion of product modulators indicates that the spectrum of this general case of narrowband FM consists of the carrier plus two sidebands, one on each side of the carrier and each having the form of the spectrum of the function $g(t)$. Narrowband FM is thus equivalent, in this sense, to AM. The bandwidth of a narrowband FM signal, in general, is $2B$ hertz, where B is the highest-frequency component of either $g(t)$ or its derivative $f(t)$, the original modulating signal. (Remember that the linear process of integration adds no new frequency components. The lower-frequency components, however, are accentuated in comparison with the higher-frequency components.) The FSK result is, of course, a special case here.

Although AM and narrowband FM have similar frequency spectra and their mathematical representations both appear in the product-modulator form, they are distinctively different methods of modulation. In the AM case we were interested in variations of the carrier envelope, its frequency remaining unchanged; in the FM case, we assumed the carrier amplitude constant, its phase (and effectively the instantaneous frequency also) varying with the signal. This distinction between the two types of modulation must be retained in the narrowband FM case also (here maximum phase shift of the carrier is assumed less than 0.2 rad).

To emphasize this distinction in the two types of modulation, note that the product modulator or sideband term in either Eq. (4-69) or Eq. (4-71) appears in phase quadrature with the carrier term ($\sin \omega_c t$ as compared with $\cos \omega_c t$). In the AM case, we had both carrier and sideband terms in phase,

$$f_c(t) = \cos \omega_c t + mf(t)\cos \omega_c t$$

For the narrowband FM case, we have

$$f_c(t) = \cos \omega_c t - K_2 g(t)\sin \omega_c t$$

That the inphase, or phase-quadrature, representation is fundamental in distinguishing between AM and narrowband FM (or, alternatively, small-angle phase modulation) is demonstrated very simply by the use of rotating vectors.

We rewrite Eq. (4-69) in its sideband-frequency form,

$$f_c(t) = \cos \omega_c t - \beta \sin \omega_m t \sin \omega_c t$$

$$= \cos \omega_c t - \frac{\beta}{2}[\cos(\omega_c - \omega_m)t - \cos(\omega_c + \omega_m)t] \quad (4\text{-}72)$$

This can also be written in the form

$$f_c(t) = \text{Re}\left[e^{j\omega_c t}\left(1 - \frac{\beta}{2}e^{-j\omega_m t} + \frac{\beta}{2}e^{j\omega_m t}\right)\right] \quad (4\text{-}73)$$

where Re[ ] represents the real part of the expression in the square brackets.

$e^{j\omega_c t}$ may be represented as a unit vector rotating counterclockwise at the rate of ω_c rad/s. Superimposed on this rotation are changes in the vector due to the three terms in parentheses. We then take the real part of the resultant vector, or its projection on the real axis. If we suppress the continuous ω_c rotation and concentrate solely on the three terms in parentheses, we may plot these as the three vectors of Fig. 4-49a. Note that the resulting vector deviates in phase from

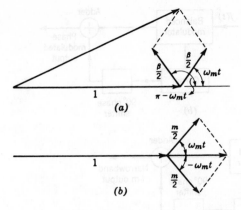

FIGURE 4-49
Vector representation. (*a*) Narrowband FM. (*b*) AM.

the unmodulated vector, while its amplitude is very nearly unchanged. (This is for the case $\beta \ll \pi/2$. Here β is shown larger for the sake of clarity.)

We can use the same vector approach for the AM case and get

$$f_c(t) = \cos \omega_c t + m \cos \omega_m t \cos \omega_c t$$

$$= \cos \omega_c t + \frac{m}{2} \left[\cos(\omega_c + \omega_m)t + \cos(\omega_c - \omega_m)t \right]$$

$$= \mathrm{Re}\left[e^{j\omega_c t}\left(1 + \frac{m}{2} e^{j\omega_m t} + \frac{m}{2} e^{-j\omega_m t} \right) \right] \tag{4-74}$$

The three quantities in parentheses here are likewise shown plotted in Fig. 4-49*b*. Note that the two sideband vectors have been rotated by $\pi/2$ radians as compared with the FM case. The resultant vector here varies in amplitude but remains in phase with the unmodulated carrier term.

We can summarize by saying that the resultant of the two sideband vectors in the FM case will always be perpendicular to (or in phase quadrature with) the unmodulated carrier, while the same resultant in the AM case is collinear with the carrier term. The FM case thus gives rise to phase variations with very little amplitude change ($\beta \ll \pi/2$), while the AM case gives amplitude variations with no phase deviation.

The distinction and similarity between AM and narrowband FM (or phase modulation as well) leads us to a commonly used method of generating a frequency-modulated wave with small modulation index ($\beta < 0.2$ rad).

We demonstrated in our discussion of AM systems that the output of a balanced modulator provides just the product or sideband term required by Eq. (4-71). For an *amplitude-modulated* output we would then add to this output the *inphase* carrier term. This is shown in block diagram form in Fig. 4-50*a*.

To obtain a *phase-modulated* output, according to our previous discussion, we must add a *phase-quadrature* carrier term to the balanced-modulator output. Such a system is shown in Fig. 4-50*b* in block-diagram form. (Remember that this is restricted to small phase variations of 0.2 rad or less.)

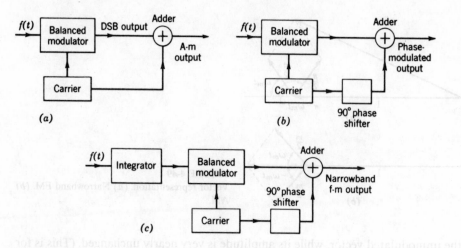

FIGURE 4-50
Evolution of a narrowband FM system. (a) Possible AM system. (b) Phase-modulation system (small phase deviations < 0.2 rad). (c) Narrowband FM system (β < 0.2 rad).

As we demonstrated previously, however, phase modulation and FM differ only by a possible integration of the input modulating signal [Eq. (4-62)]. To obtain a narrowband frequency-modulated output, then, we need only integrate our input signal and then apply it to the phase-modulation system of Fig. 4-50b. The resultant narrowband FM system (β < 0.2 rad) is shown in Fig. 4.50c.

The narrowband FM system of Fig. 4-50c is used in the Armstrong indirect FM system.

Wideband FM

We have just shown that a frequency-modulated signal with small modulation index ($\beta \ll \pi/2$) has a frequency spectrum similar to that of an amplitude-modulated signal. The significant distinction between the two cases arises from the fact that in the FM case the sidebands are in phase quadrature with the carrier, while in the AM case they are in phase with the carrier. The bandwidth of the narrowband FM signal, just like the AM signal, is thus $2B$, with B the maximum-frequency component of the modulating signal.

The noise and interference reduction advantages of FM over AM, mentioned previously, become significant, however, only for large modulation index ($\beta > \pi/2$). The bandwidths required to pass this signal become correspondingly large, as first noted in Sec. 4-2. Most FM systems in use are of this wideband type.

Here the comparison between FM and AM that was valid for small modulation index ($\beta \ll \pi/2$) ends. We shall show that the previous results for narrowband FM can be extended to the wideband case, however.

We demonstrate the increase in signal bandwidth with increasing β here for the idealized model of a sinusoidal modulating signal. The results, as noted earlier, are similar to those obtained in the binary FM case. The frequency-modulated carrier is again written in the expanded form

$$f_c(t) = \cos \omega_c t \cos(\beta \sin \omega_m t) - \sin \omega_c t \sin(\beta \sin \omega_m t) \qquad (4\text{-}75)$$

For $\beta \ll \pi/2$ we would, of course, get our previous result of a single carrier and two sideband frequencies. But now let β be somewhat larger at first. We can expand $\cos(\beta \sin \omega_m t)$ in a power series to give us

$$\cos(\beta \sin \omega_m t) \doteq 1 - \frac{\beta^2}{2}\sin^2 \omega_m t \qquad \beta^2 \ll 6 \qquad (4\text{-}76)$$

If we assume $\beta \ll \sqrt{6}$ and retain just the first two terms in the power series for the cosine, we get the additional term $\sin^2 \omega_m t \cos \omega_c t$ in the expression for $f_c(t)$. This term gives, upon trigonometric expansion, additional sideband frequencies spaced $\pm 2\omega_m$ radians from the carrier and also contributes a term $-\beta^2/4$ to the carrier. $\sin(\beta \sin \omega_m t)$ can still be represented by $\beta \sin \omega_m t$, the first term in its power-series expansion, for $\beta^2 \ll 6$, so that $f_c(t)$ becomes

$$f_c(t) \doteq \left(1 - \frac{\beta^2}{4}\right)\cos \omega_c t - \frac{\beta}{2}\left[\cos(\omega_m - \omega_c)t - \cos(\omega_m + \omega_c)t\right]$$

$$+ \frac{\beta^2}{8}\left[\cos(\omega_c + 2\omega_m)t + \cos(\omega_c - 2\omega_m)t\right] \qquad \beta^2 \ll 6 \qquad (4\text{-}77)$$

Note that the carrier term has now begun to decrease somewhat with increasing β, the first-order sidebands at $\omega_c \pm \omega_m$ increase with β, and a new set of sidebands (the second-order sidebands) appear at $\omega_c \pm 2\omega_m$. The spectrum of this signal is shown in Fig. 4-51b, while the narrowband case is plotted in Fig. 4-51a. This appearance of new sidebands with increasing modulation index corresponds to the widening of the spectrum in the binary-FM case as the two frequencies there are deviated further away from the carrier. This is distinctly different from the AM case, where the number of sideband frequencies was dependent solely on the number of modulating frequencies, and not on the amplitude of the modulating signal. Here new sets of significant sidebands appear as the modulation index increases. For a fixed modulating frequency, β is proportional to the amplitude of the modulating signal, so that increases in signal amplitude generate new sidebands. This produces a corresponding increase in bandwidth. (The bandwidth has been doubled in this case, going from $2f_m$ to $4f_m$.)

Since the average power in the frequency-modulated wave is independent of the modulating signal, increasing power in the sideband frequencies must be accompanied by a corresponding decrease in the power associated with the carrier. This accounts for the decrease in carrier amplitude that we have already noted.

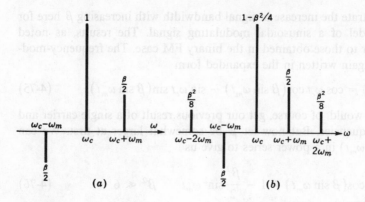

FIGURE 4-51
Effect of increasing β on FM spectrum ($\beta^2 \ll 6$). Sine-wave modulation. (a) Narrowband case, $\beta \ll \pi/2$. (b) Increasing β.

As β increases further, we require more terms in the power-series expansion for both $\cos(\beta \sin \omega_m t)$ and $\sin(\beta \sin \omega_m t)$. This gives rise to increasingly more significant sideband components, and the bandwidth begins to increase with β, or with increasing amplitude of the original modulating signal. This power-series approach can be used to explore the characteristics of wideband FM. It becomes a tedious job of trigonometric manipulation to determine the significant sideband frequencies and their associated amplitudes, however, so that we shall resort to a somewhat different approach.

We are basically interested in determining the frequency components of the frequency-modulated carrier given by

$$f_c(t) = \cos(\omega_c t + \beta \sin \omega_m t)$$

$$= \cos \omega_c t \cos(\beta \sin \omega_m t) - \sin(\beta \sin \omega_m t)\sin \omega_c t$$

But we note that both $\cos(\beta \sin \omega_m t)$ and $\sin(\beta \sin \omega_m t)$ are periodic functions of ω_m. As such, each may be expanded in a Fourier series of period $2\pi/\omega_m$. Each series will contain terms in ω_m and all its harmonic frequencies. Each harmonic term multiplied by either $\cos \omega_c t$ or $\sin \omega_c t$, as the case may be, will give rise to two sideband frequencies symmetrically situated about ω_c. We thus get a picture of a large set of sideband frequencies in general, all displaced from the carrier ω_c by integral multiples of the modulating signal ω_m. The sidebands corresponding to the $\sin \omega_c t$ term will be quadrature sidebands, while those corresponding to the $\cos \omega_c t$ term will be inphase sidebands. For small values of β, $\cos(\beta \sin \omega_m t)$ and $\sin(\beta \sin \omega_m t)$ vary slowly, and so only a small number of the sidebands about ω_c will be significant in amplitude. As β increases, these two terms vary more rapidly, and the amplitudes of the higher-frequency terms become more significant. This picture of course agrees with our previous conclusion that increasing β produces a wider-band signal and agrees as well with the binary-FM analysis. It

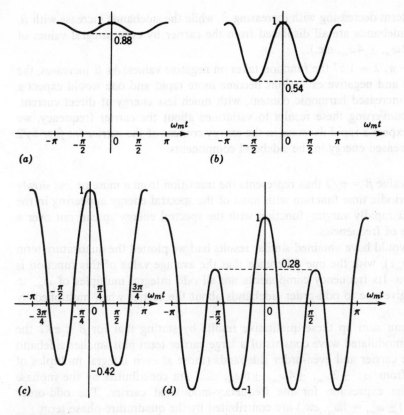

FIGURE 4-52
Plots of $\cos(\beta \sin \omega_m t)$ for various β. (a) $\beta = 0.5$, $\cos(0.5 \sin \omega_m t)$. ($b$) $\beta = 1$, $\cos(\sin \omega_m t)$. (c) $\beta = 2$, $\cos(2 \sin \omega_m t)$. (d) $\beta = 5$, $\cos(5 \sin \omega_m t)$.

is again in contrast to the AM case, where only the carrier and a single set of sidebands appear.

These remarks are given more significance by considering some plots of $\cos(\beta \sin \omega_m t)$. These are shown in Fig. 4-52 for various values of β. The four curves drawn demonstrate some interesting points:

1. For $\beta < 0.5$ the curve can be represented approximately by a dc component plus a small component at twice the fundamental frequency ω_m. But these terms multiplied by $\cos \omega_c t$ give just the carrier and the second-order sideband terms that we obtained previously for $\beta \ll \sqrt{6}$.

2. For $\beta < \pi/2 = 1.57$ the function remains positive and appears as a dc component with some ripple superimposed. One would thus expect a Fourier analysis to give a large dc component plus successively decreasing harmonics. This dc component, or average value of the function, decreases with increasing β, however. Again, if we multiply this by $\cos \omega_c t$, we obtain a picture of a

carrier term decreasing with increasing β, while the sidebands increase with β. These sidebands are all displaced from the carrier by even integral values of ω_m ($\pm 2\omega_m$, $\pm 4\omega_m$, etc.).

3. For $\beta > \pi/2 = 1.57$ the function takes on negative values. As β increases, the positive and negative excursions become more rapid and one would expect a greatly increased harmonic content, with much less energy at direct current. Again converting these results to variations about the carrier frequency, we would expect a rapid decrease in the energy content of the carrier for $\beta > \pi/2$ and increased energy in the sideband components.

The value $\beta = \pi/2$ thus represents the transition from a more or less slowly varying periodic time function with most of the spectral energy appearing in the carrier to a rapidly varying function with the spectral energy spread out over a wide range of frequencies.

We would have obtained similar results had we plotted the quadrature term $\sin(\beta \sin \omega_m t)$, with the one difference that the average value of this function is always zero. Its frequency components are all odd integral multiples of ω_m, so that they give rise to odd-order sidebands about the carrier when multiplied by $\sin \omega_c t$.

We can sum up these qualitative results by stating that for $\beta < \pi/2$ the frequency-modulated wave consists of a large carrier term plus smaller sideband terms. The carrier and even-order sidebands (those at even integral multiples of ω_m away from ω_c: $\pm 2\omega_m$, $\pm 4\omega_m$, $\pm 6\omega_m$, etc.) are contributed by the inphase term of the expression for the frequency-modulated carrier. The odd-order sidebands ($\pm \omega_m$, $\pm 3\omega_m$, etc.) are contributed by the quadrature-phase term.

For $\beta > \pi/2$, we get a picture of a wave with only a small carrier term plus increased energy in the sidebands. The bandwidth of the FM signal increases rapidly with $\beta > \pi/2$. This implies wide bandwidths and is, of course, as pointed out previously, the desirable situation in most FM systems used for their good noise- and interference-rejection properties.

By wideband FM, we shall thus mean a frequency-modulated signal with $\beta > \pi/2$.

To demonstrate these conclusions more quantitatively, we must actually determine the frequency components and their amplitudes for the frequency-modulated signal of arbitrary β and sinusoidal modulating signal. As was noted previously, this may be done by expanding both $\cos(\beta \sin \omega_m t)$ and $\sin(\beta \sin \omega_m t)$ in the respective Fourier series. Multiplying the cosine term by $\cos \omega_c t$ and the sine term by $\sin \omega_c t$ then gives us our FM signal.

Both series may be found simultaneously by considering the periodic complex exponential

$$v(t) = e^{j\beta \sin \omega_m t} \qquad -\frac{T}{2} < t < \frac{T}{2} \qquad (4\text{-}78)$$

The real part of this function gives us our cosine function; the imaginary part, the sine function. If we expand this exponential in its Fourier series, we can expect to get a real part consisting of even harmonics of ω_m and an imaginary part consisting of the odd harmonics. [This is deduced from out previous discussion of $\cos(\beta \sin \omega_m t)$ and the associated Fig. 4-52.] By equating reals and imaginaries, we shall then obtain the desired Fourier expansions for $\cos(\beta \sin \omega_m t)$ and $\sin(\beta \sin \omega_m t)$, respectively.

The Fourier coefficient of the complex Fourier series for the exponential of Eq. (4-78) is given by

$$c_n = \int_{-T/2}^{T/2} e^{j(\beta \sin \omega_m t - \omega_n t)} \, dt \qquad \omega_m = \frac{2\pi}{T} \qquad \omega_n = \frac{2\pi n}{T} = n\omega_m \quad (4\text{-}79)$$

Normalizing this integral by letting $x = \omega_m t$, we get

$$\frac{c_n}{T} = \frac{1}{2\pi} \int_{-\pi}^{\pi} e^{j(\beta \sin s - nx)} \, dx \qquad (4\text{-}80)$$

This integral can be evaluated only as an infinite series (as was the case in Chap. 2 for the sine integral Si x). It occurs very commonly in many physical problems. It is called the *Bessel function of the first kind* and is denoted by the symbol $J_n(\beta)$. [Note from Eq. (4-80) that c_n is a function of both β and n.]

In particular,

$$J_n(\beta) \equiv \frac{1}{2\pi} \int_{-\pi}^{\pi} e^{j(\beta \sin x - nx)} \, dx \qquad (4\text{-}81)$$

so that $$c_n = TJ_n(\beta) \qquad (4\text{-}82)$$

For $n = 0$, we get $c_0 = TJ_0(\beta)$, the dc component of the Fourier-series representation of the periodic complex exponential of Eq. (4-78). Increasing values of n give the corresponding Fourier coefficients for the higher-frequency terms of the Fourier series. The spectrum of the complex exponential of Eq. (4-78) (and ultimately that of the frequency-modulated signal) will thus be given by the value of the Bessel function and will depend on the parameter β. Thus

$$e^{j\beta \sin \omega_m t} = \frac{1}{T} \sum_{n=-\infty}^{\infty} c_n e^{j\omega_n t} = \sum_{n=-\infty}^{\infty} J_n(\beta) e^{j\omega_n t} \qquad \omega_n = n\omega_m \quad (4\text{-}83)$$

As an example, let $n = 0$. Then

$$J_0(\beta) \equiv \frac{1}{2\pi} \int_{-\pi}^{\pi} e^{j\beta \sin x} \, dx \qquad (4\text{-}84)$$

is the dc component of the Fourier series of Eq. (4-83). But

$$e^{j\beta \sin x} = 1 + (j\beta \sin x) + \frac{(j\beta \sin x)^2}{2!} + \frac{(j\beta \sin x)^3}{3!} + \cdots \qquad (4\text{-}85)$$

using the series expansion for the exponential.

The power terms in $\sin x$ may be rewritten as sines and cosines of integral multiples of x, so that Eq. (4-85) can also be written

$$e^{j\beta \sin x} = 1 + j\beta \sin x - \frac{\beta^2}{2}\frac{1 - \cos 2x}{2} + \cdots \qquad (4\text{-}86)$$

If we now integrate over a complete period of 2π radians [as called for by Eq. (4-84)], the terms in $\sin x$, $\cos 2x$, etc., vanish, leaving us with

$$J_0(\beta) = 1 - \frac{\beta^2}{4} + \cdots \qquad (4\text{-}87)$$

—an infinite series in β. [This is, of course, one method of evaluating the integral of Eq. (4-81).] But a comparison with Eq. (4-77) shows that this is exactly the coefficient of the carrier term of our FM signal, obtained there by a power-series expansion of $\cos(\beta \sin \omega_m t)$. The advantage of the present approach, using a Fourier-series expansion, is that the Bessel function is already tabulated so that we do not have to repeat the evaluation of Eq. (4-81) for different values of n by means of an infinite series.

From Eq. (4-83), the Fourier-series expansion of the complex exponential, we can obtain our desired Fourier series for $\cos(\beta \sin \omega_m t)$ and $\sin(\beta \sin \omega_m t)$. It can be shown, either from the integral definition of $J_n(\beta)$ [Eq. (4-81)] or from the power-series expansion of $J_n(\beta)$, that

$$J_n(\beta) = J_{-n}(\beta) \qquad n \text{ even}$$
$$= -J_{-n}(\beta) \qquad n \text{ odd} \qquad (4\text{-}88)$$

Writing out the Fourier series term by term, and using Eq. (4-88) to combine the positive and negative terms of equal magnitude of n, we get

$$e^{j\beta \sin \omega_m t} = J_0(\beta) + 2[J_2(\beta)\cos 2\omega_m t + J_4(\beta)\cos 4\omega_m t + \cdots]$$
$$+ 2j[J_1(\beta)\sin \omega_m t + J_3(\beta)\sin 3\omega_m t + \cdots] \qquad (4\text{-}89)$$

But $\qquad e^{j\beta \sin \omega_m t} = \cos(\beta \sin \omega_m t) + j \sin(\beta \sin \omega_m t) \qquad (4\text{-}90)$

Equating real and imaginary terms, we get

$$\cos(\beta \sin \omega_m t) = J_0(\beta) + 2J_2(\beta)\sin 2\omega_m t + 2J_4(\beta)\cos 4\omega_m t + \cdots \qquad (4\text{-}91)$$

and

$$\sin(\beta \sin \omega_m t) = 2J_1(\beta)\sin \omega_m t + 2J_3(\beta)\sin 3\omega_m t + \cdots \qquad (4\text{-}92)$$

Equations (4-91) and (4-92) are the desired Fourier-series expansions for the cosine and sine terms. As noted previously, the cosine term has only the even harmonics of ω_m in its series, the sine term containing the odd harmonics.

The spectral distribution of the frequency-modulated carrier is now readily obtained. As previously written,

$$f_c(t) = \cos \omega_c t \cos(\beta \sin \omega_m t) - \sin \omega_c t \sin(\beta \sin \omega_m t) \qquad (4\text{-}93)$$

Using the Fourier-series expansions for the cosine and sine terms, and then utilizing the trigonometric sum and difference formulas (as in the AM analysis), we get

$$\begin{aligned}
f_c(t) = J_0(\beta)\cos \omega_c t &- J_1(\beta)[\cos(\omega_c - \omega_m)t - \cos(\omega_c + \omega_m)t] \\
&+ J_2(\beta)[\cos(\omega_c - 2\omega_m)t + \cos(\omega_c + 2\omega_m)t] \\
&- J_3(\beta)[\cos(\omega_c - 3\omega_m)t - \cos(\omega_c + 3\omega_m)t] \\
&+ \cdots
\end{aligned}$$

$$(4\text{-}94)$$

We thus have a time function consisting of a carrier and an infinite number of sidebands, spaced at frequencies $\pm f_m$, $\pm 2f_m$, etc., away from the carrier. This is in contrast to the AM case, where the carrier and only a single set of sidebands existed. The odd sideband frequencies arise from the quadrature term of Eq. (4-93); the even sideband frequencies arise from the inphase ($\cos \omega_c t$) term. This, of course, agrees with our previous qualitative discussion based on Fig. 4-52.

The magnitudes of the carrier and sideband terms depend on β, the modulation index, this dependence being expressed by the appropriate Bessel function. Again, this is at variance with the AM case, where the carrier magnitude was fixed and the two sidebands varied only with the modulation factor.

We showed previously, from qualitative considerations of the time variation of the function $f_c(t)$, that for $\beta \ll \pi/2$, we should have primarily a carrier and one or two sideband pairs. For $\beta > \pi/2$, we should have increasingly more significant sideband pairs as β increases. The magnitude of the carrier should also decrease rapidly.

We can now verify these qualitative conclusions by referring to plots or tabulations of the Bessel function. As an example, a graph of the functions $J_0(\beta)$, $J_1(\beta)$, $J_2(\beta)$, $J_8(\beta)$, and $J_{16}(\beta)$ is shown in Fig. 4-53. Note that for $\beta > \pi/2$ the value of $J_0(\beta)$ decreases sharply. $J_0(\beta)$ represents the magnitude of the carrier term, so that this result agrees with that obtained from the curves of Fig. 4-52.

For β small ($\beta \ll \pi/2$), the only Bessel functions of significant magnitude are $J_0(\beta)$ and $J_1(\beta)$. The FM wave thus consists essentially of the carrier and the

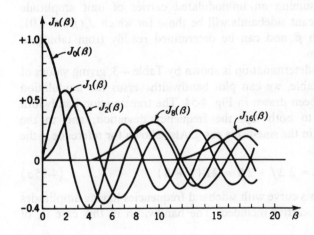

FIGURE 4-53
Examples of Bessel functions of the first kind.

two first-order sideband frequencies. This is, of course, the narrowband FM case considered previously. As β increases, however, the magnitudes of the higher-order sidebands begin to increase, the carrier magnitude begins to decrease, and the bandwidth required increases. The significant number of sideband terms depends on β, the modulation index. Note that $J_8(\beta)$ is essentially zero up to $\beta = 4$ and then begins to increase to a peak value at $\beta = 9.5$. $J_{16}(\beta)$ begins to increase significantly for $\beta > 12$ and peaks at about $\beta = 18$.

It is apparent from the curves of Fig. 4-53, and can be shown in general, that the higher-order Bessel functions, $J_n(\beta)$ with $n \gg 1$, are essentially zero to the point $\beta = n$. They then increase to a peak, decrease again, and eventually oscillate like damped sinusoids. This means that for $\beta \gg 1$ the number of significant sideband frequencies in the frequency-modulated wave is approximately equal to β. $[J_n(\beta) \doteq 0, n > \beta,$ so that the corresponding sideband terms are negligible.] Since the sidebands are all f_m hertz apart, and since there are two sets of them, on either side of the carrier, the bandwidth B_T of the FM signal is approximately

$$B_T \doteq 2\beta f_m = 2\frac{\Delta f}{f_m} f_m = 2 \Delta f \qquad \beta \gg 1 \qquad (4\text{-}95)$$

This agrees, of course, with the results of the binary-FM case. This assumes a sinusoidal modulating signal of frequency f_m hertz. Δf represents the maximum-frequency deviation away from f_c, the unmodulated carrier frequency, and depends on the amplitude of the modulating signal. So for large β the bandwidth is directly proportional to the amplitude of the modulating signal. This is again to be compared with the AM or narrowband FM case where the bandwidth is $2B$, B being the baseband bandwidth (f_m in the case of a single sine wave at that frequency).

The bandwidth is equal to $2 \Delta f$ only for very large modulation index. For smaller values of β, we can determine the bandwidth by counting the significant sidebands. The word significant is usually taken to mean those sidebands which have a magnitude of at least 1 percent of the magnitude of the unmodulated carrier. We have been assuming an unmodulated carrier of unit amplitude ($\cos \omega_c t$), so that the significant sidebands will be those for which $J_n(\beta) > 0.01$. The number will vary with β and can be determined readily from tabulated values of the Bessel function.

An example of such a determination is shown by Table 4-3, giving values of β up to 2. Using such a table, we can plot bandwidth versus the modulation index β. Such a curve has been drawn in Fig. 4-54. The transmission bandwidth B_T is shown normalized to both Δf, the frequency deviation, and to the baseband bandwidth B(f_m in the sine-wave case). Also shown for reference is the rule-of-thumb relation

$$B_T = 2 \Delta f + 2B = 2B(1 + \beta) \qquad (4\text{-}95a)$$

as well as a sine-wave analysis curve with sideband frequencies having amplitudes 10 percent or more of the carrier included. The bandwidth in this case is, of

TABLE 4-3
Significant sidebands

β	$J_0(\beta)$	$J_1(\beta)$	$J_2(\beta)$	$J_3(\beta)$	$J_4(\beta)$	No. of side-bands	Band-width
0.01	1.00	0.005	—	—	—	1	$2f_m$
0.20	0.99	0.100	—	—	—	1	$2f_m$
0.50	0.94	0.24	0.03	—	—	2	$4f_m$
1.00	0.77	0.44	0.11	0.02	—	3	$6f_m$
2.00	0.22	0.58	0.35	0.13	0.03	4	$8f_m$

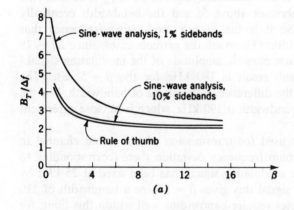

(a)

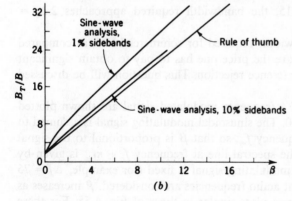

(b)

FIGURE 4-54
FM bandwidth versus modulation index. (a) Normalized to frequency deviation. (b) Normalized to baseband bandwidth.

course, less than that for 1-percent amplitude, and agrees closely with the rule-of-thumb relation. All curves show B_T equal to $2B$ for small β, and approaching $2\,\Delta f$ for large β.

We are now in a position to make some calculations of the required bandwidth for typical sinusoidal signals. Since the bandwidth ultimately varies with Δf, the frequency deviation, or the amplitude of the modulating signal, some limit must be put on this amplitude to avoid excessive bandwidth. The FCC has fixed the maximum value of Δf at 75 kHz for commercial FM broadcasting stations. What does this imply in the way of required bandwidth? If we take the modulating frequency f_m to be 15 kHz (typically the maximum audio frequency in FM transmission), then $\beta = 5$, and the required bandwidth is 240 kHz, from Fig. 4-54. (Alternatively, for $\beta = 5$, there are eight significant sideband frequencies, so $2 \times 8 \times 15 = 240$ kHz is the bandwidth required.) For $f_m < 15$ kHz (the lower audio frequencies) β increases above 5, and the bandwidth eventually approaches $2\,\Delta f = 150$ kHz. So it is the *highest* modulating frequency that determines the required bandwidth. (These are the extreme cases, since $\Delta f = 75$ kHz corresponds to the maximum possible amplitude of the modulating signal.) The corresponding rule-of-thumb result is 180 kHz for the $\beta = 5$ case. The difference is, of course, due to the difference in definition of bandwidth. For the 10-percent sideband level, the bandwidth is 190 kHz, which is in close agreement with the rule of thumb.

Frequency modulation is used for transmission of the sound channel in commercial TV, and the maximum frequency deviation there (corresponding to the maximum amplitude of the modulating signal) has been fixed at 25 kHz by the FCC. For a 15-kHz audio signal this gives $\beta = 1.7$, or a bandwidth of 110 kHz. The lower audio frequencies require bandwidths well within this limit, for with f_m decreasing and $\beta > 15$, the bandwidth required approaches $2\,\Delta f = 50$ kHz.

The relatively large bandwidths required for commercial FM, as compared with AM sound transmission, are the price one has to pay to obtain significant improvement in noise and interference rejection. This question will be discussed in detail in Chap. 6.

The amplitude spectra of a frequency-modulated signal are shown plotted in Fig. 4-55 for $\beta = 0.2, 1, 5, 10$. The sinusoidal modulating signal is assumed to be of constant modulation frequency f_m, so that β is proportional to the signal amplitude. The amplitude of the spectral line at frequency $f_c \pm nf_m$ is given by $J_n(\beta)$. If the amplitude of the modulating signal is fixed (for example, $\Delta f = 75$ kHz for all signals) and different audio frequencies are considered, β increases as f_m decreases and we get spectrum plots similar to those of Fig. 4-55. For these plots Δf is fixed, however, so that we get a picture of more and more spectral lines crowding into a fixed frequency interval. An example of such a plot is shown in Fig. 4-56. Δf has been chosen as 75 kHz, with f_m varying from 15 kHz down to 5 kHz. This plot shows clearly the lines concentrating within the $2\,\Delta f$ or 150-kHz points as β increases. (Remember again that the bandwidth approaches $2\,\Delta f$ for large β.)

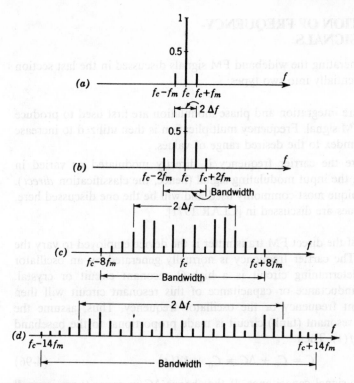

FIGURE 4-55
Amplitude–frequency spectrum, FM signal (sinusoidal modulating signal, f_m fixed, amplitude varying). (*a*) $\beta = 0.2$. (*b*) $\beta = 1$. (*c*) $\beta = 5$. (*d*) $\beta = 10$.

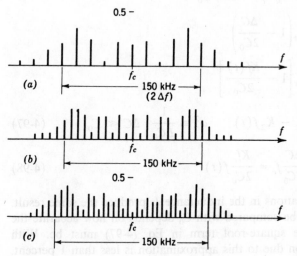

FIGURE 4-56
Amplitude–frequency spectrum, FM signal (amplitude of Δf fixed, f_m decreasing). (*a*) $f_m = 15$ kHz ($\beta = 5$). (*b*) $f_m = 7.5$ kHz ($\beta = 10$). (*c*) $f_m = 5$ kHz ($\beta = 15$).

4-10 GENERATION OF FREQUENCY-MODULATED SIGNALS

The methods of generating the wideband FM signals discussed in the last section can be grouped essentially into two types:

1. *Indirect FM.* Here integration and phase modulation are first used to produce a narrowband FM signal. Frequency multiplication is then utilized to increase the modulation index to the desired range of values.
2. *Direct FM.* Here the carrier frequency is directly modulated or varied in accordance with the input modulating signal (hence, the classification *direct*). This is the technique most commonly used and will be the one discussed here. Indirect techniques are discussed in [CLAR 1971].

At the heart of the direct FM transmitter is the device employed to vary the carrier frequency. The carrier frequency is normally generated by an oscillator whose frequency-determining circuit is a high-Q resonant circuit or crystal. Variations in the inductance or capacitance of this resonant circuit will then change the resonant frequency or the oscillator frequency. Thus, assume the capacitance of the resonant (tank) circuit is made proportional to the baseband modulating signal $f(t)$. Then

$$C = C_0 + \Delta C = C_0 + Kf(t) \qquad (4\text{-}96)$$

Here C_0 is the zero-signal capacitance. If the change ΔC in capacitance is small compared with C_0, it is simple to show that the instantaneous frequency ω_i of the tuned circuit becomes linearly proportional to $f(t)$, as desired. Specifically,

$$\omega_i = \frac{1}{\sqrt{LC}} = \frac{1}{\sqrt{LC_0}} \frac{1}{\sqrt{1 + \Delta C/C_0}}$$

$$\doteq \omega_c \left(1 - \frac{\Delta C}{2C_0}\right)$$

$$= \omega_c \left[1 - \frac{Kf(t)}{2C_0}\right]$$

$$= \omega_c - K_2 f(t) \qquad \omega_c^2 \equiv \frac{1}{LC_0} \qquad \Delta C \ll C_0 \qquad (4\text{-}97)$$

and

$$\Delta f = \frac{\Delta C}{2C_0} f_c = \frac{Kf_c}{2C_0} f(t) \qquad (4\text{-}98)$$

It is apparent that small variations in the inductance L produce the same result.

How small ΔC should be compared with C_0 depends on how accurate the linear approximation to the square-root term in Eq. (4-97) must be. With $\Delta C/C_0 < 0.013$, the distortion due to this approximation is less than 1 percent. (The reader can check this for himself by evaluating the next, nonlinear term in

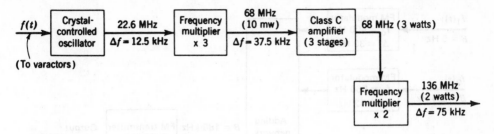

FIGURE 4-57
Typical direct FM transmitter for space telemetry. [From A. V. Balakrishnan (ed.), *Space Communications*, McGraw-Hill, New York, 1963, p. 190.]

the power-series expansion of the square root.) Although the change in capacitance is of necessity small, the frequency deviation Δf may be quite large if the zero-signal resonant frequency f_c is large enough. As an example, if $\Delta C/2C_0 = 0.005$ and $f_c = 15$ MHz, then $\Delta f = 75$ kHz, which is the maximum deviation specified for standard radio broadcasting. Generally, this method of *directly* varying the instantaneous frequency requires substantially less additional frequency multiplication and conversion than does the indirect method.

There are various ways of obtaining a capacitance (or inductance) variation proportional to the signal intelligence $f(t)$. A reverse-biased *PN* junction provides one example. Other examples appear in [CLAR 1971].

FM transmitters have been used quite commonly in space communications and telemetry. A typical block diagram of a direct-type FM transmitter for space applications is shown in Fig. 4-57 [ALLE 1963].[25] This all-solid-state system provides 2 W output power at 136 MHz. A series reactive network consisting of varactor diodes and an inductor provides the required variable capacitance in the 22.6-MHz crystal-controlled oscillator. The FM signal is then tripled in frequency and amplified to provide 3 W output at 68 MHz. A frequency doubler then provides the desired output. The initial frequency deviation is 12.5 kHz. The final Δf, after frequency multiplication by 6, is 75 kHz.

Frequency multiplexing of several data channels is quite commonly used in space telemetry.[26] In this case the individual data channels each frequency-modulate a carrier, the resultant FM signals being arranged to occupy adjacent frequency bands. These FM signals are then summed and the composite complex signal used to frequency modulate a very high-frequency sine-wave carrier for final transmission. An example of such an *FM–FM system* is shown in Fig. 4-58. (The notation FM–FM is commonly used to indicate two steps of FM. AM–FM similarly implies frequency multiplexing of multiple data channels using AM

[25][ALLE 1963] W. B. Allen, in A. V. Balakrishnan (ed.), *Space Communications*, McGraw-Hill, New York, 1963, pp. 190–192.
[26]See "FM–FM Telemetry Systems," in [GRUE, chap. 6]; also [STAM].

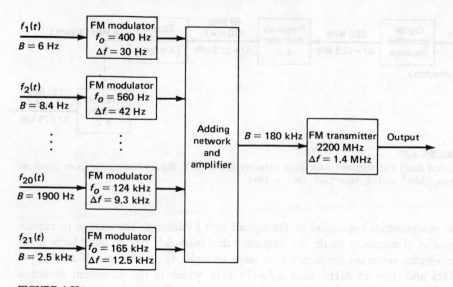

FIGURE 4-58

FM–FM system for space telemetry (proportional-bandwidth subcarrier channels).

techniques, with the composite set of AM signals then used to frequency-modulate a high-frequency carrier.) In this example, the ratio of frequency deviation to subcarrier frequency in each subchannel is held fixed at 7.5 percent. For a modulation index of 5 for each subchannel, the corresponding signal bandwidths increase with the channel number. Low-bandwidth signals would thus be used in the low-numbered channels, wider-bandwidth signals in the higher-numbered ones.

Very often one or more of the subchannels may be used for the transmission of time-multiplex digital data, or several subchannels may be combined to accommodate wider-band data signals.

Frequency multiplexing will be discussed in more detail in Sec. 4-12.

4-11 FREQUENCY DEMODULATION

Frequency demodulation, the process of converting a frequency-modulated signal back to the original modulating signal, can be carried out in a variety of ways. Ultimately, however, the process used must provide an output voltage (or current) whose *amplitude* is *linearly* proportional to the *frequency* of the input FM signal. The term *frequency discriminator* is commonly used to characterize a device providing this frequency-amplitude conversion.

Various schemes have been proposed to accomplish the task of frequency demodulation. We shall discuss two types of frequency discriminators in this section: a balanced discriminator involving the use of tuned circuits and so-called zero-crossing detectors. Others appear in [CLAR 1971].

Consider again the FM signal given by

$$F_c(t) = A \cos \theta(t) = A \cos\left[\omega_c t + K \int f(t)\, dt\right] \qquad (4\text{-}99)$$

Here $f(t)$ is the baseband or modulating signal. It is apparent that to extract $f(t)$ from this expression, we must somehow generate the instantaneous frequency

$$\omega_i(t) = \frac{d\theta(t)}{dt} = \omega_c + Kf(t) \qquad (4\text{-}100)$$

If we then balance out the constant term ω_c, we have the desired output $f(t)$.

We shall show later that zero-crossing detectors do provide a measure of ω_i and, hence, $f(t)$. The approach we consider now is that of studying Eq. (4-99) for the FM signal. Some thought indicates that ω_i may be generated from that equation by differentiating $f_c(t)$ with respect to time. Specifically, if we assume the amplitude A constant (we shall have to include a limiter to ensure this later), the derivative of $f_c(t)$ is just

$$\frac{df_c(t)}{dt} = -\left[A \sin \theta(t)\right]\frac{d\theta}{dt}$$

$$= -A\left[\omega_c + Kf(t)\right]\sin \theta(t) \qquad (4\text{-}101)$$

Note that this expression is precisely in the form of an AM signal, whose *envelope* is given by

$$A\left[\omega_c + Kf(t)\right] = A\omega_c\left[1 + \frac{Kf(t)}{\omega_c}\right]$$

Since we have been assuming the frequency deviation $\Delta\omega = Kf(t) \ll \omega_c$, the envelope never goes to zero, and, in fact, varies only slightly about the average quantity $A\omega_c$. It is then apparent that we may now obtain $f(t)$ by envelope-detecting $df_c(t)/dt$ (see Fig. 4-59).

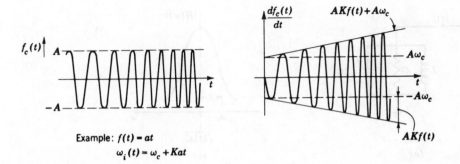

Example: $f(t) = at$

$\omega_i(t) = \omega_c + Kat$

FIGURE 4-59
Typical FM signal $f_c(t)$ and its derivative $df_c(t)/dt$ [example: $f(t) = at$].

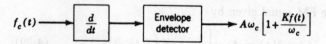

$$f_c(t) \longrightarrow \boxed{\dfrac{d}{dt}} \longrightarrow \boxed{\begin{array}{c}\text{Envelope}\\\text{detector}\end{array}} \longrightarrow A\omega_c\left[1 + \dfrac{Kf(t)}{\omega_c}\right]$$

FIGURE 4-60
FM detector.

The FM detector thus consists of a differentiating circuit followed by an envelope detector (Fig. 4-60). To ensure that the amplitude A is truly constant [otherwise additional (distortion) terms involving dA/dt appear at the output], one normally inserts a *limiter* prior to differentiation. The limiter serves to keep amplitude variations from appearing in the output. If one uses hard clipping to keep the amplitude invariant, square waves at the varying instantaneous frequency $\omega_i(t)$ are produced. It is then necessary to follow the limiter with a bandpass filter centered about ω_c to convert the square waves back to the cosinusoidal form of Eq. (4-99); i.e., terms centered about $2\omega_c$ and the other higher harmonics of ω_c are filtered out. This is commonly incorporated in the differentiator, as will be shown in the paragraphs that follow.

There are various ways of performing the necessary differentiation. We consider here only one, that involving the single-tuned circuit of Fig. 4-61.

To demonstrate that this circuit does provide the required differentiation and envelope detection, we first note that if the circuit is detuned so that the unmodulated carrier frequency ω_c lies on the sloping part of the amplitude–frequency characteristic and the frequency variations occur within a small region about the unmodulated carrier, the amplitude of the output wave will follow the instantaneous frequency of the input. This is shown in both Figs. 4-61 and 4-62. The region over which the characteristics are very nearly linear must be wide enough to cover the maximum frequency deviation.

We demonstrate this quantitatively by calculating the frequency response of the circuit. It is apparent that the magnitude of the transfer impedance is given

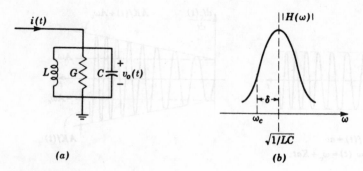

(a) (b)

FIGURE 4-61
Single-tuned circuit. (*a*) Circuit. (*b*) Amplitude response.

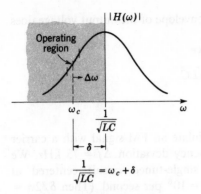

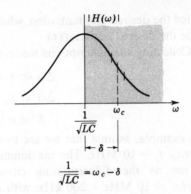

Operation along left-hand slope

Operation along right-hand slope

FIGURE 4-62
FM demodulation.

by

$$|H(\omega)| = \left| \frac{V_0(\omega)}{I(\omega)} \right| = \frac{1/G}{\sqrt{1 + (\omega C - 1/\omega L)^2/G^2}} \quad (4\text{-}102)$$

We now define $\Delta\omega = \omega - \omega_c$ as the frequency deviation away from the carrier frequency ω_c, and let $1/\sqrt{LC} = \omega_c \pm \delta$, as in Fig. 4-62. (The sign depends on the slope along which we operate.) To ensure linearity of the operating region, assume that

$$\Delta\omega \ll \omega_c$$

(This is of course normally true anyway.) Also, let $\delta \ll \omega_c$. (The carrier frequency ω_c is then close to the center frequency $1/\sqrt{LC}$.) It is then easily shown that Eq. (4-102) reduces to

$$|H| \doteq \frac{1/G}{\sqrt{1 + 4(C/G)^2(\delta - \Delta\omega)^2}} \quad (4\text{-}103)$$

in the case of operation along the left-hand slope.

Now assume further that $\delta \gg \Delta\omega$. This implies, of course, that although ω_c is close to $1/\sqrt{LC}$, we never deviate far enough away from ω_c to approach $1/\sqrt{LC}$. This is necessary to ensure linearity of the operating region. Further, assume that $\delta \ll G/2C \equiv \alpha$. Equation (4-103) then reduces to

$$|H| \doteq \frac{1}{G}\left[\left(1 - \frac{\delta^2}{2\alpha^2}\right) + \frac{\delta}{\alpha^2}\Delta\omega\right] \quad (4\text{-}104)$$

Note that with the assumptions made $|H|$ does have a component linearly proportional to $\Delta\omega$, as desired. This shows that the single-tuned circuit *has* provided the desired differentiation, while the envelope of the output voltage does provide the desired output $f(t)$.

Collecting the assumptions made, we have

$$\Delta\omega \ll \delta \ll 1/\sqrt{LC}$$

$$\Delta\omega \ll \omega_c$$

$$\delta \ll \alpha$$

As an example, assume that we are to demodulate an FM signal with a carrier frequency $f_c = 10$ MHz. The maximum frequency deviation $\Delta f = 75$ kHz. We then use as the differentiating circuit a single-tuned circuit centered at $1/2\pi\sqrt{LC} = 10$ MHz $+ 200$ kHz, with $\alpha/2\pi = 10^6$ per second. (Then $\delta/2\pi = 200$ kHz.)

The requirements on the inequalities to obtain linearity may be relaxed somewhat and the $\delta^2/2\alpha^2$ term in Eq. (4-104) (which is large compared with the $\Delta\omega$ term) eliminated by using a *balanced demodulator*, that is, two single-tuned circuits, one tuned to $\omega_c + \delta$ and the other to $\omega_c - \delta$. If the individual outputs are envelope detected and subtracted, the final output is

$$|H|_{\omega_c+\delta} - |H|_{\omega_c-\delta} = \frac{2\delta}{G\alpha^2}\Delta\omega \qquad (4\text{-}105)$$

as desired. An example of such a balanced demodulator is shown in Fig. 4-63.

A block diagram of a typical FM receiver, covering the broadcast range of 88 to 108 MHz, is shown in Fig. 4-64. Note that except for the limiter and discriminator circuits, the form of the receiver is similar to that of a conventional AM receiver. All h-f circuits prior to the discriminator must be designed for the FM bandwidth of 225 kHz, however, while the audio amplifier which amplifies the recovered modulating signal need cover only the 50- to 15-kHz range. The i-f amplifiers are tuned to a center frequency of 10.7 MHz. The audio amplifier normally includes a deemphasis circuit. This circuit, in conjunction with a preemphasis circuit in the transmitter, provides additional discrimination against noise and interference. It is discussed in detail in Chap. 6.

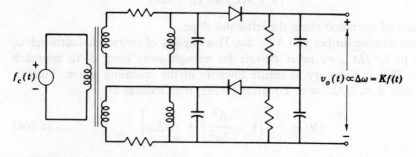

FIGURE 4-63
Balanced FM demodulator.

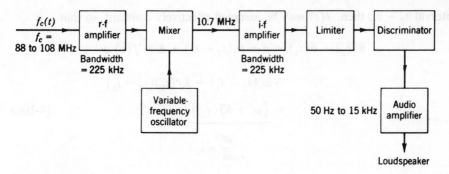

FIGURE 4-64
Typical FM receiver.

Zero-Crossing Detectors

It was noted above that FM detectors normally include hard limiters to eliminate any amplitude fluctuations that could then be converted (erroneously) to a detect FM output. It is thus apparent that the FM information must be contained in the points at which the FM signal $f_c(t)$ crosses the origin, the *zero crossings*. We shall demonstrate this statement below, providing another means of detecting FM signals.

Consider then again the FM signal given by

$$f_c(t) = A\cos\theta(t) = A\cos\left[\omega_c t + K\int f(t)\, dt\right] \qquad (4\text{-}99)$$

Again, as an example, let $f(t) = at$, $0 \le t \le T$, a repetitive ramp. Then $\omega_i = \omega_c + Kat$, $\theta(t) = \omega_c t + Kat^2/2$. Let t_1 be a zero crossing, as shown in Fig. 4-65, with $t_2 = t_1 + \Delta t$ the next zero crossing. Then $\theta(t_2) - \theta(t_1) = \pi$. Assume that the bandwidth B of $f(t)$ is much less than f_c, the carrier frequency. The information-bearing signal $f(t)$ changes much more slowly than f_c. In the

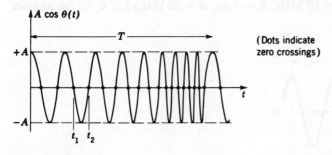

(Dots indicate zero crossings)

FIGURE 4-65
Zero-crossing determination.

interval $t_2 - t_1$, then, $f(t)$ may be assumed effectively constant, so that

$$\theta(t_2) - \theta(t_1) = \pi = \omega_c(t_2 - t_1) + K\int_{t_1}^{t_2} f(t)\, dt$$

$$\doteq \omega_c(t_2 - t_1) + Kf(t_1)(t_2 - t_1)$$

$$= \underbrace{\left[\omega_c + Kf(t_1)\right]}_{\dfrac{d\theta}{dt} \equiv \omega_i}(t_2 - t_1) \tag{4-106}$$

From Eq. (4-106) we thus have

$$\omega_i = \omega_c + Kf(t) \doteq \frac{\pi}{t_2 - t_1}$$

and

$$f_i = f_c + \frac{K}{2\pi}f(t) \doteq \frac{1}{2(t_2 - t_1)} \tag{4-107}$$

The desired output $f(t)$ may thus be found by measuring the spacing between zero crossings.

If positive-going zero crossings only are considered [those at which the slope of $f_c(t)$ is positive], we get

$$f_i \doteq \frac{1}{t_2 - t_1} \tag{4-107a}$$

A simple way of measuring the spacing of zero crossings is to actually *count* the zero crossings in a given time interval.

Thus, consider a counting interval T_c long enough so that it counts a significant number of zero crossings, yet short enough compared with $1/B$ so that $f(t)$ still does not change too much in this interval (see Fig. 4-66). Then

$$\frac{1}{f_c} < T_c \ll \frac{1}{B} \tag{4-108}$$

(As an example, let $f_c = 10$ MHz, $T_c = 1$ μs, $B = 20$ kHz.) Let n_c be the number

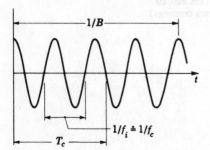

FIGURE 4-66
Counting intervals.

of positive zero crossings in T_c seconds. We then have

$$n_c \doteq \frac{T_c}{t_2 - t_1} \tag{4-109}$$

or

$$f_i = \frac{n_c}{T_c} \tag{4-110}$$

(n_c is approximately 10 in the example noted.) The instantaneous frequency f_c, and from this the derived $f(t)$, are thus found directly in terms of the measured count n_c. [In practice, one would half-wave-rectify $f_c(t)$, differentiate to accentuate the zero-crossing points, again rectify to eliminate the negative pulses due to the negative-going zero crossings, and pass the resultant sequence of positive pulses into a low-pass device with time constant T_c. The output would then be a direct measure of $f_i = f_c + Kf(t)/2\pi$. By using a balanced device one may again obtain $f(t)$ directly.]

Other types of FM detectors in addition to those described above have been developed and used in practice. One particular class, which is of particular importance in deep-space communications where power is at a premium, uses feedback techniques to improve signal detectability in the presence of noise. Among the different types of detectors in this group one may consider the phase-locked loop, the FM demodulator with feedback (FMFB), and the frequency-locked loop FM demodulator [CLAR 1971], [SCHW 1966].

4-12 FREQUENCY-DIVISION MULTIPLEXING: TELEPHONE HIERARCHY

In Secs. 3-3 and 3-8 we introduced time-division multiplexing or combining of signals as a means of transmitting multiple signals over one common signal channel. Another common technique, particularly with analog signals, for combining many independent signals so that they can be transmitted over a common channel is that of *frequency-division multiplexing* (FDM). In this procedure individual baseband signal channels are each multiplexed up in frequency, the carrier for each channel being chosen so that the resultant modulated signals occupy adjacent, nonoverlapping frequency bands. The composite signal, made up of the sum of the individual modulated signals, is then transmitted as one wider-band analog signal.

The technique is thus analogous to time-division multiplexing. There samples of individual signal channels occupy adjacent, nonoverlapping time slots. In the case of FDM the signals occupy adjacent frequency bands. In both cases the transmission bandwidth is increased in proportion to the number of signal channels multiplexed together. The advantage of multiplexing—either in time or in frequency—is that transmission facilities are *shared* among the various channels multiplexed together.

The various modulation techniques discussed in this chapter may be used to carry out the FDM process. An example of an FM–FM frequency-multiplexed scheme has already been presented briefly in Sec. 4-10 (see Fig. 4-58). AM, DSB, and SSB techniques have all been used to multiplex or combine independent signal channels. Combinations of these have been used as well. The sound signal and the video (picture) signal for TV are multiplexed together for common transmission over a given frequency band. In this case the voice signal is transmitted using FM, while the picture signal is sent using *vestigial sideband* transmission: the upper sideband plus a fraction of the lower sideband is transmitted [COUC].[27] Frequency multiplexing is used as well in FM stereo transmission to transmit two independent signals. (Details appear in Prob. 4-63, at the end of the chapter.)

To demonstrate the concept of frequency-division multiplexing in more detail, we focus in this section on a portion of the North American FDM telephone hierarchy that uses SSB techniques to transmit up to 600 voice channels over a common transmission channel [BELL 1982]. [FM FDM techniques are commonly used as well to multiplex up to 1,800 voice channels over the microwave links used for long-haul (long-distance) transmission.] Three successive levels of multiplexing, using SSB modulation at each level, are used to attain the final combination of 600 voice channels. First, 12 voice channels, of 4-kHz bandwidth, are multiplexed together to form a *group* covering the range 60 to 108 kHz. Five groups in turn are further combined to form a *supergroup* covering the range 312 to 552 kHz. Finally, 10 supergroups are combined to form a *mastergroup*. (No standard arrangement is specified for the mastergroup generation. We shall instead mention two mastergroup examples.) The FDM hierarchy is shown schematically in Fig. 4-67. Additional multiplexing levels, not discussed here, can be used to transmit as many as 13,200 voice channels [BELL 1982, pp. 322–324].

One method, adopted by AT & T for generating a group and embodied in its A5 channel bank, uses 12 carriers spaced 4 kHz apart to generate 12 SSB signals that are then summed to form the group. The lower sideband is selected in each case, resulting in *inverted* spectra compared to the baseband originals. There are various ways of generating the desired SSB signals, as noted earlier in this chapter. The A5 channel bank first generates DSB signals, using product modulators, and then filters out the upper sideband of each DSB signal. Details are shown in Fig. 4-68. The sideband inversion noted above is indicated by following two points *a* and *b* on the spectral curve. Although developed specifically for voice (telephone) transmission, any signal fitting into the voice channel band, with a spectrum from 200 to 3,400 Hz, may be transmitted in a voice channel. This enables data-modem outputs to be multiplexed as well.

An alternative method of group generation, arriving at the same output structure of Fig. 4-68, is employed by Northern Telecom of Canada. A two-step

[27][COUC] L. W. Couch II, *Digital and Analog Communication Systems*, Macmillan, New York, 1987, pp. 382, 383.

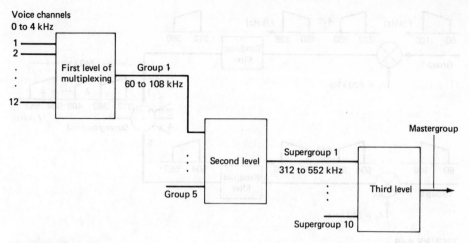

FIGURE 4-67
North American FDM hierarchy.

modulation process is used. An upper sideband SSB signal is generated for each of the 12 voice channels by first shifting all channels individually up to a common center frequency of 8.14 MHz and then filtering out the lower sidebands. Each upper sideband SSB signal is then shifted down to its appropriate frequency band in the group band by beating with one of 12 equally spaced carriers, ranging from 8.204 MHz to 8.248 MHz. It is left to the reader to demonstrate that this two-step modulation process results in the same group

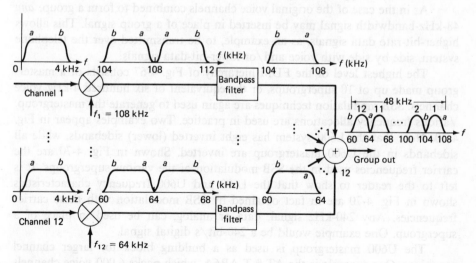

FIGURE 4-68
Group generation, AT & T A5 channel bank.

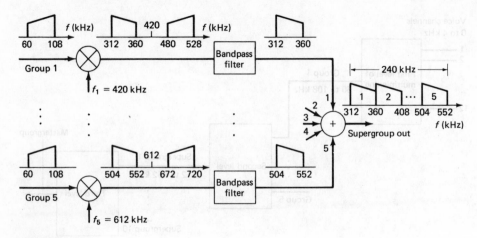

FIGURE 4-69
AT & T supergroup generation.

spectral occupancy as that of Fig. 4-68. The AT & T A6 channel bank uses a similar two-step modulation process [BELL 1982, pp. 319, 320].

The second level of this FDM hierarchy combines five groups, each in the range 60 to 108 kHz, by again using SSB modulation. The resultant supergroup (Fig. 4-67) occupies the frequency range 312 to 552 kHz. Group 1, as an example, is shifted to a center frequency of 420 kHz, and the lower (inverted) sideband, ranging from 312 to 360 kHz, is selected by again using bandpass filtering. The five carrier frequencies used, at spacings of 48 kHz, are 420, 468, 516, 564, and 612 kHz. Details appear in Fig. 4-69.

As in the case of the original voice channels combined to form a group, *any* 48-kHz-bandwidth signal may be inserted in place of a group signal. This allows higher-bit-rate data signals, as an example, to be transmitted over the telephone system, side by side with voice and/or lower-bit-data signals.

The highest level of the FDM hierarchy of Fig. 4-67 consists of a mastergroup made up of 10 supergroups, or the equivalent of six hundred 4-kHz voice channels. SSB modulation techniques are again used to generate the mastergroup. Various frequency allocations are used in practice. Two examples appear in Fig. 4-70. Note that the L600 system has eight inverted (lower) sidebands, while all sidebands in the U600 mastergroup are inverted. Shown in Fig. 4-70 are the carrier frequencies used in the SSB modulation of the various supergroups. It is left to the reader to show that the L600 and U600 frequency characteristics shown in Fig. 4-70 are in fact obtained by SSB modulation with these carrier frequencies. Any 240-kHz signal, data or analog, can be used in place of a supergroup. One example would be a 240-bit/s digital signal.

The U600 mastergroup is used as a building block for larger channel groupings. One example is the AT & T AR6A, which packs 6,000 voice channels into one wideband channel for transmission over microwave long-haul (long-dis-

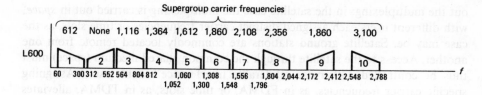

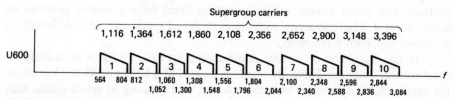

Note: All frequencies in kHz.

FIGURE 4-70
L600 and U600 mastergroups. (From *Transmission Systems for Communications*, 4th ed., Bell Telephone Laboratories, 1970, fig. 6-8, p. 135. Copyright 1970 Bell Telephone Laboratories; reprinted by permission.)

tance) radio relay links [MARK], [BELL 1982]. It does this by combining 10 U600 mastergroups. The resultant 6,000-channel signal covers the frequency range 59.844 MHz to 88.840 MHz. This very wideband signal is then modulated up to microwave frequencies (4 or 6 GHz) for transmission over microwave radio.

4-13 SATELLITE SYSTEMS APPLICATIONS

The use of satellites for both worldwide and domestic communications has expanded tremendously over the past years. Telephone (voice) traffic is now carried routinely between member nations of the Intelsat organization, augmenting international telephone communications using submarine cable strung under the various oceans of the world. (Included are the older coaxial cables and the newer fiber-optic cables, which were deployed beginning in 1988.) The transmission of TV (video) and data traffic via satellite throughout the world has become routine as well.

The prime multiplexing methods used to combine multiple simultaneous calls in satellite communications are *frequency-division multiple access* (FDMA), similar to frequency-division multiplexing (FDM) discussed in the last section, and *time-division multiple access* (TDMA), similar to time-division multiplexing (TDM), discussed at length earlier in this chapter. The crucial distinction between FDM and FDMA, as also between TDM and TDMA, lies in the fact that in the terrestrial multiplexing techniques electronic circuitry is used to carry out the multiplexing; in the satellite case the multiplexing is carried out in *space*, with different users each assigned distinct carrier frequencies or time slots, as the case may be. Satellite ground stations are commonly located remote from one another. Access to the satellite through the common shared medium (space) must thus be controlled. Otherwise intolerable interference would result. Assigning specific carrier frequencies, as in FDMA, or time slots, as in TDMA, alleviates this problem. Local area networks (LANs) using a common shared medium (twisted wire pairs, coaxial cable, or optical fiber) have a similar problem of access control. Multiple-access techniques designed specifically for LANs will be discussed in Chap. 5 following.

In the discussion of satellite communications here we focus exclusively on synchronous satellites. These are satellites located at a height of 35,860 km above the earth's surface, in orbit over the equator, and rotating in synchronism with the earth. They thus appear to be stationary as seen from the earth. These satellites are provided with receiving antennas to receive transmission from earth stations, and with transmitting antennas to relay the transmissions to other stations located geographically distant on the earth. By adjusting the antenna beam patterns one can generate global beams covering all portions of the earth in sight of a satellite. (One Intelsat satellite over the Atlantic Ocean covers portions of Africa, western Europe, South America, and the eastern part of the United States.) One can generate beams shaped to cover one country only (as in the case of domestic satellites), or multiple narrow beams that can be switched between a variety of locations.

Various frequency bands have been allocated to commercial satellite use, worldwide. The most common one consists of a 500-MHz-wide band centered at 6 GHz in the *uplink* direction (toward the satellite), and centered at 4 GHz in the *downlink* direction (toward the earth). These directions are indicated in the schematic picture of Fig. 4-71.

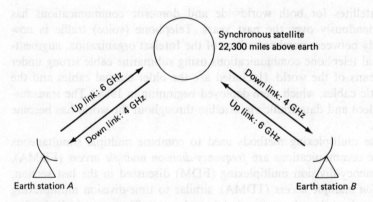

Synchronous satellite
22,300 miles above earth

Up link: 6 GHz

Down link: 4 GHz

Down link: 4 GHz

Up link: 6 GHz

Earth station *A*

Earth station *B*

FIGURE 4-71
Commercial satellite communications.

Frequency-Division Multiple Access (FDMA)

Intelsat IV, launched in 1971, used FDMA as its primary multiplexing technique. In this system the 500-MHz band at each frequency is typically subdivided into 12 bands of 36 MHz each, each covered by a separate transmitter/receiver called a *transponder*. (Spacing between the bands accounts for the missing bandwidth). Each transponder band is in turn divided into a number of frequency channels, depending on the type of application or signal to be transmitted. Earth stations are allocated specific channel assignments and must use these frequencies in transmitting or in receiving signals. An earth station will transmit a frequency-modulated signal, using a specific carrier in the 6-GHz range. The modulating or baseband signal for the transmitted FM signals consists of the frequency-division-multiplexed (FDM) sum of 4-kHz channels. All earth stations accessing a particular transponder have their FM carriers spaced so that the FM signals for each occupy adjacent bands, the composite FDMA signal at the satellite covering the entire 36-MHz transponder band. The overall access procedure is referred to as FDM/FM/FDMA.

An example appears in Fig. 4-72 [PUEN].[28] (See also [BARG].)[29] In this example, a particular country, A, is assigned sixty 4-kHz channels, divided equally among five other countries, B to F. The 12 channels assigned to each country would be frequency-multiplexed to form the 60-channel 252-kHz baseband signal shown in Fig. 4-72b [PUEN, Fig. 2]. This baseband signal frequency-modulates a carrier at the assigned carrier frequency of 6.235 GHz to produce the FM signal of 5-MHz bandwidth in Fig. 4-72c. In this example, six other countries are assumed to access the same transponder. The composite FDMA spectrum of the seven accessing signals has the form shown in Fig. 4-72d [PUEN, Fig. 12], with country A's FM signal indicated among the seven. Each of the six other countries accessing this transponder is assumed to have the channel allocation and band location shown in Fig. 4-72d.

In this typical case one of the countries has been allocated 132 channels, with an FM bandwidth of 10 MHz; another country has a 96-channel allocation with a bandwidth of 7.5 MHz; one, besides country A, has a 60-channel allocation; others have 24-channel allocations with a bandwidth of 2.5 MHz each. Bandwidth allocations in the Intelsat IV system are normally varied in increments of 2.5 MHz, as indicated in this example. Details appear in [PUEN] and [BARG].)

To complete the transmission, the 6-GHz uplink signals are rebroadcast at specified frequencies in the 4-GHz downlink range. Receiving stations select the

---

[28][PUEN] J. G. Puente and A. M Werth, "Demand-Assigned Service for the Intelsat Global Network," *IEEE Spectrum*, vol. 8, no. 1, pp. 59–69, January 1971.

[29][BARG] P. L. Bargellini (ed.), "The Intelsat IV Communications System," *Comsat Tech. Rev.*, vol. 2, no. 2, pp. 437–570, Fall 1972.

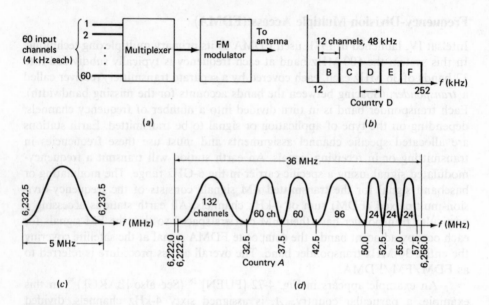

FIGURE 4-72
Typical FDMA generation, one transponder. (*a*) FDM/FM generation, earth station, country *A*. (*b*) Multiplexer output, frequency allocations. (*c*) FDM/FM output, country *A*. (*d*) Composite FDMA spectrum at transponder.

frequency band (or bands) containing the channels directed to their subscribers, use FM receivers to demodulate the appropriate multichannel baseband signals, and then further demultiplex the individual 4-kHz channels.

Time-Division Multiple Access (TDMA)

All-digital time-division multiple-access (TDMA) is used on the most recent Intelsat satellite systems, beginning with Intelsat V in 1985, and continuing with Intelsat VI. We summarize the TDMA scheme used briefly here. Details appear in [COMS 1985] and [COMS 1986].[30]

Intelsat V operates with five beams in the 4–6-GHz frequency band. One global earth-coverage beam covers all portions of the earth in sight of the satellite. An example is the Atlantic Ocean coverage mentioned earlier. This beam is used principally for carrying television, single-channel-carrier data, and low-traffic telephony. The four other beams are used principally for telephony (64-kbit/s service). Two hemi beams each cover the East and West hemispheres

---

[30][COMS 1985] "TDMA: Part I," Special issue, *Comsat Tech. Rev.*, vol. 15, no. 2B, pp. 361–525, Fall 1985. [COMS 1986] "TDMA: Part II," Special issue, *Comsat Tech. Rev.*, vol. 16, no. 1, pp. 1–298, Spring 1986.

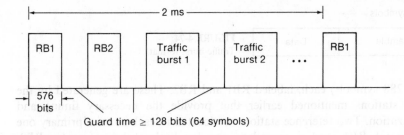

FIGURE 4-73
Intelsat TDMA frame structure.

of the earth, while two zone beams in each cover a zone within each hemisphere. In the Atlantic-region example, the east hemisphere covers Europe and Africa; the zone beam within it covers Europe and portions of North America [CAMP 1986].[31] This use of multiple overlapping beams provides added coverage to more-heavily used regions. Different polarizations are used on the zone and hemi beams to enable them to coexist simultaneously. The 500-MHz frequency band is thus reused four times, providing an effective bandwidth of 2 GHz. Reference stations located in each zone provide network timing to enable earth-station terminals to properly access the common medium with no interference.

Intelsat VI adds two additional zone beams, one within each hemisphere, for a frequency reuse of six, with an effective bandwidth of more than 3 GHz. In addition, it provides for dynamic switching between beams, as contrasted with static switching in the Intelsat V system. This is called *satellite-switched TDMA*, or SS/TDMA [CAMP 1986]. Both systems have spot beams at the 11–14-GHz frequency band as well, to provide added coverage.

Associated with each hemi and zone beam are a number of 72 MHz-wide TDMA transponders, each operating at a different frequency within the 500-MHz range, each providing a throughput of 120 Mbits/s. QPSK is the modulation technique used to provide the 120-Mbit/s data rate over the 72-MHz bandwidth. TDMA terminals located at earth stations transmit bursts of traffic on the carrier frequency assigned to them, and at a specified time within a repetitive frame structure, just as in conventional time multiplexing. Frames are 2 ms long. The TDMA frame has the structure shown in Fig. 4-73 [PONT].[32]

Note that a series of traffic bursts are shown, each generated by a different terminal. Each is separated by a guard time of at least 128 bits (64 QPSK symbols), to allow for some variation in timing. Preceding them are two bursts of

[31][CAMP 1986] S. J. Campanella, B. A. Pontano, and J. L. Dicks, "Advantages of TDMA and Satellite-Switched TDMA in Intelsat V and VI," *Comsat Tech. Rev.*, vol. 16, no. 1, pp. 207–238, Spring 1986.

[32][PONT] B. A. Pontano, S. J. Campanella, and J. L. Dicks, "The Intelsat TDMA/DSI system," *Comsat Tech. Rev.*, vol. 15, no. 2B, pp. 369–398, Fall 1985.

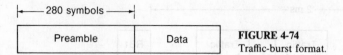

|←——— 280 symbols ———→|

Preamble	Data

FIGURE 4-74
Traffic-burst format.

576 bits (288 symbols) each, labeled RB1 and RB2. These are generated by the reference stations mentioned earlier that provide the necessary timing and synchronization. Two reference stations are located in each zone: a primary one that generates RB1, and a secondary one for backup that generates RB2. Receiving terminals lock onto RB1 only, unless the primary reference station is down.

The first 176 symbols (352 bits) of the reference burst constitute a unique sequence designed to enable receiving modems at ground terminals to acquire and synchronize to bursts. Additional symbols are used to differentiate between reference and traffic bursts, to position a burst relative to the start of a frame, and to exchange control information. The last 8 symbols (16 bits) are used to address and control each traffic terminal in sequence to enable them to appropriately locate their own burst time slot [PONT].

The traffic bursts in Fig. 4-73, each generated by a traffic terminal, consists of a 280-symbol (560-bit) preamble followed by data (Fig. 4-74). The preamble has the same format as that of the reference burst (288 symbols less the last 8 symbols used to control the traffic terminals). The data portion of the traffic burst is made up of a maximum of 8 subbursts, each in turn comprising up to 128 "satellite channels" of 64 symbols (128 bits) each. A satellite channel represents the elementary unit of data communication in this TDMA system. It provides a transmission rate of 128 bits in a 2-ms frame, or 64 kbits/s. It thus corresponds to a single voice channel for telephony or the equivalent 64-kbit/s data channel. To create this TDMA voice channel, a terminal must store up sixteen 125-μs frames' worth of 64-kbit/s PCM voice and transmit them as one burst of 128 bits at the 120-Mbit/s rate.

The subbursts within a traffic burst are of two types, generated by either of two units associated with a traffic terminal. One type of unit, called a DSI unit, is designed primarily for voice. It makes use of the well-known phenomenon that human speech consists of an alternating sequence of active or talk spurt intervals typically 400 ms long, followed by silence intervals averaging typically 600 ms. This phenomenon has been used successfully to pack two or more digital voice calls into a single 64-kbit/s voice channel. The technique is called *digital speech interpolation* (DSI) and works best with many voice channels, since the alternating talk-spurt–silence sequence is a statistical one. Silence detectors are used to determine the onset and end of a silent interval during which one or more talk spurts from other calls can be used to fill the empty channel [CAMP 1976].[33]

---

[33][CAMP 1976] S. J. Campanella, "Digital Speech Interpolation," *Comsat. Tech. Rev.*, vol. 6, no. 1, pp. 127–158, Spring 1976.

In the Intelsat TDMA system a DSI unit handles up to 240 voice channels, packing or interpolating them into a maximum of 127 satellite channels. The second type of unit, a *digital noninterpolated* (DNI) unit, is designed to handle data or small-capacity voice links where DSI would not work effectively. The DNI unit handles up to 128 satellite channels of 64 kbits/s each, or can form higher-bit-rate channels, by combining elementary 64-kbit/s channels, up to a maximum of 8.192 Mbits/s [PONT]. The DSI subburst is made up of a maximum of 127 satellite channels, with one additional channel of 128 bits, called a DSI assignment channel, used to notify the receiving system of the assignment of voice channels to satellite channels in the subburst following [PONT, Fig. 12, p. 389].

An example serves to clarify all these points. The capacity of a transponder is 120,832 QPSK (2-bit) symbols per frame. Since a frame is 2 ms long, this results in the 120-Mbit/s TDMA data rate mentioned earlier. The two reference bursts plus the minimum guard time between them and the first traffic burst (64 symbols each) leave a total of 120,128 symbols for the traffic burst. Say the first traffic burst is assigned its maximum utilization of eight subbursts of 128 satellite channels each. This first burst requires 65,880 symbols (280 symbols of preamble plus 64 symbols of guard band plus $8 \times 128 \times 64$ symbols of data). This leaves 54,248 symbols available for one additional traffic burst with a maximum of six subbursts of 128 64-kbit/s satellite channels each. If the 14 subbursts in the two traffic bursts are all DSI subbursts, i.e., all voice traffic, this represents a maximum capacity of $240 \times 14 = 3,360$ voice channels. (Recall that with DSI up to 240 voice channels can be packed into 127 satellite channels). In practice a smaller number of voice channels would normally be assigned to each transducer. The capacity of the Intelsat V system is about 40,000 voice channels; that of the Intelsat VI is 60,000 channels. Without the use of DSI these numbers would be halved.

Calculations show that the TDMA technique with DSI incorporated improves the efficiency of voice communications by a factor of three over FDMA for moderately heavy traffic terminals [PONT]. Overall costs are reduced as well [CAMP 1986]. The flexibility of TDMA and associated dynamic switching allows new communication applications to be introduced readily when needed. Examples of such applications include digital video traffic, ranging from 1 Mbit/s for video teleconferencing to 100 Mbits/s for high-definition television; low-rate TDMA (3–12 Mbits/s) for business applications; and intersatellite link technology to interconnect multiple satellite-switched TDMA satellites [CAMP 1986].

4-14 SUMMARY

As noted at the beginning of this chapter, high-frequency sine-wave transmission is necessary for effective radiation of signals through space, water, or other transmission media. It is commonly used for transmitting signals over cables and microwave links in the telephone plant. The digital signals discussed in Chap. 3 must thus modulate sine-wave carriers for transmission over a desired channel.

Both digital and analog signals will generally modulate carriers in practice. For simplicity's sake and to maintain continuity with the digital communication systems introduced in Chap. 3, we first discussed in this chapter the types of sine-wave modulation peculiar to binary signal transmission. These include, among the most common types, PSK, OOK, and FSK transmission. Discussions of implementation, both at the transmitter and at the receiver, as well as bandwidth considerations, then carried over directly to the analog signal case as well. For example, AM transmission, with OOK as a special case, was shown to require a transmission bandwidth twice that of the baseband signal, although the use of SSB transmission reduces this to just that of the baseband signal. FM transmission, with FSK as a special case, requires, in general, wider bandwidths, the transmission bandwidth being approximately given by $2\Delta f + 2B$, with Δf the frequency deviation and B the modulating signal bandwidth.

Digital modulation techniques extend the binary-modulation case to that of multisymbol signaling. Here a group of n consecutive binary digits is used to generate one of $M = 2^n$ different symbols. Examples studied in this chapter included multiple PSK (QPSK, with $M = 4$ possible signals, is one prominent example) and the combined amplitude/phase-shift variation of a sine-wave carrier used in QAM transmission. These classes of signals are used extensively in high-bit-rate transmission over band-limited telephone channels as well as digital radio. The devices that convert the digital signals to the higher-frequency analog signals used in telephone practice are called modems.

AM systems were found to require some type of product modulator for the modulation process. Both nonlinear and piecewise linear devices were shown to provide the necessary product term. Product modulators are in general used to carry out frequency conversion, the translation of signals from one frequency band to another.

We concluded the chapter with a brief discussion of frequency-division multiplexing. Both telephone and satellite systems were used as examples. Frequency-division multiplexing—with groups of signals shifted to adjacent frequency bands, the combined wider-band signal then used to modulate a higher-frequency carrier—is the analog of time-division multiplexing. In both cases a multiplicity of signals are combined for more economical transmission over a common, wider-band channel.

In these last two chapters, we have explored the basic aspects of point-to-point communication-system design. We focused first on digital baseband systems, discussing PCM and delta-modulation systems that convert analog signals to digital format, and then showing how digital signals, whether generated as such or derived from an analog form, may be combined using time-multiplexing techniques. We then studied the next step in the information transmission process, that of the modulation of a high-frequency carrier for long-range transmission. The concept of bandwidth was shown to play a fundamental role throughout. We have now seen how communication signals are handled, from generation at the transmitter to final processing at the receiver. Combining the transmitter and receiver, we have the complete point-to-point communication system first noted in Chap. 1.

We recall that we began our discussion in Chap. 1 by indicating that most point-to-point communication systems constitute parts of larger telecommunication *networks*. The communication links on which we have focused in the past two chapters represent the *physical layer* of communications in a comprehensive multilayered model of networks. In the next chapter we explore the concept of networks in more detail. We focus on local-area networks as a specific example because of their increasing deployment worldwide and the relative simplicity of their operation. Included in the discussion are an introduction to packet as well as circuit switching and some treatment of statistical multiplexing. We will attempt to be as quantitative as possible, introducing some basic material on queueing and traffic theory.

In Chaps. 6 and 7 following, we return to point-to-point communications (the physical layer), with a study of the performance of point-to-point communication systems. As noted in Chap. 1, the need for a performance evaluation arises because of possibly deleterious effects introduced by the transmission channel. To simplify the analysis in this first approach to the subject, we focus on limitations due to noise only. (The effect of intersymbol interference on signal transmission was mentioned in Chap. 3.) We model the effect of noise in digital transmission in Chap. 6, obtaining useful equations and curves for the probability of error due to noise. Both baseband and high-frequency binary transmission are considered, and PSK, FSK, and OOK techniques are compared. We then study the effect of noise on AM and FM signal reception, obtaining the well-known FM improvement factor in the presence of noise.

In Chap. 7 we specialize to digital communications, and show how the error probability due to noise may be reduced from that in channels that are limited in their transmission, with the help of more complex signaling schemes and error-correction coding. Shannon's capacity theorem, referred to previously in this book, is again introduced to provide a limit on how much improvement is possible through the use of coding techniques. Applications are drawn from telephony and from satellite and space communications systems.

PROBLEMS

4-1. The output of a PCM system consists of a binary sequence of pulses, occurring at the rate of 2×10^6 bits/s. With raised cosine shaping used for the baseband pulses, compare the transmission bandwidths required in the following two cases:

(*a*) OOK transmission, amplitude modulation of a sine-wave carrier.

(*b*) FSK, switching between two sine waves of frequencies 100 and 104 MHz. Repeat the FSK calculations if the two frequencies are 100 and 120 MHz. Sketch the spectra in all cases, and indicate assumptions made.

4-2. A binary message consists of an alternating sequence of 1's and 0's. FSK transmission is used, with the two frequencies each multiples of the binary period T and synchronized in phase (see Fig. 4-6a). Find the spectrum of the FSK wave and sketch it, verifying the expression given in the text and sketched in Fig. 4-6b.

4-3. Refer to Prob. 3-29. Find the transmission bandwidths required if the binary pulses phase-modulate a high-frequency carrier. (PSK transmission is used.)

4-4. FSK transmission is used to transmit 1,200-bit/s digital signals over a telephone channel. The FSK signals are to fit into the range 500 to 2,900 Hz. A modulation index $\beta \doteq 0.7$ is desired, so that the two carrier frequencies are taken to be 1,200 and 2,200 Hz. Find the baseband bandwidth required of the binary signals. Assuming sinusoidal roll-off shaping, what roll-off factor is required?

4-5. A telephone channel allows signal transmission in the range 600 to 3,000 Hz. The carrier frequency is taken to be 1,800 Hz.
  (a) Show that 2,400-bit/s, four-phase PSK transmission with raised cosine shaping is possible. Show that the 6-dB bandwidth about the carrier is 1,200 Hz.
  (b) 4,800 bits/s are to be transmitted over the same channel. Show that eight-phase PSK, with 50-percent sinusoidal roll-off, will accommodate the desired data rate. Show that the 6-dB bandwidth about the carrier is now 1,600 Hz.

4-6. 9,600-bit/s transmission over a telephone line is desired. For this purpose the line must be specially conditioned to allow signal transmission over the range 300 to 3,000 Hz. Show that 16-state QAM, with 12.5-percent sinusoidal roll-off shaping, will provide the desired bit rate. The carrier is chosen in the center of the band at 1,650 Hz. Show that the 6-dB bandwidth about the carrier is 2,400 Hz.

4-7. Refer to Prob. 4-6. 14.4- and 19.2-kbit/s modems are to be used for transmission over the same telephone line. Indicate what QAM constellations would be required for each. Determine the percentage of roll-off shaping required. What carrier frequency(ies) would be required?

4-8. A computer outputs data at a rate of 56 kbits/s. QAM signal transmission with appropriate signal shaping is to be used to transmit the data over a 20-kHz channel centered at 100 MHz. Which of the two signal constellations shown in Fig. P4-8 would be appropriate? Explain.

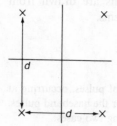
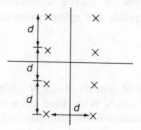

FIGURE P4-8

4-9. A single voice channel is to be transmitted via PCM techniques using satellite communications. 8000 samples/s are taken, and 7-bit quantization (128 levels) is used. 32 synchronization bits are inserted into the binary stream for every 224 data bits transmitted. The resultant binary stream is then transmitted using sinusoidal roll-off shaping for each binary pulse. The roll-off factor is 20 percent.

(a) What is the PCM bit rate in bits/s?

(b) What is the baseband (PCM signal) bandwidth?

(c) PSK is used for transmission. What is the transmission bandwidth required?

(d) QPSK is used instead: successive *pairs* of bits are used to phase-modulate a carrier. What is the transmission bandwidth required in this case?

(e) Repeat (c) if OOK transmission is used. Repeat if FSK is used with the frequency deviation chosen as 38 kHz. What is the modulation index β in this case? What is the frequency spacing of the two carriers?

4-10. Refer to Table 4-2 in the text. Calculate the roll-off factor r required for each of the digital radio systems shown, assuming sinusoidal roll-off shaping is used.

4-11. Ten 32-kbit/s delta-modulated voice channels and four 64-kbit/s computer outputs are multiplexed using TDM (time-division multiplexing). TDM frames are 125 μs long. 8 control bits per frame are added.

(a) Show the bit rate of the TDM output is 640 kbits/s.

(b) The TDM output is to be transmitted over a radio channel centered at 10 MHz. A transmission bandwidth of 240 kHz at this carrier frequency is available. Specify a modulation technique that may be used if sinusoidal roll-off shaping with $r = 0.5$ is used. Show all work.

(c) Repeat (b), using a different modulation technique, with the roll-off factor reduced to $r = 0.1$.

4-12. (a) Choose a typical sequence of 10 binary digits. Collect them in pairs, and use these to generate a set of five QPSK signals. Sketch these signals using the representation of (4-14). Let the carrier frequency be some arbitrary multiple of $1/T$. Note the points at which π-rad and $\pi/2$-rad phase shifts occur. Correlate these with the bit pair sequences.

(b) Repeat (a) using the same input bit sequence, for offset QPSK, generated using the block diagram of Fig. 4-24. Show the maximum phase shift is now $\pi/2$ rad.

4-13. Refer to Fig. 4-25 showing how an MSK signal is generated.

(a) Demonstrate that if the carrier frequency satisfies the condition of (4-16), there is no phase discontinuity at a bit transition point.

(b) Show that the MSK signal of (4-15) can be written in the equivalent forms (4-17a) and (4-17b).

(c) Let the carrier frequency $f_c = 4/T$ [$m = 8$ in (4-16)]. Sketch the MSK signal for an arbitrary sequence of 10 binary digits (five T-second intervals). Show that the signal does have a constant envelope, with no phase discontinuity at the bit transition points.

4-14. Show that the minimum frequency spacing for FSK is given by (4-19) or (4-22). (This requires filling in details of the analysis in (4-20) to (4-22), based on Fig. 4-9(b).

4-15. Show that the (baseband equivalent) spectra of MSK and QPSK signals, neglecting Nyquist shaping, are given, respectively, by (4-23) and (4-24). Superimpose sketches of the two spectra, verifying the statement made in the text that the respective first-lobe transmission bandwidths are $3/T$ and $2/T$. Show that the MSK spectrum drops off more rapidly than the QPSK spectrum.

4-16. (a) Consider the synchronous detector implementation shown in Fig. P4-16. A high-frequency signal $f(t)\cos \omega_0 t$, with $f_0 \gg B$, the bandwidth of the baseband signal $f(t)$, is sampled synchronously at the following intervals of time: $t = 0$, $\pm 2\pi/\omega_0$, $\pm 4\pi/\omega_0, \ldots$. The samples are then passed through a low-pass filter as shown. Demonstrate that $f(t)$ (this could be either a binary sequence or an analog signal) is reproduced at the filter output. *Hint*: Show this by representing the sampling operation either as multiplication by a set of periodic impulses or as multiplication by a sampling function $S(t)$. Proceed as in Chap. 3, in discussing Nyquist sampling. Find and sketch the resultant spectra at points (1) and (2). What should the frequency characteristics of the filter be?

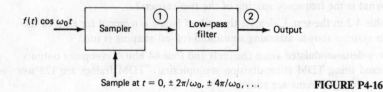

Sample at $t = 0, \pm 2\pi/\omega_0, \pm 4\pi/\omega_0, \ldots$ **FIGURE P4-16**

    (*b*) What is the output like if the sampling times are displaced by $\pi/4\omega_0$ seconds? $\pi/2\omega_0$ seconds? What does this imply about the accuracy of sampling required if $f_0 = 100$ MHz?

4-17. A 4,800-bit/s data terminal is connected to a modem. Calculate the transmission bandwidth B_T required at the modem output for each of the following schemes (50-percent roll-off shaping is used in all cases):

    (*a*) OOK transmission.

    (*b*) FSK transmission. The frequency deviates $\pm 3,600$ Hz about the carrier.

    (*c*) 16-level QAM.

4-18. A transmission channel of 1-MHz bandwidth, centered at 100 MHz, is available for signal transmission.

    (*a*) The PCM system and 240-kbit/s data source of Fig. P4-18 are time-multiplexed together, and the output then fed into a PSK modulator, as shown (25-percent roll-off shaping is used). Find the maximum number of quantization

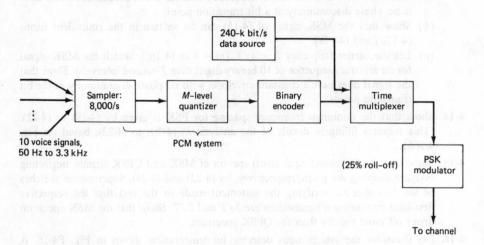

FIGURE P4-18

levels in the PCM system that may be used. (Neglect framing, signaling, and stuffing bits in this example.)

(b) The PCM system in (a) is required to have 256-level quantization. *Two* 240-kbit/s data sources are to be time-multiplexed with the PCM output. The same transmission channel must again be used. Indicate how the modulator might be modified to accomplish this.

4-19. Consider the frequency conversion system sketched in Fig. P4-19. The input signal $s_1(t)$ is a double-sideband signal with 1-MHz sidebands on either side of 10 MHz, as shown in Fig. P4-19. Specify the frequency $f_0 = \omega_0/2\pi$ of the locally generated input to the product modulator, $\cos \omega_0 t$, and sketch the filter characteristics required, for the following cases:

(a) The output is a baseband signal, 0 to 1 MHz.

(b) The output is a double-sideband signal, centered about 20 MHz.

(c) The output is a single-sideband signal with the spectral characteristic shown in Fig. P4-19.

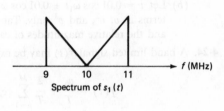
Spectrum of $s_1(t)$

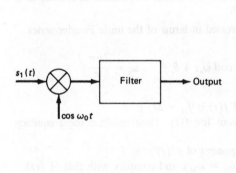
Filter → Output
$\cos \omega_0 t$

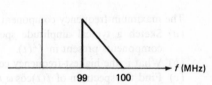
Single-sideband spectrum, part c

FIGURE P4-19

4-20. An amplifier has a slight nonlinearity, so that its output-input characteristic is given by

$$e_o = A_1 e_i + A_2 e_i^2$$

(a) $e_i = \cos \omega_m t$. Find all the frequencies present in the output. How could this device be used as a second-harmonic generator?

(b) $A_1 = 10$, $A_2/A_1 = 0.05$. Determine the ratio of second-harmonic amplitude to fundamental amplitude. (This is frequently called the *second-harmonic distortion*.)

4-21. (a) Let $e_i = 0.1 \cos 500t$ in the amplifier of Prob. 4-20. Determine the frequency terms present in the output and amplitude of each. Repeat for $e_i = 0.2 \cos 3,000t$.

(b) $e_i = 0.1 \cos 500t + 0.2 \cos 3,000t$. Determine the different frequency terms present in the output and the amplitude of each. What new frequency terms appear that were not present in the two cases of (*a*)? These are known as the *intermodulation* frequencies and are due to the nonlinear mixing of the two frequency terms.

4-22. A voltage $e_i = 0.1 \cos 2,500t + 0.2 \cos 3,000t$ is applied at the input to the amplifier of Prob. 4-20. The output voltage e_o is in turn applied to an ideal rectangular filter passing all frequencies between 50 Hz and $4,000/2\pi$ hertz with unity gain, rejecting all others. Calculate the power at the output of the filter in the frequency terms generated by the amplifier nonlinearity. Determine the ratio of power in these terms to the power in the 2,500- and 3,000-rad/s terms at the filter output.

4-23. A semiconductor diode has a current–voltage characteristic at room temperature given by

$$i = I_0 \left(e^{40v} - 1 \right)$$

(*a*) What is the maximum variation in the voltage v to ensure i linearly proportional to v, with less than 1-percent quadratic distortion?

(*b*) Let $v = 0.01 \cos \omega_1 t + 0.01 \cos \omega_2 t$. Expand i in a power series in v, retaining terms in v, v^2, and v^3 only. Tabulate the different frequencies appearing in i, and the relative magnitudes of each.

4-24. A band-limited signal $f(t)$ may be expressed in terms of the finite Fourier series

$$f(t) = \frac{c_0}{T} + \frac{2}{T} \sum_{n=1}^{M} |c_n| \cos(\omega_n t + \theta_n) \qquad \omega_n = \frac{2\pi n}{T}$$

The maximum-frequency component of $f(t)$ is $f_M = M/T$.

(*a*) Sketch a typical amplitude spectrum for $f(t)$. Then indicate the frequency components present in $f^2(t)$.

(*b*) What is the highest-frequency component of $f^2(t)$?

(*c*) Find the spectrum of $f(t)\cos \omega_c t$ ($\omega_c \gg \omega_M$), and compare with that of $f(t)$.

4-25. For each network shown in Fig. P4-25, calculate the maximum-frequency component in the output voltage.

(*a*) e_{in} has a single component of frequency f hertz.

(*b*) e_{in} has a single component of frequency $2f$ hertz.

(*c*) e_{in} has two frequency components, f and $2f$.

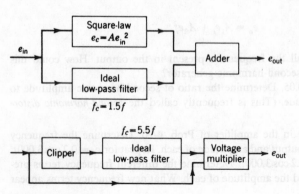

FIGURE P4-25

4-26. Spectrum of coherent radar pulses. These pulses may be generated by turning a sine-wave generator of frequency f_c on and off periodically at the same phase points. For the example shown in Fig. P4-26,

$$f_c(t) = V \cos \omega_c t \qquad \frac{-\tau}{2} < t < \frac{\tau}{2}$$

$$= 0 \qquad \text{elsewhere in a period}$$

(*a*) Find the spectrum of $f_c(t)$ by expanding the pulsed carrier in a Fourier series. (Use the exponential form of $\cos \omega_c t$.)

(*b*) Write $f_c(t) = V \cos \omega_c t \cdot S(t)$, with $S(t)$ a rectangular pulse train. Expand $S(t)$ in a Fourier series. Find the spectrum of $f_c(t)$, and compare with the result of (*a*).

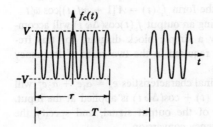

FIGURE P4-26

4-27. A periodic function $f(t)$ is band-limited to 10 kHz and has a uniform (flat) amplitude spectrum from 0 to 10 kHz. It is given by

$$f(t) = \frac{1}{2} + \sum_{n=1}^{10} \cos n\omega t \qquad \omega = 2\pi \times 1,000$$

Show that the function $f^2(t)$ has an amplitude spectrum decreasing linearly from 0 to 20 kHz. The envelope of the spectrum of $f^2(t)$ is thus triangular in shape.

4-28. A function $f(t)$ has as its Fourier transform

$$F(\omega) = K \qquad |\omega| < \omega_M$$

$$= 0 \qquad |\omega| > \omega_M$$

If $f(t)$ is the input voltage to a square-law device with the characteristics $e_o = Ae_i^2$, show that the output has the triangular spectrum of Fig. P4-28 (compare with Prob. 4-27).

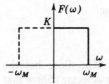

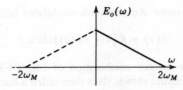

Input spectrum   Output spectrum   **FIGURE P4-28**

4-29. An AM signal consists of a carrier voltage $100 \sin(2\pi \times 10^6 t)$ plus the voltage $(20 \sin 6{,}280t + 50 \sin 12{,}560t)\sin(2\pi \times 10^6 t)$.

(a) Draw the amplitude-versus-frequency plot of the modulated signal.

(b) How much peak power will this signal deliver to a 100-Ω load?

(c) What is the average power (over a modulation cycle) delivered to a 100-Ω load?

(d) Sketch the envelope over a modulation cycle. (Indicate numerical values at key points.)

4-30. Assume that the carrier in Prob. 4-29 is suppressed after modulation. Repeat Prob. 4-29 under this condition.

4-31. *Frequency conversion.* An amplitude-modulated carrier

$$f_c(t) = A[1 + mf(t)]\cos \omega_c t$$

is to be raised or lowered in frequency to a new carrier frequency $\omega_c' = \omega_c \pm \Delta\omega$. The resultant time function will appear in the form $f_c'(t) = A'[1 + mf(t)]\cos \omega_c' t$.

(a) Show that a product modulator producing an output $f_c(t)\cos(\Delta\omega\, t)$ will accomplish this frequency conversion. Draw a simple block diagram for this frequency converter. Specify the filtering required in the two cases of frequency raised by $\Delta\omega$ and lowered by $\Delta\omega$ rad/s.

(b) Show that a nonlinear device with terminal characteristics $e_o = \alpha_1 e_i + \alpha_2 e_i^2$ will perform this frequency conversion if $f_c(t) + \cos(\Delta\omega\, t)$ is applied at the input. Sketch a typical amplitude spectrum of the output signal, and specify the filtering necessary to produce the frequency conversion.

4-32. A general nonlinear device has output–input characteristics given by $e_o = \alpha_1 e_i + \alpha_2 e_i^2 + \cdots$ (this could represent a diode, transistor, vacuum triode, etc.).

(a) Show that all combinations of sum and difference frequencies appear in the output if e_i is a sum of cosine waves.

(b) Show that this device can be used as a modulator if $e_i = f(t) + \cos \omega_c t$.

(c) The input is a normal AM wave given by $e_i = K[1 + mf(t)]\cos \omega_c t$. Show that this nonlinear device will demodulate the wave, i.e., reproduce $f(t)$.

(d) Show that this device can act as a frequency converter if

$$e_i = K[1 + mf(t)]\cos \omega_c t + \cos(\Delta\omega\, t)$$

In particular show that with proper filtering the AM wave spectrum can be shifted up or down by $\Delta\omega$ rad/s.

4-33. A function appears in the form

$$f_c(t) = \cos \omega_c t - K \sin \omega_m t \sin \omega_c t$$

Using block diagrams, show how to generate this, given $\cos \omega_c t$ and $\sin \omega_m t$ as inputs.

4-34. *Amplitude-modulation detector.* An amplitude-modulated voltage

$$f_c(t) = K[1 + mf(t)]\cos \omega_c t$$

is applied to the diode–resistor combination of Fig. P4-34. The diode has the piecewise-linear characteristics shown. (It is then called a linear detector.) Show that

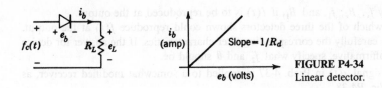

FIGURE P4-34
Linear detector.

for $|mf(t)| < 1$ the l-f components of the load voltage e_L provide a perfect replica of $f(t)$.

4-35. Repeat Prob. 4-34 for the case where the diode–resistor combination of Fig. P4-34 has the square-law characteristic $e_L = \alpha_1 e_i + \alpha_2 e_i^2$. Show that e_L contains a component proportional to $f(t)$.

4-36. (a) A DSB (suppressed-carrier) signal of the form $f(t)\cos \omega_c t$ is to be demodulated. Show that multiplying this signal by $\cos \omega_c t$ in a product modulator reproduces $f(t)$.

  (b) "The DSM demodulator is phase-sensitive." Demonstrate the validity of this statement by multiplying $f(t)\cos \omega_c t$ by $\cos(\omega_c t + \theta)$ and letting θ vary from 0 to π radians.

4-37. An AM signal has the form

$$s(t) = [1 + mf(t)]\cos \omega_0 t \qquad |mf(t)| \le 1$$

The bandwidth of $f(t)$ is $B \ll f_0$. Consider the receiver shown in Fig. P4-37.

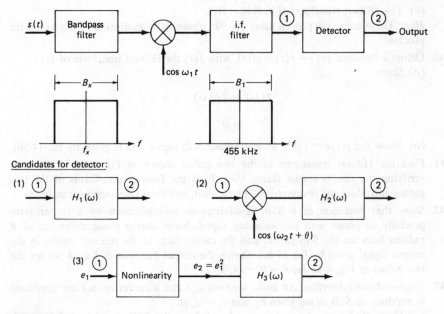

FIGURE P4-37

(a) Specify f_x, B_x, f_1, and B_1, if $f(t)$ is to be reproduced at the output.

(b) Show which of the three detectors shown could reproduce $f(t)$ at the output. Sketch carefully the corresponding filter characteristics. If the answer for device (2) is affirmative, specify what f_2 and θ should be.

4-38. The input signal $s(t)$ in Prob. 4-37 is applied to a somewhat modified receiver, as shown in Fig. P4-38.

(a) $f(t)$ is again to be reproduced at (2). What are B_y and f_1? Sketch carefully the i-f characteristic.

(b) Repeat (b) of Prob. 4-37.

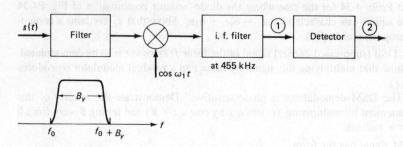

FIGURE P4-38

4-39. Prove the following properties of Hilbert transforms:

(a) If $f(t) = f(-t)$, then $\hat{f}(t) = -\hat{f}(-t)$.

(b) If $f(t) = -f(-t)$, then $\hat{f}(t) = \hat{f}(-t)$.

(c) The Hilbert transform of $\hat{f}(t)$ is $-f(t)$.

Hint: These are easily proven using the 90° phase-shift description of the transform process.

4-40. Define a function $y(t) = f(t) - j\hat{f}(t)$, with $\hat{f}(t)$ the Hilbert transform of $f(t)$.

(a) Show

$$Y(\omega) = 2F(\omega) \qquad \omega \le 0$$

$$= 0 \qquad \omega > 0$$

(b) Show $\text{Re}[y(t)e^{j\omega_c t}]$ is a *lower-sideband* SSB signal and is given by Eq. (4-50).

4-41. Find the Hilbert transforms of the two pulses shown in Fig. 4-46 in the text, verifying the results shown there. *Hint:* Find the Fourier transforms of the two pulses, introduce the necessary 90° phase shift, and then take *inverse* transforms.

4-42. Show that detection of a SSB signal requires multiplication by a carrier term precisely in phase with the incoming signal. Show that a phase difference of θ radians between the SSB carrier and the carrier term at the receiver results in the output signal given by Eq. (4-56). Sketch the output function of Eq. (4-56) for the two pulses of Fig. 4-46 for $\theta = 0$, $\pi/4$, $\pi/2$.

4-43. *Single-sideband detection.* An audio tone $\cos \omega_m t$ and a carrier $\cos \omega_c t$ are combined to produce an SSB signal given by $\cos(\omega_c - \omega_m)t$.

(a) Show that $\cos \omega_m t$ can be reproduced from the SSB signal by mixing with $\cos \omega_c t$ as a local carrier.

(b) The local carrier drifts in frequency by $\Delta\omega$ radians to $\omega_c + \Delta\omega$. What is the demodulated signal now?

(c) The local carrier shifts in phase to $\cos(\omega_c t + \theta)$. Find the audio output signal.

4-44. (a) An amplitude-modulated voltage given by

$$v_c(t) = V(1 + m\cos\omega_m t)\cos\omega_c t \qquad \text{volts}$$

is applied across a resistor R. Calculate the percentage average power in the carrier and in each of the two sideband frequencies. Calculate the peak power.

(b) The voltage $v_c(t)$ is now a suppressed-carrier voltage $v_c(t) = V\cos\omega_m t\cos\omega_c t$ applied across R ohms. What is the fraction of the total average power in each of the sideband frequencies?

4-45. An SSB radio transmitter radiates 1 kW of average power summed over the entire sideband. What total average power would the transmitter have to radiate if it were operating as a DSB (suppressed-carrier) system and the same distance coverage were required?

4-46. An AM transmitter is tested by using the dummy load and linear narrowband receiver of Fig. P4-46. The r-f amplifier portion of the receiver is swept successively and continuously over the range 100 kHz to 10 MHz. Its frequency characteristic at any frequency f_c in this range is shown in the figure. With no audio input the wattmeter reads 100 W average power. The peak-reading voltmeter (VM) and r-f amplifier tuning characteristic indicate an output of 10 V peaks at 1 MHz.

(a) With an audio input signal of 10 V peak at 1 kHz the wattmeter reads 150 W. At what frequencies are there receiver outputs? What are the various amplitudes, as read on the VM?

(b) The 1-kHz modulating signal is replaced by the composite signal $2\cos 12{,}560t + 3\cos 18{,}840t$. What is the new wattmeter reading? At what frequencies will there be receiver outputs? What are the various amplitudes?

(c) The transmitter modulator is modified so that the carrier is suppressed but the other characteristics are unchanged. An audio signal of 10 V peak at 1 kHz is applied. What is the wattmeter reading? What are the receiver output frequencies and amplitudes? Sketch the pattern that would be seen on an oscilloscope connected across the load. (The left-to-right sweep period is 2,000 μs; the return takes negligible time.)

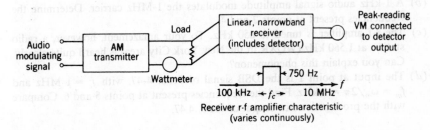

FIGURE P4-46

4-47. The radio receiver of Fig. P4-47 has the r-f amplifier and i-f amplifier characteristics shown. The mixer characteristic is given by $e_3 = e_2(\alpha_0 + \alpha_1 e_{01})$, with α_0 and α_1

constants, and $e_{01} = A \sin \omega_c' t$. The product-detector output is $e_5 = e_4 e_{02}$, with $e_{02} = B \cos(\omega_c - \omega_c')t$. Find the signals at points 4 and 6 for each of the following signals at point 1:

(a) Normal AM, $(1 + \sin \omega_m t)\sin \omega_c t$.
(b) Double sideband, suppressed carrier, $\sin \omega_m t \sin \omega_c t$.
(c) Single sideband, $\cos(\omega_c - \omega_m)t$.

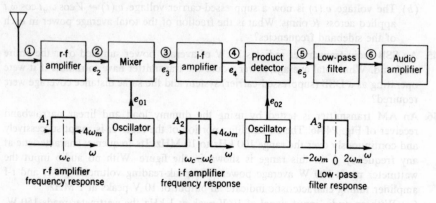

FIGURE P4-47

4-48. The product detector and oscillator II in Fig. P4-47 are replaced by an envelope detector with the characteristic $e_5 = be_4^2$. The r-f amplifier can be continuously tuned over the range $f_c = \omega_c/2\pi = 535$ to $1,605$ kHz. The tuning capacitor of oscillator I is ganged to the tuning capacitor of the r-f amplifier so that $f_c' = \omega_c'/2\pi = f_c + 455$ kHz at all times. The circuit is then that of a superheterodyne radio receiver. The passband of the amplifiers is ± 5 kHz about the center frequency.

(a) Determine all frequencies present at points 3 and 4 if the signal at 1 is a 1-MHz unmodulated carrier.
(b) A 1-kHz audio signal amplitude modulates the 1-MHz carrier. Determine the frequencies present at points 2 and 4.
(c) The r-f amplifier is tuned to 650 kHz. To your amazement, however, a radio station at 1,560 kHz (WQXR in the New York City area) is heard quite clearly. Can you explain this phenomenon?
(d) The input at point 1 is the DSB signal of Prob. 4-47, with $f_c = 1$ MHz and $f_m = \omega_m/2\pi = 1$ kHz. Find the frequencies present at points 5 and 6. Compare with the product-detector output of Prob. 4.47.

4-49. Consider the system shown in Fig. P4-49. Show that the output $g(t)$ is a SSB signal. Do this by assuming $F(\omega)$ as shown ($B \ll f_c$) and carefully sketching the transforms at the output of each device. Preserve the distinction between the shaded and unshaded halves of $F(\omega)$. Is the lower or upper half of a conventional DSB signal retained?

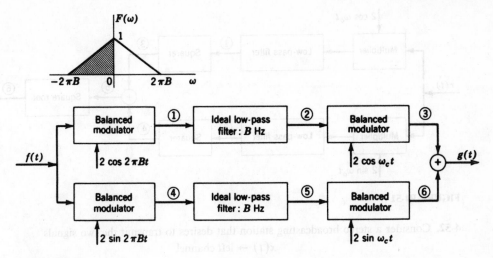

FIGURE P4-49

4-50. A DSB signal $(\cos \omega_m t + a \cos 2\omega_m t)\cos \omega_c t$ is applied to the receiver shown in Fig. P4-50. Find the signals shown at points 1, 2, and 3 if

    (a) $\omega_1 = \omega_c - 3\omega_m$

    (b) $\omega_1 = \omega_c$

    Discuss.

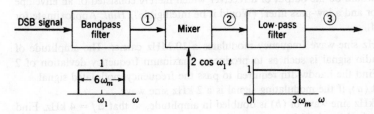

FIGURE P4-50

4-51. An AM signal is given by $r(t) = a[1 + f(t)]\cos(\omega_o t + \theta)$, where θ is a constant and $f(t)$ has a Fourier transform which is zero for $|\omega| > \Omega$. Assume that $\Omega \ll \omega_0$ and $|f(t)| \le 1$. Consider the receiver shown in Fig. P4-51. The low-pass filters have transfer functions

$$H(\omega) = 1 \qquad |\omega| < \Omega$$

$$= 0 \qquad |\omega| > \Omega$$

By calculating the signals at points 1 through 6, show that the receiver can be used to demodulate $f(t)$.

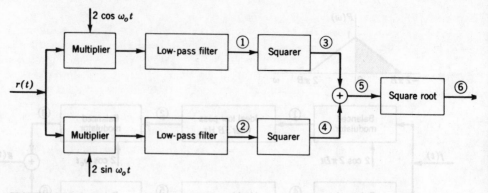

FIGURE P4-51

4-52. Consider a stereo broadcasting station that desires to transmit the two signals

$$x(t) \rightarrow \text{left channel}$$
$$y(t) \rightarrow \text{right channel}$$

Both $x(t)$ and $y(t)$ have frequency components only in the range $(2\pi)30 \le \omega \le (2\pi)10,000$. The station actually broadcasts the signal

$$[A + x(t) + y(t)]\cos \omega_0 t + [A + x(t) - y(t)]\sin \omega_0 t,$$

where $\omega_0 = 2\pi(10^6)$ and $A \gg |x(t)| + |y(t)|$.

(a) Give and discuss a block diagram of a receiving system which provides as separate outputs $x(t)$ and $y(t)$. Assume the phase and frequency of the transmitted wave are known exactly at the receiver. You may use mixers, multipliers, adders, filters, etc.

(b) What would be the output of a receiver which merely consisted of an envelope detector and a low-pass filter? (Would it be intelligible?) *Hint*: Approximate for large A.

4-53. (a) A 1-kHz sine-wave frequency modulates a 10-MHz carrier. The amplitude of this audio signal is such as to produce a maximum frequency deviation of 2 kHz. Find the bandwidth required to pass the frequency-modulated signal.

(b) Repeat (a), if the modulating signal is a 2-kHz sine wave.

(c) The 2-kHz sine wave of (b) is doubled in amplitude, so that $\Delta f = 4$ kHz. Find the required bandwidth.

4-54. A 100-MHz sine-wave carrier is to be frequency-modulated by a 10-kHz sine wave. An engineer designing the system reasons that he can minimize bandwidth by decreasing the audio amplitude. He arranges for a maximum frequency deviation Δf of only ± 10 Hz away from the 100-MHz carrier frequency and assumes that he requires only 20-Hz bandwidth.

(a) Find the fallacy in his reasoning, and specify the actual bandwidth required.

(b) Would he have been right to assume a bandwidth of 2 MHz if the audio amplitude had been chosen to produce a Δf of 1 MHz? Explain the difference between the results of (a) and (b).

4-55. An FM receiver similar to that of Fig. 4-64 is tuned to a carrier frequency of 100 MHz.

(a) A 10-kHz audio-signal frequency modulates a 100-MHz carrier, producing a β of 0.1. Find the bandwidths required of the r-f and i-f amplifiers and of the audio amplifier.

(b) Repeat (a) if $\beta = 5$.

(c) Two signals at 100 MHz are tuned in alternately. The carriers are of equal intensity. One is modulated with a 10-kHz signal and has $\beta = 5$; the other is modulated with a 2-kHz signal and has $\beta = 25$. Which requires the larger bandwidth? Explain. Compare the audio-amplifier outputs in the two cases.

(d) Two other signals are tuned in alternately. The carriers are again of equal intensity. One has a frequency deviation of 10 kHz with $\beta = 5$, the other a deviation of 2 kHz with $\beta = 25$. Which requires the larger bandwidth? Which gives the larger audio output?

4-56. A general frequency-modulated voltage has the form $f_c(t) = A_c \cos[\omega_c t + K\int f(t)\, dt]$. Show that the average power dissipated in a 1-Ω resistor is $A_c^2/2$ averaged over a modulating cycle.

4-57. (a) A modulating signal $f(t) = 0.1 \sin 2\pi \times 10^3 t$ is used to modulate a 1-MHz carrier in both an AM and an FM system. The 0.1-V amplitude produces a 100-Hz frequency deviation in the FM case. Compare the receiver r-f amplifier and audio-amplifier bandwidths required in the two systems.

(b) Repeat (a) if $f(t) = 20 \sin 2\pi \times 10^3 t$.

4-58. A sine wave is switched periodically from 10 to 11 MHz at a 5-kHz rate. Sketch the resultant waveshape. What is the form of the modulating signal if this frequency-shifted wave is considered an FSK signal? What is the approximate transmission bandwidth? Compare with the bandwidth required if the modulating signal is approximated by a 5-kHz sine wave of the same amplitude.

4-59. The tuned circuit of an oscillator is shown in Fig. P4-59. The current source $g_m e_g$ is controlled by the voltage $e_g(t)$ across R as shown.

(a) Show that with $1/\omega_c \gg RC$, the total effective capacitance of the tuned circuit is given by

$$C_T = C_0 + C + g_m RC$$

(b) What is the oscillator frequency if $g_m = 4{,}000\ \mu\text{S}$?

(c) What is the modulation index β if g_m varies from 3,000 to 5,000 μS at a 1-kHz rate?

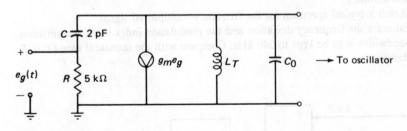

FIGURE P4-59

4-60. Consider a circuit such as the one in Fig. P4-59, but with R and C interchanged. Calculate the effective inductance introduced by the controlled source. Repeat Prob. 4-59.

4-61. A controlled source circuit similar to that of Fig. P4-59 provides an effective capacitance $C' = [-2e_g(t) + 6]10^{-12}$ F appearing in parallel with C_0 and L_T. For this case $C_0 = 14$ pF, $L_T = 50\ \mu$H, and $e_g(t) = 0.5 \sin(2\pi \times 500t)$.

(a) What is the carrier frequency?

(b) What is the frequency deviation Δf?

(c) Determine the modulation index β. Show a rough sketch of the frequency spectrum of the FM wave indicating the approximate bandwidth.

(d) Repeat (c) if the frequency deviation is reduced to 0.01 of its value in (b), with the modulating frequency unchanged.

4-62. The capacitance of a PN junction is given in terms of its reverse bias voltage V by

$$C = \frac{C_0}{(1 + V/\psi)^K}$$

with ψ the contact potential, and K and C_0 known constants. Such a reversed-bias diode is to be used as a variable capacitor.

(a) $K = 0.5$, $\psi = 0.5$, $C_0 = 300$ pF. Plot C versus the reverse-bias voltage V.

(b) The diode is to be used as the sole source of capacitance in a tuned circuit. Assume the diode is biased at -6 V and the center frequency is to be adjusted to 10 MHz. Plot frequency deviation away from 10 MHz versus voltage deviation away from -6 V. Calculate the modulation sensitivity in hertz per volt in the vicinity of -6 V (this is the initial slope of the curve plotted), and the maximum voltage excursion in either direction for a maximum of 1 percent deviation away from a linear frequency–voltage characteristic.

(c) A fixed capacitance of 100 pF is added in series with the diode. Repeat part (b) and compare.

4-63. *FM stereo.* Call the left-speaker output L, and the right-speaker output R. For stereo broadcasting the two signals are first combined (*matrixed*) to form composite signals $L + R$, and $L - R$. (As in monophonic FM, the nominal bandwidth of each signal is 15 kHz.) The $L - R$ signal is multiplied by a 38-kHz carrier in a balanced modulator to form a DSB signal, as shown in Fig. P4-63. The DSB signal, the baseband $L + R$ signal, and a 19-kHz tone from which the 38-kHz carrier is obtained are then summed to provide a frequency-multiplexed signal that in turn modulates the FM carrier. (The 19-kHz tone provides the pilot carrier for receiver synchronization.)

(a) Sketch a typical spectrum for the frequency-multiplexed signal.

(b) Estimate the frequency deviation and the modulation index if the transmission bandwidth is to be kept to 240 kHz. Compare with the monaural case ($L + R$ above).

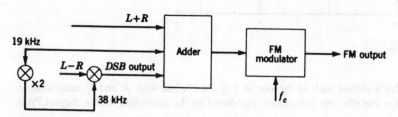

FIGURE P4-63

4-64. Consider the transmission system shown in Fig. P4-64.
   (a) Find frequencies f_1 and f_2 ($f_2 > f_1$) such that the composite (summed) signal at (1) occupies as narrow a frequency range as possible. Show that this range is 12 kHz.
   (b) The FM transmitter has a center frequency of 1 MHz. A modulation index of $\beta = 5$ is desired. Find the frequency deviation and bandwidth of the signal at (2).
   (c) With everything else unchanged the *amplitude* of the signal at (1) is increased by a factor of 2. Find the bandwidth and modulation index of the signal at (2).

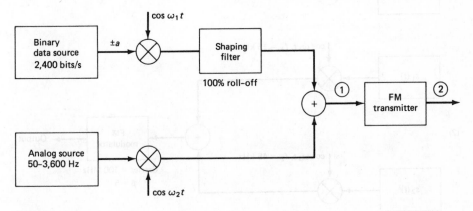

FIGURE P4-64

4-65. Two audio signals, each covering the range 50 Hz to 15 kHz, are to be combined and transmitted via FM. Two techniques shown in Fig. P4-65 are suggested.
   (a) Find the frequency deviation and transmission bandwidth of the FM output in the two cases, and compare.
   (b) Show a block diagram of the receiver in each case, indicating how $s_1(t)$ and $s_2(t)$ are reproduced.
   (c) In (b), indicate whether envelope detection can be used, after FM detection, to reproduce $s_1(t)$ and $s_2(t)$ in each case, with the two transmitters as shown. If envelope detection is *not* possible in a particular case, can the transmitter be modified (prior to the FM modulator) to allow envelope detection to be used? How? Indicate with a block diagram where appropriate.

4-66. The outputs of ten 2,400-bit/s data sources are to be frequency-multiplexed using two levels of multiplexing, as shown in Fig. P4-66. Raised-cosine shaping (100-percent roll-off) is used for the baseband binary outputs.
   (a) Compare the transmission bandwidths of the multiplexed signals in the following cases:
      (1) AM-AM (OOK transmission followed by AM).
      (2) AM-SSB (OOK transmission followed by SSB modulation).
      (3) FM-FM (FSK followed by FM).
      Choose $\Delta f = 5$ kHz in the FSK modulators; $\Delta f = 740$ kHz in the FM

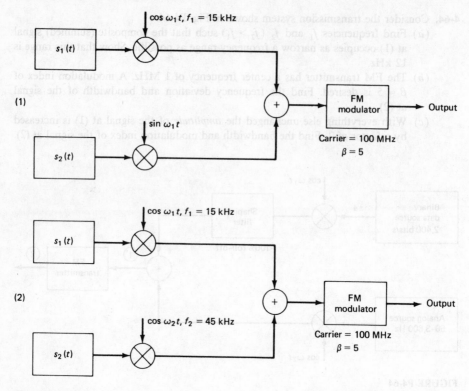

FIGURE P4-65

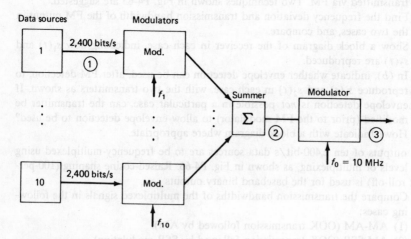

FIGURE P4-66

modulator. The carrier frequencies $f_1, \ldots, f_{10}$, are to be chosen to minimize the bandwidth in each case.

(b) Sketch typical spectra at points (1), (2), (3) for the AM–AM and AM–SSB cases.

(c) Compare the bandwidths obtained in (a) with those required if the first stage of modulation is replaced by time multiplexing. Make any reasonable assumption about synchronizing or framing information needed.

4-67. A 57-kbit/s binary signal is shaped so that it requires a 35-kHz bandwidth. Ten of these signals are then frequency-multiplexed using PSK modulation for each, as shown in Fig. P4-67a, with carriers selected to pack the signals as closely together as possible. ($f_1 = \omega_1/2\pi$ is selected as small as possible.) Ten such multiplexed outputs are now shifted in turn to the 100-MHz range using single-sideband transmission as shown in Fig. P4-67b: the first is multiplexed up to 100 MHz and its upper sideband only retained, the second is shifted up and placed as close to the first as possible, with its upper sideband retained, etc.

(a) What are the initial carrier frequencies f_1 and f_{10}?

(b) What is the final carrier frequency f_0?

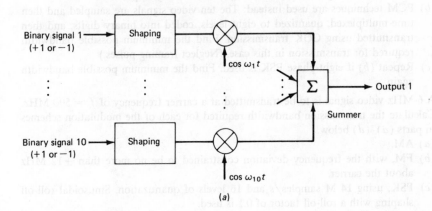

(a)

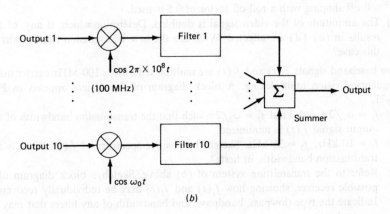

(b)

FIGURE P4-67

(c) Specify the transmission characteristics of filters 1 and 10 shown in Fig. P4-67b.

(d) Sketch the output spectrum in Fig. P4-67b.

(e) Specify a block diagram of a receiver structure for extracting the original binary signals.

Be as quantitative as possible, indicating transmission characteristics of all filters used. Assume that perfect synchronization can be maintained between transmitter and receiver.

4-68. (a) Compare the final (100-MHz) transmission bandwidth of Prob. 4-67 with that required if each group of ten 57-kbit/s binary signals is time-multiplexed rather than frequency-multiplexed. Use the same percent of roll-off shaping.

(b) Repeat (a) and compare, if two levels of time multiplexing are used, the final time-multiplexed output then fed into a 100-MHz SSB modulator.

4-69. Ten video signals, each of 4-MHz bandwidth, are to be transmitted using one carrier. Several methods of transmission are to be compared.

(a) Each signal individually amplitude-modulates a carrier. The ten AM signals are then summed, and in turn amplitude-modulate a single carrier at a high frequency. Calculate the bandwidth of this final transmitted (composite) signal, if the ten AM signals are packed together as closely as possible.

(b) PCM techniques are used instead: The ten video signals are sampled and then time-multiplexed, quantized to eight levels, coded into binary digits, and then transmitted using OOK transmission. Find the minimum possible bandwidth required for transmission in this case. (Neglect framing pulses.)

(c) Repeat (b) if eight-phase PSK is used. Find the minimum possible bandwidth again.

4-70. A 6-MHz video signal is to be transmitted at a carrier frequency of $f_c = 500$ MHz. Calculate the transmission bandwidth required for each of the modulation schemes in parts (a)–(d) below.

(a) AM.

(b) FM, with the frequency deviation constrained to be no more than ± 12 MHz about the carrier.

(c) PSK, using 14 M samples/s and 16 levels of quantization. Sinusoidal roll-off shaping with a roll-off factor of 0.1 is used.

(d) 16-QAM, using the same A/D parameters as in the PSK case above. Sinusoidal roll-off shaping with a roll-off factor of 0.5 is used.

(e) The amplitude of the video signal is doubled. Determine which, if any, of the results in (a)–(d) are affected. What are the new transmission bandwidths in this case?

4-71. Two baseband signals $f_1(t)$ and $f_2(t)$ are multiplexed onto a 100-MHz carrier using frequency-division multiplexing. A block diagram of the system appears in Fig. P4-71.

(a) $f_1 = \omega_1/2\pi = 0$. Find $f_2 = \omega_2/2\pi$ such that the transmission bandwidth of the output signal $f_c(t)$ is minimized.

(b) $f_1 = 10$ kHz, $f_2 = 35$ kHz. Sketch the positive spectrum of $f_c(t)$. What is the transmission bandwidth, in hertz?

(c) Refer to the transmitting system of (b) above. Sketch a block diagram of a possible receiver, showing how $f_1(t)$ and $f_2(t)$ may be individually recovered. Indicate the type (lowpass, bandpass) and bandwidth of any filters that may be required.

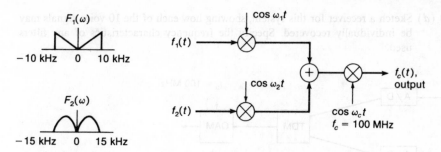

FIGURE P4-71

4-72. Ten voice sources, each covering the frequency range from 10 to 20,000 Hz, are frequency-multiplexed as shown in Fig. P4-72.

    (*a*) Find the frequencies $f_2, f_3, \ldots, f_{10}$ that minimize the overall bandwidth of the summed signal at point ①.

    (*b*) What is the bandwidth at point ② if amplitude modulation is used? Repeat for FM, with a frequency deviation $\Delta f = 620$ kHz.

    (*c*) Repeat (*b*) for both AM and FM if each of the 10 signal amplitudes is tripled.

    (*d*) Sketch a block diagram of the complete receiver needed if AM is used. Each of the 10 signals should be recovered. Put filters in where needed and indicate their characteristics.

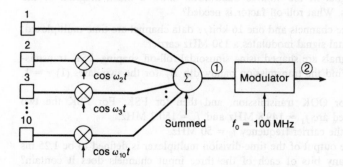

FIGURE P4-72

4-73. The 10 sources of Prob. 4-72 are each to be transmitted digitally. A/D conversion and multiplexing are used, as shown in Fig. P4-73.

    (*a*) What is the minimum sampling rate required?

    (*b*) Each signal is sampled at a rate of 44,000 samples/s. Each sample is quantized and coded into 12 bits. The 10 PCM streams are time-multiplexed into one composite PCM signal. (Neglect synchronization bits that might be required.) Find the bit rate of the composite PCM signal.

    (*c*) The composite PCM stream is fed to a 16-QAM modulator with $f_0 = 100$ MHz. Sinusoidal roll-off shaping with $r = 0.1$ is used. Find the transmission bandwidth at the output of the modulator.

(*d*) Sketch a receiver for this system, showing how each of the 10 voice signals may be individually recovered. Specify the frequency characteristics of any filters used.

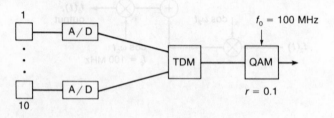

FIGURE P4-73

4-74. Show how one may generate a 12-channel group from twelve 4-kHz voice channels in the FDM hierarchy of Fig. 4-67 by the two-step modulation process used by Northern Telecom of Canada as mentioned in the text: first modulate with an 8.14-MHz carrier; select the upper sideband; then use 12 carriers, spaced equally from 8.204 to 8.248 MHz, selecting the lower sidebands. Provide a block diagram of the process. Specify the transmission characteristics of all filters used.

4-75. Computer output data at a 56-kbit/s rate is to be transmitted in one of the group channels of the FDM hierarchy of Fig. 4-67. Bipolar transmission is used to reduce low-frequency components. Sinusoidal roll-off shaping and SSB transmission are used to fit the signal in the 48-kHz bandwidth. Show a block diagram of the modulation process. What roll-off factor is needed?

4-76. Two 64-kbit/s voice channels and one 16-kbit/s data channel are time-multiplexed. The composite digital signal modulates a 150-MHz carrier.
(*a*) The output signals are shaped using sinusoidal roll-off shaping. PSK transmission is used. Find the transmission bandwidth B_T for the two cases (1) $r = 1$, (2) $r = 0.25$.
(*b*) Repeat (*a*) for OOK transmission, and then for FSK. For FSK the two frequencies used are $f_1 = 149.8$ MHz and $f_2 = 150.2$ MHz.
(*c*) Repeat (*a*) if the carrier frequency $f_c = 50$ MHz.
(*d*) A frame at the output of the time-division multiplexer is defined to be 1.25 ms long. How many bits of each of the three input channels does it contain? (Framing and control information are neglected.)
(*e*) A 56-kbit/s data channel is added at the input. 10 control bits are added per frame. Repeat (*a*).

CHAPTER

5

COMMUNICATION NETWORKS

over packet-switched networks. We return to the layered communications architecture of Sec. 1-1 (Fig. 1-2), and discuss in detail the lower (network) service layers.

In Sec. 5-2, following, we focus on local-area

5-1 INTRODUCTION: CIRCUIT AND PACKET SWITCHING

It was pointed out in Chap. 1, in introducing this book, that most communication worldwide is carried out over networks. This is clearly necessary when many users are required to communicate with one another. Dedicated connections between each pair or group of users communicating with one another are impossible to establish in this case. Consider the idealized example of such a network given by Fig. 5-1. This is similar to the example of Fig. 1-1 in Chap. 1. The network is made up of nodes and links. It enables any user to communicate with any other user (or set of users). A simple example corresponding to Fig. 5-1 would be a satellite network with each node in the network representing a satellite. The links between satellites would then be line-of-sight space connections between them. The user nodal links shown would then be the up/down ground-to-satellite links mentioned in Chap. 4 (see Fig. 4-71). Alternatively, some of the nodes could be located on the earth and others could represent satellites. The links would then be mixed space or ground (terrestrial) links. The most common configuration would have the network ground-based only, with the links then being cable, radio (including microwave), or optical fibers, as examples.

The material presented thus far in Chaps. 3 and 4 has focused on link or point-to-point communications. In this chapter we interrupt our discussion of point-to-point communications to introduce some important network concepts. In this section, in particular, we distinguish between circuit and packet switching, both techniques used in networks, with emphasis given to data communications

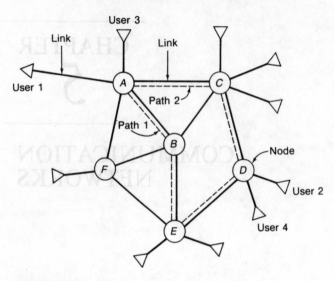

FIGURE 5-1
Example of a network.

over packet-switched networks. We return to the layered communications architecture of Sec. 1-1 (Fig. 1-2), and discuss in detail the lower (network services)
layers.

In Sec. 5-2, following, we focus on local-area networks (LANs), as one
current, extremely significant example of a network. Section 5-3 then introduces a
quantitative discussion of some of the concepts motivated by this section and
Sec. 5-2. It introduces the common Poisson model for traffic. It develops the
average-time-delay formula for a simple queue and applies this to a discussion of
the comparative time-delay performance of two types of common LANs. It then
concludes with a brief discussion of statistical multiplexing for packet switching.
Section 5-4 returns to circuit switching, discusses it in more detail than done in
this section, and develops the Erlang blocking-probability formula as one measure of performance in circuit switching.

Returning to Fig. 5-1, we start with our familiar notions of point-to-point
communications and enlarge these to include elements of networking. Take link
$A-C$ as an example. Information (traffic) moving across this link could be in
baseband form or modulated-carrier form. It could be data, voice, or video, or
combinations of these and other kinds of communication traffic types. We
assume throughout this chapter that this information has been transmitted, from
the source, in digital form. It could be single-user information, or, more likely,
over a network, information from many users multiplexed together. (The multiplexed traffic could, for example, represent information from multiple users
connected to node A, as shown, or could include multiplexed traffic from nodes
B and F, as well as other nodes, destined for node C and beyond.) The various
multiplexing and modulation techniques discussed in Chaps. 3 and 4 apply to

this example. Another type of multiplexing, called statistical multiplexing, will be discussed later in this chapter.

It is clear from Fig. 5-1 that providing a physical connection from node *A* to node *C*, or over any other link, still does not ensure communication between any set of users in the network. User traffic must be directed over an appropriate path or route. If users are machines and not human, the information must reach the receiving system(s) in a recognizable form. This is part of the complete communication process and leads to the concept of layered architectures mentioned briefly in Sec. 1-2.

Restricting ourselves to the lower, network services layers of the layered architecture of Fig. 1-2, the prime purpose of a network is to ensure that information leaving a source node arrives at the appropriate destination node(s). The source node is the one to which the source user is connected; the destination node(s) the one to which the destination user is connected. There are generically two ways of carrying out this function and, historically, two types of networks developed for this purpose. The older form is that of *circuit switching*. The more recent form is *packet switching*. Circuit-switching networks, exemplified by telephone networks worldwide, ensure that a *dedicated* path (or route, or *circuit*) is set up end to end from source to destination, before communication can begin. A path or route will in general consist of multiple concatenated links, connecting nodes, as shown in Fig. 5-1. Two possible paths are shown connecting nodes *A* and *D*. Others could be defined as well. The word *dedicated* implies that each link consists of multiple channels (or *trunks*), at least one of which is assigned exclusively to a particular connection (or call or conversation) during the connection setup phase. A channel, a *physical resource on a link*, can be a separate pair of wires, a separate spatial path over a radio link, a dedicated frequency band in the case of FDM, or, most commonly with digital communications, a dedicated time slot in a TDM frame. (The term "satellite channel" used in describing the TDMA concept in Sec. 4-13 refers to a TDMA time slot.) An example of a TDM link appears in Fig. 5-2. (We focus on the baseband case only for simplicity's sake. In the case of high-frequency transmission, one of the digital modulation techniques discussed in Chap. 4 would then be used to actually transmit the

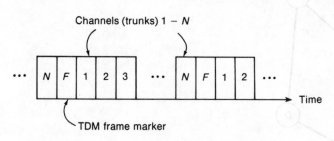

FIGURE 5-2
TDM link.

output symbols). Once the complete path, end to end, is set up, the user systems can communicate as long as they wish. On completion of a circuit-switched call the path is typically disconnected or torn down, and channels (trunks) are free to be assigned to other users. We shall have more to say about circuit switching later in this chapter.

Packet-switching networks are of much more recent vintage, having been developed commercially in the mid to late 1960s. They have been used principally for data communications. Future packet-switching networks may incorporate voice and video communications, as well as other traffic types. In these networks streams of data (messages) are blocked into smaller units called *packets* (these may range in length from tens to thousands of octets, or bytes—the two words are used interchangeably). Packets then move individually across a network. Channels are no longer dedicated in this case. They are shared by all packets accessing a particular link. In a TDM frame structure such as that of Fig. 5-2, packets would each access a slot or, if a slot were a fraction of a packet in length, would require a number of frames to be transmitted.

Packet-switching networks come in two varieties: *connectionless* (datagram) networks and *connection-oriented* (*virtual-circuit*) networks. Virtual-circuit, or connection-oriented, networks are similar to circuit-switched networks. A path or route must be set up before data transfer begins and, unless a permanent connection exists, will be torn down or disconnected once the call (conversation) is completed. Figure 5-1 could thus represent a packet-switched as well as circuit-switched network, and paths 1 and 2 could refer to two paths or virtual circuits between nodes *A* and *D*. Virtual circuits using the same link share the channels on that link. An example appears in Fig. 5-3. Two connections are shown. Virtual circuit 1 follows path 1; virtual circuit 3 follows path 2. Both virtual circuits share link *B–E*. It is clear that individual packets must carry some connection (virtual-circuit) information. Virtual circuits must thus be globally distinguishable throughout a network. Packets in Fig. 5-3 are shown carrying their virtual-circuit number. Nodes along the path in the network route these

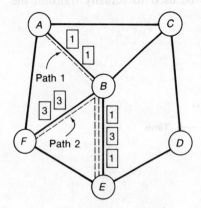

FIGURE 5-3
Connection-oriented packet-switched network.

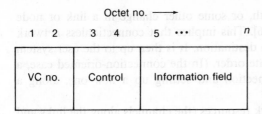

FIGURE 5-4

Example of connection-oriented packet format (VC = virtual circuit).

packets according to the virtual-circuit number, using routing tables stored at each node [SCHW 1987, Chap. 6].

An example of a connection-oriented packet appears in Fig. 5-4. The packet shown is n octets long. The first four octets in this example represent the packet *header*—the virtual-circuit number and control information added at the network source node. The rest of the packet is the information field provided to the network by the user system. The two-octet control field could be used to distinguish between data and control packets (those used to set up and tear down connections, to carry routing information from node to node, to signal different types of error conditions, etc.), to number packets sequentially, and to indicate the end of a message (a sequence of packets), among other necessary functions. The two-octet VC number implies at most $2^{16} = 65,536$ virtual circuits can be present at any one time. To increase this number, many networks number their links as well. The VC number is then applied to a given link only and is often referred to as a *logical channel number*. The global VC number is then the combination of the link number and the logical channel number [SCHW 1987, Chaps. 5, 6]. Each node along a path in a network must thus change the packet logical channel number before transmitting the packet out onto the next link.

In the case of connectionless packet networks no connection phase is needed. Packets are simply launched into the network at will. No specific path is set up beforehand, but packets must still be routed to the appropriate destination(s). The packets must thus carry complete routing information, typically their source–destination addresses. An example of such a packet, often called a datagram, appears in Fig. 5-5. Routing tables at each node are used to route each packet to the appropriate next neighbor. A routing algorithm at each node is automatically invoked to reroute packets in the event of a nodal or link failure,

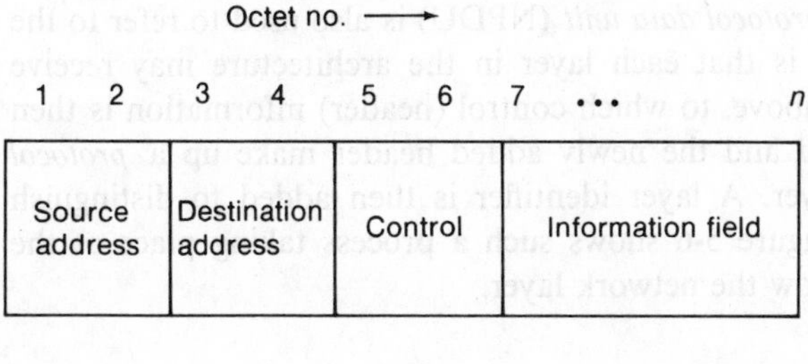

Octet no. ⟶

| 1 | 2 | 3 | 4 | 5 | 6 | 7 | ... | n |

| Source address | Destination address | Control | Information field |

FIGURE 5-5

Example of connectionless packet (datagram) format.

congestion encountered along a path, or some other change in a link or node characteristic [SCHW 1987, Chap. 6]. This implies that connectionless network packets may arrive out of order at a destination. It is then up to the user system to put them back into the appropriate order. (In the connection-oriented case, a failure implies taking down a connection and setting up a new one, along a different path.)

Since packets *share* the network resources (the channels along the links and the nodal processors) there is no guarantee of immediate processing, routing, and transmission when a packet arrives at a node as in the circuit-switched case. Packets are typically queued for transmission along the appropriate next link on a path. These could be packets newly arrived at a network node from a user terminal or packets already transiting the network, arriving on a link from a previous node. The term *store-and-forward network* is sometimes used to denote a network in which queueing takes place at each node. The queueing process introduces random delay into the transmission end to end. This turns out to be one of the performance parameters to be considered in designing and evaluating the performance of a network. For this reason we study a simple model of queueing later in this chapter.

In circuit-switched networks, on the other hand, the only delay encountered during transmission end to end is some nodal processing delay and propagation delay. The propagation delay is normally significant only in satellite links, and then principally for voice communications. Contention for resources within these networks is only encountered during the call setup (connection) phase in determining whether a free channel exists on each link along a path. Calls may be blocked if no free channel is available (this is the usual mode of operation on telephone networks), or may be queued until a free channel on a complete end-to-end path does become available. Circuit-switched networks are thus often rated on the basis of their call-blocking performance. A simplified model for calculating the blocking probability is introduced toward the end of this chapter.

Returning to packet switching, how does the discussion thus far fit into the layered communications architecture discussed briefly in Sec. 1-2 of this book? Figure 5-6 reproduces the Network Services portions of the seven-layer OSI Reference Model of Fig. 1-2. This represents the lowest three layers of that architecture. Figure 5-6 shows the packet being formed at the network layer by adding a header to the information field (user data) arriving from the user system. (See Figs. 5-4 and 5-5.) As noted above, the header contains, among other parameters, address information to be used in routing the packet through the network. The term *network protocol data unit* (NPDU) is also used to refer to the packet. The reason for this is that each layer in the architecture may receive information from the layer above, to which control (header) information is then added. The information field and the newly added header make up a *protocol data unit* (PDU) at that layer. A layer identifier is then added to distinguish PDUs at different layers. Figure 5-6 shows such a process taking place at the data-link layer, the layer below the network layer.

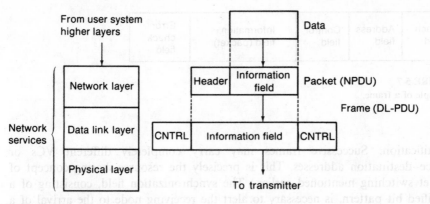

FIGURE 5-6
Layered architecture and data units.

The term *protocol* is used a great deal in the network literature. It refers to the rules of procedure by which layers at the same level in the communications architecture, but in different machines, communicate with one another. The routing process at the network layer represents a portion of the protocol at that layer, for example.

As noted in Sec. 1-2, the purpose of the data-link layer is to ensure that a packet transmitted onto a link (Fig. 5-1) arrives at the other end of the link correctly and in correct sequence of transmission. Noise and interference on the link may result in erroneous reception. (This will be discussed in detail in Chap. 6 following.) Multiple links are sometimes used between neighboring nodes, with packets using particular links alternately. This may result in out-of-sequence reception. To carry out these data-link functions, additional control information must be added, as indicated in Fig. 5-6. The resultant protocol data unit can be termed a data-link PDU, or DL-PDU. It is commonly called, for simplicity, a *frame*. (This is not to be confused with TDM frames.) A frame thus consists of a packet (the information field in the frame) plus control information. (In actual practice the situation is more complicated. Certain data-link frames are used strictly for controlling correct functioning of a data link and carry no information field. See [SCHW 1987, Chap. 4]. We ignore this added complexity here.)

An example of a data-link frame format appears in Fig. 5-7. The number of the frame, to ensure sequenced delivery at the receiving node, would appear in the control field. Each successive frame has its number incremented by 1. The address field contains the address of one or both of the sending and receiving nodes, at either end of the link. (Recall that the information field carrying a datagram, a connectionless packet, contains the network source and destination addresses. These are typically different from the addresses mentioned here. Since *all* packets, regardless of source–destination address or VC number, are transmitted as frames, the numbering of the frames has nothing to do with packet

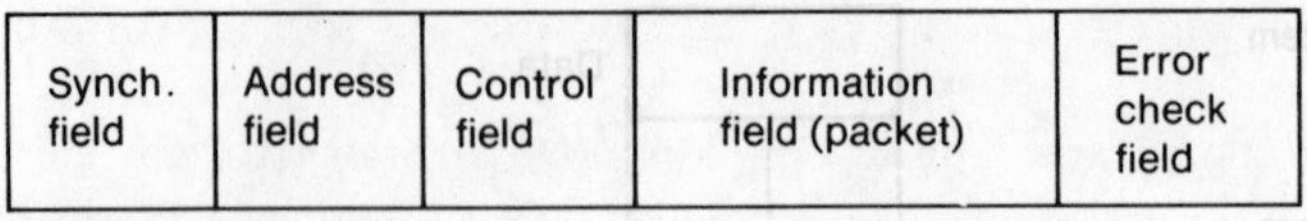

Synch. field	Address field	Control field	Information field (packet)	Error check field

FIGURE 5-7
Example of a frame.

identification. Successive frames may carry completely different VCs or source–destination addresses. This is precisely the resource-sharing concept of packet switching mentioned earlier.) The synchronization field, consisting of a specified bit pattern, is necessary to alert the receiving node to the arrival of a frame and to provide frame synchronization information. Frames are sent out asynchronously, when assembled and ready to be transmitted. Hence they must carry their own synchronization information. It is the frame that actually occupies the slots in a TDM link, for example. Although the link itself may be synchronous, the time at which a data-link frame, as assembled, is transmitted may be completely random. This implies that any given slot may or may not be occupied by a frame or portion thereof. The synchronization field carries the frame arrival information, as already noted. (A similar situation arises with character-based data transmission, as noted in Chap. 3.)

One specific example of a standard data-link protocol, with a well-defined frame structure and rules of procedure for handling frames, is the ISO-specified *high-level data-link control*, or HDLC for short. An example of an HDLC frame appears in Fig. 5-8. Synchronization here is carried out by first transmitting the 8-bit flag (F) pattern 01111110. (This is again not to be confused with the TDM frame marker of Fig. 5-2.) The end of the frame is signaled by again transmitting a flag pattern. Since the beginning and end of the frame are distinctly defined, the information field (the packet) can be uniquely identified and can be of any length. In another example to be provided in the section following, on local-area networks, the synchronization field appears at the beginning of the frame only, as in Fig. 5-7. A separate length field in that case then indicates the length of the information field following. In the HDLC case a flag (F) pattern appearing anywhere in the information field would erroneously signal the end of the frame.

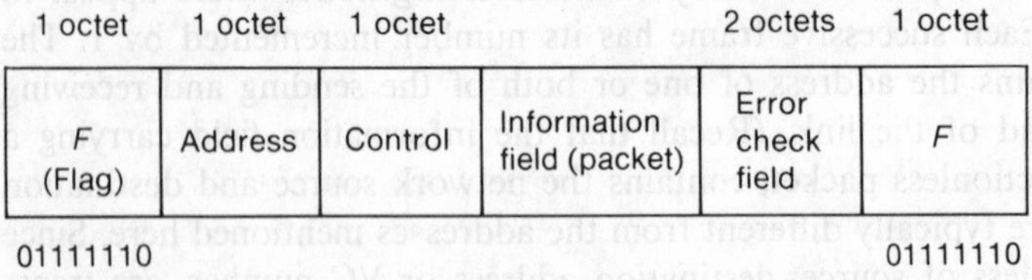

1 octet	1 octet	1 octet	2 octets	1 octet

F (Flag)	Address	Control	Information field (packet)	Error check field	F

01111110   01111110

FIGURE 5-8
HDLC frame.

To prevent this from happening, a 0 bit is inserted following any sequence of five 1s. This bit is then removed at the receiving node.

Note that both Figs. 5-7 and 5-8 show an additional error-check field. This is used to detect frame bit errors. This field is calculated as a particular modulo-2 sum of bits in the fields preceding it. The transmitting node at one end of the link carries out the calculation prescribed and puts the resultant bit pattern into the error-check field. The receiving node repeats the calculation and compares the pattern obtained with that received. If the two agree, the frame, and hence the packet contained in it, is declared to have been received correctly. If not, the frame is deemed to be in error and will, in most cases, be dropped. Details of this error-check procedure appear in Chap. 7.

The HDLC protocol provides for positive acknowledgements to be sent back to the transmitting node on receipt of a correct frame or sequence of correct frames. At the transmitter each frame's time of transmission is separately logged. If a specified timeout interval expires with no receipt of a positive acknowledgement, the frame in question and all frames following are repeated. This ensures a foolproof error-correction process. (Negative acknowledgements can also be returned to indicate detected errors.)

In local-area networks, as will be seen in the section following, errors are detected and erroneous frames dropped. An indication of error is sent up to higher layers. But errors are not corrected as in the HDLC case. It is up to higher layers in the architecture to correct or otherwise handle the error. These higher layers could be located in user systems connected to the LAN, or elsewhere in a much larger network of which the LAN is a part. With the advent of low-noise, high-bandwidth optical transmission links the LAN approach of detecting but not correcting errors is being applied to wider-area networks as well.

The chance of an error in a packet is reduced considerably with the use of fiber optics, and the much wider bandwidths available result in much faster transmission of packets. It thus becomes feasible to leave the correction of errors to the end systems, rather than have it done within the network itself as in the case of HDLC. This simplifies the data-link protocol and improves the performance of the overall network.

To summarize the discussion of packet switching thus far, consider the layered architecture superimposed on path 2 of Fig. 5-1. This path consists of nodes A, C, and D and the links connecting them. Say A is the source node, D the destination node, and C the intermediate network node. The layered architecture involving all three nodes appears in Fig. 5-9. (In many cases there is two-way communications. Nodes A and D may thus both be serving as source nodes, with the other node as destination node. We choose only one direction in Fig. 5-9 for simplicity.) Packets are formed in the network layer of node A. They are routed to the appropriate data link control at that node and are there encapsulated into frames. They are then transmitted bit by bit across the link to node C, using the physical layer transmitter at node A's side of link $A-C$. (This transmitter corresponds to one of those discussed in Chapter 4.) The receiver at node C's side of link $A-C$, located in node C's physical layer, demodulates the received

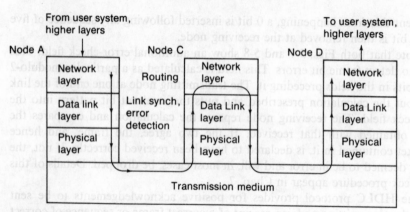

FIGURE 5-9
End-to-end communications, path 2, Fig. 5-1.

signal, passing the demodulated signal bit by bit to the data link layer. That layer synchronizes onto the received information, blocks it into the appropriate frame, and carries out an error check. If the frame has been received correctly, the frame-control information (synchronizing field, address field, error-check field, and other control fields) is stripped off and the packet itself is passed up to node C's network layer. (Otherwise the entire frame is dropped.) That layer, using a VC number or addresses in the packet header (Figs. 5-4 and 5-5), determines the appropriate outgoing link to destination D, and passes the packet to the data-link control of that link. This is also located in node C's data-link layer, as shown. The process carried out by node A is now repeated. Node D in turn repeats the receiving process carried out by node C. The only difference now is that at node D's network layer the received packet is routed to the appropriate user system connected to node D, rather than to another node in the network.

We have mentioned the "passing" of information, whether a frame, packet, or information within a packet, up or down to an adjacent layer. In the case of the OSI Reference Model discussed in Sec. 1-2 (Fig. 1-2), the international standards call for information to be passed between layers using well-defined atomic units called *primitives*. Some simple examples appear in Sec. 5-2 following, in the discussion of LANs. A detailed discussion appears in [SCHW 1987, Chaps. 3 and 7]. These primitives carry any necessary control information and data that constitute the information field of the protocol data unit in the adjacent layer. As an example, the data shown coming down from higher layers of the user system in Fig. 5-6 are carried as part of an appropriate primitive crossing the boundary between the layer above (usually the transport layer of Fig. 1-2) and the network layer. The information in the packet (the NPDU) is in turn passed as part of a primitive across the network-layer–data-link-layer boundary. The blocks of information passed will be queued if they cannot be processed immediately by the receiving layer.

This discussion thus far on packet switching has implicitly assumed that the information carried in the packets consists of terminal- or computer-generated data. This was pointed out at the beginning of this section with the comment that, historically, the older circuit-switched networks were designed for voice, while the newer (circa 1970s) packet-switched networks were designed for data traffic. There is currently a trend underway to combine various types of traffic on one network. Various techniques have been proposed or developed for this purpose. One example is *fast packet switching*, which is designed to operate over high-speed, high-bandwidth, optical links. In this technique data, voice, video, and other types of traffic are all transmitted in packet form. Specially designed fast packet switches carry out the network routing function in hardware to speed up the process, while the data-link function is reduced to a bare minimum, as already noted.

Random queueing delays may still occur in such networks. Real-time voice (and video to some extent) destined for human reception cannot be delayed more than several hundred milliseconds end to end. (Human beings conducting a two-way conversation find such delays intolerable.) Provision must thus be made in such networks for ensuring rapid delivery of real-time traffic. One technique is to provide priority to these packets.

Other techniques used to combine different traffic types in one network multiplex real-time circuit-switched voice and packet data onto the same physical transmission facilities. One example, using a TDM frame structure, allocates a fixed number of slots (channels or trunks) per TDM frame to voice, with the remainder allocated to packet data. Voice calls handled on a circuit-switched basis must be assigned dedicated slots in each frame. [Digital speech interpolation (DSI), mentioned in Sec. 4-13, may, however, be used to increase the call-handling capacity.] The data packets, on the other hand, queue for slots in each frame. If circuit-switched slots are not used, they may be occupied (temporarily) by data packets. This improves the delay performance of the data, since packets do not have to queue up as long. This technique has been called a *movable-boundary* multiplexing scheme. [SCHW 1987, Chap. 12].

These procedures are part of a strong movement underway, worldwide, toward the concept of *integrated-services digital networks* (ISDNs), in which telecommunications traffic of all types—data, voice, and video, among others—is carried transparently between users over a single user-network connection. Unified network resources of the types just noted and unified network control are used to ensure delivery of the information to the appropriate destinations, transparently to the users. The standardization, development, and deployment of ISDNs is under intensive development worldwide.

5-2 LOCAL-AREA NETWORKS

This discussion in Sec. 5-1 just concluded dealt with some networking ideas in a general sense. In this section we specialize to one specific type of network, called a *local-area network* (LAN). This provides us with specific examples of some of the concepts discussed in Sec. 5-1. LANs, as we shall see, deal only with the lowest two layers of the layered communication architecture of Figs. 1-2 and 5-6, providing the simplest example of the use of that architectural model beyond the physical layer alone, discussed in earlier chapters of this book. LANs are, in addition, of considerable technological interest because of their widespread use.

LANs, by definition, are networks covering a small area, at most several kilometers in extent. They are used principally to interconnect terminals, work-stations, and various other intelligent systems within a building or a campus that commonly belong to one organization.

Although a network of the form of Fig. 5-1 covering a small enough area could be construed to be a LAN, the designation is generally limited to the bus and ring topologies of Fig. 5-10. (Fig. 5-1, in contrast, is an example of a *mesh*-type network. Some all-optical LANs are designed in the form of a passive star.) A coaxial cable is commonly used as a bus, with stations accessing the bus through passive taps. An optical fiber with active taps (to overcome tap losses) could be used as well. Ethernet, as an example, uses a coaxial cable as its transmission medium. The physical medium in the case of the ring could be twisted-wire pair, coaxial cable, or optical fiber. In the ring topology, stations serve as *repeaters*, receiving and retransmitting all incoming information.

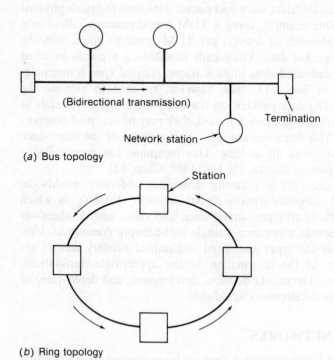

(Bidirectional transmission)

Termination

Network station

(*a*) Bus topology

Station

(*b*) Ring topology

FIGURE 5-10
Local-area networks.

The medium in both the bus and the ring is common to all stations. In the case of the bus, energy is launched through a tap in both directions simultaneously. Terminations at each end of the bus absorb energy reaching them (Fig. 5-10a). In the case of the ring one-way transmission is used to access all stations as shown in Fig. 5-10b. The shared medium allows all stations connected to it to communicate with one another. Network routing, necessary with the mesh networks of Figs. 5-1 and 5-3, is not needed here. LANs thus do not require the network layer (Figs. 5-6 and 5-9) of the communications architecture model. They incorporate the physical layer and portions of the data-link layer only, as will be seen shortly. This simplifies the multiple-user communication problem considerably and is one of the reasons for the rapid acceptance and deployment of LANs. (Another reason of course is the simple topology of either bus or ring, making it relatively easy to string wire pairs, coaxial cable, or optical fiber for either topology throughout a building or group of buildings.) The block of information transmitted across the medium is called a frame, just as in Sec. 5-1.

The common (shared) medium poses a critical problem, however. How do users access this distributed medium without interfering with one another? There are two possibilities, and both are used. One can simply transmit randomly, at will, and hope that no one else is transmitting at the same time; or a distributed control may be used, with access permission passed sequentially from user to user.

The random access scheme, with significant modifications introduced to improve the network performance, is the basis for Ethernet (introduced first by Xerox Corp.) and related LAN schemes. Distributed control is used in the token bus and token ring schemes, as well as in the more recent high-bandwidth 100-Mbit/s, optical-fiber-based FDDI system. (FDDI stands for fiber distributed data interface.) All of these schemes will be discussed in some detail in the paragraphs following.

Random Access CSMA / CD

Consider the random access mode of operation first, as applied to the bus of Fig. 5-10a. As stated above, this will work if one station only is accessing the bus. If two or more stations attempt to access the bus at the same time, a *collision* is said to occur and, clearly, no signal gets through. Provision must thus be made to recognize and resolve the collision. The simplest possible random access strategy has a station transmit at will. Collision detection is then accomplished by monitoring the medium (or channel, as it is sometimes called) and noting when the signal on the medium differs from that transmitted. On detecting a collision, the station reschedules the transmission of the frame to some later, randomly chosen time. (If the time for retransmission is not randomized, it is clear that all stations experiencing a collision will do so again.)

This simple random access strategy, called the *Aloha access* scheme (after its original use in the Aloha radio system in Hawaii in the early 1970s), works in the LAN environment but only if the traffic on the network is light enough and if the network is not too large in extent.[1] If traffic increases to the point where collisions occur more frequently, the network can actually become unstable, new transmissions causing collisions, which in turn generate more collisions at the retry time. It is in fact quite easy to show, under some simple assumptions, that the maximum bit transmission rate of the Aloha scheme is $1/2e$, or about 18%, of the bus capacity [ABRA],[2] [SCHW 1977], [SCHW 1987]. Thus if the rated bit rate on the LAN is 10 Mbits/s, the Aloha scheme allows at most an average transmission rate of 1.8 Mbits/s. The ratio of actual bit rate over the medium to the capacity is called the *utilization*.

This maximum utilization percentage (18 percent) can be improved considerably by incorporating a number of extra features. The first is to *sense* the medium for any ongoing transmission and attempt transmission only when the medium is perceived to be idle. This procedure is called *carrier sense* (CS). Second, when a collision is detected, colliding stations can abort transmission. (To ensure that all such stations notice the collision and stop transmitting, any station detecting a collision immediately transmits a so-called jam signal to force cessation of transmission.) Third, it has been found, through simulation and actual network measurements, that the random retry interval before retransmitting a given frame having undergone a collision should be doubled with each collision. The more collisions a station incurs, the longer it has to wait (until some maximum retry interval). An individual station is penalized with this technique, but the ensemble of all stations finds the potential utilization increased.

This modified random access procedure is termed a CSMA/CD access procedure. (The acronym stands for *carrier sense multiple access with collision detection*.) This is the procedure that was adopted for Ethernet, and is the one that is used in the current LAN random access bus protocol. (Details appear in a later subsection describing LAN standards).

How well does this modified procedure perform? A significant improvement over the 18-percent maximum utilization figure of Aloha is found if the bus is "short enough." It is clear that the carrier sense and transmission abort procedures will only work if stations on the bus are close enough together to quickly detect one another's transmissions. This implies that the signal propagation time from one end of the bus to the other must be short compared to the transmission

---

[1] The Aloha system was developed as a means of allowing data terminals located on various islands in Hawaii to communicate with a central computer. It was not a LAN. The central receiving system detected collisions and radioed information about them back to the sources involved. In the LAN application under discussion here there is no central monitoring system. Each LAN station must detect its own collisions. This limits the size of the network. The collision control used provides an example of *distributed* control.

[2] [ABRA] N. Abramson, "The Aloha System," in *Computer Networks*, N. Abramson and F. Kuo (eds.), Prentice-Hall, Englewood Cliffs, N.J., 1973.

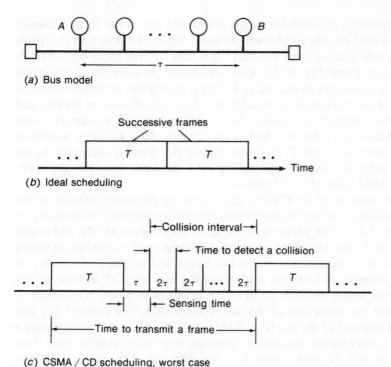

(a) Bus model

(b) Ideal scheduling

(c) CSMA / CD scheduling, worst case

FIGURE 5-11
Determination of CSMA/CD throughput.

time of a frame. As the transmission bit rate increases, the frame transmission time decreases, requiring the use of a shorter bus. This represents a critical limitation to the use of CSMA/CD buses as LANs. We now quantify these comments, showing the bus utilization can approach 100 percent if the ratio of bus propagation delay to frame transmission time is very short. Reference will be made to Fig. 5-11 in carrying out the analysis. Fig. 5-11a, showing the bus model to be analyzed, is similar to that of Fig. 5-10a.

Let the transmission time of a frame be T seconds. (Although frames in real systems vary in length, the argument is simplified considerably by taking the case of fixed-length frames.) This is just the length L of the frame, in bits, divided by the transmission bit rate C (the capacity) of the medium. For example, if the frame is 1000 bits long and C is 1 Mbit/s, then $T = 1$ ms. If the transmission rate is increased to 10 Mbits/s, then $T = 100$ μs.

Now assume that a frame is always available, somewhere on the bus, for transmission. Full utilization of the channel can clearly be obtained if the frames can be scheduled in an organized, noncolliding, manner, with frames transmitted one after another, in sequential order. This shown in Fig. 5-11b. This is precisely what is done in TDM (Chap. 3) with all data inputs available at one point.

It is impossible to schedule stations distributed over a bus in this manner, however. (It would require a "Maxwell demon," sensing random packet arrivals at stations in zero time, to carry this out).[3] It is thus referred to, in Fig. 5-11b, as *ideal scheduling*. From Fig. 5-11b ideal scheduling provides for a maximum throughput, in frames per second, of $1/T$. This is equivalent, as already noted, to transmitting at the bus (channel) capacity of C bits/s. Collisions on the bus, and retransmissions required to resolve these, will reduce the maximum frame throughput below this value. As the bus propagation delay increases relative to the frame transmission time T, the frame throughput possibly decreases. As the propagation delay is reduced, approaching zero, the maximum throughput approaches the ideal value of $1/T$ frames/s.

The performance of the CSMA/CD scheduling procedure, relative to that of ideal scheduling, can be calculated using the worst-case (smallest-throughput) model of Fig. 5-11c. The parameter τ in that figure represents the end-to-end propagation delay, the delay between stations furthest apart on the bus, as shown in Fig. 5-11a. Its value depends on the bus length and propagation velocity on the bus. For example, if the length is 1 km and the velocity is 200,000 km/s, then $\tau = 5$ μs. If the length increases to 10 km, τ increases to 50 μs. Why does Fig. 5-11c represent the worst case of the use of the CSMA/CD scheme? Say that station A, at one end of the bus (Fig. 5-11a), is in the process of transmitting a frame. The carrier sense mechanism prevents any other station from then transmitting as well. Say that station B, at the other end of the bus, is waiting to transmit. It defers transmission until A finishes. But it takes τ seconds for B to sense that A has finished. An unavoidable worst-case τ-second gap thus appears in signal occupancy on the bus, as shown in Fig. 5-11c. This reduces the throughput over the bus. The effect is negligible if $\tau/T \ll 1$, just the point made earlier.

In addition to throughput reduction because of sensing time, the collision-resolution time also reduces the throughput possible over the CSMA/CD bus. This is shown in Fig. 5-11c as well. Say station B starts to transmit once it senses A has completed transmission. Just before station B's transmission reaches station A, that station starts its own transmission, sensing the medium to be idle. As B's transmission reaches it, it detects a collision and sends a jam signal. This signal takes τ seconds to reach B, at which point B aborts its transmission. The total time, in the worst case, to detect a collision is thus 2τ second, as shown in Fig. 5-11c. After a number of such 2τ collision-detection intervals, shown in Fig. 5-11c, station B finally gets to transmit its frame. (The picture of Fig. 5-11c ignores specific-collision-retry strategies, in particular the one involving the successive doubling of retry intervals. Simulation shows that the model of

---

[3]The satellite channel discussed in Sec. 4-13 is another example of a shared medium. Reference stations, transmitting control signals, and reference bursts to denote the beginning of a TDMA frame provide centralized scheduling information to control access to the medium in that case. This contrasts with the decentralized access under discussion here.

Fig. 5-11c captures the CSMA/CD throughput result quite accurately [LAM].[4])
Fig. 5-11c now enables us to determine the throughput performance of the
CSMA/CD scheme. Clearly, if $\tau \ll T$, the scheme can approach the ideal
scheduling case of Fig. 5-11b. If $\tau \geq T$, it reduces to the simple Aloha scheme.

The maximum throughput possible is less than the capacity $1/T$ because of
the sensing and collision intervals. The collision interval is random because of the
random number of retransmissions required to finally resolve a collision. The
transmission time of a frame is then increased, in the worst case, from T to some
(random) larger value, which adds the sensing time τ and collision interval, as
shown in Fig. 5-11c. The *average* transmission time, using the symbol J to
represent the average number of 2τ-second transmission intervals, is then given
by

$$T' = T + \tau + 2\tau J \tag{5-1}$$

The worst-case maximum throughput, in the maximum number of frames per
second that can be transmitted over the bus on the average, is just $1/T'$. Dividing
this by $1/T$, the capacity of the bus, gives the desired maximum utilization ρ_m of
the CSMA/CD scheme:

$$\rho_m = \frac{1}{T'} \bigg/ \frac{1}{T} = \frac{1}{1 + a(1 + 2J)} \tag{5-2}$$

with

$$a \equiv \tau/T$$

This maximum utilization is thus always less than one because of carrier sensing
and collision resolution. The parameter controlling the maximum throughput
performance is a, the ratio of end-to-end propagation delay to frame transmission time. Increasing the bus length and/or the transmission rate C reduces the
maximum utilization, just as noted earlier. The parameter a must thus be kept
small for proper operation.

The specific values of bus length and transmission bit rate that can be
accommodated depend on the values of the parameter J, the average number of
retransmissions required to resolve a collision. We estimate this parameter with a
simple probabilistic model. In particular, say the probability of successful retransmission at the end of a 2τ-second collision detection interval is v. A
collision occurs with probability $1 - v$. The probability that the collision interval
(Fig. 5-11c) is one 2τ-second interval is then v. The probability it is two such
intervals long is $v(1 - v)$. The probability that it is j intervals long is $v(1 - v)^{j-1}$.
The average number of J of such intervals is then

$$J = \sum_{j=1}^{\infty} jv(1 - v)^{j-1} = \frac{1}{v} \tag{5-3}$$

by a simple calculation.

---

[4][LAM] S. S. Lam, "A Carrier Sense Multiple Access Protocol for Local Networks," *Comput.
Networks*, vol. 4, no. 1, pp. 21–32, January 1980.

The success probability v can itself be found in the following manner. Say n stations are active on the bus ($n \gg 1$). Let p be the probability any station wants to transmit in a 2τ-second interval. A successful transmission means only one of the n stations wants to transmit while the $n - 1$ others do not. The probability v of successful transmission is then given by the binomial probability

$$v = np(1 - p)^{n-1} \tag{5-4}$$

The form of (5-4) indicates that there is an optimum choice of p that maximizes v. Differentiating (5-4), one finds the optimum value of p to be given by

$$p_{opt} = 1/n \tag{5-5}$$

Inserting this in (5-4), one finds the maximum value of v to be given by

$$v_{max} = \left(1 - \frac{1}{n}\right)^{n-1} \rightarrow e^{-1} \qquad n \rightarrow \infty \tag{5-6}$$

From (5-3) the average number of retransmissions using this model is then $J = e$, and the final expression for the maximum bus utilization is given by

$$\rho_m \doteq \frac{1}{1 + a(1 + 2e)} = \frac{1}{1 + 6.44a} \qquad a \equiv \tau/T \tag{5-7}$$

Consider some examples. Say first that $C = 10$ Mbits/s is the bus transmission rate. Frames are 1,000 bits long, so that $T = 100$ μs. The bus length is 2 km, and the propagation velocity is 200,000 km/s. (The propagation delay is 5 μs/km.) The end-to-end delay is then $\tau = 10$ μs. The parameter a in this case is $a = \tau/T = 0.1$. From (5-7), $\rho_m \doteq 0.6$. The bus can thus be utilized to a maximum of 60 percent using the CSMA/CD access strategy. This means that at most 6 Mbits/s of data can be transmitted over it. Equivalently, at most 6,000 frames/s can be transmitted, on the average. If the transmission rate C is reduced to 1 Mbit/s, T increases to 1 ms and a reduces to 0.01. The maximum utilization increases to 0.94.

These examples point out an interesting conclusion: Although the maximum utilization for the case of $a = 0.1$ ($C = 10$ Mbits/s) is only 0.6, the throughput possible is still 6,000 thousand-bit frames per second, on the average. If 100 stations use the bus, each station can still transmit a maximum of 60 frames/s, on the average. Clearly in many situations this is much more than required. This limit on utilization poses no problem. The CSMA/CD strategy is, in fact, designed for LANs in which most stations are idle most of the time, a typical situation in many office or campus environments. As noted earlier the CSMA/CD bus system is relatively simple to install and easy to use. For a low-usage environment it provides a simple, cost-effective choice and has been adopted widely for this reason.

In those applications where higher throughput is required, or the random time required to successfully transmit a frame poses a problem, a more controlled approach must be used. Token passing serves this purpose. As an example, automated factories commonly use token-passing LANs. They require a controlled communication medium, one in which the time required to pass units of information from one machine to another is more tightly constrained then in the CSMA/CD case. We thus discuss token-passing LANs in the next subsection.

Distributed Control: Token Passing

It was noted earlier in this section that both random-access and distributed-control techniques are used to access the common (shared) medium of LANs. In the previous subsection the CSMA/CD random-access strategy was discussed at length. In this subsection we describe the token-passing distributed-control technique. In the next we provide operational details on some of the LAN standards that have been adopted. In Sec. 5-3 following we provide a performance comparison of these techniques.

As implicit in the use of the name, token passing means that permission to transmit is passed sequentially from one station to another by means of a "token," a specified bit or flag set in an information frame, or a special control frame defined as a token. There are various ways of doing this. In one technique a station, currently engaged in transmitting over the medium, passes control to the next station on conclusion of its transmission by setting a token bit in its transmitted frame. A station recognizing the token bit is then free to transmit its own information if it so desires. This means that multiple tokens may exist simultaneously on the medium. This procedure is the basis of the FDDI scheme to be described briefly later. In another procedure the currently transmitting station passes control to the next station (i.e., issues a token) only on the return of its own frame. In this case there is only one token available at any one time, simplifying management of the LAN.

Both bus and ring topologies (Fig. 5-10) are used to support the token-passing access strategy. In the case of the bus, stations have to be numbered in succession to determine which station can next receive the token. In the case of the ring the "next" station is implicit in the direction of transmission. We assume a ring topology here to simplify the discussion.

In the simplest mode of operation each station on the ring receives each frame and then passes it on (retransmits it) to its neighbor. If that station recognizes its address as the destination address, it copies the frame in addition to retransmitting it. The original sending station takes its own frame off the ring as it returns to that station after one cycle around the ring. In the single-token procedure the sending station then passes control to the next station by issuing a token after receipt of its own frame.

Figure 5-12 shows the ring topology of Fig. 5-10 redrawn to emphasize the fact that each station receives, and then transmits (regenerates), a frame. In the case of the CSMA/CD access procedure a station with a frame to transmit does so as soon as it senses the bus free. In the case of token passing a station must wait until it receives permission to do so. This access time takes, on the average, one-half a cycle time from the time a station is ready to transmit. (Why is this

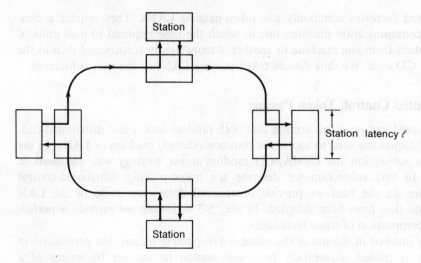

FIGURE 5-12
Token-passing ring.

so?) For simplicity, we discuss average cycle time only here. The cycle time is a randomly varying quantity, since each station in the ring, on gaining control, will require a random length of time to transmit its waiting frames. We shall see, in Sec. 5-3 following, that the cycle time represents a significant part of the time delay for a packet to get through the system.

The cycle time is made up of two components. One is the time required to physically pass the token (permission to transmit) around the ring. This time is referred to as the ring *latency L*, in units of time. The ring latency is itself the sum of the propagation delay τ required to cycle once around the ring and the latency or delay required to retransmit a frame at each station on the ring. We use the symbol l to represent the delay through a station (Fig. 5-12). This delay can range from a minimum of one bit time to many bits. For N stations on the ring the ring latency L is then

$$L = \tau + Nl \qquad (5\text{-}8)$$

The symbol τ is used here because the propagation delay is the equivalent of the end-to-end delay τ on the bus (Fig. 5-11a). Clearly, the smaller the latency is, the smaller the cycle time, the faster the access time, and the better the performance.

As an example, say $N = 50$ stations are deployed over a ring (or a bus) 2 km in length. Say the ring operates at a transmission rate of 1 Mbit/s. First take the latency per station to be one bit. This translates into $l = 1$ μs/station. Letting the propagation delay on the ring again be 5 μs/km, we have $\tau = 10$ μs. The total latency L is then 60 μs. If 100 stations access the ring, L increases to 110 μs. If it requires 8 bits/station to regenerate the incoming frame, l increases to 8 μs/station. For 50 stations on the ring we then have $L = 410$ μs. As the ring

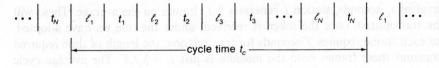

FIGURE 5-13
Cycle time in token-passing system (propagation delay included in latency).

transmission rate or capacity C increases, the latency per station l decreases, as does the ring latency L.

We indicated above the average cycle time, or time required for each station to access the ring once, is made up of two components. One is the latency L, just discussed. The other is the average time required for each station to transmit its waiting frames once it receives permission to do so. Call this time t_j for the jth station, $j = 1, 2, \ldots, N$. The cycle time t_c can then be represented as shown in Fig. 5-13. (The propagation delay τ has been included in the latency for simplicity.) The calculation of the t_j's depends on the access discipline adopted. One could, for example, allow each station to transmit only one frame per access. As another procedure, one could transmit more frames, but limit access to those frames that were waiting for transmission before permission to do so was granted. We choose the simplest discipline here: we allow each station to empty its buffer, i.e., to transmit all waiting frames, when given permission to do so. This simplifies the calculation considerably.

Let the average traffic load at station i, generated by users connected to it for transmission over the ring for bus, be λ_i frames/s (Fig. 5-14). This is also often called the frame (or packet) arrival rate. From one access to the next, an

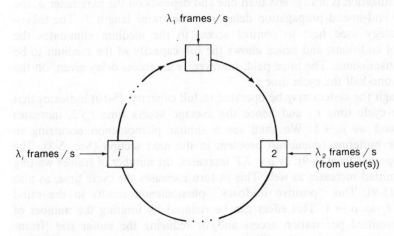

FIGURE 5-14
Average traffic through the ring.

interval of t_c seconds, station i generates $\lambda_i t_c$ frames on the average. These will all be transmitted, once the token is received, under the rule we have adopted. Since each frame requires T seconds for transmission, the length of time required to transmit these frames onto the medium is just $t_i = \lambda_i t_c T$. The average cycle time is then

$$t_c = L + \sum_{i=1}^{N} t_i$$

$$= L + t_c \lambda T \qquad (5\text{-}9)$$

using the parameter $\lambda = \sum_{i=1}^{N} \lambda_i$ to represent the total land, in frames/s, requiring transmission over the ring (Fig. 5-14). λ is also often called the average system arrival rate, in frames (packets) per second. Simplifying (5-9) we get, as the desired expression for the cycle time t_c,

$$t_c = \frac{L}{1 - \lambda T}$$

$$= \frac{L}{1 - \rho} \qquad (5\text{-}10)$$

with

$$\rho \equiv \lambda T \qquad (5\text{-}11)$$

representing the *utilization* of the ring.

Some comments are in order here. Recall first, from Fig. 5-11b, that the transmission *capacity* of the medium is $1/T$ frames/s. λ represents the *load* on the system. $\lambda/(1/T) = \lambda T \equiv \rho$ is thus the fractional utilization of the ring capacity, as stated above. Note from (5-10) that this has a maximum value of 1 (100-percent utilization), unlike the CSMA/CD case [Eq. (5-7)] in which the maximum utilization is always less than one and depends on the parameter a, the ratio of the end-to-end propagation delay τ to the frame length T. The token-passing strategy used here to control access to the medium eliminates the possibility of collisions, and hence allows the full capacity of the medium to be used for transmissions. The price paid, however, is an access delay given, on the average, by one-half the cycle time t_c.

Although the system may be operated to full capacity, (5-10) indicates that the average cycle time t_c, and hence the average access time $t_c/2$, increases beyond bound as $\rho \to 1$. We shall see a similar phenomenon occurring in studying the buffering (queueing) problem in the next section (Sec. 5-3). The reason is apparent from (5-9): as $\rho = \lambda T$ increases, the number of frames waiting to be transmitted increases as well. This in turn increases the cycle time, as also shown by (5-9). This "positive feedback" phenomenon results in the rapid increase in t_c as $\rho \to 1$. This effect can be reduced by limiting the number of frames transmitted per station access and/or reducing the buffer size (frame storage capacity) at each node. (We have implicitly assumed no limit on the number of frames that may be queued or buffered.)

Equation (5-10) indicates, as expected, that even with very low load (small λ, or $\rho \ll 1$), there is a minimum cycle time (and hence access delay) given by the latency L. This is the penalty incurred by using a distributed-control scheme such as token passing. It does not occur with a random access scheme. There, with very low traffic, the chance of a collision is small, and access is immediate. This was the point made earlier—for low traffic, random access schemes such as CSMA/CD provide somewhat better access (delay) performance than token-passing schemes. For higher traffic loads, however, the random access schemes saturate more quickly. The simple Aloha strategy allows at most 18 percent of the transmission capacity to be utilized. (In practice this is no more than 10 percent, to prevent instability.) The CSMA/CD scheme increases this value, as shown by (5-7), but the maximum utilization is typically less than that of a token-passing scheme and depends on the parameter a, the ratio of propagation delay to frame length. Wide variations in delays are expected as well with CSMA/CD in the higher utilization region because of the increased chance of collisions. We shall have more to say on these issues in Sec. 5-3, in discussing the time-delay performance of LANs in more detail.

Consider some examples of the application of (5-10) in the study of token-passing systems. Take the case of $C = 1$ Mbits/s first, as was done earlier. Let the frames be 1000 bits long again. Then $T = 1$ ms, and $1/T = 1,000$ frames/s is the maximum capacity (throughput) of this system. This also represents the maximum load in the case of a token-passing scheme. Say we limit the utilization to $\rho = 0.8$, to prevent the cycle time from getting too large. Then the maximum load with this limitation is $\lambda = 800$ frames/s. For 50 stations this represents an average load per station of $\lambda_i = 16$ frames/s. For 100 stations it becomes 8 frames/s. At this load the average cycle time is, from (5-10), $5L$. As shown previously in calculating the latency for various examples, $L = 60$ μs for a 2-km ring with a propagation delay of 5 μs/km, 50 stations, and a station latency of 1 bit. This results in a cycle time of $t_c = 300$ μs, or an average access delay of 150 μs for this case. For 100 stations we get $t_c = 550$ μs. If the latency increases to 8 bits/station, then $t_c = 2.05$ ms for 50 stations, or 4.05 ms for 100 stations.

Now say the transmission capacity of the medium is increased to $C = 5$ Mbits/s. For 1,000-bit frames, $T = 200$ μs, and a maximum number of $1/T = 5,000$ frames/s can now be transmitted, on the average. Letting $\rho = 0.8$ again, this allows $\lambda = 4,000$ frames/s to access the medium, on the average, from all stations. The latency, cycle time, and access delay are now all reduced as well. For a latency of 1 bit/station, $l = 0.2$ μs. For 50 stations and a 2-km ring, $L = 20$ μs and $t_c = 5L = 100$ μs. For 100 stations we get $L = 30$ μs and $t_c = 5L = 150$ μs. If the utilization is $\rho = 0.5$, we get $t_c = 2L$ and the cycle times are reduced accordingly. Additional examples are provided in the problems at the end of this chapter.

In this subsection we have stressed the evaluation of cycle time and access delay, since these parameters are fundamental to the operation of token-passing schemes and are easily obtained for the simplified model chosen here. In Sec. 5-3 following we point out that user packets accessing a LAN incur a queueing delay as well. This requires the knowledge of some queueing theory, which we provide in Sec. 5-3. Queueing and access delay (discussed here) both contribute to the time-delay performance of a LAN, to be discussed briefly in Sec. 5-3.

Local-Area-Network Standards

In the previous subsections we have introduced the two major LAN access strategies, with some discussion of their relative performance. More detailed performance characteristics will be provided in Sec. 5-3 following. In this subsection we survey specific LAN implementations, focusing on the CSMA/CD bus, the token-passing ring, and the FDDI 100-Mbit/s, optically based ring.

LAN standards in conformance with the OSI model were first established by a special standards committee of the Institute of Electrical and Electronics Engineers (IEEE) called the IEEE 802 Committee. They have since been adopted worldwide as well. Three standards have been defined: IEEE standard 802.3 for a CSMA/CD bus, 802.4 for a token bus, and 802.5 for a token ring. The 802.3 standard is very similar to the Ethernet specification jointly developed by Xerox, Digital Equipment Corp., and Intel. The 802.5 standard is based on work carried out by IBM in its Zurich Research Laboratory and in laboratories at Research Triangle Park, N.C. The FDDI specification has been developed by a committee of the American National Standards Institute (ANSI), as an extension of the 802.5 token-ring standard, designed specifically for much higher-bit-rate (100 Mbits/s), optical-fiber LANs.

The IEEE standards, developed in conformance with the OSI Reference Model, follow the architectural pattern of Fig. 5-15. The three standards cover the physical layer of the OSI model and a portion of the data-link layer, called the medium-access control sublayer, or MAC sublayer, for short. The physical layer and the MAC sublayer characteristics depend on the physical medium and the access method, and hence differ for each of the three standards. They come

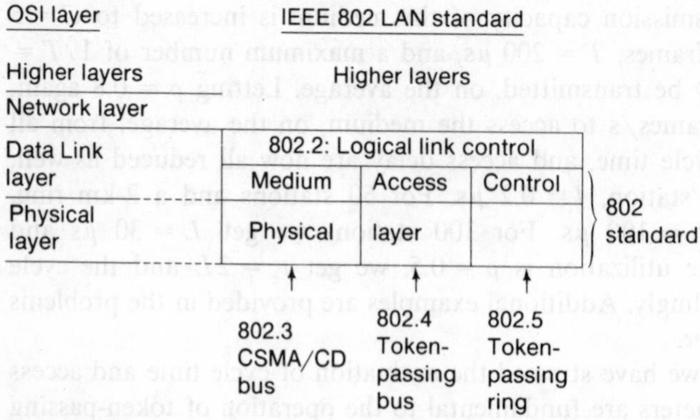

FIGURE 5-15
IEEE 802 LAN standards.

together, however, at the logical-link control level, which is the same for all three and allows all three to interact with higher OSI layers, as shown.

The physical layer's prime function, as noted a number of times in this book, is to ensure that individual bits are properly transmitted onto, and received from, the medium. It does this by generating the appropriate electrical signals on the medium. This is precisely the function we have described in detail, in Chaps. 3 and 4, in discussing point-to-point communications. All three IEEE standards use baseband communications; hence high-frequency transmitters and receivers are not required. Other, broadband LAN systems do incorporate high-frequency modulators and demodulators. The FDDI system, to be described briefly later, is designed for use with optical fibers and hence incorporates optical transmitters and receivers. Other functions are carried out by the physical layer as well. In the CSMA/CD case, for example, it is the physical layer that generates the carrier-sense and collision-detect signals that are used by the MAC sublayer above to determine when it is appropriate to transmit, or when retransmission due to a collision is necessary. We shall have more to say about this layer later in describing the actual bit-level signals transmitted onto the medium.

At this point we focus on the MAC sublayer, our first specific example of a layer above the physical layer emphasized thus far in this book. Recall from our discussion in Sec. 5-1 that the OSI data-link layer assembles a block of bits called a frame, which it then passes on to the physical layer for transmission bit by bit. (Fig. 5-6). The frame as assembled contains data (a packet) received from the layer above, plus control information necessary to get it across the link. The MAC sublayer carries out this function, among others, in the LAN standards. The "link" is in this case the LAN. (It is in fact the use of a LAN rather than a simple physical link for point-to-point communications that necessitates splitting the data link into the two sublayers of the LAN standards.) Consider the MAC sublayer of the 802.3 CSMA/CD bus as an example. The frame format for this case is shown in Fig. 5-16 [IEEE 1985a].[5] It consists of eight fields, as shown. The first field, the preamble, a sequence of seven octets, each of the form 10101010, allows the receiving physical-layer circuitry to carry out bit synchronization. (Recall that packets, and hence frames in which they are encapsulated, are transmitted asynchronously, when ready, in packet-switched networks. The receiving system must detect the arrival of a frame and lock onto it.)

The start-frame delimiter field, consisting of the bit sequence 10101011, provides frame synchronization: A receiving system (actually each station on the bus) then knows the next field following is the destination address. A receiving system recognizing its own address continues to accept the rest of the frame. Other systems on the bus ignore it. The field following is the source address, the MAC address of the sending station. The 802.3 standard allows either two- or six-octet address fields, as shown in Fig. 5-16. The 10-Mbit/s implementation is

---

[5][IEEE 1985a] *CSMA/CD Access Method*, *Standard 802.3-1985*, IEEE, New York, 1985.

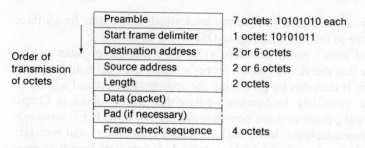

Preamble	7 octets: 10101010 each
Start frame delimiter	1 octet: 10101011
Destination address	2 or 6 octets
Source address	2 or 6 octets
Length	2 octets
Data (packet)	
Pad (if necessary)	
Frame check sequence	4 octets

Order of transmission of octets

FIGURE 5-16
802.3 CSMA/CD frame format.

required to have six-octet (48-bit) addresses, however [IEEE 1985a]. Individual or multiple stations may be addressed. The address in the latter case is referred to as a *multicast* address. (A *broadcast* address is a special case in which *all* stations on the LAN are addressed.)

Data packets may be of variable length. The length of the data-packet field, in octets, is specified by the two-octet-length field following the address fields. The data field contains the information (the packet) passed down by the logical-link-control sublayer and higher layers above. The pad field following is also of variable length and is used to pad out the data field if its length is too short to ensure a required minimum frame length. As an example, the minimum frame length for the 10-Mbit/s 802.3 standard is 64 octets (512 bits) from the beginning of the destination-address field to the end of the frame-check field in Fig. 5-16. Since the control fields account for 18 octets in this case, the data plus pad fields must be at least 46 octets (368 bits) in length. If the data field is shorter than this number, as indicated by the length field, the pad field is used to pad up to this length. Since the length field is only two octets long, there is clearly a maximum frame size as well. This is specified as 1,518 octets in the 10-Mbit/s standard.

The four-octet frame-check sequence concluding the frame is used to detect bit errors at the receiving station. As noted in Sec. 5-1, this field is generated by carrying out a prescribed modulo-2 sum of the contents of all the fields of the frame preceding, beginning with the destination-address field. The technique is called a cyclic redundancy check and uses a polynomial encoding algorithm. An example of such an algorithm appears in Chap. 7 in discussing error detection procedures. The MAC sublayers at both the sending and receiving systems carry out the same calculation. The MAC sublayer of the receiving system, producing a different value for the frame-check sequence field than the one received, knows an error or series of errors have occurred, and drops the data packet (the data field in the frame). It does not pass the data on to the logical-link-control (LLC) sublayer and layers above. It may, however, signal that an error has occurred. It makes no attempt to recover from the error. Error recovery is up to the LLC sublayer or layers above.

The 802.2 LLC standard (Fig. 5-15) specifies two possible modes of operation. In one mode, called a *connection service*, error recovery is carried out. This is done by having the sending LLC sublayer retransmit the packet in question after timing out with no receipt of a positive acknowledgement from the receiving LLC sublayer. This type of service requires that the data units at the LLC sublayer, before being formed into frames at the MAC sublayer, carry sequence numbers to enable them to be identified for retransmission. It also requires that a logical connection be set up before data transmission can begin. With this mode of operation the LLC sublayer presents the appearance of a full data-link control (an example is HDLC, mentioned in Sec. 5-1) to the network layer above.

In many applications error recovery is carried out at higher layers, most often at the transport layer (Fig. 1-2), between the end-user systems in communication with one another. If errors are infrequent (this is the case with optical-fiber connections) and communication between the user systems is fast (short distances and/or high-speed transmission make this possible), this simpler mode of recovery can be used. This is called *connectionless service*.

These procedures, defining operations carried out between the LLC sublayers in stations connected through a LAN, are examples of *protocols* specifying precise means of communication between two peer entities at the same layer in a layered communications architecture. This point has already been made in Sec. 5-1. Protocol data units (PDUs) carry the results of the protocol actions between peer entities. Two MAC sublayers, one in each of two stations connected through a LAN, also communicate through a well-defined protocol. The protocol data unit in this case is the MAC frame. The procedures for assembling and handling an 802.3 CSMA/CD frame, just discussed, represent part of the 802.3 MAC sublayer protocol. These procedures include, at the receiving side, recognizing a destination address, checking the length field, discarding the pad field if appended, and carrying out the cyclic redundancy frame check. This description in words may be represented schematically as shown in Fig. 5-17. Peer protocols are defined at all layers of the OSI Reference Model, generalizing the concept shown here for the LAN case [SCHW 1987], [HALS].[6]

Communications between peer layers in the OSI model are shown dashed in Fig. 5-17 because the peers carry out *logical* communications only. The only direct access is through the physical medium. An LLC sublayer wanting to send data to another LLC sublayer, for example, can only do so by using its MAC sublayer. It passes its data down to the MAC sublayer, which then encapsulates this information into frames. (See Fig. 5-16 for the 802.3 example.) The MAC sublayer in turn communicates with its peer sublayer logically only, actually using the services of its physical layer to generate the bit stream that will really

---

[6][HALS] F. Halsall, *Data Communications, Computer Networks and OSI*, Addison-Wesley, Wokingham, England, 1988.

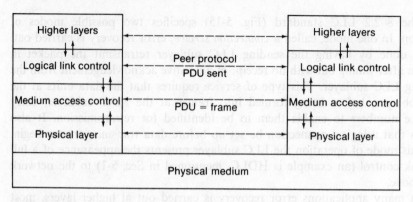

FIGURE 5-17
Communication between layers and peers: 802 standards.

propagate across the medium. Its PDU, the frame, although "sent" to the peer MAC sublayer, must actually be transmitted, bit by bit, over the physical medium.

There are thus two kinds of communications involved in the OSI Reference Model concept: logical communications between peers at the same layer, using peer protocols, and communications between adjacent layers in the same system, as indicated in Fig. 5-17 with pairs of arrows crossing adjacent layers. In the OSI concept the layer below provides a service to the layer above. It is thus called the *service provider*. The layer above, using this service, is called the *service user*. The MAC sublayer is thus the service provider for the LLC sublayer. The physical layer is the service provider for the MAC sublayer. Communication between layers is carried out by passing *service primitives* between them. These concepts are diagrammed, in general, in Fig. 5-18. They apply to any two layers in the OSI Reference Model [SCHW 1987]. The layers are diagrammed horizontally here, with time shown increasing down the page.

Four service primitives are defined for the OSI Reference Model. These are, as shown in Fig. 5-18, a request primitive at the source, from service user to service provider; an indication primitive at the destination, from service provider to service user there; a response primitive (if needed) from the destination service user to its provider; and a confirm primitive, back at the source, from provider to user. These primitives carry necessary data and control information between layers. The provider layer, on receiving a primitive from its user, carries out the prescribed protocol actions at that layer and generates a protocol data unit (PDU) if the results of that action are to be communicated to its peer provider layer.

These primitives are defined for each layer in the OSI Reference Model, for the transmission of data, as well as for setting up (connecting) and tearing down (disconnecting) logical connections at a given layer if necessary. The primitives for these different modes of operation have the labels **DATA**, **CONNECT**, and

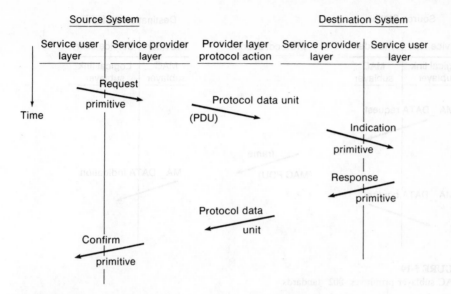

FIGURE 5-18
OSI layer primitives and PDUs.

DISCONNECT appended to them [SCHW 1987]. We focus here on the 802 logical-link control and MAC sublayers, with the MAC sublayer serving as the service provider for the LLC sublayer, to provide a simple example. The concept of logical connection is not used at the MAC sublayer, so that **DATA** primitives only need be considered. (Connections are required to be established and torn down at the logical-link control sublayer if the connection-service mode of operation is used). In addition, only three of the four primitives are required. The response primitive is not needed, since receipt of a frame (the MAC PDU) at the destination side is not acknowledged in the 802 MAC protocols. (Recall in the case of the 802.3 MAC sublayer that error detection is carried out at the destination MAC sublayer and that frames are dropped if errors are detected, but that no further action at this sublayer is taken.)[7] The service-user/provider concept of Fig. 5-18 then simplifies to the transfer of primitives and transmission of the one frame shown in Fig. 5-19. The **DATA. confirm** primitive shown has local significance only, since there is no response primitive issued at the destination system preceding it, as shown in the more general case of Fig. 5-18. Note

---

[7]Clearly the destination station may at times be expected to reply to the *data*—the packet—carried inside the MAC frame. This reply involves communication at a higher layer, however. The MAC sublayer *never* looks inside its data field. This is in fact true at all layers. A reply would then be carried as data inside another frame sometime later, moving from the previous destination system to the previous source system, with source and destination addresses now reversed.

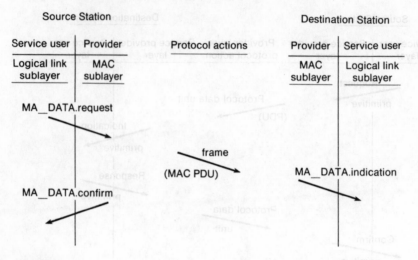

FIGURE 5-19
MAC sublayer primitives: 802 standards.

that all three primitives have an initial label designating the provider layer. **MA** in this case stands for MAC sublayer. Primitives transferred between network layer and logical-link sublayer would carry the designation **L_DATA.request**, etc. Those transferred between session and transport layers would be proceded by a **T**, etc. [SCHW 1987].

For concreteness we now describe the three 802.3 MAC sublayer primitives in detail [IEEE 1985a]. The **MA_DATA.request** service primitive is generated by the logical-link control (LLC) sublayer whenever it has data ready to be transmitted to a peer sublayer. The data can be a packet, the block of information received from higher layers, or control information required for LLC purposes. The primitive contains three parameters: the MAC destination address (an individual or group address), the data to be passed, and a quality-of-service class. (In the CSMA/CD protocol only one quality of service is provided.) The primitive is formally described as

```
MA_DATA.request(
        destination_address,
        m_sdu,
        service_class
        )
```

On receipt of this primitive the MAC sublayer creates the frame of Fig. 5-16 and passes it down to the physical layer for transmission over the LAN to the destination MAC sublayer. The parameter **m_sdu** (MAC service data unit) carries the LLC data to be incorporated in the data field of the frame. The standard specifically says that no particular implementation of the primitive is implied, nor is anything further said about its "transfer" across the layer interface. These are left up to the individual implementer. This is true of all OSI specifications, at all layers of the architecture.

The `MA_DATA.indication` primitive is similar in construct. It is passed by the destination MAC sublayer to its LLC sublayer on arrival of an error-free frame. Its description is represented as follows:

```
MA_DATA.indication(
                   destination_address,
                   source_address,
                   m_sdu,
                   reception_status
                   )
```

The `source_address` parameter is the address of the sending MAC sublayer, as provided by the source address of the incoming frame (Fig. 5-16). The reception-status parameter represents status information to be passed to the LLC sublayer. The `m_sdu` (MAC service data unit) parameter again contains the contents of the frame data field.

Finally, the `MA_DATA.confirm` primitive has, in the case of the 802.3 standard, local significance only, as already noted (Fig. 5-19). The sending MAC sublayer uses this to notify its LLC sublayer of the success or failure of the `MA_DATA.request`. (The case of excessive frame collisions represents one example of failure. In this case the MAC and physical layers essentially give up trying to transmit the frame and so notify the LLC sublayer.) This primitive carries only one parameter, `transmission_status`:

```
MA_DATA.confirm (transmission_status).
```

In the remainder of this section we describe features of each of three LAN standards briefly. These include the IEEE 802.3 CSMA/CD standard, portions of which we have already described in the preceding material, the IEEE 802.5 token-ring standard, and FDDI, the high-speed token-ring standard.

IEEE 802.3 CSMA/CD STANDARD. Recall from our discussion in the earlier part of this section that the CSMA/CD random access procedure consists of two basic features:

1. *Carrier sense.* Listen for carrier, and transmit only if the medium is quiet.

2. *Collision detection.* During transmission listen for collision; abort and reschedule transmission if collision is detected.

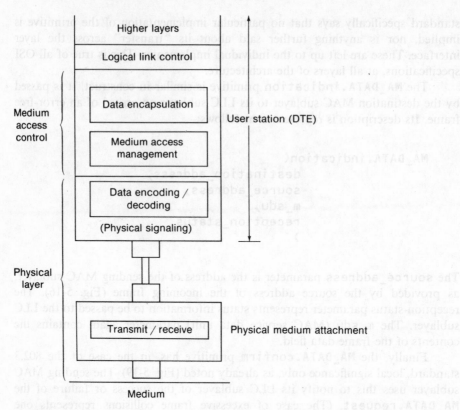

FIGURE 5-20
IEEE 802.3 CSMA/CD architecture.

These features must be implemented within the constructs of the MAC and physical layers. In addition, the physical layer must generate the appropriate signals for transmission onto the medium, while the MAC sublayer must handle the frame generation and frame reception functions described earlier. Figure 5-20 shows how these various functions are apportioned both logically and physically.

The MAC sublayer is shown divided into two parts. The data-encapsulation portion incorporates the framing, addressing, and error-detection functions of the MAC sublayer. It constructs the frame (Fig. 5-16) on receipt of a **MA_DATA.request** from the LLC layer. It then passes the frame on to medium access management for transmission. (It also tears the frame down and passes the data-field contents up to the LLC sublayer as the **m_sdu** parameter in the **MA_DATA.indication** primitive, if the frame passes its error check. See Fig. 5-19.) Medium access management is responsible for collision avoidance and collision handling (contention resolution). It uses a carrier sense signal provided by the physical signaling portion of the physical layer to determine when the medium is occupied, and it initiates transmission, passing frame bits serially to the physical layer, when the medium is deemed quiet.

Medium access management initiates the collision-handling procedure on receipt of a collision-detect signal from the physical layer. A jam signal is first transmitted, the ongoing transmission terminated, and the random interval selected for retransmission. This includes the binary backoff procedure, in which the retry interval is doubled on each retransmission until a maximum backoff limit is reached.

For the 10-Mbit/s CSMA/CD LAN, the backoff limit is 10. This means that at the nth retransmission attempt, $n \leq 10$, the delay before retransmitting after detecting a collision is a random number of units of time called the slot time, uniformly distributed between 0 and 2^n. The slot time, equivalent to the 2τ-second interval used earlier in discussing the CSMA/CD technique (Fig. 5-11), is specified to be 512 bit times for the 10-Mbit/s system. Subsequent retry intervals remain between 0 and 2^{10} until 16 transmission attempts have been recorded. This "excess collision" event is then reported as an error, via the **MA_DATA.confirm** primitive (Fig. 5-19), to higher layers, as noted above.

The physical-layer component of the 802.3 standard is also divided into two parts, as shown in Fig. 5-20. The data-encoding portion encodes the data bits received serially from the MAC sublayer into a zero-dc binary waveform suitable for the coaxial medium. The encoding technique used is called Manchester encoding. An example appears in Fig. 5-21. Note that 1's are represented by positive-going signal transitions, 0's by negative-going transitions. This waveform is then transmitted electrically onto the medium by the transmit portion of the physical layer. The physical layer monitors the medium at the same time and, on detecting a collision (reception of a signal waveshape other than the one transmitted), generates a collision-detect signal. The physical layer also generates the carrier sense signal used by the MAC sublayer in the collision-avoidance procedure.

Note from Fig. 5-20 that the MAC sublayer and the data-encoding/decoding portion of the physical layer are located physically within the station connected to the LAN. This station is termed generically a DTE (data terminal equipment). The transmit/receive or transceiver portion of the physical layer appears in the physical medium attachment, attached directly to the medium. The medium, in the case of the 10-Mbit/s standard, is a baseband coaxial cable.

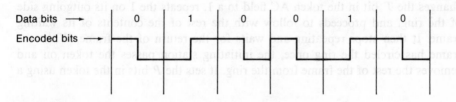

FIGURE 5-21
Manchester encoding.

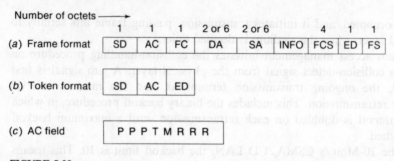

FIGURE 5-22
802.5 token-ring frame formats.

IEEE 802.5 TOKEN-RING STANDARD. The MAC sublayer protocol in this standard carries out some of the same functions as in the case of the 802.3 CSMA/CD standard. It receives a **MA_DATA.request** primitive from the LLC layer and encapsulates the LLC data included into a frame for transfer to its physical layer. The format of the frame formed by this layer appears in Fig. 5-22a. Figure 5-22b portrays the token format for this standard [IEEE 1985b].[8]

The starting delimiter (SD) and ending delimiter (ED) denote the beginning and end of a frame, respectively. An information length field is thus not needed as in the 802.3 case (Fig. 5-16). The access control (AC) field is used to implement the ring access protocol. This field is shown broken out into its eight bits in Fig. 5-22c. The token bit T is set to 1 in a frame and 0 in a token. Eight levels of data priority are provided by the three P bits. This makes the token-passing protocol differ somewhat from that described earlier in this section. There the token was assumed passed to the neighboring station on the ring. Here it is passed to the next station with priority equal to, or higher than, that indicated by the P bits. The three R bits allow a station with a frame waiting for transmission to reserve the token if the waiting frame is of higher priority than the one currently circulating, and if no station on the ring has higher priority. It does this by changing the R bits to the higher priority of its own waiting frame while regenerating a frame, or token of higher priority, but with lower-priority R bits.

The overall token-passing protocol may then be summarized as follows: a station receiving a token of priority equal to or less than that of its waiting frame changes the T bit in the token AC field to a 1, repeats the 1 on its outgoing side of the ring, and proceeds to follow with the rest of the contents of its waiting frame. It then stops repeating and waits for the return of the frame. When the frame has circled the ring once, the initiating station passes the token on and removes the rest of the frame from the ring. It sets the P bits in the token using a

[8][IEEE 1985b] *Token Ring Access Method, Standard 802.5-1985*, IEEE, New York, 1985.

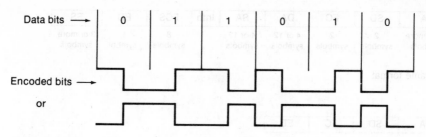

FIGURE 5-23
Differential Manchester coding.

procedure designed to have the combination of the *P* and *R* bits provide fair access to all users on the ring [IEEE 1985*b*], [HALS].

The FC (frame control) and FS (frame status) fields are used to carry out management and control functions on the ring. One of the stations on the ring serves as *active monitor* to take such supervisory actions as recovering from lost tokens or from tokens and frames circulating indefinitely around the ring. As an example, the active monitor uses the *M* bit in the AC field (Fig. 5-22*c*) to prevent the latter occurrence. This bit is initially set to 0. It is set to 1 by the active monitor station for each frame and token passing through. The *M* bit remains at this value until it reaches the initiating station, where it should be reset to 0. A token or frame reaching the monitor with its bit set to 1 is thus invalid and is purged; a new token is issued.

The encoding procedure at the 802.5 physical layer differs somewhat from that of the 802.3 standard. Differential Manchester encoding is used. An example appears in Fig. 5-23. The 0 bit produces a transition at both the beginning and the middle of the bit interval. The 1 bit keeps the same polarity in the first half of the bit interval as in the latter half of the previous bit interval. A polarity transition still takes place in the middle of the interval. Note that two encoded bit streams are thus possible, depending on the polarity of the previous bit.

FDDI (FIBER DISTRIBUTED DATA INTERFACE). The IEEE 802 LAN standards just discussed operate at transmission rates of at most 10 Mbits/s. There clearly exists a need to transmit at much higher bit rates. One example is a high-speed network interconnection between computer systems; another is a high-speed connection between mainframes and mass storage systems. As workstations become more powerful, their interconnection will require higher-speed communications. High-quality graphics and video signals require high-speed networking as well. The *fiber distributed data interface* (FDDI) was developed for these and other applications.

FDDI is designed to operate at a 100-Mbit/s bit rate, using dual (counter-rotating) fiber-optic rings. It is based on the IEEE 802.5 token-ring standard, but uses multiple tokens to improve the throughput performance. The basic FFDI standard was developed by the Accredited Standards Committee (ASC) X3T9 of

PA	SD	FC	DA	SA	Info	FCS	ED	FS
16 or more symbols	2 symbols	2 symbols	4 or 12 symbols	4 or 12 symbols		8 symbols	1 symbol	3 or more symbols

(a) Frame format

PA	SD	FC	ED
16 or more symbols	2 symbols	2 symbols	2 symbols

(b) Token format

FIGURE 5-24
Frame and token formats, MAC protocol, FDDI.

the American National Standards Institute (ANSI) [FDDI 1986a], [ROSS].[9] It is designed to conform with both the OSI Reference Model and IEEE 802 LAN standards. Like the 802.5 standard on which it is based, it consists of a MAC sublayer and a physical layer. For the transmission of data the MAC sublayer interfaces with the LLC sublayer through the set of three data primitives shown portrayed in Fig. 5-19. On receiving a **MA_DATA.request** primitive with a service data unit (**m_sdu**) embedded, the MAC sublayer forms a frame with the **m_sdu**s as the data field. The frame format for FFDI is shown in Fig. 5-24a [FDDI 1986a]. (Multiple **m_sdu**s and hence frames may be transferred with one primitive.) The token format appears in Fig. 5-24b.

Note the similarity between these formats and those of the 802.5 token ring (Fig. 5-22). Note also that there is no access-control field in the FDDI frame structure. Access control is carried out somewhat differently than in the token ring, as will be discussed shortly. The PA field is a preamble (see the CSMA/CD frame format in Fig. 5-16) that is used for bit synchronization. The starting-delimiter (SD) field is the one that provides frame synchronization. The FCS (frame check sequence) field covers all fields from FC to the information field inclusive.

Field lengths in Fig. 5-24 are expressed in units of *symbols*. The FDDI standard defines 24 symbols: 16 for data and 8 for control. Each of these is encoded into 5-bit code groups at the physical layer for transmission over the optical fiber. Table 5-1 portrays the symbol-coding table used. The data symbols

[9][FDDI 1986a] *Draft Proposed American National Standard*, *FDDI Token Ring Media Access Control* (*MAC*), ASC X3T9.5 Rev-10, ANSI, New York, February 28, 1986. [ROSS] F. E. Ross, "FDDI—A Tutorial," *IEEE Commun. Mag.*, vol. 24, no. 5, pp. 10–17, May 1986.

TABLE 5-1
FDDI Symbol-Coding Table

Control symbols	Output code group
Line state	
Q (quiet)	0 0 0 0 0
I (idle)	1 1 1 1 1
H (halt)	0 0 1 0 0
Starting delimiter	
J	1 1 0 0 0
K	1 0 0 0 1
Ending delimiter	
T	0 1 1 0 1
Control indicators	
R	0 0 1 1 1
S	1 1 0 0 1
Data symbols	
0 0 0 0	1 1 1 1 0
0 0 0 1	0 1 0 0 1
0 0 1 0	1 0 1 0 0
0 0 1 1	1 0 1 0 1
0 1 0 0	0 1 0 1 0
0 1 0 1	0 1 0 1 1
0 1 1 0	0 1 1 1 0
0 1 1 1	0 1 1 1 1
1 0 0 0	1 0 0 1 0
1 0 0 1	1 0 0 1 1
1 0 1 0	1 0 1 1 0
1 0 1 1	1 0 1 1 1
1 1 0 0	1 1 0 1 0
1 1 0 1	1 1 0 1 1
1 1 1 0	1 1 1 0 0
1 1 1 1	1 1 1 0 1

each represent a sequence of four data bits, as passed down in the `m_sdu` from the LLC sublayer to the MAC sublayer [FDDI 1986*b*].[10]

The preamble (PA) field in Fig. 5-24 consists of 16 or more *I* (idle) symbols; the starting delimiter (SD) field consists of a *J* followed by a *K* for frame synchronization, as already noted; the ending delimiter (ED) field consists of one *T* in the case of a frame, two *T*'s in the case of a token; the frame-status (FS) field consists of at least three control indicator symbols, *R* or *S*, followed by a *T*. The first three symbols, in order, are used for error-detection indication (the *S* is then set), address-recognition indication (*S* is set), and frame-copying

---

[10] [FDDI 1986*b*] *Draft Proposed American National Standard*, *FDDI Physical Layer Protocol* (*PHY*), ASC X3T9.5 Rev-14, ANSI, New York, October 20, 1986.

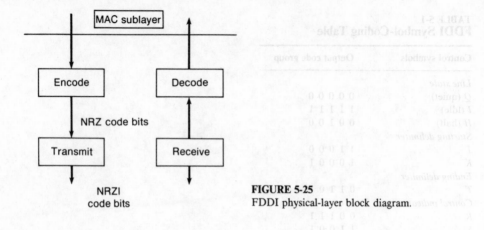

FIGURE 5-25
FDDI physical-layer block diagram.

indication (S is set). The last two indicators tell the transmitting station, on receiving its transmitted frame back, that the destination address was recognized and that the frame was then copied. If they are not returned set, the transmitting station knows a problem has occurred. The remaining frame-control (FC) field is used to define the type of frame and associated control functions.

The conversion of 4-bit data symbols to 5-bit code groups (Table 5-1) is carried out at the physical layer. This implies that the 100-Mbit/s FDDI data rate is actually transmitted at a 125-Mbit/s rate over the fiber-optic ring. The physical-layer block diagram appears in Fig. 5-25. Symbols are first encoded into 5-bit code groups and appear as a sequence of nonreturn-to-zero (NRZ) bits (see Chap. 3). The transmitter then inverts the signal level whenever a 1 appears. The resulting signal is called an NRZI (nonreturn-to-zero inverted) signal. The purpose is to ensure that synchronization (clock) information is readily extracted from the signal as transmitted. Note, for example, that the sequence of idles (I's) transmitted as the preamble (Fig. 5-24 and Table 5-1) corresponds to a sequence of all 1's. The NRZI waveform is then a sequence of alternating transitions that is readily detected at each station along the ring. In addition, the 5-bit coding pattern adopted (Table 5-1) ensures that there are at least two transitions (i.e. two 1's) per transmitted symbol, with a maximum of three 0's. This latter condition ensures a tolerable maximum dc value on the line.

As noted earlier, the FDDI token-passing scheme allows multiple tokens and frames to exist on any one ring, increasing the throughput. It allows systems with increased latency to operate effectively. FDDI systems can thus operate with more stations and/or longer rings. A token-holding timer is used to limit the time a station occupies the medium before releasing a token. Specifically, each station is assigned a *target token-rotation time* (TTRT). Different priorities may be accommodated by assigning a different TTRT for each priority level. Each station maintains a *token-rotation timer* (TRT), which is reset to zero whenever a token is received. A new token may be captured and a waiting frame transmitted if TRT < TTRT for that station and priority. When TRT reaches TTRT, token capture is not allowed. (This is true for the so-called asynchronous operation under discussion here. The FDDI standard also defines synchronous transmission, a service transmission class appropriate for traffic such as voice, which is quasiperiodic. For this type of service, service time on the ring is preallocated and the time delay is guaranteed not to exceed a specific value.) The timer procedure ensures fairness of transmission on the ring. It also provides a dynamic control for transmission on the ring—as traffic increases with a concurrent increase in delay as well, the station timer values will increase as well, increasing the average time between the capture of tokens.

A station holding a token may transmit additional frames so long as another timer, the *token-holding timer* (THT), does not exceed the TTRT for that station and priority. Whenever a station captures a new token, its current value of TRT is saved as THT. For lightly loaded rings, stations can transmit more frames per token; as the load increases, increasing TRT as well, THT will be correspondingly larger and the number of frames able to be transmitted will be reduced. The use of THT limits the time a station can hold a token to the TTRT.

Consider the procedure for frame transmission now. A station with frames queued for transmission waits for receipt and capture of a token if it is allowed to do so. It then transmits the waiting frame(s), followed immediately after by a new token. (This must be done in accordance with the TRT and THT procedures just outlined.) This procedure increases the throughput on the ring over that of the 802.5 token-ring standard, as already noted, and allows multiple tokens to exist simultaneously on the ring.

A transmitting station is responsible for removing its frame(s) from the ring. It does so by recognizing its source address on frames received on the upstream side of the ring. But note from Fig. 5-24a that the five fields PA through SA will be transmitted back on the ring before the source address is recognized. These five fields, plus idle (I) symbols the station then starts transmitting, represent frame fragments that start circulating around the ring. They will be removed on encountering a station in the process of transmitting its own frames.

5-3 PERFORMANCE ANALYSIS IN NETWORKS

The discussion thus far in this chapter, except for a brief introduction to performance questions for the CSMA/CD bus and the token ring, has been rather qualitative. We introduced the distinction between packet-switched and circuit-switched networks in Sec. 5-1, and then followed with a detailed discussion of local-area networks (LANs) in the previous section (Sec. 5-2) to provide a concrete example of packet switching and its connection to the OSI Reference Model.

In this section we study the performance question in more detail. We first introduce a common model for traffic statistics, that of Poisson arrivals. This model is used to represent the generation of packets at a user station or, equivalently, the arrival of packets at a node in a packet-switching network. It has been used for many years to represent the generation (arrival) of calls in circuit-switched networks. We apply this traffic model to the study of the simplest possible queueing model representing the buffering or queueing operation at a node in a network. This is the $M/M/1$ queue. (The notation will be defined at the appropriate time). The time-delay calculation for this queue then enables us to discuss the time-delay performance of the CSMA/CD and token-ring protocols as a function of applied load, and show how they compare with one another. We will also be able to study, using this queueing model, the performance of statistical multiplexers, commonly used in packet switching—a different type of multiplexing than the time division multiplexing first introduced in Chap. 3. This material is extended, in Sec. 5-4 following, to call-blocking calculations in circuit-switched networks.

Traffic-Arrival Model: Poisson Statistics

Consider the elementary picture of a node in a network shown in Fig. 5-26. A number of input links are shown depositing traffic into the node; an output link is shown transferring the traffic out to another node. The input traffic could be packets arriving from other nodes and/or user stations connected to the node; it could be calls in a circuit-switched network for which end-to-end connections have to be set up. The ability of the node (and the network of which it is a part) to handle these packets or calls depends on the way they are processed, the rate at which they can be transferred out of the node, and, finally, the way they arrive at the node. In particular, one would expect that if the node call- or packet-handling *capacity* is some quantity μ calls (or packets) per unit time, the number arriving per unit time (the *load*) should not exceed μ. (The actual details of how the calls or packets are transferred, for example by the TDM technique of Fig. 5-2, are not needed at this time.) This concept will be demonstrated quantitatively in this section and Sec. 5-4 following.

Focus on arrivals at the node first. One would expect, as a reasonable assumption, that the time of arrival of a call or packet is random. Users of a network generally do not notify the network when they expect to use its resources. A computer outputting a file or blocks of data as the result of some processing may be expected to do so at some random times. A human making a telephone call may generally be assumed to do so at some random time. The random arrivals of calls or packets at the node may be indicated by the marks

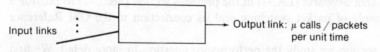

Input links ⋮

Output link: μ calls / packets per unit time

FIGURE 5-26
Representation of node in network.

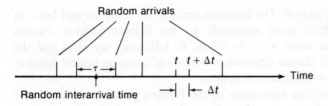

FIGURE 5-27
Arrivals at the node in Fig. 5-26.

shown in Fig. 5-27. The time between them is a random variable τ as shown. (For simplicity at this point we aggregate the arrivals from all input links.) Now zoom in on a small time interval $(t, t + \Delta t)$ in Fig. 5-27. This is shown in Fig. 5-28. The *Poisson model* of traffic arrivals (calls or packets) is defined by the following three statements:

1. The probability of one arrival in the interval $(t, t + \Delta t)$ is $\lambda \Delta t \ll 1$ with λ a proportionality constant, independent of t.
2. The probability of no arrival in that interval is $1 - \lambda \Delta t$.
3. An arrival in one time interval $(t, t + \Delta t)$ is independent of arrivals before or after that interval. This defines a *memoryless* process.

The first statement appears reasonable. It says that, for a very small interval, the chance of an arrival is correspondingly small and proportional to the length of that interval (i.e., as the interval increases, the chance of an arrival increases proportionately). The second statement says that if the interval is small enough no more than one arrival can take place. The third statement, a critical one in the model, says that an arrival does not preclude another one from immediately taking place. This is consistent with the random-arrival picture shown in Fig. 5-27. The Poisson model can be shown to be the limiting case of other models if many users access a system such as that of Fig. 5-26. Users are considered independent of one another, and hence one user initiating a call or sending a packet does not preclude another, or another input link, from doing the same.

As noted above, the Poisson process has been found to be a quite accurate representation of calls arriving at a telephone exchange. It is used, because of its simplicity and its agreement with some limited measurements, to represent packet arrivals. It is used as an appropriate statistic in many other fields of

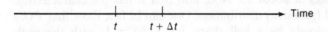

FIGURE 5-28
Enlargement of small time interval $(t, t + \Delta t)$.

science and engineering as well. The emission (arrival) of electrons and holes in semiconductors is modeled quite accurately by the Poisson process. Photon emission is modeled the same way. In Chap. 6, following, we shall use the Poisson representation of photon emission to determine limits on optical communications in fiber-optic communication systems.

Using the three defining statements of the Poisson process, we can derive the *Poisson probability distribution*. Consider a time interval $T \gg \Delta t$. For the Poisson process the probability of k arrivals in the interval T is found to be given by

$$P(k) = \frac{e^{-\lambda T}(\lambda T)^k}{k!} \qquad k = 0, 1, 2, \ldots \qquad (5\text{-}12)$$

The average number of arrivals in the interval T is then

$$E(k) = \sum_{k=0}^{\infty} kP(k) = \lambda T \qquad (5\text{-}13)$$

by a simple calculation. [As a hint, it is left to the reader to show that (5-12) is properly normalized; i.e., $\sum_k P(k) = 1$. Factoring λT out of the sum in (5-13), the resultant expression is still normalized, and (5-13) results.]

Equation (5-13) says that an alternative definition of λ, the proportionality factor for the Poisson process, is the average number of arrivals per unit time, i.e., the average arrival rate. In the case of Fig. 5-26 it represents the aggregate load at the node. It is this quantity that should be less than the capacity μ. The variance σ_k^2 of the Poisson distribution turns out to be equal to the mean value:

$$\sigma_k^2 = E[k - E(k)]^2 = E(k) = \lambda T \qquad (5\text{-}14)$$

This is also left to the reader to prove.

From (5-13) and (5-14) we have

$$\frac{\sigma_k}{E(k)} = \frac{1}{\sqrt{\lambda T}} \qquad (5\text{-}15)$$

For large T ($\lambda T \gg 1$) the distribution closes in tightly about the average value λT. This implies that if one actually measures the number of arrivals m in a large time interval T, m/T is a good estimate of λ. As an example, say 1,000 calls arrive in one hour at a telephone exchange. Then 1,000 calls/hour is a good estimate of λ, since $1/\sqrt{\lambda T} = 0.03$ represents the fractional deviation from the average value. Measurements would, with a high probability, tend to cluster about λT.

Figure 5-29 is a plot of the Poisson distribution for $E(k) = \lambda T = 10$. Note that the distribution peaks at about 10. Note also that it has the characteristic bell shape of the normal (gaussian) distribution. One can in fact show that $P(k)$ is approximated quite closely by a bell shape for $E(k) \gg 1$, with the peak occurring at $E(k)$. We shall use this result in some of the calculations on the performance of optical communication systems in Chap. 6. Note from (5-12) that

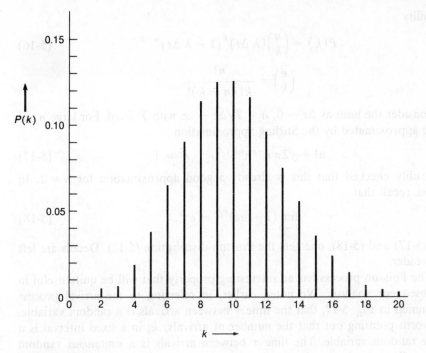

FIGURE 5-29
Poisson distribution, $E(k) = 10$.

$P(0) = e^{-\lambda T}$. As λ and/or T increase, the chance of no arrival in the interval T becomes exponentially small.

How does one derive the Poisson distribution from the three defining statements? This is readily done by choosing a fixed interval T, dividing it into subintervals Δt, and calculating the probability $P(k)$ of having k arrivals in the interval. If one then lets $\Delta t \to 0$, one obtains (5-12). Specifically, consider the interval T, containing $n = T/\Delta t$ subintervals, as shown in Fig. 5-30.

From the first two defining statements for the Poisson process, the arrival/nonarrival events in an elementary interval Δt represent a Bernoulli trial: The probability of an occurrence is $\lambda \Delta t$; that of no occurence is $1 - \lambda \Delta t$. From the third defining statement, probabilities in adjacent Δt subintervals are independent. The probability $P(k)$ of k arrivals in the interval T is then the binomial

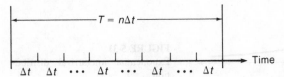

FIGURE 5-30
Derivation of Poisson distribution.

probability

$$P(k) = \binom{n}{k}(\lambda \, \Delta t)^k (1 - \lambda \, \Delta t)^{n-k} \tag{5-16}$$

with

$$\binom{n}{k} \equiv \frac{n!}{k!\,(n-k)!}$$

Now consider the limit as $\Delta t \to 0$, $n = T/\Delta t \to \infty$ with T fixed. For large n, $n!$ may be approximated by the Stirling approximation

$$n! \doteq \sqrt{2\pi}\, e^{-n} n^{n+1/2} \qquad n \gg 1 \tag{5-17}$$

It is readily checked that this is already a good approximation for $n = 2$. In addition, recall that

$$\lim_{\varepsilon \to 0} (1 + a\varepsilon)^{b/\varepsilon} = e^{ab} \tag{5-18}$$

Using (5-17) and (5-18), one gets the Poisson distribution (5-12). Details are left to the reader.

The Poisson process has an interesting property that will be quite useful in the subsequent analysis. We noted earlier, in referring to the arrival process diagrammed in Fig. 5-27, that the time τ between arrivals is a random variable. (It is worth pointing out that the number of arrivals, k, in a fixed interval is a discrete random variable. The time τ between arrivals is a *continuous* random variable.) We can show quite readily that the variable τ is exponentially distributed with its probability density function $f_\tau(\tau)$ given by

$$f_\tau(\tau) = \lambda e^{-\lambda \tau} \qquad \tau \geq 0 \tag{5-19}$$

This is diagrammed in Fig. 5-31. The average value $E(\tau)$ of the time between traffic arrivals is just

$$E(\tau) = \int_0^\infty \lambda \tau e^{-\lambda \tau}\, d\tau = \frac{1}{\lambda} \tag{5-20}$$

This is to be expected. In the example noted above, with $\lambda = 1,000$ calls/hour (on the average) arriving at a telephone exchange, the average time between arrivals is $1/\lambda = 0.001$ hour. The variance of the exponential distribution is readily shown to be

$$\sigma_\tau^2 = 1/\lambda^2 \tag{5-21}$$

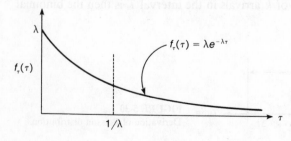

FIGURE 5-31
Exponential interarrival distribution.

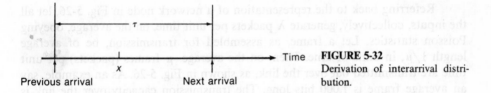

FIGURE 5-32
Derivation of interarrival distribution.

To derive the exponential interarrival distribution for the Poisson process consider the time diagram sketched in Fig. 5-32. Let τ be the (random) time between two successive arrivals. Take the origin of time as the previous arrival point. Some time x later there can have been no further arrival if $\tau > x$. The probability that $\tau > x$ is the probability there are no arrivals in the interval $(0, x)$. From (5-12) this is just

$$P(\tau > x) = P(0 \text{ arrivals in } (0, x))$$

$$= e^{-\lambda x} \tag{5-22}$$

The probability that $\tau \le x$ is just the cumulative probability distribution $F_\tau(x) = P(\tau \le x)$ and is, from (5-22), given by

$$F_\tau(x) = P(\tau \le x)$$

$$= 1 - e^{-\lambda x} \tag{5-23}$$

Differentiating this with respect to x to obtain the density function $f_\tau(x)$, we have

$$f_\tau(x) = \frac{dF_\tau(x)}{dx} = \lambda e^{-\lambda x} \tag{5-24}$$

This proves our desired relation.

The Poisson traffic model will be used throughout the rest of this chapter.

$M/M/1$ Queue and Packet Switching

We now apply the Poisson traffic model to the study of the queueing, or store-and-forward, process implicit in packet switching. Its application to circuit switching will be discussed in Sec. 5-4.

Recall from our discussion of packet switching in Sec. 5-1 that queueing of packets occurs because of the sharing of link transmission facilities. A packet, after arrival and necessary processing at a network node (Fig. 5-9), has to wait for earlier packets to complete their transmission before it can be transferred across a link. (This assumes all packets have the same priority and are served in order of arrival. We use the word packet generically here. It is the frame encapsulating a packet that is actually transmitted across a link.) The packet wait time at each node along a path in the network introduces random delay into the arrival time at the destination node, and it is this delay, due to queueing, that we would like to determine.

Referring back to the representation of a network node in Fig. 5-26, let all the inputs, collectively, generate λ packets per unit time, on the average, obeying Poisson statistics. Let a frame, as assembled for transmission, be of average length $1/\mu$, in units of time. Then, on the average, μ frames (packets) per unit time are transmitted out over the link, as shown in Fig. 5-26. As an example, say an average frame is 1,000 bits long. The transmission capacity over the link is $C = 1$ Mbits/s. Then the average frame length, in units of time, is 1 ms, and, on the average, 1,000 frames (packets) per second are transmitted. Note that the frame length $1/\mu$ is the same as the quantity T used earlier in discussing transmission over LANs. [See (5-1), (5-9) to (5-11), and Fig. 5-11.] We have changed the notation here to conform to standard queueing notation. In the earlier discussion on LANs we assumed frames were all of fixed length for simplicity. Here we generalize the discussion to include packets (and hence frames) drawn from a random length distribution, with average length $1/\mu$.

More specifically, it turns out that the simplest length distribution to choose, in this introduction to queueing, is the exponential distribution. Letting the frame length, in units of time, be a random variable m, we assume, for the analysis here, that the frame-length density function is given by

$$f_m(m) = \mu e^{-\mu m} \qquad m \geq 0 \tag{5-25}$$

Comparing with (5-20) and (5-21),

$$E(m) = 1/\mu \tag{5-26}$$

and

$$\sigma_m^2 = (1/\mu)^2 \tag{5-27}$$

This density function is sketched in Fig. 5-33. Shorter frames are thus more likely to be generated than longer ones.

This model for frame lengths can clearly not be a very accurate one: frames are assumed to be continuously varying in length. Real frames are multiples of bits and, very often, as seen in the previous section, multiples of octets. The fixed header size means that they have a minimum length, not zero as is the case with the model here. Yet despite these faults, the model is useful. For large frames the discrete variation in length is approximated quite well by a continuous variation. It also turns out that the exponential model often produces worst-case, conservative results [SCHW 1977]. Finally, the analysis is simplified considerably using

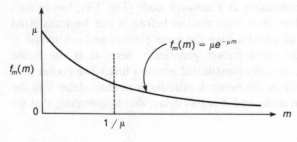

FIGURE 5-33
Exponential frame-length distribution.

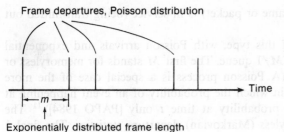

Frame departures, Poisson distribution

Time

|← m →|

↑
Exponentially distributed frame length

FIGURE 5-34
Frame departures, output of node.

this model, and it does demonstrate quantitatively the most significant effects of queueing.

The simplicity of the analysis is immediately apparent. Comparing with the Poisson traffic arrival process of Fig. 5-27, which was shown to have exponentially distributed interarrival times, exponentially distributed frames leaving a node must depart at random, Poisson-distributed, times. This result is portrayed in Fig. 5-34. (It is clear that a node must always have a frame ready for transmission for this picture to hold.)

Using this exponential length distribution and the previous model of traffic arrivals, the packet switching node of Fig. 5-26 may be represented by the queueing model of Fig. 5-35. This is the simplest model possible for a packet switch. Nodal processing implicit in the layered architecture of Fig. 5-9 (and any queueing encountered while waiting for processing) has been neglected, although it could be subsumed into the average frame transmission time $1/\mu$. The model of Fig. 5-35 shows packets arriving at a queue at an average rate λ. They are served "first come, first served," or in *FIFO order* (first in, first out), and depart one at a time at an average rate μ, over the service facility. Figure 5-35 is, more generally, applicable to a service facility that serves (transmits) customers (frames or packets) at an average rate of μ customers (frames or packets) per unit time. The average service (transmission) time is $1/\mu$. At any point in time n customers (frames or packets) are queued up for service. If n is zero the queue is empty; if

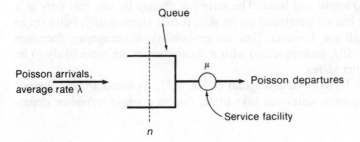

Queue

Poisson arrivals,
average rate λ

μ

Poisson departures

Service facility

n

FIGURE 5-35
$M/M/1$ queueing model, packet-switching node of Fig. 5-26.

$n = 1$, the single customer (frame or packet) is in service (being transmitted out over the link).

A queueing structure of this type, with Poisson arrivals and exponential service times, is called an $M/M/1$ queue. The first M stands for memoryless or Markovian arrival statistics. (A Poisson process is a special case of the more general Markov process, one in which the probability of an event happening at time $t + \Delta t$ depends on the probability at time t only [PAPO 1984]).[11] The second M stands for memoryless (Markovian) departure statistics. The final 1 means there is only one server (one outgoing channel). In Sec. 5-4 we shall discuss the $M/M/N$ queue, with N outgoing channels that provide service. More generally, a $G/G/N$ queue is one that has general arrival and service distributions, with N servers. (Think of a bank with one line and N tellers. Customers arrive randomly with some known distribution; the time to serve them is some other random distribution.) An $M/G/1$ queue would be one with Poisson arrivals but with some nonexponential service-time (frame-length) distribution. Frames (or packets) of constant (fixed) length have a deterministic length distribution. The queue in this case is called an $M/D/1$ queue.

The time to pass through the queue of Fig. 5-35 has two components: a random waiting time W, with average value $E(W)$, to move to the head of the queue, and the service (transmission) time once service begins. Letting the average time delay through the queue be $E(T)$, we have

$$E(T) = E(W) + \frac{1}{\mu} \qquad (5\text{-}28)$$

$E(T)$ and $E(W)$ are the quantities of interest for us. To calculate these delays we first find the probability distribution of n, the number of frames queued for service (Fig. 5-35). The number n represents the state of the system. The Poisson arrival and departure models enable us to carry out this calculation quite readily. Recall from the definition of the Poisson process that no more than one frame (customer) can enter or leave the queueing system of Fig. 5-35 at a time. A plot of the number of frames (customers) in the queue—the state of the system—as a function of time would thus have the form of Fig. 5-36. Starting from an empty state at some arbitrary time, the queue builds up and empties randomly as customers (frames) arrive and leave. The state can change by one unit only at a time. If the queue has no constraint on its size, it can, theoretically, build up to any value. We shall see, however, that the probability of occupancy decreases exponentially (actually, geometrically) with n. Lower states are more likely to be occupied than higher states.

Consider the $M/M/1$ state diagram of Fig. 5-37. As noted above, adjacent transitions only between states can take place, due to a single arrival or depar-

---

[11][PAPO 1984] A. Papoulis, *Probability, Random Variables, and Stochastic Processes*, 2nd ed., McGraw-Hill, New York, 1984.

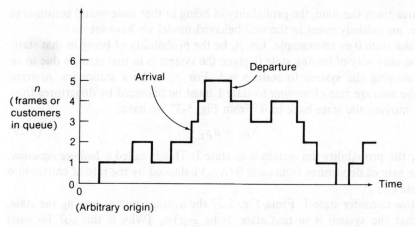

FIGURE 5-36
Random state transitions due to arrivals and departures, $M/M/1$ queue.

ture. Multiple-state transitions are ruled out because of the Poisson model used. Superimposed on the state diagram are arrival-rate transitions and departure-rate transitions, λ and μ, respectively. If the system is currently at state $n = 2$, for example, the arrival process, with average rate λ, may bring it to state $n = 3$. Alternatively, one can say that there is a probability $\lambda \, \Delta t \ll 1$ that an arrival will occur, moving the system to state $n = 3$. In contrast to an arrival, the departure (service completion) process, with average rate μ, may move the system to state $n = 1$. Equivalently, a frame (customer) may complete service with probability $\mu \, \Delta t \ll 1$, departing the queueing system, so that the system, moves to state $n = 1$.

An intuitive rate-balance argument now enables us to calculate the probability p_n that the system is in state n. Assume the system has been operating for a long time. Transitions from state to to state take place randomly, as shown in Fig. 5-36. The probability of being in a given state takes on a constant, stationary value independent of time. Each of the states in Fig. 5-37 can be assigned its probability of occupancy, $p_0, p_1, p_2, \ldots, p_{n-1}, p_n, \ldots$, with the proviso, of course, that $\sum_n p_n = 1$. For this to be true the average rate of transitions *into* any state must equal the average rate of transitions *out of* the state, given that one is in the state. (If the rate of transitions into a state were, on the average, to exceed

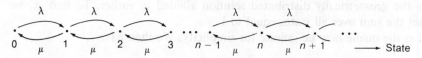

FIGURE 5-37
State diagram, $M/M/1$ queue.

departures from the state, the probability of being in that state would continue to increase, an unlikely event in the well-behaved model we have set up.)

Take state 0 as an example. Let p_0 be the probability of being in that state. Then the only way of leaving state 0, given the system is in that state, is due to an arrival moving the system to state $n = 1$. For p_0 to be a stationary, nonzero value, the average rate of moving to state 1 must be balanced by departures from state 1, moving the state back to 0. From Fig. 5-37 we have

$$\lambda p_0 = \mu p_1 \tag{5-29}$$

with p_1 the probability the system is in state 1. This is called a *balance equation*, with the rate of departures from state 0 (λp_0) balanced by the rate of entries into that state (μp_1).

Now consider state 1. From Fig. 5-37 the average rate of leaving the state, given that the system is in that state, is $(\lambda + \mu)p_1$. [Why is this so? To what state(s) can the system move?] Entry into state 1 can be from state 0, due to an arrival, or state 2, due to a departure. The average rate of entry, conditioned on being in state 0 *or* state 2, is $\lambda p_0 + \mu p_2$. [The Poisson model ensures that the probability, jointly, of both an arrival and a departure is proportional to $(\Delta t)^2$ and is hence negligible compared to the probability of one or the other.] The balance equation for this state is then given by

$$(\lambda + \mu)p_1 = \lambda p_0 + \mu p_2 \tag{5-30}$$

From (5-29) this simplifies to

$$\lambda p_1 = \mu p_2 \tag{5-31}$$

Proceeding this way, state by state, recursively, it is left to the reader to show that the balance equation for state $n - 1$ is given by

$$(\lambda + \mu)p_{n-1} = \lambda p_{n-2} + \mu p_n \qquad n \geq 2 \tag{5-32}$$

leading to the simplified balance equation

$$\lambda p_{n-1} = \mu p_n \tag{5-33}$$

Our solution for p_n, the probability of occupancy of state n, is now almost complete. From (5-33), $p_n/p_{n-1} = \lambda/\mu$. But $p_{n-1}/p_{n-2} = \lambda/\mu$ as well. Proceeding backwords recursively, until (5-29) is reached, it is left to the reader to show that

$$\frac{p_n}{p_0} = \left(\frac{\lambda}{\mu}\right)^n = \rho^n, \qquad \rho \equiv \frac{\lambda}{\mu} \tag{5-34}$$

This is the geometrically distributed solution alluded to earlier. To find p_0 we must set the sum over all states equal to 1.

Let the queue now be infinite for simplicity. We then have

$$\sum_{n=0}^{\infty} p_n = 1 \tag{5-35}$$

from which it is readily shown, taking $\rho = \lambda/\mu < 1$, that

$$p_0 = 1 - \rho \qquad (5\text{-}36)$$

and

$$p_n = (1 - \rho)\rho^n \qquad n \geq 0 \qquad (5\text{-}37)$$

The parameter $\rho \equiv \lambda/\mu$ is called the *link utilization* or *traffic intensity*. This is precisely the same parameter introduced earlier, in Sec. 5-2, in discussing the operation of the token-passing ring. [See (5-10) and (5-11).] Note again that the fixed frame length T in that case corresponds to the average frame-length paramter $1/\mu$ here. The throughput capacity of the link in this case is μ frames per unit time. To keep the queue from building up indefinitely, the load λ must be less than the capacity. The parameter ρ is the ratio of load to capacity. From (5-36) we must have $\rho < 1$ to ensure $p_0 > 0$. This is required for a stable stationary system, as assumed here. For if $\rho = 1$, with $p_0 = 0$, we have $p_1 = 0$, from (5-29). Then the probability of each state in turn becomes 0, leading to an unstable situation. A stable queue must empty occasionally, as shown in Fig. 5-36.

Equation (5-36), the geometric distribution of $M/M/1$ queue lengths, is plotted in Fig. 5-38 for the two cases of $\rho = 0.5$ and $\rho = 0.8$. An example of a system with $\rho = 0.5$ would be one with transmission capacity $\mu = 1,000$ frames/s, and load $\lambda = 500$ frames (or packets) per second, summed over arrivals from all inputs. The probability that the queue is empty is $p_0 = 1 - \rho = 0.5$. The probability that the queue has at least one frame in service and/or waiting for transmission is $1 - p_0 = \rho = 0.5$ also, in this case. The probability that there is only one frame in the system (and hence being served, i.e., undergoing transmission) is $p_1 = 0.25$. The probability that there are two frames in the queue, one

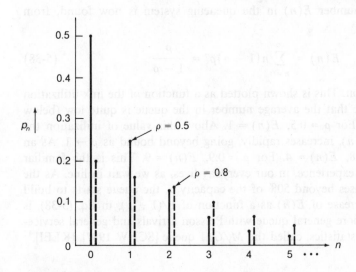

FIGURE 5-38
Probability of state, $M/M/1$ queue.

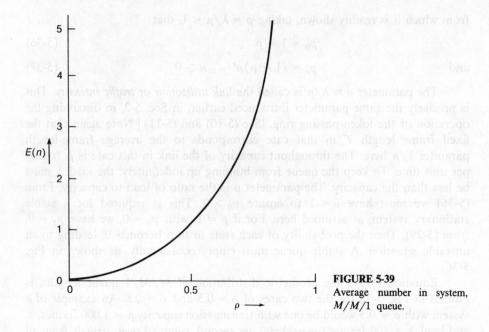

FIGURE 5-39
Average number in system, $M/M/1$ queue.

undergoing transmission, the other waiting for service, is $p_2 = 0.125$. These probabilities are shown represented by solid lines in Fig. 5-38. If the arrival rate increases to $\lambda = 800$ packets/s, in this example, ρ increases to 0.8. The probability the queue is empty drops to $p_0 = 0.2$. Higher states become more probable, i.e., the queue is more likely to have frames (customers) waiting. This case is represented by the dashed lines of Fig. 5.38.

The average number $E(n)$ in the queueing system is now found, from (5-37), to be given by

$$E(n) = \sum_{n=0}^{\infty} n(1 - \rho)\rho^n = \frac{\rho}{1 - \rho} \tag{5-38}$$

after some calculation. This is shown plotted as a function of the link utilization ρ in Fig. 5-39. Note that the average number in the queue is quite low (below one) until $\rho = 0.5$. For $\rho = 0.5$, $E(n) = 1$. Above this value of utilization the average number, $E(n)$, increases rapidly, going beyond bound as $\rho \to 1$. As an example, for $\rho = 0.8$, $E(n) = 4$. For $\rho = 0.9$, $E(n) = 9$. This is the familiar phenomenon we all experience, in our everyday lives, as we wait in line. As the traffic load λ increases beyond 50% of the capacity μ, the queue starts to build up rapidly. This increase of $E(n)$ as a function of $1/(1 - \rho)$, in Eq. (5-38), is characteristic of a more general queue with Poisson arrivals and general service-time (frame-length) statistics, called the $M/G/1$ queue [SCHW 1987], [KLEI].[12]

---

[12][KLEI] L. Kleinrock, *Queueing Systems, Volume 1: Theory*, Wiley, New York, 1975.

The $M/M/1$ model captures this important characteristic. The $M/G/1$ queue is treated briefly in one of the problems at the end of this chapter.

As an example, it may be shown that the average queue occupancy for an $M/D/1$ queue, one with fixed-length (constant-service-time) frames of length $1/\mu$, is given by

$$E(n) = \frac{\rho}{1 - \rho}\left(1 - \frac{\rho}{2}\right) \qquad \rho = \frac{\lambda}{\mu} \qquad (5\text{-}39)$$

The average occupancy is less than that of the exponentially distributed $M/M/1$ model, but note that the leading term is the $M/M/1$ result.

The average time delay $E(T)$ through the queueing system, i.e., the time $E(W)$ spent waiting for transmission plus the transmission (service) time $1/\mu$, is readily calculated from $E(n)$ by the application of the following simple formula called *Little's formula* [SCHW 1987]:

$$E(T) = \frac{E(n)}{\gamma} \qquad (5\text{-}40)$$

$E(T)$ is the average time spent in the system, $E(n)$ is the average number of customers in the system, and γ is the average throughput (customers served per unit time) of the system. This formula holds for *any* queueing system, no matter what arrival and service statistics, no matter what priority discipline, so long as the system is a *conservative* one; i.e., it serves all customers once admitted. The throughput represents the customers actually served. It is the difference between the attempted number of arrivals per unit time and those blocked or turned away for lack of room. In our case of an infinite queue, none are blocked and $\gamma = \lambda$. For a queue with blocking probability P_B and arrival rate λ, we have $\gamma = \lambda(1 - P_B)$. (Can you justify this expression?) A schematic representation of Little's formula appears in Fig. 5-40.

A finite $M/M/1$ queue, capable of holding at most N frames (customers), experiences blocking when the queue builds up to its maximum value N. Arrivals at that point are turned away. Little's formula then applies only to the net number accepted for service. We shall provide an example of the use of Little's formula in a limited-service environment in our discussion of circuit-switched blocking in Sec. 5-4 following. The finite $M/M/1$ queue is analyzed in one of the problems for this chapter.

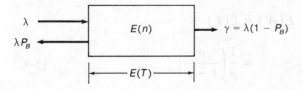

FIGURE 5-40
Environment of Little's formula.

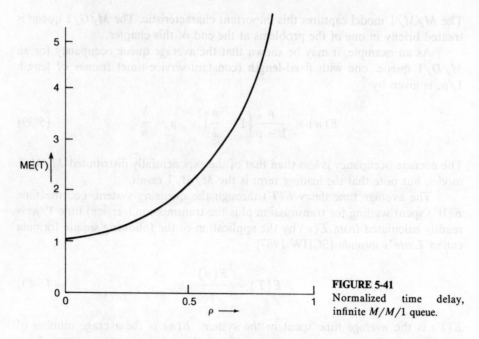

FIGURE 5-41
Normalized time delay, infinite $M/M/1$ queue.

Applying Little's formula to the infinite $M/M/1$ queue, for which $\gamma = \lambda$, we get, from (5-40) and (5-38),

$$E(T) = \frac{E(n)}{\lambda} = \frac{1}{\mu}\left(\frac{1}{1-\rho}\right) \tag{5-41}$$

(Recall that $\rho = \lambda/\mu$.) The form of (5-41) is quite instructive. For $\rho \ll 1$ (the load is much less than the capacity), a frame, once assembled, spends negligible time waiting in the queue, on the average, and its average delay is simply $1/\mu$, the time required for transmission. As the load begins to build up, the average wait time increases, and the time delay increases correspondingly. The normalized version of (5-41), $E(T)/(1/\mu) = \mu E(T)$, the time delay normalized to average transmission time, is shown plotted in Fig. 5-41. Note that the delay is $2/\mu$ at $\rho = 0.5$ and then begins to rise rapidly, following the form of $1/(1-\rho)$, as $\rho \to \infty$. As an example, if an average frame takes 1 ms (0.001 s) to be transmitted, the time delay through the queue, including transmission, will be 2 ms if $\rho = 0.5$. If ρ increases to 0.8, the delay becomes $5(1/\mu)$, or 5 ms, in this example.

Using (5-28), we can find the average waiting time $E(W)$ for the $M/M/1$ queue. This is

$$E(W) = E(T) - \frac{1}{\mu}$$

$$= \frac{1}{\mu}\left(\frac{\rho}{1-\rho}\right) \tag{5-42}$$

from (5-41). Note that except for the transmission-time factor $1/\mu$, this is identical with the equation (5-38) for $E(n)$, and explains the values for $E(T)$ shown in Fig. 5-41.

The $M/D/1$ delay and average-waiting-time expressions corresponding to those of the $M/M/1$ queue are readily found using Little's formula, (5-39), and (5-28):

$$E(T) = \frac{E(n)}{\lambda} = \frac{1}{\mu}\left(\frac{1}{1-\rho}\right)\left(1-\frac{\rho}{2}\right) \tag{5-43}$$

and

$$E(W) = E(T) - \frac{1}{\mu} = \frac{1}{2\mu}\left(\frac{\rho}{1-\rho}\right) \tag{5-44}$$

These queueing results are applied in the next two subsections to LAN performance analysis and to statistical multiplexing.

Performance of LANs

The average-time-delay equation (5-41) for the $M/M/1$ queue [and the $M/D/1$ result (5-43), if desired] enables us to interpret performance results for the token-passing and CSMA/CD access schemes. We do not derive any results here. We simply state them, as taken from the literature. The performance of a LAN is commonly defined to be the transfer time T_f required to transfer data from a source station on the LAN to a destination station [BUX].[13] This varies with the load and so is normally plotted as a function of the load. The lower the delay for a given load, the better the performance.

Consider an N-station token ring (or, equivalently, the token-passing bus) as discussed in the previous section. For this system the transfer delay T_f is found to have three components [SCHW 1987]:

$$T_f = E(T) + \frac{t_c}{2}\left(1-\frac{\rho}{N}\right) + \frac{L}{2} \tag{5-45}$$

The first term is the time delay at a station, precisely as discussed in the previous subsection. It consists of the wait time $E(W)$ plus the time to transmit the frame onto the ring. The second term is just one-half the cycle time, $t_c/2$, modified slightly by the factor $1 - \rho/N$. These two terms together constitute the access delay, the delay in getting a frame onto the ring. The ring utilization ρ is given by $\rho = \lambda/\mu = \lambda T$, in the notation used earlier in discussing the token ring. [See Eq. (5-11).] This agrees with our intuitive feeling for the performance—added to the normal queueing delay is the average time required to obtain permission to transmit. This is just $t_c/2$, one-half the cycle time, as noted in the previous section. The load or arrival rate λ is the load on the *entire* ring, the sum of the

---

[13][BUX] W. Bux, "Local-Area Subnetworks: A Performance Comparison," *IEEE Trans. Commun.*, vol. COM-29, no. 10, pp. 1465–1473, October 1981.

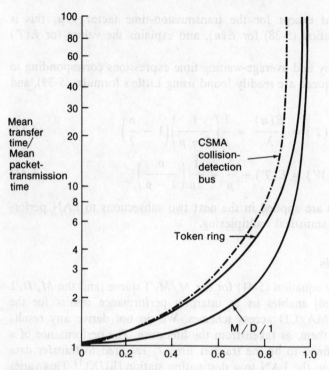

FIGURE 5-42
Transfer-delay–throughput characteristics at 1 Mbit/s (from [BUX, Fig. 8], IEEE, 1981, with permission).

traffic intensities of all the stations, since all stations contribute to the traffic on the ring and hence to the delay. The ring utilization ρ is the one used in calculating $E(T)$ as well. Since $\rho < 1$, $\rho/N \ll 1$ if there are many stations on the ring, and it may normally be neglected. Added to the access delay is the term $L/2$, one-half the latency around the ring. This is clearly the average time required for a frame to move from a transmitting station to its destination, located, on the average, one-half of the ring away.

For the special case of exponentially distributed frames we have, from (5-41),

$$T_f = \frac{1}{\mu}\frac{1}{1-\rho} + \frac{L}{2(1-\rho)}\left(1 - \frac{\rho}{N}\right) + \frac{L}{2} \qquad (5\text{-}46)$$

We have written the cycle time t_c here in terms of the ring latency L [See eq. (5-10)]. Equation (5-46), normalized to $1/\mu$, appears plotted in Fig. 5-42 for the case of a 1-Mbit/s, 2-km ring, with 50 stations connected to it. Each station is assumed to require 1 bit (1 μs) to regenerate (read in/read out) a frame as it moves around the ring. Frames are, on the average, 1,000 bits long [BUX, Fig. 8].[14] If the frames were of fixed length, the $M/D/1$ equation (5-43) would be used for $E(T)$ in (5-45), modifying that equation accordingly.

Note that Fig. 5-42 has a curve labeled "$M/D/1$." This is a plot of $E(T)/(1/\mu) = \mu E(T)$, using (5-43) directly. Why this plot? It is apparent from (5-45) that the *minimum* possible delay for the ring (or for any LAN for that matter) is the average time delay $E(T)$ due to queueing. Consider an idealized situation in which one could sense instantaneously the arrivals of packets at stations anywhere on the ring. One could tag them by time of arrival and schedule them for transmission—first in, first out—onto the common medium. This is the concept of ideal scheduling mentioned in the previous section in introducing random access and CSMA/CD performance. It was noted there that a "Maxwell demon," moving at infinite speed (zero propagation delay), would be required to carry this out. Ideal scheduling, in our current terminology, corresponds to establishing a global FIFO queue with average rate λ and transmission capacity μ. The average delay is then just the first term $E(T)$ appearing in (5-45). Given a global queue with Poisson arrivals, the *smallest* delay possible is the $M/D/1$ delay of (5-43). Any deviation from fixed frame lengths increases the average time delay $E(T)$. (One can show, for the case of an $M/G/1$ queue with general service-time distribution, that $E(T)$ increases with the variance of the distribution [SCHW 1987], [KLEI]. The constant-length frames of the $M/D/1$ queue have zero variance. The $M/G/1$, queue, as noted, is discussed in one of the problems at the end of this chapter.) This is the reason why the $M/D/1$ delay [Eq. (5-43)] is less than that of the $M/M/1$ delay [Eq. (5-41)]. The $M/D/1$ delay curve in Fig. 5-42 thus represents a bound on the lowest time delay attainable for access by competing stations onto a common medium. The difference between the token-ring delay curve and the $M/D/1$ curve represents the deterioration of performance due to the token-passing scheduling mechanism. (As noted, there is a small deterioration as well due to the assumption of the exponential distribution.)

The curve for CSMA/CD performance also appears in Fig. 5-42. This enables us to compare the CSMA/CD bus with the token ring under similar conditions. It may be shown that the transfer-delay expression for the CSMA/CD bus, assuming exponentially distributed frame lengths, is given approximately by

$$T_f \doteq \frac{1}{\mu}\frac{1}{1 - \rho(1 + 6.44a)} + \frac{\tau}{2} + \cdots \qquad (5\text{-}47)$$

τ is again the end-to-end propagation delay on the bus, and $a = \mu\tau \equiv \tau/T$, as used previously [see Eq. (5-2)]. This expression has been obtained by rewriting, in

---

[14]In the paper by Bux from which this curve is taken, the *packet* is assumed to be 1,000 bits long, exponentially distributed. A 24-bit header is added to form the frame. The frame is thus not quite exponentially distributed. Since $24 \ll 1,000$, the effect is negligible here.

a different form, an equation originally derived for the CSMA/CD bus access delay by Lam [LAM] and modified by Bux [BUX]. Bux's equation also appears in [SCHW 1987]. Note that the first term in (5-47) is our old friend the $M/M/1$ time delay, but modified in the denominator by a term involving a. The denominator expression shows that the delay increases beyond bounds at a maximum value of ρ given by

$$\rho_m = \frac{1}{1 + 6.44a}$$

This is precisely our equation (5-7), derived in the previous section using a simplified model of the collision resolution process.

The second term $\tau/2$ in (5-47) represents the time for a frame to propagate from the source to the destination station, located, on the average, one-half the bus length away. This compares with the token-ring latency term $L/2$ appearing in (5-46).

Fig. 5-42 shows how the token ring and CSMA/CD compare in average-time-delay–throughput performance, and how they both compare with the "best possible" access scheme, that corresponding to a global queue using ideal scheduling. Note that the CSMA/CD scheme performs somewhat better at low utilizations, as expected: At $\rho = 0$ the minimum transfer delay for the token ring is, from (5-46), $1/\mu + L$. (There is always a transfer delay of $1/\mu$, the transmission time of the frame, plus one-half the cycle time, plus one-half the latency around the ring.) The corresponding minimum delay for the CSMA/CD scheme is $1/\mu + \tau/2$. The propagation delay for the 2-km bus is 10 μs, using 5 μs/km as a typical propagation delay term. The term $\tau/2$ is thus 5 μs. For a 1,024-bit frame, $1/\mu = 1.024$ ms. The corresponding latency term is $L = 60$ μs for the token ring, using 1 bit (or 1 μs) of latency for each of the 50 stations and adding $\tau = 10$ μs for the round-trip propagation delay. The minimum delay is then 1.084 ms. If the latency per station is increased to 16 bits or 16 μs, L increases to 810 μs, and the minimum delay for the token ring becomes 1.81 ms. This shows the sensitivity of the token ring to latency. Increasing the number of stations increases the latency correspondingly. This does not happen with the CSMA/CD system.

At the higher utilizations the performance of the CSMA/CD bus begins to deteriorate considerably because of increased collisions. This is manifested by the denominator term in (5-47). For the example of Fig. 5-42, $a = \mu\tau \doteq 0.01$. The delay then begins to increase rapidly as the utilization approaches $\rho_m = 1/(1 + 6.44a) = 0.94$. This is borne out by the CSMA/CD curve of Fig. 5-42. The token-ring performance is dominated by the $M/M/1$ normalized time delay $\mu E(T) = 1/(1 - \rho)$ and does not rise as rapidly as that of the CSMA/CD bus.

Figure 5-43 plots the relative performance for the same systems but with the transmission capacity raised to 10 MHz. The *relative* performance $\mu E(T)$ of the token ring deteriorates somewhat at low utilization compared to that of the CSMA/CD bus, although its actual transfer delay at $\rho = 0$ is now reduced to $1/\mu + L = 115$ μs. (This shows up as $\mu T_f = 1.15$ in Fig. 5-43.) The CSMA/CD

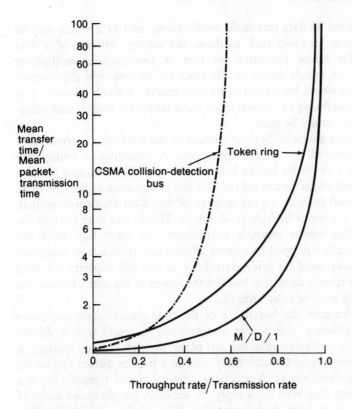

FIGURE 5-43
Transfer-delay–throughput characteristics at 10 Mbits/s (from [BUX, Fig. 9], IEEE, 1981, with permission).

performance now deteriorates as $\rho \to \rho_m \doteq 0.6$ ($a = \mu\tau = 0.1$ in this case). More detailed comparisons between the CSMA/CD and token-ring procedures appear in [BUX].

Statistical Multiplexing

In time-division multiplexing, as discussed in Chap. 3, each output time slot is assigned to one of the incoming signals. The output bit rate is then at least the sum of the incoming bit rates of all signal channels multiplexed together—it is generally run at a somewhat higher rate because of synchronization and control signals (overhead), as well as the need to accommodate expected variations in the input rates. (Recall that elastic buffering and bit stuffing were used to allow for occasional slowing down of the input bit streams.)

This may be appropriate for signals such as voice which are available for transmission most of the time, and is in fact the way digital circuit switching is carried out. It can be a wasteful and quite costly technique for bursty signals, such as those outputted by data terminals, workstations, and PCs, which may be idle much of the time. In cases such as these, the *average* bit rate of a data terminal may be far below the rated bit rate. A time-division multiplexer combining several such signals would be idle much of the time, and the communication link it drives would have most of its slots empty. A much lower-bit-rate link and/or the multiplexing of considerably more terminals than would otherwise be the case could easily be used.

Consider a simple example. Say the outputs of ten 4,800-bit/s terminals or PCs are to be multiplexed onto one outgoing line. A time-division multiplexer would probably use a 56- or 64-kbit/s link at its output. Say a human being is seated at the keyboard of each terminal (or PC) and is inputting at the rate of 60 words/min. Each word consists, on the average, of five 8-bit characters, so that, with steady typing, the input bit rate is 40 bits/s. This is less than 0.01 of the allotted bit rate. This simple example is, perhaps, not quite fair, since the terminal/PC is typically equipped to receive information from a host computer or file server that may itself be firing data back at the full capacity (or even more), so that in the reverse direction, back to the screen of the user's system, the transmission capacity may be fully utilized.

But even in this case the burstiness of the data transmission can make TDM combining inefficient. For a user almost never interacts with a distant system (the reason for multiplexing in the first place) through "steady typing." A PC does its own processing and occasionally calls on a host or distant system for some interactive communications. A user at a terminal would typically input a few lines at a time and then wait for a reply. In addition, people spend much of their time thinking, away from their terminal or PC, or otherwise leaving their system idling. Say, as an example, a user in this mode inputs two lines, a total of 20 words, in 20 s, and then waits for a reply. The host system may reply with a screenful of data at the 4,800-bit/s rate assumed here, which may require 10 s for transmission. The user then spends several minutes mulling over the reply, and may do his/her own work at the PC, or send another one- or two-line command back to the host. If we just consider the host-to-user direction, and take into account a few minutes of idle time, the 4,800-bit/s peak data rate is again reduced by a factor of 50 to 100. It is clear that much of the time the communications link is idle. The users are, however, paying for the use. This is precisely the reason for introducing statistical multiplexing.

This discussion may actually appear redundant to the reader. The reason is apparent. We have in essence described the advantage of packet switching, as compared to circuit switching, in a bursty data environment. Statistical multiplexing is one of the functions carried out by a packet switch. Figs. 5-26 and 5-35 together, providing a queueing model of a packet-switching node in a network, provide one example of the statistical multiplexing process. Statistical multiplexing is not limited to general-purpose packet switches, however. It provides an important concentration function in any data communications application in which a number of sources of bursty traffic are to be more efficiently multiplexed onto one or more communication links. Two examples appear in Fig. 5-44. In

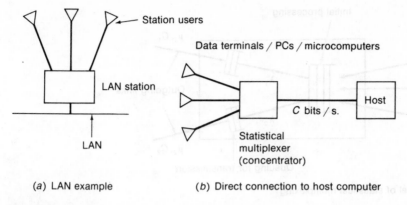

(a) LAN example (b) Direct connection to host computer

FIGURE 5-44
Examples of statistical multiplexing (in addition to Fig. 5-1).

Fig. 5-44a several users of a LAN are shown sharing a single LAN station. Blocks of data from each of the users are read into the LAN station buffer; packets and frames are formed and are then read out in some prescribed order (FIFO or other) onto the LAN, using the procedures described previously. In Fig. 5-44b several data terminals, PCs, and minicomputers are shown sharing a common transmission link to a single host computer. Statistical multiplexing would be used to more efficiently concentrate the data to and from the host. A third example would be that of a packet-switching network, exemplified by Fig. 5-1, with a given node (a packet switch) statistically multiplexing data from both external stations (users) and neighboring nodes.

In all these and other examples, the statistical multiplexing function is the same. Traffic from various sources is collected in a buffer, necessary processing of the type described earlier is carried out, individual frames are formed, and they are then transmitted out sequentially over a common outgoing link. A simplified model of this process, similar to those discussed earlier in this chapter, appears in Fig. 5-45a. Multiple outgoing links are shown, to accommodate the packet-switching network model of Fig. 5-1. (In the examples of Fig. 5-44, one outgoing link only would be required.) The transmission capacity of link i in bits/s is C_i, and in frames/s is μ_i. Two queues are shown conceptually, although in practice only one buffer might be used. The first queue represents time for processing. An example would be the LAN logical-link control and MAC sublayer functions described earlier in this chapter. In the case of a packet-switching network both data-link and network-layer (routing) functions would be carried out. (These were the functions portrayed graphically in Fig. 5-9.) As has already been noted in modeling the queueing process, both processing and wait time (waiting for frame transmission to begin) can be subsumed in one queue for simplicity, and Fig. 5-45b results. (In all of our analysis, however, we neglect processing time.) The focus here is on one of the outgoing links of Fig. 5-45a, if the statistical multioplexer has more than one outgoing link, as in the case of a packet switch.

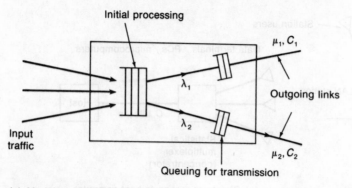

Initial processing

Input traffic

μ_1, C_1

Outgoing links

μ_2, C_2

Queuing for transmission

(a) Model of statistical multiplexing

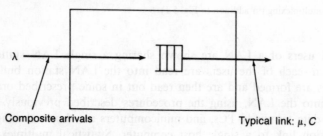

Composite arrivals

Typical link: μ, C

(b) Composite simplified model

FIGURE 5-45
Statistical multiplexing simplified.

Not shown in Fig. 5-45 is the physical-layer transmission actually required to get the bits onto the line.

It is clear, as already stated, that the statistical multiplexing process leads back directly to the queueing models discussed in the previous subsection. All that remains then is to work out some additional examples to show the effect of statistical multiplexing and its comparison with time-division multiplexing. We focus on the case of Fig. 5-44b, showing several data sources connected by a statistical multiplexer to a common host computer, since that is the one that would lend itself most directly to a comparison of statistical and time-division multiplexing. For simplicity of analysis we assume either exponentially distributed or fixed frame lengths and take the average frame lengths $(1/\mu)$ to be the same for all data sources. Allowing the frame lengths to differ by data source, although more realistic, requires the use of the $M/G/1$ model [SCHW 1987, p. 62].

Example 1. 100 PCs are each connected by a 2,400-bit/s link to a concentrator. Each transmits a message 130 octets long, on the average, once every min. The concentrator buffers these, adds a 20-octet header to each to form a frame, and transmits the frames in FIFO order to the host. If we ignore the transmission process over the local 2,400-bit/s link, and focus on the frames as they leave the concentrator, we note that the composite traffic rate over the concentrator–host link averages 100×150 octets/min., or 2,000 bits/s. (Each PC averages 20 bits/s, showing the bursty nature of the traffic process in this case.) A 4,000-bit/s concentrator–host link would provide a link utilization of $\rho = 0.5$. More realistically, one would probably select a transmission capacity of $C = 4,800$ bits/s. Then $\rho = 2,000/4,800 = 0.42$. The average transmission time for a frame is $1,200/4,800 = 0.25$ s. The inbound delay (concentrator–host direction) is, for the case of exponentially distributed frames, using (5-41),

$$E(T) = 0.25\left(\frac{1}{1 - 0.42}\right) = 0.43 \text{ s}$$

As has been pointed out a number of times, this neglects processing time at the concentrator.

The frames are processed at the host, one at a time on arrival there. Assume each frame generates a 300-octet (2,400-bit) reply from the host, including overhead. We assume *full duplex* transmission is used. In this common mode of transmission, the transmission link transmits in both directions simultaneously. The modems described in Chap. 3 were implicitly assumed to operate in this manner. (Separate cables, wires, or paths can be used for this purpose. Alternatively, different frequencies may be assigned, one for each direction, or a link operating at twice the bit rate, 9,600 bits/s in this example, could be used, transmitting half the time in one direction, half the time in the other.) The outbound traffic, from the host computer to the concentrator, must be queued up at the host for FIFO transmission back to the concentrator. It is left to the reader to show that the average return delay is

$$E(T) = 0.5\left(\frac{1}{1 - 0.84}\right) = 3.13 \text{ s}$$

(We have again ignored processing time, this time at the host.) The outbound direction clearly dominates in delay, because of the assumption that the average reply is twice the length of the inquiry. This is clearly about the limit of what the 4,800-bit/s link can handle. If the host replies were to become longer, in this example, a higher-bit-rate link would have to be used.

Consider the TDM alternative to statistical multiplexing. A TDM combining all 100 PCs would require a 240-kbit/s transmission rate in either direction. The major delays entailed, again neglecting processing time at the host, would be the single transmission delays, in either direction, required to transmit the inbound and outbound messages over the 2,400-bit/s links. (These time delays are of course also present in the statistical-multiplexer case.)

Example 2. 50 data terminals, 50 PCs, and 25 minicomputers are all connected to a host computer via a concentrator. A full-duplex 56-kbit/s link connects the concentrator and host system. Each terminal inputs a block of data once every 10 min, on the average; each PC generates a block of data for the host once every 5 min, on the average; each minicomputer transmits a block once every 2 min, on the average. Each block of data is transmitted as a constant-length frame 12,000 bits long. Replies from the host are exponentially distributed in length, with average length 12,000 bits, as assembled, including control fields.

The composite traffic load at the concentrator is

$$\lambda = 50\frac{12,000}{600} + 50\frac{12,000}{300} + 25\frac{12,000}{120}$$

$$= 5,500 \text{ bits/s}$$

The average traffic load outbound, from the host back to the concentrator, is the same. This is a light load for the 56-kbit/s link. The link utilization in either direction is $\rho = 5,500/56,000 = 0.092$. The average time delay in the concentrator, inbound, is

$$E(T) = \frac{1}{\mu}\frac{1}{1-\rho}\left(1 - \frac{\rho}{2}\right) = 0.214\frac{1}{0.908}(1 - 0.046) = 0.22 \text{ s}$$

The average delay in the host queue, outbound, is

$$E(T) = \frac{1}{\mu}\frac{1}{1-\rho} = 0.2.4\frac{1}{0.908} = 0.24 \text{ s}$$

Because the utilization is so low, both $M/M/1$ and $M/D/1$ analyses give similar results. In addition, there is a transmission delay incurred by each system in getting its data into and out of the concentrator. This depends on the local link bit rates and would be the same for either statistical or time-division multiplexing.

What concentrator–host link speed would be required if straight TDM were used in place of statistical multiplexing? This depends of course on the output bit rates of each of the devices themselves. As simple examples, say the PCs are connected via 2,400-bit/s lines, the terminals via 4,800-bit/s lines, and the minicomputers via 19.2-kbit/s lines. (Modems would probably be used in all cases.) The total transmission capacity of the concentrator–host link would then have to be at least 50(4,800) + 50(2,400) + 25(19,200) = 840 kbits/s. A T1 connection would probably be required in this case. This again demonstrates the advantage of statistical multiplexing when combining bursty data sources. (We have deliberately left out comparative cost calculations between using statistical and time-division multiplexing. This depends on comparative costs at the time of calculation for the various devices and transmission links used, and may change dramatically as new systems come on the market, or line costs change. A stab at such a comparative calculation appears in [SCHW 1977, pp. 344–347].)

5-4 AN INTRODUCTION TO CIRCUIT SWITCHING

The discussion in the past two sections has been devoted exclusively to packet switching. We now turn to circuit switching, the other principal mode of connecting user stations for communications through a network. This technique is of course historically the older technique, underlying almost all telephone voice communications worldwide.

Recall from Sec. 5-1 that in this technique a dedicated connection end to end is established between users desiring to communicate with one another. This

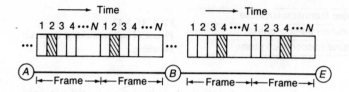

FIGURE 5-46
A TDM circuit (connection) on path 1, Fig. 5-1.

connection is said to constitute a call. As noted in Sec. 5-1, the connection consists of one or more dedicated channels (or *trunks*) on each link in the path over which the connection is made. A channel on a link can be a frequency band in the case of FDM or a time slot in the case of TDM. Time-division multiplexing is the more recently developed technique, the one most appropriate to digital communications, and the one on which we focus.

Referring back to Fig. 5-1, our basic example of a network, consider path 1, which consists of concatenated links $A-B$ and $B-E$. Say that each link carries a repetitive set of TDM frames, each holding N time slots, as shown in Fig. 5-2. A circuit in a circuit-switched connection would be allocated one or more of the time slots on each of the links, and would hold that time slot so long as the connection were maintained. As an example, say T1 lines are used. Each channel then consists of an 8-bit slot, repeating at 125-μs intervals. This is the DS0 64-kbit/s channel mentioned in Chap. 3. $N = 24$ channels constitute the link. A 128-kbit/s connection would require two such channels. Figure 5-46 shows a connection on path 1 in Fig. 5-1, using channel 2 on link $A-B$ and channel 4 on link $B-E$. These channel assignments would be maintained throughout the duration of the call.[15] This is to be compared with Fig. 5-3, which shows packets flowing over a virtual-circuit packet-switched network. (Note again that packets may use the basic TDM mode of transmission as well. The difference is that a packet does not have a dedicated slot in a TDM frame. It queues up for transmission and is sent out over the first available slot, or set of slots, if more than one is necessary, when its turn comes for transmission. On completion of transmission the next packet ready for transmission again uses the first available slot or slots for transmission. Packets—actually the data-link frames described in previous sections—must thus carry their own identification, as shown in Figs. 5-4 and 5-5. A circuit assigned to a slot does not need to be identified. The slot assignment carries the identification.)

---

[15] We disregard, in this introductory treatment, the possibility of rearranging channel assignments, if necessary, to accommodate added traffic. An example is DSI, digital speech interpolation, mentioned in Sec. 4-13, in which connections lose their channel assignment during a speech silence interval. The appearance to the users must still be that of a dedicated channel.

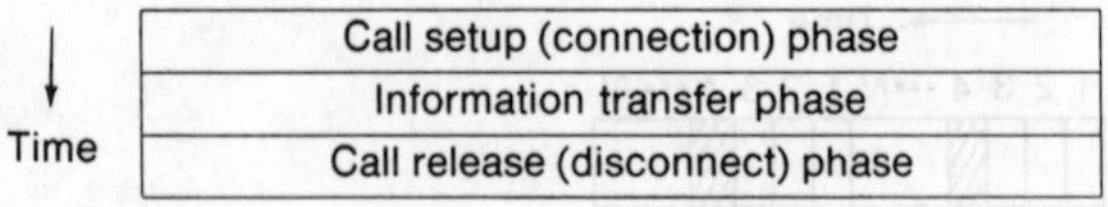

	Call setup (connection) phase
Time	Information transfer phase
	Call release (disconnect) phase

FIGURE 5-47
Phases of communication in circuit switching.

It is apparent from our discussion of statistical multiplexing in the previous section that circuit switching is a technique most appropriate to long streams of uninterrupted data transmission. The oldest example is of course voice, although with newer technologies, integrating voice and data on one common network, it may become cost-effective to transmit voice in packet form as well. Long file transfers and other types of *nonbursty* data transmission may lend themselves to circuit switching. Facsimile transmission and some types of digital video provide other examples, although packet-switched technology could be used in these cases as well.

Since channels (trunks) on end-to-end paths in circuit-switched networks are dedicated to particular calls, there must be a connection, or call-setup, phase to establish a connection before information transfer can begin. Once the call is completed, the connection must be released. These three phases of communication are diagrammed in Fig. 5-47. (Note that connection-oriented packet switching requires the same three phases of communication.) Network signals must be sent to nodes along the path selected in the process of establishing and later releasing the connection, or connections, if more than two users participate in a call.

In Fig. 5-48 we provide an example of the signals used in setting up, and later tearing down, a call in the simplest of situations, the ordinary telephone call with which we are all familiar. This is colloquially labeled a POTS call ("plain, ordinary telephone service"). Path 1 in Fig. 5-1 is again used as an illustration. In the telephone field the "nodes" in the network are generically called switching offices or exchanges and are so labeled in Fig. 5-48. Signals are indicated by arrows with labels attached.

We are all familiar with the signals between us and the local exchange (also called an end office) to which our telephones or data terminals are connected. The calling party (source) desiring to establish the call sends a *connect* signal for this purpose to the local exchange. In a POTS call this is done by taking the telephone off hook. The local exchange replies with a *dial tone*, asking the calling party to send the called party (destination) identification (telephone number). This is of course done by inputting the appropriate digits (via dial or Touch-Tone telephone). In a more complex, automated situation the initial connect message from user to exchange could of course include the destination id (address), as well as other parameters indicating the type of call desired. (Is this call to be a multiparty conference call, does it require secure facilities, what capacity—bit rate or bandwidth—is required during the information transfer phase, etc.?) In current telephone systems the dial tone may be delayed to provide a congestion control mechanism in the event of heavy traffic at the exchange or in the network [SCHW 1987, Sec. 11-3].

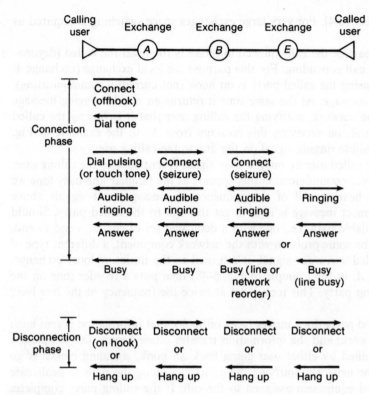

FIGURE 5-48
Examples of control signals, POTS call.

On receiving the destination id the local exchange computer system will select the appropriate path through the network to the exchange to which the called party is connected, dedicate a channel (trunk) on the link connecting it to the next node (exchange) along the path selected, and send a special *connect* message (also called a *seizure* message) to that node. This is shown in Fig. 5-48 as a connect message moving from local exchange *A* to exchange *B*, the next node on the path selected. Node *B* in this case is called a *tandem* exchange. (Exchanges may be local only; tandem only, handling calls arriving from other exchanges only; or local/tandem, connecting both to user telephones and systems, as well as to other exchanges.) Exchange *B* repeats the process, selecting a suitable channel on its link to exchange *E* along the appropriate path, and then sending a connect (seizure) message to exchange *E*. After each exchange has selected the appropriate outgoing trunk for this call, it dedicates a path through a switch at the exchange that will connect the specific incoming trunk with the outgoing one, once information transfer begins. Modern switching systems carry out time-slot interchange operations, switching the information (bits) in the specific incoming time slot to the appropriate outgoing one. Details appear in

[SCHW 1987, Sec. 10-4]. For very large exchanges space switching is required as well.

The final part of the call-connection phase is to signal the called (destination) user that a call is pending. For this purpose the local exchange (exchange E in Fig. 5-47), sensing the called party is on hook (not currently communicating), sends a *ringing* message. At the same time it returns an *audible ringing* message back through the network, notifying the calling user that it is ringing the called party. Exchange A, on receiving this message from E, in the example of Fig. 5-48, puts an audible ringing signal on the line to the calling user.

Should the called user be busy, a *busy* signal is sent back to the calling user. In the case of voice communication this appears as the familiar line-busy tone we are all used to hearing. All of this sequence of messages and signals above assumes the connect message is able to get through to the called party. Should there be no available path, i.e., one with a dedicated set of channels end to end, or should there be some problem with the network equipment, a different type of busy signal, called a *reorder* signal, is returned to the initiating local exchange. This exchange (A, in the example of Fig. 5-48) then puts a reorder tone on the line to the calling party. This tone is set at twice the frequency of the line busy tone.

If the called party does answer (goes offhook), that information is sent back through the network, and the information transfer phase begins. On completion of the call, signified by either user going back on hook, signaling messages go back through the network, notifying the exchanges along the path to deallocate the channels and equipment assigned to the call. If the calling party completes the call, a *disconnect* message is sent. If the called party terminates, a *hangup* message is sent.

How are these various control messages actually sent? In older equipment *inband signaling* is used. In this case the channels selected for the call are used to transmit the control signals. More recently, with the advent of digital telephony, the CCITT has adopted a technique called *common-channel signaling* to transmit call control signals. It is also called *out-of-band* signaling. This technique uses a separate packet-switched signaling network to handle control signals. This network may be physically different than the circuit-switched network it serves, or it may use separate portions of the same network (for example, dedicated time slots on a link between exchanges). In either case it is *logically* separate. The CCITT common-channel signaling system incorporates a layered set of protocols conforming to the OSI Reference Model, and is called the CCITT common-channel signaling (CCS) system no. 7. Message formats are defined for handling the various signals of Fig. 5-48, as well as others not appearing there [SCHW 1987, Sec. 12-2]. System no. 7 has been designed for use with both national and international traffic, for local and long-distance networks. A conceptual model of a CCS network, showing how it is associated with the circuit-switched network it serves, appears in Fig. 5-49. The packet switches of the CCS network are called signal transfer points (STPs). They may be colocated at circuit-switching exchanges, or may be connected to them via dedicated links.

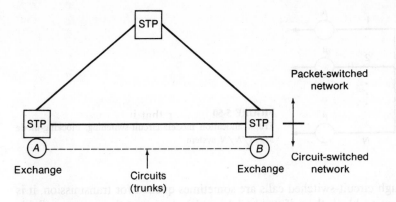

FIGURE 5-49
The CCS concept.

Although designed to handle the control signals of the circuit-switched network (for example, the signals between exchanges in the POTs scenario of Fig. 5-48), a CCS network may be used for other purposes as well. It may be used for network management, for database access and management, and for a whole variety of transaction-type services not necessarily related to the call connection/disconnection process of Fig. 5-48. Examples include the well-known 800 service, calling-card service (using a credit card to make a call without operator assistance), credit-call validation for shopping, etc. A CCS network could be used as a standalone packet-switched network, carrying packet-switched data between data end-users, in addition to its function as a network for carrying the circuit-switched network trunk signals. The combination of circuit-switching network and packet-switching CCS network brings us closer to the day of fully integrated networks, carrying all types of digital traffic, voice, video, or data, ubiquitously to the user. As noted earlier, these integrated networks providing services for all types of users and traffic are called *integrated-services digital networks* (ISDN).

Performance Issues in Circuit Switching: Blocking-Probability Calculations

In Sec. 5-3, previously, in discussing the performance of packet-switching networks, we focused on time delay, since packets arriving at a node or switch are normally queued for transmission. The analysis of the $M/M/1$ queue enabled us to quantify the delay due to queueing. We applied the queueing analysis to a discussion of the comparative performance of CSMA/CD and token-ring LANs, as well as to some example calculations of the time-delay performance of statistical multiplexers.

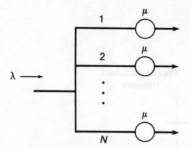

FIGURE 5-50
Trunk allocation model: circuit-switching, blocking-mode $M/M/N/N$ system.

Although circuit-switched calls are sometimes queued for transmission, it is more common to block them if trunks (channels) along a path are not available to handle them. The performance of a circuit-switched system, or *grade of service* as it is sometimes called, is then rated in terms of the blocking probability—the probability an incoming call will find all trunks occupied. We carry out calculations of this quantity in this section. As in the case of packet-switching performance we focus on one node (exchange) only. (Strictly speaking, one should calculate the probability an incoming call will not find a set of channels available along the entire end-to-end path along which it is to be routed. In the case of packet switching one should add the delays along an entire rate, end to end, to determine the delay performance.) Our analysis proceeds as follows.

Say a given outgoing link at an exchange has N channels or trunks available for information transfer. An example would be the TDM link of Fig. 5-2. We assume the call, once allocated a trunk, will hold it for a time long compared to the TDM frame length. This time is termed the call *holding time*. As an example, let the TDM frame length be 125 us, while the average length of the call is 100 s.[16] The ratio of the two is approximately 10^6, clearly a very large number. The discrete-time structure of the TDM frame may thus be ignored in carrying out the analysis. The N slots of the TDM frame then correspond to N parallel servers in the queueing system. (This is the same assumption made in developing the continuous-time $M/M/1$ queueing model for the packet-switched traffic in Sec. 5-3.) Let the holding time be exponentially distributed, with average length in time $1/\mu$. Say calls arrive at this outgoing link obeying Poisson statistics with average arrival rate λ. Since there is, by hypothesis, no queueing allowable in this simplified analysis, a call is blocked if all N channels (or servers) are occupied. Figure 5-50 portrays this model pictorially. This is to be compared with the $M/M/1$, single-server queueing model of Fig. 5-35. The holding time here is comparable to the service time there. Here there are N servers in parallel, as

---

[16]The holding time actually begins at the time the trunk is allocated to the call during the call establishment phase and ends with the disconnect phase. This corresponds to the time between sending the connect signal in Fig. 5-48 and sending the disconnect signal. For long call lengths the setup and disconnect times may be neglected.

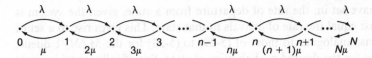

FIGURE 5-51
State diagram, $M/M/N/N$ system.

noted; the $M/M/1$ model has one server. The structure of Fig. 5-50 is called an $M/M/N/N$ system. It is also called an N-server queueing system with no waiting room. (Since there is no queueing, that word is actually extraneous.) The second N means that the system will hold a maximum of N calls (customers in the more general queueing terminology), all in service, none waiting. Calls arriving when all N servers are occupied are turned away, or *blocked*. It is the probability of this event that we would like to calculate. The assumption of exponential holding (service) time for a call means that departures from each of the trunks (servers) in Fig. 5-50, if occupied, obey a Poisson departure process: there is a probability $\mu \, \Delta t \ll 1$ that a call in progress will complete and depart the system.

One proceeds in a manner similar to that described in Sec. 5-3 in analyzing the $M/M/1$ queue. The assumption of Poisson arrivals and exponential service-time (holding-time) distribution makes this possible. Let n again represent the state of the system. In this case it represents the number of trunks (servers) occupied, or calls in progress. Clearly, from the model, we have $0 \leq n \leq N$. The state diagram of the system is then finite and is represented as in Fig. 5-51. This diagram is similar to that of Fig. 5-37 except for one critical difference. There only one server operated and the chance of a service completion in time $(t, t + \Delta t)$ was $\mu \, \Delta t \ll 1$, from the exponential service time—Poisson departure event duality. Here, with n servers occupied if n calls are in progress, the probability of one service completion in the small time interval $(t, t + \Delta t)$ is $n\mu \, \Delta t \ll 1$, i.e., it is n times as likely. The probability of no completion is $1 - n\mu\Delta t$. The reason for this is that with the Poisson departure model for each of the trunks, departures (call completions) are independent from trunk to trunk. The chance of more than one call completing in time $(t, t + \Delta t)$ is negligibly small, but there are n ways in which one call can complete, increasing the chance of completion by the factor n. If the system is in state 2, with two calls in progress, there is a probability $2\mu \, \Delta t$ of a service completion in $(t, t + \Delta t)$. The corresponding *rate* of completions, if in this state, is 2μ. Similar remarks pertain to all states n, $1 \leq n \leq N$. The rate of completion of one call at state n is thus $n\mu$, the system dropping to state $n - 1$ after a call completion. As in the case of the $M/M/1$ model, a call arriving with the system in any state $n < N$ will raise the state to $n + 1$. The probability of an arrival at time $(t, t + \Delta t)$ is $\lambda \, \Delta t \ll 1$, and the rate of moving up one state is λ.

As in the case of the $M/M/1$ queue, we can find the stationary (equilibrium) probability p_n that the system is in state n by a balance argument: For equilibrium to have set in, the rate of departure from a state, given the system is in that state, must equal the rate of arrivals to that state. This gives rise to a set of balance equations, analogous to those of (5-29) to (5-33) for the $M/M/1$ queue, that we can solve for the desired probabilities of state. Specifically, consider state p_0. From Fig. 5-51, and by analogy with (5-29), we must have

$$\lambda p_0 = \mu p_1 \tag{5-48}$$

The left-hand side is the rate of leaving state $n = 0$, given the system is in state 0. The right-hand side is the rate of entering state $n = 0$, given the system is in state $n = 1$. Proceeding state by state, as in the $M/M/1$ case, we have

$$(\lambda + \mu) p_1 = \lambda p_0 + 2\mu p_2 \tag{5-49}$$

This now differs from (5-30) for the $M/M/1$ queue because of the increased chance of a departure when the system is in state $n = 2$. Combining (5-48) and (5-49), we now have

$$\lambda p_1 = 2\mu p_2 \tag{5-50}$$

Continuing, we write, as the balance equation for state $n = 2$ (see Fig. 5-51),

$$(\lambda + 2\mu) p_2 = \lambda p_1 + 3\mu p_3 \tag{5-51}$$

Using (5-50), this simplifies to

$$\lambda p_2 = 3\mu p_3 \tag{5-52}$$

The pattern is apparent. It is left to the reader to show that the general equation relating probabilities for states $n - 1$ and n is

$$\lambda p_{n-1} = n\mu p_n \quad 1 \le n \le N \tag{5-53}$$

From this equation it is readily shown that

$$\frac{p_n}{p_0} = \frac{(\lambda/\mu)^n}{n!}$$

$$= \frac{A^n}{n!} \quad A \equiv \frac{\lambda}{\mu} \tag{5-54}$$

(We use the symbol A rather than the ρ used previously. The arrival rate λ is the total arrival rate destined for all N servers. This will be made clearer shortly.) To complete the solution, we find p_n by invoking the normalization condition

$$\sum_{n=0}^{N} p_n = 1 \tag{5-55}$$

Note that this differs from the infinite-queue $M/M/1$ case studied earlier because of the finite number of states. (The finite $M/M/1$ queue, holding at most N customers in a buffer, requires the same normalization condition for its analysis. The analysis for that queue appears in a problem at the end of this chapter.) From (5-54) and (5-55) it is readily shown that

$$p_n = \frac{A^n/n!}{\sum_{l=0}^{N} A^l/l!} \qquad A \equiv \frac{\lambda}{\mu} \qquad (5\text{-}56)$$

In particular, the blocking probability P_B is found by setting $n = N$:

$$P_B = p_N = \frac{A^N/N!}{\sum_{l=0}^{N} A^l/l!} \qquad A \equiv \frac{\lambda}{\mu} \qquad (5\text{-}57)$$

This formula for the blocking probability of an N-trunk system with Poisson arrivals is called the *Erlang loss formula* or Erlang-B formula, after the great Danish engineer A. K. Erlang, who pioneered in quantifying telephone-traffic engineering in the early part of the 20th century.

The parameter $A = \lambda/\mu$, whose units are *erlangs*, is a measure of the total load on the N-trunk link. The per-trunk utilization ρ, comparable to the ρ introduced in the $M/M/1$ analysis, is defined as $\rho \equiv A/N = \lambda/N\mu$. A is often called the *offered load* of the N-trunk system. This is really the *normalized* offered load, normalized to the trunk capacity μ, since λ, the average arrival rate, is the actual offered load, in calls per unit time. Say, as an example, that a call arrives, on the average, once every 10 s. The holding time is $1/\mu = 100$ s, on the average. The Erlang load on the system is then $A = \lambda/\mu = 10$ erlangs. If there are $N = 10$ output trunks available for the calls, the per-trunk utilization is then $\rho = A/N = 1$. One would expect the blocking probability in this case to be high. If the number of trunks is doubled to $N = 20$, $\rho = 0.5$ for the same Erlang load. The blocking probability should then be relatively low. This is in fact found to be the case. Unlike the infinite-buffer $M/M/1$ queue discussed in Sec. 5-3, where $\rho < 1$ was the condition for a stable queue, ρ can have any value here. This is true for any finite-buffer system. (The finite $M/M/1$ queue discussed in the problems can have any value of ρ.) As ρ increases, the queue fills up more often; customers are blocked or turned away, just as in the case here. But as ρ approaches 1, with the per-trunk load λ/N equaling the trunk service rate μ, blocking is found to increase rapidly.

Some example blocking-probability curves, for blocking probabilities less than 10 percent, obtained using (5-57), appear in Fig. 5-52. A blocking probability (grade of service) $P_B \leq 5$ percent is a typical design figure in most circuit-switched telephone networks. From Fig. 5-52 one can determine the appropriate link trunk size N for a given Erlang load. Consider the example just mentioned with $A = 10$ erlangs. From Fig. 5-52, it is clear that a system with $N = 20$ trunks provides very good performance ($P_B = 0.25$ percent), while $N = 10$ trunks produces a blocking probability far in excess of 10 percent. For this case $N = 15$ trunks would result in a blocking probability $P_B = 4$ percent.

Say the load now increases to $A = 20$ erlangs. This could be due to the holding time $1/\mu$ doubling to 200 s (note how critical customer behavior is to the operation of the telephone system), or to the arrival rate λ doubling from one call per 10 s, on the average, to one call per 5 s, on the average. For twenty trunks P_B

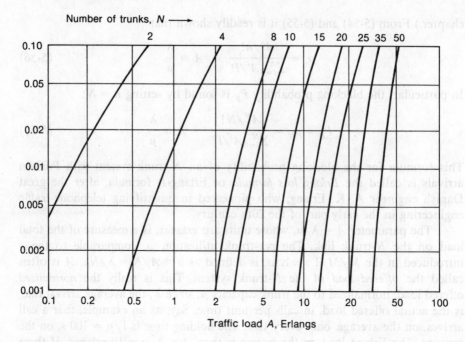

FIGURE 5-52
Erlang blocking probability.

increases from the prior value of 0.25 percent to a value in excess of 10 percent. Twenty-five trunks would now be required to bring the blocking probability to a tolerable value of 5 percent. The blocking probability P_B is very sensitive to changes in the Erlang load A for $P_B < 10$ percent.

Calculations using (5-57) are cumbersome for large N and A. The following simple recursive relation may be used to more readily determine P_B for various values of A and N:

$$\frac{1}{P_B(N)} = 1 + \frac{N}{AP_B(N-1)} \qquad P_B(0) = 1 \qquad (5\text{-}58)$$

It is left to the reader to derive this expression from (5-57).

Various parameters of interest may be found from the $M/M/N/N$ probability of state p_n, given by (5-56), and the blocking probability P_B of (5-57). For example, the average number of calls in progress is just the average number of trunks occupied, $E(n)$. From (5-56) this is given by

$$E(n) = \sum_{n=0}^{N} np_n = A(1 - P_B) \qquad (5\text{-}59)$$

after some simple manipulations, and using (5-55) and (5-57). Details are left to the reader.

As a check, let the offered load A get very large. Then clearly P_B must approach 1. From (5-57),

$$1 - P_B = \sum_{l=0}^{N-1} \frac{A^l}{l!} \bigg/ \sum_{l=0}^{N} \frac{A^l}{l!} \tag{5-60}$$

As $A \to \infty$, we have $1 - P_B \to N/A$. Then from (5-59), $E(n) \to N$. The implication is clear: For a very large offered load, the N trunks are, on the average, always occupied. More specifically, we have $p_N = P_B \to 1 - N/A$, $A \to \infty$. Hence the N trunks are fully occupied with a probability approaching 1.

What is the throughput or carried load, in calls per unit time, of the N-trunk system? Call this γ. Note from Fig. 5-40 that this is just

$$\gamma = \lambda(1 - P_B) \tag{5-61}$$

One could thus use the Erlang-B curves of Fig. 5-52, Eq. (5-58), or Eq. (5-60) to calculate the throughput. For very small blocking probability the throughput is just the offered load, in calls per unit time. As the load increases, the blocking probability P_B increases and more calls are turned away. Consider the example introduced earlier. We had $\lambda = 1$ call/(10 s), on the average. With the average holding time $1/\mu = 100$ s, $A = \lambda/\mu = 10$ erlangs. If $N = 20$ trunks are used, $P_B = 0.25$ percent, and the throughput is effectively 1 call/(10 s). If $N = 15$ trunks are used, $P_B = 4$ percent, and the throughput is now 96 percent of the load. For $P_B \leq 5$ percent, the throughput is at least 95 percent of the load.

Equation (5-61) for the throughput of any blocking system leads to a very interesting result for the $M/M/N/N$ model of the N-trunk circuit-switched system under discussion here. Normalizing the throughput γ to the per-trunk capacity μ, we have

$$\frac{\gamma}{\mu} = A(1 - P_B) = E(n) \tag{5-62}$$

from (5-59). But this is to be expected. Each trunk contributes a potential capacity of μ calls per unit time. If $E(n)$ trunks are occupied, on the average, the throughput is just $\gamma = E(n)\mu$. In particular, as the offered load λ increases, increasing the normalized offered load A correspondingly, more blocking takes place, and the throughput or *carried* load saturates at the maximum capacity of N trunks, $N\mu$. This is the maximum load the system can carry.

Equation (5-62) agrees with Little's formula as well. Recall from (5-40) that this formula provides a simple relation connecting *carried* load or throughput, average number in the system, and time delay through the system. Applying this to the $M/M/N/N$ system under discussion here, we have

$$E(T) = \frac{E(n)}{\gamma} = \frac{1}{\mu} \tag{5-63}$$

from (5-40) and (5-62). This is of course in agreement with our intuition. From the model, Fig. 5-50, of the system with no queueing (no waiting room), calls once admitted get served immediately. There is no waiting time, and the total time delay T is just the average service time, or holding time, $1/\mu$.

5-5 SUMMARY

This chapter, introducing network concepts into the discussion of communication systems, has clearly been quite different from those preceding. Except for our introduction to the book in Chap. 1, in which we introduced the concept of networks quite briefly, the material covered prior to this chapter has focused on point-to-point communications, or, in layered-network terminology, the physical layer. But, as noted both in Chap. 1 and in Sec. 5-1 of this chapter, the bulk of communications worldwide is actually carried out over networks of various types.

No network can exist without physical connections between nodal switches. Hence it is vitally important to discuss means of transmitting information between nodes (stations or exchanges) in a network. Physical-layer transmission can be carried out using baseband techniques, described both in Chap. 3 and in our discussion of LANs in Sec. 5-2 of this chapter. More commonly, for wider-area communications, modulation techniques described in Chap. 4 are used. But it is equally important to note that getting bits, or signals in general, across a link in a network is not sufficient to ensure communications is correct and understandable. Messages comprising sequences of bits in the case of digital communications have to be correctly synchronized. Errors have to be detected, and eventually corrected. Messages must be routed to the correct destination in a network, and, if transmitted as blocks (packets), delivered in the correct sequence. They must be eventually delivered to the correct end user in the correct format and in the form in which they can be correctly interpreted and understood.

All of these design questions represent networking issues and give rise, for their solution, to the concept of layered-network architectures and protocols, operating at each layer, designed to have peers at a given layer communicate correctly with one another. Accordingly, in this chapter, after distinguishing in more detail between circuit and packet switching, we focused, in Sec. 5-2, on packet-switched LANs, which make use of a portion of the data-link layer above the physical layer. In particular, using the IEEE 802 standards notation (which conforms as well with the 7-layer ISO OSI Reference Model), we focused on the medium-access (MAC) layer, which receives primitives carrying data in the form of packets from the logical link layer above and delivers the information in the form of frames to the physical layer for transmission, bit by bit, over the physical medium.

We noted that the MAC layer adds control information to the packet to form the frame (not to be confused with the TDM frame). These control fields carry synchronizing, address, and error-detection information, to be used by the receiving MAC layer in correctly interpreting a received frame. We discussed, in this context, the IEEE 802 standards on CSMA/CD and token-passing LANs. We also discussed, briefly, the much higher-bit-rate FDDI token-passing ring.

In Sec. 5-3 we turned to performance issues in networking, introducing queueing analysis as an important tool toward this end. We focused principally on the $M/M/1$ queue, with Poisson arrivals and exponential packet lengths. This enabled us to determine the delay in passing through a queue. This material was then used in comparing the time-delay–throughput performance of the CSMA/CD bus and the token-passing ring. A discussion of statistical multiplexing, as contrasted to synchronous TDM, concluded the performance section. In Sec. 5-4 we moved on to circuit switching, describing that technology in more detail, and providing an example, in terms of a POTS application, of how circuits (calls) are set up or connected. We concluded that section with an introduction to circuit-switched traffic engineering, deriving the Erlang-B blocking formula and providing examples of its use and application.

This concludes our discussion of networking issues in this book. Readers desiring more information on this subject are referred to books and papers cited in this chapter, as well as to references contained in them.

In the next two chapters we return to point-to-point (physical-layer) communications, describing the problem of errors introduced during transmission and means utilized to correct these. In the case of light-wave (fiber-optic) communication, limitations on transmission turn out to be due to statistical fluctuations in the photon arrivals themselves. These are modeled as due to Poisson statistics. At lower radio frequencies, used in terrestrial microwave systems—for example, satellite and space communications—noise encountered during transmission provides the limiting factor on correct (error-free) reception of signals. Noise modeling and the analysis of point-to-point communication systems in the presence of noise are discussed in detail in Chap. 6 following. In Chap. 7 optimum receiver structures for minimizing errors due to noise, as well as modern coding techniques for correcting errors due to noise, are discussed in detail.

PROBLEMS

5-1. Refer to Fig. 5-1, and suppose 51.2-Mbit/s links are used. A TDM frame structure is imposed on each link. A frame is 1.25 ms long and consists of 800 slots. Eight of the slots are used for framing and control information; the others are used for transmitting user data.

    (*a*) How many bits are allocated to each slot? What is the bit rate of a *circuit-switched* channel assigned to a slot? How many such channels are available?

    (*b*) The network is to be used for handling circuit-switched video. Each video channel requires a transmission rate of 1.536 Mbits/s. How many slots per frame are required for a channel? How many such channels can a link handle?

    (*c*) The network is designed to handle both circuit-switched and packet-switched traffic. For this purpose $\frac{1}{3}$ of the data slots are allocated to circuit-switched traffic; $\frac{2}{3}$ to packets. Five 1.536-Mbit/s video channels are to be accommodated in the circuit-switched portion; the remainder of that portion is allocated to 64-kbit/s voice. How many voice channels are available?

(*d*) Continuing with part (*c*), focus on the packet-switched portion. Packets vary in length, but are 8000 bits long, on the average.

    (1) Packets are transmitted at the full bit rate available to them. What is this rate? How long does it take to transmit a typical (average) packet? How many slots in a frame are required? How many packets per frame can be transmitted, on the average? What is the average capacity of a link, in packets/s?

    (2) Packets are transmitted at a rate of 1.536 Mbits/s. How many slots per frame are required per packet? [How does this result compare with that of the video channels in (*b*) above?] How many frames are required, on the average, to transmit a packet? Show that it requires 5.2 ms on the average to transmit a packet. What is the maximum number of packets that may be handled at the same time? [Note how this differs from (1) above, where only one packet at a time is transmitted.]

5-2. In describing HDLC the text makes the point that positive acknowledgements (acks) plus a timeout procedure "ensure a foolproof error-correction process."

    (*a*) The timeout interval is normally chosen to be somewhat greater than the round-trip delay, the time for a frame to propagate to the other end of the link and for a positive ack to be returned to the transmitting node. This time can sometimes be difficult to estimate. Will the procedure work if the timeout is chosen too short, so that the timeout interval expires before receipt of the positive ack? What if the interval is considerably longer than the round-trip delay? Explain your results. What is the effect of the poor choice of timeout in each case? Note that frames are numbered in sequence.

    (*b*) A negative ack can be sent back on receipt of an incorrect frame (one in error or one received out of sequence, for example). If both positive and negative acks are used, is the timeout procedure still necessary? Explain.

5-3. Refer to Fig. 5-3. That figure shows two virtual circuits, 1 and 3, sharing link *B–E*. Say that packets arrive randomly at node *B* from nodes *A* and *F*, as shown. On the average there are two VC1 packets for every VC3 packet. The packets have the format of Fig. 5-4, with the appropriate VC number included. Sketch the formats of each of a sequence of six frames moving across link *B–E*. The HDLC structure of Fig. 5-8 is used. The address is that of node *E*. Frames are numbered sequentially, starting with 0, using a 3-bit sequence number in the control field of Fig. 5-8.

5-4. Consider path 1 in Fig. 5-3, carrying VC1. A typical packet is to be followed as it moves along the path. Redraw Fig. 5-9 for this case. Sketch the format at each layer (network and data link) at each of the three nodes along the path. Use the VC format of Fig. 5-4 and the HDLC frame format of Fig. 5-8. Include a 3-bit sequence number in the HDLC control field. (*Hint*: Each link may be shared by multiple VCs as shown in Fig. 5-3 and in Prob. 5-3 above. What does this imply about the data-link sequence numbers over the two links of path 1?)

5-5. A connectionless packet-switched network cannot guarantee delivery of packets (datagrams) in sequence to a destination. Resequencing must thus be carried out at the destination. (This is typically done at layer 4, the transport layer, of Fig. 1-2.) Resequencing buffers are required for this purpose.

    (*a*) How can one arrange to detect an out-of-sequence packet? Say the packet format is that of Fig. 5-5. If this detection process is carried out at layer 4, above the network layer, where must sequencing information be carried in the packet?

   (b) The detection of out-of-sequence packets implies packets may be lost or delayed in arriving at the destination. Show how a timer-positive ack procedure may be used to correct for lost packets. (This procedure is similar to that carried out at the data-link layer, noted in the text and in Prob. 5-2 above.) Will it handle the problem of delayed packets as well? Explain.

   (c) Datagrams may sometimes be routed improperly or may be forced to be rerouted around failed links and/or nodes. In extensive networks covering large areas a datagram may arrive at a destination after a user-to-user session has been concluded, and a new one has been begun. (In the meantime the datagram in question would have been repeated by the source user and correctly received at the destination.) Can you think of a way (or ways) in which to handle this problem? Is it *always* possible to detect the original datagram and discard it on arrival?

5-6. A CSMA/CD bus has 1000 stations connected. Find the *maximum* number of frames/s *per station* that can be transmitted for the following cases:

   (a) Bus length = 1 km. Capacity $C = 1$ Mbit/s. Propagation delay = 8 μs/km. Frames are 1,000 octets (8,000 bits) long.

   (b) Same as (a), but $C = 10$ Mbits/s.

   (c) Same as (b), but bus length = 2 km. Compare (a), (b), (c), and comment on the results.

   (d) 2-km bus, $C = 10$ Mbits/s, delay = 8 μs/km. Frames are 100 octets long. Compare (c) and (d). What is the maximum utilization ρ_m in each case? What is the *maximum bus throughput*, in bits/s, for the two cases? (*Note:* This last question asks for the total traffic on the bus, not the traffic per station.)

5-7. The possibility of using CSMA/CD for a metropolitan-area network (MAN) is to be investigated. The total bus length is 40 km (25 miles). Propagation delay is 8 μs/km.

   (a) What is the maximum line capacity (transmission rate) C that can be used for data frames (1) 128 bits, (2) 1,200 bits, and (3) 12,000 bits long, if $a = \tau/T \leq 0.1$ must be maintained?

   (b) Find the maximum number of users that can be accommodated for the following three cases: (1) Each user inputs 1 data frame per 30 s, on the average; (2) 1 data frame per minute, on the average; (3) 1 data frame per 2 min, on the average. Frames are 1,200 bits long. Repeat for frames 12,000 bits long. $a \leq 0.1$ must be maintained.

5-8. A token ring is 2 km long. Propagation delay is 5 μs/km.

   (a) Find the average cycle time t_c and average access time $t_c/2$ for the following cases:

   (1) $C = 4$ Mbits/s. Frames are 1,200 bits long. There are 100 stations on the ring. Latency per station is 1 bit. The average load (arrival rate) per station is adjusted to keep $\rho = \lambda T = 0.8$.

   (2) Same as (1), but latency is increased to 16 bits/station.

   (3) Repeat (1) and (2) if ρ is reduced to 0.6.

   (b) Find the load (arrival rate), in frames/s, allowed per station in the two cases of (a), $\rho = 0.8$ and 0.6.

5-9. Refer to Prob. 5-7 above. A 40-km token ring is to be used as a MAN. Frames are 1,200 bits long. $\rho = 0.8$ is desired. Use the same propagation delay as in Prob. 5-7.

(a) $C = 360$ kbits/s. Each user inputs 1 frame per 30 s, on the average. There is 1 bit of latency per station. Find the number of users that can be accommodated and the average cycle time of the ring.

(b) Repeat (a) if the latency is 16 bits/station.

(c) Repeat (a) if the latency is 16 bits/station and usage is 1 frame per 2 min, per user. Compare the results of (a), (b), (c) with those of Prob. 5-7.

(d) Repeat (c) (latency is 16 bits/station, 1 frame per 2 min., per station) if $C = 4$ Mbits/s. Can a CSMA/CD scheme accommodate the same number of users? Explain.

5-10. Using the three statements defining the Poisson process in the subsection on the traffic-arrival model in Sec. 5-3, derive the binomial probability $P(k)$ of k arrivals in the interval T given by (5-16). Let $\Delta t \to 0$. Using (5-17) and (5-18), show that (5-12) results.

5-11. (a) Show that the Poisson distribution of (5-12) sums to 1. Show that the average number of arrivals in the interval T and the variance σ_k^2 both equal λT.

(b) What is the probability of *at least* one arrival? What is the probability of *exactly* one arrival? Under what condition is the probability of one arrival approximately equal to λT? Does this agree with the definition of the Poisson process?

(c) A packet switch in a network has an average packet arrival rate of 6 packets/min. Arrival statistics are approximated quite well by the Poisson distribution. What is the probability of *no* arrival in 1 s? in 10 s? in 1 min? What is the probability of *one* arrival for the same times? On the average, 360 packets are expected to arrive in one hour. What is the range of variation, as measured by the standard deviation σ_k, about this value?

5-12. Calculate and plot the Poisson distribution of (5-12) for $\lambda T = 0.1, 1, 5$. Compare these plots with that of Fig. 5-29 for $\lambda T = 10$.

5-13. Refer to Prob. 5-11c. The average packet arrival rate at a packet switch is $\lambda = 6$ packets/min. What is the average time *between* arrivals? What is the probability, given an arrival, that another will occur within 1 s? Within 10 s? Within 20 s? Repeat if λ doubles to 12 packets/min. For $\lambda = 6$ packets/min, find the probability, given an arrival, that another packet will arrive between 1 and 2 s later; between 9 and 10 s later.

5-14. Given Poisson arrivals, the time τ between arrivals is an exponentially distributed random variable with probability density function (5-19). Show (5-19) is properly normalized. Calculate the variance and mean value of τ, and show these are given, respectively, by (5-21) and (5-20).

5-15. Two possible networking scenarios are to be examined. In the first scenario two user stations are connected to the same CSMA/CD LAN, as shown in Fig. P5-15a. In the second scenario, one of the user stations can only be reached through a wide-area network, as shown in Fig. P5-15b. In the second scenario the LAN and the WAN are connected through a gateway G, as shown in Fig. P5-15b. Two sets of data link protocols are used in G, as shown in Fig. P5-15c. The logical-link control (LLC) on the LAN side gives the appearance of a full data-link control to the gateway network layer. The LLC is connectionless, however, with no error recovery carried out. Virtual-circuit routing is used over the WAN. In either scenario the transport layer in *A* communicates with the transport layer in *B*. These layers are not at all aware of the underlying network or networks. For communication to begin, the transport layer at *A* must first set up a transport connection with its peer at *B*. In both cases the MAC sublayer at *A* receives an **MA_DATA.request** primitive from the layer above containing the necessary connection information (including the address of *B*). The primitive carries a destination address. In the first scenario this is *B*. In the second it is *G*.

(*a*) Explain why the destination address in the primitive differs in the two cases. Why can't this be the MAC address of *B* in the WAN case? In what portion of the primitive must the WAN id or address of *B* be carried? (See the text for the composition of the primitive.)

(*b*) In the second scenario a virtual circuit through the WAN must be set up for communication to take place. In the particular situation under discussion here, when is the WAN alerted that a virtual circuit must be set up? What message must carry this information?

(*c*) Sketch a frame transmitted onto the LAN by the physical layer of *A*, in the two scenarios, indicating the *frame* addresses carried by each (Fig. 5-16).

(*d*) Sketch the frame transmitted between *G* and node 1 of the WAN, indicating the *frame* address in that case. Indicate where the virtual-circuit id must be carried.

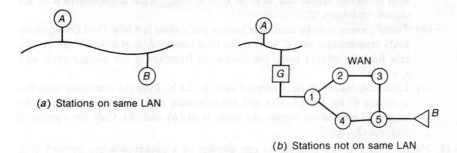

(*a*) Stations on same LAN

(*b*) Stations not on same LAN

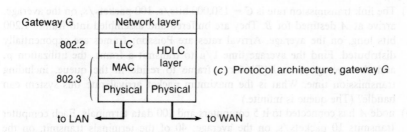

(*c*) Protocol architecture, gateway *G*

FIGURE P5-15

5-16. (*a*) Using the balance-equation argument discussed in the text, show that the balance equation relating probabilities of state in the $M/M/1$ queue is given by (5-32). Show this simplifies to (5-33), whose solution is given by (5-34). Finally, show that the probability p_n that the queue has n frames (customers) in queue (both undergoing transmission and waiting for service) is given by (5-37).

(*b*) Plot p_n for $\rho = 0.3$ and 0.9, and compare with Fig. 5-38.

5-17. (*a*) Packets arrive at a data switch, on the average, once every 0.1 s. The arrival distribution is Poisson. Frames, as assembled, are exponentially distributed in length, with average length 960 bits. They are transmitted out at a rate of 19.2 kbits/s. Show the average number of frames on queue (including the one in transmission) is $E(n) = 1$. Show the average time *waiting* on queue is 0.05 s, with a total time delay through the queue given by 0.1 s.

(*b*) Repeat (*a*) if the arrival rate (offered load) is increased to 18 packets/s, on the average.

(*c*) Repeat (*b*) if the average frame length is decreased to 640 bits; i.e., the arrival rate is still 18 packets/s on the average, and the transmission rate is still 19.2 kbits/s.

(*d*) Repeat (*a*) and (*b*) if the frames are of fixed (constant) length, 960 bits. Compare with (*a*) and (*b*).

5-18. 100 data stations are to be connected using a 3-km-long LAN. Propagation delay on the LAN is 5 μs/km. Frames transmitted by each station are 15,000 bits long.

(*a*) CSMA/CD is to be used. Specify the *maximum* bus transmission rate C, in bits/s, that may be used if $a \equiv \tau/T$ is to be at most 0.2. T is the frame length in seconds; τ is the end-to-end propagation delay. What is the maximum bus utilization ρ_m for this choice of C? The actual utilization of the bus, $\rho = \lambda T$, with λ the bus arrival rate, is to be kept to $0.8\rho_m$. What is the offered load *per station*, in frames/s?

(*b*) Token passing is to be used. The latency per station is 8 bits. Find the *minimum* LAN transmission rate C so that the total latency L is at most 215 μs. At this rate find the offered load, *per station*, in frames/s if the average cycle time $t_c = 2L$.

(*c*) 1,000 stations are to be connected over the LAN. Find the maximum transmission rate C for CSMA/CD and the minimum rate for token passing in this case. [All parameters remain the same as in (*a*) and (*b*). Only the number of stations changes.]

5-19. Nodes A and B are adjacent to one another in a packet-switched network (Fig. P5-19).

(*a*) The link transmission rate is $C = 150,000$ bits/s. 100 packets/s, on the average, arrive at A destined for B. They are buffered and assembled into frames 1,200 bits long, on the average. Arrival rates are Poisson; frames are exponentially distributed. Find the average time $1/\mu$ to transmit a frame, the utilization ρ, and the average time $E(T)$ for a frame to reside in the queue, including transmission time. What is the maximum packet arrival rate this system can handle? (The queue is infinite.)

(*b*) node A has connected to it 5 computers and 100 data terminals. Each computer transmits 10 packets/s, on the average; 40 of the terminals transmit, on the average, 1 packet/(4 s) each; 60 terminals average 1 packet/(2 s) each. Frames, as assembled, are 1,000 bits long, on the average. Show the link utilization is $\rho = 0.6$. Show the average time delay through the queue is $E(T) = 16.7$ ms.

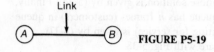

Link

FIGURE P5-19

(c) (1) HDLC is used as the data-link control. The frame carries a destination address, as does the packet within it. Can you distinguish between these two addresses?

(2) Can you explain why virtual circuit routing, with a VC id carried in each packet, requires a *connection* phase, while datagram routing, with the destination address carried in each packet, does not?

(3) Two possible transmission techniques are under study for use in this system —QAM over digital radio, and OOK using optics. Will the choice of either one affect the analysis in (*a*) and (*b*) above? Explain.

5-20. Five data terminals are connected to a packet switch. Two of the terminals generate packets at an average rate of 1 packet/min each. The other three generate packets at an average rate of 1 packet/(30 s) each. The composite packet arrival stream may be modeled as Poisson. Packets are queued for transmission in order of arrival (FIFO service). The outgoing frames, as assembled, are exponentially distributed in length, with an average length of 12,000 bits. The outgoing transmission rate is 2,400 bits/s.

(*a*) Calculate the average frame transmission time in seconds.

(*b*) Calculate the line utilization ρ.

(*c*) Find the average number of frames in queue, as well as the average delay $E(T)$ through the queue.

(*d*) It is desired to connect another terminal to the packet switch. It is estimated this terminal will generate 1 packet/(15 s) on the average. Is this acceptable? If not, state why not. If so, state the effect on the average delay.

5-21. The text and the problems given here focus implicitly on infinite queues. In real systems finite buffers are of course used. The effect of finite buffering is explored in this problem.

(*a*) An $M/M/1$ queue can accept at most N packets. If filled, additional packets arriving are dropped (blocked). Show that the probability the queue is in state n, $0 \le n \le N$, is given by $p_n = (1 - \rho)\rho^n/(1 - \rho^{N+1})$. [*Hint*: Equation (5-34) for the state probability still applies. Over what values of n must this now be summed to find p_0?]

(*b*) Show the probability a packet is blocked is given by

$$P_B = (1 - \rho)\rho^N/(1 - \rho^{N+1}).$$

Let $\rho = 0.5$. Say it is desired to keep the blocking probability to no more than 10^{-3}. What size buffer (value of N) is required? Repeat if $\rho = 0.8$. (*Hint*: The calculation may be simplified considerably by noting that $\rho^{N+1} \ll 1$ in both cases. Why is this so?) The average offered load is $\lambda = 1,000$ packets/s. What is the *throughput* (average *carried* load) in this case? How many packets are dropped per second on the average?

(*c*) Repeat (*b*) for a blocking probability of 10^{-8}.

(*d*) With a *finite* buffer the utilization ρ is not limited to 1. As ρ increases, however, the blocking probability P_B increases, approaching 1.

(1) Show that $P_B = 1/(N + 1)$ at $\rho = 1$. Calculate P_B for the two values of N found in (*b*) above. Show that the normalized throughput $\gamma/\mu = N/(N + 1)$.

(2) Show that as $\rho \to \infty$, $P_B \to 1$. Show that the throughput approaches μ in this case; i.e., as ρ increases beyond bounds, the throughput saturates at the

capacity μ. [*Hint*: $\gamma = \lambda(1 - P_B)$. Find $1 - P_B$ as $\rho \to \infty$. Show $1 - P_B \to 1/\rho$, $\rho = \lambda/\mu$.]

(3) Show that as $\rho \to \infty$, $p_n \to 0$ for $n < N$; i.e., as the offered load λ increases, the queue tends to be filled up, at its maximum value of N.

5-22. The text discusses the $M/M/1$ queue at length. Recall that in this queueing model arrivals obey a Poisson process, while the service time is exponentially distributed. In this problem we extend that discussion briefly to the $M/G/1$ queue, one with *general* service-time distribution. It may be shown [KLEI], [SCHW 1987] that the average waiting time $E(W)$ for an $M/G/1$ queue is given by

$$E(W) = \frac{\lambda E(\tau^2)}{2(1 - \rho)} \tag{1}$$

where λ is the average (Poisson) arrival rate, $E(\tau^2)$ is the second moment of the service-time distribution, and $\rho = \lambda E(\tau)$, with $E(\tau)$ the average service time, equivalent to the symbol $1/\mu$ used in the text.

(*a*) Let the service time be exponential. Show that (1) simplifies to (5-42) in the text, checking that result for the $M/M/1$ queue. (*Hint*: How are the variance and average value related for the exponential distribution? Hence how is the second moment related to the average value?)

(*b*) The service time is a constant $1/\mu$. The queue is thus the $M/D/1$ one mentioned in the text. Show from (1) that the average waiting time is given by (5-44). (*Hint*: What is the variance of the service time in this case? Hence how are the second moment and average values now related?)

(*c*) Equation (5-28) relates the average time and average waiting time in a queue. Using this equation and the results of parts (*a*) and (*b*) of this problem, show that the average time delays for the $M/M/1$ and $M/D/1$ queues are given, respectively, by (5-41) and (5-43). Applying Little's theorem to these two cases, show that the average number of customers in the queue, including the one in service, is given by (5-38) and (5-39) respectively.

(*d*) Using (5-28) and (1) above, show the average time delay for an $M/G/1$ queue is given by

$$E(T) = \frac{1}{\mu}\left(\frac{1}{1 - \rho}\right)\left[1 - \frac{\rho}{2}(1 - \mu^2\sigma^2)\right] \tag{2}$$

with $\sigma^2 = E(\tau^2) - E^2(\tau) = E(\tau^2) - (1/\mu)^2$ the variance of the service-time distribution. This is called the Pollaczek–Khinchine formula. Under what condition does one obtain the *smallest* average delay? Explain. Does this formula agree with the $M/M/1$ result of (5-41)? What does this formula predict happens to the average time delay as $\sigma^2/(1/\mu)^2$ increases? Is this in agreement with the average-waiting-time formula (1)? Explain.

(*e*) Using (1) and (2), compare the average waiting time and the average time delay $E(T)$ at a utilization of $\rho = 0.5$ for the following cases: (1) constant service time, (2) exponential service time, (3) $\sigma^2 = 5(1/\mu)^2$, (4) $\sigma^2 = 50(1/\mu)^2$. Repeat for $\rho = 0.8$.

5-23. Show that (5-53) represents the general balance equation for the $M/M/N/N$ system. Show this leads to (5-56) as the solution for the probability there are n calls in progress.

5-24. Show the Erlang blocking probability $P_B(N)$ may be recursively obtained using (5-58). Use this relation to check some of the points in Fig. 5-52. In particular, calculate $P_B(2)$, $P_B(4)$, $P_B(8)$, and $P_B(10)$ for $A = 5$ erlangs. Calculate $P_B(10)$, $P_B(15)$, and $P_B(20)$ for $A = 10$ erlangs.

5-25. A circuit-switched exchange has 10 outgoing trunks. Calculate the blocking probability if the average call holding time is 200 s and calls arrive, on the average, once every 40 s. What is the Erlang load A in this case? Repeat if the call holding time doubles to 400 s.

5-26. A PBX (private branch exchange) owned by a small business has 100 telephone extensions connected to it. The PBX has one T1 link, accommodating 24 simultaneous calls, connecting it to the public telephone network. A grade of service of $\leq$ 1-percent blocking probability is desired at the PBX. Is the one T1 link sufficient if users use their extensions, on the average, once every half hour for a period of 10 min? Explain. If one T1 link is insufficient, would adding a second T1 link alleviate the problem? Alternatively, would reducing the number of extensions help? Explain. Discuss the tradeoffs between increasing the number of "outside lines" and reducing the number of internal extensions.

5-27. Calculate the Erlang load in each of the following cases:
  (a) Average call arrival rate is 1 call/(2 s); average call holding time is 4 s.
  (b) Average call arrival rate is 1 call/(10 min); average call holding time is 20 min.
  (c) Average call arrival rate is 1 call/(5 s); average call holding time is 20 min.
  (d) Average call arrival rate is 10 calls/s; average call holding time is 10 min.
  [*Note*: Local exchanges, to which most telephones are connected, may be sized in thousands of erlangs. They are generally rated in terms of *busy-hour call attempts* (BHCA), the number of calls arriving during the busiest hour, in addition to the Erlang load.]

5-28. Refer to Problem 5-26. One-half of the 100 extensions are used by PCs equipped with voice-grade modems. The PCs typically provide the same usage pattern as users at the other extensions: They dial out, on the average, once every half hour for about 10 min. Only 10 percent of that time is actually used for transmitting data, however. The PCs are typically quiet 90 percent of the time. What is the effect on the Erlang load? Explain. What might be a more efficient way of connecting the 50 PCs to the outside world? Explain.

5-29. Show the average number of trunks (servers) occupied in the $M/M/N/N$ system of Fig. 5-50 is given by (5-59).

CHAPTER

6

PERFORMANCE OF POINT-TO-POINT COMMUNICATION SYSTEMS: LIMITATIONS DUE TO NOISE

As noted at the end of Chap. 5, on networks, we return to point-to-point communications in this chapter, discussing performance issues at the *physical* layer. Each layer in a layered network architecture typically has performance measures that must be evaluated. At higher layers performance may be measured in terms of maximum protocol data-unit throughput attainable at a given layer; it may be measured in terms of processing and/or service delay. (Recall that the LAN performance discussed in Chap. 5 focused on delay versus throughput.) Other possible measures include speed and complexity of processing, reliability and security, end-to-end response time, etc.

In the case of point-to-point communications at the physical layer deterioration in performance is principally due to noise, distortion, and interference introduced during transmission. More specifically, in digital communications, with which we are principally concerned in this book, this deterioration in performance is measured by the *probability of bit error*: the probability that an error will occur in detecting a bit. In the case of light-wave (fiber-optic) transmission we shall see that the discreteness of the photons transmitted sets a fundamental (quantum) limitation on the ability to detect bits correctly. In communication at lower frequencies, noise introduced during transmission sets a limit on correct (error-free) communication. (Noise is introduced as well during light-wave transmission; this degrades the performance beyond the error probability due to the discreteness of the photons, to be discussed here.) Error calculations for light-wave communications are easier to discuss at this stage, since they draw only on the Poisson model of statistics introduced in Chap. 5. We therefore begin our discussion with light-wave communications. We follow this with a discussion of the effect of noise on communications.

Before proceeding with the discussion of performance limitations in this chapter, however, it is worthwhile recalling our interest, in earlier chapters in this book, in the transmission bandwidth or spectral occupancy of communication signals, whether at baseband or, after modulation, transmitted at carrier frequencies. One important reason for this is that bandwidth is a resource that must be conserved. The electromagnetic spectrum used for the transmission of the overwhelming majority of communication signals is limited in its bandwidth allocation at the various frequency bands in use. It is thus important to know the bandwidth requirements of the transmission medium or channel over which the signals are to be transmitted in order to have relatively undistorted signals arriving at the receiver. Where distortion is introduced, by transmission over band-limiting channels, its effect on the signals transmitted must be determined.

Bandwidth considerations represent one element in determining the performance of a communication system. As noted briefly in Sec. 1-3, in discussing the transmission of signals through a system, noise is added as the signal moves from transmitter to receiver, in some cases signal fading is encountered, interference from other signals may be introduced, and a variety of other adverse effects may appear. All these effects must ultimately be assessed as to their relative importance, and the significant ones incorporated into a model of the overall system from which the performance may be evaluated. In this chapter, after evaluating limitations on lightwave communications, we stress the evaluation of the performance of communication systems, using the simplest model of a transmission channel that limits system performance—one that adds noise to the signal as it propagates over the channel, as well as providing the usual bandwidth limitation. We do this for several reasons. First, additive noise, as we shall note later in describing its effect on performance, represents the basic limitation on performance in many systems below light-wave frequencies. The noise is always there, whether we like it or not, and so puts a limit on any performance measure. Second, it enables us to focus on simple modeling without any complications due to a variety of other performance-limiting factors. Third, it enables us to introduce useful measures of performance that can be extended to include other limiting factors if desired.

Limitations due to bandwidth and to additive noise will be stressed throughout this chapter. Recall that they came up, in a qualitative way, in Chap. 1. They will come up again in Chap. 7, in introducing and discussing Shannon's celebrated expression that describes fundamental limits on the rate of transmission in digital communication systems.

We have already noted that the probability of bit error in digital communication systems represents a basic measure of performance. In analog systems such as AM and FM systems, the signal-to-noise ratio is found to be a critical measure of performance. We have already introduced this ratio as a measure of performance in discussing PCM and DPCM systems in Chap. 3. The discussion there focused on quantization and overload noise, both of which can be controlled by varying the quantization levels and sampling rates, with corresponding possible increases in transmission bandwidth. The discussion here will concentrate on unavoidable additive noise.

In Sec. 6-1, following, we introduce the discussion of probability of error, as already noted, by calculating the fundamental (quantum) limits on performance in light-wave transmission systems. We then move on to additive noise by first considering baseband binary signals. We then discuss the effect of additive noise on the performance of high-frequency binary-modulated signals such as PSK, OOK, and FSK. Limits on performance of heterodyned optical systems are discussed at this point as well. We conclude the discussion with AM and FM systems. QAM systems are treated in Chap. 7 following. Topics on the representation of noise are introduced where needed.

6-1 PERFORMANCE LIMITS IN DIGITAL LIGHT-WAVE SYSTEMS

Current digital light-wave (fiber-optic) transmission systems use on–off keyed (OOK) transmission with direct-detection (envelope-detection) photoreceivers. We thus discuss the performance of such systems first, then continue with coherent systems to see the potential improvement possible by introducing synchronous detection.

A typical fiber-optic transmission link is sketched schematically in Fig. 6-1. A laser transmitter is turned on and off at the binary (data) rate. The resultant OOK signal is launched into an optical fiber and is detected at the other end of the link by a photodiode detector. Both PIN photodiodes and avalanche photodiodes (APDs) are available. The PIN photodiode is very efficient, providing close to one electron out for every photon received. But it thus produces a weak signal out for a weak signal in. Noise in the electronic circuits following thus overwhelms the system in the case of weak signals. (Noise in systems will be discussed briefly later in this chapter.) APD detectors, on the other hand, provide the large

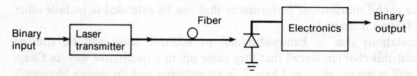

FIGURE 6-1
Direct-detection light-wave communication system.

signal power required to overcome the noise introduced in the electronic systems following, but are themselves quite noisy, due to statistical fluctuations in the gain. They are preferred in long-haul fiber-optic systems because of their high gain. Using an OOK, direct-detection system of this type, it is found experimentally that about 1,000 photons/bit at the detector are needed to attain a bit-error probability of 10^{-9}, the target error probability for lightwave systems.

Single-mode fiber provides the lowest attenuation of the optical signal. At a wavelength of 1.3 μm (1300 nm), loss due to attenuation in the fiber is about 0.4 dB/km. Minimum attentuation is attained at a wavelength of 1.55 μm, with an attenuation of about 0.25 dB/km a typical value [HENR 1985a], [HENR 1985b].[1]

Consider the implications of these numbers. A photon at 1.3 μm carries a quantum of energy given by $hf_0 = 15 \times 10^{-20}$ J, where $f_0 = 2.3 \times 10^{14}$ Hz is the frequency at this wavelength, and $h = 6.6 \times 10^{-34}$ J-s is Planck's constant. Say the desired bit rate is $R = 1/T = 1$ Gbit/s. Then the power delivered at the receiver by 1000 photons/bit (the number required to attain an error probability of 10^{-9}) is 15×10^{-8} W. Using the attenuation figure of 0.4 dB/km, a 100-km link would attenuate the transmitter power by 40 dB, or a factor of 10^4. The transmitter power required for the 100-km link is thus $15 \times 10^{-4} = 1.5$ mW. Single-mode lasers at both 1.3 and 1.55 μm provide powers of about 1 mW, so a span of about 100 km is possible. (We ignore here bit-rate limitations due to dispersion. See [HENR 1985a] and [HENR 1985b] for discussion of this question.)

These numbers are typical ones. What is the absolute *best* in performance that one could hope for? We shall show that, using OOK transmission with direct detection, 10 photons/bit are theoretically required to attain a bit-error probability $P_e = 10^{-9}$. This represents a factor-of-100 improvement over systems in the field. To calculate this limit we proceed as follows. Assume an ideal PIN photodiode is used at the receiver. Each photon striking the diode is assumed to generate one electron. (This is actually quite realistic. PIN diodes have a photon–electron conversion efficiency approaching 1.) Say that the photodiode introduces no noise and that the electronic circuits following introduce no noise either. This latter assumption is not a realistic one, but we are interested at this point in calculating the best possible performance.

The output of the PIN diode at the end of a binary interval T is a measure of the number of photons collected by the diode in that interval. (Each electron generated results in a narrow pulse of current. The total current flowing thus measures the number of electrons generated, and hence the number of photons striking the diode.) The photodiode mechanism is thus a counting one. The number measured at the end of each binary interval is compared with a threshold

---

[1][HENR 1985b] P. S. Henry, "Lightwave Primer," *IEEE J. Quantum Electronics*, vol. QE-21, no. 12, pp. 1862–1879, December 1985.

to determine whether or not a pulse of light hit the diode. Clearly, for the ideal diode envisioned here, this threshold must be zero, since the off state in an OOK system means no light striking the diode and hence zero count (with the assumption of zero noise).

Let n represent the number of photons hitting the diode when a light pulse (the on-state) is present. It turns out that this number is a random variable, since the number of photons in a light beam is known to follow the Poisson distribution equation (5-12) of Chap. 5. In particular, let the average number of photons striking the diode in an interval T be $E(n) = \lambda_p T$. Then the probability the count is n is given by

$$P(n) = (\lambda_p T)^n e^{-\lambda_p T} / n! \qquad n = 0, 1, 2, \ldots \qquad (6\text{-}1)$$

From our original discussion of Poisson statistics in Chap. 5, it is clear that photons strike the diode randomly in time. In any small time interval $(t, t + \Delta t)$ the probability a photon appears is $\lambda_p \Delta t \ll 1$; the probability no photon appears is $1 - \lambda_p \Delta t$. The parameter λ_p is a measure of the intensity of the light beam, in average number of photons per unit time impinging on the diodes. Poisson statistics imply as well that the presence or absence of a photon in any small time interval is independent of whether a photon had just been present or not, or whether one was coming just after this interval; i.e., the photon arrival process is a memoryless one.

Since each photon carries hf_0 joules of energy, the average energy E absorbed by the diode in the binary interval T is

$$E = E(n) hf_0 = \lambda_p T hf_0 \qquad (6\text{-}2)$$

with $E(n) = \lambda_p T$ the average number of photons in the binary interval T.

This represents the light particle picture. Consider the wave picture now. As noted many times in this book, OOK transmission means transmitting $A_T \cos \omega_0 t$, $0 \le t \le T$, for a 1 and nothing for a zero. (We neglect shaping here.) At the receiver, then, the attenuated on-pulse of light of frequency f_0 may be represented by $A \cos \omega_0 t$, $0 \le t \le T$, with A the attenuated amplitude. The energy in this pulse is proportional to $A^2 T$. This energy must be the same as that given by (6-2). Since the amplitude A as written here has arbitrary units, we are free to choose for it any value we wish, providing the equality with (6-2) is maintained. In particular, it turns out to be useful to let $A^2 T = \lambda_p T$, or $A^2 = \lambda_p$. This simply says that the energy in the pulse (the wave picture) is $E = A^2 T hf_0$ with hf_0 the desired proportionality constant. Since A^2 is the envelope squared of the pulse and $A^2 T$ the integral of this quantity over the binary interval, the wave picture implies that the ideal photodiode produces at its output the integral of the square of the envelope. Recall from Chap. 4 that this was in fact one way to implement envelope detection: a nonlinear diode followed by a low-pass filter. The filtering process here is given by the integral over the interval T. Summarizing the discussion thus far, the ideal diode can be represented in the particle interpretation as providing a summed count of photons impinging on it in the binary interval T. In the wave interpretation, it provides an output for each binary interval proportional to the integral of the envelope squared of the optical signal impinging on it. We shall use these dual interpretations later in discussing other types of optical transmission.

Returning now to the diode-counting argument in this ideal, noise-free situation, it is clear that an optical pulse, when present, will be detected as such if any number of photons strike the diode. An error will occur if no counts are registered over the entire interval T. From (6-1) the probability of this happening if a pulse is present is $P(0) = e^{-\lambda_p T}$. Assume pulses in an OOK system are present one-half the time, on the average. Then the probability of an error is

$$P_e = \tfrac{1}{2}P(0) = \tfrac{1}{2}e^{-\lambda_p T} \tag{6-3}$$

For $P_e = 10^{-9}$, we find $\lambda_p T = 20.7$ photons, on the average, are needed. But pulses are present one-half the time only. The average number of photons in a binary interval must then be only 10.3 if an error probability of 10^{-9} is to be maintained. The number 10.3 presents the *quantum limit* for direct detection OOK transmission with $P_e = 10^{-9}$. It is the lowest number possible, since an ideal system has been assumed: an ideal diode of unity efficiency, generating no noise to mask the photon counts, and negligible noise in the electronic circuits following. In practice, as already noted, 1000 photons/bit are actually required to attain a bit error of probability of 10^{-9}. Some improvement may be expected as improved photodiodes come on the market, but the (ideal) quantum limit using OOK transmission and photodiode direct detection is far from attainable. Instead attention has focused on the use of coherent detection techniques to improve the performance. The quantum limits for these techniques are calculated in the next subsection.

Coherent (Homodyne) Detection

Synchronous or coherent detection has been discussed in Chap. 4. It was noted there that PSK, QPSK, and QAM communication systems in general require the use of coherent detection at the receiver, since the bit information is carried in phase changes. We discuss here the application of coherent transmission to optical communication systems.

Historically, the process of synchronous or coherent detection of communication signals was called *homodyne detection* to distinguish it from heterodyne detection. Recall from Chap. 4 that in heterodyne detection incoming high-frequency signals are shifted down to a lower intermediate frequency (i-f) by multiplying by a local-oscillator signal different in frequency from the incoming carrier signal. In the synchronous detection case the local-oscillator frequency is the same as that of the incoming carrier; hence, the use of the word homodyne. Synchronous, coherent, and homodyne detection are thus all synonymous terms for the same operation [SCHW 1966]. The term homodyne detection has come back into widespread use in discussing coherent optical systems, so we use that term throughout this subsection. (Heterodyne coherent optical systems will be discussed later in this chapter.)

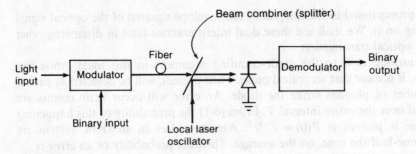

FIGURE 6-2
Coherent-light-wave communication system.

An example of a coherent optical communication system appears in Fig. 6-2. A single-frequency laser with very narrowband spectral output and good frequency stability is required as the source [BASC],[2] [LINK]. For coherent OOK transmission an optical switch, switching on and off at the binary data rate, can be used to modulate the laser output. For PSK transmission an electrooptical phase modulator can be used. In the case of coherent FSK transmission the laser current could be switched, resulting in two output light frequencies. Figure 6-2 shows these or other modulation schemes being carried out by a separate modulator. At the receiver a local laser oscillator signal coherently locked to the incoming light frequency is combined with the incoming modulated signal using a beam splitter. (This could be a partially reflecting plate or a fiber directional coupler.) Synchronously locking the local-oscillator frequency to that of the incoming optical carrier frequency can be a difficult task at optical frequencies. This synchronization is more readily carried out at microwave frequencies in the gigahertz range than at the optical frequency of 10^{14} Hz, which is one reason for using heterodyne techniques as discussed later in this chapter. Finally, the combined local-oscillator and received modulated signal are directed at a photodiode. In this coherent case a PIN diode can more readily be used than in the noncoherent case, since the large local-oscillator signal always ensures a strong signal will be present. Assumptions made previously, neglecting the effect of noise in both the diode and the electronic circuits following, are thus much more realistic.

We now carry out the performance analysis of homodyne OOK and PSK transmission. The performance of heterodyne OOK, PSK, and FSK transmission is left to a later section in this chapter. Consider the PSK case first. Let the received signal over a binary interval T seconds long be $+A \cos \omega_c t$ for a binary 1 transmitted and $-A \cos \omega_c t$ for a binary 0 transmitted. Added to this signal is

[2][BASC] E. E. Basch and T. G. Brown, "Introduction to Coherent Optical Fiber Transmission," *IEEE Commun. Mag.*, vol. 3, no. 5, pp. 23–30, May 1986.

the local-oscillator signal $B \cos \omega_c t$, where we take the amplitude $B \gg A$. The photodiode thus has $(B + A)\cos \omega_c t$ or $(B - A)\cos \omega_c t$ as its two possible inputs. The detection system carries out the same counting process as in the noncoherent case considered previously. We again assume an ideal PIN diode, with one photoelectron liberated for every photon received, and photodiode noise neglected. (Note, as already stated, that this last assumption is now much more valid because of the strong local-oscillator signal always present.)

The local-oscillator signal, interpreted as a beam of photons striking the diode, obeys Poisson statistics, just as does the received (modulated) signal. The sum of two Poisson-distributed random variables is Poisson as well, as noted in our discussion of statistical multiplexing in Chap. 5. The count or diode output at the end of each binary interval is thus Poisson-distributed. We again apply the dual wave–particle picture to equate the count to the integral of the envelope squared of the composite input wave. In this case of homodyne PSK reception we have, as the integral of the envelope squared, $(B + A)^2 T$ or $(B - A)^2 T$, depending on which binary signal has been received. These can then be interpreted as *average counts* at the photodiode. The photon count—which, because of our assumption of an ideal PIN diode, equates to the number of electrons liberated in a binary interval T seconds long—is thus a Poisson random variable with one of two possible expected (average) values: $(B + A)^2 T$ or $(B - A)^2 T$.

Recall from Chap. 5 (Fig. 5-29) that the Poisson distribution for large average value peaks at, and is centered about, its average value. It may in fact be shown that the Poisson distribution for large average value is approximated very closely by the gaussian (normal) distribution with the same mean value and variance [PAPO 1984], [ALLE 1978].[3] This can be seen from Fig. 5-29, which displays the characteristic bell shape of the gaussian distribution. This gaussian approximation to the Poisson distribution is a direct result of the central limit theorem of probability theory, which states that the gaussian distribution is the limiting distribution of the sum of independent random variables. We note from our discussion in Chap. 5 that the Poisson distribution was derived as the limit of a binomial distribution, which is in turn defined to be the distribution of the *sum* of elementary, *independent* Bernoulli variables.

Figure 6-3a portrays the distribution of the photon counts for homodyne PSK transmission. As the binary information carried shifts from a 1 to a 0, or the reverse, the photon count shifts from one curve to the other correspondingly. Since it is the shift that carries the information, the constant value $(B^2 + A^2)T$ at which the two curves intersect is immaterial to the counting process and may be removed. This is most readily done by using a balanced photodiode in Fig. 6-2 which cancels out the constant value. One is then left with the output count distribution of Fig. 6-3b. The two distributions are centered about $-2ABT$ and $+2ABT$, respectively. Since the variance of a Poisson distribution equals its

---

[3][ALLE 1978] A. O. Allen, *Probability, Statistics, and Queueing Theory*, Academic, New York, 1978.

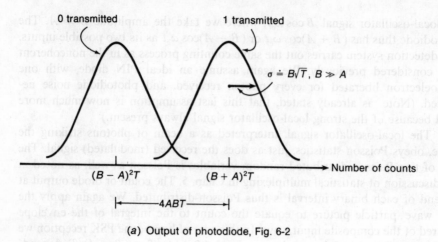

(a) Output of photodiode, Fig. 6-2

FIGURE 6-3
Photon-count statistics, binary interval, homodyne PSK transmission.

mean value, the variances of the two distributions in Fig. 6-3 are $(B - A)^2 T$ and $(B + A)^2 T$, respectively. Since we have chosen $B \gg A$ for homodyne detection, both distributions have very nearly the same variance $\sigma^2 \doteq B^2 T$. The width of the curves in Fig. 6-3 is the standard deviation $\sigma \doteq B\sqrt{T}$ and is so indicated.

Given the count at the end of each binary interval (or, equivalently, the integral of the square of the envelope), we have to decide whether a 1 or a 0 was

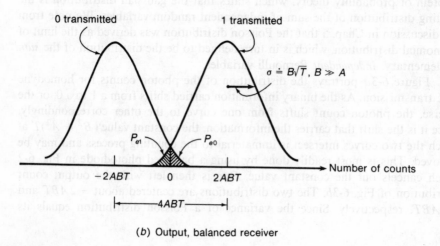

(b) Output, balanced receiver

FIGURE 6-3
Continued

transmitted. From the symmetry of Fig. 6-3b and assuming 1 or 0 equally likely to be transmitted, it is clear that a reasonable decision mechanism is to declare a 1 present if the count is positive, and a 0 present if the count is negative. This will in fact be shown in Chap. 7 to be optimum in the sense of minimum probability of error. But note from Fig. 6-3b that either decision can result in an error: Given a 0 transmitted, there is a chance the count will be positive; given a 1 transmitted, there is a chance the count will be negative. Note from Fig. 6-3b that these two error probabilities, labeled P_{e1} and P_{e0} respectively, are equal.

To calculate these error probabilities we use the gaussian approximation to the Poisson distribution. The gaussian or normal density function $f_x(x)$ with average value a and variance σ^2 is given by the familiar expression

$$f_x(x) = \frac{e^{-(x-a)^2/2\sigma^2}}{\sqrt{2\pi\sigma^2}} \tag{6-4}$$

The variance σ^2 in our case is B^2T; the average is either $-2ABT$ or $+2ABT$. From Fig. 6-3b, the probability of error, P_{e1}, given a 1 transmitted, is found by integrating the curve centered about $+2ABT$ over its tail from $-\infty$ to 0:

$$P_{e1} = \int_{-\infty}^{0} \frac{e^{-(x-2ABT)^2/2\sigma^2}}{\sqrt{2\pi\sigma^2}} \, dx \tag{6-5}$$

This is shown by the hatching in Fig. 6-3b. The corresponding error probability, P_{e0}, given a 0 transmitted, is found by integrating over the other tail.

These integrals can only be evaluated by numerical integration. Tables of the gaussian integral exist in many different forms. We will be using one standard form throughout this book. It is called the error function erf x. This is defined as

$$\text{erf } x \equiv \frac{2}{\sqrt{\pi}} \int_0^x e^{-y^2} \, dy, \tag{6-6}$$

with

$$\text{erf } \infty = 1 \tag{6-7}$$

It will frequently be of interest as well, particularly when calculating small probabilities of error, to consider $1 - \text{erf } x$. We define this quantity to be the complementary error function erfc x:

$$\text{erfc } x \equiv 1 - \text{erf } x = \frac{2}{\sqrt{\pi}} \int_x^{\infty} e^{-y^2} \, dy \tag{6-8}$$

It is left to the reader as an exercise to show that the probability P_{e1} in (6-5) is given by the expression

$$P_{e1} = \tfrac{1}{2} \, \text{erfc} \, \frac{2ABT}{\sqrt{2}\,\sigma}$$

$$= \tfrac{1}{2} \, \text{erfc} \, \sqrt{2TA^2} \tag{6-9}$$

since $\sigma^2 = B^2T$.

To find the overall bit-error probability P_e, we must in general add the two weighted error probabilities P_{e0} and P_{e1}. Thus, let the probability a binary 0 is present in general be P_0, while the probability a 1 is present is $P_1 = 1 - P_0$. These are called *a priori probabilities*. Here we have assumed $P_0 = P_1 = \frac{1}{2}$. The two probabilities P_{e0} and P_{e1} are conditional probabilities, conditioned on a 0 and a 1 being present, respectively. The overall probability of error, P_e, is found by unconditioning P_{e0} and P_{e1} and adding the two resultant probabilities of error. (Note that the two events, making an error when a 0 is present and making an error when a 1 is present, are mutually exclusive.) Specifically, we have

$$P_e = P_0 P_{e0} + P_1 P_{e1} \tag{6-10}$$

In the case under discussion here we have $P_{e1} = P_{e0}$. Equation (6-10) then simplifies to

$$P_e = P_{e1} \tag{6-10a}$$

From (6-9), letting $A^2T = \lambda_p T$, with λ_p the average photon arrival rate at the receiver, we finally have as the desired probability of bit error for homodyne PSK transmission

$$P_e = \frac{1}{2} \operatorname{erfc} \sqrt{2\lambda_p T} \tag{6-10b}$$

This may be evaluated numerically for various values of $\lambda_p T$.

A useful approximation to the complementary error function of (6-8), particularly appropriate for small probabilities of error [or large x in (6-8)], is found by integrating (6-8) by parts and retaining the leading term only. This is also left as an exercise for the reader. This approximation is given by

$$\operatorname{erfc} x \doteq \frac{e^{-x^2}}{x\sqrt{\pi}} \qquad x > 3 \tag{6-11}$$

Using this approximation, we can write the bit-error probability P_e in the form

$$P_e \doteq \frac{1}{2} \frac{e^{-2\lambda_p T}}{\sqrt{2\pi\lambda_p T}} \qquad \sqrt{2\lambda_p T} > 3 \tag{6-12}$$

Comparing this result with that of (6-3) for direct-detection OOK transmission, we see that they are comparable. In fact, if we pick $P_e = 10^{-9}$ as the desired goal, we find $\lambda_p T = 9$ photons/bit. This average photon count required at the receiver is called the quantum limit for homodyne PSK transmission. This compares with $\lambda_p T = 10.3$ photons/bit, on the average, for direct-detection OOK transmission. Since the two are comparable, why even bother with coherent transmission? There are several reasons. One is that the quantum limit for the direct-detection case is idealized. Recall that it assumes a noiseless receiver. As pointed out earlier, a weak signal at the PIN input produces a weak signal at the output. Noise can therefore not be neglected in this case. This is the reason why APD detectors have been used with long-haul, weak-signal, direct-detection systems. They provide a much higher signal output, but, as noted, are themselves noisy. The result is that real systems require received photon counts many times that of the quantum limit. A coherent system *can* use the relatively noise-free PIN diode, however, since the weak received signal has the strong local oscillator signal added to it.

A second reason for the use of binary coherent schemes is that the frequency stability of the laser transmitters used may allow multiple closely spaced carriers to be transmitted simultaneously. This is exactly the FDM technique described in Chap. 4. It would result in a tremendous increase in the total transmission capacity of a given fiber. (The wavelength range from 1.3 to 1.55 μm corresponds to approximately 0.5×10^{14} Hz. Say that 10-Gbit/s PSK transmission is desired. The transmission bandwidth required, assuming 25-percent sinusoidal roll-off shaping is used, is 12.5 GHz. Four thousand such channels could potentially be frequency-multiplexed over this wavelength range. For 2-Gbit/s transmission, 20,000 channels could be accommodated. These are enormous numbers.) Finally, APD receiver performance begins to deteriorate at bit rates above several Gbits/s. For these reasons and others, there has been a great stimulus to move to coherent lightwave systems.

One critical drawback to the introduction of homodyne PSK systems at light-wave frequencies is the fact that laser phase noise degrades the performance possible using these systems [SALZ 1985], [SALZ 1986].[4] Laser phase noise is due to spontaneous emissions within the laser cavity, causing the phase of the optical output wave to deviate randomly away from its desired value. As the bit rate is increased, this impairment can be made quite small. Analysis indicates that the degradation due to phase noise in homodyne PSK systems can be kept below 1 dB in equivalent increased power required, if the ratio of data bit rate to the laser frequency linewidth (deviation from a constant frequency output) is greater than 3,000 [SALZ 1985], [SALZ 1986]. As an example, the bit rate must be greater than 3 Gbits/s if the linewidth is kept to 1 MHz. At a frequency of 10^{14} Hz, this corresponds to 1 part in 10^8. Heterodyned PSK systems and FSK systems, to be discussed later, can reduce the problem considerably [SALZ 1986].

We have discussed homodyne PSK performance in detail. How do homodyne OOK systems perform? An analysis similar to that carried out for homodyne PSK shows that the quantum-limit performance is worse by 3 dB: two times as much power is required, on the average; i.e., the average number of photons/bit required increases to 18. Interestingly, this is poorer than the quantum limit of 10.3 photons/bit for direct-detection OOK transmission, but, following the same reasoning applied to homodyne PSK transmission, homodyne OOK transmission might still be preferred, since the quantum limit here may be approached more closely.

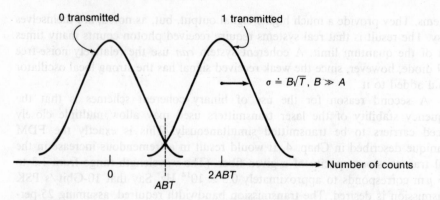

FIGURE 6-4
Photon-count statistics, balanced receiver, homodyne OOK transmission, Fig. 6-2, $B \gg A$.

We shall only outline the analysis in this case, leaving details to the reader. In the case of homodyne OOK transmission, the received signal $+A \cos \omega_0 t$ or 0 is again synchronously detected by adding a local-oscillator signal $A \cos \omega_0 t$, $B \gg A$, at the receiver. The composite light-wave signal at the photodiode is then $(B + A)\cos \omega_0 t$ or $B \cos \omega_0 t$. It is left to the reader to show, using the same arguments as used earlier for homodyne PSK, that the photon count statistics are approximated quite well by the two gaussian curves of Fig. 6-4. (Balanced detection is again assumed). The spacing between the two curves is now approximately $2ABT$ ($B \gg A$) in place of $4ABT$ (Fig. 6-3). It is clear from Fig. 6-4 that a 1 should be declared present if the number of counts following the balanced detector exceeds ABT. If the count drops below ABT a 0 should be declared present. Note how this differs from direct detection, with no local oscillator present, in which case *any* count signifies a 1 present.

The probability of error, again assuming 1's and 0's are equally likely, is now given by

$$P_e = \tfrac{1}{2} \operatorname{erfc} \sqrt{A^2 T/2}$$
$$= \tfrac{1}{2} \operatorname{erfc} \sqrt{\lambda_p T/2} \tag{6-13}$$

Using approximation (6-11) for erfc x, one now finds that

$$P_e \doteq \frac{1}{2} \frac{e^{-\lambda_p T/2}}{\sqrt{\pi \lambda_p T/2}} \tag{6-14}$$

This is the same form as (6-12) for homodyne PSK. It looks as though the required $\lambda_p T$ is four times that in the PSK case for the same P_e. But note again that power is on only one-half the time in the OOK case. This reduces the deterioration in performance to a factor of two, or 3 dB. Thus, for $P_e = 10^{-9}$, the homodyne-OOK quantum limit becomes 18 photons/bit, on the average, required at the receiver. This means twice the average power at the laser transmitter for the same fiber link length (transmitter–receiver spacing), or one-half the length for the same average transmitter power. Similar results comparing PSK with OOK transmission will be found to hold later when discussing additive noise in digital radio systems below the optical region.

The homodyne-OOK quantum limit of 18 photons/bit, on the average, needed at the receiver to attain a bit probability of error of 10^{-9} is considerably below the measured values of 1,000 photons/bit, using direct-detection OOK transmission with APO detectors. As noted above, in discussing homodyne PSK systems, this figure of 50 in potential improvement in power performance indicates that it is worthwhile pursuing the goal of coherent detection. The other reasons mentioned above, such as the ability to use FDM techniques to attain very high throughput capacities over optical fibers, are important as well.

One additional example of the calculation of a quantum limit is more of academic interest, but it does serve as an interesting example of the calculation technique employed here. The example is that of the existence of a superquantum limit [SALZ 1985], [SALZ 1986] for a special case of homodyne PSK transmission. Referring back to Fig. 6-2, we again let a synchronous local-oscillator optical signal $B \cos \omega_0 t$ be added to the received light-wave signal $\pm A \cos \omega_c t$. Instead of taking $B \gg A$ as in the previous two examples, however, we assume tight amplitude control of the local-oscillator signal, letting $B = A$. Amplitude, phase, and frequency must all be locked to the incoming signal then. The summed optical signal appearing at the (ideal) PIN diode input is then $2A \cos \omega_0 t$ in the case of a 1 transmitted, and 0 in the case of a 0 transmitted. The output of the diode is then 0 if a 0 is received, and $4A^2T = 4\lambda_p T$ if a 1 is received. This result is identical to that for direct-detection OOK, but with the effective amplitude of the on-signal doubled. Poisson statistics then apply, and, using the same argument as for direct-detection OOK, the probability of error is found to be

$$P_e = \tfrac{1}{2} e^{-4\lambda_p T} \tag{6-15}$$

Details are left to the reader. For $P_e = 10^{-9}$, this expression says that $\lambda_p T = 5.2$ photons/bit are required at the receiver, on the average. (Here, unlike the OOK case, transmitted power is on at all times, so that one doesn't further divide by two to find the average power or photon count required.)

As noted, this technique is of academic interest. *Any* count made during the transmission of a 0 ($-A \cos \omega_0 t$) produces an error. To keep P_e close to 10^{-9} the local oscillator amplitude B must be controlled tightly enough that the chance of an error during the transmission of a 0 is less then 10^{-9}. This error term is $\tfrac{1}{2}[1 - e^{-(A-B)^2 T}] \doteq \tfrac{1}{2}(A - B)^2 T$. Since $(A + B)^2 T \doteq 4A^2 T = 20.6$, this says that $(A - B)/A < 4 \times 10^{-5}$. In addition to the need for phase and frequency synchrony, the fractional deviation in amplitude must be kept to less than 0.004 percent for this limit to be attainable.

The results of this section on light-wave performance limits are summarized in Table 6-1. Also included in the table are results for heterodyne coherent detection, to be discussed later in this book. Note that the heterodyne technique produces a 3-dB (factor of two) deterioration in performance from the homodyne

TABLE 6-1
Quantum limits, light-wave transmission, $P_e = 10^{-9}$

Detection technique	Photons/bit required
Direct detection	10.3
Coherent homodyne:	
OOK	18
PSK	9
Superquantum limit	5.2
Coherent heterodyne:	
OOK	36
FSK	36
PSK	18

results obtained here, but utilizes phase and frequency control at much lower frequencies, where it is easier to attain.

6-2 BASEBAND BINARY COMMUNICATIONS: ERRORS DUE TO NOISE

In Sec. 6-1 just concluded we introduced the concept of errors in binary transmission by discussing limits on the performance of binary communications at light-wave frequencies. These limits arise from the quantum nature of the light-wave signal, manifested in a Poisson distribution of the number of photons striking a diode detector during a binary interval. Statistical fluctuations in the counts may result in errors in distinguishing between binary signals received.

At lower frequencies, for example at microwave frequencies in the gigahertz range and below, the quantum effects are no longer noticeable and errors now turn out to be due to noise added during transmission of the signals.[5] The word "added" means that, as measured at the receiver, the composite signal consists of the desired binary signal plus noise. Quantization noise, discussed in Chap. 3, was modeled as additive noise as well. The additive noise under discussion here has natural origins, rather than being introduced by equipment. We shall generically refer to both this noise and the signal as having units of voltage for simplicity's sake. We could equally well refer to current or some other physical quantity.

We shall explore the sources of this noise briefly at the end of this chapter. Suffice it to say at this point that noise is introduced in a variety of ways: Where

---

[5]As will be noted at the end of this chapter in discussing additive noise, quantum effects become negligible at a frequency $f \ll kT/h$, where k is Boltzmann's constant, and T is the absolute temperature in degrees Kelvin. At room temperature $kT/h \sim 10^{13}$ Hz, considerably below the optical frequency $f_0 \sim 10^{14}$ Hz considered in the previous section.

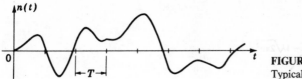

FIGURE 6-5
Typical oscillogram, noise voltage.

an antenna is used at the receiver, the antenna picks up noise radiation from the sky. Any dissipative elements generate noise as well. The dissipation in a transmission cable thus generates noise. Resistive elements in electrical circuits generate noise. All of these noise sources are temperature-dependent, and the noise generated is called generically *thermal noise*. In addition, active elements generate noise due to the random motion of current carriers (electrons and holes, for example). These two types of spontaneous fluctuation noise are always present in electrical circuits, although they may be reduced by lowering the temperature or changing the circuit design. This contrasts with "man-made" noise (electromagnetic pickup, mechanical vibrations converted to electrical disturbances, etc.), which can be eliminated or minimized with proper design, and erratic noise (effects of electrical storms, sudden and unexpected voltage change, etc.), which by its very description does not occur continuously. We focus here on the spontaneous fluctuation noise.

A typical oscillogram of the noise voltage $n(t)$ might appear as in Fig. 6-5. Although the noise is assumed random, so that we cannot specify in advance particular voltage values as a function of time, we assume we know the noise statistics. In particular, we assume first that the noise is zero-mean gaussian; i.e., it has a gaussian probability-density function, with mean $E(n) = 0$. Specifically, if we sample the noise at any arbitrary time t_1, the probability that the measured sample $n(t_1)$ will fall in the range n to $n + dn$ is given by $f(n)\, dn$, with

$$f(n) = \frac{e^{-n^2/2\sigma^2}}{\sqrt{2\pi\sigma^2}} \tag{6-16}$$

This is the most commonly used statistical model for additive noise in communications, and is in most applications a valid representation for actual noise present. We assume the noise variance σ^2 is known. (As will be demonstrated later in this chapter, σ^2 may be measured either digitally or with a long-time-constant true-power meter.) Note that this model has the same form as that used in the previous section to approximate the Poisson distribution. It is not to be confused with the other model, in which mean and variance were equal. The function is shown sketched in Fig. 6-6. It has the typical bell-shaped curve, peaking at $n = 0$ (the most probable value of the random variable). Its width is measured by the standard deviation σ. The probability that the random noise voltage n will be less than σ volts in magnitude at any time sampled is 0.68. The probability that values of n higher than several times σ will be attained falls off exponentially in n^2. The noise is equally likely to have positive and negative

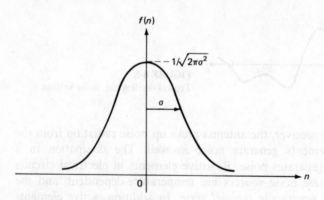

FIGURE 6-6
Gaussian probability-density function.

values. The driving force behind this gaussian model for the noise statistics (another model, that of *laplacian noise*, appears among the problems at the end of this chapter) is the *central limit theorem* of probability: the statistics of the sum of a number of random variables tends to gaussian under some rather broad conditions.

Now assume we are receiving binary pulses in a digital communication system. The noise $n(t)$ is added to the incoming group of pulses in the receiver, and there is a possibility that the noise will cause an error in the decoding of the signal. Specifically, if the system is of the NRZ on–off type, in which pulses represent 1's (or marks) in the binary code, the absence of pulses representing 0's or spaces (see Chap. 3), the error will occur if noise in the absence of a signal happens to have an instantaneous amplitude comparable with that of a pulse when present or if noise in the presence of a signal happens to have a large enough negative amplitude to destroy the pulse. In the first case the noise alone will be mistaken for a pulse signal, and a 0 will be converted to a 1; in the second case the 1 actually transmitted will appear as a 0 at the decoder output.

How often will such errors occur on the average? Is it possible to decrease the rate of errors below a tolerable maximum by increasing the pulse amplitude? If so, how much increase is necessary? What is the effect on the error rate of reducing the noise? All these questions are readily solved if we know the noise statistics or have a reasonably good model for these. We shall demonstrate this using the gaussian noise model of Eq. (6-16).

Assume that the pulse amplitudes are all A volts, as in Chap. 3. The composite sequence of binary symbols plus noise is sampled once every binary interval, and a decision is made as to whether a 1 or a 0 is present. One particularly simple way of making the decision is to decide on a 1 if the composite voltage sample exceeds $A/2$ volts, and a 0 if the sample is less than $A/2$ volts. Errors will then occur if, with a pulse present, the composite voltage sample is less than $A/2$, or, with a pulse absent, if the noise alone exceeds $A/2$.

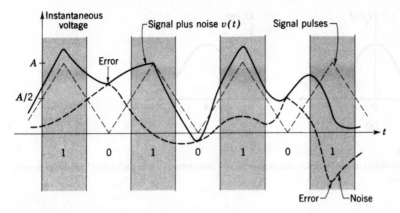

FIGURE 6-7
Effect of noise in binary-pulse transmission.

This decision criterion is similar to the one adopted in Sec. 6-1 (Fig. 6-4) in discussing errors due to photocount statistics.

An example of a possible signal sequence, indicating the two possible types of error, is shown in Fig. 6-7. The signal pulses are shown triangular for simplicity's sake. The pulses and noise are shown dashed, while the resultant or composite voltage $v(t)$ is represented by the solid line. In this case samples are taken at the *center* of each binary interval, the system decoder then responding to the amplitude of these samples.

To determine the probability of error *quantitatively* we consider the two possible types of error separately. Assume first that a 0 is sent, so that no pulse is present at the time of decoding. The probability of error in this case is just the probability that noise will exceed $A/2$ volts in amplitude and be mistaken for a pulse or a 1 in the binary code. Alternatively, since $v(t) = n(t)$ if a 0 is present, the sampled value v is a random variable with the same statistics as the noise. The probability of error is then just the probability that v will appear somewhere between $A/2$ and ∞. Thus the density function of v, assuming a 0 present, is just

$$f_0(v) = \frac{1}{\sqrt{2\pi\sigma^2}} e^{-v^2/2\sigma^2} \tag{6-17}$$

The subscript 0 denotes the presence of a 0 symbol, and the probability of error P_{e0} in this case is just the area under the $f_0(v)$ curve from $A/2$ to ∞:

$$P_{e0} = \text{Prob}\left(v > \frac{A}{2}\right) = \int_{A/2}^{\infty} f_0(v) \, dv \tag{6-18}$$

The density function $f_0(v)$ is shown sketched in Fig. 6-8a, with the probability of error indicated by the shaded area. This is of course similar to the calculations

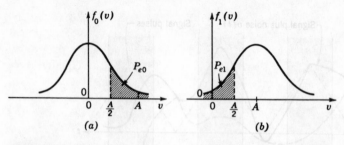

FIGURE 6-8
Probability densities in binary-pulse transmission. (*a*) Noise only (0 transmitted). (*b*) Pulse plus noise
(1 transmitted).

carried out in Sec. 6-1 for both PSK and OOK transmission (see Figs. 6-3 and
6-4).

Assume now that a 1 is transmitted by the system encoder. This appears at
the decoder as a pulse of amplitude A volts plus superimposed noise. A sample
$v(t)$ of the composite voltage taken at time t is now the random variable
$A + n(t)$. The fixed quantity A serves to shift the noise level from an average of
zero volts to an average of A volts. The random variable v has the same statistics
as n, fluctuating about A, however, rather than 0. Its density function is the same
gaussian function, with the same variance, but with an average value of A. We
have

$$f_1(v) = \frac{1}{\sqrt{2\pi\sigma^2}} e^{-(v-A)^2/2\sigma^2} \tag{6-19}$$

This is shown sketched in Fig. 6-8*b*. The probability of error now corresponds to
the chance that the sample v of signal plus noise will drop below $A/2$ volts and
be mistaken for noise only (be judged, incorrectly, a 0). This is just the area under
the $f_1(v)$ curve from $-\infty$ to $A/2$ and is given by

$$P_{e1} = \text{Prob}\left(v < \frac{A}{2}\right) = \int_{-\infty}^{A/2} f_1(v)\, dv \tag{6-20}$$

This probability of error is indicated by the shaded area in Fig. 6-8*b*.

The probability of error of the system is now found using the same
approach as in Sec. 6-1. The two possible types of error again represent mutually
exclusive events: The 0 precludes a 1 appearing, and vice versa. Letting the a
priori probability of transmitting a 0 be a known quantity P_0, while the probability of transmitting a 1 is taken to be $P_1 = 1 - P_0$, we have again, as the total
error of the system,

$$P_e = P_0 P_{e0} + P_1 P_{e1} \tag{6-21}$$

It is apparent from Fig. 6-8 and from the symmetry of the gaussian curves
that the two conditional probabilities P_{e0} and P_{e1} are equal in this example, as
they were in the previous one in Sec. 6-1. (This may also be shown mathemati-

cally by a linear translation of coordinates, letting $x = v - A$ in Eq. (6-20), or by noting that the probability that noise alone will be less than $-A/2$ is the same as the probability that it will exceed $A/2$.) If we also make the rather reasonable assumption, as previously, that the two binary signals 0 and 1 are equally likely to occur, then $P_0 = P_1 = \frac{1}{2}$, and we are left with the result that the total probability of error, P_e, is the same as P_{e0} or P_{e1}. It is left to the reader as an exercise to show that the probability of error is then again simply given by the complementary error function erfc x:

$$P_e = \frac{1}{2} \operatorname{erfc} \frac{A}{\sqrt{2}\,\sigma}$$

$$= \frac{1}{2}\left(1 - \operatorname{erf} \frac{A}{2\sqrt{2}\,\sigma}\right) \tag{6-22}$$

Here

$$\operatorname{erfc} x \equiv \frac{2}{\sqrt{\pi}} \int_x^\infty e^{-y^2} \, dy \tag{6-23}$$

and

$$\operatorname{erf} x \equiv \frac{2}{\sqrt{\pi}} \int_0^x e^{-y^2} \, dy \tag{6-24}$$

We rewrite these definitions here because of their importance in all the work to follow in this book. The complementary error function will be recurring over and over again because of our focus on additive *gaussian* noise. Because of its importance we include, in Table 6-2, a short table of erf x. The approximation (6-11) to erfc x can be used for larger values of x.

With the 1's and 0's assumed equally likely in a long message, Eq. (6-22) gives the probability of an error in the decoding of any digit. Note that P_e depends solely on A/σ, the ratio of the signal amplitude to the noise standard deviation. This latter quantity σ is commonly referred to as the *rms noise*. The ratio A/σ is then the peak *signal-to-rms-noise ratio*.

The probability of error is shown plotted versus A/σ, in decibels, in Fig. 6-9. Note that for $A/\sigma = 7.4$ (17.4 dB), P_e is 10^{-4}. This means that on the average 1 bit in 10^4 transmitted will be judged incorrectly. If 10^5 bits/s are being transmitted, this means a mistake every 0.1 s, on the average, which may not be satisfactory. However, if the signal is increased to $A/\sigma = 11.2$ (21 dB), a change of 3.6 dB, then P_e decreases to 10^{-8}. For 10^5 bits/s this means a mistake every 1,000 s or 15 min on the average, which is much more likely to be tolerable. (In nonoptical communications practice designers often use $P_e = 10^{-5}$ as a design goal for binary communication systems. Recall that in the light-wave world 10^{-9} is the design goal.)

Above $A/\sigma = 6$ or 16 dB (approximately), the probability of error decreases very rapidly with small increases in signal. In the example just cited, increasing the signal by a factor of 3.6 dB (from $A/\sigma = 7.4$ to 11.2) reduces the

TABLE 6-2
Error function $\text{erf } x \equiv (2/\sqrt{\pi})\int_0^x e^{-x^2}\, dx$

x	$\text{erf } x$	x	$\text{erf } x$	x	$\text{erf } x$
0.00	0.00000	1.05	0.86244	2.10	0.99702
0.05	0.05637	1.10	0.88021	2.15	0.99764
0.10	0.11246	1.15	0.89612	2.20	0.99814
0.15	0.16800	1.20	0.91031	2.25	0.99854
0.20	0.22270	1.25	0.92290	2.30	0.99886
0.25	0.27633	1.30	0.93401	2.35	0.99911
0.30	0.32863	1.35	0.94376	2.40	0.99931
0.35	0.37938	1.40	0.95229	2.45	0.99947
0.40	0.42839	1.45	0.95970	2.50	0.99959
0.45	0.47548	1.50	0.96611	2.6	0.99976
0.50	0.52050	1.55	0.97162	2.7	0.99987
0.55	0.56332	1.60	0.97635	2.8	0.99992
0.60	0.60386	1.65	0.98038	2.9	0.99996
0.65	0.64203	1.70	0.98379	3.0	0.99998
0.70	0.67780	1.75	0.98667		
0.75	0.71116	1.80	0.98909		
0.80	0.74210	1.85	0.99111		
0.85	0.77067	1.90	0.99279		
0.90	0.79691	1.95	0.99418		
0.95	0.82089	2.00	0.99532		
1.00	0.84270	2.05	0.99626		

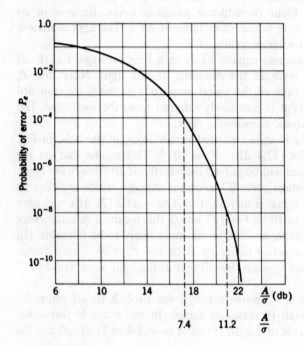

FIGURE 6-9
Probability of error for binary detection in gaussian note.

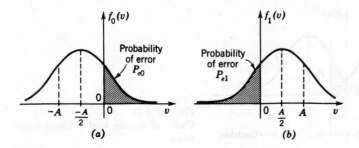

FIGURE 6-10
Probability densities in the transmission of NRZ polar binary pulses. (a) Negative pulse transmitted.
(b) Positive pulse.

error rate by 10^4. The existence of a narrow range of signal-to-noise ratios above which the error rate is tolerable, and below which errors occur quite frequently, is termed a *threshold effect*. The signal-to-noise ratio at which this effect takes place is called the threshold level. For the transmission of binary digits the threshold level is chosen somewhere between $A/\sigma = 6$ and 8 (16 to 18 dB). Note that this does not imply complete noise suppression above the threshold level. It merely indicates that for pulse amplitudes greater than 10 times the rms noise, say, errors in the transmission of binary digits will occur at a tolerable rate.

That the foregoing error analysis for the transmission of on–off binary pulses holds true for NRZ-polar pulses is shown by Fig. 6-10. We recall from Chap. 3 that the positive and negative pulses need only be transmitted at $A/2$ or $-A/2$ volts, respectively. The decoder then determines which pulse is present from the polarity of the total instantaneous voltage (signal plus noise). Figure 6-10a shows the probability-density function for the negative pulse of $-A/2$ volts plus noise. Figure 6-10b shows the corresponding curve for the positive pulse plus noise. The error probability is in each case the same, and, comparing with Fig. 6-8, the same as for the case of on–off pulses. The error curve of Fig. 6-9 thus applies to either type of binary-digit transmission. The polar signal requires only half the signal amplitude of the on–off signal, however, or one-fourth of the peak power. (The *average* power is one-half that of the on–off signal, since that signal sequence is zero half the time, on the average.) It is thus apparent that a polar signal is preferable where possible. These comparative results are the same as those found earlier in calculating light-wave quantum limits. See Table 6-1.

Optimum Decision Levels

In this discussion of the probability of error in binary transmission we have so far relied on more or less intuitive judgments in developing the expression for the probability of error. Thus we have assumed the signals to be equally likely to be transmitted, we have arbitrarily chosen as our decision level the value $A/2$ for

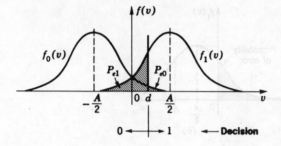

FIGURE 6-11
Choice of decision level in binary transmission.

the on–off pulse sequence, or 0 in the case of the polar sequence, etc. One may readily ask how significant these assumptions are. Is it possible to decrease the probability of error by another choice of decision level? Is there a minimum P_e one can attain? We shall consider these questions and others related to them ("best" choice of binary waveshapes, the effect of multiple sampling, extension to M-ary transmission, etc.) in a quite general way in Chap. 7.

At this point, however, we can say something about the possibility of decreasing P_e for this particular problem of binary transmission by an appropriate choice of decision level. In particular, assume a polar sequence of pulses transmitted with gaussian noise added, so that we have a composite sample $v(t)$ of signal plus noise, as previously. How shall we make the decision about whether a 1 or a 0 was transmitted? In this communications problem it is apparent that a reasonable design criterion is that of minimizing the probability of error P_e. A system with minimum P_e is then optimum from our point of view.

. Since the decoder can only base its decision on the voltage amplitude of the sample $v(t)$ taken, it is apparent that the only possible way to adjust P_e or to optimize the system is to vary the amplitude level at which the decision is made. Call this decision level d. It is apparent from Fig. 6-11, in which this level is shown superimposed on the probability-density plots for polar transmission, that increasing d positively decreases the chance of mistaking a 0 for a 1 (P_{e0}) but at the cost of increasing P_{e1}. It is also apparent from the symmetry of the figure and the form of the gaussian functions shown that an optimum solution is $d = 0$, just our previous intuitive guess, *assuming 0's and 1's equally likely*. It is equally apparent that if for some reason 0's occur more often on the average ($P_0 > P_1$), one would tend to shift d positively. If on the other hand 1's tend to occur more often ($P_1 > P_0$), one would shift d negatively. The optimum choice of d thus depends on the a priori probabilities P_0 and P_1.

To make this discussion more quantitative we must return to our original formulation of the probability of error. From Eqs. (6-18), (6-20), and (6-21), we have, with d as an arbitrary decision level,

$$P_e = P_0 \underbrace{\int_d^\infty f_0(v)\, dv}_{P_{e0}} + P_1 \underbrace{\int_{-\infty}^d f_1(v)\, dv}_{P_{e1}} \tag{6-25}$$

(Recall that the previous equations were written for the on–off-signal case. Had they been written for the polar case, 0 would have been used in place of $A/2$.)

An optimum choice of d corresponds to minimum P_e, according to our criterion. Since P_e is a function of d in Eq. (6-25), we simply differentiate with respect to d to find the optimum level. In particular, we then have

$$\frac{\partial P_e}{\partial d} = 0 = -P_0 f_0(d) + P_1 f_1(d)$$

or
$$\frac{f_1(d)}{f_0(d)} = \frac{P_0}{P_1} \tag{6-26}$$

invoking the usual rules of differentiation with respect to integrals.

It is thus apparent that the optimum d (in the sense of minimum error probability) depends on the form of the two conditional density functions [$f_0(v)$ and $f_1(v)$], as well as the a priori probabilities P_0 and P_1. If $P_0 = P_1 = \frac{1}{2}$, the optimum value of d is given by the point at which the two density functions intersect. For polar signals in gaussian noise this is just the point $d = 0$ (Fig. 6-11). For $P_0 \neq P_1$, the level shifts, as expected. Specifically, it is left for the reader to show that for the case of polar signals in additive gaussian noise (Fig. 6-11), the solution to Eq. (6-26) is given by

$$d_{opt} = \frac{\sigma^2}{A} \ln \frac{P_0}{P_1} \tag{6-27}$$

As expected, d increases positively if $P_0 > P_1$, and negatively if $P_1 > P_0$. The actual shift depends on the signal amplitude, noise variance, and P_0/P_1.

In practice this choice of optimum d is not very critical, and in the case of polar signals in additive gaussian noise one would normally pick $d = 0$ as the decision level. For one generally does not know the a priori probabilities accurately, and even if one did, the signal-to-noise ratio required for effective binary communication makes d_{opt} from Eq. (6-27) very close to zero. Specifically, if $A/\sigma = 8$ and $P_0/P_1 = 3$ (highly unlikely, since this requires $P_0 = \frac{3}{4}$, $P_1 = \frac{1}{4}$), then $d_{opt} = \sigma/8$. The optimum shift away from a $d = 0$ decision level is thus a fraction of the rms noise, an insignificant change. (Some thought would indicate that this corresponds approximately to changing the signal amplitude by the same amount, with the level held fixed. With the signal-to-noise ratio initially at 18 dB, this represents a shift of approximately 0.13 dB away. From Fig. 6-9 the change in P_e is not noticeable.)

If the optimization is inconsequential in this case, why discuss it? There are several reasons.

1. We at least know that our first, intuitive guess was a valid one. The optimization procedure tells us that *in this case* there is no sense looking for an improvement in system performance by varying the threshold level. This is very often exactly the reason for attempting to carry out system optimizations in more sophisticated situations.

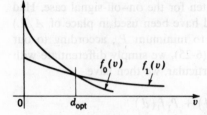

FIGURE 6-12
Example of determination of optimum decision level
($P_0 = P_1 = \frac{1}{2}$).

2. If the received signal amplitude (or noise variance for that matter) is not accurately known, or varies due to disturbances along the transmission channel, the probability of error will change as well. The sensitivity of P_e to changes in the amplitude A is obviously related to the sensitivity due to changes in d. (Alternatively, one would approach the problem of sensitivity to changes in A in a way similar to that done here.)

3. If the statistics of the received signals plus noise are *not* gaussian, and do not have the nice symmetry of the density functions of Fig. 6-11, intuition fails in determining the desired decision level. Examples of such situations will be encountered later in this book in dealing with the noncoherent detection of binary signals.[6] One must thus resort to the solution of Eq. (6-26) or of equations like it. One simple pictorial example of two conditional density functions obtained under certain conditions in noncoherent detection is shown in Fig. 6-12. Here $P_0 = P_1 = \frac{1}{2}$ is assumed, so that the optimum decision level occurs at the intersection of the two conditional density functions $f_1(v)$ and $f_0(v)$.

4. This first discussion of optimum decision levels serves as a good introduction to the more general optimization problems to be considered in Chap. 7.

6-3   INFORMATION CAPACITY OF PCM SYSTEMS: RELATIONS AMONG SIGNAL POWER, NOISE, AND BANDWIDTH

The probability of error calculations for binary transmission in the previous section enable us to develop an interesting relation for the capacity, in bits/s, of a PCM system with output power S transmitting digital signals over a channel of bandwidth B and that introduces additive gaussian noise of variance σ^2. The capacity in this case represents the bit transmission rate possible for a prescribed probability of error. It turns out that this capacity expression is in precisely the same form as the Shannon capacity expression to be discussed in Chap. 7 that provides the maximum bit rate (or capacity) for error-free performance of a channel with the same constraints. Specifically, for an error probability of 10^{-5},

---

[6]See [SCHW 1966, figs. 7-4-2 and 7-4-3], for the effect of threshold variation in on–off-keyed (OOK) signals with noncoherent detection.

we shall see that the PCM system requires seven times the power (8.5 dB) of the theoretically optimum one with error-free transmission. The expression we shall obtain is also useful because it shows, in a manner similar to the Shannon expression, how signal power may be exchanged for bandwidth.

This exchange of signal power for bandwidth was also discussed earlier in Chap. 3 in describing the possibility of reducing bandwidth by combining several binary pulses and transmitting instead one M-level signal. This brief analysis also applies to digital transmission with successive symbols coded into one of several amplitude levels.

Specifically, assume the input analog signal has been quantized to M possible amplitude levels. Assume further that the signal of B-hertz bandwidth has been sampled at the minimum Nyquist rate of $2B$ samples/s. With binary transmission, $M = 2^n$, $n = \log_2 M$ binary pulses would be transmitted for each sample, and the rate of information transmission in bits/s is then

$$C = 2B \log_2 M = 2nB \quad \text{bits/s} \tag{6-28}$$

The transmission channel must provide at least this transmission capability, or capacity. (We have implicitly assumed here that all amplitude levels are equally likely. If this is not the case, the more likely levels would be represented by fewer bits than the less likely one. See Sec. 1-6 for discussion.)

Rather than code into binary digits, however, say that the M levels are coded into n pulses of m amplitude levels each. Thus set $M = m^n$ in general. The information rate is still the same, so we now have

$$C = 2nB \log_2 m \quad \text{bits/s} \tag{6-29}$$

Let the bandwidth of the transmission channel be W hertz. With ideal Nyquist shaping we can transmit $2W$ symbols/s over this channel. Setting $2W = 2nB$, the desired symbol rate, we have

$$C = W \log_2 m^2 \quad \text{bits/s} \tag{6-30}$$

How is the number of amplitude levels m chosen? Obviously, one would like to make m as large as possible consistent with the power available for the system. Say that S watts of average power is available. With m possible levels equally likely to be transmitted and spaced a units apart (equal spacing), the average signal power is found by averaging over all possible levels. Assuming that NRZ polar transmission is used (which we have already seen provides a power improvement over the on–off case), the levels transmitted are actually $\pm a/2, +3a/2, \ldots, \pm (m-1)a/2$. The average power is then simply given by

$$S = \frac{2}{m} \left\{ \left(\frac{a}{2} \right)^2 + \left(\frac{3a}{2} \right)^2 + \cdots + \left[\frac{(m-1)a}{2} \right]^2 \right\}$$

$$= (a)^2 \frac{m^2 - 1}{12} \tag{6-31}$$

(Readers should check this relation for themselves.)

Solving for m^2 in terms of the average power S and substituting into Eq. (6-30) for the capacity, we have finally

$$C = W \log_2\left(1 + \frac{12S}{a^2}\right) \tag{6-32}$$

with W the transmission bandwidth.

For a given capacity, then, one may reduce the transmission bandwidth W by increasing the average signal power S. This is just the procedure noted previously, where successive pulses are combined into one wider pulse with increased amplitude levels. But note how inefficient this bandwidth–power exchange is. One must increase the power *exponentially* to obtain a corresponding linear decrease in bandwidth. As an example, assume that $12S/a^2 \gg 1$. Then if the power is increased eightfold, the bandwidth may be reduced by a factor of 3. Similarly, by a linear *increase* in bandwidth, the required signal power may be *reduced* exponentially.

How does one now determine the level spacing a? This ultimately depends on the noise encountered while attempting to decode the received signals at the receiver. For the case of binary transmission this spacing between levels is precisely the signal amplitude A in the example of on–off transmission or the separation between signals in the example of polar transmission (see Figs. 6-8 and 6-10). The specific choice of A in that case, or a in general, depends on the noise variance σ^2 and the error probability P_e deemed tolerable. This is made clear by Fig. 6-13, comparing m-level transmission with the two types of binary transmission. For the m-level case it is apparent that the spacing must be some constant K times the rms noise σ. In fact, if the error probability is small enough and the spacing a large enough, the chance that a given level being transmitted will be converted by noise to a level other than one of the adjacent ones is extremely small. To a good approximation the error analysis of the previous section is valid in this multilevel case also if the parameter A there is replaced by the spacing a.

In general, then, letting $a = K\sigma$, and writing N for σ^2 to emphasize *noise* power (the connection between the noise variance and the noise power will be

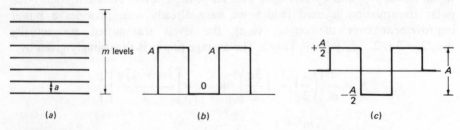

(a) (b) (c)

FIGURE 6-13
Digital pulse transmission. (a) m levels. (b) On–off pulses. (c) Polar pulses.

made clearer in Sec. 6-4), (6-32) can be rewritten as[7]

$$C = W \log_2\left(1 + \frac{12}{K^2}\frac{S}{N}\right) \qquad (6\text{-}33)$$

The quantity S/N—the ratio of average signal power to average noise power, or SNR as it is commonly abbreviated—will appear quite often in later discussions of the effect of noise on systems. At this point we simply note, as first pointed out in Chap. 1, that noise plays a role in determining system capacity through its effect on limiting the number of amplitude levels that may be used. This is exactly the reason it appears in the capacity expression of Eq. (6-33). Equation (6-33) thus emphasizes the point made in Chap. 1 that the capacity is limited by bandwidth and noise.

The capacity expression of Eq. (6-33) is interesting for another reason as well. Shannon [SHAN 1949] has shown that there is a maximum possible rate of transmission of binary digits over a channel limited in bandwidth to W hertz, with mean noise power N and mean signal power S. This rate of transmission, or capacity C, is maximum in the sense that if one tries to transmit information at a higher rate, the number of errors made in decoding the signals at the receiver begins to mount rapidly. In fact, the chance of an error in a code word of block length n can be shown to approach certainty as $n \to \infty$. On the other hand, if the information rate in bits per second is *less* than C, the chance of an error goes rapidly to zero. This maximum rate of transmission was found by Shannon to be given by

$$C = W \log_2\left(1 + \frac{S}{N}\right) \qquad (6\text{-}34)$$

Note that this is in precisely the same form as the PCM capacity expression of Eq. (6-33). Shannon's maximum-capacity expression provides an upper bound on the rate at which one can communicate over a channel of bandwidth W and signal-to-noise ratio SNR.[8] His original derivation indicated that it was theoretically possible to transmit at almost this rate with the error rate made to approach

---

[7]We are assuming throughout this discussion that the power level remains fixed at all points from transmitter to receiver. In actual practice, of course, it will vary from point to point. For example, it will normally be much less at the receiver antenna, or receiver input, than at the transmitter output. But amplifiers may of course be used, and normally are used, to bring the signal up to the desired power level. The signal amplitude *relative to the level spacing a* remains unchanged throughout transmission and reception, however, so that the ratio S/a^2 of Eq. (6-32) remains fixed. One may, therefore, just as well consider *relative* signal power, and assume it unchanging throughout the transmission path. Alternatively, the power level S refers to the signal power measured at the same point as the noise N. In a real system, as will become apparent from examples discussed later, S is directly proportional to the power made available at the transmitter output. Although S and N are, strictly speaking, mean-squared voltages, we use the common term power to represent both. They would represent the power dissipated in a 1-Ω resistor.

[8]A detailed discussion of this equation appears in Chap. 7.

zero as closely as desired, but he did not specify any particular system for so communicating. He showed only that complex encoding and indefinitely large time delays in transmission would be needed. Comparing Eqs. (6-33) and (6-34), we are now in a position to compare the PCM system with this hypothetical one transmitting at a maximum possible rate over a given channel.[9]

In particular note that the PCM system requires $K^2/12$ times the signal power of the optimum Shannon system for the same capacity, bandwidth, and noise power. For an error probability of 10^{-5}, we found in the previous section that $A/\sigma = 9.2$ for binary transmission. Using the argument described above, this should to a good approximation be the ratio of level spacing a to the rms noise σ for an m-level system. This is just the value of K required in (6-33). For this value of K, $K^2/12 = 7$, and the PCM system requires seven times as much power (8.5 dB) as the theoretically optimum one for the same channel capacity. (Note, however, that the optimum system can theoretically be made to transmit error-free at the cost of large time delays in transmission, while the PCM system, in this example, has the nonzero error rate of 10^{-5}.) Both Eqs. (6-33) and (6-34) have the form of the capacity expression (1-3) introduced in Chap. 1. They make explicit the qualitative remarks made there that both noise and bandwidth play fundamental roles in limiting the performance of communication systems. A specific transmission channel will have a bandwidth W available for communication and will introduce some known additive noise power N. The Shannon expression (6-34) then describes the maximum rate of error-free digital transmission over that channel as a function of the signal power S. Equation (6-33) says that normal digital transmission over the same channel is limited in a similar manner: the transmission bandwidth W limits the number of symbols that may be transmitted over the channel to $2W$ per second at most. The number of bits carried by a symbol, with amplitude-level variation, is then limited by the average signal power S, and the noise N introduced on the channel.

6-4 NOISE POWER AND SPECTRAL REPRESENTATION OF NOISE

In Secs. 6-2 and 6-3 we assumed the noise added to the signal to have known statistics (most commonly, gaussian), with a specified variance σ^2. This enabled us to calculate the probability of error in baseband binary signal transmission due to additive noise and to assess the performance of a PCM system. To proceed further we must indicate ways of measuring the variance σ^2, as well as other statistical parameters of the noise. More important, since the noise function $n(t)$ is a time-varying wave, like any signal it must be affected by the system through which it passes. How does one quantitatively determine the effect of

---

[9]An M-ary system to be described in Chap. 7 has a performance approaching the Shannon optimum as $M \to \infty$.

systems on noise? What happens when noise, picked up, for example, by an antenna at a high frequency, is converted down to a lower frequency or to baseband, together with the signal to which it is added? How do linear filters and nonlinear devices act on the noise? All of these questions must be answered before proceeding further with our performance analysis of communication systems.

We thus digress somewhat, in this section and in the one following, to study ways of measuring and representing the noise. In particular, we shall find it useful, as with the signals in previous chapters, to develop a spectral representation for the noise. This will provide a means of studying the effect of systems—both linear and nonlinear—on noise. Interestingly, if we return to the premise of Chap. 1 that real signals must be time-varying and unpredictable (otherwise why transmit them?), it is apparent that the analysis we shall outline in this section and the one following is not only of importance in studying noise, but is exactly the analysis one must use in studying real time-varying signals in systems.

The frequency or spectral analysis of random signals and noise will be found to differ somewhat from the spectral analysis for deterministic signals studied in Chap. 2 and used in the chapters following. It will be found to be based on the spectral distribution of the *power* in the random wave. Nonetheless, many of the results obtained in our earlier study of deterministic signals will still be found to be valid. These include such things as bandwidths, the filtering effects of linear systems, the inverse time–bandwidth relationship, etc. This indicates the usefulness of the approach we have adopted of studying deterministic signals first.

Thus, although we shall stress the spectral representation of *noise*, as well as the effect of systems on noise in these sections, the ideas and concepts introduced are applicable as well to random signals. References given later will guide the reader interested in pursuing these topics further.

As noted in Sec. 6-2, a typical oscillogram of noise would appear as in Fig. 6-14. Random-signal waveshapes would also have a similar irregular, unpredictable appearance. We call this random time-varying function a *random process* $n(t)$. [Although we shall for simplicity's sake use the notation $n(t)$ and generally refer to the random wave as noise, random signals are included as well, as noted above.] A sample of $n(t)$ taken at an arbitrary time t is a random variable with some probability-density function $f_n(n)$. In the specific case discussed in Sec. 6-2, the noise was assumed to be gaussian, with $f_n(n)$ described by the gaussian

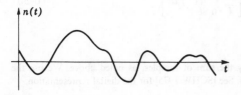

FIGURE 6-14
Random process.

function of (6-16). We shall most often assume gaussian noise in this book, but in general a random process will be described by any time function whose samples are random variables with some specified $f_n(n)$. (Consider as a simple, nongaussian example a two-level noise process: the random wave is equally likely to be either $+a$ or $-a$ when sampled. A special case is a binary pulse train, with 1's and 0's equally likely to occur. This is of course precisely the model of a binary signal randomized by the unpredictable occurrence of 1's and 0's.)

To determine $f_n(n)$ experimentally, if one did not know the underlying statistics, one could perform a histogram analysis, sampling $n(t)$ at intervals "far enough apart" to ensure the statistical independence of the samples, setting levels at n and $n + \Delta n$, and counting the number of times the samples fell in this range of n [SCHW 1975, chap. 3].

But what is meant by "independent samples"? What constitutes "far enough apart"? It is questions like this that we shall discuss in this section and the next, in dealing with noise spectral analysis. To motivate the discussion of the spectral analysis of the random process $n(t)$, we first focus attention on the measurement of some simple statistical parameters such as $E(n)$, the variance σ^2, etc. In considering how one measures these quantities, we shall be led into the more general discussion of spectral analysis.

Although the average value and variance of n can be obtained from the same histogram analysis of $n(t)$ used to find $f_n(n)$, simply by averaging measured samples appropriately, it is apparent intuitively that one should be able to make the same measurements much more simply using time-averaging meters. For example, if we were to feed the wave $n(t)$ into a dc meter, we would intuitively expect to get a measure of the expected value $E(n)$. In this case we are implicitly comparing an *expected* or *statistical* average with a *time* average, as carried out by a dc meter. Specifically[10], if the meter has an effective time constant T, its reading should give a number[10]

$$\bar{n} = \frac{1}{T} \int_0^T n(t)\, dt \tag{6-35}$$

It is apparent that as $n(t)$ varies randomly, so will $\bar{n}$. Depending on *when* we perform the indicated average, we will get different numbers $\bar{n}$. So $\bar{n}$ is a random variable, with its own expected value, variance, etc. But we would still expect to find $\bar{n}$ some measure of $E(n)$, the statistical average of $n(t)$. To indicate the connection, we take the expected value of $\bar{n}$ itself; i.e., we visualize many meter readings over different sections of $n(t)$, each T seconds long, the expected value of $\bar{n}$ then being the statistical average of these. Then

$$E(\bar{n}) = E\left[\frac{1}{T} \int_0^T n(t)\, dt \right] \tag{6-36}$$

---

[10]A digital meter would replace the integral by the sum of samples, as noted above. We use the integral representation throughout for simplicity. See [SCHW 1975] for the digital representation.

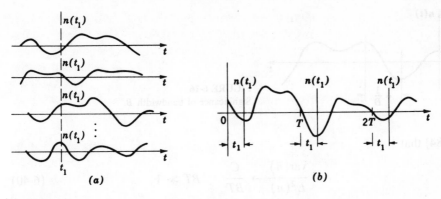

FIGURE 6-15
Ensemble averages. (*a*) Many identical sources. (*b*) By cutting one record.

It may be shown that the operations of expectation and integration are interchangeable [PAPO 1984]. We then write

$$E(\bar{n}) = \frac{1}{T} \int_0^T E[n(t)] \, dt \tag{6-37}$$

We now assume that the expected value $E[n(t)]$ is independent of time t. This is reasonable, for if the expected value *were* varying with time, one would not expect the dc meter reading to be a fixed number anyway. Alternatively, if we were to visualize many such strips of $n(t)$ each T seconds long, placed one above the other [either obtained from the same record by cutting the one strip at T-second intervals, or by visualizing many identical sources providing independent outputs $n(t)$] (see Fig. 6-15), we could perform an ensemble average of the random variable $n(t_1)$ to actually find a close approximation to $E[n(t_1)]$. One would then assume that $E[n(t_2)]$ or $E[n(t)]$ at any *other* value of t, was the same. (This would be verified by averaging at each time interval, if so desired.)

With this assumption that $E[n(t)]$ is a *constant*, independent of time, we find, from Eq. (6-37), that

$$E(\bar{n}) = E(n) \tag{6-38}$$

So our intuition is justified here, indicating that at least in an *average* sense the time average $\bar{n}$ does provide a measure of $E(n)$. But we would also expect that the time interval T should play a role here. By making T longer, or by averaging over longer sections of $n(t)$, we would expect to find $\bar{n}$ approaching $E(n)$ more closely. In fact, this is easily demonstrated by calculating the variance var($\bar{n}$) of the random variable $\bar{n}$. Thus, by definition of the variance,

$$\operatorname{var}(\bar{n}) = E[\bar{n} - E(\bar{n})]^2 = E\left\{ \frac{1}{T} \int_0^T [n(t) - E(n)]^2 \, dt \right\} \tag{6-39}$$

Although we shall not perform the calculation here, it is readily shown [PAPO

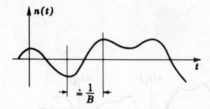

FIGURE 6-16
Significance of bandwidth B.

1984] that[11]

$$\frac{\text{var}(\bar{n})}{E^2(n)} \to \frac{C}{BT} \qquad BT \gg 1 \qquad (6\text{-}40)$$

where C is a fixed constant the order of 1, and B is the bandwidth of the process $n(t)$. [We shall define B precisely in the material to follow, but roughly speaking it is a measure of the rapidity of variation of $n(t)$, just as with the deterministic signals encountered previously. As indicated in Fig. 6-16, the time spread between successive dips and peaks in the wave is approximately the reciprocal of the bandwidth.] As an example, if $B = 100$ kHz and $T = 1$ ms (recall that this is the meter averaging time), $1/BT = 0.01$. The spread about the expected value is thus 0.1 of the expected value.

As the dc meter averages over longer and longer time intervals, its reading $\bar{n}$ approaches more and more closely the parameter $E(n)$. (In practical situations it is usually sufficient to have $T \gg 1/B$.) For the variance of the reading $\bar{n}$ goes to zero as $1/T$, indicating that the variations about $E(n)$ decrease in the same manner. Thus, in the previous example if the meter time constant is increased to 100 ms, $1/BT = 10^{-4}$. The spread about the expected value is the square root of this, or 10^{-2}. Increasing the integration time by a factor of 100 has narrowed the deviation about $E(n)$ by a factor of 10, on the average. In the limit, as $T \to \infty$, we must have

$$\lim_{T \to \infty} \bar{n} = \lim_{T \to \infty} \frac{1}{T} \int_0^T n(t)\, dt = E(n) \qquad (6\text{-}41)$$

A random waveshape or process $n(t)$ for which Eq. (6-41) is true is said to be an *ergodic process*; i.e., time and ensemble (statistical) averages may be equated. Although there are processes for which this is not true,[12] we shall henceforth assume that $\bar{n}$ and $E(n)$ may be equated.

---

[11] This assumes of course that $E(n) \neq 0$.

[12] A trivial example of a nonergodic process is that consisting of an ensemble of constant-voltage sources. Each source maintains its output absolutely constant with time. Each source provides, however, a different output. Choosing one source at random and averaging its output with time, we of course measure the particular source voltage. Measuring all sources simultaneously, however, and averaging these (the *ensemble* average), we get a different result than the time average, the ensemble average depending on the distribution of the source output.

Since we have shown that one may use a dc meter to measure $E(n)$, one may reasonably ask if it is similarly possible to measure σ^2, the variance of the noise. The answer is of course "yes," and in fact one uses a *power meter* for this purpose. Specifically, if one defines the average power P_{av} over an interval T seconds long, just as in previous chapters:

$$P_{av} \equiv \frac{1}{T} \int_0^T n^2(t) \, dt \tag{6-42}$$

one shows, again by interchanging the order of ensemble averaging and integrating, that

$$E(P_{av}) = E(n^2) = \sigma^2 + E^2(n) \tag{6-43}$$

$$\sigma^2 = E(P_{av}) - E^2(n) \tag{6-44}$$

if $E(n)^2$ is invariant with time. [Recall that $\sigma^2 = m_2 - m_1^2 = E(n^2) - E^2(n)$ for a random variable.]

Again P_{av}, as read by the power meter of time constant T, is a random variable, but *on the average* the readings will provide a measure of the second moment $E(n^2)$. Since $E^2(n)$ is very nearly the square of the dc value, it is apparent that the variance σ^2 must provide a measure of the fluctuating or non-dc power. To emphasize the fact that the variance on an ensemble-average basis is the same as the time-averaged fluctuation power, we shall henceforth use the symbol N for the latter. One often calls this the ac power, as measured by true rms meters. N would then be the *square* of the rms meter reading.

One may again show [PAPO 1984] that[13]

$$\frac{\text{var}(P_{av})}{E^2(P_{av})} = \frac{C'}{BT} \qquad BT \gg 1, \quad C' \text{ a constant} \tag{6-45}$$

Thus, as $T \to \infty$ (in practice $T \gg 1/B$ again suffices), the reading P_{av} approaches $E(n^2)$ with probability of 1, and we have

$$\lim_{T \to \infty} \left(P_{av} - \bar{n}^2 \right) = \lim_{T \to \infty} \frac{1}{T} \int_0^T \left[n(t) - \bar{n} \right]^2 dt = N \tag{6-46}$$

A process $n(t)$ for which time and ensemble averaging are equal, in the sense of Eq. (6-46), is again spoken of as an ergodic process. We assume henceforth that one may interchange these two averages, although we shall encounter at least one example later in which this is not valid.

We have just shown how one relates time and ensemble averages for a random wave or process $n(t)$. In particular, one may use a dc meter to measure $E(n)$, and, if the dc term is blocked or absent [$E(n) = 0$], one may use a true rms

---

[13] Here one must generally assume, however, that the statistics of $n(t)$ are *gaussian*; i.e., at any instant of time $f(n)$ is gaussian.

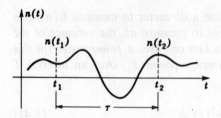

FIGURE 6-17
Autocorrelation definition.

meter to measure N, the noise power or variance. These assume, however, that the meter time constant $T \gg 1/B$, with B the "bandwidth" of the process. How does one determine B? How is B related to the actual variations in time of $n(t)$? Is it possible to calculate N, and, if so, how does this depend on the physical systems through which $n(t)$ propagates. It is also apparent, extrapolating from our discussions of deterministic signals in previous chapters, that the bandwidth B must somehow relate to the physical system in which $n(t)$ is generated or through which it propagates. For example, one would not expect to find noise with a bandwidth of 1 MHz at the output of a system whose bandwidth is 100 Hz. Any noise terms varying this rapidly just would not appear at the system output.

Basically, we require some measure of how the noise process may vary in a given time interval. Specifically, if we consider the noise wave $n(t)$ of Fig. 6-17 we note that as $t_2 \to t_1$, $n(t_2)$ as a random variable becomes more "closely related to" (or "predictable by") $n(t_1)$. As $t_2 - t_1$ increases, we expect less dependence of one upon the other. We make this concept more precise by defining the autocorrelation function $R_n(t_1, t_2)$:

$$R_n(t_1, t_2) \equiv E[n(t_1)n(t_2)] \qquad (6\text{-}47)$$

Although many different definitions of "dependence" of one random variable on one another are possible, the autocorrelation function is probably the simplest and has many desirable properties that we shall explore later. Note that it is the extension to the *same* random variable (hence the prefix *auto*) of the definition for the *covariance* of two random variables appearing in probability theory. It is apparent that if $t_2 \to t_1$, then $R_n \to E(n^2)$, or just the statistical second moment. If, at some spacing $t_2 - t_1$, $n(t_2)$ and $n(t_1)$ tend to become statistically independent (one would expect this to occur at intervals greater than $1/B$), then $R_n \to E^2(n)$, or 0 if $E(n) = 0$. Thus $R_n(t_1, t_2)$ provides one possible measure of the dependence of $n(t_2)$ and $n(t_1)$.

To simplify the discussion we shall assume that $R_n(t_1, t_2)$ depends only on the interval $(t_2 - t_1) \equiv \tau$, and not on the time origin t_1. [This is similar to our assumption, made previously, that $E(n)$ is independent of time.] Then we can write

$$R_n(\tau) \equiv E[n(t)n(t + \tau)] \qquad (6\text{-}48)$$

A process for which this is true, and for which $E(n)$ is independent of time, is called a *stationary process*.[14]

Now how would we actually measure $R_n(\tau)$? As we did previously, we set up a time integral with the property that its expected value equals $R_n(\tau)$. Consider the integral

$$\overline{R}_n(\tau) \equiv \frac{1}{T} \int_0^T n(t) n(t + \tau) \, dt \tag{6-49}$$

Note that this provides some measure of the mutual dependence, for time τ, of $n(t)$ and $n(t + \tau)$. For as $\tau \to 0$, $\overline{R}_n(0) = P_{av}$; as τ increases and $n(t)$ and $n(t + \tau)$ vary relatively independently of one another, one would expect that the product of the two would be negative as often as positive, approaching zero if $E(n) = 0$.

Again $\overline{R}_n(\tau)$ is a random variable, depending on the interval T seconds long over which evaluated. If we now ensemble-average over all possible values of this variable, we get, from Eqs. (6-49) and (6-48),

$$E\left[\overline{R}_n(\tau)\right] = R_n(\tau) \tag{6-50}$$

(Again ensemble averaging and integration are interchanged.) So in an average sense the time average of Eq. (6-49) and the ensemble average of Eq. (6-48) are the same.

As previously, one may calculate the variance of $\overline{R}_n(\tau)$ and show it goes to zero as $1/BT$ for large T.[15] We then have, as in the previous cases,

$$\lim_{T \to \infty} \overline{R}_n(\tau) = R_n(\tau) \tag{6-51}$$

[Note from Eqs. (6-48) and (6-49) that included as a special case here is the result $\lim_{T \to \infty} P_{av} = N + E^2(n) = E(n^2)$, previously shown as Eq. (6-46).]

We are now in a position to actually relate $R_n(\tau)$ to a spectral analysis of $n(t)$, and thus to a defined bandwidth. We could proceed by assuming temporarily that $n(t)$ is deterministic. We take a section of $n(t)$ T seconds long and expand it in a Fourier series. This will obviously consist of harmonics of the fundamental frequency $1/T$ (see Fig. 6-18). Thus,

$$n(t) = \frac{1}{T} \sum_{m = -\infty}^{\infty} c_m e^{j\omega_m t} \qquad \omega_m = \frac{2\pi m}{T} \tag{6-52}$$

Here

$$c_m = \int_{-T/2}^{T/2} n(t) e^{-j\omega_m t} \, dt \tag{6-53}$$

as in previous chapters. Note that c_m is a random variable because $n(t)$ is

---

[14]Strictly speaking, such a process is usually called a *wide-sense* stationary process. The term stationary process is then reserved for a more general case in which distribution functions are invariant with time. See [PAPO 1984].

[15]One must assume $n(t)$ is gaussian to actually carry out the averaging necessary.

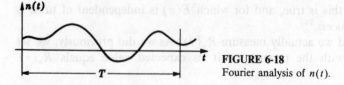

FIGURE 6-18
Fourier analysis of $n(t)$.

random. In fact, if $E(n) = 0$, it is easily shown that $E[c_m] = 0$. So we are in the peculiar situation of having a Fourier-series representation of $n(t)$ which is valid for the *particular time interval* T over which determined, but which varies statistically each time we take another strip of $n(t)$ T seconds long.

To obviate this difficulty one can calculate $|c_m|^2$, which can never go to zero, and use this to carry out a noise spectral analysis. This is in fact the approach commonly used in digital spectral analysis, as we shall see shortly. Instead, we adopt a more formal procedure at this time. Recall that the autocorrelation function $R_n(\tau)$ was introduced to provide a measure of the time variation of the random process $n(t)$. $R_n(\tau)$ thus plays the role here, in dealing with *random* processes, that the time function itself did in the deterministic case. In the deterministic case (Chap. 2) we found the spectral representation of a time function $f(t)$ by taking its Fourier transform. In the random case we formally *define* the spectral representation of $n(t)$ to be the *Fourier transform* of $R_n(\tau)$. Calling this quantity $G_n(f)$, we formally have

$$G_n(f) = \int_{-\infty}^{\infty} R_n(\tau) e^{-j\omega\tau} \, d\tau \tag{6-54}$$

This function must have the property that as $R_n(\tau)$ takes on narrower and narrower values about zero [implying that $n(t)$ and $n(t + \tau)$ become less dependent for a given τ, or that $n(t)$ varies more rapidly], it becomes wider in frequency. This property is of course consistent with the desired inverse time–bandwidth relation.

From the Fourier-transform relation connecting $G_n(f)$ and $R_n(\tau)$, it is apparent that the inverse Fourier transform exists, and that $R_n(\tau)$ may be formally found from $G_n(f)$ by writing

$$R_n(\tau) = \int_{-\infty}^{\infty} G_n(f) e^{j\omega\tau} \frac{d\omega}{2\pi}$$

$$= \int_{-\infty}^{\infty} G_n(f) e^{j\omega\tau} \, df \tag{6-55}$$

But recall that $R_n(0) = E(n^2)$ is the second moment of $n(t)$, and that $R_n(0) = P_{av}$, the total power in the noise wave, as measured by a true power meter. From (6-55), we have

$$R_n(0) = E(n^2) = \int_{-\infty}^{\infty} G_n(f) \, df \tag{6-56}$$

The function $G_n(f)$, defined formally as the Fourier transform of the autocorrelation function, thus appears to have the dimensions of a power density: its integral over all frequencies is just the total power in the noise. For this reason $G_n(f)$ is termed specifically the *power spectral density*, or frequently the *power spectrum*. It measures the distribution of noise power with frequency. A power meter tuned to a frequency f_0 and measuring the power in a narrow range Δf about f_0 would provide a good approximation to $2G_n(f)\Delta f$. [Since negative frequencies are just an artifice, one can equally well double $G_n(f)$ in (6-56) and integrate over positive frequencies only.] In the special case where the noise $n(t)$ is zero mean, $E(n) = 0$, and

$$N = \int_{-\infty}^{\infty} G_n(f)\,df \qquad E(n) = 0 \qquad (6\text{-}57)$$

The noise power or variance N, the parameter on which the probability of error in the detection of pulses in noise was found to depend, is thus directly related to the spectral density $G_n(f)$. It is the sum of the noise-power contributions at all frequencies.

Some examples of autocorrelation-function/spectral-density pairs appear in Fig. 6-19. In each case the average value of the noise has been taken as zero, and the autocorrelation function thus approaches zero for τ large enough. Note also that in each case $R_n(0)$ has been set equal to N, and that the area under the spectral density curve is correspondingly equal to N as well.

Comparing the autocorrelation-function/spectral-density pairs in each of the three cases of Fig. 6-19, the inverse correlation-time–bandwidth relation mentioned earlier becomes apparent. In particular, we define the bandwidth B of a noise wave in terms of the width of its spectral density function. The corresponding autocorrelation function then goes to zero for the spacing τ greater than $1/B$. Since $R_n(\tau) = E[n(t)n(t + \tau)]$ and $E(n) = 0$ by assumption, it is apparent that $n(t)$ and $n(t + \tau)$ (Fig. 6-20) become uncorrelated for $\tau > 1/B$. The reciprocal of the bandwidth thus plays an important role in determining the measure of correlation between a sample of $n(t)$ at time t, and a sample τ seconds later. Thus, in example 1 of Fig. 6-19, with f_0 the 3-dB bandwidth, $R_n(\pm 1/2\pi f_0) = e^{-1}R_n(0)$. [$G_n(f_0) = \frac{1}{2}G_n(0)$; this is *not* the same as half-power bandwidth, $B_{1/2}$, for which $\int_{-B_{1/2}}^{B_{1/2}} G_n(f)\,df = N/2$.] In example 2, the noise $n(t)$ is truly *band-limited* to B hertz. It is apparent that at $\tau = \pm 1/2B$, and integral multiples thereof, $n(t)$ and $n(t + \tau)$ are *always* uncorrelated. This is also the case in example 3 for $|\tau| \geq T_n$, and we note that $1/T_n$, the first zero crossing of $G_n(f)$, is a measure of the bandwidth of $n(t)$.

Specifically, if the bandwidth B is 1 MHz, samples spaced more than 1 μs apart are essentially uncorrelated in all three examples of Fig. 6-19. (In the case of example 3, if $T_n = 1$ μs, the samples *are* uncorrelated for all $\tau \geq 1$ μs.) Recall from probability theory that two uncorrelated gaussian variables are *independent* as well. If the random wave in Fig. 6-20 is then gaussian, $n(t)$ and $n(t + \tau)$ are essentially independent if $\tau > 1/B$ seconds.

Note that in examples 1 and 3 of Fig. 6-19 most of the noise power appears concentrated about the origin (dc), the bandwidths f_0 and $1/T_n$, respectively,

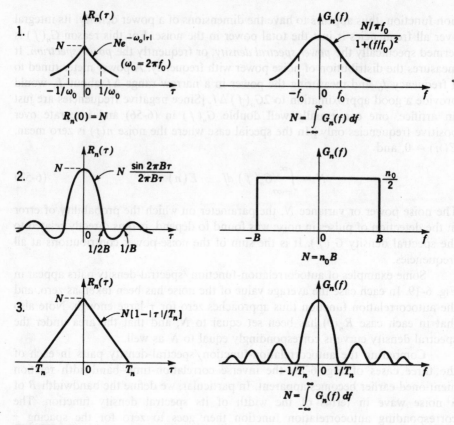

FIGURE 6-19
Correlation-function/spectral-density pairs.

then serving as measures of this concentration. The fact that relatively little noise power appears at the high frequencies thus indicates that the noise $n(t)$ rarely fluctuates at these rates, justifying our previous intuitive statements that 1/bandwidth is, roughly speaking, a measure of the time between significant changes in $n(t)$. This is of course also shown by the plots of the autocorrelation function $R_n(\tau)$; the value of τ for which $R_n(\tau)$ begins to decrease significantly is also a measure of the time between significant changes in $n(t)$ (this is in fact one possible interpretation of correlation), and is of course just 1/bandwidth, defined

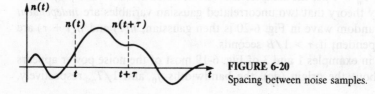

FIGURE 6-20
Spacing between noise samples.

in some arbitrary sense. In example 2 *all* the power is assumed concentrated in the range 0 to B hertz. This case is of course the random-signal equivalent of the band-limited deterministic signals of Chap. 2. $R_n(\tau)$ here is equivalent to $f(t)$ there; $G_n(f)$ is equivalent to $F(\omega)$.

One particular example of a spectral density that plays an extremely important role in communications and signal-processing analyses is that in which the spectral density $G_n(f)$ is flat or constant, say equal to $n_0/2$, over *all* frequencies:

$$G_n(f) = \frac{n_0}{2} \qquad (\text{all } f) \tag{6-58}$$

Although this is, strictly speaking, physically inadmissible, since it implies infinite noise power $[N = \int_{-\infty}^{\infty} G_n(f)\, df]$, it is a good model for many typical situations in which the noise bandwidth is so large as to be out of the range of our measuring instruments (or frequencies of interest to us). We shall describe a specific example of noise of this type later in this chapter in discussing thermal noise appearing at the input to a receiving antenna. Noise $n(t)$ with a flat spectral density $n_0/2$, as in Eq. (6-58), is called *white noise* because of its "equal jumbling" of all frequencies (compare with the common appellation "white light").

Note that in the band-limited noise case of example 2 of Fig. 6-19, one may obtain white noise by letting $B \rightarrow \infty$. The noise of example 2 is therefore often called *band-limited white noise*. It is apparent from the transform-pair relations that the autocorrelation function for white noise is just an impulse or delta function centered at the origin:

$$G_n(f) = \frac{n_0}{2} \qquad R_n(\tau) = \frac{n_0}{2}\delta(\tau) \tag{6-59}$$

The spectral-density and autocorrelation functions for white noise, as well as band-limited white noise of spectral density $G_n(f) = n_0/2$, $|f| \leq B$, $G_n(f) = 0$, $|f| > B$, appear in Fig. 6-21.

Since the autocorrelation function is an impulse in the case of white noise, this indicates that $n(t)$ is always uncorrelated with $n(t + \tau)$, no matter how small τ may be. The implication then is that $n(t)$ may vary infinitely rapidly, since it contains power at all frequencies. In practice, of course, as just noted, this simply means that the high-frequency variations are beyond the capabilities of our instruments in a particular measurement we may be making. So although the white-noise model may appear to be physically inadmissible, we could never measure the rapid variations anyway. As an example, if our measuring devices have a time response $\gg 1/B$, with B the noise bandwidth of an actual physical noise process, the noise looks to us for all practical purposes like white noise. Band-limited white noise, with $B \gg$ significant frequencies in the frequency response of our measuring devices, thus appears to us as white noise. To an oscilloscope of bandwidth 50 MHz, input noise with bandwidth 500 MHz would obviously appear like white noise.

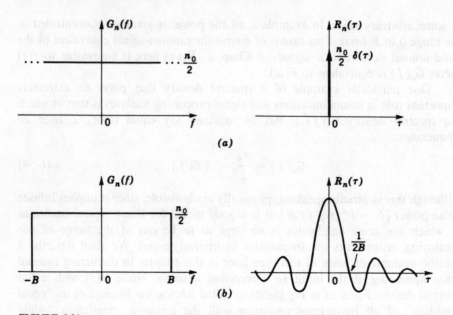

FIGURE 6-21
White-noise power spectrum and autocorrelation function. (*a*) White noise. (*b*) Band-limited white noise.

How does one measure the spectral density $G_n(f)$ in practice? One possibility is to feed the noise wave (or random signal) under investigation into a parallel bank of narrow filters, spaced Δf hertz apart, with $\Delta f \ll B$, and measure the power output of each filter. Alternatively, one may use a scanning narrowband filter, whose center frequency is shifted sequentially in steps of Δf hertz, and measure its mean-squared output as the entire frequency range is scanned. The most common approach, however, involves the Fourier analysis mentioned earlier in connection with (6-52) and (6-53). It turns out that a possible estimate (approximation) of $G_n(f_l)$, the spectral density at frequency f_l, is given by

$$\hat{G}_n(f_l) = \frac{1}{T}|c_l|^2 = \frac{1}{T}\left|\int_{-T/2}^{T/2} n(t)e^{-j\omega_l t}\,dt\right|^2 \tag{6-60}$$

with c_l just the Fourier coefficient of (6-53), using a strip of $n(t)$ that is T seconds long. Actually, one carries out the calculation of c_l digitally, taking samples of $n(t)$ spaced $< 1/2B$ seconds apart. The total number of samples processed (of the order of $2BT$) must be large to obtain good results. Fast-Fourier-transform techniques developed to speed up the calculation task have made this approach to the determination of $G_n(f)$ the one most widely used at present.[16] One caveat however: It turns out that although the average of $G_n(f_l)$ in

---

[16]See [SCHW 1975, chaps. 3, 4] for a discussion of discrete spectral estimation.

(6-60) is the desired spectral density $G_n(f_l)$ at frequency f_l, the *variance* of this estimate does not decrease with increasing T, as was the case in the discussion of $E(n)$ and σ^2 earlier. Instead one has to repeat the calculation for a number of sets of data samples (or strips T seconds long), and average them [SCHW 1975].

6-5 RANDOM SIGNALS AND NOISE THROUGH LINEAR SYSTEMS

Using the concept of power spectral density, as developed for random signals and noise, we are now in a position to consider the effect of linear filtering on these nondeterministic signals. This then parallels and extends our discussion of deterministic signals through linear systems in Chap. 2.

Consider then noise $n_i(t)$ with prescribed spectral density $G_{n_i}(f)$ and hence noise power N_i, as well as autocorrelation function $R_{n_i}(\tau)$, passed through a linear system with frequency transfer function $H(\omega)$, as shown in Fig. 6-22. What are the properties of the noise $n_o(t)$, at the output? That is, what are its spectral density $G_{n_o}(f)$, autocorrelation function $R_{n_o}(\tau)$, and output noise power N_o?

One would expect to find results similar to those obtained in Chap. 2. If the input noise $n_i(t)$ is varying roughly at a rate defined by its bandwidth B which is slow compared to the system bandwidth B_{sys}, the output noise $n_o(t)$ differs very little from $n_i(t)$. If, on the other hand, $B \gg B_{\text{sys}}$, the rapid fluctuations of $n_i(t)$ cannot get through (the system will not respond rapidly enough), and one would expect to find $n_o(t)$ varying at roughly the rate B_{sys}. We can show that these intuitive arguments are of course valid, and that the effect of the system on the noise is given, quite simply, by the following relation between input and output spectral densities:

$$G_{n_o}(f) = |H(\omega)|^2 G_{n_i}(f) \qquad (6-61)$$

The two extreme cases noted above ($B \ll B_{\text{sys}}$, $B \gg B_{\text{sys}}$) are summarized qualitatively in Fig. 6-23.

Equation (6-61) is demonstrated very simply by referring back to the definition of the spectral density as the Fourier transform of the autocorrelation function. Recall from (6-48) that $R_n(\tau)$ is the expectation of the product of $n(t)$ and $n(t + \tau)$. This is the definition of the autocorrelation function of the noise wave at both the input and the output of any linear system, with $n_i(t)$ used in place of $n(t)$ at the input, and $n_o(t)$ at the output (Fig. 6-22). We know from linear system analysis that $n_i(t)$ and $n_o(t)$ are related by the convolution

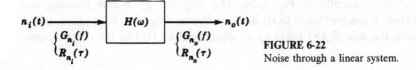

FIGURE 6-22
Noise through a linear system.

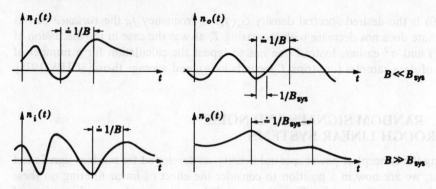

FIGURE 6-23
System response to input noise.

integral:

$$n_o(t) = \int_{-\infty}^{\infty} h(t - \tau) n_i(\tau) \, d\tau \tag{6-62}$$

Here $h(t)$, the impulse response at the system, is the inverse Fourier transform of $H(\omega)$, the system transfer function. Using (6-62) to evaluate $n_o(t)$ in the expression for the output autocorrelation function $R_{n_o}(\tau)$, rewriting in terms of the input autocorrelation function $R_{n_i}(\tau)$ and the impulse response $h(t)$, and then taking Fourier transforms, one obtains (6-61). Details are left to the reader.

Equation (6-61) is an extremely important relation, basic to the understanding of random signals and noise passing through linear systems. It further substantiates the remark made in the previous section that in dealing with random signals, $R_n(\tau)$ and $G_n(f)$ play the roles, respectively, that a time function $f(t)$ and its transform $F(\omega)$ do in dealing with deterministic signals. The spectral analysis of random signals focuses on the *power* distribution. This is related to the integrated square of signals and accounts for the $|H(\omega)|^2$ term appearing in the transfer relation of (6-61). The band-limiting effect of a linear system on an input random signal appears in the multiplication of the input spectral density by $|H(\omega)|^2$. This is directly analogous to the multiplication of the input Fourier transform by $H(\omega)$ for deterministic signals. These analogous relations account for the utility of the concepts of bandwidth and inverse time–frequency relations in studying the passage of deterministic *or* random signals through linear systems. This is precisely why deterministic models of signals can be used to represent random signals in systems, as has been done implicitly in the work thus far in this book.

The comparison of the handling of deterministic and random signals is summarized schematically in Fig. 6-24. The step in Fig. 6-24*b* showing the transition from a random wave to its autocorrelation function $R_n(\tau)$ is included to emphasize the role $R_n(\tau)$ plays as an equivalent to $f(t)$ in the deterministic

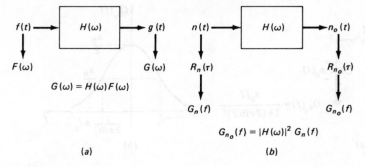

$$G(\omega) = H(\omega)F(\omega)$$

$$G_{n_o}(f) = |H(\omega)|^2 G_n(f)$$

(a) (b)

FIGURE 6-24
Handling of signals in linear systems. (a) Deterministic signals. (b) Random signals and noise.

case. One can bypass $R_n(\tau)$ completely and go directly from $n(t)$ to $G_n(f)$, if desired.

Now consider some examples of the application of (6-61). Assume first that we have white noise of spectral density $n_0/2$ applied at the input of an ideal low-pass filter of bandwidth B hertz (Fig. 6-25). The output noise is exactly the band-limited white noise of spectral density $G_n(f) = n_0/2$, $|f| \le B$, $G_n(f) = 0$, $|f| > B$, mentioned previously. The output noise power is then just

$$N_o = n_0 B \tag{6-63}$$

By increasing the filter bandwidth B, we increase the output noise power. We also increase the rate of variation of noise at the output, or decrease the correlation between $n(t)$ and $n(t + \tau)$, for a fixed τ.

As a second simple example, consider the case of white noise applied to the input of an RC filter, as shown in Fig. 6-26. Since

$$|H(\omega)|^2 = \frac{1}{1 + (\omega RC)^2} = \frac{1}{1 + (2\pi RCf)^2}$$

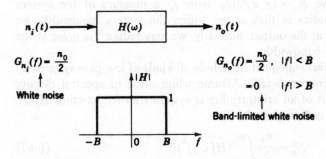

FIGURE 6-25
White noise through an ideal filter.

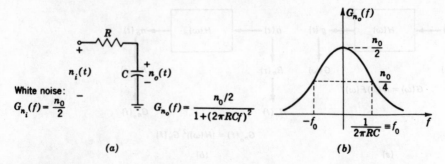

FIGURE 6-26
RC filtering of white noise. (a) Filter. (b) Output spectral density.

for this filter, we have

$$G_{n_o}(f) = \frac{n_0/2}{1 + (2\pi RCf)^2} = \frac{n_0/2}{1 + (f/f_0)^2} \tag{6-64}$$

with $f_0 \equiv 1/2\pi RC$, just as in the first example of Fig. 6-19. The bandwidth of the output noise is thus inversely proportional to the filter time constant RC, just as in the case of the deterministic signals of Chap. 2. The correlation time is also of the order of RC. For we have, as in Fig. 6-19,

$$R_{n_o}(\tau) = N_o e^{-|\tau|/RC} \tag{6-65}$$

as the Fourier transform of this spectral density. The average noise power N_o may be readily found by integrating $G_{n_o}(f)$:

$$N_o = \int_{-\infty}^{\infty} G_{n_o}(f)\, df = \int_{-\infty}^{\infty} \frac{n_0/2}{1 + (f/f_0)^2}\, df = \frac{n_0\pi}{2} f_0 \tag{6-66}$$

We now note an interesting fact shown in both of these examples—the low-pass filter and RC filter. The output noise power N_o is in both cases proportional to the system bandwidth. Thus in the first case we had $N_o = n_0 B$; in the second case we have $N_o = (n_0\pi/2)f_0$, with f_0 a measure of the system bandwidth. This thus indicates that as we widen the system bandwidth, we increase the noise power at the output. Similarly, we may reduce the noise at the output by narrowing the bandwidth.

We can generalize this statement to include all kinds of low-pass systems by defining a *noise-equivalent bandwidth*. Assume white noise of spectral density $n_0/2$ applied at the input of an arbitrary linear system transfer function $H(\omega)$. The output noise power is then given by

$$N_o = \frac{n_0}{2} \int_{-\infty}^{\infty} |H(\omega)|^2\, df \tag{6-67}$$

since $G_{n_o}(f) = (n_0/2)|H(\omega)|^2$. Assume that this same noise comes from an ideal

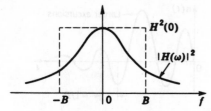

FIGURE 6-27
Noise-equivalent bandwidth.

low-pass filter of bandwidth B and amplitude $H(0)$, that is, the magnitude of the arbitrary filter transfer function at zero frequency. To have the same noise output we must then have

$$N_o = n_0 H^2(0) B = n_0 \int_0^\infty |H(\omega)|^2 \, df \qquad (6\text{-}68)$$

since $|H(\omega)|$ has even symmetry about the origin. Then we have the *noise-equivalent bandwidth* B defined as

$$B \equiv \frac{1}{H^2(0)} \int_0^\infty |H(\omega)|^2 \, df \qquad (6\text{-}69)$$

This procedure essentially corresponds to replacing the arbitrary filter $H(\omega)$ by an equivalent ideal low-pass filter of bandwidth B, as shown in Fig. 6-27. One may also do this for bandpass filters, using in place of $H(0)$ the value of $H(\omega)$ at the center frequency. As an example, for the RC filter, we have, from Eq. (6-66), $B = (\pi/2)f_0 = 1/4RC$.

To show the numerical quantities involved, assume that the white-noise spectral density at the input to a high-gain, low-pass amplifier is $n_0/2 = 10^{-14}$ V^2/Hz. The amplifier has a voltage gain of 10^3 and a high-frequency cutoff of 10 MHz. From Eq. (6-68), then, the mean-squared noise voltage at the amplifier output is $N_o = 2 \times 10^{-14} \times 10^6 \times 10^7 = 0.2 \ V^2$.

In terms of the noise-equivalent bandwidth we have then, as in Eq. (6-68), the general relation

$$N_o = n_0 H^2(0) B \propto B \qquad (6\text{-}70)$$

This indicates that the output noise power N_o is proportional to the bandwidth. As an interesting rule of thumb, then, one reduces noise in systems by narrowing the bandwidth, and increases the noise by widening the bandwidth. We include here, in the word "systems," measuring instruments, receivers, signal processors, etc.

If one attempts to detect or otherwise measure signals in the presence of noise, one thus tries to use as narrow a system bandwidth as possible—assuming that the input noise is originally much wider in bandwidth than the system. Of course one then has a limitation on the rate of variation of the signals themselves. For given classes of signals, one cannot narrow the bandwidth to the point where the signal itself is adversely affected. We shall have more to say about this

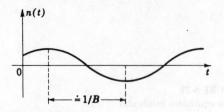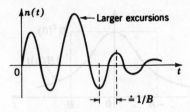

FIGURE 6-28
Effect of increased noise bandwidth.

trade-off between signal detectability and noise-power increase with increasing bandwidth shortly.

We can now summarize our study of noise thus far with two simple statements that serve as useful rules of thumb:

1. Increasing the system bandwidth increases the rate of fluctuation of the output noise (assuming the system bandwidth is initially much less than the input noise bandwidth).

2. Increasing the system bandwidth increases the output noise power. Since the output noise power N_o is a measure of the mean-squared statistical fluctuations about the average value (assumed zero here) [recall that N was the noise variance and hence a measure of the width of the noise probability-density function $f(n)$ about $E(n)$], larger instantaneous values of $n(t)$ thus become more probable as well.

These two rules appear expressed pictorially in the curves of Fig. 6-28. As the bandwidth B increases, the random process $n(t)$ is expected to deviate more often and more violently (in terms of peak excursions) from its expected or average value.

6-6 MATCHED-FILTER DETECTION: APPLICATION TO BASEBAND DIGITAL COMMUNICATIONS

In Sec. 6-2 we calculated the probability of detection in a binary communication system subject to additive gaussian noise. We implicitly assumed there that the intersymbol interference discussed in Chap. 3 (Sec. 3-10) was no problem. (In data transmission over band-limited telephone channels the reverse is usually true, as noted earlier: additive noise generally poses no problem; intersymbol interference does.)

We found there that the probability of error ultimately depended on the peak signal-amplitude-to-rms-noise ratio, A/σ or $A/\sqrt{N}$, using the present noise terminology. An interesting and very practical question that we might pose would

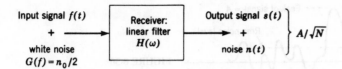

FIGURE 6-29
Matched-filter problem.

be: Is it possible to design the system up to the detector in order to maximize the ratio of peak signal amplitude to rms noise when sampled at the detector? Thus we envision white noise added to the sequence of binary pulses of known shape at the receiver input, with the composite sum passed through a linear filter (representing the system), then sampled and a decision made at the detector. Is it then possible to design the linear filter prior to detection to maximize the ratio $A/\sigma = A/\sqrt{N}$ at its output? This is shown pictorially in Fig. 6-29.

(Although we assume throughout this section that the signal is a baseband pulse, the results obtained apply also to the case of binary carrier transmission. As discussed in Chap. 4 the high-frequency pulses may be synchronously detected, reducing them to the pulse problem under consideration. Alternatively, they may be envelope-detected, if of the OOK or FSK type. This is shown in the sections that follow.)

We shall find that this problem is easily handled as an application of the power-spectrum concepts just introduced.

The results of the analysis to follow are useful in many other applications aside from binary or pulse-code-modulation (PCM) transmission. They apply as well to the design of pulse-amplitude-modulation (PAM) (nonquantized) systems. There the question posed would be: Given pulsed samples of the signal to be transmitted, how should these be filtered so as to have maximum signal-to-rms-noise ratio at the output of the system? We might alternatively state this: How should we shape our pulses (by filtering them) so that the signal-to-noise ratio will be maximized?

A similar problem is encountered in radar systems, where it is required to detect the presence of a signal echo embedded in fluctuation noise [SCHW 1975, chap. 5]. The amplitude of the signal relative to the noise should thus be maximized if possible.

In all these examples we are not specifically interested in maintaining fidelity of pulse shape. We are primarily interested in improving our ability to "see" (recognize) a pulse signal in the presence of noise. This ability to see the pulse is assumed to be related to the ratio of peak signal to rms noise. An example of such a pulse signal embedded in noise is shown in Fig. 6-30.

How do we know that the peak signal-to-noise ratio can be maximized by properly choosing the filter characteristic? This is simply answered from our discussions of Chap. 2 and the previous section.

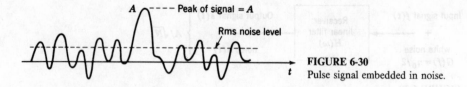

FIGURE 6-30
Pulse signal embedded in noise.

Assume, for simplicity's sake, that the input signal $f(t)$ is a rectangular pulse of width τ seconds. The system is assumed to have the idealized filter characteristics of Sec. 2-4, with a variable bandwidth B hertz.

For very small bandwidth ($B \ll 1/\tau$) the peak of the output signal is small and increases with bandwidth. This is shown by the curves of Fig. 2-35. It is also indicated by the curve of Fig. 6-31a, showing the familiar $(\sin x)/x$ spectrum with the filter cutoff frequency (B) superimposed. The output-signal amplitude is proportional to the area under the curve. For $B \ll 1/\tau$ the frequency spectrum is flat, so that the output signal increases linearly with B. The rms noise is proportional to $\sqrt{B}$ and so increases at a smaller rate than the signal for small bandwidth.

As the bandwidth increases, approaching $B = 1/\tau$, the signal amplitude begins to increase less rapidly with B. For $B > 1/\tau$ the signal remains approximately at the same amplitude as at $B = 1/\tau$ (Fig. 2-35). (Recall from Chap. 2 that increasing the bandwidth beyond $B = 1/\tau$ just served to fill out the fine details of the pulse. For a recognizable pulse a bandwidth $B = 1/\tau$ was all that was necessary.) The rms noise keeps increasing with bandwidth, however, so that the ratio of peak signal to rms noise begins to decrease inversely as $\sqrt{B}$. We would thus expect an optimum ratio at about $B = 1/\tau$. This will be borne out in the analysis to follow.

In general, not only the filter bandwidth but the shape of the filter characteristic can be adjusted to optimize the peak signal-to-noise ratio. To show this, consider $f(t)$ impressed across a linear filter with frequency transfer func-

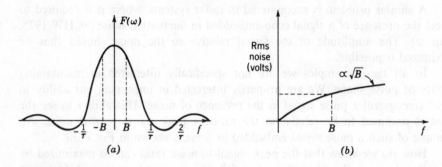

(a)

(b)

FIGURE 6-31
Rectangular pulse and noise passed through ideal filter. (a) Signal pulse spectrum, with filter cutoff superimposed. (b) Rms noise output.

tion $H(\omega)$. Defining $F(\omega)$ to be the Fourier transform of $f(t)$,

$$F(\omega) = \int_{-\infty}^{\infty} f(t) e^{-j\omega t} dt \qquad (6\text{-}71)$$

The output signal $s(t)$ is given by

$$s(t) = \frac{1}{2\pi} \int_{-\infty}^{\infty} F(\omega) H(\omega) e^{j\omega t} d\omega$$

$$= \int_{-\infty}^{\infty} F(\omega) H(\omega) e^{j\omega t} df \qquad \omega = 2\pi f \qquad (6\text{-}72)$$

The magnitude of $s(t)$ at the sampling time t_0 is just the desired output-signal amplitude A. Thus,

$$A = |s(t_0)| = \left| \int_{-\infty}^{\infty} F(\omega) H(\omega) e^{j\omega t_0} df \right|$$

The power spectrum of the white noise at the filter input is taken as

$$G(f) = \frac{n_0}{2} \qquad (6\text{-}73)$$

as in the previous section. The power spectrum at the filter output is then

$$G_n(f) = \frac{n_0}{2} |H(\omega)|^2 \qquad (6\text{-}74)$$

and the average output noise power (or mean-squared noise voltage across a 1-Ω resistor) is

$$N = \frac{n_0}{2} \int_{-\infty}^{\infty} |H(\omega)|^2 df \qquad (6\text{-}75)$$

$\sqrt{N}$ is the rms output noise in the absence of a signal.

We would now like to choose $H(\omega)$ such that the ratio $A/\sqrt{N}$ is maximized. This is the same as maximizing the square of the ratio, or A^2/N. This squared ratio is just the ratio of instantaneous peak signal power at $t = t_0$ to mean noise power, and will henceforth be referred to as the peak power signal-to-noise ratio, or peak SNR.

Since the input signal $f(t)$ is assumed given, its energy content $\int_{-\infty}^{\infty} f^2(t) \, dt$ is a constant. Calling the energy E, it is left to the reader as an exercise to show the following Fourier-transform identity is a valid one[17]

$$E = \int_{-\infty}^{\infty} f^2(t) \, dt = \int_{-\infty}^{\infty} |F(\omega)|^2 df \qquad (6\text{-}76)$$

---

[17]This relation is a basic theorem in Fourier-integral theory and is frequently called Parseval's theorem. It may be easily derived from Eq. (2-19b) in Chap. 2 by taking $(-T/2, T/2)$ as limits in the integral and letting $T \to \infty$. Alternatively, it may be proved by applying the convolution theorem. [Assume a function $f(t)$ passed through a linear filter with transfer function $H(\omega) = F^*(\omega)$.]

Dividing the ratio of peak signal power to mean noise power by the constant E will obviously not affect the determination of the maximum ratio. So we can take as our problem that of maximizing the ratio

$$\frac{A^2}{EN} = \frac{\left| \int_{-\infty}^{\infty} F(\omega) H(\omega) e^{j\omega t_0} df \right|^2}{(n_0/2) \int_{-\infty}^{\infty} |F(\omega)|^2 df \int_{-\infty}^{\infty} |H(\omega)|^2 df} \tag{6-77}$$

This is readily done by means of *Schwarz's inequality*, relating the integral of products of complex functions:

$$\left| \int_{-\infty}^{\infty} X(\omega) Y(\omega) \, d\omega \right|^2 \leq \int_{-\infty}^{\infty} |X(\omega)|^2 \, d\omega \int_{-\infty}^{\infty} |Y(\omega)|^2 \, d\omega \tag{6-78}$$

Schwarz's inequality for integrals of complex functions is just an extension of an inequality for real integrals, given by

$$\left[\int_{-\infty}^{\infty} f(t) g(t) \, dt \right]^2 \leq \int_{-\infty}^{\infty} g^2(t) \, dt \int_{-\infty}^{\infty} f^2(t) \, dt \tag{6-79}$$

It might be termed a generalization of the familiar distance relation among vectors that the magnitude of the sum of two vectors is less than or equal to the sum of the magnitudes of the two vectors:

$$|\mathbf{a} + \mathbf{b}| \leq |\mathbf{a}| + |\mathbf{b}| \tag{6-80}$$

In the vector case the equality is satisfied if $\mathbf{a} = K\mathbf{b}$, or $\mathbf{a}$ and $\mathbf{b}$ are collinear. Similarly in Eq. (6-78) the equality is satisfied if $f(t) = Kg(t)$. In the case of complex functions the equality is satisfied if

$$Y(\omega) = KX^*(\omega) \tag{6-81}$$

K is a real number.

How do we apply Schwarz's inequality to our problem of maximizing peak signal-to-noise ratio? Note that the ratio of Eq. (6-77) contains exactly the integrals of Eq. (6-78) if we let

$$X(\omega) = F(\omega) e^{j\omega t_0} \qquad Y(\omega) = H(\omega)$$

The ratio $n_0 A^2 / 2EN$ must then be less than or equal to 1, and

$$\left| \int_{-\infty}^{\infty} F(\omega) H(\omega) e^{j\omega t_0} df \right|^2 \leq \int_{-\infty}^{\infty} |F(\omega)|^2 df \int_{-\infty}^{\infty} |H(\omega)|^2 df \tag{6-82}$$

In particular, the ratio is a *maximum* when the equality holds, or

$$H(\omega) = K \left[F(\omega) e^{j\omega t_0} \right]^* = KF^*(\omega) e^{-j\omega t_0} \tag{6-83}$$

As an example, if $f(t)$ is the rectangular pulse of width τ and height V, $F(\omega) = V\tau\{[\sin(\omega\tau/2)]/(\omega\tau/2)\}$ and

$$H(\omega) = K\frac{\sin(\omega\tau/2)}{\omega\tau/2}e^{-j\omega t_0}$$

for maximum ratio of peak signal to rms noise.

Filters possessing the characteristic of Eq. (6-83) are said to be *matched filters*. The response at the output of such a filter to $f(t)$ applied at the input is

$$s(t) = \int_{-\infty}^{\infty} F(\omega)H(\omega)e^{j\omega t}\,df$$

$$= K\int_{-\infty}^{\infty} |F(\omega)|^2 e^{j\omega(t-t_0)}\,df \qquad (6\text{-}84)$$

In particular $s(t)$ will have amplitude A when $t = t_0$:

$$|s(t_0)| = K\int_{-\infty}^{\infty} |F(\omega)|^2\,df = A$$

Note that the amplitude A is thus proportional to the signal energy E.

An interesting relation for the matched-filter output signal-to-noise ratio $A/\sqrt{N}$ may be derived by applying the matched-filter condition of Eq. (6-83) to Eq. (6-77). Specifically, it is apparent that at the output of the matched filter the peak power SNR is

$$\frac{A^2}{N} = \frac{2E}{n_0}$$

or $$\frac{A}{\sqrt{N}} = \sqrt{\frac{2E}{n_0}} \qquad (6\text{-}85)$$

The signal-to-noise ratio is thus a function solely of the energy in the signal and the white-noise spectral density. *The dependence on the signal input waveshape $f(t)$ has been obliterated by use of the matched filter.* Two different signal waveshapes will provide the same probability of error in the presence of additive white noise, provided they contain the same energy and are filtered by the appropriate matched filter in each case. It is the *energy* in the signal that provides its ultimate detectability in noise. This point will be pursued further in Chap. 7.

If the input time function $f(t)$ is symmetrical in time $[f(t) = f(-t)]$, then $F(\omega)$ will be a real function of frequency. From Eq. (6-83), $H(\omega) = KF(\omega)e^{-j\omega t_0}$ for this case. This means that the impulse response $h(t)$ is $h(t) = Kf(t - t_0)$. The impulse response of a filter matched to a symmetrical input is a delayed replica of such an input.

If $f(t)$ is not symmetrical, $F(\omega)$ is complex. By using the Fourier-integral relations it may be shown that

$$h(t) = Kf\left[-(t - t_0)\right] \qquad (6\text{-}86)$$

in general. The proof is left to the reader as an exercise; it is identical to the procedure used to prove Parseval's theorem above. Since $f(t)$ is normally defined for positive t, $h(t)$ in the general case will be defined for negative t. As pointed out in Chap. 2, such a filter is physically not realizable. In the general case, then, the matched filter is not realizable.

Of what value then is this entire analysis leading to the matched-filter result? Just as in the case of the ideal filter of Chap. 2, we can approximate the matched-filter characteristics by those of an actual filter. We can also compare practical filters with the matched filter so far as the ratio of peak output signal to noise is concerned and can optimize their shape and bandwidth as far as practicable. This is the procedure we shall follow in the remainder of this section.

The input time function $f(t)$ is assumed to be a rectangular pulse of width τ seconds and height V. We assume that $V\tau = 1$. With $f(t)$ symmetrically located about $t = 0$, $F(\omega) = [\sin(\omega\tau/2)]/(\omega\tau/2)$, a real function as noted above. The impulse response of the matched filter is then also a rectangular pulse of τ seconds duration. $[H(\omega) = F(\omega)$ here.] The response of this matched filter to the rectangular pulse will then be the convolution of two rectangular pulses. This gives a triangular-pulse output. We can check this by noting that for the matched filter $F(\omega)H(\omega) = \{[\sin(\omega\tau/2)]/(\omega\tau/2)\}^2 e^{-j\omega t_0}$ ($V\tau = 1$). This is just the Fourier transform of a triangular pulse of width 2τ seconds, as shown in Chap. 2. This output pulse is τ seconds wide at the half-amplitude points.

Note that such a triangular pulse is not too different in shape from the output of the ideal low-pass filter of Sec. 2-4, with $B = 1/\tau$ (see Fig. 2-35). In fact the ideal-filter output for $B = 1/\tau$ could very well have been approximated by such a triangle. If the bandwidth of the matched filter is assumed to be the frequency of the first zero in its amplitude characteristic, the bandwidth is also just $1/\tau$ ($\sin \omega\tau/2 = 0$; $\omega\tau/2 = \pi$; $f = 1/\tau$).

This is an interesting point, for it agrees with our previous results that for producing a recognizable pulse a filter bandwidth of the order of $B = 1/\tau$ should be used. We shall see below that for an ideal low-pass filter $B\tau = 0.7$ actually gives maximum signal-to-noise ratio.

Just how significant the shapes of the filter characteristic and bandwidth are in determining the output peak signal-to-noise ratio for a rectangular-pulse input can be found by applying Eq. (6-77) to various filters. The resulting signal-to-noise ratio can then be compared with that for the optimum matched filter. We shall actually calculate $n_0 A^2/2EN$ so that the optimum value is normalized to 1. In all cases the rectangular-pulse input is assumed to have unit area ($V\tau = 1$), so that

$$F(\omega) = \frac{\sin(\omega\tau/2)}{\omega\tau/2}$$

IDEAL LOW-PASS FILTER, VARIABLE BANDWIDTH. Here

$$\begin{aligned} H(\omega) &= e^{-j\omega t_0} & |\omega| &\leq 2\pi B \\ &= 0 & |\omega| &> 2\pi B \end{aligned} \tag{6-87}$$

The peak power SNR for this case, as obtained from Eq. (6-77), becomes

$$\frac{\left| \int_{-2\pi B}^{2\pi B} \frac{\sin(\omega\tau/2)}{\omega\tau/2} \, d\omega \right|^2}{\int_{-\infty}^{\infty} \left[\frac{\sin(\omega\tau/2)}{\omega\tau/2} \right]^2 d\omega \int_{-2\pi B}^{2\pi B} d\omega} = \frac{\left(\frac{2}{\tau} \int_{-a}^{a} \frac{\sin x}{x} \, dx \right)^2}{\frac{2}{\tau} \int_{-\infty}^{\infty} \left(\frac{\sin x}{x} \right)^2 dx \, 4\pi B}$$

with $x \equiv \omega\tau/2$ and $a = \pi B\tau$. Using the relation $\int_{-\infty}^{\infty} [(\sin x)/x]^2 \, dx = \pi$, and recalling the sine-integral definition, $\text{Si } a = \int_{0}^{a} [(\sin x)/x] \, dx$, the ratio squared becomes

$$\frac{2}{\pi a} (\text{Si } a)^2$$

This expression may be plotted by using tables of the sine integral [JAHN] and is found to have a maximum at $a = \pi B\tau = 2.2$. This corresponds to $B\tau = 2.2/\pi = 0.7$. At this bandwidth the peak power SNR is found to be 0.83, as compared with 1 for the optimum filter. This corresponds to a relative deterioration of 0.8 dB.

The result for an ideal low-pass filter is plotted in Fig. 6-32 as a function of $B\tau$. The decibel scale used is relative to the 0-dB case of the optimum matched filter. Although the maximum ratio is found for $B\tau = 0.7$, the maximum is very broad and varies less than 1 dB from $B\tau = 0.4$ to $B\tau = 1$. For a pulsed carrier or OOK signal the bandwidth would be twice the bandwidth shown here, so that $B\tau = 1.5$ would be optimum for a rectangular filter.

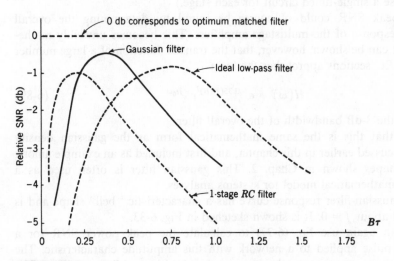

FIGURE 6-32
Peak SNR for various filters, compared with matched filter (rectangular-pulse input).

ONE-STAGE *RC* FILTER, VARIABLE BANDWIDTH.

$$H(\omega) = \frac{1}{1 + j\omega RC} \tag{6-88}$$

with $2\pi B = 1/RC$ the 3-dB radian bandwidth. The peak response of this filter to a rectangular-pulse input occurs at $t = \tau$ and is given by

$$s(\tau) = 1 - e^{-\tau/RC}$$

[This procedure is much simpler than the frequency-response method of Eq. (6-72) in this case.] The normalized signal-to-noise peak power ratio becomes for this case, after some manipulations,

$$\frac{(1 - e^{-2a})^2}{a} \qquad a = \frac{\tau}{2RC} = \pi B \tau$$

The details of this calculation are left to the reader as an exercise.

The signal-to-noise ratio for this case has also been plotted in Fig. 6-32 and shows a maximum value at $B\tau = 0.2$ ($B = 1/2\pi RC$). At this bandwidth the filter output is only 1 dB worse than that for the matched-filter case. For $B\tau = 0.5$ the S/N ratio is 2.3 dB worse than the matched-filter case, so that the variation with bandwidth is again small.

MULTISTAGE *RC* FILTERS. A signal would normally be amplified by several stages of amplifiers, with filtering included in each amplifier. It is thus of interest to compare the matched-filter output signal-to-noise ratio with that of a multistage amplifier. We assume a simple *RC* filter in each stage. (For a pulsed carrier we would use a single-tuned circuit for each stage.)

The peak SNR could of course be found by determining the overall frequency response of the multistage amplifiers. This becomes unwieldy mathematically. It can be shown, however, that the transfer function of a large number of isolated *RC* sections approaches the form

$$H(\omega) = e^{-0.35(f/B)^2} e^{-jt_0\omega} \tag{6-89}$$

where B is the 3-dB bandwidth of the overall filter.

Note that this is the same mathematical form as the gaussian density function discussed earlier in this chapter, and first included as an example among the filter shapes shown in Chap. 2. This gaussian filter is often used as a convenient mathematical model for systems analyses.

The gaussian-filter response curve has a characteristic "bell" shape and is symmetrical about $f = 0$. It is shown sketched in Fig. 6-33.

We can again use Eq. (6-77) to calculate the peak power SNR for a rectangular pulse applied to a network with this amplitude characteristic. The result will then approximate the output of a multistage *RC* amplifier. The

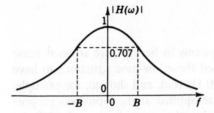

FIGURE 6-33
Frequency response, multistage amplifier (gaussian error curve).

analysis is identical to that carried out for the ideal filter. The details will not be presented here, but the results are plotted in Fig. 6-32, again compared with the optimum matched-filter case.

Actual calculations for two and three stages of amplification with RC filtering included produce results which do not differ substantially from those for the gaussian filter, so that the gaussian-error-curve analysis will be a good approximation to a multistage RC amplifier for two or more stages.

Note that the peak SNR occurs in this case for $B\tau = 0.4$. (For a two-stage amplifier the peak occurs at $B\tau = 0.3$.) The maximum is quite broad, however, varying by no more than 1 dB from $B\tau = 0.2$ to $B\tau = 0.7$.

At the maximum the ratio is only 0.5 dB less than that for the optimum matched filter. This would be quite negligible in most practical applications. The overall filter characteristic of a multistage amplifier will thus be close to optimum for transmission of rectangular pulses, with the overall bandwidth chosen as $B = 0.5/\tau$.

The filters considered here are all low-pass, and the signal and noise are both considered to be present at baseband. In practice, of course, sine-wave carrier transmission is used with all pulse systems. As shown in Chap. 4, the high-frequency circuits equivalent to the low-pass circuits here generally require twice the low-pass bandwidth ($\pm B$ about the carrier frequency). If the matched filters discussed here are included in the i-f section of a receiver, for example, all bandwidths shown in Fig. 6-32 must be multiplied by two. A multistage i-f amplifier would thus be designed to have a bandwidth of $2 \times 0.5/\tau$, or $1/\tau$ hertz, to optimize pulsed-signal detection in noise.

Such a bandwidth choice is common practice in the design of pulse radars. It is also the optimum choice in those digital or PCM systems in which noise is a more crucial factor than intersymbol interference. If intersymbol interference is a problem as well, the system bandwidth may be widened somewhat to narrow the pulses transmitted and hence decrease their overlap. The broad maxima in Fig. 6-32 indicate that the optimum bandwidth choice is not critical in combatting noise, and hence widening the bandwidths somewhat will not deteriorate the noise performance too much.

The question of i-f matched filtering as contrasted with baseband filtering will be further pursued in the sections following after a discussion of noise representations at high frequencies.

6-7 NARROWBAND NOISE REPRESENTATION

In the discussion of noise through linear systems in Sec. 6-5 we stressed noise passed through low-pass devices. We assumed these low-pass structures to have an effective bandwidth B hertz, centered at 0 Hz (dc), and showed, for example, that the output noise power with white noise applied at the input was proportional to B. In the last section, in discussing the maximization of SNR by matched filtering, we also stressed, for simplicity's sake, low-pass filtering.

We did point out that the results obtained were applicable at carrier frequencies as well, with the equivalent bandpass filters having twice the low-pass bandwidth. As a matter of fact, the discussion in Sec. 6-5 of noise (and random signals) through linear systems is general enough to enable us to handle high-frequency carrier transmission and the various narrowband bandpass circuits encountered in practice. Thus the transfer function $H(\omega)$ that appears in the spectral-density relation for input-output noise,

$$G_{n_o}(f) = |H(\omega)|^2 G_{n_i}(f) \tag{6-61}$$

is, in the case of high-frequency transmission, simply that of a filter centered at the desired center frequency.

We shall find it useful to develop a representation of noise particularly appropriate to narrowband transmission, however. This will enable us to realistically discuss the problem of detecting, at a receiver, high-frequency signals in the presence of noise. In particular, we shall use this representation for narrowband noise to discuss, in a comparative way, the detection process in various types of digital and analog systems. We shall also find this discussion helpful in calculating quantum limits on the heterodyne detection of coherent binary optical signals.

Thus we shall answer questions related to binary carrier transmission and reception that were first raised earlier in connection with our discussion of digital carrier systems: What *are* the reasons for selecting between OOK, PSK, and FSK transmission in a particular situation? What *are* the quantitative differences between synchronous (coherent) and envelope (noncoherent) detection of binary signals in noise?

In particular, we shall find that PSK systems with synchronous detection offer a distinct improvement in either probability of error or signal-to-noise ratio over the other schemes and are therefore favored *if* phase coherence may be maintained. If envelope detection *must* be used (phase coherence is either not available or the cost does not justify the additional circuitry required to maintain it), FSK is found to be superior to OOK, but again with the requirement of somewhat more complex circuitry.

Using the narrowband representation of noise, we shall also discuss AM and FM detection in the presence of noise, obtaining the well-known SNR improvement of wideband FM over AM (above the so-called FM threshold).

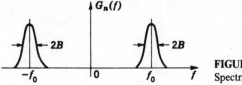

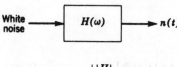

FIGURE 6-34
Spectral density, narrowband noise.

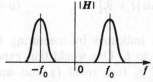

FIGURE 6-35
Generation of narrowband noise.

Consider then noise $n(t)$ at the output of a narrowband filter. Its spectral density $G_n(f)$ is centered about f_0 as in Fig. 6-34. For simplicity's sake we shall assume $G_n(f)$ symmetrical about the frequency f_0, with bandwidth $2B \ll f_0$. (The noise may be assumed to have been generated by white noise passed through a narrowband filter, as shown in Fig. 6-35. These assumptions are not necessary in a more general approach to narrowband noise representation, but are used here to simplify the discussion.[18] They are, of course, frequently encountered in practice.) It is then apparent that the noise $n(t)$, although random, will be oscillating, on the average, at frequency f_0. (As the bandwidth $2B$ is made smaller and smaller, the output should approach more and more that of a pure sine wave at frequency f_0.) We indicate this by writing $n(t)$ in the narrowband form

$$n(t) = r(t)\cos[\omega_0 t + \theta(t)] \qquad (6\text{-}90)$$

We would expect $r(t)$ and $\theta(t)$ to be varying, in a random fashion, roughly at the rate of B hertz, representing, respectively, the "envelope" and "phase" of the noise. This is indicated in Fig. 6-36.

To actually develop $n(t)$ in the form of Eq. (6-90) we use a simple artifice. We visualize the noise to be represented as the sum of many closely spaced sine

---

[18]See [SCHW 1966, pp. 35–45] for a more systematic and general approach.

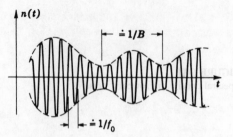

FIGURE 6-36
Narrowband noise.

waves, the spacing $\Delta f \ll B$. Thus, let

$$n(t) = \sum_{l=-\infty}^{\infty} a_l \cos[(\omega_0 + l\,\Delta\omega)t + \theta_l] \tag{6-91}$$

The variation about the center frequency f_0 is indicated by measuring the frequency of the different sine waves with respect to f_0. One would thus expect the coefficients a_l to be large in the vicinity of f_0 (i.e., small l), and small elsewhere.

Since we are not interested here in a unique representation of noise, but rather a model that will be useful in analysis, we now assume the θ_l's to be independent, uniformly distributed random variables. By the central limit theorem, $n(t)$ *then has gaussian statistics*, just the property we assumed in the error calculations earlier in this chapter. It is also apparent that $E(n) = 0$, averaging statistically over the random θ_l's. To find the coefficients a_l we now note that the sine-wave expansion of Eq. (6-91) is equivalent to assuming the continuous power spectral distribution of Fig. 6-37a to be replaced by a discrete spectrum of the same shape and power. This is shown in Fig. 6-37b. [We have concentrated on positive frequencies only, as shown, because of the form of Eq. (6-91). We then simply double the power spectral density at each frequency, as shown in the

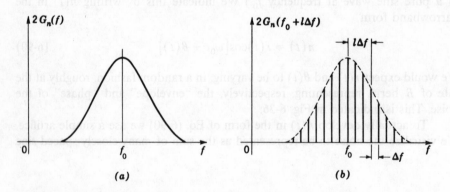

(a)   (b)

FIGURE 6-37
Discrete representation of noise spectral density. (a) One-sided (positive-frequency) spectrum. (b) Discrete equivalent.

figure. The resultant spectral density, defined for positive frequencies only, is often called the one-sided spectral density, as contrasted to the *two-sided* $G_n(f)$, symmetrical in positive and negative frequencies.]

It is apparent from both figures that the total noise power N must be given by

$$N = 2 \int_0^\infty G_n(f) \, df = \sum_{l=-\infty}^{\infty} 2G_n(f_0 + l\Delta f) \, \Delta f \qquad (6\text{-}92)$$

Again $l \Delta f$ represents the variation away from the center frequency f_0. Although $l \Delta f$ is indicated as ranging between $-\infty$ and ∞, it is of course only significant within the range $\pm B$ about f_0.

Now note that the average power in the representation $n(t)$ of Eq. (6-91) must be given by

$$N = E(n^2) = \sum_{l=-\infty}^{\infty} \frac{a_l^2}{2} \qquad (6\text{-}93)$$

a familiar result. [One may check this by multiplying together two series representations for $n(t)$ to get $n^2(t)$. Then ensemble averaging over the random variables θ_l, and noting that $E[\cos(l + m) \Delta t + \theta_l + \theta_m] = 0$, one gets Eq. (6-93).] Comparing with Eq. (6-92), we must have

$$a_l^2 = 4G_n(f_0 + l\Delta f) \, \Delta f$$
$$a_l = \sqrt{4G_n(f_0 + l\Delta f) \, \Delta f} \qquad (6\text{-}94)$$

The coefficients a_l are thus uniquely known, once the θ_l's are assumed independent and uniformly distributed.

To get Eq. (6-91) more specifically in the narrowband form of Eq. (6-90), we now expand a typical sine-wave term about f_0 in the following manner:

$$\cos[\omega_0 t + (l \Delta \omega \, t + \theta_l)] = \cos(l \Delta \omega \, t + \theta_l)\cos \omega_0 t$$
$$- \sin(l \Delta \omega \, t + \theta_l)\sin \omega_0 t \qquad (6\text{-}95)$$

Grouping the *low-frequency* terms $\cos(l \Delta \omega \, t + \theta_l)$ and $\sin(l \Delta \omega \, t + \theta_l)$ together, we then get

$$n(t) = \left[\sum_l a_l \cos(l \Delta \omega \, t + \theta_l) \right] \cos \omega_0 t - \left[\sum_l a_l \sin(l \Delta \omega \, t + \theta_l) \right] \sin \omega_0 t \qquad (6\text{-}96)$$

The resulting *low-frequency sums* shown in brackets we denote as $x(t)$ and $y(t)$, respectively:

$$x(t) = \sum_l a_l \cos(l \Delta \omega \, t + \theta_l)$$
$$y(t) = \sum_l a_l \sin(l \Delta \omega \, t + \theta_l) \qquad (6\text{-}97)$$

We then have, finally,

$$n(t) = x(t)\cos \omega_0 t - y(t)\sin \omega_0 t$$

$$= r(t)\cos[\omega_0 t + \theta(t)] \qquad (6\text{-}98)$$

as in Eq. (6-90), with

$$r^2 = x^2 + y^2 \qquad \theta = \tan^{-1}\frac{y}{x} \qquad (6\text{-}99)$$

Invoking the central limit theorem, it is apparent from Eq. (6-97) that both $x(t)$ and $y(t)$ are gaussian random processes. As a matter of fact, it is readily shown, by writing $x^2(t)$ and $y^2(t)$ as double sums and statistically averaging over the θ_l's, that

$$E(x^2) = E(y^2) = E(n^2) = N \qquad (6\text{-}100)$$

[The details are left to the reader, but note, as a hint, that

$$E\left[\cos(l\,\Delta\omega\,t + \theta_l)\cos(m\,\Delta\omega\,t + \theta_m)\right] = 0$$

with θ_l and θ_m *independent*, unless $l = m$, in which case $E(\ ) = \frac{1}{2}$.]

Both the inphase noise term $x(t)$ and the quadratic term $y(t)$ individually have the same invariance or power as the original noise $n(t)$. [It is apparent by appropriate averaging that $E(x) = E(y) = 0$.]

In addition, it is readily shown by calculating $E(xy)$, using the same series representations of Eq. (6-97), that x and y are uncorrelated and, being gaussian, independent.

It is of interest to discuss the power spectral densities of $x(t)$ and $y(t)$. Comparing Eqs. (6-91) and (6-97), it is apparent that the noise terms $x(t)$ and $y(t)$ may be visualized as the original noise $n(t)$ shifted down to zero frequency. With $n(t)$ a random noise wave, oscillating, with a bandwidth B hertz, about the center frequency f_0, the inphase and quadrature terms $x(t)$ and $y(t)$ are both noise processes centered at dc; hence they are slowly varying at the bandwidth B. The calculation of the spectral densities in fact verifies this. It is readily shown that $G_x(f)$ and $G_y(f)$ are equal, and correspond to the original noise spectral density $G_n(f)$ shifted down to dc (zero frequency). In particular, they are found to be given by [SCHW 1966, pp. 39, 40]

$$G_x(f) = G_y(f) = G_n(f + f_0) + G_n(f - f_0) \qquad -f_0 < f < f_0$$

$$= 0 \qquad\qquad\qquad\qquad \text{elsewhere} \qquad (6\text{-}101)$$

A sketch of a typical high-frequency noise spectral density and the low-frequency $G_x(f)$ are shown in Fig. 6-38.

If, as a special and very common case, $G_n(f)$ is symmetrical about the carrier frequency f_0, the positive- and negative-frequency contributions of $G_n(f)$ may be simply shifted down to zero frequency and added to give

$$G_x(f) = G_y(f) = 2G_n(f + f_0) \qquad (6\text{-}102)$$

(This is the case where the i-f filtering is symmetrical about f_0.) As an example, if

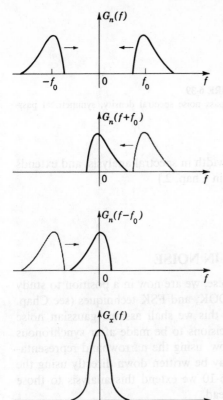

FIGURE 6-38
Inphase (low-pass) noise spectral density (asymmetric noise spectrum).

$G_n(f)$ is gaussian-shaped and given by

$$G_n(f) = \frac{N/2}{\sqrt{2\pi\sigma^2}} e^{-(f-f_0)^2/2\sigma^2} + \frac{N/2}{\sqrt{2\pi\sigma^2}} e^{-(f+f_0)^2/2\sigma^2} \qquad (6\text{-}103)$$

with $\sigma \ll f_0$, we have

$$G_x(f) = G_y(f) = \frac{N}{\sqrt{2\pi\sigma^2}} e^{-f^2/2\sigma^2} \qquad (6\text{-}104)$$

The result is sketched in Fig. 6-39. [Note that σ may be defined as an rms bandwidth. For from the properties of gaussian functions,[19] it is apparent that

$$\sigma^2 = \frac{\displaystyle\int_{-\infty}^{\infty} f^2 G_x(f)\, df}{\displaystyle\int_{-\infty}^{\infty} G_x(f)\, df} \qquad (6\text{-}105)$$

---

[19] Recall in a probabilistic context that this is just the definition of variance if the average value is zero.

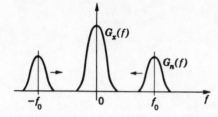

FIGURE 6-39
Low-pass noise spectral density, symmetrical pass-band.

This is often used as the definition of bandwidth in spectral analysis, and extends the various possible definitions considered in Chap. 2.]

6-8 BINARY R-F TRANSMISSION COMPARED: SYNCHRONOUS DETECTION OF BINARY SIGNALS IN NOISE

Using the narrowband representation of noise, we are now in a position to study the comparative SNR properties of PSK, OOK, and FSK techniques (see Chap. 4), as well as others if so desired. To do this we shall assume gaussian noise added during transmission and assume decisions to be made after synchronous detection at the receiver. We shall then show, using the narrowband representation of noise, that probabilities of error may be written down directly using the error calculations of Sec. 6-2. In Section 6-10 we extend this analysis to those cases where envelope detection is used instead.

Recall from Chap. 4, as well as Sec. 6-1, that synchronous detection requires carrier phase coherence to be maintained. The process of synchronous detection consists of multiplication of a received carrier signal by a locally generated sine wave of the same frequency and phase, the resultant product term then being passed through a low-pass filter to eliminate second-harmonic terms.

For a PSK binary sequence of the form $\pm A \cos \omega_0 t$, or for an OOK sequence consisting of either $A \cos \omega_0 t$ or 0,[20] we simply multiply by $\cos \omega_0 t$ and filter. A synchronous detector for these signals is shown in Fig. 6-40.

For the FSK sequence consisting of $A \cos \omega_1 t$ or $A \cos \omega_2 t$, *two* sets of synchronous detectors are needed, one operating at frequency f_1, the other at frequency f_2. The resultant FSK detector is shown in Fig. 6-41. Note that in both figures predetection (i-f) filters are shown. These are narrowband filters with bandwidths chosen wide enough to pass the respective carrier signals (generally $2B_l$ hertz, if the low-pass filter bandwidths are B_l). Actually, we shall show quite simply that they should be matched filters or reasonable approximations to these if additive noise is the primary source of error in detection.

---

[20] Rectangular pulse shaping is assumed here for simplicity. Any shape $f(t)$ could be written in place of A.

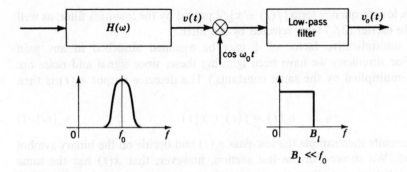

FIGURE 6-40
Synchronous detector for PSK and OOK signals.

Now assume that signal plus noise appears at the output of a particular narrowband filter. [This is labeled $v(t)$ in Fig. 6-40.] It is apparent, as pointed out in the discussion of Chap. 4, that all three binary cases are covered by assuming a signal of the form $f(t)\cos \omega_0 t$. [In the PSK case $f(t)$ is $\pm A$, in the OOK case, $+A$ or 0. In the FSK case ω_0 is either ω_1 or ω_2, and $f(t)$ is A if a signal is present in one of the two parallel channels, 0 if it is absent.] The composite signal plus noise at the input to the detector may thus be written

$$v(t) = f(t)\cos \omega_0 t + n(t)$$
$$= [f(t) + x(t)]\cos \omega_0 t - y(t)\sin \omega_0 t \qquad (6\text{-}106)$$

using the narrowband noise representation of the last section.

The noise $n(t)$ is narrowband in form, its spectral density dependent on the i-f filters $H(\omega)$ shown in Figs. 6-40 and 6-41. The low-pass noise terms $x(t)$ and $y(t)$ thus have half the i-f bandwidth, assumed small compared to the center frequency f_0. Multiplication of $v(t)$ by the locally generated $\cos \omega_0 t$ therefore

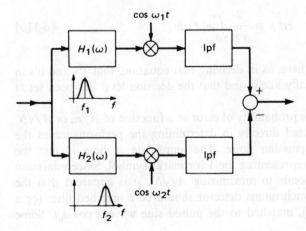

FIGURE 6-41
Synchronous detection of FSK signals.

results in a low-frequency term $[f(t) + x]/2$ passed by the low-pass filter, as well as a double carrier $(2f_0)$ term rejected by the filter.

The multiplicative factor of $\frac{1}{2}$ may be assumed absorbed in any gain factors. (For simplicity we have been ignoring these, since signal and noise are then both multiplied by the same constants.) The detector output $v_o(t)$ is then simply

$$v_o(t) = f(t) + x(t) \tag{6-107}$$

Decision circuits then sample the low-pass $v_o(t)$ and decide on the binary symbol transmitted. We showed in the last section, however, that $x(t)$ has the same gaussian statistics, as well as the same variance (power) N, as the noise $n(t)$. From the form of Eq. (6-107), it is apparent that the binary decision problem here is *identical* with that first considered in Sec. 6-2. The $x(t)$ term here is the same as the low-pass $n(t)$ included there.

The process of synchronous detection performs the same operation on noise as on signal. It merely serves to translate the center frequency down, from f_0 to 0 frequency.

In particular, in the OOK case, the detector output is just

$$v_{o,\text{OOK}}(t) = \left\{ \begin{matrix} A \\ \text{or} \\ 0 \end{matrix} \right\} + x(t) \tag{6-108}$$

Since this output is identical with that discussed in Sec. 6-2, it is apparent that the probability of error is just

$$P_{e,\text{OOK}} = \frac{1}{2}\left(1 - \text{erf}\,\frac{A}{2\sqrt{2N}}\right) = \frac{1}{2}\,\text{erfc}\,\frac{A}{2\sqrt{2N}} \tag{6-109}$$

with erf x the error function, and erfc x, the *complementary error function*, given by

$$\text{erfc}\,x = 1 - \text{erf}\,x$$

$$\text{erf}\,x \equiv \frac{2}{\sqrt{\pi}} \int_0^x e^{-y^2}\,dy \tag{6-110}$$

[See Eq. (6-22). We assume here, as in deriving that equation, that 1's and 0's in the binary sequence are equally likely, and that the decision level has been set at $A/2$.]

Figure 6-9, showing the probability of error as a function of A/σ, or $A/\sqrt{N}$ in this case, may thus be used directly in determining the performance of the OOK system in additive gaussian noise. The amplitude A here is just the amplitude of the sine wave representing the 1 (or mark) symbol. Since minimum probability of error corresponds to maximizing $A/\sqrt{N}$, it is apparent that the $H(\omega)$ filter preceding the synchronous detector should be a matched filter (or a good approximation to one), matched to the pulsed sine wave $A \cos \omega_0 t$. Some thought indicates that this is just the low-pass matched filter translated up to the center frequency f_0. This assumes white noise at the input to the i-f filter $H(\omega)$.

Alternatively, a little thought will indicate that the $H(\omega)$ filter may be widened considerably if desired, and the matched filtering performed in the low-pass filter following the multiplier. The synchronous detector merely serves to translate frequencies down, so that the *overall* filtering is effectively due to the cascaded effect of $H(\omega)$ and the low-pass filter. It is this overall filter that should be matched to the signal. The low-pass filter is often called a *postdetection* filter.

In the PSK case the synchronous detector output consists of a polar signal $\pm A$ plus noise. This thus corresponds exactly to the polar signal analysis in Sec. 6-2. Here, however, we have $\pm A$ as the signal, rather than $\pm A/2$, as assumed there. Again choosing 0 as the decision level ($v_o > 0$ is called a 1, $v_o < 0$ a 0 signal), and assuming equally likely binary symbols, the probability of error is just

$$P_{e,\text{PSK}} = \tfrac{1}{2}\,\text{erfc}\,\frac{A}{\sqrt{2N}} \tag{6-111}$$

As noted in Sec. 6-2, and as is apparent by comparing Eqs. (6-109) and (6-111), the PSK system requires only half the signal amplitude that the OOK system does, for the same probability of error. There is thus a 6-dB peak SNR improvement. On an average-power basis, however, the improvement is only 3 dB because the OOK system is off half the time, on the average, requiring only half as much power.

In the case of the FSK system the outputs of two detectors are compared. At any one time one detector has signal plus noise, the other noise only. Calling the noise output of one channel x_1, that of the other x_2, we have, on subtracting the two channel outputs, the FSK output given by

$$v_{o,\text{FSK}} = \left\{ \begin{matrix} +A \\ \text{or} \\ -A \end{matrix} \right\} + (x_1 - x_2) \tag{6-112}$$

The output signal is again polar: $+A$ appears if a 1 has been transmitted, $-A$ for a 0 transmitted. The total noise output is, however, $x_1 - x_2$. If the noises in the two channels are independent (true if the system input noise is white and the two bandpass filters $H_1(\omega)$ and $H_2(\omega)$ do not overlap [SCHW 1966, pp. 44, 45], the usual case), the variances add.[21] We have effectively doubled the noise by subtracting the two outputs. However, since the output signal is polar, the effective signal excursion, as in the PSK case, is twice that of the OOK case. The

---

[21]If $y = x_1 - x_2$ and $E(x_1) = E(x_2) = 0$, as here,

$$\text{var}(y) = E(y^2) = E(x_1 - x_2)^2 = E(x_1^2) - 2E(x_1 x_2) + E(x_1^2) = E(x_1^2) + E(x_2^2)$$

since x_1 and x_2 are independent and hence uncorrelated. More generally, readers are asked to show for themselves that if $y = a_1 x_1 + a_2 x_2$, x_1 and x_2 independent, then $\text{var}(y) = a_1^2\,\text{var}(x_1^2) + a_2^2\,\text{var}(x_2^2)$, independent of the first moments or mean values.

FSK system thus provides results intermediate between the OOK and PSK cases:

$$P_{e,\text{FSK}} = \tfrac{1}{2}\,\text{erfc}\,\frac{A}{2\sqrt{N}} \qquad (6\text{-}113)$$

For a specified probability of error the FSK system requires 3 dB more signal power than the equivalent PSK system with the same noise power, but is 3 dB better than the OOK system on a peak-power basis. (Recall from Chap. 4 that FSK requires wider transmission or channel bandwidths than either of the other two systems. The channel bandwidth is measured prior to the H_1 and H_2 filters of Fig. 6-41.)

Again a minimum probability of error requires maximization of the ratio $A/\sqrt{N}$ at the input to the synchronous detector. For this purpose the two filters H_1 and H_2 in Fig. 6-41 should be matched as closely as possible to their respective signal inputs.

It is apparent from this simple analysis of binary signals in noise that PSK transmission is to be preferred if phase coherence is available. Some of the deep-space probes have used PSK modulation successfully in their telemetry systems. Rather sophisticated techniques are of course required to establish and maintain the necessary phase synchronism. The analysis of high-frequency binary transmission with envelope detection will be considered in the next section. We shall find there, as expected, that envelope detection results in a somewhat higher probability of error, or a corresponding loss in SNR.

Optimum Matched-Filter Detection

The probability of error results appearing in Eqs. (6-109), (6-111), and (6-113) may be written in a unified way by recalling the matched-filter result of Sec. 6-6: It was shown there, in the case of the detection of a pulse in noise, that the matched-filter output SNR is given by

$$\frac{A^2}{N} = \frac{2E}{n_0} \qquad (6\text{-}114)$$

[see (6-85)]. Here E represents the energy in the signal at the point where the white gaussian noise of spectral density $n_0/2$ is added.

A little thought will indicate that the pulse to be detected in Sec. 6-6 didn't necessarily have to be baseband in nature. It could just as well have been a high-frequency pulse, corresponding to the OOK case here. The optimum matched filter would then be a bandpass filter, centered at the carrier frequency f_0 and shaped to correspond to the high-frequency pulse shape. This is precisely one of the two possibilities mentioned above in the design of the two filters of Fig. 6-40. The result of Sec. 6-6, given by (6-114), thus goes over directly to the OOK case here: the minimum-probability-of-error result, Eq. (6-109), for OOK transmission may be written by replacing $A/\sqrt{N}$ with the equivalent ratio $\sqrt{2E/n_0}$ from (6-114).

One important comment must be made, however. The energy E in the present case is the *high-frequency* signal energy, measured again at the point where the high-frequency signal and noise are added.

Using a similar argument, $A/\sqrt{N}$ in each of the other cases considered, (6-111) for PSK transmission and (6-113) for FSK transmission, may be replaced by $\sqrt{2E/n_0}$ if matched filtering is used. All three results can then be encompassed by the following single probability-of-error expression:

$$P_e = \tfrac{1}{2}\, \text{erfc}\, \frac{a}{2\sqrt{2}} \qquad (6\text{-}115)$$

The parameter a written here has the following definitions:

For OOK transmission,

$$\frac{a^2}{8} = \frac{E}{4n_0}$$

For FSK transmission,

$$\frac{a^2}{8} = \frac{E}{2n_0}$$

For PSK transmission,

$$\frac{a^2}{8} = \frac{E}{n_0}$$

E is again the *high-frequency* signal energy at the input to the receiver; $n_0/2$ is the gaussian white-noise spectral density measured at the same point.

In the case of PSK or OOK transmission,

$$E = \int_0^T [f(t)\cos \omega_0 t]^2 \, dt \qquad (6\text{-}116)$$

with T the binary interval over which the pulse is defined, and $f(t)$ the pulse shape. In the case of FSK transmission the same definition of the energy holds, except that ω_0 is replaced by ω_1 and ω_2, the FSK carrier frequencies in rad/s. If the shape factor $f(t)$ is varying slowly compared to the carrier frequencies, $(B \ll f_0, f_1, f_2)$, and many carrier cycles are encompassed in the binary interval T $(Tf_0 \gg 1)$, the energy E is given approximately by

$$E \doteq \frac{1}{2}\int_0^T f^2(t) \, dt \qquad (6\text{-}117)$$

Independent arguments leading to (6-115) as the error-probability expression for OOK, PSK, and FSK transmission, using synchronous detection with matched filtering, appear in several problems at the end of this chapter. A more general approach introduced in Chap. 7 demonstrates that (6-115) is applicable to any two binary wave shapes to be detected in the presence of additive white gaussian noise. Specifically, let $s_1(t)$ be the explicit expression for one signal and $s_2(t)$ the expression for the other, each lasting T seconds in time. Then the minimum probability of error of reception of these two waveshapes, assumed transmitted with equal probability, is found to be given by (6-115), with a^2 defined by the following expression:

$$a^2 \equiv \int_0^T \frac{(s_1 - s_2)^2 \, dt}{n_0/2} \tag{6-118}$$

It is left to the reader to show that the results for OOK, PSK, and FSK transmission are encompassed by this definition.

The unified expression for the minimum binary (bit) error probability, (6-115), is shown plotted in Fig. 6-42.

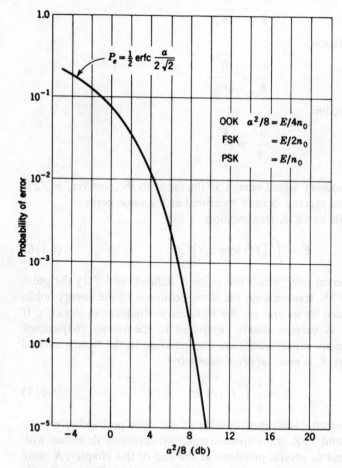

FIGURE 6-42

Probability of error, optimum binary transmission.

These results for the matched-filter, minimum-error-probability receiver are readily obtained without resort to the narrowband noise representation discussed above. It is instructive to demonstrate this approach, particularly for the case of rectangular binary waveshapes, i.e., those with no waveshaping included. The optimality of the synchronous detection receiver arises quite naturally. This approach will also be found useful in evaluating the performance of optical heterodyne detection in the next section.

Specifically, let the binary signal be of the form $f(t)\cos \omega_0 t$, $0 \leq t \leq T$, T the binary interval, with $f(t) = \pm A$ in the case of PSK, $+A$ or 0 in the case of OOK transmission. White gaussian noise $n(t)$, with spectral density $n_0/2$, is added during transmission. The signal $v(t)$ appearing at the receiver is then, as in (6-106), given by

$$v(t) = s(t) + n(t)$$
$$= f(t)\cos \omega_0 t + n(t) \qquad 0 \leq t \leq T \qquad (6\text{-}119)$$

with $s(t) = f(t)\cos \omega_0 t$ the received signal.

From the results of Sec. 6-6, the matched-filter receiver, the one that maximizes the output signal-to-noise ratio or minimizes the probability of error, has a transfer function $H(\omega)$ that is the complex conjugate of $S(\omega)$. [See (6-83).] This must be centered at the carrier frequency $f_0 = \omega_0/2\pi$. Now consider the special case under consideration, of $f(t)$ a rectangular pulse of width T, the binary interval. The impulse response of the matched filter is then just the rectangular high-frequency pulse $\cos \omega_0 t$, $0 \leq t \leq T$, ignoring a multiplicative constant. From the convolution integral the output of this filter, with $v(t)$ applied at the input, is

$$v_o = \int_o^T v(t)\cos \omega_0 t\, dt = \int_0^T s(t)\cos \omega_0 t\, dt + \int_0^T n(t)\cos \omega_0 t\, dt \qquad (6\text{-}120)$$

with $s(t) = \pm A\cos \omega_0 t$ for PSK transmission, and $A\cos \omega_0 t$ or 0 for OOK transmission. The implication of (6-120) is clear: The matched-filter receiver is one that first multiplies $v(t)$ by $\cos \omega_0 t$ and then integrates the product from 0 to T. This matched-filter receiver is portrayed in Fig. 6-43. It is sometimes called an *integrate-and-dump circuit*. Note that the matched-filter receiver for this case first carries out synchronous detection, then does the integration. The integration portion is just the low-pass filter operation of Fig. 6-40 for the special case of a rectangular signal pulse of width T.

From (6-120) the output of the matched filter has two terms: a signal term and a noise term. Consider PSK as an example. (The OOK case follows in a

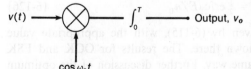

FIGURE 6-43
Matched-filter receiver, high-frequency signal plus white noise.

similar manner.) Carrying out the integration indicated, the two possible signal outputs are $\pm AT/2$, assuming the frequency f_0 high enough that $\omega_0 T \gg 1$. The noise term is given by

$$n_o = \int_0^T n(t) \cos \omega_0 t \, dt \tag{6-121}$$

Since $n(t)$ represents a random process, n_o, evaluated at one point T in time, is a random variable. As noted in Sec. 6-7, if $n(t)$ is gaussian, n_o must also be gaussian. Letting $n(t)$ be a zero-mean gaussian process, $E(n_o) = 0$ as well. The random variable n_o is thus fully determined once its variance σ_o^2 is known. This quantity is readily determined, just as in (6-39), by squaring n_o and taking the expectation of the resultant product:

$$E(n_o^2) = E\left[\int_0^T n(t) \cos \omega_0 t \, dt \cdot \int_0^T n(s) \cos \omega_0 s \, ds\right] \tag{6-122}$$

(Note that t is a dummy variable. Replacing it with s in the second integral leaves the integral unchanged.) Interchanging the order of expectation and integration, we get, using the definition (6-48) of the autocorrelation function,

$$E(n_o^2) = \int_0^T \int_0^T R_n(t - s) \cos \omega_0 t \cos \omega_0 s \, dt \, ds \tag{6-123}$$

But recall that we had assumed $n(t)$ was white noise, with spectral density $n_0/2$. From (6-59), $R_n(t - s) = n_0/2 \, \delta(t - s)$. Inserting this in (6-123), using the sifting property of the impulse function, and carrying out the indicated integration, we find that

$$\sigma_o^2 = E(n_o^2) = \frac{n_0}{2} \cdot \frac{T}{2} \tag{6-124}$$

Details are left to the reader.

The statistics of the matched filter output v_o are now completely determined. Since n_o is gaussian, $v_o = s_o + n_o$ is gaussian as well. Its average value is $s_o = \pm AT/2$, depending on which signal was transmitted. Its variance is $n_0 T/4$, from (6-124). The two distributions of v_o are plotted in Fig. 6-44. Just as in (6-111), the probability of error is given by

$$P_{e,\text{PSK}} = \tfrac{1}{2} \, \text{erfc} \, \frac{AT/2}{\sqrt{2}\,\sigma_o} = \tfrac{1}{2} \, \text{erfc} \sqrt{\frac{A^2 T}{2n_0}} \tag{6-125}$$

But note that $A^2 T/2 = E$, the energy in the PSK signal. We finally get, for the probability of error in PSK, using matched-filter detection,

$$P_{e,\text{PSK}} = \tfrac{1}{2} \, \text{erfc} \sqrt{E/n_0} \tag{6-126}$$

This is precisely the expression given by (6-115), with the appropriate value introduced for the parameter a shown there. The results for OOK and FSK transmission can be obtained the same way. Further discussion of the optimum

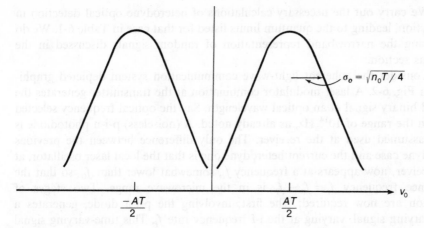

$$\sigma_o = \sqrt{n_0 T / 4}$$

FIGURE 6-44
Probability-density function, output of matched-filter receiver of Fig. 6-43, PSK transmission.

detection of digital signals in noise, including QAM transmission, appears in Chapter 7. In the next section we return to the performance of optical communication systems, focusing on heterodyne coherent detection. The analysis carried out follows, to some extent, the approach used here.

6-9 HETERODYNE DETECTION OF COHERENT LIGHT-WAVE SYSTEMS

In Sec. 6-1 we discussed performance limits in digital lightwave light-wave systems, focusing on direct-detection OOK transmission, and coherent homodyne detection of various binary optical systems. The limits obtained were quantum ones, due to variations in the photon count of a light-wave signal impinging on a photodetector. Additive noise, introduced principally at the detector and in electronic circuits following, would degrade the performance even more.

Coherent homodyne detection of optical signals, although capable potentially of providing substantial improvements over practical direct detection systems which use relatively noisy avalanche photodiodes, requires phase locking of a locally generated light-wave signal. As noted in Sec. 6-1, this can be a difficult task at light-wave frequencies. Phase synchronization at the receiver of a lightwave system is more readily carried out electronically at gigahertz frequencies, in the microwave range, using heterodyne rather than homodyne techniques. The price paid, as already noted in discussing Table 6-1, is a 3-dB or 2-to-1 deterioration in the quantum limits from those calculated for homodyne detection. These quantum limits in the case of heterodyne detection still provide potentially orders-of-magnitude improvement over direct-detection light-wave systems in current use, and so suggest that coherent heterodyne detection is a viable technique.

We carry out the necessary calculations of heterodyne optical detection in this section, leading to the quantum limits listed for that case in Table 6-1. We do this using the narrowband representation of random signals discussed in the previous section.

Consider the coherent light-wave communication system depicted graphically in Fig. 6-2. A laser-modulator combination at the transmitter generates the desired binary signal at an optical wavelength. Say the optical frequency selected is f_0, in the range of 10^{14} Hz, as already noted. A (noiseless) p-i-n photodiode is again assumed used at the receiver. The only difference between the previous homodyne case and the current heterodyne one is that the local laser oscillator, at the receiver, now appears at a frequency f_l, somewhat lower than f_0, so that the difference frequency $f_i = f_0 - f_l$ is in the microwave range. Two stages of detection are now required: The first, involving the p-i-n diode, generates a time-varying signal, varying at the i-f frequency rate f_i. This time-varying signal must now be detected using coherent techniques, but the locally generated synchronization signal required is $\cos \omega_i t$ rather than the homodyne signal of $\cos \omega_0 t$. Phase synchronization at the i-f frequency f_i can be done electronically and is much more readily carried out than at the optical frequency f_0.

We carry out the analysis, as previously, for the three basic types of binary communication: PSK, OOK, and FSK. Consider PSK first. The receiver in this case is diagrammed in Fig. 6-45. The received optical signal, neglecting shaping factors, is $\pm A \cos \omega_0 t$, using the notation of Sec. 6-1. Added to this, at the beam splitter, is the locally generated optical signal $B \cos \omega_l t$, $B \gg A$, with $\omega_0 = \omega_i + \omega_l$, $f_i = \omega_i/2\pi$ the i-f frequency.

The output of the p-i-n diode, following the analysis of Sec. 6-1, is again a count whose average value is proportional to the square of the envelope of the incoming composite signal. To determine this envelope we use simple trigonometry:

$$\pm A \cos \omega_0 t + B \cos \omega_l t = \pm A \cos (\omega_i + \omega_l)t + B \cos \omega_l t$$
$$= [\pm A \cos \omega_i + B]\cos \omega_l t \mp A \sin \omega_i t \sin \omega_l t$$
$$= c(t)\cos[\omega_l t + \beta(t)] \qquad (6\text{-}127)$$

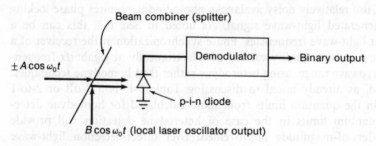

FIGURE 6-45
Heterodyne detection, coherent PSK light-wave system.

The square of the envelope $c(t)$ is given by

$$c^2(t) = (\pm A \cos \omega_i + B)^2 + A^2 \sin^2 \omega_i t$$

$$= A^2 + B^2 \pm 2AB \cos \omega_i t \qquad (6\text{-}128)$$

(The reader may note that we chose to define the envelope of a signal oscillating at radian frequency ω_i. The same result would have been obtained had we used frequency ω_0 instead.) Unlike the direct detection and homodyne analysis of Sec. 6-1, we now have a time-varying envelope, and hence a photodiode count whose average value varies with time. This translates into electron statistics, and hence current, also varying with time.

As in the case of Sec. 6-1, the statistics at the output of the detector are still Poisson. With a 1 transmitted, the average value is $A^2 + B^2 + 2AB \cos \omega_i t$. The variance is the same, but with the local-oscillator amplitude $B \gg A$, the variance is closely approximated by B^2. With a 0 transmitted, the average value decreases to $A^2 + B^2 - 2AB \cos \omega_i t$; the variance remains very nearly at B^2. Subtracting out the constant average $A^2 + B^2$, the problem becomes that of detecting a time-varying signal $+2AB \cos \omega_i t$ or $-2AB \cos \omega_i t$ in the presence of noise whose variance is B^2. This noise consists of a memoryless Poisson process which is closely modeled by white noise. (Photon arrivals may or may not occur in small intervals Δt long.) This is precisely the problem described at the end of the last section. Matched-filter detection is called for; the matched-filter receiver is the integrate-and-dump circuit of Fig. 6-43, consisting of a synchronous detector followed by an integrator, integrating over the binary interval T seconds long. The demodulator indicated in Fig. 6-45 is precisely this circuit. In Fig. 6-46 we sketch the complete PSK receiver. An actual receiver would use a balanced detector to zero out the constant bias term $A^2 + B^2$. Since frequency $f_i = \omega_i/2\pi$ would typically be in the microwave (gigahertz) range, electronic circuitry would be used to implement the demodulator.

The output of the balanced matched-filter receiver is readily determined. It is left for the reader to show that it has a signal component $\pm ABT$. The noise component is found to have a variance $B^2T/2$. [The analysis is very similar to

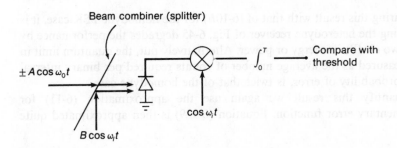

FIGURE 6-46
Matched-filter demodulator, heterodyne coherent PSK detector, $\omega_i = \omega_0 - \omega_l$.

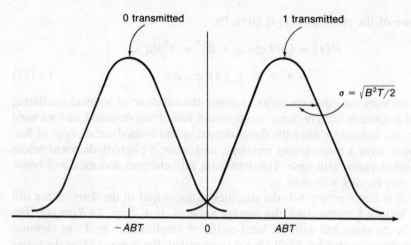

FIGURE 6-47
Calculation of probability of error, heterodyne detection, coherent PSK lightwave system.

that carried out in Eqs. (6-121) to (6-124). Here we have $E[n^2(t)] = B^2$; moreover, $E[n(t)n(s)] = 0$ because of the memoryless property of the Poisson process. Equation (6-123) simplifies to $\int_0^T B^2 \cos^2 \omega_i t \, dt$ and evaluates to $B^2 T/2$ directly.] Since Poisson statistics are again approximated quite closely by gaussian statistics for large average value, the probability distributions of current in the two cases of a 1 transmitted or a 0 transmitted are given by the bell-shaped curves of Fig. 6-47. The probability of error, assuming 1's and 0's equally likely to be transmitted, is given by

$$P_e = \tfrac{1}{2} \operatorname{erfc} \frac{ABT}{\sqrt{2}\,\sigma} = \tfrac{1}{2} \operatorname{erfc} A\sqrt{T}$$

$$= \tfrac{1}{2} \operatorname{erfc}\sqrt{\lambda_p T} \qquad (6\text{-}129)$$

again letting $A^2 T = \lambda_p T$, as done in Sec. 6-1. [See (6-2) and the discussion following.]

Comparing this result with that of (6-10b) for the homodyne PSK case, it is clear that using the heterodyne receiver of Fig. 6-45 degrades the performance by a factor of two (3 dB) in energy or power. Alternatively put, the quantum limit in this case, measured as the average number of counts required per binary interval for a given probability of error, is twice that of the homodyne case.

To quantify this result we again use the approximation (6-11) for the complementary error function. Equation (6-129) is then approximated quite well by

$$P_e \doteq \frac{\tfrac{1}{2}e^{-\lambda_p T}}{\sqrt{\pi \lambda_p T}} \qquad (6\text{-}130)$$

For $P_e = 10^{-9}$, $\lambda_p T = 18$ photons/bit. This is the result previously noted in Table 6-1. As pointed out in Sec. 6-1, heterodyne detection results theoretically in poorer performance than homodyne detection, but the quantum limit of 18 photons/bit for $P_e = 10^{-9}$ is potentially much more readily approached in practice. The phase and frequency synchronization required to carry out the coherent multiplication by cos $\omega_i t$ in Fig. 6-46 applies to the frequency f_i and not to the light-wave frequency f_0. Conventional electronic phase-lock techniques are available for this purpose [SKLA, Chap. 8].

The quantum-limit analysis for the coherent OOK lightwave system using heterodyne detection proceeds in a manner similar to that described for the PSK case above. We outline the approach here, leaving the details for a problem at the end of this chapter.

In this case the light-wave signal appearing at the p-i-n diode input is either $A \cos \omega_0 t + B \cos \omega_i t = c(t)\cos[\omega_i t + \beta(t)]$ if a 1 is transmitted, or $B \cos \omega_i t$ if a 0 is transmitted. The diode output, proportional to the envelope squared, is now either $B^2 + 2AB \cos \omega_i t$ (dropping the A^2 term, since $B \gg A$) or B^2. Again using a matched-filter demodulator to synchronously detect the cos $\omega_i t$ term, the output current distribution is very nearly gaussian with variance $B^2 T/2$. The average value with a 1 transmitted is $B^2 T/2 + ABT$; with a 0 transmitted it is $B^2 T/2$. The probability of error is then calculated to be

$$P_e = \tfrac{1}{2} \operatorname{erfc} \frac{A\sqrt{T}}{2} = \tfrac{1}{2} \operatorname{erfc} \sqrt{\frac{\lambda_p T}{4}} \tag{6-131}$$

Comparing with (6-129) and (6-130) for the PSK case, we again have the factor of 4, or 6 dB, noted previously in Secs. 6-1 and 6-2. But recall again that OOK transmission is on only 50 percent of the time, on the average. This recoups 50 percent of the power lost. Heterodyne coherent OOK light-wave transmission thus requires, on the average, twice the number of photons in a binary interval that PSK transmission does. For $P_e = 10^{-9}$, this translates into 36 photons per binary interval as the coherent OOK heterodyne quantum limit, as listed in Table 6-1.

As the final heterodyne scheme for coherent light-wave transmission, consider FSK. Here the two optical signals transmitted are $A \cos \omega_1 t$ or $A \cos \omega_2 t$, just as discussed in Chap. 4, and again in Sec. 6-8, in discussing FSK synchronous detection in noise. The receiver in this case is the one shown in Fig. 6-48: A local oscillator signal $B \cos \omega_i t$, $B \gg A$, is again added to the received signal using a beam splitter or some other type of optical combiner; the summed signal is detected using a p-i-n diode. The transmitted frequencies f_1 and f_2, as well as the local-oscillator frequency f_i, are chosen so that the difference frequencies $f_1' = f_1 - f_i$ and $f_2' = f_2 - f_i$ are both within the passband of a microwave receiver centered at $f_i = (f_1' + f_2')/2$. It is left to the reader to show that the optimum matched-filter detector in this case is the one shown in Fig. 6-48. This is to be compared with the FSK synchronous detector of Fig. 6-41.

Following the approach used in both the PSK and OOK analysis above, it is left to the reader to show that if a 1 ($A \cos \omega_1 t$) is sent, the output appearing at

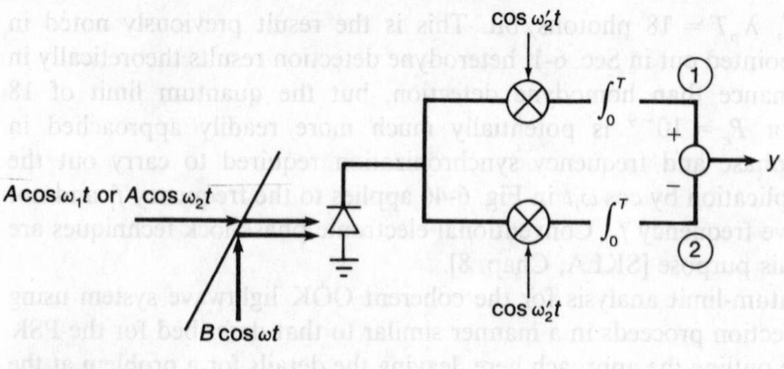

FIGURE 6-48

Matched-filter receiver, heterodyne coherent FSK lightwave system. $\omega'_1 = \omega_1 - \omega_l$; $\omega'_2 = \omega_2 - \omega_l$.

point (1) in Fig. 6-48 is approximately a gaussian random variable with average value $B^2 T/2 + ABT$, while the output at point (2) is very nearly gaussian with average value $B^2 T/2$. If a 0 ($A \cos \omega_2 T$) is sent, the outputs are just reversed. It is clear that one should subtract the two outputs to obtain the final binary output: $+1$ for a 1 transmitted, -1 for a zero transmitted. This operation is indicated in Fig. 6-48 and mirrors the FSK detector operation sketched previously in Fig. 6-41. Following the FSK synchronous-detection analysis of Sec. 6-8, it is clear that an error will occur if, given a 1 sent, the output at (2) exceeds that at (1). Let the difference of the two outputs be a random variable y, as indicated in Fig. 6-48. If a 1 ($A \cos \omega_1 t$) is sent, y will be very nearly a gaussian random variable of average value ABT and variance $B^2 T$ ($B \gg A$). If a 0 ($A \cos \omega_2 t$) is sent, y is very nearly gaussian with average value $-ABT$ and variance $B^2 T$. [Recall the discussion in Sec. 6-8 following (6-112). Just as was the case there, the variance of the difference of two random variables is the sum of the variances.]

Putting this altogether, it is left as an exercise for the reader to show that the quantum-limit probability of error for heterodyne FSK light-wave transmission is given by

$$P_e = \tfrac{1}{2} \operatorname{erfc} A\sqrt{T/2} = \tfrac{1}{2} \operatorname{erfc}\sqrt{\lambda_p T/2} \qquad (6\text{-}132)$$

Comparing with the result in (6-129) for heterodyne PSK transmission, we find that FSK transmission results in a 3-dB (factor of 2) penalty. As an example, $\lambda_p T = 36$ photons are required per binary interval to obtain a (quantum limit) probability of error $P_e = 10^{-9}$. This is the same average value obtained for OOK transmission and is listed in Table 6-1 as well.

6-10 NONCOHERENT BINARY TRANSMISSION

We now return to the discussion of the performance of binary signals with additive gaussian noise by extending the previous analysis, in Sec. 6-8, of coherent signal transmission and detection to the noncoherent case. This is the situation in which phase coherence cannot be maintained or in which it is uneconomical to incorporate phase-control circuits in the receiver. One then generally resorts to envelope detection of the high-frequency signals. Envelope detection was discussed in Chap. 4. It was also encountered in Secs. 6-1 and 6-9 above, in discussing light-wave detection systems. It was noted there that photo-diodes by their very nature carry out envelope detection. Yet, except for the case of direct detection of OOK light-wave signals, the light-wave detection analysis dealt only with coherent systems. The focus of this section, as in Secs. 6-2 and 6-8, is on binary communication systems at frequencies below the optical range in which errors are due primarily to additive gaussian noise.

We recall that if we have a high-frequency sine wave of the form $r(t)(\cos \omega_0 t + \theta)$, with $r(t)$ a positive quantity, the envelope detector provides $r(t)$ at its output. [In the previous section the symbol $c(t)$ was used to represent the envelope.] As first noted in Chap. 4, a nonlinear device plus low-pass filtering is needed to recover $r(t)$. It is apparent that PSK signals require phase coherence to be demodulated. We therefore consider here only OOK or FSK signals, detected with envelope detectors. As in Fig. 6-41, the FSK receiver consists of *two* channels, one tuned to frequency f_1, the other to frequency f_2. Each synchronous detector in Fig. 6-41 is replaced by an envelope detector. The outputs of the two detectors are then compared to determine whether one binary symbol or the other was transmitted. The FSK envelope-detection scheme is shown in Fig. 6-49b. The OOK receiver consists of one channel, tuned to the carrier frequency f_0, with one envelope detector providing the desired output.

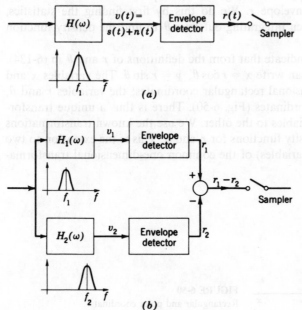

FIGURE 6-49
Noncoherent envelope detection. (a) OOK receiver. (b) Noncoherent FSK detection.

The OOK receiver is shown in Fig. 6-49a. A decision level on the output then decides whether a 1 or a 0 was transmitted.

For simplicity's sake we shall discuss first the simple OOK system. Results for the FSK case are found in a similar manner, by an extension of the analysis. If we assume an OOK sequence of symbols, the output $v(t)$ of a narrowband filter centered at f_0 is, as in (6-106), adding signal and noise,

$$v(t) = [f(t) + x(t)]\cos \omega_0 t - y(t)\sin \omega_0 t \qquad (6\text{-}133)$$

Here $f(t) = A$ or 0. Rewriting this in the equivalent form

$$v(t) = r(t)\cos[\omega_0 t + \theta(t)] \qquad (6\text{-}134)$$

with $\qquad r = \sqrt{(f + x)^2 + y^2} \quad$ and $\quad \theta = \tan^{-1}\dfrac{y}{f + x}$

it is apparent that an envelope detector will produce $r(t)$ at its output. Sampling $r(t)$ once each binary period, we then make a decision about whether a 1 or a 0 is present by noting whether the sampled $r(t) > b$ or $r(t) < b$, respectively, with b a specified decision level.

The probability of error depends on the statistics of r in the two cases, $f = A$ or 0. We develop the probability density function for these two cases in the subsection following.

Rayleigh and Rician Statistics

Consider first the case where the signal is absent. This is the noise-only case with $A = 0$. With x and y independent and gaussian, the problem is to determine the statistics of the random envelope r. We do this by first finding the statistics, jointly, of r and θ, and then integrating out over θ to find the density function of r.

A little thought will indicate that from the definitions of r and θ in (6-134), in terms of x and y, one can write $x = r\cos\theta$, $y = r\sin\theta$. The variables x and y correspond to two-dimensional rectangular coordinates; the variables r and θ, to the equivalent polar coordinates (Fig. 6-50). There is thus a unique transformation from one set of variables to the other. We use the known transformations to find the probability-density functions for r and θ. This is the extension to two dimensions (two random variables) of the common one-dimensional transformation [PAPO 1984].

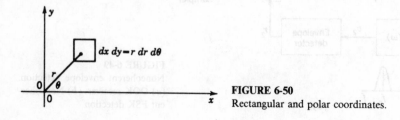

FIGURE 6-50
Rectangular and polar coordinates.

In the one-variable case we equate areas under the probability-density curves. Here too we equate probabilities:

$$\text{Prob}(x_1 < x < x_2, \; y_1 < y < y_2) = \text{Prob}(r_1 < r < r_2, \; \theta_1 < \theta < \theta_2) \quad (6\text{-}135)$$

This corresponds, however, to equating volumes under the joint probability-density curves. As noted above, we are effectively converting from rectangular (x, y) coordinates to polar (r, θ) coordinates. With $f_{r\theta}(r, \theta)$ the probability-density function for the polar coordinates, we must have

$$f_{xy}(x, y) \, dx \, dy = f_{r\theta}(r, \theta) \, dr \, d\theta \quad (6\text{-}136)$$

Recall from Sec. 6-8 that x and y are independent and gaussian. Then

$$f_{xy}(x, y) = f_x(x)f_y(y) = \frac{e^{-(x^2+y^2)/2\sigma^2}}{2\pi\sigma^2} = \frac{e^{-r^2/2\sigma^2}}{2\pi\sigma^2} \quad (6\text{-}137)$$

using σ^2 for the variances and $r^2 = x^2 + y^2$. Transforming differential areas, we have

$$dx \, dy = r \, dr \, d\theta \quad (6\text{-}138)$$

(see Fig. 6-50).

From Eq. (6-136), then, with Eqs. (6-137) ad (6-138),

$$f_{r\theta}(r, \theta) \, dr \, d\theta = \frac{re^{-r^2/2\sigma^2}}{2\pi\sigma^2} \, dr \, d\theta \quad (6\text{-}139)$$

and

$$f_{r\theta}(r, \theta) = \frac{re^{-r^2/2\sigma^2}}{2\pi\sigma^2} \quad (6\text{-}140)$$

To find the density function $f_r(r)$ for the envelope alone, we simply average Eq. (6-140) over all possible phases. Since the phase angle θ varies between 0 and 2π, we get

$$f_r(r) = \int_0^{2\pi} f_{r\theta}(r, \theta) \, d\theta = \frac{re^{-r^2/2\sigma^2}}{\sigma^2} \quad (6\text{-}141)$$

This is called the *Rayleigh distribution* and is shown sketched in Fig. 6-51. The peak of this distribution occurs at $r = \sigma$ and is equal to $e^{-1/2}/\sigma$. As σ (the standard deviation of the gaussian variables x and y) increases, the distribution flattens out, the peak decreasing and moving to the right. It is easily seen that

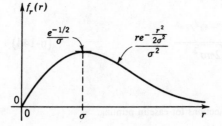

FIGURE 6-51
Rayleigh distribution.

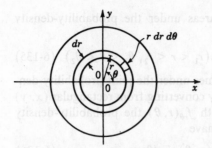

FIGURE 6-52
A target.

$f_r(r)$ is properly normalized, so that $\int_0^\infty f_r(r)\, dr = 1$. Note that the normalization is from 0 to ∞ here, instead of from $-\infty$ to ∞ for the gaussian distribution. The envelope can have only *positive* values.

The Rayleigh distribution appears in many other applications of statistics. Another simple example involves the firing of bullets at a target. Assume that the distribution of the bullets hitting the target is gaussian along the horizontal, or x, axis of the target and also gaussian along the vertical, or y, axis (i.e., a two-dimensional gaussian distribution) (Fig. 6-52). The average location of the hits is at the origin, and the standard deviation in each direction is σ. The probability that the hits will lie within an annular ring dr units wide and r units from the origin is just $f_r(r)\, dr$, with $f_r(r)$ the Rayleigh distribution. [Note from Fig. 6-52 that, if $f_{r\theta}(r, \theta)\, dr\, d\theta$ represents the probability that the bullets will lodge within the differential area $r\, dr\, d\theta$, the probability that the bullets will lodge within the concentric annular ring is found by integrating over all values of θ. This is exactly what was done in Eq. (6-141).]

The envelope of the noise-only case ($A = 0$) thus obeys Rayleigh statistics. Now consider the case where the signal is present during OOK transmission. What is the probability distribution of the envelope in this case? Equation (6-133) is now given by

$$v(t) = [A + x(t)]\cos \omega_0 t - y(t)\sin \omega_0 t \qquad (6\text{-}142)$$

where x and y are the previous gaussian-distributed terms, each with variance σ^2. Considering the factor $x + A$ alone, we note that the sum represents a gaussian variable with A the average value and σ^2 still the variance. Calling the sum a new parameter x',

$$x' \equiv x + A \qquad (6\text{-}143)$$

we have[22]

$$f(x') = \frac{e^{-(x'-A)^2/2\sigma^2}}{\sqrt{2\pi\sigma^2}} \qquad (6\text{-}144)$$

---

[22] We henceforth drop the subscript on the density functions for ease in printing.

The envelope of $v(t)$ is now given by

$$r^2 = x'^2 + y^2 = (x + A)^2 + y^2 \tag{6-145}$$

and the phase is

$$\theta = \tan^{-1} \frac{y}{x'} = \tan^{-1} \frac{y}{x + A} \tag{6-146}$$

We can again find the probability distributions for both the envelope and phase by a transformation to polar coordinates. This will give us the probability distribution at the output of an envelope detector, as well as the distribution at the output of a phase detector.

With x' and y independent random variables related to r and θ by the transformations $x' = r\cos\theta$, $y = r\sin\theta$, we have

$$f(r, \theta)\, dr\, d\theta = f(x', y)\, dx'\, dy = \frac{e^{-[(x'-A)^2 + y^2]/2\sigma^2}}{2\pi\sigma^2} dx'\, dy$$

$$= \frac{e^{-A^2/2\sigma^2} r e^{-(r^2 - 2rA\cos\theta)/2\sigma^2}}{2\pi\sigma^2} dr\, d\theta \tag{6-147}$$

Note that we cannot write $f(r, \theta)$ as a product $f(r)f(\theta)$, since a term in the equation appears with both variables multiplied together as $r\cos\theta$. This indicates that r and θ are *dependent* variables. They are connected in this case by the term $rA\cos\theta$. This is apparent from Eqs. (6-145) and (6-146) as well as Eq. (6-147). If $A \to 0$, the two variables again become independent and $f(r, \theta)$ reduces to the product $f(r)f(\theta)$ found for the zero-signal case.

We can find $f(r)$ again by integrating over all values of θ. This gives us

$$f(r) = \frac{e^{-A^2/2\sigma^2} r e^{-r^2/2\sigma^2}}{2\pi\sigma^2} \int_0^{2\pi} e^{(rA\cos\theta)/\sigma^2}\, d\theta \tag{6-148}$$

The integral in Eq. (6-148) cannot be evaluated in terms of elementary functions. Note, however, its similarity to the defining integral for the Bessel function of the first kind and zero order given by Eq. (4-84). It is in fact related to the Bessel function of the first kind. In particular,

$$I_0(z) \equiv \frac{1}{2\pi} \int_0^{2\pi} e^{z\cos\theta}\, d\theta \tag{6-149}$$

is called the *modified* Bessel function of the first kind and zero order. In terms of $I_0(z)$, Eq. (6-148) becomes

$$f(r) = \frac{r}{\sigma^2} e^{-(r^2 + A^2)/2\sigma^2} I_0\left(\frac{rA}{\sigma^2}\right) \tag{6-150}$$

The modified Bessel function can be written as an infinite series, just like the Bessel function of the first kind. This series can be shown to be

$$I_0(z) = \sum_{n=0}^{\infty} \frac{z^{2n}}{2^{2n}(n!)^2} \tag{6-151}$$

For $z \ll 1$,

$$I_0(z) \doteq 1 + \frac{z^2}{4} + \cdots \doteq e^{z^2/4} \tag{6-152}$$

Letting $A \to 0$ in Eq. (6-150), we get the Rayleigh distribution again, checking our previous result for the zero-signal case.

The envelope distribution of Eq. (6-150) is often called the *Rician distribution* in honor of S. O. Rice of Bell Telephone Laboratories, who developed and discussed the properties of this distribution in a pioneering series of papers on random noise [RICE].[23]

We have indicated that for $A^2/2\sigma^2 \to 0$, the envelope of the received signal follows the Rayleigh distribution. For large $A^2/2\sigma^2$, however, it again approaches the original gaussian distribution of the inphase (x) signal term. This is apparent from Eq. (6-142) or Eq. (6-145). For as A increases relative to σ, the inphase term dominates, the quadrature term contribution to the envelope becomes negligible, and the envelope becomes just

$$r \doteq A + x \qquad A \gg \sigma \tag{6-153}$$

This is just a gaussian random variable with average value A_c.

This can also be demonstrated from the Rician density function [Eq. (6-150)] itself. To show this we make use of a known property of the modified Bessel function—that is, that it approaches asymptotically, for large values of the argument, an exponential function. Thus for $z \gg 1$,

$$I_0(z) \doteq \frac{e^z}{\sqrt{2\pi z}} \tag{6-154}$$

Letting $rA \gg \sigma^2$ in Eq. (6-150), we make use of Eq. (6-154) to put $f(r)$ in the form

$$f(r) \doteq \frac{r}{\sqrt{2\pi r A \sigma^2}} e^{-(r-A)^2/2\sigma^2} \tag{6-155}$$

This function peaks sharply about the point $r = A$, dropping off rapidly as we move away from this point. Most of the contribution to the area under the $f(r)$ curve (or the largest values of the probability of a range of r occurring) comes from points in the vicinity of $r = A$. In this range of r, then, we can let

[23] [RICE] S. O. Rice, "Mathematical Analysis of Random Noise," *Bell System Tech. J.*, vol. 23, pp. 282–333, July 1944; vol. 24, pp. 46–156, January 1945 (reprinted in N. Wax, *Selected Papers on Noise and Stochastic Processes*, Dover, New York, 1954).

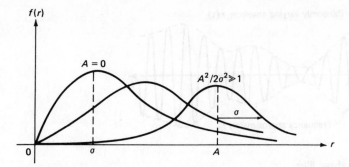

FIGURE 6-53
Rician distribution.

$r = A$ in the nonexponential (and slowly varying) portions of $f(r)$ and get

$$f(r) = \frac{1}{\sqrt{2\pi\sigma^2}} e^{-(r-A)^2/2\sigma^2} \qquad rA \gg \sigma^2 \qquad (6\text{-}156)$$

In the vicinity of the point $r = A$, then, the distribution approximates the normal (gaussian) distribution as noted above.

The Rician distribution is shown plotted in Fig. 6-53 for different values of $A^2/2\sigma^2$.

Probability-of-Error Calculations

We now use the Rayleigh and Rician distributions just derived to determine the probability of error in the case of envelope detection. The two statistical distributions are rewritten below for convenience, with the noise power N in place of the variance σ^2:

1. Noise-only case, $A = 0$:

$$f_n(r) = \frac{re^{-r^2/2N}}{N} \qquad r \geq 0 \qquad (6\text{-}157)$$

2. Signal-plus-noise case, $A > 0$:

$$f_s(r) = \frac{re^{-r^2/2N}}{N} e^{-A^2/2N} I_0\left(\frac{rA}{N}\right) \qquad r \geq 0 \qquad (6\text{-}158)$$

(The subscript n stands for noise, s for the signal plus noise.) Recall again that $I_0(x)$ is the modified Bessel function. N is of course the noise variance or the mean noise power measured at the output of the narrowband filter $H(\omega)$ in Fig. 6-49a. (Here $A^2/2$ is the average signal power with a 1 transmitted. $A^2/2N$ is thus a power signal-to-noise ratio.)

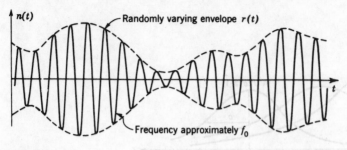

FIGURE 6-54
Noise at output of narrowband filter.

A typical sketch of noise at the output of the narrowband filter is shown in Fig. 6-54. Note that it resembles a sine wave at frequency f_0, slowly varying in amplitude and phase at a rate determined by the filter bandwidth. The envelope $r(t)$ shown dashed in Fig. 6-54 has the Rayleigh statistics of Eq. (6-157). The functional form of the noise shown is of course given by Eq. (6-133) with $A = 0$. The random phase angle $\theta(t)$ is uniformly distributed between 0 and 2π.

Using the two density functions, that of Eq. (6-157) for noise only (a 0 transmitted), and that of Eq. (6-158) for signal plus noise (a 1 transmitted), we are now in a position to calculate the probability of error for OOK signaling, with envelope detection. The analysis is similar to that of the error analysis of Sec. 6-2, the only difference being that we must now consider envelope statistics rather than the gaussian statistics assumed there.

Here we decide on a 0 transmitted if $r < b$, a 1 transmitted if $r > b$, as noted earlier. The decision level b thus corresponds to the decision level d of Sec. 6-2. Although d could take on any value, positive or negative, b is of course restricted to positive values because of the envelope characteristics. Figure 6-55 shows the two decision regions introduced by defining the decision level b.

Assume, as in Sec. 6-2, that the a priori probabilities of transmitting a 0 and a 1 are, respectively, P_0 and $P_1 = 1 - P_0$. The overall probability of error is then

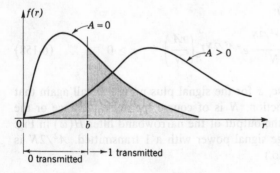

FIGURE 6-55
Decision regions with envelope-detected OOK signals.

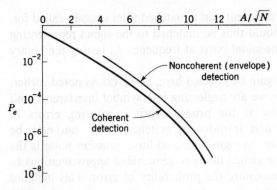

FIGURE 6-56
Binary error probabilities, OOK transmission.

given by

$$P_e = P_0 \int_b^\infty f_n(r) \, dr + P_1 \int_0^b f_s(r) \, dr \qquad (6\text{-}159)$$

with the Rayleigh-density function of Eq. (6-157) used in the first integral and the Rician-density function of Eq. (6-158) used in the second. The two integrals are indicated by the crosshatching in Fig. 6-55.

Although the first integral is directly evaluable, giving $e^{-b^2/2N}$, the second integral cannot be evaluated in closed form. It has, however, been numerically evaluated and tabulated by numerous investigators [SCHW 1966]. Carrying out the indicated integrations of Eq. (6-159) in the special case where $P_0 = P_1 = \frac{1}{2}$ and the two integrals are the same (i.e., the two crosshatched areas of Fig. 6-55 are the same), one obtains the curve of Fig. 6-56. Also shown is the comparable curve as obtained earlier for coherent (synchronous) detection. Note that the envelope-detection process is somewhat inferior to coherent detection. For the same probability of error P_e it requires somewhat more signal power (higher $A/\sqrt{N}$); for the same SNR $A/\sqrt{N}$, P_e is somewhat larger. This is as might be expected, since we are essentially throwing away useful information by ignoring the phase in envelope detection.

Actually one can again optimize the decision level b, choosing it to minimize the probability of error P_e from Eq. (6-159), as was done in Sec. 6-2. The result is not too different from that of Fig. 6-56. (As will be shown in Chap. 7, the optimum corresponds to the point at which the two density functions in Fig. 6-55 intersect. For $A^2/N \gg 1$, which is necessary to ensure low probability of error, that optimum point does not differ substantially from the values of b used in calculating Fig. 6-56.)

Note one very important point, however. Again the probability of error depends uniquely on the ratio $A/\sqrt{N}$, the ratio of peak signal at the narrowband filter output to the rms noise measured at the same point. The only way to decrease the probability of error is to increase $A/\sqrt{N}$. How does one do this, aside from the obvious ways of increasing transmitter power and trying to decrease the additive noise? It is apparent that a matched filter is again called for. The narrowband filter $[H(\omega)]$ should thus be matched to the signal representing the "1" symbol, in this case a sinusoidal burst at frequency f_0, lasting the binary interval.

A word of caution should again be injected here, however. As noted earlier, in first discussing matched filters, we are neglecting intersymbol interference and are assuming that additive noise is the prime culprit in causing errors in detection. The point made in first introducing matched filters can now be repeated. In all digital transmission systems where additive gaussian noise is the prime cause of detection errors, matched filters or reasonable approximations to them will normally be used to minimize the probability of error. This includes baseband digital systems, coherent or synchronous carrier systems, the FSK system to be discussed briefly below, search radar systems, etc. If individual pulse decisions may be considered, independent of streams of data preceding or following the pulse in question, a matched filter is usually called for. If intersymbol interference is the major problem, however, the filter design of Chap. 3 should be considered instead.

In practice, of course, the matched-filter condition is usually met by designing the filter to have the appropriate bandwidth. This is usually the reciprocal of the signal pulse width (or the reciprocal of the binary interval), as noted earlier in discussing matched filters. Again, as noted earlier, some widening of the bandwidth may be tolerated and in fact is often employed to decrease pulse overlap (intersymbol interference), without affecting the SNR critically.

How does one now determine the probability of error of the noncoherent, or envelope-detected, FSK system of Fig. 6-49b? Assume here that frequency f_1 corresponds to a 1 transmitted, f_2 to a 0. If a 1 is actually transmitted, signal plus noise will appear on channel 1, noise alone on channel 2. The sampled value of $r_1 - r_2$ should be positive for a correct decision to be made. Similarly, $r_1 - r_2$ should be negative if a 0 is transmitted. (Note that although phase synchronism is no longer assumed between transmitter and receiver, binary-interval synchronism must be maintained. This is true as well with the OOK receiver of Fig. 6-49a.)

An error will obviously be made if $r_1 - r_2$ is negative, with a 1 transmitted, or positive with a 0 transmitted. If 1's and 0's are assumed equally likely to be transmitted, the probability of either type of error is the same by the symmetry of the system of Fig. 6-49b. Assuming as an example a 1 transmitted, the probability of error is just the probability that the noise causing r_2 will exceed the signal-plus-noise envelope signal r_1. This is given by

$$P_e = \int_{r_1=0}^{\infty} f_s(r_1) \left[\int_{r_2=r_1}^{\infty} f_n(r_2)\, dr_2 \right] dr_1 \qquad (6\text{-}160)$$

with the density functions of Eqs. (6-159) and (6-158) used where indicated. [The inner integral provides the probability of error for a *fixed* value of r_1. Averaging over all possible values of r_1, one then obtains Eq. (6-160).] Since $f_n(r)$ is just the Rayleigh density, the inner integral integrates readily to $e^{-r_1^2/2N}$. The expression for the probability of error is then just

$$P_e = \int_0^\infty \frac{r_1}{N} e^{-r_1^2/N} e^{-A^2/2N} I_0\left(\frac{r_1 A}{N}\right) dr_1 \qquad (6\text{-}161)$$

To integrate this expression we use a simple trick. We define a new (dummy) variable $x = \sqrt{2}\, r_1$. Equation (6-161) then becomes, with a little manipulation,

$$P_e = \tfrac{1}{2} e^{-A^2/4N} \int_0^\infty \frac{x}{N} e^{-x^2/2N} e^{-A^2/4N} I_0\left(\frac{xA}{\sqrt{2}\,N}\right) dx \qquad (6\text{-}162)$$

But the integrand is exactly in the form of the Rician density function of Eq. (6-158) if A there is replaced by $A/\sqrt{2}$ here. The integral must then just equal 1, and we have, quite simply,

$$P_e = \tfrac{1}{2} e^{-A^2/4N} \qquad (6\text{-}163)$$

The probability of error of the noncoherent FSK system thus decreases exponentially with the power SNR $A^2/2N$. The error curve corresponding to Eq. (6-163) is plotted in Fig. 6-57, together with the corresponding curves for synchronous (coherent) PSK and FSK transmission, using the results of Sec. 6-8 and Sec. 6-2. Note that just as in the case of noncoherent versus coherent OOK (Fig. 6-56), there is a penalty paid for using envelope rather than synchronous detection. The noncoherent systems require slightly more signal power for the same probability of error.

This loss in SNR due to envelope detection becomes negligible at high SNR, however, as is apparent from Fig. 6-57, and as may be shown from the synchronous-detection results of Sec. 6-8, using the asymptotic ($x \gg 1$) form for the complementary error function,

$$\operatorname{erfc} x \doteq \frac{e^{-x^2}}{x\sqrt{\pi}} \qquad x \gg 1 \qquad (6\text{-}164)$$

The coherent FSK error probability derived in Sec. 6-8 and indicated in Fig. 6-57 is then just

$$P_e = \tfrac{1}{2} \operatorname{erfc} \frac{A}{2\sqrt{N}} \doteq \frac{1}{\sqrt{\pi}\,A/2\sqrt{N}} \frac{e^{-A^2/4N}}{2} \qquad (6\text{-}165)$$

Note that the dominating exponential behavior is just that of the noncoherent FSK expression of Eq. (6-163). At high $A^2/2N$ the other terms in the denominator rapidly become negligible, and noncoherent and coherent FSK approach one another.

It is similarly possible to show that the asymptotic (high-SNR) error probability for both coherent and noncoherent OOK is given by [SCHW 1966]

$$P_e \doteq \tfrac{1}{2} e^{-A^2/8N} \qquad (6\text{-}166)$$

Comparing this with Eqs. (6-163) and (6-165), it is apparent that the OOK systems require twice the SNR ($A^2/2N$) that the FSK systems require. Since the

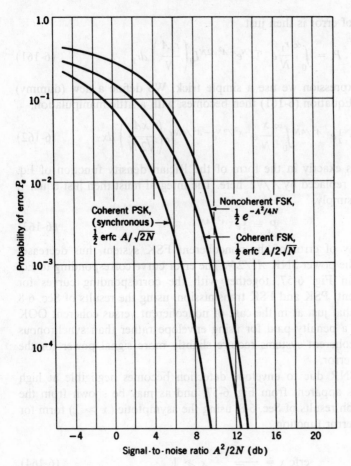

Coherent PSK, (synchronous) → $\frac{1}{2}$ erfc $A/\sqrt{2N}$

Noncoherent FSK, $\frac{1}{2}e^{-A^2/4N}$

Coherent FSK, $\frac{1}{2}$ erfc $A/2\sqrt{N}$

Signal-to-noise ratio $A^2/2N$ (db)

FIGURE 6-57
Performance curves, binary transmission.

OOK signals use power only during a 1 transmission, the two systems achieve the same error rate at the same *average signal power*.

Again, minimum probability of error is ensured by maximizing $A^2/2N$, and hence using matched filters. In the case of noncoherent FSK this means that the two narrowband filters (Fig. 6-49b) are *each* matched to their respective channel.

The stress here in the binary FSK case has been on two-filter receivers; the two frequencies transmitted are separately detected, as in Figs. 6-41 and 6-49b. In practice, discriminators and zero-crossing detectors (Chap. 4) are commonly used for binary FM detection, as well as for analog FM. The error calculations for these detectors become rather involved and are left to the references [BENN 1965].

6-11 SIGNAL-TO-NOISE RATIOS IN FM AND AM

We mentioned in Chap. 4 that wideband FM gives a significant improvement in noise or interference rejection over AM. We would now like to demonstrate this statement and see just how well, and under what conditions, FM provides an improvement over AM.

In previous sections we were able to determine system performance quite uniquely by calculating probabilities of errors. An analogous approach is more difficult to adopt here because of the *continuous* nature of the signals with which we deal. (The calculation of probabilities of errors requires discrete levels of transmission.) Instead, we shall use here a less satisfactory, although still useful, approach: continuous-wave (c-w) systems such as AM and FM will be compared on the basis of SNR at the receiver input and output. This will essentially hinge on a comparative discussion of the detection process: the envelope detector in the AM case, and the discriminator in the FM case. By comparing SNR at the input and output of the detector in the two cases, we shall find that the wideband FM system produces the well-known SNR improvement with bandwidth, while in the AM system the input and output SNR can at best be the same.

This exchange of bandwidth for SNR in the case of FM, with SNR improvement obtained at the expense of increased transmission bandwidth, is not as efficient, however, as the optimum exponential exchange predicted by the Shannon capacity expression. Since the form of the information-capacity expression for PCM is similar to that of the Shannon optimum, PCM systems provide a SNR bandwidth exchange much more efficient than that for FM. For the purpose of comparison of FM and AM we shall assume the same carrier power and noise spectral density at the input to each system. We shall calculate the SNR at the system outputs and compare.

Amplitude Modulation

A typical AM receiver to be analyzed is shown in Fig. 6-58. The amplitude-modulated carrier at the input to the envelope detector has the form

$$v(t) = A_c[1 + mf(t)]\cos \omega_0 t \qquad |mf(t)| \le 1 \qquad (6\text{-}167)$$

if noise is assumed absent. A_c is the unmodulated carrier amplitude measured at the same point.

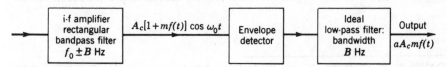

FIGURE 6-58
Idealized AM receiver.

If the modulating signal $f(t)$ is band-limited to B hertz, the intermediate-frequency (i-f) amplifier preceding the detector should have a bandwidth of at least $2B$ hertz, centered about f_0 hertz. The amplifier is assumed to have the characteristics of an ideal rectangular filter.

This AM signal is now envelope-detected and passed through an ideal filter B hertz wide. As shown in Chap. 4, the output of the envelope detector $f_d(t)$ will be proportional to $f(t)$, or

$$f_d(t) = aA_c m f(t) \qquad (6\text{-}168)$$

with a constant of proportionality of the detector. (This constant will henceforth be set equal to 1, since amplifiers can always be introduced to change the gain arbitrarily. In addition, we shall be interested in *ratios* of signal to noise, and such constants cancel out anyway.)

The actual envelope-detection process was shown in Chap. 4 to be that of a nonlinear operation on the input AM signal followed by a low-pass filter as in Fig. 6-58. Two types of nonlinearity were examined in Chap. 4: a piecewise-non-linear characteristic and one possessing smooth curvature. Both were shown to provide the desired envelope-detected output term. It turns out that the signal-to-noise analysis is most readily carried out assuming a detector with quadratic curvature. We shall for this reason concentrate on such a *quadratic envelope detector* here. Analyses for other types of detectors lead to similar results and so will not be considered in detail here [DAVE].[24]

Our study of the signal-to-noise properties of AM detection is simplified still further by considering the rather artificial case of an *unmodulated* carrier in the presence of additive noise. This zero-modulating-signal case is a common artifice (we shall use the same approach in discussing FM noise), and is useful because the major results found apply in the modulated-carrier case as well [DAVE], [SCHW 1966]. Interestingly, this implies modifying the low-pass filter somewhat. The envelope output of Eq. (6-168) assumes zero dc transmission at the filter, blocking the unmodulated-carrier portion of the AM wave of Eq. (6-167). For the unmodulated-carrier model we shall be considering, however, it is just this blocked term that will represent the output signal. But this apparent inconsistency notwithstanding, the approach does provide an understanding of, and useful quantitative information about, the signal-to-noise properties of AM detection.

Assume accordingly for a signal-to-noise analysis that the instantaneous voltage $v(t)$ at the detector input (i-f output) consists of the unmodulated carrier portions of Eq. (6-167) plus gaussian noise $n(t)$. Then, as in previous sections, we

---

[24][DAVE] W. B. Davenport, Jr., and W. L. Root, *Introduction to Random Signals and Noise*, McGraw-Hill, New York, 1958.

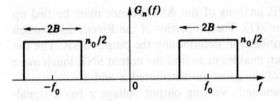

FIGURE 6-59
Noise spectral density at i-f amplifier
output.

may write $v(t)$ in the form

$$v(t) = A_c \cos \omega_0 t + n(t)$$

$$= (x + A_c)\cos \omega_0 t - y(t)\sin \omega_0 t$$

$$= r(t)\cos[\omega_0 t + \theta(t)] \qquad (6\text{-}169)$$

Here $\qquad r^2 = (x + A_c)^2 + y^2$

and $\qquad\qquad \theta = \tan^{-1}\dfrac{y}{x + A_c}$

With the noise assumed white at the input to the narrowband rectangular-shaped i-f filter, the noise spectral density $G_n(f)$ at the filter output must have the rectangular shape shown in Fig. 6-59. The mean power N is thus given by

$$E(n^2) = N = \int_{-\infty}^{\infty} G_n(f)\, df = 2n_0 B$$

We now assume $v(t)$ passed through a quadratic envelope detector, and ask for the SNR at the low-pass filter output (Fig. 6-60). Recalling from Chap. 4 that the quadratic envelope detector squares the input $v(t)$ and then passes low-frequency components only ($f \ll f_0$), we have, at the low-pass filter output,

$$z = v^2_{\text{lowpass}} = \frac{r^2}{2} = \frac{(x + A_c)^2 + y^2}{2} \qquad (6\text{-}170)$$

from Eq. (6-169). (Recall that x, y, and r are *slowly varying* random functions, with bandwidth $B \ll f_0$.) We have again ignored a detector constant with dimensions of volts/volts^2, since we shall shortly take the ratio of signal to noise powers, the constant then dropping out anyway. We shall in fact henceforth ignore the factor $\frac{1}{2}$ appearing in front of r^2, since it is similarly an immaterial constant for our purposes.

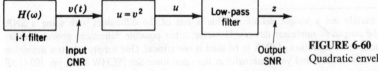

FIGURE 6-60
Quadratic envelope detector.

It is apparent that the SNR analysis of the AM detector must be tied up with the statistics of the envelope $r(t)$. The properties of the Rician distribution discussed earlier can in fact be utilized in determining the output SNR. The use of the quadratic detector, however, enables us to find the output SNR much more simply in terms of the statistics of the gaussian-distributed x and y.

Specifically, we note the randomly varying output voltage z has a signal-dependent part (providing the output signal term), as well as a noise-dependent part. We now *define* the output SNR S_o/N_o to be the ratio of the output signal power in the absence of noise to the mean noise power at the output.[25] Since z is a *voltage*, z^2 must be used to find the powers.

Setting $n(t)$ in Eq. (6-169), or, equivalently, x and y in Eq. (6-170), equal to zero, it is apparent the output signal power in the absence of noise is

$$S_o = A_c^4 \tag{6-171}$$

(Recall that we are neglecting the immaterial constant $\frac{1}{2}$.) The mean noise power at the output must then be the average power or second moment of the random variable z less the signal term:

$$N_o = E(z^2) - A_c^4 \tag{6-172}$$

From Eq. (6-170), with the factor $\frac{1}{2}$ again dropped,

$$E(z^2) = E(r^4) = E\left[(x + A_c)^2 + y^2\right]^2 \tag{6-173}$$

It is here that the simplicity of the quadratic detector becomes apparent. For the desired second moment of the output z is for this detector type just the fourth moment of the envelope r, found either by appropriate integration of the Rician density function, or, more simply, by expanding the right-hand side of Eq. (6-173) and taking the indicated average of the *gaussian* variables term by term. In this latter case we make use of the following identities:

1. The mean noise power at the i-f output, as shown previously, is

$$E(x^2) = E(y^2) = N$$

2. A known property of gaussian functions (this is easily checked either by direct integration, or by the moment-generating property of characteristic functions [PAPO 1984]) is

$$E(x^4) = E(y^4) = 3N^2$$

---

[25] This is unfortunately not a unique definition. This is one of the difficulties with using a SNR formulation at the output of nonlinear devices. However, other possible definitions provide similar results so that the specific definition of SNR to be used is not critical. One simply selects a definition simple enough to be evaluable and yet meaningful at the same time. See [SCHW 1966, pp. 102–120] for various approaches.

3. By assumption

$$E(x) = E(y) = 0$$

4. Since x and y are *independent* gaussian variables,

$$E(x^2y^2) = E(x^2)E(y^2) = N^2$$

Carrying out the indicated averaging of Eq. (6-173) then (the details are left as an exercise for the reader), we get the very simple expression

$$E(z^2) = E(r^4) = 8N^2 + 8NA_c^2 + A_c^4 \tag{6-174}$$

The mean noise power at the envelope-detector output is thus

$$N_o = \underbrace{8N^2}_{n \times n} + \underbrace{8NA_c^2}_{s \times n} \tag{6-175}$$

Note the two terms appearing. The first is often called the $n \times n$ term, and is due, as we shall see shortly, to the detector input noise nonlinearly beating with itself. The second is the so-called $s \times n$ term, which is due to the noise nonlinearly mixing with the carrier (or with a modulating signal if present). This second term obviously disappears when the unmodulated carrier goes to zero. Interestingly, this also predicts an *increase* in output noise level when an unmodulated AM carrier is tuned in. This is in fact easily noticed on commercial AM receivers. An opposite effect, a noise *suppression* or quieting effect, will be found to occur in FM.

Combining Eqs. (6-171) and (6-175), the output SNR is found to be given by

$$\frac{S_o}{N_o} = \frac{A_c^4}{8N^2 + 8NA_c^2} \tag{6-176}$$

This may be written in a more illuminating form by defining the carrier-to-noise ratio as

$$\text{CNR} \equiv \frac{A_c^2}{2N} \tag{6-177}$$

($A_c^2/2$ is of course the average power in the unmodulated sine-wave carrier.) Then the output SNR becomes

$$\frac{S_o}{N_o} = \frac{1}{2} \frac{(\text{CNR})^2}{1 + 2\,\text{CNR}} \tag{6-178}$$

Note that for the CNR $\ll 1$ (0 dB), the output SNR drops as the *square* of the carrier-to-noise ratio. This is the *suppression characteristic* of envelope detection. The output SNR deteriorates rapidly as the carrier-to-noise ratio drops below 0 dB. This quadratic SNR behavior below 0 dB is characteristic of all envelope detectors, and is due specifically to the $n \times n$ noise term dominating at low CNR.

For high CNR (CNR $\gg$ 1), on the other hand,

$$\frac{S_o}{N_o} \doteq \tfrac{1}{4} \text{CNR} \qquad \text{CNR} \gg 1 \qquad (6\text{-}179)$$

The output SNR is then linearly dependent on the carrier-to-noise ratio, again a common characteristic of envelope detectors. (Here the $s \times n$ noise term dominates so far as the output noise is concerned.) Thus *no SNR improvement is possible with AM systems*.

With FM, on the other hand, we shall find it possible to get significant improvement in output S_o/N_o by increasing the modulation index, at the expense of course of increased transmission bandwidth. Here in the AM case an increase in the transmission bandwidth beyond the bandwidth $2B$ needed to pass the AM signals serves only to increase the noise N and hence decrease the output SNR.

The complete signal-to-noise characteristic for the envelope detector, showing both the asymptotic high- and low-CNR cases, is shown sketched in Fig. 6-61. Although derived here only for the quadratic-detector case, similar characteristics may be derived for other types of nonlinearity in the detector law. The exact intersection of the two asymptotic lines depends on the detector law assumed, but the slopes, or shape of the detector signal-to-noise characteristic, will be the same for all detector laws.

It it apparent from the discussion of previous sections that a synchronous detector does not produce the quadratic suppression characteristics due to envelope detection at small CNR. The inphase or coherent carrier injection provides the same signal and noise powers at the output as at the input. The output SNR is thus everywhere linearly proportional to the input CNR. The reader is asked to demonstrate this himself to his own satisfaction.

The change from the nonlinear (quadratic) to the linear portion of the detector characteristic of Fig. 6-61 may be accounted for in an alternative and rather instructive fashion by considering the envelope Rayleigh and Rician density functions discussed previously. Referring for example to Fig. 6-53, we note that for low $A/\sqrt{N}$ (low CNR) the envelope will not deviate too far on the average from the $r = 0$ axis. Since r can never become negative by definition of

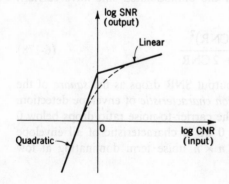

FIGURE 6-61
Asymptotic signal-to-noise characteristics, envelope detector.

an envelope, we would expect a lopsided probability distribution with most of the contribution coming in the vicinity of $r = 0$. This is just the Rayleigh distribution. As the carrier A_c increases, however, we would eventually expect the envelope to be symmetrically distributed about A_c. Although variations of the envelope above A_c have theoretically no limit, while below A_c the envelope is constrained never to become negative, the $r = 0$ axis is so remote for $A_c \gg \sqrt{N}$ that this nonzero constraint becomes insignificant and the probability-density curve approaches just the symmetrical bell-shaped characteristic of the gaussian function.

As far as the signal plus noise at the output is concerned, then, the nonlinear operation of the envelope detector has no effect on the distribution for large CNR. The same result is found to hold true for other nonlinear demodulators with high CNR: the output distribution of signal plus noise remains the same as that of the input.

This is exactly the reason why we have been assuming the noise distribution to remain gaussian as the noise progresses from the r-f stages of a receiver down to the narrowband i-f output. Even with no transmitted signal present the local oscillator injects a large enough signal voltage at the nonlinear mixer to ensure a gaussian noise distribution at the mixer output. The mixer then serves only to translate r-f energy down to the i-f spectrum. The signal and noise properties remain relatively unchanged.

As noted earlier, the local carrier injection required for suppressed-carrier demodulation produces the same result; the noise distribution remains gaussian at the demodulator output.

6-12 AM DETECTOR SPECTRAL ANALYSIS

The envelope-detector signal-to-noise characteristic may be obtained quantitatively in a completely different fashion by focusing attention on the spectral aspects of the detection process. Specifically, we determine the noise density at the output of the nonlinear device, and then investigate the filtering effect of the low-pass filter.

Not only is this approach valid in its own right, enabling us to specifically consider the low-pass filter design and its effect on the output noise, but it also enables us to introduce an extremely powerful tool in random-signal and -noise analysis—the use of correlation functions in determining the spectral properties of random signals passed through nonlinear devices or in calculating the spectra of various random signals.

We defined the power spectral density and the autocorrelation function in Sec. 6-4 to be Fourier-transform pairs. We did not pursue this point further (until the present section of course), because most of the emphasis in preceding sections has either been on noise passed through linear devices or on probability-of-error calculations. The spectral density at the output of linear filters is of course obtained by multiplying the input spectrum by the square of the magnitude of the transfer function. But how does one handle spectra at the output of nonlinear devices such as the envelope detector under consideration here? How does one calculate the spectrum of particular classes of random signals? Many techniques have been developed for handling these problems [DAVE]. One of the most common and most useful is that of calculating the autocorrelation function at the nonlinear device output, and then taking its Fourier transform to find the spectrum at the same point. We shall demonstrate this technique here. Other applications, to FM spectral analysis for example, appear in the references cited.[26]

The quadratic detector is again stressed here for simplicity's sake. The output voltage $z(t)$ will thus again contain the low-pass components of $v^2(t)$ (Fig. 6-60). We shall focus attention on the quadratic term $u = v^2$, however, from which $z(t)$ can be found by filtering.

Recall from Sec. 6-4 that the autocorrelation function of a random process $u(t)$ is simply given by taking the expected value of the product of $u(t)$ and the delayed term $u(t + \tau)$:

$$R_u(z) \equiv [u(t)u(t + \tau)] \tag{6-180}$$

Expressing $u(t)$ here in terms of the input $v(t)$, we have

$$R_u(\tau) = E\left[v^2(t)v^2(t + \tau)\right] \tag{6-181}$$

Evaluating this expression and formally taking its Fourier transform, we find the spectral density $G_u(f)$. Passing this through the low-pass filter $H_L(\omega)$, we then find of course that $G_z(f) = |H_L|^2 G_u(f)$, the desired output spectral density. Here we shall simply say that the filter is an ideal low-pass filter of bandwidth $< f_0$, but high enough to pass all low-frequency components of $u(t)$. Instead of formally writing out $G_u(f)$, we shall then go directly to $G_z(f)$ by ignoring all high-frequency terms in $G_u(f)$.

Before formally evaluating Eq. (6-181), however, we introduce one modification into the expression previously used for $v(t)$. Recall that the reason for using envelope detection in the first place was that we assumed lack of phase coherence. This implies that the received carrier signal must be of the form $A_c \cos(\omega_0 t + \phi)$, with ϕ a random, unknown phase. We have tacitly ignored this phase term so far, writing the unmodulated carrier signal as $A_c \cos \omega_0 t$, because it played no real role in the analysis, and could arbitrarily be set equal to zero without destroying the validity of the treatment. Here, however, where we are taking statistical averages to find autocorrelation functions, the fact that ϕ *is* random does affect the result. The indicated statistical averaging will thus be taken over the random carrier phase angle, as well as the noise. We shall assume, as previously, that ϕ is uniformly distributed over 2π radians, and statistically independent of the noise.

---

[26]See [SCHW 1966, chap. 3] for a summary of applications to FM noise and signal bandwidth determination.

With this modification we now write the composite signal at the i-f filter output as

$$v(t) = A_c \cos(\omega_0 t + \phi) + n(t) \qquad (6\text{-}182)$$

The expression for $v(t + \tau)$ is then of course[27]

$$v(t + \tau) = A_c \cos[\omega_0(t + \tau) + \phi] + n(t + \tau) \qquad (6\text{-}183)$$

Squaring both $v(t)$ and $v(t + \tau)$ and multiplying them together, the autocorrelation function for $u(t)$ becomes

$$R_u(\tau) = E\left\{ \left[A_c \cos(\omega_0 t + \phi) + n(t) \right]^2 \left[A_c \cos(\omega_0(t + \tau) + \phi) + n(t + \tau) \right]^2 \right\} \qquad (6\text{-}184)$$

Expanding the terms in brackets, performing the indicated ensemble averages term by term over ϕ and n, and ignoring terms that will lead to high-frequency components of the spectral density, we get, as the autocorrelation function of the low-pass z,

$$R_z(\tau) = \underbrace{\frac{A_c^4}{4}}_{s \times s} + \underbrace{N A_c^2 + 2 R_n(\tau) A_c^2 \cos \omega_0 \tau}_{s \times n} + \underbrace{R_{n^2}(\tau)}_{n \times n} \qquad (6\text{-}185)$$

Note again the various terms appearing: the signal component $A_c^4/4$ that we have labeled $s \times s$, the $s \times n$ term corresponding to signal beating (or mixing) with noise, and the $n \times n$ term $R_{n^2}(\tau)$ corresponding to noise mixing nonlinearly with itself. The $n \times n$ term is defined as

$$R_{n^2}(\tau) \equiv E\left[n^2(t) n^2(t + \tau) \right] \qquad (6\text{-}186)$$

This particular autocorrelation term may be further simplified by again using a known property of two dependent gaussian variables [$n(t)$ and $n(t + \tau)$ here]: Calling them, for ease in writing, n_1 and n_2, it may be shown [SCHW 1966], [PAPO 1984] that

$$E\left(n_1^2 n_2^2 \right) = N^2 + 2 R_n^2(\tau) \qquad (6\text{-}187)$$

---

[27]As a check the reader may find $R_v(\tau) = E[v(t)v(t + \tau)]$. Inserting Eqs. (6-182) and (6-183) into this expression, multiplying, performing the indicated ensemble average over ϕ and n, and discarding terms centered at $2f_0$, it is easy to show that

$$R_v(\tau) = \frac{A_c^2}{2} \cos \omega_0 \tau + R_n(\tau)$$

Taking Fourier transforms, we then get

$$G_v(f) = \frac{A_c^2}{4} [\delta(f - f_0) + \delta(f + f_0)] + G_n(f)$$

which is just the spectral density corresponding to the sine wave at frequency f_0 plus the additive noise.

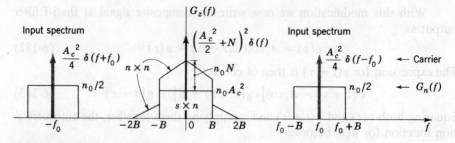

FIGURE 6-62
Low-pass spectral density, quadratic envelope detector: band-limited white noise plus carrier at input.

Then $R_z(\tau)$ simplifies to

$$R_z(\tau) = \left(\frac{A_c^2}{2} + N\right)^2 + \underbrace{2R_n(\tau)A_c^2\cos\omega_0\tau}_{s\times n} + \underbrace{2R_n^2(\tau)}_{n\times n} \quad (6\text{-}188)$$

Taking the Fourier transform of this expression term by term to find the desired spectral density $G_z(f)$, we obtain the following interesting results.

1. The first term gives rise to an impulse at dc, of area $(A_c^2/2 + N)^2$:

$$G_1(f) = \left(\frac{A_c^2}{2} + N\right)^2 \delta(f) \quad (6\text{-}189)$$

This dc terms is shown sketched in Fig. 6-62 for the rectangular-shaped $G_n(f)$ assumed here.

2. The second term results in a shift down to dc of the noise spectrum $G_n(f)$, originally centered at f_0:

$$G_2(f) = 2A_c^2 \int_{-\infty}^{\infty} R_n(\tau)\cos\omega_0\tau\, e^{-j\omega\tau}\, d\tau$$

$$= A_c^2 \int_{-\infty}^{\infty} R_n(\tau)[e^{-j(\omega-\omega_0)\tau} + e^{-j(\omega+\omega_0)\tau}]\, d\tau$$

$$= A_c^2[G_n(f - f_0) + G_n(f + f_0)] \quad (s\times n) \quad (6\text{-}190)$$

Here use is made of the Fourier-transform relation between $G_n(f)$ and $R_n(\tau)$. (The shift indicated includes one up to $2f_0$ hertz as well, but we ignore this, concentrating on the low-pass expressions.) This shift in frequency is as expected, since this $s \times n$ spectral term corresponds precisely to the spectrum of the term $n(t)\cos(\omega_0 t + \phi)$, obtained when squaring $v(t)$. Just as in previous chapters, multiplication by $\cos\omega_0 t$ corresponds to a shift up and down by f_0. Since $n(t)$ is itself centered at f_0, the resultant multiplication shifts $n(t)$ down to 0 Hz and up to $2f_0$ hertz, as shown here. This $s \times n$

contribution to the output spectral density is shown sketched in Fig. 6-62 as well.

3. The third term, $2R_n^2(\tau)$, results in a spectral contribution obtained by convolving the input noise spectral density with itself:

$$G_3(f) = 2\int_{-\infty}^{\infty} G_n(f')G_n(f-f')\,df' \qquad (n \times n) \qquad (6\text{-}191)$$

This is easily demonstrated by recalling from Chap. 2 that the Fourier transform of a product is just the convolution of the two individual Fourier transforms. Thus, if $G(\omega) = F(\omega)H(\omega)$, we have

$$g(t) = \int_{-\infty}^{\infty} f(\tau)h(t-\tau)A\tau\,d\tau$$

Here the two functions corresponding to F and H are both $R_n(\tau)$, and we are going from the τ domain to the f domain, rather than from f to t, but by the symmetry of Fourier transforms it is apparent Eq. (6-191) is valid.

Specifically, for the rectangular $G_n(f)$ centered at f_0 (and $-f_0$ as well), convolution results in the triangular-shaped $n \times n$ term shown centered at 0 Hz in Fig. 6-62. (Another contribution at $2f_0$ is again not shown.) Physically, this $n \times n$ term, the power spectrum of $n^2(t)$, appears because of the multiplication of the input $n(t)$ by itself in forming v^2. The triangular spectrum may be verified qualitatively by visualizing $n(t)$ represented by a large number of equal-amplitude sine waves, all in the vicinity of f_0 hertz. Each one, beating with itself as well as all the others, gives rise to difference frequencies extending from 0 to a maximum of $2B$ hertz. (This maximum contribution is due to the two extreme frequency terms located at $f_0 - B$ and $f_0 + B$, respectively.) Some thought will indicate that most contributions to the $n \times n$ spectrum come from sine waves closely spaced to one another. (There are proportionately more of these.) As the spacing between sine waves to be beaten together increases, there are correspondingly fewer terms involved, and the overall contribution drops. This method of approximating the spectrum by discrete lines, and determining the beat frequencies and the number of contributions to each, is an alternative (albeit much more tedious) way of determining the noise spectra at the output of this quadratic envelope detector [SCHW 1966, pp. 108–117].

The dc spectral contribution $G_1(f)$ may be checked quite easily by considering the output random process $z(t)$. We have

$$E(z) = E(v^2)_{\text{lowpass}} = \frac{A_c^2}{2} + N \qquad (6\text{-}192)$$

from Eq. (6-182) directly. (Again $E(n) = 0$; $E[\cos^2(\omega_0 t + \phi)] = \frac{1}{2}$.) Then the dc power is just $(A_c^2/2 + N)^2$, as found here.

The total spectrum $G_z(f) = G_1(f) + G_2(f) + G_3(f)$. As first noted in Sec. 6-4, the total output power is then obtained by summing $G_z(f)$ over the entire frequency range. In this case the indicated integration can be done by inspection, using Fig. 6-62, and adding up the three contributions term by term. Thus

$$E(z^2) = \int_{-\infty}^{\infty} G_z(f) \, df$$

$$= \underbrace{\left(\frac{A_c^2}{2} + N\right)^2}_{dc} + \underbrace{2Bn_0 A_c^2}_{s \times n} + \underbrace{2Bn_0 N}_{n \times n}$$

$$= \left(\frac{A_c^2}{2} + N\right)^2 + NA_c^2 + N^2 \qquad (6\text{-}193)$$

(In the last line we have replaced $2Bn_0$ by its equivalent N.)

Expanding out and collecting like terms, we have, finally,

$$4E(z^2) = A_c^4 + 8NA_c^2 + 8N^2 \qquad (6\text{-}194)$$

just as in Eq. (6-174) previously. [The apparent factor-of-4 difference is just due to the factor $\frac{1}{2}$ neglected in deriving Eq. (6-174).] The spectral approach thus provides us with the same result obtained previously. [As another check, using Eq. (6-188), $R_z(0)$ gives the same answer, noting that $R_n(0) = N$.]

But not only do we have the total noise power at the output, we also have its spectral distribution as well. As pointed out earlier, this enables us to determine the effects of different filters on the result. For example, it is apparent that the output noise we have calculated—previously, and again just now using the spectral approach—is actually somewhat more than one would get in practice using the quadratic detector and low-pass filter. For it includes noise spectral contributions out to $2B$ hertz (Fig. 6-62), whereas all that is required is a low-pass filter cutting off at B Hz. The power due to the $n \times n$ noise term is then reduced from N^2 to $0.75N^2$ (Fig. 6-62), increasing the output SNR somewhat. With a modulating signal introduced, the dc terms can also be eliminated and S_o/N_o (as redefined to include the modulated output) improved further.

A similar analysis for a piecewise-linear detector (often called a *linear envelope detector*) results in the low-frequency spectrum shown in Fig. 6-63 [RICE, fig. 9, part 4]. (The negative-frequency terms have been folded over and combined with the positive ones.) Again the two types of noise, $s \times n$ and $n \times n$, appear. As shown in the figure the parameter c determines the $n \times n$ contribution, the parameter a the $s \times n$ contribution. The two parameters depend on CNR in a rather complicated way, as shown in Fig. 6-64. For CNR > 4, however,

$$c \doteq \frac{(1/\pi)^2}{8 \, \text{CNR}} n_0$$

and

$$a \doteq \frac{1}{\pi}$$

So even for CNR = 4, the $s \times n$ contribution predominates, as in the quadratic

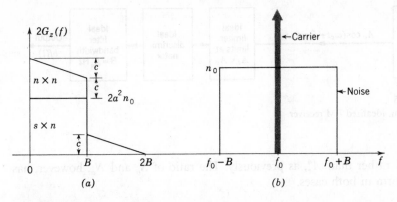

FIGURE 6-63
Low-frequency power spectrum, noise plus carrier, at output of piecewise-linear detector. (*a*) Output spectrum. (*b*) Input spectrum. (S. O. Rice, "Mathematical Analysis of Random Noise," *Bell System Tech. J.*, vol. 24, pp. 46–156, January 1945, fig. 9, part 4. Copyright, 1945, The American Telephone and Telegraph Co.; reprinted by permission.)

detector. For smaller values of CNR, the curves of Fig. 6-64 may be used to obtain c and a.

The dc contributions to the spectral density are not shown here. Note that the dimensions of the noise spectral components are not the same as those of Fig. 6-62 for the quadratic detector. But this is as it should be, since the output voltage in the linear-detector case is proportional to r, the envelope itself, rather than r^2, as in the quadratic case. In particular, the output signal here is just

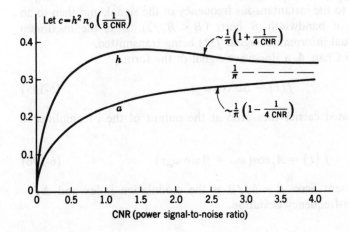

FIGURE 6-64
Coefficients for linear-detector output shown in Fig. 6-63. (S. O. Rice, "Mathematical Analysis of Random Noise," *Bell System Tech. J.*, vol. 24, pp. 45–156, January 1945, fig. 10, part 4. Copyright, 1945, The American Telephone and Telegraph Co.; reprinted by permission.)

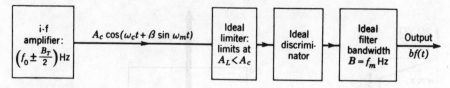

FIGURE 6-65
Block diagram, idealized FM receiver.

$S_o \doteq A_c^2/2$, rather than A_c^4, as previously. The ratio of S_o and N_o, however, has the same form in both cases.

6-13 FREQUENCY-MODULATION NOISE IMPROVEMENT

We now consider the case of frequency modulation. Again assuming the received signal to have gaussian noise added to it, we shall show that, contrary to the AM case, widening the transmission bandwidth (as is required for wideband FM) *does* improve the output SNR. As previously, the SNR will be defined as the ratio of the mean signal power with noise absent to the mean noise power in the presence of an unmodulated carrier. For simplicity's sake the analysis will be confined to the case of large carrier-to-noise ratio (CNR).[28]

The idealized FM receiver to be discussed here is shown in Fig. 6-65. A frequency-modulated signal of transmission bandwidth B_T hertz is first passed through an ideal limiter which removes all amplitude variations. The limiter output, after filtering, goes to the discriminator, assumed to give an output directly proportional to the instantaneous frequency of the signal, and then to an ideal low-pass filter of bandwidth B hertz ($B < B_T/2$). B is the maximum bandwidth of the actual information signal $f(t)$ being transmitted.

Assuming, as in Chap. 4, a sine-wave signal of the form

$$f(t) = \Delta\omega \cos \omega_m t \tag{6-195}$$

the frequency-modulated carrier measured at the output of the i-f amplifier is given by

$$f_c(t) = A_c \cos(\omega_0 t + \beta \sin \omega_m t) \tag{6-196}$$

Noise is assumed absent here. $\beta = \Delta f/B$ is the modulation index and $\Delta f = \Delta\omega/2\pi$ the maximum-frequency deviation.

---

[28]See [SCHW 1966, chap. 3] for a discussion of the complete FM noise problem, including references to the literature.

The average power of the FM wave is simply

$$S_c = \tfrac{1}{2} A_c^2 \tag{6-197}$$

independent of the modulating signal.

The instantaneous frequency is given by

$$\omega = \frac{d\theta}{dt} = \omega_0 + \beta \omega_m \cos \omega_m t = \omega_0 + \Delta\omega \cos \omega_m t$$

$$= \omega_0 + f(t) \tag{6-198}$$

The discriminator output is proportional to the instantaneous frequency deviation away from ω_0, or $\omega - \omega_0$. This frequency deviation is just $f(t)$. The output signal is then

$$f_d(t) = b\,\Delta\omega \cos \omega_m t = bf(t) \tag{6-199}$$

where b is a constant of the discriminator. As in the AM case, this constant will be set equal to 1.

The discriminator output must be filtered to eliminate higher-frequency distortion terms. Filtering will also reduce the output noise when present. The filter bandwidth is chosen as $B = f_m$ hertz in order to pass all frequency components of $f(t)$.

From Eq. (6-199) the average output signal power is simply

$$S_o = \frac{(\Delta\omega)^2}{2} \quad \text{watts} \tag{6-200}$$

if a 1-Ω normalized load resistor is assumed.

The case of noise plus unmodulated carrier (signal absent) can now be treated in a manner directly analogous to that for AM. We again assume fluctuation noise of spectral density $n_0/2$ W/Hz uniformly distributed (i.e., band-limited white noise) at the output of the i-f amplifier. Here, as shown in Fig. 6-66, the noise is uniformly distributed over the range $\pm B_T/2$ hertz about the carrier frequency f_0. (Compare with Fig. 6-59 for the AM case, where the transmission bandwidth $2B$ is generally less than the FM transmission band-

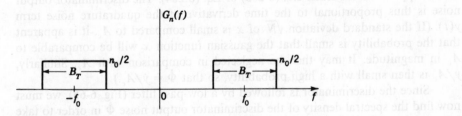

FIGURE 6-66
Noise spectral density, FM receiver.

width B_T.) The noise power at the i-f output (detector input) is thus

$$N = B_T n_0 \tag{6-201}$$

As previously, we may use the narrowband representation for the noise to write the unmodulated carrier plus noise in the form

$$
\begin{aligned}
v(t) &= A_c \cos \omega_0 t + n(t) \\
&= (A_c + x)\cos \omega_0 t - y(t)\sin \omega_0 t \\
&= r(t)\cos[\omega_0 t + \Phi(t)]
\end{aligned}
\tag{6-202}
$$

In the AM case we focused attention on the properties of the envelope $r(t)$. It is apparent that in the FM case we focus attention on the phase term $\Phi(t)$. For in this unmodulated carrier case it is apparent that $\Phi(t)$ represents the noise at the discriminator output. In particular, since

$$\Phi = \tan^{-1} \frac{y}{x + A_c} \tag{6-203}$$

the discriminator output is given by

$$\dot{\Phi} = \frac{(x + A_c)\dot{y} - y\dot{x}}{y^2 + (x + A_c)^2} \tag{6-204}$$

This is a rather formidable-looking expression and is the reason why FM noise analysis, even in the unmodulated-carrier case, is so difficult to carry out. (The straightforward, albeit mathematically difficult, way of determining the spectral density of the noise at the discriminator output is to find the autocorrelation function of the random noise process $\dot{\Phi}(t)$, relating it to the known input correlation function $R_n(\tau)$. One then takes the Fourier transform to find the output spectral density $G_{\dot{\phi}}(f)$ [SCHW 1966].)

For large CNR this expression for the discriminator output $\dot{\Phi}(t)$ simplifies considerably. Thus, recalling that $E(x^2) = E(y^2) = N$, and assuming that $A_c^2 \gg N$ (the CNR is actually $S_c/N = A_c^2/2N$), the discriminator output is given simply by

$$\dot{\Phi} \doteq \frac{1}{A_c}\dot{y} \qquad A_c^2 \gg N \tag{6-205}$$

This is apparent from either Eq. (6-203) or Eq. (6-204). The discriminator output noise is thus proportional to the time derivative of the quadrature noise term $y(t)$. (If the standard deviation $\sqrt{N}$ of x is small compared to A_c, it is apparent that the probability is small that the gaussian function x will be comparable to A_c in magnitude. It may then be neglected in comparison with A_c. Similarly, y/A_c is then small with a high probability, so that $\dot{\Phi} \doteq \dot{y}/A_c$.)

Since the discriminator is followed by a low-pass filter (Fig. 6-65), we must now find the spectral density of the discriminator output noise $\dot{\Phi}$ in order to take into account the effect of the filter. To do this we simply note that differentiation is a linear operation. Hence Eq. (6-205) indicates that $\dot{\Phi}$ may be considered the

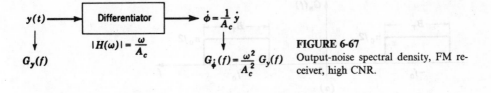

FIGURE 6-67
Output-noise spectral density, FM receiver, high CNR.

response at the output of a (linear) differentiator $H(\omega)$ with y applied at the input. From our discussion of random signals and noise we then write directly

$$G_\phi(f) = |H(\omega)|^2 G_y(f) \qquad (6\text{-}206)$$

But differentiation of a time function corresponds to multiplication of its Fourier transform by $j\omega$. Then $H(\omega) = j\omega/A_c$, $|H(\omega)|^2 = \omega^2/A_c^2$, and we have, very simply,

$$G_\phi(f) = \frac{\omega^2}{A_c^2} G_y(f) \qquad A_c^2 \gg N \qquad (6\text{-}207)$$

This is shown schematically in Fig. 6-67.

Recall from our initial discussion of the narrowband noise representation, however, that for symmetrical bandpass filters,

$$G_x(f) = G_y(f) = 2G_n(f + f_0) \qquad (6\text{-}208)$$

Thus we simply find the spectral density of the quadrature (or inphase) noise component by shifting the noise spectral density $G_n(f)$ down to 0 frequency. Then we also have

$$G_\phi(f) = \frac{2\omega^2}{A_c^2} G_n(f + f_0) \qquad A_c^2 \gg N \qquad (6\text{-}209)$$

In particular, for the band-limited white-noise case assumed here (Fig. 6-66),

$$G_\phi(f) = \frac{\omega^2 n_0}{A_c^2} \qquad -\frac{B_T}{2} < f < \frac{B_T}{2}$$

$$= 0 \qquad \text{elsewhere} \qquad (6\text{-}210)$$

This is shown schematically in Fig. 6-68.

We are now in a position to readily determine the total noise at the FM receiver output. For assuming a low-pass filter of known spectral shape $H_L(\omega)$ following the discriminator, the noise spectral density at the low-pass filter output is simply $|H_L(\omega)|^2 G_\phi(f)$. We then integrate this spectral density over all frequencies to find the output noise N_o. Again for simplicity's sake assume this final filter to be an ideal low-pass one of bandwidth $B < B_T/2$. The bandwidth B should just be sufficient to pass all signal components, yet no larger, to avoid increasing the noise passed. B is thus just the bandwidth of the original modulating signal (see Chap. 4). In the case of the sine-wave signal of frequency f_m, B is just f_m.

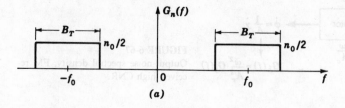

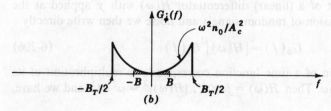

FIGURE 6-68
FM noise spectrum (high-CNR case). (a) Spectrum of i-f noise. (b) Spectral density at FM detector output.

The output noise N_o is thus found by integrating $G_\Phi(f)$ from $-B$ to B (Fig. 6-68):

$$N_o = \int_{-B}^{B} G_\Phi(f)\, df$$

$$= \frac{2(2\pi)^2 n_0}{A_c^2} \int_0^B f^2\, df$$

$$= \frac{(2\pi)^2 n_0}{3S_c} B^3 \tag{6-211}$$

Note that the output noise, although proportional to B^3, is *inversely* proportional to the carrier power $S_c = A_c^2/2$. As the carrier increases, therefore, the noise power drops. This *noise quieting* effect is of course well known in FM, and is just the opposite of the effect encountered in AM. (Recall that there the introduction of the carrier *increased* the noise.)

By using Eq. (6-200), the expression for the output signal power (the signal is assumed to be a cosine wave with noise absent), the mean SNR at the output becomes

$$\frac{S_o}{N_o} = 3\left(\frac{\Delta f}{B}\right)^2 \frac{S_c}{2n_0 B} \tag{6-212}$$

But $2n_0 B = N_c$, the average power in the AM sidebands, and $\beta = \Delta f/B$ is the modulation index. Then

$$\frac{S_o}{N_o} = 3\beta^2 \frac{S_c}{N_c} \tag{6-213}$$

Note that S_c/N_c corresponds to the CNR of an *AM system* with the same carrier power and noise spectral density. The total noise power over the transmission bandwidth B_T of the FM system is greater than N_c, since $B_T > 2B$.

For a specified carrier amplitude and noise spectral density at the i-f amplifier output Eq. (6-213) shows that the output SNR increases with the modulation index or the transmission bandwidth. This is in contrast to the AM case, where increasing the bandwidth beyond $2B$ was found only to degrade the output SNR.

We may specifically compare the FM and AM systems by assuming the same unmodulated carrier power and noise spectral density n_0 for both. (These quantities are measured here at the output of the i-f amplifier.) For a 100-percent-modulated AM signal we have

$$\left(\frac{S_o}{N_o}\right)_{AM} = \frac{S_c}{N_c}$$

Equation (6-213) may thus be modified to read

$$\left(\frac{S_o}{N_o}\right)_{FM} = 3\beta^2 \left(\frac{S_o}{N_o}\right)_{AM} \tag{6-214}$$

For large modulation index (this corresponds to a wide transmission bandwidth, for, with $\beta \gg 1$, the bandwidth approaches $2\,\Delta f$), we can presumably increase S_o/N_o significantly over the AM case. As an example, if $\beta = 5$, the FM output SNR is 75 times that of an equivalent AM system. Alternatively, for the same SNR at the output in both receivers the power of the FM carrier may be reduced 75 times. But this requires increasing the transmission bandwidth from $2B$ (AM case) to $16B$ (FM case); see Fig. 4-54. Frequency modulation thus provides a substantial improvement in SNR, but at the expense of increased bandwidth. This is of course characteristic of all noise-improvement systems.

Can we keep increasing the output SNR indefinitely by increasing the frequency deviation and hence the bandwidth? If we keep the transmitter power fixed, S_c is fixed. With the noise power per unit bandwidth $(n_0/2)$ fixed and the audio signal bandwidth B fixed, N_c presumably remains constant, but, as the frequency deviation increases and the bandwidth with it, more noise must be accepted by the limiter. Eventually, the noise power at the limiter becomes comparable with the signal power. The above simplified analysis, which assumes large carrier-to-noise power ratios, does not hold any more, and noise is found to "take over" the system.

This effect is found to depend very sharply upon the FM carrier-to-noise ratio S_c/N and is called a *threshold* effect. For this ratio greater than a specified threshold value, FM functions properly and shows the significant improvement in

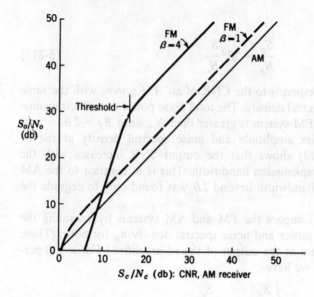

FIGURE 6-69
Measured characteristics, FM and AM receivers. (Adapted from M. G. Crosby, "Frequency Modulation Noise Characteristics," *Proc. IRE*, vol. 25, pp. 472–514, April 1937, fig. 10, by permission.)

SNR predicted by Eq. (6-214). For the ratio below this threshold level the noise improvement is found to deteriorate rapidly, and Eq. (6-214) no longer holds. The actual threshold level depends upon the FM carrier-to-noise ratio and upon β. For large β the level is usually taken as 10 dB.

This threshold phenomenon is a characteristic of all wideband noise-improvement systems and was encountered previously in discussing PCM systems.

Two conditions must thus ordinarily be satisfied for an FM system to show significant noise-quieting properties:

1. FM carrier-to-noise ratio >10 dB to avoid the threshold effect.
2. With FM carrier-to-noise ratio >10 dB, $\beta > 1/\sqrt{3}$ if $S_o/N_o > S_c/N_c$ [see Eq. (6-214)].

But $\beta > 1/\sqrt{3} \doteq 0.6$ corresponds to the transition between narrowband and wideband FM. *Narrowband FM thus provides no SNR improvement over AM.* This of course as expected, for the improvement is specifically the result of restricting the noise phase deviations of the carrier to small values, while the signal variations are assumed to be large.

Experimental and theoretical studies of FM noise characteristics show the threshold phenomenon very strikingly and also bear out the validity of Eq. (6-214) above the threshold value. Figure 6-69 is taken from some experimental work of M. G. Crosby [CROS][29] and shows a comparison of AM and FM

---

[29][CROS] M. G. Crosby, "Frequency Modulation Noise Characteristics," *Proc. IRE*, vol. 25, pp. 472–514, April 1937, fig. 10.

receivers for $\beta = 4$ and $\beta = 1$. Note that for $\beta = 4$ the FM signal-to-noise ratio deteriorates rapidly for $S_c/N_c < 13$ dB. In fact, for $S_c/N_c < 8$ dB, the AM system becomes superior. For $S_c/N_c > 15$ dB, however, the FM system shows an improvement of 14 dB. For $\beta = 4$ we would expect the theoretical improvement to be $3\beta^2 = 48$, or 17 dB. For $\beta = 1$ the threshold level is experimentally found to occur at 2 dB. Above this value of AM carrier-to-noise ratio the FM improvement over AM is 3 dB. The theoretical improvement would be expected to be $3\beta^2 = 3$, or 4.8 dB.

These characteristics measured by Crosby are of historical significance because they were among the first obtained in quantitative studies of FM noise. They have of course since been reproduced countless times by many investigators. The detailed theoretical analyses noted earlier bear these results out as well.

Much engineering time has been devoted to the development of threshold-improvement receivers designed to reduce the threshold in FM receivers. These include the FM receiver with feedback (FMFB), the phase-locked loop, and the frequency-locked loop [SCHW 1966], [VITE 1966], [CLAR 1967], [HESS].[30]

Signal-to-Noise Improvement through Deemphasis

We showed in Chap. 4 that the transmission bandwidth of an FM system is determined by the maximum frequency deviation Δf produced by the highest modulating frequency f_m to be transmitted. In particular, for $f_m = 15$ kHz and a maximum frequency deviation Δf of 75 kHz we found that the required bandwidth was 240 kHz.

In practice the higher-frequency components of the modulating signal rarely attain the amplitudes needed to produce a 75-kHz frequency deviation. Audio signals of speech and music are found to have most of their energy concentrated in the lower-frequency ranges. The instantaneous signal amplitude, limited to that required to give the 75-kHz deviation, is due most of the time to the lower-frequency components of the signal. The smaller-amplitude high-frequency (h-f) components will, on the average, provide a much smaller frequency deviation. The FM signal thus does not fully occupy the large bandwidth assigned to it.

The spectrum of the noise introduced at the receiver does, however, occupy the entire FM bandwidth. In fact, as we have just noted, the noise-power spectrum at the output of the discriminator is emphasized at the higher frequencies. (The spectrum is proportional to f^2 for a large carrier-to-noise ratio.)

This gives us a clue as to a possible procedure for improving the SNR at the discriminator output: we can artificially *emphasize* the h-f components of our input audio signal at the transmitter, *before the noise is introduced*, to the point where they produce a 75-kHz deviation most of the time. This *equalizes* in a

---

[30][CLAR 1967] K. K. Clarke and D. T. Hess, "Frequency-Locked Loop Demodulator," *IEEE Trans. Commun. Technol.*, pp. 518–524, August 1967. [HESS] D. T. Hess, "Equivalence of FM Threshold Extension Receivers," *IEEE Trans. Commun. Technol.*, October 1968.

sense the l-f and h-f portions of the audio spectrum and enables the signal fully to occupy the bandwidth assigned. Then, at the output of the receiver discriminator, we can perform the inverse operation: *deemphasize* the higher-frequency components, to restore the original signal-power distribution. But in this deemphasis process we reduce the h-f components of the noise also and so effectively increase the SNR.

Such a preemphasis and deemphasis process is commonly used in FM transmission and reception and provides, as we shall see, 13 to 16 dB of noise improvement. It is the basis of the well-known Dolby noise-reduction system in audio recording as well. Note that this procedure is a simple example of a signal-processing scheme which utilizes differences in the characteristics of the signal and the noise to process the signal more efficiently. The entire FM process is itself an example of a much more complex processing scheme in which use is made of the fact that random noise alters the instantaneous frequency of a carrier much less than it does the amplitude of the carrier (for large carrier-to-noise ratio). The noise-improvement properties of PCM and other wideband systems are again due to differences in the characteristics of random noise and signal.

A simple frequency transfer function that emphasizes the high frequencies and has been found very effective in practice is given by

$$H(\omega) = 1 + j\frac{\omega}{\omega_1} \tag{6-215}$$

An example of an *RC* network that approximates this response very closely is shown in Fig. 6-70*a*. The asymptotic logarithmic amplitude-frequency plot for this network is shown in Fig. 6-70*b*.

With $r \gg R$ the amplitude response has two break frequencies given by $\omega_1 = 1/rC$ and $\omega_2 \doteq 1/RC$. Signals in the range between ω_1 and ω_2 are thus emphasized. (Actually, the higher-frequency components are passed unaltered, and the lower-frequency components are attenuated. The attenuation can of course be made up by amplification.) The choice of $f_1 = \omega_1/2\pi$ is not critical,

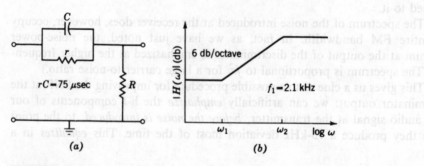

FIGURE 6-70

Example of a preemphasis network. (*a*) Preemphasis network, $r \gg R$, $rC = 75$ μs. (*b*) Asymptotic response, $\omega_1 = 1/rC$, $\omega_2 = 1/RC$.

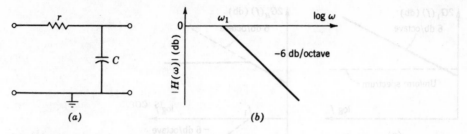

FIGURE 6-71
Example of a deemphasis network. (a) Deemphasis network, $rC = 75$ μs. (b) Asymptotic response, $f_1 = 2.1$ kHz.

but 2.1 kHz is ordinarily used in practice ($rC = 75$ μs). The frequency $f_2 = \omega_2/2\pi$ should lie above the highest audio frequency to be transmitted. $f_2 \geq 30$ kHz is a typical requirement. In the range between these two frequencies $|H(\omega)|^2 \doteq 1 + (f/f_1)^2$, and all audio frequencies above 2.1 kHz are increasingly emphasized.

The receiver deemphasis network, following the discriminator, must have the inverse characteristic given by

$$H(\omega) = \frac{1}{1 + jf/f_1} \tag{6-216}$$

with $f_1 = 2.1$ kHz as before. This then serves to restore all signals to their original relative values. The simple RC network of Fig. 6-71. ($rC = 75$ μs) provides the deemphasis characteristic.

How much does the deemphasis network improve the SNR at the discriminator output? From Eq. (6-210) of the FM noise analysis, the noise spectral density at the discriminator output (for large carrier-to-noise ratio) is

$$G_\phi(f) = \frac{n_0\omega^2}{A_c^2} = \frac{n_0\omega^2}{2S_c} \tag{6-217}$$

where n_0 is the input noise spectral density, A_c the carrier amplitude, and $S_c = A_c^2/2$ the mean carrier power at the discriminator input. If this noise is now passed through the RC deemphasis network of Fig. 6-71, the modified spectral density at the network output is

$$G_H(f) = G_\phi(f)|H(\omega)|^2 = \frac{n_0\omega^2}{2S_c}\frac{1}{1 + (f/f_1)^2} \tag{6-218}$$

The original noise-power spectrum $G_\phi(f)$ at the output of the discriminator and the modified spectrum $G_H(f)$ are shown sketched in the logarithmic plots of Fig. 6-72. (Only the one-sided spectra, defined for positive f only, are shown because of the logarithmic plots.)

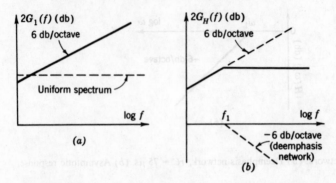

FIGURE 6-72
Logarithmic FM noise power spectrum: output of discriminator ($S_c \gg N_c$). (*a*) Spectrum without deemphasis. (*b*) Spectrum with deemphasis.

Note that for $f > f_1$ the noise spectrum with deemphasis included becomes a uniform spectrum; the deemphasis network has canceled out the ω^2 (increasing noise frequency) factor of Eq. (6-217).

The total mean noise power at the output of an ideal low-pass filter of bandwidth B hertz is given by

$$N_{oD} = \int_{-B}^{B} G_H(f)\, df$$

$$= \int_{-B}^{B} \frac{n_0 \omega^2}{2 S_c} \frac{df}{1 + (f/f_1)^2} \tag{6-219}$$

where N_{oD} represents the mean noise power with the deemphasis network included, as compared with the symbol N_o used previously for the noise power with no deemphasis network.

Equation (6-219) is readily integrated to give

$$N_{oD} = \frac{n_0}{2\pi S_c}\, \omega_1^3 \left(\frac{B}{f_1} - \tan^{-1} \frac{B}{f_1} \right) \tag{6-220}$$

Multiplying the numerator and denominator by $3/B^3$, and recalling from Eq. (6-211) that $N_o = (2\pi)^2 n_0 B^3 / 3 S_c$, the mean noise power can be written in the form

$$N_{oD} = N_o D \tag{6-221}$$

where

$$D = 3 \left(\frac{f_1}{B} \right)^3 \left(\frac{B}{f_1} - \tan^{-1} \frac{B}{f_1} \right) \tag{6-222}$$

The parameter D represents the effect of the deemphasis network and is readily seen to be less than or equal to 1 in value. The deemphasis network thus reduces the output noise. For $B \ll f_1$ (the deemphasis effect is then introduced beyond the range of the low-pass filter) we have $D \to 1$, as is to be expected. For $B \gg f_1$ we have $\tan^{-1}(B/f_1) \to \pi/2$ and

$$D \to 3\left(\frac{f_1}{B}\right)^2 \qquad f_1 \ll B \qquad (6\text{-}223)$$

The output noise power thus decreases rapidly with increasing B.

Increasing B indefinitely provides no *absolute* improvement in the output noise, however, for N_o increases as B^3. The output filter bandwidth B should thus be restricted to just the bandwidth required to pass the highest audio frequency and no more.

With $f_1 = 2.1$ kHz, as noted previously, and $B = 15$ kHz, we have $D = \frac{1}{20}$. The noise is thus reduced by a factor of 20, or 13 dB. If $B = 10f_1 = 21$ kHz, the improvement due to the deemphasis network is 16 dB.

The signal power at the output of the discriminator is $S_o = (\Delta\omega)^2/2$ [Eq. (6-200)], for a single sine wave, independent of the preemphasis and deemphasis procedure. The SNR with deemphasis is thus

$$\frac{S_o}{N_{oD}} = \frac{1}{D}\frac{S_o}{N_o} = \frac{3\beta^2}{D}\frac{S_c}{N_c} \qquad (6\text{-}224)$$

The signal-to-noise improvement in decibels is the same as the noise reduction: 13 dB for $B = 15$ kHz, 16 dB for $B = 21$ kHz.

Preemphasis and deemphasis techniques are obviously not restricted to FM. They are possible because the audio signals to be transmitted in practice are concentrated at the low end of the spectrum. All modulation systems can use deemphasis techniques to improve the SNR at the receiver output. Deemphasis networks are commonly used in FM receivers, with the corresponding preemphasis networks built into the audio section of FM transmitters. The same "equalization" principle is also used quite commonly in sound recording, and is the basis of the Dolby system, as already noted.

The discussion of SNR improvement by deemphasis has proceeded on an *ad hoc* basis. A specific deemphasis network was postulated and noise improvement demonstrated by calculation. The discussion can, however, be handled on a more general level by postulating the use of preemphasis and deemphasis networks and then finding the networks that minimize the output noise. Specifically, we shall use an approach similar to that adopted previously in discussing matched filters. Here too the Schwarz inequality will be found to play a role.[31] The one distinction is that the signal as well as the noise is now assumed random.

Specifically, let the signal at the transmitter have a known spectral density $G_s(f)$. The signal is then passed through a preemphasis network $H(\omega)$, and the resultant signal actually transmitted. This output signal now has a spectral

---

[31] This approach to deemphasis-network analysis was suggested to the author in a private communication by Dr. Robert Price.

density $G_s(f)|H|^2$, and the average transmitter power is

$$P = \int_{-\infty}^{\infty} G_s(f)|H(\omega)|^2 \, df \qquad (6\text{-}225)$$

We assume, as is usually the case in practice, that P is *fixed* at some maximum level.

Noise of spectral density $G_n(f)$ is added during transmission, and signal plus noise passed through a deemphasis network with transfer function $H^{-1}(\omega)$, just the inverse of the preemphasis network. The output signal power is then just

$$S_o = \int_{-\infty}^{\infty} G_s(f) \, df \qquad (6\text{-}226)$$

a fixed quantity, and the output noise power is

$$N_o = \int_{-\infty}^{\infty} G_n(f)|H(\omega)|^{-2} \, df \qquad (6\text{-}227)$$

How do we now choose $|H(\omega)|$ to maximize S_o/N_o (or minimize N_o, since S_o is fixed), with P a known constant? (Note that the phase of the two correction networks is arbitrary, provided, however, that the phase of the deemphasis network corrects for that of the preemphasis network to avoid signal distortion.)

Since P is constant, we can just as well minimize

$$PN_o = \int_{-\infty}^{\infty} G_s(f)|H|^2 \, df \int_{-\infty}^{\infty} G_n(f)|H|^{-2} \, df \qquad (6\text{-}228)$$

But recall that the Schwarz inequality for real integrals may be written

$$\int A^2(f) \, df \cdot \int B^2 \, df \geq \left[\int A(f)B(f) \, df \right]^2 \qquad (6\text{-}229)$$

If we let

$$G_s(f)|H|^2 \equiv A^2(f)$$

and

$$G_n(f)|H|^{-2} \equiv B^2(f)$$

we have immediately

$$PN_o \geq \left[\int \sqrt{G_s(f)G_n(f)} \, df \right]^2 \qquad (6\text{-}230)$$

with the minimum output noise attained when $A(f) = B(f)$, or

$$|H(\omega)|^2_{\text{opt}} = \sqrt{\frac{G_n(f)}{G_s(f)}} \qquad (6\text{-}231)$$

Provided that the signal and noise have *different* spectral shapes (an almost obvious consideration), preemphasis does pay off (i.e., optimum networks in the sense indicated here do exist).

As an example assume that $G_s(f)$ varies as $1/f^2$ (this is a particularly simple model for indicating lower energy at higher frequencies) and $G_n(f)$ increases over a limited frequency range as f^2. This is then the high-CNR FM case discussed earlier, where attention is focused just on the baseband portions of the system. Then the optimum $|H| \propto f$, just the preemphasis network assumed earlier (Fig. 6-70). (The nonlinear modulation portions of the FM system may be ignored here, since the discussion is based solely on the optimization of the baseband preemphasis and deemphasis networks, not on the entire system.)

This optimization may be carried one step further without assuming any particular structure for the system (i.e., the preemphasis–deemphasis network pair assumed here), and complete receivers can be designed that demodulate analog signals in some optimum sense in the presence of noise. Such criteria as least mean-squared error between transmitted and received signals, maximum SNR, maximum a posteriori probability, etc., have been adopted, and optimum, albeit not necessarily realizable, structures obtained. But approaches such as these are beyond the scope of this book [VANT],[32] [VITE 1966, chap. 5].

6-14 THERMAL-NOISE CONSIDERATIONS[33]

Up to this point in this chapter we have been assuming the white-noise spectral density $n_0/2$ either given to us, or measured using some of the techniques discussed earlier. In most communication systems this noise may be grouped into either of two types—*thermal noise*, which has a fundamental thermodynamic origin, and *shot noise* due to an average current flow in the circuits making up the systems. (Note again that we are focusing only on *spontaneous fluctuation noise*, which is ever present in the physical environment, and which results in basic limitations on the transmission of information.) We shall discuss the origin of the thermal noise at some length, because of its fundamental nature, coming up with a very simple and specific formula for the noise spectral density. Thus we shall show that the thermal-noise power spectral density may be taken as white at radio frequencies as high as 10^{13} Hz, the formula for the spectral density being given by

$$G_n(f) = \frac{n_0}{2} = \frac{kT}{2} \quad \text{W/Hz} \tag{6-232}$$

[32][VANT] H. Van Trees, *Detection, Estimation, and Modulation Theory*, vol. I, Wiley, New York, 1968.

[33]Comprehensive references to the material of this section include the following books: [BENN 1960] W. R. Bennett, *Electrical Noise*, McGraw-Hill, New York, 1960; [BELL 1960] D. A. Bell, *Electrical Noise, Fundamentals and Physical Mechanism*, Van Nostrand, London, 1960; [ZIEL] A. Van der Ziel, *Noise*, Prentice-Hall, Englewood Cliffs, N.J., 1954. See also [SCHW 1970] M. Schwartz, *Information Transmission, Modulation, and Noise*, 2nd ed., McGraw-Hill, New York, 1970, chap. 7.

or $n_0 = kT$. Here $k = 1.38 \times 10^{-23}$ J/K is the Boltzmann constant, and T is the absolute temperature of the thermal noise source, in degrees Kelvin.

Shot noise will be mentioned only briefly. We shall show that its effect, as well as the effect of other noise sources, may be included by assuming an effective noise temperature higher than the actual T in the thermal-noise equation.

In the next section we tie this material together with that of the previous chapters by working out some actual calculations of SNR and E/n_0 for space and satellite communications. This then enables us to actually evaluate the performance of some typical communication systems.

We can summarize the distinction between thermal and shot noise in the following way. *Thermal noise* is associated with random motion of particles in a force-free environment. For example, the air pressure in a given room is due to the summed effect of countless air molecules moving chaotically in all directions. The molecules are in continuous disorderly motion, striking and rebounding from one to another. When we talk of the "pressure" at a point we refer in effect to the resultant force per unit area of all molecules striking a surface located at the point in question. This force will *fluctuate*, or vary in time, as fewer or more molecules strike the wall from time to time. Since the numbers of molecules involved are ordinarily tremendously large for normal-sized surfaces, the *average* force in time will remain constant as long as the average molecular energy remains constant. The instantaneous force as a function of time, however, will vary randomly about this average value. Increasing the temperature increases the molecular energy, and the average pressure goes up, as do the fluctuations about the average. Thermodynamics and the kinetic theory of heat applied to this problem indicate that for an ideal gas (one for which intermolecular forces may be neglected), the average kinetic energy of motion per molecule in any one direction is $kT/2$, with $k = 1.38 \times 10^{-23}$ J/K the Boltzmann constant, and T the absolute temperature in degrees Kelvin. This is the reason why we find the mean-squared thermal noise proportional to kT.

In electrical work we encounter similar fluctuations which are thermally induced. Conductors contain a large number of "free" electrons together with ions strongly bound by molecular forces. The ions vibrate randomly about their equilibrium (average) positions, however, this vibration being a function of temperature. Collisions between the free electrons and the vibrating ions continually take place. There is a continuous transfer of energy between electrons and ions. This is the source of the resistance in the conductor. The freely moving electrons constitute a current, which over a long period of time averages to zero, since as many electrons on the average move in one direction as another. (This is the analog of the pressure case noted above, in which the *average* molecular velocity is zero, although chaotic motion exists.) There are random fluctuations about this average, however, and, in fact, we shall see that the mean-squared fluctuations in current are proportional to kT also.

Both cases noted—pressure fluctuations and current fluctuations—deal with the chaotic motion of particles (molecules or electrons) possessing thermal energy. There are no forces present "organizing" this motion in preferred directions. Both cases may therefore be treated by equilibrium thermodynamics, with the mean-squared fluctuations found proportional to kT.

The second type of noise noted above, *shot noise*, is also due to the discrete nature of matter, but here we assume an average flow in some direction taking place: electrons flowing between cathode and anode in a cathode-ray oscilloscope, electrons and holes flowing in semiconductors, photons emitted in laser systems, photoelectrons emitted in photodiodes, fluid moving continuously under the action of a pressure gradient, etc. Although averaging over many particles we find the average flow, or average number moving per unit time, to be a constant, there will be fluctuations about this average. The mechanism of the fluctuations depends on the particular process; in a vacuum-tube case it is the random emission of the electrons from the cathode, in a semiconductor it is the randomness in the number of electrons that continually recombine with holes, or in the number that diffuse, etc. Thus the processes that give rise to an average flow have statistical variations built in, producing fluctuations about the average.

Shot noise is modeled by the Poisson process introduced in discussing photon statistics in Sec. 6-1. It represents the generalization to these other physical processes—involving electrons, or electrons and holes, for example—of the "self-noise" described in discussing light-wave communication. Recall that in the Poisson process the variance equals the average value. The variance represents the mean-squared fluctuation about the mean value, and is the seat of the noise. Shot noise is thus characterized by a dependence of the noise on the average value of the flow, a very different characteristic than that of thermal noise.

Thermal noise was first thoroughly studied experimentally by J. B. Johnson of Bell Laboratories in 1928. His experiments, together with the accompanying theoretical studies by H. Nyquist, demonstrated that a metallic resistor could be considered the source of spontaneous fluctuation voltages with mean-squared value

$$\overline{v^2} = 4kTRB \tag{6-233}$$

where T is the temperature in degrees Kelvin of the resistor, R its resistance in ohms, k the Boltzmann constant already referred to (1.38×10^{-23} J/K), and B any arbitrary bandwidth. Johnson was able to measure the value of k fairly accurately using this equation and thus demonstrated its validity. He also showed that $\overline{v^2}$ was proportional to temperature.

This expression for the mean-squared thermal noise due to a resistor R implies that the noise is white. We shall see shortly that it is valid up to extremely high frequencies of the order of 10^{13} Hz. At these high frequencies quantum-mechanical effects set in. (This assumes of course that R is independent of frequency over this tremendous range.) We shall develop a more general relation later which includes the quantum-mechanical effects at high frequencies. (The more general expression is necessary when considering the effect of noise on

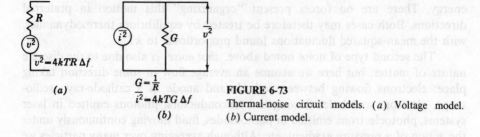

(a)

$G = \frac{1}{R}$

$\overline{i^2} = 4kTG \, \Delta f$

(b)

FIGURE 6-73
Thermal-noise circuit models. (a) Voltage model. (b) Current model.

communications at optical frequencies. Our discussion of quantum limits on digital light-wave communications in previous sections explicitly ignored noise introduced during transmission and on reception. It focused on errors due to the Poisson nature of the photon stream itself.)

For white noise $\overline{v^2}$ may be written as $n_0 B$, with $n_0/2$ the noise spectral density in volts squared (see Sec. 6-5). From Eq. (6-233) the voltage thermal-noise spectral density is thus given by the simple expression

$$G_v(f) = \frac{n_0}{2} = \frac{\overline{v^2}}{2B} = 2kTR \qquad (6\text{-}234)$$

We shall develop this white-noise spectral density as a special case of the more general relation to which reference has just been made.

Nyquist's original derivation of Eq. (6-233) [NYQU 1928b][34] was based on thermodynamic reasoning, assuming temperature equilibrium. The actual mechanism of thermal-noise generation—assumed to be due to the random interaction between the conduction electrons and ions in a metallic conductor—is not necessary for the derivation. Although this at first appears disconcerting, it is actually a blessing in disguise. For using the same thermodynamic reasoning it may be shown that *any linear passive* device, mechanical, electromechanical, microphones, antennas, etc., has associated with it thermal noise of one form or another. In some cases this may be due to random agitation of the air molecules, in others to random electrical effects in the ionosphere and atmosphere, etc. This is so because the $\frac{1}{2}kT$ term occurs generally in thermodynamics as the energy associated with any mode of oscillation (as temperature increases, gas molecules move more rapidly, ions vibrate more violently in a lattice structure, etc.). This was the basis of Nyquist's derivation. We shall use a somewhat similar approach here.

Because of this reasoning the resistors in the electrical analog of a passive linear physical device may be considered sources of noise voltage as given by Eq. (6-233). This concept is commonly used in antenna work, acoustics, etc.

A voltage-model representation of Eq. (6-233) is shown in Fig. 6-73a. R is assumed noise-free, with the noise effect lumped into the noise-voltage source

[34][NYQU 1928b] H. Nyquist, *Phys. Rev.*, no. 32, p. 110, 1928.

shown. An application of Norton's theorem gives the current-source equivalent of Fig. 6-73b. (Since $i = v/R$, we have $\overline{i^2} = \overline{v^2}/R^2 = 4kTGB$, $G = 1/R$.)

Either model may be used, although the current-source model is often more convenient, especially when calculating noise voltages across parallel elements. Some typical numbers are of interest. Let $B = 5$ kHz, $T = 293$ K (this is normal room temperature, or 20°C), and $R = 10$ kΩ. Then $\overline{v^2} = 0.8 \times 10^{-12}$ V^2, or

$$\sqrt{\overline{v^2}} = 0.90 \ \mu\text{V} \qquad \text{rms}$$

and $\sqrt{\overline{i^2}} = 0.90 \times 10^{-10}$ A rms. If the bandwidth is quadrupled to 20 kHz, the rms noise voltage and current are doubled to 1.8 μV and 1.8×10^{-10} A, respectively. The rms noise voltage is proportional to the square root of the resistance and to the square root of the bandwidth.

If the temperature is increased, the resistance value used refers to the new temperature, as does T. Since the derivation of Eq. (6-233) depends on thermal equilibrium, the equation holds only after a steady-state temperature has been reached, not during heating or cooling.

Recapitulating, both theory and experiment indicate that a resistance R at temperature T is the source of a fluctuation (noise) voltage with mean-squared value

$$\overline{v^2} = 4kTRB \tag{6-233}$$

and voltage spectral density

$$G_r(f) = 2kTR \equiv \frac{n_0}{2} \tag{6-234}$$

The corresponding mean-squared value and spectral density for the current-source model may be written, respectively,

$$\overline{i^2} = 4kTGB \tag{6-235}$$

and

$$G_i(f) = 2kTG \equiv \frac{n_0}{2} \tag{6-236}$$

As previously, B represents the noise-equivalent bandwidth of the measuring instrument or circuit used to measure these quantities.

Depending on whether we deal with voltage or current in a network we use the spectral density forms of (6-234) or (6-236). The same symbol $n_0/2$ is used here for both cases, just as was done in earlier sections of this chapter. The dimensions of $n_0/2$ depend on which physical quantity is being measured. (In earlier sections we assumed a unit resistance. Since we commonly take ratios of mean-squared signal to mean-squared noise to form the signal-to-noise ratio, the actual dimensions of $n_0/2$ do not really matter, as long as we are consistent.)

The distinction between voltage and current spectral density disappears completely when we discuss actual power generated. As is true with any power source, the power generated depends on the load impedance. In particular, maximum power is transferred when the load impedance is matched to the generator impedance, in this case just R in Fig. 6-73. The maximum power available, under matched conditions is called the *available power*. For the noise source of Fig. 6-73a, the available power in a bandwidth of B hertz is just

$$N = \frac{\overline{v^2}}{4R} = kTB \equiv n_0 B \qquad (6\text{-}237)$$

and the corresponding power spectral density, in W/Hz, is just

$$G_n(f) = \frac{n_0}{2} = \frac{kT}{2} \qquad (6\text{-}232)$$

and $n_0 = kT$. This is of course the expression written earlier. In carrying out the SNR calculations of the next section we shall use this expression to compute the noise power.

The discussion to this point of the noise spectral density, whether in units of voltage squared (6-234), current squared (6-236), or power (6-232), has been based on (6-233), an expression found experimentally by J. B. Johnson. It is now of interest to digress somewhat to discuss the actual derivation of the thermal-noise spectral density. This will enable us to determine the validity of the white-noise approximation and the frequency (in the infrared range) at which the spectral density begins to vary with frequency. It will also enable us to readily consider extensions to masers and lasers—i.e., thermal-noise calculations at infrared and optical frequencies—as well as to thermal noise generated in space and received at an antenna.

Recall again that we assume we have a resistor R sitting at an equilibrium absolute temperature T. This resistor is the source of random current (and hence voltage) fluctuations produced by the heat energy assumed provided by its surroundings. As the temperature T increases, the electrons moving freely inside the conducting material are raised to higher energy levels and the mean-squared current flow increases. (The average current of course remains zero with no electric field applied, since currents in opposite directions cancel, on the average.) The actual physical mechanism of current flow in the conductor depends on the interaction of the electrons with the thermally vibrating ions in the metallic crystal. Since the noise derivation using an assumed model for electrical conduction through a metal is rather complicated [LAWS],[35] we resort instead to the stratagem first used by H. Nyquist [NYQU 1928b] in deriving the thermal-noise equation for a resistor. This technique is based on simple equilibrium thermodynamics, avoids the problem of the specific physical mechanism involved in the noise generation, and has the advantage of easily being extended to thermal-noise calculations where physical resistors may not be present, e.g., blackbody radiation, thermal noise in microwave circuits, masers, lasers, etc.

---

[35][LAWS] J. L. Lawson and G. E. Uhlenbeck, *Threshold Signals*, McGraw-Hill, New York, 1950.

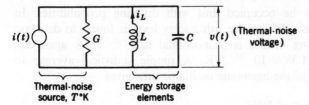

Thermal-noise
source, $T°K$

Energy storage
elements

FIGURE 6-74
Tuned circuit for thermal-noise calculations.

The stratagem consists of assuming the resistor connected electrically to one or more energy-storage elements. The elements store up the thermal energy provided by the resistors. By knowing the energy stored and equating it to the thermal energy supplied by the resistor, one then finds the mean-squared thermal-noise current (or voltage) available at the resistor terminals.

Although various combinations of energy-storage elements may be used for this calculation, we shall select the oscillatory circuit consisting of a parallel inductor and capacitor, as shown in Fig. 6-74. We do this for two reasons:

1. The stored thermal energy of the tuned circuit is readily written down.
2. The approach used enables us to extend the results to many other situations: nonelectrical systems where G, L, C are the electrical analogs (e.g., a mass–spring combination, with G representing the dissipative elements assumed at temperature T); microwave and optical circuits, with LC representing a resonant cavity and G its dissipation; etc.

This oscillatory circuit, which oscillates at the resonant frequency $f_0 = 1/2\pi\sqrt{LC}$, is an instance of the *harmonic oscillator* of modern physics. In most books on modern physics and quantum mechanics it is shown that the harmonic oscillator, resonant at frequency f_0, can possess discrete stored energies only, its discrete energy levels given by

$$E_n = \left(nh + \tfrac{1}{2}\right)f_0 \qquad n = 0, 1, 2, \ldots \tag{6-238}$$

(Fig. 6-75). The constant h is Planck's constant, $h = 6.6257 \times 10^{-34}$ J-s. If one now energizes this harmonic oscillator thermally at T degrees Kelvin, one finds

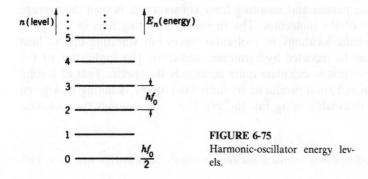

FIGURE 6-75
Harmonic-oscillator energy levels.

that all energy levels may be occupied, but with differing probabilities. In particular, the probability of exciting the nth energy level is found to decrease exponentially with increasing n, and is proportional to $e^{-E_n/kT}$, k again the Boltzmann constant, $k = 1.38 \times 10^{-23}$ J/K. A simple statistical average to provide the average energy of the harmonic oscillator then gives

$$\overline{E} = \frac{\sum\limits_{n=0}^{\infty} E_n e^{-E_n/kT}}{\sum\limits_{n=0}^{\infty} e^{-E_n/kT}} = \frac{hf_0}{2} + \frac{hf_0}{e^{hf_0/kT} - 1} \qquad (6\text{-}239)$$

after substituting in Eq. (6-238) and performing the indicated summations.

As an example, for very low temperatures, $kT \ll hf_0$, we have $\overline{E} = hf_0/2$, the zero-point energy or lowest energy level. If the thermal energy provided is very small, the harmonic oscillator will on the average remain at its lowest energy level. If the temperature is high, $kT \gg hf_0$, then $e^{-hf_0/kT} \doteq 1 - hf_0/kT$, and

$$\overline{E} = kT \qquad kT \gg f_0 \qquad (6\text{-}240)$$

This is the classical result, which says that the average energy of the oscillator is proportional to the absolute temperature. It is instructive to note that by average we again mean either of two possibilities—an ensemble or time average:

1. Many identical oscillators, oscillating independently of each other, are available. Each one will randomly occupy a particular energy level. The average energy of the *ensemble* is then given by Eq. (6-239).
2. Alternatively, *one* oscillator will occupy only one level at any one time. But over many observation times it will occupy different levels with different probabilities, the *average* being given by Eq. (6-239).

The LC circuit of Fig. 6-74 is just one of many possible harmonic oscillators to which Eq. (6-239) applies. (In most physics texts the symbol ν, rather than f_0, is used to denote the frequency of oscillation.) The oscillator may be made up of two bound atoms forming a molecule such as H_2. Heat applied to a gaseous system of such molecules tends to pull the atoms apart, and restoring forces tend to keep them together, the two atoms then vibrating at a characteristic frequency determined by their masses and restoring force constants. $\overline{E}$ is then the average vibrational energy of the molecules. The thermally vibrating ions in a crystal, bound to their specific locations by molecular forces but vibrating due to heat energy applied, may be modeled by harmonic oscillators. The application of Eq. (6-239) then enables one to calculate quite accurately the specific heat of a solid [REIF].[36] Thermal radiation produced by individual atoms radiating in a given substance is also calculable using Eq. (6-239). Here one assumes the radiation

---

[36] [REIF] F. Reif, *Fundamentals of Statistical and Thermal Physics*, McGraw-Hill, New York, 1965.

"captured" by a resonant structure of arbitrary size. Standing electromagnetic waves are set up in this structure, at frequencies appropriate to its boundary conditions. Each frequency is then assumed to correspond to a fictitious harmonic oscillator at that frequency, and has average energy given by Eq. (6-239). Summing over all possible frequencies, the thermal energy distribution is found to be exactly that of *blackbody radiation* [REIF]: the radiant energy emanated by many heated sources. It is this blackbody radiation, produced by the sun, stars, sources of radiation in the earth's atmosphere, etc., that appears as thermal noise at an antenna input in any high-frequency radio receiver.

Consider now specifically the parallel $G-L-C$ combination of Fig. 6-74. The resistor at temperature T degrees Kelvin may be an actual resistor connected across the LC circuit, or the equivalent dissipation resistance of the LC circuit, assumed connected in parallel, or the equivalent resistance of an antenna tuned to frequency $f_0 = 1/2\pi\sqrt{LC}$, etc. We visualize the resistor kept at temperature T by literally being immersed in a heat bath at that temperature; e.g., if the resistor is part of a circuit in a room, T is the normal room temperature. On being connected to the LC circuit the resistor provides the energy $\overline{E}$, given by Eq. (6-239), eventually stored in the L and C after the connection has been made for a while. The connection also enables a current to flow through the resistor, producing a power loss in that element. We relate all of these by saying that there is an average stored energy in the capacitor,

$$\overline{E}_1 = \tfrac{1}{2}C\overline{v^2}$$

equal to the stored energy $\overline{E}_2 = \tfrac{1}{2}L\overline{i_L^2}$ in the inductor. The total stored energy is then

$$\overline{E} = C\overline{v^2} = \frac{hf_o}{2} + \frac{hf_0}{e^{hf_0/kT} - 1} \tag{6-241}$$

from Eq. (6-239). The quantity $\overline{v^2}$ is just the mean-squared fluctuation of the voltage $v(t)$ appearing across the tuned circuit, and thus represents the thermal noise measured at that point. If we visualize this noise term having a spectral density $G_v(f)$, we must have

$$\overline{v^2} = \int_{-\infty}^{\infty} G_v(f)\, df \tag{6-242}$$

Assuming now that the source of the thermal noise in the resistor is represented by the current source $i(t)$ in Fig. 6-74, we must have the following relation connecting the spectral densities of $v(t)$ and $i(t)$:

$$G_v(f) = |H(\omega)|^2 G_i(f) \tag{6-243}$$

From Eqs. (6-241) to (6-243), we then get the following equation, which enables us to find the spectral density $G_i(f)$ of the noise source in terms of the known stored thermal energy of the tuned circuit:

$$\overline{v^2} = \frac{\overline{E}}{C} = \int_{-\infty}^{\infty} |H(\omega)|^2 G_i(f)\, df \qquad (6\text{-}244)$$

The transfer function appearing in (6-244) is the impedance of the parallel combination of the G, L, and C in Fig. 6-74. Letting its bandwidth be very narrow compared to the center frequency, $G_i(f)$ may be assumed to be slowly varying over that range of frequencies and may be taken out of the integral of (6-244). Carrying out the indicated integration, and then solving for $G_i(f)$, using (6-239) for the stored energy of the circuit, we get, finally,

$$G_i(f) = 2\left(\frac{hf}{2} + \frac{hf}{e^{hf/kT} - 1}\right)G \qquad (6\text{-}245)$$

as the spectral density of the resistive noise-current source. Here we have dropped the 0 subscript in the frequency term, since f_0 was an arbitrary frequency to which we assumed the oscillatory circuit tuned.

Equation (6-245) represents the general spectral-density expression for the thermal-noise current source associated with the resistor. It can of course be converted to a voltage equivalent by simply replacing G with R.

This general form for spectral density now holds for *any* dissipative element at temperature T, at any frequency, with an equivalent resistance R, or equivalent conductance $G = 1/R$.

The first term $hf/2$ in the expression for spectral density, due to the zero-point energy of the harmonic oscillator, is a strictly quantum-mechanical one. This quantum-mechanical noise is negligible at frequencies $f \ll kT/h \sim 10^{13}$ Hz. At infrared and optical frequencies, however, it begins to play a dominant role.

Note that in general the noise spectral density is *not* white. It varies with frequency, and, in particular, begins to decrease at frequencies the order of kT/h, or 10^{13} Hz at room temperature. For frequencies considerably below 10^{13} Hz, however, the quantity within the parentheses of (6-245) is approximated quite closely by kT. At these frequencies the noise is effectively white, and the noise spectral density is given by the simple expressions (6-232), (6-234), and (6-236).

As an example of the applicability of (6-245) or its approximate, white-noise form, Eq. (6-236), assume that the antenna of a radio receiver is connected directly to a tuned circuit at the desired r-f (carrier) frequency. In addition to the desired signals coming in at the antenna, thermal noise also appears. Assume that this noise is primarily due to blackbody radiation from space at an average temperature of T_s degrees Kelvin. It is well known [JORD][37] that the antenna

---

[37][JORD] E. C. Jordan, *Electromagnetic Waves and Radiating Systems*, Prentice-Hall, Englewood Cliffs, N.J., 1950.

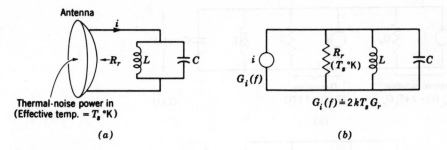

Antenna

Thermal-noise power in
(Effective temp. $= T_s$ °K)

$G_i(f)$

$G_i(f) \doteq 2kT_sG_r$

(a)

(b)

FIGURE 6-76
Thermal radiation power at antenna. (a) Actual system. (b) Noise model.

may be assumed to have an effective radiation resistance R_r such that I^2R_r = power at antenna input, with I the rms current actually measured at the antenna terminals. This is shown in Fig. 6-76a.

Using the same argument as previously, the tuned circuit must have an average stored energy $\bar{E} = kT_s$ (for frequency $f_0 \ll kT_s/h$), since it is the thermal or blackbody radiation from space, at effective temperature T_s, that provides the stored energy, by hypothesis. This is important to stress. It is *not* the temperature of the tuned circuit that determines the thermal-noise energy stored, but the temperature of whatever mechanism is responsible for providing the noise power.

Since the tuned circuit sees, effectively, the radiation resistance R_r in parallel with it, it is apparent that the noise source acts as if it were a resistance R_r at a temperature T_s. This results in the noise model shown in Fig. 6-76b.

How does one determine the effective temperature T_s? This depends of course on what the antenna "sees": it depends on the actual thermal radiators in the solid angle subtended by the antenna (these could be the earth's surface reradiating thermal energy, the atmosphere, the sun if the antenna is aimed in that direction, the galaxy, etc.), their actual temperatures, the frequency of the antenna system and the thermal noise received at this frequency, etc. All these must be measured. In practice one measures an effective rms noise current at the antenna terminals (or, perhaps, an rms noise voltage across the tuned circuit). If this is essentially due to incoming thermal radiation, and *not* to actual dissipation in the antenna itself, one must have

$$\overline{i^2} = 4kT_sG_rB \qquad (6\text{-}246)$$

with B the bandwidth of the measuring apparatus. With G_r, B, and $\overline{i^2}$ known (measured), this provides a measure of T_s.

How *does* one take into account actual antenna dissipation in the tuned circuit (including a resistor possibly put in parallel)? Let R represent the equivalent resistance corresponding to these quantities. Letting the actual temperature of the antenna system be T degrees Kelvin, and the effective temperature of space T_s degrees Kelvin, each source must independently provide energy

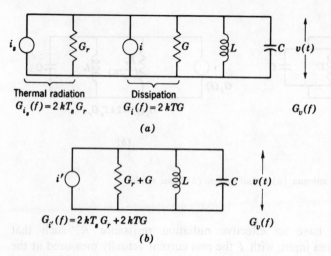

FIGURE 6-77
Multiple thermal-noise sources. (*a*) Complete model. (*b*) Reduced model.

to the tuned circuit. Assuming the frequency f low enough so that $f \ll kT/h$ and $f \ll kT_s/h$, to simplify the analysis [otherwise we use the more complicated form, Eq. (6-245), for the spectral densities], the spectral density at the tuned circuit output (or any circuit output for that matter) is given by

$$G_v(f) = |H(\omega)|^2(2kT_sG_r + 2kTG) \qquad G = \frac{1}{R}, \quad G_r = \frac{1}{R_r} \qquad (6\text{-}247)$$

One simply adds the independent noise contributions. (Recall that if independent or uncorrelated random variables are added, their variances add.) This is shown in Fig. 6-77.

More commonly, one deals with the *power* spectral density form of (6-232) in carrying out calculations involving antenna receiving systems. The noise power output of a typical receiving system then consists essentially of two quantities—the radiation from space at some equivalent source temperature T_s, plus all other noise generated within the receiving system itself. This additional noise generally contains both thermal and shot noise components. It has become common to lump all these additional noise sources together by defining an effective *noise temperature* T_e. This is the temperature of a (fictitious) thermal-noise source at the system input that would be required to produce the same added noise power at the output. If this effective temperature T_e is much less than the equivalent temperature T_s of noise sources actually producing noise power at the system input, this implies the system introduces no noise of its own. The total noise power spectral density, as measured at the antenna input, is then given by

$$G_n(f) = \frac{k(T_s + T_e)}{2} = \frac{kT_{sys}}{2} \qquad (6\text{-}248)$$

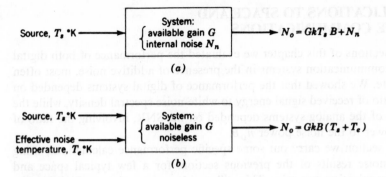

FIGURE 6-78
Definition of effective noise temperature. (*a*) Actual system noise. (*b*) Effective noise temperature.

with T_{sys} the overall system noise temperature. Figure 6-78 shows schematically how the noise temperature T_e is defined. A system with power gain G and bandwidth B is shown producing at its output the sum of two noise contributions: one due to the amplification (or attenuation, if $G < 1$) of the input source noise, the other, N_n, representing the noise power due to all the system noise sources. Reflecting these back to the input, the system noise sources are represented as arising from an equivalent thermal noise source at temperature T_e at the input.

In practice, low-noise receiving systems (e.g., maser amplifiers) are often used to reduce the effective noise temperature. In some space communication systems the resultant T_e may be reduced to as low as 2 K. In others it ranges from 10 to 30 K.

The term *noise figure* is sometimes also used to measure the noisiness of a receiving system. The noise figure F is defined as the ratio of noise power appearing at the system output to that that would appear if the system generated no noise of its own, the output noise power then being that due to the thermal noise power at the input only. A noise figure of 2 (3 dB) thus means the system noise contribution equals that introduced at the input to the system. The power spectral density, using the noise-figure concept, is then simply

$$G_n(f) = \frac{FkT_s}{2} \qquad F \geq 1 \tag{6-249}$$

Alternatively, noise figure and noise temperature are related by the expression

$$F = 1 + \frac{T_e}{T_s} \tag{6-250}$$

6-15 APPLICATIONS TO SPACE AND SATELLITE COMMUNICATIONS

In previous sections of this chapter we evaluated the performance of both digital and analog communication systems in the presence of additive noise, most often taken as white. We showed that the performance of digital systems depended on E/n_0, the ratio of received signal energy to white-noise spectral density, while the performance of the analog systems depended on the SNR, involving the ratio of the signal power to the noise power $n_0 B$.

In this section we carry out some specific performance calculations, using the thermal-noise results of the previous section, for a few typical space and satellite communication examples. This will enable us to see how noise limits the rate of transmission in the digital case, and requires the use of higher-gain antennas and/or lower-noise receivers for analog FM to ensure above-threshold operation. Trade-offs among signal power, antenna sizes, noise temperature, bandwidth, and/or digital data rate arise naturally out of the discussion. This then leads directly into the material on Chap. 7, where, focusing on digital communications, we ask whether the limitations on the rate of transmission due to noise can be reduced by more sophisticated coding. We shall in fact show there that coding can be used to improve the performance of digital communications systems limited by noise, but that the ratio E/n_0 still remains the limiting factor.

The examples to be worked out in this section deal with transmission through space from a transmitter on a space vehicle (either involved in a deep-space probe, or a synchronous satellite in orbit about the earth). The results obtained are more general, however, since they refer to radio communication between any two bodies located a known distance apart. Figure 6-79 describes the general picture. The transmitter on the space vehicle communicates with the earth station d meters away. The system operates at a known carrier frequency of

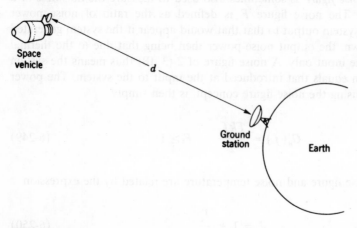

FIGURE 6-79
Space communication.

f hertz (or equivalent wavelength λ meters), and has an average transmitter output power S_T watts at that frequency. The problem is to determine the signal power and/or energy received at the earth and use this to calculate both E/n_0 and the SNR.

If the power on the vehicle were radiated isotropically, the power density (W/m^2) at a distance d would be $S_T/4\pi d^2$. An antenna on the vehicle serves to concentrate or focus the electromagnetic energy transmitted into a beam. The larger the antenna size (in wavelengths), the narrower the beam and the greater the energy concentration. Specifically, this focusing effect is represented by assigning to the antenna a gain G_T over isotropic radiation. The effective power density at a distance d from the transmitting antenna is then $(S_T/4\pi d^2)G_T$. At high frequencies aperture-type antennas (parabolas or lens antennas are examples) are commonly used, in which case it may be shown that the maximum gain attainable is proportional to the aperture area A_T (the solid angle subtended by the beam is inversely proportional to the area) and is given by $G_T = 4\pi\eta_T A_T/\lambda^2$ [ANGE].[38] Here λ is the wavelength and $\eta_T < 1$ is an efficiency parameter. At the receiver the receiving antenna of aperture area A_R ideally presents an effective area equal to A_R in picking up the received power. This area is less than A_R because of losses. An efficiency parameter η_R is introduced to account for these losses. The received power in watts is then

$$S_R = \frac{S_T}{4\pi d^2} G_T A_R \eta_R \tag{6-251}$$

This simple expression relates received and transmitted powers. (It ignores transmission losses due to attenuation along the propagation path. It assumes free-space transmission.) Quite commonly actual power calculations are carried out in decibels. This of course simplifies the calculation, and enables any additional loss or gain factors to be simply added or subtracted. (These would include antenna feed losses, propagation losses, etc.)

Consider some numbers from the Mariner 10 deep-space mission to Mercury in 1974 [EAST].[39] One of the prime objectives was to return high resolution images of Mercury via a high-bit-rate telemetry system. $S_T = 16.8$ W of transmitter power was available for this purpose. (A 20-W transmitter was used, but 15 percent of the power was required for another, low-data-rate digital channel, as well as to transmit a carrier signal used for synchronous detection at the receiver.)

The telemetry signal was transmitted at a frequency of 2,300 MHz (S band), or a wavelength of 0.13 m. The transmitted antenna had a diameter of 53 in, or

---

[38][ANGE] D. J. Angelakos and T. E. Everhart, *Microwave Communications*, McGraw-Hill, New York, 1968, sec. 5-7.

[39][EAST] M. G. Easterling, "From $8\frac{1}{3}$ Bits/s to 100,000 Bits/s in Ten Years," *Proceedings, National Telecommunications Conference*, Dallas, Texas, 1976; reprinted in *IEEE Commun. Soc. Mag.*, vol. 15, no. 6, pp. 12–15, November 1977.

1.35 m. Using an antenna efficiency parameter $\eta_T = 0.54$, the gain of the transmitting antenna is readily found to be $G_T = 575$, or, in decibels, 27.6 dB. The distance to Mercury at the time of the encounter was 99×10^6 mi, or 1.6×10^{11} m. The distance loss factor $4\pi d^2$, in (6-251), is then calculated to be 235 dB, again using decibel measure. The earth-station antennas were 64-m parabolic dishes, with an efficiency $\eta_R = 0.575$. The product $\eta_R A_R$ in decibels is then calculated to be $\eta_R A_R = 32.5$ dB.

Putting all of these numbers together, the received power, in decibels relative to a watt (dBW), is

$$S_R|_{dBW} = S_T|_{dBW} + G_T|_{dB} + \eta_R A_R|_{dB} - 4\pi d^2|_{dB} \qquad (6\text{-}252)$$

For the numbers given here this is calculated to be -162.6 dBW. This is an astoundingly small power (5.44×10^{-17} W), due of course to the extraordinarily long distances (160×10^6 km) over which communication must be carried out. But, as has been noted many times in this book, it is the ratio of the signal to the noise that determines the effectiveness of communications. In particular, the very small power by itself poses no problem—one can always introduce amplification to raise the signal to any desired level. (This is of course precisely what is done.)

The noise spectral density is thus critical. In this example of the Mariner 10 mission very low-noise maser receivers, with effective noise temperatures of 2.1 K, had been specially designed. As a result, the overall system temperature (space temperature plus noise temperature) was calculated to be 13.5 K. Again using decibel measure, it is readily shown that $n_0 = kT = -217.3$ dB at this temperature. (It is left to the reader to show that k, Boltzmann's constant, is in decibel measure -228.6 dB.) Finally, then $S_R/n_0|_{dB} = 54.7$ dB.

We now note that the average received power S_R is simply the average energy E received in a bit interval divided by the length of the bit interval. Alternatively, letting R be the bit rate in bits per second,

$$\frac{E}{n_0} = \frac{S_R}{n_0 R} \qquad (6\text{-}253)$$

Since S_R/n_0 is known in this example, E/n_0 may be calculated for any bit rate. More appropriately, choosing an acceptable probability of bit error P_e, we can calculate the E/n_0 required for a given digital modulation scheme, and from this determine the allowable binary transmission rate R. In particular, for the Mariner 10 mission it was decided that $P_e = 0.05$ was acceptable for the image telemetry channel under consideration. This relatively high error rate was specifically chosen to allow higher bit rates to be transmitted, with corresponding increases in image resolution. The fact that 5 bits in 100, on the average, would be in error was deemed acceptable for the application (picture transmission) involved in this example.

PSK transmission was used for the telemetry data. Using Fig. 6-42 to determine E/n_0 for this case, one finds that for $P_e = 0.05$, $E/n_0 = 1.4$ dB. Hence from (6-253), $R = 214,000$ bits/s is the bit transmission rate allowed. In the Mariner 10 example, a 117,600-bit/s data rate was actually used. (Additional power losses in the system not accounted for here result in the difference in transmission rates.)

The fact that it is possible to transmit digital data at rates exceeding 100 kbits/s over distances of 160×10^6 km or more must be considered a remarkable achievement. It is the result of the coordinated efforts of many engineers working jointly over a period of many years to develop higher-power transmitters at the frequency in question, larger antennas on both the space vehicle and on the ground, lower-noise receivers, better modulation and coding techniques, etc. The ratio E/n_0 as seen on the ground reflects all these inputs.

The dependence of power on distance, going inversely as d^2 [see Eq. (6-251)], is a particularly sensitive one. Note that a factor-of-2 change in distance results in a factor-of-4 (6-dB) change in power. This in turn reflects itself in a factor of four in the allowable data rate.

To show the interplay of the various factors determining the performance of these space communication systems, consider as a contrast to the Mariner 10 system the telemetry system used in the 1964 Mariner 4 mission to Mars [EAST]. The transmitting-antenna diameter was 31 in, or 0.79 m, with a gain of 23.4 dB, compared to the 27.6-dB gain of the Mariner 10 antenna. The transmitter power was 10 W, of which only 29 percent could be used directly for data transmission, the remainder being used for transmitting the carrier and a synchronizing signal. The ground antennas were 26-m (85-ft) dishes, rather than the 64-m (210-ft) antennas used with Mariner 10. This alone reduces the allowable bit rate by a factor of 6. The noise temperature at the receiver was 55 K. The distance to Mars was 216×10^6 km. All of these differences, together with other loss factors, result in a combined reduction in E/n_0 of close to 9,000, as compared to the Mariner 10 system. The Mariner 4 system was required to operate at a lower error probability as well. As a result, the data rate in 1964, in transmissions from Mars, was $8\frac{1}{3}$ bits/s. Contrast this with the 117,600-bit/s data transmission rate from Mercury just 10 years later.

Both of these space missions were to the nearby planets. The Voyager missions, to the outer planets, required additional improvements and changes to allow data to be transmitted at 100-kbit/s rates over the long distances involved [KOLD].[40] The transmitting antenna in particular was increased in size to 3.66 m (12 ft). Its efficiency parameter was improved to 0.65. The transmitting frequency was increased from 2295 MHz (S band) to 8415 MHz (X band) to take advantage of the $1/\lambda^2$ gain improvement. As a result, the gain of the Voyager antenna is 48 dB, as compared to 27.6 dB for the Mariner 10 antenna. This enabled the data rate at a distance of 750×10^6 km to be established at a design value of 115 kbits/s, with $P_e = 0.005$.

---

[40][KOLD] J. R. Kolden and V. L. Evanchuk, "Planetary Telecommunications Development during the Next Ten Years," *Proceedings, National Telecommunications Conference*, Dallas, Texas, 1976; reprinted in *IEEE Commun. Soc. Mag.*, vol. 15, no. 6, pp. 16–19, 24, November 1977.

During the Voyager encounter with Uranus, at a distance of 3.2×10^9 km from the earth, data were transmitted at a rate of about 30 kbits/s with a probability of error of 10^{-5}. Communications at this distance at such a low error probability required quite sophisticated coding techniques to be used [POSN].[41] Design details are therefore deferred until the end of Chap. 7, following the discussion of coding techniques used in communication systems.

Satellite Performance Calculations

Equation (6-251) for the received power at a distance d meters from a transmitting antenna is directly applicable to the calculation of the signal-to-noise ratio at the receiver in satellite communication systems as well. It is customary in satellite communication applications to rewrite the equation in terms of the gain of the receiving antenna, however, to focus attention on design parameters that are under the control of individual users on the earth. Recall that the Intelsat worldwide communication system has multiple users at various earth stations accessing a given synchronous satellite (see Sec. 4-13). Since the satellite parameters and frequency of transmission are fixed, the performance of the communication system as seen by individual users can only be modified by varying the receiver noise temperature and the receiver antenna size, or, equivalently, its gain G_R. The SNR at the receiver and hence the performance will be seen to depend on G_R/T. This ratio has thus come to be considered a figure of merit of a given earth station.

Equation (6-251) is easily rewritten by noting again that the antenna gain is related to the area by the expression $G_R = 4\pi \eta_R A_R / \lambda^2$. Hence replacing $\eta_R A_R$ in (6-251) by $(\lambda^2/4\pi)G_R$, one gets

$$S_R = \frac{S_T}{4\pi d^2} G_R G_T \frac{\lambda^2}{4\pi} \tag{6-254}$$

as an equivalent expression. The power-to-noise spectral density is then given by dividing S_R in (6-254) by $n_0 = kT$, just as done in the space-communication examples. Equation (6-254) does not include various losses occurring at the transmitter, during transmission, and at the receiver.

We now focus very specifically on the Intelsat IV system. The downlink frequency for this system is 4 GHz, as noted earlier in Sec. 4-13. The transponder power output is 3.2 W, and the satellite antenna gain is $G_T = 20$ dB for the 17°-wide global beam that provides maximum earth coverage [BARG]. (These numbers refer to points on the beam axis, directly below the satellite. A 3-dB loss is incurred by users located at the beam edge.) The satellite–earth distance, again considering users located directly below the satellite, is 35,788 km. It is left to the

---

[41][POSN] E. C. Posner and R. Stevens, "Deep Space Communications—Past, Present, and Future" *IEEE Commun. Mag.* (special centennial issue), vol. 22, no. 5, pp. 8–21, May 1984.

reader to show, using these numbers, that the received signal-to-noise spectral density, in decibels, is given by

$$\left.\frac{S_R}{n_0}\right|_{dB} = 58 + \left.\frac{G_R}{T}\right|_{dB} - \text{losses (dB)} \qquad (6\text{-}255)$$

This points up the significance of G_R/T as a figure of merit, as noted previously.

Frequency modulation is used as the FDMA modulation technique in the Intelsat IV system. Assuming the received power S_R is distributed uniformly across the 36-MHz transponder bandwidth, the carrier-to-noise ratio CNR is just $S_R/(36 \times 10^6)n_0$. The carrier-to-noise ratio in decibels is then given by

$$\text{CNR}|_{dB} = \left.\frac{G_R}{T}\right|_{dB} - 17.7 - \text{losses (dB)} \qquad (6\text{-}256)$$

FM reception requires the carrier-to-noise ratio to be above a threshold of about 10 dB for FM performance to be satisfactory (Sec. 6-13). This puts a lower limit on G_R/T, from (6-256). A suggested value for G_R/T that should provide good performance is 40.7 dB. Note from (6-256) that for this number $\text{CNR}_{dB} = 23 - \text{losses (dB)}$. This thus provides a loss margin of about 10 dB to ensure above-threshold operation.

Typical large earth-station antennas that provide this 40.7-dB design value for G/T include a 26-m (85.3-ft) antenna with 50-percent efficiency, operated in conjunction with a low-noise receiver at 50 K, and a 29.5-m (96.7-ft) reflector with 70-percent efficiency and a noise temperature of 78 K [BARG]. Note that very large antennas are called for. The same trade-offs are at work here as in the space communications case: were higher-power satellite transmitters to become available, the earth-station costs could be reduced correspondingly. Going to higher frequencies would also increase the satellite gain, thereby reducing the required size of earth antennas.

6-16 SUMMARY

In this chapter we began our study of the performance of communication systems. We began by developing the quantum limits for digital light-wave systems, with fluctuations in photon arrival statistics providing the inherent limit on the performance. We then explored in some depth the effect of additive noise on communication signal transmission. In the case of digital signals the noise occasionally results in a mistaken digit, and the performance is thus evaluated in terms of error probability. In the case of analog signal transmission, with AM and FM as the prime examples, the signal-to-noise ratio (SNR) serves as a comparable measure of system performance.

In order to study the effect of noise on system performance we showed how one analyzes both noise and random signals passing through systems. The mechanism of doing this was to define the autocorrelation function and its Fourier transform, the power spectral density. These two functions are central to the study of random processes and recur over and over again in more advanced treatments than that given here.

The power spectral density represents, as implied by the name, the signal (or noise) power distribution over all frequencies. If the power is concentrated in a definable range of frequencies, we can talk of the signal (or noise) bandwidth B, just as in earlier chapters. By the usual Fourier relations, the width of the corresponding autocorrelation function is proportional to $1/B$. This in turn is, by definition of the autocorrelation function, a measure of the correlation between signal samples: for a time separation $\tau < 1/B$, the samples are essentially correlated; for $\tau > 1/B$, the correlation usually goes to zero. This in turn describes, in an intuitive way, the rate of change of the signal (or noise) in time.

The effect of passing a random signal through a linear system $H(\omega)$ is to multiply the signal spectral density by $|H(\omega)|^2$. This simple relation then enabled us to determine both the band-limiting effect of systems on signals and the actual signal (noise) power at the system output.

With these basic concepts of random processes as an introduction we were able to discuss in a systematic way the comparative signal-to-noise properties of a representative group of high-frequency binary transmission systems as well as more traditional AM and FM systems. Thus, after first introducing the *matched filter* both as an application of the noise spectral analysis and because of its importance in its own right, we went on to discuss the reception of high-frequency binary signals in noise. Both synchronous and noncoherent (envelope) detection were considered, the discussion including the PSK, FSK, and OOK signals first introduced in Chap. 4. The narrowband representation of noise enabled us to actually follow through the detection process. We found that matched filtering was appropriate to *all* binary receivers to minimize probability of error, that synchronous detection provides lower error rates (for the same SNR) than envelope detection, and that, ideally, coherent PSK was the system to be preferred.

The matched filter will be encountered again in Chap. 7, where it will be shown to arise quite naturally in discussing, from a fundamental statistical viewpoint, ways of processing digital signals in the presence of additive gaussian noise to minimize probability of error. We showed here that the effect of the matched filter is to make the probability of error dependent on the ratio E/n_0 of signal energy to white-noise spectral density. This ratio will again be shown in Chap. 7 to provide the basic limitation on digital transmission.

In the case of analog modulation systems we were able to show that FM, as an example of a "wideband" modulation scheme, provides a SNR improvement over AM systems. This in turn provides an improvement in the ability to transmit information. In particular, in FM systems, an increase in bandwidth provides a proportional increase in output SNR, effectively suppressing the noise more and more relative to the signal. This is only possible above the threshold region of carrier-to-noise ratio, however. Thus, below a CNR of approximately 10 dB the output SNR plunges rapidly.

This bandwidth–SNR exchange does not occur in AM-type systems. There, above a 0-dB CNR, the output SNR is strictly proportional to the input SNR. (Below 0 dB a suppression effect is also encountered in AM.)

The SNR–bandwidth exchange of FM systems is of course not as efficient as the exponential exchange encountered with coded PCM systems in Sec. 6-3.

To actually evaluate the performance of communication systems in the presence of noise, one must know precisely what is meant by the noise appearing at the input to a receiving system. We showed at the end of the chapter that ever-present thermal noise provides the ultimate limitation on information transmission. We were able to demonstrate that the thermal-noise spectral density is proportional to the absolute temperature at frequencies well below the optical range. Other sources of noise are then commonly introduced by defining an equivalent noise temperature that incorporates their effect.

Some sample calculations drawn from space and satellite communication enabled us to apply some of the results of this chapter to real systems. We were able to show how trade-offs in signal power, noise temperature, and antenna gains affected the performance of such systems.

PROBLEMS

6-1. The quantum limit for light-wave OOK systems using direct detection is to be determined. Show, using (6-3), that the average number of photons required to be received in a binary interval is 10.3 for an error probability of 10^{-9}.

6-2. Consider a light-wave homodyne PSK system. Show the probability of error, given a 1 transmitted, is given by (6-9). Show the probability of bit error, P_e, is given by (6-10b). Use approximation (6-11) for P_e to show that the quantum limit in this case is 9 photons per bit interval for $P_e = 10^{-9}$.

6-3. Integrate (6-8) by parts to show that erfc x may be approximated by (6-11). Show the approximation is valid for $x > 3$.

6-4. Fill in the details of the analysis of light-wave homodyne OOK transmission to show that the probability of error of this (noiseless) system is given by (6-13). Show that in this case the quantum limit becomes 18 photons per bit interval if $P_e = 10^{-9}$.

6-5. Carry out the analysis of light-wave homodyne PSK transmission for the special case where the local-oscillator amplitude $B = A$, the amplitude of the received optical signal. Show the probability of error in this case is given by (6-15). Show that for $P_e = 10^{-9}$, 5.2 photons per bit interval, on the average, are required.

6-6. The output rms noise voltage of a given linear system is found to be 2 mV. The noise is gaussian fluctuation noise. What is the probability that the instantaneous noise voltage at the output of the system lies between -4 and $+4$ mV?

6-7. Repeat Prob. 6-6 if a dc voltage of 2 mV is added to the output noise.

6-8. Show that the probability of error in mistaking a binary pulse in noise for noise alone or of mistaking noise for a binary pulse is given by Eq. (6-22). Calculate this error for various values of pulse height to rms noise, and check the curve of Fig. 6-9.

6-9. A binary transmission system transmits 50,000 digits per second. Fluctuation noise is added to the signal in the process of transmission, so that at the decoder, where the digits are converted back to a desired output form, the signal pulses are 1 V in amplitude, with the rms noise voltage 0.2 V. What is the average time between mistakes of this system? How is this average time changed if the signal pulses are doubled in amplitude? *Note:* Assume that 1's and 0's are equally likely to be transmitted.

6-10. Show that the optimum decision level for polar signals in additive gaussian noise is given by Eq. (6-27).

6-11. The laplacian distribution is given by $f(x) = ke^{-|x|/c}$ (Fig. P6-11).
(a) Determine k such that $f(x)$ is properly normalized.
(b) Show the standard deviation $\sigma = \sqrt{2}\,c$.
(c) Sketch the cumulative distribution $F(x)$.
Note: This distribution is sometimes used to model the amplitude distribution of burst-type or impulse noise, occurring in high-frequency digital communications.

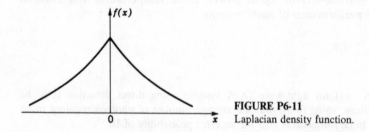

FIGURE P6-11
Laplacian density function.

6-12. Noise having the laplacian distribution of Prob. 6-11 is added to a polar signal sequence of amplitude $\pm A$. Find the probability of error in terms of A/σ (σ the noise standard deviation or rms value), if the decision level for one signal-plus-noise sample is set at zero. Plot the error curve and compare with Fig. 6-9 for gaussian noise.

6-13. The input to a binary communication channel consists of 0's with a priori probability $P_0 = 0.8$, and 1's with a priori probability $P_1 = 0.2$. The transition probabilities on the channel, i.e., the probabilities during transmission that 1's will be received as 1's, 1's received as 0's, etc., are indicated in Fig. P6-13.
(a) Find the probability of error, P_e.
(b) Find P_e if the decisions are *reversed*, i.e., received 1's are called 0's and vice versa.

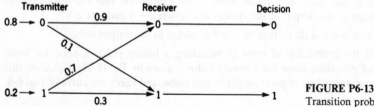

FIGURE P6-13
Transition probabilities.

(c) The decision is made to *always* call a received signal a 0. Calculate the probability of error. Which is the best decision rule of the three described in (a), (b), (c)?

(d) Repeat (a), (b), (c) if $P_0 = P_1 = 0.5$.

6-14. Consider a binary PCM system transmitting 1's with a probability $P_1 = 0.6$ and 0's with a probability $P_0 = 0.4$. The receiver recognizes 0's, 1's, and a third symbol E, called an erasure symbol. There is a probability $P(0|1) = 0.1$ that the 1's will be received (mistakenly) as 0's, $P(E|1) = 0.1$ that they will be received as E's, and $P(1|1) = 0.8$ that they will be received (correctly) as 1's. Similarly, with 0 assumed transmitted, the appropriate probabilities of events at the receiver are given by $P(1|0) = 0.1$, $P(E|0) = 0.1$, $P(0|0) = 0.8$.

(a) Sketch a diagram indicating two transmit and three receive levels, show the appropriate transitions between them, and indicate the appropriate probabilities. *Note:* In the symbolism used above, all conditioning refers to the *transmitter*.

(b) Calculate the probabilities of receiving a 0, a 1, and an E. Show these sum to 1, as required.

(c) Show that the probability of an error is 0.1, the probability of a correct decision at the receiver is 0.8, and the probability of an erasure is 0.1.

(d) Repeat (b) and (c) if the transition probabilities, with a 0 transmitted, are changed to $P(1|0) = 0.05$, $P(E|0) = 0.05$, $P(0|0) = 0.9$.

6-15. Refer to Prob. 6-14. The symbol 1 is received. What is the probability it came from a 0? From a 1? Repeat for the symbols 0, and E, as received. (It may pay to adopt new symbols such as T_0, T_1 and R_0, R_1, R_E, or A_1, A_2 and B_1, B_2, B_3, to keep the appropriate conditional probabilities straight.) Check your results by summing appropriate probabilities.

6-16. A binary source outputs bits at a 2,400-bit/s rate. Gaussian noise is added during transmission. The signal-to-noise ratio at the receiver (amplitude of received signal pulse to noise standard deviation) is 10 dB. Find the probability of error of the system in the two cases of (1) NRZ on–off transmission, and (2) polar transmission. 1's and 0's are equally likely to appear. Use (6-11) and Table 6-2 for the calculation.

6-17. It is common practice in nonoptical digital transmission systems to strive for an error probability due to noise of 10^{-5}. Find the necessary ratio of signal to noise at the receiver (signal amplitude to rms noise) in the two cases of NRZ on–off and polar transmission. Use (6-11) for the calculation.

6-18. A digital transmission channel has a bandwidth of 2,400 Hz and provides a signal-to-noise ratio (SNR or S/N) of 20 dB. Find the information transmission rate (in bits/s) possible over this channel if PCM transmission is used and an error probability of 10^{-5} is specified. Compare with the Shannon capacity for the same channel. Repeat for SNR = 10 dB; 30 dB.

6-19. A random signal $s(t)$ of zero average value has the triangular spectral density of Fig. P6-19.

(a) What is the average power (mean-squared value) $S \equiv E(s^2)$ of the signal?

(b) Show that its autocorrelation function is

$$R_s(\tau) = S\left(\frac{\sin \pi B\tau}{\pi B\tau}\right)^2$$

Hint: Refer back to Chap. 2 for the Fourier transform of a triangular pulse.

(c) $B = 1$ MHz, $K = 1$ $\mu V^2/Hz$. Show that the rms value of the signal is $\sqrt{S} = 1$ mV and that samples of $s(t)$ spaced 1 μs apart are uncorrelated.

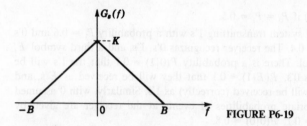

FIGURE P6-19

6-20. Band-limited white noise $n(t)$ has spectral density $G_n(f) = 10^{-6}$ V^2/Hz, over the frequency range -100 to $+100$ kHz.

(a) Show the rms value of the noise is approximately 0.45 V.

(b) Find $R_n(\tau)$. At what spacings are $n(t)$ and $n(t + \tau)$ uncorrelated?

(c) $n(t)$ is assumed gaussian. What is the probability at any time t that $n(t)$ will exceed 0.45 V? 0.9 V?

(d) The noise, again assumed gaussian, is added to polar signals of amplitude $\pm A$. What is the probability of error if the binary signals are equally likely, the decision level is taken as 0, and $A = 0.9$ V? Repeat for $A = 1.8$ V and 4.5 V.

6-21. $R_n(\tau) = N\cos \omega_0\tau$. Show $G_n(f) = (N/2)\delta(f - f_0) + (N/2)\delta(f + f_0)$. Sketch both $R_n(\tau)$ and $G_n(f)$.

6-22. Consider a random signal $s(t) = A\cos(\omega_0 t + \theta)$, with θ a uniformly distributed random variable. Show that

$$E[s(t)s(t + \tau)] = \frac{A^2}{2}\cos \omega_0\tau$$

by averaging over the random variable θ, as indicated. Compare this result with that of Prob. 6-21. Can you explain this result?

6-23. Consider a random signal

$$s(t) = \sum_{i=1}^{n} a_i\cos(\omega_i t + \theta_i)$$

with the frequencies all distinct, and the θ_i's random and independent. Calculate the autocorrelation function of $s(t)$ by averaging $s(t)s(t + \tau)$ over the random θ_i's, and show that

$$R_s(\tau) = \sum_{i=1}^{n} \frac{a_i^2}{2}\cos \omega_i\tau$$

Calculate the spectral density $G_s(f)$, and sketch. Compare this result with that of Probs. 6-21 and 6-22.

6-24. Consider the periodic rectangular pulse train of Fig. P6-24. Timing jitter causes the entire train to be shifted relative to a fixed time origin by a random variable Δ as shown. Δ may be assumed uniformly distributed over the range 0 to T. Show by averaging $s(t)s(t + \tau)$ over Δ that the autocorrelation function is a periodic sequence of triangular pulses of peak amplitude $A^2 t_0/T$, base width $2t_0$, and period T.

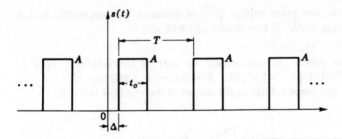

FIGURE P6-24

6-25. An autocorrelation function that frequently arises in practical problems is given by

$$R(\tau) = R(0) e^{-\alpha|\tau|}\cos \beta\tau$$

(a) Calculate the power spectrum $G(f)$.

(b) Typical values for α and β are $\alpha = 1$, $\beta = 0.6$. Plot $R(\tau)/R(0)$ and $G(f)$.

(c) Check the results of (a) by considering the two limiting cases (1) $\alpha = 0$, (2) $\beta = 0$.

6-26. White noise of spectral density $G_n(f) = n_0/2$ W/Hz is applied to an ideal low-pass filter of bandwidth B hertz and transfer amplitude A. Find the correlation function of noise at the output. Calculate the total average power at the filter output from the spectral density directly, and compare with $R(0)$.

6-27. White noise of spectral density $G(f) = 10 \ \mu V^2/Hz$ is passed through a noiseless narrowband amplifier centered at 400 Hz. The amplifier may be represented by an ideal bandpass filter of 50-Hz bandwidth about the 400-Hz center frequency and amplification factor of 1,000.

(a) Write an expression for the autocorrelation function $R(\tau)$ at the amplifier output.

(b) The output noise voltage is to be sampled at intervals far enough apart so as to ensure uncorrelated samples. How far apart should the samples be taken?

6-28. White noise of spectral density $10^{-16} \ V^2/Hz$ is applied at the input of the circuit in Fig. P6-28, as shown.

(a) Find the noise spectral densities $G_1(f)$ and $G_2(f)$, at points 1 and 2, respectively, in terms of the bandwidth $B \equiv 1/2\pi RC$.

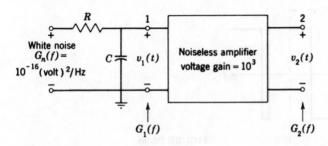

FIGURE P6-28

(b) Find the output rms noise voltage $\sqrt{N_2}$ in terms of the bandwidth B. Let $R = 10$ kΩ. What is $\sqrt{N_2}$ if $C = 0.0001$ μF? 0.01 μF?

6-29. Consider the circuit of Fig. P6-29.

(a) Show that the power spectral density of $v(t)$ at the amplifier input is
$$G_v(f) = 10^{-14}/[1 + (f/B)^2] \text{ V}^2/\text{Hz}; \quad B = G/2\pi C = 1,600 \text{ Hz}.$$

(b) Show that the rms noise voltage at the output of the amplifier is 7 mV.

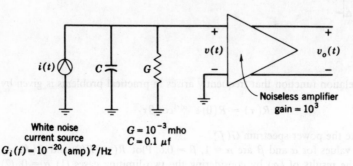

White noise
current source
$G_i(f) = 10^{-20}(\text{amp})^2/\text{Hz}$

$G = 10^{-3}$ mho
$C = 0.1$ μf

FIGURE P6-29

6-30. Consider the random signal shown in Fig. P6-30. $s(t)$ switches randomly between $+1$ and -1. The probability a switch will take place in any small interval Δt is $\lambda \Delta t \ll 1$, independent of switches in any other time interval. The probability that no switch will take place is $1 - \lambda \Delta t$. The probability of k switches in T seconds is then given by the Poisson probability

$$P(k) = \frac{1}{k!}(\lambda T)^k e^{-\lambda T} \qquad k = 0, 1, 2, \ldots$$

The average number of switches in T seconds is λT, and the parameter λ represents the average number of switches per unit time. λ thus measures the rapidity of change of $s(t)$, and one would expect the bandwidth of $s(t)$ to depend on λ. In this problem we show how one determines the spectral density of a random signal such

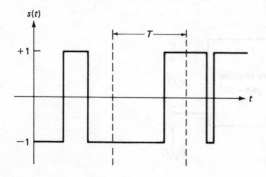

FIGURE P6-30

as $s(t)$ from a calculation of the autocorrelation function.

(a) Show that

$$R_s(\tau) \equiv E[s(t)s(t+\tau)]$$
$$= P[s(t)s(t+\tau) > 0] - P[s(t)s(t+\tau) < 0]$$

Hint: What are the four possible values of $s(t)s(t+\tau)$ that one must average over?

(b) Show that the result of (a) is equivalent to P[even number of switches in τ seconds] $-$ P[odd number of switches in τ seconds]. Use the Poisson distribution to calculate this difference and show that $R_s(\tau) = e^{-2\lambda\tau}$, $\tau > 0$. Repeating for negative τ, show that $R_s(\tau) = e^{-2\lambda|\tau|}$.

(c) Show that

$$G_s(f) = \frac{1/\lambda}{1 + (\pi f/\lambda)^2}.$$

What is the bandwidth of this signal? How does it relate to λ? Compare this result with white noise passed through an RC filter. (See Prob. 6-28, for example.)

6-31. A source $n(t)$ has an autocorrelation given by $R_n(\tau) = 3e^{-a|\tau|}$.

(a) Find $G_n(f)$. Sketch $R_n(\tau)$ and $G_n(f)$ for $a/2\pi = 10^4$ and 10^6. Compare the two sets of curves. What is the rms noise $\sqrt{N}$ in each of the two cases?

(b) Refer to Fig. P6-31. Find the output rms noise power $\sqrt{N_o}$ if $B = a/2\pi = 10^4$.

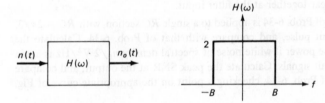

FIGURE P6-31

6-32. Refer to Fig. 6-22 describing the input–output notation for a linear system. Set up the expression for the output autocorrelation function $R_{n_o}(\tau)$ in terms of the expectation of the product of $n_o(t)$ and $n_o(t+\tau)$. Replace $n_o(t)$ and $n_o(t+\tau)$ by the respective convolution integrals relating the output time function to the input time function and the impulse response $h(t)$. Find $R_{n_o}(\tau)$ in terms of $R_{n_i}(\tau)$ and $h(t)$. Take Fourier transforms and show that (6-61), relating input and output spectral densities, results.

6-33. An on–off binary sequence $s(t)$ has white gaussian noise $n(t)$ added to it, as shown in Fig. P6-33. 1,000 bits/s are transmitted. A typical binary 1 has the shape shown in the figure (50-percent-roll-off sinusoidal shaping is used). $H(\omega)$ may be taken to have zero phase. The decision circuit shown outputs a 1 if $v > A/2$ and a 0 if $v < A/2$, with v the value of the voltage at the output of $H(\omega)$, taken once every millisecond at the expected maximum A of the signal component of $v(t)$. Find the probability of error of this system, if 1's and 0's are equally likely to be transmitted.

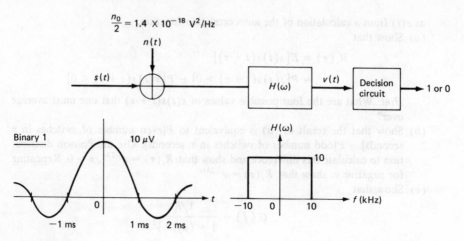

FIGURE P6-33

6-34. A rectangular pulse of amplitude V volts and width τ seconds is applied to a matched filter. Show that the output is a triangular-shaped pulse. Find the peak value of this pulse. Calculate the total noise power at the output of the filter (assumed noiseless) if white noise of spectral density $n_0/2$ V^2/Hz is applied at the input. Calculate the output signal-to-noise ratio at the peak of the signal pulse if signal and noise appear together at the filter input.

6-35. (a) The signal pulse of Prob. 6-34 is applied to a single RC section, with $RC = 2\tau/3$. Sketch the output pulse, and compare with that of Prob. 6-34. Calculate the total output noise power if white noise of spectral density $n_0/2$ V^2/Hz is again added to the input signals. Calculate the peak SNR at the output, and compare with the result of Prob. 6-34, checking a point on the appropriate curve of Fig. 6-32.

(b) Let the pulse width τ vary, and repeat (a). Calculate the peak SNR at the output, and plot as a function of τ. Compare with the appropriate curve of Fig. 6-32.

6-36. A signal pulse of unit peak amplitude and half-power width τ is given mathematically by the gaussian error curve $f(t) = e^{-0.35(2t/\tau)^2}$. Added to the signal pulse is white noise of spectral density $n_0/2$ V^2/Hz. The signal plus noise is applied to a filter. Show that the optimum filter characteristic for maximizing the peak SNR at the filter output is given by a gaussian curve in frequency.

$$|H(\omega)| = \sqrt{\frac{\pi}{1.4}} \, \tau e^{-(\omega\tau)^2/5.6}$$

(Recall that $\int_{-\infty}^{\infty} e^{-x^2} \, dx = \sqrt{\pi}$.) Sketch $f(t)$ and $|H(\omega)|$.

6-37. The gaussian pulse and white noise of Prob. 6-36 are passed through an ideal low-pass filter of cutoff frequency $2\pi B$ rad/s. Show that the maximum peak SNR at the output occurs at $2\pi B\tau = 2.4$. Show that this maximum value of the peak SNR is only 0.3 dB less than that found by using the optimum filter characteristic of Prob. 6-36.

6-38. (*a*) Prove that the impulse response of a matched filter is given in general by Eq. (6-86).

(*b*) A signal pulse given by $f(t) = e^{-\alpha t}$, $t \geq 0$, is mixed with white noise of spectral density $n_0/2$ V^2/Hz. Find the impulse response of the matched filter, and compare with $f(t)$.

6-39. The i-f section of a communications receiver consists of four identical tuned amplifiers with an overall 3-dB bandwidth of 1 MHz. The center frequency is 15 MHz. The amplifiers represent the bandpass equivalent of RC-coupled amplifiers. The input to the i-f strip consists of a 1-μs rectangular signal pulse plus fluctuation noise generated primarily in the r-f stage and mixer of the receiver. Calculate the relative difference in decibels of the peak SNR at the receiver output for the amplifier given, as compared with an optimum matched filter. Repeat for overall amplifier bandwidths of 500 kHz and 2 MHz.

6-40. (*a*) Find and sketch the matched-filter output to the two waveforms shown in Fig. P6-40.

(*b*) Compare the output of matched filter 2 at times $t = T$, $t = T - T/4n$, $t = T - T/2n$. How critical is the *phase* synchronization between transmitter and receiver in this case? Explain.

(*c*) The received signal $s(t)$ is a sinusoidal pulse at frequency $f_c = 1,000$ MHz, and pulse width $T = 1$ μs. The output of a filter matched to $s(t)$ is to be sampled precisely at the end of the pulse, $t = T = 1$ μs. Using (*b*), discuss the synchronization required.

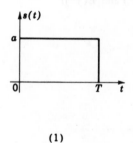

(1)

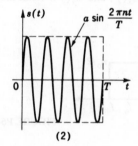

(2)

FIGURE P6-40

6-41. (*a*) Prove the Fourier-transform relationship

$$E = \int_{-\infty}^{\infty} |f(t)|^2 \, dt = \int_{-\infty}^{\infty} |F(\omega)|^2 \, df$$

Hint: Consider the special case $f(t)$ real. Let $f(t)$ be the input to a matched filter. Find and equate the outputs using the convolution integral and then Fourier transforms.

(*b*) Check this equality for $f(t)$ a rectangular pulse, a gaussian pulse (see Prob. 6-36), and $f(t) = e^{-\alpha |t|}$.

6-42. The rectangular-shaped polar binary sequence of Fig. P6-42 is received in the presence of additive gaussian white noise. A' is in volts. The bit rate is 1 Mbits/s, equally likely to be 1's and 0's. The noise spectral density is $n_0/2 = \frac{1}{2} \times 10^{-20}$ V^2/Hz.

(a) Matched filter detection is used. $A' = 0.22$ μV. Find the probability of error, P_e. What is the average time between errors?

(b) Repeat (a) if $A' = 0.3$ μV.

(c) An *RC* filter, adjusted to be 1 dB from the matched-filter result, is used at the receiver. Find P_e if $A' = 0.3$ μV.

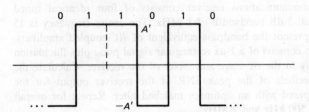

FIGURE P6-42

6-43. (a) Using Eq. (6-97), show by averaging over θ_l that

$$E(x^2) = E(y^2) = N$$

(b) Show, similarly, that $E(x) = E(y) = 0$, and that $E(xy) = 0$, as well.

6-44. A noise process $n(t)$ has the spectral density $G_n(f)$ shown in Fig. P6-44. [$E(n) = 0$.]

(a) Find the autocorrelation function and sketch for $f_0 \gg B$.

(b) Find the mean-squared value (power) of the process.

(c) $n(t)$ is written in the narrowband form $n(t) = x(t)\cos \omega_0 t - y(t)\sin \omega_0 t$. Sketch the spectral densities $G_x(f)$ and $G_y(f)$. What are $E(x^2)$ and $E(y^2)$?

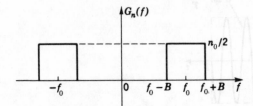

FIGURE P6-44

6-45. A binary communications system uses on–off-keyed (OOK) transmission: the transmitted signal $s(t) = f(t)\cos \omega_0 t$ or 0, repeating every $T = 1$ ms. Suppose $f_0 = 1$ MHz, and $f(t)$ is the triangle in Fig. P6-45. White gaussian noise, $n_0/2 = 10^{-20}$ V²/Hz, is added during transmission. The receiver block diagram is shown in the figure.

(a) Find the average noise power (mean-squared noise) at point 1.

(b) $H_2(\omega)$ is to be designed to maximize the signal-to-noise ratio at point 2. Write an expression for $H_2(\omega)$.

(c) An *RC* filter is used for $H_2(\omega)$:

$$|H_2(\omega)| = \frac{1}{\sqrt{1 + (f/f_c)^2}}$$

Find the average noise power at 2 for the two cases $f_c = 1$ kHz and $f_c = 10$ kHz.

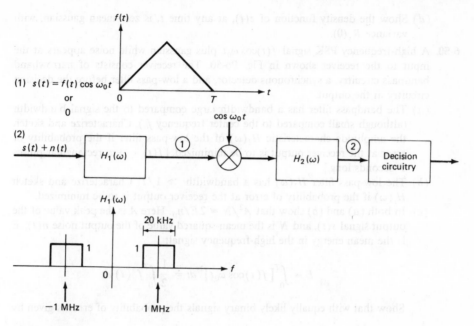

(1) $s(t) = f(t) \cos \omega_0 t$
   or
   0

(2)
   $s(t) + n(t)$

FIGURE P6-45

6-46. Find and sketch the spectral density of the derivative of the noise processes in Probs. 6-20 and 6-44. *Hint:* Differentiation is a linear operation and hence may be represented by a linear filter. What is $H(\omega)$ for this filter?

6-47. Compare the correlation functions for $n(t)$ and $x(t)$ in Prob. 6-44.

6-48. Consider the random process $z(t) = x \cos \omega_0 t - y \sin \omega_0 t$, where x and y are independent random gaussian variables with zero expected value and variance σ^2.

 (*a*) Show that $z(t)$ is also normal (gaussian) with zero expected value and variance σ^2. Show the autocorrelation function $R_z(t, t + \tau) = \sigma^2 \cos \omega_0 \tau$, independent of t. (The process is therefore *wide-sense stationary*.) *Hint:* Set up formally the expression $E[z(t)z(t + \tau)]$, and then average over both x and y.

 (*b*) Show that $z(t)$ can also be written as $r \cos(\omega_0 t + \theta)$. Find the joint density function of r and θ.

 (*c*) Repeat (*a*) for $z(t) = x \cos(\omega_0 t + \varphi) - y \sin(\omega_0 t + \varphi)$ with φ a uniformly distributed $(0, 2\pi)$ random variable independent of x and y.

6-49. Consider $z(t) = x(t)\cos \omega_0 t - y(t)\sin \omega_0 t$, where $x(t)$ and $y(t)$ are normal (gaussian), zero-mean, independent random *processes* with $R_x(\tau) = R_y(\tau)$. (They are therefore wide-sense stationary.)

 (*a*) Show $R_z(\tau) = R_x(\tau)\cos \omega_0 \tau$. (It is therefore wide-sense stationary as well.) Distinguish between this problem and Prob. 6-48. *Hint:* Again average over both $x(t)$ and $y(t)$, as in Prob. 6-48.

 (*b*) Find the power spectrum $G_z(f)$ in terms of the spectrum $G_x(f) = G_y(f)$.

 (*c*) With $R_x(\tau) = \sigma^2 e^{-\alpha|\tau|}$ evaluate the spectra of $x(t)$ and $z(t)$. Sketch. Compare with Prob. 6-25.

(d) Show the density function of $z(t)$, at any time t, is zero-mean gaussian, with variance $R_x(0)$.

6-50. A high-frequency PSK signal $f(t)\cos \omega_0 t$ plus gaussian white noise appears at the input to the receiver shown in Fig. P6-50. The receiver consists of narrowband bandpass circuitry, a synchronous detector, and a low-pass filter before the decision circuitry at the output.

(a) The bandpass filter has a bandwidth large compared to the signal bandwidth (although small compared to the center frequency f_0). Characterize and sketch the amplitude characteristic $H_2(\omega)$ of the low-pass filter if the probability of error at the receiver output is to be minimized. [$f(t) = \pm a$: rectangular pulses T seconds long.]

(b) The low-pass filter $H_2(\omega)$ has a bandwidth $\gg 1/T$. Characterize and sketch $H_1(\omega)$ if the probability of error at the receiver output is to be minimized.

(c) In both (a) and (b) show that $A^2/N = 2E/n_0$. Here A is the peak value of the output signal $s(t)$, and N is the mean-squared value of the output noise $n(t)$. E is the mean energy in the high-frequency signal:

$$E = \int_0^T \left[f(t)\cos \omega_0 t \right]^2 dt \doteq \frac{1}{2} \int_0^T f^2(t) \, dt$$

Show that with equally likely binary signals the probability of error is given by

$$P_{e,\text{PSK}} = \tfrac{1}{2} \, \text{erfc} \sqrt{\frac{E}{n_0}}$$

This is then the matched-filter error probability for PSK signals agreeing with (6-115) and the discussion relating to that equation.

(d) Filter $H_1(\omega)$ has a rectangular amplitude characteristic of bandwidth $\pm B$ about f_0. Filter $H_2(\omega)$ has a rectangular (ideal low-pass) amplitude characteristic of bandwidth B hertz. Find the peak SNR at the receiver output for $B = 0.5/T$, $0.75/T$, and $1/T$. *Hint:* Show that the ideal low-pass curve in Fig. 6-32 is applicable.

(e) $E/n_0 = 8$ dB. Find the probability of error in (c) and for the three bandwidths of (d).

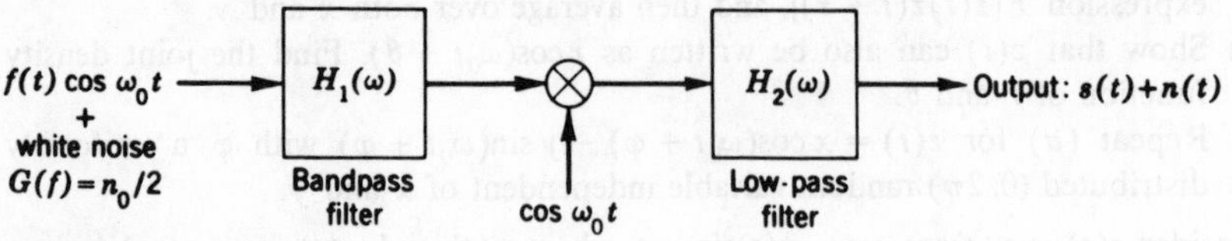

$f(t) \cos \omega_0 t$
$+$
white noise
$G(f) = n_0/2$ → $H_1(\omega)$ [Bandpass filter] → ⊗ [$\cos \omega_0 t$] → $H_2(\omega)$ [Low-pass filter] → Output: $s(t) + n(t)$

FIGURE P6-50

6-51. Repeat Prob. 6-50 for an OOK signal plus gaussian white noise at the input to the receiver of Fig. P6-50. Show that the matched-filter error probability is in this case

$$P_{e,\text{OOK}} = \tfrac{1}{2} \, \text{erfc} \left(\frac{1}{2} \sqrt{\frac{E}{n_0}} \right)$$

6-52. Draw a block diagram for an FSK matched-filter receiver with synchronous detection. Show that with additive white gaussian noise at the receiver input and equally likely binary signals the probability of error for the system is

$$P_{e,\text{FSK}} = \tfrac{1}{2}\,\text{erfc}\sqrt{\frac{E}{2n_0}}$$

E and n_0 are the same as in Probs. 6-50 and 6-51. Calculate the probability of error for $E/n_0 = 8$ dB and compare with the PSK and OOK results in Probs. 6-50 and 6-51 respectively. Replace the matched filter with the rectangular filters of Prob. 6-50d, and evaluate the probability of error for the three bandwidths given there. Compare with the PSK and OOK results in Probs. 6-50 and 6-51.

6-53. An FSK system transmits 2×10^6 bits/s. White gaussian noise is added during transmission. The amplitude of either signal at the receiver input is 0.45 μV, while the white-noise spectral density at the same point is $n_0/2 = \tfrac{1}{2} \times 10^{-20}$ V^2/Hz. Compare the probability of error for a receiver using synchronous detection with one using envelope detection. Assume matched-filter detection in both cases. Repeat for received signal amplitudes of 0.9 μV.

6.54. (*a*) Gaussian bandpass noise $n(t)$ with power spectral density $G_n(f) = n_0/2$, $f_0 - B < |f| < f_0 + B$, zero elsewhere, as in Fig. P6-44, is applied to an envelope detector. Find the probability-density function of the detector output $r(t)$, as well as its dc and rms values.

(*b*) Repeat for another noise process $n(t)$ with spectral density n_0 over the range of frequencies $f_0 - 2B < |f| < f_0 + 2B$, zero elsewhere. Sketch the two probability-density functions on the same scale, and compare dc and rms values.

6-55. Zero-mean bandpass gaussian noise $n(t)$, as in Prob. 6-54a, is applied to the RC filter shown in Fig. P6-55. The output noise $n_o(t)$ is then gaussian as well. Find and sketch the power spectral density of $n_o(t)$ for various values of RC. Find the mean and mean-squared value of $n_o(t)$ as a function of RC. Write the probability-density function of $n_o(t)$ for some value of RC.

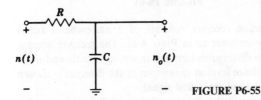

FIGURE P6-55

6-56. The object of this problem is to obtain the minimum-probability-of-error expression for PSK, OOK, and FSK, assuming matched-filter detection, without resorting to the narrowband representation of noise, the technique adopted in Sec. 6-8.

(*a*) Starting with (6-119), carry through the calculations indicated. In particular, show the noise variance at the output of the matched filter is given by (6-124). For PSK, show that the probability of error is given by (6-125) and (6-126).

(*b*) Repeat the analysis for (1) OOK transmission and (2) FSK transmission, showing that the results agree with those subsumed by (6-115).

6-57. Carry out the detailed analysis of heterodyne detection of a PSK light-wave signal sketched out in Sec. 6-9. In particular, starting with (6-127) and following the steps indicated, show the probability of error is given by (6-129). Using approximation (6-130), show that the quantum limit in this case, for $P_e = 10^{-9}$, is 18 photons per binary interval.

6-58. Carry out the analysis of heterodyne detection of an OOK light-wave signal, and show the probability of error is given by (6-131). Show that for $P_e = 10^{-9}$, the quantum limit in this case is 36 photons per binary interval.

6-59. Repeat Prob. 6-58 for the heterodyne detection of an FSK optical signal. Show the optimum receiver is the matched filter receiver of Fig. 6-48. Carry out the details of the analysis and show (6-132) is obtained. Calculate the FSK quantum limit for $P_e = 10^{-9}$, and show it is the same value as that obtained for OOK in Prob. 6-58.

6-60. (*a*) Show the Rayleigh distribution of (6-141) is properly normalized. Show its expected value and variance are $\sqrt{\pi/2}\,\sigma$ and $[2 - (\pi/2)]\sigma^2$, respectively.

(*b*) What is the probability that the envelope of narrowband gaussian noise will exceed three times its rms value? *Hint:* Use the result of part (*a*).

6-61. Gaussian bandpass noise with mean-squared value N is detected by a quadratic (or square-law) envelope detector, whose output is proportional to the square of the instantaneous envelope voltage. Thus the detector output voltage $z(t)$ is cr^2, as shown in Fig. P6-61, with c a constant of proportionality and r the envelope voltage.

(*a*) Show that the probability-density function of z at any time t is

$$f(z) = \frac{e^{-z/2cN}}{2cN} \qquad z \geq 0$$

(*b*) Calculate the voltages at the output of the detector that would be read by a long-time-constant dc meter, a long time-constant rms meter, and a long-time-constant rms meter preceded by a blocking capacitor.

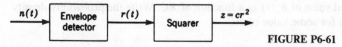

FIGURE P6-61

6-62. A non-phase-coherent communication receiver consists of a narrowband tuned amplifier and a quadratic envelope detector as in Prob. 6-61. The receiver accepts signal pulses of fixed amplitude. To distinguish between incoming signals and noise present in the receiver, a specific voltage level at the output of the detector is chosen such that all voltages exceeding this level are called signal.

(*a*) What is the probability that noise in the absence of signal will be mistaken for signal if the level is set at $2N$, with N the mean-squared noise voltage at the detector input? (Assume that the detector constant of proportionality is 1 V/V².)

(*b*) Plot the probability of error due to noise if the voltage level is varied from 0 to $20N$.

6-63. *Computer generation of gaussian random variables from uniformly distributed random numbers.*

(*a*) Assume that random numbers x_i, uniformly distributed from 0 to 1, are available. Let $y = (b/n)\sum_{i=1}^{n}(x_i - \frac{1}{2})$, n a fixed number. Show y approximates a gaussian random variable of zero average value and variance $\sigma^2 = b^2/12n$.

(b) The gaussian approximation of (a) is poor on the tails of the distribution. Why? A better approximation, using two independent uniform random numbers x and y, is obtained as follows:

(1) Let $r = \sqrt{-2\sigma^2 \log_e x}$. Show

$$f(r) = \frac{re^{-r^2/2\sigma^2}}{\sigma^2}$$

i.e., the Rayleigh distribution of (6-141).

(2) Show $z = r \cos 2\pi y$ is zero-mean gaussian, with variance σ^2. *Hint:* Refer to the derivation of the Rayleigh density function in Sec. 6-10.

6-64. Carry out the indicated statistical averaging in (6-173) to obtain (6-174).

6-65. Assume that an unmodulated carrier plus narrowband noise is synchronously detected. Show that the output SNR is proportional to the input CNR for *all* values of CNR.

6-66. (a) Gaussian bandpass noise $n(t)$ with power spectral density $G_n(f) = n_0/2$, $f_0 - B < |f| < f_0 + B$, zero elsewhere, is applied to the quadratic envelope detector of Fig. P6-61. (Assume the detector constant $c = 1$.) Find the spectral density of the output noise $z(t)$ by first finding the correlation function $R_z(\tau)$ in terms of the correlation function of the input $x(t)$ and $y(t)$. *Hint:* $r^2 = x^2 + y^2$. Assume x and y independent. Recall that $R_x(\tau) = R_y(\tau)$. Use (6-187) for gaussian processes to relate $R_{x^2}(\tau)$ or $R_x(\tau)$. The spectral density of $G_x(f)$ is given in terms of the input noise spectral density by (6-102).

(b) Repeat part (a), using the procedure of Sec. 6-12. Thus assume that quadratic envelope detection is equivalent to squaring the input $n(t)$ and passing $n^2(t)$ through a low-pass filter. Show that the resultant output spectrum is the same as that found in (a), except for the constant factor $\frac{1}{4}$ noted in Secs. 6-11 and 6-12.

6-67. An FM receiver consists of an ideal bandpass filter of 225-kHz bandwidth centered about the unmodulated carrier frequency, an ideal limiter and frequency discriminator, and an ideal low-pass filter of 10-kHz bandwidth in the output. The ratio of average carrier power to total average noise power at the input to the limiter is 40 dB. The modulating signal is 10-kHz sine wave that produces a frequency deviation Δf of 50 kHz.

(a) What is the signal-to-noise ratio S_o/N_o at the output of the low-pass filter?

(b) A deemphasis network with a time constant $rC = 75$ μs is inserted just before the output filter. Calculate S_o/N_o again.

(c) Repeat (a) and (b) if the modulating signal is a 1-kHz sine wave of the same amplitude as the 10-kHz wave. Repeat with the amplitude reduced by a factor of 2. (The carrier amplitude and filter bandwidths are unchanged.)

6-68. An audio signal is to be transmitted by either AM or FM. The signal consists of either of two equal-amplitude sine waves: one at 50 Hz, the other at 10 kHz. The amplitude is such as to provide 100-percent carrier modulation in the AM case and a frequency deviation $\Delta f = 75$ kHz in the FM case. The average carrier power and the noise-power density at the detector input are the same for the AM and FM systems.

(a) Calculate the transmission bandwidth and output filter required in the AM case and the FM case. The carrier-to-noise ratio is 30 dB for the AM system. Calculate the output S_o/N_o for each sine wave for each of the systems.

(Preemphasis and deemphasis networks are not used.)

(b) Repeat (a) if the amplitude of the 10-kHz wave is reduced by a factor of 2.

6-69. The ratio of average carrier power to noise spectral density, S_c/n_0, at the detector input is 4×10^6 for both an FM and an AM receiver. The AM carrier is 100-percent modulated by a sine-wave signal, while a sine-wave signal produces a maximum deviation of 75 kHz of the FM carrier. Calculate and compare the output signal-to-noise ratio for both the FM and the AM receivers if the bandwidth B of the low-pass filter in each receiver is successively 1, 10, and 100 kHz. Deemphasis networks are not used. (Assume that the r-f bandwidths are always at least twice the low-pass bandwidth.)

6-70. The low-pass filter bandwidth of an AM and FM receiver is 1 kHz. The ratio of average carrier power to noise spectral density, S_c/n_0, is the same in both receivers and is kept constant. The AM carrier is 100-percent modulated. Calculate the relative SNR improvement of the FM over the AM system if the frequency deviation Δf of the FM carrier is 100 Hz; 1 kHz; 10 kHz.

6-71. The time constant of an RC deemphasis network is chosen as 75 μs. Plot the improvement in output SNR due to the deemphasis network for both FM and AM detectors as a function of the bandwidth of the output low-pass filter. (Assume that S_c/n_0 is the same and constant in both cases.) What is the minimum filter bandwidth to be used if audio signals from 0 to 10 kHz are to be passed?

6-72. The received signal $s(t) = m(t)\cos(\omega_c t + \theta) - \hat{m}(t)\sin(\omega_c t + \theta)$ is embedded in white gaussian noise with spectral density $n_0/2$. [$m(t)$ is the message; $\hat{m}(t)$ its Hilbert transform.]

(a) Show that $s(t)$ is a SSB signal.

(b) Assuming that θ is known, draw a block diagram of a synchronous demodulator, including appropriate low-pass filtering.

(c) Find the output SNR if $m(t)$ is random, $E(m) = 0$, $E(m^2) = S$.

6-73. The output of a "jittery" oscillator is described by $g(t) = \cos(\omega t + \theta)$, where ω and θ are independent random variables with the following probability-density functions:

(1) θ is uniform $(0, 2\pi)$.

(2) ω has a probability-density function $f_\omega(\omega)$.

Show that the power spectral density of $g(t)$ is given by

$$G_g\left(\frac{\omega}{2\pi}\right) = \frac{\pi}{2}f_\omega(\omega)$$

Sketch for $f_\omega(\omega)$ gaussian, with expected value ω_0. *Hint:* Write the autocorrelation function for $g(t)$, averaging over *both* ω and θ. Show $R_g(\tau) = \frac{1}{2}E(\cos \omega\tau)$, referring to expectation over ω. Write out the form for this expectation in terms of $f_\omega(\omega)$, then compare with the expression for the Fourier transform of $G_g(f)$.

6-74. The output SNR and input SNR of an FM discriminator *above threshold* are related by the equation

$$\frac{S_o}{N_o} = 3\beta^2(\beta + 1)\frac{S_i}{N_i}$$

with β the modulation index. The complete SNR characteristic is shown in Fig. P6-74. An FM signal at the discriminator input has a power of 55 mW. The input noise is white with spectral density $n_0/2 = 0.25 \times 10^{-10}$ W/Hz. The maximum modulation frequency is 5 MHz. The frequency deviation is 25 MHz. If the bandwidth following the discriminator is B hertz, while that preceding the discriminator is $2(\beta + 1)B$, find

(a) S_i/N_i in decibels.

(b) S_o/N_o in decibels.

(c) Repeat if the deviation is increased to 50 MHz.

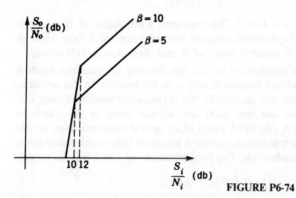

FIGURE P6-74

6-75. A communication system produces at its output an impulse term plus random noise given by

$$e_o(t) = 2\pi\delta(t - t_i) + n(t)$$

The random noise has power spectral density

$$G_n(f) = kf^2$$

up to very high positive and negative frequencies. (This is a model of impulse and random noise occurring at the output of FM receivers.) This input voltage is to be passed through a linear filter $H(\omega)$ designed to optimize the recognition of the impulse term. Determine the expression for $H(\omega)$ which maximizes, at time $t_i + t_0$, the ratio of the output due to the impulse to the rms output due to $n(t)$. *Hint:* Use the Schwarz inequality.

6-76. Band-limited white gaussian noise with spectral density $n_0/2$, $-B < f < B$, is passed through a square-law detector whose output is $n^2(t)$, and then through an ideal low-pass filter of bandwidth B. Determine the power spectrum of $n^2(t)$, the spectrum at the low-pass filter output, and the rms value of the output noise.

6-77. Calculate the rms noise voltage in a 10-kHz bandwidth across

(a) a 10-kΩ resistor at room temperature.

(b) a 100-kΩ resistor at room temperature.

Repeat for a 5-kHz bandwidth. Repeat for $T = 30$ K.

6-78. Consider a noisy resistor R at temperature T degrees Kelvin and an inductor L connected in series.

(a) Find the spectral density of the current through the inductor.

(b) Show that the average energy stored in the inductor is $\frac{1}{2}kT$.

6-79. Using Eq. (6-238), show that the average energy of the harmonic oscillator is given by Eq. (6-239).

6-80. Starting with (6-244), derive (6-245) for the spectral density of the resistive noise-current source in Fig. 6-74. To do this, first show that if the bandwidth of $H(\omega)$ is very narrow compared to the center frequency $f_0 = 1/2\pi\sqrt{LC}$, then $|H(\omega)|^2$ may be written

$$|H(\omega)|^2 \doteq \frac{1/G^2}{1 + (\delta/\alpha)^2}.$$

with $\delta = \omega - \omega_0 \ll \omega_0$ and $\alpha = G/2C$. This represents a translation of $H(\omega)$ down to $\delta = 0$. Since $G_i(f)$ may be assumed constant over all values of δ, take it out of the integral, integrate over all possible values of δ, and show that (6-245) results.

6-81. The optical-communication calculations in the text focused on quantum limiting cases, neglecting noise introduced enroute as well as at the receiver. In this problem, modeling any optical system, not necessarily the digital-communication ones discussed in the text, we show how one takes into account noise in the system in calculating an output SNR. A simplified model of an optical communication system is shown in Fig. P6-81. The transmitter produces pulses of light which travel down the optical path to the photodetector. The photodetector current i may be written

$$i = \bar{I} + i_s + i_B$$

$\bar{I}$, the *signal*, is the average current due to the transmitted light. i_s is a shot-noise component with spectral density $G_s(f) = e\bar{I}$, due to the arrival of the photons at discrete but random instants. This is precisely the Poisson-distributed "self-noise" discussed in the text. It is due to the variance in the count statistics. Recall that for Poisson statistics the variance and mean are equal. i_B is a white-noise component with spectral density $G_B(f) = \eta$, due to background radiation.

(*a*) Derive an expression for the signal-to-noise power ratio at the output of the RC filter. Assume that the resistor R is noiseless.

(*b*) Repeat if R is a source of thermal noise.

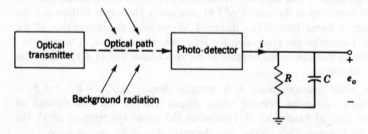

FIGURE P6-81
Optical communication system.

6-82. *Noise figure of lossy transmission line (cable).* Consider signals transmitted along a cable of length l with voltage attenuation constant α (Fig. P6-82). The ratio of power out to power in is then $L = e^{-2\alpha l}$. It can then be shown [SIEG][42] the the line introduces thermal noise due to the line losses given by $N_l = (1 - L)kTB$, $hf \ll kT$, with T the temperature of the line and B a specified bandwidth.

---

[42] [SIEG] A. E. Siegman, *Microwave Solid-State Masers*, McGraw-Hill, New York, 1964, pp. 373–375.

Show that the noise figure of the lossy cable at T degrees Kelvin is

$$F = 1 + \frac{1 - L}{L} = \frac{1}{L}$$

For a line with $L = \frac{1}{2}$, then, $F = 2$.

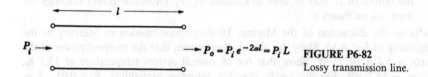

$$P_o = P_i e^{-2\alpha l} = P_i L$$

FIGURE P6-82
Lossy transmission line.

6-83. *Maser receiving systems.* Consider the low-noise maser receiver shown in Fig. P6-83. Although the low-noise (low-temperature) maser amplifier is used to decrease the system noise as much as possible, it is found in practice that the line feed from antenna to maser amplifier provides the limitation on the reduction of the system noise. To demonstrate this, consider the following examples:

(a) The line loss is $L \equiv -0.1$ dB. The maser has an effective noise temperature of 3 K. Show that the effective noise temperature at the antenna input = 10 K. (The second-stage noise contribution may be neglected.)

(b) The maser amplifier noise is now 30 K. Show that the effective noise temperature at the antenna input is $\doteq 37$ K.

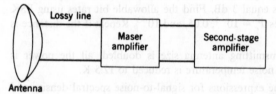

FIGURE P6-83
Maser receiver.

6-84. *Measurement of effective noise temperature.*

(a) Consider a system denoted by H in Fig. P6-84 whose effective noise temperature T_e is to be measured. Two thermal-noise sources, one at temperature T_1 degrees Kelvin, the other at temperature T_2 degrees Kelvin, as shown, are separately connected to the input of H. The output power, denoted respectively by P_1 and P_2, is measured in each case. Show that the effective noise tempera-

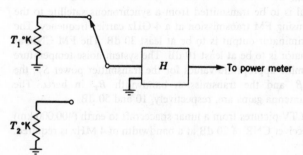

FIGURE P6-84
Measurement of effective noise temperature.

ture is then given by

$$T_e = \frac{T_1 - yT_2}{y - 1}$$

with $y \equiv P_1/P_2$ the ratio of the two powers.

(b) Show how a calibrated attenuator plus some sort of power-indicating device at the output of H may be used to measure P_1/P_2. (Absolute power readings are then not necessary.)

6-85. Refer to the discussion of the Mariner 10 deep-space mission to Mercury at the beginning of Sec. 6-15. Show, for the numbers given, that the received power at the earth is 5.4×10^{-17} W. Show that for an overall system temperature of 13.5 K, $S_R/n_0 = 54.7$ dB. Finally, verify that for bit-error probability $P_e = 0.05$, $R = 213,000$ bits/s is the bit transmission rate allowed using PSK transmission. What bit rate would be allowed if FSK transmission were used instead? What bit rate would be allowed if $P_e = 10^{-5}$ were required?

6-86. The Voyager space mission has the following design features: $f = 8415$ MHz, $S_T = 23$ W, transmitting antenna diameter is 3.66 m, $\eta_T = 0.65$, $d = 7.58 \times 10^8$ km, receiver antenna diameter is 64 m, and $\eta_R = 0.575$, $T = 21$ K. Other losses total 5.5 dB. Show that data may be transmitted at a bit rate of 115.2 kbits/s using PSK transmission with an acceptable bit-error probability of $P_e = 0.005$.

6-87. Consider a deep-space telemetry system with the following parameters: $S_T = 20$ W, with 50 percent of this power used for telemetry. The transmitting-antenna gain is $G_T = 24$ dB. The distance to the earth is 1.6×10^8 km (10^8 mi). The receiving antenna is a 64-m dish, with 57.5-percent efficiency. The system noise temperature is 25 K. Additional power losses equal 3 dB. Find the allowable bit rates using PSK transmission for the three cases $P_e = 10^{-3}, 0.05$, and 10^{-5}. Repeat if the distance is increased to 3.2×10^8 km.

6-88. Repeat Prob. 6-87 if the transmitting antenna size is doubled, all the power is devoted to telemetry, and the noise temperature is reduced to 12.5 K.

6-89. Derive (6-255) and (6-256), the expressions for signal-to-noise spectral density and CNR, respectively, for the Intelsat IV communications system.

6-90. Refer to the Intelsat IV system. Show that a 30-m ground antenna, with an efficiency of 70 percent, requires a low-noise receiver with $T = 85$ K to achieve $G_R/T = 40.7$ dB at a 4-GHz frequency.

6-91. Refer to the satellite system calculations in Sec. 6-15. The down link frequency is increased to 12 GHz, all other satellite parameters remaining the same. Comment on the G_R/T required now to maintain good performance. Find the earth-station antenna size required if $\eta_R = 0.5$ and $T = 50$ K. Compare with existing designs.

6-92. A 5-MHz baseband signal is to be transmitted from a synchronous satellite to the earth 3.6×10^7 m away, using FM transmission at a 4-GHz carrier frequency. The SNR at the receiver discriminator output is to be at least 30 dB. The FM CNR at the input to the discriminator is to be at least 10 dB. The system noise temperature is taken as 100 K. Determine appropriate values for the transmitter power S_T, the FM modulation index β, and the transmission bandwidth B_T in hertz. The transmitter and receiver antenna gains are, respectively, 10 and 50 dB.

6-93. Real-time transmission of TV pictures from a lunar spacecraft to earth (400,000 km) is to be investigated. A receiver CNR of 20 dB at a bandwidth of 4 MHz is required.

A 500-MHz carrier is to be used, with a 2-m $\times$ 2-m antenna on the spacecraft and an antenna with 45-dB gain on the earth. What is the power requirement of the transmitter on the space vehicle?

6-94. Investigate the possibility of maintaining analog voice contact with a space mission 8×10^9 km from the earth. (This represents the distance to the farthest planet of the solar system.) A receiver CNR of 20 dB is desired. A low-noise receiving system with a 5-K effective noise temperature at 2 GHz is available. The spacecraft may be allowed up to 250-W power output and can carry a large unfurlable parabolic antenna.

CHAPTER
7

STATISTICAL
COMMUNICATION
THEORY AND DIGITAL
COMMUNICATIONS

As we move into this last chapter of the book it is useful to recapitulate what we have covered thus far and to outline what will be presented in the sections following. Recall from our discussion in Chap. 1, with further elaboration in Chap. 5, that we emphasize in this book the physical layer corresponding to point-to-point communication in communication networks. Except for Chap. 5, which dealt with packet and circuit switching, using local-area networks (LANs) as a particular application, the book has focused on the principles and systems involved in transmitting information along a link connecting two neighboring nodes in a network.

After describing A/D conversion, PCM, DPCM, and time-division multiplexing in Chap. 3 and then studying various modulation techniques in Chap. 4, we began a detailed study of the comparative performance of various point-to-point communication systems in Chap. 6. In the case of optical (light-wave) communications, quantum limitations were obtained for the error performance of a number of digital systems. For systems at frequencies below the optical range, where quantum effects no longer dominate, we indicated that additive noise played a key role in limiting performance. In addition, system spectral response or bandwidth was found to play a role in limiting performance. In Chap. 1 we first pointed out qualitatively that the rate of transmission of information, in bits per second, was limited by these two basic quantities, the time response or

564

bandwidth of systems through which the information was to pass, and noise innately present in all systems.

In Chap. 6 we concentrated on the analysis and comparison of the most commonly used communication schemes, whether for the transmission of digital or analog signals. In this chapter we return to the question of information transmission from a more fundamental viewpoint. We ask whether it is possible to *optimize* the design of systems in the sense of maximizing the information-transmission rate with prescribed constraints on error probability, signal power, noise, and bandwidth. This leads us into the realm of statistical communication theory.

We have already considered some aspects of system optimization at various points in Chap. 6. Thus, in discussing binary communications, we discussed the optimum setting of a decision threshold. The concept of matched filtering arose out of the discussion of maximizing SNR in binary transmission. We applied the Schwarz inequality in considering optimum emphasis networks for FM and AM analog transmission. We discussed the SNR–bandwidth exchange in pulse-code-modulation (PCM) systems, and indicated that it was similar to that found by Shannon for a hypothetical optimum digital transmission system.

These were essentially isolated cases, however, useful in developing familiarity with existing systems and their performance. We now attack the problem of optimum information transmission in a more systematic way. We use here as a tool the elements of statistical decision theory. The emphasis throughout will be on *digital* communication, first because of its rapidly growing importance in modern technology, and second because the optimization procedures, based primarily on the minimization of probability of error, are much simpler to carry out and interpret for digital than for analog signal transmission.[1]

After a necessary introduction to statistical decision theory with specific reference to binary communication, we consider in detail the optimum design of binary communication systems, designed to perform with minimum probability of error in the presence of additive gaussian noise.[2] The specific questions to be answered are: (1) What is the optimum decision procedure at the receiver? and (2) Is is possible to optimally design signals at the transmitter?

Surprisingly, we shall find both questions answered simultaneously by our statistical-decision approach. Polar signal transmission with matched-filter decision threshold detection will be found to be the optimum binary transmission scheme. This is, of course, exactly the system analyzed earlier—the system we found theoretically superior to both frequency-shift-keyed (FSK) and on–off-keyed (OOK) transmission.

---

[1] Optimum analog transmission relies on the concepts of statistical *estimation* theory. See [VITE 1966, part 2] for an introduction and comprehensive bibliography. A detailed discussion appears in [VANT].

[2] As noted earlier in the book, this model is particularly appropriate for space communications. We ignore intersymbol interference here, the major problem in telephone data transmission. See [LUCK] for a detailed treatment of both noise and intersymbol interference.

In Chap. 4 we discussed briefly the possibility of using quadrature amplitude modulation (QAM) to increase digital transmission rates over fixed-bandwidth channels. Following the discussion of binary transmission, we extend the analysis to show how one optimally processes QAM signals received over an additive white-noise channel. It turns out that matched-filter detection is again called for, and, as predicted in Chap. 4, the error performance of these systems deteriorates from the binary case.

QAM transmission is a special case of M-ary transmission, with n binary digits encoded into one of $M = 2^n$ possible signals. It turns out that by encoding into *orthogonal* signals (M different frequencies provide one example), one can reverse the error-performance deterioration and in fact drive the error probability down as far as one likes, thus improving on the binary-system performance. The price paid is an increase in the transmission bandwidth. We show that this improvement in error performance is a special case of the Shannon capacity expression first introduced in Chap. 1, and then referred to again in Chap. 6 in studying PCM system performance. The Shannon capacity expression shows that there must exist coding schemes that reduce the probability of error.

We conclude this chapter by considering coding techniques that provide error detection and error correction as a means of improving digital-transmission performance. Here the addition of extra (redundant) data symbols to the signal binary stream enables error detection and correction to be carried out—at the cost, of course, of increased system complexity and reduction of data rate (or increased bandwidth).

7-1   STATISTICAL DECISION THEORY

It is apparent from all our discussions in this book that the problems of deciding between either of two signals transmitted in binary communication, or of appropriately processing analog signals in AM or FM, are essentially statistical in nature. The signals transmitted are, of course, random to begin with, the noise added enroute or at the receiver can generally only be described statistically, the fading and multiplicative noise possibly encountered enroute can likewise only be described statistically, etc. We must then look to the realm of statistics for techniques that may be directly carried over to the communication field to help develop schemes for optimally transmitting and processing signals.

The fields of statistical decision and estimation theory have proven particularly fruitful in handling the problem of optimum information transmission. Statistical decision theory, as is apparent from the name, deals specifically with the problem of developing statistical tests for optimally deciding between several possible hypotheses. One would expect techniques developed here to be particularly useful in digital communications, detection radar, and other systems where discrete *decisions* have to be made (which one of two signals was transmitted, which one of M signals was transmitted, is it a target or noise, etc.). Statistical estimation theory, on the other hand, deals with methods of estimating the best possible continuous random parameters or time-varying random functions. It is thus applicable to problems of analog transmission. We concentrate here only on statistical decision theory and its application to digital communications.[3] By "optimum" or "best" system we shall mean here for the most part one that minimizes the probability of error.[4]

To bring out the elements of statistical decision theory and its applicability to digital communication, consider the problem of distinguishing between either one of two possible signals received. Assume that s_1 or s_2 has been transmitted and a voltage v received. We sample v, and, based on the value of the sample measured, determine in the best way possible which of the two signals was transmitted. (Later, we shall extend this to the case of many sequential samples.)

In statistical terminology, we are given the value of a statistical sample (or group of samples) and wish to select between either of two alternative hypotheses. Call these H_1 and H_2. Hypothesis H_1 corresponds to the decision "s_1 transmitted"; H_2 of course to the decision "s_2 transmitted."

How does one establish a rule for deciding between the two hypotheses? Note that we can make two types of error. Assuming H_1 true, s_2 may have been transmitted, or alternatively, assuming H_2 true, s_1 may have been transmitted. It is apparent that the total probability of error to be minimized is based on both these errors. It is also apparent that the rule to be chosen will consist of splitting up the one-dimensional space corresponding to all possible values of v into two nonoverlapping (mutually exclusive) regions V_1 and V_2 such that the overall error probability is minimized.[5] We assume that we know the a priori probabilities P_1 and P_2 of transmitting s_1 and s_2, respectively ($P_1 + P_2 = 1$), as well as the *conditional* probability densities $f(v|1)$ and $f(v|2)$, corresponding respectively to the probability of receiving v given s_1 transmitted, and v given s_2 transmitted. A typical example is shown in Fig. 7-1.

We set up the expression for the overall probability of error and then minimize it by adjusting V_1 and V_2. This then provides the desired rule.

Just as in the error-probability calculations of Chap. 6, we may find the probability of error by considering first the probability that v will fall in region V_2 even though a 1 has been transmitted. This is simply

$$\int_{V_2} f(v|1)\, dv$$

Similarly, the probability that v will fall in V_1 even though signal 2 has been

---

[3][WOZE] J. M. Wozencraft and I. M. Jacobs, *Principles of Communication Engineering*, Wiley, New York, 1965, is a classic book that expands on the material in this and subsequent sections. See also [VITE 1966, part 3]. [VANT]; [HELS] C. W. Helstrom, *Statistical Theory of Signal Detection*, Pergamon, New York, 1968; and [SCHW 1975] discuss communications and other application areas.

[4]It is important to keep in mind that the word *optimum* is usually meant in a restricted sense; it refers to the "best" system according to the particular criterion adopted for evaluating the system performance.

[5]More general cost functions than simple error probability can be developed. Generally, the resultant rule is a simple extension of the one developed here, however.

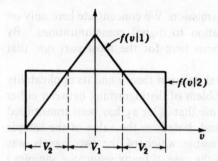

FIGURE 7-1
Choice of binary-decision regions.

transmitted is given by

$$\int_{V_1} f(v|2)\, dv$$

Again, as in Chap. 6, the overall probability P_e that is to be minimized by adjusting V_1 (or V_2) is found by weighting each of the integrals above by its respective a priori probability and then summing the two:

$$P_e = P_1 \int_{V_2} f(v|1)\, dv + P_2 \int_{V_1} f(v|2)\, dv \qquad (7\text{-}1)$$

We use a little trick now to perform the minimization quite directly. Since $V_1 + V_2$ covers all possible values of v, we have

$$\int_{V_1 + V_2} f(v|1)\, dv = 1 = \int_{V_1} f(v|1)\, dv + \int_{V_2} f(v|1)\, dv \qquad (7\text{-}2)$$

We can then eliminate the integral over V_2 in Eq. (7-1), writing instead

$$P_e = P_1 + \int_{V_1} [P_2 f(v|2) - P_1 f(v|1)]\, dv \qquad (7\text{-}3)$$

Since P_1 is a specified number and assumed known, P_e is minimized by choosing the region V_1 appropriately. A little thought indicates that this is done by adjusting V_1 to have the integral term in Eq. (7-3) negative and as large numerically as possible. But we recall that probabilities and density functions are always positive. The solution then corresponds quite simply to picking V_1 as the regions of v corresponding to

$$P_1 f(v|1) > P_2 f(v|2) \qquad (7\text{-}4)$$

This is then the desired decision rule. As an example, let $P_1 = P_2 = \frac{1}{2}$. The region V_1 then corresponds to all values of v where $f(v|1) > f(v|2)$. Three examples are shown in Fig. 7-2.

Note that the first example resembles that of choosing between two gaussian distributions, and shows the optimum decision level occurring precisely at the intersection of the two functions. This agrees of course with the optimum threshold location found in Chap. 6. Some simple mathematics will verify this result. Assume that the two signals transmitted are A and 0, with a priori

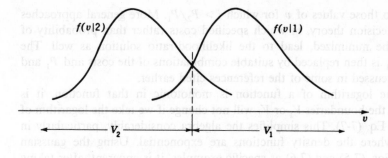

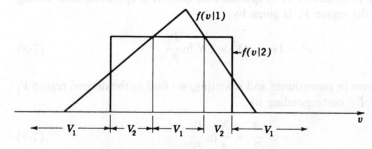

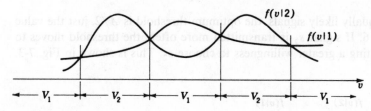

FIGURE 7-2
Examples of binary-decision regions, $P_1 = P_2 = \frac{1}{2}$.

probabilities P_1 and P_2, respectively. Gaussian noise of zero average value and variance N (mean noise power) is added on reception. As in Chap. 6, the two conditional density functions are, respectively,

$$f(v|1) = \frac{1}{\sqrt{2\pi N}} e^{-(v-A)^2/2N} \qquad (7\text{-}5)$$

and

$$f(v|2) = \frac{1}{\sqrt{2\pi N}} e^{-v^2/2N} \qquad (7\text{-}6)$$

The optimum threshold level is now found by substituting into Eq. (7-4).

The optimum decision rule often is written in the equivalent form

$$l \equiv \frac{f(v|1)}{f(v|2)} > \frac{P_2}{P_1} \qquad (7\text{-}7)$$

The parameter l, a function of the sample value v, is called the *likelihood ratio*. The region V_1 corresponding to the decision that S_1 was transmitted then corresponds to those values of v for which $l > P_2/P_1$. More general approaches to optimum-decision theory, in which specified costs rather than probability of error are to be minimized, lead to the likelihood-ratio solution as well. The number P_2/P_1 is then replaced by suitable combinations of the costs and P_1 and P_2. This is discussed in some of the references cited earlier.

Since the logarithm of a function is monotonic in that function, it is apparent that the boundaries V_1 or V_2 will not change if we take the logarithm of both sides of Eq. (7-7). This simplifies the algebra considerably, particularly in those cases where the density functions are exponential. Using the gaussian functions of Eqs. (7-5) and (7-6) as specific examples, it is apparent, after taking logarithms, that the region V_1 is given by

$$v^2 - (v - A)^2 > 2N \ln \frac{P_2}{P_1} \tag{7-8}$$

Expanding the term in parentheses and rewriting, we find as the desired region V_1 all those values of v corresponding to

$$v > \frac{A}{2} + \frac{N}{A} \ln \frac{P_2}{P_1} \tag{7-9}$$

Note that for equally likely signals, the optimum threshold is $A/2$, just the value found in Chap. 6. If signal s_2 is transmitted more often, the threshold moves to the right, indicating a greater willingness to choose s_2. This is shown in Fig. 7-3.

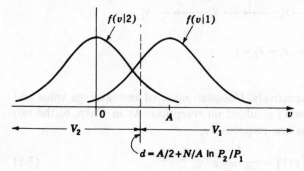

FIGURE 7-3
On–off signals plus gaussian noise.

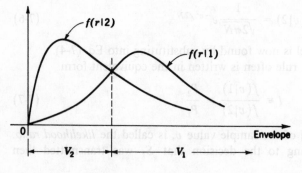

FIGURE 7-4
Envelope-detected signals, optimum decision regions.

As another example, assume OOK transmission, additive gaussian noise, and envelope detection at the receiver. From our discussion in Chap. 6 it is apparent that the detected envelope r is Rayleigh-distributed when a 0 is transmitted, Rician-distributed when a 1 is transmitted. The two envelope density functions are shown sketched in Fig. 7-4, with the optimum decision level shown at their intersection in the case of equally probable transmission.

7-2 SIGNAL VECTORS—MULTIPLE-SAMPLE DETECTION

We have shown how one optimally decides between two signals received on the basis of one received sample. It is apparent that one should be able to improve the signal detectability by making available more received samples. The obvious questions then are:

1. How much improvement is to be expected?
2. What is the optimum decision rule?

In this latter case one alternatively ask: What is the optimum way of processing the samples?

We shall assume for simplicity that we have n *independent* samples on which to base the decision. [For the case of binary pulses in additive gaussian noise this corresponds generally to sampling at intervals $> 1/($bandwidth of the noise). As shown in Chap. 6, the correlation rapidly decreases to zero beyond this point.] These are generated by sequentially sampling the received waveform as in Fig. 7-5. Alternatively, a particular pulse could be repeated n times, each repetition then being sampled once.

The n samples define n-fold density functions. In particular, if signal s_1 is transmitted, we get the n-dimensional conditional-density function

$$f(v_1, v_2, \ldots, v_j, \ldots, v_n|1) = \prod_{j=1}^{n} f(v_j|1)$$

with successive samples assumed independent. Similarly, if s_2 is transmitted, we

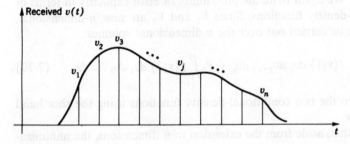

FIGURE 7-5
Generation of n samples for processing.

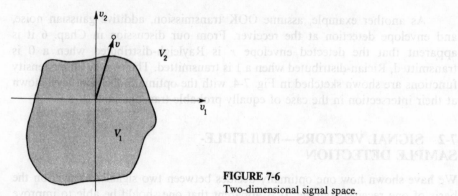

FIGURE 7-6
Two-dimensional signal space.

may write the alternative n-fold conditional-density function

$$f(v_1, v_2, \ldots, v_j, \ldots, v_n | 2) = \prod_{j=1}^{n} f(v_j | 2)$$

As in the one-sample case, we have to assume these functions known. Note that the n samples may be visualized as describing an n-dimensional space, the possible range of values of each serving to define the range of that particular dimension. A little thought indicates that our statistical decision problem now boils down to dividing the n-dimensional space into two mutually exclusive regions V_1 and V_2 ($V_1 + V_2$ corresponding to the entire space of the n samples). We would like to choose the boundary between these two regimes such that the probability of error is minimized. If the n samples fall into region V_1, we declare signal s_1 present, if into region V_2, we declare s_2 present.

The composite samples $v_1, v_2, \ldots, v_j, \ldots, v_n$ now constitute an n-dimensional vector **v**. This geometric and vector approach often simplifies quite considerably the analysis and optimum design of communication systems, and has been widely adopted by communication theorists. An example of the two-dimensional region corresponding to $n = 2$ samples is shown in Fig. 7-6. The received vector **v** is shown falling in region V_2, so that signal s_2 would be declared present.

How do we choose V_1 and V_2 optimally now, in the sense of minimizing the error probability P_e? We again write the probability of error explicitly in terms of the two conditional-density functions. Since V_1 and V_2 are now n-dimensional, the integration must be carried out over the n-dimensional volumes:

$$P_e = P_1 \int_{V_2} f(\mathbf{v}|1) \, dv_1 \, dv_2 \ldots dv_n + P_2 \int_{V_1} f(\mathbf{v}|2) \, dv_1 \, dv_2 \ldots dv_n \quad (7\text{-}10)$$

Here we have written the two conditional-density functions using the shorthand vector notation for **v**.

But note now that, aside from the extension to n dimensions, the minimization process here is identical to that carried out earlier for one dimension. The optimum choice for the region V_1 is thus given by the likelihood ratio

$$l \equiv \frac{f(\mathbf{v}|1)}{f(\mathbf{v}|2)} > \frac{P_2}{P_1} \tag{7-11}$$

As an example assume we again transmit an on–off signal of amplitude A or 0, and gaussian noise is added at the receiver. The received signal-plus-noise voltage $v(t)$ is sampled n times (alternatively, the signal may be assumed repeated n times), and the n samples $v_1, \ldots, v_n$ used to make the decision. The conditional-density functions for the jth sample (assuming the samples independent) are given respectively by

$$f(v_j|1) = \frac{e^{-(v_j - A)^2/2N}}{\sqrt{2\pi N}} \tag{7-12}$$

and

$$f(v_j|2) = \frac{e^{-v_j^2/2N}}{\sqrt{2\pi N}} \tag{7-13}$$

The n-dimensional density functions are products of these individual sample functions. Again, taking logarithms to simplify, we find

$$\ln l = \frac{1}{2N} \left[\sum_{j=1}^{n} v_j^2 - \sum_{j=1}^{n} (v_j - A)^2 \right] > \ln \frac{P_2}{P_1} \tag{7-14}$$

In the special case where $P_2 = P_1 = \frac{1}{2}$, we have the region V_1 defined by

$$\sum_{j=1}^{n} v_j^2 > \sum_{j=1}^{n} (v_j - A)^2 \tag{7-15}$$

Note, however, that not only can we define a vector $\mathbf{v} \equiv (v_1, v_2, \ldots, v_n)$, but we can talk of two n-dimensional vectors $\mathbf{s}_1 \equiv (s_1^{(1)}, s_2^{(1)}, \ldots, s_n^{(1)})$ and $\mathbf{s}_2 \equiv (s_1^{(2)}, s_2^{(2)}, \ldots, s_n^{(2)})$, where the subscripts represent the sample number and the superscripts the particular signal, 1 or 2, under consideration. In this special case $\mathbf{s}_1 \equiv (A, A, A, \ldots, A)$ and $\mathbf{s}_2 \equiv (0, 0, 0, 0, \ldots, 0)$, since we have assumed a rectangular pulse of height A throughout the n-sample interval (Fig. 7-7).

In is now apparent that the right-hand side of Eq. (7-15) represents the squared length of the vector $\mathbf{v} - \mathbf{s}_1$, and the left-hand side the squared length of the vector $\mathbf{v} - \mathbf{s}_2$. In terms of the usual vector notation we have the squared length of a vector $\mathbf{a}$ given by the dot product $\mathbf{a} \cdot \mathbf{a}$, so that Eq. (7-15) may be equally well given by

$$(\mathbf{v} - \mathbf{s}_2) \cdot (\mathbf{v} - \mathbf{s}_2) > (\mathbf{v} - \mathbf{s}_1) \cdot (\mathbf{v} - \mathbf{s}_1) \tag{7-16}$$

The n-dimensional vector notation with dot product is just the extension to n dimensions of the common three-dimensional vector notation. [The reader may find it instructive to use arbitrary but known pulse shapes $s_1(t)$ and $s_2(t)$ for the two signals. Vectors $\mathbf{s}_1$ and $\mathbf{s}_2$ can then again be defined as the composite of the n samples for each, and Eq. (7-16) obtained in this more general case.] The interpretation of the optimum decision rule in this case of two signals plus

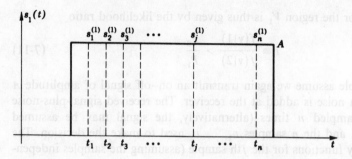

FIGURE 7-7
n-dimensional signal s_1.

gaussian noise is now apparent from Eq. (7-16). Pick signal s_1 if the distance between the received vector v and the known vector s_1 is less than the distance between v and s_2. This is shown graphically in Fig. 7-8 for the special case of two dimensions.

Note that the receiver must have stored replicas of both vectors s_1 and s_2 [or, equivalently, the n sample values of $s_1(t)$ and of $s_2(t)$]. It measures the received vector v, and then forms the necessary dot products and decides on s_1 or s_2, following the rule of Eq. (7-16).

The rule may be simplified in this case, however. For note that in both Eqs. (7-15) and (7-16) a common factor

$$\mathbf{v} \cdot \mathbf{v} = \sum_{j=1}^{n} v_j^2$$

may be canceled out on left- and right-hand sides. We then have remaining the

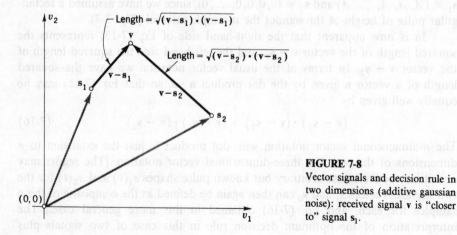

FIGURE 7-8
Vector signals and decision rule in two dimensions (additive gaussian noise): received signal v is "closer to" signal s_1.

rather simple expression

$$\sum_{j=1}^{n} v_j > \frac{nA}{2} \tag{7-17}$$

for the special case of on–off signals. In words: Sum the n received samples and see if the sum exceeds the specified threshold $nA/2$. Note that this is just the extension to n dimensions of the one-dimensional result obtained earlier. The interesting point here is that the rule calls for the *sum* of the received samples. This is specifically due to the assumption of known binary signals in additive gaussian noise. In examples to follow we shall find different rules for different assumed statistics.

More generally, if instead of on–off binary signals we assume two *arbitrary*, equally likely binary signals $s_1(t)$ and $s_2(t)$, the n samples of each define, respectively, the two vectors s_1 and s_2. In this case, the optimum decision rule from Eq. (7-16) becomes, after expanding the dot products and dropping the common term $v \cdot v$,

$$v \cdot (s_1 - s_2) > \frac{s_1 \cdot s_1 - s_2 \cdot s_2}{2} \tag{7-18}$$

In terms of the samples themselves, we have

$$\sum_{j=1}^{n} v_j \left[s_j^{(1)} - s_j^{(2)} \right] > \sum_{j=1}^{n} \frac{s_j^{(1)^2} - s_j^{(2)^2}}{2} \tag{7-19}$$

The receiver now evaluates a weighted sum, weighting each received sample v_j with the stored samples $s_j^{(1)} - s_j^{(2)}$ before adding. The final sum is then compared with a known threshold.

The boundary between regions V_1 and V_2 is found by replacing the inequalities in the equations above by equalities. In n dimensions the boundary between regions V_1 and V_2, given for additive gaussian noise by either Eq. (7-17), Eq. (7-18), or Eq. (7-19), is called a *hyperplane*. For the special case of on–off signals in two dimensions this degenerates into the line $v_1 + v_2 = A$, shown sketched in Fig. 7-9.

How much improvement does the use of the n samples provide over one sample? The answer of course depends on the particular signal shapes and noise statistics assumed. Consider, however, the on–off case as a specific example. If the two signals are assumed equally likely for simplicity, either signal is equally likely as well to be mistaken for the other. The probability of an error is then the probability that vector v, with s_1 transmitted, appears in region V_2. From Eq. (7-17) this corresponds to the sum of the samples falling *below* the threshold level $nA/2$. Rather than calculate the probability of the n-dimensional gaussian vector v falling into the region V_2, we can deal with the much simpler sum of the v_j's. We note that with the v_j's each gaussian, the sum must be gaussian as well. In particular, the variance of the sum is the sum of the variances, or just nN in this

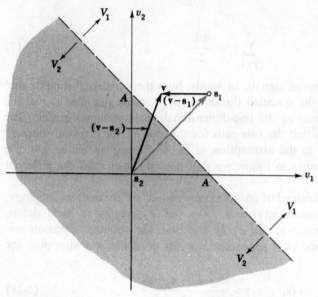

FIGURE 7-9
Decision rule for on–off signals ($s_2 = 0$) in two dimensions (additive gaussian noise).

case, while the expected values add as well.

Letting

$$y \equiv \sum_{j=1}^{n} v_j$$

we then have the two conditional-density functions, one for signal s_1, the other for s_2,

$$f(y|1) = \frac{e^{-(y-nA)^2/2nN}}{\sqrt{2\pi nN}} \qquad (7\text{-}20)$$

and

$$f(y|2) = \frac{e^{-y^2/2nN}}{\sqrt{2\pi nN}} \qquad (7\text{-}21)$$

These are shown sketched in Fig. 7-10. The decision level $nA/2$ is of course just at the intersection of the two curves. The probability of error is then just that of the single-sample case, but with the signal amplitude A replaced by nA, the noise power N replaced by nN. The improvement obtained by using the n samples optimally (adding the received samples and requiring the sum to exceed a threshold level) corresponds to a net increase in the single sample signal-to-noise ratio $A/\sqrt{N}$ by a factor of $\sqrt{n}$. The n-sample system thus corresponds to a single-sample system with effective SNR given by $\sqrt{n}\,A/\sqrt{N}$. The SNR in power improves linearly with n.

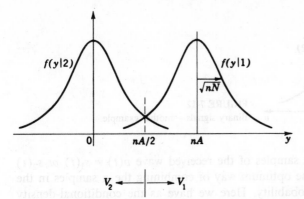

FIGURE 7-10
Alternative error calculation, additive gaussian noise.

Alternatively, for the same probability of error the peak signal power A^2 may be reduced by a factor of n if n samples are added. There is thus an exchange of power and time (or bandwidth). For to obtain large numbers of independent samples, the signal duration must be increased accordingly. The bit rate must thus be decreased. (The same is true if instead of lengthening the signal duration the signal pulses are always repeated n times.) Note, however, that the signal *energy* $E = \int s^2(t)\,dt$ remains fixed. For if the basic bit interval is τ and the pulse height $\sqrt{n}\,A$, then $E = nA^2\tau$. If pulses of height A and duration $n\tau$ are now transmitted, E remains the same (Fig. 7-11). Ultimately, then, it is the signal energy that determines the probability of error. This was first noted in discussing matched filters in Chap. 6. We shall return to these points and tie them together once and for all in the next section.

We have spent substantial time on the gaussian case because of its great utility and importance in communication problems. We shall also extend the ideas further in the next section as well as those following. We now consider some other examples of optimum signal processing for minimum probability of error.

Assume as the first example that the two signals s_1 and s_2 are zero-mean gaussian-distributed variables, but with differing variances σ_1^2, and σ_2^2, respec-

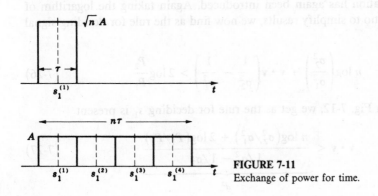

FIGURE 7-11
Exchange of power for time.

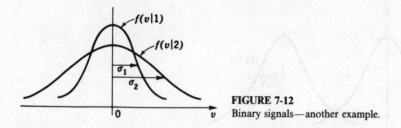

FIGURE 7-12
Binary signals—another example.

tively. Again n independent samples of the received wave $v(t) = s_1(t)$ *or* $s_2(t)$ are taken, and we require the optimum way of combining the n samples in the sense of minimum error probability. Here we have as the conditional-density functions for the jth sample,

$$f(v_j|1) = \frac{e^{-v_j^2/2\sigma_1^2}}{\sqrt{2\pi\sigma_1^2}} \tag{7-22}$$

and

$$f(v_j|2) = \frac{e^{-v_j^2/2\sigma_2^2}}{\sqrt{2\pi\sigma_2^2}} \tag{7-23}$$

These are sketched in Fig. 7-12.

The n-dimensional density functions needed for calculating the likelihood ratio of Eq. (7-11) are then, with independent samples assumed,

$$f(\mathbf{v}|1) = \frac{\exp\left[-\dfrac{1}{2\sigma_1^2}\displaystyle\sum_{j=1}^{n} v_j^2\right]}{\left(2\pi\sigma_1^2\right)^{n/2}} = \frac{e^{-(1/2\sigma_1^2)\mathbf{v}\cdot\mathbf{v}}}{\left(2\pi\sigma_1^2\right)^{n/2}} \tag{7-24}$$

and

$$f(\mathbf{v}|2) = \frac{\exp\left[-\dfrac{1}{2\sigma_2^2}\displaystyle\sum_{j=1}^{n} v_j^2\right]}{\left(2\pi\sigma_2^2\right)^{n/2}} = \frac{e^{-(1/2\sigma_2^2)\mathbf{v}\cdot\mathbf{v}}}{\left(2\pi\sigma_2^2\right)^{n/2}} \tag{7-25}$$

Here vector notation has again been introduced. Again taking the logarithm of the likelihood ratio to simplify results, we now find as the rule for deciding signal s_1 present,

$$n\log\left(\frac{\sigma_2^2}{\sigma_1^2}\right) + \mathbf{v}\cdot\mathbf{v}\left(\frac{1}{\sigma_2^2} - \frac{1}{\sigma_1^2}\right) > 2\log\frac{P_2}{P_1} \tag{7-26}$$

If $\sigma_1^2 < \sigma_2^2$, as in Fig. 7-12, we get as the rule for deciding s_1 is present

$$\mathbf{v}\cdot\mathbf{v} < \underbrace{\frac{n\log(\sigma_2^2/\sigma_1^2) + 2\log(P_1/P_2)}{1/\sigma_1^2 - 1/\sigma_2^2}}_{d^2} \tag{7-27}$$

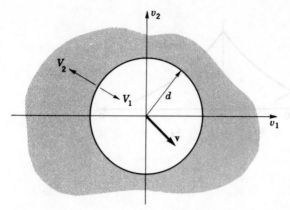

FIGURE 7-13
Decision regions for case of Fig. 7-12.

The square of the length of vector **v** is to be compared with a threshold. If

$$\mathbf{v} \cdot \mathbf{v} \equiv \sum_{j=1}^{n} v_j^2 > d^2$$

we declare s_2 present; if $< d^2$, we declare s_1 present. The geometry here is again shown in the two-dimensional case in Fig. 7-13. In the n-dimensional case the boundary between V_1 and V_2 corresponds to a hypersphere concentric with the origin. Points inside the sphere correspond to s_1, those outside to s_2. This is consistent with our intuition, for with s_1 and s_2 the random gaussian variables of Fig. 7-12, it is apparent that polarity should play no role in detection here. One would expect signal s_2 to have larger amplitudes, on the average, than signal s_1. Squaring the received samples eliminates polarity from consideration. We then compare the sum of the squared values with the threshold d^2.

As a second additional example we assume polar signals of amplitude $\pm A$ transmitted. Noise is again added, but this time the noise probability-density function is given by the laplacian function

$$f(n) = \frac{1}{2c} e^{-|n|/c} \tag{7-28}$$

This is sketched in Fig. 7-14. It is left to the reader to show that the function is

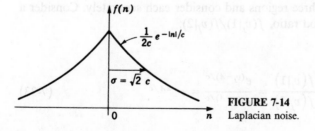

FIGURE 7-14
Laplacian noise.

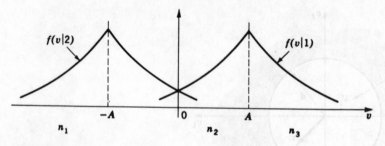

FIGURE 7-15
Polar signals in laplacian noise.

properly normalized and that the standard deviation (rms noise) is given by

$$\sigma = \sqrt{2}\,c \tag{7-29}$$

This density function is sometimes used to model additive impulse or burst-type noise. The simple exponential behavior, rather than the quadratic exponential of the gaussian density function, means higher amplitudes have correspondingly higher probabilities of appearing, a characteristic of this type of impulse noise.

The received signal sample v is then

$$v = \begin{Bmatrix} s_1 \\ \text{or} \\ s_2 \end{Bmatrix} + n \tag{7-30}$$

The two conditional-density functions are given by

$$f(v|1) = \frac{e^{-|v-A|/c}}{2c} \tag{7-31}$$

and

$$f(v|2) = \frac{e^{-|v+A|/c}}{2c} \tag{7-32}$$

as sketched in Fig. 7-15.

We now sample the received signal v n times and again ask for the optimum processing procedure. With independent samples assumed we again set up the likelihood ratio as in Eq. (7-11) and proceed to crank out the result. Here we have to be somewhat careful, however, because of the shape of $f(n)$. To take into account the abrupt change in the form of $f(v|1)$ and $f(v|2)$ at $v = \pm A$, we break the range of v into three regions and consider each separately. Consider a typical term in the likelihood ratio, $f(v_j|1)/f(v_j|2)$:

1. $v_j < -A$. Then

$$\frac{f(v_j|1)}{f(v_j|2)} = \frac{e^{(v_j-A)/c}}{e^{(v_j+A)/c}} = e^{-2A/c} \tag{7-33}$$

Note that the dependence on v_j cancels out. The only knowledge retained is the fact that $v_j < -A$. Assume now that n_1 of the n samples available fall in this range of v_j. There are then n_1 terms like Eq. (7-33) in the likelihood ratio, all to be multiplied together. Again taking the natural logarithm of the likelihood ratio to simplify results, it is apparent that these n_1 terms in the likelihood ratio contribute

$$-\frac{2n_1 A}{c}$$

to the total log l.

2. $v_j > A$. Here

$$\frac{f(v_j|1)}{f(v_j|2)} = \frac{e^{-(v_j - A)/c}}{e^{-(v_j + A)/c}} = e^{2A/c} \tag{7-34}$$

Again the dependence on v_j cancels out, and each term in log l that corresponds to $v_j > A$ contributes $+2A/c$ to the total. Assuming that n_3 of n samples have $v_j > A$, we get as the contribution to log l,

$$+\frac{2n_3 A}{c}$$

3. $-A < v_j < A$. Here

$$\frac{f(v_j|1)}{f(v_j|2)} = \frac{e^{(v_j - A)/c}}{e^{-(v_j + A)/c}} = e^{2v_j/c} \tag{7-35}$$

Assume that n_2 of the n samples fall in this range. Taking logarithms, we find these n_2 terms in the likelihood ratio contribute the term

$$\frac{2}{c} \sum_{j=1}^{n_2} v_j$$

to the total.

The three numbers n_1, n_2, and n_3 are indicated in Fig. 7-15. It is apparent that we have the constraint

$$n_1 + n_2 + n_3 = n \tag{7-36}$$

Combining all three terms, the rule for deciding on signal s_1 now becomes

$$(n_3 - n_1)A + \sum_{j=1}^{n_2} v_j > \frac{c}{2}\ln\frac{P_2}{P_1} \tag{7-37}$$

The interpretation here is quite interesting. The optimum processor consists of three-level threshold circuitry followed by an appropriate counter and an adding device. If the threshold circuitry detects a sample in the $v_j > A$ region, a positive count of A is added to the counter. If a sample in the range $v_j < -A$ appears, A is *subtracted* from the counter. If $-A < v_j < A$, the sample value is stored in the adding circuit. At the end of the n samples, the counter and adder outputs are summed. If they exceed the decision level $(c/2)\ln(P_2/P_1)$, s_1 is declared present; otherwise s_2 is assumed present. Note that such a processor lends itself nicely to digital circuitry. Note also that if A/σ is small (small SNR), the number of samples n_2 falling in the central region will tend to be small, the adder output will become negligible, and the counter alone will suffice.

7-3   OPTIMUM BINARY TRANSMISSION

We now focus attention on one particular case of binary transmission: the transmission of binary symbols $s_1(t)$ or $s_2(t)$ in additive gaussian noise. We assume a fixed binary interval T seconds long and ask for both the optimum receiver structure and optimum signal shapes $s_1(t)$ and $s_2(t)$. Part of the answer is already available to us. We showed in the previous section that with n samples of the received signal plus noise the optimum processing was that described by the vector Eq. (7-18), or its equivalent Eq. (7-19). Thus choose $s_1(t)$ if

$$\mathbf{v}\cdot(\mathbf{s}_1 - \mathbf{s}_2) > \frac{\|\mathbf{s}_1\|^2 - \|\mathbf{s}_2\|^2}{2} \tag{7-38}$$

(Here we use the symbol $\|\ \|$ for magnitude of a vector. Also recall the assumption that the a priori probabilities P_1 and P_2 are equal.)

We now ask the obvious question: In a given interval T, how many samples n should we use? To answer this we assume the noise is band-limited white noise, with spectral density $G_n(f) = n_0/2$, over the range of frequencies $\pm B_n$ hertz. The total noise power is then $N = n_0 B_n$. We assume the two signals $s_1(t)$ and $s_2(t)$ band-limited over the band B, $B \ll B_n$.

For this model of noise we recall the autocorrelation function, the Fourier transform of the spectral density, is just

$$R_n(\tau) = N\frac{\sin 2\pi\tau B_n}{2\pi\tau B_n} \tag{7-39}$$

Both $G_n(f)$ and $R_n(\tau)$ are shown sketched in Fig. 7-16. Note that there is zero correlation between samples spaced multiples of $1/2B_n$ seconds apart. For gaussian noise this further indicates the samples are *independent*. There are thus $n = 2B_n T$ independent samples available to us. Recall also from the sampling theorem in Chap. 3 that samples spaced $1/2B_n$ seconds apart suffice to uniquely characterize a band-limited signal. In fact, we indicated that with the sample values $n(j/2B_n)$, $j = 0, \pm 1, \pm 2, \ldots$, known, we could reproduce the original wave $n(t)$ as

$$n(t) = \sum_j n\!\left(\frac{j}{2B_n}\right)\frac{\sin 2\pi B_n(t - j/2B_n)}{2\pi B_n(t - j/2B_n)} \tag{7-40}$$

The one catch here is that all samples $j = (-\infty, +\infty)$ must be known, whereas we only have $n = 2B_n T$ of them. For $B_n T \gg 1$, however, Eq. (7-40)

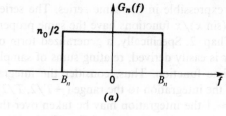

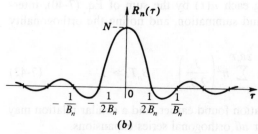

FIGURE 7-16
Band-limited white noise. (*a*) Spectral density. (*b*) Autocorrelation function.

provides a good approximation to $n(t)$ in the binary interval T, and we shall make this assumption.

The $(\sin x)/x$ functions in Eq. (7-40) have an interesting property that proves extremely useful to us. They are examples of orthogonal functions, with the property that

$$\int_{-\infty}^{\infty} \frac{\sin \pi (2B_n t - k)}{\pi (2B_n t - k)} \cdot \frac{\sin \pi (2B_n t - m)}{\pi (2B_n t - m)} \, dt = \frac{1}{2B_n} \delta_{km} \qquad (7\text{-}41)$$

Here δ_{km} is the Kronecker delta

$$\delta_{km} = 1 \qquad k = m$$
$$= 0 \qquad k \neq m$$

The integral of the product of two $(\sin x)/x$ functions displaced in time is thus zero. The Fourier series of Chap. 2 is another example of a set of orthogonal functions, in which the integral of the product over a specified interval (finite or infinite) is zero.

The proof of the orthogonality of the $(\sin x)/x$ functions is left as an exercise for the reader. [As a hint, consider the integral of Eq. (7-41) to be a convolution integral. It is then equal to the integral containing the product of the Fourier transforms of the two $(\sin x)/x$ functions. These are just constants over the range $\pm B_n$, with appropriate exponential phase factors. It is then easy to show the integral of the resultant exponential terms goes to zero.]

Now consider the two binary signals $s_1(t)$ and $s_2(t)$. As noted above, these are assumed bandlimited to a bandwidth $B < B_n$. Say these are oversampled at a rate of B_n samples/s. Then, from the discussion of Chap. 3, they too are representable by a $(\sin x)/x$ series of the form of (7-40), with the samples of $s_1(t)$ and $s_2(t)$, respectively, replacing those of $n(t)$. The received signal $v(t) =$

$[s_1(t)$ or $s_2(t)] + n(t)$ is thus equally expressible in the same series. The series expansions in terms of the orthogonal $(\sin x)/x$ functions have the same properties as those of the Fourier series of Chap. 2. Specifically, a generalized form of the Parseval theorem mentioned earlier is easily derived, relating sums of sample values to an integral of the analog time function. Thus, consider the integral $\int n^2(t)\, dt$. [Although we should restrict the integration to the range $(-T/2, T/2)$, over which $n(t)$ is defined, with $B_n T \gg 1$ the integration may be taken over the infinite range $(-\infty, \infty)$.] Replacing each $n(t)$ by the sum of Eq. (7-40), interchanging the order of integration and summation, and noting the orthogonality relation of Eq. (7-41), we find

$$\int_0^T n^2(t)\, dt \doteq \frac{1}{2B_n} \sum_{j=1}^{2B_n T} n^2\left(\frac{j}{2B_n}\right) \qquad B_n T \gg 1 \qquad (7\text{-}42)$$

This is the same as the Parseval relation found earlier, and a similar relation may readily be derived the same way for *all* orthogonal series expansions.

If we now consider two time functions $v(t)$ and $s(t)$, representable by (7-40) as well, we readily demonstrate in the same way that

$$\int_0^T v(t)s(t)\, dt \doteq \frac{1}{2B_n} \sum_{j=1}^{2B_n T} v\left(\frac{j}{2B_n}\right) s\left(\frac{j}{2B_n}\right) \qquad (7\text{-}43)$$

But this is quite interesting, for if we look at the optimum processor for binary signals in gaussian noise, Eq. (7-38), we note that the vector products shown are just in the form of the right-hand side of Eq. (7-43). Specifically, then, applying Parseval's theorem to both sides of Eq. (7-38), we find the optimum processor to be equally well given by

$$\int_0^T v(t)[s_1(t) - s_2(t)]\, dt > \frac{1}{2}\int_0^T \left[s_1^2(t) - s_2^2(t)\right] dt \qquad (7\text{-}44)$$

Alternatively, note that the integrals on the right-hand side above are just the respective energies in the signals. The inequality can thus be written

$$\int_0^T v(t)[s_1(t) - s_2(t)]\, dt > \frac{E_1 - E_2}{2} \qquad (7\text{-}44a)$$

with $\qquad E_1 \equiv \int_0^T s_1^2(t)\, dt \qquad E_2 \equiv \int_0^T s_2^2(t)\, dt$

The interpretation here is quite interesting. It says that instead of the digital operations on the samples indicated by Eq. (7-38), one may equally well take the incoming signal $v(t)$, multiply it by two stored replicas of $s_1(t)$ and $s_2(t)$, integrate, and sample the resultant output every T seconds to see if it exceeds a specified threshold. Note that the $s_1(t)$ and $s_2(t)$ inserted at the receiver must be precisely in phase with the $s_1(t)$ or $s_2(t)$ portion of the received $v(t)$. The resultant operation is nothing more than our old friend coherent or synchronous detection. In the general form of Eq. (7-44a) it is also often called correlation

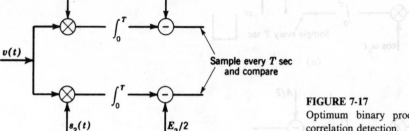

FIGURE 7-17
Optimum binary processor—
correlation detection.

detection. A further alternative form may be obtained by separating the s_1 and s_2 terms:

$$\int_0^T v(t)s_1(t) - \frac{E_1}{2} > \int_0^T v(t)s_2(t)\,dt - \frac{E_2}{2} \qquad (7\text{-}44b)$$

The E_1 and E_2 thus serve as fixed-bias terms to equalize the detector outputs. The correlation detector and sampler of Eq. (7-44b) is shown sketched in Fig. 7-17.

The discussion above has focused on baseband signals and noise. What if the signals are the high-frequency modulated carriers of Chaps. 4 and 6? Let the additive noise now be band-limited white noise centered at the carrier frequency f_0 of the signal. Prob. 6-44a shows that the autocorrelation function of this noise process is given by

$$R_n(\tau) = N\frac{\sin \pi B_T \tau}{\pi B_T \tau}\cos 2\pi f_0\tau \qquad B_T = 2B_n$$

This again has the $(\sin x)/x$ form, modulating the carrier term, and goes to zero at values of τ spaced $1/B_T = 1/2B_n$ apart. This high-frequency band-limited white-noise model thus has the same property as that of the narrowband case, and all of the analysis above still applies.

As an example, let $s_1(t) = \cos \omega_0 t$, $s_2(t) = -\cos \omega_0 t$, just the PSK signals of Chap. 4. Then $E_1 = E_2$, and the correlation detector of Fig. 7-17 becomes the synchronous detector discussed previously. This is shown in Fig. 7-18a. The integrator shown following synchronous detection is the integrate-and-dump circuit first encountered in Sec. 6-8 in discussing matched filtering. It was encountered again in Sec. 6-9 in discussing heterodyne detection of coherent light-wave systems. As noted there, the integrator provides the necessary low-pass filtering as part of the synchronous detection process. If $s_1(t) = A\cos \omega_0 t$, $s_2(t) = 0$, we have the OOK signal of Chap. 4. Then

$$E_1 = \int_0^T A^2\cos^2 \omega_0 t \doteq \frac{A^2T}{2}$$

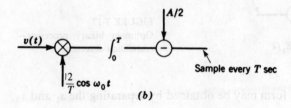

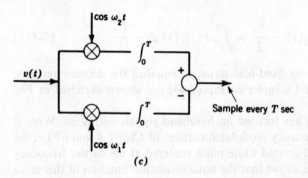

FIGURE 7-18
Examples of Fig. 7-17. (a) PSK synchronous detector. (b) OOK synchronous detector. (c) FSK synchronous detector.

if $\omega_0 T \gg 2\pi$, and the processing called for is just

$$\frac{2}{T}\int_0^T v(t)\cos\omega_0 t\, dt > \frac{A}{2}$$

This corresponds of course to synchronous detection, followed by the $A/2$ decision level (Fig. 7-18b). Finally, if $s_1(t) = \cos\omega_1 t$, $s_2(t) = \cos\omega_2 t$, $E_1 = E_2$, we get the FSK synchronous detector of Fig. 7-18c.

There is still a further interpretation of the optimum processor that leads directly to the matched filter of Chap. 6. The integral of Eq. (7-44a) may be rewritten as the following convolution integral:

$$\int_0^T v(t)[h_1(T - t) - h_2(T - t)]\, dt > \frac{E_1 - E_2}{2} \qquad (7\text{-}44c)$$

where
$$h_1(T - t) \equiv s_1(t)$$
$$h_1(t) = s_1(T - t)$$
and
$$h_2(T - t) \equiv s_2(t) \qquad (7\text{-}45)$$
$$h_2(t) = s_2(T - t)$$

By taking Fourier transforms of both sides of Eq. (7-45), it is apparent that we

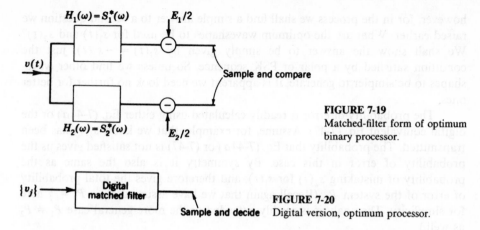

FIGURE 7-19
Matched-filter form of optimum binary processor.

FIGURE 7-20 Sample and decide   Digital version, optimum processor.

must have

$$H_1(\omega) = e^{-j\omega T} S_1^*(\omega) \tag{7-46}$$

and

$$H_2(\omega) = e^{-j\omega T} S_2^*(\omega)$$

—just our earlier (Chap. 6) conditions for a matched filter. The optimum processor may thus be drawn in the matched-filter form of Fig. 7-19. This, in the special cases referred to above, is identical with the matched-filter formulation we obtained in Chap. 6. There we wanted to maximize a SNR in order to decrease the probability of error. Here we have shown that one can do no better—provided that the assumptions made in Chap. 6 are valid. Thus we assume negligible intersymbol interference, with band-limited white gaussian noise the only possible source of binary error.

   Although we have stressed the analog processors of Figs. 7-17 and 7-19, it is apparent that with modern integrated circuits digital processing is often to be preferred. One then seeks ways of implementing Eq. (7-38), or its digital equivalents, directly. One may consider carrying out the process

$$\frac{1}{2B_n} \sum_{j=1}^{n=2B_nT} v_j \left[s_1\left(\frac{j}{2B_n}\right) - s_2\left(\frac{j}{2B_n}\right) \right] > \frac{E_1 - E_2}{2} \tag{7-47}$$

directly, using the incoming samples v_j and stored signal samples, or, alternatively, pass the successive incoming samples v_j through a *digital* matched filter for processing. This is indicated in Fig. 7-20.

Optimum Waveshapes

It is apparent that the calculation of probability of error for the optimum binary processor must lead to the same erfc x curves obtained in Chap. 6, since we have just demonstrated the equivalence of the *ad hoc* detectors discussed there to the optimum processors studied here. It is still useful to repeat the calculation, however, for in the process we shall find a simple answer to a second question we raised earlier. What are the optimum waveshapes to be used for $s_1(t)$ and $s_2(t)$? We shall show the answer to be simply given by $s_1(t) = -s_2(t)$, just the condition satisfied by a polar or PSK sequence. So unless we find other wave-shapes to be simpler to generate, it is apparent we need look no further for better ones.

The probability of error is readily calculated using either Eq. (7-44a) or the digital equivalent Eq. (7-47). Assume, for example, that we know $s_1(t)$ has been transmitted. The probability that Eq. (7-44a) or (7-47) is not satisfied gives us the probability of error in this case. By symmetry it is also the same as the probability of mistaking $s_2(t)$ for $s_1(t)$, and therefore gives the total probability of error of the system P_e. (Recall again that we have assumed $P_1 = P_2 = \frac{1}{2}$ here for simplicity. The analysis is readily extended to the more general case $P_1 \neq P_2$ as well.)

With $s_1(t)$ transmitted, the received signal $v(t)$ is

$$v(t) = s_1(t) + n(t) \tag{7-48}$$

The probability of error is then simply the probability that

$$\int_0^T [n(t) + s_1(t)][s_1(t) - s_2(t)]\, dt < \frac{E_1 - E_2}{2}$$

or, alternatively, using the Parseval identity,

$$\frac{1}{2B_n} \sum_{j=1}^{2B_nT} (n_j + s_{1j})(s_{1j} - s_{2j}) < \frac{E_1 - E_2}{2}$$

[We have used the simpler notation s_{1j} and s_{2j} to represent the jth samples of $s_1(t)$ and $s_2(t)$, respectively.] Simplifying by leaving the $n(t)$ term only on the left-hand side, and recalling the definitions of E_1 and E_2,

$$E_1 \equiv \int_0^T s_1^2(t)\, dt \doteq \frac{1}{2B_n} \sum_{j=1}^{2B_nT} s_{1j}^2$$

$$\tag{7-49}$$

$$E_2 \equiv \int_0^T s_2^2(t)\, dt \doteq \frac{1}{2B_n} \sum_{j=1}^{2B_nT} s_{2j}^2$$

we get as the condition for an error to occur

$$y \equiv \int_0^T n(t)[s_1(t) - s_2(t)\, dt] < -b \equiv -\frac{1}{2} \int_0^T [s_1(t) - s_2(t)]^2\, dt \tag{7-50}$$

Equivalently, using the sample values, an error occurs if

$$y \equiv \frac{1}{2B_n} \sum_{j=1}^{2B_nT} n_j(s_{1j} - s_{2j}) < -b \tag{7-51}$$

But the noise $n(t)$ is assumed gaussian. The random variable y is then gaussian as well. [This is apparent either from Eq. (7-51), where y is defined as the weighted sum of $2B_nT$ gaussian variables n_j, or equally well from Eq. (7-50), describing y as the output of a *linear* matched filter with $n(t)$ applied at the input.] The expected value and variance of y are given very simply by

$$E(y) = \frac{1}{2B_n} \sum_{j=1}^{2B_n T} E(n_j)(s_{1j} - s_{2j}) = 0 \tag{7-52}$$

(we have assumed zero-mean noise), and

$$\sigma_y^2 = E[y - E(y)]^2$$

$$= \left(\frac{1}{2B_n}\right)^2 E\left[\sum_i \sum_j n_i n_j (s_{1i} - s_{2i})(s_{1j} - s_{2j})\right]$$

$$= \left(\frac{1}{2B_n}\right)^2 \sum_i \sum_j E(n_i n_j)(s_{1i} - s_{2i})(s_{1j} - s_{2j}) \tag{7-53}$$

interchanging summation and expectation.

Recall, however, that for band-limited white noise, the samples spaced $1/2B_n$ seconds apart are *uncorrelated*. Also, $E(n_i^2) = N$ [see Eq. (7-39)]. Therefore, $E(n_i n_j) = N\delta_{ij}$. Equation (7-53) then simplifies to

$$\sigma_y^2 = \frac{N}{(2B_n)^2} \sum_{j=1}^{2B_n T} (s_{1j} - s_{2j})^2 = \frac{N}{2B_n} \int_0^T [s_1(t) - s_2(t)]^2 \, dt$$

$$= \frac{n_0}{2} \int_0^T [s_1(t) - s_2(t)]^2 \, dt \tag{7-53a}$$

again using the Parseval relation. Here we have also put $N = n_0 B_n$ for the band-limited white noise. (Recall that $n_0/2$ is the band-limited spectral density. See Fig. 7-16a.)

The probability density of the variable y defined by Eqs. (7-50) and (7-51) is then

$$f(y) = \frac{1}{\sqrt{2\pi\sigma_y^2}} e^{-y^2/2\sigma_y^2} \tag{7-54}$$

and the probability of error is just

$$P_e = \int_{-\infty}^{-b} \frac{e^{-y^2/2\sigma_y^2} \, dy}{\sqrt{2\pi\sigma_y^2}}$$

$$= \int_{-\infty}^{-b/\sqrt{2}\,\sigma_y} \frac{e^{-x^2} \, dx}{\sqrt{\pi}}$$

$$= \tfrac{1}{2} \operatorname{erfc} \frac{b}{\sqrt{2}\,\sigma_y} \tag{7-55}$$

The appropriate integration to obtain P_e is indicated by the shaded area in Fig. 7-21.

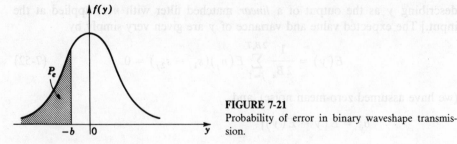

FIGURE 7-21
Probability of error in binary waveshape transmission.

Using the definition of b in Eq. (7-50) and that of σ_y^2 in Eq. (7-53a), we have as the final result for P_e,

$$P_e = \tfrac{1}{2}\operatorname{erfc}\frac{a}{2\sqrt{2}} \qquad (7\text{-}55a)$$

where the new parameter a is defined by

$$a^2 \equiv \int_0^T \frac{(s_1 - s_2)^2\, dt}{n_0/2} \qquad (7\text{-}56)$$

This is precisely the result obtained earlier in Chap. 6, in discussing high-frequency binary transmission. There it was obtained in a rather *ad hoc* fashion, by showing that the three cases considered, OOK, PSK, and FSK transmission, could all be subsumed in a probability-of-error expression identical to $(7\text{-}55a)$ [see Eq. (6-115)], with the parameter a defined appropriately in each case. Here we have shown that $(7\text{-}55a)$ is in fact more general: *any* form of binary communication in the presence of additive gaussian noise will have a probability-of-error expression given by $(7\text{-}55a)$, with the parameter a defined in terms of the two signals by (7-56).

As a check, consider the three types of high-frequency binary transmission considered in Chap. 6. For each of these we first write the probability-of-error expression obtained, assuming matched filtering, in Chap. 6, and then show it is in fact given by Eqs. $(7\text{-}55a)$ and (7-56). This thus repeats the calculations of Chap. 6. We then point out more generally that these two equations enable us to determine the *optimum* waveshapes to be used in the presence of additive gaussian noise.

In all three examples below we assume rectangular shaping for simplicity. Sinusoidal roll-off shaping, or Nyquist shaping more generally, as described in Chaps. 3 and 4, could be handled just as well by incorporating it in the expressions for $s_1(t)$ and $s_2(t)$.

1. OOK:

$$P_e = \tfrac{1}{2}\operatorname{erfc}\left(\frac{1}{2}\sqrt{\frac{E}{n_0}}\right) \qquad (7\text{-}57)$$

To show this is included in $(7\text{-}55a)$, let $s_2(t) = 0$ in Eq. (7-56), and $s_1(t) =$

$A \cos \omega_0 t$, just the OOK case. Then the parameter

$$a^2 = \frac{2}{n_0} \int_0^T A^2 \cos^2 \omega_0 t \, dt = \frac{2E}{n_0}$$

and

$$\frac{a}{2\sqrt{2}} = \frac{1}{2\sqrt{2}} \sqrt{\frac{2E}{n_0}} = \frac{1}{2} \sqrt{\frac{E}{n_0}}$$

just as in Eq. (7-57).

2. **FSK**:

$$P_e = \tfrac{1}{2} \operatorname{erfc} \sqrt{\frac{E}{2n_0}} \qquad (7\text{-}58)$$

Here we have $s_1(t) = A \cos \omega_1 t$ and

$$s_2(t) = A \cos \omega_2 t$$

If $\omega_1 T \gg 2\pi$, $\omega_2 T \gg 2\pi$, and $(\omega_1 - \omega_2)T \geq 2\pi$, it is readily shown that $\int_0^T s_1(t) s_2(t) \, dt \doteq 0$. [The signals $s_1(t)$ and $s_2(t)$ are examples of orthogonal signals.] Equation (7-56) then simplifies to

$$a^2 = \frac{2}{n_0} \int_0^T \left[s_1^2(t) + s_2^2(t) \right] dt = \frac{4E}{n_0}$$

since here $E_1 = E_2 = E$. Then we also have $a/2\sqrt{2} = \sqrt{E/2n_0}$, just as in Eq. (7-58).

3. **PSK**:

$$P_e = \tfrac{1}{2} \operatorname{erfc} \sqrt{\frac{E}{n_0}} \qquad (7\text{-}59)$$

Here we have $s_1(t) = -s_2(t)$, and $a^2 = 8E/n_0$, from Eq. (7-56). Then $a/2\sqrt{2} = \sqrt{E/n_0}$, agreeing of course with Eq. (7-59).

The optimum waveshapes to be used in binary signal transmission in additive gaussian white noise are also readily obtained from Eqs. (7-55a) and (7-56), as already noted. Since $\operatorname{erfc}(a/2\sqrt{2})$ decreases with increasing a, the larger a is, the smaller the probability of error P_e. A little thought will indicate that a is maximized and P_e minimized by setting $s_1(t) = -s_2(t)$. The PSK signals of course satisfy these conditions. Other pairs of polar signals would serve just as well. Since $a^2 = 8E/n_0$ for this case, with

$$E = \int_0^T s_1^2 \, dt = \int_0^T s_2^2 \, dt$$

it is again the ratio of average energy E to noise spectral density n_0 that determines the probability of error. This is the point we made in discussing

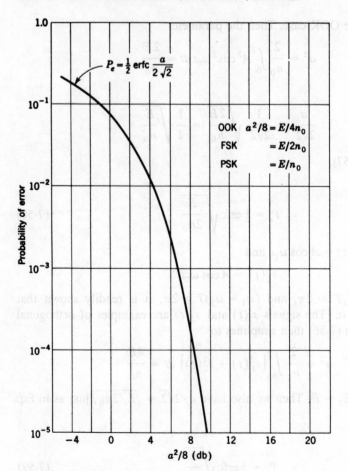

FIGURE 7-22
Probability of error, optimum binary transmission.

matched filters in Chap. 6. To minimize error probability, one should use signals with as high an average energy content as allowable. In passing the signals through the matched filter, the specific dependence on the details of the wave-shape disappears. The matched-filter signal-power output is proportional to the average energy E.

A universal probability-of-error curve for optimum binary transmission in additive white gaussian noise is shown in Fig. 7-22. This is precisely the curve plotted earlier as Fig. 6-42 and is repeated here for ease of access. It is just a plot of Eq. (7-55a). As indicated above and again in the figure, the parameter $a^2/8$ on which the probability of error depends is a function only of E/n_0, the ratio of signal energy to noise spectral density.

In this discussion, synchronous or phase-coherent detection is again assumed available, as in Chap. 6. If it is not possible to maintain phase synchro-

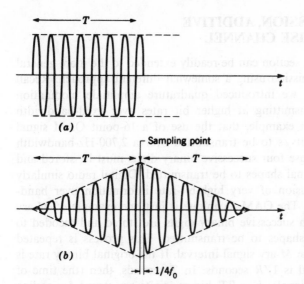

(a)

Sampling point

(b)

$1/4f_0$

FIGURE 7-23
Matched-filter output for input sinusoidal pulse. (*a*) Input pulse. (*b*) Output pulse (ignoring a constant time delay).

nism, one must again resort to envelope detection with its attendant SNR deterioration. The need for synchronous detection is implicit in the correlation or matched-filter detection circuits of Figs. 7-17 and 7-19. As an example assume the input to the matched filter is $A \cos \omega_0 t$, defined over the binary interval T as in the examples just cited. The matched filter must then be a bandpass filter centered at f_0, and of bandwidth $\sim 1/T$. Alternatively, its impulse response is the same high-frequency rectangular pulse $\cos \omega_0 t$, of pulse width T, although turned around in time. The output of the filter, the convolution of signal and impulse response, is then just a high-frequency sinusoidal pulse $2T$ seconds long, at the same frequency f_0, but with a *triangular* envelope, reaching its peak at the T-second interval. (Recall that the convolution of two rectangles is a triangle.) This is shown in Fig. 7-23.

Note that the output peaks up, as expected, at the sampling time T. But it is crucial that sampling take place *exactly* at T. If sampling takes place a quarter of a cycle ($1/4f_0$ seconds) early or late, the output drops to zero. This synchronism must be maintained to within a fraction of $1/4f_0$ seconds, which is no mean task if the carrier frequency f_0 is in the VHF, UHF, or microwave range.

Actually, in practice one would not allow the output pulse to extend $2T$ seconds. For then successive binary pulses spaced $1/T$ seconds apart would interfere with one another. The integrator-plus-comparator circuits shown in Fig. 7-18 indicate that decisions are to be made every T seconds. The word *dump* in the appellation *integrate-and-dump* circuit used to represent this matched-filter implementation implies that the stored energy is to be released (dumped) every T seconds [WOZE, pp. 235, 236]. A practical implementation of the integrate-and-dump circuit consists of a resonant circuit tuned to frequency f_0, with provision for shorting out the tuned circuit every T seconds just before receiving a signal input, to dump energy stored from previous intervals.

7-4   *M*-ARY TRANSMISSION, ADDITIVE WHITE-GAUSSIAN-NOISE CHANNEL

The material of the previous section can be readily extended to the more general case of *M*-ary signal transmission using a somewhat different approach. Recall that in Chap. 4 (Sec. 4-3) we introduced quadrature amplitude modulation (QAM) as a means of transmitting at higher bit rates over fixed-bandwidth channels. We showed, as an example, that the use of a 16-point QAM signal constellation allows 9,600 bits/s to be transmitted over a 2,700-Hz-bandwidth telephone channel. In this case four successive binary digits must be stored and recoded as one of the 16 signal shapes to be transmitted. Digital radio similarly uses QAM for the transmission of very high-bit-rate information over band-limited microwave channels. The QAM technique is just one example of *M*-ary signal transmission, in which successive binary digits are stored and recoded to allow one of $M = 2^k$ waveshapes to be transmitted. This process is repeated every T seconds, T being the *M*-ary signal interval. If the original binary rate is R bits/s, the binary interval is $1/R$ seconds. In T seconds, then (the time of transmission of an *M*-ary signal), $k = RT$ binary digits are stored for coding into one of $M = 2^{RT}$ possible signals. As an example, two binary symbols in succession result in $M = 4$ possible waveshapes. If four binary signals are stored, they give rise to $M = 16$ possible waveshapes. Details appear in Sec. 4-3 in the discussion of QAM signaling. Figure 7-24 reviews the general concept of *M*-ary transmission. Figure 7-24*b* provides an example of five successive binary digits being stored, for which $M = 2^5 = 32$ possible output signals.

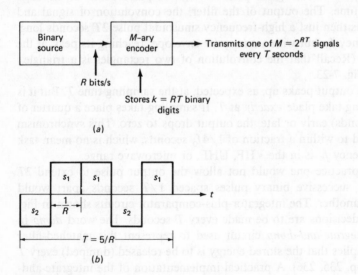

FIGURE 7-24
Binary-to-*M*-ary conversion. (*a*) *M*-ary encoding. (*b*) Example with $M = 2^5 = 32$.

One problem noted in Chap. 4 with the use of the QAM technique was that as more signal points in the two-dimensional constellation are used for higher rate transmission over the same bandwidth channel, they crowd more closely together and become more vulnerable to noise and other disturbances on reception. We shall show in this section how probability-of-error calculations can be carried out for various QAM signal sets verifying quantitatively the conjectures made in Chap. 4.

The general idea of M-ary transmission can be extended in another direction as well. We shall show that by choosing M *orthogonal* signals (one example is M-ary FSK, a set of M carrier frequencies spaced wide enough apart to ensure orthogonality), one can actually *reduce* the probability of error below that of optimum binary (PSK) transmission. The price paid is that the transmission bandwidth and complexity of the system increases as M increases. The use of M orthogonal signals is thus suggested for relatively wideband channels, where the increased bandwidth required may not pose too severe a problem, but where power limitations necessitate some such coding of binary signals to reduce the error probability below that obtained for the binary signals in the previous section. Space communication channels serve as one possible example of such channels. The M-ary QAM signals, on the other hand, which show an *increase* in error rate as M increases, are appropriate for such band-limited channels as the telephone channel or digital radio, where there may not be a severe E/n_0 limitation, but the bandwidth limitation restricts high-speed binary symbol transmission.

To discuss the performance of M-ary signal sets in detail, we choose the simplest model of a transmission channel: one that introduces additive white gaussian noise only. This turns out to be a fairly realistic model for many space communication systems. Although telephone channels are limited more by intersymbol interference and impulsive noise than by additive gaussian noise, the results obtained for the QAM signals are useful in the telephony case, since they do provide an upper limit on the performance and suggest useful receiver structures. They are useful as well in the case of digital radio. This additive-white-gaussian-noise model was used briefly at the end of Sec. 6-8 in analyzing the matched-filter performance of high-frequency binary waveshapes (PSK, OOK, FSK) in additive noise. The technique used there is generalized to M-ary communication in this section.

The additive-white-gaussian-noise model is often referred to as the AWGN channel. To study the performance of M-ary signals transmitted over this channel we again apply the basic concepts of statistical decision theory, but approach the problem somewhat differently than in the previous section. The approach adopted here does not rely on sampling the signal plus noise to generate independent statistical samples, as assumed in the previous section. In the case of $M = 2$ or binary transmission, the results turn out to be identical to those of the previous section. This is to be expected, since the optimum binary processor and its error performance, as expressed by (7-44), (7-55a), and (7-56), depend neither on the bandwidth B_n of the band-limited noise model chosen, nor on the samples of the various waveshapes. These were in a sense artificially introduced to enable the calculations to be made. The approach of this section thus provides an alternative way of generating the matched-filter–correlation-detector results of the previous section, allowing extension to more general cases as well. The key result of this section is that we demonstrate that M-ary signal detection may be studied by working with the signal waveshapes directly.

To motivate the approach to be used, consider first, as an example, the case of four QAM signals. (Recall from Chap. 4 that these can also be called QPSK signals.) As shown in Chap. 4, the set of four signals may be expressed as

$$s_1(t) = \sqrt{\frac{2}{T}}\, a \cos \omega_0 t + \sqrt{\frac{2}{T}}\, a \sin \omega_0 t$$

$$s_2(t) = \sqrt{\frac{2}{T}}\, a \cos \omega_0 t - \sqrt{\frac{2}{T}}\, a \sin \omega_0 t$$

$$s_3(t) = -\sqrt{\frac{2}{T}}\, a \cos \omega_0 t - \sqrt{\frac{2}{T}}\, a \sin \omega_0 t \qquad (7\text{-}60)$$

$$s_4(t) = -\sqrt{\frac{2}{T}}\, a \cos \omega_0 t + \sqrt{\frac{2}{T}}\, a \sin \omega_0 t$$

(Rectangular waveshapes are again assumed for simplicity.) The $\cos \omega_0 t$ carrier term is called the *inphase term*, and the $\sin \omega_0 t$ term the *quadrature term*. The information carried in the signal is then the sign of each of these terms.

The carriers in (7-60) have each been written with a factor $\sqrt{2/T}$ for normalization purposes: $\sqrt{2/T} \cos \omega_0 t$ and $\sqrt{2/T} \sin \omega_0 t$ are then orthonormal with respect to one another. To make this more explicit, we can rewrite (7-60) in the form

$$s_i(t) = \sum_{j=1}^{2} s_{ij} \phi_j(t) \qquad i = 1, 2, 3, 4 \qquad (7\text{-}61)$$

Here $\phi_1(t) = \sqrt{2/T} \cos \omega_0 t$ and $\phi_2(t) = \sqrt{2/T} \sin \omega_0 t$ are orthonormal functions, defined by the usual integral expression,

$$\int_0^T \phi_i(t)\phi_j(t)\, dt = \delta_{ij} \qquad (7\text{-}62)$$

The coefficients s_{ij} are just the appropriate values of a or $-a$, from (7-60). As an example, $s_{11} = a$, $s_{12} = a$, $s_{21} = a$, $s_{22} = -a$, etc. Just as in Chap. 4, we may define a signal plane whose two axes represent the coefficients, respectively, of $\phi_1(t)$ and $\phi_2(t)$, in (7-61) or (7-60). The four signals $s_1(t)$, $s_2(t)$, $s_3(t)$, $s_4(t)$, may then be represented by four points in the plane. The set of points, as noted in Chap. 4, comprises a signal constellation. We denote them, in this example, by $\mathbf{s}_1 = (s_{11}, s_{12}) = (a, a)$, $\mathbf{s}_2 = (s_{21}, s_{22}) = (a, -a)$, $\mathbf{s}_3 = (s_{31}, s_{32}) = (-a, -a)$, and $\mathbf{s}_4 = (s_{41}, s_{42}) = (-a, a)$. These are shown plotted in Fig. 7-25.

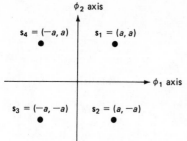

FIGURE 7-25
QAM signal constellation, $M = 4$.

The critical thing to note now is that the information carried in the particular signal $s_i(t)$ transmitted is given by the value of the corresponding vector $\mathbf{s}_i$, or, equivalently, the two numbers, (s_{i1}, s_{i2}). Since the orthonormal carriers $\phi_1(t)$ and $\phi_2(t)$ are common to all four signals and hence carry no information, they can be stripped away at the receiver without affecting in any way the optimum processing of the received signal. This is exactly the extension to this somewhat more general case of the processes of frequency conversion and synchronous detection discussed in both Chaps. 4 and 6. Shifting baseband signals up in frequency for transmission and then back again to baseband at reception does not affect the system performance in noise.

How does one carry out the process of stripping away the orthonormal carriers? This is obviously done, making use of the orthogonality property of (7-62), and generalizing the concept of synchronous detection, by multiplying the particular $s_i(t)$ transmitted by both $\phi_1(t)$ and $\phi_2(t)$, and then integrating over the T-second interval. The resultant correlator is shown in Fig. 7-26. The output of each of the two branches is $+a$ or $-a$, depending on the signal $s_i(t)$ transmitted.

Now assume that noise has been added during transmission. The received signal over a T-second interval is then

$$v(t) = s_i(t) + n(t) \qquad 0 \le t \le T \qquad (7\text{-}63)$$

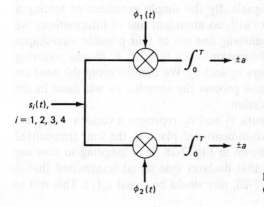

FIGURE 7-26
Correlator, $M = 4$ signals.

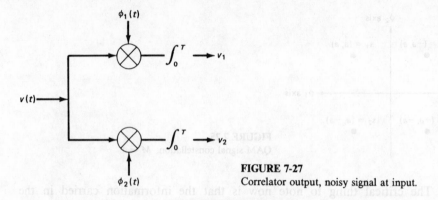

FIGURE 7-27
Correlator output, noisy signal at input.

if $s_i(t)$ is the particular one of the four signals transmitted. Applying $v(t)$ to the correlator of Fig. 7-26, it is apparent that there are two noisy outputs. These are shown in Fig. 7-27, labeled v_1 and v_2 respectively. From the form of $v(t)$ in (7-63), and from the correlator operations of Fig. 7-26, it is apparent that these two outputs may be written

$$v_1 = s_{i1} + n_1$$

and

$$v_2 = s_{i2} + n_2 \tag{7-64}$$

with s_{i1} and s_{i2} precisely the components of $s_i(t)$ appearing in (7-61). The two noise terms, n_1 and n_2, are given by

$$n_j = \int_0^T n(t)\phi_j(t)\, dt \tag{7-65}$$

They are thus, mathematically, the orthonormal projections of the noise wave $n(t)$.

Since no information has been lost in carrying out the correlation operation of Fig. 7-26, the optimum way of processing the received waveshape $v(t)$ must correspond to optimum processing of the two numbers v_1 and v_2. By "optimum" we of course mean the processing procedure that minimizes the probability of error in transmitting these QAM signals. By the simple expedient of forcing a correlator to be used at the receiver (with no attendant loss of information), we have reduced the problem of distinguishing one out of four possible waveshapes on the basis of complete analog information, $v(t)$, $0 \le t \le T$, to one involving the best way of handling two numbers v_1 and v_2. We thereby avoid the need (at least theoretically) to sample $v(t)$ and process the samples, as was done in the preceding section for binary transmission.

It is apparent that the two outputs, v_1 and v_2, represent a vector $\mathbf{v} = (v_1, v_2)$ that can be plotted on the same two-dimensional plane as the four transmitted signal vectors s_1, s_2, s_3, s_4. This is shown in Fig. 7-28. It is tempting to now say that the optimum processor is one that declares that signal transmitted that is closest to $\mathbf{v}$. In the example of Fig. 7-28, this would be signal $s_4(t)$. This will in

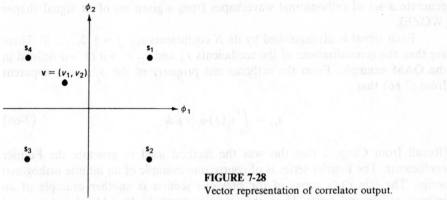

FIGURE 7-28
Vector representation of correlator output.

fact be shown to be the case for equally likely signals transmitted over the AWGN channel, extending the equivalent result of the binary case (see Fig. 7-8).

Before proceeding to carry out the calculations involving additive white gaussian noise, we generalize the QAM example to the M-ary transmission case. Consider now that one of M signals, $s_i(t)$, $i = 1, 2, \ldots, M$, is transmitted every T seconds, as shown in Fig. 7-24. [These can correspond to the general QAM case, to M different frequencies, to baseband transmission, or to any choice of M known waveshapes. Signal shaping is also included, since it reflects itself in the specific form of the $s_i(t)$.] Let these M signals be transmitted over a channel using $N \leq M$ carriers. Without loss of generality we take these carriers to be orthonormal signals, $\phi_1(t), \phi_2(t), \ldots, \phi_N(t)$. We then have, as a representation of $s_i(t)$,

$$s_i(t) = \sum_{j=1}^{N} s_{ij}\phi_j(t) \qquad i = 1, 2, \ldots, M \qquad (7\text{-}66)$$

Here, as previously,

$$\int_0^T \phi_i(t)\phi_j(t)\, dt = \delta_{ij} \qquad (7\text{-}67)$$

This then extends the QAM example, with $N = 2$ carriers ($\cos \omega_0 t$ and $\sin \omega_0 t$) needed, to more general cases. For example, if the $s_i(t)$'s are themselves orthogonal signals (as noted, M-ary FSK is exactly this case), $N = M$, $s_i(t) = a\phi_i(t)$, and $s_{ij} = 0$, $i \neq j$. Time-displaced (nonoverlapping) pulses as well as other types of waveshapes could be used as these carriers.

That only $N \leq M$ orthogonal carriers are needed in general may be proven by invoking the standard Gram–Schmidt orthogonalization procedure [WOZE]. The precise form of the carriers is not important at this point. (The specific choice *is* important, as is apparent from previous chapters of the book, in determining the transmission bandwidth, peak power requirements, cost and ease of implementation, etc.) In fact, the Gram–Schmidt procedure may be invoked to generate a set of orthonormal waveshapes from a given set of M signal shapes [WOZE].

Each signal is distinguished by its N coefficients s_{ij}, $j = 1, 2, \ldots, N$. These are then the generalizations of the coefficients s_{i1} and $s_{i2} = +a$ or $-a$ defined in the QAM example. From the orthonormal property of the ϕ_j's, it is apparent from (7-66) that

$$s_{ij} = \int_0^T s_i(t)\phi_j(t)\, dt \tag{7-68}$$

[Recall from Chap. 2 that this was the method used to generate the Fourier coefficients. The Fourier series is of course one example of an infinite orthogonal series. The $(\sin x)/x$ series of the previous section is another example of an infinite orthogonal series. Here only a finite number, $N \leq M$, of orthonormal functions is needed.]

As in the QAM case, the information as to which of the M signals is being transmitted is carried by the N coefficients s_{ij}. For a particular signal $s_i(t)$ the N coefficients may be visualized as representing an N-dimensional vector $\mathbf{s}_i = (s_{i_1}, s_{i_2}, \ldots, s_{iN})$. They can also be plotted as points in an N-dimensional space, each of whose axes corresponds to one of the orthonormal functions. s_{ij} is then the projection of $s_i(t)$ along the $\phi_j(t)$ axis.

Generalizing the QAM approach, then, the carriers $\phi_j(t)$, $i = 1, 2, \ldots, N$, may be stripped off at the receiver by carrying out a correlation process. This leaves just the N coefficients s_{ij} at the correlator output. With noise $n(t)$ added during transmission, the received signal, just as in the QAM case, is given by

$$v(t) = s_i(t) + n(t) \qquad 0 \leq t \leq T \tag{7-69}$$

and the output of the correlation receiver is given by N numbers $v_1, v_2, \ldots, v_N$. They make up the vector

$$\mathbf{v} = (v_1, v_2, \ldots, v_N) = \mathbf{s}_i + \mathbf{n} \tag{7-70}$$

The noise vector $\mathbf{n} = (n_1, n_2, \ldots, n_N)$, with

$$n_j = \int_0^T n(t)\phi_j(t)\, dt \tag{7-71}$$

exactly as in (7-65). A block diagram of this correlator receiver, consisting of a bank of N correlation operations, with $\mathbf{v}$ appearing at the output, is shown in Fig. 7-29. This is shown followed by an optimum processor for determining, with minimum probability of error, which of the M signals is transmitted every T seconds. The N numbers making up the vector $\mathbf{v}$ play the role of the n samples described in Sec. 7-2.

How does one now extend the optimum binary detection case of the previous sections to the case of M-ary detection? This is done quite simply by first returning to the optimum-likelihood-ratio test for binary hypothesis testing, given by (7-11). It is apparent that the optimum choice for region V_1 in that case

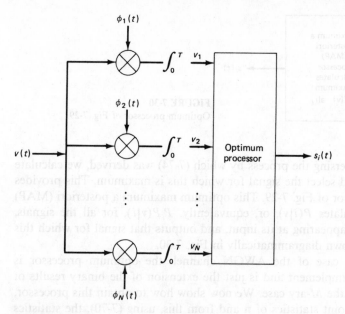

FIGURE 7-29
Correlation receiver, N orthonormal carriers.

is equally well given by

$$P_1 f(\mathbf{v}|1) > P_2 f(\mathbf{v}|2) \tag{7-72}$$

From probability theory each side of the inequality in (7-72) is the joint probability of two events. Letting $i = 1$ or 2, we may thus write

$$P_i f(\mathbf{v}|i) = P(\mathbf{v}, i) = P(i|\mathbf{v}) f(\mathbf{v}) \tag{7-73}$$

Introducing the right-hand side of (7-73) into (7-72), and canceling the factor $f(\mathbf{v})$ common to both sides, we have, as an alternative optimum decision procedure, the rule: choose hypothesis H_1 if

$$P(1|\mathbf{v}) > P(2|\mathbf{v}) \tag{7-74}$$

The two probabilities, $P(1|\mathbf{v})$ and $P(2|\mathbf{v})$, are called *a posteriori* probabilities. They represent, respectively, the probability that signal s_1 was transmitted, and that s_2 was transmitted, *given* the vector $\mathbf{v}$ received. The rule of (7-74) says simply that one is to select the signal more likely to have been transmitted. This guarantees minimum probability of error. Now extend this to one of M signals transmitted. Calculate the a posteriori probabilities $P(i|\mathbf{v})$, $i = 1, 2, \ldots, M$, for each of the signals. The obvious extension of the optimum rule to this case is to select the most probable event, or the signal with *maximum a posteriori probability*. Signal $s_i(t)$ is thus declared present, at the receiver, if

$$P(i|\mathbf{v}) > P(j|\mathbf{v}) \qquad \text{all} \quad j \neq i \tag{7-75}$$

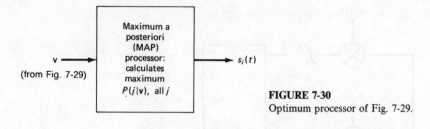

FIGURE 7-30
Optimum processor of Fig. 7-29.

Alternatively, by reversing the process by which (7-74) was derived, we calculate $P_i P(\mathbf{v}|i)$ for all i and select the signal for which this is maximum. This provides the optimum processor of Fig. 7-29. This optimum maximum a posteriori (MAP) processor thus calculates $P(i|\mathbf{v})$, or, equivalently, $P_i P(\mathbf{v}|i)$, for all the signals, using the value of $\mathbf{v}$ appearing at its input, and outputs that signal for which this is largest. This is shown diagrammatically in Fig. 7-30.

In the special case of the AWGN channel, the optimum processor is particularly easy to implement and is just the extension of the binary results of Secs. 7-2 and 7-3 to the M-ary case. We now show how to obtain this processor, by first finding the joint statistics of $\mathbf{n}$ and from this, using (7-70), the statistics of $\mathbf{v}$.

Recall from Chap. 6 that the spectral density of zero-mean white noise is given by

$$G_n(f) = \frac{n_0}{2} \quad \text{W/Hz} \tag{7-76}$$

The corresponding autocorrelation function is

$$R_n(t, s) = E[n(t)n(s)] = \frac{n_0}{2}\delta(t - s) \tag{7-77}$$

We have already noted in the previous section that with $n(t)$ gaussian the noise coefficient n_j given by a linear operation on $n(t)$ of the form of (7-71) is gaussian as well. [It may be readily shown, from the theory of random processes, that any linear operation on a gaussian process produces another gaussian process [PAPO 1984]. This was utilized in Chap. 6 in describing the statistics of narrowband noise, as an example. This notion was also used in Chap. 6 in evaluating the performance of a high-frequency binary signal using matched-filter detection. See (6-121) as an example. The linear operation of (7-71) thus produces a gaussian random variable.] All one needs in order to write its probability-density function explicitly is its mean value and variance. In like manner the joint statistics of the N random variables n_j, $j = 1, 2, \ldots, N$, making up $\mathbf{n}$ are completely defined by their mean values, variances, and cross-correlations. To find these quantities we use (7-71) and the zero-mean, white-noise attribute of $n(t)$. Specifically, taking the expectation of n_j in (7-71), interchanging the expectation and integration operations [PAPO 1984, chap. 9] and noting that $n(t)$ is by definition zero mean, we have first that n_j is a zero-mean random variable:

$$E(n_j) = 0$$

Also,

$$\sigma_j^2 = E\left(n_j^2\right) = E\left[\int_0^T \int_0^T n(t)n(s)\phi_j(t)\phi_j(s)\,dt\,ds\right]$$

$$= \int_0^T \int_0^T E[n(t)n(s)]\phi_j(t)\phi_j(s)\,dt\,ds$$

$$= \frac{n_0}{2} \tag{7-78}$$

again interchanging expectation and integration operations, and then using both the white-noise definition of (7-77) and the orthonormality property [Eq. (7-67)] of the $\phi_j(t)$'s. Details are left to the reader. It is also left to the reader to show in a similar manner that

$$E[n_i n_j] = 0 \qquad i \neq j \tag{7-79}$$

The same procedure was used in Chap. 6 in studying the performance of PSK in additive white gaussian noise. See (6-122), (6-123), and (6-124). This points out the advantage of using the AWGN model where appropriate on physical grounds. It simplifies analysis considerably.

The white-gaussian-noise assumption thus leads to very simple results for the statistics of the noise samples at the outputs of the n correlators of Fig. 7-29. The noise samples are all gaussian, with mean and equal variance, and are pairwise uncorrelated. From the properties of gaussian random variables as well, they are then *independent* random variables. The joint statistics of the N noise samples are then simply written. They represent a multidimensional set of independent gaussian random variables. Thus,

$$f(n_1, n_2, \ldots, n_N) = f(\mathbf{n}) = \prod_{j=1}^N f(n_j)$$

$$= \frac{e^{-\mathbf{n} \cdot \mathbf{n}/n_0}}{(\pi n_0)^{N/2}} \tag{7-80}$$

The vector dot product $\mathbf{n} \cdot \mathbf{n}$ is simply the shorthand notation for $\sum_{j=1}^N n_j^2$. The simplicity of the form for the joint statistics of $\mathbf{n}$ is the reason for the desire to model channels as having additive white gaussian noise.

Since $\mathbf{v} = \mathbf{s}_i + \mathbf{n}$ is the vector representation of the correlator output in Fig. 7-29, it is apparent that the probability density of $\mathbf{v}$, *conditioned* on $\mathbf{s}_i$ being present, is given simply by replacing $\mathbf{n}$ in (7-80) with $\mathbf{v} - \mathbf{s}_i$. Hence we have, for the AWGN channel,

$$f(\mathbf{v}|\mathbf{s}_i) = \frac{e^{-(\mathbf{v}-\mathbf{s}_i)\cdot(\mathbf{v}-\mathbf{s}_i)/n_0}}{(\pi n_0)^{N/2}} \tag{7-81}$$

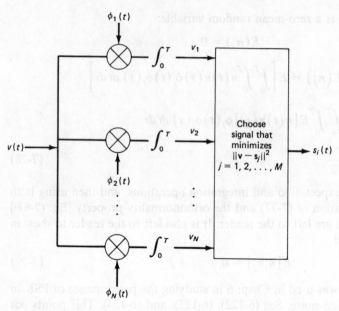

FIGURE 7-31
Optimum correlation receiver, equally likely signals, AWGN channel.

This is exactly the expression needed to determine the a posteriori probabilities of (7-75).

Now consider the special but common case in which the M signals are equally likely to appear. We then have $P_1 = P_2 = \cdots P_M = 1/M$. From (7-75) the MAP detector in this case thus simply selects the signal with the largest conditional probability density function $f(\mathbf{v}|\mathbf{s}_i)$. Note from (7-81) that this is just the signal with the smallest exponent, or the one that minimizes

$$(\mathbf{v} - \mathbf{s}_i) \cdot (\mathbf{v} - \mathbf{s}_i) \equiv \|\mathbf{v} - \mathbf{s}_i\|^2 = \sum_{j=1}^{N} (v_j - s_{ij})^2 \qquad (7\text{-}82)$$

This is precisely the expression for the squared distance between $\mathbf{v}$ and $\mathbf{s}_i$ in the N-dimensional Euclidean sense. We have thus shown that for the AWGN channel with one of M equally likely signals transmitted the optimum detector is the one that selects the signal "closest to" the received signal vector $\mathbf{v}$. The MAP processor of Fig. 7-30 thus calculates the distance between $\mathbf{v}$ and all stored signal vectors $\mathbf{s}_j$, $j = 1, 2, \ldots, M$, and selects the $\mathbf{s}_i$ that is closest to $\mathbf{v}$. This is shown schematically in Fig. 7-31. In the two-dimensional example of Fig. 7-28 with one of four signals transmitted, $\mathbf{s}_4$ would be selected as the one most likely to have been transmitted. The results of this section extend those of Sec. 7-3.

Matched-Filter Detection

The optimum receiver structure of Fig. 7-31 may be redrawn in two alternative but equivalent ways. One structure replaces the distance calculation of the MAP processor by a dot-product calculation. The second structure is completely different: the correlator receiver is replaced by a completely equivalent *matched-filter* structure, with the received signal $v(t)$ correlated against stored versions of each of the M possible signals transmitted, rather than the N orthogonal carriers of Fig. 7-31. Both of these structures extend the results of the previous sections. The matched-filter structure has of course already been discussed in connection with binary signaling in Sec. 7-3. The dot-product processing is similar to that given by (7-18) in Sec. 7-2. There samples of $v(t)$ were being considered. Here, more generally, $\mathbf{v}$ represents the result of correlating $v(t)$ against the N orthonormal $\phi_j(t)$'s, as provided by the N correlation outputs in Fig. 7-31.

To demonstrate the validity of these statements consider the quadratic distance measure of (7-82). Expanding this quadratic form term by term, we get

$$(\mathbf{v} - \mathbf{s}_i) \cdot (\mathbf{v} - \mathbf{s}_i) = \|\mathbf{v}\|^2 - 2\left(\mathbf{v} \cdot \mathbf{s}_i - \frac{\|\mathbf{s}_i\|^2}{2}\right) \qquad (7\text{-}82a)$$

Since $\|\mathbf{v}\|^2$ is independent of the transmitted signal, it is apparent that minimizing the distance corresponds precisely to *maximizing*

$$\left(\mathbf{v} \cdot \mathbf{s}_i - \frac{\|\mathbf{s}_i\|^2}{2}\right)$$

Consider now the term $\mathbf{s}_i \cdot \mathbf{s}_i = \|\mathbf{s}_i\|^2 = \sum_{j=1}^{N} s_{ij}^2$. It is easily shown that this is just the expression $\int_0^T s_i^2(t)\,dt = E_i$, the *energy* in the signal $s_i(t)$. For, using the orthogonal expansion of $s_i(t)$, we have

$$\int_0^T s_i^2(t)\,dt = \int_0^T \left[\sum_{j=1}^{N} s_{ij}\phi_j(t)\right]\left[\sum_{k=1}^{N} s_{ik}\phi_k(t)\right] dt$$

Interchanging summation and integration, and recalling that the functions $\phi_j(t)$ were defined to be orthonormal over the interval $(0, T)$, it is left to the reader to show that

$$\|\mathbf{s}_i\|^2 = \sum_{j=1}^{N} s_{ij}^2 = \int_0^T s_i^2(t)\,dt = E_i \qquad (7\text{-}83)$$

This is just a special case of the general Parseval theorem discussed earlier (see Sec. 7-3, for example), relating integrals of time functions to the sums of their Fourier (orthogonal function) coefficients. It is thus apparent that the MAP processor of Fig. 7-31 for the AWGN channel can be replaced by the equivalent processor shown in Fig. 7-32. The energy terms shown subtracted out in the figure have a physical justification. They eliminate a bias in favor of higher-energy signals when comparing them on the basis of the decision parameter $\mathbf{v} \cdot \mathbf{s}_i$.

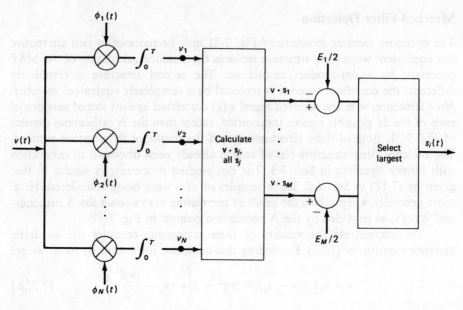

FIGURE 7-32
Equivalent receiver, AWGN channel.

As an additional by-product of these manipulations, note from (7-83) that the points in the signal constellation are all located at distances from the origin corresponding to the square root of their respective energies. The signal $\mathbf{s}_i$ is located at a distance $\sqrt{E_i}$, for example (see Fig. 7-25). We shall use this result in the next section in evaluating probabilities of error.

The optimum matched-filter receiver for the AWGN channel mentioned above is also readily obtained by applying Parseval's theorem to the distance decision function of Eq. (7-82). Specifically, it is left to the reader to show, in a manner similar to that used in proving (7-83), that

$$\mathbf{v} \cdot \mathbf{s}_i \equiv \sum_{j=1}^{N} v_j s_{ij} = \int_0^T v(t) s_i(t) \, dt \qquad (7\text{-}84)$$

Since it is the quantity $\mathbf{v} \cdot \mathbf{s}_i - E_i/2$ that is to be maximized in deciding on the most probable signal transmitted, it is apparent from (7-83) and (7-84) that one could equally well operate *directly* on the received signal waveshape $v(t)$ rather than first correlating against the carriers as in Figs. 7-31 and 7-32. The resultant optimum receiver that maximizes $\mathbf{v} \cdot \mathbf{s}_i - \|\mathbf{s}_i\|^2/2$ directly is shown sketched in Fig. 7-33. This is called a *matched-filter* receiver since the incoming received signal $v(t)$ is correlated with or matched against stored replicas of the M possible signal waveshapes. This extends the binary matched-filter results of Sec. 7-3 to M-ary signals. Rather than carry out the correlation function involving multiplication and integration, one can show as in the binary case that this is

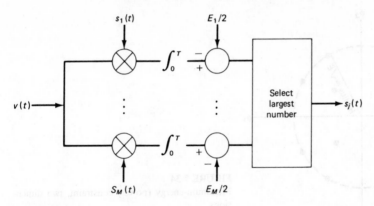

FIGURE 7-33
Matched-filter receiver, AWGN channel.

identical to passing $v(t)$ through a bank of *filters* and comparing outputs every T seconds.

The choice as to which implementation to use—that of Fig. 7-32, say, or that of Fig. 7-33—depends on the complexity of the signals transmitted, how easily generated, their number, the number N of carriers, and how easily these are generated. Consider as an example the case in which the two carriers are quadrature sine waves $\sqrt{2/T} \cos \omega_0 t$ and $\sqrt{2/T} \sin \omega_0 t$. If there are four possible signals transmitted, as in Fig. 7-25, the correlation receiver of Fig. 7-26 requires just two reference signals at the receiver. The equivalent matched-filter receiver would thus involve correlating against the four possible signals, $\sqrt{2/T} a \cos(\omega_0 t + \theta_i)$, with $\theta_i = \pm\pi/4$ and $\pm 3\pi/4$. In practice, all four waveshapes at the receiver would be derived from one sine wave. Note that the correlation receiver requires N correlations or filtering operations, that of the matched filter M such operations. In practice, there is of course always some shaping of the amplitude term multiplying the carrier. (It is not just a fixed number or rectangular shaping, as assumed up to now.) This is particularly true at the transition regions separating the beginning and end of successive T-second intervals. Matched filtering may then be used to account for this shaping. The distinction between the correlation and matched-filter receivers of Figs. 7-32 and 7-33 is in fact often blurred (particularly in the case where the carriers are simple sines and cosines), and both are often called matched-filter devices.

7-5 SIGNAL CONSTELLATIONS AND PROBABILITY-OF-ERROR CALCULATION

The vector-space representation of signals and the optimum detector solution as that which chooses the signal "closest to" the received signal is particularly useful in signal design as well as in probability-of-error calculations. Geometric concepts and results can very often be brought to bear successfully in handling these

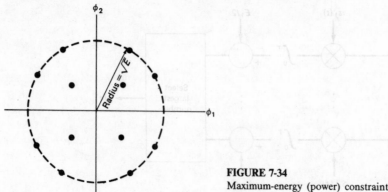

FIGURE 7-34
Maximum-energy (power) constraint, two dimensions.

questions. The comments made earlier as to the distinction between power-limited and band-limited channels are readily verified in terms of a geometric picture. A power-limited channel (or its equivalent, an energy-limited channel) corresponds to one in which signal points are all constrained to lie on or within a sphere of radius $\sqrt{E}$, with E the maximum energy. ($E = ST$, with S the maximum power allowed for transmission; see Fig. 7-34.)

Consider first the case in which $N = 2$ carriers are used. (This is again the example of either two quadrature sine waves or two orthogonal sine waves of different frequencies.) It is apparent that when one tries to transmit at higher and higher bit rates, with correspondingly larger numbers of signals used, the signals become packed closer together and the probability of error must increase.

The only way to avoid this dilemma of increasing error probability—or, alternatively, the only way to *reduce* the probability of error by purposely choosing larger values of M— is by going to higher dimensions. A three-dimensional example with three orthogonal signals appears in Fig. 7-35. These signals are now "farther apart" than they are in two dimensions, so one would expect the probability of error to decrease. We shall demonstrate this quantitatively in the

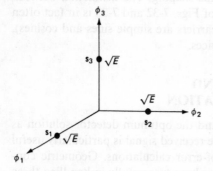

FIGURE 7-35
Orthogonal signals. three dimensions.

next section. As we add more *orthogonal signals*, increasing the dimensionality of the vector space, the signals move farther apart and the error probability decreases. However, as noted earlier, this requires correspondingly wider bandwidths for transmission.

Now consider the band-limited channel. In this case we are restricted to the two dimensions of Fig. 7-34. One would also use quadrature carriers rather than orthogonal sine-wave carriers of different frequencies to reduce the bandwidth. This is precisely what was described in Chap. 4, in discussing QAM transmission. As noted above, the probability of error increases if more signals must be packed into a given (energy-limited) region. However, if there is no specific power constraint (at least within limits), the signal points can always be moved farther apart. Equivalently, if the signal-to-noise ratio is sufficiently high (as will be shown shortly), signal points may be added without deteriorating the system too much.

An interesting design problem to which approximate answers only can be given is that of determining a set of M signals, constrained in power and in bandwidth, that minimizes the probability of error. The corresponding geometric picture is quite apparent. In the case of two dimensions, for example, how does one choose the optimum location of M points within the circle of Fig. 7-34? Rather than answer this question directly, we shall focus on the calculation of probability of error once a constellation (location of signal points) has been specified. Even here we shall have to restrict ourselves to simple locations of points (most commonly spanning a rectangular region in two dimensions) to keep the problem from becoming computationally too complex. This leads directly to probability-of-error calculations for QAM signals.

The reason for this is readily apparent using the geometric picture. Consider, for example, the three cases of $M = 3$, 4, and 8 signals located in a two-dimensional plane as portrayed in Fig. 7-36. The minimum-error-probability decision rule for the AWGN channel with equally probable signals assigns the decision to the signal "closest to" the received signal point [Eq. (7-82)]. This then defines a *decision region* around each signal point. Three sets of decision regions appear in the examples of Fig. 7-36. It is apparent that one finds these by locating the perpendicular bisector between pairs of signal points, as shown in Fig. 7-36a, for example. Details are left to the reader.

How does one now calculate the probability of error? One can determine the probability that the received signal vector **v** falls *outside* the specified decision region for a particular signal transmitted, and then average appropriately over the entire signal set, after weighting by the probability of occurrence of the given signal. Alternatively (and this is the approach we shall adopt), one can calculate the probability that the received signal vector **v** falls (correctly) within the desired decision region for each signal and again average appropriately. In either case it is apparent that the evaluation of probabilities over irregular regions, as in Fig. 7-36a, can be quite difficult. The rectangular regions of Fig. 7-36b and c are much simpler to handle, however, and we shall focus on these.

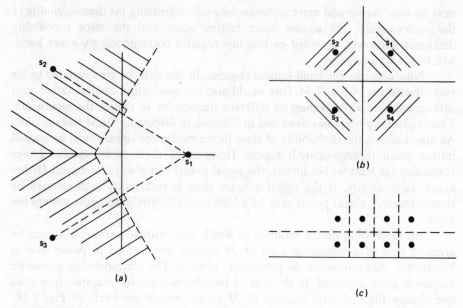

FIGURE 7-36
Examples of signal constellations and optimum decision regions. (a) $M = 3$. (b) $M = 4$. (c) $M = 8$.

Binary Signals

Before proceeding with the probability-of-error calculations for M-ary signaling with rectangular signal constellations (QAM provides a practical example of one such set of signals), we calculate the probability of error for binary signals. The results found agree of course with those already obtained in Sec. 7-3, as well as in Chap. 6. They provide an alternative and instructive way of carrying out the error-probability calculations, and serve to introduce the approach used for more complex signal constellations.

As the first example of the calculation of the probability of error, consider the polar or antipodal signals of Fig. 7-37 spaced d units apart. With the two signals equally likely to be transmitted (as assumed here) it suffices to determine the probability of error for either one. By symmetry this is the same as for the

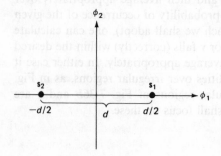

FIGURE 7-37
Polar (antipodal) signal set.

other, and, averaging over both, it is the system probability of error as well. In this case it is apparent that one correlator only in Fig. 7-27 need be used, since the output of the second branch should be zero and could equally well be closed. Alternatively, it could just as well be ignored. This shows up in the decision regions of Fig. 7-37 as well, since it is apparent that $\mathbf{v}$ anywhere in the right half plane should be associated with $\mathbf{s}_1$, while any value in the left half plane is associated with $\mathbf{s}_2$. It is thus the noise n_1 at the ϕ_1 correlator output of Fig. 7-27 only that can cause an error. Specifically, then, let $\mathbf{s}_2$ be transmitted. An error occurs only if $n_1 > d/2$, for then the vector $\mathbf{v} = \mathbf{s}_2 + \mathbf{n}$ (or the scalar $v_1 = s_{21} + n_1$) moves into the $\mathbf{s}_1$ decision region. The probability of this happening is easily calculated as

$$P_e = \int_{d/2}^{\infty} \frac{e^{-x^2/n_0}}{\sqrt{\pi n_0}} \, dx$$

$$= \tfrac{1}{2} \operatorname{erfc} \frac{d}{2\sqrt{n_0}} \tag{7-85}$$

using the known statistics of the gaussian random variable n_1 [see (7-78) and (7-80)]. Here $\operatorname{erfc} x$ is again the *complementary* error function defined as

$$\operatorname{erfc} x \equiv \frac{2}{\sqrt{\pi}} \int_x^{\infty} e^{-y^2} \, dy \tag{7-86}$$

Obviously, the probability of error depends on the signal separation d. For $d/\sqrt{n_0}$ large enough (approximately > 3), P_e decreases exponentially with d^2/n_0. To demonstrate the connection between the error probability P_e and the signal energy E, it is instructive to rewrite P_e in (7-85) in terms of the energy E. (We shall do this in fact with all error calculations.) It is apparent that $d/2 = \sqrt{E}$ in this case. (Recall that $\mathbf{s}_i \cdot \mathbf{s}_i = E$.) Hence for the antipodal signal set of Fig. 7-37,

$$\text{PSK:} \qquad P_e = \tfrac{1}{2} \operatorname{erfc} \sqrt{\frac{E}{n_0}} \tag{7-85a}$$

This agrees of course with the results of Sec. 7-3 and Chap. 6.

Now take the two signal points of Fig. 7-37, keep their distance apart at d units, and move them arbitrarily over the (ϕ_1, ϕ_2) plane. An example is shown in Fig. 7-38a. A little thought will indicate that the probability of error remains the same: the points are still spaced the same distance apart. An error will occur if noise added to one signal point moves the sum more than halfway to the other point. This is exactly the calculation made in obtaining Eq. (7-85). Alternatively, one may choose two other orthonormal signals, ϕ_1' and ϕ_2', linearly dependent on ϕ_1 and ϕ_2, in terms of whose coordinates the $\mathbf{s}_1$ and $\mathbf{s}_2$ of Fig. 7-38a look just like those of Fig. 7-37. This obviously corresponds to rotating and translating the axes of Fig. 7-38 to line up appropriately with $\mathbf{s}_1$ and $\mathbf{s}_2$. The choice of axes does not affect the probability of error. So rotation and translation of a constellation does not affect P_e as long as the points in the constellation all move together. This is a very useful observation in the calculation of probability of error.

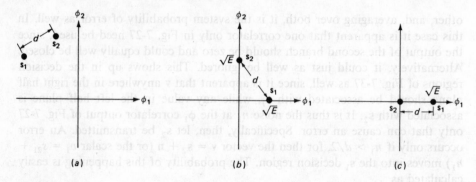

FIGURE 7-38
Translation and rotation of two-signal set. (a) Arbitrary location. (b) FSK. (c) OOK.

What *is* affected is the energy (and hence power) requirement. For as the points move farther away from the origin, the energy required increases. A little thought will in fact indicate that the minimum-energy location of the two signal points of Fig. 7-38a is exactly that of Fig. 7-37 (or the rotated equivalent). In general, the minimum-energy location of any constellation has its center of gravity located at the origin. As an example, consider the two special orientations of the two-signal set shown in Fig. 7-38. The one in Fig. 7-38b has its two signals orthogonal to one another. This thus corresponds to the binary FSK case, with the two frequencies chosen orthogonal to one another. In Fig. 7-38c one signal is always zero. This thus corresponds to on–off or on–off-keyed (OOK) transmission. It is apparent that the FSK signal set requires twice the energy of the polar set for the same probability of error, while the nonzero component of the OOK set requires four times the signal energy. (Its *average* energy, assuming equally likely signals, is only twice as much.)

If the energy in these two examples is kept *fixed*, the spacing d must decrease. This is reflected in the following error-probability equations for the FSK and OOK signals, respectively, obtained from (7-85) by substituting in the appropriate values for d from Fig. 7-38b and c:

$$\text{FSK:} \qquad P_e = \tfrac{1}{2}\,\text{erfc}\sqrt{\frac{E}{2n_0}} \qquad (7\text{-}85b)$$

$$\text{OOK:} \qquad P_e = \tfrac{1}{2}\,\text{erfc}\sqrt{\frac{E}{4n_0}} \qquad (7\text{-}85c)$$

These results agree of course with those found earlier in Chap. 6 and in Sec. 7-3 [see (7-57) to (7-59)]. But note again that the energy E in the case of OOK transmission is the energy of the on-pulse only. Since zero energy is used in the off-case, the *average* energy is $\bar{E} = E/2$, and the performance of OOK transmission, in an average-energy sense, is the same as that for FSK, or 3 dB worse than

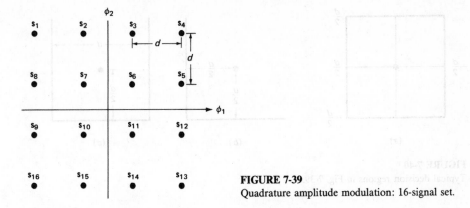

FIGURE 7-39
Quadrature amplitude modulation: 16-signal set.

for PSK. This point has already been made a number of times earlier, particularly in Chap. 6, in discussing both coherent optical transmission and transmission in the presence of additive gaussian noise, as is the case here.

Quadrature Amplitude Modulation (QAM)

The probability-of-error calculation is easily generalized to signals in two dimensions that occupy a rectangular region as in Fig. 7-36c. One particular example is the class of QAM (quadrature-amplitude-modulated) signals. These signals were discussed in some detail in Sec. 4-3 in connection with the need to transmit at high bit rates over band-limited channels such as a telephone or digital-radio channel. As noted in that chapter, QAM signal sets have been implemented in high-speed modems. The binary-signal probability-of-error calculations are easily extended to cover this class of signals. In terms of the notation of the previous section, this class has in general M signals and $N = 2$ orthogonal carriers. Hence the receiver of Fig. 7-26 applies here.

Consider the $M = 16$ signal set of Fig. 7-39 as an example. The signal points are shown spaced d units apart and symmetrically oriented about the origin. This is thus a minimum energy set.

The signals are of varying energy (and hence power) in this type of signal set. This contrasts with a pure M-ary PSK signal set in which the signals are all of equal energy, spaced at different angles around a circle in the (ϕ_1, ϕ_2) plane. Since the signals are of varying amplitude, one can only evaluate the transmission-energy requirements in a statistical sense. For M signals equally likely to be transmitted, the *average* energy is given by

$$\bar{E} = \frac{1}{M} \sum_{i=1}^{M} E_i \tag{7-87}$$

with E_i the energy of signal s_i. For the specific case of Fig. 7-39 with the signals

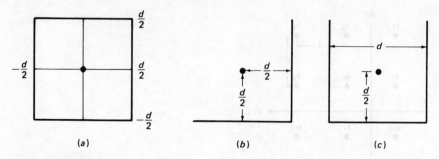

FIGURE 7-40
Typical decision regions in Fig. 7-39.

spaced d units apart,

$$\bar{E} = \frac{1}{16}\left(\frac{4d^2}{2} + \frac{8 \times 10d^2}{4} + \frac{4 \times 18d^2}{4}\right)$$

$$= \tfrac{5}{2}d^2 \tag{7-88}$$

Hence in terms of the average energy,

$$d^2 = \tfrac{2}{5}\bar{E}$$

This serves to connect the spacing d with the average energy.

Now consider the calculation of probability of error of this set. As noted earlier, it is simpler to first find the probability P_c of *correct* reception. Then $P_e = 1 - P_c$. It is apparent from Fig. 7-39 that the decision region for each signal is of rectangular shape. Three types of regions appear in Fig. 7-39. These are indicated in Fig. 7-40. The signal point in question appears at the center of the region in each case.

Consider region a in Fig. 7-40 as an example. It is apparent from Fig. 7-39 that this corresponds to the decision region for signals s_6, s_7, s_{10}, and s_{11}. A received signal vector $\mathbf{v}$ falling inside one of the these regions would result in that signal being declared present. In corresponding fashion, *if* one of these signals s_i *is* transmitted, the probability $P(c|s_i)$ that the signal is received correctly corresponds to the probability that the received signal vector $\mathbf{v}$ lies within the square of Fig. 7-40a. For the QAM signal in question, with $N = 2$ carriers, the correlation detector of Fig. 7-27 produces two output samples with independent gaussian noise terms n_1 and n_2, respectively. For $\mathbf{v}$ to lie within the square of Fig. 7-40a, it is apparent that both n_1 and n_2 must lie within the range $0 \pm d/2$. The probability of correct reception, conditioned on s_i being transmitted ($i = 6, 7, 10$, or 11), is thus

$$P(c|s_i) = \text{Prob}\left(-\frac{d}{2} < n_1 < \frac{d}{2}\right)\text{Prob}\left(-\frac{d}{2} < n_2 < \frac{d}{2}\right)$$

$$= p^2 \tag{7-89}$$

with

$$p = 2 \int_0^{d/2} \frac{e^{-x^2/n_0}}{\sqrt{\pi n_0}} \, dx$$

$$= 2 \int_0^{d/2\sqrt{n_0}} \frac{e^{-x^2}}{\sqrt{\pi}} \, dx$$

$$= \text{erf} \frac{d}{2\sqrt{n_0}} \tag{7-90}$$

Here the property, previously proved, that each of the random variables n_1 and n_2 has variance $n_0/2$ has been used.

In similar manner, the probability of correct reception of signals s_1, s_4, s_{13}, and s_{16} in Fig. 7-39 with the decision region of Fig. 7-40b is readily shown to be

$$P(c|s_i) = r^2 \tag{7-91}$$

$$r = \int_{-d/2}^{\infty} \frac{e^{-x^2/n_0}}{\sqrt{\pi n_0}} \, dx$$

$$= \frac{1}{2} + \frac{p}{2} \tag{7-92}$$

Finally, the probability of correct reception of signals s_2, s_3, s_5, s_{12}, s_{14}, s_{15}, s_8, and s_9 is found from Fig. 7-40c to be given by

$$P(c|s_i) = pr \tag{7-93}$$

The probability of correct reception of an entire signal set is found in general by multiplying the conditional probabilities by the a priori probabilities of transmission and summing:

$$P_c = \sum_{i=1}^{M} P(s_i) P(c|s_i) \tag{7-94}$$

In the special case of the 16-signal set of Fig. 7-39 with the signals equally likely to be transmitted, the probability of correct reception is given simply by

$$P_c = \frac{1}{16} \left[4p^2 + 4p(1 + p) + 4 \left(\frac{1 + p}{2} \right)^2 \right]$$

$$= \frac{(3p + 1)^2}{16} \tag{7-95}$$

with p defined by Eq. (7-90). As a check, if the signals all move far apart, with $d \to \infty$, then $p \to 1$ and $P_c \to 1$.

As in the two-signal case considered previously, it is of interest to write the probability of error directly in terms of energy and noise spectral density. From (7-88), $d^2 = \frac{2}{5}\overline{E}$. Using this in (7-90) for p, letting $P_e = 1 - P_c$, and assuming

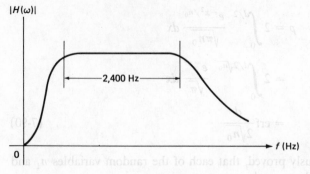

FIGURE 7-41
Amplitude–frequency characteristic, typical telephone channel.

that $P_e \ll 1$ (the desired case), it is readily shown from (7-95) that

$$P_e \doteq \tfrac{3}{2}(1 - p) = \tfrac{3}{2}\,\mathrm{erfc}\sqrt{\frac{\bar{E}}{10n_0}} \qquad (7\text{-}96)$$

Comparing with (7-85a), it is apparent that the 16-signal QAM constellation of Fig. 7-39 requires somewhat more than 10 times the signal power of the PSK signals for the same probability of error. On the other hand, the system is effectively transmitting at four times the bit rate possible with PSK alone. This is the price one pays for packing more signals into the same "signal space."

An example serves to put this in perspective. Assume that we have a telephone channel over which data are to be transmitted for which the useful transmission bandwidth is 2,400 Hz (see Fig. 7-41). If PSK or OOK transmission were to be used, the carrier would be centered in the useful band. Depending on the Nyquist signal shaping used, 1,200- to just under 2,400-bit/s signals could then be transmitted. Vestigial-sideband techniques, with the carrier located at either the upper or the lower part of the band, could be used to increase the bit rate allowable to almost 4,800 bits/s. If FSK transmission were used instead, two carriers with a modulation index of $\beta = 0.7$ could be chosen within the bandwidth. In this case the modulation bandwidth available would be about 700 Hz, and the *maximum* bit rate possible 1,400 bits/s.

But assume now that 16-signal QAM is used instead. If noise is no problem on the channel, the data rate allowable can range from 4,800 to just under 9,600 bits/s, depending on the signal shaping used. From Eq. (7-96), however, the signal-to-noise ratio $\bar{E}/n_0$ should be at least 100 or 20 dB to have $P_e \leq 10^{-5}$. This signal-to-noise ratio is quite acceptable for the telephone channel, with 30-dB signal-to-noise ratios commonly measured. In the case of the telephone channel, limitations on data transmission arise not from gaussian noise but from such other factors as intersymbol interference, phase jitter, and impulse noise. This has already been noted. As was also noted in Sec. 4-3, data modems allowing up to 19.2-kbit/s transmission over telephone channels are available, but only over specially conditioned channels to widen the bandwidth available.

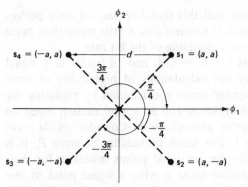

FIGURE 7-42
Four-signal set.

They also incorporate adaptive equalizers to further shape or equalize the channel characteristics to reduce intersymbol interference, and the signal constellation used may be chosen to reduce errors due to phase jitter rather than to improve the error performance due to noise.

Although the AWGN channel model is thus not a very accurate one for the telephone channel, the concepts developed here are nonetheless quite useful in describing data transmission over that channel. Matched filtering is used, in addition to further equalization to reduce intersymbol interference. QAM transmission is commonly used, and the signal-constellation description is found extremely useful as well. In addition, as the effects of intersymbol interference and phase jitter are reduced, the ultimate limitations due to thermal noise eventually come into focus. The AWGN channel model thus serves as a bound on the transmission capability of a channel such as the band-limited telephone channel. We shall return to this point shortly in discussing the Shannon capacity bound. The example of digital radio will be discussed separately at the end of this section.

Another example of a signal set whose error performance in additive white gaussian noise is easily evaluated is the $M = 4$ QAM set used to motivate this material, and plotted in Fig. 7-25. The signal-constellation plot is repeated here in Fig. 7-42. It may also be considered as an example of a QPSK (four-phase PSK) signal set.

Letting the spacing between pairs of points again be d units, it is apparent that the four decision regions are identically those of Fig. 7-40b. The probability of correct reception is thus given, because of the symmetry, by

$$P_c = r^2 \tag{7-97}$$

as in (7-91) and (7-92). Since $E = d^2/2$ in this case, as may be noted from Fig. 7-42, it is left to the reader to show that

$$P_e = 2 \int_{\sqrt{E/2n_0}}^{\infty} \frac{e^{-x^2}}{\sqrt{\pi}} \, dx = \mathrm{erfc} \sqrt{\frac{E}{2n_0}} \tag{7-98}$$

Comparing with (7-85b), it is apparent that this signal set has an error performance similar to that of an FSK signal. It requires just a little more than twice the energy of the PSK signal but allows a doubling of the bit rate.

Can one generalize these results for $M = 2$, 4, and 16 points in a signal constellation? Clearly, one can carry out calculations of probability of error versus average energy for any rectangular signal constellation by repeating the technique just described. A simple observation, and an approximation based on it, do lead to an interesting and useful generalization. Consider an M-point rectangular constellation with $M \gg 1$. For small probability of error P_e it is apparent that errors will be primarily due to signal points mistaken for their nearest neighbors. The chance of additive noise moving a signal point to one closest to a nonneighboring point is truly miniscule. As an example, in Fig. 7-39 for 16-QAM, the transmission of signal s_4 might occasionally be detected as s_3 or s_5, due to noise, but its detection as s_{12} or s_2 is extremely unlikely. For $P_e \leq 10^{-4}$, say, the spacing d (and hence the average energy $\bar{E}$) is large enough to keep the probability that s_4 is detected as s_{12} or s_3 very small. Even its detection as s_6 is an unlikely event, occurring with probability $\ll P_e$.

Say M now quadruples. 16-QAM now becomes 64-QAM, as an example. To maintain the same probability of error the spacing between the signal points must remain about the same. The new constellation now covers about four times the area it did before. To a first approximation, the average energy $\bar{E}$ is proportional to the area covered by the points and must quadruple as well. We thus have, for P_e fixed and $M \gg 1$,

$$\bar{E} \doteq MKd^2 \tag{7-99}$$

with d the spacing between the points (Figs. 7-38, 7-39, 7-42) and K a constant.

Take the two cases already discussed as examples. For QPSK (4-QAM), we had $\bar{E} = d^2/2$ from Fig. 7-42, while from (7-88), we have $\bar{E} = 5d^2/2$ for 16-QAM. The factor of 5 here is close to 4, the ratio of the number of signal points in the two cases.

Continuing with the approximation we have suggested, we have, for small P_e,

$$P_e \doteq \operatorname{erfc} \frac{d}{2\sqrt{n_0}} \tag{7-100}$$

This generalizes, in an approximate fashion, (7-85) for the binary signal case. A multiplicative factor in front of the erfc has been left out in this approximation, since it is typically of the order of unity. The erfc, which varies exponentially with d for small P_e, clearly dominates the error-probability calculation. Using (7-99), we then get, as an approximation for the probability of error for an M-QAM system, with $M \gg 1$ and $P_e \ll 1$,

$$P_e \doteq \operatorname{erfc} C\sqrt{\frac{\bar{E}}{Mn_0}} \qquad M \gg 1, \quad P_e \ll 1 \tag{7-101}$$

The constant C is used to subsume both K and the factor of 2 appearing in (7-100).

How accurate is this approximation? Calculations carried out for large M for digital-radio applications show that it is indeed quite good for design purposes. To check the validity of the approximation it is useful to reinterpret the ratio E/n_0 in terms of the more commonly used signal-power-to-noise-power ratio. Specifically, say sinusoidal roll-off shaping is used with the QAM transmission, as first discussed in Sec. 4-3. The signal transmission bandwidth, from our discussion in Sec. 4-3, is

$$B_T = \frac{1}{T}(1 + r) \qquad (7\text{-}102)$$

with $1/T$ the QAM signal rate and r the roll-off factor. The matched filter used at the receiver will have this bandwidth as well, and will effectively convert the additive white noise at its input to band-limited noise with average power $N = n_0 B_T$. Letting S be the average signal power, we must have $\bar{E} = ST$, since a QAM signal lasts T units of time. Putting all of this together, we have

$$\frac{\bar{E}}{n_0} = \frac{ST}{n_0} = \frac{S(1 + r)}{n_0 B_T} = \frac{S}{N}(1 + r) \qquad (7\text{-}103)$$

All E/n_0 values can thus be converted directly to signal-to-noise ratios, with due account taken of the roll-off factor r. Equation (7-101) for the probability of error can be written, using (7-103), in terms of S/N.

As an example, take 16-QAM, for which P_e was given by (7-96). For $P_e = 10^{-4}$, it is readily shown that $E/n_0 = 69.5$, or 18.4 dB. As a check, one can use Fig. 7-22. This shows that PSK requires $E/n_0 = 8.3$ dB for $P_e = 10^{-4}$. Comparing (7-96) with (7-85a) for PSK and ignoring the factors in front of the erfc, it is noted that 16-QAM requires 10 times as much signal energy. This produces a value of $E/n_0 = 18.3$ dB, quite close to the calculated value. For a roll-off factor $r = 0.5$, the signal-to-noise ratio required is 16.5 dB. This compares with a value of about 18 dB appearing in a paper on digital radio [KOHI].[6] The same paper indicates that for $P_e = 10^{-4}$ and $r = 0.5$, the conditions chosen above, 64-QAM requires a S/N of over 24 dB, 256-QAM a S/N of 31 dB, and 1024-QAM a S/N of 37 dB. Since 6 dB corresponds to a factor of 4, these numbers validate the original assumption (7-99), as well as the approximation (7-101) based on it: As the number of points in the signal constellation increases by M, the energy (and hence S/N) required, for the same error probability, increases by the same factor. This relationship will be exploited further in Sec. 7-7, after discussing the Shannon capacity expression in more detail.

---

[6][KOHI] K. Kohiyama and O. Kurita, "Future Trends in Microwave Digital Radio: A View from Asia," *IEEE Commun. Mag.*, vol. 25, no. 2, pp. 41–46, February 1987.

The approximation (7-101) for the probability of error of QAM systems with large constellations is further validated by a figure appearing in [MEYE].[7] Figure 2 in that paper, for the case $P_e = 10^{-6}$ and $r = \frac{1}{3}$, also shows a 6-dB, or factor-of-4, increase in S/N required as M increases by a factor of 4. That figure will also be discussed in Sec. 7-7.

7-6 *M*-ARY ORTHOGONAL SIGNALS

We now consider the case of M orthogonal signals. As noted earlier in this chapter, this class of signals is most useful for a power-limited channel: as M increases, the transmission bandwidth goes up in proportion, but the probability of error is found to decrease exponentially. An example of such a signal set for $M = 3$ has already been shown in Fig. 7-35. More generally, we have $N = M$ carriers required, and we can write

$$s_1(t) = \sqrt{E}\,\phi_1(t), \quad s_2(t) = \sqrt{E}\,\phi_2(t), \quad \ldots, \quad s_M(t) = \sqrt{E}\,\phi_M(t) \quad (7\text{-}104)$$

(The signals are all taken to be of equal energy.) In vector form, we have

$$\mathbf{s}_1 = (\sqrt{E}, 0, \ldots, 0)$$
$$\mathbf{s}_2 = (0, \sqrt{E}, \ldots, 0)$$
$$\mathbf{s}_M = (0, 0, \ldots, \sqrt{E}) \qquad (7\text{-}105)$$

Such signals satisfy the orthogonality condition

$$\int_0^T s_i(t)s_j(t)\,dt = E\delta_{ij} \qquad (7\text{-}106)$$

with δ_{ij} the Kronecker delta:

$$\delta_{ij} = 1 \qquad i = j$$
$$= 0 \qquad i \le j$$

In the vector-space formulation,

$$\mathbf{s}_i \cdot \mathbf{s}_j = E\delta_{ij} \qquad (7\text{-}107)$$

Examples of such signals are M frequencies, displaced roughly $1/T$ hertz to make them orthogonal; M pulses or pulsed sine waves, each lasting T/M seconds, each displaced from one another in time by T/M seconds (see Fig. 7-43); and coded orthogonal signals (Fig. 7-44). The M pulses of Fig. 7-43 are quite inefficient in their use of power, since they only occupy $1/M$ of the entire time interval T seconds long. For the same energy (or average power) the peak power must be M times as large. Figure 7-44 shows an example of three signals lasting the entire T-second interval that are orthogonal to one another. These are

---

[7][MEYE] M. H. Meyers and V. K. Prabhu, "Future Trends in Microwave Digital Radio; a View from North America," *IEEE Commun. Mag.*, vol. 25, no. 2, pp. 46–49, February 1987.

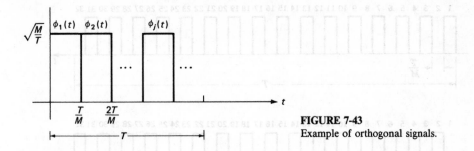

FIGURE 7-43
Example of orthogonal signals.

more efficient than the pulses of Fig. 7-43. Generally, one divides the T-second interval into M subintervals T/M seconds apart. If binary transmission is used on each one of these subintervals, there are 2^M possible signal variations. One would then select M of these that are orthogonal. The pulse at each subinterval could then be used to modulate a sine-wave carrier or either of two quadrature carriers. An example of two orthogonal signals for the case of $M = 32$ appears in Fig. 7-45.

It is apparent that the bandwidth requirements for a set of M baseband orthogonal signals ranges from $M/2T$ to M/T, depending on the pulse shaping used. For a bit rate of R bits/s, $k = RT$ bits are encoded to form the M-ary signals. We thus have $M = 2^{RT}$, and the bandwidth actually increases exponentially with the encoding time T. This is one major drawback in the use of M-ary orthogonal signals. For high-frequency M-ary transmission the bandwidth dou-

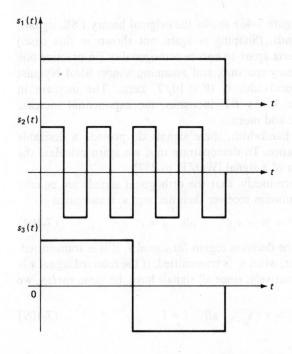

FIGURE 7-44
Another example of orthogonal signals.

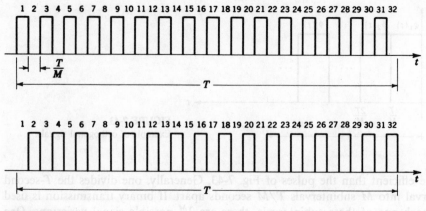

FIGURE 7-45
Orthogonal signals, $M = 32$.

bles. Consider as an example M-ary FSK transmission, with one of $M = 32$ different frequencies to be transmitted every T seconds. A typical sine wave is shown in Fig. 7-46a. Assuming almost optimum Nyquist shaping in this case (the shaping is not shown in Fig. 7-46a), and spacing signals $1/T$ hertz apart to ensure orthogonal signaling, one gets as the overall transmission bandwidth for this M-ary signal set

$$W = \frac{32}{T}$$

This is shown in Fig. 7-46b. Figure 7-46c shows the original binary FSK signals, each lasting $1/R = T/5$ seconds. (Shaping is again not shown in this case.) Spacing these two signals R hertz apart to ensure orthogonality (in practice one might pick $0.7 R$ as the frequency spacing), and assuming almost ideal Nyquist shaping again, the original bandwidth is $W = 10/T$ hertz. The increase in bandwidth is thus about 3 to 1. As RT increases, the exponential increase $M = 2^{RT}$ comes into play more and more.

Despite this increase in bandwidth, these signals do provide a desirable improvement in error performance. To demonstrate this, we again calculate the probability of *correct* reception of a signal [WOZE, p. 257].

Specifically, assume, as previously, that the orthogonal signals are equally likely to be transmitted. An optimum receiver then declares $\mathbf{s}_i$ transmitted if

$$\|\mathbf{v} - \mathbf{s}_i\|^2 < \|\mathbf{v} - \mathbf{s}_j\|^2 \quad \text{all} \quad j \neq i \tag{7-108}$$

Equation (7-108) then defines the decision region for signal $\mathbf{s}_i$ if it is transmitted. The decision will thus be correct, when $\mathbf{s}_i$ is transmitted, if the received signal $\mathbf{v}$ is such as to satisfy (7-108). Alternatively, since all signals have the same energy, we must have

$$\mathbf{v} \cdot \mathbf{s}_i > \mathbf{v} \cdot \mathbf{s}_j \quad \text{all} \quad j \neq i \tag{7-109}$$

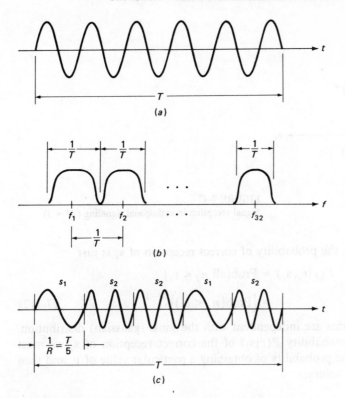

FIGURE 7-46
M-ary FSK transmission, $M = 32$, minimum bandwidths. (a) 1 of 32 frequencies. (b) Bandwidth $W \doteq 32/T$ hertz. (c) Original binary signals: Bandwidth $\doteq 10/T$ hertz.

This is exactly the receiver implementation of Fig. 7-32 if all the signals have the same energy. But $\mathbf{s}_i$ may be written $\mathbf{s}_i = \sqrt{E}\, \phi_i$ with ϕ_i a unit vector in the ϕ_i direction (see Fig. 7-47). Then $\mathbf{v} \cdot \mathbf{s}_i = v_i \sqrt{E}$, with v_i the projection of $\mathbf{v}$ along the $\mathbf{s}_i$ axis. (v_2 is shown, for example, in Fig. 7-47). The optimum receiver for the orthogonal signal case thus declares signal $\mathbf{s}_i$ present if

$$v_i > v_j \quad \text{all} \quad j \neq i \tag{7-110}$$

This also defines the region of correct reception of $\mathbf{s}_i$ if that is the signal transmitted.

In words, signal $\mathbf{s}_i$ is correctly received if the component of $\mathbf{v}$ along the i axis is greater than the components along all the other axes. But with $\mathbf{s}_i$ transmitted,

$$v_i = \sqrt{E} + n_i \qquad v_j = n_j \quad \text{all} \quad j \neq i \tag{7-111}$$

(see Fig. 7-48). As previously, the n_j's are all zero-mean, independent gaussian variables, with variance $= n_0/2$. Note from (7-110) and (7-111) that the signal $\mathbf{s}_i$ will be correctly received if, given v_i, all $n_j < v_i$. Thus, *conditioned* on a

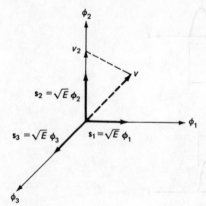

FIGURE 7-47
Signal reception in orthogonal signaling ($M = 3$).

particular value of v_i, the probability of correct reception of $\mathbf{s}_i$ is just

$$P(c|v_i, \mathbf{s}_i) = \text{Prob}(\text{all } n_j < v_i)$$

$$= \left[\text{Prob}(n_j < v_i)\right]^{M-1} \tag{7-112}$$

since all the noise terms are independent with the same (gaussian) distribution. To find the desired probability $P(c|\mathbf{s}_i)$ of the correct reception of $\mathbf{s}_i$ we must multiply (7-112) by the probability of obtaining a particular value of v_i and then sum over all possible values:

$$P(c|\mathbf{s}_i) = \int P(c|v_i, \mathbf{s}_i) f(v_i) \, dv_i \tag{7-113}$$

From (7-111), however, v_i is gaussian with average value $\sqrt{E}$. Using this plus the fact that n_j is zero-mean gaussian, it is left to the reader to show that (7-113) becomes

$$P(c|\mathbf{s}_i) = \int_{-\infty}^{\infty} \frac{e^{-(y-\sqrt{E})^2/n_0}}{\sqrt{\pi n_0}} \left[P(n < y)\right]^{M-1} dy \tag{7-114}$$

where

$$P(n < y) = \int_{-\infty}^{y} \frac{1}{\sqrt{\pi n_0}} e^{-x^2/n_0} \, dx \tag{7-115}$$

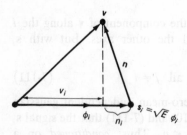

FIGURE 7-48
Geometry of received signal, M-ary signaling.

Since the signals are assumed equally likely, and all have the same probability $P(c|s_i)$ of being received correctly, (7-114) represents the probability of an error-free transmission for the M orthogonal signals transmitted over the AWGN channel. Note that it depends on E/n_0 and M. Equation (7-114) cannot be integrated exactly. Tables and curves for $P_e = 1 - P_c$ have been obtained numerically. One such set of curves appears in Fig. 7-49 [VITE 1966, fig. 8.3]. Here, in

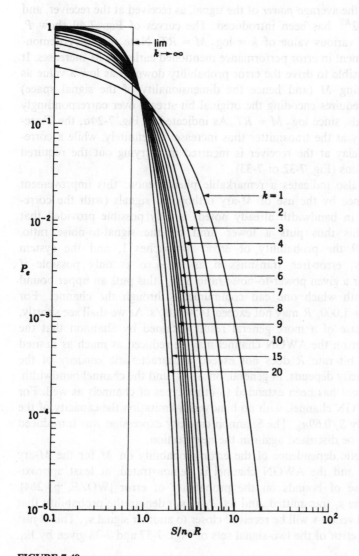

FIGURE 7-49
Error probability for orthogonal signals ($k = \log_2 M$). (From A. J. Viterbi, *Principles of Coherent Communication*, McGraw-Hill, New York, 1966, fig. 8.3, with permission.)

place of E/n_0 and M, use has been made of the relation

$$\frac{E}{n_0} = \frac{ST}{n_0} = \frac{S}{n_0 R}(RT)$$

$$= \frac{S \log_2 M}{n_0 R} \tag{7-116}$$

S again represents the average *power* of the signal, as received at the receiver, and the relation $M = 2^{RT}$ has been introduced. The curves of Fig. 7-49 show P_e versus $S/n_0 R$ for various value of $k = \log_2 M = RT$. Note that they demonstrate the improvement in error performance mentioned earlier as M increases. It is theoretically possible to drive the error probability down to as low a value as desired by increasing M (and hence the dimensionality of the signal space) indefinitely. This requires encoding the original bit stream over correspondingly longer time intervals, since $\log_2 M = RT$. As indicated in Fig. 7-24a, the T-second encoding delay at the transmitter thus increases indefinitely, while a correspondingly long delay at the receiver is incurred in carrying out the required correlation operations (Fig. 7-32 or 7-33).

Figure 7-49 also indicates a remarkable phenomenon: this improvement in error performance by the use of M-ary orthogonal signals (with the corresponding increase in bandwidth already noted) is only possible provided that $S/n_0 R > 0.69$. This thus puts a lower limit on the signal-to-noise ratio. For $S/n_0 R < 0.69$ the probability of error approaches 1, and the system fails. Alternatively, error-free transmission as $M \to \infty$ is only possible if $R < S/0.69 n_0$. For a given power-to-noise ratio S/n_0, this puts an upper bound on the rate R with which one can communicate through the channel. For example, if $S/n_0 = 1,000$, R may not exceed 1450 bits/s. As we shall see shortly, this is a special case of a more general result obtained by Shannon that the probability of error on the AWGN channel may be reduced as much as desired *provided* that the bit rate R does not exceed a characteristic *capacity* of the channel. This capacity depends, in general, on S, n_0, and the channel bandwidth. The capacity concept has been extended to other types of channels as well. For the case of an AWGN channel, with no bandwidth limitation the capacity of the channel is precisely $S/0.69 n_0$. The Shannon capacity expression was introduced in Sec. 6-3. It will be discussed again in the next section.

The asymptotic dependence of the error probability on M for the M-ary orthogonal signal and the AWGN channel is demonstrated, at least approximately, by the use of bounds on the probability of error [WOZE, p. 264]. Specifically, assume $\mathbf{s}_i$ transmitted, and let $P_e(\mathbf{s}_i, \mathbf{s}_k)$ denote the probability that the received signal vector $\mathbf{v}$ will be received closer to another signal $\mathbf{s}_k$. This is just the probability of error of the two-signal sets of Figs. 7-37 and 7-38 given by Eq. (7-85):

$$P_e(\mathbf{s}_i, \mathbf{s}_k) = \tfrac{1}{2} \operatorname{erfc} \frac{d}{2\sqrt{n_0}} \tag{7-117}$$

If we now have one of M signals present, as is the case here, an error will occur if $\mathbf{v}$ is closer to $\mathbf{s}_k$ than to the transmitted $\mathbf{s}_i$ for at least one such signal $\mathbf{s}_k$, $k \neq i$. As a loose upper bound we can say the probability of this happening is just the sum of $M - 1$ terms like that of (7-117). Thus

$$P_e \leq \sum_{k=1}^{M-1} P_e(\mathbf{s}_i, \mathbf{s}_k)$$

$$= \frac{M-1}{2} \operatorname{erfc} \frac{d}{2\sqrt{n_0}} \tag{7-118}$$

But the orthogonal signals under consideration are pairwise $d = \sqrt{2E}$ units apart (see Fig. 7-47). Hence we have

$$P_e < \frac{M}{2} \operatorname{erfc} \sqrt{\frac{E}{2n_0}} \tag{7-119}$$

and the right-hand term is a loose upper bound on the exact expression found from (7-114).

A simple bound on $\operatorname{erfc} x$ is readily found to be given by

$$\tfrac{1}{2} \operatorname{erfc} x < e^{-x^2} \tag{7-120}$$

Hence

$$P_e < M e^{-E/2n_0} \tag{7-121}$$

from (7-119). Letting $M = 2^{RT} = e^{0.69RT}$ and $E = ST$, with S the average power of the signals, (7-121) becomes

$$P_e < e^{-T[(S/2n_0) - 0.69R]} \tag{7-122}$$

This is the desired bound. It indicates that P_e decreases exponentially with increasing T *provided* that the bit rate R is less than a specified number. The number shown here is half that noted earlier and indicated in Fig. 7-49. This is due to the looseness of the original bound of (7-118). A tighter bound actually provides the desired result that $P_e \to 0$ exponentially in T, provided that $R < S/0.69n_0$.

This exponential decrease in the probability of error for orthogonal signals is obviously quite desirable, since it shows that power-limited channels may be used effectively in the presence of noise by proper coding of signals. The improvement in error performance is not as dramatic or practical as might at first be expected, however, because of the extremely large values of M required. Specifically, consider that $P_e = 10^{-5}$. From Fig. 7-49 note that the signal-to-noise ratio required to attain this error probability decreases very slowly with increasing M. Thus in going from $M = 2$ ($k = 1$), or binary FSK, to $M = 32$ ($k = 5$) orthogonal signals, the signal-to-noise ratio required is reduced only 6 dB, from $S/n_0 R = 20$ to 5. A 10-dB reduction to $S/n_0 R = 2$ would require the storage and coding of 20 consecutive bits. This by itself is not too difficult (as we shall see, practical binary codes store far more than 20 bits), but the system then requires the generation of 2^{20} different orthogonal signals, as well as a bandwidth expansion of this order. For this reason error-reduction techniques for use with power-limited channels have moved more in the direction of sophisticated coding procedures, to be discussed in a later section.

The geometric reason for the error improvement with increasing T goes as follows. The signal points are each located at the point $\sqrt{E}$ on one axis of an $N = M$-dimensional space. As T increases, so does $E = ST$. The noise variance remains the same, however, so the possibility of noise moving a given signal point to another decreases. Alternatively, if the received signal is divided by $\sqrt{T}$, renormalizing the geometric hyperplane of $M = N$ dimensions, all signal points remain at a fixed distance $\sqrt{S}$ from the origin. The noise variance is reduced by T, however. As the dimensionality of the signal space increases, then, the noise tends to cluster more about the signal point corresponding to the one transmitted. The noise terms tend to fall within spheres more and more tightly packed about the signal points. As long as $S/n_0 R > 0.69$, these spheres do not overlap, and the probability of an error becomes rarer as T gets larger.

Space-Channel Applications

The discussion of M-ary orthogonal signaling and its comparison with binary signaling can be clarified further by considering a few simple examples drawn from space communication. Recall that in Sec. 6-15 of Chap. 6 we obtained a simple expression (6-251) for the received power intercepted by a receiving antenna of area A_R, with efficiency η_R, located at a distance d meters from the transmitter. Repeating that expression here, we have

$$S_R = \frac{S_T}{4\pi d^2} G_T A_R \eta_R \tag{7-123}$$

G_T represents the transmitter antenna again over an isotropic radiator and is in turn given by

$$G_T = \frac{4\pi \eta_T A_T}{\lambda^2} \tag{7-124}$$

with A_T the transmitting antenna area (cross-sectional aperture), η_T the antenna efficiency, and λ the wavelength of the transmission.

Given the various parameters of the transmitter–receiver system, and the known spacing d between them, we can calculate the received power. For a given bit rate of transmission this enables us to calculate the energy E intercepted by the receiver. Recall that the noise spectral density was given by $n_0 = kT$. Knowing the system temperature T and the energy, we can then calculate the fundamental ratio E/n_0 that determines the performance of the system.

Alternatively, and more properly, we use the approach of Sec. 6-15. We *specify* the performance desired (bit-error probability tolerable), and from this determine the bit transmission rate R (in bits/s) allowable. In particular, how much improvement does the introduction of M-ary orthogonal signaling provide us? We have already seen that this improvement increases rather slowly with M, but the use of some examples makes this point more dramatic.

Example 1. $T = 100$ K, $S_T = 100$ W. Let the antenna efficiencies be 1, for simplicity. We also neglect system power losses. The frequency is

$$f = 2,000 \text{ MHz} \quad (\lambda = 0.15 \text{ m})$$

and

$$d = 10^6 \text{ mi} = 1.6 \times 10^9 \text{ m}$$

The receiving antenna has a 13-by-13-ft aperture, so that $A_R \doteq 19$ m^2 and $G_R \sim 10^4$. Let the transmitting antenna be much smaller, with $G_T \sim 100$. Then from (7-123), $S_R \doteq 6 \times 10^{-15}$ W and $S_R/n_0 \doteq 3.5 \times 10^6$.

If binary PSK transmission is used, and $P_e \leq 10^{-5}$ desired, we must have $E/n_0 \geq 10$. It is then apparent, since $E = S_R/R$, with R the binary transmission rate in bits/s, that $R \leq 3.5 \times 10^5$ bits/s. So the use of binary transmission, with no additional encoding, limits the rate of transmission to less than 3.5×10^5 bits/s in order to provide a tolerable error probability. Note again that in all examples discussed in this chapter it was E/n_0 that determined the probability of error. The only way to increase the effective signal energy E received at the antenna, and reduce P_e, without resorting to further signal encoding, is by slowing down the signal rate, allowing the signal to be received over a longer interval of time.

The use of M-ary orthogonal signaling can improve this situation. Thus, for $M = 32$ ($RT = 5$ input binary symbols must be stored), and $P_e \leq 10^{-5}$, Figure 7-49 indicates that $S_R/n_0 R \geq 5$. Hence $R \leq 700,000$ bits/s.[8] This is an improvement of $2:1$ over the previous maximum binary rate. Although there is improvement with increasing M, it is quite slow, as already noted. The resultant system is also much more complex than the binary system, requiring, in addition to the encoder and decoder, a transmitter capable of producing 32 orthogonal signals and a 32-bank correlation receiver. The bandwidth required is also several times that for the binary signal. Continuing to increase M by storing additional binary digits (with a corresponding increase in complexity and bandwidth), one finds from Fig. 7-49 that for $M = 2^{10} = 1,024$, $E/n_0 = S_R/n_0 R \geq 3.2$ for $P_e \leq 10^{-5}$. For the example given here, $R \leq 1.09 \times 10^6$ bits/s. In the limit as M gets very large, $S_R/n_0 R = 0.69$ is required to drive P_e to as low a value as possible. In this example the *maximum* rate of transmission, with M very large, is $R = 5 \times 10^6$ bits/s, an increase of $10/0.69 = 14.5$ in the transmission rate over binary PSK transmission, but clearly impractical using M-ary orthogonal signaling techniques.

Example 2. This is the same as the previous example, but with receiving antennas increased considerably to 55-by-55-ft dishes. Then $A_R \doteq 300$ m^2, $G_R \doteq 1.5 \times 10^5$, $S_R/n_0 \doteq 18 \times 10^6$, and $R \leq 5.3 \times 10^6$ bits/s for binary transmission with $P_e \leq 10^{-5}$. The 15-fold increase in antenna size leads to a corresponding 15-fold increase in the binary transmission rate. The $M = 32$ signaling rate can be increased 15-fold as well to $R \leq 10.5 \times 10^6$ bits/s.

---

[8] The curves of Fig. 7-49 actually refer to the *character*-error probability, i.e., the probability that one of the M signals will be in error. This may be readily converted to bit-error probability, if so desired. See [VITE 1966, p. 227, fig. 8.6]. For $M \gg 1$, there is no essential difference between the two.

Example 3. Let $f = 500$ MHz, and use the same receiving antenna as in (2) above. Then G_R is approximately 10^4. Assume that the transmitter average power is now 1 W, let the temperature be 200 K, and let $G_T = 10$ at this lower transmitting frequency. Then, with $d = 10^6$ mi again, 2,900 bits/s is the maximum data transmission rate at $P_e = 10^{-5}$ if PSK transmission is used. It can be increased to 5,800 bits/s with $M = 32$-orthogonal-signal transmission and in the limit approaches 42 kbits/s for very large M. If the transmission distance increases to $d = 10^7$ mi, it is apparent that the received power drops by 100, and the maximum data rate drops to 29 bits/s using PSK transmission.

Example 4. $f = 2,000$ MHz, $S_T = 8$ W, and $d = 8 \times 10^{11}$ m. (This is the distance to Jupiter.) Assume that the effective temperature of the sky plus noise from the antenna and receiving system is $T = 50$ K. A 45-by-45-ft ground antenna is used, and its efficiency is $\eta = 0.6$. Then $G_R = 8 \times 10^4$. Let the space antenna gain be $G_T = 8 \times 10^{13}$. (This corresponds to a 15-by-15-ft or 5-by-5-m dish, much larger than in the previous example.) It is left to the reader to show that $R \leq 140$ bits/s for binary transmission and $R \leq 280$ bits/s for 32-orthogonal-signal transmission, if $P_e = 10^{-5}$ is desired, while the limiting bit rate using M-ary signaling is 2,000 bits/s.[9]

These numbers indicate the dilemma a designer faces in a power-limited AWGN channel as exemplified by the space channel. As distances between the earth and the space probe increase, it appears that the data transmission rate must decrease correspondingly (going as $1/d^2$), unless the power and antenna size can be increased. These are precisely the trade-offs that were discussed earlier in Sec. 6-15. Alternatively, it is possible to get some further improvement by appropriate encoding of data symbols.

This is of course the procedure adopted in going to M-ary orthogonal signal transmission. We showed in this case that it was in fact possible to improve the bit rate, at a given error probability, by using large values of M, but that the rate of improvement was rather slow. As $M \to \infty$, however, an improvement of 14.5 in the bit rate is possible at $P_e = 10^{-5}$, and the error probability in fact can be reduced as low as desired in this case. The question then raised is: Are there other encoding schemes, perhaps more effective than M-ary orthogonal signaling, that can provide a desired improvement over binary signaling alone with no further encoding? The answer is "yes." There exist many such schemes, and we shall explore some of these in following sections. Interestingly, however, the best possible encoding scheme can do no better than the M-ary orthogonal signal case with $M \to \infty$. To demonstrate this we discuss next the famous Shannon capacity expression that puts a bound on the rate of *error-free* digital signal transmission.

---

[9]Note that by adjusting the various design parameters appropriately, as discussed in Sec. 6-15, communication with Jupiter at a rate of 115 kbits/s has actually been achieved. The example here is purely hypothetical.

An important point to note, however: we look for encoding schemes because theory indicates that they might provide more than 10 times the bit rate allowed by noncoded binary transmission. (The number, again, is $10/0.69 = 14.5$ at $P_e = 10^{-5}$.) However, just as in the case of M-ary orthogonal signaling, very wide bandwidths are required. This is obviously not acceptable with band-limited channels such as the telephone channel. Complex coders and decoders may thus not be appropriate in that case. It is for power-limited channels such as the space channel, with relatively wide bandwidths allowed, that one thinks in terms of sophisticated coding techniques to improve digital-transmission capability.

7-7 THE SHANNON CAPACITY EXPRESSION

Although the Shannon capacity expression has been referred to previously in this book (see Sec. 6-3, for example), we now explain its significance in detail, in order to motivate the need for encoding techniques for digital communications.

Figure 7-22 indicates the best performance possible using binary signals in the presence of additive white gaussian noise. Figure 7-49 shows that one may improve the performance by going to M-ary orthogonal signaling, although large improvements are obviously impractical, since they require enormous values of M. Is it then possible to improve the performance in some other way, using some other form of signaling?

This question was essentially answered in Chap. 6 in discussing the Shannon capacity expression (6-34). We indicated there that Shannon had proven that virtually error-free digital transmission was possible over a channel with additive gaussian noise, providing one did not try to exceed the channel capacity in bits per second. Specifically, assume as in Chap. 6 an available transmission bandwidth of W hertz. Band-limited gaussian noise of spectral density $n_0/2$ is added during transmission. (This is just the assumption made in the cases of optimum binary and M-ary transmission). Then Shannon was able to show that by appropriately *coding* a binary message sequence before transmission it should be possible to achieve as low an error rate as possible provided the channel capacity C was not exceeded. The capacity expression in this case of band-limited white noise was found by Shannon to be given by[10]

$$C = W \log_2\left(1 + \frac{S}{N}\right) \qquad \text{bits/s} \qquad (7\text{-}125)$$

with S the average signal power and $N = n_0 W$ the average noise power. (S/N is then the signal-to-noise ratio at the receiver.)

Thus, provided one did not attempt to transmit more than C bits/s over such a channel, one could hope to attain tolerable error rates. Specifically, if the

---

[10][SHAN 1949]. See also [WOZE, p. 323] and [GALL] R. G. Gallager, *Information Theory and Reliable Communication*, Wiley, New York, 1968, pp. 373, 389.

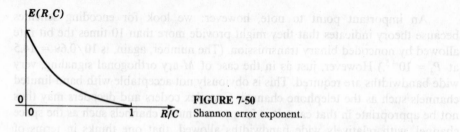

FIGURE 7-50 Shannon error exponent.

binary transmission rate is R bits/s (the binary interval is then $1/R$ seconds), and if $R < C$, it may be shown that the error probability is bounded by

$$P_e \leq 2^{-E(C, R)T} \qquad R < C \qquad (7\text{-}126)$$

with $E(C, R)$ a positive function such as the one shown in Fig. 7-50. As the transmission R approaches C the probability of error $\rightarrow 1$. This is apparent from (7-126) and Fig. 7-50.

The parameter T appearing in (7-126) indicates the time required to transmit the *encoded* signal. With binary transmission rate R and channel capacity C fixed, the probability of error may be reduced by increasing T. Although Shannon proved the capacity expression (7-125) quite generally for the *gaussian channel*, he did not provide a formula for actually designing the required encoder. His proof indicates that it is *possible* to transmit at as low an error rate as possible, but does not show how. A great deal of research in the years since Shannon developed his capacity expression has been devoted to the investigation of various types of encoders.

Not only does the need to design encoders provide a drawback to the application of Shannon's theorem, but an additional complication enters into the picture. As one tries for lower and lower probabilities of error, the encoding time T becomes longer and longer. A delay of T seconds in transmission is then incurred at the transmitter. A corresponding delay of T seconds at the receiver is incurred in decoding the actual transmitted message, for a total delay of $2T$ seconds. As usual, then, a price must be paid for the required decrease in SNR. The circuitry becomes much more complex, and large time delays are incurred. This is precisely what was found with the case of M-ary orthogonal signals. Larger values of M require correspondingly more binary digits to be stored ($\log_2 M = RT$), and the same T-second delay at both the transmitter and receiver is encountered there as well. As will be seen shortly, the M-ary orthogonal signal set, with $M \rightarrow \infty$, provides in fact an example of a Shannon-type encoder.

The general form of the encoding scheme suggested by Shannon's work appears in Fig. 7-51. Note that it is similar to the binary-M-ary encoder of Fig. 7-24. The basic difference is that the encoder and decoder of Fig. 7-51 are left completely unspecified. A modulator is not shown in Fig. 7-51.

Note that in the encoding-decoding process the same bit rate of R bits/s is always maintained. There is no increase or decrease in rate of transmission. A

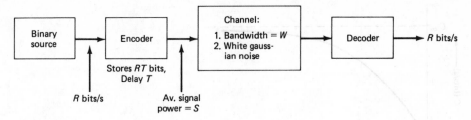

FIGURE 7-51
Encoding for optimum transmission.

total delay of $2T$ seconds is entailed, however, because of the encoding at the transmitter (time taken to examine RT bits) and the decoding at the receiver (time taken to examine the encoded message T seconds long).

Aside from providing a stimulus for work in the area of coding, the Shannon formulation does provide another concurrent result: it enables us to compare transmission over real channels with the maximum possible rate of error-free transmission. One can thus judge the capability of a particular transmission scheme and determine how close one is to the ideal scheme. Consider, for example, the band-limited telephone channel already mentioned several times in passing in this chapter. We have noted that the key impairments for data transmission over this channel are intersymbol interference, signal phase jitter, and impulse noise. It has been found experimentally that the additive gaussian noise on this channel is such as to provide a signal-to-noise ratio S/N of 10^3 (30 dB). If the other impairments were eliminated, this would then provide the remaining, irreducible limit on transmission. The Shannon capacity bound applied to this channel, assuming the other impairments not present, thus provides an upper bound on the maximum rate of error-free transmission. If we assume $W \sim 3$ kHz for this channel, a reasonable figure, (7-125) indicates that the capacity is about $C = 30,000$ bits/s. Actually, the ideal band-limited frequency model assumed in Shannon's derivation is not quite appropriate for the telephone channel. Shannon's analysis can be extended to include nonideal frequency characteristics as well, and the application of this work to the telephone channel [LUCK, pp. 35–38] indicates that its capacity is closer to 23,000 bits/s. The 19.2-kbit/s modems using trellis coding, to be discussed later in this chapter, come close to this capacity.

The Shannon capacity expression applied to the power-limited channel produces quite a different conclusion. It indicates that coding *can* play a role in improving the transmission rate over such channels, with the error probability maintained at a tolerable value. We have already noted this fact in our discussion of M-ary orthogonal transmission.

Consider, for example, the capacity expression (7-125) applied to a channel with no limits on bandwidth. It is apparent that if S/N is held fixed, then capacity is directly proportional to bandwidth. So increasing the bandwidth

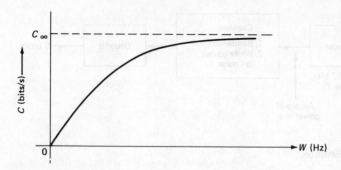

FIGURE 7-52
Capacity variation with bandwidth.

should provide an improvement in transmission capability. (Note that for a fixed bandwidth an increase in power only provides a logarithmic increase in the capacity. For example, in the telephone case cited earlier, if S/N were doubled to 2,000, the capacity would only increase by 10 percent.) Actually, the noise increases with bandwidth as well, since $N = n_0 W$.

In particular, for large W the capacity levels off and approaches a limiting value C_∞ given by

$$C_\infty = \lim_{W \to \infty} C = \frac{S}{n_0 \ln 2} = \frac{S}{0.69 n_0} \qquad (7\text{-}127)$$

This is shown in Fig. 7-52. Note that this is precisely the bound discussed earlier under M-ary transmission. It appears in Fig. 7-49 as well. [This limiting value of C is obtained from (7-125) by noting that $\log_e(1 + \epsilon) \doteq \epsilon, \; \epsilon \ll 1.$]

There is thus a limit on the rate at which one can transmit error-free over a power-limited channel with the bandwidth allowed to get as large as desired. It is still significantly higher than the data rates attainable with binary PSK and $M = 32$ orthogonal-signal transmission, as noted in the examples at the end of the previous section, accounting for the great interest in coding techniques for space channels to which reference has already been made. Although transmission at a rate of C_∞ bits/s is clearly unattainable (just as in the case of M-ary orthogonal transmission with $M \to \infty$), transmission at one-half this rate is a realistic goal. This is still seven times the uncoded-PSK rate and is therefore in many cases a desirable goal. As an example, in the hypothetical space problem of Example 4 in the previous section, we found digital transmission with an error probability of 10^{-5} could only be carried out at a rate of 140 bits/s, using uncoded PSK transmission. Since $C_\infty = 2,000$ bits/s for this example, a transmission rate of 1,000 bits/s could be considered a realistic figure for which to strive.

Space missions have used these concepts and have adopted coding techniques widely in an effort to come close to the Shannon limit. We shall use the

1986 Voyager Uranus encounter as an example in a later section, after first introducing the fundamental ideas of coding.

Now consider the digital radio systems with large signal constellations discussed earlier in Sec. 7-5 in connection with QAM probability-of-error calculations. How well do these compare to the Shannon limit? Recall our approximation (7-101) which indicates that, for large M, the energy in the signal should be proportional to M for a given probability of error. With a fixed transmission bandwidth B_T and hence signaling rate $1/T$, the signal-to-noise ratio S/N is proportional to E/n_0, as shown in (7-103). We thus have S/N proportional to M as well for a given probability of error. This enables us to derive an approximate rate-versus-S/N equation describing QAM performance, similar to that of the Shannon capacity expression of (7-125).

Specifically, recall that with QAM transmission at R bits/s, one of $M = 2^{RT}$ QAM signals is transmitted every T seconds. The bit-rate–bandwidth relationship, first discussed in Chap. 4, is thus given by

$$R = \frac{\log_2 M}{T} = \frac{B_T}{1 + r}\log_2 M \tag{7-128}$$

using (7-102) to replace $1/T$ by the transmission bandwidth B_T. Replacing M by the signal-to-noise ratio S/N times a constant K we have, finally,

$$R = \frac{B_T}{1 + r}\log_2\left(K\frac{S}{N}\right) \tag{7-129}$$

Comparing this with the Shannon capacity expression (7-125), we see that it is of similar form. (The transmission bandwidth B_T in the QAM case is the same as the parameter W in the Shannon expression.) Both expressions have the bit rate linearly proportional to the bandwidth, but proportional only to the logarithm of the signal-to-noise ratio. Equation (6-33) in Chap. 6, describing the performance of baseband PCM systems in additive gaussian noise, was of the same form. Note, however, that the Shannon capacity expression provides an idealized *zero-probability* capacity. The constant K in (7-129), as well as the constant in the PCM performance expression (6-33), varies with the error probability.

Figure 7-53 summarizes this discussion. The normalized Shannon transmission capacity, C/B_T, in bits per hertz, is plotted versus signal-to-noise ratio. (The symbol B_T has been used here in place of W to facilitate comparison with QAM.) This provides an absolute limit on error-free performance of any point-to-point communication system in the presence of additive gaussian noise. (Recall that the actual transmission rate R must always be less than C.) Also plotted is a curve of normalized bit rate R/B_T versus S/n for a series of QAM systems, for the special case of $P_e = 10^{-6}$ and roll-off factor $r = \frac{1}{3}$. This curve has been reproduced from fig. 2 of [MEYE]. Plotting R/B_T versus S/N in dB produces precisely the linear curve predicted by (7-129). The slope of the line is in fact $1/(1 + r) = \frac{3}{4}$ times that of the Shannon capacity curve, as predicted by (7-129). A similar curve for the case of $P_e = 10^{-4}$ and $r = \frac{1}{2}$ appears in [KOHI] (see fig. 2 in that paper). There is clearly a sizable gap between the QAM system

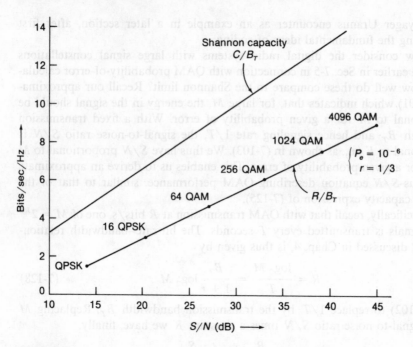

FIGURE 7-53
QAM systems and Shannon capacity compared. (Based on [MEYE, fig. 2, p. 47] with permission.)

performance and the Shannon limit. As an example, the 64-QAM system in Fig. 7-53 provides 4.5 bits/s per hertz of bandwidth; Shannon's theorem predicts that one should be able to transmit at close to twice that rate, 9 bits/s per hertz, with an error as small as desired, for the same signal-to-noise ratio. The 64-QAM system in Fig. 7-53 provides an error probability of 10^{-6}. Reducing this probability would require a higher S/N.

Coding techniques must be used to close this gap. The remaining sections of this book introduce the basic concepts of forward error-correction coding.

7-8 BLOCK CODING FOR ERROR DETECTION AND CORRECTION

Introduction

In previous sections on the additive-white-gaussian-noise (AWGN) channel, we discussed probability-of-error calculations at length and showed that it is possible, by encoding k binary digits into one of $M = 2^k$ orthogonal signals, to reduce the probability of error P_e as low as we like by increasing k indefinitely. The binary source rate R had to be less than the channel capacity C, in bits/s. We found the transmission bandwidth increasing with M, or *exponentially* with k, however. We also found the improvement, or reduction of P_e, rather slow with M. In discussing Shannon's capacity theorem in the last section, we indicated that M-ary orthogonal signaling is just one possible way of encoding binary digits to reduce the error rate.

In this section we discuss a class of encoding procedures on which a great deal of work has been carried out since Shannon's pioneering efforts in the area. This is the class of parity-check block codes, in which r parity-check bits, formed by linear operations on the k data bits, are appended to each block of k bits. These codes can be used to both detect and correct errors in transmission. We shall focus here on a particular class of block codes, cyclic codes, for which relatively simple digital encoders and decoders may be found. Such codes are commonly used not only for data transmission but for such applications as magnetic-tape encoding, enhanced computer system reliability, etc. However, as was the case with orthogonal signals, the forward error-correcting properties of such codes have not found a great deal of utilization in band-limited channels. Instead, there the prime application has been in the error-*detecting* properties of these codes. If an error is detected anywhere in the received code block, the transmitter is notified to repeat the signal.

Space and satellite channels have made extensive use of the forward error-correcting capabilities of codes. In addition to block codes, convolution codes have been used a great deal. In these codes a sliding sequence of past data bits is used to generate several code bits. Distinct blocks are no longer sent, and successive transmitted bits contain in them the history of a sequence of data bits. Various decoding algorithms have been developed for such codes, and it has been found possible to get quite respectable improvements in error performance by using relatively short encoders. These are discussed in Sec. 7-9 following.

Block Coding[11]

Recall from our previous discussion of the AWGN channel that we store up k successive binary digits and use these to generate a new set of signal waveshapes. In the previous discussion we considered one encoder–modulator device that carried out this operation. We now separate these two functions, as shown in Fig. 7-54. The encoder takes a block of k successive binary digits and converts this to an equivalent block of $n > k$ binary digits. These digits are in turn fed into a modulator which generates the analog waveshapes for transmission. This modulator can group several bits or all of the n-bit block in outputting the transmitted signals, just like the modulators discussed in the AWGN sections. More com-

---

[11]References in this area include the following books and papers: [BLAH] R. E. Blahut, *Theory and Practice of Error Control Codes*, Addison-Wesley, Reading, Mass., 1983; [MICH] A. M. Michelson and A. H. Levesque, *Error-Control Techniques for Digital Communications*, Wiley-Interscience, New York, 1985; [LIN] S. Lin and D. J. Costello, Jr., *Error Control Coding: Fundamentals and Applications*, Prentice-Hall, Englewood Cliffs, N.J., 1983; [LUCK, chaps. 10, 11]; [PETE] W. W. Peterson and E. J. Weldon, Jr., *Error-Correcting Codes*, MIT Press, Cambridge, Mass., 2nd ed., 1972; [BERL 1980] E. R. Berlekamp, "The Technology of Error-Correcting Codes," *Proc. IEEE*, vol. 68, no. 5, pp. 564–592, May 1980; [BERL 1987] E. R. Berlekamp, R. E. Peile, and S. P. Pope, "The Application of Error Control to Communications," *IEEE Commun. Mag.*, vol. 25, no. 4, pp. 44–57, April 1987.

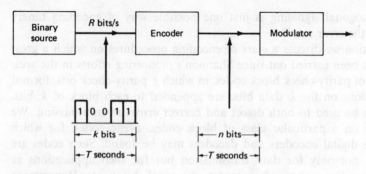

FIGURE 7-54
Binary encoding operation.

monly, each individual bit of the code block is used to modulate a carrier, resulting in binary PSK, FSK, or other of the common binary transmission signals mentioned in Chap. 4. (For space communication applications PSK transmission is used because of its inherently better error performance.)

In this section we focus on the encoder design. One simple example is that of a single-parity-check device, used to detect an odd number of errors. Here $n = k + 1$, and for every k data bits one bit is added. Most commonly, this bit represents the modulo-2 (mod-2) sum of the data bits (in which case it is called an even-parity bit, since the total number of 1's in the code word is even) or the complement of this sum (called an odd-parity bit).

By mod-2 sum we recall that we mean the following definitions:

$$
\begin{aligned}
0 \oplus 0 &= 0 \\
0 \oplus 1 &= 1 \\
1 \oplus 0 &= 1 \\
1 \oplus 1 &= 0
\end{aligned}
\tag{7-130}
$$

The symbol $\oplus$ will henceforth represent the mod-2 sum operation. This notation has already been introduced in Sec. 3-4 in connection with the Gray code [Eq. (3-25)]. More than two bits may similarly be combined. As an example, the mod-2 sum of the data sequence $1\,0\,0\,1\,0\,1$ is 1. An even-parity check code word would thus be

$$
\overbrace{1\ 0\ 0\ 1\ 0\ 1}^{k\ \text{data bits}}{}^{\displaystyle\overbrace{}^{n\text{-bit code word}}}_{}1
$$

while an odd-parity check code word would be

$$
1\ 0\ 0\ 1\ 0\ 1\ 0
$$

(The bit stream will be assumed read in from left to right. The first three bits in order are then $1, 0, 0$.) Either code word could be used to detect an odd number of errors at the receiver by simply repeating the parity-check calculation and comparing with the received parity bit, or by carrying out the mod-2 sum

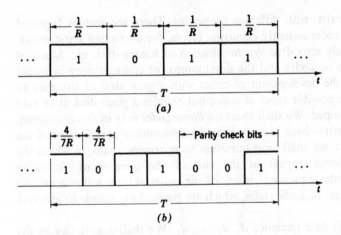

FIGURE 7-55
$(7, 4)$ error-correcting code. (a) Original binary stream. (b) Encoded binary word.

(exclusive-or) operation over *all* the received bits and checking to see if the resultant sum is 0 (even parity) or 1 (odd parity), as the case may be.

More generally with codes, $r = n - k$ check bits are added to every k bits input. One thus speaks of (n, k) codes. Here n represents the total number of bits in a code word, while k is the original block size. An encoder outputs a unique n-bit code word for each of the 2^k possible input k-bit blocks. As an example, a $(15, 11)$ code has $r = 4$ parity-check bits for every 11 data bits. A $(7, 4)$ code would be one generating $r = 3$ parity-check bits for every 4 data bits. A little thought will indicate that as the number of parity-check bits r increases it should be possible to correct more and more errors. (Recall again that with $r = 1$ error correction is not possible. The code will only detect an odd number of errors.) In addition, as k increases, Shannon's theorem indicates the overall probability of error should decrease. Long codes with a relatively large number of parity-check bits should thus provide better performance. Such codes are more difficult and more costly to implement, however. As r increases the required transmission bandwidth goes up as well ($n = k + r$ bits are now packed into a time slot previously allocated to k bits). The efficiency of transmission, k/n, goes down accordingly, since fewer data bits are using a given channel. An example of a $(7, 4)$ code with 3 parity-check bits and 4 data bits appears in Fig. 7-55. This example demonstrates the time compaction noted above.

A critical objective is therefore to choose the parity-check bits to correct as many errors as possible, but with the efficiency kept as high as possible.[12]

---

[12]Although increasing r, and hence n, results in more errors corrected, the resultant required increase in bandwidth introduces more noise and hence increases the probability of error among the uncorrectable error sequences. The net result is to reduce the error-probability gain expected. We shall carry out some sample calculations shortly to demonstrate this effect.

Innumerable codes exist, with different properties. There are various types of codes for correcting independently occurring errors, for correcting burst errors, for providing relatively error-free synchronization of binary data, etc. Much of the effort in research on codes and the development of coding theory in recent years has gone into the development of codes with a great deal of structure to them. This limits the possible types of codes but enables a great deal to be said about the coder developed. We shall focus on *linear codes* only in this discussion. In these codes the parity-check bits are given by appropriate mod-2 sums of the data bits. In addition, we shall limit ourselves to *systematic codes*, in which the parity-check bits always appear at the end of the code word, following the original binary data sequence.[13] Much of the material later will concentrate still further on the class of *cyclic codes*, which are particularly simple to generate and decode.

Consider a k-bit data sequence $d_1, d_2, \ldots, d_k$. We shall denote this by the vector **d**:

$$\mathbf{d} = (d_1, d_2, \ldots, d_k)$$

The corresponding code word will be denoted by the n-bit vector **c**:

$$\mathbf{c} = (c_1, c_2, \ldots, c_k, c_{k+1}, \ldots, c_n)$$

For a systematic code $c_1 = d_1, c_2 = d_2, \ldots, c_k = d_k$. The r parity-check bits, $c_{k+1}, c_{k+2}, \ldots, c_n$, are in turn given by the weighted mod-2 sum of the data bits:

$$c_{k+1} = h_{11}d_1 \oplus h_{12}d_2 \oplus \cdots \oplus h_{1k}d_k$$

$$c_{k+2} = h_{21}d_1 \oplus h_{22}d_2 \oplus \cdots \oplus h_{2k}d_k$$

$$\vdots \tag{7-131}$$

$$c_n = h_{r1}d_1 \oplus h_{r2}d_2 \oplus \cdots \oplus h_{rk}d_k$$

The coefficients h_{ij} are either 0 or 1. It is the choice of these coefficients that determines the properties of the particular code.

As an example, consider a $(15, 11)$ code with the following parity-check equations:

$$c_{12} = d_1 \oplus d_2 \oplus d_3 \oplus d_4 \qquad \oplus d_6 \qquad \oplus d_8 \oplus d_9$$

$$c_{13} = \qquad d_2 \oplus d_3 \oplus d_4 \oplus d_5 \qquad \oplus d_7 \qquad \oplus d_9 \oplus d_{10}$$

$$c_{14} = \qquad d_3 \oplus d_4 \oplus d_5 \oplus d_6 \qquad \oplus d_8 \qquad \oplus d_{10} \oplus d_{11} \tag{7-132}$$

$$c_{15} = d_1 \oplus d_2 \oplus d_3 \qquad \oplus d_5 \qquad \oplus d_7 \oplus d_8 \qquad \oplus d_{11}$$

It is left for the reader to show that if the data vector is $\mathbf{d} = (0\,1\,0\,1\,1\,1\,0\,1\,0\,1\,1)$, the 4 check bits are, respectively, $c_{12} = 0$, $c_{13} = 0$, $c_{14} = 0$, $c_{15} = 0$.

---

[13] It can be shown that this restriction does not affect the performance of the resultant code.

With the parity-check bits given by (7-131) it is apparent that the vector form **c** for a systematic code word can be written as a matrix operation on the data word **d**:

$$\mathbf{c} = \mathbf{d}G \tag{7-133}$$

G must be a $k \times n$ matrix, with the first k columns an identity matrix I_k representing the fact that the first k bits of **c** are just the original data bits. The remaining r columns of G represent the transposed array of coefficients h_{ij} of (7-131). Thus we must have

$$G = [I_k \quad P] \tag{7-134}$$

with
$$P = \begin{bmatrix} h_{11} & h_{21} & \cdots & h_{r1} \\ h_{12} & h_{22} & \cdots & h_{r2} \\ \vdots & \vdots & & \vdots \\ h_{1k} & h_{2k} & \cdots & h_{rk} \end{bmatrix} \tag{7-135}$$

G is called the *code-generator matrix*.

For the (15, 11) code example of (7-132), we have

$$P = \begin{bmatrix} 1 & 0 & 0 & 1 \\ 1 & 1 & 0 & 1 \\ 1 & 1 & 1 & 1 \\ 1 & 1 & 1 & 0 \\ 0 & 1 & 1 & 1 \\ 1 & 0 & 1 & 0 \\ 0 & 1 & 0 & 1 \\ 1 & 0 & 1 & 1 \\ 1 & 1 & 0 & 0 \\ 0 & 1 & 1 & 0 \\ 0 & 0 & 1 & 1 \end{bmatrix} \tag{7-136}$$

The G matrix is similarly given by

$$G = \begin{bmatrix} 1 & 0 & 0 & 0 & 0 & 0 & 0 & 0 & 0 & 0 & 0 & 1 & 0 & 0 & 1 \\ 0 & 1 & 0 & 0 & 0 & 0 & 0 & 0 & 0 & 0 & 0 & 1 & 1 & 0 & 1 \\ 0 & 0 & 1 & 0 & 0 & 0 & 0 & 0 & 0 & 0 & 0 & 1 & 1 & 1 & 1 \\ 0 & 0 & 0 & 1 & 0 & 0 & 0 & 0 & 0 & 0 & 0 & 1 & 1 & 1 & 0 \\ 0 & 0 & 0 & 0 & 1 & 0 & 0 & 0 & 0 & 0 & 0 & 0 & 1 & 1 & 1 \\ 0 & 0 & 0 & 0 & 0 & 1 & 0 & 0 & 0 & 0 & 0 & 1 & 0 & 1 & 0 \\ 0 & 0 & 0 & 0 & 0 & 0 & 1 & 0 & 0 & 0 & 0 & 0 & 1 & 0 & 1 \\ 0 & 0 & 0 & 0 & 0 & 0 & 0 & 1 & 0 & 0 & 0 & 1 & 0 & 1 & 1 \\ 0 & 0 & 0 & 0 & 0 & 0 & 0 & 0 & 1 & 0 & 0 & 1 & 1 & 0 & 0 \\ 0 & 0 & 0 & 0 & 0 & 0 & 0 & 0 & 0 & 1 & 0 & 0 & 1 & 1 & 0 \\ 0 & 0 & 0 & 0 & 0 & 0 & 0 & 0 & 0 & 0 & 1 & 0 & 0 & 1 & 1 \end{bmatrix} \tag{7-137}$$

It is apparent from (7-135) and (7-136) that no columns of P can be alike, for then the same parity-check bit would be generated by these columns, defeating the purpose of the encoding operation.

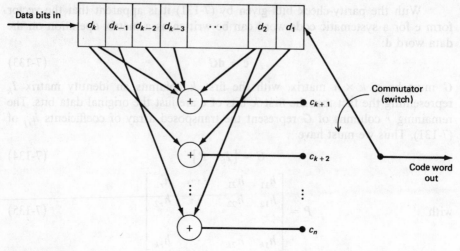

FIGURE 7-56
One possible encoder (commutator rests on register for k time slots, then moves to other positions for one time slot each).

The encoding operation, represented in equation form by (7-131) and in matrix form by (7-133), may be schematized by the block diagram of Fig. 7-56. Other encoder representations, using mod-2 operations on shift-register outputs, will be considered later. The commutator in Fig. 7-56 must rest on the register for k time slots while the k data bits are being read out. Note that the k data bits plus r parity-check bits must all be read out during the time the k bits are being read in.

Another example of a code is a $(7, 3)$ code with the P matrix

$$P = \begin{bmatrix} 1 & 1 & 0 & 0 \\ 0 & 1 & 1 & 0 \\ 1 & 1 & 1 & 1 \end{bmatrix} \qquad (7\text{-}138)$$

Note that there are 4 check bits. The code efficiency is thus $\frac{3}{7}$. There are eight possible code words:

$\mathbf{d}$	$\mathbf{c} = \mathbf{d}G = \mathbf{d}[I_k \; P]$
000	000 0000
001	001 1111
010	010 0110
011	011 1001
100	100 1100
101	101 0011
110	110 1010
111	111 0101

A close look at these indicates that they differ in at least three positions. Any *one* error should then be correctable, since the resultant code word will still be closer to the correct (transmitted) one, in the sense of the number of bit positions in which they agree, then to any other. This is thus an example of a *single-error-correcting code*. The difference in the number of positions between any two code words is called the *Hamming distance*. The Hamming distance plays a key role in assessing the error-correcting capability of codes. For two errors to be correctible (other error patterns may be detectable as well) the Hamming distance d should be at least 5. In general, for t errors correctible, $d \geq 2t + 1$, or $t = [(d - 1)/2]$, where $[x]$ refers to the integer less than or equal to x.

What decoding operation is now required at the receiver? One simple procedure is to repeat the parity-check calculation of the encoder and compare the resultant $r = n - k$ parity-check pattern with that actually received. If the calculated and received patterns do not agree, one or more errors are indicated. Appropriate error-correction procedures can then be initiated. (The simplest error-correction procedure conceptually is to compare the received code word against a stored table of code words, selecting the one most likely to have been transmitted. It is apparent that this table grows exponentially with k, however, so that for long codes this method proves self-defeating.)

More precisely, consider a systematic code word $\mathbf{c} = \mathbf{d}G$, with $\mathbf{d}$ the k-bit data sequence. It is apparent that this may be written

$$\mathbf{c} = [\mathbf{d} \quad \mathbf{d}P] = [\mathbf{d} \quad \mathbf{c}_P] \tag{7-139}$$

from (7-133) and (7-134). The parity-check bit sequence $\mathbf{c}_P$ is simply given by

$$\mathbf{c}_P = \mathbf{d}P \tag{7-140}$$

Assume now that $\mathbf{c}$ represents a received sequence of n digits. The first k digits representing some vector $\mathbf{d}$ must be part of a transmitted code word, since they always represent one of 2^k possible sequences of k digits. To check to see whether the full n-bit sequence $\mathbf{c}$ represents a possible code word, the decoder can carry out the operation $\mathbf{d}P$ and compare with the received parity-check sequence $\mathbf{c}_P$. Since mod-2 subtraction is the same as addition, we must have

$$\underset{\substack{\text{calculated} \\ \text{at} \\ \text{the decoder}}}{\mathbf{d}P} \quad \oplus \quad \underset{\substack{\text{received} \\ \text{parity-check} \\ \text{sequence}}}{\mathbf{c}_P} \quad = 0 \tag{7-141}$$

if the received sequence is a proper code word. The vector summation in (7-141) implies a mod-2 comparison bit by bit. This conceptual way of checking for possible errors is sketched in Fig. 7-57. [Note that the mere fact that (7-141) is found valid does not guarantee error-free reception. Any code word can obviously have error patterns occur which are not detectable.]

Equation (7-141) may be rewritten in matrix form as follows:

$$\mathbf{d}P + \mathbf{c}_P = [\mathbf{d} \quad \mathbf{c}_P] \begin{bmatrix} P \\ I_{n-k} \end{bmatrix} = 0 \tag{7-142}$$

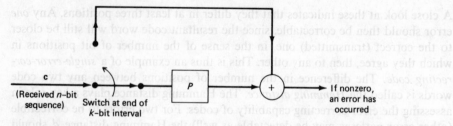

FIGURE 7-57
Conceptualized decoder.

Here I_{n-k} is an identity matrix of order $n - k$. Very generally, then, for any code word **c**, we must have

$$\mathbf{c}H^T = 0 \tag{7-143}$$

Then $n \times r$ matrix H^T is given by

$$H^T = \begin{bmatrix} P \\ I_{n-k} \end{bmatrix} \tag{7-144}$$

Its transpose

$$H = \begin{bmatrix} P^T & I_{n-k} \end{bmatrix} \tag{7-145}$$

is called the *parity-check* matrix. This matrix plays an important role in the theory of error-correcting codes. Note from (7-135) and (7-145) that H is in general given by

$$H = \begin{bmatrix} h_{11} & h_{12} & \cdots & h_{1k} & 1 & 0 & \cdots & 0 \\ h_{21} & h_{22} & \cdots & h_{2k} & 0 & 1 & \cdots & 0 \\ \vdots & \vdots & & \vdots & \vdots & \vdots & & \vdots \\ h_{r1} & h_{r2} & \cdots & h_{rk} & 0 & 0 & \cdots & 1 \end{bmatrix} \tag{7-146}$$

Consider as an example the (7, 3) code mentioned earlier, whose P matrix was given by (7-138). For this code we have

$$H^T = \begin{bmatrix} 1 & 1 & 0 & 0 \\ 0 & 1 & 1 & 0 \\ 1 & 1 & 1 & 1 \\ 1 & 0 & 0 & 0 \\ 0 & 1 & 0 & 0 \\ 0 & 0 & 1 & 0 \\ 0 & 0 & 0 & 1 \end{bmatrix} \tag{7-147}$$

and
$$H = \begin{bmatrix} 1 & 0 & 1 & 1 & 0 & 0 & 0 \\ 1 & 1 & 1 & 0 & 1 & 0 & 0 \\ 0 & 1 & 1 & 0 & 0 & 1 & 0 \\ 0 & 0 & 1 & 0 & 0 & 0 & 1 \end{bmatrix} \qquad (7\text{-}148)$$

Summarizing what has been said thus far, we can generate a code word by carrying out the operation

$$c = dG \qquad (7\text{-}133)$$

A code word must in turn satisfy the condition

$$cH^T = 0 \qquad (7\text{-}143)$$

Now say that an error occurs in one or more of the digits c. The received vector r may then be written in the form

$$r = c \oplus e \qquad (7\text{-}149)$$

with e an n-bit vector representing the error pattern. [If errors occur in the second and third bits, for example, then $e = (0\,1\,1\,0\,0\,\cdots\,0)$.] Operating on r with the matrix H^T, we have

$$rH^T = (c \oplus e)H^T = eH^T = s \qquad (7\text{-}150)$$

The r-element vector s, called the *syndrome*, will be nonzero if an error has occurred. (Conversely, since not all error patterns are detectable by any code, the condition $s = 0$ is no guarantee of error-free transmission.)

Assume now, as an example, that a *single* error has occurred in the ith digit of the n-bit code word transmitted. Then

$$e = (0\,0\,0\,\cdots\,\underset{\substack{i\text{th} \\ \text{digit}}}{1}\,\cdots\,0) \qquad (7\text{-}151)$$

From the defining relation for the syndrome it is then easy to show that

$$s = (h_{1i}\,h_{2i}\,\cdots\,h_{ri}) \qquad (7\text{-}152)$$

Comparing with (7-146), this is just the ith column of the parity-check matrix H. So the error is not only detectable, but correctable as well, provided that all columns of H (or corresponding rows of H^T) are uniquely defined. Any code satisfying this condition is a single-error-correcting code.

The (7, 3) code again provides a simple example. Say that 1101010 is the code word that was transmitted, while the received code word is 1111010 (there is an error in the third position). The e vector then has the elements 0010000, and the syndrome vector is $s = (1111)$, after postmultiplying $r = (1111010)$ by the matrix H^T of (7-147). It is apparent that s is just the third row of H^T or the third column of the parity-check matrix H [Eq. (7-148)] for this code.

What kind of constraint is put on codes to satisfy the single-error-correcting condition that all columns of H are uniquely defined? This says that the first k columns of (7-146) must be unique. They must also differ from the last r columns containing a single 1 in each column, and cannot include an all-0 column. (Why is this so?) It is thus apparent that to have each of the k r-bit columns uniquely defined, we must have

$$2^r - (r + 1) \geq k \qquad (7\text{-}153)$$

(r bits can be arranged in 2^r possible ways, $r + 1$ of which must be ruled out because of the stipulation on the all-zero column and the r single-one columns.) This inequality that must be satisfied by a single-error-correcting code is a special case of the Hamming inequality for a more general t-error correcting code, to be discussed briefly below. As an example of the use of this inequality, note that the $(7, 3)$ code has $r = 4$. Hence $2^4 - 5 = 11 > k = 3$. The code should therefore be single-error-correcting, as we have already seen. A $(7, 4)$ code, with $r = 3$, is also single-error-correcting. The $(15, 11)$ code of (7-136) is obviously single-error-correcting, since all 11 rows of P (corresponding to the 11 columns of H^T that must be uniquely defined) *are* unique, nonzero, and with no single 1's. Note that this code has $r = 4$ check bits. Hence it satisfies (7-153) as an equality. It is left for the reader to show that a $(6, 3)$ code is single-error-correcting, while a $(6, 4)$ code cannot be designed for this purpose.

More generally, what can we say about the parity-check requirements for higher-order error-correcting codes? This is obviously quite useful in beginning the selection process for appropriate codes. More precisely, for a code to correct *at least* t errors, what values of k and n are required, and what efficiencies are possible? Various bounds are available to help in this selection process, but we focus only on the Hamming bound, a special case of which appeared in (7-153). This bound says simply that the number of possible check-bit patterns must at least equal the number of ways in which up to t errors can occur. For an (n, k) code, then, we have

$$2^{n-k} \geq \sum_{i=0}^{t} \binom{n}{i} \qquad (7\text{-}154)$$

[Note that with $t = 1$, and $n = r + k$, we get just Eq. (7-153).] Table 7-1 shows some typical (n, k) representations and their efficiencies, found by solving (7-154) and selecting the codes with the largest k value only. The $t = 1$, or single-error-correcting cases, are those already discussed. The (n, k) doublets shown represent possible candidates for error correction. Systematic ways of finding (n, k) codes will be described later. These codes must then be investigated further to see whether they in fact have the desired error-correction capability, as well as other desirable properties. Note that the efficiency decreases as the requirement on the error-correcting capability increases. Longer codes are then needed to recoup this efficiency.

It was pointed out earlier that it is not sufficient to characterize a code by its error-correcting capability only. By introducing r parity-check bits the bit rate must of necessity increase by a factor of n/k, or fractionally by r/k, to maintain real-time transmission. There is thus an increased bandwidth requirement that must be charged against the code. Additional noise is also let into the system. Alternatively, because of the shorter time interval over which a bit is transmitted,

TABLE 7-1
Examples of error-correcting codes

n	k_{max}	Code	Efficiency
Single-error-correcting codes: $t = 1$ ($d = 3$)			
4	1		
5	2	(5, 2)	0.4
6	3	(6, 3)	0.5
7	4	(7, 4)	0.57
15	11	(15, 11)	0.73
Double-error-correcting codes: $t = 2$ ($d = 5$)			
10	4	(10, 4)	0.4
11	4	(11, 4)	0.36
15	8	(15, 8)	0.53
Triple-error-correcting codes: $t = 3$ ($d = 7$)			
10	2	(10, 2)	0.2
15	5	(15, 5)	0.33
23	12	(23, 12)	0.52
24	12	(24, 12)	0.5

there is correspondingly less energy in the received signal bit. The critical detection parameter E/n_0, with E the signal energy in each received bit and n_0 the noise spectral density for white noise, is thus reduced. This tends to *increase* the probability of error, partially reducing the effectiveness of the code in correcting errors. A complete study of a code must take this reduced E/n_0 into account.

To demonstrate this procedure, we consider a simple example. Assume that a $(7, 4)$ single-error-correcting block code is used. Binary PSK is used for transmitting the successive bits in each code word. The AWGN channel is assumed for simplicity. It is desired to compare the probability of error in the coded case with that in the uncoded case. We do this by comparing the error probability of a *block* in the two cases, coded and uncoded.

Specifically, let the probability of error of a bit in the uncoded case be P_{el}. For the AWGN channel with PSK transmission this is just Eq. (7-59) found earlier in this chapter, as well as in Chap. 6:

$$P_{el} = \tfrac{1}{2}\,\mathrm{erfc}\sqrt{\frac{E}{n_0}} \qquad (7\text{-}155)$$

The probability of error of the uncoded block in the $(7, 4)$ case is just the probability that at least one bit in four will be in error, and is thus given by

$$P_{e,\,\mathrm{uncoded}} = 1 - (1 - P_{el})^4 \doteq 4P_{el} \qquad P_{el} \ll 1 \qquad (7\text{-}156)$$

Now consider the coded case. Let the corresponding bit-error probability be p. This must be of the same form as P_{el}, but with the signal-to-noise ratio E/n_0

TABLE 7-2
Comparison of block error probability, coded and uncoded, (7, 4) code

E/n_0, dB	P_{e1}	$P_{e,\text{uncoded}}$	$P_{e,\text{coded}}$
-1	10^{-1}	0.344	0.34
4.2	10^{-2}	0.0394	0.026
6.8	10^{-3}	4×10^{-3}	1.9×10^{-3}
8.3	10^{-4}	4×10^{-4}	1.6×10^{-4}
9.6	10^{-5}	4×10^{-5}	8.6×10^{-6}

reduced by a factor $\frac{7}{4}$. Hence

$$p = \tfrac{1}{2}\operatorname{erfc}\sqrt{\frac{4E}{7n_0}} \tag{7-157}$$

The probability of an error in this coded case in now the probability that at least two independent errors will occur in a pattern of 7 bits. This is given by the cumulative binomial probability

$$P_{e,\text{coded}} = \sum_{j=2}^{7} \binom{7}{j} p^j (1-p)^{7-j}$$

$$\doteq 21p^2 \qquad p \ll 1 \tag{7-158}$$

Using (7-155) and (7-157), we may compare (7-156) and (7-158). A comparison for various values of E/n_0 appears in Table 7-2. The (7, 4) block code thus does not provide significant improvement in the error probability until $P_{e1} = 10^{-5}$ or less. One would have to go to much longer codes to demonstrate appreciable improvement.

Hamming Distance and the Binary Symmetric Channel

Implicit in the discussion of errors and their detection and correction, thus far, has been the assumption that signals in each binary interval at the receiver, prior to decoding, were individually detected and decisions made on each as to whether it was a 1 or a 0. The incoming signal, even though analog in nature because of distortion and additive noise encountered during transmission, is thus assumed converted to a sequence of binary digits before entering the decoder. This process of bit-by-bit quantization into either of two levels is called *hard limiting*. It is not at all obvious that this is a good procedure, particularly if there is memory in the channel. One can in fact show—using convolutional decoders, for example—that it is possible to improve system performance in that case by retaining a sequence of analog received signals, and making binary decisions on the composite set

Transmitter   Receiver

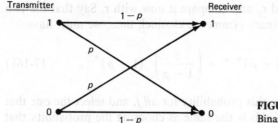

FIGURE 7-58
Binary symmetric channel.

[HELLE].[14] This procedure of basing decisions on the analog signals (or at least a finely quantized version of these) is called *soft limiting*. A comparison of soft and hard limiting, in the context of convolutional decoding, appears in the next section.

We noted in passing, earlier, that the Hamming distance d (the minimum number of bit positions by which code words for a given code differ) appears to play a critical role in the performance of block codes. In fact, we indicated that the error-correcting capability t was simply $[(d-1)/2]$. Here too we were implicitly assuming bit-by-bit hard limiting. If the 2^k possible code words differ in at least d bit positions, a hard-limited received block should be correctable if fewer than $(d-1)/2$ bits have been changed during the transmission. This procedure of assigning a hard-limited received block to the code word to which it is closest in the Hamming-distance sense can in fact be shown to be optimum for a particular class of *memoryless* channels called the *binary symmetric channel* (BSC). The AWGN channel with hard limiting is one example of this class.

The binary symmetric channel is, as its name indicates, a channel for which only two digits (0 and 1) appear at the transmitter and receiver (hence the emphasis on hard limiting). Either digit is assumed converted to the other during transmission with the same probability $p \leq \frac{1}{2}$. (This is the reason for the word "symmetry" in the title.) Since the channel is assumed memoryless, *each* digit in a sequence has the same probability p of being received in error. A schematic representation of the BSC appears in Fig. 7-58. To demonstrate the optimality of the Hamming distance rule for this set of channels, say a specific n-bit code word c_i of the 2^k possible is transmitted. An n-bit binary sequence $\mathbf{r}$ is received. Then for the minimum probability of error we must use the maximum a posteriori (MAP) rule discussed earlier in this chapter. Specifically, we select code word c_i if

$$P(c_i|\mathbf{r}) > P(c_j|\mathbf{r}) \qquad \text{all } j, \quad j \neq i \tag{7-159}$$

Now assume all 2^k code words equally likely. The rule (7-159) is then converted to the equivalent maximum-likelihood rule that selects c_i if

$$P(\mathbf{r}|c_i) > P(\mathbf{r}|c_j) \qquad \text{all } j, \quad j \neq i \tag{7-160}$$

---

[14][HELLE] A. J. Heller and I. M. Jacobs, "Viterbi Decoding for Satellite and Space Communications," *IEEE Trans. Commun. Technol.*, vol. COM-19, no. 5, part II, p. 835, October 1971.

Consider a particular code word $\mathbf{c}_j$ and compare it now with $\mathbf{r}$. Say that the two differ in n' positions. For the binary symmetric channel, then, we must have

$$p(\mathbf{r}|\mathbf{c}_j) = p^{n'}(1 - p)^{n-n'} = \left(\frac{p}{1 - p}\right)^{n'} (1 - p)^n \qquad (7\text{-}161)$$

From (7-160) we are to calculate this probability for *all j*, and select the one that is largest. Since $p/(1 - p) < 1$, this is the same as choosing the probability that has the smallest n'. Hence the best rule, in the sense of minimizing the probability of error, is to select as the appropriate code word of the 2^k available the one that is closest to $\mathbf{r}$ in the Hamming-distance sense. This type of decoder is optimum for the BSC. It is *not* optimum for burst-type channels (in which a series of successive bit changes occur), or for channels using convolutional coding, in which memory is introduced into the transmission, and other examples of channels with memory.

Cyclic Codes

The Hamming bound discussed earlier is one example of a technique used to help us determine the size of a code needed to check for a specified error-correction capability. We pointed out earlier as well that any (n, k) code satisfying the Hamming inequality will automatically provide single-error-correcting capability provided that the columns of the parity-check matrix H (or, equivalently, the rows of the matrix G) are uniquely defined. To go further with higher-order error-correction capability in a systematic way, it is necessary to introduce additional structure into the code formulation. Although this of necessity limits the choice of codes, as pointed out previously, it at least provides a systematic way to select codes. We therefore focus on the class of codes called *cyclic codes* [BLAH], [MICH], [LIN], [PETE]. These are codes such that code vectors are simple lateral shifts of one another.

For example, if $\mathbf{c} = (c_1, c_2, \ldots, c_{n-1}, c_n)$ is a possible code vector, then so are $(c_2, c_3, \ldots, c_n, c_1)$ and $(c_3, c_4, \ldots, c_n, c_1, c_2)$, etc. Consider $\mathbf{c} = (1\,0\,1\,1\,0\,1)$. Then it is apparent that $(0\,1\,1\,0\,1\,1)$ and $(1\,1\,0\,1\,1\,0)$ are cyclic shifts and must serve as code words as well. These cyclic codes have a great deal of structure, and specific rules of generation may be set up for them. They are commonly used, not only for error correction, but in error detection as well, since they are easily implementable.

An interesting property of the generator matrix of a cyclic code is that its last element, in the kth row and nth column, must always be a 1. For consider the data-bit sequence $\mathbf{d} = (0\,0\,0 \cdots 0\,1)$ operated on by a generator matrix G whose last element is 0. Then the code word is

$$\mathbf{c} = \underbrace{(0\,0\,0 \cdots 0\,1}_{\substack{\text{information} \\ \text{bits}}} \underbrace{\cdots 0)}_{\substack{\text{parity} \\ \text{bits}}}$$

Shifting this once to the right, we obtain

$$\mathbf{c}' = \underbrace{(0\,0\,0\,\cdots\,0\,0}_{\text{information bits}}\ \underbrace{1\,\cdots\,)}_{\text{parity bits}}$$

This is obviously impossible, for our codes are such that the all-zero data sequence must produce an all-zero parity sequence. For a systematic cyclic code we must thus have the generator matrix of the form

$$G = \underbrace{\begin{bmatrix} 1 & 0 & 0 & \cdots & 0 & \vdots & \cdots & \\ 0 & 1 & 0 & \cdots & 0 & \vdots & \cdots & \\ 0 & 0 & 1 & \cdots & 0 & \vdots & \cdots & \\ \vdots & \vdots & \vdots & & \vdots & \vdots & & \vdots \\ 0 & 0 & 0 & \cdots & 1 & \vdots & \cdots & 1 \end{bmatrix}}_{I_k} \tag{7-162}$$

We shall see shortly that it is the last row of the matrix that determines the properties of the code.

Cyclic codes are describable in polynomial form, a property that is extremely useful in their analysis and implementation. The code word $\mathbf{c} = (c_1, c_2, \ldots, c_n)$ may be expressed as the $(n-1)$-degree polynomial

$$c(x) = c_1 x^{n-1} + c_2 x^{n-2} + \cdots + c_{n-1} x + c_n \tag{7-163}$$

Each power of x represents a one-bit shift in time. The highest-order coefficient c_1 in the polynomial represents the first bit of the code word; the last coefficient c_n, the last bit of the code words. Successive shifts to generate other code words are then repeated by the operation $xc(x) \bmod (x^n + 1)$. Thus, shifting once, we have

$$xc(x) \bmod (x^n + 1) = c_2 x^{n-1} + c_3 x^{n-2} + \cdots + c_{n-1} x^2 + c_n x + c_1 \tag{7-164}$$

Shifting a second time, we have

$$x^2 c(x) \bmod (x^n + 1) = c_3 x^{n-1} + c_4 x^{n-2} + \cdots + c_n x^2 + c_1 x + c_2 \tag{7-165}$$

Using this polynomial representation, the G matrix may be represented with polynomials of x as well. Specifically, we insert the appropriate power of x in any element with a 1, and leave blank the elements containing a zero. Thus, as an example, consider the following matrix for a $(7, 3)$ code:

$$G = \begin{bmatrix} 1 & 0 & 0 & 1 & 1 & 1 & 0 \\ 0 & 1 & 0 & 0 & 1 & 1 & 1 \\ 0 & 0 & 1 & 1 & 1 & 0 & 1 \end{bmatrix} \tag{7-166}$$

Its polynomial representation is then

$$G = \begin{bmatrix} x^6 & - & - & x^3 & x^2 & x & - \\ - & x^5 & - & - & x^2 & x & 1 \\ - & - & x^4 & x^3 & x^2 & - & 1 \end{bmatrix} \tag{7-166a}$$

More generally, for an (n, k) cyclic code, we must have

$$
G = \begin{bmatrix}
x^{n-1} & - & - & - & 0 & - & \cdots & \\
- & x^{n-2} & - & - & - & - & \cdots & \\
- & - & \cdot & & & - & \cdots & \\
- & - & & \cdot & & - & \cdots & \\
- & - & & & \cdot & - & \cdots & \\
- & - & - & - & - & x^{n-k} & \cdots & 1
\end{bmatrix} \leftarrow g(x)
\tag{7-167}
$$

Note that the last row must always be representable by a polynomial of the form

$$
g(x) = x^{n-k} + \cdots + 1
\tag{7-168}
$$

by our observation earlier that for cyclic codes the last element must always be a 1.

This polynomial, called the *generator polynomial* of the code, determines the characteristics of the code. For consider a matrix G' made up of k rows generated by successive multiplications of $g(x)$ by x:

$$
G' = \begin{bmatrix}
x^{k-1}g(x) \\
\vdots \\
x^2 g(x) \\
x g(x) \\
g(x)
\end{bmatrix}
\tag{7-169}
$$

Operating on G' by the vector $\mathbf{d} = (d_1, \ldots, d_{k-1}, d_k)$, with d_1 the first bit in the k-bit data sequence and d_k the last, we get as a code polynomial

$$
\begin{aligned}
c(x) &= d_1 x^{k-1}g(x) + d_2 x^{k-2}g(x) + \cdots + d_k g(x) \\
&= d(x)g(x)
\end{aligned}
\tag{7-170}
$$

with $d(x)$ a $(k-1)$-degree (or lower) polynomial whose coefficients are the components of $\mathbf{d}$. Note that $c(x)$ is a cyclic polynomial of degree $n-1$ or less, and there are just 2^k possible code words, corresponding to the 2^k possible k-bit data sequences. The code words are not systematic, however, in the sense that the first k bits represent the information bits and the remaining $r = n - k$ bits the parity bits. To generate the systematic form matrix, G' must be transformed into a new matrix G which has the identity matrix I_k in the first k columns. This is called the *standard form* of G and turns out to be exactly the desired matrix of the type of (7-167).

The recipe for doing this goes as follows:

1. Use $g(x)$ as the kth row.
2. To generate the $(k-1)$st row, cyclically shift the kth row one column to the left. This corresponds of course to the operation $xg(x)$. But the kth column entry must be zero to have the standard form. If this entry is 1, add the kth row to it. Thus the $(k-1)$st row is $xg(x)$ if the coefficient of x^{n-k-1} in $g(x)$ is 0, or $xg(x) + g(x)$ (assuming mod-2 addition again) if the coefficient is 1.

3. To generate the $(k - 2)$nd row repeat the same process: shift the $(k - 1)$st row entries one column to the left. Add $g(x)$ if the kth column entry is not zero. Repeat this for all the rows until the topmost one is reached. Note that this corresponds to successive row additions on G' until the appropriate standard form of G is reached.

As an example, say that $g(x) = x^4 + x^3 + x^2 + 1$, and let $n = 7$. [This is thus a $(7, 3)$ code.] Then

$$G' = \begin{bmatrix} x^6 & x^5 & x^4 & - & x^2 & - & - \\ - & x^5 & x^4 & x^3 & - & x & - \\ - & - & x^4 & x^3 & x^2 & - & 1 \end{bmatrix} \qquad (7\text{-}171)$$

This of course does not have the appropriate identity form in the first $k = 3$ columns. To generate the standard form of G, we follow the rules above and find precisely the matrix shown previously in (7-166a):

$$G = \begin{bmatrix} x[xg(x) + g(x)] \\ xg(x) + g(x) \\ g(x) \end{bmatrix} = \begin{bmatrix} x^6 & - & - & x^3 & x^2 & x & - \\ - & x^5 & - & - & x^2 & x & 1 \\ - & - & x^4 & x^3 & x^2 & - & 1 \end{bmatrix} \quad (7\text{-}166a)$$

The generator matrix for this code, replacing x's by 1's and blanks by 0's in (7-166a), is of course the one given earlier by (7-166):

$$G = \begin{bmatrix} 1 & 0 & 0 & 1 & 1 & 1 & 0 \\ 0 & 1 & 0 & 0 & 1 & 1 & 1 \\ 0 & 0 & 1 & 1 & 1 & 0 & 1 \end{bmatrix} \qquad (7\text{-}166)$$

It is apparent that the standard form of G is obtained from G' by successive addition of rows. That this does not change the code words but corresponds simply to their reordering is readily demonstrated. Consider an arbitrary matrix G_1 with n-element row vectors $r_1, r_2, \ldots, r_k$. Specifically, let

$$G_1 = \begin{bmatrix} r_1 \\ r_2 \\ \vdots \\ r_k \end{bmatrix} \qquad (7\text{-}172)$$

These row vectors are said to serve as the *basis vectors* for the code words. For consider a data vector

$$d_1 = (d_1, d_2, \ldots, d_{k-1}, d_k) \qquad (7\text{-}173)$$

Then the code word corresponding to this vector is given by

$$c_1 = d_1 G_1 = d_1 r_1 + d_2 r_2 + \cdots + d_k r_k \qquad (7\text{-}174)$$

Another matrix, G_2 is now formed by adding the jth row of G_1 to the ith row to form a new ith row. Hence

$$G_2 = \begin{bmatrix} \mathbf{r}_1 \\ \mathbf{r}_2 \\ \vdots \\ \mathbf{r}_i + \mathbf{r}_j \\ \vdots \\ \mathbf{r}_k \end{bmatrix} \tag{7-175}$$

The code word for the same k-bit data word $\mathbf{d}_1$ is now

$$
\begin{aligned}
\mathbf{c}_2 = \mathbf{d}_1 G_2 &= d_1 \mathbf{r}_1 + \cdots + d_i(\mathbf{r}_i + \mathbf{r}_j) + \cdots + d_k \mathbf{r}_k \\
&= d_1 \mathbf{r}_1 + \cdots + d_i \mathbf{r}_i + \cdots + (d_j + d_i)\mathbf{r}_j + \cdots \\
&= \mathbf{d}' G_1
\end{aligned} \tag{7-176}
$$

Since every one of the 2^k possible sequences k bits long must be a data word, the sum of two words must give rise to a new code word:

$$\mathbf{d}_1 + \mathbf{d}_2 = \mathbf{d}_3 \tag{7-177}$$

It is apparent that $\mathbf{d}'$ in (7-176) must be a data word, and hence $\mathbf{c}_2$ is one of the 2^k code words. Both matrices G_1 and G_2, the latter obtained by linear transformations on the former, give rise to the same code-word set. Hence both G and G' discussed earlier produce the same set of code words. The only difference is that G produces a *systematic* set, with information bits always corresponding to the first k bits.

Each cyclic code is thus derivable from a generator matrix $g(x)$. A code word $c(x)$, in polynomial form, may always be written in the form

$$c(x) = a(x)g(x) \tag{7-178}$$

since, from the rules for finding G, each row of the generator matrix must be a polynomial times $g(x)$. As a check, the polynomial $a(x)$ must be of the $(k-1)$st order to have $c(x)$ an $(n-1)$st-order polynomial. There are thus k coefficients of this polynomial with a total of 2^k possible code words.

Since all cyclic codes are generated by an appropriate generator polynomial $g(x)$, all that remains to determine them is to indicate how one finds $g(x)$. This turns out to be very straightforward. We state without proof the following theorem [PETE]: *the generator polynomial $g(x)$ for an (n, k) cyclic code is a divisor of $x^n + 1$.*

As an example, consider the class of $(7, k)$ codes. We have already indicated that the $(7, 4)$ and $(7, 3)$ codes are single-error-correcting. To find the cyclic codes of this group we need the appropriate divisors of $x^7 + 1$. It is left for the reader to show that

$$x^7 + 1 = (x + 1)(x^3 + x + 1)(x^3 + x^2 + 1) \tag{7-179}$$

Products of divisors are divisors as well. This has two polynomials of the fourth order that can serve as generator polynomials of a $(7, 3)$ code. [Recall that $g(x)$ is of $(n - k)$ order.] Consider, in particular, the generator polynomial

$$g(x) = (x + 1)(x^3 + x + 1) = x^4 + x^3 + x^2 + 1 \qquad (7\text{-}180)$$

This is precisely the example used in (7-171) and (7-166a). The generator matrix for this code is given by (7-166a). Its eight possible code words, found using (7-133), are

$$
\begin{array}{cc}
000 & 0000 \\
001 & 1101 \\
010 & 0111 \\
011 & 1010 \\
100 & 1110 \\
101 & 0011 \\
110 & 1001 \\
111 & 0100 \\
\end{array}
$$

Note that except for the all-zero code word these are all cyclic versions of one another. Note also that the minimum Hamming distance is 4, corresponding to a single-error-correction capability. This code has a limited burst-error-correction capability as well [LUCK, p. 373].

To summarize our results thus far for cyclic codes, we have shown that the Hamming inequality of (7-154) can be used to find an appropriate (n, k) combination as a possible candidate for specified error-correction capability. A divisor of $x^n + 1$ of order $n - k$ will then serve as the generator polynomial $g(x)$. Using the rules outlined earlier, we can then find the generator matrix G. The resultant codes found must then be tested to see if they in fact possess the desired error-correction capability. We shall demonstrate some simple procedures shortly for generating the code words directly from $g(x)$. This is in fact one of the reasons for focusing on cyclic codes: they are often easily implemented. In addition to the random-error-correction capability stressed thus far, one can get other properties as well by choosing $g(x)$ appropriately. These include, among others, burst-error-correction capability, synchronization capability, ability to detect (but not correct) various error patterns, etc. We shall discuss the error-detection property of cyclic codes later in this section.

As another example of a set of cyclic codes, consider the class of $(15, k)$ codes. These must be generated by divisors of $x^{15} + 1$. Carrying out the division, one finds

$$x^{15} + 1 = (x + 1)(x^2 + x + 1)(x^4 + x + 1)$$
$$\times (x^4 + x^3 + 1)(x^4 + x^3 + x^2 + x + 1) \qquad (7\text{-}181)$$

These five divisors may in turn be multiplied together to form new divisors. In all, there are

$$\binom{5}{1} + \binom{5}{2} + \binom{5}{3} + \binom{5}{4} = 30$$

possible polynomials from which generator polynomials may be obtained. It

TABLE 7-3
Some $(15, k)$ cyclic codes

k	Error-correction capability t	Hamming distance d	g(x)
14	0	2	$(1, 0) \equiv x + 1$
11	1	3	$(4, 1, 0) \equiv x^4 + x + 1$
10	1	4	$(1, 0)(4, 1, 0)$
7	2	5	$(4, 1, 0)(4, 3, 2, 1, 0)$
6	2	6	$(1, 0)(4, 1, 0)(4, 3, 2, 1, 0)$
5	3	7	$(4, 1, 0)(4, 3, 2, 1, 0)(2, 1, 0)$
4	3	8	$(1, 0)(4, 1, 0)(4, 3, 2, 1, 0)(2, 1, 0)$
2	4	10	$(1, 0)(4, 1, 0)(4, 3, 2, 1, 0)(4, 3, 0)$
1	7	15	$(4, 1, 0)(4, 3, 2, 1, 0)(4, 3, 0)(2, 1, 0)$

turns out 26 of these are nontrivial. Some of these 26 codes and their generator polynomials are given in Table 7-3.[15]

Cyclic-Code Generation: Polynomial Encoding

It has already been noted above that cyclic codes lend themselves readily to generation directly from the generator polynomial $g(x)$. Shift-register implementation can be used to carry out the code generation serially, if desired. To demonstrate this, recall from (7-178) that a code-word polynomial $c(x)$ must be divisible by the generator polynomial $g(x)$. It is also of degree $n - 1$ or less. Consider now a data sequence $d_1, d_2, \ldots, d_{k-1}, d_k$, and write this as the polynomial

$$d(x) = d_1 x^{k-1} + \cdots + d_{k-1} x + d_k \qquad (7\text{-}182)$$

of degree $k - 1$ or less. The operation $x^{n-k} d(x)$ then generates a polynomial of degree $n - 1$ or less. We now take $x^{n-k} d(x)$ and divide this by the polynomial $g(x)$ of degree $n - k$:

$$\frac{x^{n-k} d(x)}{g(x)} = q(x) + \frac{r(x)}{g(x)} \qquad (7\text{-}183)$$

The division results in a polynomial $q(x)$ of degree $k - 1$ or less and a remainder polynomial $r(x)$. Since $r(x) + r(x) = 0$ under mod-2 addition, it is apparent that the $(n - 1)$-degree polynomial $x^{n-k} d(x) + r(x)$ is divisible by

---

[15][LUCK, p. 295, table 10-1]. To simplify the notation, $(2, 1, 0)$ is used to represent $x^2 + x + 1$, etc.; thus $(1, 0)(4, 1, 0)$ is $(x + 1)(x^4 + x + 1) = x^5 + x^4 + x^2 + 1$.

$g(x)$ and must therefore be a code word, from (7-178). Thus

$$c(x) = a(x)g(x) = x^{n-k}d(x) + r(x) \qquad (7\text{-}184)$$

But $x^{n-k}d(x)$ corresponds to a simple left shift by $n - k$ units of the data bits. Hence the remainder $r(x)$ must represent the parity check bits. Specifically, then,

$$r(x) = \text{rem} \frac{x^{n-k}d(x)}{g(x)} \qquad (7\text{-}185)$$

with "rem" denoting remainder.

As an example, consider the $(7,3)$ code with generator polynomial $g(x) = x^4 + x^3 + x^2 + 1$ discussed earlier [see Eqs. (7-166), (7-166a), and (7-180)]. Say that the data word is $\mathbf{d} = (0\,0\,1)$, or $d(x) = 1$. Then it is left for the reader to show that

$$r(x) = \text{rem} \frac{x^4}{x^4 + x^3 + x^2 + 1} = x^3 + x^2 + 1 \qquad (7\text{-}186)$$

The code word is thus

$$\mathbf{c} = (0\,0\,1\,1\,1\,0\,1) \qquad (7\text{-}187)$$

agreeing with the second code word in the set of eight tabulated earlier. Similarly, say that $\mathbf{d} = (1\,1\,1)$ or $d(x) = x^2 + x + 1$. Then

$$r(x) = \text{rem} \frac{x^6 + x^5 + x^4}{x^4 + x^3 + x^2 + 1} = x^4 \qquad (7\text{-}188)$$

and $\mathbf{c} = (1\,1\,1\,0\,1\,0\,0)$, just the last code word listed in the set of eight.

The polynomial representation of cyclic codes and the calculation of the parity-check-bit remainder polynomial $r(x)$ by dividing the left-shifted $d(x)$ by the generator polynomial $g(x)$ suggest various ways of implementing the parity-check-bit calculation. These give rise to simple shift-register encoders. One such scheme, using $r = n - k$ shift register stages, is shown in Fig. 7-59. With the switch at the right held in the O position, as shown, the k data bits are shifted in, one at a time. The shift register elements are designated by the 1-bit delay symbol

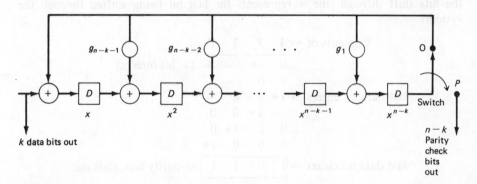

FIGURE 7-59
Cyclic-code encoder, $r = n - k$ registers.

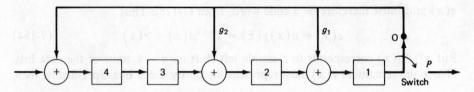

FIGURE 7-60
Encoder, $(7, 3)$ code, $g(x) = x^4 + x^3 + x^2 + 1$.

D. As these k bits are moving through the encoder, they are being shifted out onto the output line as well, since they form the first k bits of the n-bit code word. The data bits continue moving through the shift registers until the last (kth) data bit clears the last ($n - k$th) register. The mod-2 addition units shown are exclusive-or devices. The gain controls $g_{n-k-1}, g_{n-k-2}, \cdots, g_1$ are either present (a 1) or absent (a 0), depending upon whether the corresponding coefficients in the $g(x)$ polynomial given by $g(x) = x^{n-k} + g_1 x^{n-k-1} + \cdots + g_{n-k-1} x + 1$ are 1 or 0. At the time the last data bit clears the last register, the $r = n - k$ registers contain the parity-check bits. The switch is now thrown to position P, and the r check bits are shifted out, one at a time, onto the line. In effect, multiplication through the feedback elements shown in Fig. 7-59 provides the division called for by (7-185) in the calculation of the remainder polynomial.

The encoder for the $(7, 3)$ code discussed previously as an example appears in Fig. 7-60. Since

$$g(x) = x^4 + x^3 + x^2 + 1 = x^4 + g_1 x^3 + g_2 x^2 + 1$$

we have

$$g_1 = g_2 = 1, \qquad g_{n-k-1} = g_3 = 0$$

in this case. To check the operation of the encoder in this case, consider the data sequence $0\,0\,1$, applied in that order to the input of the encoder. We trace the operation of the device by indicating the contents of each of the four registers as the bits shift through (the $*$ represents the last bit being shifted through the system):

	Contents of →	4	3	2	1		
		0	—	—	—	↓	bit interval
		0	0	—	—		
last data bit enters →		1*	0	0	—		
		—	1*	0	0		
		0	0	1*	0		
		0	0	0	1*		
last data bit clears →		1	0	1	1	→	parity bits, shift out

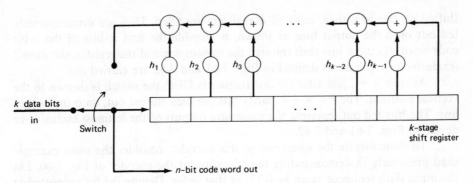

FIGURE 7-61
Alternative encoder, cyclic codes.

Note that the output bit sequence, $1\,1\,0\,1$, in that order, is in fact the desired parity bit sequence for the data sequence $0\,0\,1$.

An alternative encoder implementation is found by noting that since $g(x)$ is a divisor of $x^n + 1$, from the theorem quoted earlier, we can always write

$$g(x)h(x) = x^n + 1 \qquad (7\text{-}189)$$

The polynomial $h(x)$ as defined is called the *parity-check polynomial*. $h(x)$ must be a polynomial of order k, and hence can always be written in the form

$$h(x) = x^k + h_1 x^{k-1} + h_2 x^{k-2} + \cdots + h_{k-1} + 1 \qquad (7\text{-}190)$$

The coefficients h_j, $1 \le j \le k - 1$, are either 1 or 0, depending on whether the corresponding term in the polynomial appears or not. As an example, for the $(7, 3)$ code discussed above, it is readily shown that $h(x) = (x^7 + 1)/g(x) = x^3 + x^2 + 1$.

It turns out that a cyclic-code encoder may be implemented using a k-stage shift register with mod-2 operations involving the $k - 1$ coefficients in the expansion of (7-190). The specific implementation appears in Fig. 7-61. We state this without proof, relying on the $(7, 3)$ code to provide a specific example.

For that code, with $g(x) = x^4 + x^3 + x^2 + 1$ and $h(x) = x^3 + x^2 + 1$, as noted above, the encoder takes the form of Fig. 7-62. The device operates as follows. With the switch in the horizontal position, as shown, the k data bits are

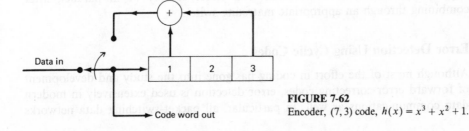

FIGURE 7-62
Encoder, $(7, 3)$ code, $h(x) = x^3 + x^2 + 1$.

shifted in, one at a time, until all k registers are filled. They are simultaneously fed out onto the output line, as shown, to provide the first k bits of the n-bit code word. As the k bits shift through the various steps of the register, the mod-2 (exclusive-or) operations defined in Figs. 7-61 and 7-62 are carried out.

At time $k +$, just after the last register is filled, the switch is thrown to the vertical position. The $r = n - k$ parity bits are then shifted out, onto the output line. The bits fed out represent the successive outputs of the leftmost exclusive-or device in Figs. 7-61 and 7-62.

To demonstrate the operation of this encoder, consider the same example used previously in demonstrating the operation of the encoder of Fig. 7-60. Let the input data sequence again be $0\,0\,1$, in that order. Denote the bit outputted at time j by c_j (the output of the mod-2 adder in Fig. 7-62 after the switch is thrown up). The contents of the three registers in Fig. 7-62, as well as c_j, at successive intervals following the throwing of the switch appear as follows:

Time j	Contents of → 1 2 3	c_j
3 +	1 0 0	← switch up
4	1 1 0 1	
5	1 1 1 1	
6	0 1 1 0	
7	1 0 1 1	parity-check bits, in sequence

Note that the parity-check sequence agrees with that found previously using the encoder of Fig. 7-60.

As another example, consider the $(15, 11)$ code appearing in Table 7-3, with generator polynomial $g(x) = x^4 + x + 1$. It is left to the reader to show that

$$h(x) = x^{11} + x^8 + x^7 + x^5 + x^3 + x^2 + x + 1$$

for this code. The two encoders, one corresponding to operations with $g(x)$, the other to operations with $h(x)$, appear in Fig. 7-63. It is left as an exercise to the reader to trace through the operation of these two encoders and to show that they do in fact provide the same parity-check outputs.

Note that the two encoder implementations discussed here operate on the serial data to provide serial output. The implementation of Fig. 7-56, with $r = n - k$ output leads, each connected in a different manner to the k registers, could provide either serial or parallel output. Figure 7-56 may also be looked on as an implementation in which the k information (data) bits are read in sequentially, stored, and then read out, either serially or in parallel, after combining through an appropriate matrixing switch.

Error Detection Using Cyclic Codes

Although most of the effort in coding has gone into the study and development of forward error-correcting codes, error detection is used extensively in modern data communications as well. In particular, all packet-switching data networks

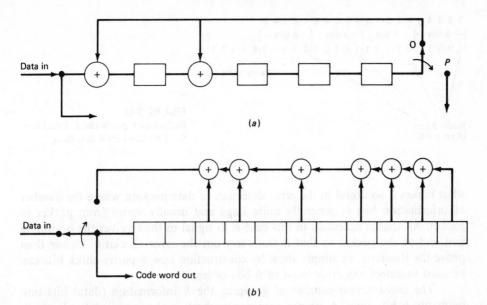

FIGURE 7-63
Encoders, $(15, 11)$ code. (a) $g(x) = x^4 + x + 1$.
(b) $h(x) = x^{11} + x^8 + x^7 + x^5 + x^3 + x^2 + x + 1$.

and computer networks use error detection with retransmission in the event of an error detected. We have already commented on this protocol function in our discussion of networks in Chap. 5. Cyclic codes are used most frequently in performing the error-detection function.

Recall that packets, and the link-level frames encapsulating them, can be hundreds and even thousands of bits in length. It is apparent that error correction for code words of this length can be a formidable task. Error detection, with a fixed number of parity-check bits appended, is easily carried out, however.

We have already noted a simple form of error detection—the use of a single added bit to determine whether an odd number of bits have been received in error. More generally, r parity-check bits enable any burst of errors r bits or less in length to be detected. This is independent of the length of the packet, accounting for the utility of the technique. Since $r \ll k$ most commonly, the $g(x)$ or remainder-type cyclic encoder is generally used in the error-detection application. (Recall that this requires an r-stage shift register.)

Burst errors are, as the name implies, those errors that wipe out some or all of a sequential set of bits. A burst of length b by definition consists of a sequence of bits in which the first and the bth bits are in error, with the $b - 2$ bits in between either in error or received correctly. A theorem then states that b parity-check symbols as part of a linear block code are necessary and sufficient for detecting all burst errors of length b or less in a block of length n [PETE]. Note, as stated earlier, that this detection capability is independent of n, which is

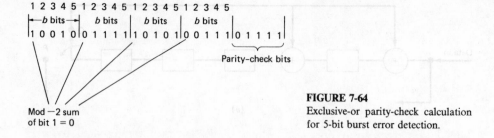

FIGURE 7-64
Exclusive-or parity-check calculation for 5-bit burst error detection.

what makes it so useful in the error detection of data packets, where the number of information bits is generally quite large and usually varies from packet to packet. All that is necessary in this case is to signal to the receiver the beginning and end of the packet so that it can carry out the error checking. Rather than prove the theorem, we simply show by construction how b parity-check bits can be used to detect any error burst of b bits or less.

The construction consists of grouping the k information (data) bits into segments b bits long. A simple even-parity check is then applied to all equal-numbered bits in each of the segments. (This is equivalent to taking the mod-2 sum of equal-numbered bits and then adding a parity-check bit that equals the mod-2 sum.) The b parity-check bits so formed are then placed at the end of the entire code word. This thus generates a systematic linear code. An example with $b = 5$ appears in Fig. 7-64. As shown in the figure, the mod-2 sum of the number 1 bits is 0. The mod-2 sum of the number 2 bits is similarly found to be 1, etc. The full 5-bit parity-check vector is then 0 1 1 1 1, as shown.

Now note from this construction that only one bit in any burst of b bits or less will affect any parity-check bit, and will thus be detected. This is true whether the burst appears in one of the b-bit segments into which the data sequence has been grouped, or overlaps two such segments. This simple code thus detects any burst of b bits or less.

In addition to detecting a burst of b bits or less, a linear code with $r = b$ parity-check bits will detect a high percentage of longer bursts as well. This is what makes the error-detection property so useful. In particular, a theorem we prove below states that the fraction of bursts of length $b > r$ that remain *undetected* by a *cyclic (n, k) code $(n - k = r)$* is 2^{-r} if $b > r + 1$, or is $2^{-(r-1)}$ if $b = r + 1$. If the number of parity bits, r, is large enough, almost all errors are detected. As an example, if $r = 16$ bits, all bursts of length 16 bits or less will be detected and the fraction of bursts of length $b > 17$ remaining undetected is $2^{-16} \sim 4 \times 10^{-6}$, an extremely small number.

To prove this theorem, say that a burst of length b starts with the ith bit and ends with the $(i + b - 1)$th bit. Again using powers of x to represent shifts in time, we can define a burst polynomial $b(x)$, such that

$$b(x) = x^i b_1(x) \tag{7-191}$$

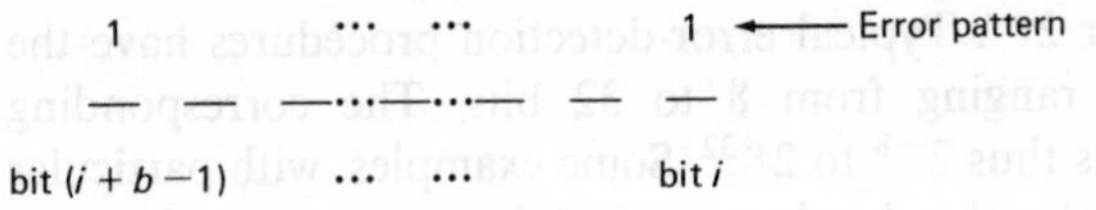

FIGURE 7-65
Error pattern, burst of length b.

and $b_1(x)$ is a polynomial of degree $b - 1$:

$$b_1(x) = x^{b-1} + \cdots + 1 \qquad (7\text{-}192)$$

This is apparent from Fig. 7-65, which shows an error, represented by a 1, appearing at bit i, and an error appearing at bit $i + b - 1$, at the end of the burst. The error burst b bits long can have 2^{b-2} possible symbols (1 or 0) between its beginning and end, each constrained, by definition, to be a 1. This corresponds to 2^{b-2} possible burst patterns each b bits long, or 2^{b-2} possible forms of the polynomial $b_1(x)$.

Since the parity-check calculation at the receiver will be carried out by dividing by the generator polynomial $g(x)$, an error will remain undetected if and only if $b_1(x)$ is divisible by $g(x)$. (Why is this so?) Hence the condition for a burst-error pattern to remain undetected is that $b_1(x)$ has $g(x)$ as a factor. In this case $b_1(x)$ must take on the form

$$b_1(x) = g(x)Q(x) \qquad (7\text{-}193)$$

$Q(x)$ is a polynomial of degree $(b - 1) - r$, since $g(x)$ is of degree r and $b_1(x)$ is of degree $b - 1$. There are two possible cases to consider. In the first case the burst length is such that $b - 1 = r$. Then $Q(x) = 1$, and there is only *one* undetected burst pattern. The fraction of undetected bursts is then simply given by

$$\text{fraction of undetected bursts} = \frac{1}{2^{b-2}}$$

$$= 2^{-(r-1)} \qquad b - 1 = r \qquad (7\text{-}194)$$

In the second case, $b - 1 > r$. Since the polynomial $Q(x)$ is of degree $(b - 1) - r$ and must end with a 1, it has $(b - 1) - r - 1$ terms, whose coefficients can be 1 or 0. The number of undetected burst patterns in this case is therefore $2^{(b-1)-r-1}$, and

$$\text{fraction of undetected bursts} = \frac{2^{b-1-r-1}}{2^{b-2}}$$

$$= 2^{-r} \qquad b - 1 > r \qquad (7\text{-}195)$$

These two results prove the theorem cited above. They verify the statement made earlier that an error-detecting code with a moderate number of parity-check bits will detect the occurrence of a large majority of error burst patterns. As noted previously, and as discussed in Chap. 5, all modern data and computer networks use some form of error detection with requests for repeats of incorrectly received packets. The use of an error-detection scheme reduces the raw probability of error of a packet by the factor 2^{-r}. Typical error-detection procedures have the number of parity-check bits ranging from 8 to 32 bits. The corresponding reduction in error probability is thus 2^{-8} to 2^{-32}. Some examples, with particular reference to the MAC layer protocol in local-area networks, appeared in Chap. 5. The international standard for data link control, HDLC, mentioned briefly in Chap. 5, uses a 16-bit cyclic check sequence. The generator polynomial for this standard is prescribed to be

$$g(x) = x^{16} + x^{12} + x^5 + 1 \qquad (7\text{-}196)$$

The actual calculation of the probability of error of a packet or block of data protected by a cyclic check scheme is difficult to carry out because of a lack of detailed knowledge of the mechanisms producing typical bursts. If the underlying mechanism is the ever-present thermal noise and its effect may be modeled as additive white gaussian noise, successive bit errors in a burst are independent of one another. The probability that a packet or block n bits long is then received in error is $[1 - (1 - p)^n] \doteq np$, $np \ll 1$, with p the bit-error probability. It has already been noted, however, that the band-limited telephone channel, which is used most frequently as the backbone communication link for data networks, is not modeled accurately as an AWGN channel. Error bursts on this channel do have memory and do introduce error dependence into successive bits in a data stream. This makes the calculation of error probabilities quite difficult. Nevertheless, tests have shown that the effect of error on blocks of data is to make a block error more likely as the block length n increases and that a reasonable model for the block error probability has it proportional to block length [BURT].[16] Thus

$$P_b \doteq np \qquad (7\text{-}197)$$

with p a parameter to be determined from experiment. This simple result agrees with the intuitive feeling that the chance of an error should go up as the block length increases.

If cyclic error checking is now carried out, our simple result says that 2^{-r} of the error events will be undetected as such. (This assumes the burst length $b > r$, or that $r \gg 1$.) The overall block error probability can thus be written, approximately, as

$$P_e \doteq np \, 2^{-r} \qquad (7\text{-}198)$$

This equation is useful in assessing the performance of various block checking schemes. Some examples follow.

1. $p = 10^{-5}$, $n = 500$ bits, $r = 8$ bits. Then

$$P_e \doteq 2 \times 10^{-5}$$

---

[16][BURT] H. O. Burton and D. D. Sullivan, "Errors and Error Control," *Proc. IEEE*, vol. 60, no. 11, pp. 1293–1301, November 1972.

2. $p = 10^{-5}$, $n = 500$ bits, $r = 16$ bits:

$$P_e \doteq 10^{-7}$$

The effect of adding another 8 bits to the parity check scheme is to reduce the error probability by $2^{-8} = 1/256$.

3. $p = 10^{-5}$, $n = 1,000$ bits, $r = 16$ bits:

$$P_e \doteq 2 \times 10^{-7}$$

4. $p = 10^{-5}$, $n = 1,000$ bits, $r = 32$ bits:

$$P_e \doteq 4 \times 10^{-12}$$

It is apparent from these simple calculations that effective error protection is obtained for long data blocks using comparatively few parity-check bits. (Note that the ratio r/n remains small in all these cases.)

Reed–Solomon (RS) Codes

Forward error-correcting block codes have begun to be used increasingly in recent years for error control in communication systems because of the advent of relatively low-cost IC and VLSI technology. In particular, Reed–Solomon (RS) codes, a class of cyclic codes with particularly powerful error-control properties, have found widespread acceptance in fields as diverse as space communications and the compact-disc digital audio system. RS codes represent a special case of the BCH (Bose–Chaudhuri–Hocquenghem) class of cyclic codes designed to provide multiple-error correction. We summarize the basic properties of these codes only. Details on their design and implementation appear in [MICH] and most of the other references cited on coding. [BERL 1980] and [BERL 1987] make a particularly strong case for the RS codes and discuss their error performance in detail. The widest application of RS codes has been in their nonbinary form, with multiple bits constituting a symbol, treated as a unit. As we shall see, it is this *symbol* correction property that makes them particularly powerful.

Consider the so-called primitive binary BCH codes first [MICH]. They will correct up to t errors per code word, with $t < n/2$. In particular, let $n = 2^m - 1$. Then no more than $r = mt$ parity check bits are required. As an example, let $m = 3$, $n = 7$. Say double-error correction is desired, so that $t = 2$. Then a BCH code exists with at most $r = mt = 6$ parity-check bits required. It is left to the reader to show that $r \geq 5$ does in fact satisfy the Hamming bound of (7-154). A $(7, 2)$ code can thus correct up to two errors. A trivial example of another multiple-error-correcting code is the $(7, 1)$ code. This is an example of a binary repetitive code: the single information bit is simply repeated another six times. It is clear that this can correct up to $(n - 1)/2 = 3$ errors.

Say we now choose $m = 4$ and $n = 15$. Say up to $t = 2$ errors are again to be corrected. Then no more than $r = mt = 8$ parity-check bits are required. It is again left to the reader to show that the resultant $(15, 7)$ code satisfies the Hamming bound of (7-154).

The $(23, 12)$ Golay code will correct up to $t = 3$ errors and is an example of a nonprimitive BCH code [MICH]. It is the only nontrivial multiple-error-correcting code which satisfies the Hamming bound of (7-154) with an equality. Such a code is called a *perfect* code, since it provides the minimum length n for a given error-correction capability t. [Single-error-correcting codes satisfying the Hamming bound with an equality are called binary Hamming codes. The $(7, 4)$ and $(15, 11)$ codes are examples. Binary repetition codes provide the only other class of perfect codes.]

We now shift our focus to Reed–Solomon codes. As noted, these are *nonbinary*, multisymbol codes. In particular, let a symbol comprise b bits. There are then $q = 2^b$ possible symbols defining the code alphabet. As an example, if $b = 8$ bits (an octet), there are $q = 2^8 = 256$ possible symbols. An (n, k) RS code is a block code with k information symbols and n code-word symbols. RS codes have the property that the code word n is limited to at most $q + 1$ symbols in length. (Most typically, $n \le q - 1$ is a design constraint, but RS codes may be extended to $n = q$ and $q + 1$.) For example, if symbols are made up of 6-bit groups, $(64, k)$ RS codes can be generated. In particular, a $(64, 40)$ code would consist of $64 \times 6 = 384$ bit code words, each containing 240 information bits treated as 40 6-bit symbols.

Consider the definition of the Hamming distance d, now extended to represent the minimum number of places in which *symbols* of code words differ. Then the error-correcting capability of a nonbinary (symbol) code is clearly $t = d/2$ *symbols*. As an example, say a 4-symbol code is used. Let the four symbols be $0, 1, 2, 3$. (In this case each symbol would be represented by two bits.) The two code words $c_1 = 0123$ and $c_2 = 0321$ differ in two places. It may then be shown [MICH] that for the RS class of codes, the distance d_{RS} is

$$d_{RS} = n - k + 1 = r + 1 \tag{7-199}$$

with $r = n - k$ the number of parity-check symbols. Alternatively, since the error-correction capability of a code is $t < d/2$, the RS codes will correct up to t *symbol* errors, provided

$$r \ge 2t_{RS} \tag{7-200}$$

As an example, consider a $(64, 40)$ RS code. This will correct up to 12 symbol errors.

It is clear that large multisymbol codes have, potentially, extremely powerful error-correction capability. Given q symbols from which to choose, there are q^n possible combinations for a code word n symbols long. Of these, only q^k are valid code words. The ratio $q^k/q^n = q^{-r}$ represents the fraction of potential code words that are actually used. This drops rapidly with increasing r, indicating that large Hamming distances are obtainable by appropriate choice of the set of code words. As an example, consider the $(64, 40)$ code noted above. In this case $q = 2^6 = 64$. The fraction of possible words 64 symbols long actually used as code words is $64^{-24} = 2^{-144}$, clearly an extremely small number. This makes words differing from a code word readily detectable and correctable, and is the reason for the large error-correcting capability of $t = r/2 = 12$ symbols.

The 1986 Voyager Uranus space mission used a (255, 223) RS code, combined with convolutional coding (to be discussed in the next section), to attain a bit-error rate of 10^{-5} while transmitting at approximately 30 kbits/s [POSN]. Eight-bit symbols were used, so that $q = 256$. This code is capable of correcting up to $r/2 = 16$ symbols. A discussion of the signal-to-noise requirements for this space mission appears at the end of the next section.

In some coding applications symbols may be received garbled beyond recognition. As an example, individual bits may not be interpretable as 1's or 0's. They are then "erased" and are called erasure bits. (A binary channel with this property is often called a binary erasure channel.) Nonbinary symbols may similarly be labeled "erasure" symbols. It is then simply proven that a code with distance d may correct any combination of t errors and e erasures providing $2t + e < d$ [MICH].[17] Alternatively, if one corrects e erasures, the error-correcting capability of a code is reduced to $t < (d - e)/2$. In particular, for RS codes, which correct both errors and erasures, we have, modifying (7-200),

$$r \geq 2t_{RS} + e_{RS} \qquad (7\text{-}201)$$

There is thus a tradeoff possible between error correction and erasure correction.

The compact-disc digital audio system provides an example of the use of RS codes for both error correction and erasure [PEEK]. Two RS encoders in tandem are used to encode the original audio samples. The reverse process of decoding is carried out in playing the disc. Specifically, call the two decoders used in tandem (concatenated) C_1 and C_2. Both decoders use 8-bit symbols. The first code is of the form (32, 28); the second is of the form (28, 24). The parity-check length is thus $r = 4$ symbols in each case. Decoder C_1 attempts to detect and correct single-symbol errors only. It attempts to detect, but not correct, multiple error patterns, and assigns erasure flags to all symbols of a word so detected. It may then be shown that this decoder will detect double and triple symbol errors with certainty, while the probability of an undetected error pattern (with from 4 to 32 error symbols per code word) is approximately 1.9×10^{-6} [PEEK].

Leaving C_1, the 28 information symbols of a single word (parity-check symbols are dropped) are separated by delay lines so that each is assigned to a different word entering C_2. Errors in one word leaving C_1 are thus spread out over multiple words entering C_2. Decoder C_2 again attempts to detect and correct single errors. It tries to correct double erasures, so designated by the erasure flag appended in C_1. Interpolation is then used to replace errors remaining that are detected as such but are not corrected. (The use of interpolated samples can

---

[17]In the case of an erasure, the *location* of a bad symbol is known. Hence less effort is required to correct it. An error first has to be detected before being corrected. Alternatively put, only half as many errors can be corrected as can erasures.

provide inaudible results,, while undetected errors produce audible clicks. This is the reason for using a combination of error and erasure correction [PEEK].)

7-9   CONVOLUTIONAL CODING

As noted at the beginning of the previous section, coding techniques fall into two major classes: the block codes just discussed, in which blocks of k bits (or symbols, more generally) have r parity-check bits (or symbols) added to form a code word; and convolutional codes, in which a sliding sequence of data bits is used to generate a coded stream of bits. Convolutional codes can be designed to operate on symbols as well. We focus on binary coding for simplicity.

As we shall see in carrying out a performance analysis of some convolutional codes, they have the property similar to that of block codes of being able to correct errors and improve the performance of point-to-point communication systems significantly. They thus provide another example of a set of codes designed to have a communication system approach the Shannon limit in performance. They have been used extensively in both space and satellite communication applications. More recently both convolutional and block (Reed–Solomon) codes have been used together to attain performance better than possible with either alone. We shall provide an example of this technique applied to the Voyager Uranus space mission at the end of this section.

The convolutional coder consists of a K-stage shift register. Input data bits are shifted along the register one bit at a time. (A q-ary coder would have each b-bit symbol shifted along.) Modulo-2 sums of the contents of the shift-register stages are shifted out at a rate v times as fast. There are thus v bits out for every bit in. (In a symbol encoder, v symbols are shifted out for every symbol in.) An R-bit/s input data stream thus gives rise to an Rv-bit/s coded output stream.

An example of a $K = 3$, $v = 2$ convolutional coder appears in Fig. 7-66 [VITE 1971].[18] Each time a data bit is shifted in, two encoded data bits are read out in sequence. Calling the data bits in each of the three stages of Fig. 7-66 d_1, d_2, d_3, with the output coded bits labeled c_1 and c_2 corresponding to the two outputs, we have

$$c_1 = d_1 \oplus d_2 \oplus d_3$$
$$c_1 = d_1 \qquad \oplus d_3 \tag{7-202}$$

This coding is carried out continuously, on all data bits as they are shifted through the register. A typical input bit stream with corresponding output bits is shown in Fig. 7-66b.

K is called the constraint length of the convolutional coder. A coder outputting v bits for every bit in is called a rate-$1/v$ coder. More generally, a

---

[18][VITE 1971] A. J. Viterbi, "Convolutional Codes and Their Performance in Communication Systems," *IEEE Trans. Commun. Technol.*, vol. COM-19, no. 5, pp. 751–771, October 1971.

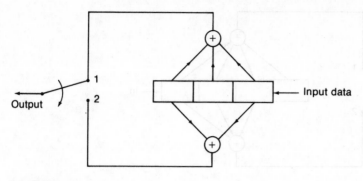

Output

Input data

(a) Coder

Time interval $\longrightarrow$

	1	2	3	4	5	6	7	8
Input bits:	0	1	1	0	1	0	0	1

Output bits:	0 0	1 1	0	1	0	1	0 0	1 0	1 1	1 1
Switch positions $\longrightarrow$	1 2	1 2	1 2	1 2	1 2	1 2	1 2	1 2

Initialization

(b) Sample bit stream

FIGURE 7-66
Example of a $K = 3$, $v = 2$ convolutional coder.

constraint-length-K, rate-$1/v$ coder would have its output (coded) bits appearing in the form

$$c_1 = h_{11}d_1 \oplus h_{12}d_2 \oplus \cdots \oplus h_{1K}d_K$$
$$c_2 = h_{21}d_1 \oplus h_{22}d_2 \oplus \cdots \oplus h_{2K}d_K$$
$$\vdots \tag{7-203}$$
$$c_v = h_{v1}d_1 \oplus h_{v2}d_2 \oplus \cdots \oplus h_{vK}d_K$$

The h_{ij}'s are 1 or 0, depending on whether a connection is made or not. The v encoded bits (or symbols in a more general encoder) are outputted sequentially after each input shift. The form of (7-203) represents a modulo-2 convolution of the input data bits with the h_{ij}'s, whence the name convolutional coder.

A particular input bit is carried along, in coded fashion, for K stages, and in v output bits per stage. This introduces redundancy into the system. Since K represents the memory of the system, it is intuitively apparent that the larger the value of K, the more readily a decoder at the receiver will be able to correct errors in the output bit stream introduced during transmission. We shall provide quantitative estimates, in terms of bounds on the error probability, of this observation.

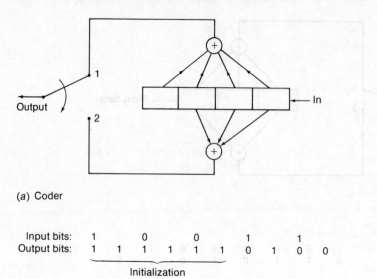

(a) Coder

Input bits:	1		0		0		1		1	
Output bits:	1	1	1	1	1	1	0	1	0	0

Initialization

(b) Sample bit stream

FIGURE 7-67
A $K = 4$, $v = 2$ convolutional coder.

Another example, this time a constraint-length-4, rate-$\frac{1}{2}$ coder, appears in Fig. 7-67. The output bit stream is again shown for a sample input bit sequence. Other connections of the shift-register stages would produce other output bit sequences for the same input data-bit sequence.

If we now refer back to the $K = 3$, rate-$\frac{1}{2}$ coder of Fig. 7-66, we note that the output bit sequence in any time interval after initialization, uniquely determined by the bits in the stages of the shift register, may also be considered as being determined by the bits in the $K - 1 = 2$ leftmost stages plus the new data bit arriving to fill the last stage. Thus, for example, in interval 3 the leftmost $K - 1 = 2$ stages contain 0 1 in that order; a 1 arriving in interval 3 produces 0 1 as the two output bits. Had a 0 arrived, the output would have been 1 0, as shown in interval 6. The output of the coder at any time interval may be represented as due to the state of the $K - 1$ leftmost stages (defined by the $K - 1$ previous input data bits) plus the incoming data bit (0 or 1) in that interval. The coder may be visualized as moving from one state, represented by $K - 1$ shift-register stages, to another. Transitions between states are governed by the particular incoming bit (0 or 1). This leads to the representation of the coder as a finite-state machine. The machine has 2^{K-1} possible states (recall again that we are focusing on *binary* inputs here); transitions between states are determined, as noted above, by the incoming bit. The finite-state-machine representation of the coder of Fig. 7-66, as an example, appears in Fig. 7-68. It has four states, labeled a, b, c, d, each corresponding to one of the $2^{K-1} = 4$ possible arrangements of

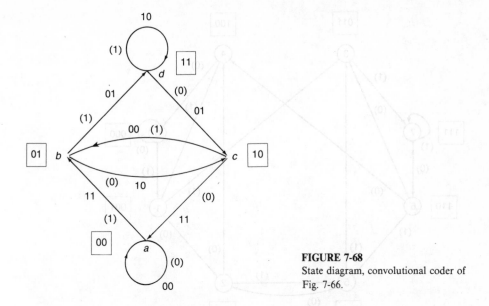

FIGURE 7-68
State diagram, convolutional coder of Fig. 7-66.

bits in the $K - 1 = 2$ leftmost stages of the $K = 3$ shift register. These four two-bit arrangements, each corresponding to the two stages read from left to right, appear in the rectangular boxes appended to the state labels. Arrows indicate the direction of the transitions. The 1 or 0 in parentheses next to the transitions represent the input bit; the two bits following represent the output bits. Thus, with the coder in state a ($\boxed{00}$), a 1 appearing at the input produces 1 1 at the output. The system moves to state b ($\boxed{01}$). If in state b, a 1 at the input produces 0 1 as the output bits. The system then moves to state d ($\boxed{11}$) as shown. If a 0 appears at the input while the system is in state b, the bit sequence 10 will appear at the output, and the system will move to state c ($\boxed{10}$).

All $K = 3$, rate-$\frac{1}{2}$ coders are representable by the state diagram of Fig. 7-68; different modulo-2 connections among the stages [the h_{ij}'s of (7-203)] just change the output bits. Figure 7-69 represents the corresponding state diagram of the $K = 4$, rate-$\frac{1}{2}$ convolutional coder. Output bits have been left out. The coder shown in Fig. 7-67a would be represented by the diagram of Fig. 7-69 with the output bits included. States in Fig. 7-69 have been represented by numbers, rather than letters, for simplicity.

The coder operation may be representable two other ways: as a trellis or as an ever-expanding tree. The trellis representation of the $K = 3$, rate-$\frac{1}{2}$ coder of Fig. 7-66 appears in Fig. 7-70. The four states of this coder (2^{K-1} in general) appear along the vertical axis; transitions between the states are represented in time along the horizontal axis. The transition due to a 0 input bit is always graphed as the upper one of the two leaving any state. (Output bits appear along each transition, as in Fig. 7-68.) The trellis representation demonstrates at a glance the repetitive nature of the coder finite-state machine: starting at any state

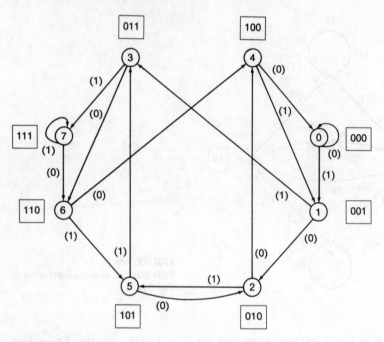

FIGURE 7-69
State diagram, $K = 4$, rate-$\frac{1}{2}$ coder.

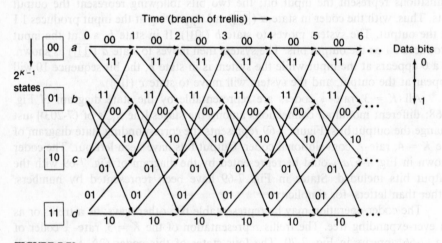

FIGURE 7-70
Trellis representation, coder, Fig. 7-66.

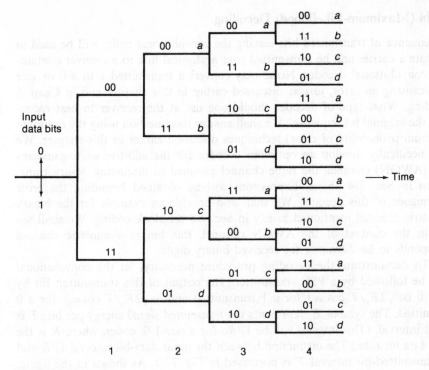

FIGURE 7-71
Tree representation, coder, Fig. 7-66.

at a given point in time, the machine eventually returns to that state. We shall use this representation shortly to evaluate the performance of the convolutional coder. Trellis coding in the next section will use a similar representation.

The tree representation of convolutional coders appears in Fig. 7-71, again using the $K = 3$, rate-$\frac{1}{2}$ coder of Fig. 7-66 as an example. This too demonstrates the cyclic nature of the coder operation: From state a, as an example, the coder can remain at a or move to state b; from state b it can shift to state c or d; from c it can move to a or b; and, finally, from d it can move to c or stay at d. The rule used in obtaining the tree structure of Fig. 7-71 is the same as that adopted for the trellis of Fig. 7-70: upward transitions correspond to a 0 data bit at the input; downward transitions correspond to a 1. Note that although the four states are entered and reentered as time progresses, the number of possible sequences (*paths*) of transmitted bits increases exponentially with time. The Hamming distance between paths increases as well. This, we shall see shortly, provides the basis for the improved performance of a system using convolutional coding. As a given path increases in length, it is more readily distinguishable from other paths. One or more errors in transmission are thus more readily detected and corrected. We shall show that the probability of error in fact decreases exponentially with increasing constraint length K of the coder.

Viterbi (Maximum-Likelihood) Decoding

The sequence of transmitted bits leaving the convolutional coder will be used to modulate a carrier and be transmitted over a physical link to a receiver containing a convolutional decoder. Noise may convert a transmitted 1 to a 0 or vice versa, causing an error, just as discussed earlier in this chapter and in Chap. 6 preceding. What type of decoder should one use at the receiver to best reconstruct the original bit sequence? We shall answer this question using the optimum (minimum probability of error) techniques discussed earlier in this chapter. We shall specifically develop an optimum decoder for the additive-white-gaussian-noise (AWGN) channel, the same channel assumed in discussing M-ary transmission in Sec. 7-4 above. Expressions will be obtained bounding the error performance of this decoder. We shall also provide an example for the binary symmetric channel mentioned briefly in Sec. 7-8 on block coding. We shall see that, in the context of the AWGN channel, this binary symmetric channel corresponds to *hard-limiting* the received binary digits.

To demonstrate the decoding procedure necessary, let the convolutional coder be followed by a PSK transmitter. The output of this transmitter, bit by bit, will be $\sqrt{2E_s/T} \cos \omega_0 t$ for a 1 transmitted and $-\sqrt{2E_s/T} \cos \omega_0 t$ for a 0 transmitted. The symbol E_s represents the *transmitted* signal energy per bit; T is the bit interval. (This interval will be $1/Rv$ for a rate-$1/v$ coder, where R is the input data bit rate.) The distinction between the input data-bit interval $1/R$ and the transmitted-bit interval T is portrayed in Fig. 7-72. As shown in the figure, $E_b = vE_s$ is the equivalent energy required to transmit the v bits over the original data-bit interval.

Say this sequence of PSK signals is transmitted over an AWGN channel. At the receiver a matched-filter detector is first used on a bit-by-bit basis to retrieve the individual bits, as transmitted. The signal component at the output of the matched filter will be $+\sqrt{E_s}$ or $-\sqrt{E_s}$, depending on whether a 1 or a 0 was transmitted. [See (7-83).] For a rate-$1/v$ coder the v transmitted signal components at the output of the matched filter during the jth data-bit interval may then be represented as $\sqrt{E_s} x_{j1}, \sqrt{E_s} x_{j2}, \ldots, \sqrt{E_s} x_{jv}$, with $x_{jk} = \pm 1$, $k = 1, \ldots, v$, depending on whether a 1 or a 0 was transmitted. As an example, consider the rate-$\frac{1}{2}$

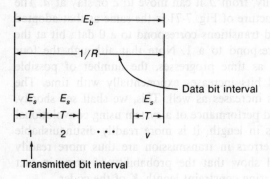

Data bit interval

Transmitted bit interval

FIGURE 7-72
Data bit and transmitted bit intervals.

($v = 2$) coder of Fig. 7-66. The data-bit interval is shown ranging from $j = 1$ to $j = 8$. For $j = 4$, then, as a typical interval, $(x_{41}, x_{42}) = (-1, +1)$, corresponding to 0 1 transmitted.

For the AWGN channel assumed here, the output of the matched filter has a gaussian noise component as well. The noise component in the kth transmitted bit of the jth data-bit interval will be labeled n_{jk}. Its variance is $n_0/2$, corresponding to a white-noise spectral density of $n_0/2$. [(See (7-76) and (7-78).] For the AWGN channel, the individual noise components are all independent, with the probability density of n_{jk} given by

$$f(n_{jk}) = \frac{e^{-n_{jk}^2/n_0}}{\sqrt{\pi n_0}} \tag{7-204}$$

The total output of the matched filter at the kth transmitted bit of the jth data interval will then be a gaussian random variable

$$y_{jk} = \sqrt{E_s}\, x_{jk} + n_{jk} \tag{7-205}$$

with probability density function

$$f(y_{jk}|x_{jk}) = \frac{e^{-\left(y_{jk} - \sqrt{E_s}\, x_{jk}\right)^2/n_0}}{\sqrt{\pi n_0}} \tag{7-206}$$

(We use the symbol y_{jk} to represent the received signal plus noise in place of v_j used previously.)

Given a sequence of received signal values y_{jk} at the matched filter output ($1 \le k \le v$, $1 \le j \le L$ say), we would like to find the corresponding values of transmitted x_{jk}, and from these, reproduce the input data stream, that minimize the probability of error. Because of the convolutional encoding the transmitted bits depend on the past history and persist some time in the future as well. There is thus no natural stopping place to consider in choosing the number of input data intervals, L. For the time being we assume some specific value of L. With L fixed there are 2^L possible signal paths in a tree such as that of Fig. 7-71 that the transmitted sequence (or corresponding input data sequence) could have taken, given the received sequence y_{jk}, $1 \le k \le v$, $1 \le j \le L$. It is clear that maximum a posteriori (MAP) processing, as in (7-75), is called for. Here the MAP probability for each of the 2^L paths is to be calculated, and the path with the largest value selected as the most probable. Specifically, let the vector $\mathbf{y}_j \equiv (y_{j1}, y_{j2}, \ldots, y_{jv})$ represent the ensemble of received signal values at the matched-filter output in input data interval j. Consider any one of the 2^L possible paths in the tree, and call this the mth path, $1 \le m \le 2^L$. For this particular path we define a vector $\mathbf{x}_j^m \equiv (x_{j1}^m, x_{j2}^m, \ldots, x_{jv}^m)$ as the sequence of transmitted bits in the jth interval of that path. As an example, in the tree of Fig. 7-71, the bottommost path has the sequence 1 0 in the fourth interval shown there. Using (7-206) and noting that $\mathbf{y}_j$ consists of v independent random variables $y_{j1}, \ldots, y_{jv}$, because of the AWGN channel postulated here, we can readily calculate $f(\mathbf{y}_j|\mathbf{x}_j^m)$ for the known vector $\mathbf{x}_j^m$. This will be a product of gaussian functions, each of the form of (7-206). Repeating this over all L intervals of path m, we can calculate $\prod_{j=1}^{L} f(\mathbf{y}_j|\mathbf{x}_j^m)$ over the entire path. (We again make use of the fact that probabilities over intervals are independent as well.) This is the conditional probability density function for path m. Multiplying this by the a priori probability P_m of path m, we have the a posteriori probability to be maximized.

We now invoke the same simplification used earlier in discussing the optimum M-ary processor in Sec. 7-4. [See the discussion following (7-81).] We assume each of the 2^L paths is equally likely to be transmitted. (In Fig. 7-71, as an example, at the end of interval 4 there are 16 possible paths going back to interval 1. There is clearly no reason why any one of these paths should have been more likely to have been transmitted than any other.) The a priori probabilities are thus equal, and the MAP processor simplifies to calculating $\prod_{j=1}^{L} f(\mathbf{y}_j|\mathbf{x}_j^m)$ for each of the 2^L paths and selecting the path with the largest value. This conditional probability-density function is also called the *likelihood function*, and the test that maximizes this function (occurring both here and in Sec. 7-4) the *maximum-likelihood* test. [If we refer back to (7-11) describing the likelihood-ratio test for two hypotheses, the two functions $f(\mathbf{v}|1)$ and $f(\mathbf{v}|2)$ are the likelihood functions in that case. Setting $P_2 = P_1$, we get the same result as here: select the signal corresponding to the maximum likelihood function.]

Instead of comparing 2^L likelihood functions, we can take logarithms and compare *log-likelihood functions*. The log-likelihood function for path m is

$$\sum_{j=1}^{L} \log f(\mathbf{y}_j|\mathbf{x}_j^m).$$

Using (7-206) to evaluate this quantity for the AWGN channel with bit-by-bit PSK signal modulation, we find, finally, that the most probable path is the one among the 2^L paths possible that maximizes

$$\sum_{j=1}^{L} \left[-\frac{1}{n_0} \sum_{k=1}^{v} \left(y_{jk} - \sqrt{E_s}\, x_{jk}^m \right)^2 - \frac{v}{2} \log \sqrt{\pi n_0} \right]$$

Leaving out constant values and values common to all paths, we have two possible ways of interpreting this result. Both of these are familiar to us from the previous analysis in Sec. 7-4:

1. Choose as the most likely path the one with the *smallest* mean-squared distance measure

$$\sum_{j=1}^{L} \sum_{j=1}^{v} \left(y_{jk} - \sqrt{E_s}\, x_{jk}^m \right)^2$$

Thus, given the received sequence y_{jk}, $j = 1, \ldots, L$, $k = 1, \ldots, v$, choose the transmitted sequence x_{jk}^m to which it is the closest in mean-squared distance.

2. Choose as the most likely path the one with the *largest* correlation value or inner product

$$\sum_{j=1}^{L} \sum_{k=1}^{v} y_{jk} x_{jk}^m$$

This result is obtained by expanding the squared distance measure and noting that $x_{jk}^2 = 1$.

As noted, both metrics 1 and 2 extend the work in Sec. 7-4. Equation (7-82) in that section corresponds to metric 1 (see Fig. 7-31 as well). Figure 7-32 corresponds to metric 2.

A problem with designing decoders that implement either one of these two metrics directly is that the number of paths grows exponentially with L. Various techniques and algorithms have been developed to cope with this problem. Examples and discussions of such techniques appear in the references, e.g., [MICH, chaps. 8–10]. We focus here on a maximum-likelihood decoding algorithm due to Viterbi [VITE 1967],[19] [VITE 1971] that has found widespread commercial use in satellite and space communications, and is particularly effective for short-constraint-length ($K \leq 7$) codes.

The basic concept behind the Viterbi algorithm is quite simple. Focus for simplicity on the correlation (inner-product) metric

$$\sum_{j=1}^{L} \sum_{k=1}^{v} y_{jk} x_{jk}^m$$

This says the decoder has been operating for L data input intervals, each containing v transmitted bits. At the end of the next interval ($j = L + 1$), the quantity $\sum_{k=1}^{v} y_{L+1k} x_{L+1k}$ is calculated for each possible path and added to the previous stored value. This then results in the new metric $\sum_{j=1}^{L+1} \sum_{k=1}^{v} y_{jk} x_{jk}^m$, with m having 2^{L+1} possible values. As an example, consider the tree structure of Fig. 7-71. There are 8 possible paths, hence 8 possible values for $\sum_{j=1}^{3} \sum_{k=1}^{v} y_{jk} x_{jk}^m$, at the end of interval 3. At the end of interval 4 there are 16 new calculations made, corresponding to 16 possible paths the coder could have taken up to that time. Two of these are each associated with one of the previous 8 paths.

But now refer back to Fig. 7-68, portraying the finite-state-machine diagram for the same coder. Note that during each new data input interval the machine must move from one state to the next one following. Focus on a particular state, say b, as an example. For the system to be at this state at time $L + 1$ it must have been either at state c at time L, moving to b after emitting 0 0 as the two transmitted bits, or at state a previously, moving to b with 1 1 transmitted. Similar observations can be made for each of the $2^{K-1} = 4$ states in this example.

---

[19][VITE 1967] A. J. Viterbi, "Error Bounds for Convolutional Codes and an Asymptotically Optimum Decoding Algorithm," *IEEE Trans. Inform. Theory*, vol. IT-13, pp. 260–269, April 1967.

An alternative and completely equivalent way of updating the correlation metric is to calculate this metric for each path coming in to each state. Referring back to Fig. 7-71 with the tree representation, note that this just represents a reordering of the update calculations. It leads directly to the Viterbi algorithm, however. The algorithm simply chooses the larger of the two updated metrics homing on a given state and discards the smaller of the two. This process is repeated each data input interval. The metric retained is called the *survivor*.

Since the maximum-likelihood solution is to always select the path with the largest correlation metric, a path with a smaller metric that has been rejected could never have caught up with the survivor. Pruning the number of paths by always selecting the survivor of the two entering each state thus retains the maximum-likelihood character of the solution. The number of surviving paths always remains at 2^{K-1}, never increasing exponentially, yet retaining the optimum (maximum-likelihood) path among the survivors. Since there are 2^{K-1} paths to evaluate, K cannot be too large, as noted earlier. (For binary encoders there are clearly only two possible ways of leaving or entering a state. Figure 7-69 provides another example.)

We can summarize the Viterbi algorithm for the binary convolutional decoder by studying Fig. 7-73. There are two surviving paths entering each current state. Call these two paths l and m, as shown. Increment the metric on each path by adding $\sum_{k=1}^{v} y_{Lk} x_{Lk}^{l}$ and $\sum_{k=1}^{v} y_{Lk} x_{Lk}^{m}$ respectively. Drop the metric that is smaller. This calculation is carried out for each of the 2^{K-1} states. As an example, consider state d in Fig. 7-68. This is reached from state b with $0\,1$ transmitted or from state d itself with $1\,0$ transmitted. The two increments to the metrics, respectively, would then be $-y_{L1} + y_{L2}$ and $y_{L1} - y_{L2}$. (Recall that the output of the receiver matched filter is $\pm\sqrt{E_s}$, with $-\sqrt{E_s}$ corresponding to a 0.) The path metric

$$\sum_{j=1}^{L} \sum_{k=1}^{v} y_{jk} x_{jk}^{m}$$

is kept for each of the 2^{K-1} survivors, and the process is repeated at the end of the next input data interval. For L intervals (the term "branches" is often used), there are a total of $2^{K-1}L$ comparisons carried out. This grows linearly with L.

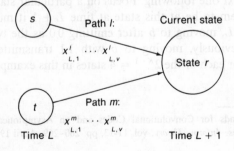

Previous two states

FIGURE 7-73
Binary-convolutional-coder state diagram: each state is reached from two other states.

Without the Viterbi algorithm the total number of comparisons at the end of L intervals is $2^{L+1} - 1$. The Viterbi algorithm represents a substantial improvement in computation (as well as memory required) for large L and K not too large.

Although we have focused on maximization of the correlation metric to carry out maximum-likelihood (minimum-error-probability) decoding, we could equally well have discussed minimization of the mean-squared quantity $\sum_{j=1}^{L}\sum_{k=1}^{v}(y_{jk} - \sqrt{E_s}\,x_{jk}^m)^2$ to provide the maximum-likelihood decoder. (Recall that both metrics appeared as equivalent solutions for the AWGN channel.) An analogous metric, involving minimization of the Hamming distance, appears as the maximum-likelihood solution for the convolution decoder in the case of the binary symmetric channel. Recall that this channel and the Hamming-distance rule as the one that minimizes the probability of error for the channel were discussed briefly in the last section. [See Fig. 7-58 and the discussion following (7-161).] As noted in that discussion, the binary symmetric channel arises when the received signals are first quantized into either of two binary digits before entering the decoder. In the example of the AWGN channel we have been pursuing in this section, this corresponds to hard-limiting the analog signal plus noise term y_{jk}. The resultant binary sequence is then compared with the various paths the transmitted sequence could have taken, and the one to which the received sequence is closest in a Hamming sense is selected as the most likely to have been transmitted. The application of the Viterbi algorithm to this maximum-likelihood decoding for the binary symmetric channel is straightforward and enables us to provide a simple, concrete example of the algorithm's use.

Specifically, refer again to the constraint-length-$K = 3$, rate-$\frac{1}{2}$ convolution coder of Fig. 7-66. Let the hard-limited received bit sequence, starting with $j = 1$, be the following set of bit pairs:

Received sequence:	01	01	00	11	10	$\cdots$
Interval (branch) j:	1	2	3	4	5	$\cdots$

We shall apply the Viterbi algorithm successively, for each new value of j, selecting the four survivors, one for each state, and then incrementing the (Hamming distance) metric at the next interval.

Recall from our previous discussion, as shown in Fig. 7-66b, that $K - 1 = 2$ intervals are required to carry out initialization. Hence the Viterbi algorithm can only be begun at the third interval ($j = 3$). To initialize we assume here that the encoder started in state a (Fig. 7-68) at time $j = 0$. All paths must have started with the system in that state. By the third interval there are 8 possible paths that the system could have taken (two each entering each of the four states). These are listed in Table 7-4 (see Fig. 7-71 as well). They are arranged by current state, and, for each current state, the path corresponding to the state from which it could have come. (This corresponds to rearranging the 8 states at interval 3 in Fig. 7-71.) Also indicated is the Hamming distance between each of the 8 paths and the received bit sequence noted above.

TABLE 7-4
Viterbi-algorithm initialization (j = 3)

		Possible paths				
$j =$	1	2	3	Previous	Current	Hamming
Received sequence =	01	01	00	state	state	distance
	00	00	00	a	a	2*
	11	10	11	c		5
	00	00	11	a	b	4
	11	10	00	c		3*
	00	11	10	b	c	3
	11	01	01	d		2*
	00	11	01	b	d	3
	11	01	10	d		2*

*Survivor.

For each of the $2^{K-1} = 4$ states, the path with the smaller Hamming distance (compared to the received sequence) is selected as the survivor. This initializes the Viterbi algorithm. At interval $j = 4$ the algorithm is repeated. The Hamming distance (the metric used here) is updated by comparing the two new received bits 1 1 with the pair of bits in each of the 8 paths, and the survivor again selected: The complete history of the survivors is always retained.

We now carry out the Viterbi algorithm at interval 4. The new received signal pair is, as indicated above, 1 1, as shown in Table 7-5.

We repeat this process once more, at $j = 5$, to ensure the example is well understood. The new received bit pair is now 1 0, as shown in Table 7-6.

How long does one keep repeating the algorithm? When does one finally make a decision? How is that decision made? To reduce the cost of a Viterbi

TABLE 7-5
Viterbi-algorithm (j = 4)

		Possible paths (previous survivors)					
$j =$	1	2	3	4	Previous	Current	Hamming
Received sequence =	01	01	00	11	state	state	distance
	00	00	00	00	a	a	2 + 2 = 4
	11	01	01	11	c		2 + 0 = 2*
	00	00	00	11	a	b	2 + 0 = 2*
	11	01	01	00	c		2 + 2 = 4
	11	10	00	10	b	c	3 + 1 = 4
	11	01	10	01	d		2 + 1 = 3*
	11	10	00	01	b	d	3 + 1 = 4
	11	01	10	10	d		2 + 1 = 3*

*Survivor.

TABLE 7-6
Viterbi-algorithm ($j = 5$)

			Possible paths					
$j =$	1	2	3	4	5	Previous	Current	Hamming
Received bits =	01	01	00	11	10	state	state	distance
	11	01	01	11	00	a		$2 + 1 = 3$*
	11	01	10	01	11	c	a	$3 + 1 = 4$
	11	01	01	11	11	a		$2 + 1 = 3$*
	11	01	10	01	00	c	b	$3 + 1 = 4$
	00	00	00	11	10	b		$2 + 0 = 2$*
	11	01	10	10	01	d	c	$3 + 2 = 5$
	00	00	00	11	01	b		$2 + 2 = 4$
	11	01	10	10	10	d	d	$3 + 0 = 3$*

*Survivor.

decoder the path memory should be kept as small as possible. Studies have shown that a length L approximately 4 or 5 times K is sufficient to produce performance close to optimum [HELLE]. At this point it has been found, through theory and simulation, that the oldest bits on the surviving paths will, with high probability, be identical [HELLE]. One simple procedure is then to output the oldest bit on the most likely of the surviving paths. At each iteration, then, after selecting the 2^{K-1} survivors, the one with the smallest metric is used to output a bit; the oldest interval of each of the survivors is dropped from the path memory and the algorithm repeated at the next interval with the history variable L fixed. In the example above, the survivor with the smallest distance at the end of interval 5 is the one with the distance 2. Its path would then be used to determine the original data bit at interval 1 if 5 were the path history interval L used.

Consider a Viterbi decoder with a constraint length $K = 7$. For $L = 4K$ or $5K$ its path length would be 28 to 35. Using $L = 35$ as a specific case, the number of comparisons required to output a bit would then be $2^{K-1}L = 2240$. This compares with $2^{L+1} = 2^{36}$ comparisons required if the Viterbi algorithm had not been used. In practice the metric updates and path comparisons are done digitally. This implies the analog received signal plus noise terms y_{jk} must be quantized to some set of levels. It has been found that 8-level (3-bit) quantization provides bit-error-probability performances within 0.2–0.25 dB of those obtained using the analog value of y_{jk}. Hard-limiting (two-level quantization) results in a 2-dB performance loss [HELLE]. This loss represents the added signal power required to attain the same bit-error probability. Detailed performance results involving a number of other practical factors, including many bit-error probability curves for a variety of Viterbi decodes, appear in [HELLE].

In the next subsection we carry out a theoretical study of the performance of convolutional coding, showing very specifically how the bit-error probability depends on constraint length and signal-to-noise ratio.

Performance of Convolutional Coders

The material up to this point has dealt with the basic concepts of convolutional coding as well as describing the Viterbi algorithm for carrying out maximum-likelihood decoding. In this subsection we evaluate the performance of convolutional coders.

To do this we note that an error occurs when the path selected differs from the correct one. Hence the probability of error is found by calculating the probability of deviating from a specified correct path and averaging over all such paths. As noted earlier, however, we assume all paths equally likely. Hence any path may be chosen as the correct one and the probability of deviating from it calculated to determine the probability of error. For simplicity, and without loss of generality, let this be the all-0 path. This is the upper horizontal path, as an example, in the trellis of Fig. 7-70. Alternatively, this corresponds to starting in state a in the state diagram of Fig. 7-68 (an all-0 data sequence and the corresponding all-0 transmitted bit sequence), or in state 0 of the state diagram of Fig. 7-69. To calculate the probability of error we must then determine the possible ways in which the decoder can deviate from this path and the probability of doing so.

Take the constraint length $K = 3$, rate-$\frac{1}{2}$ coder of Fig. 7-66 as an example. Refer to the trellis representation of Fig. 7-70. It is clear from the cyclic reentry properties of the trellis that any point in time on the all-0 path can be used as a point at which a deviation from the path due to an error could take place. All points shifted by one data interval look alike. Focusing on one of these, point 0 for example, we start listing the various paths that could be taken in leaving the all-0 transmitted bit path and then returning to it later, in order of increasing Hamming distance for the transmitted bit sequence. A hard look indicates that the path with the smallest Hamming distance is the path $a-b-c-a$. This has a Hamming distance of 5. This is shown redrawn by itself in Fig. 7-74a to avoid clutter. Another look at the trellis of Fig. 7-70 indicates that the path with the next larger value of Hamming distance that leaves the all-0 path and then returns to it some time later has a Hamming distance of 6. Two such paths exist. They are $a-b-c-b-c-a$ and $a-b-d-c-a$, and are sketched in Fig. 7-74b. One could alternatively determine these paths by studying the state diagram of Fig. 7-66. Many more such paths, of distance $7, 8, \ldots$, can be found by studying either the trellis or the state diagram. (It is left to the reader to show that there are four paths of distance 7. These are $a-b-d-d-c-a$, $a-b-c-b-c-b-c-a$, $a-b-d-c-b-c-a$, and $a-b-c-b-d-c-a$.)

Why list the paths in order of increasing Hamming distance? The larger the distance, the more transmitted bits there are in error, and the less likely that particular event is to be selected. The path with the smallest Hamming distance away from the all-0 path thus represents the most-probable-error event and dominates the error-probability computation. The smallest Hamming distance is termed the *minimum free distance* d_F. Clearly the larger d_F is, the better the performance. We shall in fact see later that for the AWGN channel the error

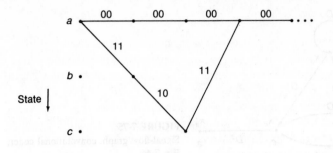

(a) Path with minimum Hamming distance: minimum free distance

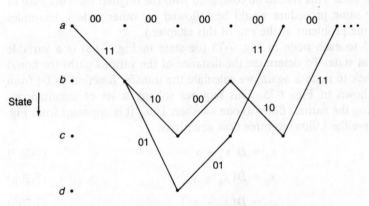

(b) Two possible paths with Hamming distance of 6

FIGURE 7-74
Determination of paths deviating from all-0 path, convolutional coder, Fig. 7-66.

probability decreases exponentially with increasing distance. Given a specified constraint length K, one searches for the coder configuration (shift-register connections) that results in the largest value of d_F. It is found that d_F increases with K. The error performance thus improves with the constraint length, as expected.

It is computationally cumbersome to enumerate the various paths of increasing Hamming distance. A simple transform-like technique related to signal-flow calculations enables us to carry out the computation readily. By extension it also enables us to find a tight bound for the error probability. We introduce this technique by example, again using the coder of Fig. 7-66. Refer to the coder state diagram of Fig. 7-68. Let each transmitted (output) 1 in the diagram be represented by a D. Two 1's correspond to D^2. Since we are interested in paths deviating from and then returning to state a, we redraw the

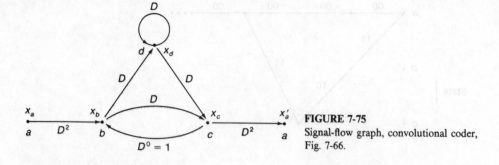

FIGURE 7-75
Signal-flow graph, convolutional coder,
Fig. 7-66.

state diagram of Fig. 7-68 with the starting node a split apart to put it in a flow form. The resulting signal-flow diagram for the coder of Fig. 7-66 is shown sketched in Fig. 7-75. This should be compared with the original state diagram of Fig. 7-68. (The same procedure would be followed for other coders. Examples appear among the problems at the end of this chapter.)

Appended to each node in Fig. 7-75 (or state in Fig. 7-68) is a variable labeled with that state. To determine the distance of the various paths (or flows) from node a back to node a again, we calculate the transfer function $T(D)$ from x_a to x_a', as shown in Fig. 7-75. This requires solving a set of simultaneous equations relating the various flows to one another. Thus, it is apparent from Fig. 7-75 that we have the following three flow equations:

$$x_b = D^2 x_a + x_c \qquad (7\text{-}207)$$

$$x_c = D(x_b + x_d) \qquad (7\text{-}208)$$

$$x_d = D(x_d + x_b) \qquad (7\text{-}209)$$

Solving these to obtain x_c in terms of x_a, and then noting from Fig. 7-75 that $x_a' = D^2 x_c$, we have, finally,

$$T(D) \equiv \frac{x_a'}{x_a} = \frac{D^2 x_c}{x_a} = \frac{D^5}{1 - 2D} \qquad (7\text{-}210)$$

We observe that the exponent of D in the numerator is 5, just the minimum free distance d_F.

But note that the term $1/(1 - 2D)$ may be expanded in the infinite series

$$\frac{1}{1 - 2D} = 1 + 2D + (2D)^2 + (2D)^3 + \cdots \qquad (7\text{-}211)$$

The transfer function $T(D)$ can thus be rewritten in the equivalent form

$$T(D) = D^5 + 2D^6 + 4D^7 + 8D^8 + \cdots$$

$$= \sum_{d=5}^{\infty} 2^{d-5} D^d \qquad (7\text{-}212)$$

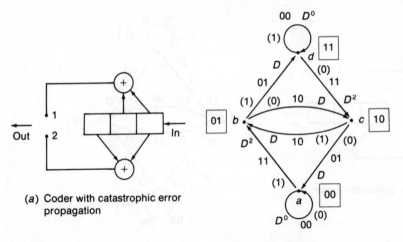

(a) Coder with catastrophic error propagation

(b) State diagram for coder of a

FIGURE 7-76
A coder exhibiting catastrophic error propagation.

The interpretation is apparent. For this convolutional coder, there is one path from a back to a at distance 5 (the minimum free distance d_F), two paths at distance 6, four paths at distance 7, and, in general, 2^{d-5} paths at distance d. The signal-flow approach, calculating the transfer function $T(D)$, has enabled us to come up with a closed-form solution for the number of ways in which the system can "flow" from, or leave, state a, returning to that state.

This signal-flow approach, calculating the transfer function in closed form, and then expanding it in an infinite series to determine the set of (error) paths that can be followed in deviating from the correct path, is valid for most convolutional coders. There is one exception. It is possible by improper design to come up with a coder that exhibits what is called *catastrophic error propagation*. This is a coder for which a finite number of symbol errors causes an infinite number of bit errors to be decoded. For a coder such as this the calculation of $T(D)$ leads to no solution. An example of a coder exhibiting catastrophic error propagation appears in Fig. 7-76a [VITE 1971, pp. 763, 764]. The corresponding state diagram is sketched in Fig. 7-76b. The powers of D corresponding to the number of 1's in the transmitted bit pairs during each transition have been indicated in this figure.

Say that the input data sequence is again the all-zero one. The correct path thus corresponds to staying in state a. The incorrect path $a–b–d–d–\cdots–d–c–a$ has a distance of 6, independent of the number of times the self-loop at state d is traversed. A decoder selecting this path as the correct one would incorrectly decode the data-bit sequence as two 1's (the $a–b$ and $b–d$ portions of the path) plus a 1 for each time the self-loop at d was traversed. This could thus lead to catastrophic error propagation. A necessary and sufficient condition for this

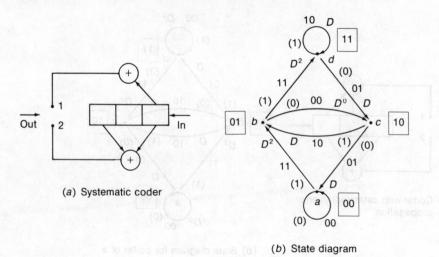

(a) Systematic coder

(b) State diagram

FIGURE 7-77
Example of systematic coder.

problem to occur is that a closed-loop path in the state diagram, other than the one due to an all-0 input data sequence, has a weight of $D^0 = 1$, i.e., exhibits an output (transmitted) sequence of all 0's in this path [VITE 1971]. The coder of Fig. 7-76 demonstrates this condition.

This problem can always be eliminated by using a *systematic* coder. A systematic coder is one for which one of the v output bits is identical to the input bit. In the example of Fig. 7-76, eliminating the middle top connection or the left-hand bottom connection converts the coder to a systematic one. Figure 7-77 shows a systematic coder equivalent to the nonsystematic one of Fig. 7-76. Note now that there is no self-loop of weight $D^0 = 1$. Note also that the minimum free distance d_F for this $K = 3$, rate-$\frac{1}{2}$ coder is 3 (path a–b–c–a), less than that of the nonsystematic $K = 3$, rate-$\frac{1}{2}$ coder of Fig. 7-66. A systematic coder will always have a minimum free distance less than that of a nonsystematic coder, and will thus provide poorer error performance. (This is obviously due to the fact that one of the output bits has no coding built into it.)

The transfer function of any binary convolutional coder not exhibiting catastrophic error propagation can always be expanded in the form

$$T(D) = \sum_{d=d_F}^{\infty} a(d) D^d \qquad (7\text{-}213)$$

Here $a(d)$ represents the number of paths at distance d from the "typical" all-0 path. Given the number of such paths, the error probability P_e of deviating from the correct path is then readily upper-bounded by

$$P_e < \sum_{d=d_F}^{\infty} a(d) P_d \tag{7-214}$$

Here P_d represents the probability that d transmitted bits are received in error. Why an upper bound? Many of the error paths may overlap. Hence they are not mutually exclusive as assumed by (7-214). Figure 7-74 provides a simple example. The branch $a\text{-}b$ is common to all three paths shown. Hence the probabilities of moving along each path cannot simply be added together. The state diagram in Fig. 7-68 and the trellis representation of Fig. 7-70 for this coder provide other examples of paths that share branches and are thus not mutually exclusive. We shall use (7-214) to calculate the error probability for the AWGN channel. But note first that P_e does not represent the bit-error probability P_B for the convolutional coder, which is what is really desired. (It represents the path error probability, as noted.) We now show how the transfer-function approach can be modified somewhat to obtain the bit-error probability as well [VITE 1971]. Actually, in specific examples for the AWGN channel, P_e and P_B will be found not to differ by very much, since the dominant factor in determining the probability in both cases will be a term varying exponentially with the minimum free distance d_F.

The bit-error probability P_B differs from the error probability P_e in weighting the probability of each path by the number of data bits resulting in error along that path. Since, by hypothesis, the all-0 path is the correct one, any branch of a path with a data bit 1 on it would result in a data-bit error were that path to be selected as the correct one. We must thus count the number of data 1's on each path other than the all-0 one, and weight the probability of moving onto that path by the number of data 1's. This is again a tedious problem that is bypassed by resorting to the signal-flow approach. As previously, we refer to the trellis or state representation of a given coder and now let the symbol N be attached to any branch of a path produced by a data 1. This is similar to letting the symbol D represent the occurrence of any transmitted 1. We again use the $K = 3$ rate-$\frac{1}{2}$ coder of Fig. 7-66 as an example to calculate the modified transfer function $T(D, N)$ that will provide the solution to our problem.

Figure 7-78a shows the state diagram of Fig. 7-68 modified to include N wherever a data 1 occurs. Figure 7-78b shows the resultant signal-flow diagram with N multiplying the power of D along any path on which it appears. The modified transfer function $T(D, N) \equiv x_a'/x_a$ is now calculated using Fig. 7-78b. Specifically, the signal-flow equations corresponding to (7-207) to (7-209), but including the value N where it appears, are now written as follows:

$$x_b = D^2 N x_a + N x_c \tag{7-215}$$

$$x_c = D(x_d + x_b) \tag{7-216}$$

$$x_d = DN x_d + DN x_b \tag{7-217}$$

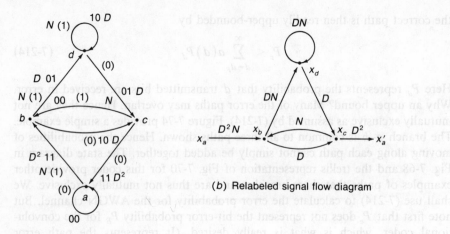

(a) Relabeled state diagram

(b) Relabeled signal flow diagram

FIGURE 7-78
Calculation of bit-error probability, convolutional coder, Fig. 7-66.

Solving these simultaneously for x_c in terms of x_a, and then letting $x_a' = D^2 x_a$ from Fig. 7-78b, it is readily shown that

$$T(D, N) \equiv \frac{x_a'}{x_a} = \frac{D^5 N}{1 - 2DN} \tag{7-218}$$

This clearly agrees with the prior calculation of $T(D)$ [Equation (7-210)] if we let $N = 1$.

As previously, we now expand (7-218) into its equivalent infinite series [compare with (7-212)] to obtain

$$T(D, N) = \sum_{d=5}^{\infty} 2^{d-5} N^{d-4} D^d \tag{7-219}$$

The exponent of N represents the number of data bits in error for that particular path. Thus, the path with the minimum free distance $d_F = 5$ would produce one erroneous data bit if selected by mistake. The path with a distance of $d = 6$ would result in two data bits being received erroneously, etc. This agrees with the state and signal-flow diagram in Figs. 7-68 and 7-78, as well as the trellis of Fig. 7-70: there would be one data bit in error if path $a-b-c-a$ were erroneously selected as part of the complete data bit path; two bits in error if $a-b-c-b-c-a$ or $a-b-d-c-a$ were detected as part of the data path, etc.

How do we now use this infinite-series expansion of $T(D, N)$ to calculate the bit error probability P_B? For the example just worked out, an upper bound on

P_B would be given by

$$P_B < \sum_{d=5}^{\infty} (d-4)2^{d-5}P_d \tag{7-220}$$

since 2^{d-5} represents the number of paths at distance d from the (correct) all-0 one and $d-4$ the desired weighting of the path by the data bits in error if that path were selected. P_d, as defined previously, is the probability of selecting the path at distance d. We can obtain (7-220) directly from $T(D, N)$ by noting that the multiplicative term $(d-4)$ is obtained by differentiating $T(D, N)$ with respect to N and then setting $N = 1$.

In general, then, we have, for a binary convolutional encoder,

$$P_B < \sum_{d=d_F}^{\infty} b(d)P_d \tag{7-221}$$

where the factor $b(d)$ multiplying P_d is found by differentiating $T(D, N)$ with respect to N, setting $N = 1$, and expanding the resultant expression in an infinite series in D:

$$\left. \frac{dT(D, N)}{dN} \right|_{N=1} = \sum_{d=d_F}^{\infty} b(d)D^d \tag{7-222}$$

As an example, consider the coder just discussed. Differentiating (7-218) with respect to N, setting $N = 1$, and then expanding in an infinite series, we have

$$\left. \frac{dT(D, N)}{dN} \right|_{N=1} = \frac{D^5}{(1-2D)^2}$$

$$= D^5 \left[1 + 2(2D) + 3(2D)^2 + 4(2D)^3 + \cdots \right]$$

$$= \sum_{d=5}^{\infty} (d-4)2^{d-5}D^d \tag{7-223}$$

This is of course the same result obtained earlier on differentiating (7-219) term by term.

We now apply these general results to the calculation of error probabilities when transmitting over an AWGN channel. (Equivalent results for the general binary symmetric channel are obtained and discussed in [VITE 1971].) Recall that maximum-likelihood detection over this channel required selecting the path with the largest metric $\sum_{j=1}^{L}\sum_{k=1}^{v} y_{jk}x_{jk}^m$, $1 \le m \le 2^L$. The parameter $x_{jk} = \pm 1$ represents the transmitted bit appearing at the output of the receiver matched filter, with PSK on each bit used as the modulation technique. The received signal plus noise term y_{jk} is given by

$$y_{jk} = \sqrt{E_s}\, x_{jk} + n_{jk} \tag{7-205}$$

E_s represents the energy over the transmitted bit interval (Fig. 7-72).

Changing the notation slightly, let x_{jk}^0 represent a transmitted bit on the all-0 (correct) path. Then $x_{jk}^0 = -1$, all j and k. Let x_{jk}^d be a transmitted bit on another path with a Hamming distance of d. This implies that d of the transmitted bits differ from those of the all-0 path. Call this path d. Path d will be chosen as the correct path, with a path error made, if its metric is greater than that of the all-0 path. An error is thus made if

$$\sum_{j=1}^{L} \sum_{k=1}^{v} y_{jk} x_{jk}^d > \sum_{j=1}^{L} \sum_{k=1}^{v} y_{jk} x_{jk}^0 \qquad (7\text{-}224)$$

Alternately, an error is made if

$$z_d' \equiv \sum_{j=1}^{L} \sum_{k=1}^{v} y_{jk} \left(x_{jk}^d - x_{jk}^0 \right) > 0 \qquad (7\text{-}225)$$

But, as noted above, $x_{jk}^0 = -1$ and $x_{jk}^d = -1$ in all but d bit positions, in which it has the value $+1$. We thus have, as the conditions for an error,

$$z_d' = 2 \sum_{l=1}^{d} y_l > 0$$

or

$$z_d = \sum_{l=1}^{d} y_l > 0 \qquad (7\text{-}226)$$

with

$$y_l = -\sqrt{E_s} + n_l \qquad (7\text{-}227)$$

from (7-205), since $x_{jk}^0 = -1$, by hypothesis. We have replaced the double subscripts jk by the single subscript l to indicate that it is a particular sequence of d bits that is involved here.

The condition (7-226) for d transmitted bits to be received in error is precisely the condition required to calculate the probability P_d appearing in (7-214) and (7-221). Specifically, we have, for the AWGN channel,

$$P_d = \text{Prob}\left[z_d = \sum_{l=1}^{d} y_l > 0 \right] \qquad (7\text{-}228)$$

Note from (7-227) that y_l is gaussian with variance $n_0/2$ and average value $-\sqrt{E_s}$. The random variable z_d, the sum of gaussian variables, is then also gaussian with expected value $-d\sqrt{E_s}$ and variance $dn_0/2$. The calculation of P_d is diagrammed in Fig. 7-79. It is left for the reader to show that this probability may be written in the familiar form

$$P_d = \tfrac{1}{2} \, \text{erfc} \sqrt{\frac{dE_s}{n_0}} \qquad (7\text{-}229)$$

with

$$\text{erfc } x \equiv \frac{2}{\sqrt{\pi}} \int_x^{\infty} e^{-y^2} \, dy$$

The transmitted signal energy E_s may be replaced, if desired, by the data-bit

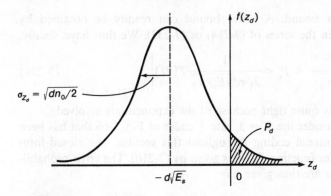

FIGURE 7-79
Calculation of path-error probability P_d.

energy $E_b = vE_s$ (Fig. 7-72). We shall in fact do this when comparing convolutional coding with uncoded M-ary modulation.

Using this expression for P_d, we are now in a position to actually calculate error and bit-error probabilities using convolutional coding over the AWGN channel. To do this we utilize the asymptotic form of the complementary error function first introduced in (6-11):

$$\operatorname{erfc} x \doteq \frac{1}{x\sqrt{\pi}} e^{-x^2} \qquad x > 3 \tag{7-230}$$

We then have

$$P_d \doteq \frac{1}{2\sqrt{\pi dE_s/n_0}} e^{-dE_s/n_0} \tag{7-231}$$

For the small error probabilities of interest to us this approximation will always be valid.

Consider the expression (7-214) for the error probability P_e first. Using (7-231) for P_d, and than noting that $d \geq d_F$, we can replace d by the constant value d_F in the nonexponential part of (7-231), obtaining as a looser upper bound for P_e

$$P_e < \frac{1}{2\sqrt{\pi d_F E_s/n_0}} \sum_{d=d_F}^{\infty} a(d) e^{-dE_s/n_0} \tag{7-232}$$

Comparing this with the expression (7-213) for the coder transfer function $T(D)$, we note that the infinite sums are precisely of the same form. The infinite-series bound on P_e can thus be replaced by the closed-form expression

$$P_e < \frac{1}{2\sqrt{\pi d_F E_s/n_0}} T(D) \Big|_{D=\exp(-E_s/n_0)} \tag{7-233}$$

This gives us an upper bound. A lower bound can readily be obtained by retaining the first term in the series of (7-214) or (7-232). We thus have, finally,

$$\frac{a(d_F)e^{-d_F E_s/n_0}}{2\sqrt{\pi d_F E_s/n_0}} < P_e < \frac{1}{2\sqrt{\pi d_F E_s/n_0}}T(D)\bigg|_{D=\exp(-E_s/n_0)} \quad (7\text{-}234)$$

These bounds are usually quite tight because of the exponentials involved.

As an example, consider the $K = 3$, rate-$\frac{1}{2}$ coder of Fig. 7-66 that has been used to explain convolutional coding throughout this section. The closed-form expression for the transfer function $T(D)$ is given by (7-210). The error-probability bounds for this coder are thus given by

$$\frac{1}{2\sqrt{5\pi E_s/n_0}}e^{-5E_s/n_0} < P_e < \frac{1}{2\sqrt{5\pi E_s/n_0}}\frac{e^{-5E_s/n_0}}{(1-2e^{-E_s/n_0})} \quad (7\text{-}235)$$

For large E_s/n_0 such that $e^{-E_s/n_0} \ll \frac{1}{2}$, these bounds are quite tight. To test this conclusion, let $E_s/n_0 = 2$. We then have

$$4 \times 10^{-6} < P_e < 5.5 \times 10^{-6}$$

For larger values of E_s/n_0 the bounds are tighter still.

To calculate the bounds on the bit-error probability P_B we proceed in the same manner. We now use (7-221), (7-222), and (7-229) to carry out the calculations. The asymptotic approximation (7-231) again provides simple, closed-form bounds, however. Comparing (7-221) and (7-222), with (7-231) used to calculate P_d, we readily find

$$P_B < \frac{1}{2\sqrt{\pi d_F E_s/n_0}}\frac{dT(D,N)}{dN}\bigg|_{N=1, D=\exp(-E_s/n_0)} \quad (7\text{-}236)$$

We can again get a lower bound by using the first term in the series of (7-221). We thus have, as the final bounds for the bit-error probability

$$\frac{b(d_F)e^{-d_F E_s/n_0}}{2\sqrt{\pi E_s/n_0}} < P_B < \frac{1}{2\sqrt{\pi d_F E_s/n_0}}\frac{dT(D,N)}{dN}\bigg|_{N=1, D=\exp(-E_s/n_0)} \quad (7\text{-}237)$$

These bounds are again generally tight and, as a matter of fact, quite close to those found for the error probability P_e. Since the exponential behavior with E_s/n_0 dominates all of these expressions, the two probabilities P_e and P_B are generally quite close to one another.

Consider the $K = 3$, rate-$\frac{1}{2}$ coder of Fig. 7-66 again. For this coder we have, from (7-223),

$$\frac{dT(D,N)}{dN}\bigg|_{N=1, D=\exp(-E_s/n_0)} = \frac{e^{-5E_s/n_0}}{(1-2e^{-E_s/n_0})^2}$$

Comparing this with (7-235), which uses $T(D)$ to calculate the upper bound, we note that the only difference is in the additional factor in the denominator. For

TABLE 7-7
Comparison of modulation and coding schemes for $P_e = 10^{-5}$

Scheme	E_b / n_0, dB
PSK	9.6
Rate-$\frac{1}{2}$ convolutional code: $K = 3$	6
5	5
7	4.2
M-ary orthogonal signaling: $M = 2^5$	7
2^7	6
2^{10}	5
2^{20}	4

$E_s/n_0 = 2$, the value used before, this factor is 0.73, increasing the probability by a factor of 1.37. Specifically, we have, as the bounds for the bit-error probability for this coder,

$$4 \times 10^{-6} < P_B < 7.5 \times 10^{-6}$$

These are to be compared with the previous bounds for P_e.

Using these probability-of-error results for convolutional coders, one can compare various modulation and/or coding schemes with convolutional coding. An example of such a comparison for an error probability of $P_e = 10^{-5}$ appears in Table 7-7. Convolutional coders with maximum values of the minimum free distance d_F have been assumed for the comparison. The use of phase-shift keying (PSK) by itself, with no coding, requires a signal energy-to-noise spectral-density ratio E_b/n_0 of 9.6 dB to attain that error probability. This has been noted a number of times already in this book. Using a $K = 3$, rate-$\frac{1}{2}$ decoder, the performance is improved by 3.6 dB. This checks our own results above. We found that using $E_s/n_0 = 2$, the probability of error is about 0.5×10^{-5}. This translates to a *data*-bit signal-to-noise ratio of $E_b/n_0 = 4$, or 6 dB, just as shown in the table. Note, however, that, since the table has been constructed for rate-$\frac{1}{2}$ coders, the actual bit rate and hence bandwidth required for transmission is twice that required when using PSK alone.

The signal-to-noise ratios shown for the M-ary orthogonal modulation schemes are taken from Fig. 7-49, using (7-116) to convert from signal power to signal energy. Note that an orthogonal modulation scheme with $2^7 = 128$ orthogonal signals would be required to duplicate the performance of the rate-$\frac{1}{2}$ convolutional coder. The bandwidth required is considerably greater as well. The performance of a $K = 7$ coder is 2 dB better than the $K = 3$ coder and is equivalent to that of an M-ary modulation system with 2^{20} orthogonal signals.

How are these numbers applied in the design of a communication system? We take a space-communications example to further compare convolutional coding with PSK and an $M = 32$ orthogonal signal system. The example is outlined in Table 7-8. The space vehicle is assumed to transmit at a frequency of

TABLE 7-8
Space-communications example*

Distance		Information bit rate R, bits / s[†]			
d, km	S_R / n_0	PSK	32-FSK	$K = 7$, rate-$\frac{1}{2}$ coder	C_∞
1.5×10^5	10^7	10^6	2×10^6	4×10^6	14.5×10^6
1.5×10^6	10^5	10,000	20,000	40,000	145,000
1.5×10^7	10^3	100	200	400	1450

* $S_T = 1$ W, $f_0 = 500$ MHz, $G_T = 10$ dB, $G_R = 40$ dB, $n_0 = 10^{-21}$ W/Hz.
[†] $P_e = 10^{-5}$.

500 MHz. The transmitting antenna has a gain $G_T = 10$ dB, as shown; the transmitted power is $S_T = 1$ W. The receiving antenna gain is 40 dB. The noise spectral density is $n_0 = 10^{-21}$ W/Hz, equivalent to an effective temperature of 72 K. Given these parameters, what is the maximum bit rate at which the vehicle can communicate? (Bandwidth is assumed to be no problem.) Using (6-251), the received signal power S_R, on the ground, is readily calculated at various distances between the space vehicle and earth. The resultant ratio of received signal power to noise spectral density, S_R/n_0, is shown tabulated in Table 7-8 for three different vehicle–earth distances. Since PSK transmission requires an energy-to-noise-spectral-density ratio $E_b/n_0 = 10$ for $P_e = 10^{-5}$, the PSK bit rate is energy-limited to the rates shown in Table 7-8. A $K = 7$, rate-$\frac{1}{2}$ convolutional coder provides a 6-dB, or 4-to-1, improvement over PSK at $P_e = 10^{-5}$ from Table 7-7. The resultant *information* rates for the $K = 7$, rate-$\frac{1}{2}$ coder are tabulated in Table 7-8 as well. Note that the actual transmission rate is double the information rate. Also shown in the table are the approximate bit rates achievable using $M = 32$ orthogonal (FSK) signaling. The maximum channel capacity (the maximum possible rate achievable with zero error probability) is tabulated as well for comparison [see (7-127)]. The performance of the $K = 7$, rate-$\frac{1}{2}$ convolutional coder at $P_e = 10^{-5}$ comes within a factor of 3.6 (-5.6 dB) of channel capacity. At lower error probabilities this performance would be correspondingly poorer.

In the next subsection we consider a specific application of convolutional coding to the Voyager Uranus space mission.

Application to Voyager Uranus Encounter

We conclude this section with a brief discussion of the application of convolutional coding, as well as Reed–Solomon block coding, to deep-space communications.

Constraint-length-7, rate-$\frac{1}{2}$ convolutional coding, incorporating Viterbi-algorithm decoding, was used on the U.S. Voyager space mission to the outer planets in 1980. The mission to Uranus in 1986 incorporated both convolutional coding and a (255, 223) 8-bit-symbol RS code. In this case the data symbols were first block-encoded using the RS code. The coded sequence was then passed through the convolutional coder for final transmission over the telemetry downlink from the space vehicle to earth. At the receiver, on earth, the reverse decoding operations were carried out: Viterbi decoding followed by RS decoding. The resultant concatenated code combination was calculated to provide 8-dB signal-to-noise advantage at a bit-error rate of 10^{-6} over uncoded PSK transmission [POSN]. The Voyager Uranus mission was specifically designed to attain a data (information) bit transmission rate of 29.9 kbits/s at an error rate of 10^{-5}. We focus on the detailed signal-to-noise calculations for this mission to show how this transmission rate was made possible over a space communication distance of 3×10^9 km. We use the parameters tabulated in [POSN, Table 1, p. 10].[20]

The downlink telemetry system operated at a carrier frequency of 8.4 GHz (wavelength $\lambda = 0.0357$ m.) Transmitted power was 18.2 W, or 12.6 dBW (dB relative to a watt). A 3.6-m-diameter transmitting antenna with an efficiency of $\eta_T = 0.62$ provided a gain of $G_T = 4\pi n_T A_T/\lambda^2 = 48$ dB. The space loss $(\lambda/4\pi d)^2$ [see (6-251)] was -301 dB at the distance of 3×10^9 km.

On earth the basic 64-m receiving antenna located in Canberra, Australia provided a gain of $G_R = 72$ dB. Added to this was 3.6-dB additional array gain provided by combining the Canberra antenna with three other antennas to form a four-element receiving array [POSN, Fig. 2, p. 11]. Losses were calculated to be -1.8 dB. (Table 1 in [POSN] lists the losses as -4.6 dB). Using (6-251), and converting the terms therein to dB measure, one finds the received power to be given by $S_R = -166.6$ dBW (dB relative to a watt). The system noise temperature was calculated to be 25 K, taking into account atmospheric noise, the cosmic 3-K background noise, ground-antenna sidelobes "seeing" a warm earth, and the receiver front-end feed, microwave components, and amplifiers. (This has been corrected from the figure of 36 K listed in [POSN, Table 1].) At this temperature the noise spectral density $n_0 = kT$ is readily found to be -214.6 dBW. Combining received signal and noise, we find

$$\left.\frac{S_R}{n_0}\right|_{dB} = 48 \text{ dB}$$

If encoded PSK transmission were used, the maximum data-transmission rate possible at a bit-error rate of 10^{-5} would have been $R = 6,900$ bits/s. (Recall that the required $E_b/n_0 = S_R/Rn_0$ is 9.6 dB at this error probability.) The Shannon capacity, assuming very wide bandwidths are possible, is 91,200 bits/s. (The bandwidth allocated to this mission at the carrier frequency of 8.4 GHz was 10 MHz, clearly much larger than the bandwidth of roughly 8 kHz required to transmit uncoded PSK. The system is thus power-limited, and the

---

[20] There are some errors in the table as published. Corrections have been made based on personal correspondence with Dr. E. C. Posner.

bandwidth available appears effectively infinite.) Constraint-length-7, rate-$\frac{1}{2}$ convolutional coding provides a coding gain of 5.4 dB over uncoded PSK at $P_e = 10^{-5}$ (see Table 7-7). Convolutional coding alone would thus have allowed transmission at a data bit rate of $R = 24$ kbits/s. Reed–Solomon coding concatenated with convolutional coding was used to bring the rate up to the desired data bit rate of 29.9 kbits/s, as already noted.

Calculations indicated that the concatenated coding schemes would require a ratio of signal energy to noise spectral density ratio equal to $E_b/n_0 = 2.6$ dB for an error probability of 10^{-5} [POSN]. Note that this is within 4 dB of the Shannon capacity limit of $10 \log_{10} 0.69 = -1.6$ dB. [See Fig. 7-49 or (7-127).] For this value of E_b/n_0 the ratio of received signal power to noise spectral density, S_R/n_0, at the desired bit rate $R = 29.9$ kbits/s turns out to be 47.4 dB. This leaves a margin of only 0.6 dB or 15 percent from the value of $S_R/n_0 = 48$ dB calculated above. This is an astonishingly low margin of error. It is truly amazing, and a tribute to outstanding engineering, that the predicted performance values of space communication systems have always come as close as they have to the actual values measured.

Figure 7-80, taken from [POSN, Fig. 6, p. 17], summarizes the progress made over the years in deep-space communications using various types of coding techniques. The Viking orbiters and landers were missions to Mars, launched in 1975 and encountering Mars in 1976. The dashed line projects coding improvements into the 1990s, showing how it is hoped to narrow the gap with the Shannon limit further. The steepness of the Voyager 1986 (the Uranus mission)

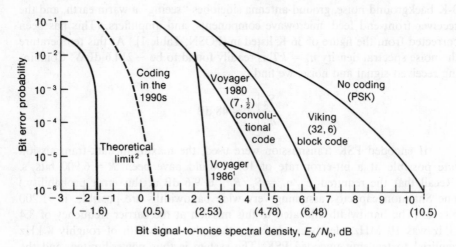

[1] $(7, \frac{1}{2})$ convolutional code (Viterbi decoding) concatenated with a Reed – Solomon (255, 223) outer code.
[2] Infinite bandwidth expansion, Shannon capacity.

FIGURE 7-80

Impact of coding on deep-space communications over the years (from [POSN, Fig. 6], by permission).

curve is characteristic of the performance of block codes such as the Reed–Solomon codes [BERL 1987].

7-10 TRELLIS-CODED MODULATION

A discerning reader will have noted that, in the discussion thus far in this book, we have treated modulation and coding separately. QAM techniques were introduced and shown to provide improved bit-rate performance over band-limited channels. Coding techniques were introduced as a means of providing improved error-rate performance over power-limited channels. In this concluding section of the book we provide an introduction to trellis coding, a recent technique combining both coding and modulation to improve performance over band-limited channels. It has been applied to the design of high-bit-rate tele-phone channel (modems) operating at 14.4 and 19.2 kbits/s over the 2,400-Hz telephone channel. This approaches the Shannon limit of 23 kbits/s for that channel. (See Sec. 7-7.) Similar improvements in performance are possible in satellite, digital microwave, and mobile communications.

The basic idea behind combining coding and modulation is to introduce controlled redundancy, in the form of coding, to reduce channel error rates (or, the equivalent, improve the signal-to-noise ratio) while at the same time using our familiar QAM techniques to increase the information bit rate over a band-limited channel. [Recall from our discussion in Sec. 7-7 that increasing the bit rate over a band-limited channel normally requires additional signal power. See (7-129) and Fig. 7-53.] Both block and convolutional coding can be used. It has been found that convolutional coding is somewhat simpler to use and provides somewhat better performance.

The trellis-coding technique employing convolutional coding that we discuss was developed by Dr. Gottfried Ungerboeck of IBM Zurich Research Laboratory [UNGE 1982], [UNGE 1987].[21] This technique introduces redundancy by doubling the usual number of QAM signals transmitted. Thus, where M-ary QAM would normally employ a signal set of $M = 2^k$ symbols to reduce the symbol rate, and hence the bandwidth, by a factor of M (or, alternatively, to increase the bit rate over a given channel by a factor of M), Ungerboeck's technique employs $2M$ or 2^{k+1} possible symbols for the same factor-of-M reduction of bandwidth or increase in bit rate. The resultant system is found to provide 3–6-dB improvement in SNR over normal QAM transmission.

As an example, the first commercial implementation of a trellis-coded modem, introduced in 1984, used a 128-QAM structure for 14.4-kbit/s transmission. This is based on a 64-QAM signal constellation [FORN].[22] Earlier 14.4-

---

[21][UNGE 1982] G. Ungerboeck, "Channel Coding with Multilevel/Phase Signals," *IEEE Trans. Inform. Theory*, vol. IT-28, no. 1, pp. 55–67, January 1982. [UNGE 1987] G. Ungerboeck, "Trellis-Coded Modulation with Redundant Signal Sets," *IEEE Commun. Mag.*, vol. 25, no. 2, pp. 5–11, 12–21, February 1987.

[22][FORN] G. D. Forney, Jr., et al., "Efficient Modulation for Band-Limited Channels," *IEEE J. Selected Areas Commun.*, vol. SAC-2, no. 5, pp. 632–647, September 1984.

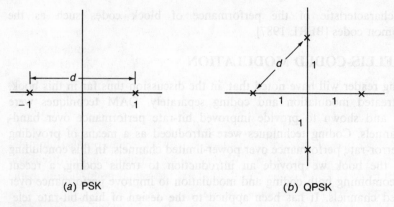

(a) PSK   (b) QPSK

FIGURE 7-81
Comparison of PSK and QPSK signal constellations, equal energy signals.

kbit/s modems using a non-trellis-coded 64-QAM signal constellation were introduced in 1980–1981. The trellis-coded modem requires less signal power or, conversely, for the same power, results in a lower bit-error rate.

We demonstrate the basic idea behind trellis coding using QPSK as an example [UNGE 1982]. Eight signals (8-PSK) will thus be found to be required for transmission rather than the four used for QPSK. We review first the problem encountered in Sec. 7-5 and 7-7 in using QAM techniques. As we add more points to the two-dimensional signal constellation space the probability of error increases because of signal-point crowding, or, to keep the probability of error fixed, signal power or energy must increase [see (7-129) and Fig. 7-53]. This is no different from what is predicted by the Shannon capacity expression (7-125). We would, however, like to narrow the gap between QAM performance and Shannon capacity. Consider the relative performance of PSK and QPSK as an example. Figure 7-81 provides a review of the earlier discussion in Sec. 7-5. The signal points in both cases are located at a (normalized) distance of unity. The energy required to transmit these two signal sets is thus the same. (The normalization consists of dividing through by $\sqrt{E}$. Recall that actual distances are proportional to $\sqrt{E}$.) The signal points for PSK are located a distance $d = 2$ apart; for QPSK they are $d = \sqrt{2} = 1.414$ apart. The probability of error is thus higher in the QPSK case. The distance d in both cases is measured in a Euclidean sense.

Specifically, we have, from (7-85) and (7-85a), introducing $\sqrt{E}$ back into the calculations,

$$P_e = \tfrac{1}{2} \operatorname{erfc} \frac{d\sqrt{E}}{2\sqrt{n_0}} = \tfrac{1}{2} \operatorname{erfc} \sqrt{\frac{E}{n_0}} \tag{7-238}$$

for the case of PSK. For the case of QPSK, we find that

$$P_e = \operatorname{erfc} \frac{d\sqrt{E}}{2\sqrt{n_0}} = \operatorname{erfc} \sqrt{\frac{E}{2n_0}} \tag{7-239}$$

[See (7-98) and the discussion leading to it.] Ignoring the constant factor in front of the erfc, both error functions have the same dependence on the signal spacing d. Since the QPSK spacing is less, its error probability, for fixed signal energy E, is correspondingly higher. Alternatively, the QPSK scheme requires approximately 3 dB more signal power (or energy) to attain the same error probability. This is immediately apparent from (7-239) and (7-238), since the ratio of the signal spacings in the two cases is $\sqrt{2} = 1.414$. Trellis coding allows us to recoup this loss.

The reason that the Euclidean distance d between signal points dominates the error probability is that for the AWGN channel implicitly under discussion here the optimum detector is the one that selects the signal point closest to the noisy received signal in a mean-square sense. [See (7-82) as well as the discussion in the previous section on MAP and maximum-likelihood decoding.] Trellis coding enlarges on this basic concept. It introduces redundant signal points and codes the resultant signal set in such a way as to make the error events depend on the Euclidean distance of signal *paths*, rather than signal points. By appropriate coding this Euclidean path distance can be increased over the Euclidean distance d between signal points. Binary convolutional coding discussed in the previous section operated in a similar fashion, although there it was the Hamming distance between sequences of binary signals that determined the chance of an error event.

As noted earlier, the trellis-coding technique under discussion here doubles the number of signals used. For the QPSK example this means adding four more signal points to form an 8-PSK signal set. The resultant signal constellation appears in Fig. 7-82. All points have again been chosen to be a (normalized) distance of unity from the origin. (All points are actually a distance $\sqrt{E}$ from the origin, as noted previously.) Three distances are defined in the trellis-coding discussion and are labeled in Fig. 7-82. The pairs of points (0, 4), (1, 5), (3, 7), and (2, 6) are all $\Delta_2 = 2$ units apart. Note that the 8-PSK constellation actually consists of two sets of interspersed QPSK signals. Signal points in each of the QPSK sets are a distance $\Delta_1 = \sqrt{2} = 1.414$ units apart (compare with d in Fig. 7-81b). Finally, neighboring points in the 8-PSK constellation are $\Delta_0 = 2\sin(\pi/8) = 0.765$ units apart. Without coding, the performance of this 8-PSK system would depend primarily on Δ_0, resulting in a further reduction in

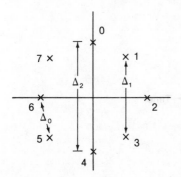

FIGURE 7-82
8-PSK signal constellation used in trellis coding on QPSK signal set.

performance from that of QPSK. The use of coding will be shown to *improve* the performance, with the Euclidean distance that determines the probability of error increasing from 1.414 (Fig. 7-81*b*) to as much as 2.274, an improvement of 4.1 dB for this example.

Trellis coding in this example consists of transmitting one of the eight possible signals, 0–7 of Fig. 7-82 in each *QPSK interval*, according to predetermined states and transitions between them. (Since the system in this example is derived from QPSK transmission, two bits at a time will determine the signal transmitted. For a binary data rate of R bits/s, one of eight signals is transmitted every $T = 2/R$ seconds.) To demonstrate the scheme we define, first, two states of a trellis. One state has the label 0426, corresponding to those four signal points in Fig. 7-82. The other state is labeled 1537. Note that these correspond, respectively, to points in the two embedded QPSK constellations. These states and the transitions defined between them result in the trellis shown in Fig. 7-83. We should, strictly speaking, use as labels the symbols $s_0, s_1, \ldots, s_7$, corresponding to the eight different, phase-shifted signals, $s_0(t), s_1(t), \ldots, s_7(t)$. We use the numbers only for simplicity and to keep from cluttering up the diagrams. We shall however, use the signal symbols s_j, $j = 0, \ldots, 7$, where necessary later to avoid confusion.

The meaning of the trellis structure of Fig. 7-83 is almost obvious: if the system is in state 0426 and signal 0 or signal 4 is transmitted over the interval T, the system remains in that state. If a 2 or a 6 is transmitted, the system switches to the other state 1537. Once in that state, only one of those four signals can be transmitted. Transmitting a 3 or a 7 keeps it in that state; transmitting a 1 or a 6 switches the system back to the first state. Some possible convolutional-coder implementations of this system, using two input (QPSK) bits, will be described later.

We now assume, as we have done in all the previous work in this chapter (particularly in the previous section on convolutional coding), that all input signal sequences are equally likely. As in convolutional coding, various signal paths, moving along the trellis in time, will be traced out. An error event occurs

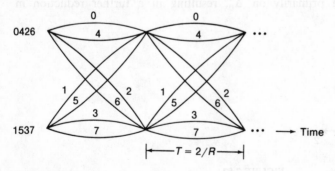

FIGURE 7-83
Two-state trellis, 8-PSK system of Fig. 7-82.

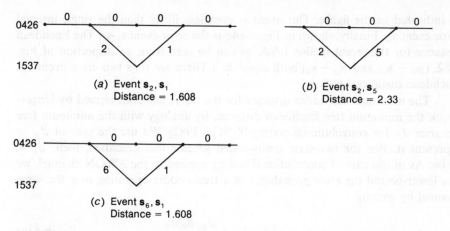

(a) Event s_2, s_1
Distance = 1.608

(b) Event s_2, s_5
Distance = 2.33

(c) Event s_6, s_1
Distance = 1.608

FIGURE 7-84
Possible error events, two-state trellis of Fig. 7-83.

if, given a particular path being followed, the decoder makes a decision on a different path. The chance of an error will clearly be dominated by paths that are "closest" together. But here the measure of closeness will be a Euclidean distance rather than the Hamming distance arising in binary convolutional coding. Since the various paths are equally likely, we focus on the all-0 path as having been transmitted and determine the various error paths that deviate from it. We again caution the reader that "all-0" means continuous transmission, over each interval T, of the phase-shifted signal s_0 of Fig. 7-82, *not* a binary sequence of 0's as in the previous section.

Given this signal path having been transmitted, what *are* the possible error events? An obvious one from Fig. 7-83 is the erroneous decision that signal 4 was transmitted in any interval T. The Euclidean distance for this, from Fig. 7-82, is $|s_0 - s_4| = \Delta_2 = 2$. Consider the following possible signal path in the trellis of Fig. 7-83, however: $s_0-s_2-s_1-s_0 \ldots$. In this case s_2 followed by s_1 are declared to have been transmitted in place of s_0 in both intervals. This error-event path is shown sketched in Fig. 7-84a. The Euclidean distance of this path is

$$\sqrt{d^2(0,2) + d^2(0,1)} = \sqrt{\Delta_1^2 + \Delta_0^2} = 1.608,$$

where $d(0,2) \equiv |s_0 - s_2| = \Delta_1$ and $d(0,1) \equiv |s_0 - s_1| = \Delta_0$, from Fig. 7-82. The mean-squared Euclidean distance over a two-interval path is the sum of the squares of the distances of each interval. This Euclidean distance of 1.608 is less than that of the single interval error event s_4 declared transmitted instead of s_0; hence it is more likely to occur. It turns out that this Euclidean distance is the smallest path distance for the trellis of Fig. 7-83. (The reader is welcome to check this assertion by carrying out the calculation for all possible paths!) As another example, Fig. 7-84b shows another two-interval error event: s_2 followed by s_5, in place of s_0-s_0. It is left to the reader to show that the Euclidean distance is 2.33, as indicated in the figure. This event is even less likely than the single-interval error event s_4. Finally, shown in Fig. 7-84c is the error event s_6-s_1. The Euclidean distance for this event is also 1.608, as can be seen from an inspection of Fig. 7-82. ($|s_6 - s_0|$ and $|s_2 - s_0|$ both equal Δ_1.) There are thus two error events of Euclidean distance 1.608.

The minimum Euclidean distance for the trellis has been termed by Unger-boeck the minimum free Euclidean distance, by analogy with the minimum free distance d_F for convolutional coding [UNGE 1982]. We use the symbol d_E to represent it. For the two-state trellis-coded scheme just described, then, $d_E = 1.608$. As in the case of convolutional coding applied to the AWGN channel, we can lower-bound the error probability of a trellis coder operating over the same channel by writing

$$P_e \geq a(d_E) \, \tfrac{1}{2} \, \mathrm{erfc} \frac{d_E\sqrt{E/n_0}}{2} \qquad (7\text{-}240)$$

Here $a(d_E)$ is the number of error paths at distance d_E. [See, for example, (7-214) and (7-234). The lower bound in (7-234) is obtained from the upper bound of (7-214) by calculating the probability of the minimum-distance path only. But again note the distinction in distance measure: in the case of (7-214) and (7-234) the distance d_F is a *Hamming* distance. Here d_E is the normalized *Euclidean* distance and, in the two-dimensional QAM signal sets under discussion here, multiplies the square root of the signal energy.] Simulations by Ungerboeck indicate that this lower bound is asymptotically achieved at high E/n_0 [UNGE 1982], [UNGE 1987].

In particular, for the two-state trellis of Fig. 7-83 under discussion here, we have $a(d_E) = 2$, and the probability of error is lower-bounded by

$$P_e \geq \mathrm{erfc}\left(\frac{1.608}{2} \sqrt{\frac{E}{n_0}} \right) \qquad (7\text{-}241)$$

Comparing this with the original QPSK error-probability expression (7-239), we note that there *is* an improvement in performance of 1.608/1.414, or 1.1 dB. Equivalently, in the original QPSK scheme, errors occur independently on an interval-to-interval basis, and are determined by the spacing between signal points of 1.414 units (see Fig. 7-81). In trellis coding the error path may be any number of signal intervals long and the Euclidean distance over a path now determines the probability that it is an error event.

Can this performance gain for trellis-coded QPSK be improved? The answer is "yes—by going to more trellis states," i.e., by introducing more complex coding. Consider the four-state trellis structure of Fig. 7-85. The meaning is the same as that of the two-state trellis of Fig. 7-83 discussed earlier. Again taking the all-0 signal path as a "typical" one, one searches various error paths, calculating the Euclidean distance for each. One such path, s_2-s_1-s_2, leaving and returning to s_0, is shown in Fig. 7-85. A similar path, apparent from Fig. 7-85, would be s_6-s_1-s_2. The minimum free Euclidean distance, generalizing

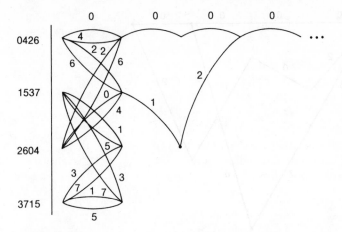

FIGURE 7-85
Four-state trellis, 8-PSK system of Fig. 7-82, with one possible error path.

the two-state trellis discussion above, is given by

$$d_E = \min_{s_l^n \neq s_0^n} \left[\sum_n |s_0^n - s_l^n|^2 \right]^{1/2} \tag{7-242}$$

This assumes the all-0 signal path has been the one transmitted. The parameter n runs over all branches of an error event, and s_l^n is the signal s_l transmitted on branch n. For the three-branch error event s_2–s_1–s_2 shown in Fig. 7-85 the Euclidean distance is readily found to be (referring to Fig. 7-82) $\sqrt{\Delta_1^2 + \Delta_0^2 + \Delta_1^2} = 2.141$. The events s_6–s_1–s_2 has the same distance, as do s_6–s_1–s_6 and s_2–s_1–s_6. But note that here the single-branch error event s_4 detected as transmitted instead of s_0 has the Euclidean distance $|s_4 - s_0| = 2$. (See Fig. 7-82.) It turns out that this is the minimum free Euclidean distance for the four-state trellis of Fig. 7-85 and occurs in this one way only. Hence $a(d_E) = 1$, and

$$P_e \geq \tfrac{1}{2} \operatorname{erfc} \sqrt{\frac{E}{n_0}} \tag{7-243}$$

from (7-240). Note from (7-238) that this expression is identical to that for PSK. Using this four-state trellis code for QPSK, one can asymptotically attain the same error probability as for PSK, yet transmit at twice the bit rate over a given band-limited channel. Comparing with (7-239) and ignoring the multiplicative factor in front of erfc, this trellis code provides a 2 : 1, or 3-dB, improvement in energy over uncoded QPSK. This represents a sizable improvement over the 1.1-dB performance gain obtained by using the two-state trellis code of Fig. 7-83.

Still further improvement is possible by going to 8, and then to 16, trellis states. We demonstrate the 8-state solution only, leaving the 16-state case to the reference [UNGE 1982, Fig. 7, p. 59]. Figure 7-86 depicts the 8-state trellis for

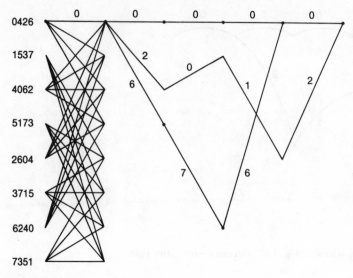

FIGURE 7-86
Eight-state trellis, 8-PSK system of Fig. 7-82. Two minimum-distance error paths shown.

the 8-PSK trellis-coded system under discussion here. Signal labels are omitted, but they can easily be put in by the reader: each state has four outgoing transitions to other states. The signal transmitted at each transition corresponds to a signal number at the state, left to right, with corresponding transitions moving down in the same order. A systematic search through the various error paths, with the all-0 path again chosen as the typical one, shows that there are two paths with a minimum free Euclidean distance $d_E = 2.141$. These two paths are depicted in Fig. 7-86. To demonstrate this result, note that the path s_6-s_7-s_6 has the Euclidean distance $\sqrt{\Delta_1^2 + \Delta_0^2 + \Delta_1^2} = 2.141$, referring to distances in Fig. 7-82. The paths s_2-s_0-s_1-s_2 has the same distance, since the second branch in the path, containing s_0, contributes zero to the Euclidean distance. The lower bound on the error probability for this trellis code is thus

$$P_e \geq \text{erfc}\left(\frac{2.141}{2} \sqrt{\frac{E}{n_0}} \right) \tag{7-244}$$

Its performance gain is $2.141/\sqrt{2}$, or 3.6 dB, over the uncoded QPSK signal set [compare with (7-239)]. The 16-state trellis provides a 4.1-dB gain [UNGE 1982].

Convolutional coders can be used to generate these codes. Viterbi decoding is then used at the receiver to select the most likely sequence of bits transmitted. Examples of three such convolutional coders for the 8-PSK system used as an example here appear in Fig. 7-87 [UNGE 1982, Figs. 9, 11]. Two are coders for the four-state trellis of Fig. 7-85. Both of these are examples of systematic coders, with one of the input data bits connected directly to the output. The third

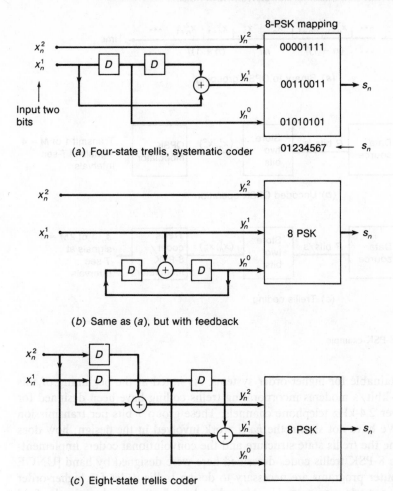

FIGURE 7-87
Examples of 8-PSK trellis coders.

example is a coder for the eight-state trellis of Fig. 7-86. In all cases there are two input data bits, labeled x_n^1 and x_n^2, since these coders are designed to improve the performance, in this example, of a QPSK system. The subscript n refers to the nth QPSK interval $T = 2/R$ seconds long. The boxes labeled D are shift registers shifting at the rate $1/T = R/2$. The coders generate three outputs y_n^0, y_n^1, y_n^2 each T-second interval, as shown. These three outputs in turn determine which one of the eight phase-shifted signals is to be transmitted. The signal selected in interval n is labeled s_n, as shown. Figure 7-88 is keyed to Fig. 7-87 and compares the trellis-coding operation with the uncoded QPSK system.

We have demonstrated the improvement due to trellis coding over uncoded QPSK in this section. Similar results, providing as much as 6-dB performance

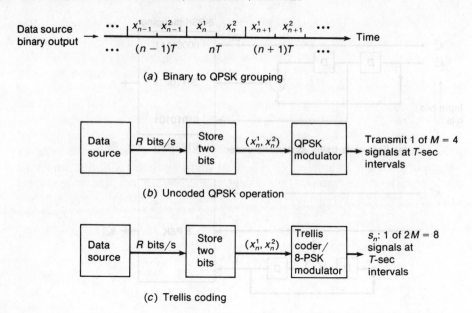

(a) Binary to QPSK grouping

(b) Uncoded QPSK operation

(c) Trellis coding

FIGURE 7-88
Trellis coding, 8-PSK example.

gain, are obtainable for higher-order systems. As noted at the beginning of this section, 19.2-kbit/s modems incorporating trellis coding have been designed for operation over 2.4-kHz telephone channels. These group 7 bits per transmission interval T. We have not shown the *hard* work involved in the design: how does one determine the trellis state structure and the convolutional coders implementing this? The 8-PSK trellis codes described here were designed by hand [UNGE 1982]. Computer programs are necessary to design trellis codes for higher-order systems that provide maximum d_E. Ungerboeck and other workers in the field have developed systematic ways for designing trellis codes. Details appear in the references.

7-11 SUMMARY

This chapter concludes the discussion, in this book, of point-to-point digital communications. Recall, as first noted in Chap. 1, that point-to-point communication is carried out by the physical layer in the layered model for network communications. This is the layer that is finally responsible for ensuring that information bits required to be transmitted over a distance, whether originally emanating from voice, video, data, facsimile, or some other communication traffic source, do in fact arrive at the receiving system.

The focus in this chapter, extending the discussion in Chap. 6, has been on communication over a channel introducing noise. The effect of other types of disturbance such as interference or fading may be modeled and handled in a related manner, and is considered in some of the references cited throughout this chapter, as well as in the current periodical literature. Light-wave (optical) communications in particular, discussed in Chap. 6, is clearly of current interest, and papers on this subject, extending the discussion in Chap. 6, appear regularly in technical journals and conference proceedings.

The specific attempt in this chapter has been to unify and extend the discussion in Chap. 6. Starting first with binary signals, we asked the question: Are there optimum binary waveshapes and optimum receiver mechanizations or processing techniques to minimize the error probability? To answer this question we applied known techniques of statistical decision theory. Starting first with single-received-signal samples and then generalizing to multiple independent samples drawn from known probability distributions, we found that the optimum processing procedure consisted of setting up a likelihood ratio and determining whether this ratio was greater than or smaller than a known constant. Alternatively, the optimum procedure consisted of subdividing the m-dimensional space of the m received signal samples into two disjoint decision regions, one corresponding to one binary signal transmitted, the other to the other signal. In most cases considered, the likelihood ratio could be simplified considerably to provide simple processing procedures for the m samples.

Specializing to the important case of additive white gaussian noise as the disturbance on the channel, we found that the optimum processor consisted of a pair of matched filters, one for each signal transmitted for binary transmission. In the digital version of these filters, each received signal sample is weighted by the corresponding stored transmitted sample, all m weighted samples then being added together. The optimum signal shapes then turned out to be any pair of equal and opposite signals. As shown first in Chap. 6, the error probability then depends solely on the ratio of signal energy to noise spectral density.

The analysis of binary signal transmission in the presence of noise was then generalized to M-ary symbol transmission in the presence of additive white gaussian noise. This analysis of the additive-white-gaussian-noise (AWGN) channel led naturally to the use of matched filters, or equivalently, correlation detection at the receiver. As an application of this material, we showed how one calculates the probability of error for the QAM signal constellations first introduced in Chap. 4. (It must again be noted, however, that these error calculations provide the effect of gaussian noise only. In telephone practice, where such signaling schemes are commonly used for higher-speed data transmission, errors are more often due to other sources. Digital radio techniques also suffer from occasional signal fading, and special measures, such as diversity, must be taken to recoup their performance.) As expected, the packing of more signal points into a two-dimensional space results in deteriorating performance.

By going to multidimensional signaling, however, using M-ary orthogonal signals, we found that the error probability could be reduced. The price paid is increased bandwidth and complexity. This reduction in error probability using M-ary orthogonal signaling was then shown to be a special case of the Shannon channel-capacity theorem. This theorem demonstrates that it is theoretically possible to drive the probability of error in the presence of additive gaussian noise to as low a value as desired by appropriate encoding and decoding operations at the transmitter and receiver, respectively. This is possible provided the binary transmission rate R in bits per second does not exceed the channel capacity, a number determined by the channel bandwidth, average signal power, and noise spectral density.

We concluded this chapter by examining some methods of detecting and correcting binary errors as a means of further improving the performance of binary systems. Three methods were considered. The first was block coding, with check bits inserted regularly in the binary stream to enable a specified number of errors to be detected and/or corrected. The second was convolutional coding, with input bits continually encoded using a shift-register operation, and read out at a higher bit rate. The Viterbi algorithm was introduced as an optimum (maximum-likelihood) decoding technique in this case. The use of block and convolutional coding results in a wider transmission requirement. Trellis coding has been developed as a technique appropriate to band-limited channels, with QAM signal transmission and coding procedures combined to improve the performance over these channels.

PROBLEMS

7-1. Consider the received-signal conditional-density functions $f(v|1)$ and $f(v|2)$ shown in Fig. P7-1.
  (a) Indicate the two decision regions V_1 and V_2 for the following values of P_1, the a priori probability of transmitting a 1: 0.3, 0.5, 0.7.
  (b) Calculate the probability of error in each of the three cases of (a).

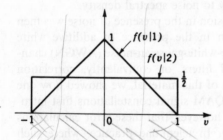

FIGURE P7-1

7-2. The probability-density function of a sample of received signal v corresponding to $s_1(t)$ transmitted is given by

$$f(v|1) = k_1 e^{-|v|} \qquad -\infty < v < \infty$$

while the corresponding density function corresponding to the signal $s_2(t)$ is

$$f(v|2) = k_2 e^{-2|v|} \qquad -\infty < v < \infty$$

  (a) Find the appropriate values of k_1 and k_2.
  (b) The a priori probabilities are $P_1 = \frac{3}{4}$, $P_2 = \frac{1}{4}$. Find the values of v for which we choose s_1, and the values for which we choose s_2.

7-3. An OOK signal is transmitted over a fading medium, and gaussian noise of mean-squared value N added at the receiver. The composite signal plus noise is envelope-detected before binary decisions are made. It may then be shown [SCHW 1966] that at the decision point the sampled envelope r has either one of the two density functions

$$f(r|1) = \frac{re^{-r^2/2N_T}}{N_T} \quad \text{or} \quad f(r|2) = \frac{re^{-r^2/2N}}{N}$$

corresponding, respectively, to signal plus noise received, and to noise alone (zero signal). Here $N_T = N + S$, with S the mean signal power averaged over the fading $(0 < r < \infty)$.

(a) Show that in the case of equally likely binary signal transmission the optimum decision test consists of deciding on a 1 ("on" signal) transmitted if the envelope r exceeds a threshold $b = \sqrt{2N(1 + N/S)\log_e(1 + S/N)}$.

(b) $S/N = 10$. Calculate b and evaluate the overall probability of error. Repeat for $S/N = 1$.

(c) m independent samples r_j, $j = 1, \ldots, m$, of r are taken before a decision is made. Show that the optimum test consists of determining whether $\sum_{j=1}^{m} r_j^2$ is greater or less than $2mN(1 + N/S)\log_e(1 + S/N)$.

7-4. A polar binary signal $\pm A$ is received in the presence of additive gaussian noise of variance N. Find the appropriate decision levels if one sample of signal plus noise is taken, for $P_1 = 0.3, 0.5$, and 0.7.

7-5. A polar binary signal of amplitude ± 1 has added to it noise $n(t)$ with density function $f(n) = \frac{3}{32}(4 - n^2)$. Find the minimum probability of error if the a priori probabilities are $P_1 = \frac{2}{5}$ and $P_{-1} = \frac{3}{5}$.

7-6. The received voltage for binary transmission has the two conditional-density functions $f(v|1)$ and $f(v|2)$ shown in Fig. P7-6. Find the optimum decision rule and minimum probability of error in the three cases $P_1 = \frac{1}{2}, \frac{2}{3}, \frac{1}{3}$.

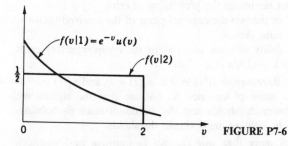

FIGURE P7-6

7-7. A received waveform $v(t)$ is of the form

$$v(t) = \left\{ \begin{array}{c} +2E \\ \text{or} \\ -E \end{array} \right\} + n(t)$$

with $n(t)$ zero-mean gaussian noise of variance N. The a priori signal probabilities are $P(+2E) = \frac{1}{3}$, $P(-E) = \frac{2}{3}$. A single sample of $v(t)$ is taken.

(a) For what values of v should we choose $+2E$ in order to minimize the overall probability of error?

(b) Give an expression for the overall probability of error.

7-8. One of two signals is transmitted over a noisy channel. The conditional-density functions of the received random variable v are

$$f(v|1) = \frac{1}{2\pi} \qquad |v| \leq \pi$$

$$= 0 \qquad \text{otherwise}$$

$$f(v|2) = \frac{1}{2\pi}(1 + \cos v) \qquad |v| \leq \pi$$

$$= 0 \qquad \text{otherwise}$$

  (a) With $P_1 = P_2 = \frac{1}{2}$, find the decision region of v corresponding to minimum probability of error.
  (b) Find the minimum probability of error in (a).
  (c) Find the values of P_1 and P_2 such that the optimum decision rule says *always* decide on signal 1. What is the probability of error in this case?

7-9. Either one of two noiselike signals is transmitted. The density functions of the received signal are

$$f(v|1) = \frac{e^{-v^2/2\sigma_1^2}}{\sqrt{2\pi\sigma_1^2}} \qquad f(v|2) = \frac{e^{-v^2/2\sigma_2^2}}{\sqrt{2\pi\sigma_2^2}}$$

$P_1 = P_2 = \frac{1}{2}$. Find the optimum receiver processing in the case of one, and then two, independent samples. Show in this latter case that signal 1 is declared present if $v_1^2 + v_2^2 > d$, d a prescribed decision level. What are the two-dimensional regions V_1 and V_2 in this latter case?

7-10. Binary signals with $P_1 = P_2 = \frac{1}{2}$ are received in additive gaussian noise of rms value 0.5 V. Two independent samples are used at the receiver to decide on signal s_1 or s_2. At the (known) sampling times the two-dimensional signal vectors are, respectively, $\mathbf{s}_1 = (+15 \text{ V}, +15 \text{ V})$ and $\mathbf{s}_2 = (-7 \text{ V}, -7 \text{ V})$.
  (a) Find the decision rule that minimizes the probability of error.
  (b) Sketch regions V_1 and V_2 in the two-dimensional plane of the received vector $\mathbf{v}$. Indicate $\mathbf{s}_1$ and $\mathbf{s}_2$ in the same sketch.
  (c) Find the minimum probability of error in terms of the complementary error function erfc x defined as $1 - (2/\sqrt{\pi})\int_0^x e^{-x^2} dx$.

7-11. Devise a detection scheme for *three* signals $s_1(t) = +a$, $s_2(t) = 0$, and $s_3(t) = -a$, received in additive gaussian noise of variance N. Assume that the signals are equiprobable. Find the optimum thresholds and the minimum error probability. *Hint:* Symmetry may be used in locating the optimum thresholds.

7-12. *Diversity transmission* (use of more than one channel to improve performance). Consider the system shown in Fig. P7-12. Polar signals $\pm a$ are sent out, in parallel over two channels as shown. Because of differing attenuation (or fading) along the two paths, the signals arrive as $\pm a_1$ and $\pm a_2$, respectively, at each receiver. Gaussian noise of variance N_1 and N_2, respectively, is added at each receiver as shown.
  (a) Show that the summed output v is a gaussian variable of expected value $\pm(A_1 a_1 + A_2 a_2)$, and variance $A_1^2 N_1 + A_2^2 N_2$.
  (b) Show that the probability of error depends on the effective SNR $(a_1 + Ka_2)^2/(N_1 + K^2 N_2)$, with $K = A_2/A_1$. Here $K = 0$ ($A_2 = 0$) and $K = \infty$ ($A_1 = 0$)

correspond to the single-receiver case. Show that the diversity system provides SNR, and hence error-probability, improvement over the single-receiver case.

(*c*) Show that the optimum choice of the gain ratio K is given by

$$K_{\text{opt}} = \left(\frac{a_2}{a_1}\right)\left(\frac{N_1}{N_2}\right)$$

This is equivalent to setting $A_1 = (a_1/N_1)g$, $A_2 = (a_2/N_2)g$, g some arbitrary gain constant. The optimum diversity system hence weights each receiver input by the ratio of signal to noise (a_i/N_i) measured at that input. This type of combining is called *maximal-ratio combining* [SCHW 1966]. Show that the effective SNR for this case is given by $a_1^2/N_1 + a_2^2/N_2$, the sum of the two SNR's.

(*d*) As a special case of diversity combining, assume that the two signal terms a_1 and a_2 represent samples in *time* of a transmitted signal. Let $N_1 = N_2 = N$ be the variance of the noise added, the two noise samples assumed independent. Show that the optimal processing of the two signal-plus-noise samples, in the sense of minimum probability of error, consists of adding them after weighting the first by a_1, the second by a_2. A little thought indicates this is the same as matched filtering. Compare this matched filtering for time diversity with maximal-ratio combining for diversity techniques in general.

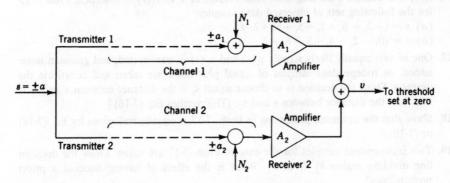

FIGURE P7-12

7-13. A binary message (0 or 1) is to be transmitted in the following manner. The transmitter has two coins labeled C_0 and C_1. For coin C_0 the probability of a head is p_0, and for coin C_1 it is p_1. If message i ($i = 0$ or 1) is to be transmitted, coin C_1 is flipped n times (independent tosses) and the sequence of heads and tails is observed by the receiver.

(*a*) Assuming the two messages are equally likely, find the optimum (minimum probability of error) decision rule for deciding between the two messages. Indicate one simple method for implementing this rule.

(*b*) Set up an expression for the resultant probability of error.

7-14. Consider the binary detection problem where we receive (after processing) the random variable v given by

$$v = s + n$$

where s, the signal, is either equal to 0 or 1 with equal prior probabilities. n is an exponential random variable with density

$$f(n) = \tfrac{1}{2} e^{-|n|} \qquad -\infty < n < \infty$$

Find:

(a) The decision rule which leads to the minimum probability of error.

(b) The resultant minimum probability of error.

7-15. One of two equally likely signals is transmitted and received in additive gaussian noise of variance 2 V^2. The signals are $s_1(t) = 4$ V $= -s_2(t)$, the binary interval being 1 ms long. Eight equispaced independent samples of the received signal

$$v(t) = \begin{cases} s_1(t) \\ \text{or} \\ s_2(t) \end{cases} + n(t)$$

are taken, and constitute an 8-vector **v**.

(a) For the following sets of observed data **v** which signal would you decide was sent?

(1) $\mathbf{v} = (4.5, 0, -1.5, 2, -6, 10, 1, -4)$.

(2) $\mathbf{v} = (-5, -3, -4, -5, -3, 20, 15, 5)$.

(b) What is the probability of error?

7-16. $s_1(t)$ is a triangle 1 ms long with peak voltage of 4 V. $s_2(t) = 0$. Repeat Prob. 7-15 for the following sets of observed data samples:

(a) $\mathbf{v} = (-2, -6, +1, +5, +6, +2, +1, -8)$.

(b) $\mathbf{v} = (0, -2, -4, +5, +6, +2, -4, -2)$.

7-17. One of two equally likely signals $s_1(t)$ and $s_2(t)$ is transmitted, and gaussian noise added. m independent samples of signal plus noise are taken and constitute the vector **v**. Show the decision is to choose signal $\mathbf{s}_1$ if the distance between **v** and $\mathbf{s}_1$ is less than the distance between **v** and $\mathbf{s}_2$. [This verifies Eq. (7-16).]

7-18. Show that the optimum processing in Prob. 7-17 is equally well given by Eq. (7-18) or (7-19).

7-19. Two independent samples for the case of Prob. 7-17 are taken. Draw the decision line dividing region V_1 from V_2. What is the effect of having unequal a priori probabilities?

7-20. Consider the integral

$$\int_{-\infty}^{\infty} \frac{\sin \pi (2Bt - k)}{\pi (2Bt - k)} \cdot \frac{\sin \pi (2Bt - m)}{\pi (2Bt - m)} \, dt$$

[See Eq. (7-41).] Show by a simple change of variables that this may be written as the convolution integral

$$\frac{1}{2B\pi} \int_{-\infty}^{\infty} \frac{\sin(\tau - x)}{\tau - x} \frac{\sin x}{x} \, dx$$

with $\tau \equiv (k - m)\pi$. Recalling that the Fourier transform of $(\sin ax)/\pi x$ is 1, $|\omega| \le a$; 0, $|\omega| > 0$, take Fourier transforms, and show that the integral is $(1/2B)\delta_{km}$, where δ_{km} is the Kronecker delta. The $(\sin x)/x$ functions are thus examples of *orthogonal* functions.

7-21. (*a*) As a generalization of Prob. 7-20 above, prove that

$$\int_{-\infty}^{\infty} \frac{\sin \omega_1(t-x)}{\pi(t-x)} \frac{\sin \omega_2 x}{\pi x} \, dx = \frac{\sin \omega_1 t}{\pi t}$$

assuming $\omega_1 \le \omega_2$. *Hint:* This is already in the form of a convolution integral. Use the approach suggested in Prob. 7-20.

(*b*) As a special case let $\omega_1 = \omega_2 = 2\pi B$; $t = (k - m)/2B$. Show that this gives the same result as in Prob. 7-20.

7-22. *Orthogonal functions.* Consider a set of functions $\phi_i(t)$ with the property

$$\int_a^b \phi_i(t)\phi_j(t) \, dt = \delta_{ij}$$

The $\phi_i(t)$'s then constitute a normalized orthogonal, or *orthonormal*, set of funct ons over the integration range (a, b).

(*a*) We desire to approximate an arbitrary function $f(t)$ by a linear sum of orthonormal functions:

$$f(t) \sim \sum_{j=1}^{n} b_j\phi_j(t) \equiv f_n(t)$$

Show that the mean-squared error between $f(t)$ and $f_n(t)$,

$$\epsilon^2 \equiv \int_a^b [f(t) - f_n(t)]^2 \, dt$$

is minimized by choosing

$$b_j = \int_a^b f(t)\phi_j(t) \, dt$$

Use the symbol a_j to denote this special case of b_j. Then $\sum_{j=1}^{n} a_j\phi_j(t)$ approximates $f(t)$ best in a least-mean-square sense. The a_j's are sometimes called the generalized Fourier coefficients.

(*b*) The orthogonal set $\phi_j(t)$ is said to be *complete* if, using the Fourier coefficients a_j, that is,

$$f_n(t) = \sum_{j=1}^{n} a_j\phi_j(t)$$

one has $\epsilon^2 \to 0$ as $n \to \infty$. Show that for this case

$$\int_a^b f^2(t) \, dt = \sum_{j=1}^{\infty} a_j^2$$

This is a generalized form of Parseval's theorem, first met in Chap. 2. That is, the energy in the signal equals the energy in the orthogonal functions. We then write

$$f(t) = \sum_{j=1}^{\infty} a_j\phi_j(t)$$

where the equality is meant in this sense of equal energy.

(*c*) Let the interval (a, b) be $(-T/2, +T/2)$. Find the normalized set of sines and cosines that are orthogonal over this interval.

(*d*) According to Prob. 7-20 [and Eq. (7-41)], the $(\sin x)/x$ functions are orthogonal over the interval $(-\infty, \infty)$. Normalize these functions and show how the coefficients a_j are related to the sampled values $f(j/2B)$ of a function $f(t)$

expanded in terms of the $(\sin x)/x$ functions [see Eq. (7-40)]. Show that the Parseval theorem in this case is given by

$$\int_{-\infty}^{\infty} f^2(t)\, dt = \frac{1}{2B} \sum_{j=-\infty}^{\infty} f^2\left(\frac{j}{2B}\right)$$

(e) Let

$$f_1(t) = \sum_{j=1}^{\infty} a_j \phi_j(t)$$

$$a_j = \int_a^b f_1(t)\phi_j(t)\, dt$$

$$f_2(t) = \sum_{j=1}^{\infty} b_j \phi_j(t)$$

$$b_j = \int_a^b f_2(t)\phi_j(t)\, dt$$

Show that

$$\int_a^b f_1(t) f_2(t)\, dt = \sum_{j=1}^{\infty} a_j b_j$$

Use this to verify Eq. (7-43) as a special case.

7-23. Equally likely polar signals of amplitude $\pm A$ are received in the presence of additive gaussian noise of variance σ^2. Suppose $A/\sigma = 1$.

(a) One sample of the received signal plus noise is taken and optimally processed. Show that the error probability $P_e = 0.159$. Show that taking three independent samples and optimally processing these reduces P_e to 0.0418.

(b) A suboptimum processor is used for the three samples of (a): each sample is independently checked for polarity. If two or three samples are positive, $+A$ is declared present. Otherwise, $-A$ is declared present. Show $P_e = 0.068$. Compare this procedure and its performance with that of the optimum processor in (a).

Note: In Probs. 7-24 to 7-32, appropriate signal shaping factors normally included are not shown explicitly.

7-24. A binary source outputs 7,200 bits/s. A modem is used to convert the binary symbols to a format capable of being transmitted over a telephone channel of 2,400-Hz bandwidth.

(a) Determine which of the following signal sets is suitable for this purpose.

(1) The QAM set of Fig. P7-24,

$$\phi_1 = \sqrt{\frac{2}{T}} \cos \omega_0 t \qquad \phi_2 = \sqrt{\frac{2}{T}} \sin \omega_0 t$$

(2) The set is the same as that of (1), but

$$\phi_1 = \sqrt{\frac{2}{T}} \cos \omega_1 t \qquad \phi_2 = \sqrt{\frac{2}{T}} \cos \omega_2 t$$

The spacing $\Delta f = f_2 - f_1 = 0.7/T$. (This is the minimum spacing possible to keep ϕ_1 and ϕ_2 orthogonal.)

(3) The M-ary AM set of Fig. P7-24. $\phi_1 = \sqrt{2/T}\cos\omega_0 t$. All points are spaced d apart.

(4) The set of Fig. P7-24. Here $\phi_1 = \sqrt{2/T}\cos\omega_1 t$, $\phi_2 = \sqrt{2/T}\cos\omega_2 t$, $\phi_3 = \sqrt{2/T}\cos\omega_3 t$, and the eight signal points appear at the vertices of a cube: $(d/2, d/2, -d/2)$, $(d/2, -d/2, -d/2)$, etc.

(b) Write specific expressions, as a function of time, for each of the signals in those signal sets deemed suitable.

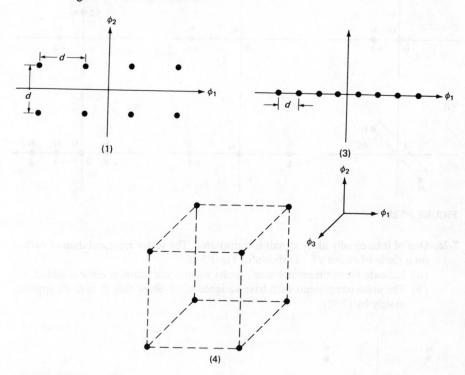

FIGURE P7-24

7-25. Two equally likely polar signal vectors s_1 and s_2 appear as in Fig. P7-25.

$$v = s_i + n \qquad i = 1 \text{ or } 2$$

n is zero-mean white gaussian. We find $P_e = 0.01$. *Note:* Why are v and n written as scalars here?

(a) Find P_e for each of the six cases shown in the figure, and compare with that for the polar signals. Compare powers as well. All signals are equally likely. The

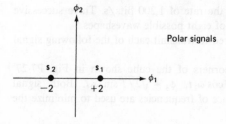

Polar signals

noise is the same in all cases. *Hint:* In (5) and (6), find P_c first. Show that $P_e = 0.013$ in (5) and 0.015 in (6).

(*b*) What is the effect on P_e and the power in all cases if all signals are shifted *up* by 2 units? *Down* by 2 units?

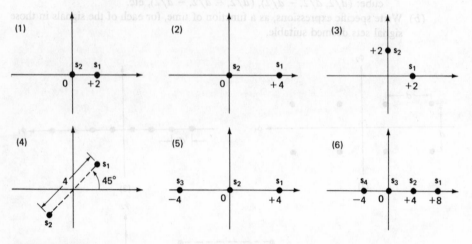

FIGURE P7-25

7-26. One of four equally likely signals is transmitted. The vector representation of each is on a circle of radius $\sqrt{E}$, as shown in Fig. P7-26.

(*a*) Indicate the optimum decision regions when white gaussian noise is added.

(*b*) The noise components each have variance $n_0/2$. Show that P_e is given approximately by (7-98).

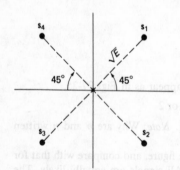

FIGURE P7-26

7-27. A data terminal outputs information at the rate of 1,200 bits/s. Three successive bits are stored and used to generate one of eight possible waveshapes.

(*a*) Find the minimum bandwidth required to transmit each of the following signal sets:

(1) The signal vectors are at the corners of the cube shown in Fig. P7-27 $\phi_1 = \sqrt{2/T}\cos\omega_1 t$, $\phi_2 = \sqrt{2/T}\cos\omega_2 t$, $\phi_3 = \sqrt{2/T}\sin\omega_2 t$. Both signal shaping and the appropriate choice of frequencies are used to minimize the bandwidth.

(2) Same as (1), but $\phi_3 = \sqrt{2/T}\cos\omega_3 t$, with all three frequencies chosen to minimize the bandwidth.

(3) See the figure. $\phi_1 = \sqrt{2/T}\cos\omega_0 t$, $\phi_2 = \sqrt{2/T}\sin\omega_0 t$.

(4) A cosinusoidal pulse $T/3$ seconds long of amplitude $+a$ or $-a$ is transmitted in each of three adjacent time slots. Then $s_i(t) = \pm a\phi_1(t) \pm a\phi_2(t) \pm a\phi_3(t)$. Each orthogonal function is given by $\sqrt{6/T}\cos\omega_0 t$, but defined in the ranges $0 \le t < T/3$, $T/3 \le t < 2T/3$, and $2T/3 \le t < T$, respectively.

(b) White gaussian noise of spectral density $n_0/2$ is added during transmission. The eight signals are equally likely to be transmitted. Find the probability of error of each signal set in terms of E/n_0. *Note:* For signal set (3), assume that a point at the origin is present in calculating P_e.

(c) Can you find a set of signals equivalent to set (1) that yields the same P_e but with less average energy?

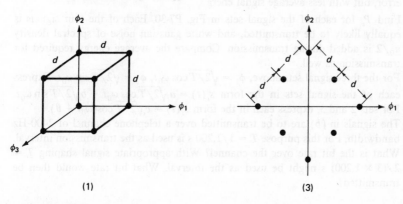

(1) (3)

FIGURE P7-27

7-28. A data source outputs digits at a rate of R bits/s. These are to be transmitted over a telephone line using a modem. The modem outputs one of the following eight signals every T_0 seconds:

$$s_i(t) = \begin{array}{ll} a\phi_1(t) + a\phi_2(t) & -a\phi_1(t) + a\phi_2(t) \\ 3a\phi_1(t) + a\phi_2(t) & -3a\phi_1(t) + a\phi_2(t) \\ a\phi_1(t) - a\phi_2(t) & -a\phi_1(t) - a\phi_2(t) \\ 3a\phi_1(t) - a\phi_2(t) & -3a\phi_1(t) - a\phi_2(t) \end{array}$$

Here $\phi_1(t) = \sqrt{\dfrac{2}{T_0}}\cos\omega_c t \quad \phi_2(t) = \sqrt{\dfrac{2}{T_0}}\sin\omega_c t \quad 0 \le t \le T_0$.

Shaping parameters, not shown here, are also used to pack $s_i(t)$ into the minimum possible bandwidth. The eight signals are equally likely to be transmitted.

(a) What are the telephone-channel bandwidth B, T_0, and R if the modem output rate is 7,200 bits/s?

(b) White gaussian noise with spectral density $n_0/2$ is added during transmission. Indicate the optimum receiver structure schematically. Show the optimum decision regions. Find an expression for the probability of error. Show this may be written in terms of E/n_0, with E the average signal energy in the T_0-second interval.

7-29. A transmitter sends one of four possible waveforms (with equal probability) over an additive-white-gaussian-noise channel with spectral density $n_0/2$. Each waveform is constructed as a combination of three possible "tones":

$$\phi_i(t) = E \cos \omega_i t \quad \omega_i = \frac{2\pi i}{T} \quad i = 1, 2, 3$$

The signal duration is T seconds. The four signals are given by

$$s_1(t) = \phi_1 \quad s_2(t) = \phi_2 \quad s_3(t) = \phi_3 \quad s_4(t) = \phi_1 + \phi_2 + \phi_3$$

(a) Do the ϕ_i's constitute an orthogonal set?

(b) Sketch the form of an optimal receiver for this system.

(c) What geometric figure do the s_i's form in the signal space?

(d) Find an equivalent set of signals which would yield the same probability of error, but with less average signal energy.

7-30. (a) Find P_e for each of the signal sets in Fig. P7-30. Each of the four signals is equally likely to be transmitted, and white gaussian noise of spectral density $n_0/2$ is added during transmission. Compare the average energy required for transmission as well.

(b) For the three signal sets above, $\phi_1 = \sqrt{2/T} \cos \omega_0 t$, $\phi_2 = \sqrt{2/T} \sin \omega_0 t$. Express each of the signal sets in the form $s_i(t) = a_i\sqrt{2/T} \cos \omega_0 t + b_i\sqrt{2/T} \sin \omega_0 t$. For sets 2 and 3, express each in the form $s_i(t) = c_i\sqrt{2/T} \cos(\omega_0 t + \theta)$.

(c) The signals in (b) are to be transmitted over a telephone channel of 2400-Hz bandwidth. For this purpose $T = 1/1,200$ s is used as the transmission interval. What is the bit rate over the channel? With appropriate signal shaping $T = 2/(3 \times 1,200)$ s might be used as the interval. What bit rate would then be transmitted?

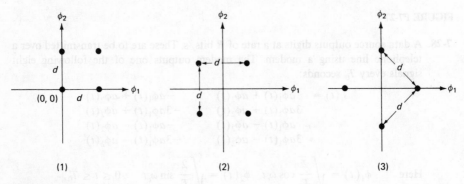

(1)   (2)   (3)

FIGURE P7-30

7-31. $N = 3$ orthogonal waveshapes are used to transmit $M = 2^3 = 8$ equally likely signals. Two possible sets of such signals appear in Figs. P7-24(4) and P7-27(1).

(a) Find P_e for those two sets in white gaussian noise of spectral density $n_0/2$. *Hint:* Show that P_e is of the form r^3, while in Prob. 7-30 it is given by r^2. Can you extend this to $M = 2^N$ signals located at the vertices of a hypercube in N dimensions?

(b) Which of the two signals requires less energy to transmit? If the spacing d is the same in this problem and Prob. 7-30, which signal sets in the two problems have a smaller probability of error?

(c) $T = 1/1,200$ s in this problem. Let $\phi_1 = \sqrt{2/T}\cos \omega_1 t$, $\phi_2 = \sqrt{2/T}\sin \omega_1 t$, $\phi_3 = \sqrt{2/T}\cos \omega_2 t$, $f_2 - f_1 = 1/T$. What bandwidth is required for transmission? What is the bit rate?

(d) $P_e = 10^{-5}$ is desired. Find E/n_0 required for the eight signals in Fig. P7-24(4). How does this compare to E/n_0 for PSK transmission, for the same $P_e = 10^{-5}$? *Hint:* With $P_e \ll 1$, as here, $r \doteq 1 - \epsilon$. Then $P_e \doteq 3\epsilon$. (Why?) Use the approximation

$$\int_a^\infty \frac{e^{-x^2}\, dx}{\sqrt{\pi}} \doteq \frac{e^{-a^2}}{2a\sqrt{\pi}} \qquad a > 1$$

and show that

$$P_e \doteq \frac{3}{2} \frac{e^{-E/3n_0}}{\sqrt{\pi E/3n_0}}$$

Solve for E/n_0.

7-32. A binary stream is to be encoded into one of four signals. Various signal sets are available for this purpose. Compare the following signal sets in terms of probability of error and bandwidth required. The signal energy is the same in all cases. The encoded signal is transmitted over a white-gaussian-noise channel. T is the transmission interval.

(1) $\pm\sqrt{2/T}\,a\cos \omega_0 t \pm \sqrt{2/T}\,a\sin \omega_0 t$

(2) $\pm\sqrt{2/T}\,a\sin \omega_0 t$, $\sqrt{2/T}\,a\cos \omega_0 t \pm \sqrt{2/T}\,a\sin \omega_0 t$

(3) $\sqrt{2/T}\sqrt{2}\,a\cos(\omega_0 t + \theta)$, $\theta = \pm\pi/4, \pm 3\pi/4$

(4) $\pm\sqrt{2/T}\,a\cos \omega_0 t \pm \sqrt{2/T}\,a\cos(\omega_0 + 2\pi/T)t$

7-33. Refer to Prob. 7-24. Find and compare P_e for sets (1), (2), and (3), if $E/n_0 = 24$.

7-34. A computer outputs data at a rate of 48 kbits/s. An 8-QAM modem, with the constellation shown in Fig. P7-34(1), is used to transmit the data.

(a) Nyquist shaping, with roll-off factor $r = 0.25$, is used. Find the bandwidth B_T required to transmit the QAM signals.

(b) The QAM signals are transmitted over an additive-white-gaussian-noise (AWGN) channel. They are equally probable.

  (1) Show the probability of correct reception is

  $$P(c) = \tfrac{1}{8}(1 + p)(3p + 1), \qquad p = \operatorname{erf}\frac{d}{2\sqrt{n_0}}.$$

  (2) The error probability $P_e = 1 - P(c)$ is very small. Hence $p \doteq 1 - \epsilon$, $\epsilon \ll 1$. Show

  $$P_e \doteq \tfrac{5}{4} \operatorname{erfc}\frac{d}{2\sqrt{n_0}} \qquad \operatorname{erfc} x = 1 - \operatorname{erf} x$$

  (3) Finally, show $P_e \doteq \tfrac{5}{4}\operatorname{erfc}\sqrt{E/6n_0}$, E the average signal energy. Compare with (7-98) and (7-96) for 4-QAM and 16-QAM respectively.

  Do these results agree with the approximation (7-100) in the text?

(c) The signal constellations (2) and (3) in Fig. P7-34 are to be considered instead of (1).

  (1) Find expressions for P_e as a function of E/n_0 for each.

  (2) $\phi_1(t) = \sqrt{2/T}\cos \omega_0 t$, $\phi_2(t) = \sqrt{2/T}\sin \omega_0 t$. Express $s_1(t)$ in terms of $\phi_1(t)$ and $\phi_2(t)$ for each of the two constellations.

(1)

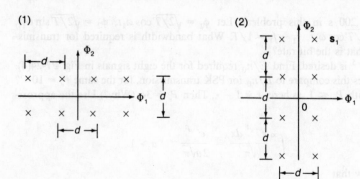

(2)

(3)

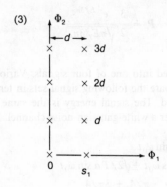

FIGURE P7-34

7-35. (*a*) Communication between a space vehicle and the earth is under investigation. A probability of error $P_e \le 10^{-5}$ is to be maintained. Compare the binary rates R (bits/s) and the approximate transmission bandwidths required for the following modes of transmission: (1) PSK; (2) binary FSK; (3) one of 32 orthogonal signals. $S/n_0 = 800$, with S the received signal power and $n_0/2$ the gaussian noise spectral density.

   (*b*) Repeat if the distance between space vehicle and·earth doubles.

   (*c*) It is desired to transmit at a rate of 320 bits/s, with $P_e = 10^{-5}$. Once again $S/n_0 = 800$. Indicate if this is possible and, if so, how it may be done. What is the *maximum* possible rate, with the probability of error reduced as low as desired?

7-36. A digital communication channel has $S/n_0 = 10$ at the receiver. With PSK transmission and $P_e \le 10^{-5}$ required, at most a 1-bit/s transmission rate is possible.

   (*a*) What is the *maximum* bit rate allowed over this channel if arbitrarily wide bandwidths are allowed and $P_e \to 0$?

   (*b*) A bandwidth of 1 kHz is available. $P_e = 10^{-5}$ is required. Indicate the maximum bit rate attainable using M orthogonal signals. What value of M is required? How many bits are encoded per M-ary signal transmitted?

7-37. (*a*) Plot the capacity in bits per second versus the bandwidth W of a channel with additive band-limited gaussian noise of spectral density $n_0/2$ and average power S, where $S/n_0 = 100$.

(b) $S/n_0 = 100$. Find the maximum rate of transmission of binary information if PSK is used and a maximum probability of error of 10^{-5} is to be maintained. Repeat for $P_e = 10^{-4}$. What is the maximum rate in both cases if FSK transmission is used?

(c) $S/n_0 = 100$ again. The channel bandwidth is $W = 10$ Hz. If the binary digits of (b) may be encoded using as complicated a digital scheme as desired, what is the maximum rate of transmission in bits per second with a probability of error as small as desired? Compare with (b). What is the SNR in this case?

(d) $S/n_0 = 100$. The channel bandwidth may be made as large as necessary. Repeat (c), and again compare with (b).

7-38. Digital communications for a deep-space probe (10^8 miles from earth) is to be investigated. Assume 500-MHz transmission with space-vehicle and earth antenna gains of 10 and 40 dB, respectively. The transmitter power is limited to 10 W. $T = 100$ K. Bit-error probability is to be less than 10^{-5}.

(a) Find the maximum rate of binary transmission if a PSK system with synchronous detection is considered.

(b) The binary data are to be encoded into one of 64 orthogonal signals. Find the maximum binary rate in this case. What is the encoding or storage time required at both transmitter and receiver?

(c) What is the maximum possible transmission rate if an arbitrarily large bandwidth and complex encoding are allowed, and the probability of error is to be made as small as desired? Compare (a), (b), (c).

(d) The antenna sizes are fixed. Repeat the problem for two different frequencies: 2,000 MHz and 1,000 MHz.

(e) Repeat if a maser receiver providing an overall temperature of 30 K is used on earth.

7-39. Refer to the discussion of the Mariner 10 deep-space mission in Sec. 6-15. Find the allowable bit transmission rate if $M = 32$ orthogonal signals were to be used. What is the Shannon capacity ($W \to \infty$) for this channel?

7-40. Repeat Prob. 7-39 for the Voyager mission (see Prob. 6-86 for the necessary parameters).

7-41. Refer to Fig. 7-53 in the text comparing various QAM systems with the Shannon capacity. Check QAM points using the approximations (7-100) to (7-103), as well as (7-129). Repeat for $P_e = 10^{-4}$ and the roll-off factor $r = \frac{1}{2}$. Do the probability-of-error equations given by (7-98), Prob. 7-34, and (7-96) for 4-QAM (QPSK), 8-QAM, and 16-QAM, respectively, agree with Fig. 7-53?

7-42. Consider the binary code with the P matrix

$$P = \begin{bmatrix} 1 & 0 & 1 \\ 0 & 1 & 1 \\ 1 & 1 & 1 \end{bmatrix}$$

(a) Is the word $(1\,0\,1\,0\,1\,0)$ a code word?

(b) A code word is of the form $(X\,1\,1\,1\,0\,0)$. Is X a 0 or a 1?

(c) Suppose the code word $(0\,0\,1\,1\,1\,1)$ is transmitted, but $(0\,0\,1\,1\,0\,1)$ is received. What is the resultant syndrome? Where would this syndrome indicate an error had occurred?

(d) How many code words are in this code? List them.

(e) What is the smallest number of errors that could change one code word into another code word? Why?

7-43. Consider a binary communication system consisting of two links as shown in Fig. P7-43. The noise in *each* channel is such that (1) errors occur independently, and (2) the probability that a 1 is received when a 0 is transmitted is p. The probability that a 0 is received when a 1 is transmitted is also p.

(a) Find the following four probabilities for the entire system:

> A 0 is received when a 0 is transmitted
> A 1 is received when a 0 is transmitted
> A 0 is received when a 1 is transmitted
> A 1 is received when a 1 is transmitted

(b) Assume that a simple coding scheme is used such that a 0 is transmitted as three successive 0's and a 1 as three successive 1's. At the detector, the following (majority) decision rule is used:

$$\left\{ \begin{array}{l} \text{Decide 0 if } 000, 001, 010, \text{ or } 100 \text{ is received} \\ \text{Decide 1 if } 111, 110, 101, \text{ or } 011 \text{ is received} \end{array} \right\}$$

If a 0 and 1 are equally likely, what is the probability of deciding incorrectly? Evaluate for $p = \frac{1}{3}$.

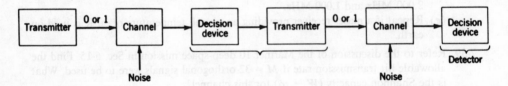

FIGURE P7-43

7-44. A binary message consists of words which are 5 bits long. The message words are to be encoded using a single-error-correcting code. The first 5 bits of each code word must be the message bits d_1, d_2, d_3, d_4, d_5, while the remaining bits are check bits.
(a) What is the minimum number of check bits? What are the P and G matrices?
(b) Construct an appropriate H matrix for this code.
(c) Find the syndrome at the receiver if there is an error in d_5.
(d) How does this code respond to double errors?

7-45. Show, by construction of an appropriate H matrix, that a $(6,3)$ code is single-error-correcting. Show that this agrees as well with the single-error-correcting inequality of Eq. (7-153). Show that a $(6,4)$ code cannot be designed to provide a single-error-correcting capability.

7-46. Consider a single-error-correcting code for 11 message bits.
(a) How many check bits are required?
(b) Find a suitable G matrix.
(c) Find the syndrome if the single error occurs in the seventh position.

7-47. A code consists of three message digits d_1, d_2, d_3 and three check digits c_4, c_5, c_6. The transmitted sequence is $d_1 \, d_2 \, d_3 \, c_4 \, c_5 \, c_6$. At the transmitter the check digits are formed from the following equations:

$$c_4 = d_1 \oplus d_3$$
$$c_5 = d_1 \oplus d_2$$
$$c_6 = d_1 \oplus d_2 \oplus d_3$$

(a) For the message $d_1 = 0$, $d_2 = 1$, $d_3 = 1$, find the transmitted sequence.

(b) Write down the G matrix.

(c) Will this code correct single errors? Why?

(d) Assume that the sequence 0 1 1 1 0 0 is received and that no more than one error has occurred. Decode this sequence: find the location of the error and the transmitted message d_1, d_2, d_3.

7-48. Consider a binary code with three message digits and three check digits in each code word. The code word is of the form

$$d_1 \, d_2 \, d_3 \, c_4 \, c_5 \, c_6$$

where the d_i's are the message digits and the c_i's are the check digits. Assume that the check digits are computed from the set of equations

$$c_4 = d_1 \oplus d_2 \oplus d_3$$
$$c_5 = d_1 \oplus d_3$$
$$c_6 = d_2 \oplus d_3$$

(a) How many code words are there in the code?

(b) Find the code word that begins 1 1 0 . . . .

(c) Suppose that the received word is 0 1 0 1 1 1. Decode to the closest code word (i.e., the code word that differs from the received word in the fewest positions).

7-49. Calculate the probability of error for the following binary codes and compare:

(n, k)	t
(7, 4)	1
(15, 11)	1
(15, 7)	2
(15, 5)	3
(31, 26)	1
(31, 21)	2
(31, 16)	3
(31, 11)	5
(31, 6)	7

where n is the total number of digits (data digits plus check digits), k is the number of data digits, and t is the error-correcting capability of the code; that is, t or fewer errors can be corrected. Assume that the probability of bit error when no coding is used is 10^{-5}. Adjust the duration of the binary digits in each code so that the transmission rate (message digits per second) is constant. *Hint:*

$$P_e = \binom{n}{t+1} p^{t+1} (1-p)^{n-(t+1)} + \binom{n}{t+2} p^{t+2} (1-p)^{n-(t+2)} + \cdots + p^n$$

Why? For very small p, as true here,

$$P_e \doteq \binom{n}{t+1} p^{t+1}.$$

7-50. A $(7, 4)$ code is to be used.

(a) Using the Hamming bound, find the potential random-error-correcting capability of such a code.

(b) The 16 code words are 0000000, 1111111, and cyclic variations of 0001011 and 0011101. List the 16 code words and show that the minimum distance d agrees with (a).

(c) Show that these are generated by the G matrix

$$G = \begin{bmatrix} 1 & 0 & 0 & 0 & 1 & 0 & 1 \\ 0 & 1 & 0 & 0 & 1 & 1 & 1 \\ 0 & 0 & 1 & 0 & 1 & 1 & 0 \\ 0 & 0 & 0 & 1 & 0 & 1 & 1 \end{bmatrix}$$

(d) Find the matrix H^T and show, for a few of the code words of (b), that $cH^T = 0$.

7-51. Use the Hamming bound of Eq. (7-154) to:

(a) Show that a $(15, 11)$ code may correct one error.

(b) Show that $(10, 4)$ and $(11, 4)$ codes may correct two errors.

(c) Find the error-correcting capability of the following $(15, k)$ codes: $k = 14, 11, 10, 7, 6, 5, 4, 2, 1$.

7-52. Verify the potential error-correcting capabilities of the codes listed in Table 7-1.

7-53. (a) Show that $x^3 + x + 1$, $x + 1$, and $x^3 + x^2 + 1$ are divisors of $x^7 + 1$. *Note:* Additions are all mod 2. $x^i \oplus x^i = 0$.

(b) Show that $x^2 + 1$ and $x^4 + x^2 + 1$ are divisors of $x^6 + 1$.

(c) Consider the polynomial $g(x) = x^4 + x + 1$. Divide this into $x^{15} + 1$ to show that

$$h(x) = \frac{x^{15} + 1}{g(x)} = x^{11} + x^8 + x^7 + x^5 + x^3 + x^2 + x + 1$$

7-54. In Prob. 7-53 it is shown $x^3 + x + 1$ is a divisor of $x^7 + 1$. Use this as a generating polynomial $g(x)$.

(a) What (n, k) code will this give rise to?

(b) Using $g(x) = x^3 + x + 1$, find the G matrix. Compare this matrix with that given in Prob. 7-50c.

7-55. (a) A systematic $(6, 2)$ cyclic code is to be generated. Given $x^6 + 1 = (x^2 + 1)(x^4 + x^2 + 1)$.

(1) Find the G matrix for this code.

(2) List the code words, indicating which represent cyclic shifts.

(3) Find the error-correcting capability t of this code two ways: from the code words themselves, and from the Hamming bound (7-154). Does this agree with the G matrix? Explain.

(b) Consider the following G matrices representing $(6, k)$ codes:

$$G_1 = \begin{bmatrix} 1 & 0 & 0 & 0 & 0 & 1 \\ 0 & 1 & 0 & 0 & 1 & 1 \\ 0 & 0 & 1 & 1 & 0 & 1 \end{bmatrix} \qquad G_2 = \begin{bmatrix} 1 & 0 & 0 & 0 & 1 & 1 \\ 0 & 1 & 0 & 1 & 0 & 1 \\ 0 & 0 & 1 & 1 & 1 & 1 \end{bmatrix}$$

$$G_3 = \begin{bmatrix} 1 & 0 & 0 & 0 & 1 & 0 \\ 0 & 1 & 0 & 0 & 0 & 1 \\ 0 & 0 & 1 & 0 & 1 & 0 \\ 0 & 0 & 0 & 1 & 0 & 1 \end{bmatrix}$$

For each indicate the value of k, whether cyclic, and whether single-error-correcting.

7-56. Refer to Prob. 7-54. Generate a new matrix G' by writing $g(x)$, $xg(x)$, $x^2g(x)$, etc., for successive rows. Use this matrix to generate the 16 code words. Compare them with the ones found in Prob. 7-50. Show that G' found here can be put into the form of G by adding rows appropriately.

7-57. Take any three 4-bit information vectors $\mathbf{d}$. Write these as $d(x)$. These are to be encoded into the appropriate $(7,4)$ code words of Prob. 7-54. For this purpose use $g(x) = x^3 + x + 1$. Calculate

$$r(x) = \text{rem}\ \frac{x^{n-k}d(x)}{g(x)} = \text{rem}\ \frac{x^3 d(x)}{g(x)}$$

in this case. Show that $x^{n-k}d(x) + r(x) = c(x)$, the appropriate code words for this case. The polynomial $r(x)$ thus provides the parity-check bits for these three information vectors. The three code words should of course agree with those found using the G matrix in Prob. 7-50.

7-58. Consider the $(7,3)$ code with generator polynomial $g(x) = x^4 + x^3 + x^2 + 1$. Find the parity-check bits for each of the seven nonzero data sequences by calculating the remainder polynomial $r(x)$ for each.

7-59. Consider the $(15,11)$ cyclic code listed in Table 7-3.
   (a) Show that the generator polynomial $g(x)$ generates the G matrix of Eq. (7-137).
   (b) Using the G matrix, find the 15-bit code word for the information vector

$$\mathbf{d} = [10001001010]$$

   (c) Check the result of (b), first finding the data polynomial $d(x)$, and then the remainder polynomial $r(x)$.

7-60. Consider the $(7,4)$ code with $g(x) = x^3 + x + 1$ of Prob. 7-54. Find $h(x)$ for this code. Implement the two encoders discussed in the text. Pick any 4-bit data sequence. Calculate the parity-check bits using both encoders. Compare with the results of the G matrix in Prob. 7-50 or Prob. 7-57.

7-61. Consider the $(15,11)$ cyclic code with generator polynomial $g(x) = x^4 + x + 1$ discussed in the text.
   (a) Find the parity-check polynomial $h(x)$.
   (b) Verify that the shift-register devices of Fig. 7-63 do represent encoders for this code. Take any 11-bit data word, find the parity-check bits obtained with the two encoders, and verify that they are the same.
   (c) Find the G matrix for this code, and show that it is the G matrix given by (7-137). Use the G (or P) matrix to calculate the parity-check bits for the same data word user in part (b). It should agree with the parity bits found there.

7-62. Refer to the two encoder implementations for the $(15,11)$ cyclic code shown in Fig. 7-63. Apply the 11-bit data sequence $\mathbf{d} = [10001001010]$ to the input of each encoder, trace through the calculation of the four parity-check bits for each, and show that they agree. Show that they are the same as would be calculated using the G matrix and polynomial-remainder calculations.

7-63. Consider a code word made up of ten 8-bit characters. The last (parity) character has as each of its bits the exclusive-or of all 9 previous bits in the same time slot. Using the block-error-probability model described in the text, calculate P_e if $p = 10^{-5}$. Show, by example, that bursts of 8 bits or less will be detected. Take any burst pattern at random, of more than 8 bits, and test to see if it is detected. Pick any code word at random for this purpose.

7-64. Refer to Prob. 7-63. The performance of the exclusive-or error-detection scheme is to be determined through simulation. For this purpose write a computer program that provides the exclusive-or parity check of all information bits in the same time slot. Randomly generate information sequences nine or more characters long; perturb these with random burst patterns of varying length, including patterns greater than 8 bits in length. Run your program enough times to verify the error-detecting capability of the code.

7-65. A code word consists of eight 8-bit information characters and parity-check bits generated by the polynomial

$$g(x) = x^{16} + x^{12} + x^5 + 1$$

(a) What burst lengths is this code guaranteed to detect? For longer burst lengths, what is the fraction remaining undetected?

(b) Using the error model described in the text, with block error probability proportional to block length, determine the block error probability if $p = 10^{-4}$.

(c) Repeat (a) and (b) if the information sequence is 1,000 bits long. How could one improve the detection capability of this system?

7-66. Refer to the generator polynomial of Eq. (7-196) used in data-link control. (See also Prob. 7-65.) Pick any information sequence two characters long. Use the remainder theorem to calculate the parity-check bits. Repeat for an information sequence four characters long. In both cases show the complete code word to be transmitted.

7-67. A cyclic $(7, 3)$ code has as its generator polynomial $g(x) = x^4 + x^2 + x + 1$.

(a) Find the G matrix for this code.

(b) Find all possible code words. What is the minimum distance of this code? Show that it is single-error-correcting.

(c) Select any 3-bit data sequence. Use the remainder theorem to find the parity-check bits, and compare with the corresponding code word in (b).

(d) Data bits are transmitted over a satellite link using PSK transmission. Matched filtering is used at the receiver. $E/n_0 = 9.1$ without encoding. The corresponding *bit*-error probability is then

$$p = \tfrac{1}{2} \operatorname{erfc} \sqrt{\frac{E}{n_0}} \doteq \frac{e^{-E/n_0}}{2\sqrt{\pi E/n_0}} = 10^{-5}$$

Calculate P_e for an uncoded 3-bit sequence and compare with P_e for the coded 7-bit sequence. Make all reasonable approximations. *Hint:* You showed in (b) that the code was single-error-correcting.

7-68. Show that $(7, 2)$ and $(15, 7)$ codes can provide double-error correction. Show a $(23, 12)$ code can correct up to three errors.

7-69. Show that the $K = 4$, rate-$\tfrac{1}{2}$ convolutional coder of Fig. 7-67a is represented by the state diagram of Fig. 7-69. Complete the diagram by including the output bits generated on each transition. Provide the trellis representation for this coder.

7-70. Consider the convolutional coders sketched in Fig. P7-70.

(a) Sketch the state-machine diagram for each coder, incorporating four nodal points and connecting branches between them.

    (*b*) For both coders find the output bit sequence for the following input data sequence: $1\,0\,0\,1\,1\,1\,0\,1\,0\,0$ (time increases from left to right).

    (*c*) Sketch the trellis structure for both coders for at least five time intervals.

(1) Constraint length = 3, rate $\frac{1}{2}$ (2) Constraint length = 3, rate $\frac{1}{3}$

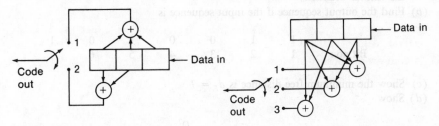

FIGURE P7-70

7-71. Refer to Prob. 7-70.

    (*a*) The 3rd and 7th bits of the output (coded) sequence of part (*b*) are changed during transmission. (This is assumed to happen in both cases, for both coder outputs.) Use the Viterbi decoding algorithm, assuming a hard-limiting decision device is used, to find the four minimum-distance survivors after the last received bit. Do this for both devices.

    (*b*) Select the survivor with the minimum distance, and use this to generate the most likely input bit sequence. Compare with the original sequence of Prob. 7-70*b*.

    (*c*) Repeat part (*b*) by artificially inserting two 0 input bits into the coder, after the last bit in the sequence of Prob. 7-70*b*. This forces the coder to end up in the $a = 0\,0$ state. (Why is this so?) The survivor in state *a* at this time should then provide the most likely path. Compare with part (*b*).

7-72. (*a*) Show the transmission function $T(D)$ for the rate-$\frac{1}{2}$ coder of Prob. 7-70 [coder number (1)] is given by

$$T(D) = \frac{D^4 + D^5 - D^6}{1 - D - D^2 - D^3 + D^4} \doteq D^4 + 2D^5 + D^6 + \cdots$$

    (*b*) Check the possible paths deviating from the all-0 path, using either the state diagram or the trellis. Show that the minimum free distance is, in fact, $d_F = 4$ and that there are two paths at distance 5 and one at distance 6 away from the all-0 path.

    (*c*) Show the error probability is bounded loosely by $P_e < e^{-2E_b/n_0}$. Find this bound for $E_b/n_0 = 5$ (7 dB). Compare this performance with that of the coder of Fig. 7-66.

7-73. Refer to the rate-$\frac{1}{2}$ coder of Prob. 7-70 [coder (1)]. Show

$$T(D, N) = \frac{D^4 N^2 + D^5 N - D^6 N^2}{1 - DN - D^2 N^2 - D^3 N + D^4 N^2}$$

Use this to calculate the upper and lower bounds for P_e and P_B for the two cases $E_s/n_0 = 1$ and 2. Comment on the tightness of the bounds. What is E_b/n_0 in each case?

7-74. Show that if the upper middle connection in coder (1) of Fig. P7-70 is left out, the resultant coder exhibits catastrophic error propagation.

7-75. Consider the constraint-length-$K = 3$, rate-$\frac{1}{3}$ convolutional encorder shown in Fig. P7-75.

(*a*) Sketch the state diagram for this encoder, indicating input and output bits in the various branches.

(*b*) Find the output sequence if the input sequence is

	1	1	0	0	1	0	1
Bit no.:	1	2	3	4	5	6	7

(*c*) Show the minimum free distance is $d_F = 7$.

(*d*) Show

$$T(D) = \frac{D^7}{1 - D - D^3}$$

(*e*) Show the error probability bound over an AWGN channel is of the form

$$P_e < e^{-CE_b/n_0}(1 + \cdots),$$

E_b = bit energy of the input bits. What is the value of C in this case?

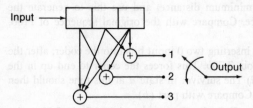

FIGURE P7-75

7-76. A constraint-length-$K = 3$, rate-$\frac{1}{3}$ convolutional encoder is designed as shown in Fig. P7-76.

(*a*) Sketch the state diagram, indicating transitions between states, and labeling them with the data input bit as well as the output (transmitted) bits.

(*b*) Show the minimum free distance is $d_F = 6$. Show there are two paths at distance $d = 8$.

(*c*) Show the transfer function is $T(D) = D^6/(1 - 2D^2)$. Show this agrees with part (*b*) above. How many paths are there at distance 10?

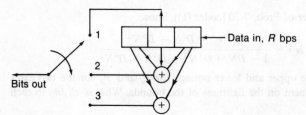

FIGURE P7-76

(d) (1) For a PSK system *without* coding the probability of bit error is

$$\frac{1}{2}\,\text{erfc}\,\sqrt{\frac{E_b}{n_0}} \doteq \frac{1}{2}\,\frac{e^{-E_b/n_0}}{\sqrt{\pi E_b/n_0}}$$

Using a convolutional encoder plus PSK, the bit-error probability is approximately $\frac{1}{2}e^{-d_F E_s/n_0}/\sqrt{\pi d_F E_s/n_0}$. E_b is the data-bit energy; E_s is the transmitted-bit energy. Compare the data-bit energy required, for the same probability of error, for the convolutional coder of this problem and PSK without coding. Compare the relative transmission bandwidths as well.

(2) The $K = 3$, rate-$\frac{1}{2}$ convolutional encoder discussed in the text (Fig. 7-66) had $d_F = 5$. Compare its performance with that of this problem with regard to relative data-bit energy E_b and transmission bandwidths. Compare with the performance of the coder of Prob. 7-75.

7-77. PSK, 16-QAM, and $K = 7$, rate-$\frac{1}{2}$ convolutional coding are being considered for use over an AWGN channel. $P_e \leq 10^{-5}$ is required. Then

(1) for PSK, $E_b/n_0 \geq 10$, E_b = received bit energy;
(2) for 16-QAM, $E/n_0 \geq 100$, E = average received symbol energy;
(3) for convolutional coding, $E_s/n_0 \geq 1.25$, E_s = received symbol energy.

Find the maximum allowable data bit rate R for each of the three possibilities for the following channels:

(a) $S_R/n_0 = 10^5$, S_R = average received signal power. Transmission bandwidth $W = 100$ kHz; assume up to W symbols/s can be handled.

(b) $S_R/n_0 = 10^5$, $W = 2500$ Hz.

(c) $S_R/n_0 = 10^7$, $W = 100$ kHz.

Explain your results.

7-78. A communications system has $S_R/n_0 = 10^3$ at the receiver (S_R = received noise power; $n_0/2$ = noise spectral density). $P_e = 10^{-5}$ is desired.

(a) The bandwidth is constrained to 1000 Hz. Find the *maximum* bit rate allowed for each of the following transmission schemes, consistent with the power and bandwidth limitation:

(1) PSK
(2) M-ary orthogonal signaling; check from among the group $M = 2, 4, 8, 16, 32, 64$.
(3) A rate-$\frac{1}{2}$ convolutional encoder, with PSK used on the output bit stream (refer to Table 7-7).

(b) The bandwidth limitation is relaxed. Repeat (a). Find the maximum Shannon capacity C_∞ as well.

7-79. Refer to Prob. 7-38. For the numbers given there compare the following communication systems:

(1) PSK with no coding.
(2) 64 orthogonal signals.
(3) Viterbi convolutional encoder, $K = 3$, rate-$\frac{1}{2}$, plus PSK. Repeat for a $K = 7$, rate-$\frac{1}{2}$ encoder.

The comparison is on the basis of the bit rate possible as well as transmission bandwidth required (use 25% roll-off). Do the comparisons for 500- and 2,000-MHz transmission frequencies. What are the Shannon capacities in these two cases, assuming very large bandwidths are possible?

7-80. Refer to the discussion of the Mariner 10 deep-space mission in Sec. 6-15. A probability of error $P_e = 10^{-5}$ is desired. Compare the use of PSK with no coding, $M = 32$ orthogonal signals, and two types of convolutional coders: $K = 3$ and $K = 7$, both at rate $\frac{1}{2}$. What is the Shannon capacity in this case?

7-81. Carry out the downlink calculations for the Voyager Uranus encounter discussed at the end of Sec. 7-9. For the numbers given there show

$$S_R/n_0 = 48 \text{ dB}$$

Show that for a bit-error probability of 10^{-5}, uncoded PSK transmission would allow a maximum transmission rate of 6,900 bits/s. Show that $K = 7$, rate-$\frac{1}{2}$ convolutional coding increases this rate to 24 kbits/s. Show the maximum error-free capacity is 91.2 kbits/s.

7-82. Refer to the two-state trellis of Fig. 7-83. Show that the minimum-distance error path has a Euclidean distance of 1.608. Do this by calculating the Euclidean distance of a number of error paths and showing that they all exceed the distance of the two paths (a) and (c) in Fig. 7-84.

7-83. Refer to the four-state trellis of Fig. 7-85. Calculate the Euclidean distance of a number of error paths. Show the minimum distance is 2 and that there is only one path with this distance.

7-84. Repeat Prob. 7-83 for the eight-state trellis of Fig. 7-86. Show, as indicated there, that there are two minimum-distance paths, with a Euclidean distance of 2.141.

7-85. Refer to Fig. 7-87. Show that the coders in (a) and (b) do in fact generate the four-state trellis of Fig. 7-85. (Refer to Fig. 7-82 for the definition of the signal points.) Pick an arbitrary input bit sequence, and trace out the corresponding output (8-PSK) signals, interval by interval, using both the trellis of Fig. 7-85 and the two coders of Fig. 7-87. Repeat for the eight-state trellis of Fig. 7-87 and the coder of Fig. 7-87c.

REFERENCES

[ABAT] J. E. Abate, "Linear and Adaptive Delta Modulation," *Proc. IEEE*, vol. 55, no. 3, pp. 290–308, March 1967.

[ABRA] N. Abramson, "The Aloha System," in *Computer Networks*, N. Abramson and F. Kuo (eds.), Prentice-Hall, Englewood Cliffs, N.J., 1973.

[ALLE 1963] W. B. Allen, in A. V. Balakrishnan (ed.), *Space Communications*, McGraw-Hill, New York, 1963, pp. 190–192.

[ALLE 1978] A. O. Allen, *Probability, Statistics, and Queueing Theory*, Academic Press, New York, 1978.

[ANGE] D. J. Angelakos and T. E. Everhart, *Microwave Communications*, McGraw-Hill, New York, 1968.

[ANSI] *American National Standard for Telecommunications—Digital Optical Interface Rates and Formats Specification*, ANSI T1.105-1988, American National Standards Inst., New York, Draft, March 10, 1988.

[BALL] R. Ballert and Y.-C. Ching, "SONET: Now It's the Standard Optical Interface," *IEEE Commun. Mag.*, Vol. 29, No. 3, pp. 8–15, March 1989.

[BARG] P. L. Bargellini (ed.) "The Intelsat IV Communications System," *Comsat Tech. Rev.*, vol. 2, no. 2, pp. 437–570, Fall 1972.

[BASC] E. E. Basch and T. G. Brown, "Introduction to Coherent Optical Fiber Transmission," *IEEE Commun. Mag.*, vol. 3, no. 5, pp. 23–30, May 1986.

[BELC] *Asynchronous Digital Multiplexes: Requirements and Objectives*, Technical Reference TR-TSY-000009, Bell Communications Research, Issue 1, May 1986.

[BELL 1960] D. A. Bell, *Electrical Noise, Fundamentals and Physical Mechanism*, Van Nostrand, London, 1960.

[BELL 1982] Bell Telephone Laboratories, *Transmission Systems for Communications*, 5th ed., 1982.

[BENN 1960] W. R. Bennett, *Electrical Noise*, McGraw-Hill, New York, 1960.

[BENN 1965] W. R. Bennett and J. R. Davey, *Data Transmission*, McGraw-Hill, New York, 1965, chap. 9.

[BENV] N. Benvenuto et al., "The 32 kbit/s ADPCM Coding Standard," *AT&T Tech. J.*, vol. 65, no. 5, pp. 12–22, September/October 1986.

[BERL 1980] E. R. Berlekamp, "The Technology of Error-Correcting Codes," *Proc. IEEE*, vol. 68, no. 5, pp. 564–592, May 1980.

[BERL 1987] E. R. Berlekamp, R. E. Peile, and S. P. Pope, "The Application of Error Control to Communications," *IEEE Commun. Mag.*, vol. 25, no. 4, pp. 44–57, April 1987.

[BLAC] H. S. Black, *Modulation Theory*, Van Nostrand, Princeton, N.J., 1955.

[BLAH] R. E. Blahut, *Theory and Practice of Error Control Codes*, Addison-Wesley, Reading, Mass., 1983.

[BOEH] R. J. Boehm et al., "Standardized Fiber Optic Transmission Systems—A Synchronous Optical Network View," *IEEE J. Selected Areas Commun.*, special issue on fiber optical systems for terrestrial applications, vol. SAC-4, no. 9, pp. 1424–1431, Dec. 1986.

[BURT] H. O. Burton and D. D. Sullivan, "Errors and Error Control," *Proc. IEEE*, vol. 60, no. 11, pp. 1293–1301, November 1972.

[BUX] W. Bux, "Local-Area Subnetworks: A Performance Comparison," *IEEE Trans. Commun.*, Vol. COM-29, no. 10, pp. 1465–1473, October 1981.

[CAMP 1976] S. J. Campanella, "Digital Speech Interpolation," *Comsat Tech. Rev.*, vol. 6, no. 1, pp. 127–158, Spring 1976.

[CAMP 1986] S. J. Campanella, B. A. Pontano, and J. L. Dicks, "Advantages of TDMA and Satellite-Switched TDMA in Intelsat V and VI," *Comsat Tech. Rev.*, vol. 16, no. 1, pp. 207–238, Spring 1986.

[CATT] K. W. Cattermole, *Principles of Pulse Code Modulation*, Illiffe, London, 1969; American Elsevier, New York, 1975.

[CLAR 1967] K. K. Clarke and D. T. Hess, "Frequency-Locked Loop Demodulator," *IEEE Trans. Commun. Technol.*, pp. 518–525, August 1967.

[CLAR 1971] K. K. Clarke and D. T. Hess, *Communic tion Circuits: Analysis and Design*, Addison-Wesley, Reading, Mass., 1971.

[COMS 1985] TDMA: Part I, Special issue, *Comsat Tech. Rev.*, vol. 15, no. 2B, pp. 361–525, Fall 1985.

[COMS 1986] TDMA: Part II, Special issue, *Comsat Tech. Rev.*, vol. 16, no. 1, pp. 1–298, Spring 1986.

[COUC] L. W. Couch II, *Digital and Analog Communication Systems*, Macmillan, New York, 1987, pp. 382–383.

[CROS] M. G. Crosby, "Frequency Modulation Noise Characteristics," *Proc. IRE*, vol. 25, pp. 472–514, April 1937, fig. 10.

[DAVE] W. B. Davenport, Jr., and W. L. Root, *Introduction to Random Signals and Noise*, McGraw-Hill, New York, 1958.

[DECI] M. Decina and G. Modena, "CCITT Standards on Digital Speech Processing," *IEEE J. Selected Areas Commun.*, special issue on voice coding for communications, Vol. 6, No. 2, pp. 227–234, February 1988.

[EAST] M. G. Easterling, "From $8\frac{1}{3}$ bits/s to 100,000 bits/s in Ten Years," in *Proceedings, National Telecommunications Conference*, Dallas, Texas, 1976; reprinted in *IEEE Commun. Soc. Mag.*, vol. 15, no. 6, pp. 12–15, November 1977.

[EVAN] J. B. Evans, Jr., and W. B. Gaunt, "The D3 Channel Bank," in *Conference Record, International Conference on Communications*, Minneapolis, Minn., June 1974, pp. 7D-1–7D-5.

[FDDI 1986a] *Draft Proposed American National Standard, FDDI Token Ring Media Access Control (MAC)*, ASC X3TR.5 Rev-10, ANSI, New York, February 28, 1986.

[FDDI 1986b] *Draft Proposed American National Standard, FDDI Physical Layer Protocol (PHY)*, ASCS3T9.5 Rev-14, ANSI, New York, October 20, 1986.

[FISK] B. Fisk and C. L. Spencer, "Synthesizer Stabilized Single-Sideband Systems," *Proc. IRE*, vol. 44, no. 12, p. 1680, December 1956.

[FLEU] B. Fleury, "Asynchronous High Speed Digital Multiplexing," *IEEE Commun. Mag.*, vol. 24, no. 8, pp. 17–25, August 1988.

[FORN] G. D. Forney, Jr., et al., "Efficient Modulation for Band-Limited Channels," *IEEE J. Selected Areas Commun.*, vol. SAC-2, no. 5, pp. 632–647, September 1984.

[GALL] R. G. Gallager, *Information Theory and Reliable Communication*, Wiley, New York, 1968.

[GAUN] W. B. Gaunt and J. B. Evans, Jr., "The D3 Channel Bank," *Bell Lab. Rec.*, vol. 50, pp. 329–333, August 1972.

[GOLD 1948] S. Goldman, *Frequency Analysis, Modulation, and Noise*, McGraw-Hill, New York, 1948.

[GOLD 1953] S. Goldman, *Information Theory*, Prentice-Hall, Englewood Cliffs, N.J., 1953.

[GRUE] E. L. Gruenberg (ed.), *Handbook of Telemetry and Remote Control*, McGraw-Hill, New York, 1967.

[HALS] F. Halsall, *Data Communications, Computer Networks and OSI*, Addison-Wesley, Wokinham, England, 1988.

[HART] G. Hart and J. A. Steinkamp, "Future Trends in Microwave Digital Radio: A View from Europe," *IEEE Commun. Mag.*, vol. 25, no. 2, pp. 49–52, February 1987.

[HELLE] A. J. Heller and I. M. Jacobs, "Viterbi Decoding for Satellite and Space Communications," *IEEE Trans. Commun. Technol.*, vol. COM-19, no. 5, part II, p. 835, October 1971.

[HELS] C. W. Helstrom, *Statistical Theory of Signal Detection*, Pergamon, New York, 1968.

[HENR 1985a] P. S. Henry, "Introduction to Lightwave Transmission," *IEEE Commun. Mag.*, vol. 23, no. 5, pp. 12–16, May 1985.

[HENR 1985b] P. S. Henry, "Lightwave Primer," *IEEE J. Quantum Electron.*, vol. QE-21, no. 12, pp. 1862–1879, December 1985.

[HESS] D. T. Hess, "Equivalence of FM Threshold Extension Receivers," *IEEE Trans. Commun. Technol.*, October 1968.

[IEEE 1981] Special section on combined modulation and coding, *IEEE Trans. Commun.*, vol. COM-29, no. 3, March 1981.

[IEEE 1985a] *CSMA/CD Access Method*, Standard 802.3-1985, IEEE, New York, 1985.

[IEEE 1985b] *Token Ring Access Method*, Standard 802.5-1985, IEEE, New York, 1985.

[IEEE 1987a] "Future Trends in Microwave Digital Radio, Views from Asia, North America, and Europe," *IEEE Commun. Mag.*, vol. 25, no. 2, pp. 40–52, February 1987.

[IEEE 1987b] "Advances in Digital Communications Radio," *IEEE J. Selected Areas Commun.*, vol. SAC-5, no. 3, April 1987.

[IRME] T. Irmer, "An Overview of Digital Hierarchies in the World Today," in *Conference Record, IEEE International Conference on Communications*, San Francisco, June 1975, pp. 16-1–16-4.

[JAGE] F. de Jager and C. B. Dekker, "Tamed Frequency Modulation, a Novel Method to Achieve Spectrum Economy in Digital Transmission," *IEEE Trans. Commun.*, vol. COM-26, no. 5, pp. 534–542, May 1978.

[JAHN] E. Jahnke and F. Emde, *Tables of Functions*, Dover, New York, 1945.

[JAYA 1974] N. S. Jayant, "Digital Coding of Speech Waveforms; PCM, DPCM, and DM Quantizers," *Proc. IEEE*, vol. 62, no. 5, pp. 611–632, May 1974.

[JAYA 1984] N. S. Jayant and P. Noll, *Digital Coding Waveforms*, Prentice-Hall, Englewood Cliffs, N.J., 1984.

[JERR] A. J. Jerri, "The Shannon Sampling Theorem—Its Various Extensions and Applications: A Tutorial Review," *Proc. IEEE*, vol. 65, no. 11, pp. 1565–1596, November 1977.

[JOHA] V. I. Johannes and R. H. McCullough, "Multiplexing of Asynchronous Digital Signals Using Pulse Stuffing with Added-Bit Signaling," *IEEE Trans. Commun. Tech.*, vol. COM-14, no. 5, pp. 562–568, October 1966.

[JORD] E. C. Jordan, *Electromagnetic Waves and Radiating Systems*, Prentice-Hall, Englewood Cliffs, N.J., 1950.

[KLEI] L. Kleinrock, *Queueing Systems, Volume 1: Theory*, Wiley, New York, 1976.

[KOHI] K. Kohiyama and O. Kurita, "Future Trends in Microwave Digital Radio: A View from Asia," *IEEE Commun. Mag.*, Vol. 25, no. 2, pp. 41–46, February 1987.

[KOLD] J. R. Kolden and V. L. Evanchuk, "Planetary Telecommunications Development During the Next Ten Years," in *Proceedings, National Telecommunications Conference*, Dallas, Texas, 1976; reprinted in *IEEE Commun. Soc. Mag.*, vol. 15, no. 6, pp. 16–19, 24, November 1977.

[KRET] E. R. Kretzmer, "The Evolution of Techniques for Data Communication over Voiceband Channels," *IEEE Commun. Soc. Mag.*, vol. 16, no. 1, pp. 10–14, January 1978.

[LAM] S. S. Lam, "A Carrier Sense Multiple Access Protocol for Local Networks," *Computer Networks*, vol. 4, no. 1, pp. 21–32, January 1980.

[LAWS] J. L. Lawson and G. E. Uhlenbeck, *Threshold Signals*, McGraw-Hill, New York, 1950.

[LIN] S. Lin and D. J. Costello, Jr., *Error Control Coding: Fundamentals and Applications*, Prentice-Hall, Englewood Cliffs, N.J. 1983.

[LINK] R. A. Linke and P. S. Henry, "Coherent Optical Detection: A Thousand Calls on One Circuit," *IEEE Spectrum*, pp. 52–57, February 1987.

[LUCK] R. W. Lucky, J. Salz, and E. J. Weldon, *Principles of Data Communication*, McGraw-Hill, New York, 1968.

[MAIT] X. Maitre, "7 kHz Audio Coding with 64 kbit/s," *IEEE J. Selected Areas Commun.*, special issue on voice coding for communications, Vol. 6, No. 2, pp. 283–298, February 1988.

[MARK] R. E. Markle, "Single Sideband Triples Microwave Radio Route Capacity," *Bell Lab. Rec.*, vol. 56, no. 4, pp. 105–110, April 1978.

[MAYE] H. F. Mayer, "Pulse Code Modulation," summary chapter in L. Martin (ed.), *Advances in Electronics*, vol. III, Academic Press, New York, 1951, pp. 221–260.

[MAYO] J. S. Mayo, "Pulse Code Modulation," *Electro-Technol.*, pp. 87–98, November 1962.

[MERM] P. Mermelstein, "G. 722, A New CCITT Coding Standard for Digital Transmission of Wideband Audio Signals," *IEEE Commun. Mag.*, Vol. 26, No. 1, pp. 8–15, January 1988.

[MEYE] M. H. Meyers and V. K. Prabhu, "Future Trends in Microwave Digital Radio; a View from North America," *IEEE Commun. Mag.*, vol. 25, no. 2, pp. 46–49, February 1987.

[MICH] A. M. Michelson and A. H. Levesque, *Error-Control Techniques for Digital Communications*, Wiley-Interscience, New York, 1985.

[MIDD] D. Middleton, *An Introduction to Statistical Communication Theory*, McGraw-Hill, New York, 1960.

[NYQU 1928a] H. Nyquist, "Certain Topics in Telegraph Transmission Theory," *Trans. AIEE*, vol. 47, pp. 617–644, April 1928.

[NYQU 1928b] H. Nyquist, *Phys. Rev.*, no. 32, p. 110, 1928.

[OLIV] B. M. Oliver, J. R. Pierce, and C. E. Shannon, "Philosophy of PCM," *Proc. IRE*, vol. 36, no. 11, p. 1324, November 1948.

[ONEA 1966a] J. B. O'Neal, "Delta Modulation Quantizing Noise, Analytical and Computer Simulation Results for Gaussian and Television Input Signals," *Bell System Tech. J.*, vol. 45, pp. 117–141, January 1966.

[ONEA 1966b] J. B. O'Neal, "Predictive Quantizing Systems (Differential PCM) for the Transmission of Television Signals," *Bell System Tech. J.*, vol. 45, pp. 1023–1036, May–June 1966.

[PAHL] K. Pahlavan and J. L. Holsinger, "Voice-Band Data Communication Modems—A. Historical Review: 1919–1988," *IEEE Commun. Mag.*, vol. 26, no. 1, pp. 16–27, January 1988.

[PAPO 1962] A. Papoulis, *The Fourier Integral and Its Applications*, McGraw-Hill, New York, 1962.

[PAPO 1968] A. Papoulis, *Systems and Transforms with Applications in Optics*, McGraw-Hill, New York, 1968.

[PAPO 1984] A. Papoulis, *Probability, Random Variables, and Stochastic Processes*, 2nd ed., McGraw-Hill, New York, 1984.

[PASU] S. Pasupathy, "Minimum Shift Keying: A Spectrally Efficient Modulation," *IEEE Commun. Mag.*, vol. 17, no. 4, pp. 14–22, July 1979.

[PEEK] J. B. H. Peek, "Communications Aspects of the Compact Disc Digital Audio System," *IEEE Commun. Mag.*, vol. 23, no. 2, pp. 7–15, February 1985.

[PETE] W. W. Peterson and E. J. Weldon, Jr., *Error-Correcting Codes*, MIT Press, Cambridge, Mass., 2nd ed., 1972.

[PONT] B. A. Pontano, S. J. Campanella, and J. L. Dicks, "The Intelsat TDMA/DSI system," *Comsat Tech. Rev.*, vol. 15, no. 2B, pp. 369–398, Fall 1985.

[POSN] E. C. Posner and R. Stevens, "Deep Space Communications—Past, Present, and Future," *IEEE Commun. Mag.* (special centennial issue), vol. 22, no. 5, pp. 8–21, May 1984.

[PRAT] Fletcher Pratt, *Secret and Urgent*, Doubleday, Garden City Books, New York, 1942.

[PUEN] J. G. Puente and A. M. Werth, "Demand-Assigned Service for the Intelsat Global Network," *IEEE Spectrum*, vol. 8, no. 1, pp. 59–69, January 1971.

[REIF] F. Reif, *Fundamentals of Statistical and Thermal Physics*, McGraw-Hill, New York, 1965.

[RICE] S. O. Rice, "Mathematical Analysis of Random Noise," *Bell System Tech. J.*, vol. 23, pp. 282–333, July 1944; vol. 24, pp. 46–156, January 1945 (reprinted in N. Wax (ed.), *Selected Papers on Noise and Stochastic Processes*, Dover, New York, 1954).

[RITC] G. R. Ritchie, "SYNTRAN—A New Direction for Digital Transmission Terminals," *IEEE Commun. Mag.*, vol. 23, no. 11, pp. 20–25, November 1985.

[ROSS] F. E. Ross, "FDDI—A Tutorial," *IEEE Commun. Mag.*, vol. 24, no. 5, pp. 10–17, May 1986.

[SALZ 1985] J. Salz, "Coherent Lightwave Communications," *AT&T Tech. J.*, vol. 64, no. 10, pp. 2153–2208, December 1985.

[SALZ 1986] J. Salz, "Modulation and Detection for Coherent Lightwave Communications," *IEEE Commun. Mag.*, vol. 24, no. 6, pp. 38–49, June 1986.

[SCHW 1966] M. Schwartz, W. R. Bennett, and S. Stein, *Communication Systems and Techniques*, McGraw-Hill, New York, 1966.

[SCHW 1970] M. Schwartz, *Information Transmission, Modulation, and Noise*, 2nd ed., McGraw-Hill, New York, 1970.

[SCHW 1975] M. Schwartz and L. Shaw, *Signal Processing: Discrete Spectral Analysis, Detection, and Estimation*, McGraw-Hill, New York, 1975.

[SCHW 1977] M. Schwartz, *Computer Communication Network Design and Analysis*, Prentice-Hall, Englewood Cliffs, N.J. 1977.

[SCHW 1980] M. Schwartz, *Information Transmission, Modulation, and Noise*, 3rd ed., McGraw-Hill, New York, 1980.

[SCHW 1987] M. Schwartz, *Telecommunication Networks: Protocols, Modeling, and Analysis*, Addison-Wesley, Reading, Mass., 1987.

[SHAN 1948] C. E. Shannon, "A Mathematical Theory of Communication," *Bell System Tech. J.*, vol. 27, pp. 379–423, July 1948; pp. 623–656, October 1948.

[SHAN 1949] C. E. Shannon, "Communication in the Presence of Noise," *Proc. IRE*, vol. 37, pp. 10–21, January 1949.

[SIEG] A. E. Siegman, *Microwave Solid-State Masers*, McGraw-Hill, New York, 1964, pp. 373–375.

[SKLA] B. Sklar, *Digital Communications*, Prentice-Hall, Englewood Cliffs, N.J., 1988, chap. 8.

[SPIL] James J. Spilker, Jr., *Digital Communications by Satellite*, Prentice-Hall, Englewood Cliffs, N.J., 1977.

[STAM] R. Stampfl, in A. V. Balakrishnan (ed.), *Space Communications*, McGraw-Hill, New York, 1963, chap. 18.

[STIF] J. J. Stiffler, *Theory of Synchronous Communication*, Prentice-Hall, Englewood Cliffs, N.J., 1971.

[SUND] C.-E. Sundberg, "Continuous Phase Modulation," *IEEE Commun. Mag.*, vol. 24, no. 4, pp. 25–38, April 1986.

[TANE 1989] A. Tanenbaum, *Computer Networks*, Prentice-Hall, Englewood Cliffs, N.J., 1989.

[UNGE 1982] G. Ungerboeck, "Channel Coding with Multilevel/Phase Signals," *IEEE Trans. Inform. Theory*, vol. IT-28, no. 1, pp. 55–67, January 1982.

[UNGE 1987] G. Ungerboeck, "Trellis-Coded Modulation with Redundant Signal Sets," *IEEE Comun. Mag.*, vol. 25, no. 2, pp. 5–11, 12–21, February 1987.

[VAN] J. B. Van der Mey, "The Architecture of a Transparent Intelligent Network," in *Conference Record, IEEE National Telecommunications Conference*, Dallas, Texas, December 1976, pp. 7.2.1–7.2.5.

[VANT] H. L. Van Trees, *Detection, Estimation, and Modulation Theory*, vol. I, Wiley, New York, 1968.

[VITE 1966] A. J. Viterbi, *Principles of Coherent Communication*, McGraw-Hill, New York, 1966.

[VITE 1967] A. J. Viterbi, "Error bounds for convolutional codes and an asymptotically optimum decoding algorithm," *IEEE Trans. Inform. Theory*, vol. IT-13, pp. 260–269, April 1967.

[VITE 1971] A. J. Viterbi, "Convolutional Codes and Their Performance in Communication Systems," *IEEE Trans. Commun. Technol.*, vol. COM-19, no. 5, pp. 751–771, October 1971.

[WOOD] G. E. Wood and T. Risa, "Design of the Mariner Jupiter/Saturn 1977 Telemetry System," in *Proceedings, International Telemetry Conference*, Los Angeles, vol. 10, 1974, pp. 606–615.

[WOZE] J. M. Wozencraft and I. M. Jacobs, *Principles of Communication Engineering*, Wiley, New York, 1965.

[ZIEL] A. Van der Ziel, *Noise*, Prentice-Hall, Englewood Cliffs, N.J., 1954.